VERTEBRATE PALEONTOLOGY IN UTAH

David D. Gillette, Editor

Utah Geological Survey

ISBN 1-55791-634-9

MISCELLANEOUS PUBLICATION 99-1
UTAH GEOLOGICAL SURVEY
a division of
UTAH DEPARTMENT OF NATURAL RESOURCES

UTAH GEOLOGICAL SURVEY

The **UTAH GEOLOGICAL SURVEY** is organized into five geologic programs with Administration, Editorial, and Computer Resources providing necessary support to the programs. The **ECONOMIC GEOLOGY PROGRAM** undertakes studies to identify coal, geothermal, uranium, hydrocarbon, and industrial and metallic resources; initiates detailed studies of these resources including mining district and field studies; develops computerized resource data bases, to answer state, federal, and industry requests for information; and encourages the prudent development of Utah's geologic resources. The **APPLIED GEOLOGY PROGRAM** responds to requests from local and state governmental entities for engineering-geologic investigations; and identifies, documents, and interprets Utah's geologic hazards. The **GEOLOGIC MAPPING PROGRAM** maps the bedrock and surficial geology of the state at a regional scale by county and at a more detailed scale by quadrangle. The **GEOLOGIC EXTENSION SERVICE** answers inquiries from the public and provides information about Utah's geology in a non-technical format. The **ENVIRONMENTAL SCIENCES PROGRAM** maintains and publishes records of Utah's fossil resources, provides paleontological and archeological recovery services to state and local governments, conducts studies of environmental change to aid resource management, and evaluates the quantity and quality of Utah's ground-water resources.

The UGS Library is open to the public and contains many reference works on Utah geology and many unpublished documents on aspects of Utah geology by UGS staff and others. The UGS has several computer data bases with information on mineral and energy resources, geologic hazards, stratigraphic sections, and bibliographic references. Most files may be viewed by using the UGS Library. The UGS also manages a sample library which contains core, cuttings, and soil samples from mineral and petroleum drill holes and engineering geology investigations. Samples may be viewed at the Sample Library or requested as a loan for outside study.

The UGS publishes the results of its investigations in the form of maps, reports, and compilations of data that are accessible to the public. For information on UGS publications, contact the Natural Resources Map/Bookstore, 1594 W. North Temple, Salt Lake City, Utah 84116, (801) 537-3320 or 1-888-UTAH MAP. E-mail: nrugs.geostore@state.ut.us and visit our web site at http://www.ugs.state.ut.us.

The Utah Friends of Paleontology is a volunteer organization dedicated to preserving Utah's fossil resources through public education and volunteer support. As part of this support, the statewide chapter and the Great Basin Chapter, through generous donations, have provided funding to help defray some of the publication costs of *Vertebrate Paleontology in Utah* and thus reduce the retail price, hopefully making it more acces-sible to a larger audience.

We would also like to acknowledge *Brian Maebius* who donated the many sketches that appear throughout the book between papers. They were chosen for graphic purposes and were not meant to be particularly representative of any species referred to in this collection. The cover art is also by Brian Maebius and was used as a poster commemorating *Utah Prehistory and Heritage Week*, May 1-8, 1999. He has a degree in art with a geology minor and has been an educator in various museums. An upcoming publication by Badlands National Park also features his fossil sketches: *Badlands: the story behind the scenery*.

Cover design and book layout by Sharon Hamre, graphic designer at the Utah Geological Survey.

About the Editor

David D. Gillette is the former State Paleontologist for Utah, Distinguished Lecturer 1994-1995 for the American Association of Petroleum Geologists, Trustee and Principal Investigator for the Southwest Paleontological Foundation in Albuquerque, New Mexico, and has received the James H. Shea Award of the National Association of Geology Teachers for communications to the general public. He is coeditor of Dinosaur *Tracks and Traces*, coauthor of *Glyphodonts of North America*, and author of *Seismosaurus: the Earth Shaker*. Dr. Gillette is currently with the Museum of Northern Arizona in Flagstaff where he is Colbert Curator of Vertebrate Paleontology.

TABLE OF CONTENTS

PALEOZOIC ERA

MESOZOIC ERA

CENOZOIC ERA

INTRODUCTION

Vertebrate Paleontology in Utah was conceived several years ago, in anticipation of annual meetings of three professional societies, all hosted by the Utah Geological Survey: The American Association of Petroleum Geologists (1997), The Geological Society of America (1997), and the Society of Vertebrate Paleontology (1998). As editor, I hoped to have this volume in print for the 1997 meetings, and felt certain that it would be completed prior to the Snowbird meeting of the SVP in October, 1998. The gestation period was longer than the doctors all predicted. Now, in 1999, I am pleased to get it published before the turn of the millennium.

I solicited contributions from all researchers in my acquaintance who were conducting vertebrate paleontological research in Utah. Optimistically expecting maybe 20 papers, at one point the numbers grew to more than 70 proposed manuscripts. The 52 papers in this book more than double my initial expectations. They vary in content from summaries or "state-of-knowledge" treatments, to detailed contributions that describe new species. Although the distinction is subtle, the title (Vertebrate Paleontology in Utah) indicates the science of paleontology in the state of Utah, rather than the even more ambitious intent if it were given the title "Vertebrate Paleontology of Utah" which would promise an en-cyclopedic treatment of the subject. The science of vertebrate paleontology in Utah is robust and intense. It has grown prodigiously in the past decade, and promises to continue to grow indefinitely. This research benefits everyone in the state, through Utah's muse ums and educational institutions, which are the direct beneficiaries.

David D. Gillette, Editor

ACKNOWLEDGMENTS

Most of the authors I know personally, an indication that ours is still a small group of dedicated researchers. All contributors have been patient, helpful, and cooperative; for their support in this task I am especially grateful. Many others, whose names do not appear as authors, have been intimately involved in the production of this book. Every paper was read critically by peer reviewers. Some of them are identified in acknowledgments, others remain anonymous. I thank all of them, for their selfless contribution to the improvement of this volume. Every manuscript was improved by their thoughtful, con structive comments.

The internal review process in the Utah Geological Survey brought improved consistency in style and content; UGS reviewers were Mike Lowe, Mike Hylland, Kimm Harty, and Lee Allison. UGS editorial staff were equally supportive, especially Sharon Hamre, Vicki Clark, Jim Parker, and editor Jim Stringfellow. Utah Geological Survey Director M. Lee Allison gave me unwavering support and encouragement throughout the production of this volume. Through the entire process, Martha C. Hayden helped, coordinated, kept records, wrote drafts, managed computer files, and made this volume, withal, possible.

For constant encouragement and unflagging assistance in all aspects of my former position at the Utah Geological Survey, I thank all members of the Utah Friends of Paleontology. This remarkable group of volunteers has expanded Utah paleontology many times over by taking our work to the general public.

I dedicate this volume to
Martha C. Hayden,
the best assistant a state paleontologist
could ever ask for. I thank her for ten years of
extraordinary support and friendship.

David D. Gillette, former State Paleontologist of Utah,
Utah Geological Survey,
presently Colbert Curator of Vertebrate Paleontology,
Museum of Northern Arizona,
Flagstaff, June 29, 1999

VERTEBRATE PALEONTOLOGY IN UTAH

David G. Gillette, Editor
Utah Geological Survey

PALEOZOIC ERA

THE DEVONIAN VERTEBRATES OF UTAH

David K. Elliott, Randal C. Reed, and Heidemarie G. Johnson
Department of Geology, Northern Arizona University, Flagstaff, AZ 86011-4099

ABSTRACT

Vertebrates occur throughout the Devonian of Utah, although at present they are better known from the Lower Devonian than from the Middle or Upper. The Early Devonian fauna is an endemic one, but does show sufficient similarity to faunas in surrounding states to enable correlation schemes to be developed and dating to be attempted. The well-known fauna from the lower Grassy Flat Member of the Water Canyon Formation is thus shown to be Emsian, and a new fauna from the Sevy Dolomite is correlated with it. The Middle Devonian faunas are more cosmopolitan and thus the upper Grassy Flat Member, which contains only a sparse fauna, cannot yet be correlated with others in western North America. Late Devonian vertebrates are known from only one locality, which is thought to be Frasnian.

INTRODUCTION

Pre-Devonian vertebrates are unknown in Utah. Although the Ordovician Swan Peak Formation has been reported to contain vertebrates (Oaks and others, 1977), collections made by the senior author show that the phosphatic material derives from inarticulate brachiopods. The vertebrate record starts in the Devonian, therefore, and is extensive, ranging throughout the "Age of Fishes" and providing important evidence towards an understanding of the early evolution of vertebrates.

The first reports of vertebrates from Utah were made by Cooley (1928), Branson (1929), and Branson and Mehl (1930), and the first descriptions were published by Branson and Mehl in 1931. These reports dealt with material from the northeast of Utah, from rocks subsequently named as the Water Canyon Formation and now known to be Early and Middle Devonian in age. At about the same time the vertebrate fauna of the Beartooth Butte Formation of Wyoming was described by Bryant (1932, 1933, 1934, 1935). These two faunas showed close similarities and their description was undertaken by Denison in a series of classic papers (1952, 1953, 1958, 1966, 1967, 1968a,b, 1970). In 1961 Ørvig described a Middle Devonian fauna from the Water Canyon Forma-

tion, but since then little has been published on these organisms until recently (Elliott,1994). Descriptions of new Early Devonian faunas from Nevada (Ilyes and Elliott, 1994) and California (Elliott and Ilyes, 1996a) have now shown the utility of these organisms in biostratigraphy, and several correlations for Lower and Middle Devonian rocks in the western U.S. have been proposed recently (Elliott and Ilyes, 1996b; Elliott and Johnson, 1997). Despite the undoubted presence of vertebrates in the Upper Devonian rocks of Utah, almost no work has been carried out on them beyond the report of their presence by Denison (1951), and Knight and Cooper (1955) and it has not yet been possible to use them in correlation.

OUTLINE OF THE MAIN VERTEBRATE GROUPS

During the Paleozoic several major vertebrate groups rose, diversified, and in some cases became extinct. These were all fish groups except for the emergence of tetrapods in the Late Devonian. However, as tetrapods have not yet been reported from the Devonian of Utah, this section will deal only with the major groups that make the Devonian "The Age of Fishes".

All fishes are divided into two superclasses, the Agnatha or jawless vertebrates and the Gnathostomata or jawed vertebrates. The Agnatha are now represented by two groups, the lampreys and the hagfishes, which are eel-like animals specialised for parasitic and scavenging modes of life in freshwater and marine environments. However, during the Devonian numerous and diverse Agnatha existed with an armor of external bony plates. These animals had a world-wide distribution in environments ranging from marine to freshwater, and have been used extensively in biostratigraphy.

The gnathostomes comprise all the jawed groups, and include the Chondrichthyes, or sharks and rays, together with the Osteichthyes, and two extinct groups, the Acanthodii and the Placodermi. The latter two groups, together with the extant Actinopterygii and Sarcopterygii, comprise the bony fish, and several members of this group are also found in the Devonian rocks of Utah.

Agnatha

Osteostraci

These are armored agnathans in which the head is covered by a large bony shield and the body by large scales. They are exemplified by the genus *Cephalaspis* (figure 1H), several species of which are known from the Lower Devonian of Utah. The headshields are triangular in outline and bear dorsally directed orbits and a nasohypophysial opening. In addition, dorsal and lateral sensory fields are present. They are thought to have been bottom-dwelling, detritus-feeding animals, similar in lifestyle and appearance to the modern catfish *Plecostomus*.

Heterostraci

These agnathans had external armor consisting of a number of bony plates, usually median dorsal and ventral plates, and a varying number of paired lateral plates including an orbital, branchial, and cornual sequence in some cases, as well as smaller plates around the mouth and eyes. The external surface of the bone is ornamented with complex ridge patterns, and these are also seen on the scales that cover the posterior part of the body. These animals probably inhabited a variety of benthonic habitats as their lack of fins and restrictive armor would have made them poor swimmers.

In Utah, the heterostracans are represented by cyathaspidids such as *Allocryptaspis* (figure 1D) in which the armor is relatively simple, and pteraspidids (figure 1E) such as *Oreaspis*, in which it is more complex. An additional group is represented by *Cardipeltis* (figure 1G), a genus of uncertain affinity in which the armor is ornamented by a complex ridge pattern of distinctive appearance. The thelodonts, a group in which the armor is composed of small scale-like elements, is also known from the Lower Devonian. These may be of particular importance in the future as, in Utah and elsewhere, they become used more widely in correlation schemes.

Gnathostomata

Chondrichthyes

These include all sharks and rays. However, none have been reported from the Devonian of Utah as yet although their fossil record extends back into at least the Silurian elsewhere.

Acanthodii

These were primitive jawed vertebrates in which the fins were preceded by fin-spines which served a protective function (figure 1A). They were also covered by small bony scales that had swollen bases. Although uncommon as articulated individuals, they are very abundant as microfossils and the scales, which exhibit a variety of morphologies, are being used more frequently in biostratigraphy as more is learned about their ranges.

Placodermi

These early gnathostomes were characterised by having a bony headshield and body armor that were articulated at a neck joint. They are generally represented by isolated plates in Devonian sequences, although articulated individuals do occur. Several different groups of placoderms are recognised. The most important is the Arthrodira, which accounts for almost 75 percent of all placoderms. Actinolepid arthrodires (figure 1C), which are early members of the group, are fairly common in the Lower Devonian of Utah, where *Simblaspis, Aethaspis,* and *Bryantolepis*, are recognised. More advanced genera are known from the Middle Devonian. Arthrodires were mostly active pelagic predators. The Antiarcha are the next most numerous group of placoderms and are represented by *Asterolepis* in the Middle and Upper Devonian of Utah (figure 1F). These benthonic detritus feeders are very distinctive, as the pectoral fins have been replaced by limb-like appendages.

Osteichthyes

Bony fishes represent the largest living group of vertebrates. Although they originated in the Silurian they had already divided into a number of distinct lineages by the Early Devonian. Of these the most important is the Actinopterygii, or ray-finned fishes, which are by far the most widespread and numerous group of modern fish. However, actinopterygians have been reported only from the Upper Devonian of Utah.

The second main lineage is the Sarcopterygii, or lobe-finned fishes, which are rare now although they were much more common during the Devonian. They include the Dipnoi, or lungfish, as well as the rhipidistians, a group of predatory fish represented in Utah by the Osteolepiformes. All sarcopterygians are characterised by the presence of the dermal tissue cosmine which forms a shiny layer over the external bones and scales.

Actinopterygii

These ray-finned fishes are primitively fusiform in shape, and have anteriorly positioned orbits and large mouths. Characteristically they have thick, rhombic scales that overlap the surrounding scales and articulate with them by means of a dorsal peg fitting into a socket

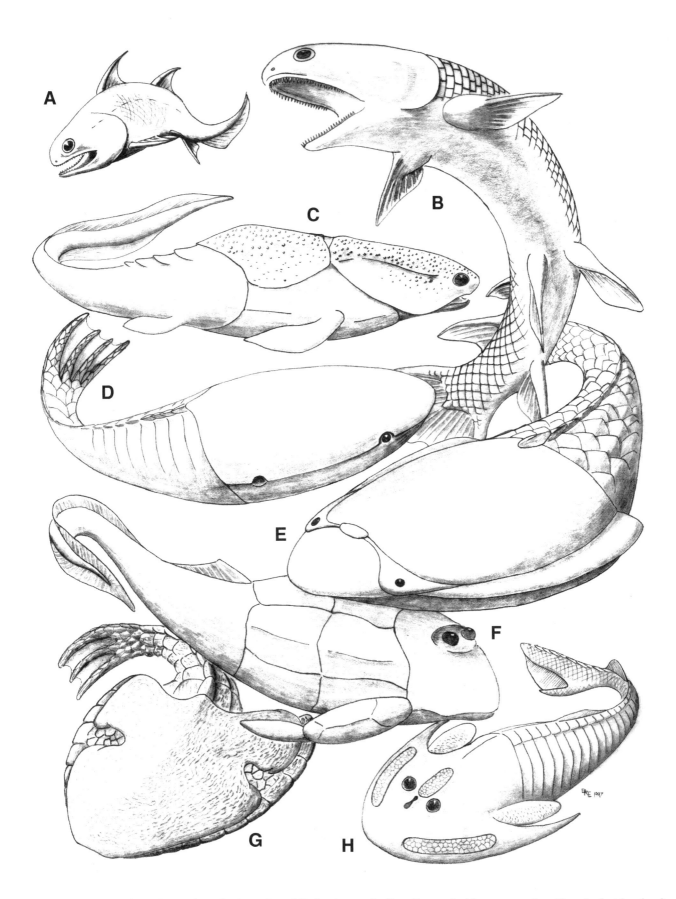

Figure 1. *Reconstructions of vertebrates from the Devonian of Utah. A, acanthodian; B, osteolepid sarcopterygian; C, actinolepid arthrodire; D, cyathaspidid heterostracan; E, pteraspidid heterostracan; F, antiarch placoderm; G, cardipeltid heterostracan; H, cephalaspid osteostracan. All drawn to the same scale, the cyathaspidid is approximately 20 cm long.*

in the scale above. They first occur in the late Silurian, and become more common through the Devonian. The only indication of their presence is in the Upper Devonian of Utah from drill cores containing fragments of the paleoniscid actinopterygian *Rhadinichthys*.

Sarcopterygii

This group includes the lungfish, which are characterised by the presence of large, ridged tooth-plates in the upper and lower jaws. These are modified in different species to provide varied feeding mechanisms, from crushing to suctorial and tritoral. Although they were marine in the Early Devonian they invaded freshwater habitats in the Middle Devonian. The genera *Uranolophus* and *Dipterus* are known from the Lower Devonian in Utah, and remains are also known from the Middle Devonian.

Osteolepiformes have also been reported from the Middle Devonian of Utah. These lobe-finned predatory fishes originated in the Middle Devonian and have thick, rhombic, cosmine-covered scales (figure 1B). They were slender and elongated, lived in shallow waters, and probably employed a lie-in-wait method of predation.

STRATIGRAPHY AND SEDIMENTOLOGY

Introduction

Devonian rocks in Utah generally represent platform deposition, with associated transitional environments (deltaic, estuarine and tidal-flat). Three main factors controlled sedimentation: sea level; crustal interactions (tectonics); and geography. Overall, the sea level rose steadily during the Devonian until the middle of the Late Devonian when the transgression reached its maximum extent and began to regress (Johnson and others, 1985). These general trends were punctuated by numerous short-term fluctuations, which often had dramatic effects on the low-relief platform. Additionally, tectonism played an important role in shaping the distribution of sediments, as well as influencing subsidence, which allowed for the great accumulation of Devonian strata. By the close of the Devonian, tectonism associated with the Antler Orogeny dominated sediment distributions. Finally, geographic features of the Devonian coastline contributed to climatic and ecological conditions and, therefore, sediment distribution.

Utah was positioned at a southern subtropical latitude and protected from prevailing ocean currents by a large emergent platform in what is now western Arizona (figure 2). As a result, much of Devonian deposition in

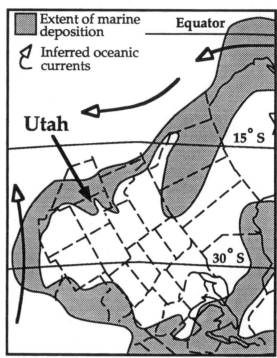

Figure 2. *Generalized paleogeography of western North America during the Early and Middle Devonian (modified from Witzke and Heckel, 1988).*

Utah occurred in a geographically restricted setting, isolated from open-marine waters. Additional features such as natural barriers along the edge of the carbonate platform and coastal prominences also restricted circulation.

Early Devonian

Deposition of Lower Devonian strata in Utah was mainly controlled by sea-level fluctuations (eustasy), and is represented by the Sevy Dolomite in southwestern Utah, and the Card and lower Grassy Flat members of the Water Canyon Formation in northern Utah (figure 3A). The Sevy and lower Card were deposited in response to transgressing seas and are dominated by laminated, non-laminated, and fenestral dolomicrites, which represent peritidal deposition on a restricted and broad carbonate tidal flat.

The Sevy Dolomite is widespread in Nevada and, as originally described by Osmond (1954), includes an upper Sandy Member that has yielded vertebrates (Ilyes and Elliott, 1994). Smith (1989) evaluated the Sevy in eastern Nevada near the Utah border, and concluded that the sands represented tidal or fluvial channels within a tidal-flat environment. Johnson and Sandberg (1977) recognised a regressive interval capping the dolomicrite portion of the Sevy and considered the Sandy Member to represent transgressive sands, equivalent to the Oxyoke Canyon Formation of east-central Nevada. Transgression at the end of the Lower Devonian spread the verte-

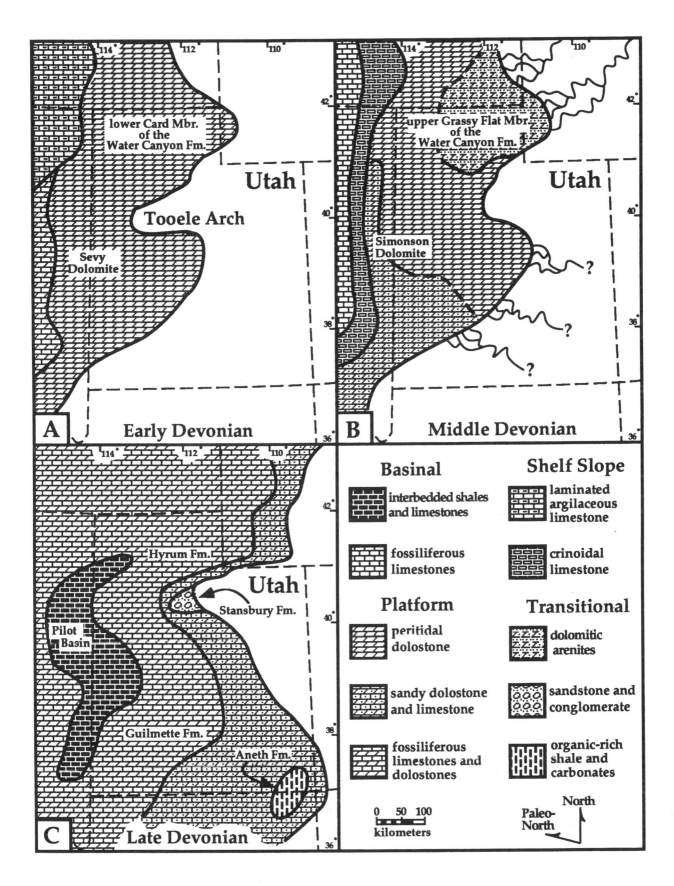

Figure 3. *Generalized lithofacies distribution during the Devonian. A, Early Devonian; B, Middle Devonian; C, Late Devonian. Facies distributions indicate general transgression throughout the Devonian and the approach of the Antler Orogeny during the Middle and Upper Devonian (modified from Johnson and Sandberg, 1977; Sandberg and Poole, 1977; Johnson and others, 1988; and Sandberg and others, 1988).*

brate-bearing sands eastward into Utah.

A vertebrate fauna was initially reported from the Sevy Formation in the Pahvant Range of west-central Utah by Davis (1983). Additional work on this locality has demonstrated the presence of a typical Early Devonian fauna that includes some of the same vertebrates known from the Sevy in Nevada, and from Death Valley, California (figure 4E) (Elliott and Johnson, 1997). Of particular importance is the abundance of thelodonts which may be of value in correlation once their distribution in western North America is better understood (Elliott, unpublished information).

The best and most complete record of Early Devonian vertebrates in Utah comes from the Water Canyon Formation, which is widespread in northern Utah and extends into Idaho. It was named by Williams (1948) for a sequence of carbonates lying between the Silurian Laketown Dolomite and the Middle Devonian Jefferson Formation. Subsequently, it was divided into a lower Card Member and an upper Grassy Flat Member (Williams and Taylor, 1964). Current work (Elliott and Johnson, 1997) indicates that the Card Member and the lower part of the Grassy Flat Member are Early Devonian in age. The lower part of the Card Member may record the same transgressive-regressive pulse as is seen in the dolomicrite portion of the Sevy Dolomite. The upper Card and lower Grassy Flat Members would then be equivalent to the transgressing sands associated with the upper Sandy Member of the Sevy Dolomite (equivalent to the Oxyoke Canyon sandstones). The upper Card Member coarsens upward from silty and sandy dolomicrites into dolomitic and vertebrate-bearing, dolomicritic, quartz arenites of the lower Grassy Flat Member. The arenites of the lower Grassy Flat are interpreted as tidally influenced distributary channels, associated with a prograding delta or estuary, within a restricted embayment (Reed, 1997).

The vertebrates come from the lower Grassy Flat Member, and were described first by Branson and Mehl in 1931, following reports by Cooley (1928), Branson (1929), and Branson and Mehl (1930). However, the major work was carried out by R. H. Denison, who collected in the Bear River Range of northern Utah during the late 1940s and early 1950s. He recognised the presence of an extensive Early Devonian fauna and reported and described it in a series of papers. The fauna includes representatives of the Osteostraci (Denison, 1952), represented by three species of *Cephalaspis*: *C. wyomingensis*, *C. utahensis* (figure 4A), and *C. brevirostris*. The heterostracans (Denison, 1953), include the enigmatic heterostracan *Cardipeltis wallacii* (figure 4B), and the cyathaspidid *Allocryptaspis utahensis*, together with sev-

eral species of the pteraspidids *Cosmaspis*, and *Oreaspis*. To this list Denison (1967) added *Protaspis errolli*, and recent work has added the pteraspidid *Clydonaspis faberensis* (Elliott, 1994), which was originally described by Denison (1953) as a member of an unknown heterostracan family, and *Blieckaspis priscillae* (Elliott and Ilyes, 1996a), originally attributed to *Protaspis* by Denison (1953). Undescribed material represents a new species of *Allocryptaspis* (figure 4D), together with at least four new cyathaspidid species (figure 4C) (Elliott, unpublished information), and nikoliviid thelodonts (J. Evans, verbal communication, 1996).

Gnathostomes are represented by the actinolepid arthrodires *Simblaspis cachensis*, *Aethaspis major*, and *A. utahensis* (Denison, 1958). Denison (1958) also described fragmentary material of *Bryantolepis*, and new material shows that this clearly represents a new species (figures 4F and 4G) (Johnson, unpublished information). Acanthodians are numerous, both as spines that have been attributed to *Onchus*, and scales that are as yet unidentified. Sarcopterygians are represented by fragmentary material of the lungfish *Uranolophus* and *Dipterus* (Denison, 1968a).

Middle Devonian

Most of Middle Devonian sedimentation was again influenced by eustatic events. By the close of the Middle Devonian, tectonic influences had profound effects on deposition. The middle and upper parts of the Grassy Flat Member of the Water Canyon Formation contain alternating dolomicrite and quartz arenites, with common vertebrate remains. The crudely cyclic strata may represent transgressive and regressive pulses or, alternatively, they may represent migrating distributary channels and interdistributary basins, within a restricted embayment (figure 3B). The top of the Grassy Flat Member, and the Water Canyon Formation as a whole, is capped by a thick intraformational breccia that is interpreted as tectonically induced karst or slumping. A similar, and potentially equivalent breccia, was described by Osmond (1954) within the Simonson Dolomite, which follows the Sevy Dolomite in Nevada and Utah. Tectonism responsible for the brecciation is interpreted as an early Antler orogenic signature (Reed, 1995, 1997). Brecciation may also be associated with a pronounced regression during the late Middle Devonian (Johnson and others, 1988).

Few vertebrates have been reported from the Middle Devonian part of the Water Canyon Formation. Ørvig (1961) described the pteraspidid *Psephaspis williamsi* from the upper Grassy Flat Member, and noted the presence of arthrodires, antiarchs, and sarcopterygians in his collection; however, these latter have never been de-

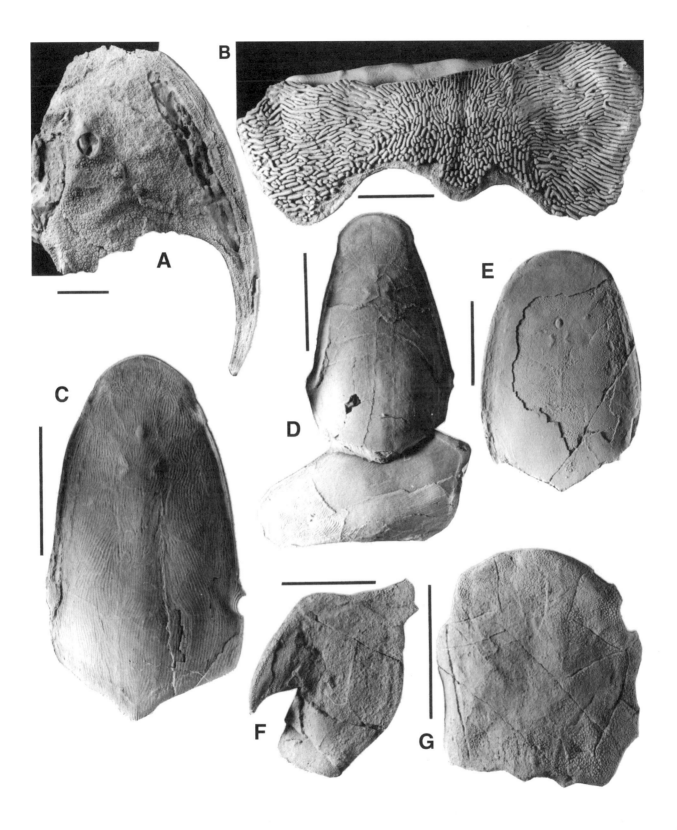

Figure 4. *Representative vertebrates from the Lower Devonian of Utah. Lower Grassy Flat Member of the Water Canyon Formation: A,* Cephalaspis utahensis, *dorsal view of headshield; B,* Cardipeltis wallacii, *posterior part of median dorsal plate; C, undescribed cyathaspidid, dorsal shield; D,* Allocryptaspis *(undescribed species), dorsal and ventral shields ; F and G,* Bryantolepis *(undescribed species), anterior ventrolateral plate and skull roof. Sevy Dolomite: E, undescribed cyathaspidid, dorsal shield. Scale bars, 2 cm. (All specimens will be deposited in the Field Museum of Natural History, Chicago, following description.)*

scribed. Denison (1968b) also included new material of *Psephaspis* from the Water Canyon Formation in his redescription of the genus. An *Asterolepis* anterior dorsolateral plate (figure 5B), collected by C. A. Sandberg from the upper Grassy Flat Member at Logan Canyon, verifies the presence of antiarchs, while our discovery of articulated osteolepids in the same area shows that sarcopterygians are indeed present (figure 5A).

Figure 5. *Representative vertebrates from the Middle Devonian of Utah. Upper Grassy Flat Member of the Water Canyon Formation: A, undescribed osteolepid; B, Asterolepis sp., anterior dorsolateral plate. Scale bars, 2 cm. (All specimens will be deposited in the Field Museum of Natural History, Chicago, following description.)*

Late Devonian

Tectonic influences are obscured by continued carbonate platform development during the late Middle and early Late Devonian. The Guilmette and Hyrum formations, which contain some vertebrate remains, represent shallow, subtidal platform limestones with some dissolution breccias and evaporite beds indicating subaerial exposure (Johnson and others, 1988). The Bay State barrier in eastern Nevada likely provided the restriction needed during regressive events to aid in the formation of platform evaporites and karst.

Central-western Utah and eastern Nevada record the deepest portions of the Antler foreland basin (figure 3C). The Pilot Basin contains deep-water turbidites of interbedded black limestones and shales (Sandberg and others, 1988). To the east, platform carbonates of the Guilmette Formation flank the basin, and provided a likely source of turbiditic sediments.

The Upper Devonian of central and southeastern Utah is characterised by mixed peritidal to supratidal siliciclastic and carbonate rocks, and local coarse conglomerates (Sandberg and Poole, 1977). The distribution of the former is mainly interpretative based on subsurface logs of the estuarine to lagoonal, vertebrate-bearing, Aneth Formation in the Paradox basin (Four Corners area) (Sandberg and others, 1988). The latter refers to the conglomerates of the Stansbury Formation in central Utah, which straddles the Tooele Arch, and represents intense local uplift. Uplift of the arch may have been a tectonic response to the further encroachment of the Antler orogenic belt. The Stansbury uplift may be the source of shallow subtidal sands found to the north and south of the Tooele Arch (Sandberg and others, 1988). Vertebrates have been reported from the Aneth Formation by Knight and Cooper (1955), who note that cores from the type well yielded fragments of the antiarch *Bothriolepis coloradensis*, the actinopterygian *Rhadinichthys devonicus*, and the rhipidistian *Holoptychius giganteus*.

Uppermost Devonian rocks in Utah record the further development of the Pilot Basin and the widespread distribution of platform carbonates, again in response to tectonism and eustacy. In the north, the Beirdneau and Leatham formations record a transition from tidal flats to basinal shales (Sandberg and others, 1988). The Pinyon Peak Limestone is distributed from central to southwestern Utah and is interpreted as peritidal to subtidal carbonate sedimentation. The Elbert and Ouray formations record a similar progression in the southeastern portions of Utah (Sandberg and others, 1988). Although *Bothriolepis coloradensis*, *Holoptychius giganteus*, and *Dipterus mordax* have been reported from the Elbert and Parting formations in Colorado (Denison, 1951), there are no reported vertebrate occurrences from the same formations in Utah.

BIOSTRATIGRAPHY

Introduction

The vertebrate-bearing rocks in the Devonian of Utah were deposited mostly in marginal marine or nonmarine environments, and generally lack age-diagnostic invertebrates. Hence the vertebrates have been pressed into service as biostratigraphic indicators. Although they have been used widely in the past to date non-marine rocks of Old Red Sandstone facies (see Long, 1993 and references therein), they are not ideal organisms for the task for a number of reasons. Good index fossils should be widespread and represent short-lived taxa. From this point of view the Devonian vertebrates of Utah are too endemic to allow correlation across more than local areas, as they are distinct to at least generic level from the Devonian vertebrates that have been studied in the Canadian Arctic, Spitsbergen and western Europe. Even at a local level some of the groups are more valuable than others, and it appears that the cyathaspidids may be most useful locally, while thelodonts may be the key to wider stratigraphic correlation. The time ranges of all these groups are insufficiently known, although work in progress to document their distribution should slowly improve this picture.

A good index fossil also should be easy to identify. This implies both that descriptive work has been carried out and that there is a sound taxonomic basis for the identification. Unfortunately, Devonian vertebrates in the western United States have been neglected since the work by Denison in the 1950s to 1970s, and there is, therefore, a considerable backlog of descriptive work that needs to be carried out before a clear biostratigraphic picture can be developed. Despite these problems initial attempts are being made to use vertebrates to date and correlate marginal and non-marine rocks of Early and Middle Devonian age in Utah and the western United States, with varying degrees of success (Elliott and Ilyes, 1996b; Elliott and Johnson, 1997).

Lower Devonian

Vertebrates are best known from the Lower Devonian of Utah, and it is at this level that correlation and dating have been most successful. Current studies have successfully linked the Water Canyon Formation of Utah with the Lost Burro Formation of California, the Sevy Formation of Nevada, and the Beartooth Butte Formation of Wyoming (Elliott and Ilyes, 1996b; Elliott and Johnson, 1997).

The Water Canyon Formation contains an extensive fauna documented chiefly by Denison (see references in the Introduction to this paper), which comes almost entirely from the lower part of the Grassy Flat Member. The provenance of the material was unclear for some time due to misunderstandings about the stratigraphic levels from which it was collected (Elliott and Ilyes, 1996b), but this has now been resolved (Elliott and Johnson, 1997). The vertebrates show some similarities with those from the Beartooth Butte Formation of Beartooth Butte, which has been dated as mid-late Emsian based on

spore determinations (Tanner, 1983). In particular *Cephalaspis wyomingensis* and *Cardipeltis wallacii* are found at both localities, together with different species of *Oreaspis, Allocryptaspis*, and *Bryantolepis* (figure 6). However, an unresolved problem is the relationship of the Grassy Flat fauna to the fauna of the Cottonwood Canyon locality of the Beartooth Butte Formation, which is late Lochkovian to early Pragian based on spore determinations (Tanner, 1983). These two faunas also show similarities at the generic level with the heterostracans *Cosmaspis* and *Cardipeltis,* and the placoderms *Simblaspis* and *Aethaspis* in common (figure 6). At present a correlation with the Beartooth Butte locality is preferred owing to the presence of the same species; however, the accumulation of more data as further descriptive work is carried out may require a reappraisal.

Correlation between the Grassy Flat Member of the Water Canyon Formation and the Sevy Dolomite is based on the presence of the same undescribed cyatha-spidid in the Grassy Flat, in the Sandy Member of the Sevy Dolomite in the Pahvant Range, Utah, and in the Northern Egan Range, Nevada (figure 6). In addition the pteraspidid *Pirumaspis* occurs both in Nevada and in the Grassy Flat Member.

In the Trail Canyon area of the Panamint Range, Death Valley, a large channel contains rocks that appear to be equivalent to the lower part of the Lippincott Member of the Lost Burro Formation (Elliott and Ilyes, 1996a). This seems to be equivalent to the "cherty argillaceous unit" (Johnson and others, 1988), which has been given a late Emsian age based on age-diagnostic conodonts. Although many of the vertebrates from the Lippincott Member are yet to be described, one of the pteraspidids, *Blieckaspis priscillae*, occurs also in the Grassy Flat Member of the Water Canyon Formation. It is also clear from personal observation that several of the cyathaspidids in this fauna are the same as those from the Sevy Dolomite in Utah and Nevada.

Nikoliviid thelodonts are now recognised from all of these formations except the Beartooth Butte (Elliott, unpublished information). However, a considerable amount of descriptive work remains to be done before their value to biostratigraphy can be fully realized.

Middle Devonian

Middle Devonian vertebrates appear to be much more cosmopolitan than those in the Early Devonian, which suggests that it should be possible to develop effective correlation schemes based on them, once more work on their distribution has been carried out.

The upper part of the Grassy Flat Member of the

	Lost Burro Formation Lippincott Member Death Valley	Sevy Dolomite Sandy Member		Water Canyon Formation Lower Grassy Flat Member Bear River Range	Beartooth Butte Formation	
		Pahvant Range	Northern Egan Range		Beartooth Butte	Cottonwood Canyon
Osteostraci	Cephalaspis sp. _ _ _	Cephalaspis sp. _ _ _ _	Cephalaspis sp. _ _ _ _	Cephalaspis? wyomingensis ...... Cephalaspis utahensis Cephalaspis brevirostris	Cephalaspis wyomingensis _	_ Cephalaspis sp.
Heterostraci Pteraspididae		New genus and species A & B	Tuberculaspis elyensis Lamiaspis longiripa	Oreaspis dunklei _ _ _ _ Oreaspis williamsi Oreaspis? tenuistriata Oreaspis sp.	Oreaspis ampla Protaspis bucheri _ _ _ _ Protaspis dorfi Cyrtaspidichthys ovata Cyrtaspidichthys sculpta	Protaspis mcgrewi Protaspis brevispina
	Blieckaspis priscillae .... Panamintaspis snowi		Pirumaspis lancasteri _ _	Blieckaspis priscillae Clydonaspis faberensis Pirumaspis sp. Cosmaspis sp. _ _ _ _ _		Cosmaspis transversa Lampraspis tuberculata
Cardipeltidae	Cardipeltis wallacii			Cardipeltis wallacii ......:........ Cardipeltis wallacii _ _ _		Cardipeltis richardsoni Cardipeltis bryanti
Cyathaspididae	New genus and species B .... New genus and species C	New genus and species B ..... New genus and species C	Ctenaspis sp. New genus and species A New genus and species B New genus and species C	Allocryptaspis utahensis _ Allocryptaspis n. sp.	Allocryptaspis flabelliformis Allocryptaspis ellipticus	
Thelodonti	Nikoliviids _ _ _ _	Nikoliviids _ _ _ _ _ _ _ _		_ Nikoliviids Canonia? sp.		
Placodermi Actinolepidae	New genus and species_	_ New genus and species _	_ New genus and species	Simblaspis cachensis _ _ _ _ _ Aethaspis major_ _ _ _ _ _ _ Aethaspis utahensis Bryantolepis sp. _ _ _ _	Anarthraspis montana Anarthraspis chamberlini Bryantolepis brachycephala Bryantolepis cristata	Simblaspis sp. Aethaspis sp.
Acanthodii	Onchus sp._ _ _ _ _	Cheiracanthoides sp.	_ Onchus sp. _ _ _ _	Onchus sp. _ _ _ _	_ Onchus sp.	
Dipnoi				Uranolophus sp.- _ _ _ _ Dipterus sp. _	-Uranolophus wyomingensis ...... Uranolophus wyomingensis	

generic similarity _ _ _   specific similarity ....

Figure 6. *Vertebrate faunal lists from the Lower Devonian of the western United States (modified from Elliott and Ilyes, 1996b).*

Water Canyon Formation is now considered to be Middle Devonian based on the vertebrates present. Although the fauna is not very extensive, comprising only *Asterolepis*, osteolepids, and the pteraspidid *Psephaspis*, similar faunas are present in the Lemhi Range of Idaho and the Yahatinda Formation of Alberta, as well as the Denay Limestone and Mountain Springs Formation of Nevada (figure 7).

The age determination of the Yahatinda Formation, which contains a vertebrate fauna similar to that in the upper Grassy Flat (Elliott, unpublished information), is based on spore identifications by McGregor (1963, 1964) which point to a late Givetian to very early Frasnian age; however, the overlying rocks contain conodonts of latest Givetian age (Geldsetzer and Mallamo,1991; Uyeno,1991) constraining the date to the late Givetian. The Red Hill and Roberts Mountains localities (figure 7) also support this age date as both vertebrate faunas are associated with conodonts of late Givetian age (Morgan, 1980; Ziegler and others, 1976). The upper part of the Water Canyon Formation is constrained in age by the overlying Hyrum and Jefferson formations which are dated as middle to late Givetian based on their invertebrate fauna (Sandberg and others, 1988). Thus the upper part of the Grassy Flat Member must be Eitelian or earliest Givetian in age.

Upper Devonian

Late Devonian vertebrates have been recorded only

from the Aneth Formation in southeastern Utah. It is entirely subsurface, and Knight and Cooper (1955) reported finding fragments of *Bothriolepis coloradensis*, *Rhadinichthys devonicus*, and *Holoptychius giganteus* in cores from the type well. A fauna that also includes *B. coloradensis* and *Rhadinichthys* has been reported by Sandberg (1963) from the Souris River Formation, at Cottonwood Canyon in northern Wyoming. The spores from this locality indicate a late Givetian or possibly earliest Frasnian age (D. C. McGregor, written communication, 1992). *Bothriolepis coloradensis* is also recorded from the Parting and Elbert formations of Colorado (Denison, 1951, and references therein) and also extends as far south as Arizona, where it occurs in the Temple Butte Formation of the Grand Canyon (Denison, 1951). These occurrences are considered to be Famennian in age (Sandberg and others, 1988), and suggest that *B. coloradensis* is widespread temporally as well as spatially.

As the Parting and Elbert formations are also present in Utah, it is likely that they contain identifiable vertebrates, and that a vertebrate-based correlation scheme could be developed. However, a considerable amount of collecting and identification remains to be done before that could be accomplished.

CONCLUSIONS

Devonian vertebrates are widespread in Utah, initial-

	Upper Grassy Flat Member Water Canyon Fm. N. Utah	Spring Mt. Channel Lemhi Range Idaho	Denay Lst. Red Hill Nevada	Denay Lst. Roberts Mts. Nevada	Yahatinda Fm. Alberta Canada	Mountain Springs Fm. Virgin Mts. Nevada
Heterostraci Pteraspididae	*Psephaspis williamsi* "*Psephaspis*" n.sp.	*Psephaspis idahoensis* "*Psephaspis*" n.sp.			"*Psephaspis*" 2 spp.	
Placodermi Arthrodira		*Holonema haiti*		*Holonema* Pachyosteina Dinichthyidae *Coccosteus*	*Holonema*	*Holonema*
Antiarcha	*Asterolepis*	*Asterolepis*	*Asterolepis*	*Asterolepis*	*Asterolepis*	*Asterolepis*
Ptyctodontida				*Ptyctodus* *Rhynchodus*		
Petalichthyida				*Macropetalichthys*		
Osteichthyes Actinopterygii Sarcopterygii			*Cheirolepis*	*Cheirolepis*		
Osteolepiformes Porolepiformes Onychodontida Dipnoi Acanthodii	Osteolepiform dipnoan		*Eusthenopteron* ?*Glyptolepis* dipnoan *Persacanthus simpsonensis*	*Onychodus* *Persacanthus*	?*Eusthenopteron*	Osteolepiform
Chondrichthyes Holocephali incertae sedis		Holocephali?		*Synthetodus*? Petalodontida		

Figure 7. *Vertebrate faunal lists from the Middle Devonian of the western United States (modified from Elliott and Johnson, 1997).*

ly in nearshore marine and non-marine environments and subsequently in the marine environments. Although they are best-known from the Lower Devonian at present, this occurrence is mostly an artifact of the areas in which study has been concentrated. As work continues both Middle and Late Devonian faunas should become more extensively recognized. The vertebrates of the Early Devonian, and to a lesser extent the Middle Devonian, are already showing their usefulness in correlation and dating of nearshore and non-marine environments, and it is expected that their value will increase as they become better known and understanding of their ranges improves.

ACKNOWLEDGMENTS

We would like to thank the editor of this volume, Dave Gillette, for giving us the opportunity to summarize the current state of our knowledge on the Devonian vertebrates of Utah, and Charles Sandberg and Mark Wilson for their helpful reviews. Part of this work was carried out with the help of financial support from the National Geographic Society and from the Organized Research program of Northern Arizona University to DKE, and from G.S.A. and Sigma Xi to RCR, and we would like to express our gratitude to those bodies.

REFERENCES

Branson, E. B., 1929, New localities for Devonian fishes: Geological Society of America Bulletin, v. 40, p. 245.

Branson, E. B., and Mehl, M. G., 1930, Primitive fishes from the Devonian of Utah and Wyoming: Geological Society of America Bulletin, v. 41, p.180.

1931, Fishes of the Jefferson Formation of Utah: Journal of Geology, v. 39, p. 509-531.

Bryant, W. L., 1932, Lower Devonian fishes of Beartooth Butte, Wyoming: Proceedings of the American Philosophical Society, v. 17, p. 225-254.

—1933, The fish fauna of Beartooth Butte, Wyoming. Part I-The Heterostraci and Osteostraci: Proceedings of the American Philosophical Society, v. 72, p. 285-314.

—1934, The fish fauna of Beartooth Butte, Wyoming-Parts II and III: Proceedings of the American Philosophical Society, v. 73, p. 127-167.

—1935, *Cryptaspis* and other Devonian fossil fish from Beartooth Butte, Wyoming: Proceedings of the American Philosophical Society, v. 75, p. 111-141.

Cooley, I. L., 1928, The Devonian of the Bear River Range, Utah: Logan, Utah State Agricultural College, M.S. thesis, 23 p.

Davis, R. L., 1983, Geology of the Dog Valley-Red Ridge Area, Southern Pavant Mountains, Millard County, Utah: Brigham Young University Geology Studies, v. 30(1), p. 19-36.

Denison, R. H., 1951, Late Devonian fresh-water fishes from the western United States: Fieldiana-Geology, v. 11(5), p. 221-261.

—1952, Early Devonian Fishes from Utah-Part I. Osteostraci: Fieldiana-Geology, v. 11(6), p. 265-287.

—1953, Early Devonian Fishes from Utah-Part II. Heterostraci: Fieldiana-Geology, v. 11(7), p. 291-355.

—1958, Early Devonian Fishes from Utah-Part III. Arthrodira: Fieldiana-Geology, v. 11(9), p. 461-551.

—1966, *Cardipeltis*, an Early Devonian Agnathan of the Order Heterostraci: Fieldiana-Geology, v. 16(4), p. 89-116.

—1967, A new *Protaspis* from the Devonian of Utah, with notes on the classification of Pteraspididae: Journal of the Linnean Society of London-Zoology, v. 47(311), p. 31-37.

—1968a, Early Devonian lungfishes from Wyoming, Utah, and Idaho: Fieldiana-Geology, v. 17(4), p. 353-413.

—1968b, Middle Devonian fishes from the Lemhi Range of Idaho: Fieldiana-Geology, v. 16(10), p. 260-288.

—1970, Revised classification of the Pteraspididae with description of new forms from Wyoming: Fieldiana-Geology, v. 20(1), p. 1-41.

Elliott, D. K., 1994, A new pteraspidid (Agnatha-Heterostraci) from the Lower Devonian Water Canyon Formation of Utah: Journal of Paleontology, v. 68(1), p. 176-179.

Elliott, D. K., and Ilyes, R. R., 1996a, New Early Devonian pteraspidids (Agnatha, Heterostraci) from Death Valley National Monument, southeastern California: Journal of Paleontology, v. 70(1), p. 152-161.

—1996b, Lower Devonian vertebrate biostratigraphy of the western United States: Modern Geology, v. 20, p. 253-262.

Elliott, D. K., and Johnson, H. G., 1997, Use of vertebrates to solve biostratigraphic problems: Examples from the Lower and Middle Devonian of western North America, *in* Klapper, Gilbert, Murphy, M. A., and Talent, J. A., editors, Geological Society of America Special Paper 321, Paleozoic sequence stratigraphy, biostratigraphy, and biogeography - studies in honor of J. Granville ("Jess") Johnson, p, 179-188.

Geldsetzer, H. H. J., and Mallamo, M. P., 1991, The Devonian of the southern Rocky Mountains - the Canmore area, *in* Smith, P. L., editor, A field guide to the paleontology of southwestern Canada - the first Canadian paleontology conference: Vancouver, University of British Columbia, p. 83-102.

Ilyes, R. R., and Elliott, D. K., 1994, New Early Devonian pteraspidids (Agnatha-Heterostraci) from east-central Nevada: Journal of Paleontology, v. 68, p. 878-892.

Johnson, J. G., and Sandberg, C. A., 1977, Lower and Middle Devonian continental-shelf rocks of the western United States, *in* Murphy, M. A., Berry, W. B. N., and Sandberg, C. A., editors, Western North America - Devonian: University of California Riverside, Campus Museum Contribution 4, p. 121-143.

Johnson, J. G., Klapper, Gilbert, and Sandberg, C. A., 1985, Devonian eustatic fluctuations in Euramerica: Geological Society of America Bulletin, v. 96(5), p. 567-587.

Johnson, J. G., Sandberg, C. A., and Poole, F. G., 1988, Early Devonian paleogeography of western United States, *in* McMillan, N. J., Embry, A. F., and Glass, D. J., editors, Devonian of the world, volume I - regional syntheses: Canadian Society of Petroleum Geologists, p. 161-182.

Knight, R. L., and Cooper, J. C., 1955, Suggested changes in the Devonian terminology of the Four Corners area, *in* Four Corners Geological Society Ist Annual Field Conference Guidebook, p. 56-58.

Long, J. A., 1993, Paleozoic vertebrate biostratigraphy and biogeography: Baltimore, The Johns Hopkins University Press, 369 p.

McGregor, D. C., 1963, Paleobotanical evidence for the age of basal Devonian strata at Ghost River, Alberta: Bulletin of Canadian Petroleum Geology, v. 11(3), p. 299-303.

—1964, Devonian miospores from the Ghost River Formation, Alberta: Geological Survey of Canada Bulletin, v. 109, p. 1-31.

Morgan, T. G., 1980, The Middle Devonian fish faunas of central Nevada: Berkeley, University of California, Ph.D. dissertation, 250 p.

Oaks, R. Q., James, W. C., Francis, G. C., and Schulingkamp, W. J. III, 1977, Summary of Middle Ordovician stratigraphy and tectonics, northern Utah, southern and central Idaho: Wyoming Geological Association Guidebook, v. 29, p. 101-118.

Ørvig, Tor, 1961, Notes on some early representatives of the Drepanaspida (Pteraspidomorphi, Heterostraci): Arkiv for Zoologi, v. 12(33), p.515-535.

Osmond, J. C., 1954, Dolomites in Silurian and Devonian of east-central Nevada: American Association of Petroleum Geologists Bulletin, v. 38(9), p. 1911-1956.

Reed, R. C., 1995, Early Paleozoic tectonic subsidence and coastal embayments of the western United States: Arizona-Nevada Academy of Sciences, Proceedings Supplement, v. 30, p. 38.

Reed, R.C., 1997, Stratigraphy and sedimentology of the Lower and Middle Devonain Water Canyon Formation, northern Utah. Unpublished MS thesis, Northern Arizona University, Flagstaff, 322 p.

Sandberg, C. A., 1963, Spirorbal limestone in the Souris River (?) Formation of Late Devonian age at Cottonwood Canyon, Bighorn Mountains, Wyoming: U. S. Geological Survey Professional Paper 475-C, article 63, p. C14-C16.

Sandberg, C. A., and Poole, F. G., 1977, Conodont biostratigraphy and depositional complexes of Upper Devonian cratonic-platform and continental-shelf rocks in the western United States, *in* Murphy, M. A., Berry, W. B. N., and Sandberg, C. A., editors, Western North America-Devonian: University of California Riverside, Campus Museum Contribution 4, p. 144-182.

Sandberg, C. A., Poole, F. G., and Johnson, J. G., 1988, Upper Devonian of western United States, *in* McMillan, D. J., Embry, A. F., and Glass, D. J., editors, Devonian of the world, volume I-regional syntheses: Canadian Society of Petroleum Geologists, p. 183-220.

Smith, C. D., 1989, Paleoenvironment of a new Lower Devonian vertebrate fauna, Sevy Dolomite, east-central Nevada: Flagstaff, Northern Arizona University, M.S. thesis, 176 p.

Tanner, William, 1983, A fossil flora from the Beartooth Butte Formation of northern Wyoming: Carbondale, Southern Illinois University, Ph. D. dissertation, 208 p.

Uyeno, T. T., 1991, Pre-Famennian Devonian conodont biostratigraphy of selected intervals in the Canadian Cordillera, *in* Orchard, M. J., and McCracken, A. D., editors, Ordovician to Triassic conodont paleontology of the Canadian Cordillera, Geological Survey of Canada Bulletin 417, p. 129-161.

Williams, J. S., 1948, Geology of the Paleozoic rocks, Logan Quadrangle, Utah: Geological Society of America Bulletin, v. 59, p. 1121-1164.

Williams, J. S., and Taylor, M. E., 1964, The Lower Devonian Water Canyon Formation of northern Utah: Contributions to Geology of the University of Wyoming, v. 3, p. 38-53.

Witzke, B. J., and Heckel, P. H., 1988, Paleoclimatic indicators and inferred Devonian paleolatitudes of Euramerica, *in* McMillan, N. J., Embry, A. F., and Glass, D. J., editors, Devonian of the world, volume I-regional syntheses: Canadian Society of Petroleum Geologists, p. 49-63.

Ziegler, Willi, Klapper, Gilbert, and Johnson, J. G., 1976, Redefinition and subdivision of the varcus Zone (conodonts, Middle-?Upper Devonian) in Europe and North America: Geologica et Palaeontologica, v. 10, p. 109-140.

LATE PALEOZOIC FISHES OF UTAH

Stuart S. Sumida
Department of Biology
California State University San Bernardino
5500 University Parkway
San Bernardino, California 92407
ssumida@mail.csusb.edu

Gavan M. Albright
Department of Biology
California State University San Bernardino
5500 University Parkway
San Bernardino, California 92407

Elizabeth A. Rega
Joint Science Department
The Claremont Colleges
925 North Mills Avenue
Claremont, California 91711
erega@jsd.claremont.edu

ABSTRACT

Only two fish taxa are known to be unique to Utah: the acanthodian *Utahacanthus guntheri* from the earliest Pennsylvanian age Manning Canyon Formation of central Utah, and the rhipdistian crossopterygian *Lohsania utahensis* from the (probably) late Pennsylvanian Halgaito Shale in southeastern San Juan County. The majority of the Late Paleozoic fish fauna from Utah are derived from sediments of the Halgaito Shale, a rock unit recently reassigned to the Late Pennsylvanian on the basis of invertebrate evidence. Elements of the Halgaito fauna include: two xenacanthid sharks, *Orthacanthus compressus* and *O. texensis*; at least one crossopterygian, *L. utahensis*, and possibly another, *Ectosteorhachis*; the lungfishes *Sagenodus* and *Gnathoriza*; many reports of palaeoniscoid scales and vertebral centra; and a platysomid phyllodont. Only isolated palaeoniscoid scales are known from definitively Lower Permian sediments in Utah. These elements conflict with the biostratigraphic assignments based on invertebrate markers. This conflict suggests that the complete fauna and flora found in sediments of these ages must be critically re-examined to provide an accurate age determination for many of the redbed localities of Utah.

INTRODUCTION

Much of the work on Late Paleozoic fishes of Utah has been indirectly associated with the search for terrestrial vertebrates. Many of the fish materials are incomplete, or have been recorded from deposits that might also produce tetrapods - depositional environments such as stream channel conglomerates or transitional facies between aquatic and terrestrial sediments. Not surprisingly, the diversity of known Late Pennsylvanian and Early Permian fishes in Utah is not high.

Geological Context

Most of the fossil fishes considered in this review have been recovered from sediments very close to the Permo-Pennsylvanian boundary of southeastern Utah. A clear understanding of the temporal assignments of these rock units is critical to an accurate picture of the distribution of Late Paleozoic fishes in the state. Thus, a brief review of the associated stratigraphy follows.

Redbed exposures in southeastern Utah have long been considered to be Early Permian sediments which lay uncomformably on limestones of the Pennsylvanian Honaker Trail Formation. Certain authors (Vaughn, 1962; Frede and others, 1993) regard the successive rock units as members of the larger Cutler Group or equivalent to the undifferentiated Cutler Formation. Others (for example, Baars, 1995) break this series of rocks into formally named formations, as adopted herein. A more complete discussion of the stratigraphic correlations of this area is presented by Sumida and others (this volume) in their discussion of Late Paleozoic amniotes. The most basal of these rock units, the Halgaito Shale, includes terrestrial to semi-terrestrial redbed deposits and stream

channel conglomerates. Most significant to
this review, it has yielded the majority of
fish fossils from southeastern Utah. The
Halgaito Shale is followed by the monumen-
tal deposits of the Cedar Mesa Sandstone, a
formation in which no fish fossils have been
found to date and whose paleoenvironmental
reconstruction is subject to a variety of interpretations as summarized below. Fish fossils
are found, though less frequently than in the
Halgaito, in the succeeding Organ Rock
Shale, a formation that likely signaled the
return of lowland or intertidal environments
(Baars, 1962, 1995).

The Halgaito Shale and the Organ Rock
Shale are redbeds, lithologically continuous
to the east with the undifferentiated Cutler
Formation. The intervening Cedar Mesa
Sandstone has been interpreted in a variety
of ways. Baars (1962) and Vaughn (1966)
felt that it is of a primarily shallow marine
origin. However, Stanesco and Campbell
(1989) suggested that it was deposited as a complex aeolian unit bordered to the east by fluvial environments and
the south by sabkha environments. Most recently, Baars
(1995) interpreted the Cedar Mesa as sands (possibly)
deposited in a coastal environment. Given the size and
geographic range of the formation, these hypotheses do
not need to be mutually exclusive. The interpretations of
coastal aeolian and sabkha environments might explain
why no fish fossils have been found in the Cedar Mesa to
date. The youngest of the named rock units in southeastern Utah is the DeChelly Sandstone. Conditions during
deposition of the DeChelly reflect a return to an aeolian
environment.

The more northerly marine carbonates of the Elephant Canyon Formation (= Rico Formation in Stanesco
and Campbell, 1989) are also important to an understanding of the redbed sediments of southeastern Utah.
Until recently, the Elephant Canyon was considered to be
Early Permian in age. However, interpretation of
fusulinids indicates a Late Pennsylvanian assignment for
the Elephant Canyon (Baars, 1991, 1995). The Elephant
Canyon interfingers southward with the earliest terrestrial
redbeds of the Halgaito Shale (Vaughn, 1967; Baars,
1962, 1995). If the Late Pennsylvanian assignment of
the Elephant Canyon is correct, then the Halgaito must
also be considered Late Pennsylvanian. These assignments effectively move the Pennsylvanian-Permian
boundary from the base of the Halgaito Shale to a position between the Halgaito Shale and overlying Cedar
Mesa Sandstone (figure 1). This is significant inasmuch

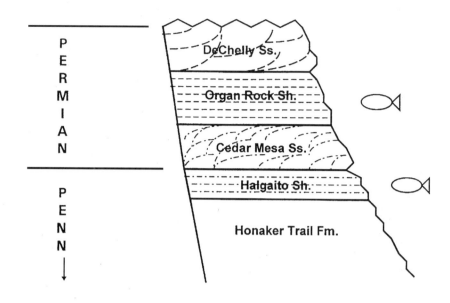

*Figure 1. Stratigraphic section showing named rock units known to produce fish fossils in
southeastern Utah. Scheme partially after Baars (1995).*

as the majority of the fossils discussed here are from
either the Halgaito Shale, or from transitional facies
between the marine beds of the Elephant Canyon and the
terrestrial beds of the Halgaito (tables 1 and 2). Thus,
the vast majority of fish fossils known from the Late
Paleozoic of southeastern Utah (table 1) may now actually be interpreted as Latest Pennsylvanian (Virgilian) in
age.

FISH FAUNA

The known fish fauna in southeastern Utah is summarized in table 1 and includes only a few taxa that are
unambiguously identifiable to the level of genus or
species. Although palaeoniscoid remains are common,
they are not represented by materials complete enough to
allow confident identification beyond the order
Palaeoniscoidea. However, acanthodian, chondrichthian,
crossopterygian, and dipnoan elements are somewhat
more diagnostic. The following discussion is organized
along the taxonomic scheme of Carroll (1988).

Acanthodii

The oldest known, and among the best characterized,
of Late Paleozoic fish from Utah is the acanthodian *Utahacanthus guntheri*. Unlike the majority of Late Paleozoic fish fossils from Utah, *Utahacanthus* is known only
from the earliest Pennsylvanian age Manning Canyon
Formation of the south side of the Traverse Range in

Table 1. Late Paleozoic fishes from Utah. Upper level classification is based primarily on the scheme of Carroll (1988). Institutional abbreviations: BYUVP, Brigham Young University Paleontological Collections; CMNH, Carnegie Museum of Natural History; CSUSB VP, California State University San Bernardino Vertebrate Paleontology; UCLA VP, University of California Los Angeles (some materials transferred and accessioned into collections of the Carnegie Museum of Natural History and The University of California); YPM, Yale Peabody Museum of Natural History.

Late Pennsylvanian

	Taxon	Rock Unit or Formation	Locality	Reference	Depository
Acanthodii	Utahacanthus guntheri	Manning Canyon Formation	Five miles west of Lehi	Schultze (1990)	BYUVP 10279
Chondrichthyes	Orthacanthus compressus	Halgaito Shale	Valley of the Gods	Vaughn (1962); Frede and others (1993)	CMNH
	O. compressus	Halgaito Shale	John's Canyon (i and ii)	Frede and others (1993)	CMNH
	Orthacanthus texensis	Halgaito Shale	Valley of the Gods (i)	Vaughn (1962); Frede and others (1993)	CMNH
	O. texensis	Halgaito Shale	John's Canyon (i and ii)	Frede and others (1993)	CMNH
	O. texensis	Halgaito Shale	Mexican Hat Rock (i and ii)	Vaughn (1962)	UCLA VP
	O. texensis	Halgaito Shale	Lisbon Valley	Vaughn (1965)	UCLA VP
	xenacanth	Halgaito equivalent of Cutler Formation	Lime Creek	This report	CMNH, CSUSB VP
	xenacanth	Halgaito Shale	Valley of the Gods (i, iii)	This report	CMNH, CSUSB VP
	xenacanth	Halgaito\Elephant Canyon transitional facies	Arch Canyon	Vaughn (1967)	UCLA VP
	xenacanth	Halgaito\Elephant Canyon transitional facies	Cane Creek Anticline	Vaughn (1967)	UCLA VP
	xenacanth	Halgaito\Elephant Canyon transitional facies	Indian Creek	Vaughn (1967)	UCLA VP
Crossopterygii	Lohsania utchensis (?)	Halgaito Shale	Valley of the Gods (ii, iii)	This report	CMNH, CSUSB VP, YPM 5701, 5702, 5703; UCLA VP 1688
	Lohsania utchensis	Halgaito Shale	John's Canyon (iii)	Thomson and Vaughn (1968)	UCLA VP 1620
	Ectosteorhachis (?) aff. E. nitidus	Halgaito Shale	Mexican Hat Rock (i)	Vaughn (1962)	
	Ectosteorhachis (?) aff. E. nitidus	Halgaito\Elephant Canyon transitional facies	Arch Canyon	Vaughn (1967)	UCLA VP 1681
	Ectosteorhachis (?)	Halgaito equivalent of Cutler Formation	Lisbon Valley	Vaughn (1966)	UCLA VP
Dipnoi	Sagenodus sp.	Halgaito Shale	Valley of the Gods (i)	Frede and others (1993)	CMNH
	Gnathoriza	Halgaito Shale	Snake Canyon	Vaughn (1966)	UCLA VP 1678
	Gnathoriza	Halgaito equivalent of Cutler Formation	Lisbon Valley	Vaughn (1966)	UCLA VP 1680
Actinopterygii	palaeoniscoid	Manning Canyon Formation	Five miles west of Lehi	Schultze (1990)	BYUVP
	palaeoniscoid	Halgaito Shale	Mexican Hat Rock (ii)	Vaughn (1962)	UCLA VP
	palaeoniscoid	Halgaito Shale	Valley of the Gods (i, iii)	This report	CMNH, CSUSB VP
	palaeoniscoid	Halgaito\Elephant Canyon transitional facies	Arch Canyon	Vaughn (1967)	UCLA VP
	palaeoniscoid	Halgaito\Elephant Canyon transitional facies	Cane Creek Anticline	Vaughn (1967)	UCLA VP
	palaeoniscoid	Elephant Canyon Formation	Comb Wash	Vaughn (1967)	UCLA VP
	palaeoniscoid	Halgaito\Elephant Canyon transitional facies	Indian Creek	Vaughn (1967)	UCLA VP
	palaeoniscoid	Elephant Canyon Formation	Green and Colorado Rivers confluence	Vaughn (1967)	UCLA VP
	palaeoniscoid	Elephant Canyon Formation	Peavine and Dark Canyons	Vaughn (1967)	UCLA VP
	palaeoniscoid	Halgaito equivalent of Cutler Formation	Lisbon Valley	Vaughn (1965)	UCLA VP
	phyllodont	Halgaito Shale	Valley of the Gods (i)	Frede and others (1993)	CMNH

Early Permian

	Taxon	Rock Unit or Formation	Locality	Reference	Depository
Chondrichthyes	xenacanth (?)	Organ Rock Shale	Red House Cliffs eastern face	This report	CSUSB VP
Actinopterygii	palaeoniscoid	Organ Rock Shale	Monument Pass	Vaughn (1964)	UCLA VP 1649

Table 2. *Section, township, and range (Salt Lake Base Line) data for localities yielding Late Paleozoic fish fossils in Utah.*

Locality	Section, Township, Range
Pennsylvanian	
Arch Canyon	NE1/4 sec. 21, T.37S., R.20E.
Cane Creek Anticline	between secs. 35 & 36, T.26S., R.20E.
Comb Wash	SE1/4 sec. 35, T.38S., R.20E.
Green and Colorado Rivers confluence	between secs. 9 &16, T.30S., R.19E.
Indian Creek	NE1/4 sec. 1, T.30S., R.20E.
John's Canyon (i)	NE1/4 NE1/4 sec. 19, T.40S., R.18E.
John's Canyon (ii)	NW1/4 NE1/4 sec. 18, T.40S., R.18E.
John's Canyon (iii)	NW1/4 NE1/4 sec. 34, T.40S., R.19E.
Lehi, five miles west	Sec. 9, T.5S., R.1W.
Lime Creek	NW1/4, sec. 29, T.41S., R.19E.
Lisbon Valley	SE1/4 SE1/4 sec. 20, T.30S., R.25E.
Mexican Hat Rock (i)	SE1/4 sec. 21, T.41S., R.19E.
Mexican Hat Rock (ii)	NW1/4 sec. 29, T.41S., R.19E.
Peavine and Dark Canyons	SW corner of T.34S., R.19E.
Snake Canyon	SW1/4 sec. 26, T.40 S., R.20E.
Valley of the Gods (i)	NE1/4 NW1/4 sec. 29, T.40S., R19E.
Valley of the Gods (ii)	SE1/4 sec. 27, T.40S., R.19E.
Valley of the Gods (iii)	NE1/4 SE1/4 sec. 24, T.40S., R.18E.
Permian	
Monument Pass	Sec. 20, T.43S., R.17E.
Red House Cliffs eastern face	NE1/4 sec. 23, T.36S., R.16E.

central Utah (Tidwell, 1967; Schultze, 1990). *Utahacanthus* is significant in that it is the earliest post-Devonian acanthodian found in North America that does not belong to the genus *Acanthodes*. It is known from a single but fairly complete specimen that provides a reasonable basis for reconstruction of cranial morphology and body outline. Schultze (1990) assigned it confidently to the Acanthodii, though he noted that it is unique in its possession of strongly developed gill rays and a very long pectoral fin spine.

Chondrichthyes

The remains of xenacanth sharks (figure 2A, B) are nearly ubiquitous among Halgaito Shale localities of southeastern Utah. Most of the remains are fragmentary or isolated teeth recovered from stream channel conglomerates, identifiable only as probably xenacanthid. However, in a separate study, Gary Johnson aided Frede and others (1993) in the identification of two different taxa - *Orthacanthus compressus* and *O. texensis* from the Halgaito samples. The two taxa are closely related and generally considered to be indicators of freshwater environments (Sander, 1989; Johnson, 1991). Johnson (1991) noted that the temporal distribution of *O. compressus* is restricted to Wolfcampian and older sediments, whereas *O. texensis* is of much greater distribution, ranging well into the Leonardian. Although consistent with previously published records of xenacanth shark distributions, the presence of these two taxa does little to shed

light on the age assignment of the Halgaito Shale.

A single partial tooth found in the Lower Permian Organ Rock Shale may be tentatively identified as chondrichthian. It was found in one of a series of heavily conglomeratic stream channel lenses on the eastern face of the Red House Cliffs south of Utah State Highway 95, near Fry Canyon.

Crossopterygii

Two rhipidistian crossopterygian genera have been reported from southeastern Utah, *Ectosteorhachis* and *Lohsania*. Earlier studies (Vaughn, 1962, 1965, 1966, 1967) assigned crossopterygian remains to *Ectosteorhachis*, aff. *E. nitidus*. These earlier reports were based exclusively on the presence of isolated scales that are indistinguishable from those associated with complete body fossils of *Ectosteorhachis*. In a later report, Thomson and Vaughn (1968) described a crossopterygian unique to southeastern Utah, *Lohsania utahensis*. It was the first crossopterygian from Utah to be represented by more than just scales and included cranial materials as well as fragments of the trunk in partial articulation.

Lohsania is distinctive in that its vertebral segments are composed of three elements: a principal centrum, an accessory centrum, and the neural arch (figure 2E, F). This is in clear distinction to the condition in *Ectosteorhachis* in which the vertebral centrum is a single, ring-like structure. The principal centrum in *Lohsania* narrows dorsally and is uniquely associated with an accessory central element that articulates with, or is fused to, its anterodorsal aspect. Given the unique nature of the central elements in *Lohsania*, Thomson and Vaughn (1968) were not able to homologize the individual elements with those of tetrapods or other crossopterygians, including *Ectosteorhachis*.

Thomson and Vaughn (1968) noted that scales found in clear association with the holotype and paratypes of *Lohsania* cannot be differentiated from those in *Ectosteorhachis*. This observation casts doubt on earlier reports of the presence of *Ectosteorhachis* in southeastern Utah, with the possiblity that they are really indications of the presence of *Lohsania*. *Ectosteorhachis* is a common component of Late Paleozoic faunal communities, so its presence would not be surprising, but diagnostic elements are lacking. Here we take the somewhat conservative stance of reporting its possible presence.

Dipnoi

Only isolated toothplates of lungfishes have been recovered from the Halgaito Shale; however, toothplates are adequate for identification of two different genera. The triradiate blades of the toothplates in *Gnathoriza* are easily distinguished from those of *Sagenodus* in which five to six denticulate ridges are present (figure 2G). *Sagenodus* is known from one of four localities in the Valley of the Gods (Valley of the Gods i in table 1), interpreted by Frede and others (1993) as a small pond deposit. *Gnathoriza* is known from the Lisbon Valley locality, which Vaughn (1966) suggested was possibly subject to seasonal dessication. Vaughn cited the presence of *Gnathoriza* at the Lisbon Valley locality to support his hypothesis of seasonal drying; however, it must be noted that aestivation burrows attributable to *Gnathoriza* have not yet been found.

Actinopterygii

A platysomid tooth plate with phyllodont structure has been discovered at an unambiguously non-marine locality in the Valley of the Gods. Although the single tooth plate cannot be identified confidently to genus, its presence is reasonable given the broad distribution of phyllodonts in other Late Paleozoic sediments (Johnson and Zidek, 1981).

The vast majority of actinopterygian remains are those of palaeoniscoid fishes. Scales and vertebral elements (figure 2C, D) have been recovered from a wide range of localities (table 1). Vaughn (1967) was the first to collect the vertebral elements, all centra, and he described them as resembling those of "holostean-grade"

actinopterygians. Schultze and Chorn (1986) compared these with those of similar vertebrae from across North America, and although they agreed that the centra were indeed actinopterygian in nature, these authors pointed out that they should not be considered as "holostean." The centra are slightly taller than they are long, and are approximately "hourglass-shaped." Schultze and Chorn (1986) acknowledged that it is extremely difficult to distinguish the anterior and posterior faces of the vertebrae (figure 2C). However, they did indicate (essentially following Berman, 1970) that the dorsal aspect is marked by deep, elongated sockets for attachment of the neural arches, whereas the more ventral sockets for rib attachment are somewhat shallower.

Palaeoniscoids are known from a variety of localities, ranging from the marine Elephant Canyon Formation, to transitional facies, to stream channels within the more terrestrial to semiterrestrial redbeds of the Halgaito Shale. Unfortunately, given that the remains are not assignable to any specific group, they could represent one or many taxa. Thus, their utility in distinguishing depositional environments is extremely limited. Palaeoniscoid scales are among the few fish elements that can be identified confidently from the Lower Permian Organ Rock Shale of southeastern Utah (Vaughn, 1964).

SUMMARY AND DISCUSSION

Minimally, two different taxa of fishes are known from the Early Pennsylvanian Manning Canyon Formation of central Utah, the acanthodian *Utahacanthus* and remains of palaeonscoids. At least seven, and possibly eight, fish taxa are known from the Late Paleozoic Halgaito Shale of southeastern Utah. These include two sharks, two lungfish, at least two different actinopterygians, and at least one but possibly two crossopterygians. The Halgaito and its redbed equivalents appear to include more than a single, generalized type of depositional environment. The presence of *Gnathoriza* at the Lisbon Valley locality may indicate that at least some of the regions during this time were subject to seasonal drought, whereas other localities that include sharks, palaeoniscoids, and the non-aestivating *Sagenodus* may reflect more consistently available aquatic environments. As most of the materials have been recovered from terrestrial to semi-terrestrial deposits of the Halgaito Shale, future concentration on the more clearly aquatic or semi-aquatic environments associated with stream channel deposits might yield additional information. Deposits of the definitively Lower Permian Organ Rock Shale

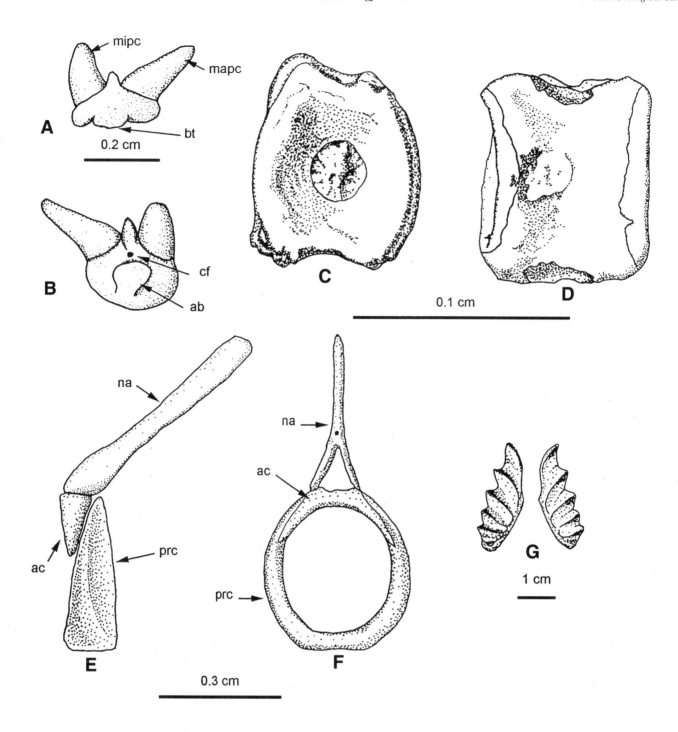

Figure 2. *Representative fishes from Late Paleozoic exposures of southeastern Utah: A and B, labial and lingual-occlusal views of a tooth of the xenacanthid shark* Orthacanthus texensis; *C and D, vertebral centrum of palaeoniscoid actinopterygian in end and lateral views; E and F, vertebral elements of the rhipidistian crossopterygian* Lohsania utahensis *in lateral and anterior views; G, mandibular toothplates of the dipnoan* Sagenodus. *C and D after Schultze and Chorn (1986). E and F after Thomson and Vaughn (1968). Abbreviations: ab, apical button; ac, accessory centrum; bt, basal tubercle; cf, central foramen; mipc, minor principle cusp; mapc, major principle cusp; na, neural arch; prc, principle centrum.*

include precious few examples of fish materials. Most have been found in coprolites only, with an isolated record of a possible chondrichthian. The Halgaito and the Organ Rock are often regarded similarly in terms of depositional environments. Vertebrate fossils are rarely found in the Organ Rock north of Monument Valley, and the pronounced differences in the frequency and distribution of fish fossils indicates significant differences between the two, particularly farther north. A clearer interpretation of these differences might be facilitated with additional collection and analysis of aquatic vertebrates. Conversely, the paucity of fish finds from the Organ Rock might simply be a reflection of collecting bias toward terrestrial vertebrates.

Of the fishes known from southeastern Utah, only the rhipidistean crossopterygian *Lohsania* is unique to the region. Late Paleozoic deposits of southeastern Utah contain little that is unique, but the fauna that they share in common with other regions does allow useful comparisions. This is of particular significance given the recent proposal that the Halgaito Shale be reassigned from the Lower Permian to the Upper Pennsylvanian (Baars, 1995). Although phyllodonts and both lungfish genera discussed above are known from the Pennsylvanian, *Orthacanthus compressus*, *O. texensis*, *Sagenodus*, and *Gnathoriza* are common elements of Early Permian faunas recorded from north-central Texas, northern New Mexico, and the Dunkard Basin. *Ectosteorhachis* is well known from the Lower Permian of north-central Texas; however, its equivocal presence in the Utah localities makes it stratigraphically less useful than other taxa. On balance, the invertebrate record supports a latest Pennsylvanian age for the Halgaito Shale, whereas the vertebrate fossil record retains some indications of an earliest Permian assignment. This inconsistency will perhaps necessitate a re-examination of both North American and European strata that have up to now been considered to be earliest Permian (Wolfcampian) in age (Sumida and others, 1996). Of particular significance would be examination of north-central Texas deposits where datable marine facies exist (Hentz, 1988). Analysis of the Halgaito and Elephant Canyon formations of Utah will be of central importance in the ultimate understanding of this biostratigraphic problem.

ACKNOWLEDGMENTS

The authors would like to thank David D. Gillette for the invitation to contribute this manuscript. New information on materials from the Halgaito Shale was collected during collaborative fieldwork with David S Berman and R. Eric Lombard. We thank the members of our hard-working field parties from 1989 to 1993 and 1997: Luisa Abukarma, John Balsley, John Bolt, Angela Dudeck, Brette Greenwood, Amy Henrici, Tom Hetherington, Jeff Janovets, Matthew Kosnik, Johanna Lombard, Mary Lombard, Stefan Lombard, Robert Lombard, Debra McPhearson, Dennis and Robin O'Keefe, Laura Panko, Sally Parker-Johnson, and Natalie Seel. Gary Johnson and Sebastian Frede provided thorough information regarding identification of the xenacanth shark materials. Peter P. Vaughn was an invaluable source of information on the geology, geography, and paleontology of the Four Corners region and, during the 1990 field season, directed us to a number of the localities reported upon in table 2. David Berman provided helpful discussion that influenced and improved the manuscript substantially. Careful and thoughtful review by John Chorn and Gary Johnson also improved the manuscipt significantly. James Walliser proofread the manuscript. This work was supported by a California State University San Bernardino Minigrant (to SSS) and a California State University San Bernardino Associated Students Grant (to GA).

REFERENCES

Baars, D. L., 1962, Permian system of the Colorado Plateau: American Association of Petroleum Geologists Bulletin, v. 46, p.149-218.

—1991, Redefinition of the Pennsylvanian-Permian boundary in Kansas, Midcontinent, U.S.A.: Program with Abstracts, International Congress of the Permian System of the World, Perm USSR, p. A3.

—1995, Navajo Country, A geology and natural history of the Four Corners Region: Albuquerque, University of New Mexico Press, 255 p.

Berman, D. S, 1970, Vertebrate fossils from the Leuders Formation, Lower Permian of north-central Texas: University of California Publications in Geological Sciences, no. 86, 61 p.

Carroll, R. L., 1988, Vertebrate Paleontology and Evolution: New York, W. H. Freeman and Company, 698 p.

Frede, Sebastian, Sumida, S. S., and Berman, D. S, 1993, New information on early Permian vertebrates from the Halgaito Tongue of the Cutler Formation of southeastern Utah: Journal of Vertebrate Paleontology, v. 13 (supplement to no. 3), p. 36A.

Hentz, Tucker, 1988, Lithostratigraphy and paleoenvironments of upper Paleozoic continental redbeds, North-Central Texas: Bowie (new) and Wichita (revised) Groups: The University of Texas at Austin, Bureau of Economic Geology Report of Investigations 170, 55 p.

Johnson, G. D., 1991, Chondrichthyan biostratigraphy of the North American Permian System: Contributions to Eurasian Geology, Occasional Publications ESRI, Series No. 8B, p. 41-50.

Johnson, G. D., and Zidek, Jiri, 1981, Late Paleozoic phyllodont tooth plates: Journal of Paleontology, v. 55, p. 524-536.

Sander, Martin, 1989, Early Permian depositional environments and pond bonebeds in central Archer County, Texas: Palaeogeography, Palaeoclimatology, and Palaeoecology, v. 69, p. 1-21.

Schultze, H.-P., 1990, A new acanthodian from the Pennsylvanian of Utah, U.S.A., and the distribution of otoliths in gnathostomes: Journal of Vertebrate Paleontology, v. 10, p. 49-58.

Schultze, H.-P., and Chorn, John, 1986, Palaeoniscoid (Actinopterygii, Pisces) vertebrae from the Late Paleozoic of central North America, Journal of Paleontology, v. 60, p. 744-757.

Stanesco, J. D., and Campbell, J. A., 1989, Eolian and noneolian facies of the Lower Permian Cedar Mesa Sandstone Member of the Cutler Formation, southeastern Utah: U.S. Geological Survey Bulletin, 1808, p. F1-F13.

Sumida, S. S., Berman, D. S, and Martens, Thomas, 1996, Biostratigraphic correlations between the Lower Permian of North America and central Europe using the first record of an assemblage of terrestrial tetrapods from Germany: PaleoBios, v. 17, p. 1-12.

Thomson, K. S., and Vaughn, P. P., 1968, Vertebral structure in Rhipidistia (Osteichthyes, Crossopterygii) with description of a new Permian genus: Postilla, no. 127, p. 1-19.

Tidwell, W. D., 1967, Flora of Manning Canyon Shale. Part I: A lowermost Pennsylvanian flora from the Manning Canyon Shale, and its stratigraphic significance: Brigham Young University Geology Studies, v. 14, p. 3-66.

Vaughn, P. P., 1962, Vertebrates from the Halgaito Tongue of the Cutler Formation, Permian of San Juan County, Utah: Journal of Paleontology, v. 36, p.529-539.

—1964, Vertebrates from the Organ Rock Shale of the Cutler Group, Permian of Monument Valley and vicinity, Utah and Arizona: Journal of Paleontology, v. 38, p. 567-583.

—1965, Frog-like vertebrae from the Lower Permian of southeastern Utah: Los Angeles County Museum Contributions in Science, no. 87, p. 1-18.

—1966, Comparison of the early Permian vertebrate faunas of the Four Corners region and North Central Texas: Los Angeles County Museum Contributions in Science, no. 105, p. 1-13.

—1967, Evidence of ossified vertebrae in actinopterygian fish of the Early Permian age from southeastern Utah, Journal of Paleontology, v. 41, p. 151-160.

LATE PALEOZOIC AMPHIBIAN-GRADE TETRAPODS OF UTAH

Stuart S. Sumida
Department of Biology
California State University San Bernardino
5500 University Parkway
San Bernardino, California 92407
ssumida@mail.csusb.edu

James B. D. Walliser
Department of Biology
California State University San Bernardino
5500 University Parkway
San Bernardino, California 92407
jwallise@prodigy.net

R. Eric Lombard
Department of Organismal Biology and Anatomy
The University of Chicago
1027 East 57th Street
Chicago, Illinois 60637
elombard@midway.uchicago.edu

ABSTRACT

Amphibian-grade tetrapods from Utah include representatives of most of the major groups known from the Late Paleozoic. Microsaurs, nectridians, and äistopods are known only from the Late Pennsylvanian and include the (possibly) microsaurian *Utaherpeton franklini*, the nectridian *Diplocaulus*, and the äistopod *Phlegethontia*. Remains of temnospondylous labyrinthodont amphibians are more widespread, with trimerorhachid and eryopid temnospondyls known from both Upper Pennsylvanian and Lower Permian sediments. Records of the temnospondyl *Platyhystrix* appear to be restricted to the Late Pennsylvanian Halgaito Shale, whereas the only evidence of a zatracheid temnospondyl comes from the Early Permian Organ Rock Shale. Anthracosaurian amphibians are considerably rarer. There is a single Late Pennsylvanian record of the embolomerous amphibian *Archeria* in Utah. The seymouriamorph *Seymouria sanjuanensis* is known primarily from Lower Permian sediments of the Organ Rock Shale. The progressive decrease in amphibian fossils with time in southeastern Utah may provide support for hypotheses suggesting a drying trend in this part of the world during the Early Permian. However, caution is urged as additional prospecting and collection always hold the potential to modify this scenario.

INTRODUCTION

The search for tetrapod fossils in Late Paleozoic sediments of Utah has been focused primarily on the southeastern part of the state. In that region, the Monument Upwarp has brought to the surface vast exposures of Upper Paleozoic redbeds that hold promise for the recovery of semi-terrestrial to terrestrial animals. Indeed, with one exception from the sediments near Lehi in the north-central part of the state, all the Paleozoic tetrapods so far found in Utah come from that region. Consideration of organisms recovered from these sediments is complicated, however, by two issues, both of which involve the determination of boundaries: (1) the phylogenetic boundary defining the transition between amphibian-grade tetrapods and amniotes; and (2) the geologic boundary defining the transition between the Pennsylvanian and Permian.

Phylogenetic Considerations

The advent of cladistic analysis has led to a much more rigorous definition of taxonomic groupings. However, it has also relegated long-standing paraphyletic terms such as "amphibian" to an awkward limbo. Although careful wording such as "amphibian-grade tetrapods" is perhaps a correct characterization of the taxa surveyed in this report, the less-precise term "amphibian" will be utilized from this point forward as a shorthand for these organisms. Included in this paraphyletic group are any tetrapods that cannot be included within the crown group Amniota.

Geological Considerations

The earliest known tetrapod fossil from Utah is a microsaur from the Manning Canyon Shale of the north-central portion of the state. Tidwell (1967) considered the Manning Canyon Shale to be lowermost Pennsylvanian according to the associated flora. However, Carroll and others (1991) have characterized these strata as transitional between the Upper Mississippian and lowermost Pennsylvanian.

The majority of amphibian remains from the Late Paleozoic of Utah come from members of the Cutler Formation in the southeastern part of the state. From oldest to youngest they are the Halgaito Shale, Cedar Mesa Sandstone, Organ Rock Shale, and DeChelly Sandstone. The age of the Halgaito Shale has recently been revised (Baars, 1991, 1995). The data for this revision are examined in detail by Sumida and others (this volume). Essentially, evidence from fusulinid fossils in the geographically contiguous and time-equivalent Elephant Canyon Formation appear to indicate a Late Pennsylvanian age. This interpretation is contrary to a previous, long-standing designation for the Halgaito as the lowest component of the Permian system in southeastern Utah, sitting unconformably on marine limestones of the Late Pennsylvanian. If this new age assignment is correct, many of the fossils previously considered to be Early Permian in age must now be considered to be Late Pennsylvanian instead. Significantly, the similarity of the tetrapod fossils from the Halgaito Shale to Early Permian fossils from Oklahoma, north-central Texas, the tri-state area of Ohio-Pennsylvania-West Virginia, and eastern Germany (Sumida and others, 1996) is one of the reasons for the slow acceptance of this scheme. Despite these cautions, we follow the revised time assignment here.

Very few tetrapod fossils are known from the younger Cedar Mesa Sandstone. All authors agree that it is Early Permian. However, the depositional environment has been variously interpreted. Baars (1962) and Vaughn (1966a) considered it to be of a primarily shallow, marine origin. Stanesco and Campbell (1989) have suggested that it was deposited as a complex aeolian unit bordered to the east by fluvial environments and to the south by sabkha environments; more recently, Baars (1995) interpreted the Cedar Mesa as sands deposited in a coastal environment.

The Organ Rock Shale is often considered to be lithologically similar to the Halgaito (Baars, 1962, 1995), and it has yielded a small number of amphibians.

No tetrapod body fossils have been recovered from the DeChelly Sandstone (Vaughn, 1963, 1973), a unit generally interpreted as aeolian. Tetrapod trackways are known from the DeChelly, however the taxonomic identity of these ichnofossils is impossible to determine at present.

SURVEY OF TAXA

In classical systematics and in present imprecise casual convention, Late Paleozoic amphibians have been divided into two large groupings, the Labyrinthodontia and the Lepospondyli, each containing several subtaxa. As is typical of polyphyletic or paraphyletic groups, neither has robust synapomorphies. As systematic analyses have become more precise, the confusion these older terms engender has become a hindrance to communication. In this transitional period during which a new consensus of relationships is being forged, not even a provisional 'least controversial' systematic organizaion of higher level taxa is possible. However, present systematic work confirms the recognition of some higher taxonomic groups and we use these to organize the presentation of amphibian fossils from Utah.

Microsauria

Only one tetrapod from Utah has been assigned to the order Microsauria, *Utaherpeton franklini* from the Manning Canyon Shale of Utah County in central Utah (Carroll and others, 1991). Carroll and others (1991) interpreted the Manning Canyon Shale from which the specimen was recovered to be transitional in age between the latest Mississippian and earliest Pennsylvanian; however Schultze (1990) in a description of an acanthodian from the same sediments, suggested that deposits are of a definitively Early Pennsylvanian age.

Carroll and his coworkers were severely restricted by the incomplete nature of the specimen and its position of preservation. However, they tentatively assigned *Utaherpeton* to the microsaurian suborder Microbrachomorpha based on a single clearly visible character: the shortness of the nasal bones. Unfortunately, no other unambiguous synapomorphies can be used to characterize *Utaherpeton*. One of the most diagnostic features of microsaurs, the configuration of the first cervical vertebra, was not available to Carroll and his coworkers for analysis, as an attempt to see it would have necessitated the destruction of a large portion of the specimen. The skull as reconstructed appears to be microsaurian in nature; however, Carroll and others (1991) note:

> The skull has been restored according to the pattern of small early microsaurs such as members of the families Hylopesiontidae, Tuditanidae, and Hapsidopareiontidae. Unfortunately, the temporal region is not well enough exposed to document the typical microsaurian configuration in which a large tabular is in contact with the postorbital.

Many of the other characters utilized to describe the genus appear to be primitive for tetrapods in general. Carroll and his coworkers do note that there are features of *Utaherpeton* that are shared with äistopods and nectridians: holospondylous vertebrae, teeth without labyrinthine infolding, no squamosal embayment, and no palatal tusks and pit pairs. These features are derived with respect to stem tetrapods but are all losses, a difficult class of characters to understand in any group, but especially amphibians. It is best to state that *Utaherpeton* is clearly a tetrapod and that it gives one a sense of having microsaurian affinities.

Nectridia

Although the presence of a microsaur in Utah is equivocal, the presence of a nectridian is unquestionable. Complete body fossils are lacking; however, isolated vertebrae (figure 1) display the typical bicipital transverse processes of *Diplocaulus*, well known from numerous localities and specimens from the southwestern United States. Several partial vertebral elements of *Diplocaulus* have been recovered from undifferentiated Cutler Formation in Lisbon Valley, San Juan County (Vaughn, 1966a). The presence of the aestivating lungfish *Gnathoriza* (Vaughn, 1966a; Sumida and others, this volume) suggests that the Lisbon Valley locality is likely one that was subject to seasonal periods of drying.

Äistopoda

The presence of äistopods can also be reported with confidence. Short strings of articulated vertebrae as well as many disarticulated elements have been recovered from both undifferentiated Cutler Formation both in Lisbon Valley and Arch Canyon, San Juan County. These materials are also extremely fragmentary; however, they are similar enough to materials referable to *Phlegethontia* from nearby Halgaito Shale deposits of Monument Valley, San Juan County, to make a reasonably clear taxonomic assignment (Vaughn, 1973).

Temnospondyli

The trimerorhachid amphibian *Trimerorhachis* is known from both Late Pennsylvanian and Early Permian localities but is not common. Fragmentary remains of characteristically sculptured dermal skull bones have been found in the Valley of the Gods, San Juan County; Frede and others (1993) have interpreted this Late Pennsylvanian locality as a small pond deposit. Vaughn (1973) reported other fragmentary materials as well as a reasonably diagnostic lower jaw from an Early Permian deposit of the Organ Rock Shale near Arch Canyon, San Juan County. The pattern of dermal sculpture is like that of *Trimerorhachis*, but because of the limited amount of material taxonomic assignment is problematic. *Trimerorhachis* is a common component of pond margin faunas from the Lower Permian (Olson, 1952; Sander, 1989) and is known also from northern New Mexico (Berman and Reisz, 1980), but the only unequivocal trimerorhachid described from definitively Late Pennsylvanian sediments of the Four Corners region is *Lafonia lehmani* from the Madera Formation of the Manzano Mountains of north-central New Mexico (Berman, 1973). To suggest that the materials from the Valley of the Gods may be *Lafonia* and those from Monument Pass might be *Trimerorhachis* is tempting, but prudence dictates the conservative reportage of unassignable trimerorhachids from both until more complete specimens are recovered.

Of all the amphibians known from the Late Paleozoic of Utah, *Eryops* is easily the most common, accounting for as many reports as most other amphibians combined. *Eryops* has been found in more rock units in southeastern Utah than any other amphibian, including sediments of the Halgaito, Cedar Mesa, and Organ Rock formations. Pennsylvanian records of *Eryops* in southeastern Utah include the Valley of the Gods, just inside the mouth of John's Canyon, San Juan County, and at a locality designated the "*Platyhystrix* pocket" by Vaughn (1962) near U. S. Highway 163 between three and four miles north of the town of Mexican Hat, also in San Juan County. The Valley of the Gods locality preserves the most complete *Eryops* specimen which includes a partial skull, lower jaws, and a partial postcranium. These materials are among those most strongly suggesting *Eryops*, given the relatively large interpterygoid vacuities and relatively flattened skull as compared to forms such as *Edops*. (No identifiable specimens of the latter have ever been found in Utah, so the conservative assignment to *Eryops* is adopted here.) Most recently, a partial lower jaw plus impression was recovered from near the mouth of John's Canyon. Potentially diagnostic features of the symphyseal region are missing; the incomplete-

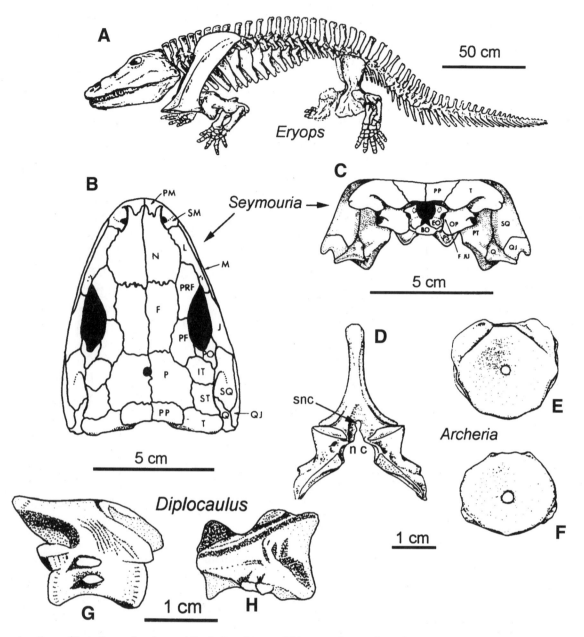

Figure 1. *Reconstructions of Late Pennsylvanian and Early Permian amphibian taxa known from the state of Utah. A, whole body reconstruction of the eryopid temnospondyl* Eryops; *B and C, skull of the seymouriamorph* Seymouria sanjuanensis *in dorsal and occipital views; D-F, reconstructions of the neural arch, pleurocentrum, and intercentrum of the anthracosaur embolomere,* Archeria, *in cranial view; G and H, dorsal vertebra of the nectridian* Diplocaulus *in lateral and dorsal views. A after Romer (1966); B and C after Berman and others (1992); D-F after Holmes (1989). Abbreviations: BO, basioccipital; EO, exoccipital; F, frontal; F JU, jugular foramen; IT, intertemporal; M, maxilla; N, nasal; n c, neural canal; OP, opisthotic; P, parietal; PF, postfrontal; PM, premaxilla; PO, postorbital; PP, postparietal; PRF, prefrontal; PT, pterygoid; Q, quadrate; QJ, quadratojugal; SM, septomaxilla; snc supraneural canal; SQ, squamosal; ST, supratemporal; T, tabular.*

ness of the specimen demands that the possibility of another taxon be entertained. However, generic identification of the specimen is not possible at this time, but it is worth noting that on the basis of size of the dermal sculpture, the specimen might be assignable to *Eryops*.

To date, no amphibians are known from the aeolian deposits of the Cedar Mesa Sandstone; however, a remarkable stream-channel deposit cutting through those deposits is worthy of note. In their analysis of the depositional environments of the Cedar Mesa Sandstone,

Stanesco and Campbell (1989) reported the discovery of vertebrate bone in what appeared to be an immense, fossilized log jam within a broad stream-channel deposit. The assemblage included petrified logs approaching one meter in diameter, as well as the remains of *Eryops* and pelycosaurian-grade synapsid amniotes. This remarkable locality was located just east of Canyonlands National Park, but recent vandalism resulted in the complete destruction of the site: all previously exposed plant and animal remains are now gone. The loss is tragic, and the first and third authors of this review were indeed fortunate to record the presence of certain taxa before its destruction.

Only fragmentary elements referable to *Eryops* have been recovered from the Organ Rock Shale (Vaughn, 1964). In fact, most of those are from Organ Rock sediments in Arizona, just south of the border to San Juan County. Although not actually from Utah, their remarkably close proximity to the state is indicative of their presence at a time when state boundaries were irrelevant.

Cranial materials confidently referable to the temnospondyl amphibian *Platyhystrix* are extremely rare (Berman and others, 1981). However, the vertebrae and their elongate, tuberculated neural spines are more commonly found. They are highly diagnostic, making generic documentation fairly easy. In Utah, *Platyhystrix* is known only from Pennsylvanian-age Halgaito Shale sediments. Vaughn (1962) documented so many specimens from a locality north of the town of Mexican Hat that he named it the "*Platyhystrix* pocket." At the Cedar Point locality overlooking the San Juan River Canyon where it winds through the Glen Canyon National Recreation Area, a nearly complete dorsal sail has been recovered. The Cedar Point locality is a heavily conglomeratic stream channel approximately thirty meters upslope from the valley floor (equivalent in elevation to the Floor of the Valley of the Gods). In this case, and in the case of the specimens recovered by Vaughn, a fairly confident determination of *Platyhystrix* sp., cf. *P. rugosus* may be made.

Vaughn (1964) reported the possible presence of a zatracheid temnospondyl from the Lower Permian Organ Rock Shale just southeast of Train Rock in Monument Valley. Notably, the materials were recovered from conglomeratic sediments, possibly from a stream. As the spiked and stellate pattern of dermal skull bones in *Zatrachys* is easily recognizable, Vaughn's tentative assignment is accepted here. *Zatrachys* is not known from earlier deposits in Utah or the nearby Arizona component of Monument Valley.

Anthracosauria

The diversity of anthracosaurians from the Late Paleozoic of Utah is much lower than that of temnospondyls. However, two notable taxa are present, the embolomere *Archeria*, and the seymouriamorph *Seymouria*. *Archeria* is known with reasonable certainty from a single vertebral centrum. Despite the evidence being restricted to a single element, the solid, disc-like nature of *Archeria* centra allows an fairly confident identification. The specimen was recovered from Late Pennsylvanian sediments of the Halgaito Shale in the Valley of the Gods, San Juan County. The centrum is small, probably that of a juvenile. Materials recovered during the 1997 field season suggest an additional *Archeria* specimen. A stream channel in the Valley of the Gods has yielded the caudal end of what appears to be a large embolomerous amphibian, most closely conforming to the pattern seen in *Archeria*. Additional preparation will be necessary to allow confident taxonomic assignment, but this together with the vertebral element suggests that *Archeria* might be a somewhat more common component of the Late Pennsylvanian to Early Permian assemblages than previously thought.

Perhaps the best characterized of Late Paleozoic amphibians from Utah is *Seymouria*. A small vertebra from the Late Pennsylvanian Halgaito Shale in John's Canyon, San Juan County, is probably referable to a seymouriid, but far more complete specimens are known from the Navajo Reservation of the southeastern-most part of the state. These materials represent the type and paratypes of *Seymouria sanjuanensis* (Vaughn, 1966b). A broad range of studies now provide a fairly precise understanding of the genus and species (Vaughn, 1966b; Berman and others, 1987; Berman and Martens, 1993).

Vaughn (1966b) described *Seymouria sanjuanensis* on the basis of three different skulls, skull roof impressions, and associated postcranial materials. *Seymouria* demonstrates characteristically anthracosaurian and seymouriamorph features: a well-developed otic notch combined with parietal-tabular contact and narrow interpterygoid vacuities, exclusion of the atlantal pleurocentrum from ventral exposure via articulation between the atlantal and axial intercentra, vertebrae dominated by large pleurocentra, and terrestrially adapted limbs. *Seymouria sanjuanensis* is distinguished from other species of the genus by: (1) a narrow, chevron-shaped postorbital that extends far along the dorsal and ventral margins of the orbit and a posteriorly projecting apex that partially separates the intertemporal and squamosal; and (2) separation of the maxilla and quadratojugal by the jugal along the ventral margin of the skull.

Although originally described from Utah specimens, *S. sanjuanensis* appears to have a greater geographic range than any other seymouriamorph, and perhaps any other Paleozoic tetrapod. *Seymouria sanjuanensis* is known from numerous specimens from north-central New Mexico (Berman and others, 1987) as well as from central Europe (Berman and Martens, 1993).

Amphibian of Unknown Affinities

Perhaps the most enigmatic of Late Paleozoic

amphibians recovered from Utah are the two small verte-brae that represent the holotypic and referred specimens of *Lasalia cutlerensis* from the undifferentiated Cutler Formation of Lisbon Valley, San Juan County. Vaughn (1965) could not place *Lasalia* in any known Paleozoic group. The vertebrae bear a striking resemblance to those normally found in anurans. The cancellous cen-trum is amphicoelous but not notochordal. Transverse processes are elongate, circular in cross-section and hol-low. The neural spine is low and unlike those of known lepospondyls or labyrinthodonts. Clear assignment to the Lissamphibia would require cranial and dental ele-ments which are lacking.

Jenkins and Shubin (1995) have suggested that an as yet unnamed specimen from the Jurassic Kayenta Forma-tion on the Navajo Reservation in northeastern Arizona is the earliest known unequivocal frog. Piveteau (1937), Estes and Reig (1973), Bolt (1991), and Laurin and Reisz (1997) have suggested that *Triadobatrachus* from the early Triassic of Madagascar must be closely related to the Anura. However, the Paleozoic has produced no other examples of anuran fossils. In this regard, Vaughn's (1965) finding is intriguing. If *Lasalia* is not an anuran, it points out an even greater diversity of prim-itive lepospondyls or labyrinthodonts than previously thought. If it is somehow related to primitive lissam-phibians, the origins of lissamphibians must be sought in the Late Pennsylvanian or earlier.

Diadectomorpha

Diadectomorphs are reviewed in detail in the section on Amniota and their close relatives (Sumida and others, this volume) and are mentioned here only briefly. Diad-ectomorpha, as currently recognized, includes three fami-lies: Limnoscelidae, Tseajaiidae, and Diadectidae (Ber-man and others, 1992; Sumida and others, 1992; Laurin and Reisz,1997; and Lee and Spencer, 1997). Vaughn reported the presence of a limnoscelid from the "*Platy-hystrix* pocket" north of Mexican Hat, but could provide no more precise an identification. *Tseajaia campi* was originally collected by Charles Camp in 1942 from the Organ Rock Shale in the Utah portion of Monument Val-ley on the Navajo Reservation; however it was not until Vaughn's (1964) description that it became the basis of the monospecific Tseajaiidae. Fragmentary specimens from a number of localities in both the Halgaito and Organ Rock are identifiable as pertaining to the Diadecti-dae. Most are almost certainly indications of the pres-ence of *Diadectes*, the best known member of the family. *Diadectes* in Utah comes from the Late Pennsylvanian (Valley of the Gods) as well as Lower Permian (Monu-ment Valley).

Trackways

A number of putative tetrapod trackways have been reported from San Juan County, particularly in the DeChelly Sandstone. Vaughn (1963, 1973) and Sadler (1993) have noted these, but definitive correlation between trackway types and osteologically represented taxa is extremely difficult. Their presence is noteworthy if for nothing else than to emphasize the presence of tetrapods in post-Organ Rock sediments.

SUMMARY AND DISCUSSION

More taxa and specimens are known from Late Pennsylvanian localities, particularly those of the Hal-gaito Shale, than from the Early Permian. Tables 2 and 3 indicate this disparity. Only *Eryops* and trimerorhachids span the Pennsylvanian and Permian localities. Microsaurs, nectridians, and äistopods appear to be exclusively of Pennsylvanian age in Utah.

The only amphibian unique to Utah is the tentatively assigned, Early Pennsylvanian microsaur *Utaherpeton franklini*. Most of the fauna is otherwise similar to those of surrounding Four Corners states, a condition Vaughn (1966a) suggested was due simply to their close proximi-ty; or it is similar to assemblages known from north-cen-tral Texas. This lack of uniqueness does not diminish the importance of certain taxa, however. The broad geologi-cal range of *Eryops* in Utah confirms Vaughn's (1958) analysis which concluded that the genus was the most consistently cosmopolitan in the Late Paleozoic. The presence of *Seymouria sanjuanensis* in what are still con-sidered to be definitively Lower Permian sediments is an important element in world-wide biostratigraphic correla-tions. The presence of the same species in redbed sedi-ments of central Germany (Berman and Martens, 1993) has in part allowed, for the first time, confident correla-tion between Lower Permian redbeds of North America and the Late Paleozoic redbeds of the German Upper Rotleigend (Sumida and others, 1996).

Vaughn (1966a, 1973) drew comparisons between the Late Paleozoic vertebrate assemblages within the Four Corners Region, as well as with those of north-cen-tral Texas. As amphibians span a diversity of life history strategies, they played an important role in his compara-tive analysis. Vaughn (1966a) suggested that both north-central Texas and southeastern Utah were primarily deltaic environments. However, the presence of the nec-tridian *Diplocaulus*, as well as the aestivating lungfish *Gnathoriza*, from Lisbon Valley, may indicate that the Late Pennsylvanian Halgaito Shale and its equivalents included some regions of extreme seasonality in water availability. Vaughn (1973) further suggested that the Lower Permian was a period of progressive drying. A synthesis of the amphibian and fish data would tend to support this hypothesis. Very few fish fossils are found in Lower Permian sediments in southeastern Utah. Similarly, most aquatically adapted amphibians from Utah are known mainly from Pennsylvanian sediments. Conversely, Lower Permian sediments yield *Seymouria*, a terrestrially adapted genus, closely related to amniotes, and *Eryops*, an ubiquitous faunal element not particularly useful in paleoenvironmental reconstruction. The only other amphibians from the Lower Permian are rarely found zatracheid and trimerorhachid specimens. However, caution must be exercised when suggesting paleoenvironmental conclusions. The paucity of amphibian fossils in Cedar Mesa, Organ Rock, and DeChelly units may be due to sampling bias. Further exploration is clearly warranted, particularly in the Cedar Mesa Sandstone and Organ Rock Shale. A similar lesson was dramatically provided with the discovery of *Seymouria sanjuanensis* in central Europe. Its previous absence was simply due to the sampling bias away from redbed exposures; however, now an animal previously thought exclusive to Utah and New Mexico is known to have a remarkably wide distribution. Care must be exercised to avoid similar prejudices when analyzing the amphibian assemblages through the succession of Late Paleozoic sediments in Utah.

ACKNOWLEDGMENTS

The authors would like to thank David D. Gillette for the invitation to contribute this manuscript. New information on materials from the Halgaito Shale were collected during the first and third authors' collaborative field seasons with David S Berman. We thank the members of our hard-working field parties from 1989 to 1993 and 1997: Luisa Abukarma, John Balsley, John Bolt, Angela Dudeck, Brette Greenwood, Amy Henrici, Tom Hetherington, Jeff Janovets, Matthew Kosnik, Johanna Lombard, Mary Lombard, Stefan Lombard, Robert Lombard, Debra McPhearson, Dennis and Robin O'Keefe, Laura Panko, Sally Parker-Johnson, Elizabeth Rega, and Natalie Seel. Amy Henrici prepared much of the materials recovered during those field seasons. Sebastian Frede, at the time an undergraduate at the University of Chicago, also prepared and identified some of the material reported on in this study. The Monticello, Utah, office of the BLM has been especially helpful to our fieldwork and we particularly thank Robert Turri for facilitating our progress. Colonel Richard and Jacqualine Lombard were gracious hosts during parts of our field seasons. As always, Peter P. Vaughn was an invaluable source of information on the geology, geography, and paleontology of the Four Corners region. This work was supported by a California State University San Bernardino Minigrant (to SSS) and a California State University San Bernardino Associated Students Grant (to JBDW).

Table 1. *Geographic data for localities that have yielded Late Pennsylvanian and Early Permian amphibian fossils in Utah.*

Locality	Section, Township, Range
Uppermost Mississippian to lowermost Pennsylvanian	
Lehi, 16 km west northwest	Sec. 9, T.5S., R.1W.
Pennsylvanian	
Arch Canyon	NE1/4 sec. 21, T.37S., R.20E.
Cedar Point	NE 1/4 SE 1/4 sec. 17, T.41S., R.18E.
John's Canyon (i)	NE1/4 NE1/4 sec. 19, T.40S., R.18E.
John's Canyon (ii)	NE1/4 NE1/4 sec. 18, T.40S., R.18E.
John's Canyon (iii)	NW1/4 NE1/4 sec. 34, T.40S., R.18E.
Lisbon Valley	SE1/4 SE1/4 sec. 20, T.30S., R.25E.
"*Platyhystrix* pocket"	SE 1/4 sec. 21, T.41S., R.19E.
Valley of the Gods (i)	NE1/4 NW1/4 sec. 29, T.40S., R19E.
Valley of the Gods (ii)	SE1/4 sec. 27, T.40S., R.19E.
Valley of the Gods (iii)	NE1/4 SE1/4 sec. 24, T.40S., R.19E.
Valley of the Gods (iv)	E border of secs. 27&34, T.40S., R.19E.
Valley of the Gods 1997	NE1/4 sec. 30, T.40S., R.19E.
Permian	
Monument Pass	Sec. 20, T.43S., R.17 E.
Saddleback and Stagecoach Buttes	Intersection of secs. 17,18,19,20, T.43S., R.17E. (Arizona)
Train Rock	SE1/4 sec. 4, T.43S., R.15E.

Table 2. Amphibian-grade tetrapods known from Pennsylvanian and earlier age sediments of Utah. Institutional abbreviations: BYUVP, Brigham Young University Paleontological Collections; CMNH, Carnegie Museum of Natural History; CSUSB VP; California State University San Bernardino Vertebrate Paleontology Collections; NTM, Navajo Tribal Museum, collections on extended loan to the Carnegie Museum of Natural History; UCLA VP, University of California Los Angeles (some materials transferred and accessioned into collections of the Carnegie Museum of Natural History and the University of California).

Latest Mississippian to Earliest Pennsylvanian

Taxon	Rock Unit or Formation	Locality	Reference	Depository
Microsauria				
Utaherpeton franklini	Manning Canyon Shale Formation	16 km. WNW of Lehi	Carroll and others (1991)	BYU VP 3050

Late Pennsylvanian

Taxon	Rock Unit or Formation	Locality	Reference	Depository
Nectridia				
Diplocaulus sp.	Halgaito Shale equivalent of Cutler Formation	Lisbon Valley	Vaughn (1965, 1966a)	UCLA VP 1674
Diplocaulus (?)	Halgaito Shale	"*Platyhystrix* pocket"	Vaughn (1962)	UCLA VP 1623
Äistopoda				
Phlegethontia (?)	Halgaito Shale equivalent of Cutler Formation	Lisbon Valley	Vaughn (1965, 1966a)	UCLA VP 1688
Phlegethontia (?)	Halgaito Shale	Arch Canyon	This report	UCLA VP 1681
Temnospondyli				
Trimerorhachoidea				
trimerorhachid	Halgaito Shale	Valley of the Gods (i)	Frede and others (1993)	CMNH
Eryopoidea				
Eryops	Halgaito Shale	Valley of the Gods (i and iii)	Frede and others (1993)	CMNH
Eryops	Halgaito Shale	"*Platyhystrix* pocket"	Vaughn (1962)	UCLA VP 1621, 1622
Eryops	Halgaito Shale	John's Canyon (iii)	This report	CMNH
Eryops	Halgaito Shale	Lisbon Valley	This report	UCLA VP 1668
Eryops (?)	Halgaito Shale	Valley of the Gods 1997	This report	CSUSB VP
Platyhystrix cf. *P. rugosus*	Halgaito Shale	Cedar Point	Vaughn (1962)	CMNH
Platyhystrix cf. *P. rugosus*	Halgaito Shale	"*Platyhystrix* pocket"	This report	
Platyhystrix cf. *P. rugosus*	Halgaito Shale equivalent of Cutler Formation	Lisbon Valley	This report	UCLA VP 1677
Platyhystrix	Halgaito Shale	Valley of the Gods (ii)	This report	CMNH
Anthracosauria				
Embolomeri				
Archeria	Halgaito Shale	Valley of the Gods (iv)	This report	CSUSB VP
Archeria (?)	Halgaito Shale	Valley of the Gods 1997	This report	CSUSB VP
Seymouriamorpha				
Seymouria ?	Halgaito Shale	John's Canyon	This report	CSUSB VP

Unknown

Taxon	Rock Unit or Formation	Locality	Reference	Depository
?				
Lasalia cutlerensis	Halgaito Shale equivalent of Cutler Formation	Lisbon Valley	Vaughn (1965)	UCLA VP 1670, 1673

Table 3. Amphibian-grade tetrapods known from Early Permian age sediments of Utah and north-eastern Arizona. Institutional abbreviations as in table 2.

Early Permian

Taxon	Rock Unit or Formation	Locality	Reference	Depository
Temnospondyli				
Trimerorhachoidea				
trimerorhachid	Organ Rock Shale	Monument Pass	Vaughn (1973)	UCLA VP
Eryopoidea				
Eryops	Cedar Mesa Sandstone	East of Canyonlands	This report	CSUSB VP
Eryops	Organ Rock Shale	Monument Valley, Arizona	Vaughn (1964)	UCLA VP 1642, 1643
zatracheid	Organ Rock Shale	Train Rock, Monument Valley	Vaughn (1964)	UCLA VP 1644
Anthracosauria				
Seymouriamorpha				
Seymouria sanjuanensis	Organ Rock Shale	Saddleback & Stagecoach	Vaughn (1966b)	NTM 1023, 1024, 1025, 1026
Unknown Tetrapoda				
Ichnofossils				
footprints	DeChelly Sandstone	Numerous	Vaughn (1963, 1973); Sadler (1993)	

REFERENCES

Baars, D. L., 1962, Permian system of the Colorado Plateau: American Association of Petroleum Geologists Bulletin, v. 46, p. 149-218.

—1991, Redefinition of the Pennsylvanian-Permian boundary in Kansas, midcontinent, U.S.A.: Program with Abstracts, International Congress of the Permian System of the World, Perm USSR, p. A3.

—1995, Navajo country, a geology and natural history of the Four Corners Region: Albuquerque, University of New Mexico Press, 255 p.

Berman, D. S, 1973, A trimerorhachid amphibian from the Upper Pennsylvanian of New Mexico: Journal of Paleontology, v. 47, p. 932-945.

Berman, D. S, and Martens, Thomas,1993, First occurrence of Seymouria (Amphibia: Batrachosauria) from the Lower Permian Rotleigend of central Germany, Annals of Carnegie Museum, v. 62, p. 63-79.

Berman, D. S, and Reisz, R. R., 1980, A new species of *Trimerorhachis* (Amphibia: Temnospondyli) from the Lower Permian Abo Formation of New Mexico, with discussion of Permian faunal distributions in that state: Annals of Carnegie Museum, v. 49, p. 455-485.

Berman, D. S, Reisz, R. R., and Eberth, D. A., 1987, *Seymouria sanjuanensis* (Amphibia, Batrachosauria) from the Lower Permian Cutler Formation of north-central New Mexico and the occurrence of sexual dimorphism in that genus questioned, Canadian Journal of Earth Sciences, v. 24, p. 1769-1784.

Berman, D. S, Reisz, R. R., and Fracasso, M. A., 1981, Skull of the Lower Permian dissorophid amphibian *Platyhystrix rugosus*: Annals of Carnegie Museum, v. 50, p. 391-416.

Berman, D. S, Sumida, S. S., and Lombard, R. E., 1992, Reinterpretation of the temporal and occipital regions in *Diadectes* and the relationships of diadectomorphs: Journal of Paleontology, v. 66, p. 481-499.

Bolt, J. R., 1991, Lissamphibian origins, *in* Schultze, H.-P., and Trueb, Linda, editors, Origins of the higher groups of tetrapods, consensus and controversy: Ithaca, New York, Cornell University Press, p. 194-222.

Carroll, R. L., Bybee, Paul, and Tidwell, W. D., 1991, The oldest microsaur (Amphibia): Journal of Paleontology, v. 65, p. 314-322.

Estes, Richard, and Reig, Oscar, 1973, The early fossil record of frogs--a review of the evidence, *in* Vial, J. L., editor, Evolutionary biology of the anurans: Columbia, University of Missouri Press, p. 11-63.

Frede, Sebastian, Sumida, S. S., and Berman, D. S, 1993, New information on early Permian vertebrates from the Halgaito Tongue of the Cutler Formation of southeastern Utah: Journal of Vertebrate Paleontology, v. 13, p. 36A.

Holmes, Robert, 1989, The skull and axial skeleton of the Lower Permian anthracosauroid amphibian *Archeria crassidisca* Cope: Palaeontographica, v. 207, p. 161-206.

Jenkins, F. A., and Shubin, N. H., 1995, An early Jurassic jumping frog: the evolution of the anuran pelvis: Journal of Vertebrate Paleontology, v. 15, p. 38A

Laurin, Michel, and Reisz, R. R., 1995, A reevaluation of early amniote phylogeny: Zoological Journal of the Linnean Society, v. 113, p. 165-223.

—1997, A new perspective on tetrapod phylogeny, *in* Sumida, S. S., and Martin, K. L. M., editors, Amniote origins, completing the transition to land: San Diego, Academic

Press, p. 9-60.

Lee, M. Y. S., and Spencer, P. S., 1997, Crown-clades, key characters and taxonomic stability: When is an amniote not an amniote?, *in* Sumida, S. S., and Martin, K. L. M., editors, Amniote origins, completing the transition to land: San Diego, Academic Press, p. 61-84.

Olson, E. C., 1952, The evolution of a Permian vertebrate chronofauna: Evolution, v. 6, p. 181-196.

Piveteau, J., 1937, Un amphibien du Trias Inférieur, Essai sur l'origine et l'évolution des amphibiens anoures: Annales Palaeontologie, v. 26, p. 135-177.

Romer, A. S., 1966, Vertebrate paleontology, third edition: Chicago, The University of Chicago Press, 468 p.

Sadler, C. J., 1993, Arthropod trace fossils from the Permian De Chelly Sandstone, Northeastern Arizona: Journal of Paleontology, v. 67, p. 240-249.

Sander, Martin, 1989, Early Permian depositional environments and pond bonebeds in central Archer County, Texas: Palaeogeography, Palaeoclimatology, and Palaeoecology, v. 69, p. 1-21.

Schultze, H.-P., 1990, A new acanthodian from the Pennsylvanian of Utah, U.S.A., and the distribution of otoliths in gnathostomes: Journal of Vertebrate Paleontology, v. 10, p. 49-58.

Stanesco, J. D., and J. A. Campbell. 1989, Eolian and noneolian facies of the Lower Permian Cedar Mesa Sandstone Member of the Cutler Formation, southeastern Utah: U. S. Geological Survey Bulletin 1808, p. F1-F13.

Sumida, S. S., Lombard, R. E., and Berman, D. S, 1992, Morphology of the atlas axis complex of the late Palaeozoic tetrapod suborders Diadectomorpha and Seymouriamorpha: Philosophical Transactions of the Royal Society of London, v. 336, p. 259-273.

Sumida, S. S., Berman, D. S, and Martens, Thomas, 1996, Biostratigraphic correlations between the Lower Permian of North America and central Europe using the first record of an assemblage of terrestrial tetrapods from Germany: PaleoBios, v. 17, p. 1-12.

Tidwell, W. D., 1967, Flora of the Manning Canyon Shale, Pt. 1, a lowermost Pennsylvanian flora from the Manning Canyon Shale, Utah and its stratigraphic sequence: Brigham Young University Geological Studies, v. 21, p. 1-66.

Vaughn, P. P., 1958, On the geologic range of the labyrinthodont amphibian *Eryops*: Journal of Paleontology, v. 32, p. 918-922.

—1962, Vertebrates from the Halgaito Tongue of the Cutler Formation, Permian of San Juan County, Utah: Journal of Paleontology, v. 36, p.529-539.

—1963, A downslope trackway in the DeChelly Sandstone, Permian of Monument Valley: Plateau, v. 36, p. 25-28.

—1964, Vertebrates from the Organ Rock Shale of the Cutler Group, Permian of Monument Valley and vicinity, Utah and Arizona: Journal of Paleontology, v. 38, p. 567-583.

—1965, Frog-like vertebrae from the Lower Permian of southeastern Utah: Los Angeles County Museum Contributions in Science, no. 87, p. 1-18.

—1966a, Comparison of the early Permian vertebrate faunas of the Four Corners region and North Central Texas: Los Angeles County Museum Contributions in Science, No. 105, p. 1-13.

—1966b, *Seymouria* from the Lower Permian of southeastern

Utah and possible sexual dimorphism in that genus: Journal of Paleontology, v. 40, p. 603-612.

—1973, Vertebrates from the Cutler Group of Monument Valley and vicinity, Utah and Arizona, *in* James, H. L. editor, Guidebook of Monument Valley and Vicinity: New Mexico Geological Society Field Conference Volume, no. 24, p. 99-105.

LATE PALEOZOIC AMNIOTES AND THEIR NEAR RELATIVES FROM UTAH AND NORTHEASTERN ARIZONA, WITH COMMENTS ON THE PERMIAN-PENNSYLVANIAN BOUNDARY IN UTAH AND NORTHERN ARIZONA

Stuart S. Sumida
Department of Biology
California State University San Bernardino
5500 University Parkway
San Bernardino, California 92407
ssumida@mail.csusb.edu

R. Eric Lombard
Department of Organismal Biology and Anatomy
The University of Chicago
1027 East 57th Street
Chicago, Illinois 60637
elombard@midway.uchicago.edu

David S Berman
Section of Vertebrate Paleontology
Carnegie Museum of Natural History
4400 Forbes Avenue
Pittsburgh, Pennsylvania 15213
bermand@clp2.clpgh.org

Amy C. Henrici
Section of Vertebrate Paleontology
Carnegie Museum of Natural History
4400 Forbes Avenue
Pittsburgh, Pennsylvania 15213
henricia@clp2.clpgh.org

ABSTRACT

All Late Paleozoic amniote taxa and their near relatives known from Utah have been recovered from deposits in San Juan County in the southeastern corner of the state that extend into the northeastern corner of adjacent Arizona. Also noted herein are those members of this assemblage which have been found in the portion of the Cutler Group of Monument Valley that is distributed in neighboring northeastern Arizona. The Late Paleozoic amniotes of this region are dominated by at least five different pelycosaurian genera: the sphenacodontids *Sphenacodon*, *Dimetrodon*, and *Ctenospondylus*, the edaphosaurid *Edaphosaurus*, and the ophiacodontid *Ophiacodon*. Of these, *Sphenacodon* and *Ophiacodon* are the most common. Eureptilian tetrapods are less common both in number of specimens and number of taxa. Although having a world-wide Late Paleozoic distribution, captorhinomorph reptiles appear to be conspicuously absent. Disarticulated but associated remains of numerous individuals from a single site represent an as yet unnamed taxon that may be an araeoscelidian reptile. Members of the Diadectomorpha are generally regarded as closely related to amniotes, and the group is represented by the commonly occurring *Diadectes*. Only a few specimens possibly assignable to the more primitive diadectomorph family Limnoscelidae are present. The extremely rare *Tseajaia* is known from a nearly complete specimen from the San Juan County portion of Monument Valley.

INTRODUCTION

Phylogenetic Context

Rigorous cladistic analyses over the past two decades have begun to result in widely accepted and nearly consistent hypotheses of relationship among basal members of the Amniota (figure 1). Most authors including Reisz (1980, 1986), Heaton and Reisz (1986), Gauthier and others (1988), Berman and others (1992), and Laurin and Reisz (1995, 1997) regard the Synapsida as the basal member of Amniota. Many of the same authors regard the "Parareptilia" to be a relatively early branch of the Amniota, although the relationship of the possibly related turtles remains a matter of contention. Successively more derived are the eureptilian taxa Captorhinidae, Protorothyrididae, and Araeoscelidia.

Most of the phylogenetic analyses noted above regard the Late Paleozoic Diadectomorpha as the sister group of Amniota. Modesto (1992), Berman and others (1992), and Lee and Spencer (1997) have recently presented characters that indicate diadectomorphs might be crown-group amniotes; however, these analyses have acknowledged the limitation of the inability to demonstrate the mode of reproduction in the Paleozoic members of either group. Regardless of the phylogenetic hypothesis accepted, the close link between Diadectomorpha and taxa traditionally regarded as Amniota is the reason for the inclusion of the former in this survey.

Geological and Geographic Considerations

All of the diadectomorph and amniote taxa known from Utah have been recovered from deposits in San Juan County in the southeastern corner of the state. Because these deposits have continuous exposure in the northeastern corner of adjacent Arizona, this additional area is also considered here. This extensive area has been the subject of study by a series of field parties. In the 1940s, Charles Camp lead field crews from the University of California at Berkeley. Joint Harvard University and U. S. Geological Survey field crews followed in the mid-1950s. Peter Vaughn lead crews from the University of California at Los Angeles in the 1960s. Most recently, this region has been explored in a collaborative study by the authors.

The Cutler Group redbeds in southeastern Utah and adjacent area of Arizona are impressively exposed in this area as a consequence of the Monument Upwarp and canyon-cutting by the Colorado River and its tributaries. Traditionally, these redbeds have been subdivided into a series of smaller rock units that lie unconformably above the Pennsylvanian marine limestone Honaker Trail Formation. Tetrapod fossils have been recovered from semiterrestrial to terrestrial deposits within these rock units; from oldest to youngest they include the Halgaito Shale, Cedar Mesa Sandstone, Organ Rock Shale, and DeChelly

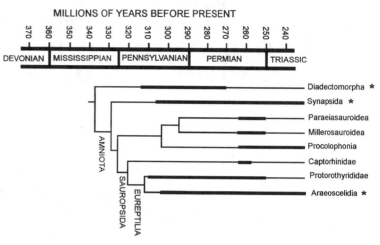

Figure 1. *Hypothesis of relationships of amniote taxa and their nearest sister-groups based primarily on Lombard and Sumida (1992) and Sumida (1997). Thicker lines indicate approximate known temporal distribution of representative fossils of each lineage. Asterisk (*) indicates taxa known from Upper Pennsylvanian and Lower Permian sediments of Utah and northeastern Arizona.*

Sandstone. Until recently, the Halgaito Shale and its equivalents were considered to be earliest Permian Wolfcampian in age. However, a recent re-evaluation and consensus on the beds defining the base of the Permian at its type section in the Ural Mountains of Russia (Baars, 1991, 1995; Davydov and others, 1995; Chernykh and others, 1997) have resulted in a change in placement of the Permo-Pennsylvanian boundary in the Four Corners region. A re-evaluation of invertebrate marker fossils indicates that the more northerly Elephant Canyon Formation must be latest Pennsylvanian, Virgilian in age. As the Elephant Canyon interfingers with the Halgaito Shale, the latter is effectively reassigned to the latest Pennsylvanian and the Permo-Pennsylvanian boundary is moved to a position between the Halgaito Shale and the Cedar Mesa Sandstone. The majority of the fossils included in this survey have been recovered from the Halgaito Shale. Thus, it appears that many of the Late Paleozoic fossils known from Utah and nearby regions that had previously been interpreted as earliest Permian in age are actually latest Pennsylvanian.

The Halgaito Shale may be characterized as fluvial redbeds that include elements of a variety of microenvironments. It consists of slope-forming, thin-bedded, reddish-brown shales, siltstones, sandstones, and some conglomerate lenses (Baars, 1962). Proposed depositional environments for this unit are: (1) deltaic in which drainage was to the north (Vaughn, 1962, 1966), or (2) a coastal lowland and/or intertidal flat in which channels were either stream-generated or tidal (Baars, 1962, 1995). Sumida and others (1999) noted that portions of the Halgaito appear to have experienced a fairly constant presence of water, whereas other regions may have been subject to more seasonal desiccation. It should be noted that these ancient environments can be difficult to distinguish from one another (Miall, 1984; Baars, 1995). Vertebrate fossils tend to be fragmentary and occur mainly in conglomerate lenses and associated crossbedded sandstones and siltstones (Vaughn, 1962, 1970). A new vertebrate locality was discovered recently in the Valley of the Gods in a siltstone resting on a conglomerate, preserving articulated and disarticulated remains of several taxa (Frede and others, 1993). The deposition suggests that a current acted on the bones as they came to their final resting position. One of the blocks collected from this locality includes a portion of the distal end of an articulated tail of the pelycosaur *Ophiacodon* resting on its right side, whereas the remainder of the skeleton is weathered away. Numerous bones of a small reptile are preserved between and adjacent to the distal tips of the neural spines of the tail. Very few bones of the small, possibly araeoscelidian, reptile are found on the opposite side of the tail. This suggests that a stream current may have deposited the disarticulated bones against the *Ophiacodon* tail where they became trapped. The presence of mudcracks which originate above the bone layer and penetrate through it suggests that the deposit represents a channel which silted in and subsequently dried.

The overlying Cedar Mesa Sandstone consists primarily of light-colored, resistant, cliff-forming, and commonly crossbedded sandstones that form a gradational contact with the underlying Halgaito Shale and interfingering Elephant Canyon Formation (Baars, 1962). Proposed depositional environments include a shallow-water, marginal marine to beach deposit (Baars, 1962; Vaughn, 1962, 1966) in which the sand was deposited as near-shore bars and coastal dunes (Baars, 1995). Stanesco and Campbell (1989) suggested that the Cedar Mesa was deposited as a complex aeolian unit bordered to the east by fluvial environments and to the south by sabkha environments. Tetrapod trackways have been discovered, but vertebrate fossils are known from only one locality (Stanesco and Campbell, 1989).

The slope-forming Organ Rock Shale has been described as lithologically similar to the Halgaito Shale (Baars, 1962, 1995; Vaughn, 1964), and has yielded a small but important assemblage of amniotes which are more numerous and generally more complete than those of the Halgaito Shale. A gradational contact exists between the Cedar Mesa Sandstone and the Organ Rock Shale.

The orangish-red DeChelly Sandstone forms massive crossbedded cliffs (Baars, 1962). Its depositional environment is generally interpreted as aeolian with wind direction and sand transport to the southwest (Baars,

1962, 1995). Tetrapod trackways are known from the DeChelly, though assignment of ichnofossils to either Amphibia or Amniota is impossible at this time. No skeletal remains have been found.

SURVEY OF TAXA

Diadectomorpha

Berman and others (1992), Sumida and others (1992), and Lee and Spencer (1997) have affirmed the monophyly of the Diadectomorpha based on cranial characters and characters of the atlas-axis complex. It is composed of three families, the Diadectidae and monogeneric Tseajaiidae sharing a more recent common ancestor with one another than with Limnoscelidae (Berman and others, 1992; Sumida and others, 1992). Specimens representative of all three families are known from Late Paleozoic rocks of southeastern Utah and northeastern Arizona. As the nearest outgroup of Amniota, a thorough understanding of the diadectomorphs is of particular importance.

Limnoscelidae

Scattered remains assignable to the Limnoscelidae are known from many Late Paleozoic localities in North America, but only one complete skeleton and the majority of another individual comprise the majority of our knowledge of the genus *Limnoscelis* (one specimen from northern New Mexico and one from central Colorado) (Berman and Sumida, 1990). Many other genera have been described on the basis of minimal materials. Upon closer examination many of these could likely be considered nomina dubia.

Only one reasonably confident report of a limnoscelid is known from Utah. Vaughn (1962) reported the presence of vertebral material possibly assignable to the family from a locality he described as the "*Platyhystrix* pocket" in the Halgaito Shale near the town of Mexican Hat in southeastern San Juan County. (See table 1 for exact geographic data of all localities described in this report.) Additionally, according to Vaughn (1962, p. 563), "a badly weathered vertebra found by the Harvard University-U.S. Geological Survey party in 1954 nine miles to the north-northeast seems to belong to [*Limnoscelis*]." Despite the paucity of materials, features of these vertebrae provide ample reason for at least tentative assignment to the Limnoscelidae (Vaughn, 1962; Berman and Sumida, 1990; Sumida, 1991).

Tseajaiidae

Possibly the most unique tetrapod recovered from the

Paleozoic sediments of Utah is *Tseajaia campi*. The type and referred specimens were recovered by Charles Camp in the Organ Rock Shale in southeastern San Juan County in 1942 (Vaughn, 1964) at narrowly separated sites from the same horizon in the Organ Rock Shale in San Juan County. Vaughn (1964) provided the initial description of *Tseajaia*; however, he never designated a locality name for the discovery site of holotype and paratype; thus, the basis of the generic name may be adopted for this purpose. It is derived from the Navajo name "Tse Ajai," meaning "rock heart," that identifies a nearby igneous plug (Baker, 1936, p. 63). Subsequent discoveries of *Tseajaia* have been made in the Lower Permian Cutler Formation of north-central New Mexico (Berman and others, 1992; Berman, 1993).

Vaughn (1964) and Moss (1972) suggested *Tseajaia* was intermediate between amphibian-grade seymouriamorphs and diadectids—ultimately assigning it to the Seymouriamorpha. However, re-evaluation of the holotype in light of discoveries of new materials (Berman and others, 1992), as well as conclusions reached in other studies (Heaton, 1980; Sumida and others, 1992) clearly indicate that *Tseajaia* is a member of the Diadectomorpha. Characters uniting the Diadectomorpha (and visible in the Utah *Tseajaia* specimen) include: projection of the supraoccipital beyond the margin of the otic capsule, the presence of an anteriorly directed midventral projection of the axial intercentrum, and a corresponding midventral trough of the atlantal intercentrum for articulation with the process. Among the features *Tseajaia* shares with diadectomorphs and more traditionally defined amniotes is the lack of an intertemporal bone. However, *Tseajaia* is autapomorphic within diadectomorphs in that it has secondarily lost contact between the parietal and tabular due to a lateral expansion of the postparietal (Berman and others, 1992).

Postcranial features found in the Utah specimen of *Tseajaia* (as well as the New Mexico specimens) are also distinctive; Sumida and others (1992) and Sumida (1997) point out that *Tseajaia* and other diadectomorphs share a number of postcranial features with amniotes. These include: fusion of the axial neural arch and centrum,

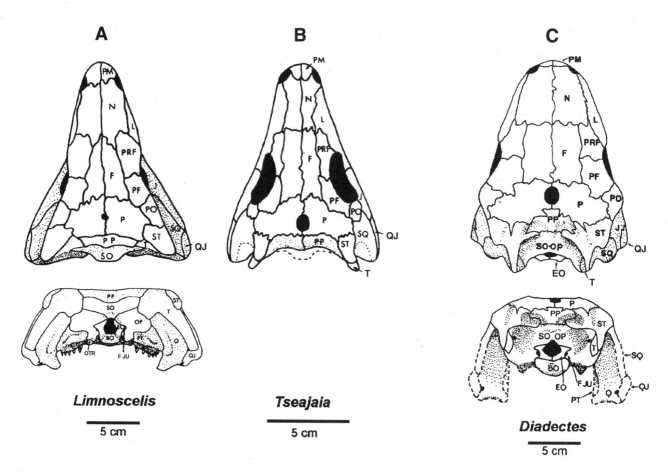

A **B** **C**

Limnoscelis

5 cm

Tseajaia

5 cm

Diadectes

5 cm

Figure 2. *Reconstructions of Late Pennsylvanian and Early Permian Diadectomorpha known from southeastern Utah and northern Arizona. A, dorsal and occipital view of the skull of* Limnoscelis; *B, dorsal view of* Tseajaia; *C, dorsal and occipital view of* Diadectes. *Illustrations after Berman and others (1992). Abbreviations: a, angular; bo, basioccipital; d, dentary; eo, exoccipital; f, frontal; f ju, jugular foramen; it, intertemporal; j, jugal; m, maxilla; n, nasal; op, opisthotic; p, parietal; pf, postfrontal; pm, premaxilla; po, postorbital; pp, postparietal; prf, prefrontal; pt, pterygoid; q, quadrate; qj, quadratojugal; sa, surangular; sm, septomaxilla; sp, splenial; sq, squamosal; st, supratemporal; t, tabular.*

Table 1. *Geographic data for localities that have yielded Late Pennsylvanian and Early Permian amniotes and their near relatives in Utah and northeastern Arizona. *Exact locality data for the Canyonlands locality is omitted due to problems associated with vandalism.*

Locality	Section, Township, Range
Pennsylvanian	
Arch Canyon	NE1/4 sec. 21, T.37S., R.20E.
Cedar Point	NE 1/4 SE 1/4 sec. 17, T.41S., R.18E.
John's Canyon (i)	NE1/4 NE1/4 sec. 19, T.40S., R.18E.
John's Canyon (ii)	NE1/4 NE1/4 sec. 18, T.40S., R.18E.
John's Canyon (iii)	NW1/4 NE1/4 sec. 34, T.40S., R.18E.
Lime Creek	NW1/4, sec. 29, T.41S., R.19E.
Lisbon Valley (i)	SE1/4 SE1/4 sec. 20, T.30S., R.25E.
Lisbon Valley (ii)	SW1/4 NE1/4 sec. 34, T.30S., R.25E.
"*Platyhystrix* pocket"	SE 1/4 sec. 21, T.41S., R.19E.
Valley of the Gods (i)	NW1/4 NW1/4 sec. 29, T.40S., R.19E.
Valley of the Gods (ii)	SE1/4 sec. 27, T.40S., R.19E.
Valley of the Gods (iii)	NE1/4 SE1/4 sec. 24, T.40S., R.19E.
Valley of the Gods (iv)	E border of secs. 27&34, T.40S., R.19E.
Valley of the Gods 1997	NE1/4 sec. 30, T.40S., R.19E.
Permian	
Canyonlands	*
Hoskinnini Mesa, nearby butte	SW1/4, sec. 7, T.43S., R.14E.
Hoskinnini Mesa, north slope	NW1/4 sec. 13, T.43S., R.14E.
Hoskinnini Mesa, north slope	NW1/4 sec. 8, T.43S., R.14E.
Mitchell Butte, Arizona (i)	NE1/4 sec 11, T. 43S., R.16E.
Mitchell Butte, Arizona (ii)	SW1/4 sec. 12, T.43S., R.16E.
Mitten Buttes, Arizona	T.41N., R.21E.
Monument Pass	Sec. 20, T. 43S., R.17 E.
Monument Pass, 2 mi. SE	S1/2 sec. 17, T.43S., R.17E.
Organ Rock	N1/2 sec. 16, T.42S., R.14E.
Saddleback and Stagecoach Buttes	Intersection of secs. 17,18,19,20, T.43S., R.17E.
Train Rock	SE 1/4 sec. 4, T.43S., R.15E.
Tse Ajai	NW1/4 sec. 20, T.43S., R.17E.
Tse Ajai referred	NW1/4, sec. 13, T.43S., R.16E.

fusion of the atlantal pleurocentrum to the dorsal aspect of the axial intercentrum, bracketing of the axial neural spine by posteriorly directed atlantal neural arches, a well-developed process for the latissimus dorsi on the humerus, a distinctively large olecranon process on the ulna, and tibial length greater than half that of the femur (usually approaching 70%).

Diadectidae

Diadectes is the only identifiable representative of the Diadectidae known from the area of this report, however no specimens of the degree of completeness seen in *Tseajaia* are known. Fragments that are unquestionably diadectid are common components of both Late Pennsylvanian and Early Permian assemblages, though most are isolated vertebrae or teeth. Diadectid vertebrae are distinctive for their possession of laterally expanded ("swollen") neural arches, occasionally in combination with accessory intervertebral articulations known as hyposphenes and hypantra. The marginal dentitions are unique in their anterior, chisel-like incisiform teeth,

whereas the molariform teeth are transversely expanded.

Vertebral materials that may be provisionally assigned to *Diadectes* span the Permo-Pennsylvanian boundary. Specimens are known from the Late Pennsylvanian Halgaito Shale in the Valley of the Gods (Frede and others, 1993) and the "*Platyhystrix* pocket" of Vaughn (1962) near the town of Mexican Hat in southeastern San Juan County. *Diadectes* is found at a greater number of Early Permian localities, all of which occur in the Organ Rock Shale. The most complete specimens have been those of at least two individuals comprising partial axial columns, pectoral girdles and limbs "from the southeast side of a small bell-shaped butte just north of Hoskinnini Mesa" (Vaughn, 1964) in San Juan County. Additionally, *Diadectes* has been identified from a variety of other Lower Permian localities in Utah: (1) southeast of Monument Pass, (2) near the base of the northern slope of Hoskinnini Mesa, (3) about one mile north of Organ Rock Monument, and (4) southeast of Train Rock. It is also known from the Arizona portion of Monument Valley, near the base of the Mitten Buttes (Baker, 1936; Vaughn, 1964).

Pelycosaurian-grade Synapsida

In both quantity and variety, pelycosaurian-grade synapsids dominate Late Pennsylvanian and Early Permian terrestrial tetrapod assemblages in southeastern Utah. At least five genera from three families are known, most commonly identifiable as the ophiacodontid *Ophiacodon* or the sphenacodont *Sphenacodon*. Occasionally, material identifiable only as pelycosaurian is encountered, such as near Lime Creek, north of the town of Mexican Hat in San Juan County.

Ophiacodontidae

Remains of ophiacodontid pelycosaurs are found in both Late Pennsylvanian and Early Permian sediments. Late Pennsylvanian specimens from John's Canyon and the Valley of the Gods are confidently assignable to the genus *Ophiacodon*, but specific determination is not possible. These are most readily identified by their vertebral structure that is typically pelycosaurian in nature but lacking the distinctive lateral excavations of the neural arch seen in sphenacodontids or edaphosaurids. Vaughn (1962) used relative size and structure of several dorsal vertebrae, parts of four scapulocoracoids, and a portion of a humerus to suggest the possible presence of *Ophiacodon navajovicus* (Williston, 1914; Romer and Price, 1940) from his locality known as the "*Platyhystrix* pocket."

Rare, fragmentary remains of *Ophiacodon*, comparable to *O. retroversus* of Texas, are known from Organ Rock Shale localities near Monument Pass and just east of Mitchell Butte (Vaughn, 1964). This is the largest representative of the genus from the Four Corners region, and together with the Halgaito specimens exhibits a consistent increase in size with ascent through the stratigraphic column in a manner similar to that seen in Early Permian forms from Texas. This and the lack of adequate materials to allow a clearer picture of the relationship with forms from New Mexico led Vaughn (1964) to decide that is was inappropriate to name a new species based on the Utah materials.

Edaphosauridae

Though not as frequently encountered as those of *Ophiacodon* or *Sphenacodon*, remains of edaphosaurid pelycosaurs are not uncommon. Vertebral elements found in three different locations in the Halgaito Shale of the Valley of the Gods are easily identifiable as *Edaphosaurus* by the tuberculate cross-bars found on the elongate neural spines. Although rolled up on itself, at least one specimen includes nearly a complete dorsal sail

with centra. Although the vertebrae are apparently completely ossified, they are extremely small, as the entire sail could not have been longer than 20 centimeters or taller than fifteen. No cranial material is known from the Halgaito localities, and confident specific assignment is not possible. Extensive prospecting by Vaughn (1964, 1966, 1973) and later by the authors of this report has not yielded *Edaphosaurus* from post-Halgaito deposits. It is unclear whether this is a reflection of a true faunal distribution or collecting bias. Given the frequency with which *Edaphosaurus* is found in other Four Corners Region sediments, the latter may very well be the case.

Sphenacodontidae

Pelycosaurian synapsids are the most dominant component of the Late Paleozoic tetrapod assemblages of southeastern Utah, and they are most prominently represented by sphenacodontids. Sphenacodontids are easily recognizable by their tall, narrow skulls, short postorbital region, and aggressively caniniform teeth (Romer and Price, 1940; Eberth, 1985) (figure 3). Eberth (1985) has pointed out that, based on cranial morphology alone, the different genera of sphenacodonts are essentially indistinguishable. Indeed, most are defined by the relative development of the vertebral neural spines. Of those known from Utah and nearby deposits, the spines of *Sphenacodon* are relatively shortest. Those of *Dimetrodon* are the longest and have fore and aft grooves for most of their length giving them a "dumbbell" or "figure-8" shaped cross section. *Ctenospondylus* has neural spines of intermediate length. Given the similarity of cranial and appendicular materials, confident identification of sphenacodontid materials could be difficult; fortunately, vertebral elements are among those most commonly found.

Sphenacodontid specimens most likely assignable to *Sphenacodon* are found through much of the Late Paleozoic sequence exposed in southeastern Utah, with representatives known from the Halgaito, Cedar Mesa, and Organ Rock units. *Sphenacodon* is especially ubiquitous in Late Pennsylvanian localities of the Halgaito Shale; examples are known from the "*Platyhystrix* pocket", two different localities in the Valley of the Gods, John's Canyon, and two different localities in the Lisbon Valley. Most of these reports are based on axial elements, easily identifiable by the deeply excavated fossae at the bases of the vertebral neural spines; however, the associated remains of a single individual are known from the Lisbon Valley site, and partial articulated postcranial remains are known from the Valley of the Gods.

Characteristic cranial and vertebral materials have also been recovered from an extraordinary locality in the

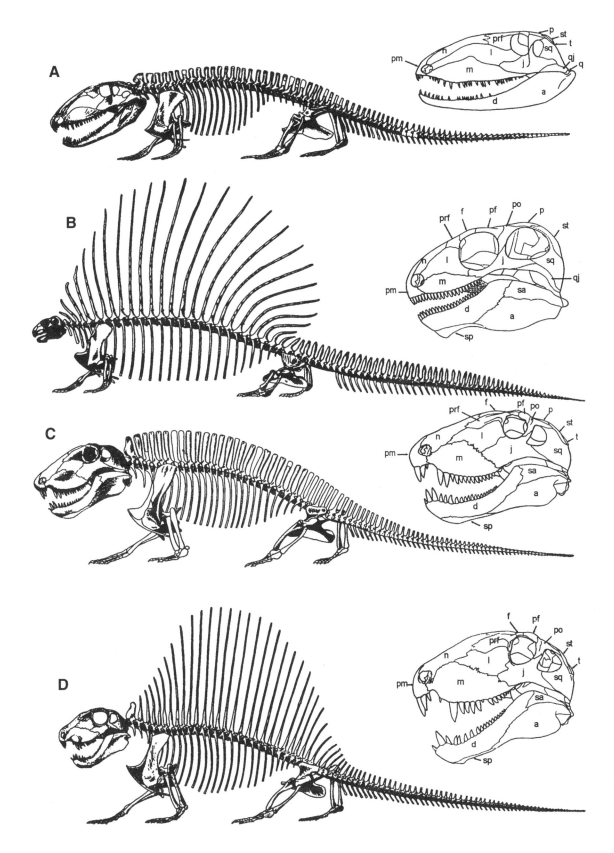

Figure 3. *Reconstructions of Late Pennsylvanian and Early Permian Synapsida known from southeastern Utah and northern Arizona. A, left lateral view of the skull and whole body reconstruction of the ophiacodontid pelycosaur* Ophiacodon; *B, left lateral view of the skull and whole body reconstruction of the edaphosaurid pelycosaur* Edaphosaurus; *C, left lateral view of the skull and whole body reconstruction of the sphenacodontid pelycosaur* Sphenacodon; *D, left lateral view of the skull and whole body reconstruction of the sphenacodontid pelycosaur* Dimetrodon. *A and B after Romer and Price (1940) and Reisz (1986), C and D after Romer and Price (1940), Reisz (1986), and Eberth (1985). Abbreviations as in figure 2.*

Table 2. Diadectomorph and amniote tetrapods known from Pennsylvanian-age sediments of Utah. Institutional abbreviations: CMNH, Carnegie Museum of Natural History; CSUSB VP, California State University San Bernardino Vertebrate Paleontology Collections; NTM, Navajo Tribal Museum, collections on extended loan to the Carnegie Museum of Natural History; UCLA VP, University of California Los Angeles (some materials transferred and accessioned into collections of the Carnegie Museum of Natural History and the University of California); USNM, United States National Museum, Washington, D.C.

Late Pennsylvanian

Taxon	Rock Unit or Formation	Locality	Reference	Depository
DIADECTOMORPHA				
Limnoscelidae				
limnoscelid	Halgaito Shale	"*Platyhystrix* pocket"	Vaughn (1962)	UCLA VP 1626
Diadectidae				
Diadectes sp.	Halgaito Shale	Valley of the Gods (i)	Frede and others (1993)	CMNH
Diadectes sp.	Halgaito Shale	"*Platyhystrix* pocket"	Vaughn (1962)	UCLA VP 1624, 1625
SYNAPSIDA				
pelycosaur indeterminate	Halgaito Shale	Lime Creek	This report	not removable from locality
Ophiacodontidae				
Ophiacodon cf. *O. navajovicus*	Halgaito Shale	"*Platyhystrix* pocket"	Vaughn (1962)	UCLA VP1627-1635
Ophiacodon	Halgaito Shale	John's Canyon (i)	This report	CMNH
Ophiacodon	Halgaito Shale	Valley of the Gods (i)	This report	CMNH
Edaphosauridae				
Edaphosaurus sp.	Halgaito Shale	Valley of the Gods (i)	Frede and others (1993)	CMNH
Edaphosaurus sp.	Halgaito Shale	Valley of the Gods (ii)	This report	CMNH
Edaphosaurus sp.	Halgaito Shale	Valley of the Gods 1997	This report	CSUSB VP
Sphenacodontidae				
Sphenacodon sp.	Halgaito Shale	John's Canyon (i)	This report	CMNH
Sphenacodon sp.	Halgaito Shale equivalent of Cutler Formation	Lisbon Valley (i)	This report	UCLA VP 1671
Sphenacodon sp.	Halgaito Shale equivalent of Cutler Formation	Lisbon Valley (ii)	This report	UCLA VP 1672
Sphenacodon sp.	Halgaito Shale	"*Platyhystrix* pocket"	Vaughn (1962)	UCLA VP 1636, 1637
Sphenacodon sp.	Halgaito Shale	Valley of the Gods (i)	This report	CMNH
Sphenacodon sp.	Halgaito Shale	Valley of the Gods (ii)	This report	CMNH
sphenacodontid	Halgaito Shale	Valley of the Gods 1997	This report	CSUSB VP
ARAEOSCELIDIA				
araeoscelid (?)	Halgaito Shale	Valley of the Gods (i)	This report	CMNH

Table 3. *Diadectomorph and amniote tetrapods known from Early Permian-age sediments of Utah and northeastern Arizona. Abbreviations as in table 2.*

Early Permian

Taxon	Rock Unit or Formation	Locality	Reference	Depository
DIADECTOMORPHA				
Tseajaiidae				
Tseajaia campi	Organ Rock Shale	Tse Ajai	Vaughn (1964)	UCMP V4225/59012
Tseajaia campi	Organ Rock Shale	Tse Ajai referred	Vaughn (1964)	UCMP V4216/63841
Diadectidae				
Diadectes sp.	Organ Rock Shale	Mitchell Butte, Arizona (i)	Vaughn (1964)	NTM 1008
Diadectes sp.	Organ Rock Shale	Monument Pass	Vaughn (1964)	USNM 11929
Diadectes sp.	Organ Rock Shale	Train Rock	Vaughn (1964)	
Diadectes sp.	Organ Rock Shale	Organ Rock Monument	Vaughn (1964)	NTM 1003, 1005, 1006, 1007
Diadectes sp.	Organ Rock Shale	Hoskinnini Mesa north	Vaughn (1964)	NTM 1002
Diadectes sp.	Organ Rock Shale	Hoskinnini Mesa nearby butte	Vaughn (1964)	
Diadectes sp.	Organ Rock Shale	Mitten Buttes, Arizona	Baker (1936)	UCMP V4217/59002, V4218; UCMP V4222/ 58999, V4222/59000
SYNAPSIDA				
Ophiacodontidae				
Ophiacodon sp.	Organ Rock Shale	Monument Pass	Vaughn (1964)	NTM 1009, 1010, 1011, 1012, 1013; UCMP V4217/59004
Sphenacodontidae				
Ophiacodon sp.	Organ Rock Shale	Mitchell Butte, Arizona (i)	Vaughn (1964)	UCLA VP1645
Ctenospondylus cf. *C. casei*	Organ Rock Shale	Hoskinnini Mesa, north slope	Vaughn (1964, 1966)	NTM 1018
Ctenospondylus cf. *C. casei*	Organ Rock Shale	Hoskinnini Mesa, nearby butte	Vaughn (1964, 1966)	NTM 1001, 1014, 1015
Ctenospondylus cf. *C. casei* (?)	Organ Rock Shale	Monument Pass	Vaughn (1964, 1966)	UCMP
Dimetrodon sp.	Organ Rock Shale	Mitchell Butte, Arizona (i)	Vaughn (1966)	UCLA VP 1675
Dimetrodon sp.	Organ Rock Shale	Mitchell Butte, Arizona (ii)	Vaughn (1966)	NTM 1039
Dimetrodon sp.	Organ Rock Shale	Monument Pass	Vaughn (1966)	NTM 1040
Dimetrodon sp.	Organ Rock Shale	Monument Pass south	Vaughn (1966)	NTM 1041
Sphenacodon sp.	Cedar Mesa Sandstone	Near Canyonlands National Park	This report	CSUSB VP
Sphenacodon cf. *S. ferocior*	Organ Rock Shale	Mitchell Butte, Arizona (i)	Vaughn (1964)	UCLA VP1646, 1647
UNKNOWN TETRAPODA				
Ichnofossils				
footprints	Cedar Mesa Sandstone	(?)	This report	
footprints	LeChelly Sandstone	Numerous	Vaughn (1963, 1973); Sadler (1993)	

Cedar Mesa Sandstone in the Indian Creek drainage near the eastern border of Canyonlands National Park. This locality preserved what appeared to be a log jam that contained several large, current-oriented, silicified conifer logs, the largest being eight meters long and a meter in diameter. Within this deposit, vertebral and cranial elements of *Sphenacodon* (as well as the temnospondyl amphibian *Eryops*) were recorded. Unfortunately, this locality was vandalized and stripped of fossils completely in 1995. [In 1996 the large petrified logs were recovered; however, the tetrapod materials remain lost to science.]

Sphenacodon continues into Organ Rock Shale deposits, but is not as common as in the Halgaito Shale. Axial elements referable to *Sphenacodon* sp., cf. *S. ferocior* were identified by Vaughn (1964) from just east of Mitchell Butte in northeastern Arizona. He proposed the possible assignment to *S. ferocior* based on size comparisons with similar materials described by Case and Williston (1913) and Romer and Price (1940). Given the presence of other sphenacodontids in Organ Rock deposits, this assignment must be viewed with some caution. However, this genus is present in older Utah sediments, and in older and equivalent sediments in other Four Corners regions.

Whereas *Sphenacodon* is a common member of Late Paleozoic assemblages in both Pennsylvanian and Permian sediments of southeastern Utah, two other sphenacodontids are restricted to the Early Permian Organ Rock Shale. Only fragmentary remains are known for *Dimetrodon* in Utah, but the specimens can identified with confidence given the distinctive nature of the extremely elongate neural spines in that genus. Vaughn (1966) reported *Dimetrodon* from four different localities: near Monument Pass as well as approximately two miles south of Monument Pass in San Juan County, Utah and two localities near Mitchell Butte in Arizona. The presence of *Dimetrodon* in Utah is not surprising given its occurrence in fluvial redbed sediments of approximately the same age in north-central New Mexico (Berman, 1977). The New Mexican material of *Dimetrodon* was complete enough to recognize a new species, *D. occidentalis* (Berman, 1977). It is tempting to assign the Utah specimens to that species as this is the only species currently known from facies approximating the Organ Rock either temporally and geographically (Eberth and Miall, 1991; Berman, 1993). It is logical to consider this taxon as a candidate for the Utah materials, however *D. occidentalis* is based on details of neural spines not available in those from Utah.

The second sphenacodontid genus known from the Organ Rock Shale is also defined primarily by its neural spine morphology. *Ctenospondylus* possesses elongate neural spines and, while they are laterally compressed as in *Sphenacodon*, they are clearly longer for a given size individual. Conversely, they are considerably shorter than those in *Dimetrodon* even in completely mature individuals and do not possess the subcircular or dumbbell shaped cross section found in the various species of that genus. *Ctenospondylus* had been very poorly known until Vaughn's (1964) discovery of remains of the genus in southeastern San Juan County just north of Hoskinnini Mesa and near the base of the Mesa. Vaughn speculated that materials from near Monument Pass might also be referable to the genus. The best of these confirms the difficulty in distinguishing sphenacodontid taxa on the basis of any data other than axial characters. Among the remains is a skull virtually identical to the configuration found in *Dimetrodon* and *Sphenacodon* (Eberth, 1985).

Araeoscelidia

Basal members of the Eureptilia are unexpectedly absent in the Late Paleozoic deposits of southeastern Utah. Unlike sediments of comparable deposits in New Mexico, Oklahoma, and north-central Texas, there are no reported occurrences of captorhinomorph reptiles in Utah. However, in one of the Late Pennsylvanian localities of the Halgaito Shale in the Valley of the Gods a small, possibly araeoscelidian reptile is represented by scattered remains of numerous individuals preserved in what is believed to be a silted-in stream-channel deposit (Frede and others, 1993).

The materials may represent an as yet unnamed new taxon, or may be referable to a previously described member of the Araeoscelidia. Unfortunately, very little cranial material has been found thus far and despite a large amount of postcranial material present, it is nearly completely disarticulated. Features that suggest assignment to Araeoscelidia include (1) extremely elongate "cervical" vertebrae, typical of the condition found in *Araeoscelis* from the Lower Permian of north-central Texas, *Petrolacosaurus* from the Upper Pennsylvanian of Kansas, and *Zarcasaurus* from the Lower Permian of northern New Mexico (Sumida, 1991); (2) an isolated parietal that suggests the presence of a temporal opening; (3) the appendicular elements that are lightly built as in other gracile araeoscelids; and (4) propodial and epipodial elements that approximate *Araeoscelis* and *Petrolacosaurus* in proportions. Assignment of the Valley of the Gods reptile to Araeoscelidia is, however, considered speculative until more complete and articulated specimens can be found.

Trackways

A number of vertebrate trackways have been reported, particularly in the DeChelly Sandstone. Vaughn (1963, 1973) and Sadler (1993) have noted these, but definitive correlation between trackway types and osteologically represented taxa is extremely difficult. The presence of the trackways is noteworthy if for nothing else to emphasize the possible presence of amniotes in post-Organ Rock sediments. Vaughn's (1963) report of a downslope trackway from DeChelly sediments was most likely made by an amniote of proportions similar to that of a small living lizard. Additional trackways have been discovered by the authors in rocks resting on Halgaito Shale sediments. The best preserved example is in a block that that had rolled downslope from the higher Cedar Mesa Sandstone near the mouth of John's Canyon. This particular trackway is noteworthy in that the footprints are large, nearly five centimeters across, yet the right and left sides are unusually close to each other. They are separated by less than ten centimeters at most and the stride length was very short.

COMMENTS ON PERMIAN-PENNSYLVANIAN BOUNDARY

Because the base of the Permian at its type section in the Ural Mountains has recently been redefined (Baars, 1991, 1995; Davydov and others, 1995; Chernykh and others, 1997) the position of the Permo-Pennsylvanian boundary in the Four Corners regions needs to be re-evaluated. Placement of the Permo-Pennsylvanian boundary in southeastern Utah and northeastern Arizona can now be recognized at the contact of the Halgaito Shale and Cedar Mesa Sandstone. The former interfingers with the marine Elephant Canyon Formation which contains marine fusulinids and conodonts that are currently being considered as latest Pennsylvanian, Virgilian age (Baars, 1995; Chernykh and others, 1997). The age of the Organ Rock Shale, which overlies the Cedar Mesa Sandstone, was previously considered to be earliest Leonardian based on correlation with the upper portion of the Wichita Group of Texas (Vaughn, 1964). More recently, the lower part of the Organ Rock Shale in the region of the fossil localities described here was considered upper Leonardian (Eberth and Berman, 1993; Sumida and others, 1996). Accepting the current placement of the Permo-Pennsylvanian boundary, all of the Organ Rock Shale may be Wolfcampian.

Fossil localities in the nearby, undifferentiated redbed deposits of the Cutler and Abo formations in central and north-central New Mexico have most recently been judged as spanning the Permo-Pennsylvanian transition (Eberth and Berman, 1993; Eberth and Miall, 1991). Comparison of vertebrate assemblages from these regions with the Halgaito Shale and Organ Rock Shale in Utah and Arizona should help in determining the Permo-Pennsylvanian boundary in New Mexico. However, the currently described Halgaito assemblage is very fragmentary, and in most cases elements cannot be confidently identified below the generic level. Fortunately, new localities in the Valley of the Gods include articulated, as well as disarticulated but closely associated remains of several taxa. Further study of these will undoubtedly provide a better understanding of the Halgaito fauna. It is hoped that eventually a better understanding of these North American deposits will allow a more precise age assignment of European localities that preserve taxa remarkably like those from the southwestern United States (Berman and Martens, 1993; Sumida and others, 1996).

SUMMARY

Other studies in this volume have demonstrated that fishes and amphibians were considerably more diverse in Late Pennsylvanian deposits than in Early Permian. Even if ichnofossils are excluded, a comparable summary for amniotes indicates the reverse: a slightly higher diversity of taxa in Early Permian assemblages relative to those of the Late Pennsylvanian. This could be explained in two ways. It might suggest that more terrestrial amniotes became somewhat more abundant with time as fishes and amphibians became less common. This would support Vaughn's (1966, 1973) hypothesis that gradual drying might have occurred through the Early Permian. The slight increase in amniotes and their near relatives might simply be a byproduct of collection or collection bias. The search for vertebrate fossils has been focused on terrestrial to semiterrestrial deposits, or stream channel lenses that might yield terrestrial tetrapods.

The diversity of Early Permian synapsids in southeastern Utah derives in part from the discovery of the rarely occurring *Dimetrodon* and *Ctenospondylus* in the Organ Rock Shale. It is reasonable to assume that similarly rare taxa might still be discovered in Late Pennsylvanian sediments. Indeed, the recent discovery of a new araeoscelid at a Late Pennsylvanian locality in the Valley of the Gods attests to the continued potential for new discoveries in this region.

ACKNOWLEDGMENTS

The authors thank David Gillette for the invitation to contribute to this volume. We thank the members of our hard-working field parties from 1989 to 1993 and 1997: Luisa Abukarma, John Balsley, John Bolt, Angela Dudeck, Brette Greenwood, Tom Hetherington, Jeff Janovets, Matthew Kosnik, Johanna Lombard, Mary Lombard, Stefan Lombard, Robert Lombard, Debra McPhearson, Dennis and Robin O'Keefe, Laura Panko, Sally Parker-Johnson, Elizabeth Rega, and Natalie Seel. Sebastian Frede prepared and identified some of the material reported on in this study. The Monticello, Utah, office of the BLM has been especially helpful to our fieldwork and we particularly thank Robert Turri for facilitating our progress. The late Colonel Richard and Jacqualine Lombard were gracious hosts during parts of our field seasons, and it is with fond memories that we acknowledge their immeasurable support and enthusiasm for our work. Elizabeth Rega read the manuscript, offering insightful and helpful commentary. As always, Peter Vaughn was an invaluable source of information on the geology, geography, and paleontology of the Four Corners region. Without his hard work and ground-breaking effort, the authors would not have been able to pursue this project. This work was supported by a California State University San Bernardino Minigrant (to SSS). This paper is dedicated to the fond memory of Luke, a trusting and caring canine friend.

REFERENCES

Baars, D. L., 1962, Permian system of the Colorado Plateau: American Association of Petroleum Geologists Bulletin, v. 46, p.149-218.

—1991, Redefinition of the Pennsylvanian-Permian boundary in Kansas, Midcontinent, U.S.A.: Program with Abstracts, International Congress of the Permian System of the World, Perm USSR, p. A3.

—1995, Navajo country, a geology and natural history of the Four Corners Region: Albuquerque, University of New Mexico Press, 255 p.

Baker, A. A., 1936, Geology of the Monument Valley-Navajo Mountain region, San Juan County, Utah: U. S. Geological Survey Bulletin, no. 865, p. 1-106.

Berman, D. S, 1977, A new species of *Dimetrodon* (Reptilia, Pelycosauria) from a non-deltaic facies in the Lower Permian of north-central New Mexico: Journal of Paleontology, v. 51, p. 108-115.

—1993, Lower Permian vertebrate localities of New Mexico and their assemblages, *in* Lucas, S. G., and Zidek, Jeri, editors, Vertebrate paleontology in New Mexico: New Mexico Museum of Natural History and Science Bulletin, no. 2, p. 11-21.

Berman, D. S, and Martens, Thomas, 1993, First occurrence of *Seymouria* (Amphibia: Batrachosauria) in the Lower Permian of central Germany: Annals of Carnegie Museum, v. 62, p. 63-79.

Berman, D. S, and Sumida, S. S., 1990, A new species of *Limnoscelis* (Amphibia, Diadectomorpha) from the Late Pennsylvanian Sangre de Cristo Formation of central Colorado: Annals of Carnegie Museum, v. 59, p. 303-341.

Berman, D. S, Sumida, S. S., and Lombard, R. E., 1992, Reinterpretation of the temporal and occipital regions in *Diadectes* and the relationships of diadectomorphs: Journal of Paleontology, v. 66, p. 481-499.

Case, E. C., and Williston, S. W., 1913, A description of a certain collection of bones referred to *Sphenacodon* Marsh: Carnegie Institute of Washington Publication no. 181, p. 61-70.

Chernykh, V. V., Ritter, S. M., and Wardlaw, B. R., 1997, *Streptognathus isolatus* new species (Conodonta)-- proposed index for the Carboniferous-Permian boundary: Journal of Paleontology, v. 71, p. 162-164.

Davydov, V. I., Glenister, B. F., Spinosa, Claude, Ritter, S. M., Chernykh, V. V., Wardlaw, B. R., and Snyder, W. S., 1995, Proposal of Aidaralash as GSSP for the base of the Permian system: Permofiles, v. 26, p. 1-9.

Eberth, D. A., 1985, The skull of *Sphenacodon ferocior*, and comparisons with other sphenacodontines (Reptilia: Pelycosauria): New Mexico Bureau of Mines and Mineral Resources Circular 190, p. 1-39.

Eberth, D. A., and Berman, D. S, 1993, Stratigraphy, sedimentology, and vertebrate paleoecology of the Cutler Formation redbeds (Pennsylvanian-Permian) of north-central New Mexico, *in* Lucas, S. G., and Zidek, Jeri, editors, Vertebrate paleontology in New Mexico: New Mexico Museum of Natural History and Science Bulletin, no. 2, p. 33-48.

Eberth, D. A., and Miall, A. D., 1991, Stratigraphy, sedimentology and evolution of a vertebrate-bearing, braided to anastomosed fluvial system, Cutler Formation (Permian-Pennsylvanian), north-central New Mexico: Sedimentary Geology, v. 72, p. 225-252.

Frede, Sebastian, Sumida, S. S., and Berman, D. S, 1993, New information on early Permian vertebrates from the Halgaito Tongue of the Cutler Formation of southeastern Utah: Journal of Vertebrate Paleontology, v. 13 (Supplement to No. 3), p. 36A.

Gauthier, J. A., Kluge, A. G., and Rowe, Timothy, 1988, The early evolution of the Amniota, *in* Benton, M. J., editor, The phylogeny and classification of tetrapods, volume 1, amphibans, reptiles, birds, Systematics Association Special Volume No. 35A: Oxford, Clarendon Press, p. 103-155.

Heaton, M. J., 1980, The Cotylosauria: a reconsideration of a group of archaic tetrapods, *in* Panchen, A. L., editor, The terrestrial environment and the origin of land vertebrates: London, Academic Press, p. 497-551.

Heaton, M. J., and Reisz, R. R., 1986, Phylogenetic relationships of captorhinomorph reptiles: Canadian Journal of Earth Sciences, v. 23, p. 402-418.

Laurin, Michel, and Reisz, R. R., 1995, A reevaluation of early amniote phylogeny: Zoological Journal of the Linnean

Society: v. 113, p. 165-223.

—1997, A new perspective on tetrapod phylogeny, *in* Sumida, S. S., and Martin, K. L. M., editors, Amniote origins, completing the transition to land: San Diego, Academic Press, p. 9-60.

Lee, M. Y. S., and Spencer, P. S., 1997, Crown-clades, key characters and taxonomic stability-- when is an amniote not an amniote?, *in* Sumida, S. S., and Martin, K. L. M., editors, Amniote origins, completing the transition to land: San Diego, Academic Press, p. 61-84.

Lombard, R. E., and Sumida, S. S., 1992, Recent progress in understanding early tetrapods: American Zoologist, v. 32, p. 609-622.

Miall, A. D., 1984, Deltas, *in* Walker, R. G., editor, Facies models, Second Edition, Geological Association of Canada, 317 p.

Modesto, S. P., 1992, Did herbivory foster early amniote diversification?: Journal of Vertebrate Paleontology, v. 12, (Supplement to no. 3) p. 44A.

Moss, J. L., 1972, The morphology and phylogenetic relationships of the Lower Permian tetrapod *Tseajaia campi* Vaughn (Amphibia: Seymouriamorpha): University of California Publications in Geological Sciences, v. 98, p. 1-72.

Reisz, R. R., 1980, The Pelycosauria- a review of the phylogenetic relationships, *in* Panchen, A. L., editor, The terrestrial environment and the origin of land vertebrates, Systematics Association Special Volume No. 15: London, Academic Press, p. 553-592.

—1986, Pelycosauria: Handbuch der Palaeoperpetologie, v. 17, p. 1-102.

Romer, A. S., and Price, L. I., 1940, Review of the Pelycosauria, Geological Society of America Special Paper, no. 28, 538 p.

Sadler, C. J., 1993, Arthropod trace fossils from the Permian De Chelly Sandstone, northeastern Arizona: Journal of Paleontology, v. 67, p. 240-249.

Stanesco, J. D., and Campbell, J. A., 1989, Eolian and noneolian facies of the Lower Permian Cedar Mesa Sandstone Member of the Cutler Formation, southeastern Utah: U. S. Geological Survey Bulletin, no. 1808, p. F1-F13.

Sumida, S. S., 1991, Vertebral morphology, alternation of neural spine height, and structure in Permo-Carboniferous

tetrapods, and a reappraisal of primitive modes of terrestrial locomotion: University of California Publications in Zoology, v. 122, p. 1-133.

—1997, Locomotor features of taxa spanning the origin of amniotes, *in* Sumida, S. S., and Martin, K. L. M., editors, Amniote origins, completing the transition to land: San Diego, Academic Press, p. 353-398.

Sumida, S. S., Albright, G. A., and Rega, E. A., 1999, Late Paleozoic fishes of Utah, *in* Gillette, D. D., editor, this volume.

Sumida, S. S., Berman, D. S, and Martens, Thomas, 1996, Biostratigraphic correlations between the Lower Permian of North America and central Europe using the first record of an assemblage of terrestrial tetrapods from Germany: PaleoBios, v. 17, p. 1-12.

Sumida, S. S., Lombard, R. E., and Berman, D. S, 1992, Morphology of the atlas axis complex of the late Palaeozoic tetrapod suborders Diadectomorpha and Seymouriamorpha: Philosophical Transactions of the Royal Society of London, v. 336, p. 259-273.

Vaughn, P. P., 1962, Vertebrates from the Halgaito Tongue of the Cutler Formation, Permian of San Juan County, Utah: Journal of Paleontology, v. 36, p.529-539.

—1963, A downslope trackway in the DeChelly Sandstone, Permian of Monument Valley: Plateau, v. 36, p. 25-28.

—1964, Vertebrates from the Organ Rock Shale of the Cutler Group, Permian of Monument Valley and vicinity, Utah and Arizona: Journal of Paleontology, v. 38, p. 567-583.

—1966, Comparison of the early Permian vertebrate faunas of the Four Corners region and North Central Texas: Los Angeles County Museum Contributions in Science, no. 105, p. 1-13.

—1970, Alternation of neural spine height in certain Early Permian tetrapods: Bulletin of the Southern California Academy of Sciences, v. 69, p. 80-86.

—1973, Vertebrates from the Cutler Group of Monument Valley and vicinity. Utah and Arizona, *in* James, H. L., editor, Guidebook of Monument Valley and vicinity: New Mexico Geological Society Field Conference Volume, No. 24, p. 99-105.

Williston, S. W., 1914, The osteology of some American Permian vertebrate: Journal of Geology, v. 22, p. 364-419.

MESOZOIC ERA

SMALL FOSSIL VERTEBRATES FROM THE CHINLE FORMATION (UPPER TRIASSIC) OF SOUTHERN UTAH

J. Michael Parrish
Biological Sciences,
Northern Illinois University
DeKalb, Illinois 60115

ABSTRACT

Although the Upper Triassic Chinle Formation has produced extensive vertebrate faunas in Arizona and New Mexico, vertebrate faunas from this formation in Utah are rare. Paleontological reconnaissance between 1983 and 1988 produced macrovertebrates, which have been described elsewhere, and small vertebrates that are the subject of this report. They were recovered from two localities in southeastern Utah, at two different stratigraphic positions.

INTRODUCTION

The Chinle Formation has produced a rich, diverse assemblage of fossil vertebrates, although the most familiar localities, and most of the well-preserved tetrapod material comes from Arizona and New Mexico (summaries in Parrish, 1989; Long and Murry, 1995). The Chinle Formation is exposed extensively throughout much of Utah, but its tendency to crop out as steep, near-vertical exposures rather than badlands, along with the relative inaccessibility of many of the exposures, has rendered the prospecting of Utah's Chinle more difficult than the more southern parts of the formation. Between 1983 and 1988, a paleontological reconnaissance of the Chinle in much of southern Utah was undertaken by the author, along with Steven Good and Russell Dubiel (Dubiel, 1987; Parrish and Good, 1987; Good and others, 1987). Although a preliminary report (Parrish and Good, 1987) was published on the fossil macrovertebrates discovered during these studies, the small vertebrate material collected was not described in detail. This report describes material collected from two different localities in southeastern Utah, representing two distinct stratigraphic levels in the Chinle. The material discussed here is reposited at the University of Colorado, Boulder, Museum of Paleontology. (Abbreviations: AMNH, American Museum of Natural History, New York; UCM, University of Colorado Museum).

BIOSTRATIGRAPHY/SYSTEMATIC PALEONTOLOGY

Monitor Butte Member
Blue Lizard Mine Locality

A concentration of small vertebrate bones was found in the Monitor Butte Member of the Chinle Formation in Red Canyon (Parrish and Good, 1987) (San Juan County, 37°33'33"N, 110°16'57"W, T. 37 S., R. 15 E., NE1/4 section 20). The fossiliferous locality was roughly five meters above the contact with the Shinarump Conglomerate, near the Blue Lizard Mine, which gives the locality its name. The small bones were weathering out of several limestone lenses within a tan to brown mudstone. In addition to the bones of small vertebrates discussed here, the locality yielded abundant coprolites and unionid bivalves. The bones, which are a distinctive bright blue in color, weather out of the limestone as near-complete but disarticulated elements.

The bulk of the material represents what appears to be a single taxon of crocodylomorph. The occurrence of the proximal ends of two right humeri indicates a minimum of two individuals.

Monophyletic Hierarchy: Diapsida, Archosauromorpha, Archosauria, Pseudosuchia, Crocodylomorpha indeterminate

The crocodylomorph material (UCM 76191-76195) from the Blue Lizard Mine locality represents individuals of relatively uniform, small size. Precise size estimates are difficult, because few complete elements are preserved. Comparisons of comparable elements (caudal centra, proximal end of femur, humerus), indicate that the Blue Lizard crocodylomorph represents individuals just a bit smaller in size than the holotype of *Hesperosuchus agilis* (AMNH 6758; Colbert, 1952). Identifiable elements preserved include many paramedian and lateral armor plates (UCM 76195, figure 1), a series of vertebrae (UCM 76195, figure 2), the proximal ends of two right humeri (UCM 76193), the distal end of a right

Figure 1. *Armor plates of the crocodylomorph from the Blue Lizard locality. Scale = 1 cm.*

humerus (UCM 76193), the proximal end of a left femur (UCM 76192, figure 3) , and the proximal and distal ends of a left fibula (UCM 76192, figure 3). Correspondence of the vertebral and armor material is established because one of the caudal vertebrae (UCM 76191, figure 2) has a piece of armor attached to it.

The armor plates are unique among small diapsids from the Chinle Formation in several ways. First, the paramedian plates appear to be considerably broader than long, a feature only characteristic of aetosaurs, *Doswellia*, and protosuchian crocodyliforms among Triassic-Jurassic archosauromorphs. Second, they have a unique pattern of widely spaced, deep, subcircular pits that have the greatest similarities with those found in protosuchian crocodyliforms such as *Protosuchus* (Colbert and Mook, 1951) and *Orthosuchus* (Nash, 1968). The protosuchians are also the only Triassic-Jurassic crocodyliforms with paramedian armor that is wider than it is long, and with lateral plates in addition to paramedians. The earliest protosuchian known to date is *Hemiprotosuchus*, from the Norian facies of the Los Colorados Formation, Argentina (Bonaparte, 1972). It

would be premature to extend the range of the protosuchians down to the early Carnian on the basis of this fragmentary material, but the resemblances are striking, although the gracile limb bones are more similar to those of 'sphenosuchians' like *Saltoposuchus* and *Hesperosuchus* than they are to protosuchians.

Taxonomic Hierarchy: Diapsida, Archosauromorpha, Archosauriformes indeterminate

A second distinctive form of armor comes from the Blue Lizard Mine locality, representing another small, armored form that presumably represents a different small archosaur (UCM 76194, figure 4). The three relatively complete plates are subrectangular in shape, with gently rounded outlines. All three plates are covered with small, deep pits that are so closely spaced that they are separated from one another only by small ridges. Two of the plates seem clearly to represent paramedian armor, as they have an articular facet along their median edges for articulation with a counterpart. What appears to be the more cranial of these two is longer than it is broad, and gently bowed in a mediolateral direction. The more caudal of the two is 1.5X as broad as it is long, and

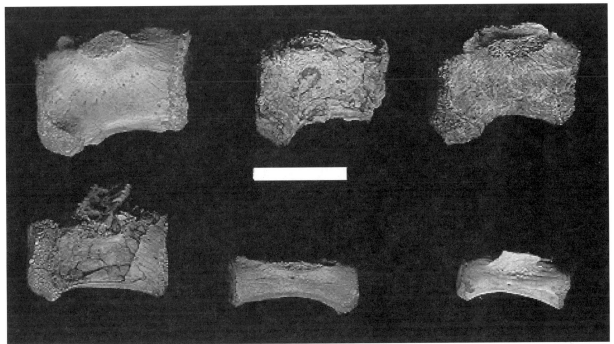

Figure 2. *Six caudal vertebrae of the crocodylomorph from the Blue Lizard locality. Note the armor plate attached to the fourth vertebra in the series. Scale = 1 cm.*

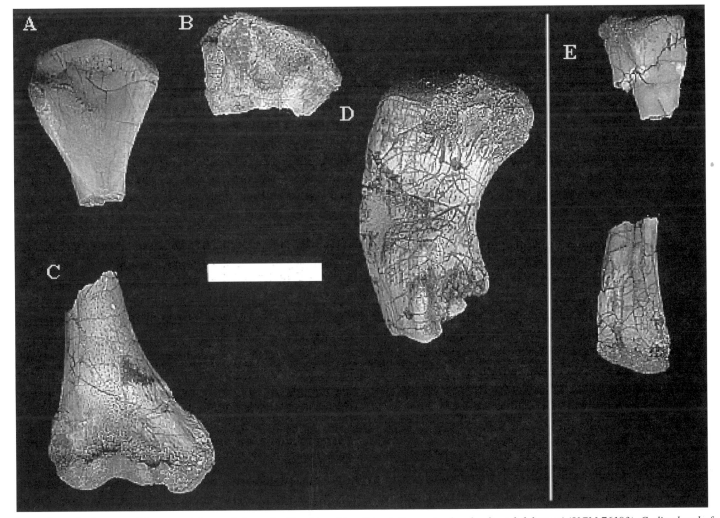

Figure 3. *Limb elements of the crocodylomorph from the Blue Lizard locality. A,B, proximal ends of two left humeri (UCM 76193). C, distal end of a right humerus (UCM 76193). D, proximal end of a left femur (UCM 76192). E, proximal and distal ends of a left fibula (UCM 76192). Scale = 1 cm.*

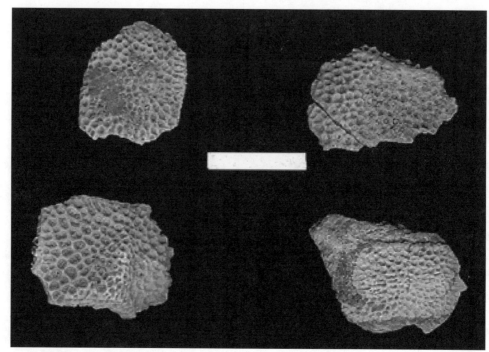

Figure 4. *Paramedian armor of the indeterminate archosauriform from the Blue Lizard locality. Scale = 1 cm.*

it has a parasagittally aligned ridge on its dorsal surface just lateral to the midline. Rather than being gently convex upwards like the more cranial element, it has two nearly straight planes that meet at an obtuse (nearly 170°) angle. The third plate is not as well preserved, but appears to also be a more cranial paramedian roughly the same size as the first element described. This material does not closely resemble comparably sized aetosaurs or crocodylomorphs, two other groups that also exhibit broad paramedian armor. More similarity is seen between this material and *Doswellia*, an archosauro-morph known from the Dockum Formation of Texas (Long and Murry, 1995) and the Doswell Formation of Virginia (Weems, 1980). The Blue Lizard locality armor shares with *Doswellia* the pattern of pitting, the downward angulation of the lateral part of the larger paramedians, and the presence of a rugose articular facet on the midline for the element's counterpart. Differences include the presence of a non-pitted articular flange on the caudal end of the dorsal surface in the armor of *Doswellia* that is absent in these specimens, and differences in the shape of the elements, which have straighter edges in *Doswellia* than in the Chinle armor.

Petrified Forest Member

Four Aces Mine Locality

A second occurrence of isolated elements of small vertebrates occurs in the Petrified Forest Member of the Chinle Formation at the mouth of White Canyon, near

the Four Aces Mine (San Juan County, 37°47'55"N, 110°19'40"W, T.34S., R.4E., NW1/4NE1/4 section 25). The preservation of the fossils from this locality is virtually identical to that at the Blue Lizard site, with small blue bones weathering out of a limestone matrix. Although the material from this locality is fragmentary, it includes some forms, including a theropod dinosaur and a possible ornithischian, that are otherwise unknown from the Chinle of Utah. In addition to the material described here, this locality has yielded lungfish teeth (UCM 76502) and a partial vertebral column of a large phytosaur (UCM 76199).

Monophyletic hierarchy: Diapsida, Archosauria, Dinosauria, Saurischia, Theropoda

Theropod dinosaurs are represented by several incomplete ungual phalanges (UCM 76197, figure 5). Several caudal vertebrae (UCM 76198) may be referable to the Theropoda as well, on the basis of the distinctive, subhexagonal cross section that they share with *Coelophysis*. The phalanges represent two types, a thick, rounded morph with a sharply curved claw, and a straighter form that is more compressed from side to side.

Monophyletic hierarchy: Diapsida, Archosauria, indeterminate

A partial lower jaw, lacking preserved teeth, does not appear to be referable to any familiar Chinle taxa. On the basis of the element's deep profile, the shape of the tall, wide alveoli, and the shape and position of the mandibu-

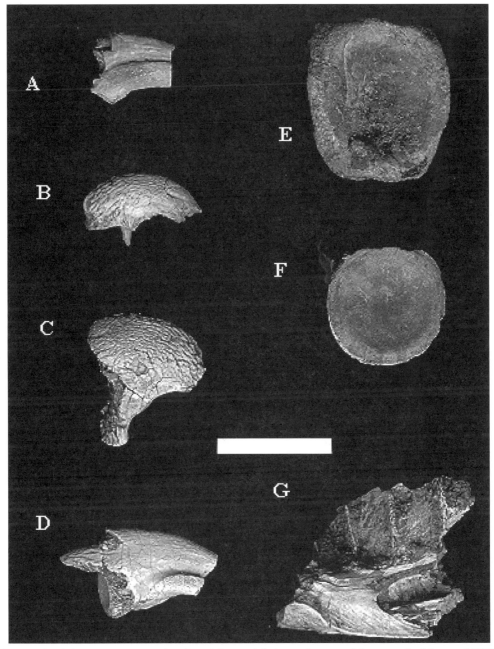

Figure 5. *Dinosaur elements from the Four Aces Mine locality. A,B, cranial views of two caudal centra of a ?theropod (UCM 76198). C-E, rounded ungual claws of ?theropod type 1 (UCM 76197). F, flattened ungual claw of ?theropod type 2 (UCM 76197). G, fragmentary right mandible of ?ornithischian (UCM 76501). Scale = 1 cm.*

lar fenestra, it most closely resembles those of Triassic-Jurassic ornithischians, but it would be imprudent to make a taxonomic identification without dentition (UCM 76501, figure 5).

DISCUSSION

Relatively few sites containing abundant bones of small tetrapods have been found in the Upper Triassic Chinle Formation. These two localities provide a tantalizing, if incomplete, view of the small vertebrate faunas of the Late Triassic of southern Utah. The most significant parts of the fauna include the ?protosuchian crocodylomorphs from the Blue Lizard locality and the theropod and possible ornithischian dinosaurs from the Four Aces Mine locality.

REFERENCES

Bonaparte, J.F., 1972, Los tetrapodos del sector Superior de la Formación Los Colorados (Triásico Superior): Opera Lilloana, v. 22, p. 1-183.

Colbert, E.H., 1952, A pseudosuchian reptile from northern Arizona: Bulletin of theAmerican Museum of Natural History, v. 99, p. 563-592.

Colbert, E.H., and Mook, C.C., 1951, The ancestral crocodilian, *Protosuchus*: Bulletin of the American Museum of Natural History, v. 97, p. 143-182.

Dubiel, R.F., 1987, Sedimentology and new fossil occurrences of the Upper Triassic Chinle Formation, southeastern Utah, *in* Campbell, J.A., editor, Four Corners Geological Society Guidebook, 10th Field Conference, Cataract Canyon, Durango, Colorado, p. 99-107.

Good, Steven, Parrish, J.M., and Dubiel, R.F., 1987, Paleoenvironmental synthesis of the Chinle Formation (Upper Triassic), southeastern Utah, *in* Campbell, J.A., editor, Four Corners Geological Society Guidebook, 10th Field Conference, Cataract Canyon, Durango, Colorado. p. 117-118.

Long, R.A., and Murry, P.A., 1995, Late Triassic (Carnian and Norian) tetrapods from the southwestern United States: New Mexico Museum of Natural History and Science Bulletin, v. 4, p. 1-254.

Nash, D.S., 1968, The morphology and relationships of a crocodilian, *Orthosuchus stormbergi*, from the Upper Triassic of Lesotho: Annals of the South African Museum v. 67, no. 7, p. 227-329.

Parrish, J.M., 1989, Vertebrate paleoecology and taphonomy of the Chinle Formation (Late Triassic) of the Southwestern United States: Palaeogeography, Palaeoclimatology, Palaeoecology, v. 72, p. 227-247.

Parrish, J.M., and Good, Steven, 1987, Preliminary report on vertebrate and invertebrate fossil occurrences, Chinle Formation (Upper Triassic), southeastern Utah, *in* Campbell, J.A. , editor, Four Corners Geological Society Guidebook, 10th Field Conference, Cataract Canyon, Durango, Colorado. p. 117-118.

Weems, R.E., 1980, An unusual newly discovered archosaur from the Upper Triassic of Virginia: Philosophical Transactions of the American Philosophical Society, v. 70, no. 7, p. 1-53.

A DINOSAUR TRACK SITE IN THE NAVAJO-NUGGET SAND-STONE, RED FLEET RESERVOIR, UINTAH COUNTY, UTAH

Alden H. Hamblin
Grand Staircase-Escalante National Monument
337 South Main
Cedar City, Utah 84720
and
Sue Ann Bilbey
Utah Field House of Natural History
235 East Main
Vernal, Utah 84078

ABSTRACT

A vertebrate track site in the Navajo/Nugget Sandstone (Upper Triassic - Lower Jurassic) on the shore of Red Fleet Reservoir near Vernal, Utah, includes more than 350 tracks of bipedal dinosaurs in nine distinct layers of horizontally bedded, calcareous sandstone. These tridactyl tracks occur in two general size ranges. The smaller of the two types (*Grallator*) has an average heel to middle toe length of 15.2 cm and an average width of 9.8 cm. The larger tracks (*Eubrontes*) average 36.6 cm in length and 23.5 cm in width.

INTRODUCTION

Until recently, the Navajo/Nugget Sandstone in northeastern Utah has been notably deficient in fossil localities. In a paleontologic evaluation of the Red Fleet Reservoir Site, the Navajo Sandstone was listed as unfossiliferous with no mention of previously known track occurrences here or elsewhere (Sloan and others, 1980). In 1987, seven years after construction of Red Fleet Reservoir was completed, dinosaur tracks were discovered in the Navajo-Nugget Sandstone along the shoreline.

The exact age of the Navajo/Nugget Sandstone is still debated due to the paucity of guide fossils, but is generally considered Late Triassic and/or Early Jurassic (Pacht, 1977; Poole and Stewart, 1964; Haubold, 1986; Olsen and Sues, 1986). Notably, animal tracks (ichnofossils) are the most common fossils in this generally unfossiliferous formation (Kayser, 1964; Stokes, 1978; Lockley and Hunt, 1995). The presence of the ichnogenera *Eubrontes* and *Grallator* allow correlation with ichnofossils from the Connecticut Valley which recently have been established as Liassic (Early Jurassic) (Haubold, 1986; Lockley and Hunt, 1995).

The purposes of this paper are to describe the Red Fleet dinosaur track site, to report the geology and paleoenvironments of the associated strata, and to briefly consider the behavioral aspects and population dynamics implied by the tracks. Further study of nearby correlative strata is necessary to more fully understand the paleoecology of the Navajo/Nugget Sandstone in this area.

LOCATION

Red Fleet Reservoir is located 12 miles northeast of Vernal, Utah and is accessible via U.S. highway 191 (figure 1). The track site is located in NE$\frac{1}{4}$NW$\frac{1}{4}$SW$\frac{1}{4}$, of section 3, T. 3 S., R. 22 E., Salt Lake Base Line and Meridian. The rock ledge containing the tracks can be seen looking east from the boat ramp (figure 2). Elevation of the lake when full is 1,712 meters (Sloan and others, 1980).

METHODS

The section of the Navajo/Nugget Sandstone lying above the track site was measured using a Jacob's staff, hand level, and Brunton compass. The track-bearing unit lies approximately 80 meters below the top of the Navajo-Nugget Sandstone, approximately two-thirds of the way up the formation. Fred Peterson of the U. S. Geological Survey measured a total of 222.8 meters of Navajo-Nugget Sandstone in this area (personal communication, 1988). Previous studies reported estimates only (Kinney, 1955; Untermann and Untermann, 1964).

The site was mapped during the fall of 1987 before the annual rise of the lake level. The rock surface was checked at differing daylight hours, because low-angle light frequently revealed tracks invisible at noon. A 5 X 5 meter grid was measured over the site with screws set at each 5 meter interval. One meter squares were marked with chalk within this grid. Mobile one meter

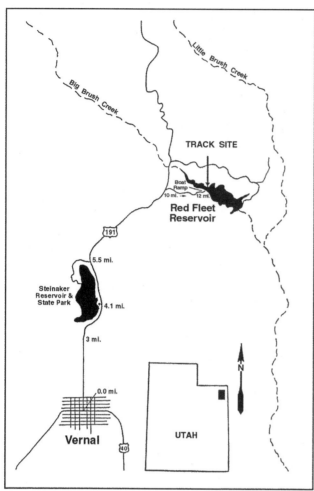

Figure 1. The track locality site at Red Fleet Reservoir State Park.

frames subdivided into 20 X 20 centimeter squares were laid over the tracks to facilitate mapping on grid paper. Tracks occur in nine different layers totaling over one and a half meters in thickness (table 1). Major track-bearing layers were mapped where exposed (figure 3). Trackways were counted and track directions were measured from the map. The map also serves as an indicator of damage at the site by water, ice, and human activity.

SITE DESCRIPTION

The track-bearing area exposed by the lake measures 60 meters east to west and 15 meters north to south (figure 3). Part of the surface is covered by loose rock material. The bedding dips 18° south, with a strike of north 70° east. Track-bearing layers continue upslope another 40 meters above the high water line of the lake, but most are covered by colluvium. Where planar rock exposures occur, however, tracks have been found. A stratigraphic cross section and descriptive table delineate the track-bearing units (table 1).

The Navajo/Nugget Sandstone at the Red Fleet track site is composed of layers of sandstone and calcareous sandstone. These are alternating, sometimes very thin, layers of pale brown (5YR5/1) and very pale orange (10YR8/2) with the brown tending to be more sandy and the orange more calcareous. These beds originally formed horizontal bedding planes between large-scale cross-bedded sandstones characteristic of the eolian Navajo-Nugget Sandstone.

Figure 2. Photograph of the track locality on a south-facing shoreline as seen from the boat ramp at Red Fleet Reservoir.

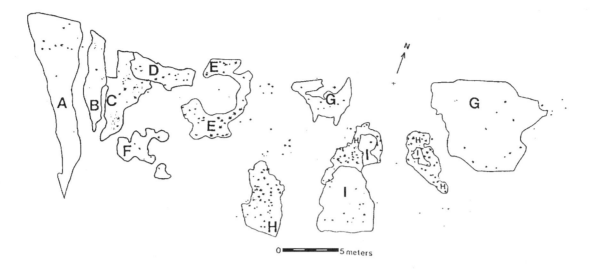

Figure 3. *Map of the track site with track-bearing units identified.*

Table 1. *A Stratigraphic cross section of the track-bearing layers plus ichnospecies information.*

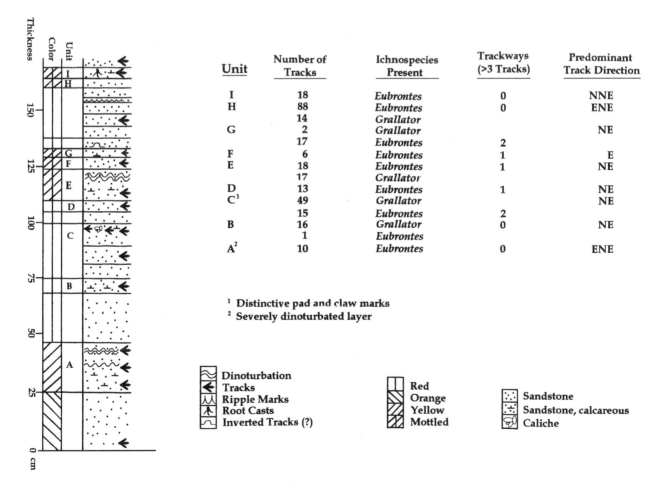

Unit	Number of Tracks	Ichnospecies Present	Trackways (>3 Tracks)	Predominant Track Direction
I	18	*Eubrontes*	0	NNE
H	88	*Eubrontes*	0	ENE
	14	*Grallator*		
G	2	*Grallator*		NE
	17	*Eubrontes*	2	
F	6	*Eubrontes*	1	E
E	18	*Eubrontes*	1	NE
	17	*Grallator*		
D	13	*Eubrontes*	1	NE
C[1]	49	*Grallator*		NE
	15	*Eubrontes*	2	
B	16	*Grallator*	0	NE
	1	*Eubrontes*		
A[2]	10	*Eubrontes*	0	ENE

[1] Distinctive pad and claw marks
[2] Severely dinoturbated layer

Dinoturbation
Tracks
Ripple Marks
Root Casts
Inverted Tracks (?)

Red
Orange
Yellow
Mottled

Sandstone
Sandstone, calcareous
Caliche

A correlative remnant of the track-bearing unit appears as a red band in a high Navajo-Nugget outcrop about 900 meters west of the site. No tracks have been found in this area. This remnant can also be identified several hundred meters to the east. Several tracks have been found in the eastward extension. Two other outcrops of similar lithology have been reported from this region, one about 4.8 km east and another about 12.9 km west on Neal Dome (Kinney, 1955). These lie near the same horizon as the Red Fleet site, but no tracks have been reported from them.

TRACKS

Approximately 350 tracks have been mapped and over 50 other tracks have been observed in unmapped areas (figure 3 and table 1). All mapped tracks appear to have been made by bipedal, tridactyl dinosaurs. They occur in two general size ranges, but considerable variation has been noticed and it is possible that more than two ichnogenera are represented. The average measurements given below are from surfaces "C" and "D" where detail of the tracks is best.

The smaller tracks average 15.2 cm from the heel to tip of the central toe (digit III) with a range of 12.5 cm to 21 cm. The width, measured perpendicular to the central toe, averages 9.8 cm. The range of small track widths is 8 cm to 14 cm. These small tracks (figure 4) appear similar to the coelurosaur tracks of the ichnogenus *Grallator* from the Upper Triassic of the Connecticut Valley described by Lull (1953). The *Grallator* tracks have an average length to width ratio of 1.55.

Average heel to tip of the central toe measurement of the larger tracks is 36.6 cm. The range of this measurement is 34 cm to 43 cm. Track width average is 23.5 cm with a range of 22 cm to 28.5 cm. The length-to-width ratio of the larger tracks averages 1.56. These tracks

(figure 5) are similar to the ichnogenus Eubrontes which was also described by Lull (1953). A comparison of the tracks shows that Eubrontes is 2.4X larger than Grallator.

Coombs (1980) attempted to distinguish claw types of bipedal dinosaurs, but found that *Eubrontes* tracks, particularly the claw marks, were significantly diverse. Therefore he was unwilling to identify with certainty whether these tridactyl tracks were theropod or ornithopod. Thulborn (1989) suggested that *Eubrontes* tracks may have been made by a theropod, but Miller and others (1989) proposed that they were made by a prosauropod similar to a plateosaurid, although it must have been bipedal. Olsen (1980) proposed that *Grallator, Anchisa-*

Figure 4. *Photograph of small tracks assigned to the ichnogenus* Grallator.

Figure 5. *Photograph of large tracks assigned to the ichnogenus* Eubrontes.

A Dinosaur Track Site - Hamblin, Bilbey

uripus, and *Eubrontes* were a growth series within a single species of theropod. Lockley and Hunt (1995) attributed species characteristics to both ichnogenera, but proposed that both are types of theropods. They also noted the abundance of *Grallator* with fewer *Eubrontes*, suggesting that if they were the same species, there should be far more *Eubrontes* tracks. Certainly there is a trend toward larger dinosaurs in the Early Jurassic, as suggested by the occurrence of *Dilophosaurus*, a possible candidate for producing the *Eubrontes* tracks (Lockley and Hunt, 1995), or perhaps one even larger, as noted by Morales and Bulkley (1996).

ENVIRONMENT

The Navajo-Nugget Sandstone generally is interpreted as having formed in an eolian depositional environment, although some have suggested a marine-dominated environment (see the review by Stokes, 1978). Carbonate-rich sandstone or limestone lenses among the cross-bedded sandstone beds have been considered lacustrine or marginal marine in origin (Gilluly and Reeside, 1928; Gilland, 1979; Picard, 1976). Gilland (1979) interpreted a carbonate lens near Moab as a freshwater lake deposit. This carbonate lens contains dinosaur tracks described

TRACKWAYS

Due to the number of track-bearing layers and their restricted exposure, only seven trackways have been positively identified. Most of the trackways consist of only three tracks. Two trackways occur on surface "C," one trackway each on surfaces "D," "E," and "F," and two trackways on surface "G" (table 1). All seven trackways were made by the larger animals. The stride lengths vary from 1.1 to 1.4 meters. Further study of the surfaces and additional mapping will undoubtedly reveal more trackways. Figure 6 is a composite rose diagram showing all the trackway directions. Figure 7 quantifies the track orientations for each stratigraphic unit. Trackways and track orientations in six of the nine units show dominant trends toward the northeast.

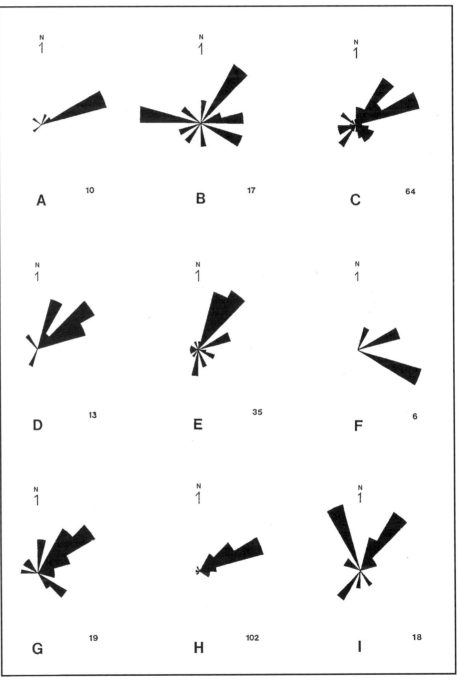

Figure 7. *Rose diagrams of track orientations by unit. Units are keyed to table 1.*

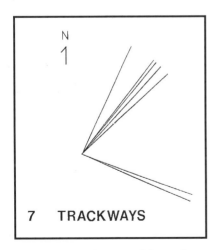

Figure 6. *Rose diagram of the trackway directions.*

by Lockley (1986, p. 16-18). Another newly discovered track site in the Navajo Sandstone in northeastern Arizona is also in a lacustrine unit, composed of a limestone bed that extends over 250,000 m² (Nations and others, 1996). Apparently, lakes formed occasionally among the dunes of the Navajo Sandstone.

The track-bearing beds at Red Fleet Reservoir are horizontally bedded sandstone or carbonate-cemented sandstone. Oscillating wave ripple marks and varying densities of dinoturbation (dinoturbation index from 10 to 75%, after Lockley and Conrad, 1989) imply standing water, whereas calcareous nodules and mottled coloration suggest a fluctuating water table. Without a more extensive investigation, it is difficult to imply more than the presence of an ephemeral playa lake. The occurrence of ripple marks striking northeasterly and a greater density of dinoturbation to the northwest suggests that a lake lay to the northwest of this tracksite. Unfortunately there is little variation in thickness of individual units in the correlative beds nearby and little sedimentologic evidence to suggest either deeper or shallower water. Similar beds at or near this horizon elsewhere may indicate the presence of a large lake. Further field evaluation is necessary to determine the regional extent of this lake.

BEHAVIOR

Abundance and parallel orientation of tracks have been used as evidence to suggest gregarious behavior (Lockley, 1986). This evidence can also be used to suggest shorelines of lakes, rivers, or seaways (Lockley, 1987). Most of the tracks at the Red Fleet track site are oriented in a northeast direction (figures 6 and 7). The gaits of the dinosaurs in the trackways (ratios of 0.79 to 1.2 as calculated by dividing the length of a stride by the track maker's height at the hip as described by Thulborn, 1989) suggest a slow walking speed for bipedal dinosaurs, perhaps indicative of browsing or drinking. These facts and interpretations, along with the carbonate nature of the rock, horizontal bedding with ripple marks on a track-bearing surface, and the placement of the calcareous sandstone units between eolian cross-bedded sandstones, suggest the movement of dinosaurs along the edge of a playa lake in an arid desert region. The lake must have persisted over an extended time as a watering hole, as suggested by the abundance of tracks in successive layers of rock.

There are several possible interpretations for the faunal assemblage or population dynamics represented in the tracks:

(1) If the assignment of *Eubrontes* as a prosauropod is correct as presented by Miller and others (1989), we see nearly equal numbers of carnivores (*Grallator*) and herbivores visiting this lake (table 1). However unit H, which reveals the largest number of footprints, has a far greater number of *Eubrontes*. Perhaps this is more representative of a normal population of dinosaurs living at that time (a predator to prey ratio of approximately 1 : 5).

(2) The length-to-width ratios for the tracks of *Grallator* and *Eubrontes* suggest that the animals that made them may be part of a monospecific group. The ratios are very similar (1.55 *Grallator* to 1.56 *Eubrontes*), suggesting a growth series within one species. Annual hatchings might produce the size differentiation of *Eubrontes* individuals being 2.4 times larger than those of the *Grallator*. The variety of sizes within both types of tracks indicates social behavior between young adults and older individuals as they moved in a northeasterly direction. The absence of very small tracks suggests that the very young were kept segregated from the older group.

(3) The different track types could represent two species of theropod that visited the watering hole. There does not appear to be any hostile behavior recorded in the rocks although overprinting might have obscured such activity. Theropods seem to be the prominent dinosaurs from the Late Triassic and Early Jurassic. However, bone material is scant, so hypotheses about the population dynamics are difficult to test. A population of only carnivorous dinosaurs seems difficult to imagine. What were they eating?

CONCLUSIONS

The Red Fleet track site is a new locality important both for the number of individual dinosaur tracks present and the number of strata containing them. These animals were living in an arid region near a large playa lake which persisted over an extended time. Sahara-like sand dunes dominated the landscape. Further studies are necessary to delineate the lake boundaries and other associated paleoenvironments of the Navajo/Nugget Sandstone of northeastern Utah. Unfortunately no vertebrate skeletal fossils are known from the Navajo/Nugget Sandstone in this area. Discovery of bones from the track makers or their relatives could help clarify the population dynamics as well as the species diversity of the site.

ACKNOWLEDGMENTS

We wish to express appreciation to the following for assistance in field work and preparation of this paper: Peter Laraba, Shanna Whitbeck, and Ilene Hamblin.

Appreciation also goes to the senior author's children, particularly Flint, whose birthday party at Red Fleet Reservoir led to the discovery of the track site. Martin Lockley and David D. Gillette gave suggestions for the update and improvement of the document. The original paper was presented orally by the senior author at the Symposium on Vertebrate Behavior as Derived from the Fossil Record at Bozeman, Montana in September, 1988.

REFERENCES

Coombs, W. P., 1980, Swimming ability of carnivorous dinosaurs: Science, v. 207, p. 1198-1200.

Gilland, J. K., 1979, Paleoenvironment of a carbonate lens in the Lower Navajo Sandstone near Moab, Utah: Utah Geology, v. 6, p. 29-37.

Gilluly, James, and Reeside, J. B., Jr., 1928, Sedimentary rocks of the San Rafael Swell and some adjacent areas in eastern Utah: U. S. Geological Survey Professional Paper 150, p. 61-110.

Haubold, H. H., 1986, Archosaur footprints at the terrestrial Triassic - Jurassic transition, *in* Padian, Kevin, editor, The beginning of the age of dinosaurs - faunal change across the Triassic - Jurassic boundary: Cambridge, Cambridge University Press, p. 189-201.

Kayser, R. B., 1964, Petrology of the Nugget-Navajo Sandstone at outcrops near Hanna, Utah, and Dinosaur National Monument *in* Sabatka, E. F., editor, Guidebook 13th Annual Field Conference: Intermountain Association of Petroleum Geologists, p. 105-108.

Kinney, D. M., 1955, Geology of the Uinta River-Brush Creek area Duchesne and Uintah Counties, Utah: U. S. Geological Survey Bulletin 1007, 185 pp.

Lockley, M. G., 1986, A Guide to Dinosaur Tracks of the Colorado Plateau and American Southwest: Denver, University of Colorado at Denver Geology Department Magazine, Special Issue, v. 1, p. 1-56.

—1987, Dinosaur trackways, *in* Czerkas S. J., and Olsen, E. C., editors, Dinosaurs past and present: Seattle and London, Natural History Museum of Los Angeles County in association with University of Washington Press, v. 1, p. 81-95.

—1991, Tracking dinosaurs: Cambridge, Cambridge University Press, 238 p.

Lockley, M. G., and Conrad, Kelley, 1989, The paleoenvironmental context, preservation, and paleoecological significance of dinosaur tracksites in the western USA, *in* Gillette, D. D., and Lockley, M. G., editors, Dinosaur tracks and traces: Cambridge, Cambridge University Press, p. 121-134.

Lockley, M. G., and Hunt, A. P., 1995, Dinosaur tracks and other fossil footprints of the western United States: New York, Columbia University Press, 338 p.

Lull, R. S., 1953, Triassic life of the Connecticut Valley: Connecticut State Geological Natural History Survey, v. 81, p. 1-331.

Morales, Michael, and Bulkley, Scott, 1996, Paleoichnological evidence for a theropod dinosaur larger than *Dilophosaurus* in the Lower Jurassic Kayenta Formation, *in* Morales, Michael, editor, The continental Jurassic: Flagstaff, Transactions of the Continental Jurassic Symposium, Museum of Northern Arizona, Bulletin 60, p. 143-146.

Miller, W. E., Britt B. B., and Stadtman, K. L., 1989, Tridactyl tracks from the Moenave Formation of southwestern Utah, *in* Gillette, D. D., and Lockley, M. G., editors, Dinosaur tracks and traces: Cambridge, Cambridge University Press, p. 209-215.

Nations, J. D., Swift, R. L., and Selestewa, Nathan, 1996, A newly discovered dinosaur tracksite in the Lower Jurassic Navajo Sandstone, northeastern Arizona, *in* Morales, Michael, editor, The continental Jurassic: Flagstaff, Transactions of the Continental Jurassic Symposium, Museum of Northern Arizona, Bulletin 60, p. 141.

Olsen, P. E., 1980, Fossil great lakes of the Newark supergroup in New Jersey, *in* Manspeizer, Warren, editor, Field studies of New Jersey geology and guide to field trips: New York State Geological Association, 52nd Annual Meeting, p. 352-398.

Olsen, P. E., and Sues H.-D., 1986, Correlation of continental Late Triassic and Early Jurassic sediments, and patterns of the Triassic - Jurassic tetrapod transition, *in* Padian, Kevin, editor, The beginning of the age of dinosaurs - faunal change across the Triassic - Jurassic boundary: Cambridge, Cambridge University Press, p. 321-351.

Pacht, J. A., 1977, Diagenesis of the Nugget Sandstone, western Wyoming and north-central Utah, *in* Heisey, E. L., editor, Guidebook 29th annual field conference: Wyoming Geological Association, p. 207-219.

Picard, M. D., 1976, Oil and gas potential of Nugget Sandstone, southeastern Wyoming and northeastern Utah: American Association of Petroleum Geologists Bulletin, v. 60, no. 8, p. 1406.

Poole, F. G., and Stewart, J. H., 1964, Chinle Formation and Glen Canyon Sandstone in northeast Utah and northwest Colorado, *in* Sabatka, E. F., editor, Guidebook 13th Annual Field Conference: Intermountain Association of Petroleum Geologists, p. 93-104.

Sloan, R. E., Hartman, J. H., Dempsey, L. J., Jordan, M. E., and Robertson, E. B., 1980, Paleontological resources evaluation--Red Fleet Reservoir: Salt Lake City, Utah, U. S. Bureau of Reclamation, 47 p.

Stokes, W. L., 1978, Animal tracks in the Navajo-Nugget Sandstone: Contributions to Geology, University of Wyoming, v. 16, no. 2, p. 103-107.

Thulborn, R. A., 1989, The gait of dinosaurs, *in* Gillette, D. D., and Lockley, M. G., editors, Dinosaur tracks and traces: Cambridge, Cambridge University Press, p. 39-50.

Untermann, G. E., and Untermann, B. R., 1964, Geology of Uintah County: Utah Geological and Mineralogical Survey Bulletin 72, p. 1-112.

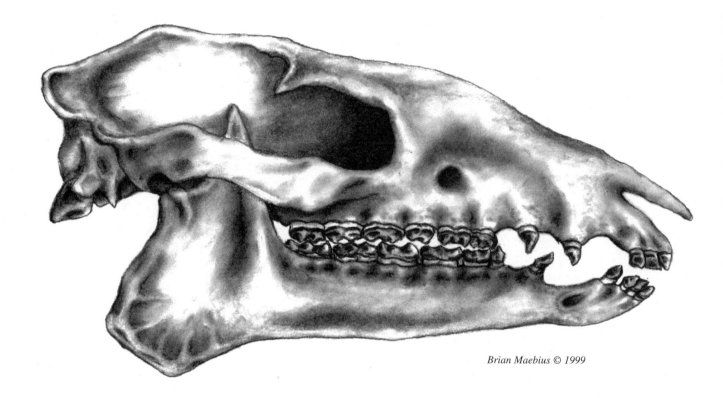

Brian Maebius © 1999

Eohippus

THE FIRST DISCOVERIES OF DINOSAURS IN THE AMERICAN WEST

Brent H. Breithaupt
Geological Museum, University of Wyoming, Laramie, WY 82071-3006

ABSTRACT

While dinosaurs are quite well known from the western United States today, hints of the paleontological potential of this region were evident for over 70 years prior to any major discoveries. Dinosaur remains were first noted from the Rocky Mountain West in 1806 when a large bone was found in Cretaceous rocks of present-day Montana by William Clark during the Lewis and Clark expedition. A half century later, Joseph Leidy assigned various teeth found by Ferdinand V. Hayden, during his explorations of the West, to several new Cretaceous taxa (for example, *Trachodon*, *Troodon*, *Palaeoscincus*, *Deinodon*, and *Thespesius*). In 1859 John S. Newberry, while part of Captain John N. Macomb's survey of areas of present-day Utah, discovered the remains of a herbivorous dinosaur later described by Edward D. Cope as the Jurassic sauropod *Dystrophaeus*. With the opening of the West facilitated by the railroad, a dramatic number of new dinosaur discoveries were made. Othniel C. Marsh is reputed to have been shown a large bone from southeastern Wyoming Territory in 1868. This bone likely represents the first discovery of a Jurassic dinosaur from the now famous Como Bluff area. Later that same year, Hayden wrote of the presence of "huge bird" tracks (probably those of a Cretaceous dinosaur) along the Union Pacific Railroad line in western Wyoming Territory. A "petrified horse hoof" given to Hayden in 1869 from northern Colorado Territory was later described by Leidy as the vertebra of the Jurassic theropod *Poicilopleuron*. The 1870s were a time of a tremendous number of dinosaur discoveries in the West. One of the earliest discoveries that decade was a partial skeleton from western Wyoming Territory of one of the largest, terrestrial, prehistoric animals known at the time, the first ceratopsian dinosaur (*Agathaumas*), collected and described by Cope in 1872. Later that decade, important dinosaur discoveries were made in the frontier West, as Marsh and Cope began collecting in earnest in this region. The year 1877 marked the first major dinosaur sites discovered in the Morrison Formation of Colorado and Wyoming, foreshadowing the abundant dinosaur fossils later to be found in this region of North America. Today, nearly 200 years after the first dinosaurs were noted in the Rocky Mountain West, significant paleontological discoveries continue to be made.

INTRODUCTION

Dinosaur remains have been found on every continent. In North America, the Rocky Mountain West is exceptionally well known for the diversity of dinosaurian material found there. However, prior to the middle 19th century, American paleontology was in its infancy, only a handful of dinosaurs had been found in North America, and dinosaurs were virtually unknown from the West. Those dinosaurs that were known were described primarily from isolated or very incomplete skeletal material. Although abundant dinosaur remains were not recovered from the American West until 1877, dinosaurs were reported almost a century earlier (1787) from the eastern part of the United States (Colbert, 1968) and two centuries earlier (1677) from Europe (Buffetaut, 1987).

With the development of vertebrate paleontology in the West, as a result of the opening of the region for exploration and travel, the 1870s provided a wonderful glimpse of past life, especially that of the Age of Reptiles. The documentation of giant saurian remains from rock units of the West in the late 1870s ignited interest in the scientific community that eventually led to numerous discoveries in the paleontological wonderland of the American frontier.

FIRST DISCOVERIES

Native Americans undoubtedly were the first to encounter dinosaur fossils in the Rocky Mountain West. These people must have noticed the petrified remains which had been weathering out of the Mesozoic rock units for thousands of years in this area of North America, but probably did not understand how these remains came to be nor their importance. Although much is still to be learned about how Native Americans perceived fossils, it is known that some tribes believed that prehistoric animal remains represented a race of giants from long ago (Betts, 1871), while others believed that they were the ancient remains of huge, unholy serpents that burrowed into the earth and were hunted and killed by a Great Spirit wielding lightning bolts (Colbert, 1968).

Dinosaur remains were first documented from the Rocky Mountain West in 1806 when a large bone was found by William Clark of the famous Lewis and Clark expedition in the bank of the Missouri River in present-day Montana. This bone, described in Clark's journal (Friday, July 25, 1806) as a large fish rib, was most likely a poorly mineralized, Late Cretaceous dinosaur rib from the Hell Creek Formation. However, the specimen and other records concerning it are not locatable. Clark's journal entry follows (from Simpson, 1942: p. 171-172, with Simpson's annotations in brackets, and with original spelling):

> . . . dureing [sic] the time the men were getting the two big horns [sheep, shot for food] which I had killed to the river I employed my self in getting pieces of the rib of a fish which was Semented within the face of the rock this rib is (about 3) inches in Secumpherence about the middle it is 3 feet in length tho a part of the end appears to have been broken off (the fallen rock is near the water--the face of the rock where rib is is perpend[icula]r - 4 i[nch]s lengthwise, a little barb projects I have several pieces of this rib the bone is neither decayed nor petrified but very rotten. the part which I could not get out may be seen, it is about 6 or 7 Miles below Pompys Tower in the face of the Lar[boar]d [north] Clift about 20 feet above the water.

DISCOVERIES OF THE 1850s

Almost a half century after Clark's discovery, the eminent scientist Ferdinand Vandiveer Hayden came to the West as part of the Geological and Geographical Survey of the Territories. Hayden collected many of the first invertebrate and vertebrate fossils described from the Western Territories. Native Americans called him the "man who picks up stones running," as he often collected geological specimens while in hostile Indian territory. Many of the fossil fishes, reptiles, and mammals discovered by Hayden were described by Philadelphia paleontologist Joseph Leidy.

In 1855 Hayden collected numerous teeth from Cretaceous rocks at the confluence of the Missouri and Judith rivers in present-day Montana. The following year Leidy (1856) described these fossils and assigned the "lacertilian-like" teeth to three new taxa of prehistoric beasts, *Palaeoscincus costatus, Troodon formosus*, and *Trachodon mirabilis*. From another suite of tooth types he designated the name *Deinodon horridus* (a relative of the carnivorous dinosaur *Megalosaurus*), but later erected another species *Aublysodon mirandus*, from this suite (Leidy, 1868). Also, in 1856, Leidy named the dinosaur

Thespesius occidentalis from two caudal vertebrae and a first phalanx given him by Hayden from the "Great Lignite" Formation, Grand River, Nebraska Territory (now part of the state of South Dakota). Although based only on isolated teeth, *Troodon* and *Aublysodon* remain valid genera. *Deinodon* has been synonymized with the better known *Albertosaurus*. *Palaeoscincus* and *Thespesius* are considered nomina dubia, but represent some of the earliest western discoveries of ankylosaurs and hadrosaurs, respectively. Leidy assigned many of the teeth brought back by Hayden to *Trachodon*. Later some of these hadrosaurian teeth were shown to actually be from the ceratopsian *Monoclonius* and the genus *Trachodon* was synonymized with *Edmontosaurus*.

In 1859 John Strong Newberry (geologist for the U.S. Department of Engineering associated with Captain John N. Macomb's survey in the area of modern-day Utah) discovered the remains of a giant, herbivorous dinosaur (Gillette, 1996a, 1996b). The 150 million-year-old partial skeleton was packed out of the East Canyon upstream from the junction of the Green and Colorado Rivers and turned over to Leidy (Miller and Hall, 1990). Eighteen years later, another Philadelphia paleontologist, Edward Drinker Cope (1877), described this new sauropod, *Dystrophaeus viaemalae*. Although there has been some question as to whether or not this taxon is synonymous with *Camarasaurus, Dystrophaeus* appears to be valid.

Also in 1859, Hayden observed some large reptile remains in what is now northern Wyoming. Hayden (1869, p. 113) wrote:

> On the eastern slope of the Big Horn Mountains I observed this same series of beds in the summer of 1859, holding a position between cretaceous No. 2 and the jurassic marls, with a considerable thickness of earthy lignite, large quantities of petrified wood, and numerous large uncharacteristic bones, which Dr. Leidy regarded as belonging to some huge saurian.

Unfortunately, further information on this material and its locality are not available.

On one of his expeditions in the late 1850s, Hayden collected a fragment of "dermal armor" and "distal phalanx" from "Black Foot Country at the head of the Missouri River" (probably from Late Cretaceous units in southeastern Montana). Leidy (1872) assigned the "armor" and possibly the phalanx to a new saurian, *Tylosteus ornatus*. Baird (1979) identified the "dermal armor" as a squamosal node-cluster from the skull of a pachycephalosaur. He synonomized *Tylosteus ornatus* with the better known *Pachycephalosaurus wyomingensis*. The ungual phalanx was assigned to the hadrosaur *Edmontosaurus* (Baird, 1979).

DISCOVERIES OF THE 1860s

On his first trip to the West, noted paleontologist Othniel Charles Marsh of Yale University is reputed to have been shown fossilized bone material at the Union Pacific Railroad's Como Station in eastern Wyoming Territory in 1868. Later, Samuel Wendell Williston (1915) wrote that the station agent at the time was William Edward Carlin, but this may be in error. Carlin and the section foreman, William Harlow Reed, who ignited Marsh's interest in the abundant vertebrate fossils of the region in 1877 (Breithaupt, 1990), can be traced to the nearby Carbon Station only as early as 1874. There is little evidence that either individual was at Como Station in 1868. Williston's account may be confusing a number of incidents, as Marsh traveled past Como Bluff several times on his collecting trips to the Tertiary deposits of western Wyoming Territory in the early 1870s. Only the mention of Marsh's (1868) paper on salamander metamorphosis suggests that this visit occurred in 1868, while other parts of Williston's account indicate an event that occurred in the early 1870s. Williston's (1915, p. 127-128) account follows:

> A few years earlier Professor Marsh, on his way east from the Tertiary deposits of western Wyoming, had stopped at Como, Wyoming, to observe the strange salamanders, or 'fish with legs' as they were widely known, so abundant in the lake at that place, about whose transformations he later wrote a paper, perhaps the only one on modern vertebrates that he ever published. While there Mr. Carlin, the station agent, showed him some fossil bone fragments, so Mr. Reed told me, that they had picked up in the vicinity, and about which Professor Marsh made some comments. But he was so engrossed with the other discoveries he was then making that he did not follow up the suggestion. Had he done so the discovery of the 'Jurassic Dinosaurs' would have been made five years earlier.

Approximately 60 miles south of Como Station another intriguing account is provided by Hayden (1868: p. 81) of ancient reptile remains

> . . . at the Big Laramie stage-station, six miles west of Fort Sanders. In the broad, level plain-country west of this point, No. 3 attains a thickness of 50 to 100 feet, sometimes exhibiting its usual chalky character, but mostly composed of thinly laminated calcareous shale. All through are thin layers of fibrous carbonate of lime. The fibers are at right angles to the plane surface, and attached to these masses or layers are myriads of the little oyster, *Ostrea congesta*. I also found a number of vertebrae of a saurian animal.

Again, other documentation of this find is nonexistent.

In 1868, the same year that the rails were laid for the first transcontinental railroad in the United States, Hayden documented dinosaurian traces in the rocks between Black Butte Station and Green River in western Wyoming Territory along the Union Pacific Railroad route in the Bitter Creek Valley. Hayden (1868: p. 99) wrote:

> The railroad passes down the Bitter Creek Valley, which has worn through the Tertiary beds, and on the east side the high walls can be seen inclining at small angles. As we pass down the valley toward Green River, the inclination brings to view lower and lower beds. These are all plainly marine Tertiaries, while an abundance of impressions of plants are found everywhere; no strictly fresh-water shells occur, but seams of *Ostrea* of various species. There are also extensive beds of hard, flat table-rocks, which would make the best of flagging-stones. On the surface are most excellent illustrations of wave-ripple marks, and at one locality what appears to be tracks of a most singular character. One of the tracks appears to have been made by a soliped, and closely resembles the tracks of mules in the soft ground on the river-bottom. Others seem to belong to a huge bird; another to a four-toed pachydermatous animal. I have obtained careful drawings of these tracks, as well as specimens of them.

As the specimens and drawings have yet to be found, the identity of the tracks is difficult to ascertain. Those described as tracks of a large bird in units that are now considered fluvial deposits of the latest Cretaceous Lance Formation are probably dinosaur tracks.

Whereas dinosaur footprints were tentatively assigned to giant bird tracks in Wyoming Territory in the late 1860s, local residents of Middle Park, Colorado Territory, were identifying unusual shaped fossils in their region as "petrified horse hooves." Hayden obtained one of these "hooves" in 1869. The following year, this specimen was identified by Joseph Leidy (1870) as a vertebral fragment of the carnivorous dinosaur *Poicilopleuron valens*. Leidy (1870, p. 3) wrote of the discovery of *Poicilopleuron*:

> A specimen, consisting of less than half of a vertebral body, was submitted to my examination by Professor Hayden, who obtained it last summer during his geological survey. It is from Middle Park, Colorado, and Professor Hayden thinks was derived from a cretaceous formation. Similar specimens were reported to be not unfrequent, and were known under the appellative of 'petrified horse hoofs.' The fossil indicates an elongated form of caudal vertebra of some large saurian. Much constricted toward the middle, such specimens would be most liable to break in this position, and the halves from their form might readily be taken, by the inexperienced in such matters, for what they are called.

This specimen was later found to represent one of the first known discoveries of the famous Jurassic theropod *Allosaurus*. Although many fossils of *Allosaurus* have been collected over the years (Gilmore, 1920; Madsen, 1976), one of the most complete *Allosaurus* skeletons ever found was uncovered in 1991 from the Bighorn

Basin of northern Wyoming (Breithaupt, 1996). This discovery signifies the potential for important finds to be made even of relatively well-known dinosaurs.

DISCOVERIES OF THE 1870s

On one of his early Yale College expeditions, Marsh traveled south out of Fort Bridger into Utah Territory in 1870 in search of gigantic petrified bones that Indians and hunters rumored to exist there (Schuchert and LeVene, 1940). On the northern rim of the Uinta Basin, Marsh (1871) found a fossil turtle and some teeth which he believed to be Cretaceous forms. The teeth were reported to have resembled those of the English theropod *Megalosaurus*. Miller and Hall (1990) suggested that these specimens actually came from the Late Jurassic Morrison Formation and that the teeth belong to *Allosaurus*. In 1871, on his second major expedition west, Marsh found a partial, articulated, postcranial dinosaur skeleton with some associated skull fragments in the Niobrara Cretaceous of Kansas near Smoky Hill River. Marsh described this material the following year, naming it *Hadrosaurus agilis* (Marsh, 1872). Later, Marsh (1890) erected the hadrosaur species *Claosaurus agilis* based on this material.

Continuing his explorations of the West in the 1870s, Hayden reported another interesting occurrence of gigantic reptile remains in southeastern Wyoming Territory. Although at a similar stratigraphic level to his 1869 discovery, this site appears to be located farther to the northwest on the Laramie Plains. Hayden (1871: p. 123) wrote:

> Near the middle of these plains, on Cooper's Creek, are some quite remarkable exhibitions of the chalk cliffs of the middle cretaceous period, in which are oyster-shells, fish scales, and the bones of a huge Saurian reptile. A little farther to the west is a long line of yellow sandstone bluffs two hundred to three hundred feet high, forming beds of transition or passage between the cretaceous and tertiary periods; and still farther west are more rugged hills in which are found beds of coal.

Also in the early 1870s, G. M. Dawson, while working for the British North American Boundary Commission, collected dinosaurian material (later referred by Cope to the hadrosaurs *Hadrosaurus* and *Cionodon*) from deposits in British America (now Saskatchewan) along the Milk River (Lull and Wright, 1942).

Not until 1872 in western Wyoming Territory was another major discovery made in the Rocky Mountain west as important as the earlier discovery of *Dystrophaeus* in southern Utah. Drs. F. B. Meek and H. M. Bannister found the remains of a large fossilized reptile near Black Butte Railroad Station while working for Hayden's Geological Survey of the Territories. Professor Cope arrived that same year to collect these remains and would name the "marvelous" remains *Agathaumas sylvestris* (Cope, 1872). *A. sylvestris* was one of the largest, best preserved, and most complete dinosaurs known at that time from North America. Meek and Bannister discovered the bones in a dark gray sandstone between two thin beds of coal in the Laramie Formation. This discovery was pivotal in discussions of the so-called "Laramie Problem", a raging, late 1800s debate regarding the age of western Cretaceous units (Knowlton, 1922; Breithaupt, 1982; 1994). Currently the Laramie Formation in Wyoming is known as the Lance Formation and is considered Late Cretaceous in age. *Agathaumas sylvestris* consisted of 16 vertebrae, part of the pelvis, and ribs. It was found embedded with leaves and sticks of dicotyledonous plants and cemented together with sand and clay.

Cope (1873: p. 523) wrote an interesting account of the discovery and importance of *Agathaumas*:

> One day the writer climbed the sandstone bluffs that rise above the flats of Bitter Creek, nearby opposite the Black Butte, in search of some bones that his predecessor Mr. Meek, was said to have discovered in searching for shells. Reaching to near the line of the highest beds of coal, fragments of huge bones were found projecting from the rocks. Picks and shovels were called into requisition. In course of time the wreck of one of the princes among giants lay piled around this desecrated grave. His single vertebra was too feet four inches from spine to body, and one hip-bone four feet from front to rear along the edge. But the chief interest attached to the fact that he told a certain story of the age of the coal beds. Like Samson he slew more in his death than he ever had in his life. He was a Dinosaur, known to Philadelphians by the examples in our Academy of herbivorous (*Hadrosaurus*), and the carnivorous (*Laelaps*), those bird-like lizards that strode about on the banks of the Delaware, when as yet New Jersey was not. These creatures were no tertiary chickens; they belong to the dim old ages of the Trias, Jura and Cretaceous, and ended their days with the last period, for a finality. So old *Agathaumas* (for so was he named), said the Bitter Creek Coal was cretaceous, and his word will be hard to contradict.

Cope's excitement with the discovery of bones near Black Butte Station was manifested in his name *Agathaumas sylvestris* meaning "marvelous forest-dweller." Although its relationship to other dinosaurs was unknown at the time, *Agathaumas* is now thought to be a large, heavily-built ceratopsian, provisionally identified as *Triceratops*. Unfortunately, it is only known from postcranial skeletal material. It is estimated to have been 30 feet long and weighed 6 tons. Later, *Agathaumids* were also reported from Late Cretaceous units in Colorado and the Dakotas. In 1873 Cope collected fragmentary horn cores and limb bones from Colorado. He named these remains *Polyonax mortuarius* later that year (Hatcher and others, 1907). *Polyonax* is now considered an indeterminate ceratopsian from the Late Cretaceous Denver Formation of Colorado (Weishampel and others, 1990).

Agathaumas sylvestris was one of the first ceratopsian skeletons discovered. When it was found, "this species was no doubt equal in dimensions to the largest known terrestrial saurians or mammals" (Cope, 1875: p. 56). Therefore, it was considered in the early 1870s to be one of the largest animals ever to walk the earth. *Agathaumas'* designation as the largest dinosaur was short-lived, as the massive, herbivorous Jurassic sauropods found in the latter half of the 1870s easily eclipsed *Agathaumas* in size.

The discovery of *Agathaumas* heralded in a dramatic time for dinosaur discoveries in the West. The remainder of the 1870s saw a plethora of new dinosaur remains discovered, as Cope and Marsh expanded their spheres of influence and interest into the newly available western frontier. Cope's summary of North American dinosaurs in 1870 consisted of only eighteen species and thirteen genera. Only three of these genera (all from the east coast) were known to any extent. Of the thirteen genera, five were known by teeth, one by a jaw, and two by vertebrae. The North American Jurassic had not yet yielded any dinosaur skeletons other than the still undescribed bones of *Dystrophaeus viaemalae*, which were considered Triassic in age until early in the twentieth century.

With major discoveries in the Cretaceous Judith River Formation of Montana Territory by Cope in 1876 and those in the Jurassic Morrison Formation in Colorado and Wyoming Territory, (that is, Morrison, Garden Park and Como Bluff areas) by both Cope and Marsh the following year, the race to discover dinosaurs in North America had begun (Cope, 1878; 1879; Marsh, 1896; Ostrom and McIntosh, 1966). And though these areas of the West have continued to be collected for the past 120 years, this race continues today. Skilled fossil hunter Samuel Wendell Williston (1915: p. 124) wrote about the discoveries of dinosaurs in the Jurassic deposits of the West in 1877:

> Most great discoveries are due rather to a state of mind, if I may use such an expression, than to accident. The discovery of the immense dinosaur deposits in the Rocky Mountains in March, 1877, may truthfully be called great, for nothing in paleontology has equaled it, and that it was made by three observers simultaneously can not be called purely an accident.

In the autumn of 1878 (no more than eighteen months after the first major discoveries of dinosaurs in the Morrison Formation of Wyoming Territory and Colorado), Williston (1878: p. 43) wrote the following regarding the discovery of dinosaurs:

> The history of their discovery is both interesting and remarkable. For years the beds containing them had been studied by geologists of experience, under surveys of Hayden and King, but, with the possible exception of the half of a caudal vertebra, obtained by Hayden and described by Leidy as a species of *Poikilopleuron*, not a single fragment had been recognized. This is all the more remarkable from the fact that in several of the localities I have observed acres literally strewn with fragments of bones, many of them extremely characteristic and so large as to have taxed the strength of a strong man to lift them. Three of the localities known to me are in the immediate vicinity, if not upon the actual townsites of thriving villages, and for years numerous fragments have been collected by tourists and exhibited as fossil wood. The quantities hitherto obtained, though apparently so vast, are wholly unimportant in comparison with those awaiting the researches of geologists throughout the Rocky Mountain region. I doubt not that many hundreds of tons will eventually be exhumed.

The remainder of the 19th century was filled with numerous collectors venturing to the Rocky Mountain West in search of the rich Mesozoic fauna preserved there (McIntosh, 1990; Breithaupt, 1990). Museums around the world acquired this material and as more discoveries were made, the field of vertebrate paleontology grew dramatically. Thirty-eight years after the discovery of the major Jurassic dinosaur sites in the Morrison Formation of the West, Williston (1915: p. 131) wrote:

> How many tons of these fossils have since been dug up from these deposits in the Rocky Mountains is beyond computation. My prophecy of hundreds of tons has been fulfilled; and they are preserved in many museums of the world.

DISCUSSION

Dinosaurs are currently found worldwide. The Rocky Mountain West is exceptionally well known for the diversity of dinosaurian material that occurs there. The opening of the western frontier to commerce and settlement also opened the doors to the frontiers of science in vertebrate paleontology. The 19th century studies done by Hayden, Leidy, Cope, and Marsh bolstered the emergence of vertebrate paleontology worldwide and laid the foundation for the next century of study. Prehistoric reptiles continue to be popular today. People, young and old, marvel at restorations and reconstructions of these fascinating beasts that once roamed ancient landscapes. Dinosaurs can be seen in many business establishments, being used to sell everything from pasta to postage stamps. The public's recognition of Mesozoic reptiles is the result of over 150 years of research, especially the foundational studies done in western North America in the late 1800s.

Although some reports were made of the discoveries of dinosaurs prior to the 1870s, not until the opening of the western frontier associated with the railroad was the vast paleontological wonderland of western North America suspected. Further exploration by scientists from eastern institutions lead to the cornucopia of discoveries made in the 1870s. Dinosaur collecting in the early days of the West was filled with hardships. Only a select few were drawn to this line of work. But despite the obstacles, the reward of uncovering a fantastic prehistoric beast for the first time increasingly drove more and more individuals into the field of dinosaur paleontology. Famed dinosaur hunter Richard Swan Lull (1926: p. 457) provided a colorful description of collecting in the Old West:

> The old-time expeditions were staged in the real West, at a time when lack of means of transportation and the presence of Indian menace, together with the very intimate contact every fossil hunter must have with his physical surroundings -- with fatigue, heat and cold, hunger and thirst -- made the search for the prehistoric a real adventure suited to red-blooded men. Big game was then abundant, but the good was offset by days of labor through rolling sandhills, with infrequent streams, often alkaline, little vegetation, and the menace of the occasional prairie fire and Indian attack, in spite of which material by the ton was collected with unflagging zeal.

Since the discoveries of *Deinodon, Poicilopleuron,* and *Agathaumas* in the 1850s, 1860s, and 1870s, respectively, literally thousands of dinosaur remains have been uncovered in the West. Whereas only a handful of

dinosaurs were well-known in the middle 19th century, today entire dinosaur dictionaries (for example, Glut, 1982), encyclopedias (for example, Norman, 1985; Lessem and Glut, 1993; Glut, 1997; Currie and Padian, 1997), and texts (Weishampel and others, 1990) have been compiled. Originally known from only isolated teeth and fragmentary skeletal remains, dinosaurs are now known from complete articulated skeletons, some with skin impressions. Dinosaurs are so well recognized from deposits in the West that many western states have dinosaurs as state symbols (either state fossils or state dinosaurs) (for example, Utah - *Allosaurus*, Montana - *Maiasaura*, Colorado - *Stegosaurus*, New Mexico - *Coelophysis*, and Wyoming - *Triceratops*). And whereas the early sites only produced a few fragmentary remains, today mass death assemblages (for example, Cleveland-Lloyd Quarry, Howe Quarry) are known, some resulting in such national treasures as Dinosaur Provincial Park in Alberta and Dinosaur National Monument in Utah and Colorado. In addition, dinosaur fossils from the American West currently highlight exhibit and research collections in museums throughout the world. And, even after more than a century of work, important vertebrate paleontological discoveries are still being made in the West.

ACKNOWLEDGMENTS

Appreciation is extended to the Wyoming Council for the Humanities for their help in funding parts of this project. Thanks to David Gillette, Gustav Winterfeld, and Michael Leite for their assistance in critically evaluating this manuscript.

REFERENCES

Baird, Donald, 1979, The dome - headed dinosaur Tylosteus ornatus Leidy 1872 (Reptilia: Ornithischia: Pachycephalosauridae): Academy of Natural Sciences, Notulae Naturae, v. 456, p. 1-11.

Betts, C. W, 1871, The Yale College Expedition of 1870: Harper's New Monthly Magazine, October, p. 663-671.

Breithaupt, B. H., 1982, Paleontology and paleoecology of the Lance Formation (Maastrichtian), east flank of Rock Springs Uplift, Sweetwater County, Wyoming: Contributions to Geology, v. 21, no. 2, p. 123-151.

—1990, Biography of William Harlow Reed--the story of a frontier fossil collector: Earth Sciences History, v. 9, no. 1, p. 6-13.

—1994, The first dinosaur discovered in Wyoming, *in* Nelson, G. E., editor, Forty-fourth Annual Field Conference, Wyoming Geological Association Guidebook: Casper, Wyoming Geological Association, p. 15-23.

—1996, The discovery of a nearly complete *Allosaurus* from the Jurassic Morrison Formation, eastern Bighorn Basin, Wyoming, *in* Bowen, C. E., Kirkwood, S. C., and Miller, T. S., editors, Forty-seventh Annual Field Conference, Wyoming Geological Association Guidebook: Casper, Wyoming Geological Association, p. 309-312.

Buffetaut, Eric, 1987, A short history of vertebrate paleontology: London, Croom Helm Ltd., 223 p.

Colbert, E. H., 1968, Men and dinosaurs: New York, E. P. Dutton and Co., Inc., 283 p.

Cope, E. D., 1870, Synopsis of the extinct Batrachia, Reptilia, and Aves of North America: Transactions of the American Philosophical Society, v. 14, p. 86-122.

—1872, On the existence of Dinosauria in the Transition Beds of Wyoming: American Philosophical Society, Proceedings, v. 12, p. 481-483.

—1873, The monster of Mammoth Buttes: Pennsylvania Monthly, v. 4, p. 521-534.

—1875, The Vertebrata of the Cretaceous formations of the West, *in* Hayden, F. V. (U.S. geologist in charge), Report of the U.S. Geological Survey of the Territories: Washington, D.C., Department of the Interior, U. S. Government Printing Office, v. 2, 302 p.

—1876, Descriptions of some vertebrate remains from the Fort Union beds of Montana: Academy of Natural Sciences, Proceedings, v. 28, p. 255-256.

—1877, On a dinosaurian from the Trias of Utah: American Philosophical Society, Proceedings, v. 16, p. 579-587.

—1878, The principal characteristics of the American Cretaceous dinosaurs: American Naturalist, v. 12, p. 811-812.

—1879, New Jurassic Dinosauria: American Naturalist, v. 13, p. 402-404.

Currie, P. J., and Padian, Kevin, 1997, Encyclopedia of dinosaurs: San Diego, Academic Press, 869 p.

Gillette, D. D., 1996a, Origin and early evolution of the sauropod dinosaurs of North America - - the type locality and stratigraphic position of *Dystrophaeus viaemalae* Cope 1877, *in* Huffman, A. C., Lund, W. R., and Godwin, L. H., editors, Geology and resources of the Paradox Basin: Utah Geological Association Guidebook 25, p. 313-324.

—1996b, Stratigraphic position of the sauropod *Dystrophaeus viaemalae* Cope and implications, in Morales, Michael, editor, The Continental Jurassic: Flagstaff, Museum of Northern Arizona Press,. Museum of Northern Arizona Bulletin 60, p. 59-68.

Gilmore, C. W., 1920, Osteology of the carnivorous Dinosauria in the United States National Museum, with special reference to the genera *Antrodemus* (*Allosaurus*) and *Ceratosaurus*: Smithsonian Institution, United States National Museum, Bulletin 110, p. 1-159.

Glut, D. F., 1982, The new dinosaur dictionary: Secaucus, New Jersey, Citadel Press, 288 p.

—1997, Dinosaurs--the encyclopedia: Jefferson, North Carolina, McFarland and Company, Inc., 1076 p.

Hatcher J. B., Marsh, O. C., and Lull, R. S., 1907, The Ceratopsia: Washington, D. C., U. S. Geological Survey, Monograph, v. 49, U. S. Government Printing Office, 300 p.

Hayden, F. V., 1868, Second annual report of the United States Geological Survey of the Territories, embracing Wyoming, *in* Hayden, F. V., U. S. geologist, 1873, First, second, and third annual reports of the United States Geological Survey of the Territories for the years 1867, 1868, and 1869 under the Department of the Interior: Washington, D. C., Government Printing Office, p. 65-102.

—1869, Third annual report of the United States Geological Survey of the Territories, embracing Colorado and New Mexico, *in* Hayden, F. V., U.S. geologist, 1873, First, second, and third annual reports of the United States Geological Survey of the Territories for the years 1867, 1868, and 1869 under the Department of the Interior: Washington, D. C., Government Printing Office, p. 103-251.

—1871, Preliminary report of the United States Geological Survey of Wyoming and portions of contiguous territories, (being a second annual report of progress) conducted under the authority of the Secretary of the Interior: Washington, D. C., Government Printing Office, 511 p.

Knowlton, F. H., 1922, The Laramie Flora of the Denver Basin: Washington, D. C., United States Geological Survey, Professional Paper 130, U. S. Government Printing Office, 175 p.

Leidy, Joseph, 1856, Notices of the remains of extinct reptiles and fishes, discovered by Dr. F. V. Hayden in the badlands of the Judith River, Nebraska Territory: Academy of Natural Sciences, Proceedings, v. 1856, p. 72-73.

—1868, (Remarks on a jaw fragment of *Megalosaurus*): National Academy of Sciences, Proceedings, v. 187, p. 197-200.

—1870, (Proposal of *Poicilopleuron valens*): Academy of Natural Sciences, Proceedings, v. 22, p. 3-4.

—1872, Remarks on some extinct vertebrates: Academy of Natural Sciences, Proceedings, v. 1872, p. 38-40.

Lessem, Donald, and Glut, D. F., 1993, The Dinosaur Society dinosaur encyclopedia: New York, Random House, Inc., 533 p.

Lull, R. S., 1926, Early fossil hunting in the Rocky Mountains: Natural History, v. 26, no. 5, p. 455-461.

Lull, R. S., and Wright, N. E., 1942, Hadrosaurian dinosaurs of North America: Geological Society of America, Special Paper, no. 40, 242 p.

Madsen, J. H., 1976, *Allosaurus fragilis* -- a revised osteology: Utah Geological and Mineral Survey, Bulletin 109, 163 p.

Marsh, O. C., 1868, Observations on the metamorphosis of *Siredon* into *Amblystoma*: American Journal of Science, series 2, v. 46, p. 364-374.

—1871, On the geology of the eastern Uinta Mountains: American Journal of Science and Arts, series 3, v. 1, p. 191-198.

—1872, Notice of new American Dinosauria: American Journal of Science, series 3., v. 3, p. 301.

—1890, Additional characters of the Ceratopsidae, with notice of new Cretaceous dinosaurs: American Journal of Science, series 3., v. 39, p. 418-426.

—1896, The dinosaurs of North America: 16th Annual Report, United States Geological Survey, Part I, p. 133-244.

McIntosh, J. S., 1990, The second Jurassic dinosaur rush: Earth Sciences History, v. 9, no. 1, p. 22-27.

Miller, W. E., and Hall, D. E., 1990, Earliest history of vertebrate paleontology in Utah: Earth Sciences History, v. 9, no. 1, p. 28-33.

Norman, D. B., 1985, The illustrated encyclopedia of dinosaurs: New York, Crescent Books, 208 p.

Ostrom, J. H., and McIntosh, J. S., 1966, Marsh's dinosaurs: New Haven, Yale University Press, 288 p.

Schuchert, Charles, and LeVene, C. M., 1940, O. C. Marsh: Pioneer in paleontology: New Haven, Connecticut, Yale University Press, 541 p.

Simpson, G. G., 1942, The beginnings of vertebrate paleontology in North America: American Philosophical Society, Proceedings, v. 86, no. 1, p. 130-188.

Weishampel, D. B., Dodson, Peter, and Osmolska, Halszka, 1990, The Dinosauria: Berkeley, University of California Press, 733 p.

Williston, S. W., 1878, American Jurassic dinosaurs: Kansas Academy of Sciences, Transactions, v. 6, p. 42-46.

—1915, The first discovery of dinosaurs in the West, *in* Matthew, W. D., editor, Dinosaurs, with special reference to the American Museum collections: New York, American Museum of Natural History, Handbook, no. 5, p. 124-131.

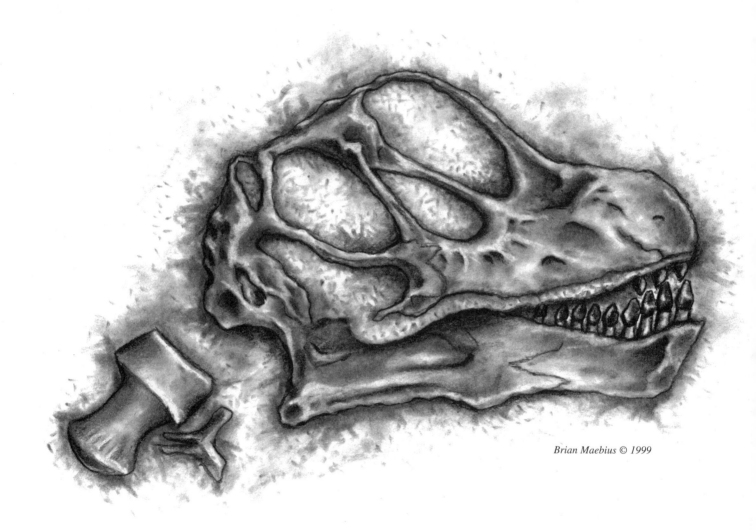

Brian Maebius © 1999

Camarasaurus

MARSH AND "MEGALOSAURUS" - UTAH'S FIRST THEROPOD DINOSAUR

Sue Ann Bilbey and James Evan Hall
Utah Field House of Natural History,
235 East Main,
Vernal, Utah 84078

ABSTRACT

During the latter half of the 19th century, Othniel Charles Marsh, the great vertebrate paleontologist from the Yale University Peabody Museum, published more than a thousand papers on paleontology, most of them on fossils of the American west. Although most of his work was done in other states, Marsh's forays into Utah are recognized for his significant discoveries of Eocene mammals from eastern Utah in a place he named the "Uintah basin." Less known and obscured by mistakes is his discovery of the first theropod dinosaur material in Utah from a site near, but not in, Dinosaur National Monument.

A TRIP TO UTAH - 1870

With 12 students from Yale University in the summer of 1870, Professor Othniel C. Marsh journeyed from Ft. Bridger (Wyoming) southward into modern-day Utah to the eastern Uinta Mountains, and on to the confluence of the Green and White Rivers. Several renditions of this excursion were reported in the contemporary press, and in professional publications (Marsh, 1871; Emmons, 1877). Although limited to the immediate route due to time constraints, Marsh commented, "The region passed over proved to be one of the most interesting fields for geological research yet discovered in this country . . ." (Marsh, 1871, p. 192).

Marsh (1871) briefly discussed the fossils and sediments of the units now known as the Wasatch, Green River, and Bridger Formations in Wyoming, all recognized today as Eocene in age. Ascending the Uinta Mountains, he reported encountering Mesozoic and older rocks. He identified ripple-marked, reddish sandstones and quartzites near the center of the range, in what today is recognized as the Precambrian Uinta Mountain Group, as "at least Silurian age" due to the occurrence of fossil remains in an overlying limestone that he identified as Carboniferous. The Carboniferous unit that unconformably overlies the Uinta Mountain Group is the Mississippian Lodgepole Formation in the northeastern Uinta Mountains.

Marsh's route from Browns Park ascended onto and crossed the Precambrian rocks on the high plateau known as Diamond Mountain then descended through upper Paleozoic rocks and extensive Mesozoic strata into the Tertiary of the Uinta Basin. C. W. Bett, one of Marsh's students, described the scenery as they continued through the mountains to overlook the basin to the south:

> We therefore forded just above the mouth of Vermilion Creek, and ascended the eastern end of the Uinta Mountains to the altitude of snow. After crossing an extensive tableland a grand scene burst upon us. Fifteen hundred feet below us lay the beds of another great tertiary [sic] lake. We stood upon the brink of a vast basin so desolate, wild, and broken, so lifeless and silent, that it seemed like the ruins of a world . . . At the White River we had ample reward for all the hardships we had experienced in reaching this goal of our journey. Though we found none of the gigantic bones of which we had heard so much from hunters and Indians, yet, as we ascended the river, the fossils increased in number, until from one point of view we counted eleven shells of pliocene tortoises which had weathered from the bluffs. (*Harpers New Monthly Magazine*, October, 1871, p. 663-671 as quoted in Schuchert and LeVene, 1940, p. 111).

In comparing the Green River Basin north of the Uinta Mountains to the basin on the south side of the Uinta Mountains, Marsh noted the similarity of the fossils and considered the lacustrine units synchronous. However, he recognized that these areas belonged to separate lake basins:

> To distinguish this ancient lake-region from the Green River Tertiary-basin north of the mountains, the former may appropriately be called the Uintah basin. (Marsh, 1881, p. 196).

The name, Uinta Basin, has endured, identifying the geographical and synclinal area between the Uinta Mountains and the Book Cliffs of eastern Utah.

Marsh (1871) elaborated on the descent from the Uinta Mountains, with a serendipitous account of the Mesozoic rocks on the north side of Split Mountain, just outside the present-day Dinosaur National Monument:

> Near Brush Creek, and about six miles from Green River, a seam of bituminous coal was discovered in the side of a dry gorge, which cuts through a high

ridge of sandstones and shales . . . The strata containing the coal where first seen dip about **65° to the north**, and form part of a denuded anticlinal. The weathering of the thickly bedded sandstone above the coal had developed huge concretionary masses . . . In the shales directly below the coal bed, cycloidal fish scales and coprolites were abundant; and lower down, remains of Turtles of Cretaceous types, and teeth of a Dinosaurian reptile, resembling those of *Megalosaurus*, were discovered. (Marsh, 1871, p. 195).

Emmons (1877) restated and unfortunately obscured the account of the discovery of the first theropod dinosaur material in Utah by contradicting Marsh's description of the angle of dip and orientation of the strata in which these fossils were found:

Near the point where the Indian trail crosses Brush Creek, a coal seam is found, which probably corresponds to that already mentioned on Ashley Creek. Cretaceous fossils, such as Ostrea congesta . . . just above, a new and very interesting crinoid . . . and Professor Marsh mentions the discovery below it of cycloidal fish-scales, . . . Cretaceous turtles, and teeth of a Dinosaur . . . a fragment of the unique Cretaceous crinoid, the Uintacrinus socialis . . . We are here on the southern side of the synclinal, or near the point of the Split Mountain anticlinal, and the beds enclosing coal have a dip of 45° to 50° to the northeast. S. F. Emmons, 1877, p. 296.

The Marsh paper (1871) is the first published report regarding a dinosaur from Utah although it was the second dinosaur discovery. The first dinosaur discovered in Utah was *Dystrophaeus viaemalae*, a poorly known sauropod, found by J. S. Newberry in 1859 (Gillette, 1996a and b), but not described until two decades later. Other Jurassic theropod dinosaurs were found in Colorado and Wyoming, but the next reference to a Utah theropod was by W. J. Holland in his 1915 annual report for paleontology from the Carnegie quarry, which is now part of Dinosaur National Monument (Holland, 1916). In that report he described the discovery of a nearly complete *Allosaurus*.

We recently re-identified Marsh's theropod dinosaur site near the Questar Pipeline corridor that cuts the plunging nose of Split Mountain near the western boundary of Dinosaur National Monument. A hogback with a resistant unit of conglomerate in the Brushy Basin Member of the Morrison Formation dips approximately 65° to the north (figure 1), an angle and orientation that corresponds to Marsh's original description. In this rock we found theropod dinosaur bone similar in form to "Megalosaurus." In addition, shell fragments of the Morrison turtle, *Glyptops*, also have been found scattered on the southern slope below the conglomerate.

Nearby in a dry gulch approximately 400 meters northwest, huge cannonball concretions are exposed above a seam of coal in the Cretaceous Frontier Forma-

Figure 1. *An aerial view of the area of Marsh's "Megalosaurus" site near Dinosaur National Monument. Exposed are steeply dipping beds of the Cretaceous Frontier, Mowry, Dakota, and Cedar Mountain Formations and the Jurassic Morrison Formation.*

tion. Overlying this unit is the Mowry Shale, well known for the abundant fish scales preserved in it, corresponding to the type locality of the *Uintacrinus socialis* described in the quote by Emmons, above. Although more specimens of the *Uintacrinus* are known from Grand Junction, Colorado and in Kansas, no more have been found in the Uinta Mountains, the type locality for this unique crinoid. David L. Meyer and the authors searched this area in 1997, but found no *Uintacrinus* fossils. Meyer agrees, however, that we have discovered the original Marsh type locality (Meyer, 1997 written communication) of this crinoid.

SUMMARY

O. C. Marsh made several geological excursions into the American west, including a short visit to northeastern Utah in 1870. This trip took him through the unexplored region of the eastern Uinta Mountains into the vast Tertiary syncline that he named the "Uintah basin." His discoveries included many firsts for Utah: a theropod dinosaur, numerous Tertiary mammals and turtles, and the first and only Utah occurrence of *Uintacrinus*, a unique Cretaceous crinoid.

REFERENCES

Emmons, S. F., 1877, Chapter II, Green river basin, *in* King, Clarence, Report of the geological exploration of the Fortieth Parallel, descriptive geology by Arnold Hague and S. F. Emmons: Professional Paper of the Engineering Department, United States Army, no. 18, p. 191-309.

Gillette, D. D., 1996a, Origin and early evolution of the sauropod dinosaurs of North America--the type locality and stratigraphic position of *Dystrophaeus viaemalae* Cope 1877, *in* Huffman, A. C., Lund, W. R., and Godwin, L. H., editors, Geology and resources of the Paradox Basin: Utah Geological Association Guidebook 25, p. 313-324.

—1996b, Stratigraphic position of the sauropod *Dystrophaeus viaemalae* Cope and implications, *in* Morales, Michael, editor, The continental Jurassic: Museum of Northern Arizona Bulletin 60, p. 59-68.

Holland, W. J., 1916, Paleontology: Annual Report of the Carnegie Museum for 1915, p. 38-42.

Marsh, O. C., 1871, On the geology of the eastern Uintah Mountains: American Journal of Science and Arts, Third Series, v. 1, nos. 1-6, p. 191-198.

Schuchert, Charles, and C. M. LeVene, 1940, O. C. Marsh - pioneer in paleontology: New Haven, Yale University Press, 541 p.

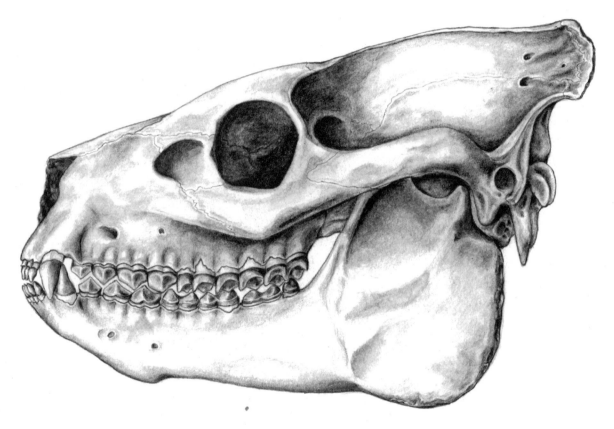

Brian Maebius © 1999

Oreodont

THE HISTORY OF DINOSAUR NATIONAL MONUMENT'S DOUGLASS QUARRY: THE PARK SERVICE YEARS

Ann S. Elder
Dinosaur National Monument,
P.O. Box 128, Jensen, UT 84035

ABSTRACT

The Douglass Quarry, in northeastern Utah, has produced many significant Jurassic vertebrate specimens since its discovery in 1909. Dinosaur National Monument was established in 1915 to ensure that the public benefited from the gigantic, reptilian remains found in the Douglass Quarry. Though many other highly significant quarries have been found within the boundaries of Dinosaur National Monument over the past 80 years, the Douglass Quarry remains the heart of the monument. Approximately 500,000 visitors gaze upon the quarry every year, contemplating the wonders of paleontology as represented by the more than 1,400 dinosaur bones still embedded in the Jurassic Morrison Formation which makes up one wall of the Quarry Visitor Center.

The Douglass Quarry is today both a locality of great scientific interest to the paleontological community, and a unit of the National Park Service. Both roles have shaped its past. This paper focuses on the history of the Douglass Quarry from 1915 when the American public became its owners, to 1958 when the National Park Service dedicated the present day in situ museum, the Quarry Visitor Center.

INTRODUCTION

Dinosaur National Monument is one of over 360 units of the National Park Service (NPS), areas set aside to preserve national treasures and provide for the enjoyment of those treasures by future generations. Dinosaur National Monument is one of only a few NPS units specifically established to preserve paleontological resources. It is the only one where a visitor center has been built over an internationally significant fossil site, the Douglass Quarry, where visitors can see over 1,400 dinosaur bones left in place as nature deposited them 150 million years ago. Approximately 500,000 visitors every year leave with a greater appreciation for the science of paleontology after visiting the quarry. In seeing the Douglass Quarry today, it is hard to imagine an area more deserving of National Monument status, but getting from a working fossil excavation to a national treasure was not an easy road.

BECOMING A NATIONAL MONUMENT

The Douglass Quarry site was discovered in 1909 by Carnegie Museum paleontologist Earl Douglass. (Details of the discovery can be found in Good and others [1958], West and Chure ([1984], Chure and McIntosh [1990], and Harvey [1991].) The Carnegie Museum quickly realized the value of the find. Many significant specimens were excavated in the first five years of quarrying, including what was then considered the most complete sauropod ever found (Douglass, n.d.). This skeleton of a new species of dinosaur, *Apatosaurus louisae* (named in honor of Andrew Carnegie's wife), was mounted in the Carnegie Museum in Pittsburgh in 1915.

The Carnegie Museum officials soon began to worry about the unprotected status of the quarry. They feared that without legal title to the fossil resources, other institutions or private citizens would compete for the bonanza of bones. In 1913, Earl Douglass, on behalf of the Carnegie Museum, filed a placer claim at the local U. S. Land Office. It was not until 1915 that a final decision was made on the claim. The First Assistant Secretary, Department of the Interior, ruled that fossil deposits were not subject to mining claims (Jones, 1915). Though the Carnegie Museum continued to appeal the decision, representatives of the Department of Interior were moving to protect the site in another way.

The National Monument Act of 1906 had been used before to protect sensitive areas of public interest. It required only the signature of the President of the United States, not an act of Congress, to set aside valuable lands. Some government officials considered the Douglass Quarry a candidate for protection under this act, but not everyone thought it worthy of National Monument status. In a memorandum dated August 21, 1915, Frank Bond, Chief Clerk of the General Land Office, expressed his concerns to his commissioner:

> I think the National Monument Act, while broad enough in its expression to cover this case, was not intended to protect objects solely for the time it would take to remove them. A fossil quarry can have no interest or value other than that which attaches to the objects removed there from and when this removal is accomplished there will remain no excuse for perpetuating the reservation. (Bond, 1915)

Luckily, other thoughts prevailed. On October 4, 1915, President Woodrow Wilson signed the legislation designating the Douglass Quarry and 80 surrounding acres as Dinosaur National Monument, stating:

> ...there is located [in Utah] an extraordinary deposit of Dinosaurian and other gigantic reptilian remains of the Juratrias period, which are of great scientific interest and value, and it appears that the public interest would be promoted by reserving these deposits as a National Monument...(Wilson, 1915)

The quarry now belonged to all of the citizens of the United States.

THOUGHTS OF AN IN SITU MUSEUM

The Douglass Quarry was indeed now protected. But with a stroke of the pen, it changed from a museum's quarry to a public trust. Immediately, questions arose. Should the Carnegie Museum be allowed to continue quarrying? Should at least some of the specimens from the site reside in the U. S. National Museum, the Smithsonian Institution in Washington, D.C.? Should a museum be built at the site?

George Smith, Assistant Secretary of the Interior and Director of the U. S. Geological Survey, expressed his opinion on the subject of an in situ museum in a letter to NPS Director Stephen Mather dated January, 1916:

> One can conceive of the impressiveness and instructiveness to the tourist of seeing partly uncovered and, in some cases, protruding from the surfaces and edges of the strata the bones and skeletons of the monsters, lying where they were buried many millions of years ago in deposits of mud and sand which now are mere strata beneath thousands of feet of outer beds from which the mountains and mesas of the region have been carved. There is, therefore, reason for the perpetuation of the Dinosaur National Monument as fact rather than name. (Smith, 1916)

Smith's interest in the area prompted Mather to request that the U. S. Geological Survey conduct a survey of the Douglass Quarry to determine what the possibilities of an in situ display really were. The survey was conducted in 1916. Visitation to the quarry at this point had already reached 500 people per year (Beidlemann, 1956).

Though the U. S. Geological Survey had been encouraging, the in situ museum remained just an idea for nearly a decade. Earl Douglass, who continued to supervise the Carnegie's excavation after monument status had been achieved, campaigned for a museum: In an article in a local Utah newspaper, the Vernal Express on December 12, 1919, entitled " The Dinosaur Quarry - A Prophecy," Douglass wrote of a great museum being built around the exposed dinosaur remains. Yet not

everyone in the paleontology profession supported the idea. W.J. Holland, Carnegie Museum Director, summed up his thoughts on the matter in a letter to NPS Assistant Director Arno B. Cammerer in November, 1921:

> ...Douglass, who is of a somewhat poetic temperament...wrote to me suggesting that the scene of his immortal labors ought to be marked by the erection on the ground of a stately edifice in which there should be assembled plaster-casts of the dinosaurs which we have extracted from the spot. ...No doubt the erection of such a building would give employment to some of the unemployed in Vernal [Utah] and might enhance the value of certain acres at present covered with sage-brush in that vicinity, I do not, however, think that the people of the United States would be justified in undertaking any such wild scheme. When we get done with our work of taking up the bones which we find in the quarry there will be nothing left there, and in my humble judgement, as a citizen of the United States and as a heavy tax-payer, I could think of nothing more scandalous than a proposal to do what has been suggested, unless the method of the "Pork barrel" is to prevail ...[T]he whole thing sums itself up in saying that it is questionable whether the United States Government would be justified in appropriating money simply to preserve intact what is in truth only a "hole in the ground", so that the people living twenty-five miles away may have a place to which to resort to gratify their curiosity when they have nothing else to do. (Holland, 1921)

Despite a lack of enthusiasm from some professionals, Douglass was persistent. His own thoughts to NPS Assistant Director Cammerer (recounted in a letter by Cammerer) were indeed prophetic:

> The uncovered area should be housed to protect the specimens and provide shelter for sight-seers and students. The north side would be a natural wall, of course, with the skeletons in place. The south side would probably be a natural wall also but the ends would have to be built and a roof with ample sky lights would cover the whole. The extra space and walls could be utilized for many other exhibits from this most interesting geological and paleontological region... At the Monument, if the skeletons are exposed as outlined, one can see the remains as they were buried many millions of years ago... [H]ere we will be able to better study out the geological history and modes of life... Those who have charge of museums have found that, to most of us, there is far more interest [in] seeing a skeleton mounted on a slab as it was found than in seeing [it] stand on its feet. (Cammerer, 1924)

Finally, in 1924, House of Representatives Bill 9064 was introduced to the U. S. Congress which would fund an in situ museum at Dinosaur National Monument. But not even the NPS supported the bill. Too many questions remained unanswered. Concerns ran high whether there were still enough bones left to make an educational exhibit. The bill did not pass. Over 1,000 visitors journeyed to the monument that year (Beidlemann, 1956).

DOUGLASS QUARRY OPERATIONS: 1915 - 1922

Meanwhile, the Carnegie Museum continued removing specimens (figure 1), though now they needed a permit. The Department of Interior had invited the Carnegie Museum to apply for a permit, recognizing that the Smithsonian could not afford a large-scale excavation at that time. The permit process required that the Carnegie Museum provide a list of the specimens collected, and a quarry map, to the Secretary of the Smithsonian every year. The permit was exclusive, granted on a yearly basis. Though the Smithsonian hoped to get at least some of the bones from the Carnegie's excavation, no such provision was made in the permit.

Figure 1. *Carnegie Museum excavation operations (photo courtesy of Sue Ann Bilbey and Evan Hall).*

By 1919, both the NPS and U. S. Geological Survey were expressing concerns about the Carnegie Museum's monopoly on the Douglass Quarry. Frustrations grew. Finally in 1922, Department of the Interior Assistant Secretary F. M. Goodwin spelled out the growing sentiment:

I venture to suggest that Dr. Holland be advised that the ethics of the case would seem to demand that he deposit a portion of his duplicate material in the National Museum. It seems very unfortunate that the Government, by reason of lack of funds for the particular purpose, should be deprived of the opportunity of securing and preserving for education and research work the treasures of its own domain. At the same time it would be both ungracious and unwise to refuse to accord permission to a properly constituted organi-

zation to do the work which we cannot do ourselves. In view of all the circumstances, however, it seems unfair that a private organization should be permitted to practically exhaust the resources of a portion of the national domain without rendering some return to the Government. [Goodwin, 1922]

Whether from governmental pressure, a change in directors, lack of funds, or a sense of having all the dinosaur bones the museum needed, 1922 was to be the last year that the Carnegie Museum collected specimens from the Douglass Quarry. The University of Utah, University of Michigan, and the Smithsonian all collected briefly over the next two years. Earl Douglass' era had ended and the quarry then fell silent for eight years. Meanwhile, another prominent museum and the Federal government debated what would happen next.

RELIEF LABOR AND THE DOUGLASS QUARRY

In the early 1930s, the American Museum of Natural History in New York City had become interested in the development of the Douglass Quarry. So had their curator, Barnum Brown. Though the American Museum and the NPS failed in their efforts to come up with a mutually beneficial development plan, the government did hire Brown as a consultant for three weeks to evaluate the quarry. Brown is credited with recommending to NPS Director Horace Albright that relief labor from the newly created New Deal programs be used to continue the work at Dinosaur National Monument (Brown, 1933).

In 1933, A.C. Boyle Jr. was hired to supervise the relief labor. Boyle was a former geologist with the Union Pacific Railroad and professor of geology at the Wyoming School of Mines. Like Earl Douglass before him, he had a high degree of personal devotion and unbridled enthusiasm for the fossil resources of Dinosaur National Monument. Likewise, he periodically ran afoul of authority because of his informal and independent mode of operation (Beidlemann, 1956). Still, Boyle was made the "acting custodian" of Dinosaur National Monument by the NPS, a position he would hold until 1938.

Boyle's first laborers consisted of 19 local men under the Civil Works Administration (CWA) program. By mid-1934, the CWA had pulled out, and 32 men staffed the Quarry as part of the Transient Relief Service. By 1936, the Transient Relief Service was transferred to the Works Progress Administration (WPA). The mission on the WPA was to remove the overburden from above the fossiliferous layer and enlarge the trench in front of the quarry for future development (figure 2).

Boyle took his duties very seriously. Not only did he see himself responsible for the removal of the overburden, he also felt an obligation to educate the visitors who

continued to find the quarry despite poor roads and no signs. By mid-1935, visitation had climbed to over 400 tourists per month with only 6% from Utah (Beidlemann, 1956). Boyle saw the WPA crew not only as laborers, but as interpreters. To that end he spent much of his time educating them so that they could inform the visitors. He gave nightly lectures to his men, and took them on Saturday field trips where they collected samples to be used for educational purposes. He encouraged them to compose songs and write poetry, hoping they might be impassioned as well as informed. One Park Service geologist commented "Dr. Boyle read some of the poetry to me and it was almost unbelievable that these men had written it" (Vandiver, 1935).

Because of Boyle's efforts, morale was high in the quarry camp. The men stayed as long as they could and accomplished their work with a unique sense of pride and ownership which they shared with the more than 6,000 people who were now visiting the quarry annually (Beidlemann, 1956). Boyle set up exhibits of bones and Indian artifacts, established visiting hours of 6:00 AM - 10:00 PM (7:00 AM - 6:00 PM in the winter), and in later years, held annual Memorial Day services for Earl Douglass, who had since passed away. Work progressed well.

Figure 2. WPA laborers remove overburden (NPS photo).

With the beginning of World War II, the relief labor programs were no longer needed and neither was Boyle. Visitation plummeted as America's attention turned to winning the war. The Douglass Quarry fell silent for a second time (figure 3).

MISSION 66

By the early 1950s, Americans were once again ready to vacation in their National Parks. To meet the demands of the returning visitors, the NPS embarked on a new development plan, Mission 66, which was

Figure 3. The Douglass Quarry in the early 1940s after the withdrawal of the WPA camp (NPS photo).

to increase the meager infrastructure in many park areas by the year 1966.

The Douglass Quarry once again came to life. Paleontologist Theodore E. White (figure 4), formerly of the Smithsonian Institution and Harvard University, was hired by the NPS in 1953 to oversee the reliefing of the bone-bearing layer, which the WPA crews had uncovered (Good and others, 1958). White trained other employees, who had no previous experience, in the delicate work of fossil preparation (figure 5). Two of these employees, Floyd "Tobe" Wilkins and Jim Adams, devoted their careers to the Douglass Quarry, each spending about 30 years reliefing the bones that can be seen today.

This was an exciting time at Dinosaur National Monument. With Mission 66 funding, an in situ museum seemed almost certain. But how many bones really remained in the fossil- bearing layer? It was the job of Dr. White and his co-workers to find out. Pneumatic tools were used in the quarry for the first time (Good and others, 1958). Large jackhammers were used to remove the remaining overburden, while smaller chipping hammers were used within the fossiliferous layer itself. A tin shed was built over a portion of the quarry, making year-round work more comfortable. Still more visitors came, and as had been the case since the day of Earl Douglass, the work remained a balance of hard labor and time spent educating the visitors (figure 6).

Development was occurring throughout the monument. A new headquarters facility was built in Dinosaur, Colorado. Employee housing areas were built near the Quarry and near Artesia, Colorado. Access roads were paved and repaired. But most exciting of all, the long awaited in situ museum became a reality, built much as Earl Douglass had envisioned it nearly half a century before. A lot had happened at the Douglass Quarry in the 40 years leading up to the 1958 dedication of the Quarry Visitor Center. Many individuals were responsible for the final success. But simply stated, Earl Douglass' dream had finally come true.

CONCLUSIONS

The Douglass Quarry is an internationally significant fossil site. It is also the most visited dinosaur quarry in the U. S. Combining these factors creates an educational opportunity unequalled in any museum. Woodrow Wilson was correct when he wrote that the public interest would be served by

Figure 4. Dr. Theodore E. White (NPS photo).

Figure 5. "Tobe" Wilkins (bottom) and Gil Stucker (top) reliefing bones in the 1950s (NPS photo).

Figure 6. Dr. White pauses from work to answer a question from a group of visitors (NPS photo).

preserving the Douglass Quarry. It is a place where the paleontological community and the NPS have met for the good of the American public.

ACKNOWLEDGMENTS

Support for this paper was provided by Dinosaur National Monument. Linda West, Scott Madsen, Dan Chure, Donna Breslin, F.A. Barnes, George Engelmann, and David Whitman reviewed early versions. A special thanks to Mrs. Theodore E. White, Sue Ann Bilbey, Evan Hall, Dave Gillette and retired Dinosaur National Monument Superintendent Denny Huffman.

REFERENCES

Beidlemann, R. G., 1956, Administrative History, Dinosaur National Monument: Unpublished report for Dinosaur National Monument, Dinosaur National Monument Quarry Library Number 979 B4.

Bond, Frank, 1915, Memorandum to Commissioner of the General Land Office, August 21,1915: Dinosaur National Monument Archive File 580.

Brown, Barnum, 1933, Letter to Horace Albright, Director National Park Service, June 26, 1933: Dinosaur National Monument Archive File 2159.

Cammerer, A. B., 1924, Letter to Case, December 30, 1924: Dinosaur National Monument Archives File 580.

Chure, D. J. and McIntosh, J. S., 1990, Stranger in a strange land--a brief history of paleontological operations at Dinosaur National Monument: Earth Sciences History, v. 9, no.1, p. 34-40.

Douglass, Earl, n.d. (ca 1916), Manuscript, The Carnegie Museum dinosaur quarry and National Monument: Dinosaur National Monument Archives.

Good, J. M., White, T. E., and Stucker, G. F., 1958, The dinosaur quarry: Washington , D. C., National Park Service, 47 p.

Goodwin, F. M., 1922, Letter to W. J. Holland, Carnegie Museum Director, January 31,1922: Dinosaur National Monument

Archives File 580.

Harvey, M. W., 1991, Utah, the National Park Service, and Dinosaur National Monument, 1909-1956: Utah Historical Quarterly, v. 59, no. 3, p. 243-263.

Holland, W. J., 1921, Letter to Arno B. Cammerer, Assistant Director, National Park Service, November 8, 1921: Dinosaur National Monument Archives File 580.

Jones, A. A., 1915, Letter to Commissioner of the General Land Office, August 6, 1915: Dinosaur National Monument Archives File 580.

Smith, George, 1916, Letter to Stephen Mather, Director, National Park Service, January 15, 1916: Dinosaur National Monument Archives File 580.

Vandiver, 1935, Letter to Trager, October 21, 1935: Dinosaur National Monument Archives File 2159.

West, Linda and Chure, D. J., 1984, Dinosaurs--Dinosaur National Monument Quarry: Jensen, Utah, Dinosaur Nature Association, 40 p.

Wilson, Woodrow, 1915, Presidential Proclamation Number 1313, 39 Strat. 2454, October 4, 1915: Dinosaur National Monument Archives.

BIOSTRATIGRAPHY OF DINOSAURS IN THE UPPER JURASSIC MORRISON FORMATION OF THE WESTERN INTERIOR, U.S.A.

Christine E. Turner and Fred Peterson
U. S. Geological Survey,
Box 25046, MS-939,
Denver, CO 80225-0046

ABSTRACT

The biostratigraphy of dinosaur remains in the Upper Jurassic Morrison Formation and related beds was studied throughout the Western Interior in an effort to place as many dinosaur localities as possible in their relative chronostratigraphic positions. First, we established a regional stratigraphic framework for the Morrison Formation throughout the Western Interior. Three primary stratigraphic markers in the formation aided in regional correlations. An important marker in about the middle or upper middle part of the formation, known as the clay change, marks the abrupt transition from predominantly non-smectitic clays below to predominantly smectitic clays above. This surface, as well as the J-5 unconformable to conformable surface at the base of the Morrison and the K-1 unconformity at the top of the Morrison, comprise the basis for most of the correlations.

After the stratigraphic framework was established, a total of 128 dinosaur sites were placed in the stratigraphic framework and then were correlated to a primary reference section (DQW) near the Carnegie Quarry at Dinosaur National Monument in northeastern Utah. Where the clay change is not evident (Black Hills and Montana), the correlations are more tenuous so the 13 localities in these areas are treated separately, even though other evidence from the regional stratigraphy and calcareous microfossils help relate these sites to the primary reference section.

The biostratigraphic distribution of the dinosaurs allows the Morrison Formation and related beds to be divided into four biozones, numbered one through four from oldest to youngest. The zones are based on the stratigraphic (vertical) distribution of long-ranging taxa (mostly genera and species), which are taxa that extend through two or more different stratigraphic positions in the formation. Single-site taxa that are only found at one locality in one stratigraphic level are not used in the zonation. Dinosaur Zone 1 extends from the base of the formation to the middle of the Salt Wash Member. Dinosaur Zone 2 extends upward to about 30 ft (9.1 m) above the clay change in the primary reference section (DQW). Dinosaur Zone 3 extends up to about the middle of the upper part of the Brushy Basin Member. Dinosaur Zone 4 extends to the top of the formation. Based on age information from palynomorphs, charophytes and ostracodes, isotopic dates, and paleomagnetic studies, Dinosaur Zones 1, 2, and 3 are Kimmeridgian in age and the Kimmeridgian-Tithonian boundary is in the lower part of Dinosaur Zone 4.

The biostratigraphic distribution shows a vertical trend of increasing faunal diversity followed by decreasing diversity during deposition of the Morrison Formation. First, it is noteworthy that dinosaurs were scarce during earliest Morrison deposition—the earliest fauna consists of only a few taxa (Zone 1, Tidwell and lower Salt Wash Members). Diversity increased dramatically near the middle of the Salt Wash Member (low in Zone 2) and continued to increase, reaching a peak in diversity just above the clay change (high in Zone 2, near the base of the upper part of the Brushy Basin Member) where the first of the long-ranging taxa began to die out. Diversity continued to decrease gradually to about the middle of the upper Brushy Basin Member where a fairly sharp decline occurred (high in Zone 3). Another fairly sharp decline in diversity occurred higher in the same member (middle of Zone 4), followed by a gradual decline, with the few remaining taxa dying out toward the end of Morrison deposition.

The changes in diversity low in Zone 2, high in Zone 3, and toward the middle of Zone 4 coincide fairly well with similar changes in the diversity of charophytes and ostracodes. This suggests that any environmental changes that occurred at these stratigraphic positions were ubiquitous and of sufficient character to exert a strong influence on markedly different types of organisms.

The scarcity of dinosaurs at the beginning of Morrison deposition may reflect a continuation of the harsh conditions that persisted during Middle Jurassic time. Dinosaurs were scarce just before Morrison deposition, or at least only sparse footprint evidence exists in Middle Jurassic rocks. It is likely that the arid climate that persisted during deposition of the eolian ergs and evaporites of the Middle Jurassic was inimical to the dinosaurs. Conditions during earliest Morrison deposition may have remained inhospitable to the dinosaurs, judging from the presence of eolian and evaporite deposits in the lowermost part of the Morrison. The development of the extensive river systems of the Salt Wash Member may have established a more equable habitat, enticing dinosaurs into the area. They seem to have flourished and reached their heyday at about the middle of the Morrison. The change from greater to lesser diversity occurs just above the clay change and thus coincides with the tremendous increase in the output of volcanic ash in the source area. What role the increase in volcanic ash may have played in dinosaur diversity, either direct or indirect, is uncertain.

Taken together with the biostratigraphic data from some of the other organisms in the Morrison ecosystem (for example, charophytes and ostracodes), the newly established biostratigraphic synthesis forms the basis for evaluating widespread paleoecological changes in the Western Interior during the Late Jurassic. Moreover, this synthesis provides, for the first time, a biostratigraphic foundation for the evaluation of taxonomic lineages and evolutionary trends among the dinosaurs in the Morrison Formation.

INTRODUCTION

Two of the more perplexing problems related to the numerous dinosaur remains recovered from the Upper Jurassic Morrison Formation of the Western Interior (figure 1) have been their age in terms of the standard geologic time scale and their relative age with respect to each another. The age of the formation has been resolved rather well in several recent publications (Kowallis and others, 1998; Litwin and others, 1998; Schudack and others, 1998), but the relative stratigraphic position of the numerous dinosaur quarries and sites that are scattered throughout seven of the Western Interior states remained an enigma. Recent advances in understanding the stratigraphy of the Morrison Formation and related beds as well as its lower and upper boundaries (Peterson and Turner, 1998) now allow many of the quarries and sites to be placed in a relative stratigraphic framework. Although new sites are discovered with each field season, we estimate that perhaps as many as about 30 presently known and mostly minor sites remain to be positioned stratigraphically and the data from most if not all of these probably would not significantly change the findings given in the present report. Thus, for this investigation, we present the results of data thus far accumu-

lated in which 141 dinosaur quarries and sites throughout the Western Interior are positioned within the formation and with respect to each other. The information presented here may prove helpful in understanding and distinguishing evolutionary relationships and biogeographic diversity, as well as in making paleoecological reconstructions.

METHODOLOGY

The goal of positioning Morrison dinosaur localities is hampered considerably by the numerous facies changes that are common in continental deposits, by the scarcity of reliable and widespread isochronous or nearly isochronous stratigraphic markers, and by the lack of abundant micropaleontological material that could aid in establishing a detailed microfossil-based biostratigraphy of the formation. Although there are a fair number of local stratigraphic markers in the formation (Peterson and Turner, 1998), most of these vary too much in stratigraphic position or are regionally too discontinuous to be useful for positioning the quarries and were only used where other means of correlation were not available. The primary stratigraphic markers that we used are the J–5 surface (Pipiringos and O'Sullivan, 1978) and the K–1 unconformity (Peterson, 1988cd, 1994) at the base and top, respectively, of the Morrison Formation (and related beds where other stratigraphic units are involved) and a prominent vertical change in clay mineralogy at or near the middle of the formation (Owen and others, 1989; Turner and Fishman, 1991). The J–5 surface is an unconformity in some localities and its correlative conformity in other places; the K–1 surface is an unconformity at the base of Lower Cretaceous rocks, but in some places, Lower Cretaceous rocks are missing and the K–2 unconformity at the base of uppermost Lower Cretaceous or lowermost Upper Cretaceous strata must be used. The vertical change in clay mineralogy within the Morrison is from largely nonsmectitic mudstone below to predominantly smectitic mudstone above (Owen and others, 1989). X-Ray analyses indicate that the clay minerals below the clay change may include some swelling (smectitic) clays but, if present, they are much less abundant and generally do not produce the "popcorn" texture in soils that typically develop on claystones and mudstones that contain abundant smectite-rich clays. An additional stratigraphic marker found by Demko and others (1996) is a persistent and well developed paleosol zone in the lowermost strata of the lower part of the Brushy Basin Member and in correlative strata in other areas. Because it was discovered after many of the dinosaur localities had been positioned, it has not been used extensively in this report although it has considerable potential as another widespread stratigraphic marker that could aid in extending correlations into areas where the clay change is not present.

For convenience of discussion, we refer to the entire assemblage of strata between the J–5 surface and the K–1 unconformity (or the K–2 unconformity in some places) as the Morrison package of beds or the Morrison Formation and related beds. Also for convenience, all strata between the J–5 surface and the clay change are herein referred to informally as the lower Morrison and all strata between the clay change and the K–1 unconformity are referred to informally as the upper Morrison. We use the term "site" for a place where a few bones identifiable to genus level were picked up or otherwise

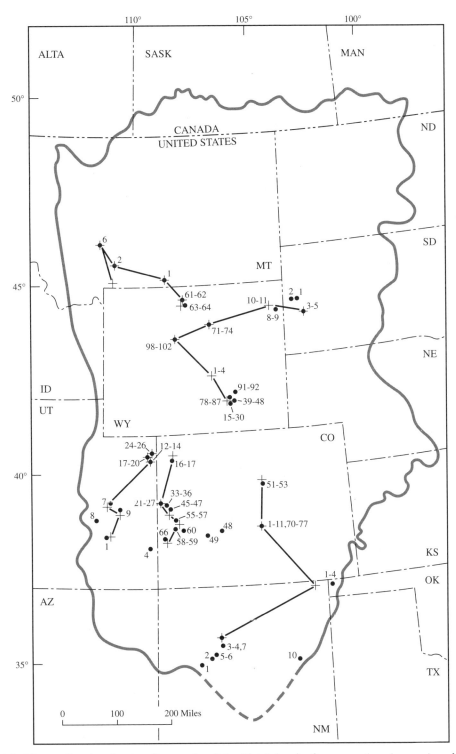

Figure 1. *Index map of the Western Interior showing dinosaur localities (dots), local reference sections (crosses), and lines of stratigraphic sec-*

A

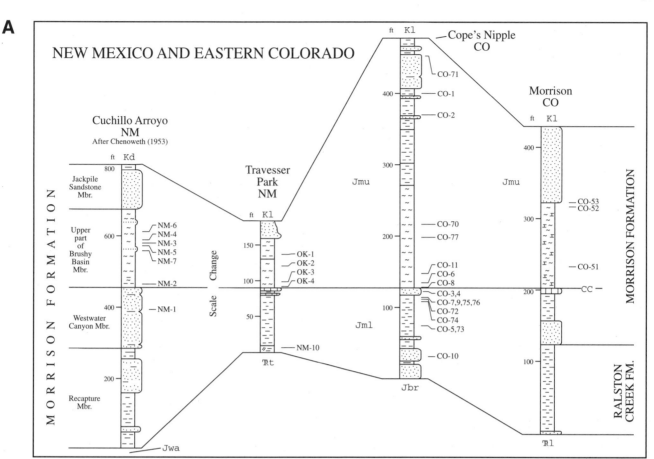

B

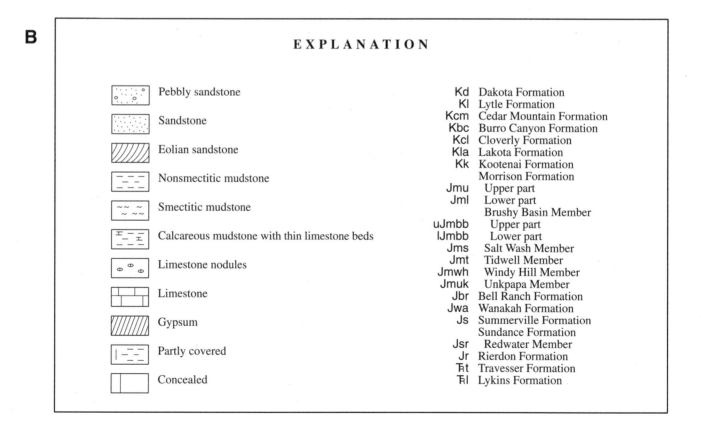

Figure 2. **A**, *Stratigraphic section showing stratigraphic position of dinosaur localities in New Mexico, Oklahoma, and eastern Colorado. Line of section shown on figure 1.* **B**, *The explanation applies to this and figures 3, 4, 5, 6, 7, 10, 11, 12, and 13.*

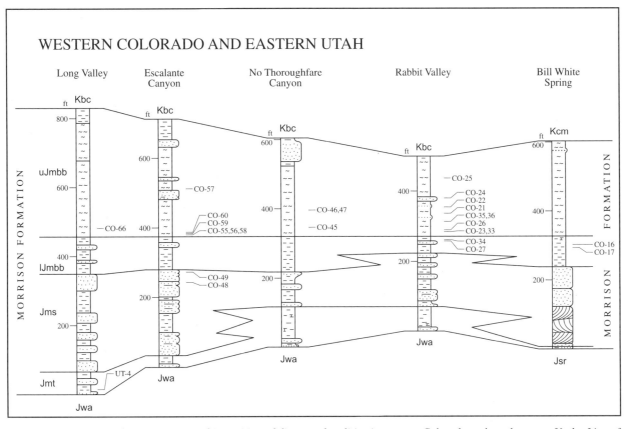

Figure 3. *Stratigraphic section showing stratigraphic position of dinosaur localities in western Colorado and southeastern Utah. Line of section shown on figure 1.*

easily extracted from the rock with minimal digging, or in rare cases where bones were identified in place by a competent paleontologist, and we use the term "locality" for either a site or a quarry where moderate to considerable excavation has occurred.

Complete or partial sections of the Morrison Formation were measured at each of the locations we recovered. In rare cases, dinosaur localities were adequately located geographically and stratigraphically in the published literature so no additional work was required; those sections not measured by us are cited in appendix 1. Throughout most of the region where the clay change is present, we measured a complete section of the Morrison, or at least a partial section from the clay change to the appropriate upper or lower contact of the part of the formation that included the dinosaur locality. Where it was only possible to measure a partial section, the locality was positioned with respect to one of the three key marker surfaces or, rarely, to some other stratigraphic marker and then correlated to the nearest available measured section. The nearest available measured section with the correlated dinosaur locality was then tied to the nearest local reference section that was more complete or representative of the local area. The local reference sections are shown in figures 2-6.

Correlating the various quarries in the local reference

sections to the primary reference section at Dinosaur National Monument (designated as the DQW or Dinosaur Quarry West section) was accomplished by positioning the quarries in proportion to their stratigraphic positions within the lower Morrison or upper Morrison units. This was done largely by graphic correlation methodology (Shaw, 1964), which is simply a way of doing it proportionately. Because we employ the proportional method of correlating the localities, it does not matter that some of the measured sections on various figures in this report are plotted at different scales.

There are obvious shortcomings in the methodology we used in trying to correlate the dinosaur localities to a single master reference section, but, given that the thickness of the Morrison was influenced by slight but nevertheless significant crustal movements, and that widespread stratigraphic markers are scarce, it is the best that can be accomplished at present.

At the base, the lowermost strata of the Morrison onlap paleotopographic highs in some places, which could lead to incorrect positioning of a locality. Fortunately, the areas where this occurs are fairly well known and appropriate measures can be taken to correct for it. A good example of this is the Cabin Creek Quarry (CO-48) near Gunnison, Colorado, where the Morrison onlapped Precambrian crystalline rocks and only the

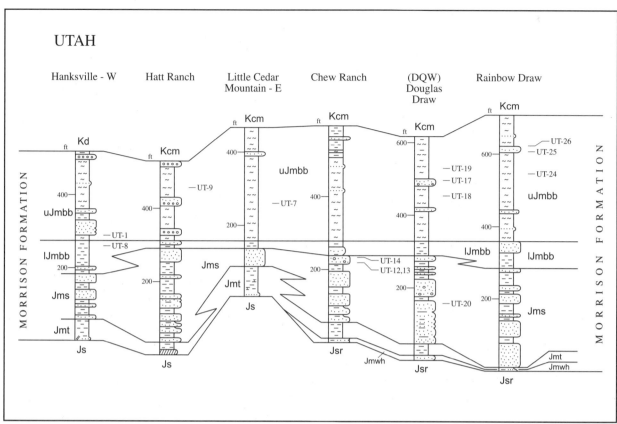

Figure 4. *Stratigraphic section showing stratigraphic position of dinosaur localities in eastern Utah. Line of section shown on figure 1.*

upper strata of the lower Morrison are present and exposed. The quarry is in the Salt Wash Member. The overlying Brushy Basin Member is concealed by a deep cover of alluvium so that the locality could not be positioned with respect to the clay change and could only be positioned with respect to the Salt Wash elsewhere. Because of the known onlap in this area and known pinchout of the lower part of the Salt Wash Member farther west (up the depositional slope) of the Gunnison area, we knew that the lowermost strata of the Salt Wash were not present there, and therefore only the uppermost beds of the Salt Wash Member were present. With this knowledge, we could position the quarry with respect to the upper contact of the Salt Wash Member and then we correlated that contact to the local reference section.

The upper contact of the Morrison is more intractable for a variety of reasons, depending on the locality. It is difficult to estimate the amount of scour beneath Lower Cretaceous rocks. An important clue is the thick, locally present, paleosol zone at the top of the Morrison Formation that is most likely at places where deep scour did not occur (T.M. Demko, oral communication, 1996). This suggests that the areas with the paleosols retained the greatest original thickness of the upper Morrison. Because we tried to refer the localities to the thickest local reference sections, an area that has a thick

paleosol at the top of the formation was considered ideal. These were also the areas where we felt most confident in our identification of the upper contact.

The "Breakfast Bench beds" at the top of the upper Morrison in the Como Bluff region of Wyoming deserve special mention because of their important dinosaur fauna and the thought that they could be Early Cretaceous in age (Bakker and others, 1990). The beds are as much as 71 ft (21.6 m) thick and consist largely of black mudstone that is smectitic to nonsmectitic and carbonaceous or noncarbonaceous. We found that the carbonaceous mudstone strata (zero to about 15 ft or zero to about 4.6 m thick) locally present at the top of the Morrison Formation in the Como Bluff area interfinger with the basal fluvial sandstone bed of the Lower Cretaceous Cloverly Formation and therefore are Early Cretaceous in age and not part of the Morrison Formation. However, we also found a paleosol beneath the carbonaceous black mudstone beds that separates them from noncarbonaceous black mudstone below. This suggests that the black noncarbonaceous mudstone beds are Late Jurassic in age and part of the Morrison Formation whereas the black carbonaceous mudstone beds above are Early Cretaceous in age and more closely allied to the Cloverly Formation. Because the Breakfast Bench fauna is restricted to the noncarbonaceous strata below the pale-

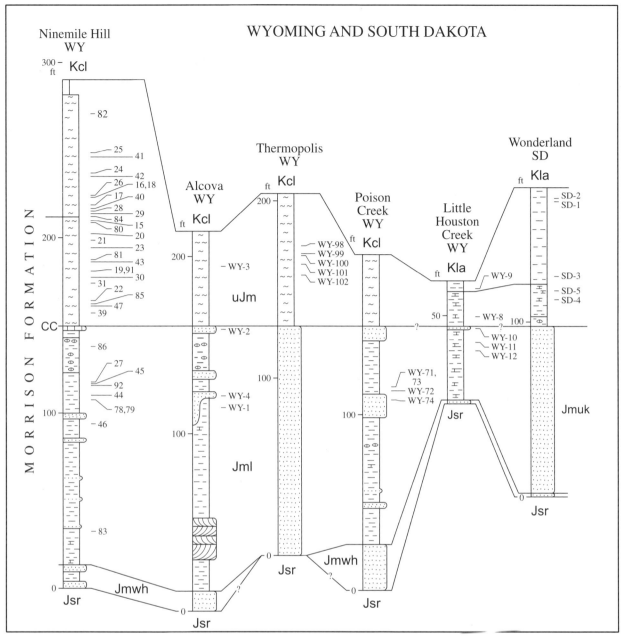

Figure 5. *Stratigraphic section showing stratigraphic position of dinosaur localities in Wyoming and South Dakota. Line of section shown on figure 1. WY omitted from locality codes on Ninemile Hill section for space considerations.*

osol, we suggest that the Breakfast Bench fauna is Late Jurassic in age. Black mudstone beds are locally present at or near the top of the Morrison at scattered localities from Montana south through Wyoming and into central Colorado near the town of Morrison so their occurrence at Como Bluff is not unusual. An important clarification here is that black carbonaceous mudstone does occur locally in beds that we consider Morrison, even though noncarbonaceous black mudstone is more commonly found at the top of the Morrison. This is based on other criteria, mentioned earlier in this report, that are used to identify the upper contact of the Morrison Formation.

Another problem with the upper contact is abrupt regional beveling to the east and west beneath Lower Cretaceous rocks. No dinosaur localities are close to the western edge of the Upper Jurassic Western Interior depositional basin and thus westward beveling is not a problem. However, localities in westernmost Oklahoma and in the Black Hills are near the eastern limit of the Morrison depositional basin and the degree of eastward beveling at the top of the formation in some of those areas, especially the Black Hills, is difficult to evaluate. In western Oklahoma, a fairly thick series of fluvial sandstone beds is present at the top of the Morrison above a thick series of smectitic mudstone beds. The fluvial beds appear to correspond in stratigraphic position to an interval in the uppermost Morrison farther west that also includes several thick fluvial sandstone beds,

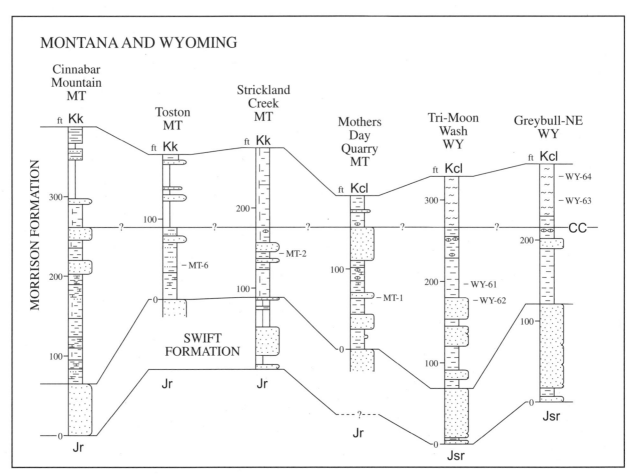

Figure 6. *Stratigraphic section showing stratigraphic position of dinosaur localities in north-central Wyoming and southern Montana. Line of section shown on figure 1.*

such as the Jackpile Sandstone Member in the southern San Juan Basin of northwestern New Mexico and the fairly thick sandstone unit at the top of the undifferentiated Morrison in northeastern New Mexico (Holbrook and others, 1987). This suggests that the entire Morrison thins eastward in the western Oklahoma area and that no inordinate amount of beveling has occurred at the top of the formation near the dinosaur localities.

Regional eastward thinning of the Morrison in the Black Hills is more difficult to evaluate. Thick fluvial sandstone beds generally are lacking at the top of the formation there, so sandstone petrology cannot be used as a guide. Furthermore, the clays throughout the formation in the Black Hills area lack smectite, so that the most reliable stratigraphic marker in the middle of the formation—the clay change—is absent. However, another basis for stratigraphic correlation permits evaluation of Morrison stratigraphy in the Black Hills area. Eolian sandstone units are fairly common in the Morrison of Wyoming and especially on the Colorado Plateau; thus far they have only been found in lower Morrison strata and not above the clay change. This suggests that the eolian Unkpapa Sandstone Member of the Morrison in

the Black Hills also is entirely within the lower Morrison and that the horizon in the Black Hills that is equivalent to the clay change elsewhere should be above the Unkpapa. Thus, we speculate that the Morrison is reasonably complete on the east side of the Black Hills where the Wonderland local reference section was measured (figure 5) and that the distinct thinning of the formation on the west side of the Black Hills is a local phenomenon.

The ostracode *Theriosynoecum wyomingense* apparently is restricted to Morrison strata below the clay change (Sohn and Peck, 1963). More recent studies by Schudack and others (1998) support this conclusion and indicate that this species occurs in their charophyte/ostracode Zones 1-3 below the clay change. The stratigraphically highest known occurrence of this species in the Black Hills is in the northeastern part of that region where it was estimated to be about 45 ft (13.7 m) below the top of the Morrison (Sohn and Peck, 1963, p. A8, Locality 11) in the lower part of the first "limy" unit. Based on correlation to a nearby measured section of the Morrison about 3 mi (5 km) southeast of the fossil locality (Foster, 1996a, Figure 4, Sturgis Area section), the lowest limestone unit is about 60 ft (18.3 m) below the top of the formation. When projected into our Wonderland local reference section (figure 11), that position is about 3 ft (1 m) above the projected position indicated for dinosaur locality WY-11 and, therefore, within uppermost strata of the Unkpapa Sandstone Member. [It should be noted that the thickness of the Wonderland section reported by Foster (1996a, Figure 4) is in error (J.R. Foster, oral communication, 1997)]. We measured the Morrison Formation at the same locality (figure 5) and obtained 176 ft (53.6 m) for the entire Morrison, including the Unkpapa Sandstone and Windy Hill Members.

The foregoing suggests that the horizon equivalent to the clay change elsewhere is above the top of the Unkpapa Sandstone Member in the Black Hills area, but how much higher is uncertain. We collected two samples for calcareous microfossils 1 ft (0.3 m) and 11 ft (3.4 m) above the top of the Unkpapa at the Wonderland section. These samples yielded an excellent suite of nine charophyte and ostracode species (Schudack, 1994) that indicate charophyte/ostracode Zone 3 or the lower part of Zone 4 (see figure 7). Neither sample contained *Theriosynoecum wyomingense*, which suggests that the samples most likely indicate the lower part of charophyte/ostracode Zone 4, the base of which is at the clay change elsewhere in the Western Interior (Schudack and others, 1998). This interpretation also suggests that the top of the calcareous strata there is within and not at the base of the upper Morrison. As discussed in a later section, the biostratigraphy of the dinosaur fauna of the Black Hills, when compared with the biostratigraphy of the dinosaur fauna elsewhere in the Western Interior, also tends to support these correlations. If correct, our analysis suggests that the top of the Morrison is not excessively beveled on the east side of the Black Hills.

Szigeti and Fox (1981, p. 344) reported *Theriosynoecum wyomingense* from the level of the Wonderland Quarry (SD-4), which is higher stratigraphically than reported by Schudack and others (in press). If correctly identified, this would suggest that the stratigraphic horizon equivalent to the clay change is higher in the Black Hills area and perhaps at the level of the highest calcareous beds. This may also suggest that there was some significant amount of eastward regional beveling at the top of the Morrison in the Black Hills region. This contrast with the tentative conclusions of our research cannot be resolved without further study.

Our tentative analysis of Morrison stratigraphy on the west side of the Black Hills suggests that the uppermost part of the formation was rather deeply eroded prior to deposition of Lower Cretaceous strata. The Windy Hill Member is present at the base of the Morrison there,

which indicates that thinning of the Morrison cannot be attributed to onlap against a significant paleotopographic high. The top of the calcareous mudstone strata appears to correlate with the top of the calcareous mudstone beds farther east at the Wonderland section (figure 5), which suggests that this horizon is above the base of upper Morrison strata. We arbitrarily positioned the horizon of the clay change at the top of the thin sandstone bed near the upper-middle part of the Morrison at Little Houston Creek (figure 5) because sandstone is more commonly found below the clay change than just above it in other areas. If our tentative assignment is correct, based largely on correlation of the top of the calcareous strata, a significant amount of pre-Cretaceous erosion occurred at the top of the Morrison on the west side of the Black Hills, which would largely but not entirely account for the considerable thinning of the formation there. These correlations suggest that some degree of internal thinning also occurred within the Morrison in this area. Accordingly, we correlated all of the dinosaur localities on the west side of the Black Hills to the Little Houston Creek local reference section (figure 5) and suggest that the top of the formation was truncated more there than elsewhere. The dinosaur localities were then correlated to the Wonderland local reference section on the east side of the Black Hills (figure 11).

A somewhat similar problem exists in Montana, but that area lacks the charophyte and ostracode information that helps to determine the internal stratigraphy of the Morrison Formation. The localities we studied are near the middle of the depositional basin where regional beveling at the top of the formation is most likely minimal. We also found a thick zone of paleosols in the upper-middle part of the formation in the section near Bridger, Montana, which most likely correlates with the middle Morrison paleosol zone farther south. Another guide to the stratigraphy in Montana is that most of the thick fluvial sandstone beds in the middle of the formation tend to occur below the clay change in areas where the clay change is present. A final guide is that black, carbonaceous mudstone beds associated with the coal deposits in the Great Falls-Lewistown Coal Field appear to correlate reasonably well with black carbonaceous and(or) black noncarbonaceous mudstone beds that are locally present at or near the top of the Morrison elsewhere in Montana and Wyoming, and as far south as Morrison, Colorado. Although the dinosaur fauna in Montana has not yet been well analyzed or described, the biostratigraphy of those genera that have been identified also supports the conclusion that the formation is more or less complete there and is neither significantly older nor younger than elsewhere in the Western Interior.

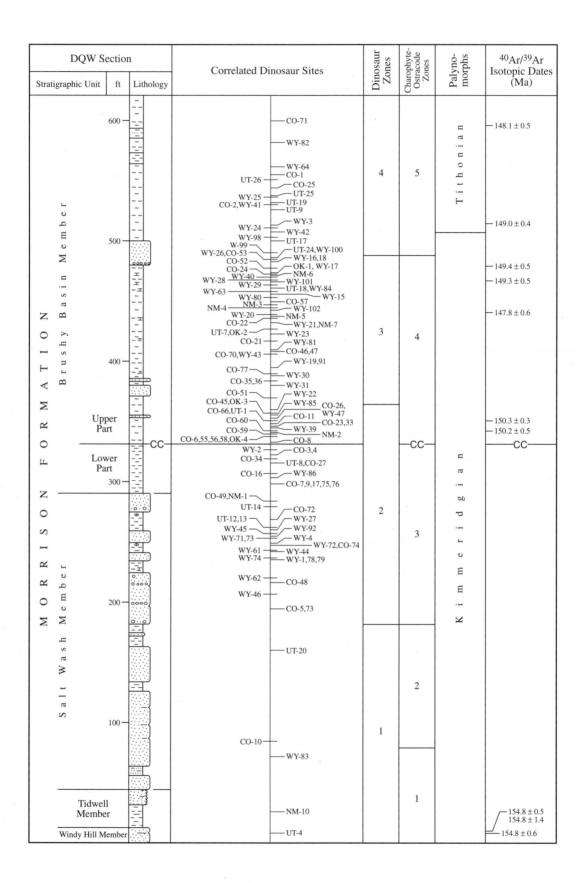

Figure 7. *Primary reference section (DQW) in western Dinosaur National Monument, Utah, showing dinosaur zonation of this report and other age-diagnostic criteria. Charophyte-ostracode zonation from Schudack and others (1998), Kimmeridgian-Tithonian boundary from Litwin and others (1998), isotopic dates from Kowallis and others (1998).*

Several illustrations in this report show the stratigraphic positions of the dinosaur localities as correlated to the primary reference section DQW at Dinosaur National Monument (figures 7-9). We plotted the localities as the methodology dictated, but the close vertical spacing of the localities on some of those illustrations implies a greater accuracy in stratigraphic positioning than is merited by the methodology. Although it is difficult to evaluate the degree of error that is involved in the methodology, we estimate that the error should be less than about plus or minus 20 ft (6 m) in most cases. The error should be less for those localities near the clay change, but it could be more in Montana and the Black Hills where the clay change is not present.

Quite often, where numerous bones are present, they are within an interval as much as 3 to 6 ft (1-2 m) in stratigraphic thickness. For this study, we used the lowest level of the bones or the quarry floor as the quarry level. In some cases, such as Cope's Quarries 2-8 at Cope's Nipple in Garden Park near Cañon City, Colorado (CO-2), we grouped all of the quarries into a single locality because the quarries are at the same stratigraphic level adjacent to each other. In other cases, such as the Bone Cabin Quarries in Wyoming where two quarries are present at the same stratigraphic level but separated laterally by a few hundred feet (about a hundred meters), we gave each quarry a separate designation, in this case WY-78 and WY-79, because they were excavated at significantly different times by entirely different parties.

One source of error that could not be compensated for adequately, but may not be a serious concern, is the stratigraphic position of the quarries in the lowermost parts of fluvial channel sandstone beds, such as the Dry Mesa and Carnegie Quarries. We positioned these and similar quarries where they occurred in the overall stratigraphy of the formation, but to be more accurate, one would have to position them with respect to a slightly higher stratigraphic level because the fluvial channels had scoured down into preexisting strata, generally overbank floodplain beds. In many cases, the depth of scour is unknown, either because the upper half or more of the fluvial channel sandstone bed is missing or concealed, as at the Carnegie Quarry, or detailed correlation of the bone-bearing strata within the channel with overbank floodplain strata outside the channel cannot be determined precisely, as at the Dry Mesa Quarry. We estimate that in most of these situations, the resulting error in positioning the quarry floor could be as much as 10 ft (3 m) too low stratigraphically.

The Carnegie Quarry (UT-18) deserves special mention because it is well known to be within a fluvial sandstone bed and this aspect is not indicated on the master

reference section (figure 10), which was measured nearby but not directly at the quarry. The master reference section (DQW) was measured about 2,000 ft (610 m) west of the Carnegie Quarry in a small drainage locally known as "Douglass Draw." Although the quarry is in a fluvial channel sandstone bed, that bed is not the same fluvial channel sandstone bed that is present at "Douglass Draw" at the higher stratigraphic level shown on figure 10. We positioned the quarry with respect to its true stratigraphic position as correlated to the master reference section DQW in "Douglass Draw" despite the fact that there is no fluvial sandstone bed at the precise level of the quarry in the master reference section.

Some of the localities are on private land and, in most cases, access was freely given by the landowners. Unfortunately, we were denied access to the land that includes the two quarries on the Red Fork of the Powder River, which accounts for why those important localities were not included in this study.

The location of the famous Stego 99 Quarry in the Como Bluff region of Wyoming has been lost, according to R.T. Bakker (oral communication, 1993). Several more recently opened quarries are in the vicinity and one of these could be the site of the old quarry.

An alphabetical list of all the dinosaur species included in this study is in appendix 2. A complete listing of the quarries and sites with their faunas and credits for the identifications are in appendix 3. Tables 1 and 2 contain a checklist of the dinosaur genera and species (including some higher taxonomic categories where necessary) found at the localities and arranged as closely as possible in their stratigraphic order.

The figure showing diversity of genera and species (figure 13) requires an explanation because both formally named species and informally named species (for example, *Allosaurus* sp.) were included in the count. If the range of a genus extended vertically across any particular locality, that locality was considered to represent a species even though the first occurrence of a formally named species was above that locality (for example, *Allosaurus* sp. below the lowest horizon of *A. fragilis* was considered as a species). In contrast, if a formally named species is present at any particular locality, no additional count was given for an identification only to genus level (for example, if a locality includes dinosaurs identified as *Allosaurus* sp. and *A. fragilis*, only the latter was counted).

In many cases, it is inappropriate to publish a scientific report without locations, but we follow procedures established by the vertebrate paleontology community by not publishing the detailed locations of the sites because of the possibility that bone hunters, rock hounds, or vandals would recover the locations and either remove any remaining material or destroy it. Also, many people freely contributed the site locations with the provision that those locations would not be published. Accordingly, no locations other than state and county are given in this report. Following accepted procedures, the locations have been given to responsible institutions or appropriate federal land-holding agencies so that responsible researchers can contact those institutions or agencies for this information.

STRATIGRAPHY

The Upper Jurassic Morrison Formation is recognized throughout most of the Western Interior of the United States (figure 1), extending from central New Mexico northward into Canada where correlative strata exist but are given different names. The formation consists predominantly of sandstone and mudstone, but it also includes a wide variety of other lithologies including conglomerate, claystone, tuff (including bentonite beds), limestone, dolomite, gypsum, anhydrite, and coal. The formation has been divided into members or other stratigraphic units in several areas. Thus far ten formally named members have been proposed on the Colorado Plateau (Brushy Basin, Bluff Sandstone, Fiftymile, Jackpile Sandstone, Junction Creek, Recapture, Salt Wash, Tidwell, Westwater Canyon, and Windy Hill Members). Along the east side of the Black Hills in South Dakota, Szigeti and Fox (1981) recognize the Unkpapa Sandstone Member at the base of the Morrison. Three other members were proposed for central Wyoming (from oldest to youngest these are the Lake Como, Talking Rocks, and Indian Fort Members of Allen, 1996) but, for the present, they must be considered informal units because type localities were never specified, type measured sections were not given, and because the publication medium has a highly restricted distribution.

Lower Contact

The lower contact of the sequence of beds that includes the Morrison Formation and related beds is the J-5 unconformity of Pipiringos and O'Sullivan (1978) or an equivalent conformable surface where evidence suggests that deposition was continuous. On the Colorado Plateau, slightly angular truncation of underlying strata has been documented at this contact in several places by Gilluly and Reeside (1928, p. 81), Pipiringos (1972), Pipiringos and O'Sullivan (1976, 1978), and Peterson (1988a). Broadly angular southward beveling of strata

beneath the J-5 unconformity along the east front of the Rocky Mountains in eastern Colorado and Wyoming was documented by Pipiringos and O'Sullivan (1976). Near Denver, the J-5 unconformity separates the Upper Jurassic Ralston Creek Formation, which correlates with basal Morrison strata elsewhere, from the underlying Triassic(?) and Permian Lykins Formation. We thus include the Ralston Creek Formation in the Morrison package of beds (Peterson and Turner, 1998).

Upper Contact

The upper contact has been enigmatic ever since the Morrison Formation was established by Cross in 1894. Under ideal circumstances, this contact is placed at the top of a thick paleosol zone (Demko and others, 1996). Because this zone was removed by erosion prior to deposition of overlying Lower Cretaceous beds at many localities, the position of the contact is based largely on a combination of other characteristics summarized by Peterson and Turner (1998).

In many places, especially northeastern New Mexico and eastern Colorado, the upper contact of the Morrison is between sandstone beds and is difficult to identify for those not familiar with the distinguishing characteristics of these lithologies. We follow Holbrook and others (1987) who showed that upper Morrison sandstone beds tend to be clay-rich, feldspathic sandstones, more properly called feldspathic wackes, whereas basal Cretaceous sandstone beds tend to be quartz rich with little feldspar or interstitial clay and may be classified as quartz arenites. The feldspar in Morrison sandstones tends to weather to clay, thereby filling the pore spaces in upper Morrison sandstone beds with clay, whereas basal Cretaceous sandstone beds tend to have considerably less interstitial clay and are more porous and permeable. Locally, as at Garden Park near Cañon City, Colorado, the basal Cretaceous sandstone bed contains appreciable quantities of interstitial clay. However, this clay is white (kaolinite?) and contrasts markedly with the light brown color of interstitial clay in the Morrison Formation.

In Montana and northern Wyoming, the upper contact is traditionally placed at the base of the lowest thick and laterally continuous sandstone bed above Morrison mudstone strata, especially if the bed is a "salt and pepper" type sandstone bed containing abundant black chert grains. However, our studies suggest that this is not a valid criterion. For example, carbonaceous mudstone is a common component of the coal zone at the top of the Morrison in the Great Falls-Lewistown Coal Field of west-central Montana. At the town of Belt, which is about 20 mi (30 km) east of Great Falls, we found carbonaceous mudstone interbedded with sandstone beds that contain abundant black chert grains and the sandstone beds are beneath a prominent (15.0 ft or 4.6 m thick) paleosol that we consider to mark the upper contact of the Morrison Formation. Similar findings elsewhere have lead us to conclude that fluvial sandstone beds, with or without appreciable quantities of black chert grains, may be present at or near the top of the Morrison in Wyoming and Montana, similar to the upper Morrison farther south on the Colorado Plateau, and in eastern Colorado, northeastern New Mexico, and western Oklahoma.

Other Stratigraphic Units

Throughout most of the southern part of the study area, the J-5 and K-1 surfaces define the lower and upper limits of the Morrison Formation. However, locally, some units historically assigned to other formations now are recognized as part of the interval between the J-5 and K-1 surfaces, and thus are Morrison equivalents.

Near the type locality of the Morrison Formation just west of Denver, Colorado, the type Ralston Creek Formation lies above the J–5 unconformity. Age determinations for the Ralston Creek Formation in the Denver area that are based on calcareous microfossils (charophytes and ostracodes; Scott, 1963, p. 92; M.E. Schudack, unpublished data, written communication, 1996) indicate that the type Ralston Creek Formation is Kimmeridgian (middle Late Jurassic) in age. This age designation, together with recognition of stratigraphic markers found in the Ralston Creek and the lower part of the Morrison Formation elsewhere, suggests that the Ralston Creek Formation correlates with the lower part of the Morrison Formation elsewhere (Peterson and Turner, 1998).

South of Denver in the vicinity of Cañon City, and in southeastern Colorado, the term Ralston Creek has been misapplied to include Middle Jurassic strata. Instead, we assign the Middle Jurassic strata to the Bell Ranch Formation and the Upper Jurassic strata, which contain recognizable stratigraphic markers, to the Morrison Formation (Peterson and Turner, 1998).

The lowest beds of the Burro Canyon Formation, formerly considered entirely Early Cretaceous in age, interfinger in some localities in southwestern Colorado and southeastern Utah with the uppermost beds of the Morrison Formation (Ekren and Houser, 1959, 1965) and lie below stratigraphic markers that indicate the top of the Morrison elsewhere (Aubrey, 1996). Accordingly, some beds, traditionally included in the lowermost Burro Canyon, are here included in the Morrison.

North of northern Utah and northern Colorado,

where lower Morrison beds include marine strata of the Windy Hill Member, it is unclear if an unconformity separates lower Morrison beds from underlying strata. In many places, the marine beds of the lower Morrison appear to be part of a conformable sequence of a shoaling upward package of marine strata.

Because marine beds of the Swift Formation in Montana and northernmost Wyoming are thought to be conformable or interfinger with basal Morrison strata (Imlay, 1980, p. 82; Richards, 1955, p. 41; Way and others, 1994) and have an unconformity at their base (Imlay, 1980), we include the Swift in the Morrison package of beds and use the unconformity at the base of the Swift as the basal surface of the Morrison package of beds.

AGE

The age of the Morrison Formation and related beds has been debated considerably in the literature but is now rather well understood. One of the objectives of the recent research on the Morrison Formation and related beds by us and our associates was to determine the age of the formation independently from what the dinosaurs might suggest. The results of those studies were recently published and are only briefly discussed below. In figure 7, we show a summary of the various age-determination studies by using the same methodology that was employed for positioning the dinosaur localities.

Palynological studies by Litwin and others (1998) indicate that the Morrison Formation and related beds are largely Kimmeridgian in age and that only the uppermost part is early Tithonian in age (figure 7). The Kimmeridgian-Tithonian boundary is within the upper part of the Brushy Basin Member of the Morrison as shown in figure 7.

The calcareous microfossils (charophytes and ostracodes) were studied by Schudack (1994, 1995) and Schudack and others (1998) who proposed five charophyte and ostracode zones shown in figure 7. The age determined by these organisms is similar to that obtained from the palynomorphs. The calcareous microfossils indicate that Zones 1-4 of Schudack and others (1998), which comprise the bulk of the formation, are Kimmeridgian in age. The Kimmeridgian-Tithonian boundary could not be identified clearly but the calcareous microfossils indicate that charophyte and ostracode Zone 5 at the top of the Morrison is definitely not Cretaceous in age and therefore could only be Kimmeridgian and (or) Tithonian in age. Charophyte and ostracode Zone 5 was tentatively considered Tithonian(?) in age based on fairly close correspondence of its lower boundary with the

Kimmeridgian-Tithonian boundary as determined by palynomorphs.

Isotopic age determinations on sanidine separates from bentonite beds were made by Kowallis and others (1998); these dates are shown in their correct stratigraphic position in figure 7. Dating was by the single-crystal laser-fusion ^{40}Ar/^{39}Ar methodology, although the ^{40}Ar/^{39}Ar plateau methodology was used for a few duplicate samples. The dates indicate that the Morrison package of beds spans a period of time of about 8 million years and ranges in age from about 155 to 148 Ma (figure 7). The Jurassic-Cretaceous boundary is about 141 Ma (Bralower and others, 1990) so these studies indicate that the top of the Morrison is about 7 million years older than the end of the Jurassic Period.

Paleomagnetic data, when evaluated in light of recent paleontologic and isotopic age determinations as well as the regional stratigraphic correlations, can be reinterpreted to be consistent with the paleontologic data. That is to say, we find some of the paleomagnetic data useful when reinterpreted, but we disagree with some of the paleomagnetic age conclusions drawn in the literature because the earlier workers did not have the benefit of the most recent paleontologic age assignments.

Several magnetostratigraphic sections through parts or most of the Morrison Formation on or near the Colorado Plateau are given by Steiner and others (1994), the most important of which are those measured at Norwood and Slick Rock, Colorado. They interpret the approximately lower third of the formation as Oxfordian in age in these sections whereas the age evidence from palynomorphs and calcareous microfossils cited above demonstrates that the lower third of the formation is Kimmeridgian in age.

The inferred paleomagnetic age for approximately the upper fourth of the formation at Slick Rock is Tithonian (Steiner and others, 1994), which is consistent with the palynological age determinations by Litwin and others (1998). The magnetic anomaly at the top of the Morrison in the Slick Rock magnetostratigraphic section correlates best with the M-22 magnetochron in the marine magnetic anomaly sequence. Because the Jurassic-Cretaceous boundary (that is, the end of the Tithonian Age) is at or very near the base of magnetochron M-18, the paleomagnetic studies suggest that about three latest Jurassic magnetochrons are missing at the Slick Rock section and therefore that the top of the Morrison there is significantly older than the end of the Jurassic Period. It should be noted that the clay change within the Morrison Formation is about 486 ft (148 m) above the base of the Salt Wash Member in their Norwood section and about 535 ft (163 m) above the base of the Salt Wash in their

Slick Rock section. Assuming, as we do, that the clay change marks an isochronous or nearly isochronous surface, the magnetostratigraphic correlations between the Norwood and Slick Rock sections as proposed by Steiner and others (1994) are not tenable. We suggest that the uppermost Morrison at the Norwood section is anomalously thin and has only Kimmeridgian strata remaining. This may be the result of any of several causes or combination of causes: the upper part of the Brushy Basin Member may have been more deeply eroded during development of the K-1 unconformity, the top of the Morrison may not have been sampled or included when the section was measured for paleomagnetic studies, or the upper Morrison there may be more compressed than is apparent.

Another paleomagnetic study of the Morrison Formation was undertaken in north-central Wyoming by Swierc and Johnson (1996) in which they concluded that the Morrison Formation there is entirely Tithonian in age. It appears that they were influenced by a fission-track date of 149 Ma near the base of the Morrison in one of their measured sections and this date is within the Tithonian Age according to the time scale of Harland and others (1990). Based on problems with fission-track dates in the Morrison Formation (B.J. Kowallis, oral communication, 1997) and the greater reliability of the ^{40}Ar/^{39}Ar dates (Kowallis and others, 1998), we discount the fission-track dates and rely, instead, on the ^{40}Ar/^{39}Ar dates elsewhere in the Morrison Formation, which are more consistent with the paleontological age designations. Furthermore, the clay change can be identified in most of Wyoming and permits correlation with the better dated Morrison on the Colorado Plateau. The clay change occurs in essentially the same measured section northeast of Greybull, Wyoming, (the Greybull NE section in figure 6) as one of the sections studied by Swierc and Johnson (1996, their South Sheep Mountain section SS). The clay change there is 95 ft (29.0 m) above the base of the Morrison and the entire Morrison is 175 ft (53.3 m) thick. The microfossil studies by Litwin and others (1998) and Schudack and others (1998) indicate that the clay change is about middle Kimmeridgian in age (figure 7), which conflicts considerably with the inferred Tithonian age for the entire Morrison that was suggested by Swierc and Johnson (1996) for strata in north-central Wyoming. Reevaluating the paleomagnetic studies in north-central Wyoming in light of the age and position of the clay change on the Colorado Plateau leads us to conclude that magnetochron M-22 is at the top of the formation in north-central Wyoming and that the Morrison in Wyoming includes both Kimmeridgian and lower Tithonian strata.

DEPOSITIONAL ENVIRONMENTS

The Morrison Formation was deposited in a wide variety of depositional environments. It is commonly thought of as an entirely nonmarine formation, but the presence of marine organisms and glauconite in Morrison strata suggests otherwise. Marine dinoflagellates were recovered from the Tidwell Member near the Carnegie Quarry in western Dinosaur National Monument, Utah (R.J. Litwin, oral communication, 1994). Glauconite occurs in sandstone beds in about the middle of the formation in northern Montana (Knechtel, 1959). The Windy Hill Member (Pipiringos, 1968; Peterson, 1994) locally contains glauconite, oolites, and brackish-water to marine bivalves that indicate deposition in shallow marine waters (this is member A of the Sundance Formation of Pipiringos, 1957). Most of the formation is interpreted to have been deposited in a variety of continental environments including eolian dune fields, sabkhas, fluvial channels, overbank floodplains, alluvial plains, saline-alkaline and freshwater lakes or ponds, evaporite basins, and coal swamps (Turner and Fishman, 1991; Turner-Peterson, 1986; Peterson, 1994). Summaries of the geology and paleogeography during deposition of the Morrison Formation and related beds were published recently by Turner and Fishman (1991), Peterson (1994) and Brenner and Peterson (1994). A good impression of the stratigraphy of the Morrison Formation and related beds throughout the region can be obtained from the various stratigraphic sections in this report (figures 2-6).

BIOSTRATIGRAPHY OF THE DINOSAURS

Localities Where the Clay Change is Present

The clay change within the Morrison Formation is recognizable in most of the Western Interior and thus in most of the areas that contain dinosaur quarries. The area in which the clay change is readily identified includes New Mexico, Colorado, Utah, and Wyoming excluding the northeast corner of that state around the Black Hills. Recognition of the clay change facilitates considerably the relative positioning of the dinosaur localities in these areas.

Although dinosaur bones have been recovered from nearly all stratigraphic levels in the Morrison Formation, the majority of the localities are in about the middle or upper middle half of the formation (figure 8). Ten quarries indicated on figure 10 dominate Morrison biostratigraphy and are the quarries that contain, or at least appear to have the potential to contain, about a thousand or

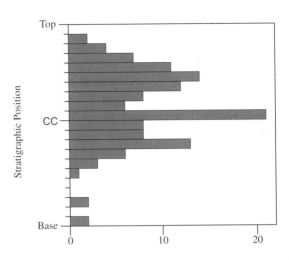

Figure 8. *Number of correlated dinosaur localities in each 30 ft (9.1 m) increment of stratigraphic thickness at the primary reference section (DQW) in western Dinosaur National Monument, Utah. Localities in the Black Hills and Montana not included. CC = clay change.*

more bones, judging from an estimate by us or by our colleagues. For the most part, these are well-known and famous quarries that include, from lowest to highest stratigraphic position, Reed's Quarry 13 at Como Bluff (WY-46), Howe Quarry (WY-62), Bone Cabin Quarry (WY-78,79), Marsh-Felch Quarry (CO-3), Dry Mesa Quarry (CO-58), Mygatt-Moore Quarry (CO-21), Cleveland-Lloyd Quarry (UT-7), Carnegie Quarry (UT-18), Stovall's Pit 1 (OK-1), and Cope's Quarries at the Nipple in Garden Park (CO-2). Additional work may demonstrate that two additional localities, the Poison Creek Quarries (WY-71, 73) and Mother's Day Quarry (MT-1), have the potential to also be included in this category. Although these ten quarries dominate Morrison biostratigraphy, there are approximately 131 other localities in the formation that have yielded bones identifiable to genus or species level. According to the numbers of dinosaur taxa recovered from each of the localities, about two-thirds of the localities contain only one or two taxa and nearly half contain only a single taxon (figure 9).

We divided the taxonomic units into several broad groupings to facilitate discussion: 1, Long-ranging taxa (mostly genera and species but also including the ankylosaurs), and 2, Single-locality species occurrences. Long-ranging taxa are those that range stratigraphically through two or more different stratigraphic levels in the master reference section (figure 7). Single-locality species are those that have only been reported from one locality and, hence, are rare and extremely restricted stratigraphically and geographically. The ankylosaurs (undivided) are also included in the long-ranging category because they are a fairly recent addition to the Morrison fauna and some have not yet been described to the genus or species level.

The stratigraphic distribution of the dinosaurs is divided most logically into four faunal zones (figure 10).

Zone 1

Zone 1 is poorly defined and marked by the beginning of the three long-ranging genera *Allosaurus*, *Stegosaurus*, and *Haplocanthosaurus*. It also includes the rare occurrence of *Dystrophaeus viaemalae* and the new allosaurid from Dinosaur National Monument (UT-20) that is currently under study by D.J. Chure (oral communication, 1997).

Zone 2

Zone 2 is marked by the abrupt beginning of many new long-ranging taxa and by the end of the ranges of several taxa toward the top of the zone. New taxa at the genus or higher level include: *Torvosaurus, Coelurus, Diplodocus, Camptosaurus, Camarasaurus, Apatosaurus, Barosaurus, Brachiosaurus,* the ankylosaurs, *Dryosaurus, Elaphrosaurus, Othnielia, Ceratosaurus, Supersaurus, Marshosaurus,* and *Edmarka* (figure 10). In addition, Zone 2 includes the lowest occurrences of 17 new long-ranging species and 14 single-site taxa shown in figure 10. The highest known occurrences of several taxa in Dinosaur Zone 2 include those of *Brachiosaurus, Elaphrosaurus, Supersaurus, Edmarka,* and *Edmarka rex*. Thus, Zone 2 marks the addition of many new taxa to the Morrison dinosaur fauna and, toward the top, the beginning of a decline in the taxa.

Zone 3

Zone 3 contains several new additions to the dinosaur fauna but, more importantly, it includes the end ranges of many taxa. The new long-ranging higher taxa are *Mymoorapelta* and *Drinker* and the new species are *Apatosaurus ajax, Mymoorapelta maysi, Marshosaurus bicentesimus,* and *Drinker nisti*. The highest levels of the following long-ranging taxa are in the upper part of this zone: *Haplocanthosaurus, Torvosaurus, Coelurus, Barosaurus,* the ankylosaurs, *Othnielia, Ceratosaurus, Marshosaurus,* and *Mymoorapelta*. In addition, 17 species die out before the end of the zone and there are five single-site taxa within it (figure 10).

Zone 4

Zone 4 marks the end of the stratigraphic ranges of the remaining dinosaur genera and species in the Morrison. *Amphicoelias* is the only new long-ranging genus to appear in this zone. The genera whose ranges end in Zone 4 include *Allosaurus, Stegosaurus, Diplodocus, Camptosaurus, Camarasaurus, Apatosaurus, Dryosaurus, Drinker,* and *Amphicoelias*. Five single-site species are also present.

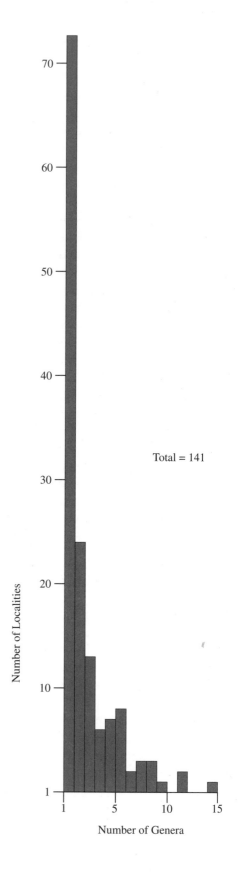

Figure 9. *Number of different dinosaur genera at each of the localities studied. Includes the broader category of ankylosaurs if no ankylosaur genus was identified. Fifty-one percent have only one genus identified, 67 percent have only one or two genera identified.*

The Black Hills and Montana

Dinosaur material recovered from Montana and the Black Hills region of northeastern Wyoming and western South Dakota occurs where a lack of smectitic clays in the upper Morrison does not permit accurate positioning with respect to the clay change. We attempted to determine a stratigraphic position that might correlate with the clay change elsewhere (figures 5, 6), but the result must be considered tentative.

The biostratigraphic distribution of the dinosaurs in areas where the clay change is present (figure 10, Table 1) offers clues to the dinosaur zonation in areas such as the Black Hills, where the clay change is not readily identified (figure 11). The ranges of the following genera in the Black Hills begin in Zone 2 in areas where the clay change is present: *Dryosaurus, Apatosaurus, Camarasaurus, Barosaurus*, and *Diplodocus*. Furthermore, *Othnielia*, present in the Black Hills (figure 11), is questionably identified low in Zone 2, although the first appearance where it is clearly identified is high in Zone 2. The highest occurrences of *Othnielia* and *Barosaurus* extend no higher than near the top of Zone 3 in areas that contain the clay change, and thus the top of Zone 3 in the Black Hills should be above the highest occurrence of these genera. *Barosaurus* extends highest in the Wyoming part of the Black Hills (locality WY-9) where it has been identified as cf. *Barosaurus*. Assuming the generic identification is satisfactory, Zone 3 in the Black Hills should extend upward to at least the position of that locality, which is why we tentatively place the upper boundary of Zone 3 as indicated on figure 11. Such a correlation accords with our earlier conclusion that the top of the Morrison in the eastern part of the Black Hills has not been eroded more deeply than most of the other localities in the Western Interior. Hence, the positioning of the eastern Black Hills dinosaur localities with respect to the projected horizon of the clay change as well as to the upper or lower boundaries of the Morrison seems reasonable.

The zonal stratigraphy of the dinosaurs in Montana is more difficult to determine for several reasons: the clay change is absent, many of the dinosaur remains that have been recovered have not yet been identified, and there is a scarcity of age-diagnostic microfossils in much of the formation. All three of the dinosaur localities are in the lower half of the Morrison and below the stratigraphic level that we tentatively correlate with the clay change farther south (figure 12). The stratigraphically highest calcareous microfossil collection that we obtained came from at or very near the level of dinosaur locality MT-2 (figure 12). The most stratigraphically restricted charophyte species that this sample contained was *Aclistochara obovata*, which ranges from the upper half of dinosaur Zone 1 through dinosaur Zone 3 in the Morrison elsewhere in the Western Interior (Schudack and others, 1998). Most of the dinosaurs recovered from Montana are long ranging. However, the lowest dinosaur collection (MT-1) yielded one individual tentatively identified as either *Diplodocus* or *Barosaurus*, both of which range from dinosaur Zone 2 upward through Zone 3 (*Barosaurus*) or Zone 4 (*Diplodocus*). Taken together, the calcareous microfossils and dinosaurs could only coexist in dinosaur Zones 2 and 3, which are of Kimmeridgian age. The uppermost strata of the Morrison are Tithonian in age because the carbonaceous mudstone and coal unit at the top of the Cinnabar Mountain local reference section (figure 12) correlates with the Tithonian age palynomorph collections obtained from a similar carbonaceous mudstone and coal unit at the top of the Morrison about 37 miles (60 km) farther northeast at West Boulder Creek, Montana (Litwin and others, 1998). Putting all of this together, a tentative evaluation of the dinosaur zonation at Cinnabar Mountain is illustrated in figure 12.

DISCUSSION AND CONCLUSIONS

The role of the major quarries in the biostratigraphy of the dinosaurs in the Morrison and related beds is considerable. Because most of these quarries have yielded numerous bones and have been studied extensively, they account for the dramatic increase in the taxonomic diversity at or near the base of Zone 2. The major quarries also account for significant increases in the faunal diversity higher in Zone 2 (figures 10, 13). The taxonomic diversity reaches a maximum high in Zone 2 (figure 13). The diversity begins to decline gradually near the top of Zone 2 and rather abruptly declines near the top of Zone 3 and again in the middle of Zone 4. Because the major quarries above the point of maximum diversity high in Zone 2 (figure 13) contain a substantial number of taxa, these quarries tend to confirm that the decline in diversity is real and probably is not biased by the numerous sites containing only one or a few taxa.

An important question is whether or not the dramatic increase in taxonomic diversity at or near the base of Zone 2 reflects a sharp change in the composition of the dinosaur fauna or if the change is largely if not entirely a function of the lack of major quarries below that level. Quite likely the marked increase in diversity largely reflects the lack of major quarries in Zone 1, but this is not necessarily the entire explanation. It seems noteworthy that the boundary between dinosaur Zones 1 and 2

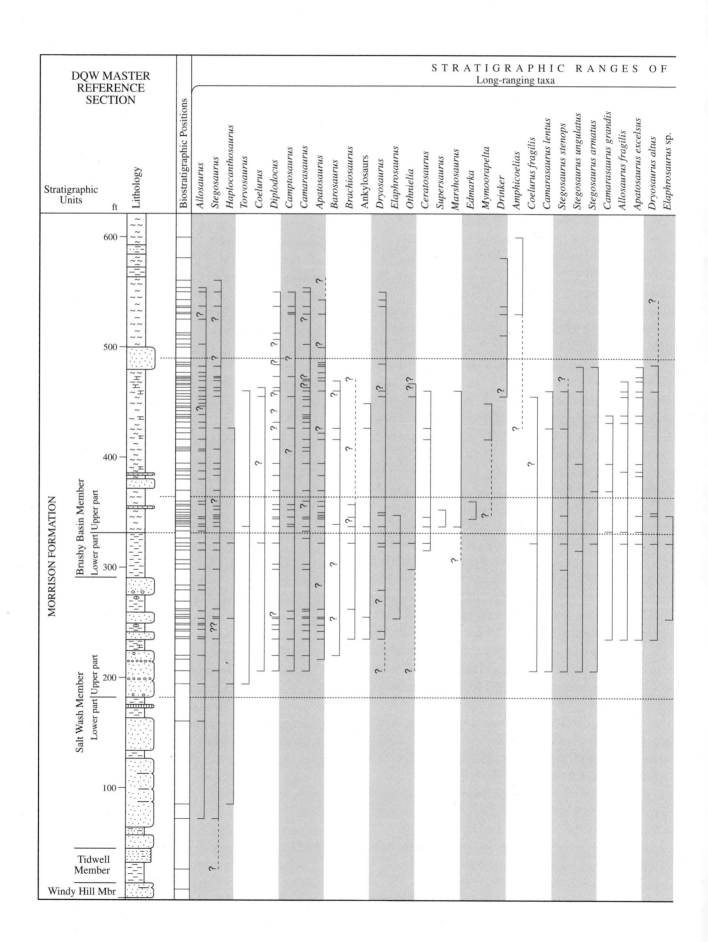

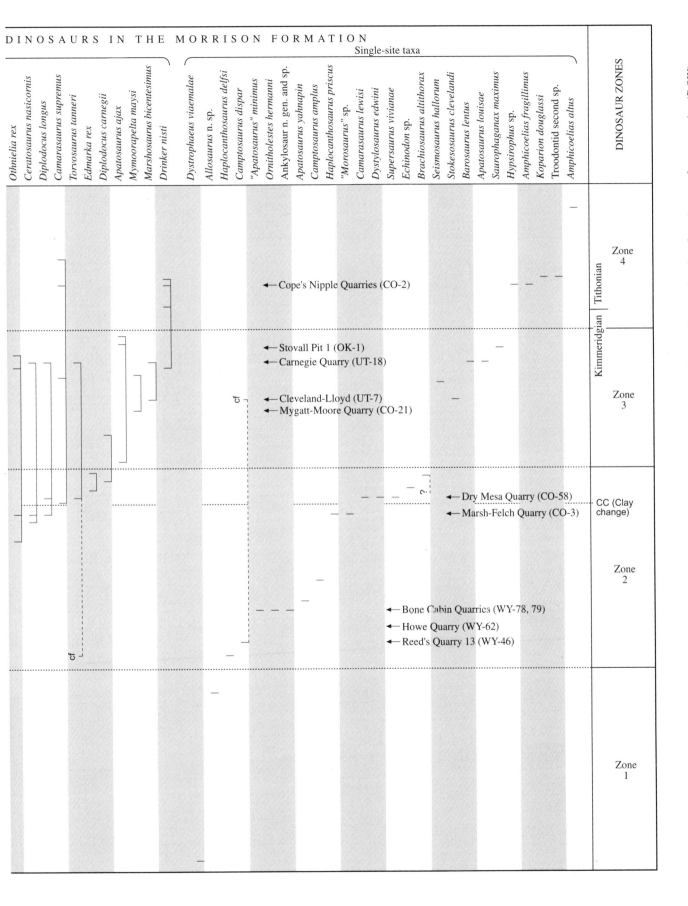

Figure 10. *Biostratigraphic ranges of dinosaurs in the Morrison Formation from localities that can be correlated to the primary reference section (DQW). The four dinosaur faunal zones are indicated on the right.*

TAXON / ID NO.	Allosaurus (1)	Stegosaurus (2)	Haplocanthosaurus (3)	Torvosaurus (4)	Coelurus (5)	Diplodocus (6)	Camptosaurus (7)	Camarasaurus (8)	Apatosaurus (9)	Barosaurus (10)	Brachiosaurus (11)	Ankylosaurus (12)	Dryosaurus (13)	Elaphrosaurus (14)	Othnielia (15)	Ceratosaurus (16)	Supersaurus (17)	Marshosaurus (18)	Edmarka (19)	Mymoorapelta (20)	Drinker (21)	Amphicoelias (22)	Coelurus fragilis (31)	Camarasaurus lentus (32)	Stegosaurus stenops (33)	Stegosaurus ungulatus (34)	Stegosaurus armatus (35)	Camarasaurus grandis (36)	Allosaurus fragilis (37)	Apatosaurus excelsus (38)	Dryosaurus altus (39)	Elaphrosaurus sp. (40)	Othnielia rex (41)	Ceratosaurus nasicornis (42)	Diplodocus longus (43)	Camarasaurus supremus (44)	Torvosaurus tanneri (45)	Edmarka rex (46)	Diplodocus carnegii (47)	Apatosaurus ajax (48)	Mymoorapelta maysi (49)	Marshosaurus bicentesimus (50)	Drinker nisti (51)
CO-71																						X																					
WY-82																					X																						
WY-64		X						?																																			
CO-1						X																													X								
UT-26	X	X				X	X	X					X																														
CO-25								X					X																							?							
UT-25	X	X				X	X	X					X																														
WY-25																					X																						X
UT-19							X																																				
CO-2, WY-41	?						X	X	X												X	X																	X				X
UT-9	X	?							?																																		
WY-3							X																																				
WY-24																					X																						X
WY-42								X																																			
WY-98	X						?		X	?																																	
UT-17													X																														
WY-99		?						?																																			
UT-24, WY-100							?		X																																		
WY-26, CO-53						X			X				X																						X					X			
WY-16, 18	X	X							X																	X					X											
CO-52	X								X																															X			
OK-1, WY-17	X	X				X	X		?	Xc?																					X												
CO-24	X	X									?					?										?																	
NM-6						X																																					
WY-40	X	X				X	X	X																					X														
WY-28															X																			X								
WY-101						?																																					
WY-29	X	X			X	X		X					?	?														X														
UT-18, WY-84	XX	X		X		XX	X	XX	X		X		X							?			X		X	X			X		X			X	X		X				X	
WY-63							?			?																																	
WY-15	X	X			X		X	X					X			X				X			X						X					X							X	
WY-80	X							X																																			
CO-57	X												X						X																					X		
NM-3	X							X																											X							
NM-4	cf																																										
WY-102							?																																				
WY-20	X							X																								X	X									
NM-5								X																																			
CO-22								X																																			
WY-21, NM-7	X					XX		X																								X	X									
UT-7, OK-2	XX	X?	X			?		X?	XX	?	X		X							?											X									X		
WY-23													X																														
CO-21	X					X		X	X	X			X			X			X																					X		
WY-81								X																																			
CO-46, 47	X	X									?																																
CO-70, WY-43	X																																										
WY-19, 91	X	XX			?	XX		XX	X														?		X		X		X								X					
CO-77		X																																									
WY-30	X																														X											
CO-35, 36		X				X		X																							X											
WY-31	X																																										
CO-51		X				X		X	X																	X													X			
WY-22	X	?						X										X															X						X			
CO-45, OK-3	X					X	X	?	X		X																																
WY-85		X																																									
CO-26, WY-47	X					X	X										X																				X						
CO-66, UT-1								X					X																		X												
CO-11		X						X					?	X	X					?					X							X	X									
CO-23, 33	X	X				X	X	X			X					X																											
WY-39	X	X				X		X	X									X																					X			
CO-60									?																																		
NM-2		X																																									
CO-59	X					X					X																																
CO-6, 55, 56, 58, OK-4	X	XX		X	?	XX	X?	3X	XX		X	X	X	X		X	X	X																					X	X			
CO-8 Clay	X								X																X		X								X	X						
WY-2 Change									X																																		
CO-3, 4	XX	X	X		X			X					X	X	X								X		X		X		X					X		X	X	X	X				
CO-34													X																														
UT-8, CO-27	X	X														X										X											X						
CO-16																	?																										
WY-86						X		X		?																																	
CO-7, 9, 17, 75, 76	XX	3X				X		XX							X										Xc												X					
CO-49, NM-1	XX							X																																			
UT-14	X												X																														
CO-72													?																														
UT-12, 13		X					X	X	X																																		
WY-27	X						X	X																																			
WY-45							?																																				
WY-92		X				X		X			X																																
WY-71, 73	X	X	X			X	X	XX	?				X																														
WY-4	X																																										
WY-72, CO-74	X	?				XX		X	X																																		
WY-61	X	?				X																																					
WY-44								X					X																														
WY-74	X																																										
WY-1, 78, 79	XX	XX				XX	XX	XX	XX		X	X	XXc												XX				X		XX	X	X									
WY-62	X					X	X	X		X																																	
CO-48									X																																		
WY-46		X		X	X	X	X						?			?							X		X				X		X											
CO-5, 73	X		X	X																																						cf
UT-20	X																																										
CO-10			X																																								
WY-83	X	X																																									
NM-10		?																																									
UT-4																																											

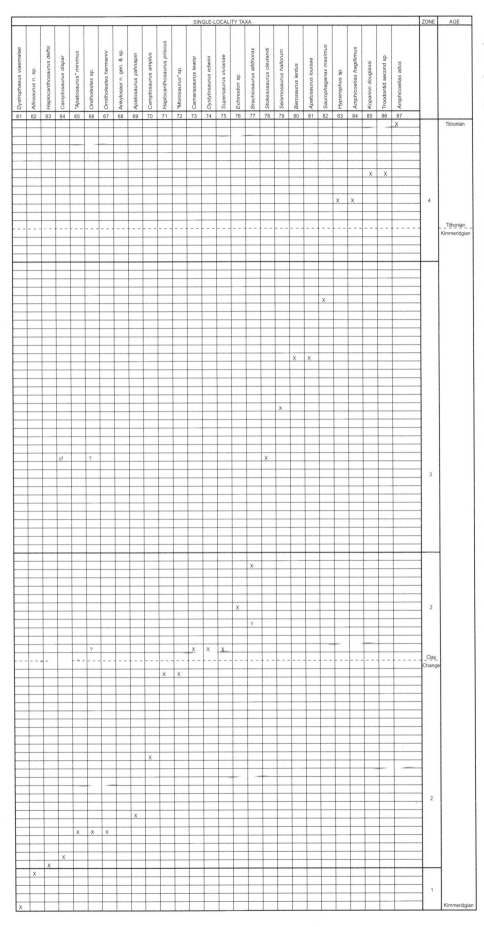

Table 1. *Biostratigraphy of dinosaur taxa at various localities in the Morrison Formation of the Western Interior excluding the Black Hills and Montana. XX or 3X indicate the number of localities that have the indicated taxon at a stratigraphic level that includes two or three localities, respectively; c represents cf where space is crowded.*

Table 2. *Biostratigraphy of dinosaur taxa at various localities in the Morrison Formation in the Black Hills and Montana. The clay change is not present in these areas but its tentatively correlated position is indicated.*

TAXON	Allosaurus	Stegosaurus	Diplodocus	Camarasaurus	Apatosaurus	Barosaurus	Dryosaurus	Othnielia	Diplodocus or Barosaurus	Barosaurus lentus	MONTANA	Allosaurus	Stegosaurus	Diplodocus or Barosaurus
TAXON IDENTITY NO.	1	2	5	7	8	9	13	14	22	84		1	2	22
SD-2	X			X	X									
SD-1 (Tithonian?)					X						(Tithonian?)			
SD-3 (Kimmeridgian?)	X					X				X	(Kimmeridgian?)			
WY-9						cf								
SD-5		X												
SD-4	X				X	X				X				
WY-8 (Clay)	?										(Clay)			
WY-10 (Change?)								X			(Change?)			
WY-11	X	X		X	X		X	X	X					
											MT-2	X		
WY-12						?								
											MT-6	?		
											MT-1	X	?	X

coincides with the change in the calcareous microfossil assemblages at the boundary between charophyte and ostracode Zones 2 and 3 of Schudack and others (1998). Also noteworthy is a lithostratigraphic change in the Salt Wash Member at the boundary between dinosaur Zones 1 and 2. This is marked by the change from fluvial sandstone beds that lack pebbles or contain very few pebbles to overlying fluvial strata that contain pebbly or conglomeratic sandstone beds or conglomerate. This occurs in the Salt Wash throughout a large part of the Colorado Plateau and is present at measured section DQW at Dinosaur National Monument (Figure 10). The lithologic change apparently correlates with the boundary between the middle and upper sequences of the Salt Wash Member farther south on the west side of the Colorado Plateau (Peterson, 1980, 1984). The lithologic change also coincides with the boundary between the upper sandstone-dominated interval and the middle mudstone-dominated interval of the Salt Wash on the east side of the Colorado Plateau (Peterson and Turner-Peterson, 1987). The coincidence of vertical sedimentologic changes with other biostratigraphic changes, such as with the charophytes and ostracodes, suggests that a marked evolutionary change may have occurred at this horizon. These evolutionary changes may have been in response to changes in habitat, depositional environment, climate,

or a combination of these factors. The lithologic change at this horizon is thus far only recognized in the Salt Wash Member, which is restricted to the Colorado Plateau. An analogous lithologic change elsewhere in the Western Interior has not yet been recognized.

The biostratigraphic distribution of the dinosaurs shows a vertical trend of increasing faunal diversity followed by decreasing diversity during deposition of the Morrison Formation. It is noteworthy that dinosaurs were scarce during earliest Morrison deposition—the earliest fauna consists of only a few taxa (Zone 1, Tidwell and lower Salt Wash Members). Diversity increased dramatically near the middle of the Salt Wash Member (low in Zone 2) and continued to increase, reaching a peak in diversity just above the clay change (high in Zone 2, near the base of the upper part of the Brushy Basin Member) where the first of the long-ranging taxa began to die out. Diversity continued to decrease gradually to about the middle of the upper part of the Brushy Basin Member where a fairly sharp decline occurred (high in Zone 3). Another fairly sharp decline in diversity occurred higher in the same member (middle of Zone 4), followed by a gradual decline, with the few remaining taxa dying out toward the end of Morrison deposition.

The changes in diversity low in Zone 2, high in Zone

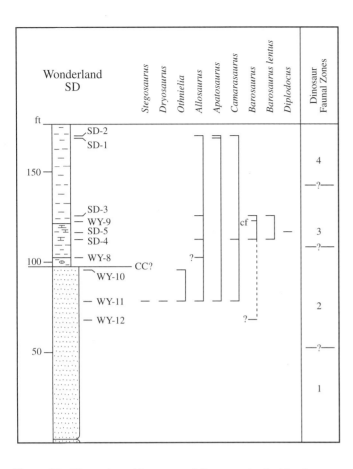

Figure 11. *Biostratigraphic ranges of dinosaurs in the Morrison Formation of the Black Hills of South Dakota and Wyoming. The correlated position of the clay change (CC?) is conjectural.*

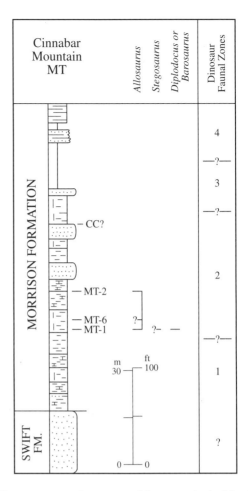

Figure 12. *Biostratigraphic ranges of dinosaurs in the Morrison Formation of southern Montana. The correlated position of the clay change (CC?) is conjectural.*

3, and toward the middle of Zone 4 coincide fairly well with similar changes in the diversity of charophytes and ostracodes. This suggests that any environmental changes that occurred at these stratigraphic positions were ubiquitous and of sufficient character to exert a strong influence on markedly different types of organisms.

The scarcity of dinosaurs at the beginning of Morrison deposition may reflect a continuation of the harsh conditions that persisted during Middle Jurassic time. Dinosaurs were scarce just before Morrison deposition, or at least only sparse footprint evidence exists in Middle Jurassic rocks. It is likely that the arid climate that persisted during deposition of the eolian ergs and evaporites of the Middle Jurassic was inimical to the dinosaurs. Conditions during earliest Morrison deposition may have remained inhospitable to the dinosaurs, judging from the presence of eolian and evaporite deposits in the lowermost part of the Morrison. The development of the extensive river systems of the Salt Wash Member may have established a more equable habitat, enticing dinosaurs into the area. They seem to have flourished and reached their heyday at about the middle of the

Morrison. The change from greater to lesser diversity occurs just above the clay change and thus coincides with the tremendous increase in the output of volcanic ash in the source area. What role the increase in volcanic ash may have played in dinosaur diversity, either direct or indirect, is uncertain.

Taken together with the biostratigraphic data from some of the other organisms in the Morrison ecosystem (for example, the charophytes and ostracodes), the newly established biostratigraphic synthesis forms the basis for evaluating widespread paleoecological changes in the Western Interior during the Late Jurassic. Moreover, this synthesis provides a biostratigraphic foundation for the evaluation of taxonomic lineages and evolutionary trends among the dinosaurs in the Morrison Formation.

The data suggest that there was essentially no change in the dinosaur fauna at the Kimmeridgian-Tithonian boundary (figures 10, 13), but with so little Tithonian Age strata preserved in the Morrison, we cannot rule out the possibility that a change in the fauna would be apparent if more specimens were available from dinosaur Zone 4.

The foregoing conclusions, based largely upon the

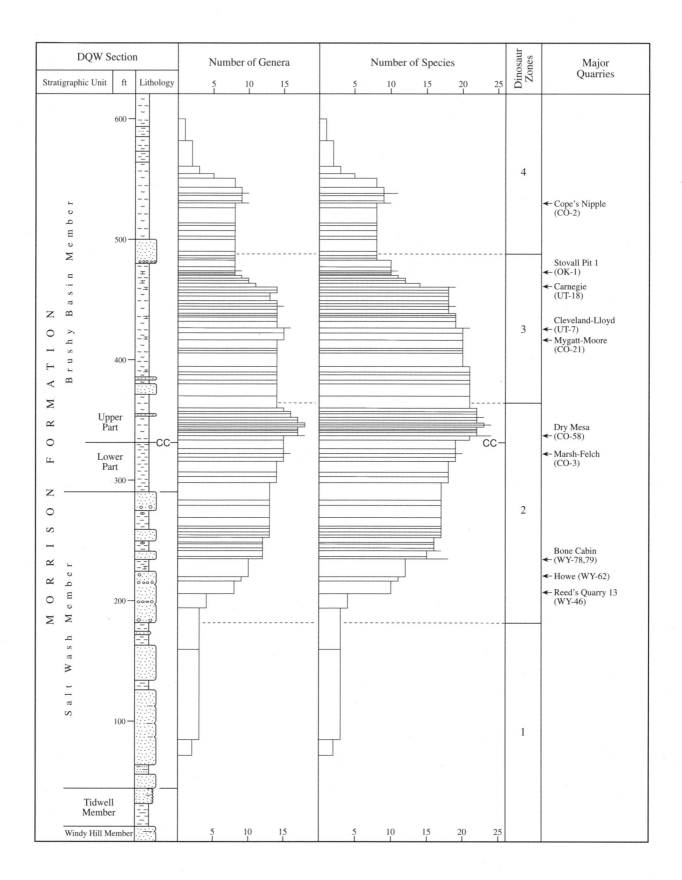

Figure 13. *Taxonomic diversity at the genus and species levels for dinosaurs in the Morrison Formation at localities correlated to the primary reference section (DQW).*

biostratigraphic distribution of the entire dinosaur fauna throughout an extensive region (figure 10), are biased considerably by the faunas thus far recovered from the ten major quarries. In view of the well-known biogeographic diversity of modern but pre-human faunas in a similarly large area, such as the Great Plains region of the United States, a single major quarry, no matter how large and diversified the recovered fauna, may contain a poor representation of the overall fauna that existed throughout the Western Interior during any specific time of Morrison deposition.

On the other hand, the fauna recovered from a major quarry could be fairly representative of the overall fauna if the factors that were responsible for the demise of the animals encouraged them to congregate in a few places just before their deaths. The most plausible scenario for this would be the concentration of animals, who ordinarily ranged over a broad area, around the last of the waterholes before those too dried up during a major drought. Extensive droughts are plausible in light of the overall semi-arid interpretation for much of the Morrison Formation. Evidence of overall dryness includes extensive evaporite deposits (gypsum-anhydrite) in the lowermost part of the Morrison and related beds in the Colorado Plateau and eastern Colorado (O'Sullivan, 1992; Peterson and Turner, 1998), large eolian dune fields in the lower Morrison in the central and southern parts of the Colorado Plateau and smaller dune fields as far north as north-central Wyoming and western South Dakota (Szigeti and Fox, 1981; Blakey and others, 1988; Peterson, 1988b, 1994), and extensive saline-alkaline or playa lake deposits in the upper Morrison (Brushy Basin Member) on the east side of the Colorado Plateau (Turner and Fishman, 1991).

With additional study by paleontologists, it may become clear that some faunal trends in this report indicate evolutionary progressions, and other taxonomic relationships may come to light. For example, the biostratigraphic ranges of *Stegosaurus stenops* , *S. ungulatus*, and *S. armatus* are so similar as to suggest an unusually close relationship between the three species. Apparently sexual dimorphism does not appear to be a reasonable explanation for some of this (P.M. Galton, oral communication, 1997). Also, more work might establish that *Hypsirophus* is an evolutionary descendant of one of the stegosaurs. Our study also shows an upward progression in the first occurrences of species in some of the genera, a progression that might reflect evolutionary lineages, which can only be clarified by further and more detailed examination by specialists. These include the vertical progression of first occurrences of the camarasaurs, including *Camarasaurus lentus*, *C. grandis*, *C. supremus*,

and *C. lewisi* (figure 10). Similarly, in the genus *Diplodocus*, the vertical progression is *D. longus*, and *D. carnegii* (the relative position of *D. hayi* is unknown because we were unable to obtain permission to enter the property containing the quarry that yielded that species). In the allosaurs, the vertical progression is *Allosaurus* n. sp. (from Dinosaur National Monument) followed by *A. fragilis*. In the genus *Apatosaurus*, the vertical progression of first appearances is *A. excelsus*, *A. yahnapin*, *A. ajax*, and *A. louisae*. "*Apatosaurus*" *minimus* is considered "a valid species, but not belonging to *Apatosaurus*" (J.S. McIntosh, written communication, 1997).

The ten major quarries, either singly or grouped, are positioned at about six different stratigraphic levels, which is intriguingly periodic. The various stratigraphic positions with their included major quarries are shown on figure 10 and are, from oldest to youngest: 1, Reed's Quarry 13 (WY-46), Howe Quarry (WY-62), and Bone Cabin Quarries (WY-78, 79); 2, Marsh-Felch Quarry (CO-3); 3, Dry Mesa Quarry (UT-58), 4, Mygatt-Moore Quarry (CO-21) and Cleveland-Lloyd Quarry (UT-7); 5, Carnegie Quarry (UT-18), and Stovall Pit 1 (OK-1); and 6, Cope's Nipple Quarries (CO-2). The six stratigraphic positions marked by these groupings of the major quarries could mark periodic recurrences of prolonged or intermittent environmental stress. The periodicity may have been related to Milankovitch cycles (De Boer and Smith, 1994), but insufficient time resolution precludes drawing any conclusions along these lines. Clearly, further research on this aspect is necessary.

RECOMMENDATIONS

A valuable contribution to understanding Morrison dinosaur faunas would be for more paleontologic research to be focused on Zone 1. Excavation of localities already known in that part of the formation and searching for more sites to enlarge the faunal base would be most helpful. The goal would be to enlarge the number of taxa to the extent that it would be sufficient to adequately represent that part of the formation. In this regard, the East Canyon (UT-4) and Meilyn (WY-83) Quarries seem most promising. A similar need exists for new sites or additional work on existing sites high in Zone 4, but the need is not as great as with Zone 1.

Additional paleontologic work is also needed in Montana, so that sufficient information becomes available to provide the basis for interpreting biogeographic diversity or paleolatitudinal variations in the overall fauna.

ACKNOWLEDGMENTS

Numerous individuals generously contributed their knowledge of the quarry locations or furnished up-to-date faunal lists in the interest of helping us determine the biostratigraphic relationships of the dinosaur fauna in the Morrison Formation and related beds. Others freely contributed additional information that helped considerably, one way or another, in facilitating this endeavor. To these many individuals we express our thanks. They include: H.J. Armstrong, W.M. Aubrey, R.T. Bakker, B.L. Bartleson, M.K. Brett-Surman, B.B. Britt, George Callison, Kenneth Carpenter, D.J. Chure, R.L. Cifelli, M.V. Connely, J.T. Cooley, B.S. Currie, Kristi Curry, L.E. Davis, T.M. Demko, Ann Elder, D.J. Engard, G.F. Engelmann, B.R. Erickson, B.J. Filla, A.R. Fiorillo, J.R. Foster, D.D. Gillette, J.T. Gregory, Daniel Grenard, J.R. Horner, Vivian Jones, J.I. Kirkland, R.L. Kolb, B.J. Kowallis, P.E. Kvale, R.J. Litwin, David Lopez, S.G. Lucas, J.H. Madsen, Jr., S.K. Madsen, J.E. Masura, J.S. McIntosh, W.E. Miller, Pat Monaco, C.A. (Bjoraker) Naus, M.T, Naus, P.D. Redman, R.D. Scheetz, R.J. Schiller, M.E. Schudack, J.D. Siegwarth, Matthew Smith, E.H. Southwell, K.L. Stadtman, C.J. Weege, and T.E. Williamson. We also thank the many private landholders who kindly gave us permission to enter their land. The report was improved by thoughtful and constructive technical reviews by K. Carpenter, J.R. Foster, J.S. McIntosh, and D.J. Nichols. The figures were drafted by cartographer Jim Parker (UGS).

The research was done in 1990 through 1996 and supported under a cooperative agreement between the U.S. Geological Survey and the U.S. National Park Service under Contract Number CA-1463-5-0001 and Interagency Agreement Number 1443-IA-1200-94-003.

REFERENCES

Allen, Al, 1994, The dinosaur beds of the Morrison Formation (Jurassic), Alcova Lake, Wyoming: Tate Museum Publication, Casper College, Wyoming, 35 p. (includes Cross Sections 1 and 2 as separates).

—1996, Morrison Formation stratigraphy between the classic Como Bluff and Thermopolis areas, Wyoming, *in* Hunter, R.A., editor, Tate '96-- paleoenvironments of the Jurassic: Casper, Wyoming, Tate Geological Museum, Tate Museum Guidebook No. 1, p. 19-28.

Anderson, O.J., and Lucas, S.G., 1996, Stratigraphy and depositional environments of Middle and Upper Jurassic rocks, southeastern San Juan Basin, New Mexico, *in* Goff, F., Kues, B.S., Rogers, M.A., McFadden, L.D., and Gardner, J.N., editors, The Jemez Mountains Region: New Mexico Geological Society Guidebook, 47th Annual Field Conference, p. 205-210.

Armstrong, H.J., and McReynolds, E.S. 1987, Stratigraphic correlation of dinosaur quarries near Grand Junction, Colorado, *in* Averett, W.R., editor, Paleontology and geology of the Dinosaur Triangle: Grand Junction, Colorado, Grand Junction Geological Society Guidebook, p. 103-106.

Aubrey, W.M., 1996, Stratigraphic architecture and deformational history of Early Cretaceous foreland basin, eastern Utah and southwestern Colorado, *in* Huffman, A.C., Jr., Lund, W.R., and Godwin, L.H., editors, Utah Geological Association Guidebook 25, p. 211-220.

Bakker, R.T., Galton, Peter, Siegwarth, James, and Filla, James, 1990, A new latest Jurassic vertebrate fauna, from the highest levels of the Morrison Formation at Como Bluff, Wyoming, part IV-- the dinosaurs-- a new *Othnielia*-like hypsilophodontoid: Hunteria, v. 2, no. 6, p. 8-19.

Bakker, R.T., Siegwarth, James, Kralis, Donald, and Filla, James, 1992, *Edmarka rex*, a new, gigantic theropod dinosaur from the middle Morrison Formation, Late Jurassic of the Como Bluff outcrop region, with comments on the evolution of the chest region and shoulder in theropods and birds, and a discussion of the five cycles of origin and extinction among giant dinosaurian predators: Hunteria, v. 2, no. 9, 24 p.

Bartleson, B.L., and Jensen, J.A., 1988, The oldest (?) Morrison Formation dinosaur, Gunnison, Colorado: The Mountain Geologist, v. 25, no. 3, p. 129-139.

Bilbey, S.A., and Hamblin, A.H., 1992, An articulated partial skeleton of *Stegosaurus* from the Salt Wash Member of the Morrison Formation near Jensen, Utah: Geological Society of America, Abstracts with Programs, v. 24, no. 6, p. 4.

Bjoraker, C.A., and Naus, M.T., 1996, A summary of Morrison Formation (Jurassic: Kimmeridgian-Tithonian) geology and paleontology, with notice of a new dinosaur locality in the Bighorn Basin (USA), *in* Bowen, C.E., Kirkwood, S.C., and Miller, T.S., editors, Resources of the Bighorn Basin: Wyoming Geological Association, 47th Guidebook, p. 297-303.

Blakey, R.C., Peterson, Fred, and Kocurek, Gary, 1988, Synthesis of late Paleozoic and Mesozoic eolian deposits of the Western Interior of the United States: Sedimentary Geology, v. 56, p. 3-125.

Bollan, H.R., 1991, The Bollan *Stegosaurus*, *in* Averett, W.R., editor, Guidebook for dinosaur quarries and tracksites tour: Grand Junction, Colorado, Grand Junction Geological Society, p. 53-54.

Bralower, T.J., Ludwig, K.R., Obradovich, J.D., and Jones, D.L., 1990, Berriasian (Early Cretaceous) radiometric ages from the Grindstone Creek section, Sacramento Valley, California: Earth and Planetary Sciences Letters, v. 98, no. 1, p. 62-73.

Brenner, R.L., and Peterson, J.A., 1994, Jurassic sedimentary history of the northern portion of the Western Interior Seaway, USA, *in* Caputo, M.V., Peterson, J.A., and Franczyk, K.J., editors, Mesozoic systems of the Rocky Mountain Region: Rocky Mountain Section of the SEPM (Society for Sedimentary Geology), p. 217-232.

Britt, B.B., 1991, Theropods of Dry Mesa Quarry (Morrison Formation, Late Jurassic), Colorado, with emphasis on the osteology of *Torvosaurus tanneri*: Brigham Young University Geology Studies, v. 37, p. 1-72.

Callison, George, 1987, Fruita-- a place for wee fossils, *in* Averett,

W.R., editor, Paleontology and geology of the Dinosaur Triangle: Grand Junction, Colorado, Grand Junction Geological Society, Guidebook, p. 91-96.

Carpenter, Kenneth, 1998, Vertebrate biostratigraphy of the Morrison Formation near Cañon City, Colorado: Modern Geology v. 28, pt. 2, p. 407-426.

Chenoweth, W.L., 1953, The variegated member of the Morrison Formation in the southeastern part of the San Juan Basin, Valencia County, New Mexico: Albuquerque, University of New Mexico, M.S. thesis, 86 p.

—1987, The Riggs Hill and Dinosaur Hill sites, Mesa County, Colorado, *in* Averett, W.R., editor, Paleontology and geology of the Dinosaur Triangle: Grand Junction, Colorado, Grand Junction Geological Society, Guidebook, p. 97-100.

Chure, D.J., 1989. The fauna of the Morrison Formation in Dinosaur National Monument, *in* Flynn, J.J., and McKenna, M.C., leaders, Mesozoic/Cenozoic vertebrate paleontology-- classic localities, contemporary approaches: 28th International Geological Congress, Field Trip T-322, p. 8-14.

—1994, *Koparion douglassi*, a new dinosaur from the Morrison Formation (Upper Jurassic) of Dinosaur National Monument-- the oldest troodontid (Theropoda: Maniraptora): BrighamYoung University Geology Studies, v. 40, p. 11-15.

—1995, A reassessment of the gigantic theropod *Saurophagus maximus* from the Morrison Formation (Upper Jurassic) of Oklahoma, USA, *in* Sun, Ailing L., and Wang, Y, editors, Sixth symposium on Mesozoic terrestrial ecosystems and biota, short papers: Beijing, China Ocean Press, p. 103-106.

Chure, D.J., Turner, C.E., and Peterson, Fred, 1994, An embryo of *Camptosaurus* from the Morrison Formation (Jurassic, Middle Tithonian) in Dinosaur National Monument, Utah, *in* Carpenter, Kenneth, Hirsch, K.F., and Horner, J.R., editors, Dinosaur eggs and babies: New York, Cambridge University Press, p. 298-311.

Cooley, J.T., 1993, Fluvial systems of the Upper Jurassic Morrison Formation, northern Beartooth and Gallatin Ranges, southwest Montana: Bozeman, Montana State University, M.S. thesis, 55 p.

Cope, E.D., 1877, On a dinosaurian from the Trias of Utah: American Philosophical Society, Proceedings, v. 16, p. 579-584.

Craig, L.C., Holmes, C.N., Freeman, V.L., Mullens, T.E., and others, 1959, Measured sections of the Morrison and adjacent formations: U.S. Geological Survey Open-File Report.

Cross, Whitman, 1894, Pikes Peak Folio, Colorado: U.S. Geological Survey Folio 7, 5 p., 4 maps (1:125,000).

Curtice, B.D., and Wilhite, D.R., 1996, A re-evaluation of the Dry Mesa Dinosaur Quarry sauropod fauna with a description of juvenile sauropod elements, *in* Huffman, A.C., Jr., Lund, W.R., and Godwin, L.H., editors, Geology and resources of the Paradox Basin: Utah Geological Association Guidebook 25, p. 325-338.

Curtice, B.D., Stadtman, K.L., and Curtice, L.J., 1996, A reassessment of *Ultrasauros macintoshi* (Jensen, 1985), *in* Morales, Michael, The continental Jurassic: Museum of Northern Arizona Bulletin 60, p. 87-95.

De Boer, P.L., and Smith, D.G., 1994, Orbital forcing and cyclic sequences: International Association of Sedimentologists Special Publication 19, p. 1-14.

Demko, T.M., Currie, B.S., and Nicoll, K.A., 1996, Paleosols at sequence boundaries in the Upper Jurassic Morrison Formation, Colorado Plateau and Rocky Mountain regions, USA: Geological Society of America, Abstracts with Programs, v. 28, no. 7, p. A-185.

Dodson, Peter, Behrensmeyer, A.K., and Bakker, R.T., 1980, Taphonomy of the Morrison Formation (Kimmeridgian-Portlandian) and Cloverly Formation (Aptian-Albian) of the western United States: Mémoires de la Société Géologique de France (Nouvelle Série), Mémoire No. 139, Ecosystémes Continentaux du Mésozoïque, p. 87-93.

Ekren, E.B., and Houser, F.N., 1959, Relations of Lower Cretaceous and Upper Jurassic rocks in the Four Corners area, Colorado: American Association of Petroleum Geologists Bulletin, v. 43, no. 1, p. 190-201.

—1965, Geology and petrology of the Ute Mountains area, Colorado: U.S. Geological Survey Professional Paper 481, 74 p.

Filla, B.J., and Redman, P.D., 1994, *Apatosaurus yahnahpin* - a preliminary description of a new species of diplodocid dinosaur from the Late Jurassic Morrison Formation of southern Wyoming, the first sauropod dinosaur found with a complete set of "belly ribs," *in* Nelson, G.E., editor, The dinosaurs of Wyoming: Wyoming Geological Association Guidebook, 44th Annual Field Conference, p. 159-178.

Fiorillo, A.R., and May, C.L., 1996, Preliminary report on the taphonomy and depositional setting of a new dinosaur locality in the Morrison Formation (Brushy Basin Member) of Curecanti National Recreation Area, Colorado, *in* Morales, Michael, editor, The continental Jurassic: Museum of Northern Arizona Bulletin 60, p. 555-561.

Foster, J.R., 1992, Fossil vertebrates of the Morrison Formation (Upper Jurassic) of the Black Hills, South Dakota and Wyoming: Rapid City, South Dakota School of Mines and Technology, M.S. thesis, 178 p.

—1996a, Fossil vertebrate localities in the Morrison Formation (Upper Jurassic) of western South Dakota, *in* Morales, Michael, editor, The continental Jurassic: Museum of Northern Arizona Bulletin 60, p. 255-263.

---1996b, Sauropod dinosaurs of the Morrison Formation (Upper Jurassic), Black Hills, South Dakota and Wyoming: Contributions to Geology, University of Wyoming, v. 31, no. 1, p. 1-25.

Foster, J.R. and Martin, J.E., 1994, Late Jurassic dinosaur localities in the Morrison Formation of northeastern Wyoming, *in* Nelson, G.E., editor, The dinosaurs of Wyoming: Wyoming Geological Association Guidebook, 44th Annual Field Conference, p. 115-126.

Fraser, G.D., Waldrop, H.A., and Hyden, H.J., 1969, Geology of the Gardiner area, Park County, Montana: U.S. Geological Survey Bulletin 1277, 118 p.

Galton, P.M., 1990, Stegosauria, *in* Weishampel, D.B., Dodson, Peter, and Osmólska, Halszka, editors, 1990, The Dinosauria: Berkeley, University of California Press, p. 435-455.

Galton, P.M., and Jensen, J.A., 1973, Small bones of the hypsilophodontid dinosaur *Dryosaurus altus* from the Upper Jurassic of Colorado: The Great Basin Naturalist, v. 33, no. 2, p. 129-132.

Gillette, D.D., 1991, *Seismosaurus halli*, gen. et sp. nov., a new sauropod dinosaur from the Morrison Formation (Upper Jurassic/Lower Cretaceous) of New Mexico, USA: Journal of Vertebrate Paleontology, v. 11, no. 4, p. 417-433.

—1996a, Origin and early evolution of the sauropod dinosaurs of North America-- the type locality and stratigraphic position of *Dystrophaeus viaemalae* Cope 1877, *in* Huffman, A.C., Jr., Lund, W.R., and Godwin, L.H., editors, Geology and resources of the Paradox Basin: Utah Geological Association Guidebook 25, p. 313-324.

—1996b, Stratigraphic position of the sauropod *Dystrophaeus viaemalae* Cope and implications, in Morales, Michael, editor, The continental Jurassic: Museum of Northern Arizona Bulletin 60, p. 59-68.

Gilluly, James, and Reeside, J.B., Jr., 1928, Sedimentary rocks of the San Rafael Swell and some adjacent areas in eastern Utah: U.S. Geological Survey Professional Paper 150-D, p. 61-110.

Goodknight, C.S., Chenoweth, W.L., and Girdley, W.A., 1991, First day road log from Grand Junction to Moab, *in* Averett, W.R., editor, Guidebook for dinosaur quarries and tracksites tour: Grand Junction, Colorado, Grand Junction Geological Society, p. 71-81.

Harland, W.B., Armstrong, R.L., Cox, A.V., Craig, L.E., Smith, A.G., and Smith, D.G., 1990, A geologic time scale 1989: New York, Cambridge University Press, 263 p.

Holbrook, J.M., Wright, Robyn, and Kietzke, K.K., 1987, Stratigraphic relationships at the Jurassic-Cretaceous boundary in east-central New Mexico, *in* Lucas, S.G., and Hunt, A.P., editors, Northeastern New Mexico: New Mexico Geological Society Guidebook, 38th Annual Field Conference, p. 161-165.

Holt, E.L., 1940, The Morrison and Summerville Formations of the Grand River Valley and their vertebrate and invertebrate fauna:

Boulder, University of Colorado, M.S. thesis, 71 p.

Imlay, R.W., 1980, Jurassic paleobiogeography of the conterminous United States in its continental setting: U.S. Geological Survey Professional Paper 1062, 134 p.

Jensen, J.A., 1985, Three new sauropod dinosaurs from the Upper Jurassic of Colorado: The Great Basin Naturalist, v. 45, no. 4, p. 697-709.

—1987, New brachiosaur material from the Late Jurassic of Utah and Colorado: The Great Basin Naturalist, v. 47, no. 4, p. 592-608.

—1988, A fourth new sauropod dinosaur from the Upper Jurassic of the Colorado Plateau and sauropod bepedalism: The Great Basin Naturalist, v. 48, no. 2, p. 121-145.

Kirkland, J.I., and Carpenter, Kenneth, 1994, North America's first pre-Cretaceous ankylosaur (Dinosauria) from the Upper Jurassic Morrison Formation of western Colorado: Brigham Young University Geology Studies, v. 40, p. 25-42.

Knechtel, M.M., 1959, Stratigraphy of the Little Rocky Mountains and encircling foothills, Montana: U.S. Geological Survey Bulletin 1072-N, p. 723-752.

Kolb, R.L., Davis, L.E., and Gillette, D.D., 1996, The theropod dinosaur *Allosaurus* Marsh from the upper part of the Brushy Basin Member of the Morrison Formation (Upper Jurassic) near Green River, Utah, *in* Huffman, A.C., Jr., Lund, W.R., and Godwin, L.H., editors, Geology and resources of the Paradox Basin: Utah Geological Association Guidebook 25, 1996 field symposium, p. 339-349.

Kowallis, B.J., Christiansen, E.H., Deino, A.L., Peterson, Fred, Turner, C.E., Kunk, M.J., and Obradovich, J.D., 1998, The age of the Morrison Formation, *in* Carpenter, Kenneth, Chure, D.J., and Kirkland, J.I., editors, The Upper Jurassic Morrison Formation - an interdisciplinary study: Modern Geology v. 23, pt. 1, p. 235-260.

Langston, Wann, Jr., 1989, A history of vertebrate paleontology at the University of Oklahoma: Norman, Oklahoma, University of Oklahoma, Museum of Paleontology, unpublished document, 92 p., plus Appendix IV of 24 p.

Litwin, R.J., Turner, C.E., and Peterson, Fred, 1998, Palynological evidence on the age of the Morrison Formation, Western Interior U.S.: a preliminary report, *in* Carpenter, Kenneth, Chure, D.J., and Kirkland, J.I., editors, The Upper Jurassic Morrison Formation - an interdisciplinary study: Modern Geology v. 23, pt. 1, p. 292-319.

Lucas, S.G., and Hunt, Adrian, 1985, Dinosaurs from the Upper Jurassic Morrison Formation in New Mexico: New Mexico Journal of Science, v. 25, p. 1-12.

Lucas, S.G., Kietzke, K.K., and Hunt, A.P., 1985, The Jurassic System in east-central New Mexico, *in* Lucas. S.G., editor, Santa Rosa-- Tucumcari region: New Mexico Geological Society Guidebook, 36th Annual Field Conference, p. 213-242.

Lull, R.S., 1919, The sauropod dinosaur *Barosaurus* Marsh: Connecticut Academy of Arts and Sciences, New Haven, v. 6, 42 p.

Madsen, J.H., Jr., 1976, *Allosaurus fragilis* - a revised osteology: Utah Geological and Mineral Survey Bulletin 109, 163 p.

Maxwell, C.H., 1976, Geologic map of the Acoma Pueblo quadrangle, Valencia County, New Mexico: U.S. Geological Survey Geologic Quadrangle Map GQ-1298, scale 1:24,000.

McIntosh, J.S., 1981, Annotated catalogue of the dinosaurs (Reptilia, Archosauria) in the collections of Carnegie Museum of Natural History: Bulletin of Carnegie Museum of Natural History, no. 18, 67 p.

—1990a, Sauropoda, *in* Weishampel, D.B., Dodson, Peter, and Osmólska, Halszka, editors, The Dinosauria: Berkeley, University of California Press, p. 345-401.

—1990b, The second Jurassic dinosaur rush: Earth Sciences History, v. 9, no. 1, p. 22-27.

McIntosh, J.S., Miller, W.E., Stadtman, K.L., and Gillette, D.D., 1996, The osteology of *Camarasaurus lewisi* (Jensen, 1988): Brigham Young University Studies in Geology, v. 41, p. 73-115.

Meyers, J.H., and Schwartz, R.K., 1994, Summary of depositional environments, paleogeography, and structural control on sedimentation in the Late Jurassic (Oxfordian) Sundance foreland basin, western Montana, *in* Caputo, M.V., Peterson, J.A., and Franczyk, K.J., editors, Mesozoic systems of the Rocky Mountain Region: Rocky Mountain Section of the SEPM (Society for

Sedimentary Geology), p. 331-349.

Miller, W.E., Baer, J.L., Stadtman, K.L., and Britt, B.B., 1991, The Dry Mesa dinosaur quarry, Mesa County, Colorado, *in* Averett, W.R., editor, Guidebook for dinosaur quarries and tracksites tour: Grand Junction, Colorado, Grand Junction Geological Society, p. 31-46.

Miller, W.E., Horricks, R.D., and Madsen, J.H., Jr, 1996, The Cleveland-Lloyd Dinosaur Quarry, Emery County, Utah-- a U.S. Natural Landmark (including history and quarry map): Brigham Young Univeristy Studies in Geology, v. 41, p. 3-24.

Molnar, R.E., Kurzanov, A.M., and Dong, Zhiming, 1990, Carnosauria, *in* Weishampel, D.B., Dodson, Peter, and Osmólska, Halszka, editors, The Dinosauria: Berkeley, University of California Press, p. 169-209.

Norman, D.B., and Weishampel, D.B., 1990, Iguanodontidae and related ornithopods, *in* Weishampel, D.B., Dodson, Peter, and Osmólska, Halszka, editors, 1990, The Dinosauria: Berkeley, University of California Press, p. 510-533.

Osborn, H.F., and Mook, C.C., 1921, *Camarasaurus, Amphicoelias,* and other sauropods of Cope: American Museum of Natural History, Memoir, New Series, v. 3, part 3, p. 247-387.

Ostrom, J.H., and McIntosh, J.S., 1966, Marsh's dinosaurs-- the collections from Como Bluff: New Haven, Yale University Press, 388 p.

O'Sullivan, R.B., 1980, Stratigraphic sections of Middle Jurassic San Rafael Group from Wilson Arch to Bluff in southeastern Utah: U.S. Geological Survey Oil and Gas Investigations Chart OC-102.

—1992, The Jurassic Wanakah and Morrison Formations in the Telluride-Ouray-western Black Canyon area of southwestern Colorado: U.S. Geological Survey Bulletin 1927, 24 p.

Owen, D.E., Turner-Peterson, C.E., and Fishman, N.S., 1989, X-Ray diffraction studies of the <0.5-μm fraction from the Brushy Basin Member of the Upper Jurassic Morrison Formation, Colorado Plateau: U.S. Geological Survey Bulletin 1808-G, p. G1-G25.

Paul, G.S., 1988, The small predatory dinosaurs of the Mid-Mesozoic - the horned theropods of the Morrison and Great Oolite - *Ornitholestes* and *Proceratosaurus* - and the sickle-claw theropods of the Cloverly, Djadokhta and Judith River-- *Deinonychus, Velociraptor* and *Saurornitholestes*: Hunteria, v. 2, no. 4, 9 p.

Peterson, Fred, 1980, Sedimentology of the uranium-bearing Salt Wash Member and Tidwell unit of the Morrison Formation in the Henry and Kaiparowits basins, Utah, *in* Picard, M.D., editor, Henry Mountains symposium: Utah Geological Association Publication 8, p. 305-322.

—1984, Fluvial sedimentation on a quivering craton-- influence of slight crustal movements on fluvial processes, Upper Jurassic Morrison Formation, western Colorado Plateau: Sedimentary Geology, v. 38, no. 1/4, p. 21-49.

—1988a, Stratigraphy and nomenclature of Middle and Upper Jurassic rocks, western Colorado Plateau, Utah and Arizona: U.S. Geological Survey Bulletin 1633-B, p. 17-56.

—1988b, Pennsylvanian to Jurassic eolian transportation systems in the western United States: Sedimentary Geology, v. 56, p. 207-260.

—1988c, A synthesis of the Jurassic System in the southern Rocky Mountain region, *in* Sloss, L.L., editor, Sedimentary cover-- North American craton, U.S.: Geological Society of America, The Geology of North America, v. D-2, p. 65-76.

—1988d, Sedimentologic and paleotectonic analysis of the Henry, Kaiparowits, and Black Mesa Basins, Utah and Arizona, *in* Sloss, L.L., editor, Sedimentary cover-- North American craton, U.S.: Geological Society of America, The Geology of North America, v. D-2, p. 134-144.

—1994, Sand dunes, sabkhas, streams, and shallow seas-- Jurassic paleogeography in the southern part of the Western Interior Basin, *in* Caputo, M.V., Peterson, J.A., and Franczyk, K.J., editors, Mesozoic Systems of the Rocky Mountain Region: Rocky Mountain Section of the SEPM (Society for Sedimentary Geology), p. 233-272.

Peterson, Fred, and Turner-Peterson, C.E., 1987, The Morrison Formation of the Colorado Plateau-- recent advances in sedimentol-

ogy, stratigraphy, and paleotectonics: Hunteria, v. 2, no. 1, 18 p.

Peterson, Fred and Turner, C.E., 1998, Stratigraphy of the Ralston Creek and Morrison Formations (Upper Jurassic) near Denver, Colorado, *in* Carpenter, Kenneth, Chure, D.J., and Kirkland, J.I., editors, The Upper Jurassic Morrison Formation - an interdisciplinary study: Modern Geology v. 23, pt. 1, p. 3-38.

Pillmore, C.L., and Mapel, W.J., 1963, Geology of the Nefsy Divide quadrangle, Crook County, Wyoming: U.S. Geological Survey Bulletin 1121-E, p. E1-E52.

Pipiringos, G.N., 1957, Stratigraphy of the Sundance, Nugget and Jelm Formations in the Laramie Basin, Wyoming: Geological Survey of Wyoming Bulletin No. 47, 63 p.

—1968, Correlation and nomenclature of some Triassic and Jurassic rocks in south-central Wyoming: U.S. Geological Survey Professional Paper 594-D, p. D1-D26.

—1972, Upper Triassic and pre-Morrison Jurassic rocks, *in* Segerstrom, Kenneth, and Young, E.J., General geology of the Hahns Peak and Farwell Mountain Quadrangles, Routt County, Colorado: U.S. Geological Survey Bulletin 1349, p. 18-29.

Pipiringos, G.N., and O'Sullivan, R.B., 1976, Stratigraphic sections of some Triassic and Jurassic rocks from Douglas, Wyoming, to Boulder, Colorado: U.S. Geological Survey Oil and Gas Investigations Chart OC-69.

—1978, Principal unconformities in Triassic and Jurassic rocks, Western Interior United States-- a preliminary survey: U.S. Geological Survey Professional Paper 1035-A, p. A1-A29.

Richards, P.W., 1955, Geology of the Bighorn Canyon–Hardin area, Montana and Wyoming: U.S. Geological Survey Bulletin 1026, 93 p.

Richmond, D.R., and Stadtman, K.L., 1996, Sedimentology of a *Ceratosaurus* site in the San Rafael Swell, Emery County, Utah: Brigham Young University Geology Studies, v. 41, p. 117-124.

Rigby, J.K., Jr., 1982, *Camarasaurus* cf. *supremus* from the Morrison Formation near San Ysidro, New Mexico-- the San Ysidro dinosaur, *in* Callender, J.F., editor, Albuquerque country II: New Mexico Geological Society Guidebook, 33rd Annual Field Conference, p. 271-272.

Riggs, E.E., 1903, *Brachiosaurus altithorax*, the largest known dinosaur: American Journal of Science, v. 4, p. 15, p. 299-306.

Scheetz, R.D., 1991, Progress report of juvenile and embryonic *Dryosaurus* remains from the Upper Jurassic Morrison Formation of Colorado, *in* Averett, W.R., editor, Guidebook for dinosaur quarries and tracksites tour: Grand Junction, Colorado, Grand Junction Geological Society, p. 27-29.

Schmude, D.E., and Weege, C.J., 1996, Stratigraphic relationship, sedimentology, and taphonomy of Meilyn, a dinosaur quarry in the basal Morrison Formation of Wyoming, *in* Morales, Michael, editor, The continental Jurassic: Museum of Northern Arizona Bulletin 60, p. 547-554.

Schudack, M.E., 1994, Die ostracoden und charophyten der Morrison-Formation (Oberjura, westliche USA)-- systematik, biostratigraphie, ökologie, biogeographie: Deutsche Forschungsgemeinschaft, Abschlußbericht zur DFG–Sachbeihilfe Schu 694/4-1, Institut für Paläontologie der Freien Universität Berlin, 139 s.

—1995, Neue mikropälontologische beitrage (ostracoda, charophyta) zum Morrison- ökosystem (Oberjura des Western Interior, USA): Berliner Geowiss. Abh, E. 16, Gundolf-Ernst-Festschrift, s. 389-407.

Schudack, M.E., Turner, C.E., and Peterson, Fred, 1998, Biostratigraphy, paleoecology, and biogeography of charophytes and ostracodes from the Upper Jurassic Morrison Formation, Western Interior, U.S.A, *in* Carpenter, Kenneth, Chure, D.J., and Kirkland, J.I., editors, The Upper Jurassic Morrison Formation - an interdisciplinary study: Modern Geology v. 23, pt.1, p. 379-414.

Schwartz, H.L., and Manley, Kim, 1992, Geology and stratigraphy of the Seismosaurus locality, Sandoval County, New Mexico: New Mexico Geology, v. 14, no. 2, p. 25-30.

Scott, G.R., 1963, Bedrock geology of the Kassler Quadrangle, Colorado: U.S. Geological Survey Professional Paper 421-B, p. 71-125.

Shaw, A.B., 1964, Time in stratigraphy: New York, McGraw-Hill Publishing Co., 365 p.

Shepard, J.D., Galton, P.M., and Jensen, J.A., 1977, Additional specimens of the hypsilophodontid dinosaur *Dryosaurus altus* from the Upper Jurassic of western North America: Brigham Young University Geology Studies, v. 24, pt. 2, p. 11-15.

Sohn, I.G., and Peck, R.E., 1963, *Theriosynoecum wyomingense* (Branson, 1935), a possible guide ostracode to the Salt Wash Member of the Morrison Formation: U.S. Geological Survey Bulletin 1161-A, p. A1-A10.

Steiner, M.B., Lucas, S.G., and Shoemaker, E.M., 1994, Correlation and age of the Upper Jurassic Morrison Formation from magnetostratigraphic analysis, *in* Caputo, M.V., Peterson, J.A., and Franczyk, K.J., editors, Mesozoic Systems of the Rocky Mountain Region: Rocky Mountain Section of the SEPM (Society for Sedimentary Geology), p. 315-330.

Swierc, J.E., and Johnson, G.D., 1996, A local chronostratigraphy for the Morrison Formation, northeastern Bighorn Basin, Wyoming, *in* Bowen, C.E., Kirkwood, S.C., and Miller, T.S., editors, Resources of the Bighorn Basin: Wyoming Geological Association, 47th Guidebook, p. 315-327.

Sues, H.-D., and Norman, D.B., 1990, Hypsilophodontidae, Tenontosaurus, Dryosauridae, *in* Weishampel, D.B., Dodson, Peter, and Osmólska, Halszka, editors, The Dinosauria: Berkeley, University of California Press, p. 498-509.

Szigeti, G.J., and Fox, J.E., 1981, Unkpapa Sandstone (Jurassic), Black Hills, South Dakota-- an eolian facies of the Morrison Formation, *in* Ethridge, F.G., and Flores, R.M., editors, Recent and ancient nonmarine depositional environments-- models for exploration: Society of Economic Paleontologists and Mineralogists, Special Publication No. 31, p. 331-349.

Turner-Peterson, C.E., 1986, Fluvial sedimentology of a major uranium-bearing sandstone-- a study of the Westwater Canyon Member of the Morrison Formation, San Juan Basin, New Mexico, *in* Turner-Peterson, C.E., Santos, E.S., and Fishman, N.S., editors, A basin analysis case study-- the Morrison Formation, Grants Uranium Region, New Mexico: American Association of Petroleum Geologists, Studies in Geology No. 22, p. 47-75.

Turner, C.E., and Fishman, N.S., 1991, Jurassic Lake T'oo'dichi'-- a large alkaline, saline lake, Morrison Formation, eastern Colorado Plateau: Geological Society of America Bulletin, v. 103, no. 4, p. 538-558.

Ver Ploeg, A.J., 1991, Rare dinosaur skeleton found near Greybull: Wyoming Geo-Notes, no. 32, p. 40-41.

Way, J.N., O'Malley, P.J., Furer, L.C., Suttner, L.J., Kvale, E.P., and Meyers, J.H., 1994, Correlations of the Upper Jurassic- Lower Cretaceous nonmarine and transitional rocks in the northern Rocky Mountain foreland, *in* Caputo, M.V., Peterson, J.A., and Franczyk, K.J., editors, Mesozoic Systems of the Rocky Mountain Region: Rocky Mountain Section of the SEPM (Society for Sedimentary Geology), p. 351-364.

Weege, Christopher, and Schmude, D.E., 1996, The stratigraphic relationship, sedimentology, and taphonomy of Meilyn-- a dinosaur quarry in the basal Morrison Formation of Wyoming, *in* Hunter, R.A., editor, Tate '96-- paleoenvironments of the Jurassic: Tate Museum Guidebook No. 1, Casper, Wyoming, p. 52-58.

West, E.S., 1978, Biostratigraphy and paleoecology of the lower Morrison Formation of Cimarron County, Oklahoma: Wichita, Kansas, Wichita State University, M.S. thesis, 61 p.

APPENDIX 1

Credits for sections measured by others that were used in the compilation.

MONTANA

The Cinnabar Mountain local reference section is from Fraser and others (1969, p. 93-95) and partly revised in further work by us.

The position of the T and J Quarry (MT-6) was correlated to a nearby section of the entire Morrison Formation that was measured by J.T. Cooley (unpublished data) and was used in figure 6 as the Toston local reference section.

The Tithonian palynomorph samples were positioned in a partial section at the top of the Morrison Formation measured by us and tied in to a complete section of the Morrison measured in essentially the same area by Cooley (1993, p. 39, section B at West Boulder River).

NEW MEXICO

The localities at Acoma (NM-1) and Concho Springs (NM-2) were correlated to measured sections in Chenoweth (1953) by Lucas and Hunt (1985), which were then correlated by us to the Cuchillo Arroyo local reference section of Craig and others (1959, section 49).

OKLAHOMA

A measured section through the lower part of the Morrison Formation by West (1978, measured section 1) was used along with our measured sections through the remainder of the Morrison Formation to help with the initial positioning of sites in western Oklahoma. These were then correlated to our Travesser Park local reference section in northeastern New Mexico.

SOUTH DAKOTA

Measured sections by Foster (1996a,b) were used to initially position several sites in the eastern Black Hills. These were then correlated to our Wonderland local reference section.

UTAH

The Green River Quarry (UT-9) was positioned in a measured section by Kolb and others (1996, p. 341, figure 2, section 3) and correlated by us to our nearby Hatt Ranch section.

WYOMING

The Thermopolis local reference section is from Bjoraker and Naus (1996, p. 303, Column 5).

We correlated the Little Houston Creek Quarry (WY-11) to a nearby and more complete local reference section in Pillmore and Mapel (1963, Plate 2, section 42). Other sites on the west side of the Black Hills were related to measured sections by Foster (1992) and Foster and Martin (1994) and correlated by us to the Little Houston Creek local reference section.

The Meilyn (WY-83) and Lynn (WY-84) sites were positioned in measured sections by Weege and Schmude (1996, Figure 2, sections A and B) and Schmude and Weege (1996, p. 550, Figure 2, sections A and B) and correlated by us to our nearby measured section at Ninemile Hill.

APPENDIX 2

Alphabetical list of taxa, with identification number. See table 1 for a listing by numerical order
that also includes selected genera.

Taxon Identity No.	Species
37	*Allosaurus fragilis* Marsh
62	*Allosaurus* n. sp. (N.A.A.)
87	*Amphicoelias altus* Cope
84	*Amphicoelias fragillimus* Cope
68	Ankylosaur new genus and species
48	*Apatosaurus ajax* Marsh
38	*Apatosaurus excelsus* Marsh
81	*Apatosaurus louisae* Holland
69	*Apatosaurus yahnapin* Filla and Redman
65	*"Apatosaurus" minimus* Mook
80	*Barosaurus lentus* Marsh
77	*Brachiosaurus altithorax* Riggs
36	*Camarasaurus grandis* (Marsh)
32	*Camarasaurus lentus* (Marsh)
73	*Camarasaurus lewisi* (Jensen)
44	*Camarasaurus supremus* Cope
70	*Camptosaurus amplus* (Marsh)
64	*Camptosaurus dispar* (Marsh)
42	*Ceratosaurus nasicornis* Marsh
31	*Coelurus fragilis* Marsh
47	*Diplodocus carnegii* Hatcher
43	*Diplodocus longus* Marsh
51	*Drinker nisti* Bakker, Galton, Siegwarth, and Filla
39	*Dryosaurus altus* (Marsh)
61	*Dystrophaeus viaemalae* Cope

Taxon Identity No.	Species
74	*Dystylosaurus edwini* Jensen
76	*Echinodon* sp.
46	*Edmarka rex* Bakker, Siegwarth, Kralis, and Filla
40	*Elaphrosaurus* sp.
63	*Haplocanthosaurus delfsi* McIntosh and Williams
71	*Haplocanthosaurus priscus* (Hatcher)
83	*Hypsirophus* sp.
85	*Koparion douglassi* Chure
50	*Marshosaurus bicentesimus* Madsen
72	*"Morosaurus"* sp.
49	*Mymoorapelta maysi* Kirkland and Carpenter
66	*Ornitholestes* sp.
67	*Ornitholestes hermanni* Osborn
41	*Othnielia rex* (Marsh)
82	*Saurophaganax maximus* Chure
78	*Seismosaurus hallorum* Gillette
35	*Stegosaurus armatus* Marsh
33	*Stegosaurus stenops* Marsh
34	*Stegosaurus ungulatus* Marsh
79	*Stokesosaurus clevelandi* Madsen
75	*Supersaurus vivianae* Jensen
45	*Torvosaurus tanneri* Galton and Jensen
86	Troodontid second sp.

APPENDIX 3

Morrison dinosaur sites and faunal lists.

The various dinosaur sites are listed by state and general locality within that state. This is followed by a code having the accepted two-letter abbreviation for the state, followed by an identifying number (for example, CO-11), the name(s) applied to the locality, and the county. The sites are listed sequentially by their identifying numbers but the numerical sequence may be broken to allow for flexibility in compilation. Credits for the identifications and faunal lists are included. Brief notes are added in places for clarity and understanding. Abbreviations follow: **AMNH**: American Museum of Natural History, **CMNH**: Cleveland Museum of Natural History; **DMNH**: Denver Museum of Natural History; **DNM**: Dinosaur National Monument, **FPA**: Fruita Paleontological Area, **LACM**: Los Angeles County Museum, **RVRNA**: Rabbit Valley Research Natural Area.

COLORADO

CAÑON CITY (Garden Park area)

CO-1   Cope's Quarry 8 (about 500 feet southwest of Cope's Nipple) Fremont County, CO; Carpenter (1998); according to K. Carpenter, (oral communication, 1997), this locality is Quarry 8 in Cope's original notes. Cope also referred to it as Camarasaurus Quarry No. 2. Osborn and Mook (1921) incorrectly called it Cope Quarry No. 1.
Sauropoda: *Camarasaurus supremus*

CO-2   Cope's Quarries 1-7 (at Cope's Nipple, or Saurian Hill) Fremont County, CO; Carpenter (1998); Osborn and Mook (1921) incorrectly called this Cope Quarry No. 2.
Theropoda: *Allosaurus?* sp.
Sauropoda: *Camarasaurus* sp., *Camarasaurus supremus*, *Amphicoelias fragillimus*, *Apatosaurus* sp.
Thyreophora: *Hypsirophus* sp. (stegosaur genus tentatively accepted pending further study; Carpenter, 1998)
Ornithopoda: *Camptosaurus* sp.

CO-3   Marsh-Felch Quarry 1, Fremont County, CO; K. Carpenter (1998; oral communication, 1991, 1997), Ostrom and McIntosh (1966)
Theropoda: *Ceratosaurus nasicornis, Allosaurus fragilis, Elaphrosaurus* sp., *Coelurus fragilis*
Sauropoda: *Haplocanthosaurus priscus, Brachiosaurus* sp., "*Morosaurus*" sp., *Diplodocus longus, Apatosaurus* sp.
Thyreophora: *Stegosaurus armatus, Stegosaurus stenops*,
Ornithopoda: *Othnielia rex, Dryosaurus altus*

CO-4   Marsh-Felch Quarry 2, Fremont County, CO; K. Carpenter (oral communication, 1991), J.S. McIntosh (written communication, 1997)
Theropoda: *Allosaurus* sp.

CO-5   CMNH Quarry (Delfs' Quarry), Fremont County, CO; K. Carpenter (oral communication, 1991)
Sauropoda: *Haplocanthosaurus delfsi*

CO-6   DMNH Quarry 1 (Dall DeWeese's 1915 Quarry), Fremont County, CO; K. Carpenter (oral communication, 1991)
Sauropoda: *Diplodocus longus*

CO-7   DMNH Quarry 2 (Kessler's 1937 Quarry), Fremont County, CO; K. Carpenter (1998; oral communication, 1991)
Theropoda: *Allosaurus* sp.
Thyreophora: *Stegosaurus stenops*

CO-8   DMNH Quarry 3 (Lindsey's 1977 Quarry), Fremont County, CO; K. Carpenter (1998; oral communication, 1991)
Theropoda: *Allosaurus fragilis*
Sauropoda: *Camarasaurus grandis*

CO-9   DMNH Quarry 4 (Carpenter's 1990 Quarry or Valley of Death 5 Quarry), Fremont County, CO; K. Carpenter (1998; oral communication, 1991)
Sauropoda: *Diplodocus* sp.
Ornithopoda: *Othnielia rex*

CO-10   DMNH Quarry 5 (Carpenter's 1991 Quarry, or Shaw's Park 1 Quarry), Fremont County, CO; K. Carpenter (1998; oral communication, 1992)
Sauropoda: *Haplocanthosaurus* sp.

CO-11   DMNH Quarry 6 (Small's Quarry), Fremont County, CO; K. Carpenter (oral communication, 1992, 1997)
Theropoda: *Elaphrosaurus* sp.
Sauropoda: *Apatosaurus excelsus*
Thyreophora: *Stegosaurus stenops*, ?*Mymoorapelta* sp.
Ornithopoda: *Dryosaurus altus*

DINOSAUR NATIONAL MONUMENT EAST

CO-16   Homestead Quarry, Moffat County, CO; D.J. Chure (oral communication, 1993)
Theropoda: *Marshosaurus*(?) sp.

CO-17   Wolf Creek Quarry, Moffat County, CO; J.R. Foster (oral communication, 1997)
Theropoda: *Allosaurus* sp.
Sauropoda: *Camarasaurus* sp., indeterminate diplodocid
Thyreophora: *Stegosaurus* sp.

GRAND JUNCTION-FRUITA AREA

(Rabbit Valley locality)

CO-21   Mygatt-Moore Quarry (M&M Quarry), Mesa County, CO; Kirkland and Carpenter (1994)
Theropoda: *Ceratosaurus* sp., *Allosaurus* sp.,
Sauropoda: *Camarasaurus* sp., *Diplodocus* sp., *Barosaurus* sp., *Apatosaurus* sp.
Thyreophora: *Mymoorapelta maysi*

CO-22   RVRNA-2 (Trail Through Time Stop 2), Mesa County, CO; Armstrong and McReynolds (1987)
Sauropoda: *Camarasaurus* sp.

CO-23   RVRNA-13 (Trail Through Time Stop 13), Mesa County, CO; K. Carpenter (written communication, 1997)
Ornithopoda: *Camptosaurus* sp.

CO-24   Lower Split Rock Site 1 (in lower sandstone bed), Mesa County, CO; J.I. Kirkland (oral communication, 1993)
Theropoda: *Allosaurus* sp.
Sauropoda: *Brachiosaurus*(?) sp.
Thyreophora: *Stegosaurus* sp., *Stegosaurus stenops*(?)
Ornithopoda: *Othnielia*(?) sp.

CO-25   Upper Split Rock Site 2 (in upper sandstone bed), Mesa County, CO; J.I. Kirkland (oral communication, 1993)
Sauropoda: *Apatosaurus* sp.
Ornithopoda: *Dryosaurus altus*(?)

CO-26   Rabbit Valley-E Site, Mesa County, CO; J.I. Kirkland (oral communication, 1993)
Sauropoda: *Supersaurus* sp.

CO-27　Bollan's Site, Mesa County, CO; Bollan (1991), J.I. Kirkland (oral communication, 1993)
Theropoda: *Allosaurus* sp. (tooth)
Thyreophora: *Stegosaurus ungulatus*

FRUITA PALEONTOLOGICAL AREA

CO-33　Callison's Quarries (includes four sites at same stratigraphic level, all nearby), Mesa County, CO; (Callison 1987), J.I. Kirkland (oral communication, 1993, 1997)
Theropoda: *Ceratosaurus* sp., *Allosaurus* sp., undetermined coelurosaur
Sauropoda: *Brachiosaurus* sp., *Camarasaurus* sp., *Diplodocus* sp., *Apatosaurus* sp.
Thyreophora: *Echinodon* sp., *Stegosaurus* sp.

CO-34　Fruita Paleontological Area Dryosaur Nesting Site, Mesa County, CO; J.I. Kirkland (oral communication, 1993)
Ornithopoda: *Dryosaurus* sp.

CO-35　LACM Quarry (Clark's Quarry), Mesa County, CO; J.I. Kirkland (oral communication, 1993)
Thyreophora: *Stegosaurus* sp

CO-36　Riggs' Quarry 15 (Dinosaur Hill Quarry), Mesa County, CO; Chenoweth (1987), Goodknight and others (1991)
Sauropoda: *Diplodocus* sp., *Apatosaurus excelsus*

RIGGS HILL AREA

CO-45　Riggs' Quarry 13 (Riggs Hill), Mesa County, CO; Riggs (1903)
Sauropoda: *Brachiosaurus altithorax*

CO-46　Holt's Quarry 1, Mesa County, CO; Holt (1940)
Thyreophora: *Stegosaurus* sp.

CO-47　Holt's Quarry 2, Mesa County, CO; Holt (1940)
Theropoda: *Allosaurus* sp.
Sauropoda: *Brachiosaurus*(?) sp.

GUNNISON AREA

CO-48　Cabin Creek Quarry, Gunnison County, CO; Bartleson and Jensen (1988)
Sauropoda: *Apatosaurus* sp.

CO-49　Curecanti-Red Creek Quarry, Gunnison County, CO; Fiorillo and May (1996)
Theropoda: *Allosaurus* sp.
Sauropoda: *Apatosaurus*(?) sp.

MORRISON AREA

CO-51　Lake's Quarries 1, 5, 8, Jefferson County, CO; Ostrom and McIntosh (1966), J.S. McIntosh (written communication, 1997)
Sauropoda: *Camarasaurus* sp., *Diplodocus* sp., *Apatosaurus ajax*
Thyreophora: *Stegosaurus armatus*

CO-52　Lake's Quarry 10-L (in black mudstone bed), Jefferson County, CO; Ostrom and McIntosh (1966)
Theropoda: *Allosaurus* sp.
Sauropoda: *Apatosaurus ajax*

CO-53　Lake's Quarry 10-U (in buff sandstone bed), Jefferson County, CO; Ostrom and McIntosh (1966)
Sauropoda: *Apatosaurus ajax*

UNCOMPAHGRE PLATEAU

CO-55　Cactus Park Quarry (of J.A. Jensen), Mesa County, CO; J.R. Foster (written communication, 1997), J.S. McIntosh (written communication, 1997)
Sauropoda: *Camarasaurus* sp., *Apatosaurus* sp.
Thyreophora: *Stegosaurus* sp.

CO-56　Dominguez-Jones Quarry (Pit 1 of J.A. Jensen), Mesa County, CO; Jensen (1988), McIntosh and others (1996)
Sauropoda: *Camarasaurus lewisi*

CO-57　Hups' Cactus Park Quarry, Mesa County, CO; K. Carpenter (written communication, 1997), J.R. Foster (written communication, 1997)
Theropoda: *Allosaurus* sp.
Thyreophora: *Mymoorapelta maysi*

CO-58　Dry Mesa Quarry 1, Mesa County, CO; Jensen (1985, 1987), Britt (1991), Miller and others (1991), W.E. Miller (oral communication, 1992), Curtice and Wilhite (1996), Curtice and others (1996)
Theropoda: *Ceratosaurus* sp., *Allosaurus* sp., *Torvosaurus tanneri*, ?*Ornitholestes* sp. and (or) *Coelurus* sp., *Marshosaurus* sp.
Sauropoda: *Brachiosaurus* sp., *Dystylosaurus edwini*, *Camarasaurus* sp., *Diplodocus* sp., *Apatosaurus* sp., *Supersaurus vivianae*
Thyreophora: *Stegosaurus* sp., ankylosaur undetermined
Ornithopoda: *Dryosaurus* sp., *Camptosaurus* sp.

CO-59　Dry Mesa Quarry 2 (Jones Hole Quarry); Mesa County, CO; W.E. Miller (oral communication, 1992), J.S. McIntosh, written communication, 1997)
Theropoda: *Allosaurus* sp.
Sauropoda: *Barosaurus* sp.
Ornithopoda: *Camptosaurus* sp.

CO-60　Potter Creek Quarry, Montrose County, CO; Jensen (1985, 1987)
Sauropoda: ?*Brachiosaurus altithorax*

URAVAN AREA

CO-66　Sheetz' Quarry 1, Montrose County, CO, Galton and Jensen (1973), Scheetz (1991)
Ornithopoda: *Dryosaurus altus* (baby)

CAÑON CITY (Garden Park area)

CO-70 to **CO-77** from Carpenter (1998)

CO-70　Shaw's Park 3, Fremont County, CO
Theropoda: *Allosaurus* sp.

CO-71　Cope's Quarry 12, Fremont County, CO
Sauropoda: *Amphicoelias altus*

CO-72　Egg Gulch, Fremont County, CO
Ornithopoda: *Dryosaurus*? sp.

CO-73　Meyer Sites 1 and 2, Fremont County, CO
Theropoda: *Allosaurus* sp., *Torvosaurus* cf. *T. tanneri*

CO-74　Meyer Site 3, Fremont County, CO
Sauropoda: *Diplodocus* sp.

CO-75　Kenny's Stegosaurus Site, Fremont County, CO
Thyreophora: *Stegosaurus* cf. *S. stenops*

CO-76　Cope's Quarry 15 (Oil Tract), Fremont County, CO; stratigraphic position approximate
Sauropoda: *Camarasaurus* sp.

CO-77　Gregg's Bone Site, Fremont County, CO
Thyreophora: *Stegosaurus* sp.

MONTANA

BRIDGER AREA

MT-1 Mothers Day Quarry, Carbon County, MT; Kristi Curry (oral communication, 1996)
Theropoda: *Allosaurus* sp., dromaeosaur (tooth)
Sauropoda: *Diplodocus* or *Barosaurus* (not *Apatosaurus*)
Thyreophora: *Stegosaurus*(?) sp.

LIVINGSTON AREA

MT-2 Upper Strickland Creek Quarry, Park County, MT; Matthew Smith (oral communication, 1992)
Theropoda: *Allosaurus* sp.
Sauropoda: Family Diplodocidae (genus and species undetermined)

TOSTON AREA

MT-6 T and J Quarry (Ted and Jane Quarry), Gallatin County, MT; R.D. Scheetz (oral communication, 1995)
Theropoda: *Allosaurus*? sp.
Sauropoda: small mature sauropods

NEW MEXICO

SOUTHEASTERN SAN JUAN BASIN AREA

NM-1 Acoma Quarry, Cibola County, NM; Chenoweth (1953), Lucas and Hunt (1985)
Theropoda: *Allosaurus* sp.

NM-2 Concho Springs Quarry, Cibola County, NM; Chenoweth (1953), Lucas and Hunt (1985)
Thyreophora: *Stegosaurus* sp.

NM-3 San Ysidro Camarasaur Quarry, Sandoval County, NM; Rigby (1982), Lucas and Hunt (1985)
Theropoda: *Allosaurus* sp. (teeth)
Sauropoda: *Camarasaurus supremus*

NM-4 Seismosaur Quarry, Bernalillo County, NM; Gillette (1991), Schwartz and Manley (1992)
Theropoda: cf. *Allosaurus* sp. (teeth)
Sauropoda: *Seismosaurus hallorum*

NM-5 Boney Canyon Quarry, Bernalillo County, NM; T.E. Williamson (oral communication, 1997)
Theropoda: large allosaurid (partial skeleton)
Sauropoda: diplodocid (partial skull), *Camarasaurus* sp. (partial skull)

NM-6 Boney Canyon-NE Site, Bernalillo County, NM; T.E. Williamson (oral communication, 1997)
Sauropoda: *Camarasaurus* sp. (tooth)

NM-7 San Ysidro Diplodocid Quarry, Bernalillo County, NM; Anderson and Lucas (1996), T.E. Williamson (oral communication, 1997)
Sauropoda: *Diplodocus* sp.

NORTHEASTERN NEW MEXICO AREA

NM-10 Bull Canyon Site, Guadalupe County, NM; Lucas and others (1985)
Thyreophora: ?*Stegosaurus* sp.

OKLAHOMA

KENTON AREA

OK-1 Stovall's Pit 1, Cimarron County, OK; Langston (1989), Chure (1995)
Theropoda: *Allosaurus* sp., *Saurophaganax maximus*
Sauropoda: *Diplodocus* sp., *Diplodocus* or *Barosaurus* sp. (may pertain to *Amphicoelias* sp.), cf. *Apatosaurus* sp., *Apatosaurus*? sp. or *Camarasaurus*? sp.
Thyreophora: *Stegosaurus* sp.
Ornithopoda: *Camptosaurus* sp.

OK-2 Stovall's Pit 5, Cimarron County, OK; Langston (1989)
Theropoda: *Allosaurus* sp.
Sauropoda: *Camarasaurus* sp., ?*Diplodocus* sp., ?*Apatosaurus* sp.
Thyreophora: ?*Stegosaurus* sp.
Ornithopoda: ?*Camptosaurus* sp.

OK-3 Stovall's Pit 6, Cimarron County, OK; Langston (1989)
Theropoda: *Allosaurus* sp.
Sauropoda: ?*Camarasaurus* sp., *Diplodocus* sp., *Apatosaurus* sp.
Ornithopoda: *Camptosaurus* sp.

OK-4 Stovall's Pit 8, Cimarron County, OK; Langston (1989)
Theropoda: ?Coelurosaurian dinosaur
Ornithopoda: ?*Camptosaurus* sp.

SOUTH DAKOTA

BLACK HILLS EAST AREA

SD-1 Bear Butte Quarry, Meade County, SD; Foster (1996a,b)
Sauropoda: *Apatosaurus* sp.

SD-2 Fuller's 351 (Spearfish) Quarry, Lawrence County, SD; Foster (1996a,b), J.R. Foster (written communication, 1997)
Theropoda: *Allosaurus* sp.
Sauropoda: *Camarasaurus* sp., *Apatosaurus* sp.

SD-3 Piedmont Quarry, Meade County, SD; Lull (1919), Dodson and others (1980)
Theropoda: *Allosaurus* sp.
Sauropoda: *Barosaurus lentus*

SD-4 Wonderland Quarry, Meade County, SD; Foster (1996a,b)
Theropoda: *Allosaurus* sp., unidentified theropod (ilium, resembles *Stokesosaurus* or *Marshosaurus*)
Sauropoda: *Camarasaurus* sp. (teeth), *Barosaurus lentus*

SD-5 Wonderland North Quarry, Meade County, SD; Foster (1996a,b)
Sauropoda: *Diplodocus* sp.

UTAH

HANKSVILLE AREA

UT-1 Hanksville Quarry, Wayne County, UT; J.S. McIntosh (written communication, 1997)
Theropoda: unidentified new(?) theropod
Sauropoda: *Apatosaurus* sp. (originally thought to be *Camptosaurus* sp. according to J.T. Gregory, written communication, 1992)

MOAB AREA

UT-4　East Canyon Quarry, San Juan County, UT; Cope (1877),
D.D. Gillette (oral communication, 1995, 1996a,b)
Sauropoda: *Dystrophaeus viaemalae*

SAN RAFAEL SWELL AREA

UT-7　Cleveland-Lloyd Quarry, Emery County, UT; Madsen (1976),
J.H. Madsen (written communication, 1994, oral commu-
nication, 1997), Miller and others (1996)
Theropoda: *Ceratosaurus* sp., *Allosaurus fragilis, Stokeso-
saurus clevelandi, Ornitholestes?, Marshosaurus bicen-
tesimus*
Sauropoda: *Haplocanthosaurus* sp., *Camarasaurus lentus,
Barosaurus* sp., *Amphicoelias?* sp.
Thyreophora: *Stegosaurus stenops*, nodosaur undetermined
Ornithopoda: *Camptosaurus* cf. *C. dispar*

UT-8　Sand Bench Site, Emery County, UT; Richmond and Stadtman (1996)
Theropoda: *Ceratosaurus nasicornis*

UT-9　Green River Quarry, Emery County, UT; Kolb and others
(1996), L.E. Davis (oral communication, 1996)
Theropoda: *Allosaurus* sp.
Sauropoda: *Camarasaurus(?)* sp.
Thyreophora: *Stegosaurus(?)* sp.

DINOSAUR NATIONAL MONUMENT WEST　(South of Green River)

UT-12　Jensen/Jensen Quarry, Uintah County, UT; Jensen (1987),
D.J. Chure (oral communication, 1993)
Sauropoda: *Brachiosaurus* sp., *Camarasaurus* sp.,
Apatosaurus sp.

UT-13　Utah Field House of Natural History Quarry, Uintah County,
UT; Bilbey and Hamblin (1992), D.J. Chure (oral com-
munication, 1993)
Thyreophora: *Stegosaurus* sp.

UT-14　DNM-5, Uintah County, UT; D.J. Chure (oral communica-
tion, 1993)
Theropoda: *Allosaurus* sp.
Ornithopoda: *Dryosaurus* sp.

DINOSAUR NATIONAL MONUMENT WEST　(Near Carnegie Quarry)

UT-17　DNM-15, Uintah County, UT; D.J. Chure (oral communication, 1993)
Sauropoda: *Apatosaurus* sp.

UT-18　Carnegie Quarry, Uintah County, UT; D.J. Chure (written
communication, 1991), J.S. Mcintosh (written communi-
cation, 1997)
Theropoda: *Ceratosaurus nasicornis, Allosaurus fragilis,
Torvosaurus tanneri, Marshosaurus bicentesimus*
Sauropoda: *Camarasaurus lentus, Diplodocus longus,
Barosaurus lentus, Apatosaurus louisae*
Thyreophora: *Stegosaurus ungulatus, Stegosaurus stenops*
Ornithopoda: *Dryosaurus altus;* ornithischian, unidentified

UT-19　DNM-315, Uintah County, UT; Chure and others (1994)
Ornithopoda: *Camptosaurus* sp. (embryo)

UT-20　DNM-116 (N.A.A. Quarry), Uintah County, UT; D.J. Chure
(oral communication, 1997)
Theropoda: *Allosaurus* n. sp. (possibly new genus)

DINOSAUR NATIONAL MONUMENT WEST　(Rainbow Park area)

UT-24　DNM-8 (Soft Sauropod Quarry), Uintah County, UT; D.J.
Chure (oral communication, 1991)
Sauropoda: *Apatosaurus* sp.

UT-25　DNM-94 (Quarry 94, Rainbow Park microsite), Uintah
County, UT; Chure (1989; 1994), D.J. Chure (oral com-
munication, 1997)
Theropoda: *Allosaurus* sp., *Koparion douglassi*, Troodontid
second sp.
Sauropoda: *Camarasaurus* sp., *Diplodocus* sp.
Thyreophora: *Stegosaurus* sp.
Ornithopoda: *Dryosaurus* sp., *Camptosaurus* sp.

UT-26　DNM-96 (Quarry 96, Rainbow Park microsite), Uintah
County, UT; D.J. Chure (oral communication, 1997)
Theropoda: *Allosaurus* sp.
Sauropoda: *Camarasaurus* sp., *Diplodocus* sp.
Thyreophora: *Stegosaurus* sp.
Ornithischia: *Dryosaurus* sp., *Camptosaurus* sp.

WYOMING

ALCOVA AREA

WY-1　Cottonwood Creek Site-1, Natrona County, WY; Allen
(1994)
Ornithopoda: cf. *Dryosaurus* sp.

WY-2　Cottonwood Creek Site-2, Natrona County, WY; Allen (1994)
Sauropoda: *Camarasaurus* sp.

WY-3　Cottonwood Creek Site-3, Natrona County, WY; Allen (1994)
Sauropoda: *Diplodocus* sp.

WY-4　Allen's (1994) Allosaur Site, Natrona County, WY; Allen
(1994)
Theropoda: *Allosaurus* sp.

BLACK HILLS NORTHWEST

WY-8　Lower Dillon's Corner Site, Crook County, WY; Foster and
Martin (1994)
Theropoda: *?Allosaurus* sp.

WY-9　Upper Dillon's Corner Site, Crook County, WY; Foster and
Martin (1994)
Sauropoda: cf. *Barosaurus* sp.

WY-10　Lightning Rod Butte Quarry, Crook County, WY; Foster and
Martin (1994)
Ornithopoda: *Othnielia* sp.

WY-11　Little Houston Quarry, Crook County, WY; Foster and Mar-
tin (1994), Foster (1996a,b)
Theropoda: *Allosaurus* sp.
Sauropoda: *Camarasaurus* sp. *Diplodocus* or *Barosaurus* sp.,
Apatosaurus sp.
Thyreophora: *Stegosaurus* sp.
Ornithopoda: *Othnielia* sp., *Dryosaurus* sp., ornithischian
indeterminate

WY-12　MIA Quarry, Crook County, WY; Foster and Martin (1994),
J.R. Foster, written communication (1997)
Sauropoda: *Barosaurus* sp.

COMO BLUFF WEST　(West of Marshall Road)

WY-15　Reed's Quarry 9, Albany County, WY; Ostrom and McIntosh

(1966), Bakker and others (1990), Sues and Norman (1990)
Theropoda: *Allosaurus fragilis, Coelurus fragilis*
Sauropoda: *Camarasaurus* sp.
Thyreophora: *Stegosaurus* sp.
Ornithopoda: *Othnielia rex* (may not be from this quarry), *Drinker nisti, Dryosaurus* sp., *Camptosaurus* sp.

WY-16 Reed's Quarry 14, Albany County, WY; Ostrom and McIntosh (1966)
Theropoda: *Allosaurus* sp.

WY-17 Reed's Quarry 10, Albany County, WY; Ostrom and McIntosh (1966)
Sauropoda: *Apatosaurus excelsus*

WY-18 Reed's Quarry 11, Albany County, WY; Ostrom and McIntosh (1966), Galton (1990), J.S. McIntosh (written communication, 1997)
Sauropoda: *Apatosaurus excelsus*
Thyreophora: *Stegosaurus ungulatus*

WY-19 Reed's Quarry 8, Albany County, WY; Ostrom and McIntosh (1966)
Theropoda: *Allosaurus* sp., *"Coelurus fragilis"*
Sauropoda: *Camarasaurus* sp., *Diplodocus* sp.
Thyreophora: *Stegosaurus* sp.

WY-20 Reed's Quarry 3, Albany County, WY; Ostrom and McIntosh (1966), Molnar and others (1990)
Theropoda: *Allosaurus fragilis*
Sauropoda: *Camarasaurus grandis*

WY-21 Reed's Quarry 1, Albany County, WY; Ostrom and McIntosh (1966), Molnar and others (1990)
Theropoda: *Allosaurus fragilis*
Sauropoda: *Camarasaurus grandis, Diplodocus* sp.

WY-22 Louise Quarry, Albany County, WY; Bakker and others (1992), J. Filla (oral communication, 1993)
Theropoda: *Allosaurus* sp., *Edmarka rex*
Sauropoda: *Camarasaurus* sp., *Apatosaurus* sp.
Thyreophora: *Stegosaurus*(?) sp.

WY-23 Reed's Quarry 2 (Fishplate Quarry), Albany County, WY; Ostrom and McIntosh (1966)
Sauropoda: *Apatosaurus* sp.

WY-24 Drinker Nisti Quarry-L (Lower Big Nose Quarry?), Albany County, WY; Bakker and others (1990)
Ornithopoda: *Drinker nisti*

WY-25 Drinker Nisti Quarry-U (Upper Big Nose Quarry?), Albany County, WY; Bakker and others (1990)
Ornithopoda: *Drinker nisti*

WY-26 Reed's Quarry 5, Carbon County, WY; Ostrom and McIntosh (1966)
Sauropoda: *Diplodocus* sp.
Ornithopoda: *Dryosaurus altus*

WY-27 Lake's Quarry 1A (Big Canyon Quarry), Carbon County, WY; Ostrom and McIntosh (1966)
Theropoda: *Allosaurus* sp.
Sauropoda: *Camarasaurus* sp.
Ornithopoda: *Camptosaurus amplus*

WY-28 Reed's Quarry 7 (Three Trees Quarry), Carbon County, WY; Ostrom and McIntosh (1966)
Ornithopoda: *Othnielia rex*

WY-29 Reed's Quarry 12, Carbon County, WY; Ostrom and McIntosh (1966), (Galton (1990), J.S. McIntosh (written communication, 1997)
Theropoda: *Allosaurus* sp., *Coelurus* sp.
Sauropoda: *Camarasaurus* sp., *Diplodocus* sp.
Thyreophora: *Stegosaurus ungulatus*

Ornithopoda: *Othnielia*? sp. or *Dryosaurus*? sp.

WY-30 Reed's Quarry 1¹/₂, Carbon County, WY; Ostrom and McIntosh (1966), Molnar and others (1990)
Theropoda: *Allosaurus fragilis*
Sauropoda: unidentified taxon

WY-31 Cope's Quarry 3, Carbon County, WY; J.S. McIntosh (oral communication, 1997)
Theropoda: *Allosaurus* sp.

COMO BLUFF EAST (East of Marshall Road)

WY-39 Nail Quarry, Albany County, WY; Bakker and others (1992)
Theropoda: *Allosaurus* sp., *Edmarka rex*
Sauropoda: *Camarasaurus* sp., *Diplodocus* sp., *Apatosaurus* sp.
Thyreophora: *Stegosaurus* sp.

WY-40 Reed's Quarry 4 (Truckstop Quarry), Albany County, WY; Ostrom and McIntosh (1966)
Theropoda: *Allosaurus fragilis*
Sauropoda: *Camarasaurus* sp., *Barosaurus* sp., *Apatosaurus* sp.
Thyreophora: *Stegosaurus* sp.

WY-41 Two Thigh Quarry, Albany County, WY; R.T. Bakker (oral communication, 1993)
Ornithopoda: *Drinker nisti*

WY-42 Bernice Quarry, Albany County, WY; J. Filla (oral communication, 1993)
Sauropoda: *Diplodocus* sp.

WY-43 Cam Bench Quarries (West, Middle, and East Sites), Albany County, WY; J. Filla (oral communication, 1993)
Sauropoda: *Camarasaurus* sp.
Ornithopoda: *Camptosaurus*(?) sp.

WY-44 Bertha Quarry, Albany County, WY; J. Filla (oral commun, 1993), R.T. Bakker (oral communication, 1993), Filla and Redmond (1994)
Sauropoda: *Apatosaurus yahnahpin*
Ornithopoda: *Dryosaurus* sp.

WY-45 Zippy Quarry, Albany County, WY; J. Filla (oral communication, 1993)
Sauropoda: *Diplodocus*? sp.

WY-46 Reed's Quarry 13, Albany County, WY; Ostrom and McIntosh (1966), Norman and Weishampel (1990), K. Carpenter (oral communication, 1997), J.S. McIntosh (written communication, 1997)
Theropoda: *Coelurus fragilis*
Sauropoda: *Camarasaurus lentus, Diplodocus* sp.
Thyreophora: *Stegosaurus armatus, Stegosaurus ungulatus*
Ornithopoda: *Othnielia*? sp. or *Dryosaurus*? sp., *Camptosaurus dispar*

WY-47 E.P. Thompson's Quarry, Albany County, WY; R.T. Bakker (oral communication, 1993)
Sauropoda: *Diplodocus carnegii*
Thyreophora: *Stegosaurus* sp.
Ornithopoda: *Camptosaurus* sp.

GREYBULL-SHELL AREA

WY-61 Big Al Quarry, Big Horn County, WY; D. Maxwell (oral communication, 1992), R. Harmon (oral communication, 1993), Ver Ploeg (1991)
Theropoda: *Allosaurus* sp.
Sauropoda: *Diplodocus* sp.
Thyreophora: *Stegosaurus*(?) sp.

WY-62 Howe Quarry, Big Horn County, WY; Dodson and others (1980)

Theropoda: *Allosaurus* sp.
Sauropoda: *Camarasaurus* sp., *Diplodocus* sp., *Barosaurus* sp.
Ornithopoda: *Camptosaurus* sp.

WY-63 Little Butte Quarry (Smithsonian "Quarry 2"), Big Horn County, WY; M. Brett- Surman (oral communication, 1997)
Sauropoda: *Barosaurus*? sp. or *Diplodocus*? sp.

WY-64 Big Butte Quarry (Smithsonian "Quarry 4"), Big Horn County, WY; M. Brett- Surman (oral communication, 1997)
Sauropoda: *Apatosaurus*? sp.
Thyreophora: *Stegosaurus* sp.

KAYCEE

WY-71 Poison Creek (Erickson) Quarry, Johnson County, WY; B.R. Erickson (written communication, 1994), J.R. Foster (written communication, 1997)
Theropoda: *Allosaurus* sp., *Elaphrosaurus* sp.
Sauropoda: *Haplocanthosaurus* sp., *Camarasaurus* sp., *Diplodocus* sp., diplodocid genus and species undetermined, *Barosaurus*(?) sp., *Apatosaurus* sp.
Thyreophora: *Stegosaurus* sp.
Ornithopoda: *Camptosaurus* sp.

WY-72 Poison Creek (Flynn) Quarry-1, Johnson County, WY; J.R. Foster (written communication, 1997)
Theropoda: *Allosaurus* sp.
Sauropoda: *Camarasaurus* sp., *Diplodocus* sp., *Apatosaurus* sp.
Thyreophora: ?*Stegosaurus* sp.

WY-73 Poison Creek (Flynn) Quarry-2, Johnson County, WY; J.R. Foster (written communication, 1997)
Theropoda: large theropod (huge tooth) possibly megalosaurid or large allosaur
Sauropoda: *Camarasaurus* sp.

WY-74 Poison Creek (Flynn) Quarry-3, Johnson County, WY; J.R. Foster (written communication, 1997)
Theropoda: *Allosaurus* sp.

MEDICINE BOW ANTICLINE (also called Flat Top Anticline)

WY-78 Bone Cabin Quarry, Albany County, WY; Shepard and others (1977), Dodson and others (1980), McIntosh (1981, 1990a), Paul (1988)
Theropoda: *Allosaurus fragilis*, *Ornitholestes hermanni*
Sauropoda: *Camarasaurus* sp., *Diplodocus* sp., *Apatosaurus excelsus*, "*Apatosaurus*" *minimus* "...a valid species, but not belonging to *Apatosaurus*" according to J.S. McIntosh (1997, written communication); also, McIntosh; 1990)
Thyreophora: *Stegosaurus stenops*
Ornithopoda: *Dryosaurus altus*, *Camptosaurus* sp.

WY-79 Bone Cabin Quarry-E (eastward extension of old Bone Cabin Quarry), Albany County, WY; Jeff Parker (oral communication, 1997), K. Carpenter (written communication, 1997)
Theropoda: *Allosaurus fragilis*
Sauropoda: *Brachiosaurus* sp., *Camarasaurus grandis*, *Diplodocus* sp., *Apatosaurus* sp.
Thyreophora: *Stegosaurus stenops*, ankylosaur new genus and new species (K. Carpenter, oral communication, 1997)
Ornithopoda: *Dryosaurus* sp., *Camptosaurus* sp.

WY-80 Jeff Parker's Quarry (near Stego 99 site), Albany County, WY; Jeff Parker (oral communication, 1992, 1997)
Theropoda: *Allosaurus* sp. (teeth)
Sauropoda: *Camarasaurus* sp.

WY-81 Pat McSherry's Quarry, Albany County, WY; R.T. Bakker (oral communication, 1992)
Sauropoda: *Camarasaurus* sp.

WY-82 Ninemile Hill Site, Carbon County, WY; R.T. Bakker (oral communication, 1992)
Ornithopoda: *Drinker* sp. (tooth)

WY-83 Meilyn Quarry, Carbon County, WY; C.J. Weege (written communication, 1997)
Theropoda: *Allosaurus* sp.
Thyreophora: *Stegosaurus* sp.

WY-84 Lynn Quarry, Carbon County, WY; C.J. Weege (written communication, 1997)
Theropoda: *Allosaurus* sp.
Sauropoda: *Camarasaurus* sp., *Diplodocus* sp.
Ornithopoda: *Drinker*? sp.

WY-85 Weege Boys Quarry, Carbon County, WY; C.J. Weege (written communication, 1997)
Thyreophora: *Stegosaurus* sp.

WY-86 Camarasaurus 1993 Quarry, Carbon County, WY; C.J. Weege (oral communication, 1997)
Sauropoda: *Camarasaurus* sp., *Diplodocus* sp., *Barosaurus*? sp.

SHEEP CREEK AREA

WY-91 AMNH Sheep Creek Quarry D, Albany County, WY; McIntosh (1981, 1990b), J.S. McIntosh (written communication, 1997)
Sauropoda: *Camarasaurus grandis*, *Diplodocus carnegii*, *Apatosaurus excelsus*
Thyreophora: *Stegosaurus ungulatus*

WY-92 Zane Quarries 1- 4, Albany County, WY; R.T. Bakker (oral communication, 1992, 1993, Bakker and others, 1992). The quarries are at four stratigraphic levels within a 16.5 ft (5.0 m) thick interval; a faunal list for the individual quarries was not available.
Theropoda: megalosaurid
Sauropoda: *Apatosaurus* sp., *Diplodocus* sp.
Thyreophora: *Stegosaurus* sp., nodosaur genus and species undetermined

THERMOPOLIS AREA

WY-98 BS (Beside Sauropod) Quarry, Hot Springs County, WY; Bjoraker and Naus (1996), C.A. Naus (written communication, 1997)
Theropoda: *Allosaurus* sp. (teeth)
Sauropoda: *Camarasaurus* sp., ?*Diplodocus* sp., ?*Apatosaurus* sp.

WY-99-102 RB (RoadBone) Quarries Hot Springs County, WY The name applies to the locality as well as to one of the producing stratigraphic levels. Bjoraker and Naus (1996), C.A. Naus (written communication, 1997)

WY-99 PL Site
Thyreophora: ?*Stegosaurus* sp.
Ornithopoda: ?*Camptosaurus* sp.

WY-100 AD Site
Sauropoda: ?*Diplodocus* sp.

WY-101 RB Site
Sauropoda: ?*Camarasaurus* sp.,

WY-102 TH Site
Sauropoda: ?*Diplodocus* sp.

STRATIGRAPHIC AND GEOGRAPHIC DISTRIBUTION OF FOSSILS IN THE UPPER PART OF THE UPPER JURASSIC MORRISON FORMATION OF THE ROCKY MOUNTAIN REGION

George F. Engelmann
Department of Geography and Geology
University of Nebraska at Omaha
Omaha, NE 68182

ABSTRACT

A paleontological survey of the Morrison Formation in the vicinity of National Park Service units within the Rocky Mountain region has documented over 500 localities at which fossil material is exposed at the surface. Although taxonomic identifications are crude, the data provide quantitative information concerning the geographic and stratigraphic distribution of fossils in this unit, as well as information about the lithologies of the sites and nature of the occurrences.

INTRODUCTION

The Upper Jurassic Morrison Formation has long been well known as a source of abundant and diverse dinosaur fossils. It has also produced one of the richest mammal faunas of the Mesozoic. Less publicized, but equally impressive, are the other elements of a diverse biota that includes plant macrofossils, invertebrates, lower vertebrates, and trace fossils. The Morrison was deposited over a large geographic area from Canada to New Mexico and from Utah to Nebraska, and is well exposed in many areas around the Rocky Mountains.

A systematic paleontological survey of the Morrison Formation exposed within Dinosaur National Monument was conducted to characterize and assess the paleontological resources of this unit within the monument for use in resource management and paleoecological interpretation. All Morrison exposures within the monument were closely inspected for surface occurrences of fossils, and the location of each site found in this way, as well as localities known prior to the survey, was documented along with information about lithologic characteristics of the site, and stratigraphic position, as determined in cooperation with a study of the stratigraphy and sedimentology of the Morrison conducted by Christine Turner and Fred Peterson. Site documentation produced by this survey is archived at Dinosaur National Monument.

A further study of the Morrison Formation in other National Park Service units surveyed the formation in a similar manner, documenting the localities in the same way. Surveys conducted in these parks were not exhaustive, as at Dinosaur National Monument, but covered only a part of the outcrop present in the area. Portions of the Morrison exposures within the following parks were examined as part of this survey: Arches National Park, Capitol Reef National Park, and Glen Canyon National Recreation Area in Utah, Colorado National Monument in Colorado, and Bighorn Canyon National Recreation Area in Wyoming (figure 1). As with Dinosaur National Monument, the locality data collected are deposited in the records of the individual National Park Service units involved.

Most of the localities documented occurred in or around the National Park Service units within the Colorado Plateau, Dinosaur National Monument, Colorado National Monument, Arches National Park, and Capitol Reef National Park, and most of those were at Dinosaur National Monument, which was the most intensively surveyed.

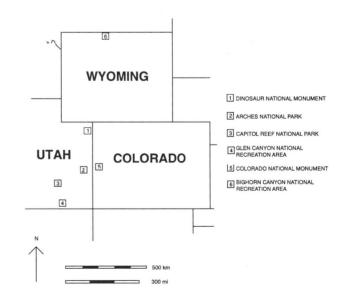

Figure 1. *National Park Service units with Morrison Formation exposures included in this survey.*

LOCALITY RECOGNITION

We documented 573 localities by these surveys. The sites recorded were not localities in the same sense that the term is often applied, as a site where collections were made. Rather, collection of specimens during the survey was minimal, and was only done to preserve specimens at risk in the field. Specimens were collected at some sites at a later date, and may be collected from others of the sites in the future, but there is no immediate plan to sample many of the sites. Localities were designated for any occurrence of fossil material at the surface where the fossils could be observed to be, or inferred to be in situ at the site. Thus, fossil material at a locality may consist of anything from bone fragments to a complete skeleton, and from plant material to trace fossils.

The criteria used to recognize localities were broadly inclusive. Any site at which one or more fossil specimens could be observed in situ in the rock was considered a locality. Where exposures were poor, as where thick soils were developed, this determination was not always obvious. If the fossil(s) continued beneath the surface, into the soil, as determined by shallow excavation or probing, it was regarded as being in place. Even fragmentary material occurring on the surface that could not be observed in place was designated as a locality if the fragments were sufficiently abundant and concentrated to imply a very localized source. In this way, even specimens that had been degraded beyond collectibility by erosion or other processes were documented. As a rule, isolated fossils occurring only on the surface, apparently as float, were not regarded as indicative of a locality at that spot. Fossil quarries and previously known localities where collections have been made and that are well documented were not included in the survey.

For the most part, localities represent the occurrence of a single or multiple specimens within a very localized area (usually several square meters or less) easily distinguished from the next nearest locality. In a small number of cases, fossils occurred throughout a distinguishable horizon over a distance of several meters or more. In such cases, a single locality was designated for the horizon, within a given area of exposures. Trace fossils are particularly likely to occur within localities recognized in this way, and so might be considered to be under-represented in terms of raw numbers. However, in the case of trace fossils, the pattern of their distribution is more informative than simple abundance.

As noted above, the primary objective of this study was not collection of fossils discovered, but documentation of localities. Consequently, extensive excavations were not conducted, in part because of time constraints,

and in part because further exposure of specimens left in the field would increase the risk of their destruction by the elements or by other means. Some shallow excavations, limited to what might be accomplished during a single visit to the site, were conducted to gather more information about the nature and extent of the occurrences. In addition, some shallow excavations or trenches were dug to expose unweathered rock even in the absence of any surface indication of the presence of fossils. This strategy was directed primarily to certain facies within the mudstones, and was adopted because experience has shown that, in these facies, some fossils, especially small vertebrates, do not survive the weathering process and provide no surface indication of their presence. A number of microvertebrate localities in the Morrison have been discovered by blind excavations carried out for other purposes (for example, to expose unweathered rock to aid in the description of a measured stratigraphic section).

STRATIGRAPHIC FRAMEWORK

Most of the areas surveyed are located in and around the Colorado Plateau, and the members that comprise the Morrison Formation in this area can be recognized throughout the region. In this we followed the stratigraphic interpretation of Turner and Peterson (1996). The units that were recognized are: the Windy Hill, Tidwell, Salt Wash, and Brushy Basin. We have found that, in most cases, one can recognize whether one is in the lower, middle, or upper part of the Salt Wash Member and have reported the stratigraphic position of localities in terms of these informal units. The distinction between the basal red beds and the upper mudstones of the Brushy Basin discussed by Peterson and Turner-Peterson (1987) could be recognized as well, and were differentiated as lower and upper Brushy Basin in locality data. In addition, distinctive facies in the uppermost part of the upper Brushy Basin made it further divisible into lower and upper parts. Although all of the units listed above were surveyed in this study, no localities could be reliably attributed to the Windy Hill and Tidwell Members of the Morrison. Away from the Colorado Plateau, the Morrison is undifferentiated, and for this study, the position within the formation of localities there must be estimated in terms of the members listed above.

FOSSILS

Fossils found during the survey were commonly quite fragmentary, and even where more complete specimens were or may be present, the fact that they were not collected nor even completely exposed means that identifications were only very rough and at high taxonomic levels for the most part. Fossils from some localities are being studied now, and others will provide collections for study in the future. However, for our purposes, crude classification of the fossils can provide some useful information (figure 2).

Dinosaur Fossils

The observation that dinosaur bone is sufficiently abundant to be used as an indicator fossil for the Morrison Formation is supported by this survey. Dinosaur bone is the most common fossil in the Morrison, occurring at 353 (62%) of the localities. It is not only the most common fossil overall, but also the most common fossil within each of the study areas. Of course, not all of these sites represent well-preserved specimens. At 164 of the localities only fragments of dinosaur bone were observed on the surface. Some of these could lead to more complete specimens, but many could, and probably do, mark only fragmentary remains. At 30 other sites bone fragments were observed in situ in the rock where they were little more than bone pebbles. On the other hand, 126 sites had at least one reasonably complete bone, and 27 more had definite evidence of more than one bone. Good evidence of partial or complete dinosaur skeletons was observed at six localities. This includes one site that produced a complete, articulated theropod. Most of the specimens that could be identified more specifically than dinosaur bone were certainly or probably sauropod bones.

Dinosaur bones were found in all stratigraphic intervals of the Salt Wash and Brushy Basin Members. However, most of these occurred from the middle part of the Salt Wash through the lower part of the upper Brushy Basin. This includes all of the sites where partial skeletons were found. Dinosaurs were particularly scarce in the lower Salt Wash where only eight localities were found. Dinosaur bone occurrences of all degrees of completeness are most abundant in the middle (86 sites) and upper (96 sites) parts of the Salt Wash, and the lower part of the upper Brushy Basin (75 sites). The number of dinosaur bone localities within the uppermost Brushy Basin (38 sites) was comparable to the number in the lower Brushy Basin (32 sites).

Other Vertebrates

Small bone that could represent non-dinosaurian vertebrates was found at 56 sites (about 10% of the locali-

	Upper Brushy Basin: upper	Upper Brushy Basin: lower	Lower Brushy Basin	Upper Salt Wash	Middle Salt Wash	Lower Salt Wash
Dinosaur fossils:						
Bone	11	13	12	43	36	5
Bones	3	12	1	4	5	
Fragments *in situ*	4	5	4	12	4	
Fragments	20	43	14	35	39	3
Skeleton		2	1	2	2	
Small vertebrates:						
Mammal		3				
Crocodilian		5			1	1
Turtle	2	8			5	
Lungfish			1	1	1	
unidentified	5	12	1		5	1
Invertebrate:						
Gastropod	2	6			6	
Unionid clam	1	5			12	
Plant fossils						
Silicified log		5		10	8	11
Silicified wood		15		12	30	17
Other		2	1			
Trace fossils:						
Dinosaur track			1	2	2	
Scoyenia		1	2	1	3	
Termite nest			4	6	2	
Ant nest		1	2	1		
Vertical burrows	1	2	5	4	3	
Invertebrate traces	1	1	2	3	4	
Rhizocretions		3	2			1

Figure 2. *Stratigraphic distribution of localities within National Park Service units as documented by this survey. Localities are listed for the Salt Wash and Brushy Basin Members according to the type of fossil material present.*

ties). At 24 of these sites, little could be said of the fragmentary specimens beyond that they represented small vertebrates, possibly including small dinosaurs. But, fragments identifiable as turtle were present at 16 sites, crocodilian at eight, and lungfish at three. Mammal fossils were found at five of the sites documented, although these sites were recognized because of the presence of other material at the surface, or by excavation for other purposes. Mammal remains were never found at the surface.

Most of the small vertebrate sites (28), including all of those at which mammals occurred, were within the lower part of the upper Brushy Basin. The next greatest number of such sites was within the middle Salt Wash (12), with much fewer in other parts of the Salt Wash and Brushy Basin.

Invertebrates

Gastropods were found at 16 sites and unionid pelecypods at 19. At the localities where they were found, specimens of these mollusks were usually abundant, although laterally restricted to a relatively small area. These localities occurred only within the upper Brushy Basin, both upper and lower parts, and the middle Salt Wash. The greatest number of unionid clam localities was found in the vicinity of Colorado National Monument in the middle Salt Wash. The middle Salt Wash in this area is dominated by fine, shaly sediments which appear to represent conditions favorable to the preservation of these invertebrates (see the discussion of lithology below).

Plant Fossils

After dinosaurs, the most common fossil in the Morrison was silicified wood, which occurred at 113 of the localities. Most of these sites were recognized by concentrations of fragments, but at 35 of them, the specimens were segments of logs. Some of the logs were quite large, as much as a meter or more in diameter, but usually not more than a few meters long, although one specimen was more than 20 meters in length. Coalified wood was found at only six sites. A very small number of sites (only three) included smaller plant structures preserved by silicification. There were small twigs and seeds and one well-preserved cone.

Silicified wood and logs occurred in the lower part of the upper Brushy Basin (22 sites) and throughout the Salt Wash (88 sites). Fossil wood was most common in the Salt Wash, especially in the lower and middle parts of the unit. But, the preservation typical of the wood found in the Salt Wash was poor, with light-colored silica preserving little of the internal structure of the wood. Although less common, wood found in the lower part of the upper Brushy Basin was often replaced by fine-grained, dark silica that preserved fine details of the cell structure.

Trace Fossils

A variety of invertebrate and vertebrate trace fossils were observed (see also Hasiotis and Demko, 1996). *Scoyenia* and similar feeding trails on bedding planes were found at seven localities. More common were burrows of diverse morphology. As noted above, in many cases the localities documented for such traces indicate horizons within the area of exposures rather than a single, localized occurrence. Perhaps the most common trace fossils were vertical burrows approximately 1 centimeter in diameter that were probably produced by some kind of insect. These burrows sometimes penetrated the entire thickness of small, red-weathering, cross-bedded sandstones less than 1 m in thickness, but often were only apparent as abundant holes on the upper or lower surfaces of such sandstones, which were thoroughly bioturbated so that no structure was preserved within the bed. Eighteen such localities were recorded.

Termite nests were present at 12 localities, some of which indicate a horizon rather than a single specimen. These nests occurred as vertical burrows 10 centimeters or more in diameter with irregular walls indicating a structure of smaller anastamosing burrows. At one locality in Glen Canyon National Recreation Area, the nests had been preserved by preferential cementation, so that they appeared as cylindrical concretions about 20 centimeters in diameter that stood 30-40 centimeters in relief above an erosional surface developed on a massive sandstone.

Crayfish burrows and ant nests were found at a small number of sites (four each). At 18 other sites, invertebrate traces were observed that could not be confidently assigned to any of the types described above. This includes possible insect pupae and subvertical structures that may be variants or poorly preserved specimens of the vertical burrows described above, or may represent something different.

Finally, sauropod tracks preserved as sole marks on sandstones overlying mudstones were observed at five localities (see Engelmann and Hasiotis, this volume). Rhizocretions were observed at six sites.

There is a definite tendency for trace fossil horizons to be concentrated at certain stratigraphic levels. Specifically, most of the trace fossil sites documented occurred in the lower Brushy Basin (18 sites) or the upper part of the Salt Wash (17 sites), with somewhat fewer sites (14) in the middle part of the Salt Wash. Eight sites were identified in the lower part of the upper Brushy Basin, and only two in the upper part, and only one rhizocretion locality was found in the lower part of the Salt Wash.

Termite nests plainly show this stratigraphic distribution, with four sites in the lower Brushy Basin, six in the upper part of the Salt Wash, only two in the middle Salt Wash, and none at higher or lower levels.

LITHOLOGY

Fossils occurred within the three common lithologies of the Morrison: sandstones, mudstones, and carbonates. Of these, however, occurrences were overwhelmingly more common in the sandstones, 423 localities. Only 109 localities were found in mudstones, and only 22 in carbonates. This is undoubtedly because the most common fossils, dinosaur bone and silicified wood, were much more likely to occur within sandstones than other lithologies. This even appeared to be the case in sections dominated by the mudstones, where the fossils would occur within thin sands or sandy layers. No simple explanation for this is immediately apparent. It may reflect a preservational bias, with bone and wood being more likely to be buried and preserved by an environment in which sand was being deposited. Or, it may be that the biota was more abundant in environments where sands accumulated.

On the other hand, most of the small vertebrate sites, including all of the fossil mammal localities, occurred within mudstones, as did most of the unionid clam localities. As noted above, the small vertebrate localities were virtually confined to the mudstone-dominated upper Brushy Basin, while the unionids were common in the middle shaly unit of the Salt Wash at Colorado National Monument. The former situation probably is best explained as a preservational bias created by the poor survival of small bones in moderately or highly energetic environments, while the latter may be the result of the presence, at that time and place, of the wetter environmental conditions needed by these organisms.

The small number of localities found in carbonates include many of the gastropod sites. The wet conditions needed to produce these sediments were undoubtedly a key factor in determining the presence of these invertebrates.

CONCLUSIONS

Although the results of this survey have been presented in a very generalized manner, it should be remembered that they are the result of a survey of selected areas that represent only a small fraction of the vast expanse of Morrison outcrop. The Morrison may be locally unfossiliferous or unusually rich in fossils in any part of the section at any particular location. As is characteristic

for terrestrial depositional environments, fossils are not uniformly distributed throughout the unit. Nevertheless, the sample areas are widely separated, and may provide some indication of a general pattern. The diverse fossil biota of the Morrison Formation is geographically widespread within the formation and is found throughout the Salt Wash and Brushy Basin Members and their lateral equivalents. The most common fossils by far are dinosaur bone and silicified wood. This may reflect the long survival of such materials when subjected to exposure and transport prior to burial, as compared to other elements of the biota. These fossils occur primarily within sandstones, although they were also found in mudstones. It is interesting to note that evidence of dinosaurs is as abundant in the Salt Wash as in the Brushy Basin, although many of the historic dinosaur quarries have been found in the Brushy Basin or the equivalent part of the section.

Small vertebrates, on the other hand, were found most often in mudstones and were most common in the upper Brushy Basin, and this was the case exclusively, for the fossil mammals. Gastropods and pelecypods exhibit a similar distribution, although possibly for different reasons.

A diverse fauna of trace fossils, some of which can be identified with specific organisms, such as termite nests, occurs in the Morrison. The traces are concentrated within a fairly narrow stratigraphic interval, being most common within the lower Brushy Basin and the uppermost Salt Wash.

Further analysis of these data, together with information from historic fossil localities in the Morrison, and stratigraphic, sedimentologic, and other types of information may help constrain models of the paleoenvironment of the Morrison Formation.

ACKNOWLEDGMENTS

These projects were supported by grants from the University of Wyoming - National Park Service Research Center and the National Park Service. In addition, the cooperation and help provided by National Park Service employees at the parks visited was invaluable. Capable field assistants, Earendil Engelmann, Tom Fowler, Jeff Honke, and Larry Bradley, were responsible for much of the data collection. Colleagues working on the Morrison Ecosystem Project have exchanged information freely making field work more efficient and aiding in analysis of the results. In particular, Dan Chure, Tim Demko, Stephen Hasiotis, Fred Peterson, and Christine Turner have contributed immeasurably to the work summarized here.

REFERENCES

Engelmann, G.F., and Hasiotis, S.T., Deep dinosaur tracks in the Morrison - sole marks that are really sole marks, *in* Gillette, D.D., editor, this volume.

Hasiotis., S. T., and Demko, T. M., 1996, Terrestrial and freshwater trace fossils, Upper Jurassic Morrison Formation, Colorado Plateau, *in* Morales, Michael, editor, The continental Jurassic: Museum of Northern Arizona Bulletin 60, p. 355-370.

Peterson, Fred and Turner-Peterson, C. E., 1987. The Morrison Formation of the Colorado Plateau - recent advances in sedimentology, stratigraphy, and paleotectonics: Hunteria, v. 2, no. 1, 18 p.

Turner, Christine, and Peterson, Fred, 1996, Morrison ecosystem project, *in* Harlow, H. J. and Harlow, M. A., editors, 18th Annual Report 1994: University of Wyoming-National Park Service Research Center, p. 152-155.

TAPHONOMY OF THE CLEVELAND-LLOYD DINOSAUR QUARRY IN THE MORRISON FORMATION, CENTRAL UTAH - A LETHAL SPRING-FED POND

Sue Ann Bilbey
Utah Field House of Natural History State Park
235 East Main
Vernal, Utah 84078

ABSTRACT

The Cleveland-Lloyd Dinosaur Quarry is a paleontologically important but extremely perplexing dinosaur site. It is located in the Upper Jurassic Brushy Basin Member of the Morrison Formation of central Utah. It was a predator trap, as is evident from the individuals represented--an abundance of *Allosaurus* with few herbivores. Numerous hypotheses have been proposed to explain the death assemblage at this site.

Dinosaur bones at the quarry are in a severely disturbed calcareous mudstone directly below a lacustrine micritic limestone, the Cleveland-Lloyd lentil. Petrologic analyses and descriptions of four cores that penetrate the fossil-bearing layer suggest the dinosaur bones accumulated in a spring-fed pond or seep. There is some evidence for periodic flooding of undisturbed deposits in core A-7, but reworking by dinoturbation or spring flow in the calcareous muds has obscured those events in the quarry horizon. The disarticulation of the skeletons, the occurrence of a single, fairly well-preserved dinosaur egg, and the presence of calcareous mudstone nodules imply that the animals sank into the volcanic ash-rich mud before scavenging could take place. Subsequent disruption of the mud and disarticulation of the skeletons occurred as a result of (1) up-welling water circulating through volcanic ash, and (2) the struggling of newly trapped animals as they attempted to free themselves from the mud.

INTRODUCTION

The Cleveland-Lloyd Dinosaur Quarry (CLQ) is located in the Upper Jurassic Brushy Basin Member of the Morrison Formation of central Utah (figure 1). It was a predator trap, as is evident from the species assemblage--an abundance of *Allosaurus* with few herbivores. It is the intent of this paper to review previously proposed hypotheses for the death assemblage, discuss the petrology of the rocks closely associated with the quarry and their depositional environments, and review the paragenetic processes involved in the lithification of the rocks and the preservation of the bones. A new hypothesis, a lethal spring-fed pond, is proposed for the origin of the fossil assemblage in the quarry with suggestions for further research.

The Cleveland-Lloyd Dinosaur Quarry, a United States Natural Landmark, is located approximately 13 km east of Cleveland, Emery County, Utah in the SE1/4 section 21 and NE 1/4 section 28, T. 17 S., R. 11 E., Salt Lake Base and Meridian, Latitude 39° 19' 26" North, Longitude 110° 41' 11" West (figure 1).

The Cleveland-Lloyd Dinosaur Quarry is on the north end of the San Rafael Swell, stratigraphically in the middle of the Brushy Basin Member of the Morrison Formation. Locally, the strata dip from 2° to 7° in a north to north 45° west direction. Ephemeral stream erosion has created dip slopes on resistant sandstone and limestone layers with associated cliffs, and gently to steeply sloping hillsides of claystone. Resistant rock detritus litters much of the poorly vegetated slopes of this desert region.

The Morrison Formation is a heterogeneous continental deposit of variegated claystone, limestone, and sandstone, recognized throughout an area of 1,500,000 km² of the western interior of the United States (Peterson, 1972). In the vicinity of the Cleveland-Lloyd Dinosaur Quarry, the formation rests, generally unconformably, on strata of the Middle Jurassic (lower Oxfordian) Summerville Formation. Disconformably overlying the Morrison in the San Rafael Swell is the Lower Cretaceous (Aptian) Cedar Mountain Formation.

The geology of the area, including the Cleveland-Lloyd Dinosaur Quarry, has been mapped by Condon and Miller (1955), Stokes and Cohenour (1956), and Witkind (1988). Miller and others (1996) compiled the quarry maps and reviewed the quarry activities since 1929.

METHODS

At the Cleveland-Lloyd Dinosaur Quarry, three partial sections were measured totaling 142 meters through the Morrison Formation. Unweathered samples were collected and described every 5 meters and at lithologic changes. Ingram's (1954) scale of stratigraphic thickness was used to delineate individual beds. In addition, four drill cores (A-1, B-1, A-4, A-7; figure 2) taken by the U. S. Bureau of Land Management (BLM) in the quarry

were described, and each lithologic change in the longest core was sampled and analyzed petrologically. Mineral suites were identified by X-ray diffraction analyses, and mineralogical relationships were determined petrograph-

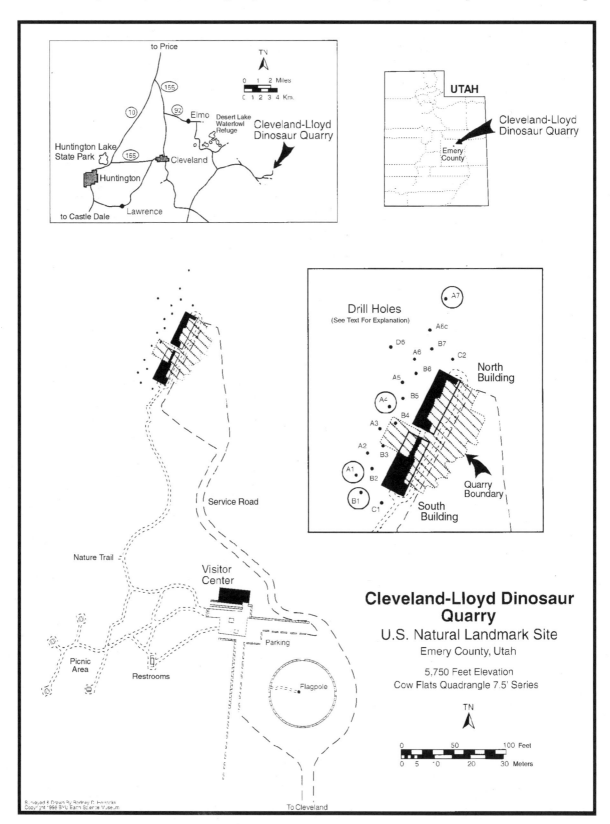

Figure 1. *Index map of the Cleveland-Lloyd Dinosaur Quarry, Emery County, Utah. Taken from Miller and others, 1996. Inset of the quarry area shows the positions of the BLM core sites. Analyzed cores are circled. Copyright 1995, Brigham Young University; used with permission.*

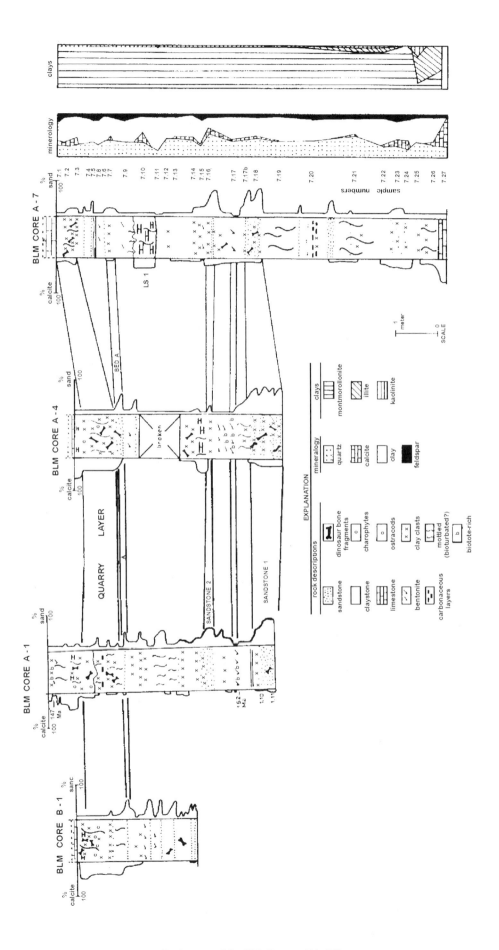

Figure 2. *Stratigraphic sections of BLM cores through the Cleveland-Lloyd Dinosaur Quarry. Correlation alignment was calculated relative to dip. Graphic representations are semi-quantitative analyses of powder and clay samples from Core A-7.*

ically and by scanning electron microscopy. Biotite samples from the volcaniclastic-rich clay layer one meter above the quarry capstone were dated by conventional K-Ar methods. More complete petrographic and petrologic descriptions of individual samples and their stratigraphic relationships are detailed in Bilbey (1992).

A Siemens Crystalloflex system with 750-watt, CU-target tube operate at 35 KV, 18 ma was used for X-ray diffraction analyses. The scan rate was 2°θ per minute. Powder samples were ground to >3.0θ by a SPEX Mixer/Ball Mill and a Fisher mortar-grinder. Clay samples were withdrawn at >0.0θ . and were separated by the use of Stokes' law of settling velocities (Folk, 1974). The 2-θm fraction was sedimented onto glass slides and scanned from 2° 2θ to 30° 2θ. These slides were then exposed to a saturated atmosphere of ethylene glycol and rescanned. Relative abundances of powdered minerals and clays were calculated following procedures developed by Schultz (1964), Biscaye (1965), and Brindley and Brown (1980).

CLEVELAND-LLOYD DINOSAUR QUARRY

Historical Overview

The discovery date of dinosaur bones at the quarry is unknown, but records show the area was worked as early as 1927 by F. F. Hintze and Golden York of the Department of Geology at the University of Utah in Salt Lake City (Madsen, 1976). In 1939, W. L. Stokes led a group from Princeton University to the area to collect dinosaur bones. The group returned the two following summers with the financial aid of Malcolm Lloyd, Jr., of Philadelphia, for whom the quarry was subsequently named (Stokes, 1945). Work has continued intermittently under the auspices of the University of Utah and the Utah Division of State History, and in cooperation with Brigham Young University (Miller and others, 1996). In 1968, the quarry was declared a United States Natural Landmark, administered and protected by the United States Bureau of Land Management.

Dinosaurs and Other Fossils

According to Madsen (1976) and Miller and others (1996), only part of the large collection of vertebrate fossil specimens from the quarry has been identified and more remain to be found. Miller and others (1996) list genera identified so far, the majority of the 70 individuals being of the species *Allosaurus fragilis* (table 1) . Identifications of vertebrate fossils were made by Madsen (1976), Stokes (1985), and Miller and others (1996),

---

Table 1.
List of fossil genera from the Cleveland-Lloyd Dinosaur Quarry. Numerals indicate estimated number of individuals.

DINOSAURS
Carnivores
   Allosaurus - 44
   Torvosaurus - 1
   Ceratosaurus - 1
   Marshosaurus - 2
   Stokesosaurus - 2
   ?Ornitholoides - 1
Herbivores
   Camarasaurus - 5
   Haplocanthosaurus - 1
   Barosaurus -1
   ?Amphicoelius - 1
   ?Mongolosaurus - 1
   Unidentified sauropod - 1
   Camptosaurus - 5
   Stegosaurus - 5
   ?Ankylosaurid or Nodosaurid - 1
   Unidentified ornithopod - 1

OTHER PLANTS AND ANIMALS
Reptilia
   Goniopholis? (crocodile) - 1
   Glyptops (turtle) - 2?
Gastropoda (fresh water)
   Amplovalvata
   Valvata
   Viviparus
Charophyta (fresh water)
   Aclistochara bransoni
   Latochara concinna
   Latochara latitruncata
   Stellatochara obovata

---

invertebrates by Sohl and Hanley (*in* Madsen, 1976), and charophytes by Peck (*in* Madsen, 1976).

The distribution of more than 10,000 dinosaur bones in the quarry is distinctive: the larger bones lie nearly horizontal in the lower portion of the quarry layer; smaller bones are scattered higher in the clay, some protruding into the overlying limestone (Madsen, 1976). The bones are generally disarticulated, the elements from one identifiable individual being scattered over more than 60 m^2 (Madsen, 1976). The preservation of the bone is generally excellent. A few breaks in some fragile bones resemble "green" fractures, perhaps due to trampling (Madsen, 1976). A few eroded or abraded bones (loss of perichondral bone in regions of high relief) are thought to be evidence of minor predation or scavenging (Madsen, 1976).

Several exposures of weathered fossil bones occur near resistant limestone and sandstone beds in the lower portion of the Brushy Basin Member near the Cleveland-Lloyd Dinosaur Quarry. In the gully east of the quarry, a weathered dinosaur rib is exposed in a channel sandstone. Also, directly below the limestone that caps the quarry (here named the Cleveland-Lloyd lentil), fossil bone fragments are scattered over several square kilometers. One set of these fragments obviously represents cross section portions of a sauropod femur. Therefore dinosaur fossils below the lentil are not confined within the boundary of the Natural Landmark.

Age

A biotite-rich, smectitic claystone lies approximately 0.5 to 1.0 meters above the limestone that caps the quarry (figure 3). It is the remnant of a graded volcanic tuff containing clasts of euhedral biotite, sanidine crystals, and quartz in a ground mass of waxy, concoidally fracturing smectite. Two independent samples of biotite from this claystone bed gave K-Ar age estimates of 146.8 ± 1 Ma with 10.4% atmospheric argon and 147.2 ± 1 Ma with 12.1% atmospheric argon (Bilbey-Bowman and others, 1986; Bilbey, 1998). Another similar biotite-rich claystone was identified approximately 3 meters below the quarry. Biotite from this unit was sampled and dated at 152 Ma by K-Ar analysis (Obradovich *in* Kowallis and others, 1986).

Figure 3. Photograph from the upper portion of the Cleveland-Lloyd Dinosaur Quarry (CLQ) into the overlying limestone (LS) and biotite-rich claystone (TUFF). Rods are 1.5 meters long.

Sedimentary Petrology

Fine-Grained Rocks

The quarry layer, a calcareous smectitic claystone, is severely disrupted, with scattered flattened intraclasts, calcareous nodules, and dinosaur bones dispersed throughout. There are several sandy stringers, but they are not continuous among the cores. Six rock samples, three each from two sites, were analyzed by X-ray diffractometry. These sample sites are more than 30 meters apart, at approximately the same depth below the base of the capping limestone. Those samples taken from the horizon directly beneath the limestone are remarkably similar mineralogically, with a significant abundance of feldspar (each nearly 20%). Those samples analyzed from deeper in the quarry layer are more variable, although they are internally more similar to each other than they are to those immediately below the bone-bearing zone. The quartz content is fairly uniform, 22 to 36%. The calcite content of the claystone beds ranges from 8 to 18%. Concretions contain calcite, from 24% in the solitary nodule to 38% in the nodule attached to a dinosaur bone. Barite, although not abundant, occurs as radial needles in some concretions.

One sample of the quarry layer, a calcareous claystone, and one solitary concretion were studied petrographically. Both are sandy claystones whose detrital grains have a feldspathic litharenite composition. Floating grains comprise 27% and 34% of these samples, respectively. Smectite is the predominant clay, constituting approximately 44% of the nodule and 53% of the claystone. The smectite is partially matrix material and partially intraclast. Calcite is a major component of the matrix of the concretion, but is a minor component in the claystone. Whereas calcite in the concretion is largely authigenic, calcite in the claystone appears to be bioclastic as suggested by the abundance of charophyte oogonia and debris. Bone fragments were encountered in both samples. Euhedral biotite is fairly common, especially in claystone where it comprises 14% of the detrital grains. It is rarer in the concretion, comprising only 7% of the grains. The abundance of biotite in this claystone is similar to that seen in the dated volcaniclastic claystone which contain nearly 21%.

Smectite, with very minor amounts of kaolinite, is the primary constituent of the matrix in the fine-grained rocks below the quarry. In the claystones, smectite is as abundant as it is in the volcaniclastic rocks, although there is no aggregate polarization of the clays, suggesting either a fluvially dispersed ash or disruption after deposition.

Disseminated microcrystalline quartz derived from the alteration of volcanic ash to smectite constitutes a major part of the authigenic components of these fine-grained rocks. Calcite (micrite to spar) is rare in the non-quarry claystones. It probably is diagenetic, but some calcite may have been derived from organic calcareous algae or by the rotting of dinosaur flesh (Weeks, 1953; Berner, 1968). Micrite is dispersed throughout the concretions, and is much more abundant than in the claystones. Dispersed micrite also occurs in the concretion attached to the dinosaur bone, although it contains even more calcite. Some barite needles are present in this concretion. Dendritic patterns of hematite and pyrolusite stain some of the fine-grained rocks.

The fine-grained rocks sampled from the BLM cores below the quarry-capping limestone are all smectitic, ranging from waxy claystone (with few detrital grains) to mudstone, sandy claystone, and siltstone. Notable is the lack of fissility in these rocks, which grade one to another with few bedding planes. A few silty claystone beds near channel sandstones contain thin, coarsening-upward sequences that suggest crevasse-splay deposits.

Sandstone

The compositions of the sandstones of the Brushy Basin Member are diverse. According to the Folk (1974) sandstone classification, the mean sandstone for the Brushy Basin is a feldspathic litharenite. If one assumes that the smectite fraction is devitrified from sand-sized volcanic detritus, the classification changes to a litharenite. However, the precise origin of the interstitial clay is difficult to determine.

The sandstone units of the Brushy Basin Member are easily differentiated from those of contiguous units by the abundance of smectitic matrix (figure 4). If the clay matrix is detrital, the sandstone beds range from very poorly to poorly sorted, and from clayey to very fine-grained sandstone. Conversely, if the matrix is pseudomatrix (that is, smectite devitrified from sand-sized volcanic detritus), the original textural classifications are quite different--poorly to well-sorted, silty to medium-grained sandstone. Calcite cements most of the sandstone beds in the lower Brushy Basin Member, particularly the coarser, better sorted types like some of those directly below the quarry. The framework is 61% to 84% detrital grains, mean of 65.2%, with point and long-axis contacts in the lower beds and concavo-convex contacts in the uppermost beds. The clay fraction comprises 12% to 31% of these sandstones. The initial porosity may have been quite high, but devitrification of the volcanic

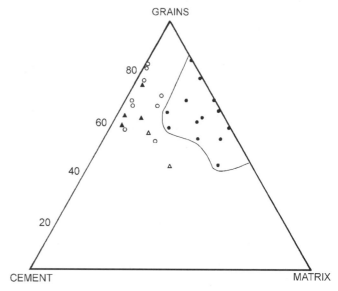

Figure 4. *Ternary diagram of sandstones in the Morrison and Cedar Mountain Formations showing percentages of grains, cement, and matrix. The line differentiates the Brushy Basin Member from the other units.*

ash, mechanical compaction, and infiltration have substantially reduced pore space to less than 5%.

The devitrification of volcanic ash to smectite was followed by precipitation of quartz overgrowths on quartz grains and microcrystalline quartz on the clay (figure 5). Subsequent cementation by calcite is seen as a progression from micrite to microspar and finally to spar.

Figure 5. *Scanning electron micrograph of a Brushy Basin sandstone, showing authigenic smectite (S) and quartz (Q) overgrowths. Bar length is 10 -μm.*

Carbonate Rocks

The texture of the Cleveland-Loyd lentil is similar to most of the other calcareous rocks in the Morrison Formation: a clayey micrite with scattered detrital grains (21%) and fossil fragments (figures 6 and 7). The grains range from medium silt to fine-grained sand, with a med-ian of 4 phi. They are generally subequant, subangular, and oriented randomly. There are coarse sand to pebble-size bone fragments through-out the lentil, with greater abundance near the top. Charophyte gyronites and ostracode carapaces are also common throughout (table 2). Calcite spar has replaced the original organic carbonate in these fossils.

At the quarry, the meter-thick lentil is remarkably homogeneous, as determined by XRD, with 52% to 56% calcite. Quartz comprises 16% to 21%, clay 13% to 23%, and feldspar 9% to 17%. Feldspar content is relatively high, comparable to the volcaniclastic beds. The clays are primarily smectite, with minor kaolinite. Compositionally this rock is classified as a slightly fossiliferous, muddy micrite.

The carbonate fraction of this rock is primarily micrite, with a few zones of recrystallized spar. Smec-tite is mixed with the micrite, suggesting that ash was mixed with carbonate ooze. A few small authigenic calcite nodules with radial barite crystals are found in CL200A. Some grains are replaced slightly by calcite. Chert and microcrystalline quartz in the limestone are detrital although some are authigenic.

Dinosaur Bones

The dinosaur bones found at the quarry, or weath-ering out in nearby gullies, are generally well pre-served, with much of their original microstructures

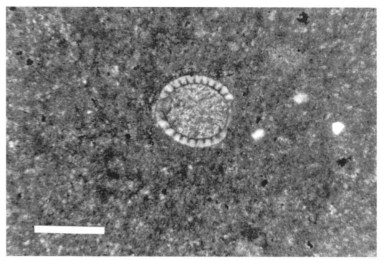

Figure 6. *Photomicrograph of the quarry capstone, a micrite. Note the rari-ty of detrital grains and the presence of a charophyte in the center of the image. Bar length is 0.2 mm.*

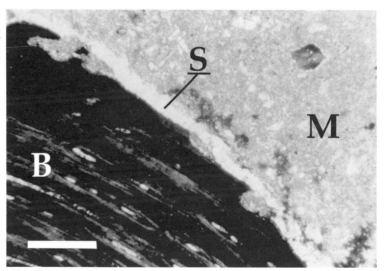

Figure 7. *Photomicrograph of the quarry micrite capstone (M) with includ-ed dinosaur bone (B). Note the abundance of spar (S) near the bone. Bar length is 0.5 mm.*

Table 2. *Fossil and carbonate data from the quarry bed and the capping limestone lentil. A 40 centimeter section of the Cleveland-Lloyd lentil was sampled and standard thin sections were cut sequentially. Each thin section was cut perpendicular to the bedding, approximately four centimeters apart. The arrangement of the 200 series reflects the stratigraphy of the specimens top (H) to bottom (A). Total occurrences in each thin section are noted. Calcium carbonate percentiles were determined from insoluble residue analyses from associated rock fragments.*

Sample Number	Bone Fragments "small" ≤ cse sand "large" ≥ pebble	Charophyta Oogonia	Ostracode Carapaces	Percent CaCO₃
200H-Capstone	8 small	2	2	52%
200G-Capstone	18 small	3	1	55%
200F-Capstone	13 small	2	0	55%
200E-Capstone	2 small	5	0	53%
200D-Capstone	4 small	0	0	56%
200C-Capstone	3 large	1	0	54%
200B-Capstone	4 large	2	0	53%
200A-Capstone	2 large	2	0	53%
37-Capstone - random sample	11 small	1	7	no data
207B - nodule on bone from quarry horizon	1 large	0	0	33%
203 - Free nodule from quarry horizon	2 small	1	0	20%

intact. The quarry bones are black and weather to gray.

Thin sections reveal finely laminated bone and numerous haversian canals filled with calcite spar (figure 7). The internal marrow cavities of most bones are completely filled by authigenic minerals, with no remaining bone structure. These cavities were filled like geodes, with initially small calcite crystals, followed by progressively larger calcite crystals and, subsequently, by large quartz crystals (figure 8). In some cases, amethyst and very small crystals of barite are also present. X-ray diffractometry suggests that Morrison Formation dinosaur fossil bone material is largely francolite (carbonate fluorapatite) with only minor amounts of dahlite (carbonate hydroxyapatite) (Hubert and others, 1996).

Figure 8. *Photograph of a dinosaur limb bone showing crystalline in-filling of calcite (C) then quartz (Q). Photo by James H. Madsen, Jr.*

Depositional Environments

Paleoenvironments of the Morrison Formation - Overview

The Upper Jurassic Morrison Formation was deposited in a variety of terrestrial environments including fluvial channel and overbank, lacustrine, and pedogenic. A detailed description of the depositional environments in the Morrison and associated formations at the Cleveland-Lloyd Dinosaur Quarry was elaborated by Bilbey (1992, 1998).

Dodson and others (1980) reviewed the paleoecology of the Morrison Formation with emphasis on the taphonomy of numerous dinosaur quarries. They identified four distinct facies consistent with a low-gradient alluvial complex: (1) "coarse clastic and sand-lens facies" - clearly fluvial, (2) "variegated mudstone facies" - soils, (3) "drab mudstone facies" - reducing environment with a high water table, and (4) "limestone-marl facies" - lake deposits.

Other distinctive minor facies include: (1) eolianites (Mook, 1916; Stokes, 1944; Peterson, 1972; Peterson and Turner-Peterson, 1986; 1987), (2) relatively pure volcanic ash deposits now devitrified to smectite (Stokes, 1944, 1945; Armstrong and Suppe, 1973; Kowallis and others, 1986), (3) alkaline lake deposits typified by bedded magadiite-type chert deposits (Surdam and others, 1972; Dodson and others, 1980), and (4) a playa lake complex defined by concentric zones of authigenic alkaline minerals in volcanic ash (Bell, 1983, 1986; Peterson and Turner-Peterson, 1986; Turner and Fishman, 1991).

Cleveland-Lloyd Dinosaur Quarry

The rock sequence in the BLM cores and in the immediate vicinity of the Cleveland-Lloyd Dinosaur Quarry is interpreted as an aggrading fluvial sequence, consisting primarily of smectitic claystone with and without interstitial calcite, minor mudstone, siltstone, sandstone, and limestone (figure 2). Locally exposed are lenticular, clayey sandstones that interfinger with greenish-gray smectitic claystone. These sandstones show characteristics of a rapidly aggrading, volcanic-ash choked, fluvial system.

A total of 4.4 meters of noncalcareous smectitic floodplain deposits overlie these fluvial sandstone beds between the last channel sandstone and the quarry layer. An intermediate calcareous horizon (figure 2, LS-1) in core A-7 appears to be proximal to the sandy sequence in A-4, but it is not directly underlain by channel deposits. Lacustrine calcareous claystone beds are adjacent to, but do not directly overlie, channel deposits suggesting flood-basin ponds.

Interspersed in the smectitic mudstone units are thin lenticular beds of fine-grained sandstone with numerous clay intraclasts. This sequence is interpreted as distal crevasse-splay deposits. The clay clasts are mostly well rounded; some are flattened by compression. One such deposit occurs near the base of the dinosaur bone-bearing layer in all cores except A-7 (bed A; figure 2). In A-7, a correlative sandy layer is 65 cm below the anomalously thin bone-bearing bed.

Below the bone-bearing layer in core A-7, but correlative with the bone-bearing layer in other cores, is a sequence of noncalcareous, light olive-gray, blocky smectitic claystone with disseminated silt and sand. There are also several very thin sandy lenses; a fissile, moderately yellowish-brown, feldspar-rich claystone; and a feldspar-rich, smectitic, blocky, gray claystone (figure 2). These units suggest deposition in a reducing environment with a high water table in the vicinity of core A-7. However, there may have been at least one period of sub-aerial exposure, for example, the moderately yellowish-brown claystone. There is no evidence for catastrophic flooding recorded in the cores, instead there are only minor pulses of distal crevasse-splay deposition below the quarry horizon, typical of streams with variable discharge.

The quarry horizon appears to be lenticular, ranging in thickness in excavated areas from 1.5 to 0.3 meters in core A-7. The bone-bearing layer is readily identifiable in the BLM cores and in the quarry by the common occurrence of the capping clayey limestone, ubiquitous disseminated calcite in a ground mass of smectite, scattered complete bone and bone fragments, scattered flattened clay intraclasts, and calcite nodules. Maps of the distribution of disarticulated dinosaur bone show larger elements lying near the base of the quarry layer and the smaller bones and fragments disseminated throughout the layer (Miller and others, 1996). This implies density stratification. There is only minor evidence of scavenging. The relatively fresh appearance of the bone (Madsen, 1976) also suggests they were not exposed to surface weathering for extended periods of time, as discussed by Behrensmeyer (1978) and Hill and Behrensmeyer (1984).

Numerous calcareous nodules are attached to many of the bones implying that they retained attached ligaments, cartilage and, perhaps, muscles because calcite concretions commonly form in the vicinity of decomposing organic matter (Weeks, 1953; Berner, 1968). A localized high pH concentration can be generated in a reducing environment, causing the precipitation of calcium soaps (for example, adipocere) that subsequently convert to calcite (Berner, 1968). Decay of the marrow, with subsequent deposition of calcite, may account for the geode-like appearance of many bones. Later, ground water rich in silica chemically released during devitrification of the volcanic ash to smectite penetrated the bones, partially to completely filling remaining vugs with quartz, some of the amethystene variety.

The charophytes, ostracodes, fresh-water gastropods, and ubiquitous calcite in the quarry horizon imply the presence of a fresh-water lake or swamp for a significant period of time. This inference is also suggested by the possible shoreline deposits in core A-7. Two previous periods of lacustrine deposition are preserved in clayey clast-rich, calcareous lenses (Core A-7, figure 5).

The quarry is overlain by the lentil, a bed of massive, homogeneous, clayey micrite which contains tiny fragments of dinosaur bones, charophyte oogonia, and ostracode carapaces. As seen in the quarry and in many pho-

tographs of previous stages of excavation, there is an abrupt, undulatory transition between the bone-bearing claystone and the overlying limestone.

Two rock samples from directly below the limestone/mudstone contact, and 30 meters apart, are similar mineralogically. Particularly important is the abundant feldspar, which comprises nearly 20% of the two samples--an abundance similar to nearby volcaniclastic beds. In addition, the uppermost portion of the limestone contains comparable quantities of feldspar. The sharp upper contact of the limestone is easily identified in the extensive dip slopes. The limestone is overlain by an extensive layer of volcanic ash that may have filled in the lake basin.

Diagenesis

Diagenetic processes are placed into a format of clastic diagenesis as defined by Burley and others (1985), namely: (1) eogenesis--the depositional or geochemical environment, (2) mesogenesis--burial processes, and (3) telogenesis--weathering or other processes related to surface conditions. Table 3 shows the paragenetic sequence for the sandstone and siltstones of the quarry.

Table 3. *Paragenetic sequences of sandstone and calcareous siltstone (meandering streams) near the Cleveland-Lloyd Dinosaur Quarry. Numbers indicate a chronologic sequence of diagenetic events.*

Eogenesis
1. Formation of calcium soaps associated with bones.

Late Eogenesis - Early Mesogenesis
2. Devitrification of volcanic ash to smectite.
3. Authigenic quartz (overgrowths and interstitial pore filling).

Mesogenesis
4. Minor illite alteration of smectite.
5a. Calcite cementation in interstitial pore space.
5b. Calcite alteration of feldspar.

Telogenesis
6a. "Vertisol" formation as rock is reexposed to surface weathering
6b. Oxidation of iron-bearing minerals to hematite and localized staining along fractures.

The vertical increase in volcaniclastic debris in the Brushy Basin Member accounts for the overwhelming abundance of smectite, for the subsequent quartz overgrowths, and for the disseminated microcrystalline quartz. Quartz grains in the clayey sandstones have minor quartz overgrowths. Calcite cement filled pore spaces not completely filled with clay.

In the calcareous fine-grained rocks, calcite is derived primarily from calcareous algae, for example, charophytes, that were abundant in Jurassic lakes. Eogenetic formation of calcite concretions associated with dinosaur bone is attributed to the anaerobic decay of flesh, which created a highly alkaline environment conducive to the formation of calcium soaps (for example, adipocere) that later converted to micrite (Weeks, 1953; Berner, 1968). Anaerobic bacteria may have destroyed the marrow, increasing space for subsequent calcite deposition. Quartz crystals filled or partially filled any remaining marrow cavities.

The claystone units appear to have been altered as telogenetic vertisols, a soil characterized by swelling smectitic clays, slickensides, and clastic dikes (Retallack, 1988). The slickenside fractures are mostly filled with gypsum, limonite, and pyrolucite, probably precipitated from cation-rich meteoric waters in the modern arid climate.

DISCUSSION

Review of Paleoenvironmental Interpretations for the Quarry

A number of paleontologists and sedimentologists have interpreted the paleoenvironment for the death assemblage at the quarry. Stokes (1945) was the first to publish paleontological information and a brief petrologic description of the quarry and the rocks immediately above the capping limestone. He described the disarticulated bones as occurring in a calcareous mudstone capped by a lacustrine limestone bed:

> Characteristics of the enclosing sediments and the condition of the bones suggest that the dinosaurs died on the bed of an evaporating pond or lake and that the remains of animals already dead were trampled and disarranged by other dinosaurs in scavenging activities in efforts to reach the last shallow pools of water....overlying the bone bed is a 3- to 4-foot layer of almost pure bentonite...heavy fall of volcanic ash which could choke and absorb streams of water, overwhelm vegetation and cause widespread destruction. Volcanic activity may have contributed to the death of the dinosaurs... (Stokes, 1945, p. 116).

There is little evidence for scavenging (mastication) or trampling (green breaks) of the bones. The quarry horizon lacks evaporite minerals and shrinkage cracks; the overlying micritic limestone implies the presence of a lake. The volcanic ash layer is above the Cleveland-Lloyd lentil limestone and almost certainly ended the lake. The dinosaurs were already encased in the quarry muds before the ashes fell.

As a result of the Cooperative Dinosaur Project at the University of Utah, Madsen (1976) published a monograph on the most abundant species in the quarry,

Allosaurus fragilis. He briefly described the death assemblage at the quarry, noting the association of some bones with various types of matrix and the arrangements of disarticulated bones and bone fragments. A few bones were masticated or ingested by scavengers or predators. Of particular importance is the presence of a disproportionately large number of specimens of carnivorous dinosaurs (>50 theropods) compared to a much smaller number of herbivores (5 sauropods and 11 ornithischians) (Madsen and Stokes, 1972). Madsen (1976) also noted the infrequent occurrence of freshwater mollusks and algae including charophytes. He suggested freshwater deposition of the mudstone and overlying limestone, but did not infer the depositional environment of the quarry layer:

> Although the scattering appears random, most elements with a significantly long dimension tend to be oriented in a horizontal or nearly horizontal plane relative to bedding, which indicates that perhaps disassociation of skeletons took place prior to their subsequent burial on a relatively flat substratum... (Madsen, 1976, p. 6 and 7).

Madsen's main inference was freshwater deposition of the sediments. Disassociation of the bones prior to burial might imply a period of surface exposure, which is not likely considering the pristine condition of most bones. The horizontal arrangement of the long bones might suggest flowing water or just resting on a flat surface. Otherwise they are randomly oriented in plan view, which rules out deposition by a flood event.

Dodson and others (1980) compared the depositional environment of the Morrison Formation at the quarry to other Morrison sites in the western United States. They described the quarry facies as limestone and calcareous mudstone, intercalated with facies of drab mudstone. In addition they reported the occurrence of stringers of gravelly sandstone in the mudstone. Their conclusion, based on their work and analysis of Madsen's data, was that the quarry is a "predator trap," or bog formed by an ox-bow lake.

Fluvial sandstones lie more than 4.4 meters below the quarry horizon and none is seen laterally. Although there are stringers of sandstone and silty claystone in the cores, most are well below the quarry. Centimeter-scale sandstones occur in the quarry, but they are not continuous among the cores. Rip-up clasts appear to be randomly distributed, except for a small layer of them near the bottom of the quarry horizon (Bed A, figure 2), or several centimeters below it in core A-7, suggesting a short interval of crevasse-splay deposition prior to the main depositional phase of the quarry horizon. None of this evidence uniquely identifies an ox-bow lake.

Stokes (1985) revised his thinking regarding the deposition of the quarry:

> Since the bones are not distributed in distinct layers, are not spread very widely, and show little evidence of having been exposed on the surface, I conclude that the dinosaurs sank into the sediment so that it enclosed them rather than being deposited on top of them. Any naturally water-saturated area where a heavy object such as a large animal may sink below the surface is by definition a bog. In my opinion the Cleveland-Lloyd site represents a prehistoric bog into which dinosaurs sank on an individual basis over a considerable period of time....as the bodies inevitably decayed, the bones were released and dispersed by the internal movement or 'working' of the bog...They slowly bubble and boil due to the circulation of water rising into them. (Stokes, 1985, p. 6)

This hypothesis was not completely developed. An upwards decrease in size of the bones suggests circulation within the muds, which is consistent with this hypothesis. Larger bones are near the bottom, smaller ones like phalanges are near the middle, and even smaller bone fragments are in the overlying limestone. However, what is the source of the water? Mudstones lateral to the quarry do not contain ground-water calcite, and yellow-stained beds contain mud cracks, suggesting exposure around a local wet area.

Hunt (1986) proposed two possible origins for the accumulation of the bones:

> A "miring" origin is suggested by the abundance of carnivore remains and the presence of complete disarticulated skeletons preserving delicate elements. A "catastrophic" origin is suggested by intraformational rip-up clasts in the bone bed, the sheet geometry of the deposit and the subhorizontal orientation of most bones. Subsequent to the bone accumulating event, certain elements further disarticulated in low energy conditions (Hunt, 1986, p. A21).

There is no sedimentological evidence for a catastrophic depositional origin for the quarry. The geometry of the quarry is lenticular, not a sheet. The minor intraformational rip-up clasts resemble the enclosing bed, inferring bioturbation(?) or internal reworking of the sediment at the depositional site. The sub-horizontal alignment of the larger bones is probably due to settling onto a horizontal surface within wet, unconsolidated mud.

Recently, Richmond and Morris (1996) combined sedimentological observations, overburden analyses, compaction ratios, and smectitic clay swelling potential to theorize:

> The fossil deposit consists of calcareous smectitic mudstone, which accumulated on the floodplain of an anastomosing fluvial system. The quarry floodpond facies was deposited between anastomosing channel levees... Dinosaurs became entrapped in the cohesive and adhesive mud as they drank and hunted near the floodpond...The expansive properties of the smectitic mud in which the dinosaurs became entombed account for the disarticulation of the dinosaur remains

and the random bone orientation within the quarry (Richmond and Morris, 1996, p. 533).

Many of the arguments of Richmond and Morris (1996) are valid. The sedimentological evaluations, overburden analyses, and compaction ratios clearly define the extent of the quarry horizon as it is now known. However, several problems arise. An anastomosing river as defined by Nadon (1994) does not match the sedimentological evidence in this portion of the Morrison Formation at the quarry. The lenticular sandstone beds are less than 2 meters thick, and extend less than 100 meters along the exposures. Sheet sandstones comprise a minor proportion of the section. There is no evidence for the amalgamation of crevasse splay deposits that formed levees or for fine lamination of the sediment within the overbank facies. Instead the dominant lithology is blocky smectitic claystone with rare interbedded lenticular sandstone and siltstone beds, for example, a rapidly aggrading fluvial system choked with volcanic ash that was eventually overwhelmed by the influx of ash.

Another major problem is their implied mechanism for the distribution of the bones, that is, the shrinking and swelling of smectitic clays in a floodpond during wet and dry cycles. The quarry horizon, as well as the surrounding sediments, were not composed originally of smectitic clay. Volcanic debris was the primary constituent in tuff layers or as reworked fluvial sediment. Thin section and SEM analyses show that devitrification of ash to smectite was a post-burial process. Excess silica derived from the devitrification of ash to smectite led to the precipitation of quartz on the clay (figure 5). Deposition of quartz in the marrow cavities of the dinosaur bones occurred after the precipitation of calcite (figure 8). Therefore devitrification of ash took place after the deposition of the bones.

A New Hypothesis

I propose that the dinosaurs became mired in a spring-fed pond or seep (not a floodpond of an anastomosing river) that had a cumulative depositional depth of about 7 meters (Richmond and Morris, 1996). The bones were distributed by (1) "dinoturbation" as the subsequent live animals attempted to escape from the mire, and (2) fluctuating groundwater movement through saturated volcanic ash, which has a high permeability (Lander and Hay, 1993). The spring was in a topographic low surrounded by a high ground-water table. Eventually regional base level rose allowing water to fill the basin and form the lake recorded by the Cleveland-Lloyd lentil. The underlying sandstone beds were local conduits for rising water, centralizing the upward circulation and forming a seep with essentially no bottom. Upwelling of water through the ash allowed the heavier bones to settle, kept moderate-sized bones suspended in the mud, and distributed small bone fragments into the overlying algal-rich lake. Decaying flesh in the anaerobic environment of the saturated ash increased the pH adjacent to the bones, producing calcareous soaps, such as adipocere (Berner, 1968) that subsequently converted to the calcite that encases many bones. Eventually an ash fall mantled the area, filling the lake and preserving the bones in the calcareous mud.

CONCLUSIONS

The lower portion of the Brushy Basin Member at the Cleveland-Lloyd Quarry records primarily lacustrine and wet overbank facies deposited on a floodplain paleoslope with a relatively low gradient. The few fluvial sandstones contain intraclasts and tuff fragments, suggesting streams that transported channel-choking loads of volcanic ash.

Dinosaur bones at the quarry are in a severely disturbed calcareous mudstone directly below a lacustrine micritic limestone, the Cleveland-Lloyd lentil. Petrologic analyses and descriptions of four cores that penetrate the fossil-bearing layer suggest the dinosaur bones accumulated in a spring-fed pond or seep. There is some evidence for periodic flooding in undisturbed deposits in core A-7, but reworking by dinoturbation or spring flow of the calcareous muds has obscured those events in the quarry horizon. The disarticulation of the skeletons, the occurrence of a single, fairly well-preserved dinosaur egg (Hirsch and others, 1989; Hirsch, 1994), and the presence of calcareous mudstone nodules imply the animals sank into the volcanic ash-rich mud before scavenging could take place. Subsequent disruption of the mud and disarticulation of the skeletons occurred as a result of (1) up-welling water circulating through the volcanic ash, and (2) the struggling of newly trapped animals as they attempted to free themselves from the mud.

SUGGESTIONS FOR FURTHER RESEARCH

(1) Further mapping is needed. The boundaries of the Cleveland-Lloyd lentil should be defined. Several new quarries have been identified in the area and their proximity relative to the Cleveland-Lloyd Quarry should be determined stratigraphically and temporally.

(2) Further petrographic analyses could be done to determine regional and local changes in the lake.

(3) Beds below the lentil should be carefully examined, especially for calcite. Calcite in these mudstones could be associated with additional dinosaur bones.

(4) The lentil should be examined for dinosaur tracks. Clearly delineated signs of "dinoturbation" would further verify my hypothesis.

(5) A seismic survey of the area might help identify the association of sandstone lenses and the quarry in the area covered by the upper Morrison Formation. Penecontemporaneous fractures or faults might be found that were conduits for ground water to the inferred spring and lake.

(6) As further quarrying proceeds, three-dimensional mapping may reveal definitively the presence or lack of paleocurrent orientation for the bones.

(7) Discovery of a modern analog of a spring-fed seep in a tectonically active area similar to that inferred for the quarry site would be helpful.

ACKNOWLEDGMENTS

This study originated as part of a Ph.D. dissertation completed at the University of Utah (Bilbey, 1992). Financial and research assistance came from a University of Utah Research Grant Program, Women's Auxiliary of the American Institute of Mining Engineers, and the Departments of Geology and Biology at Utah State University. K-Ar analyses of biotite were done by Robert Drake at the University of California at Berkeley and Francis Brown at the University of Utah. The U.S. Bureau of Land Management and the U.S. National Park Service provided drill cores from the quarry and federal antiquity permits required for this research. For permission to use the maps shown in figure 1, I thank the Brigham Young University Earth Science Museum and Kenneth Stadtman.

W. L. Stokes, M. D. Picard, A. A. Ekdale, P. Roth, J. H. Madsen, Jr., and G. Edmunds advised me during preparation of my dissertation. D. Gillette, E. Evanoff, and J. Hubert gave valuable suggestions for the improvement of this document. Numerous family members have provided financial and loving support as well as sturdy backs. To all these people and institutions, I wish to express my gratitude. Particularly I dedicate this paper to my nephew, Rick Bilbey, without whom much of the field work would not have been done, and whose loss will be felt forever.

REFERENCES

Armstrong, R. L., and Suppe, John, 1973, Potassium-argon geochemistry of Mesozoic igneous rocks in Nevada, Utah, and southern California: Geological Society of America Bulletin, v. 84, p. 1375-1392.

Behrensmeyer, A. K., 1978, Taphonomic and ecologic information from bone weathering: Paleobiology, v. 4, p. 150-162.

Bell, T. E., 1983, Deposition and diagenesis of the Brushy Basin and upper Westwater Canyon members of the Morrison Formation in Northwest New Mexico and its relationship to uranium mineralization: Berkeley, University of California, Ph. D. dissertation, 102 p.

—1986, Deposition and diagenesis of the Brushy Basin Member and upper part of the Westwater Canyon Member of the Morrison Formation, San Juan Basin, New Mexico, *in* Turner- Peterson, C. E., Santos, E. S., and Fishman, N. S., editors, A basin analysis case study-- the Morrison Formation, Grants uranium region, New Mexico: American Association Petroleum Geologists Studies in Geology, v. 22, p. 77-91.

Berner, R. A., 1968, Calcium carbonate concretions formed by the decomposition of organic matter: Science, v. 159, p. 195-197.

Bilbey, S. A., 1992, Stratigraphy and sedimentary petrology of the Upper Jurassic-Lower Cretaceous rocks at the Cleveland-Lloyd Dinosaur Quarry with a comparison to the Dinosaur National Monument Quarry, Utah: Salt Lake City, Utah, University of Utah, Ph. D. Dissertation, 295 p.

—1998, Cleveland-Lloyd Dinosaur Quarry - age, stratigraphy and depositional environments: *in* Carpenter, Kenneth, editor, The Morrison Formation-- an interdisciplinary study: Modern Geology - Special Paper, v. 22, p. 87-120.

Bilbey-Bowman, S. A., Bowman, J. T., and Drake, R. E., 1986, Interpretation of the Morrison Formation as a time-transgressive unit: Fourth North American Paleontological Congress, Abstract Program, p. 5.

Biscaye, P. E., 1965, Mineralogy and sedimentation of recent deep-sea clay in the Atlantic Ocean and adjacent seas and oceans: Geological Society of America Bulletin, v. 76, p. 803-832.

Brindley, G. W., and Brown, G., editors, 1980, Crystal structures of clay minerals and their X-ray identification: Mineralogical Society of London, 359 p.

Burley, S. D., Kantorowicz, J. D., and Waugh, Brian, 1985, Clastic diagenesis. *in* Brenchley, P. J., and Williams, B. P. J., editors, Sedimentology-- recent developments and applied aspects: Oxford, England, The Geological Society, Blackwell Scientific Publications, p. 189-226.

Condon, W. H., and Miller, C. F., 1955, Desert Lake-7.5 Minute Quadrangle, Emery County, Utah: U. S. Geological Survey Miscellaneous Geologic Investigations, Photogeologic Map I-102, scale 1:24,000.

Dodson, Peter, Behrensmeyer, A K., Bakker, R. T., and McIntosh, J. S., 1980, Taphonomy and paleoecology of the dinosaur beds of the Jurassic Morrison Formation: Paleobiology, v. 6, no. 2, p. 208-232.

Folk, R. L., 1974, Petrology of sedimentary rocks: Austin, Texas, Hemphill Publishing Company, 182 p.

Hill, Andrew, and Behrensmeyer, A. K., 1984, Disarticulation patterns of some modern East African mammals: Paleobiology, v. 10, p. 366-376.

Hirsch, K. F., 1994, Upper Jurassic eggshells from the western interior of North America, *in* Carpenter, Kenneth, editor, Dinosaur eggs and babies: Cambridge, United Kingdom, Cambridge University Press, p. 137-150.

Hirsch, K. F., Stadtman, K. L., Miller, W. E., and Madsen, J. H., Jr., 1989, Upper Jurassic dinosaur egg from Utah: Science, v. 243, p. 1711-1713.

Hubert, J. F., Panish P.T., Chure, D. J., and Prostak, K. S., 1996, Chemistry, microstructure, petrology, and diagenetic model of Jurassic dinosaur bones, Dinosaur National Monument, Utah: Journal of Sedimentary Research, v. 66, no. 3, p. 531-547.

Hunt, A. P., 1986, Taphonomy of the Cleveland-Lloyd Dinosaur Quarry, Morrison Formation (Late Jurassic), Emery County,

Utah-- a preliminary report: Fourth North American Paleontological Convention, p. A21.

Ingram, R. L., 1954, Terminology for the thickness of stratification and parting units in sedimentary rocks: Geological Society of America Bulletin, v. 65, p. 937-938.

Kowallis, B. J., Heaton, J. S., and Bringhurst, Kelly, 1986, Fission-track dating of volcanically derived sedimentary rocks: Geology, v. 14, p. 19-22.

Lander, R. H., and Hay, R. L., 1993, Hydrogeologic control on zeolitic diagenesis of the White River sequence: Geological Society of America Bulletin, v. 105, p. 361-376.

Madsen, J. H., Jr., 1976, *Allosaurus fragilis* - a revised osteology: Utah Geology and Mineral Survey, Bulletin 109, 163 p.

Madsen, J. H., Jr., and Stokes,W. L., 1972, University of Utah cooperative dinosaur project, a progress report: Utah Academy of Science Proceedings, v. 49, p. 49-50.

Miller, W. E., Horrocks, R. D., and Madsen, J. H., Jr., 1996, The Cleveland-Lloyd Dinosaur Quarry, Emery County, Utah-- a U. S. National Landmark (including history and quarry map): Brigham Young University Geology Studies 1996, vol. 41, p. 3-24.

Mook, C. C., 1916, A study of the Morrison Formation: New York Academy of Science Annals, v. 27, p. 39-191.

Nadon, G. C., 1994, The genesis and recognition of anastomosed fluvial deposits--data from the St. Mary River Formation, southwestern Alberta, Canada: Journal of Sedimentary Research, v. B64, p. 451-463.

Peterson, Fred, and Turner-Peterson, C. E., 1986, Recent advances in Morrison sedimentology on the Colorado Plateau: Fourth North American Paleontological Convention, p. A35.

—1987, The Morrison Formation of the Colorado Plateau--recent advances in sedimentology, stratigraphy, and paleotectonics: Hunteria, v. 2, no. 1, 18 p.

Peterson, J. A., 1972, Jurassic System, in Mallory, W. W., editor, Geologic atlas of the Rocky Mountain region: Denver, Rocky Mountain Association Geologists, p. 177-189.

Retallack, G. J., 1988, Field recognition of paleosols *in* Reinhardt, Juergen, and Sigleo, W. R., editors, Paleosol and weathering through geologic time: principles and applications: Geological Society America Special Paper 216, p. 1-20.

Richmond, D. R., and Morris, T. H., 1996, The dinosaur death-trap of the Cleveland-Lloyd Quarry, Emery County, Utah, *in* Morales, Michael, editor, The continental Jurassic: Museum of Northern Arizona Bulletin 60, p. 533-545.

Schultz, L. G., 1964, Quantitative interpretation of mineralogical composition from X-ray and chemical data for the Pierre Shale: U. S. Geological Survey Professional Paper 391-C, 31 p.

Stokes, W L., 1944, Morrison Formation and related deposits in and adjacent to the Colorado Plateau: Geological Society of America Bulletin, v. 55, no. 8, p. 951-992.

—1945, A new quarry for Jurassic dinosaurs: Science, v. 101, p. 115-117.

—1985, The Cleveland-Lloyd Dinosaur Quarry: United States Government Printing Office, 27 p.

Stokes, W. L., and Cohenour, R. E., 1956, Geologic atlas of Utah - Emery County: Utah Geologic and Mineral Survey Bulletin 52, p. 1-92.

Surdam, R. C., Eugster, H. P., and Mariner, R. H., 1972, Magadi-type chert in Jurassic and Eocene to Pleistocene rocks, Wyoming: Geological Society of America Bulletin, v. 83, p. 2261-2266.

Turner, C. E., and Fishman, N. S., 1991, Jurassic Lake T'oo'dichi' - a large alkaline, saline lake, Morrison Formation, eastern Colorado Plateau: Geological Society America Bulletin, v. 103, p. 538-558.

Weeks, I. G., 1953, Environment and mode of origin and facies relationships of carbonate concretions in shales: Journal of Sedimentary Petrology, v. 23, p. 162-173.

Witkind, I. J., 1988, Geologic map of the Huntington 30' x 60' quadrangle, Carbon, Emery, Grand, and Uintah Counties, Utah: U. S. Geological Survey Miscellaneous Investigations Series Map I-1764, scale 1:100,000.

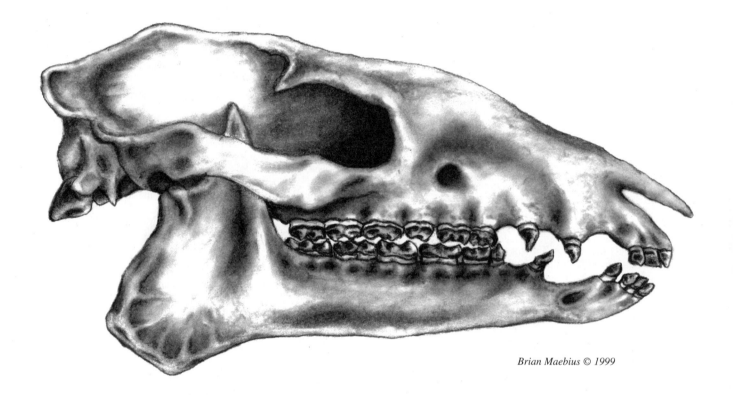

Brian Maebius © 1999

Eohippus

MORPHOLOGICAL VARIATION IN A LARGE SPECIMEN OF *ALLOSAURUS FRAGILIS*, UPPER JURASSIC MORRISON FORMATION, EASTERN UTAH

David K. Smith
Earth Science Museum, Brigham Young University, Provo, Utah 84602

Dean R. Richmond
Geology Department, Brigham Young University, Provo, Utah 84602

Paul J. Bybee
Science Department, Utah Valley State College, Orem, Utah 84058

ABSTRACT

A large articulated theropod cranium with associated postcranial material (BYU 571/8901) was found by the Hinkle family in eastern Utah at a site heretofore referred to as the Hinkle site. It was recovered by James Jensen. On the basis of comparisons with corresponding elements from the Dry Mesa Dinosaur Quarry, Grand Junction County, Colorado and the Cleveland-Lloyd Dinosaur Quarry, Emery County, Utah, we refer this material to *Allosaurus fragilis*. It is being used to document the extent of morphological variation within this taxon. The results indicate that variation in the Hinkle specimen and other material was mainly a result of allometry and individual differences without systematic importance. *Allosaurus fragilis* is a shape-conservative but size-variable taxon.

INTRODUCTION

A nearly complete theropod skull with associated postcranial material housed at the Earth Science Museum of Brigham Young University (BYU 571/8901) was found in Grand County, Utah, near the Colorado border, by the Hinkle family of Grand Junction and collected by Jim Jensen of Brigham Young University. The locality, subsequently referred to as the Hinkle Site, is about 40 kilometers from, and structurally related to, the dinosaur quarry in Rabbit Valley, Colorado near Interstate 70. The Hinkle site is in the upper Brushy Basin Member of the Jurassic Morrison Formation. The skull is nearly complete (figure 1), except for the absence of the nasal, frontal, part of

the jugal, and dorsal process of the lacrimal. Due to compression after burial, the posterior skull elements were rotated counterclockwise relative to the anterior, and the palatal elements were displaced at the ectopterygoid cranial kinetic articulation. The atlas-axis complex (figure 2), a coracoid, a humerus (figure 3), and partial scapula, pubis, femur, tibia, and metatarsal II were found associated with the skull. This theropod can easily be identified as *Allosaurus* (Madsen, 1976). Therefore, it was primarily compared with *Allosaurus* elements from Cleveland-Lloyd Dinosaur Quarry, Emery County, Utah and Dry Mesa Dinosaur Quarry, Mesa County, Colorado.

The most common theropod species in the Morrison Formation is *Allosaurus fragilis*. The type material for this taxon was found at Cañon City, Colorado in the Garden Park Quarry (Marsh, 1877), and is now curated at

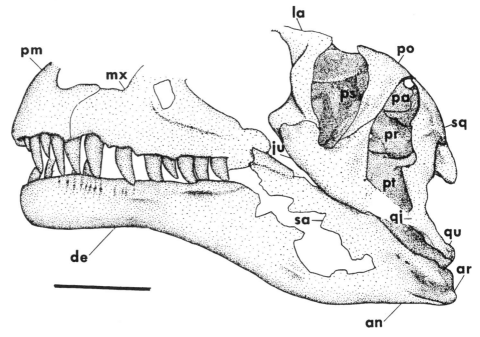

Figure 1. *Lateral view of Hinkle* Allosaurus *cranium. Abbreviations (after Madsen, 1976): an: angular; ar: articular; de: dentary; ju: jugal; la: lacrimal; mx: maxilla; po: postorbital; pm: premaxilla; pr; prootic; ps: parasphenoid; pt: pterygoid; qj: quadratojugal; qu: quadrate; sq: squamosal. Scale line equals 1.5 cm.*

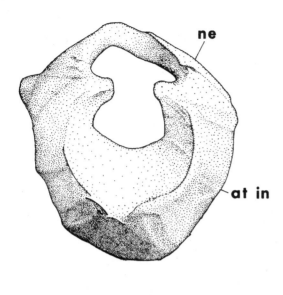

Figure 2. *Anterior view of Hinkle* Allosaurus *atlantal intercentrum and neurapophyses. Abbreviations (after Madsen, 1976): at in: atlantal intercentrum; ne: neurapophysis. Scale line equals 5 cm.*

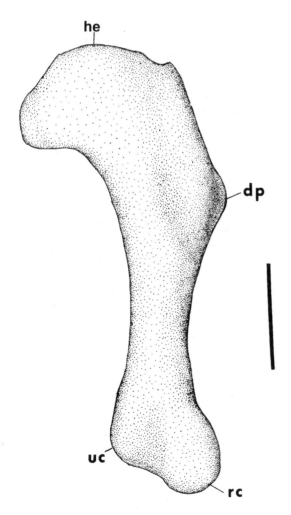

Figure 3. *Posterior view of Hinkle* Allosaurus *humerus. Abbreviations (after Madsen, 1976): dp: deltopectoral crest; he: head; rc: radial condyle; uc: ulnar condyle. Scale line equals 2.5 cm.*

the Yale-Peabody Museum (YPM 1930). The first reasonably complete specimen consisted of an individual, also from Cañon City, now housed at the Smithsonian Institution (USNM 4734). Gilmore (1920) described this specimen, but placed it within the genus *Antrodemus*, a dubious taxon based on a single vertebral centrum. Madsen (1976) described the abundant disarticulated elements from the Cleveland-Lloyd Quarry and placed almost all of the theropod material from that quarry, and from Cañon City, within *Allosaurus fragilis* and provided an updated diagnosis for this species. The only other known North American allosaurid is *Allosaurus maximus* from Oklahoma (Smith, 1999), known by some as *Saurophaganax maximus* (Chure, 1995). Daniel Chure is currently studying the systematics of the Allosauridae.

The purposes of this report are to document the presence of a large (table 1), well-preserved theropod, confirm its identity as *Allosaurus fragilis*, and to identify non-allometric peculiarities present in this specimen that have not been observed in Cleveland-Lloyd and Dry Mesa elements. However, to avoid unnecessary repetition of Madsen (1976), the osteology of this specimen will not be completely described except where it differs with material from other localities.

Table 1. *Selected element measurements (mm).*

Element	Measurement 1	Measurement 2
Dentary	210	87.0
Postorbital	170	58.5
Coracoid	82.6	175
Humerus	420	63.6

ABBREVIATIONS

AMNH, American Museum of Natural History, New York, New York; BMS, Buffalo Museum of Science, Buffalo, New York; BYU, Brigham Young University, Provo, Utah; CEU, College of Eastern Utah, Price, Utah; CM, Carnegie Museum, Pittsburgh, Pennsylvania; CMN, Canadian National Museum, Ottawa, Ontario; DNM, Dinosaur National Monument, Jensen, Utah; MOR, Museum of the Rockies, Bozeman, Montana; OMNH, Oklahoma Museum of Natural History, Oklahoma City, Oklahoma; PU, Princeton University (now curated at Yale-Peabody Museum), Princeton, New Jersey; ROM, Royal Ontario Museum, Toronto, Ontario; SMM, Science Museum of Minnesota, Saint Paul, Minnesota; UNL, University of Nebraska at Lincoln, Lincoln, Nebraska; UB, University of Bridgeport, Bridgeport, Connecticut; UGS, Utah Geological Survey, Salt Lake City, Utah; UMP, University of Michigan Exhibit Museum, Ann Arbor, Michigan; USNM, United States National Museum, Washington, DC; UUVP, University of Utah Vertebrate Paleontology (now curated at BYU Earth Science Museum), Salt Lake City, Utah; YPM, Yale-Peabody Museum, New Haven, Connecticut.

METHODS AND MATERIALS

A bone-by-bone comparison was made between the Hinkle specimen (BYU 571/8901) (figures 1-3) and corresponding elements of *Allosaurus fragilis* from an incomplete, articulated specimen from the Red Seeps Site (BYUVP 9466) in the San Rafael Swell region of Utah, elements from the Cleveland-Lloyd and Dry Mesa dinosaur quarries, and figured specimens (Madsen, 1976) to confirm the identity of the Hinkle theropod. Dentaries included in the analysis are: UUVP 1898, 200, 1905, 1908, 10093, 3389, 1909, 1906, 1904, 3810, 2456, 1910, 1907, 699, 702, 1896, 10250, 2903, 1895, 4029, 1900, 2001, 5748, 1903; BYU 725/10602; DNM 2560; UNL (unnumbered); USNM 4734, PU 6, 11, 12; AMNH 851; NMC 38454; ROM 5091; and CM 11844. Postorbitals included in the analysis are UUVP 2175, 5160, 652, 3758, 5582, 40607, 1685, 4674, 40610, 40609, 10111, 2758, 1936, 1934, 1862, 4556, 4122; BYU 725/9249; USNM 4734; and PU 7. Humeri included in the analysis are OMNH 01935; USNM 8423, 4734; BYU 725/5098, /5097, /(unnumbered), /10296, 4878; AMNH 1894, 5753; UUVP 273, 4387, 5501, 10154, 10161, 30,778, 4908, 5496, 4792, 3607; DNM 4818; UMEM (unnumbered); UNL 50038, 50039; SMM 66-42-1; CEU 1719; YPM 1931, 4944; PU 7, 3, 4; NMC 38454; ROM 5091; BMS E25840; CM1254; and CMNH 10936.

Possible sources of variation within any taxon can include individual, geographic, ontogenetic, sexual, pathological, systematic, and/or taphonomic processes (Molnar, 1990). Morphological comparisons of specimens from Cleveland-Lloyd, Dry Mesa, and Hinkle sites were performed to identify variable or gradational characters in an attempt to determine which of these processes affected the osteology of *Allosaurus*. The range of possible variation in morphology in the genus *Allosaurus* should be documented as its systematic importance is assessed. Characters that have been noted as being variable, such as the shape of the jugal (figures 1 and 4) and the location and development of pleurocoels on the axis (Madsen, 1976; Chure, personal communication 1995), were compared on both sides of the Hinkle cranium and among reference specimens from the other sites.

The Hinkle specimen was measured using landmarks corresponding with previous *Allosaurus* projects. The raw variables were converted into natural logarithms and incorporated into existing morphometric data sets including specimens from Dry Mesa, Cleveland-Lloyd, Como

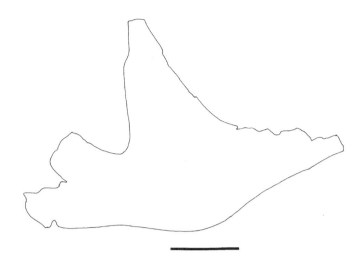

Figure 4. *Scaled lateral view of* Allosaurus *jugal from Cleveland-Lloyd. Compare with Hinkle jugal in figure 1. Scale line equals 5 cm.*

Bluff, and other sites. The Hinkle specimen data did not, however, significantly alter the multivariate results presented elsewhere (Smith, 1999). Bivariate plots (figures 7-9) of the dentary, postorbital, and humerus including the Hinkle specimen were created from these data. The bivariate allometric plot for the humerus was constructed using diameter as one of the variables. If the diameter had a higher than predicted value using a best-fit line, it was defined as robust, otherwise it was considered gracile. Therefore, robust versus gracile elements could be identified independently of size.

RESULTS

There are few non-size-related differences in the *Allosaurus* specimens examined. The descriptions of the elements involved follow the osteology established by Madsen (1976). Based on information from previous analyses (Smith, 1999), most of the non-allometric variation observed is in the skull, as expected. The relative development of crests, horns, or similar structures is gradational in the morphometric plots. The relative development and placement of cranial and post-cranial foramina, and some other structures, vary from side to side and among individuals in some bones. Otherwise, the post-cranial skeletons in *Allosaurus* are very uniform in shape. Fusion of individual elements was previously found to be unusual in all *Allosaurus* post-cranial elements.

Within the skull, the jugal was represented by specimens from Dry Mesa (BYU 725/), Cleveland-Lloyd (UUVP 01403 and 10173), and Hinkle (BYU 571/8901) (figure 4). Gilmore (1920) noted the presence of an external jugular foramen in the Cañon City specimen, but none of the observed specimens has one. Chure (personal communication, 1995) noted that this character is extremely variable both within theropod species and individuals. Therefore, this foramen cannot be considered diagnostically important. The ventral margin of the jugal is more angular in lateral view in the Cleveland-Lloyd specimen than either the Hinkle or Dry Mesa specimens. This element bowed laterally in the Cleveland-Lloyd specimen but the Dry Mesa and Hinkle specimens were flat. Bakker (personal communication, 1995) suggested that the Hinkle theropod might be a distinct species of *Allosaurus* based on the shape of the quadrate. However, our comparison of the Hinkle quadrate with corresponding specimens from Cleveland-Lloyd (UUVP 3082 and 2153) and Dry Mesa (BYU 12795) revealed no differences that could not be attributed to allometry or taphonomic distortion. The ectopterygoid and pterygoid are very consistently shaped in all of the specimens observed, except for the Hinkle specimen. In this specimen, these two elements were fused on the right side, while remaining unfused on the left. Given this asymmetry, we consider this fusion pathological.

Britt (1991) distinguished low- and high-crested lacrimal forms in *Allosaurus* samples from Dry Mesa and Cleveland-Lloyd quarries and suggested that this character in combination with some others may be of systematic importance. Unfortunately, the Hinkle *Allosaurus* lacks the lacrimal crest.

There is a considerable amount of fusion in the individual elements of the atlas-axis complex in the Hinkle material that may be related to size (figure 2). None of these elements are fused in a small Cleveland-Lloyd reconstruction incorporating real bone (UUVP 30-465, and 30-466). In a larger Cleveland-Lloyd reconstruction (UUVP 1245, 1025) and a Dry Mesa specimen (BYU 725/15599), the axis is fused to the axial intercentrum. However, the neurapophyses are rather unusual in the Hinkle specimen in that they are fused to each other and to the atlantal intercentrum forming a complete ring. This complex remains distinct from the axial intercentrum (figure 2). The degree of development of pleurocoels and parapophyses varies from specimen to specimen and from side to side on individual vertebrae (figure 5).

The preserved appendicular elements associated with the Hinkle skull are morphologically typical for *Allosaurus fragilis*. Almost all of the variation observed can be accounted for by allometry. The Hinkle coracoid is larger than typical Cleveland-Lloyd specimens, but the biceps tubercle is more indistinct. This result supports Madsen's (1976) observation that there is considerable variation in this character that is not related to size. The

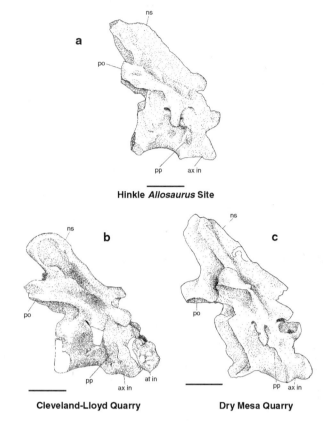

Figure 5. *Right view of* Allosaurus *atlas-axis complex from a, Hinkle; b, Cleveland-Lloyd; and c, Dry Mesa. The elements from Cleveland-Lloyd have been reconstructed and probably do not actually go together. The Dry Mesa specimen has been taphonomically distorted. Abbreviations (after Madsen, 1976): at in - atlantal intercentrum; ax in - axial intercentrum; ns - neural spine; po - postzygapophysis; pp - parapophysis. Scale line = 5 centimeters.*

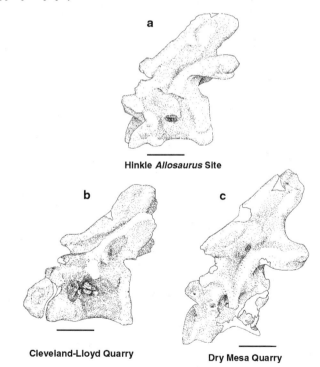

Figure 6. *Left view of* Allosaurus *atlas-axis complex from a, Hinkle; b, Cleveland-Lloyd; and c, Dry Mesa. The elements from Cleveland-Lloyd have been reconstructed and probably do not actually go together. The Dry Mesa specimen has been taphonomically distorted. The elements are drawn to the same scale as Figure 5.*

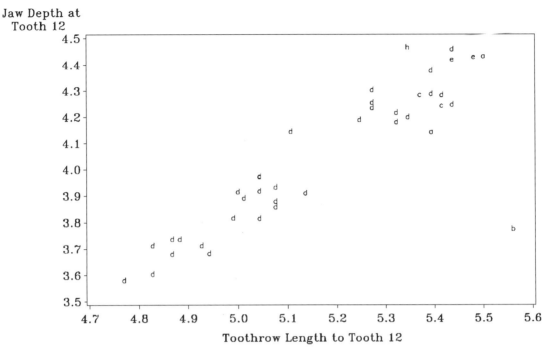

Figure 7. *Bivariate plot of dentary toothrow length versus depth. a, Canyon City; b, Dry Mesa; c, Como Bluff; d, Cleveland-Lloyd; e, Dinosaur National Monument; s, Oklahoma* Allosaurus maximus; *and h, Hinkle Site. Not all of these sites may be represented in every plot.*

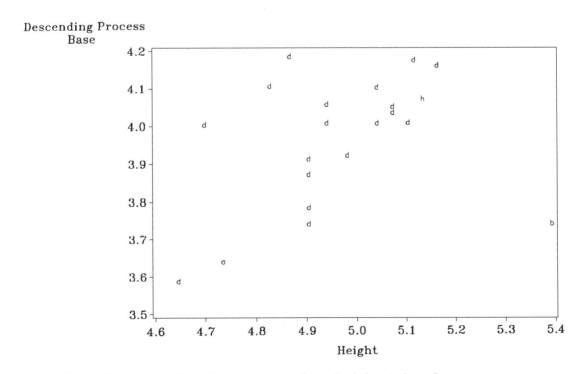

Figure 8. *Bivariate plot of postorbital height at descending process versus base. Symbols as in figure 7.*

Hinkle humerus is very similar to Cleveland-Lloyd and Dry Mesa material. Although it appears more robust than some other specimens, the scatter plot reveals that it is not extreme for a specimen of that size (figure 9). More torsion is present in the shaft of the Hinkle *Allosaurus* than was observed in the other humeri.

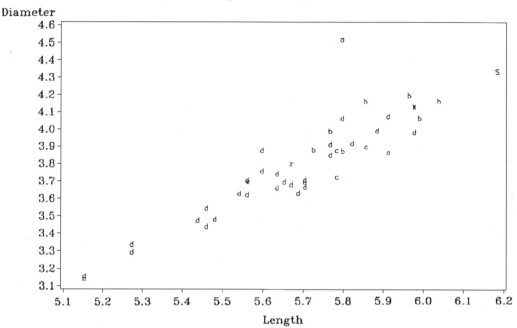

Figure 9. *Bivariate plot of humerus length versus diameter. Symbols as in figure 7.*

DISCUSSION

Most of the consistent variation observed within *Allosaurus fragilis* was ascribed to ontogeny using principal components analyses (Smith, 1999). Up to 95% of the observed variation can be ascribed to ontogeny within this species and can account for most of the variation observed within the Hinkle *Allosaurus*. It is very large and but not more robust than would be predicted by the allometric curves. However, specimens from non-Cleveland-Lloyd sites generally tend to attain a larger size than those from Cleveland-Lloyd. This generality includes the Hinkle specimen. When size is included as a factor, a discriminant analysis can identify specimens from Cleveland-Lloyd, but not those from the other quarries, using just a few variables (Smith, 1996).

The remaining variation that could not be ascribed to allometry was determined to be a result of individual variation, since it could not be used to define discrete clusters and is not consistent from site to site. Many non-allometrically related shape-variable characters are subtle. In the Hinkle *Allosaurus*, some are more similar to the specimens from Cleveland-Lloyd and others to those from Dry Mesa. For example, the amount of torsion in the shaft of the humerus was variable from individual to individual. Additionally, the development of the biceps tubercle on the coracoid varies. In some individuals, such as the Hinkle specimen, the biceps tubercle is indistinct, while in others it is well developed.

We refer the Hinkle theropod to a typical *Allosaurus fragilis* in spite of its large size and the presence of some unusual characters that are considered to be the result of individual variation, probably in conjunction with allo-

metric effects. Characters peculiar to this specimen include pathological fusion of the right ectopterygoid with the pterygoid and the axial complex fusion which may be related to allometry. The patterns of variation for each morphometric variable and morphological character indicate the presence of only a single shape-conservative, size variable, species at Dry Mesa, Cleveland-Lloyd, and the Hinkle site. This interpretation can be contrasted with that for lambeosaurine hadrosaurs and *Protoceratops* (Dodson 1975a and b) which have considerable and consistent non-allometric skull variation.

ACKNOWLEDGMENTS

We wish to thank Kenneth Stadtman (BYU) and Dee Hall for permitting access to the Hinkle, specimen preparation by one of us (D. R.), and comparative *Allosaurus* material within the BYU collection. Daniel Chure (DNM) allowed access to material at Dinosaur National Monument and photographs of other specimens. Jack Horner (MOR) permitted observation of the articulated specimen at Museum of the Rockies. James Madsen, Jr., Jack Horner, and Daniel Chure provided many useful comments. Wade Miller (BYU), David Gillette (UGS), James Madsen Jr., and Peter Galton (UB) read the manuscript. Figures 5 and 6 were prepared by Ray Johnson.

REFERENCES

Britt, B. B., 1991, Theropods of Dry Mesa Quarry (Morrison Formation, Late Jurassic), Colorado, with emphasis on the osteology of *Torvosaurus tanneri*: Brigham Young University Geology Studies v. 37, p. 1-72.

Chure, D. J., 1995, A reassessment of the gigantic theropod *Saurophagus maximus* from the Morrison Formation (Upper Jurassic) of Oklahoma, USA, *in* Sun, Ailing and Wang, Yang, editors, Sixth symposium on Mesozoic terrestrial ecosystems and biota, short papers: Beijing, China, China Ocean Press, p. 103-106.

Dodson, Peter, 1975a, Taxonomic implications of relative growth in lambeosaurine hadrosaurs: Systematic Zoology, v. 24, p. 37-54.

—1975b, Quantitative aspects of relative growth in *Protoceratops*: Journal of Paleontology v. 59, p. 929-940.

Gilmore, C. W., 1920, Osteology of the carnivorous Dinosauria in the United States National Museum, with special reference to the genera *Antrodemus* (*Allosaurus*) and *Ceratosaurus*: U. S. National Museum, Bulletin 110, p. 1-159.

Madsen, J. H., Jr., 1976, *Allosaurus fragilis* - a revised osteology: Utah Geology and Mineral Survey, Bulletin 109, 163 p.

Marsh, O. C., 1877, Notice of new dinosaurian reptiles from the Jurassic of Colorado: American Journal of Science, v. 3, p. 514-516.

Molnar, R. E., 1990, Variation in theory and in theropods, *in* Carpenter, Kenneth, and Currie, P. J., editors, Dinosaur systematics--approaches and perspectives: New York, Cambridge University Press, p. 71-80.

Smith, D. K., 1996, A discriminant analysis of *Allosaurus* populations using quarries as the operational units, *in* Morales, Michael, editor, The continental Jurassic: Museum of Northern Arizona Bulletin, v. 60, p. 69-72.

—1999, A morphometric analysis of *Allosaurus fragilis*: Journal of Vertebrate Paleontology, v. 18, p. 126-142.

Brian Maebius © 1999

Lepisosteus

THE BEAKED JAWS OF STEGOSAURS AND THEIR IMPLICATIONS FOR OTHER ORNITHISCHIANS

Stephen A. Czerkas

The Dinosaur Museum, P.O. Box 277, Monticello, Utah 84535

ABSTRACT

Unlike typical reptiles which have lips or beaks, the Ornithischia is composed of herbivorous dinosaurs that have been characterized as possessing cheeks. Contradicting this widely held belief is the reinterpretation of the dentary of *Stegosaurus* which has morphological characteristics remarkably similar to that of the Chelonia, which all have beaks. This raises considerable doubt as to whether all other ornithischians could have had cheeks.

INTRODUCTION

The earliest observation that ornithischians were peculiar reptiles in possibly having cheek pouches was made by British paleontologist Gideon Mantell. He inferred from the worn teeth of *Iguanodon*, and other details of its jaws, that this dinosaur might have had mammalian-like lips, or cheeks (Mantell, 1851). Much later, Richard Swan Lull attributed powerful muscular cheeks for ceratopsians (Lull, 1903, 1905, 1908, 1910a, 1933). Some leading paleontologists also agreed with Lull in thinking that ceratopsians had cheeks (Russell, 1935; Sternberg, 1951). Furthermore, Lull suspected that many types of ornithischians had cheeks, including stegosaurs (Lull, 1910b) and hadrosaurs (Lull and Wright, 1938). However, not all paleontologists accepted the uncharacteristic idea of reptiles, or more specifically dinosaurs, as having been equipped with cheeks (Brown and Schlaikjer, 1940). Lull's contemporary, Charles Gilmore steadfastly maintained that ornithischians had lips instead of cheeks and went so far as to create sculptures of dinosaurs depicting how the lips might have looked (Gilmore, 1920). The concept that ornithischians could have had cheeks remained largely unresolved until Peter Galton presented the most in-depth examination of the issue which concluded that virtually all ornithischians were equipped with cheeks (Galton, 1973). The only exception was that of the basal ornithischian, *Fabrosaurus*, which is now called *Lesothosaurus* (Sereno, 1991). Greg Paul went further, attributing muscular cheeks to literally all ornithischians, including *Fabrosaurus* (= *Lesothosaurus*), and to even some saurischians, including the segnosaur, *Erlikosaurus* and prosauropods such as *Plateosaurus* (Paul, 1984). The

cladistic analysis by Benton (1990) includes the supposition of cheeks suggested by the "buccal emargination" of the upper and lower jaws as an ornithischian autapomorphy. All of the above interpretations of ornithischians having cheeks were based largely upon the recessed margins of the jaws, apparent tooth wear caused by a masticating process, and the inference that cheeks would have been essential to contain the food in the animal's mouth during the masticating process. However, while now almost universally accepted by paleontologists and paleo-artists, the concept of cheeks as an ornithischian trait is once again highly suspect with this reinterpretation of the jaws of stegosaurs.

ABBREVIATIONS

CM, Carnegie Museum of Natural History; DM, The Dinosaur Museum, Blanding, Utah; GI SPS, Geological Institute Section of Palaeontology and Stratigraphy, the Academy of Sciences of the Mongolian Peoples Republic, Ulan Bator; SGWG, Sektion Geologische Wissenschaften der Ernst-Moritz-Arndt-Universitat Greifswald; USNM, National Museum of Natural History, Smithsonian Institution; ZDM, Zigong Dinosaur Museum, Zigong.

DESCRIPTION AND COMPARISON

The jaws of *Stegosaurus stenops* (USNM 4934) have been described briefly by Marsh (1887) who illustrated the skull and lower jaw articulated in a closed position. Marsh noted that the teeth were not visible in the lateral view, as shown in figure 1A. The skull and lower jaw have to this day remained joined together as originally preserved with the mouth in a closed position. The remaining matrix has prevented observation of much of the dorsal surface of the lower jaw. Gilmore (1914) elaborated much further in his description of the same specimen and included additional observations made possible by a partial dentary (USNM 4935). Referring to the dentary, Gilmore (1914, p. 37) stated that the

> ...dorsal border is comparatively wide, the tooth row being placed on the extreme internal border. Along its external border, beginning opposite the first tooth, a ridge gradually rises from this surface until opposite the last tooth it attains a height of 17 millimeters

above the border of the alveolus. Between this ridge and the dental series is a row of foramina, which evidently correspond to those on the external surface of the *Camptosaurus* dentary, and which doubtless served for the transmission of nerves and nutrient blood vessels to the lips.

Clearly, Gilmore believed that the *Stegosaurus* was equipped with a lip on the dentary, although he did not comment on why the foramina on the dentary are located on the dorsal surface of the dentary as compared to the typical lip line on the lateral surface.

In his text, Galton (1973) did not specifically describe morphological details as to why *Stegosaurus* would have had cheeks. Instead, he provided two drawings. One was of the skull in palatal view which illustrated the inset teeth, or emargination of the maxilla. The other was a lateral view of the skull and jaw with a shaded area representing where the cheeks would have been located, as shown in figure 1B.

Berman and McIntosh (1986) presented the first in-depth analysis solely dedicated to that of a lower jaw from a *Stegosaurus* (CM 41681). Berman and McIntosh described the dorsal shelf on the dentary as having a series of about nine foramina of varied sizes along most of its length, which independently complies with Gilmore's original description (see above). They also mentioned that the medial dorsal surface on the edentulous, anterior portion of the dentary has a "knife-like ridge." This ridge is in line with the tooth row and, in effect, continues the cutting function without the benefit of actual teeth. This medial ridge, as well as the lateral ridge noted by Gilmore, are morphologically and functionally analogous to the internal and external cutting edges that are found on the jaws of members of the Chelonia.

As shown in figure 1C, the lower jaw of *Stegosaurus* is unique among dinosaurs in that the dorsal flange of the dentary rises above the tooth row obscuring all of the teeth in lateral view (contra Sereno and Dong, 1992, figure 10A). As Gilmore noted, there is a distinct ridge along the dorsal, exterior margin of the dentary, as shown in figure 2A, which prevents the teeth from being visible in lateral view. Between this lateral ridge and the tooth row is a transversely wide, dorsal shelf which is slightly concave, as can be seen in figures 2B and 2C. The posterior portion of this concave shelf is steeply inclined, facing in a dorsomedial direction. The angle of inclination reduces anteriorly causing the con-

cave shelf to face dorsally. The teeth are medial to the dorsal shelf, and posteriorly they are well below the upper margin of the lateral ridge. Anteriorly, the upper margin of the lateral ridge remains above the tooth row but to a much less degree. In front of the first tooth is where the knife-like ridge appears and continues anteriorly, nearly parallel to the lateral ridge. Marsh (1887), Lull (1910b), Gilmore (1914), and Galton (1990) were all correct in stating that no teeth would have been visible in lateral view. In medial view, as shown in figure 2D, the orientation of the teeth is well below the dorsal margin.

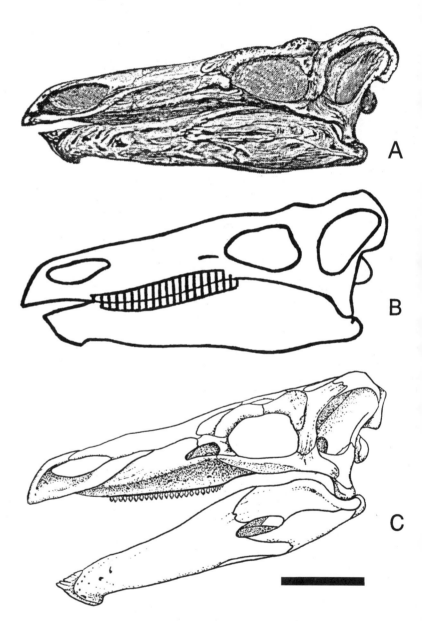

Figure 1. *Reconstructions of the skull of* Stegosaurus stenops *based on USNM 4934. A, The first skeletal reconstruction in lateral view of the skull and lower jaw (after Marsh, 1887); note that the teeth are not visible. B, Galton's (1973) drawing of the skull and lower jaw indicating where cheeks would have been (after Galton, 1973). C, The skull and lower jaw restored with the mouth in an open position; note that the teeth of the lower jaw are not visible (after Sereno and Dong, 1992); scale bar equals 10 cm.*

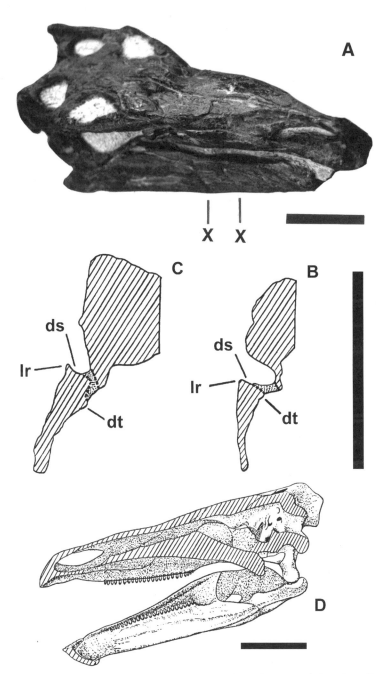

Figure 2. Comparative views illustrating the lateral ridge and dorsal shelf of Stegosaurus stenops *based on USNM 4934. A, The right side of a cast of the skull and lower jaw in dorsolateral view; note the exterior ridge of the dorsal margin of the dentary, as well as the dorsal shelf; X marks position of cross sections in B and C. B, A cross section from a cast of the skull and dentary representing the anterior position marked in figure 2A. C, A cross-section from a cast of the skull and dentary representing the posterior position marked in figure 2A. Abbreviations for 2B and 2C: ds, dorsal shelf; lr, lateral ridge; dt, dentary teeth. Stippled areas represent intervening matrix. To same scale as figure 2B. D, A longitudinal cross section of the skull and lower jaw in medial view; note that the teeth in the dentary are well below the margin of the dorsal shelf (modified from Gilmore, 1914). Scale bars equal 10 cm.*

With the exception of the retention of teeth among stegosaurs, the characteristics cited above are convergent with the morphology of beaks found among the Chelonia. Specific details of these characteristics may vary even among the Chelonia. A medial ridge may or may not be present in the beaks of the Chelonia (Romer, 1956), but the wide, slightly concave dorsal shelf, an exterior dorsal ridge, and a medial ridge are physical characteristics directly pertaining to the shape of beaks found among the Chelonia. The *Stegosaurus* dentary possesses a similar suite of characters that indicate the lower jaw was equipped in life with a horny beak. None of these characters are consistent with that of a muscular cheek. The principal difference between the lower jaws of stegosaurs and turtles is the retention of teeth in stegosaurs. The stegosaur teeth, however, are the functional equivalent to the cutting edge of the knife-like, medial ridge seen on the jaws of turtles. Altogether, the strong resemblance to the beaks of the Chelonia indicates that the mouth of *Stegosaurus* was equipped with a beak instead of cheeks.

EVOLUTION OF THE STEGOSAURIAN BEAK AND DISCUSSION

Among the Onithischia, the elevated dorsal flange of the dentary rising above most or all of the tooth row is a characteristic found only in highly derived stegosaurs, such as *Stegosaurus, Chungkingosaurus,* and *Kentrosaurus* (Galton, 1990). The beak-like characters of the *Stegosaurus* dentary are highly derived from the earliest basal ornithischians, which are known from the Triassic. Less derived plesiomorphic morphology and a developmental pattern in which the *Stegosaurus* beak may have evolved can be traced to basal stegosaurs, such as *Huayangosaurus,* and eventually back to even the most primitive ornithischians, such as *Lesothosaurus* (= *Fabrosaurus*) and *Scutellosaurus*.

Based on the presence of plesiomorphic characters, including premaxillary teeth, *Huayangosaurus* (ZDM 7001) was identified as a basal stegosaur (Dong and others, 1982). Additional plesiomorphic characters such as comparatively small spike-like plates suggest that *Huayangosaurus* was ancestral to more derived forms, culminating in those with enormous armored plates as seen in *Stegosaurus*. However direct the ancestral relationship was, the mouth region of *Huayangosaurus* possesses incipient characters that are consistent with what could have occurred before the more fully formed beak of *Stegosaurus* had developed. As shown in figure 3A, the teeth of *Huayangosaurus* are not restricted posteriorly by an edentulous anterior margin as seen in *Stegosaurus*. Instead, the teeth continue for the length of the dentary to the anterior margin where the predentary conjoins. The maxillary teeth of *Huayangosaurus* are present for the length of the maxilla, including up to its anterior margin where the tooth row then continues along the premaxilla. The elevated dorsal flange of the dentary of *Stegosaurus* is much less developed in *Huayangosaurus* (Sereno and Dong, 1992). The dorsal flange of the *Huayangosaurus* dentary is so small that most of the dentary teeth are visible in lateral view, except for portions of the last few. On the dorsal flange is an incipient lateral ridge that gradually becomes more prominent posteriorly as it rises up to the coronoid process. This lateral ridge is more strongly developed in *Stegosaurus* where it represents the exterior cropping edge of the beak. As shown in figure 3B, the lateral ridge is even smaller in less derived basal ornithischians (Haubold, 1990) such as *Emausaurus* (SGWG 85). As shown in figure 4A, the dorsal shelf of the *Stegosaurus* dentary is transversely wide for its entire length but, as shown in figure 4B, the wider posterior part of the dentary in *Emausaurus* narrows anteriorly which reflects a more plesiomorphic con-

dition. The lateral ridge is less pronounced than that of *Huayangosaurus* and is restricted posteriorly to where the dentary broadens. By comparing the lesser developed characters of a beak in *Huayangosaurus* and *Emausaurus* to those of the highly derived *Stegosaurus*, a sequential pattern of development can be seen illustrating how the beak of stegosaurs evolved. The beak takes shape with the reduction of the tooth series, increasing prominence of the dorsal flange, a thickening of the dorsal shelf, the extension of the lateral ridge along the dentary and the development of a medial ridge anterior to the teeth.

Among the most basal ornithischians are *Scutellosaurus* (Colbert, 1981) and *Lesothosaurus*. They both have teeth that are only slightly inset from the outer margin of the maxilla and dentary. Paul (1984) interpreted *Fabrosaurus* (= *Lesothosaurus*) as having cheeks based on the slightly inset teeth and large "nerve foramina" associated with cheek muscles. However, the inset tooth margins of these basal ornithischians is so slight that, as shown in figures 4C, and 4D, it is barely beyond the range which can be found among various members of the Lacertilia, including the common iguana and various *Cyclura*. It is reasonable then to attribute lacertilian style lips posterior to the beaked snout of the most primitive ornithischians.

In addition to inset teeth, the size and number of the foramina in the dentary are also not reliable indicators of the existence of a muscular cheek. The foramina in the dentary of lizards can be of various sizes and number. Foramina, even of large size, are often found in the jaws of reptiles and especially throughout the highly vascular predentary of many ornithischians. In particular, as shown in figure 5A, the predentary of the ankylosaur, *Saichania* (GI SPS 100/151) has comparatively large foramina (Maryanska, 1977; plate 29, figure 2) along the dorsal surface which certainly would have been covered by a keratinous sheath in life. The surface texture of the dentary may also be highly variable regarding the presence of a keratinous beak. Among the Chelonia, the dentary may either have vascular grooves or foramina suggesting the presence of a keratinous sheath, or have a smooth surface texture which by itself belies the fact that it would be covered by a thick, horny sheath in life. As shown in figure 5B, there is a series of foramina along the surface of the dorsal shelf on the dentary of the snapping turtle, *Chelydra serpentina* (DM S4) which otherwise has a remarkably smooth surface texture. Therefore, the surface texture of the outside of the *Stegosaurus* dentary, as well as that of its dorsal shelf, is consistent with having a keratinous beak.

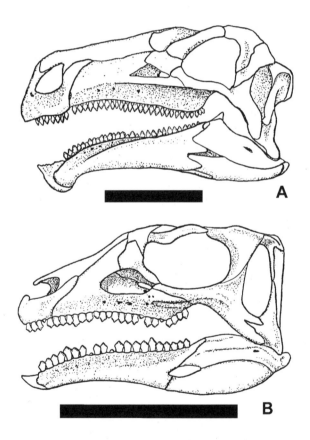

Figure 3. *Lateral views of skull and lower jaw of a basal stegosaur and a primitive ornithischian. A,* Huayangosaurus *(ZDM 7001); note that the exterior ridge of the dorsal shelf of the mandible reaches forward from the apex of the coronoid process without rising above the entire tooth row of the dentary, that there are premaxillary teeth, and that the dentary and maxillary teeth continue for the length of their anterior margins, unlike the edentulous margins in* S. stenops *in figure 1C and 2D (modified from Sereno and Dong, 1992). B,* Emausaurus *(SGWG 85); note that on the dentary, the lateral ridge is less developed, but continues up to the coronoid process while remaining well below the tooth row (after Haubold, 1990); scale bars equal 10 cm.*

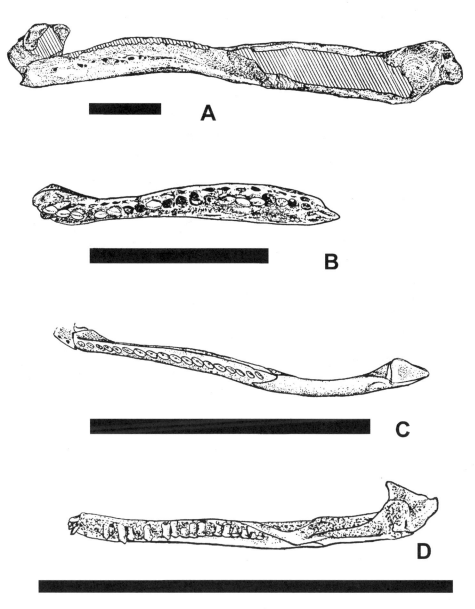

Figure 4. *Comparative dorsal views of the left lower jaws of* Stegosaurus, *primitive ornithischians and a lizard. A,* Stegosaurus *(CM 41681); note that the width of the dorsal shelf continues from the coronoid process to the anterior margin where the predentary would conjoin (after Berman and McIntosh, 1986). B, The primitive armored ornithischian,* Emausaurus *(SGWG 85); note that the dorsal shelf is widest posteriorly und constricted anteriorly (after Haubold, 1990). C, The primitive ornithischian,* Lesothosaurus; *note that the teeth are only slightly inset from the lateral margin (after Sereno and Dong, 1992). D, The lizard,* Cyclura cornuta *(DM S3); note that the posterior half of the tooth row is slightly inset and compare to the same area on the jaw in C. Scale bars for A, B, C equal 5 cm, and D equals 10 cm.*

nous sheath pertaining to the upper beak have been found on several hadrosaurs (Cope, 1883; Sternberg, 1935; Morris, 1970) suggesting that most, if not all, ornithischians did in fact have an upper beak corresponding to the predentary. While hardly indicated by the morphology of the premaxilla, the fossilized impressions of the actual beaks extend well beyond the bone and can even be equipped with a crenulated cropping edge. Even though the maxilla of *Stegosaurus* appears to be less derived by not having obvious beak-like characteristics, the evidence from the premaxillary beaks of hadrosaurs makes it reasonable to assert that the highly derived dentary beak of *Stegosaurus* probably had some sort of complimentary beak on the maxilla.

The beaked jaws of *Stegosaurus* make it all the more evident that the concept of any ornithischians having cheeks is highly problematic and unsubstantiated. Inset teeth, lateral shelves or foramina along the dentary or maxilla do not indicate conclusively that cheeks were present. Highly abraded, worn teeth may be suggestive but by themselves do not confirm whether highly derived ornithischians, such as hadrosaurs or ceratopsians, had cheeks. Fossilized skin impressions would provide the most conclusive evidence that could verify whether any ornithischians actually had cheeks, but no such impressions have been found. In lieu of conclusive evidence to the contrary, it may remain somewhat appealing to think that some ornithischians which had

In contrast to the lower jaw of *Stegosaurus*, the upper jaw is less derived and has fewer indications of a beak morphology. Within the Ornithischia, only the Ceratopsia have a rostral bone that unequivocally represents an upper beak. The premaxilla of all other ornithischians, including stegosaurs, remains less derived with indistinct indications of a beak compared to that of the predentary. Consequently, based solely upon the osteology, the indications of an upper beak are far less obvious than that displayed by the distinctive morphology of the predentary. However, fossil impressions of the kerati-

highly occluding teeth could have been further equipped with cheeks of some sort to help retain food in the mouth during the masticating process. However, the logical inference may well be flawed in overly idealizing the function of the teeth as being truly that of chewing as compared to simply cutting. In either case, the argument that onithischians must have been equipped with cheeks in order to prevent the food from falling out of the animal's mouth is not applicable to all ornithischians. Many types of ornithischians, including stegosaurs, were

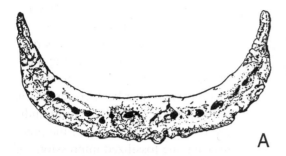

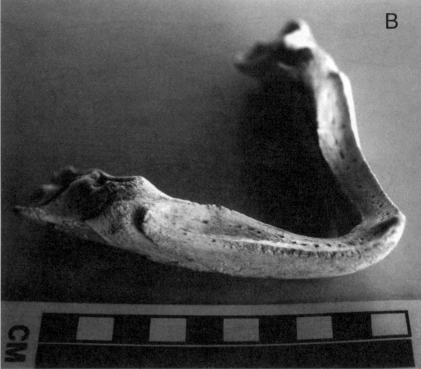

Figure 5. *Comparative views of an ornithischian predentary and Chelonia jaws. A, The predentary of the ankylosaur,* Saichania *(GI SPS 100/151) in dorsal view; note the large foramina which would have been covered by a keratinous sheath in life. B, The right side of the lower jaws of a snapping turtle,* Chelydra serpentina *(DM S4) in a dorsolateral view; note the wide dorsal shelf with formina between the interior and exterior ridges pertaining to the cutting edges of the beak. Scale bars equal 10 cm.*

equipped with diminutive teeth that could not have been effectively used for true mastication and thereby should not have required cheeks comparable to those of mammals. Cheeks would have provided little or no benefit for ornithischians with small, non-masticating teeth. For onithischians that used their teeth for cutting or cropping, cheeks could have even been more of a detriment by restricting the gape of the mouth and direct access to the teeth.

The most basal ornithischian ancestor had non-abrading teeth aligned in jaws which probably had lips resembling those of typical lacertilians. From such an ancestor, the many different groups of ornithischians diversified, often evolving more highly derived beak-like characteristics of the jaws. In some ornithischians, such as the stegosaurs, the lips were replaced by a more beak-like morphology. The *Stegosaurus* represents the most derived example known in which this occurred. Most ornithischians apparently did not progress as far as the stegosaurs in evolving a true beak-like morphology. Instead, the jaws of most ornithischians retained variations of lips posterior to their beaked snouts. However, it should be noted that the evolution of beaks is certainly not unique to *Stegosaurus*, or necessarily the Ornithischia. Various groups within the Saurischia had beaks, including the Ornithomimosauria (Barsbold and Osmolska, 1990) and the Oviraptorosauria (Barsbold and others, 1990). Marsh (1896) even commented on the reduced dentition of

the sauropod, *Diplodocus*, as suggesting that derived members of this group could have been edentulous, and thus he implied that a beak-like condition was developing in the diplodocid sauropods.

CONCLUSIONS

Stegosaurus is one of the most popular dinosaurs known from Utah, Colorado and Wyoming. As shown in figure 6A, the life restoration of a *Stegosaurus* equipped

Figure 6. *Life restoration of a* Stegosaurus. *A, Profile depicting the probable appearance of a* Stegosaurus *with beaked jaws. The model is by the author.*

with a beak, instead of cheeks, presents a dramatically vivid interpretation that is in keeping with its reptilian characteristics.

In a cladistic analysis, the recognition that the *Stegosaurus* has an extended beak along the dentary excludes the possession of cheeks as an autapomorphy within the Ornithischia. Posterior to the actual beak of the predentary and premaxilla, basal ornithischians had lips that resembled those of typical lacertilians. The variation of plesiomorphic morphologies from basal ornithischians, including basal stegosaurs, provide a sequential pattern that demonstrates how a "turtle-like" beak may have evolved. Derived characteristics indicating that the *Stegosaurus* was equipped with a beak, comparable to that of the Chelonia, includes the elevated dorsal flange above the tooth row that is expanded transversely into a wide, dorsal shelf with both a distinct exterior dorsal ridge, as well as a medial ridge.

The identification of *Stegosaurus* as having a beaked jaw makes it much more difficult to support the claim that other kinds of ornithischians had cheeks. Fossil skin impressions could possibly provide the most unequivocal evidence that might resolve the issue, but otherwise it remains inconclusive as to whether any ornithischians may have been equipped with some sort of an actual cheek. It appears to be more likely that no ornithischians had cheeks, and that other alternatives, related to the evolution of beaks as seen among stegosaurs, were employed by ornithischians with even more highly derived dental structures.

ACKNOWLEDGMENTS

I thank David Gillette, Ken Carpenter, and an anonymous reviewer for their insightful and constructive criticism. Also, I thank Paul Sereno for his encouraging comments, and Sylvia Czerkas for her dedication, patience and continual collaboration.

REFERENCES

Barsbold, Rinchen, and Osmolska, Halszka, 1990, Ornithomimosauria *in* Weishampel, D.B., Dodson, Peter, and Osmolska, Halszka, editors, The Dinosauria: Berkeley, University of California Press, p. 225-244.

Barsbold, Rinchen, Maryanska, Teresa, and Osmolska, Halszka, 1990, Oviraptorosauria *in* Weishampel, D. B., Dodson, Peter, and Osmolska, Halszka, editors, The Dinosauria: Berkeley, University of California Press, p. 249-258.

Benton, M. J., 1990, Origin and interrelationships of dinosaurs *in* Weishampel, D. B., Dodson, Peter, and Osmolska, Halszka, editors, The Dinosauria: Berkeley, University of California Press, p. 11-30.

Berman, D. S., and McIntosh, J. S., 1986, Description of the lower jaw of *Stegosaurus* (Reptilia, Ornithischia): Annals of Carnegie Museum of Natural History, v. 55, p. 29-40.

Brown, Barnum, and Schlaikjer, E. M., 1940, The structure and relationships of *Protoceratops*: Annals of the New York Academy of Sciences, v. 40, p. 133-266.

Colbert, E. H., 1981, A primitive ornithischian dinosaur from the Kayenta Formation of Arizona: Museum of Northern Arizona Press Bulletin Series, v. 53, 61 p.

Cope, E. D., 1883, On the characters of the skull of the Hadrosauridae: Proceedings of the Academy of Natural Sciences Philadelphia, v. 35, p. 97-107.

Dong, Z. M., Tang, Z. L., and Zhou, S. W., 1982 [Note on the new mid-Jurassic stegosaur from Sichuan Basin, China:] Vertebrata Palasiatica, v. 20, p. 83-87 (Chinese).

Galton, P. M., 1973, The cheeks of ornithischian dinosaurs: Lethaia, v. 6, p. 67-89.

—1990, Stegosauria *in* Weishampel, D. B., Dodson, Peter, and Osmolska, Halszka, editors, The Dinosauria: Berkeley, University of California Press, p. 435-455.

Gilmore, C. W., 1914, Osteology of the armored Dinosauria in the United States National Museum, with special reference to the genus *Stegosaurus*: U. S. National Museum Bulletin 89, 143 p.

---1920, Reptile reconstructions in the United States National Museum: Report Smithsonian Institution for 1917 (1920), p. 271-280.

Haubold, Hartmut, 1990, Ein neuer dinosauier (Ornithischia, Thyreophora) aus dem Unteren Jura des Nordlichen Mitteleuropa: Revue de Paleobiologie, v. 9, no. 1, p. 149-177.

Lull, R.S., 1903, Skull of *Triceratops serratus*: Bulletin of American Museum of Natural History, v. 29, p. 685-695.

—1905, Restoration of the horned dinosaur *Diceratops*: American Journal of Science, fourth series, v. 20, p. 420-422.

—1908, The cranial musculature and the origin of the frill in the ceratopsian dinosaurs: American Journal of Science, fourth series, v. 25, p. 387-399.

—1910a, The evolution of the Ceratopsia: Proceedings of the International Zoological Congress, v. 7, Boston, 1907, p. 771-777.

—1910b, *Stegosaurus ungulatus* Marsh, recently mounted at the Peabody Museum of Yale University: American Journal of Science, fourth series, v. 30, no. 180: p. 361-377.

—1933, A revision of the Ceratopsia or horned dinosaurs: Memoirs of the Peabody Museum of Natural History, v. 3, part 3, 175 p.

Lull, R. S., and Wright, N. E., 1942, Hadrosaurian dinosaurs of North America: Geological Society of America, Special Papers, v. 40, 242 p.

Mantell, G. A., 1851, Petrifications and their teachings; or a handbook to the gallery of organic remains of the British Museum: London, Henry G. Bohn, 496 p.

Marsh, O.C., 1887, Principal characters of American Jurassic dinosaurs. Part IX. The skull and dermal armor of *Stegosaurus*: American Journal of Science, third series, v. 34, p. 413- 417.

—1896, The dinosaurs of North America: Annual Report, U.S. Geological Survey, v. 16, part 1, p. 133-244.

Maryanska, Teresa, 1977, Ankylosauridae (Dinosauria) from Mongolia: Palaeontologica Polonica, v. 37, p. 85-151.

Morris, W. J., 1970, Hadrosaurian dinosaur bills--morphology and function: Contributions in Science, Los Angeles County Museum of Natural History, no. 193, 14 p.

Paul, G. S., 1984, The segnosaurian dinosaurs-- relics of the prosauropod-ornithischian transition?: Journal of Vertebrate Paleontology, v. 4, no. 4, p. 507-515.

Romer, A. S., 1956, Osteology of the reptiles: Chicago, University of Chicago Press, 772 p.

Russell, L. S., 1935, Musculature and function in the ceratopsia: Ottowa, Canada, Department of Mines, National Museum Bulletin, no. 77, Geological Series, no. 52, p. 39-48.

Sereno, P. C., 1991, *Lesothosaurus*, "fabrosaurids," and the early evolution of Ornithischia: Journal of Vertebrate Paleontology, v. 11, no. 2, p. 168-197.

Sereno, P. C., and Dong, Z. M., 1992, The skull of the basal stegosaur *Huayangosaurus taibaii* and a cladistic diagnosis of Stegosauria: Journal of Vertebrate Paleontology, v. 12, no. 3, p. 318-343.

Sternberg, C.M., 1935, Hooded hadrosaurs of the Belly River series of the Upper Cretaceous: A comparison with descriptions of new species: Ottowa, Canada, Department of Mines, National Museum Bulletin, v. 77, Geological Series, no. 52, 37 p.

—1951, Complete skeleton of *Leptoceratops gracilis* Brown from the Upper Edmonton member on Red Deer River, Alberta: Ottowa, Bulletin National Museums of Canada, v. 123, p. 225-255.

UPPER JURASSIC LIZARDS FROM THE MORRISON FORMATION OF DINOSAUR NATIONAL MONUMENT, UTAH

Susan E. Evans
Department of Anatomy and Developmental Biology, University College London,
Gower Street, London WC1E 6BT, U.K.
Email: ucgasue@ucl.ac.uk

Daniel J. Chure
U. S. Department of the Interior, National Parks Service,
Dinosaur National Monument, P.O. Box 128, Jensen, Utah 84035, USA.
Email: Dan_Chure@nps.gov

ABSTRACT

Late Jurassic lizard remains have been recovered from the Brushy Basin Member of the Morrison Formation at several localities in Dinosaur National Monument, Utah. These lizards include the scincomorph *Paramacellodus* and the anguimorph *Dorsetisaurus*. The dorsetisaur record is based on a single fragmentary jaw, but the paramacellodid material includes the first good skull material of this widely distributed Jurassic/Cretaceous genus, as well as a partial postcranium. In addition to the established taxa, a third genus is represented by a small block bearing the disarticulated remains of a small lizard. The elements preserved show a novel combination of features (including paired parietals, amphicoelous vertebrae and an elongated femur) which support the erection of a new genus, here named *Schilleria utahensis* new genus and species. Together these fossils contribute to a better understanding of the Morrison lizard fauna as a whole, and permit more detailed comparison between Morrison assemblages and those in other parts of the world.

INTRODUCTION

Lizards, snakes and their relatives (Squamata) form a large and complex group with over 6,000 living species. Most, however, are small animals with delicate skeletons and their fossil record is consequently very patchy. The earliest recorded lizards are from the Middle Jurassic of Britain (Evans, 1994a; 1998) and Kazakhstan (Nessov, 1988), but their relative diversity at this time (anguimorphs, scincomorphs and basal taxa), suggests a long Triassic and Early Jurassic history as yet unknown. The Late Jurassic record of squamates is somewhat better, but most specimens come from a relatively small number of localities - for example, Solnhofen (Germany), Cerin (France), Guimarota (Portugal), Karatau (Kazakhstan), Gansu (China) and those of the Morrison Formation of western North America.

Although Gilmore (1928) described lizards from the Morrison Formation at Como Bluff, Montana, this record was based on the jaws of *Cteniogenys*, now known to be a small early choristoderan (Evans, 1990). True lizards were not described until 1980 (Prothero and Estes, 1980) with the recovery of the genera *Paramacellodus* (Scincomorpha) and *Dorsetisaurus* (Anguimorpha) from Quarry 9, Como Bluff. Subsequently, lizard remains have been discovered at four other localities - Fruita in Colorado (George Callison, personal communication, 1994; Evans, 1996), the Black Hills region of Wyoming (John Foster, personal communication, 1994); Wolfe Creek, Colorado (Chure, unpublished information) and Dinosaur National Monument (Chure, 1992; Evans and Chure, 1998a,b). The present account concerns localities in Dinosaur National Monument (DNM), all of which are in the western Utah section of the Park.

Lizard remains have now been found at several localities in Dinosaur National Monument (most notably DNM 96, 317, 375 and 412), generally in association with other small vertebrates including mammals, frogs, salamanders and rhynchocephalians. As in many Late Jurassic assemblages, rhynchocephalians are more abundant than lizards, but the lizard remains from Dinosaur National Monument include some exceptional specimens which make an important contribution to our knowledge of lizard evolution at this time.

ABBREVIATIONS

Institutional abbreviations: AMNH - American Museum of Natural History, New York; BMNH - Natural History Museum, London; DNM, DINO - localities/collections of Dinosaur National Monument, Utah and Colorado; LACM - Los Angeles County Museum.

Abbreviations used in figures: a, possible astragalus; cl, clavicle; cv, caudal vertebrae; d, dentary; e, epiphysis; ecp, ectopterygoid process; f, femur; fi, fibula; ft, foot; il, ilium; j, jugal; mt5, fifth metatarsal; p, parietal; pa, palatine; po, postorbital; pp, palpebral; prf, prefrontal; pt, pterygoid; qpr, quadrate process; ru, possible radius and ulna; sp, splenial embayment; sv, sacral vertebra; t, tibia; v, vertebra.

THE MATERIAL

Dorsetisaurus

The holotype of the anguimorph lizard *Dorsetisaurus* (BMNH R.8129) is a partial skull and postcranial skeleton from an Early Cretaceous (Berriasian) horizon in the Purbeck Limestone Formation of Dorset, England (Hoffstetter, 1967; Allen and Wimbledon, 1991). The same genus has subsequently been recorded from the Late Jurassic (Oxfordian/ Kimmeridgian) Lignite Beds of Guimarota, Portugal (Seiffert, 1973; Estes, 1983). Prothero and Estes (1980) gave the first record of *Dorsetisaurus* from the Morrison Formation on the basis of two dentaries (AMNH 27646, 27647) from Quarry 9, Como Bluff, Wyoming. More recently, the genus has been reported from two localities in Colorado - Fruita (George Callison, personal communication, 1994; Evans, work in progress) and Wolfe Creek (Chure, unpublished information based on uncatalogued material in the Denver Museum of Natural History).

The *Dorsetisaurus* specimen from Dinosaur National Monument (DINO 15915, DNM locality 96) is a single left dentary with 12 tooth positions (out of an estimated total of 15-16). The teeth have the same distinctive lanceolate form as those from the Purbeck Lime-

stone Formation, with tapering tips, sharp anterior and posterior keels and wider, rounded lingual and labial ridges (figure 1A,B). The lingual ridge is somewhat more prominent in DINO 15915, with weaker anterior and posterior flanges and no obvious striations, but some of these differences may be artifacts of preservation. The dorsetisaur dentary from Fruita (LACM 5572/120504) is of similar general shape but the teeth are more rounded in cross section and lack the strong lingual and labial ridges. In this respect they more closely resemble the teeth of the type and only specimen of *D. hebetidens* (BMNH R.8109, Hoffstetter, 1967) from the Purbeck Limestone Formation, although this specimen is poorly preserved. If the Fruita specimen is congeneric with other *Dorsetisaurus* (and there can be striking interspecific differences in tooth morphology in lizards - for example, the serrated blade-like teeth of *Varanus komodoensis* by comparison with the more robust, rounded teeth of *Varanus exanthematicus*), then the strong lingual and labial ridges may characterize the teeth of *D. purbeckensis*, permitting attribution of the Dinosaur National Monument specimen to that species despite the small differences noted above.

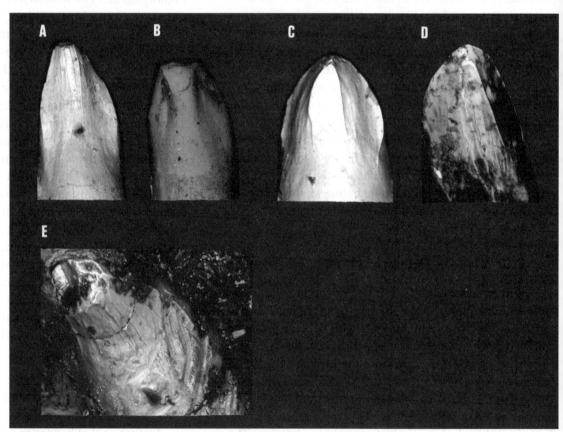

Figure 1. *Scanning electron micrographs of individual teeth of A,* Dorsetisaurus, *Purbeck Limestone Formation, uncatalogued specimen, Dorset County Museum, Dorchester, England, x50; B,* Dorsetisaurus, *Morrison Formation, Dinosaur National Park, DINO 15915, x75; C,* Paramacellodus, *Purbeck Limestone Formation, uncatalogued specimen, Dorset County Museum, Dorchester, England, x350; D,* Paramacellodus, *Morrison Formation, Dinosaur National Park, DINO 14864, x200; E,* Schilleria utahensis *new genus and species, holotype, Morrison Formation, Dinosaur National Monument, DINO 14720, x500.*

Paramacellodus

The genus *Paramacellodus* was also origi-nally described from the Purbeck Limestone Formation (*Paramacellodus oweni* Hoffstetter 1966), but it has subsequently been recorded from a wide range of localities including the Late Jurassic of Tanzania (Tendagaru, Zils and others, 1995) and North America (Prothero and Estes, 1980; Chure, 1992; Evans and Chure, 1998a,b), and the Early Cretaceous of Spain and Morocco (Richter, 1994). Other genera current-ly attributed to the family Paramacellodidae include *Becklesius* (Britain, Early Cretaceous, Hoffstetter, 1967; Portugal, Late Jurassic, Seif-fert, 1973); *Sharovisaurus* (Kazakhstan, Late Jurassic, Hecht and Hecht, 1984); and *Mimobecklesisaurus* (Late Jurassic, China, Li, 1985), making this a successful and widespread group of early Mesozoic lizards.

The paramacellodid material from Dinosaur National Monument consists of three specimens, two partial skulls (DINO 14864 and DINO 15914 [DNM localities 412 and 317, respective-ly]) and a small block (DINO 13861[DNM locality 96]) bearing the posterior trunk verte-brae and hind limbs of a small lizard in associa-tion with a few ventral osteoscutes which sug-gest attribution to *Paramacellodus*.

The two skull specimens (figure 2A,B) rep-resent the most complete paramacellodid cranial material currently available. Most of the speci-mens from other localities are isolated jaw ele-ments and osteoscutes. The original Purbeck material includes vertebrae and limb bones and a partial skull with fragments of the palate, but no details of either the skull roof or temporal region are preserved. This limited material has hampered comparison between localities, and has also prevented detailed cladistic analysis of para-macellodid relationships.

The new paramacellodid material has been described in detail elsewhere (Evans and Chure, 1998a,b), but the main features can be summarized here. The skull is gracile and lightly sculptured, with paired nasals and frontals and a single, square parietal. The upper temp-oral opening is reduced by a postorbitofrontal mass which seems to be composed of a large upper postfrontal and a small lower postorbital. The jugal and squamosal are slender. DINO 14864 provides the first evidence of a palpebral in the anterior margin of the orbit and there was apparently also a small lacrimal. The palatine and pterygoid bones are lightly built but both bear teeth. The marginal dentition is homodont and pleurodont, with

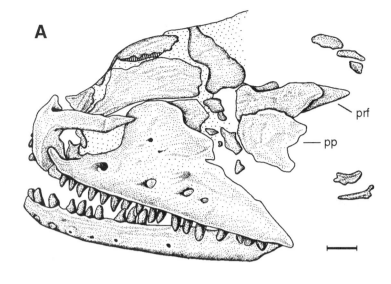

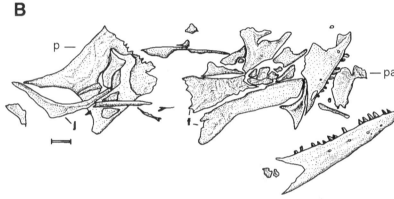

Figure 2. Paramacellodus, *Dinosaur National Park. A, DINO 14864, left lateral view; B, DINO 15914, dorsal view of specimen. Scale bars = 1 mm.*

around 20 tooth positions on the maxilla, nine on the median premaxilla, and 22-23 on the dentary. The teeth have tapered, lingually inflected tips like those of their Purbeck counterparts, smooth labially, striated lingually (figure 1C,D). Richter (1994) gave detailed illustrations of the teeth of paramacellodids, describing a prominent central region, flanked anteriorly and posteriorly by flange-like facetted regions and variable numbers of weaker striae. This arrangement is clearly seen in the teeth of both the Purbeck *Paramacellodus* and those of DINO 14864 (figure 1C,D), although there are small dif-ferences in the number and arrangement of the striae. There is also close correspondence between the Purbeck and Morrison specimens in the shape of the maxilla (high, nearly vertical narial margin; tapering upturned premaxillary process; wide medial flange).

DINO 13861 is a small block bearing the right and left hind limbs of a small lizard (figure 3) with six dorsal vertebrae, a few fragments of the hand and a small num-ber of narrow osteoscutes which probably pertained to

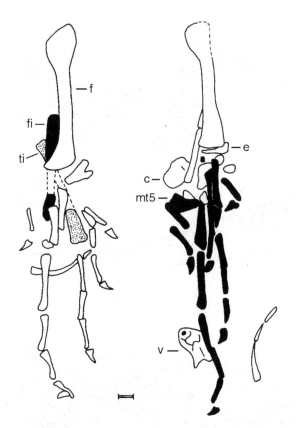

Figure 3. Paramacellodus, *Dinosaur National Park, partial postcranial skeleton, DINO 13861. Scale bar = 1 mm.*

the ventral surface of the animal. The osteoscutes, as well as the general form of the femur and vertebrae, suggest attribution to *Paramacellodus* although this assignment is tentative pending the recovery of associated skull and postcranial material. The vertebrae are typical of other small scincomorph lizards of this period, procoelous with small but distinct condylar and cotylar surfaces on the centrum, relatively long, low, posteriorly placed neural spines, and weak accessory facets (zygosphenes and zygantra) on the zyapophyseal surfaces. Of the two hind limbs, the right is the better preserved. The femur is relatively short with robust proximal and distal heads. The distal epiphysis is detached, suggesting this was an immature animal. During preservation, the femur telescoped down over the crural bones, which now lie under and slightly to the left of the femur so that only a right fibula is visible (the tibia and fibula are preserved on the left leg). In the ankle, the unfused astragalus and calcaneum provide further evidence of immaturity. The distal tarsal row cannot be reconstructed. In the foot, the first four metatarsals are relatively short and robust, the fifth is rotated inwards but is clearly hooked in two planes, as is typical for lizards. The phalangeal formula is 2:3:4:5:3 and the claws are strong with slender pointed tips. *Paramacellodus* was probably a predominantly ground dwelling lizard. The epipod-

ial/propodial proportions (Ti/Fe = 0.77) are similar to those of the modern scincid lizard *Mabuya*, but the foot is relatively longer (Foot/Fe = 1.5).

Taking the skeletal remains as a whole, the bones of the Morrison paramacellodids are generally smaller and more gracile than those from Purbeck, but the overall structure is very similar. There are no secure criteria on which to base a new specific diagnosis. For this reason the Morrison *Paramacellodus* material is referred to *Paramacellodus* sp., cf. *P. oweni*.

Systematics

Lepidosauria
    Squamata
        Family indeterminate

New Genus

In addition to material of *Dorsetisaurus* and *Paramacellodus*, one additional lizard specimen (DNM 14720) has been recovered from Dinosaur National Monument. A second specimen, probably of the same kind, is currently under preparation and will be discussed elsewhere. DNM 14720 preserves the disarticulated but associated remains of a small lizard showing a unique combination of character states which not only distinguish it clearly from both *Paramacellodus* and *Dorsetisaurus*, but also from early lizards described from other localities.

Schilleria new genus

Type species: *Schilleria utahensis.*
Etymology: To honour Dr. Robert Schiller, Chief Scientist for Grand Teton National Park and active supporter of research on the Morrison Formation.
Holoype: As for the type and only species.
Type locality: DNM locality 375, Dinosaur National Monument, Utah.
Type Horizon: Brushy Basin Member, Morrison Formation (Kimmeridgian).
Diagnosis: As for type and only species.

Schilleria utahensis new species

Etymology: For Utah
Holoype: DNM 14720, part and counterpart of a dissociated skeleton (figures 1E, 4, 5)
Diagnosis: A small (SV length estimated at 80 mm) gracile lizard characterized by the following combination of character states: shallow pleurodont dentary with weak subdental ridge; open ventrally placed Meckelian fossa, and pronounced subdental gutter; homodont, unicuspid teeth with striated tips; parietals paired, apparent-

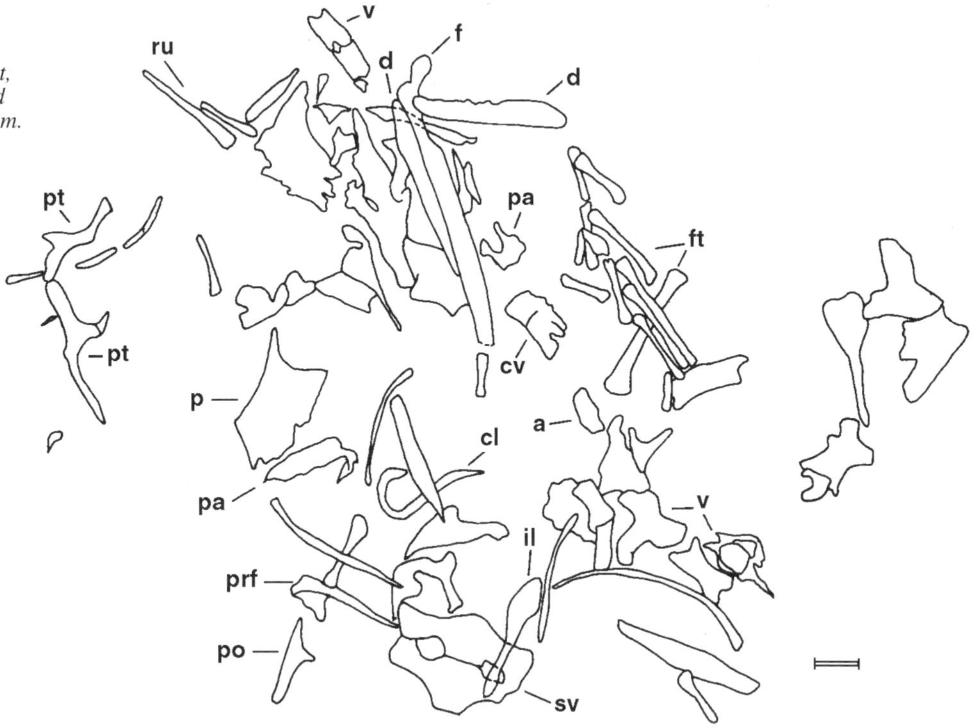

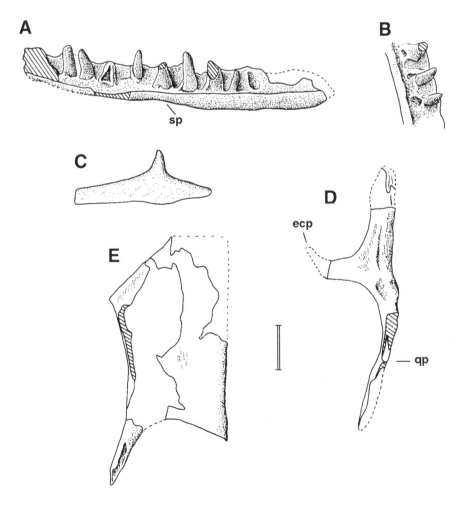

Figure 4. Schilleria utahensis *new genus and species, holotype, DINO 14720, Dinosaur National Monument, plan of specimen taken from part and counterpart blocks. Scale bar = 1 mm.*

Figure 5. Schilleria utahensis *new genus and species, holotype, DINO 14720, A, left jaw ramus, lingual view; B, left jaw ramus, partial occlusal view to show width of subdental gutter; C, possible left postorbital bone; D, left pterygoid, dorsal view; E, left parietal, dorsal view. Scale bar = 1 mm.*

ly without sculpture; parietals with short straight posterolateral processes and short triangular posteromedian
process, shallow lateral adductor muscle surfaces;
frontals apparently narrower than parietals leaving
anterolateral shoulders on the latter; palatines and pterygoids slender, apparently toothless, and probably enclosing broad interpterygoid vacuity; palatine with relatively
deep choanal groove; pterygoid deeply emarginated by
suborbital fenestra; amphicoelous vertebral centra, apparently without intercentra; caudal vertebrae autotomous;
clavicles medially expanded and perforate; femur long
and slender (at least 6.5x length of typical vertebral centrum); long metatarsals contributing to a foot roughly
twice the femoral length.

Distinguished from a majority of early lizards
described to date by the presence of amphicoelous and
not procoelous vertebrae; distinguished from the amphicoelous Solnhofen genus *Bavarisaurus* by the shallow
dentary and smaller teeth (those of *Bavarisaurus* are long
and recurved); distinguished from the Solnhofen genera
Eichstaettisaurus and *Ardeosaurus* by the length of the
femur and the shape of the frontoparietal suture.

Description

The dissociated skeletal remains of this small lizard
are preserved on a small part and counterpart block
(DINO 14720A and B), with a few limb bone fragments
on a third block (DINO 14720C). Much of the skeleton
remains indecipherable since many of the small crushed
bones were split when the blocks were separated. However, recognizable elements include parts of the skull roof,
circumorbital series, palate and mandible, with isolated
vertebrae, and parts of the girdles and limbs. A preliminary description of the specimen has been given elsewhere (Evans and Chure, 1998a), but further work has
revealed new details and permitted some reinterpretation.

The skull roof is represented by a single element
(figure 5E) - previously interpreted as a possible postorbitofrontal (Evans and Chure, 1998a) - but now revealed
(through exposure of its medial part) as one half of a
paired parietal. The bone is flat and unsculptured, with a
short postparietal process, facetted for the supratemporal,
relatively parallel medial and lateral margins, and shallow lateral surfaces for the adductor muscles. Medially,
the left and right parietals contributed to the formation of
a triangular posteromedian process. The central part of
the bone is partly damaged and the presence or absence
of a parietal foramen cannot be determined. The shape
of the anterior region is also problematical in that there
appear to have been strong anterolateral 'shoulders.'
These suggest either that the frontal had unusual posterolateral processes or that the frontal was significantly nar-

rower than the parietal. The latter condition is seen in
some living agamid lizards (for example, *Uromastyx*)
where a strongly triradiate postorbital meets the parietal
'shoulder.' Unfortunately, the frontals are almost certainly amongst the mass of broken, split bones lying to the
side of the femur, and their shape remains unknown.

Two bones are tentatively attributed to the circumorbital series. The first is an element with a strong facetted
horizontal margin and a deep ventral flange (prf, figure
4) which may be a prefrontal. The second (figure 5C) is
a small triradiate bone with two long processes (connected by an apparently horizontal margin whose thin bipar-
tite edge suggests the presence of two underlying facets)
and a third short process whose axis is at right angles to
the other two. The borders which converge onto this
process are smooth and rounded, suggesting they were
free margins. No postcranial bone, and few cranial elements could match this shape. The most likely candidate is a right postorbital or postorbitofrontal. Under this
interpretation, the long margin would have been ventral,
with the shorter ventral process meeting the jugal and the
longer one contacting the squamosal. The short dorsal
process would have contacted the parietal 'shoulder.'

The palate is represented by paired pterygoids and
palatines. One palatine (the left) lies to the right of the
femur, its posterior part is missing but a deep choanal
groove and medial maxillary process are clearly visible.
The other bone is broken but is preserved in dorsal view,
showing the relatively long, slender, posterior palatal
plate. Neither bone shows any trace of palatal teeth (for
example, where the palatal plate of the right bone has
been stripped away). Of the pterygoids, the left is most
completely preserved (figure 5D). It is a gracile bone
with a slender palatal process, a deep suborbital embayment, and narrow ectopterygoid and quadrate flanges.
Again, where parts of the anterior palatal plate have been
stripped away, there is no trace of teeth.

Both dentaries are preserved, the left in lingual view,
the right in ventrolateral view, but this element is largely
obscured by the adjacent femur and overlying skull fragments. At its anterior end, the Meckelian groove is seen
to be open and ventrally placed. The left element (figure
5A,B) is relatively long and shallow, with a weak subdental ridge. A sharp narrowing of this ridge in the central part of the bone suggests the presence of a splenial
facet. There are at least twenty tooth positions separated
from the subdental shelf by a strong subdental gutter
(figure 5B). The teeth are small and fully pleurodont,
separated by large gaps suggestive of rapid replacement
(thus the individual may have been immature). One
tooth tip is almost complete. With a conventional stere-
omicroscope, no details are visible, but scanning electron

microscopy (low vacuum, uncoated) reveals a slightly inturned tip, almost circular in cross section (figure 1E). The lingual surface is striated and limited anteriorly and posteriorly by weak keels. Centrally there is a raised portion delimited by pronounced striae. In these features, the tooth of *Schilleria* resembles that of *Paramacellodus* but the tip is longer, narrower, and less mediolaterally compressed.

Vertebrae and slender single-headed ribs are scattered over the block. The most complete vertebrae are the robust sacrals which lie in articulation (and were probably fused) with their ribs enclosing a foramen sacrale. The centra are clearly visible (the anterior one is broken open) and are amphicoelous and notochordal. There is no intervening intercentrum. Of the caudals, fragmentary anterior elements show strong caudal ribs, while the posterior caudals (figure 4, cv) are elongated, with long, low spines and fracture planes which divide the vertebra into roughly equal halves.

The only remnant of the pectoral girdle is a slender hook-like clavicle with an expanded perforate medial head (figure 4, cl). None of the forelimb elements can be identified with confidence, although two slender bones at the upper left corner of the block may be parts of the radius and ulna (figure 4, ru), and there is a short bone close to the clavicle which resembles a first metacarpal. Fragments of the ilia lie adjacent to the sacrum but provide no detail. The hindlimb and foot are somewhat better preserved. The most conspicuous element is a long, slender femur, most of which lies on the counterpart block. The proximal head lies below the left dentary (figure 4, f), the distal end is missing, but between them is a long, nearly straight shaft. The femur is at least 12 mm in length (6.4x, where x is the length of the second sacral centrum, itself roughly equal to the length of a standard dorsal vertebral centrum), but may have been somewhat longer than this. The crus is not preserved, but elements of the foot are distributed on both blocks. Metatarsals 1-3 are aligned, with the elongated MT 4 crossing below them. The relative lengths MT 4 to MT 1 suggest a strongly asymmetric foot, with a long fourth digit. Several phalanges are preserved (the first toe appears complete) and allowing for a normal phalangeal formula of 2:3:4:5;3/4, the foot length was probably about 17 mm, equal or longer than the femur. A small nodular element near the base of MT4 may be either a reduced fifth metatarsal, or an isolated (unfused) astragalus (figure 4, a).

Lifestyle

The small tapering teeth and shallow jaw argue for a diet of small insects. The proportions of the hindlimb

(for example, femur, 6.4x; MT4, 2.3x) match those of conventional terrestrial lepidosaurs (for example, *Sphenodon*, femur 6.8x; MT4 2.9x; *Agama agama*, femur 5.7x; MT4, 2.4x), although the femur is relatively more gracile in *Schilleria*.

Relationships

As with many Jurassic and Early Cretaceous lizards, *Schilleria* shows a mosaic of characters, the most significant of which are the paired parietals, notochordal vertebrae and expanded perforate clavicles. The latter are uniquely squamate. Notochordal vertebrae are found, on the one hand, in primitive lepidosaurs (*Sphenodon*), but also in the derived gekkotans (procoely is the primitive state for crown-group lizards), while paired parietals are found both in primitive lepidosauromorphs (kuehneosaurs) and some derived lizards (gekkotans, xantusiids). Recent work on early lizards, however, has shown that both paired parietal and notochordal amphicoelous vertebrae are also found in some primitive squamates that lie outside the crown-group (for example, the Late Jurassic Solnhofen genus *Bavarisaurus*, Evans, 1994b, and some Early Cretaceous lizards from Mexico, Reynoso, 1996; and Spain, Evans and Barbadillo, work in progress). Most of these taxa also have a perforate clavicle. *Schilleria* is very fragmentary and can be coded for too few character states to permit a rigorous cladistic analysis. As a preliminary step, we entered it into a matrix of living and fossil lepidosauromorphs (Evans, work in progress) and explored its position using Paup 3.1 (Swofford, 1993). The best fit (coded for only 42 out of 254 character states, on a tree of 33 included taxa) placed *Schilleria* consistently outside the squamate crown group (defined as the common ancestor of Iguania and Scleroglossa, and all its descendents), one step crownward of *Bavarisaurus*.

CONCLUSIONS

The Dinosaur National Monument small reptile assemblage resembles that of other Morrison localities in containing three established genera - the lizards *Paramacellodus* and *Dorsetisaurus*, and the rhynchocephalian *Opisthias*. The small choristoderan *Cteniogenys*, abundant in Quarry 9, Como Bluff, is represented at Dinosaur National Monument by a single very fragmentary specimen. *Schilleria* is currently unknown from other localities, while a second anguimorph *Parviraptor* (Evans, 1994c, 1996) and the aberrant scincomorph *Saurillodon* (Seiffert, 1973; Evans, 1994a), now recorded from Fruita, Colorado (Evans, 1996) have yet to be found at

Dinosaur National Monument (table 1). To the extent that many Morrison assemblages are still incompletely known, these differences may be largely artifact.

In general terms, the Morrison small vertebrate assemblages show many resemblances to that of the Purbeck Limestone Formation of England, and the two horizons were once thought to be roughly contemporaneous. More recent work, however, suggests the Purbeck Limestone Formation to be slightly younger (Berriasian, Allen and Wimbledon, 1991) than the Brushy Basin Member of the Morrison (Kimmeridgian/Tithonian, Turner and Peterson, 1992). However, the Middle Jurassic (Bathonian) small reptile assemblages of Britain (for example, Kirtlington, Oxfordshire; Skye, Scotland, Waldman and Evans, 1994) and the Late Jurassic (Oxfordian/Kimmeridgian) assemblage of Guimarota in Portugal (Seiffert, 1973) also contain several components in common with those of the Morrison (*Parviraptor, Saurillodon, Cteniogenys*), although the lepidosauromorph *Marmoretta* (Evans, 1991) has yet to be recovered from North America (table 1). It is clear that some small reptile genera had a long temporal range and should not be used as biostratigraphic indicators.

ACKNOWLEDGMENTS

We would like to record our thanks to Scott Madsen and Ann Elder of Dinosaur National Monument who found the material described here, and especially to Scott Madsen for his careful preparation of these delicate fossils. Angela Milner (BNHM, London), Sam McLeod (LACM) and Mark Norell (AMNH) permitted access to comparative material, while Olivier Rieppel (Chicago) and Nick Fraser (Virginia) provided helpful comments on an earlier draft of the manuscript. Aysha Raza, University College London, prepared figures 2-4, and contributed to the data on limb bone ratios. This work was partially funded by a grant from the University of London Central Research Fund.

Table 1. *Comparison of small reptile assemblages in horizons of the Brushy Basin Member, Morrison Formation with those of Jurassic and Early Cretaceous localities from Europe.* **Explanation:** *Common, one of the most abundant small reptiles in the assemblage; Present, represented by several specimens; Rare, only one or two specimens known.*

Locality	Kirtlington/ Skye	Guimarota	Morrison/ Como Bluff	Morrison DNM	Morrison Fruita	Morrison Wolfe Creek	Purbeck
Age	Bathonian	Oxfordian/ Kimmeridgian	Kimmeridgian	Kimmeridgian	Kimmeridgian	Kimmeridgian	Berriasian
Marmoretta	Common	Common	Unrecorded	Unrecorded	Unrecorded	Unrecorded	Unrecorded
Cteniogenys	Common	Common	Common	Rare	Unrecorded	Unrecorded	Unrecorded
Sphenodontians	Rare	Unrecorded	Present - mostly *Opisthias*	Common - mostly *Opisthias*	Common - mostly *Opisthias*	Unrecorded	Rare - includes *Opisthias*
Paramacellodus	Rare	Unrecorded	Present	Present	Rare	Unrecorded	Present
Becklesius	Unrecorded	Present	Unrecorded	Unrecorded	Unrecorded	Unrecorded	Common
Dorsetisaurus	Unrecorded	Present	Rare	Rare	Rare	Present	Common
Parviraptor	Present	Present	Unrecorded	Unrecorded	Present	Unrecorded	Present
Saurillodon	Present	Present	Unrecorded	Unrecorded	Rare	Unrecorded	Unrecorded

REFERENCES

Allen, Perce, and Wimbledon, W. A., 1991, Correlation of NW European Purbeck-Wealden (non- marine Cretaceous) as seen from the English type areas: Cretaceous Research, v. 12, p. 511- 526.

Chure, D. J., 1992, Lepidosaurian reptiles from the Brushy Basin Member of the Morrison Formation (Upper Jurassic) of Dinosaur National Monument, Utah and Colorado, USA: Journal of Vertebrate Paleontology, v. 12 (supplement 3), p. 24A.

Estes, Richard, 1983, Sauria terrestria, Amphisbaenia, *in* Wellnhofer, Peter, editor, Handbüch der Paläoherpetologie, v. 10A: Stuttgart and New York, Gustav Fischer Verlag, 249 p.

Evans, S. E., 1990, The skull of *Cteniogenys*, a choristodere (Reptilia: Archosauromorpha) from the Middle Jurassic of Oxfordshire: Zoological Journal of the Linnean Society, v. 99, p. .205-237.

—1991, A new lizard-like reptile (Diapsida: Lepidosauromorpha) from the Middle Jurassic of England: Zoological Journal of the Linnean Society, v. 103, p. 391-412.

—1994a, Jurassic lizard assemblages: Revue de Paleobiologie, v. 7, p. 55-65.

—1994b. The Solnhofen (Jurassic: Tithonian) lizard genus *Bavarisaurus*: new skull material and a reinterpretation: Neues Jahrbuch für Geologie und Paläontologie Abhandlungen, v. 192, p. 71-88.

—1994c. A new anguimorph lizard from the Jurassic and early Cretaceous of England: Palaeontology, v. 37, p. 33-49.

—1996, *Parviraptor* (Squamata: Anguimorpha) and other lizards from the Morrison Formation at Fruita, Colorado, *in* Morales, Michael, editor, The continental Jurassic: Museum of Northern Arizona Bulletin, v. 60, p. 243-248.

—1998, Crown-group lizards from the Middle Jurassic of Britain: Palaeontographica, v. 250, p 123-154.

Evans, S. E., and Chure, D. J., 1998a, Morrison lizards - structure, relationships and biogeography, *in* Carpenter, Kenneth, Chure, D. J., and Kirkland, James, editors, The Upper Jurassic Morrison Formation - an interdisciplinary study: Modern Geology v. 23, p. 35-48.

—1998b, Paramacellodid lizard skulls from the Jurassic Morrison Formation at Dinosaur National Monument, Utah: Journal of Vertebrate Paleontology, v. 18, p. 99-114.

Gilmore, Charles, 1928, Fossil lizards of North America: Memoirs of the National Academy of Sciences, v. 22, p. 1-169.

Hecht, M. K., and Hecht, B. M., 1984, A new lizard from Jurassic deposits of middle Asia: Paleontological Journal, v. 3, p. 133-136.

Hoffstetter, Robert, 1967, Coup d'oeil sur les Sauriens (=lacertiliens) des couches de Purbeck (Jurassique supérieur d'Angleterre), Colloques Internationaux: Centre National de la Recherche Scientifique, v. 163, p. 349-371.

Li, J-L., 1985, A new lizard from the Late Jurassic of Subei, Gansu: Vertebrata PalAsiatica, v. 23, p. 13-18.

Nessov, L. A., 1988, Late Mesozoic amphibians and lizards of Soviet Central Asia: Acta Zoologica Cracoviensis, v. 31, p. 475-486.

Prothero, D. R., and Estes, Richard, 1980, Late Jurassic lizards from Como Bluff, Wyoming, and their palaeobiogeographic significance: Nature, v. 286, p. 484-486.

Reynoso, V. H., 1996, A primitive lizard from the Early Cretaceous of Mexico and the phylogenetic position of early lizards: Journal of Vertebrate Paleontology, v. 16, p. 60A.

Richter, Annette, 1994, Lacertilia aus der Unteren Kreide von Uña und Galve (Spanien) und Anoual (Marokko): Berliner Geowissenschaftliche Abhandlungen, v. 14, p. 1-147.

Seiffert, Juergen, 1973, Upper Jurassic lizards from central Portugal: Memorias Serviços Geológicos de Portugal, v. 22, p. 1-85.

Swofford, D. L., 1993, PAUP - Phylogenetic analysis using parsimony, version 3.1: Computer Program distributed by Illinois Natural History Survey.

Turner, C. E., and Peterson, Fred, 1992, Sedimentology and stratigraphy of the Morrison Formation in Dinosaur National Monument, Utah and Colorado: U. S. Geological Survey, Denver, Annual Report for Period May 1, 1991-April 30th, 1992.

Waldman, Michael, and Evans, S. E., 1994, Lepidosaurian reptiles from the Middle Jurassic of Skye: Zoological Journal of the Linnean Society, v. 112, p. 135-150.

Zils, Wolfgang, Werner, Christa, Moritz, Andrea, and Saanane, Charles, 1995, Tendagaru, the most famous dinosaur locality of Africa - review, survey and future prospects: Documenta Naturae, Munich, v. 97, p. 1-41.

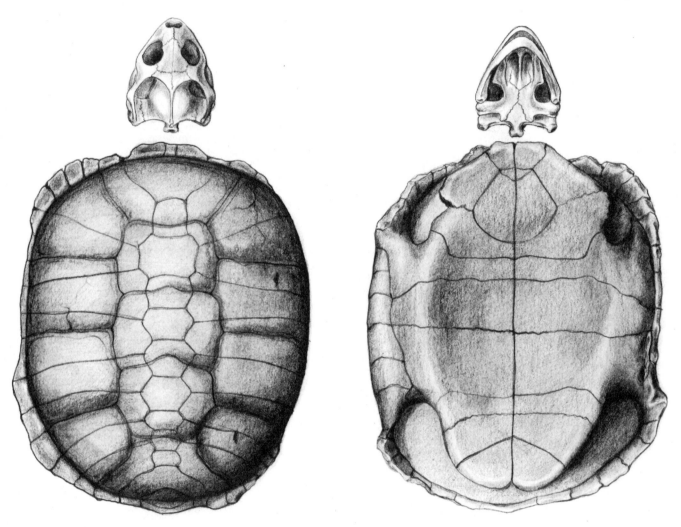

Brian Maebius © 1999

Eocene turtle

GLIRODON GRANDIS, A NEW MULTITUBERCULATE MAMMAL FROM THE UPPER JURASSIC MORRISON FORMATION

George F. Engelmann
Department of Geography and Geology
University of Nebraska at Omaha
Omaha, NE 68182

George Callison
Dinamation International Society
550 Jurassic Court
Fruita, CO 81521

ABSTRACT

Two partial skulls and some other material collected from the Morrison Formation at Dinosaur National Monument in Utah and the Fruita Paleontological Area in Colorado represent the new genus and species *Glirodon grandis*. Much of the morphology of the anterior part of the skull is preserved including a complete dentition. Many of the features of the taxon appear to be relatively primitive among multituberculates. These include: a primitive dental formula of three upper and one lower incisors, an upper canine, five upper and four lower premolars, and two upper and two lower molars; and tooth crown morphology of most cheek teeth very similar to that of *Ctenacodon*. At the same time, the dentition exhibits the relatively advanced characteristics of having restricted enamel on both the second upper and the lower incisors, and the development of a third, labial row of cusps on the second upper molars. This combination of characters makes it difficult to determine the phylogenetic relationships of the taxon, and we refer it to the Plagiaulacoidea because the solution to this problem depends on resolution of relationships among the members of this undoubtedly paraphyletic group.

INTRODUCTION

One of the most diverse Mesozoic mammalian faunas has been collected from the Late Jurassic Morrison Formation (Clemens and others, 1979). However, most of that diversity has been provided by a single locality at Como Bluff in Wyoming. Although exposures of the Morrison are widespread throughout the Colorado Plateau, it is only recently that fossil mammals have been collected in Utah and Colorado from this formation (Chure and Engelmann, 1989; Rasmussen and Callison, 1981).

Among collections that have been made at the Fruita Paleontological Area in Colorado and Dinosaur National Monument in Utah are two partial skulls of a multituberculate mammal. Comparison of the two partial skulls, LACM (Los Angeles County Museum) 120453 from Fruita, Colorado, and DINO (Dinosaur National Monument) 10822, leads us to conclude that although they are not exactly identical, they cannot be distinguished as separate taxa, even at the species level. Therefore, the description that follows is based on both specimens. The two specimens are somewhat complementary. The Fruita specimen is less crushed and preserves better the shape of the snout and palate, but the anterior part of the braincase is preserved in the DINO specimen and the dentition is more complete and much better preserved. Various details of individual bones of the skull are preserved better in one or the other of the two specimens, and in some points the skulls corroborate each other on interpretations that would be much less convincing if only observed in a single specimen. A very poorly preserved mandible associated with the DINO specimen permits identification of a mandible (LACM 120452) and partial mandible (LACM 120688) from Fruita. In addition, a maxilla (LACM 120458) from Fruita is assigned to this taxon as is a fragment of a mandible (LACM 120746).

SYSTEMATICS

Suborder Plagiaulacoidea
   Plagiaulacoidea *incertae sedis*
      Genus *Glirodon* new genus
Etymology: Greek, glires, meaning rodent, referring to the rodent-like incisors and Greek odons, meaning tooth.
Diagnosis: As for the only species *Glirodon grandis* new species
Glirodon grandis new species
Etymology: Latin, grand, referring to the relatively large

size of the species among Jurassic mammals.
Diagnosis: Differs from other plagiaulacoids in having restricted enamel on both the lower incisors and on I^2; differs from all Cimolodonta in having a complete primitive dental formula of 3,1,5,2/1,0,4,2. Holotype, DINO 10822. Referred specimens: LACM 120453, LACM 120452, LACM 120688, LACM 120458, LACM 120746.

Anatomy of the Skull

Dorsal Aspect

In overall view, the snout is rather short, broadening rapidly at the anterior zygomata which arise far forward on the maxilla. This gives the muzzle a triangular appearance in dorsal view (figures 1,2,3, and 4). The nasal bones are much longer than they are wide. Beginning as narrow elements that project slightly anterior to the incisors, they broaden very gradually posteriorly for most of their length before widening abruptly to their widest point just anterior to the suture with the frontal bones, and then narrow again posteriorly to the oblique naso-frontal suture. This appears to be an overlapping suture in which the nasals overlap the frontals with the surface expression of the suture extending postero-laterally from the median suture. One prominent feature evident in the DINO specimen is a pair of large foramina occurring within the middle of the nasals. There is one of these large foramina on each of the right and left nasals. They are situated slightly lateral to the long axis of each bone and open broadly antero-laterally. Breakage through the left foramen reveals that within the bone the narrow (but still quite easily distinguished) canal trends medially and slightly anteriorly. It is not clear whether this canal perforates the bone or if it continues within the bone for some distance. A similar, but much smaller foramen is centered within the right nasal bone anterior to the larger foramen. In lateral view (figures 3 and 4), the nasal is in contact with the premaxilla and the maxilla. The premaxilla has a broad expression on the side of the snout. The suture between it and the maxilla arises anterior to the canines and curves slightly anteriorly at first and then gradually posteriorly as it ascends to the suture with the nasal, which it contacts approximately over the canine. The widest point of the nasals occurs approximately at the point where the zygomatic processes of the maxilla arise from the main body of the maxilla. Posterior to this point, the lateral contact of the nasal is with a flat, triangular, bony shelf that covers the space between the main body of the maxilla and the zygomatic process as it diverges posteriorly. This bony plate could be referred to as a supraorbital shelf.

The supraorbital shelf is a relatively thin bony shelf apparently attached anteriorly to the snout and laterally to the zygomatic arch. The posterior margin is free and appears to be intact, as a similar outline is preserved on both right and left sides of the DINO skull. The posterior margin has a broad, lobate shape, with a relatively acute notch separating the lobe from the cranium. The medial margin of this notch forms a fairly sharp ridge which gradually merges with the flexure between the dorsal and lateral surfaces of the cranium and becomes indistinguishable at about the anteriormost of two foramina on the flexure (see below). It is not clear what bone this represents. It could be part of the maxilla, but a separation between the zygomatic arch and this bone in similar places in both specimens as a result of crushing suggests a sutural contact at that point. It could be a lacrimal bone, an interpretation consistent with Kielan-Jaworowska's (1974) identification of this element in *Nemegtbaatar* and *Chulsanbaatar*, but it is a very thin plate situated dorsally over the antorbital space and there is no indication of a lacrimal foramen to support such an interpretation. Another possible interpretation is that it is an anterior extension of the frontal bone. Because of crushing it is not clear whether there is continuity between this bony shelf and the portion of the frontal bone that participates in the cranial roof, but they do come in contact immediately posterior to the most posterior point of the naso-frontal suture.

The anterior half of the frontal bone is preserved in the Fruita specimen and virtually all of it is present in the DINO specimen, albeit somewhat crushed. We interpret the frontal bone to include a dorsal exposure, which forms part of the cranial roof and is overlapped posteriorly by the parietal bone, a lateral portion, which participates in the cranial wall, and possibly the supraorbital shelf described above.

The portion of the frontal bone on the cranial roof is separated from the supraorbital shelf by the posterior extension of the nasal bone. On this surface of the frontal bone in the DINO specimen, two small nutrient foramina open anteriorly into very straight, parallel grooves. Another small foramen opens laterally at the point where the supraorbital shelf meets the cranial roof. Although the Fruita specimen is damaged in this area, it appears to have similar morphology. Posterior to the supraorbital shelf, the nearly flat cranial roof passes by a strong, nearly right-angle flexure to a nearly vertical lateral cranial wall. At or just below the flexure, there appear to be two rather substantial foramina, aligned antero-posteriorly in the DINO specimen, the more anterior slightly dorsal to the other in the Fruita specimen. Because of breakage, little can be said of the frontal

Figure 1. *Dorsal view of the skull roof of the holotype of* Glirodon grandis *DINO 10822, stereo pair. Scale bar equals 1 mm in this and all subsequent figures.*

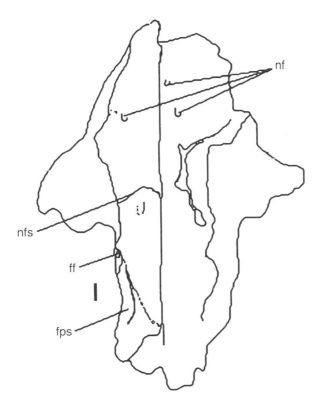

Figure 2. *Line drawing of dorsal view of skull roof of the holotype of* Glirodon grandis *DINO 10822. ff - frontal foramina; fps - fronto-parietal suture; nf - nasal foramina; nfs - nasal-frontal suture.*

Glirodon grandis - *Engelmann, Callison*

Figure 3. *Dorsal view of the Fruita specimen of* Glirodon grandis, *LACM 120453, stereo pair.*

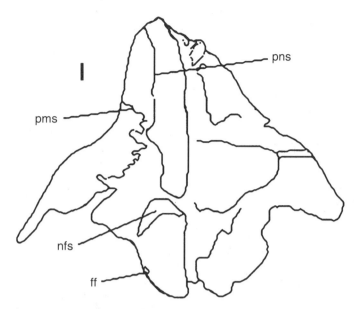

Figure 4. *Line drawing of dorsal view of the Fruita specimen of* Glirodon grandis, *LACM 120453. ff - frontal foramina; nfs - nasal-frontal suture; pms - premaxillary-maxillary suture; pns - premaxillary-nasal suture.*

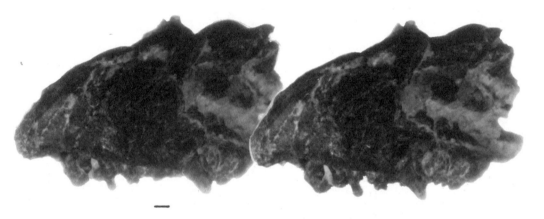

Figure 5. *Lateral view of the left side of the snout of the Fruita specimen of* Glirodon grandis, *LACM 120453, stereo pair.*

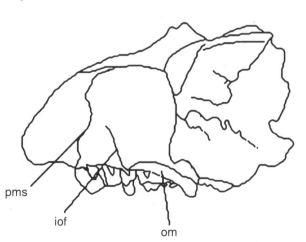

Figure 6. *Line drawing of lateral view of the left side of the snout of the Fruita specimen of* Glirodon grandis, *LACM 120453. iof - infraorbital foramina; om - origin of masseter musculature; pms - premaxillary-maxillary suture.*

bone, ventral to these foramina. The bone along the length of the flexure is rather complexly sculptured. A shallow groove bounded by low ridges begins immediately medial to the more posterior of the two foramina and opens broadly as it continues posteriorly and a bit medially. There may be a second groove medial and parallel to the first, but it is not clear. Although more poorly preserved, the right side of the cranium does appear to exhibit features similar in location and orientation to the groove(s). It seems likely that this sculptured surface represents the sutural contact with the parietal bone, which must have overlapped the frontal bone broadly. Posteriorly, the frontal flares or broadens gradually just before it is terminated by breakage.

Lateral Aspect

The Fruita skull (figures 5 and 6) is relatively uncrushed dorso-ventrally and provides the best evidence of the shape of the snout, although the anteriormost portion of the otherwise flattened DINO skull (figures 7 and 8) may be relatively uncrushed as well thanks to the presence of the robust root of I^2. The snout appears to

Figure 7. *Lateral view of the left side of the holotype of* Glirodon grandis *DINO 10822.*

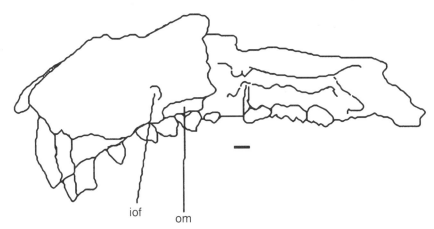

Figure 8. *Line drawing of lateral view of the left side of the holotype of* Glirodon grandis *DINO 10822. iof - infraorbital foramina; om - origin of masseter musculature.*

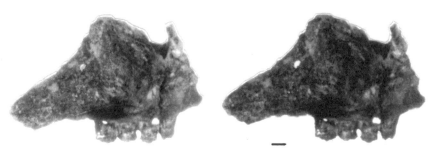

Figure 9. *Lateral view of right maxillary fragment LACM 120458, stereo pair.*

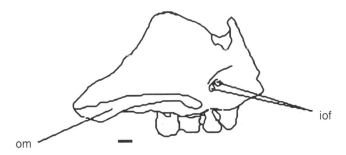

Figure 10. *Line drawing of lateral view of right maxillary fragment LACM 120458. iof - infraorbital foramina; om - origin of masseter musculature.*

slope anteriorly with a fairly rapid change from a low pointed muzzle to a moderately high skull at the frontals. As noted above, the premaxillary-maxillary suture indicates a relatively broad exposure of the premaxilla on the muzzle.

The zygomatic process of the maxilla arises approximately over P^1, only a short distance posterior to the suture with the premaxilla, and is directed rather strongly laterally. It is strap-like in form, with a deep, nearly vertical, external surface, and relatively thin in the horizontal dimension. The zygomatic process curves dorsally as it diverges from the rest of the maxilla and then ventrally, as it continues posteriorly, forming a distinct arcuate shape. This structure is best preserved on the right maxillary fragment LACM 120458 (see figures 9, 10, and 11), in which the zygomatic process turns more directly posteriorly after it has diverged from the rest of the maxilla. The zygomatic process tapers posteriorly to its termination in both LACM 120458 and LACM 120453, but this is the result of breakage in each case and there is no indication of the nature of the contact of the maxillary portion of the zygomatic arch with any more posterior components. Along the ventral margin of the zygomatic arch, as far as it is preserved, is a distinct raised surface that undoubtedly represents a site of attachment for masseter musculature. This attachment surface does not extend onto the snout, but is separated from it by a short gap at the base of the zygomatic process. At the junction of the zygomatic process with the body of the maxilla and low on the zygomatic process there are two, sub-

Figure 11. *Ventral view of right maxillary fragment LACM 120458, stereo pair.*

Glirodon grandis - *Engelmann, Callison*

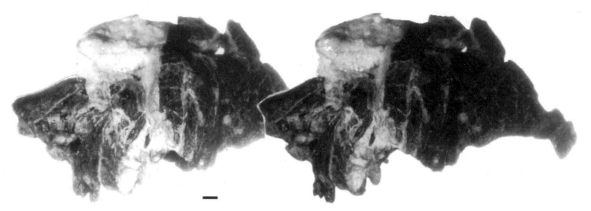

Figure 12. *Anterior view of the snout of the Fruita specimen of* Glirodon grandis, *LACM 120453, stereo pair.*

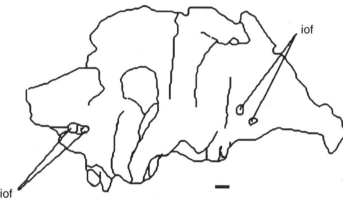

Figure 13. *Line drawing of anterior view of the snout of the Fruita specimen of* Glirodon grandis, *LACM 120453. iof - infraorbital foramina.*

Palate

In spite of some fractures and displacement of parts of the skull, the Fruita specimen (figures 14 and 15) provides considerable information about the shape of the palate and the arrangement of the dentition around it. Except for a large fracture, the effect of which can be compensated for in interpretation, the right side of the palate seems to be relatively undamaged as far back as P^5. It indicates that the tooth row curved outward from the first incisors at the midline to the second premolar. Posterior to this tooth, the tooth row seems to be aligned nearly directly antero-posteriorly, as indicated by the posterior premolars and the well-aligned posterior dentition of the DINO specimen (figures 16 and 17) (see below). The palatal roof itself exhibits a gentle concavity both across the palate and along its length, so that its highest point was approximately in the middle, rather like a gently cupped hand. This is very similar in appearance to the palate of *Kamptobaatar* as described and illustrated by Kielan-Jaworowska (1970). The left and right sides of the palate are displaced vertically across the median suture, which is a simple vertical plane, thus making it possible to view the palatal bones in cross section. The bones of the palate are rather thick along the midline, reaching their greatest thickness approximately at the middle of the palatal axis. This makes the vault of the palatal roof a rather robust, gentle arch.

The suture between the premaxilla and the maxilla on the palate is clearly indicated in both specimens. A narrow medial process of the maxilla extends anteriorly medial to the premaxilla as far forward as the I^3. At its anterior margin, the maxillary process terminates short of the margin of the premaxilla, which continues anteriorly a short distance and then abruptly turns back posteromedially to the midline leaving a poorly defined, notch-like incisive foramen. Small nutrient foramina invest this part of the premaxilla posterior to I^2. The limits of

equal infraorbital foramina which open anteriorly and slightly laterally. Both foramina are preserved on both the left and right sides of the Fruita skull (figures 12 and 13) and on the maxillary fragment. On the DINO specimen, only on the left side is a single, large infraorbital foramen well preserved, but a broad, shallow concavity of the surface anterior to the large infraorbital foramen may be an indication of a second infraorbital foramen dorsal to and smaller than the first. The inner, posterior surface of the zygomatic arch, roofed over by the supraorbital shelf, presents a flat, vertical surface. The posterior opening of the infraorbital canal is a single, large opening in all specimens.

Unfortunately, because of crushing or other damage, neither skull is very informative concerning features of the lateral wall of the braincase. Smoothly curving, seemingly finished margins on fragments of bone floating in matrix tantalizingly suggest the margins of cranial openings, but do not provide enough information to identify them with confidence. The sphenopalatine foramen and the sphenorbital fissure may be indicated in this way. Apparently the cranial wall was constructed of very delicate bone or was poorly ossified and was easily damaged by burial processes.

Figure 14. *Ventral view of the palate of the Fruita specimen of* Glirodon grandis, *LACM 120453, stereo pair.*

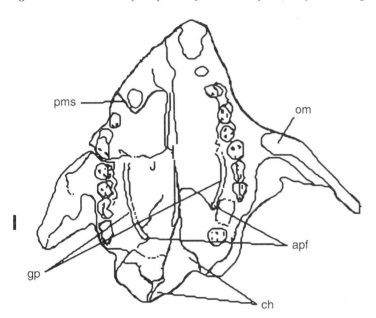

Figure 15. *Line drawing of ventral view of the palate of the Fruita specimen of* Glirodon grandis, *LACM 120453. apf - anterior palatine foramina; ch - choanae; gp - palatine grooves; om - origin of masseter musculature; pms - premaxillary-maxillary suture.*

the palatine contribution to the palate are not so easily defined among the fractures. However, we think that we can discern sutures that indicate the palatine bones to be roughly rectangular elements with the anterior suture with the maxilla nearly straight across, approximately at the level of the end of the premolar series, and the lateral suture paralleling the tooth row about half way between the teeth and the midline. This is similar to the extent of the palatine in *Lambdopsalis* (Miao, 1988), and the presence of a large foramen at the interpreted anterior margin of the palatine on both sides of the palate in both of the specimens reinforces this interpretation. This foramen is

referred to by Miao (1988) as the major palatine foramen. In the Fruita specimen, a shallow but well-defined groove curves anteriorly from this foramen as far as the P^2 on each side of the palate. The groove maintains a constant width equal to the diameter of the foramen. Short segments of a similar groove can be discerned on the right side of the badly crushed palate of the DINO specimen. The posterior margin of the palatine bones, and of the palate at this point, occurs at about the level of the M^2. Lateral to the palatine, the posterior maxillary palatal margin curves postero-laterally to a point behind the M^2. The posterior margins of these bones define the choanae.

UPPER DENTITION

The formula for the upper dentition appears to be I^{1-3}, C, P^{1-5}, M^{1-2}. This is a complete primitive multituberculate dental formula.

Of all the tooth loci, the only one for which identification is at all questionable is I^1. I^1 is very small, nearly vestigial, in this species. It is preserved only in the holotype and without the crown there because of crushing. Nevertheless, medial and very slightly anterior to the large I^2s there are two somewhat cylindrical structures which we interpret to be the roots of the I^1s. The I^2s are quite large and close together leaving little room between them for the I^1s. The crowns could not have been very large.

The I^2s are quite large, the largest of the upper teeth, in fact, and are especially remarkable for the extensive apical wear of the tooth and the restricted enamel which gives it a distinctive rodent-like appearance. Wear has

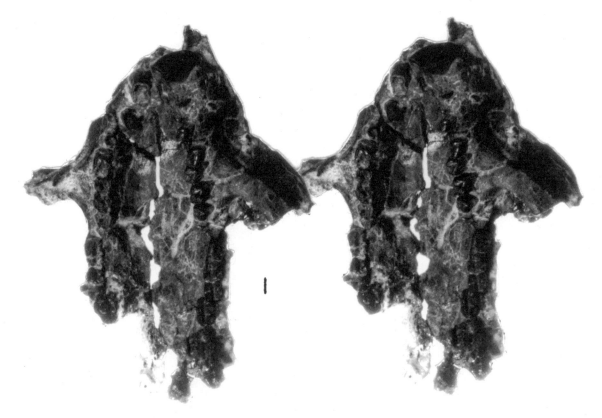

Figure 16. *Ventral view of the palate of the holotype of* Glirodon grandis *DINO 10822, stereo pair.*

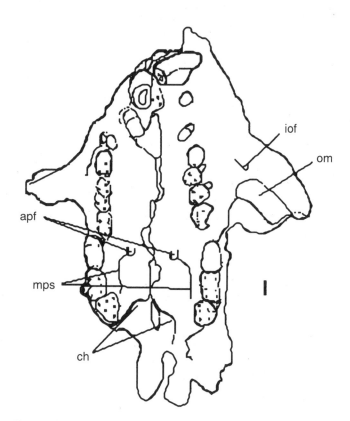

Figure 17. *Line drawing of ventral view of the palate of the holotype of* Glirodon grandis *DINO 10822. apf - anterior palatine foramina; ch - choanae; iof - infraorbital foramina; mps - maxillary-palatine suture; om - origin of masseter musculature.*

obliterated the tip of the crown so that no cusps are discernible. What remains of the crown is a simple, curving, tapering columnar structure with a more or less oval cross section (somewhat flattened on the medial side). The crown must have tapered to the tip, as what remains increases in antero-posterior diameter toward the root. The root, although quite large, does not appear to extend far posteriorly and probably was not open-rooted. A shallow groove runs the length of the tooth on the lateral side. Enamel is least developed along this groove so that it is less extensive along the length of the tooth here than it is either along the posterior, inside curve of the tooth or the anterior, outside curve where it extends furthest. Not only does enamel covering the anterior surface of I^2 extend further along the length of the tooth (further toward the root) than on other surfaces, but it is also notably thicker there as well. Because of the thicker enamel along the anterior edge, apical wear has produced a small step, forming a chisel-like edge. Posterior to this edge, the wear surface is broad, gently curving, and nearly normal to the long axis of the tooth.

The third incisor is much smaller than I^2 but still appears quite functional. It is a simple blade-like peg with the crest oriented transversely. Although the crest is strongly developed across the tip, the shape of the tooth becomes more rounded toward the root which has an antero-posteriorly elongate oval cross section. There is considerable apical wear along the crest and the wear surface (or possibly enlargement of the wear surface by breakage) extends onto the posterior surface of the tooth.

Both left and right canines are preserved and are similar in form in all important points. The canine is a small conical tooth with a single cusp modified by a few simple crests. Anterior and posterior crests curve slightly labially away from the cusp, dividing the crown into lingual and labial sides. The lingual surface is very smooth and broadly curved. It reminds one of the lingual surface of the anterior premolars. The labial surface is divided unequally by a crest which extends labially and slightly posteriorly from the cusp. Between this lateral crest and the posterior crest is a small but pronounced depression. Between the lateral and anterior crests, the surface is relatively flat or slightly convex. There is a single root with a circular cross section. The cusp is worn slightly apically.

The canine teeth in the Fruita specimen differ only slightly in that, in the left canine, the cusp appears to be divided, forming two closely appressed cusps while the right canine definitely exhibits two subequal cusps, albeit close together. The postero-labial cusp appears to be the different cusp. Because of that additional cusp, the crown of the tooth is slightly irregular, not so neatly conical.

Small diastemata separate I^2, I^3, C^1 and P^1 by about equal amounts, whereas there is no significant gap between any of the more posterior cheek teeth.

The first three upper premolars (figures 18 and 19) are, for the most part, quite similar in size and morphology in the type and referred specimens, with a single exception. In the holotype specimen, the left P^1 differs quite markedly from the right P^1 and from that tooth, left or right, in the referred specimens. With the exception of the left P^1 on the holotype, the P^1 in the type and referred specimens have three distinct cusps. The single labial cusp is the largest of the three. It is the tallest cusp above the occlusal surface and is broadly conical. The two lingual cusps are aligned antero-posteriorly and this lingual row of cusps is aligned for P^{1-3} as well. The two lingual cusps are subequal in size with the more posterior cusp consistently very slightly the larger of the two. The cusps appear to be equal in height, but the posterior cusp appears to have a slightly broader base on the crown.

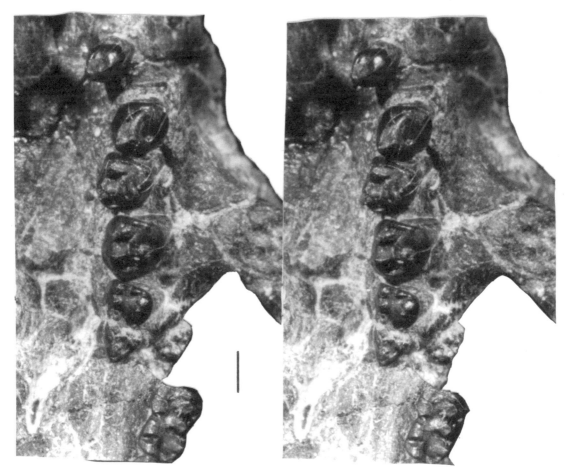

Figure 18. *Occlusal view of the anterior cheek teeth on the left side of the palate of the holotype of* Glirodon grandis *DINO 10822, including C and P1-P5, stereo pair.*

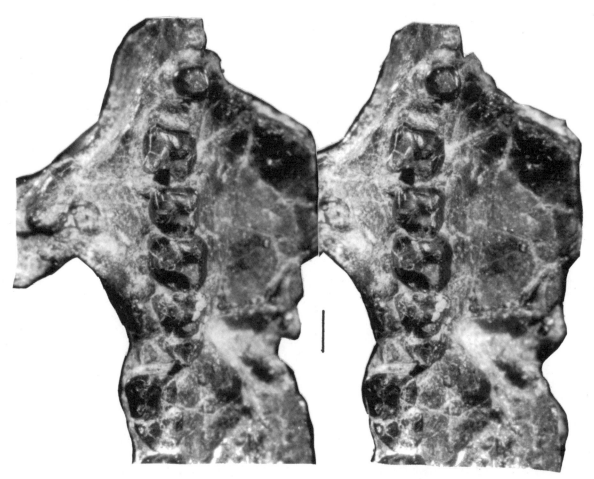

Figure 19. *Occlusal view of the anterior cheek teeth on the right side of the palate of the holotype of* Glirodon grandis *DINO 10822, including C and P1-P5, stereo pair.*

This impression of larger size for the posterior cusp is also apparent in lingual view, as the margin of the enamel extends further below the posterior cusp than below the anterior cusp. The lingual cusps are connected by antero-posteriorly oriented crests which descend from the apex of each cusp. Aligned with these crests, a crest descends anteriorly from the anterior cusp, curving labially across the anterior margin of the crown to terminate against the base of the labial cusp. This creates a small shelf anterior to and between the antero-lingual and labial cusps. A similar crest descends from the postero-lingual cusp, curves labially and terminates against the labial cusp creating a small shelf. The tooth is not quite symmetrical about a transverse axis passing between the two lingual cusps, as the labial cusp falls slightly posterior to such an axis.

Between the labial and lingual cusps is a valley where the cusp bases intersect. A faint crest descends lingually from the labial cusp into this valley and then ascends the postero-lingual cusp connecting these two cusps. No similar crest connects the labial and antero-lingual cusps. The only indications of wear are apical wear surfaces on the cusps. The tooth has two broad

roots, anterior and posterior.

The left P^1 in the holotype specimen is quite different in form. It has only two subequal cusps, one labial, one lingual, with the labial cusp the taller of the two. A crest curves antero-labially from the lingual cusp to the anterior margin of the base of the tooth. A low crest descends from the apex of each cusp to meet at the intervening valley, connecting the two. In fact, in all respects, the two cusps of P^1 compare closely with the labial and postero-lingual cusps of the other 3-cusped anterior premolars. It appears that it is the antero-lingual cusp that has failed to develop, leaving only an antero-labially descending crest.

P^4 has the premolar morphology that is commonly referred to as an upper blade. The tooth is longer than it is wide, and a single row of four small cusps runs the entire length of the tooth linked by a continuous crest. On the lingual surface of the tooth the cusps merge toward their base into a common, broad surface that is nearly flat and vertical. This surface of the crown of the tooth extends to its deepest point over the posterior of the two roots, curving upward between the roots and descending not quite so deeply over the anterior root.

The row of cusps appears to be aligned with the lingual cusps of the more anterior premolars. The widest point of the tooth is over the anterior root because of the presence of a conical labial cusp, the largest of the tooth, in this position. The tooth tapers posteriorly in spite of a second, small labial cusp there.

P^5 could be described as molariform. It is more or less rectangular in shape. Because of heavy wear and breakage caused by crushing, the morphology of the cusps is difficult to discern. There are two rows of at least three and possibly four subequal cusps. Uncertainty concerning the fourth cusp arises from the presence of a prominent anterior cingulum which is heavily worn and which may have been resolvable as two cusps when unworn. The best preserved tooth in this position, the left P^5, suggests that the most likely arrangement is four cusps in the lingual row with the most anterior continuous with the anterior cingulum, and three cusps on the labial row. The anterior cingulum is continuous with a well-developed labial cingulum which contacts the base of each of the cusps in the labial row progressively more closely posteriorly, giving the impression that the row of cusps is oblique to the axis of the tooth as determined by its labial margin. The lingual cusps are all relatively heavily worn with the greatest wear on the anterior cusps. In fact, the cusps seem divisible into two units, with the two anterior cusps situated over the anterior root closely connected such that their bases merge broadly, and the two most posterior cusps, over the posterior root, similarly broadly connected, while the second and third cusps are connected by a narrow crest and there is a slight lingual constriction at the middle of the tooth where there is no root.

M^1 (figures 20 and 21) is very similar in form to P^5, but it is slightly larger, the cusps are more robust, and there is no cingulum. The labial row consists of three similarly robust cusps with a slightly greater separation between the first and second cusps than between the second and third. The lingual row of cusps, however, is quite similar to that of P^5 in having the four cusps grouped into an anterior pair in which the anteriormost cusp is quite the smallest in the row, and a posterior pair of similar cusps with a slight narrowing at the base of the crown between the second and third cusps.

M^2 is perhaps the most surprising tooth in the dentition of this Jurassic multituberculate, in that it exhibits the beginnings of a third labial row of cusps. The labial row resembles a cingulum but there is a distinct division that defines two cusps. A crest from the anterior cusp continues as an anterior cingulum which connects to the anteriormost cusp of the lingual row. A crest from the posterior cusp extends postero-lingually to the posterior cusp of the middle row. The middle row of cusps consists of the two largest cusps of the tooth. They are subequal with the posterior slightly more robust than the anterior. The lingual row consists of three cusps increasing in size posteriorly. The first and smallest cusp, which is connected to the anterior cingulum, is closely connected to the slightly larger second cusp. A deeper notch, however, sets off the third and largest cusp from the other two. The length of the lingual row of cusps is very nearly the same as the middle row, and the greatest length of the tooth is actually between these rows because the posterior margin of the tooth is most extended there.

Figure 20. *Occlusal view of the posterior cheek teeth on the left side of the palate of the holotype of* Glirodon grandis *DINO 10822, including P4, P5, M1, and M2, stereo pair.*

Glirodon grandis - *Engelmann, Callison*

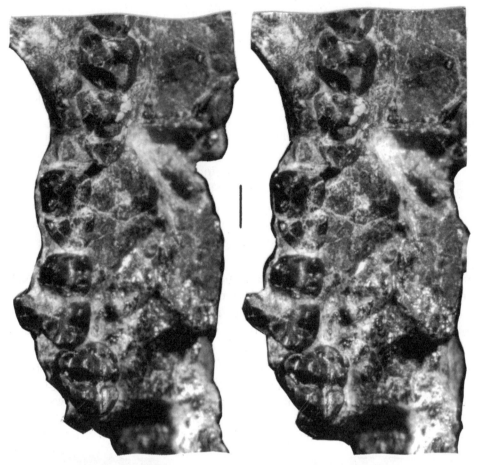

Figure 21. *Occlusal view of the posterior cheek teeth on the right side of the palate of the holotype of* Glirodon grandis *DINO 10822, including P3, P4, P5, M1, and M2, stereo pair.*

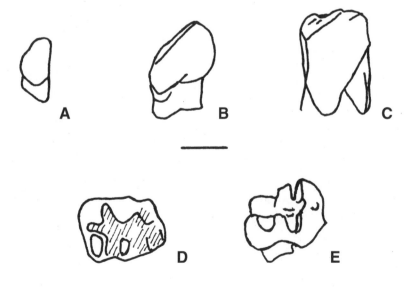

Figure 22. *Lower teeth associated with the crushed mandible of the holotype of* Glirodon grandis *DINO 10822. Only the P3 was rooted in the jaw; all others were detached, but closely associated. A. left P1, labial view. B. left P2, labial view. C. left P3, labial view. D. left M1, occlusal view, anterior to left. E. left M2, oblique labial view.*

Glirodon grandis - *Engelmann, Callison*

The best preserved example of the cheek tooth series is on the left side of the holotype specimen. Breakage and displacement have separated the dentition between the fourth and fifth premolars, but the two segments of the dentition, the anterior premolars, and the fifth premolars and the molars, each appear to have preserved the natural relative position of the teeth. It is interesting that differences in the wear patterns on the teeth in each of these segments suggests that they constituted two different functional units. The first four premolars show little wear, and that predominantly apical. The lingual cusps of these teeth are all aligned in a row, as are the labial cusps. In the posterior functional unit a pattern of wear that produced planar facets predominates. The lingual row of cusps in the fifth premolar is directly aligned with the lingual row of the first molar and that, in turn, with the middle row of the last molar. Likewise, the labial rows of cusps in these teeth are aligned. The most lingual row of cusps of the last molar is not aligned with that of any other tooth. The wear facets on each row of cusps on a tooth in this series can be described by a single, slightly curving plane, which, when extended, is continuous with a similar plane on the next tooth in the series. Such planar wear surfaces spanning the teeth of the series occur along the lingual side of the lingual and labial tooth rows on the first two teeth and the middle and labial rows of the last. There also appears to be a similar surface on the labial side of the cusps of the lingual row of the last molar. A weakly developed wear surface is distinguishable on the labial side of the lingual cusp rows of P^3 and M^1 and the middle row of M^2. This wear pattern indicates strong propalinal motion in chewing with the molars in occlusion as has been shown for other multituberculates (Gambaryan and Kielan-Jaworowska, 1995).

In lateral view (figure 7), the teeth within each of two segments of the cheek tooth series exhibit a continuity that appears natural. The displacement between the two segments can be easily restored mentally, suggesting that the cheek teeth formed a single, gentle, concave-downward arc.

MANDIBLE

As noted above, part of the holotype specimen is a partial left mandible that is so badly crushed as to be virtually unrecognizable, but for the presence of teeth. These teeth (figure 22), however, not only permit identification of the element, but also allow us to refer an excellently preserved mandible from Fruita (LACM 120452) to this taxon. First and second lower molars and P^1 and P^2 were detached but closely associated with the mandible, and P^3 is preserved in place. The molars are indistinguishable from those of the Fruita mandible. The premolars are also similar to those in the Fruita specimen to the extent that they are preserved.

The Fruita specimen (figures 23 and 24), a right mandible, is very complete and preserves much information in spite of fine fractures that run throughout the specimen. For the purpose of simplifying our description and illustrations, we have oriented the mandible with its straight ventral margin horizontal, even though the orientation of the teeth and the articular surface leads us to conclude that it would not be so oriented when in articulation with the skull. In overall form, the mandible resembles that of other plagiaulacoid multituberculates. There is a large incisor that achieves the highest point above the ventral margin of the mandible in this orientation. The incisor is separated from the cheek teeth by a pronounced diastema. A single, large, circular mental foramen opens anteriorly beneath the diastema at about mid-depth in the mandible. The cheek teeth consist of four premolars arranged to form a continuous, arcuate, blade-like edge which reaches its highest point at the fourth premolar, followed by two molars that differ little from each other morphologically. The coronoid process is broad and low relative to the dentition, equal in height to the highest point of the cheek tooth series. The exact shape of the coronoid process cannot be determined because its posterior margin may be a broken edge. However, it appears that the coronoid process thinned

Figure 23. *Right mandible of* Glirodon grandis, *LACM 120452. A. lateral view. B. medial view.*

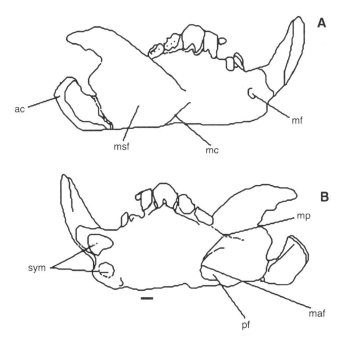

Figure 24. *Line drawings of right mandible of* Glirodon grandis, *LACM 120452. A. lateral view. B. medial view. ac - articular condyle; maf - mandibular foramen; mc - masseteric crest; mf - mental foramen; msf - masseteric fossa; pf - pterygoid fossa; sym - symphysis.*

considerably posteriorly. The articular process is the most posterior point on the mandible and is connected directly to the mandibular ramus anteriorly by a stout neck. The articular surface is an extensive, broadly curved surface covering most of the posterior articular process. The surface changes its orientation gradually from postero-dorsal, to posterior, to postero-ventral, and the entire surface is oriented postero-laterally, giving it a conspicuous lateral exposure. Although the limits of the articular surface are well defined for the most part, it merges antero-ventrally with a prominent ventro-lateral ridge or shelf that defines the ventral margin of the masseteric fossa. The masseteric fossa is an extensive and deep, triangular feature that covers the entire lateral surface of the coronoid process and virtually all of the lateral surface of the mandibular ramus ventral to the coronoid. It is bounded along the ventral margin of the mandible by a prominent ridge or shelf as noted above. This ridge rises slightly dorsal to the ventral margin of the mandible at its anterior end and converges with a ridge descending from the anterior margin of the coronoid process. The two ridges meet approximately below the last premolar and form a well-defined apex of the masseteric fossa.

Features visible only on the medial surface of the mandible (figures 23B and 24B) include the mandibular symphysis, the pterygoid fossa, and the mandibular foramen. A deep pterygoid fossa occupies more than half of the depth of the mandible beneath the last molar. This area is well defined anteriorly and ventrally by a distinct semicircular ridge that arises from the ventral margin at a point below the end of the last molar, curves anteriorly and dorsally to a point slightly below the mid-depth of the mandible and below the anterior part of the last molar, and then upward and posteriorly, to a prominent point that terminates the alveolar body of the mandible posterior to the last molar. A low, broad ridge extends posteriorly from this point across the lower part of the coronoid process. The ridge that defines the semicircular "pocket" is sharp along the anteroventral margin, and is particularly pronounced at its most anterior point, where the fossa is excavated anteriorly. Above this point, the ridge becomes broader and gentler. The fossa is approximately equally divided horizontally by a low, gentle ridge. This division appears to mark the presence of the mandibular foramen in the upper half of the depression. The mandibular symphysis is a fairly large feature. Much deeper than it is long, the symphysis extends from the ventral margin of the mandible to the alveolar margin of the incisor. But its greatest antero-posterior length is less than half its vertical extent. The upper part of the symphysis is a flat, roughly triangular surface. The more ventral part is marked by a shallow circular depression, possibly for a ligament. The symphysis appears to have been unfused.

A dorsal or occlusal view of the mandible (figures 25 and 26) is informative. One of the most striking features in this view is the size of the prominent lateral shelf

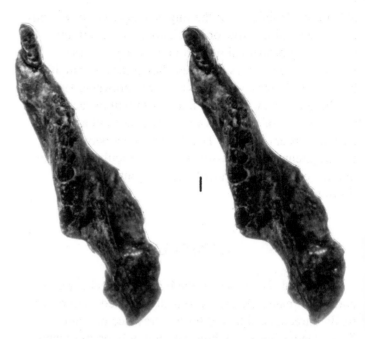

Figure 25. *Occlusal view of right mandible of* Glirodon grandis, *LACM 120452, stereo pair.*

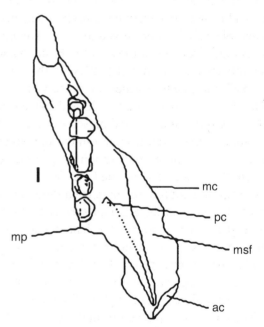

Figure 26. *Line drawing of occlusal view of right mandible of* Glirodon grandis, *LACM 120452. ac - articular condyle; mc - masseteric crest; msf - masseteric fossa; mp - medial prominence; pc - coronoid pit.*

of the masseteric fossa noted above. Also visible in this view is a small pit opening postero-dorsally between the base of the coronoid process and the last molar. This may represent a point of insertion for part of the temporalis musculature. If one uses the mandibular symphysis to determine the mid-sagittal plane, it is apparent that the mandible diverges from this at an angle of about 30°. The coronoid process falls within the same plane as the mandibular ramus, but the cheek tooth row is roughly parallel with the midline and therefore crosses the mandible at an oblique angle. The distinct postero-lateral orientation of the articular surface can be seen clearly in this view.

LOWER DENTITION

The lower dentition is similar to that found in other plagiaulacoids and in morphology compares favorably to that of *Ctenacodon* with one striking exception. The incisor is unlike any known plagiaulacoid in that the enamel is restricted to the anterior and antero-lateral surfaces of the tooth. The tooth is robust and an extensive wear surface causes it to taper very gradually to the tip, which is worn to a chisel edge much as a rodent incisor. It could not be determined whether the root of the incisor is open or closed, but the enamel surface does terminate short of the alveolar margin in both the complete mandible and the fragment (LACM 120746) which bears only this tooth. We believe that this implies that the tooth did not continue to grow once erupted.

The cheek teeth (figure 27), on the other hand, are virtually indistinguishable from those of *Ctenacodon*, except for their larger size, which is intermediate between that of *Ctenacodon* and *Psalodon*.

P_1 is a simple button with a slight occlusal crest that ascends the crown as it arcs posteriorly, separating the curved buccal and lingual surfaces of the tooth. There are no serrations. A similar tooth was found with the mangled mandible from DINO 10288.

P_2 is largely missing from the Fruita mandible, with only a small fragment at the base of the crown attached to the anterior of two roots and a small fragment of the posterior part of the crest attached to the P_3 by matrix. However, a tooth that appears to be the P_2 is present in the DINO specimen. The crown is about twice as long and twice as high as that of P_1, but it is still a very simple tooth. As is typical of multituberculates, the enamel of the crown extends lower over the anterior root than it does over the posterior root. This is also the case for each of the following lower premolars as well, with the most marked difference in P_3. This gives the tooth a dis-

tinct appearance of being sharply anteriorly inclined. A single, straight serration arises low on the anterior margin of the crown and ascends posteriorly to the highest point of the tooth, over the posterior root. The occlusal crest of the tooth curves only slightly higher than the serration as it ascends posteriorly to the same high point.

P_3 is a distinctive tooth with a very high crown (at least anteriorly) and a short but straight occlusal crest. The crown extends much lower on the anterior root than on the posterior root; so much so that the crown height over the anterior root is very nearly twice that over the posterior root. This effect is particularly striking because the nearly straight occlusal crest is oriented approximately at right angles to the roots along the entire length of the tooth. Three serrations are distinguishable near the crest but they are otherwise obliterated by a single large wear facet that covers nearly the entire labial surface of the tooth.

P_4 is a two-rooted tooth longer than it is high with the enamel of the crown extending lower over the roots than at the midlength of the tooth (slightly lower over the anterior root than over the posterior root). Five serrations

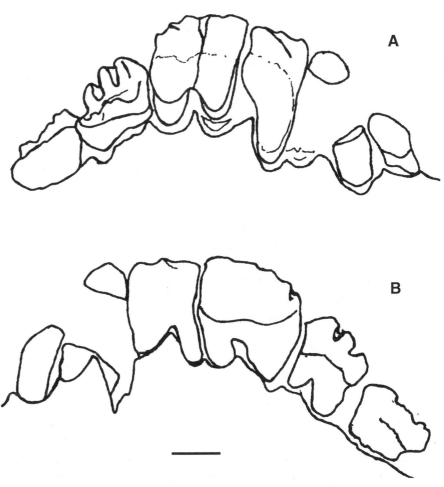

Figure 27. *Line drawing of lower cheek teeth of* Glirodon grandis, *LACM 120452, showing P1-4 and M1-2. A. labial aspect. B. lingual aspect.*

Glirodon grandis - *Engelmann, Callison*

are distinguishable on the occlusal crest. A row of small cuspules existed on the postero-labial surface of the tooth extending from the posterior margin at about mid-crown height forward over the posterior root, slightly more than a quarter the length of the tooth. There appear to have been at least three distinct cuspules in this labial row, but they have merged into a single, wavy, wear facet. The wear facet covers much of the labial surface of the tooth and is in the same plane as the wear facet observed on P_3.

As in other multituberculates, the occlusal crests of all four premolars are aligned to form a functionally single, continuous "blade," as can be seen clearly in the occlusal view of the jaw.

The two molars are very similar to each other both in size and morphology and can only be distinguished with difficulty when found in isolation. Both are subrectangular in occlusal view and have three cusps on each of the lingual and buccal rows with the anterior two cusps of each row slightly closer together than the second and third cusps which are well separated basally. The antero-labial cusps of M_1 are nearly obliterated by a wear facet that appears to be continuous with the wear facet noted on P_4. There is a distinct buccal tilt to the occlusal surface such that if the cusps themselves are held to be vertical, the buccal cusp rows will be slightly lower than the lingual rows. A well-worn antero-posterior groove separates the two cusp rows. The molars have two roots.

CONCLUSIONS

The specimens of *Glirodon* provide a welcome glimpse of the morphology of Late Jurassic multituberculates. However, as is so often the case with vertebrate fossils, rather than clarifying phylogenetic relationships of the multituberculates, the new information just adds to the complexity of the problem. We have chosen to assign this taxon to the plagiaulacoids as a temporary measure. In our view, the plagiaulacoids are undoubtedly a paraphyletic group that will be broken up and distributed among well-defined, monophyletic taxa as multituberculate phylogeny is better resolved. But *Glirodon* does not fit comfortably within existing monophyletic groups and must await revision at this high level before it can be properly placed.

The difficulty in assessing the phylogenetic relationships of *Glirodon* arises from the mixture of characters found in advanced, apparently monophyletic groups, with relatively primitive features characteristic of more remote sister groups. The strict consensus tree analysis

of Simmons (1993), which includes this taxon, places it in a polychotomy that also includes the Cimolodonta and many low-level plagiaulacoid taxa. This placement reflects the large suite of characters that are plesiomorphic relative to the well-supported Cimolodonta. By conducting sequential analyses with the addition of more poorly known taxa, Simmons (1993) was able to resolve this polychotomy further. In this hypothesis, *Glirodon* (referred to as Morrison Multituberculate), is grouped with *Monobaatar*, *Eobaatar*, and *Bolodon* in a group for which she uses the name Bolodontidae. However, this grouping is not strongly supported. In it, *Glirodon* is the sister taxon to all remaining members of the Bolodontidae, which is one member of a trichotomy with *Plagiaulax* and Cimolodonta plus *Arginbaatar*. Even in this position, features of *Glirodon* that are plesiomorphic must be regarded as character reversals. Only a few characters support the inclusion of *Glirodon* in the Bolodontidae, and one, restricted enamel on the lower incisor, is shared only with *Eobaatar*. Furthermore, the Plagiaulacidae, as redefined by Kielan-Jaworowska and Ensom (1992) and diagnosed by a convincingly apomorphic, distinctive pattern on the crown of the M_2 (not present in *Glirodon*), includes *Plagiaulax*, *Eobaatar*, and *Bolodon*. This grouping cannot be congruent with the construction of Bolodontidae of Simmons (1993). Therefore, we do not believe *Glirodon* should be referred to the Bolodontidae of Simmons (1993). Both Kielan-Jaworowska and Ensom (1992) and Simmons (1993) recognize an Allodontidae of similar construction (including *Ctenacodon* and *Psalodon*). Because of the similarity of much of the dentition of *Glirodon* to that of *Ctenacodon*, it is tempting to refer *Glirodon* to the Allodontidae. However, these similarities may be plesiomorphic and not indicative of close relationship. Thus, we believe that the strict consensus tree of Simmons (1993) best represents our current understanding of the placement of *Glirodon* within the Multituberculata.

ACKNOWLEDGMENTS

The field projects that produced the specimens described in this paper were supported by grants from the National Science Foundation (Callison) and the Center for Field Research (Callison and Engelmann and Chure). These specimens are only a few of many collected at these sites and much of the work in the field and in the lab was done by Earthwatch volunteers who found many specimens and supported the discovery of many more. The holotype specimen was found by Scott Madsen, who also performed the virtuoso work of meticulous preparation that made it available for study. Support and cooperation were provided by other employees of the National Park Service as well. In particular, research at Dinosaur National Monument which has contributed to this work has occurred largely through the efforts of Daniel J. Chure, the Park Paleontologist. Nancy Simmons, whose comprehensive work on multituberculate phylogeny is referred to in our discussion, contributed to our interpretation of the morphology of the specimens.

REFERENCES

Chure, D. J., and Engelmann, G.F., 1989, The fauna of the Morrison Formation in Dinosaur National Monument, *in* Flynn, J. J., editor, Mesozoic/Cenozoic vertebrate paleontology-- classic localities, contemporary approaches: 28th International Geological Congress Field Trip Guidebook T322, Washington, D.C., American Geophysical Union, p. 8-14.

Clemens, W. A., Lillegraven, J. A., Lindsay, E. H., and Simpson, G. G., 1979, Where, when, and what - a survey of known Mesozoic mammal distribution, *in* Lillegraven, J. A., Kielan-Jaworowska, Zophia, and Clemens, W. A., editors, Mesozoic mammals, the first two-thirds of mammalian history: Berkeley, University of California Press, p. 7-58.

Gambaryan, P. P., and Kielan-Jaworowska, Zofia, 1995, Masticatory musculature of Asian taeniolabidoid multituberculate mammals: Acta Palaeontologica Polonica, v. 40, no. 1, p. 45-108.

Kielan-Jaworowska, Zofia, 1970, New Upper Cretaceous multituberculate genera from Bayn Dzak, Gobi Desert, *in* Kielan-Jaworowska, Zofia, editor, Results of the Polish-Mongolian Palaeontological Expeditions, Part II: Palaeontologica Polonica, v. 21, p. 35-49.

—1974, Multituberculate succession in the Late Cretaceous of the Gobi Desert (Mongolia), *in* Kielan-Jaworowska, Zofia, editor, Results of the Polish-Mongolian Palaeontological Expeditions, Part V: Palaeontologica Polonica, v. 30, p. 23-44.

Kielan-Jaworowska, Zofia, and Ensom, P.C., 1992, Multituberculate mammals from the Upper Jurassic Purbeck Limestone Formation of southern England: Palaeontology, v. 35, p. 95-126.

Miao, Desui, 1988, Skull morphology of *Lambdopsalis bulla* (Mammalia, Multituberculata) and its implications to mammalian evolution: Contributions to Geology, University of Wyoming, Special Paper 4, p. 1-104.

Rasmussen, T. E., and Callison, George, 1981, A new species of triconodontid mammal from the Upper Jurassic of Colorado: Journal of Paleontology, v. 55, p. 628-634.

Simmons, N. B., 1993, Phylogeny of Multituberculata, *in* Szalay, F. S., Novacek, M. J., and McKenna, M. C., editors, Mammal phylogeny - Mesozoic differentiation, multituberculates, monotremes, early therians, and marsupials: New York, Springer-Verlag, p. 146-164.

Glirodon grandis - *Engelmann, Callison*

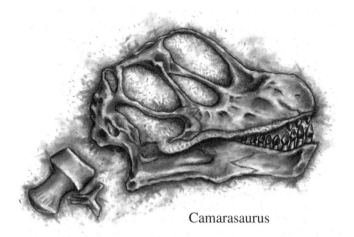

Camarasaurus

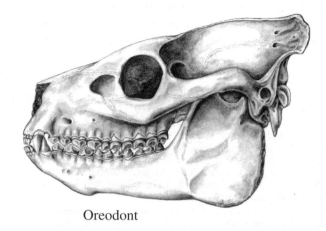

Oreodont

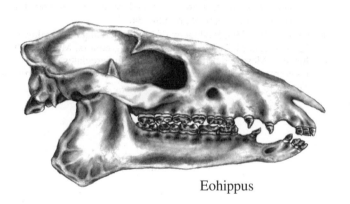

Eohippus

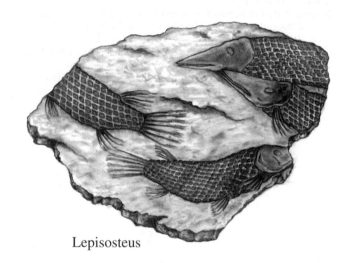

Lepisosteus

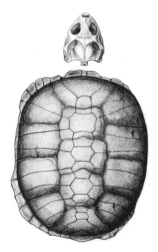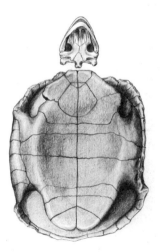

Eocene turtle

Brian Maebius © 1999

DEEP DINOSAUR TRACKS IN THE MORRISON FORMATION: SOLE MARKS THAT ARE REALLY SOLE MARKS

George F. Engelmann
Department of Geography and Geology, University of Nebraska at Omaha
Omaha, NE 68182

Stephen T. Hasiotis
Department of Geological Sciences, University of Colorado
Boulder, CO, 80309-0250

ABSTRACT

Dinosaur track sites have been found in the Upper Jurassic Morrison Formation in widely separated geographic areas. The tracks are preserved as infillings on the underside of sandstones overlying mudstones in which the tracks were made. The sites occur within the Salt Wash and lower Brushy Basin Members, and always within sedimentary facies characterized by alternating sandstones and mudstones. Details of remarkable specimens of deep tracks at sites near Arches National Park and Colorado National Monument support the interpretation of these features as sauropod tracks.

INTRODUCTION

Tracks are among the earliest fossils of dinosaurs to be well studied and, although long neglected, are the subject of careful scrutiny once again (Gillette and Lockley, 1989; Lockley, 1991). Tracks that are most commonly recognized are those that appear in plan view on the exposed bedding planes of resistant rock units, such as limestones and sandstones. Some recent work has suggested that tracks commonly occur within resistant units, but are more difficult to recognize because they are exposed in cross section and are often attributed to soft sediment deformation by physical processes of sedimentation (Loope, 1986). Occasionally, tracks have been preserved as sole marks in the underside of resistant units that filled depressions in underlying softer sediment (Lockley, 1991; Parker and Balsley, 1989).

In a paleontological survey of the Upper Jurassic Morrison Formation conducted over the last few years, we have identified several sites at which tracks are preserved on the underside of sandstone ledges. These sites add to the record of Morrison track sites reviewed by Lockley and Hunt (1995). They are located near Arches National Park in Utah, within Colorado National Monument in Colorado, at Bighorn Canyon National Recreation Area in Wyoming, and at a site in south-central Montana. In every case, they occur in the base of laterally discontinuous sandstones one meter or less in thickness that overlie mudstones of varying thickness where the section is characterized by repeated sandstone-mudstone sequences (figure 1). These features resemble ball and pillow structures or other load structures at first glance, but in some cases there is sufficient exposure area to observe the repetition of the features to form a trackway, and, in others, details of individual tracks provide compelling evidence of their origin. All of the sites occur within the lower part of the Morrison Formation, in the upper part of the Salt Wash Member, or in the lower part of the Brushy Basin Member, where these units are differentiated.

Figure 1. Sauropod track (arrow) on the underside of a sandstone at Bighorn Canyon National Recreation Area. Locality is in Morrison exposures on the west side of Sykes Mountain (Big Horn County, Wyoming, NW$\frac{1}{4}$SW$\frac{1}{4}$, Section 2, T. 57 N., R. 35 W.).

Two of the more interesting sites are those near Arches National Park and Colorado National Monument. In both cases, the track(s) were deep depressions which have been filled with sand to produce pillar-shaped or more complex structures. We will describe these two sites in greater detail.

TRACKS IN THE VICINITY OF ARCHES NATIONAL PARK

This locality occurs in an area of extensive Morrison exposures immediately to the west of Arches National Park near Dalton Well (Grand County, Utah, NE^1/$_4$SE^1/$_4$, section 11, T. 24 S., R. 20 E., Salt Lake Base Line and Meridian). Exact locality data is archived at Arches National Park with the results of the survey as L-GFE-94-64. In this area, the Brushy Basin Member of the Morrison forms a slope dominated by mudstones, interrupted by laterally discontinuous, resistant sandstone ledges, and capped by the Cedar Mountain Formation. Slope retreat has exposed the upper sandstones of the Salt Wash Member of the Morrison forming a broad bench throughout this area where the dip of the beds is relatively shallow. The lower Brushy Basin Member is well exposed in the lower part of the slope. It is characterized by red, non-smectitic mudstones and siltstones with laterally discontinuous sandstones that are seldom greater than, and usually less than one meter in thickness. The pale gray, smectitic mudstones of the upper Brushy Basin Member comprise most of the slope above. Salmon-colored, clinoptilite beds attributed to a saline-alkaline lake (Peterson and Turner-Peterson, 1987) can be seen in the upper slopes.

The tracks occur at or near the top of the lower Brushy Basin Member in the uppermost of the most prominent sandstone layers within this unit. Erosion of the finer sediment underlying the sandstone has created an overhanging ledge that exposes the base of the sandstone along several meters of outcrop (figure 2). The tracks appear as sole marks, several downward protrusions on the underside of the sandstone (figure 3). They are irregular and variable in shape with a roughly circular cross section. The smallest is approximately 20 centimeters in diameter and the largest about twice that. Most extend to a depth of about 10 to 20 centimeters below the base of the sandstone. There is no clear indication of toes or claws, and the area of exposure does not cover sufficient area to distinguish a definite trackway. However, a single track at this site exhibits characteristics that provide strong evidence that it, and therefore the other similar features at the site, are indeed tracks. This track (figure 4) is deeper than most others, extending to a depth of about 30 centimeters below the base of the sandstone. The track filling resembles a pillar extending vertically downward from the sandstone and has been completely freed from the mudstone by erosion. The feature is about 20 centimeters

in diameter at the bottom, widening gradually to about 30 centimeters where it becomes part of the sandstone bed. The outward-facing surface of the feature is very smooth overall and preserves the interface between the sand and mud. On this otherwise smooth surface, are vertical striations that were made by subtle irregularities on the side of the dinosaur's foot and toes, as the foot was driven into the soft, but cohesive mud. The striations, of varying depth and sharpness, are parallel along their entire length. They are nearly vertical, paralleling the axis of the track for most of their length but curving slightly near the bottom, perhaps as a result of the foot slipping forward in the track. Although there is not a

Figure 2. *Upper part of the Morrison Formation near Dalton Well, adjacent to Arches National Park (Grand County, Utah, NE^1/$_4$SE^1/$_4$, Section 11, T. 24 S., R. 20 E.). The prominent ledge near the base of the slope is the track horizon (arrow), and is at or near the top of the Lower Brushy Basin Member.*

Figure 3. *Closer view of the track site near Arches National Park shown in figure 2. Track fillings are visible as downward protrusions on the underside of the sandstone ledge (arrows).*

Figure 4. *Close-up of deep track filling at site near Arches National Park shown in figure 2. Note the striations on the vertical surface. The scale bar is 13 centimeters long.*

clear impression of a foot, the slightly asymmetrical, lobate shape of the track is consistent with having been made by the manus of a sauropod dinosaur, as determined from trackways seen in plan view at other sites (Farlow, and others 1989). Based on the generally round cross-sectional shape of these tracks and the shape of this track in particular, we think it is likely that the track makers were sauropods.

As noted above, this part of the section is characterized by dominantly red mudstones interrupted by laterally discontinuous sandstones. These beds probably represent recurring sequences of channel and overbank sediments. At the track site, approximately two meters of red mudstone underlie the sandstone ledge. Thin, irregularly bedded sandstones, no more than a few centimeters thick, occur throughout the mudstone, with greatest frequency near the top. One of the thickest of these thin sandstones is only about 15 centimeters below the sand-

stone that preserves the tracks, and most of the tracks stop at and do not penetrate below this horizon. Perhaps this layer of sand in the mud had sufficient strength to permit the dinosaurs to walk on this surface in spite of the soft mud. A rooted horizon in the mudstone immediately beneath the sandstone ledge is revealed by numerous gray traces created by gleying around roots. Desiccation cracks in the mudstone were, like the tracks, filled by sand and preserved on the underside of the ledge. The ledge-forming sandstone is itself riddled by traces, including vertical traces about 1 centimeter in diameter and termite nests about 10 centimeters in diameter that penetrate the entire thickness of this sandstone (figure 5). Such traces occurring at this horizon have been described by Hasiotis and Demko (1996).

Figure 5. *Detail of the track site near Arches National Park shown in figure 2. Tracks (A) can be seen on the underside of the sandstone, and termite nests (B) penetrate the sandstone.*

TRACK SITE AT COLORADO NATIONAL MONUMENT

Three small track sites were discovered in or adjacent to Colorado National Monument. All occurred within the middle shaly unit of the Salt Wash Member of the Morrison Formation. All tracks were preserved as infillings on the underside of sandstones overlying a mudstone in which the tracks were made. One site in particular merits further description (figure 6). At this site, which is at the north end of Black Ridge (Mesa County, Colorado, NE^1/$_4$SW^1/$_4$, section 13, T. 11 S., R. 2 W.), just west of the monument boundary, large, lobate structures rest on a slope, where they are associated with a thin, discontinuous sandstone ledge near the base of the erosional slope. The larger of the structures retains its connection to the 0.5 meter-thick sandstone below which it extends; the smaller has become completely detached, but is probably not displaced far from its original position.

Figure 6. *Track site near Colorado National Monument (Mesa County, Colorado, NE¹/₄, SW¹/₄, Sec. 13, T. 11 S., R. 2 W.). Lobate structures are interpreted as infilled tracks. Pick is approximately 0.6 meter long.*

Figure 7. *Detail of the left side of the large structure in figure 6. Note the vertical features on the left side of the track, probably created by the heel of the foot, and the lobate character of the structure, possibly resulting from the separation between toes or the shape of the side of the foot.*

the structure, and it may represent superimposed tracks or a single, very large track of a sauropod pes deformed by slipping in the track or on withdrawal of the foot from the mud. Only about half of the structure is exposed, and excavation of the other side, now buried in the hillside, could possibly reveal some useful information. However, a number of observations support the interpretation of the structure as an infilled track. Although the surfaces of the structure have been roughened by bioturbation and weathering, they are relatively smooth and distinct. Parallel, sub-vertical striations that conform to the orientation of the feature are evident on the surfaces, particularly on the left side (figure 7). The volume of sediment filling the track far exceeds the amount that could be reasonably expected to have been provided by the relatively thin sand as a post-depositional, soft sediment deformation structure.

The smaller of the structures (nearly 0.5 meter across and 0.3 meter deep) provides corroborating evidence. When viewed from the upslope side (figure 8), it is apparent that the shape of this feature is like that of the larger one in being asymmetrically lobate, with the long axis inclined in the same direction. In addition, a small part of the structure, distinguished by a deep cleft, is visible in this view. This appears to be the impression of a claw or a toe. We interpret this, the smaller of the two structures at the site, as the track of a sauropod pes.

Figure 8. *Structures depicted in figure 6, viewed from upslope. Note the impression of a toe or claw on the near side (arrow), well separated from the main body of the track filling, and the curving, lobate margin of the rest of the smaller structure that may reflect the shape and separation between other toes. The pick is approximately 0.6 meter long.*

CONCLUSIONS

Footprints, and trace fossils in general, are important because an organism can make thousands of traces in a lifetime, increasing the preservation potential of the evi-

The larger structure is enormous. It is greater than 1 meter across and extends more than 1 meter below the base of the sandstone at its deepest point. The morphology of the foot of the track maker is not obvious from

dence of its occurrence in the geologic record. Body fossils are often not preserved, and when they are, isolated skeletal elements are usually the only evidence of an organism.

The tracks we have described above have been selected for description because they are remarkable for their size, depth, or details of their preservation, but tracks of this type may be more common than has been supposed. Identification of tracks of this nature is important to the study of sauropod paleoecology. The tracks reveal information about where the sauropods lived in the terrestrial environment, and how they traveled as implied by the intensity of trampling.

The tracks appear to be associated with a sedimentary facies in which recurring sequences of channel and overbank fluvial sediments are characterized by 0.5- to 1-meter-thick sandstones overlying mudstone intervals up to 2 meters thick. Such facies commonly occur within the Salt Wash and lower Brushy Basin Members of the Morrison Formation. This relationship may be attributable to preservational and/or ecological control. Invertebrate traces, such as those mentioned in the description of the Arches National Park site, exhibit a similar association and may be subject to the same controls. Further study of these and other such track sites may yield information about the biology of the track makers.

ACKNOWLEDGMENTS

These sites were discovered as part of a survey supported by a grant from the National Park Service. The large track at Colorado National Monument was actually discovered by Tim Demko, one of our colleagues on the Morrison Ecosystem Project. That we were able to find our way around in the stratigraphy of the Morrison is largely the result of help from Fred Peterson and Christine Turner.

REFERENCES

Farlow, J. O., Pittman, J.G. and Hawthorne, J. M., 1989, *Brontopodus birdi*, Lower Cretaceous sauropod footprints from the U.S. Gulf Coastal Plain, *in* Gillette, D. D., and Lockley, M.G., editors, 1989, Dinosaur tracks and traces: Cambridge University Press, Cambridge. p. 371-394.

Gillette, D. D., and Lockley, M.G., editors, 1989, Dinosaur tracks and traces: Cambridge University Press, Cambridge. pp. 454.

Hasiotis., S. T., and Demko, T. M., 1996, Terrestrial and freshwater trace fossils, Upper Jurassic Morrison Formation, Colorado Plateau, *in* Morales, Michael, editor, The continental Jurassic: Museum of Northern Arizona Bulletin 60, p. 355-370.

Lockley, Martin, 1991, Tracking dinosaurs--A new look at an ancient world: Cambridge, England, Cambridge University Press, p. 238

Lockley, Martin and Hunt, A. P., 1995, Dinosaur tracks and other fossil footprints of the western United States: New York, Columbia University Press, p. 338.

Loope, D. B., 1986, Recognizing and utilizing tracks in cross section-Cenozoic hoofprints from Nebraska: Palaios, v. 1, p. 141-151.

Parker, L. R., and Balsley, J. K., 1989, Coal mines as localities for studying dinosaur trace fossils, *in* Gillette, D. D., and Lockley, M.G., editors, 1989, Dinosaur tracks and traces: Cambridge, England, Cambridge University Press, p. 353-359.

Peterson, Fred, and Turner-Peterson, C. E., 1987. The Morrison Formation of the Colorado Plateau -- recent advances in sedimentology, stratigraphy, and paleotectonics: Hunteria, v. 2, no. 1, 18 p.

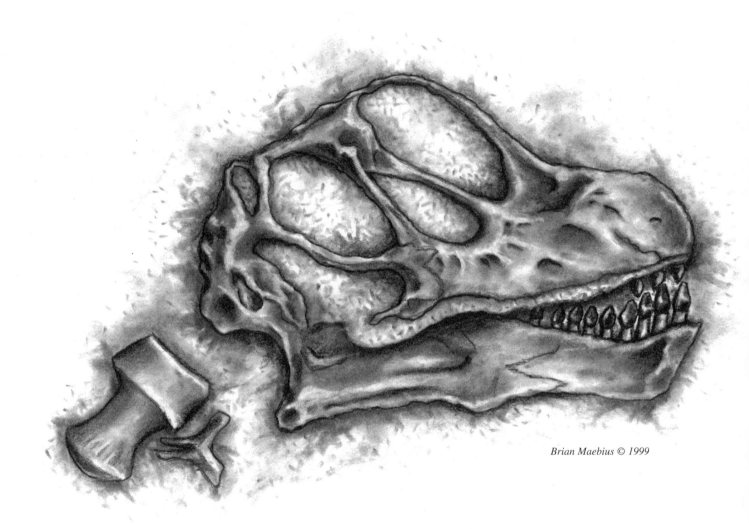

Brian Maebius © 1999

Camarasaurus

POSSIBLE TURTLE TRACKS FROM THE MORRISON FORMATION OF SOUTHERN UTAH

John R. Foster
Department of Geology and Geophysics, University of Wyoming, Laramie, WY 82071-3006

Martin G. Lockley, and Janet Brockett
Department of Geology, University of Colorado at Denver,
P.O. Box 173364, Denver, CO 80217

ABSTRACT

Tracks found in the lower Salt Wash Member of the Morrison Formation in southern Utah were made by a small, unidentified vertebrate, most probably a turtle. Twenty-nine tracks have been identified as natural casts in a unit of Salt Wash sandstone at a site north of Lake Powell. The tracks are part of at least two partial trackways made in a channel environment. The tracks are tridactyl or tetradactyl, and many have rather long digit impressions or scrape marks, parallel to the trackway axis. Most tracks are 2 to 3 centimeters in length. The longest single segment of trackway consists of at least five closely spaced tracks which represent consecutive impressions from one side. The trackways are not complete nor well-preserved enough to allow confident attribution to a trackmaker, but we tentatively attribute them to turtles. Observations on modern turtle trackways reveal that they are similar to purported trackways of walking turtles from the fossil record.

INTRODUCTION

The Upper Jurassic Morrison Formation of the western United States has long been famous for its fossil vertebrates, especially large dinosaurs, but it is now known to contain more than 45 vertebrate tracksites as well, though only a few of these sites were known until fairly recently. These sites contain tracks of a variety of vertebrate taxa. Most are of dinosaurs, but several sites include tracks of pterosaurs, crocodilians, and possibly lizards.

The first report of vertebrate tracks in the Morrison Formation was that of Marsh (1899), who described tridactyl prints from the southern Black Hills of South Dakota. Hatcher (1903) figured a tetradactyl print found near the Garden Park, Colorado, dinosaur quarries. R. T. Bird (1939a, 1939b) briefly mentioned a sauropod track site in Colorado which he never fully described, as he soon afterward diverted his attention to Lower Cretaceous sauropod tracks in Texas. These Colorado tracks were restudied nearly 50 years later, at which time the current increase in Morrison vertebrate ichnological research began (Lockley and others, 1986). Schoff and Stovall (1943) mentioned a couple of tracksites in the Morrison of the Oklahoma Panhandle found during Stovall's dinosaur excavations in the area in the late 1930s.

In 1957, W. L. Stokes described tracks from the lower Salt Wash Member of the Morrison in Arizona, which he attributed to pterosaurs. The identity of the trackmaker responsible for these prints, and others subsequently found lower in the Jurassic section, is currently debated. A crocodilian trackmaker is inferred by Padian and Olsen (1984). The majority of subsequent work indicates that these tracks may belong to pterosaurs after all (Lockley and others, 1995; Mazin and others, 1995; Unwin, 1997; Bennett, 1997).

Although tracks of theropods and sauropods are known from more than two dozen sites in the Morrison Formation, tracks of non-dinosaurian vertebrates are fairly rare. The pterosaur tracks of Stokes (1957) reportedly came from the Salt Wash Member of the Morrison, but the stratigraphic origin of tracks at this site has not yet been precisely relocated. A source from the underlying Tidwell Member or the Summerville Formation is possible, as confirmed by the discovery of new footprints from those units ascribed to pterosaurs (Lockley and Mickelson, 1997). Pterosaur tracks from low in the Morrison have recently been found in central Wyoming, but not described. They are also known from the Tidwell Member at several localities; debate about whether this member belongs in the Morrison or Summerville continues (Peterson, 1988; Anderson and Lucas, 1996). The track figured by Hatcher (1903) from Garden Park, Colorado, and a similar track from the Salt Wash of eastern Utah probably are attributable to crocodilians (Foster and Lockley, 1997), although Harris (1998) believes the Garden Park track may be that of a camptosaurid. A pair of small tracks from a sandstone at the Fruita Paleontological Area may belong to a lizard, though this occurrence needs to be investigated further.

During the 1996 field season, Jeff Pittman (CU Denver) and Debra Mickelson each independently observed the tracks described herein at a dinosaur track locality low in the Morrison Formation (Salt Wash Member). The tracks are small and do not appear to be attributable to dinosaurian trackmakers, nor are they obviously attributable to crocodilians (see Foster and Lockley, 1997, for a description of purported crocodilian tracks).

The abbreviation CU-MWC indicates joint collections of the University of Colorado at Denver and the Museum of Western Colorado.

LOCALITY

The site containing the tracks is in Copper Canyon, approximately 20 kilometers north of Lake Powell, in eastern Garfield County, Utah (figure 1). Exact locality information is in the files of the University of Colorado-Museum of Western Colorado joint collections at the University of Colorado at Denver. The site is low in the Salt Wash Member of the Morrison Formation, and occurs at the base of a thick sandstone above a thin mudstone unit. The tracks occur as natural casts on the bottom of a sandstone overhang several meters off the ground and were molded and replicated in summer, 1996, using latex rubber and plaster of Paris. In beds a few meters below, a trampled surface containing casts of sauropod manus and pes impressions has been observed, and several kilometers to the south-southeast is the Lost Spring locality which contains two large, well-preserved sauropod pes casts near the middle of the Salt Wash Member (Meyer and others, 1994; Lockley and Hunt, 1995).

TRACK DESCRIPTIONS

The tracks are preserved as CU-MWC 197.3, a plaster replica slab of the overhang surface containing 29 natural casts (figure 2). The general bearing of the tracks is toward the northeast (figure 3). All are preserved as tridactyl or tetradactyl casts. Most consist of shallow but distinct digit traces and deeper, connected "heel" impressions (figure 4). The digit impressions are in some cases significantly longer than would be expected for chelonian digits, and these may represent scrape marks of the digits made immediately prior to full implantation of the manus or pes, separately or as overprinted pairs, or as the result of the motion of the foot as it leaves the substrate and swings forward. The digit impressions indicate that the digits were all of roughly similar lengths and were oriented more or less anteriorly with little divarication. The tracks range from 1 to 5 centimeters in length, but most are 1.5 to 3 centimeters. The width of the tracks is less variable and ranges up to 3 centimeters, with most in the 1.5 to 2.0 centimeter range. This greater degree of variation in track length is to be expected, if they represent "scrape" marks or if manus and pes digit impressions are superimposed to varying degrees.

Depths of the tracks are generally 0.5-1.0 centimeter. One segment of the slab contains five consecutive tracks and perhaps two additional tracks, which may represent a manus and pes impression trackway of a single individual; other tracks are randomly distributed or are on another part of the slab and of slightly larger size and thus probably represent other individuals. The five consecutive tracks are oriented in the same direction, but the first two and last three tracks are aligned on parallel but closely spaced trends, creating a slight offset. The tracks in the series are all 1.5 to 2.0 centimeters in

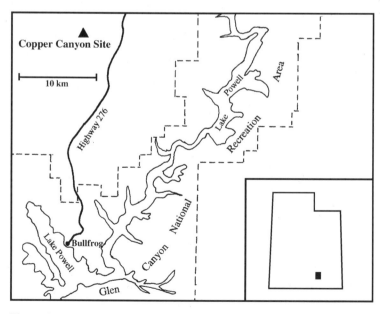

Figure 1. *Map of part of the Lake Powell region showing the Copper Canyon locality (triangle), which contains non-dinosaurian vertebrate tracks in the Salt Wash Member of the Morrison Formation, north of Bullfrog, Garfield County, Utah.*

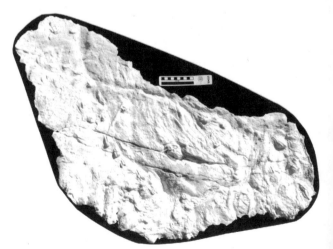

Figure 2. *Photograph of CU-MWC 197.3, a plaster replica of the sandstone overhang surface containing 29 natural track casts. Scale = 10 centimeters.*

Figure 3. *Map of the tracks at the Copper Canyon site. Reversed from a tracing of the casts so that the surface can be seen as it would have appeared from above. Tracks at bottom left are larger than others and likely represent a separate trackway. All tracks from map are contained in plaster replica in figure ?*

Figure 4. *Close-up photograph of the best-preserved tracks from CU-MWC 197.3, showing "scrape" marks of digits. From middle right area of figure 3.*

width, and the length of the trackway from the posterior edge of the first track "heel" to that of the fifth track is 19 centimeters. The spacing between the tracks in order is 5.5 centimeters, 6.0 centimeters, 3.0 centimeters, and 4.0 centimeters, respectively.

COMPARATIVE MATERIAL

The tracks from the Copper Canyon site most closely resemble a set of tracks reported by Moratalla (1993) from the Lower Cretaceous Enciso Group of the Cameros Basin, Spain (figures 5 and 6). The tridactyl and tetradactyl morphology of individual tracks, track-way configuration as consecutive rows, and size are simi-

lar to the Copper Canyon footprints. The Enciso tracks occur in a unit that has produced body fossils of turtles, possibly supporting the interpretation of a chelonian origin (Moratalla, 1993). While we are inclined to agree with this interpretation, which offers support for arguing that the Copper Canyon tracks display chelonian characteristics, the Spanish site has also yielded tracks that have been attributed to dinosaurs, pterosaurs, and birds (Moratalla, 1993; Lockley and others, 1995; and Moratalla, and others, 1992, respectively). Although such evidence suggests a diverse cross section of possible track-making groups, the purported chelonian tracks from Spain (figures 5 and 6) are morphologically distinct from tracks attributed to the other groups.

Turtle tracks have been described from France by Bernier and others (1982, 1984; also Bernier, 1985). These tracks are found in Late Jurassic limestones and are significantly larger than the Copper Canyon specimens. The French tracks fall into two categories, those made by swimming turtles which have been named

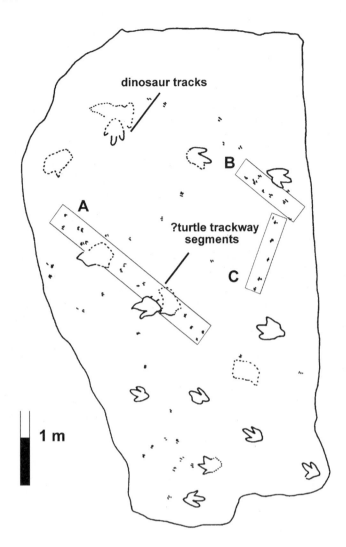

Figure 5. *Surface with chelonian tracks and dinosaur tracks from the Enciso Group (Cretaceous), Spain (after Moratalla, 1993).*

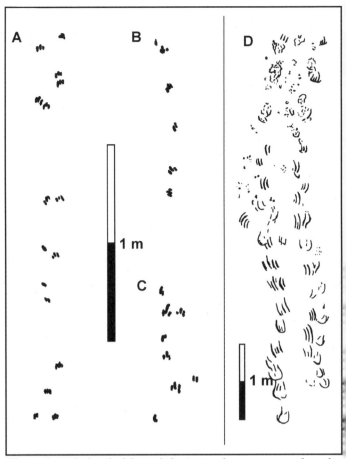

Figure 6. *A-C, detail of three chelonian trackway segments from the Enciso Group (Cretaceous), Spain (after Moratalla, 1993). D, detail of chelonian trackway from the late Jurassic of Cerin, France (after Bernier and others, 1982).*

Saltosauropus latus, and attributed incorrectly to hopping dinosaurs (Thulborn, 1990), and *Chelonichnium carinense*, considered by Bernier and others (1982) to have been made by "walking" turtles. The hopping dinosaurs debate need not concern us here. Examination of the *Chelonichnium* tracks, however, reveals configurations comparable to the Copper Canyon and Enciso Group trackways (figure 6). These similarities include overall shape which consists of parallel to subparallel mainly tridactyl and tetradactyl elongate scrape marks oriented subparallel to the trackway axis. In all trackway examples at least some of the footprints show a rounded to transverse heel impression posterior to the digit impressions. Track spacing is also close in all examples, and it is hard to distinguish manus from pes traces.

MODERN TURTLE TRACKS

Walker (1971) analyzed the gait of the modern turtle

Chrysemys picta marginata, and demonstrated that while walking it produces a wide trackway in which individual footprints reveal elongate digit scrape marks (Walker, 1971, figure 3). "Sometimes" the posterior edge of the plastron produces a trace but at other times it does not. We analyzed his drawings from cinephotographs (Walker, 1971, figure 2) in order to reconstruct a trackway (figure 7 herein). This exercise allowed us to demonstrate that the trackway of *Chrysemys* is wide and that the individual tracks are closely spaced. This configuration is similar to the trackway patterns recorded for the fossil examples from Utah, Spain and France. These observations were further substantiated by examination of the trackway of a modern ornate box turtle (*Terrapene ornata ornata*) in its natural habitat in Baca County, southeastern Colorado. Two of us (M.G. L. and J. B.) observed an individual of this species (Prichard, 1979) crossing several sections of sandy substrate. We obtained photographs of the trackways and traced these to produce the line drawing shown in figure 8. This illustration clearly shows a wide trackway with closely spaced individual footprints, many of which appear elon-

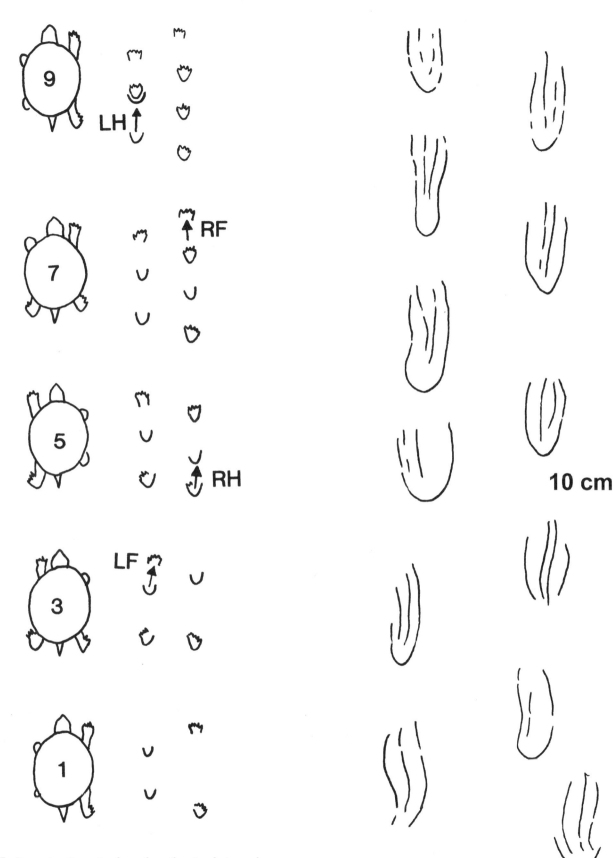

10 cm

Figure 7. *Reconstructing a trackway from the cinephotograph sequence of Walker (1971, figure 2). Position 1 (after Walker) represents the animal (genus* Chrysemys*) with all four feet on the ground. The footprints produced as it progresses through subsequent positions are shown (left front, right hind, right front and left hind = LF, RH, RF and LH respectively).*

Figure 8. Line drawing of a Terrapene *trackway from southeastern Colorado.*

gated owing to foot dragging or overprinting. Our preliminary analyses of these photographs indicate that many of the "footprints" represent superimposed manus and pes tracks. We also observed no plastron drag marks. We conclude therefore that the general trackway pattern of this particular *Terrapene* is also reminiscent of the fossil examples, though we note that this lineage was not represented in the Jurassic

We should note that there are differences between trackways made by animals walking on land and those walking under water (terrestrial and aquatic locomotion of Zug, 1971). Zug called the aquatic locomotion of turtles "bottom walking." To the best of our knowledge, there have been no studies in which fossil trackways of bottom walking (aquatic locomotion) have been recorded, or distinguished from trackways made during terrestrial locomotion. In short, there is a need for detailed studies in which trackways can be recorded and related to various styles of terrestrial and aquatic locomotion. Such studies would have the potential to reveal differences between trackways generated in such different habitats. For example, the incompleteness of the sequence of footprints on one side of the trackway segments from Spain and Utah (figures 3-6), might reflect bottom walking, as the inferred, subaqueous habitat would suggest. Owing to the difficulties involved in getting a turtle to walk underwater (rather than on land) in controlled conditions, and successfully produce a trackway that can be preserved and replicated, this experiment has not yet been attempted. However, in addition to obtaining illustrations of the *Terrapene* trackway, we have obtained footprints of modern turtles *Kinosternon craeseri*, made by pressing their feet into clay, which allow us to investigate the morphology of individual footprints (figure 9).

Haubold (1971) illustrated the supposed turtle tracks Chelonipus, which are vaguely similar to the Copper Canyon tracks, but he also illustrated the indeterminate tracks Serripes, Ruecklinichnium, and Procolophonichnium. All of these tracks could represent turtles, but this is far from certain, and these ichnogenera are not well

known, nor is an evaluation of their morphology and affinity within the scope of the present discussion.

We know of two other tracksites which reveal footprints similar to those at Copper Canyon. Both are associated with the Upper Cretaceous to Paleocene fluviatile sequences in Colorado. Although they have yet to be studied, they indicate the potential for discovering additional comparative material.

DISCUSSION

The Copper Canyon tracks are unlike any others previously reported from the Morrison Formation. The size and morphology are significantly different from all known dinosaurian and pterosaur tracks from the formation. There are some minor similarities to tracks attributed to crocodilians (Foster and Lockley, 1997) in terms of the relative lengths of digits, but the similarity is not compelling. The tracks preserved at the Copper Canyon site are similar in some respects to impressions made by the manus and pes of modern turtles as represented by *Kinosternon creaseri* (figure 9), which in turn are similar in size, and general morphology, to the purported turtle tracks described by Moratalla (1993) from the Cretaceous of Spain (figure 9). When coupled with the similarity between the Copper Canyon tracks and those already interpreted as chelonian tracks from Spain and France, the possibility of a chelonian origin is persuasive. When we also consider the configuration of trackways produced by *Terrapene* and *Chrysemys* (figures 7 and 8) we consider the chelonian explanation of the fossil trackways to be compelling. However, track-making experiments with modern turtles that may support this interpretation have not yet been undertaken. Such experimentation should be undertaken to evaluate further the possibility that the fossil tracks are chelonian. In the meantime, we must conclude that the remote possibility remains that the Utah tracks may have been made by some other vertebrate such as a small crocodilian.

This is approximately the forty-fifth vertebrate track site discovered in the Morrison Formation, but only the sixth with non-dinosaurian vertebrates. Thus, ongoing ichnological research continues to reveal traces not previously recorded in the ichnological record. We do not yet fully understand Morrison vertebrate tracks, despite the significant progress of recent years. Hence, we can expect further new discoveries such as this one.

ACKNOWLEDGMENTS

Partial sponsorship for this project was provided by a grant from the National Science Foundation to M. Lock-

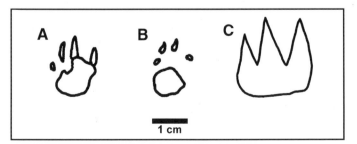

Figure 9. *Impressions of (A) the right manus and (B) the right pes of a modern* Kinosternon craeseri. *C, outline drawing of chelonian track from the Enciso Group (Cretaceous), Spain (after Moratalla, 1993). Scale = 1 cm.*

ley. Thanks to Jeff Pittman and John Kamm for help in the field and to the Bureau of Land Management for permission to work in the area. We appreciate the helpful comments of reviewers Jim Madsen, Dino Lab, Salt Lake City, Utah, and Eugene Gaffney of the American Museum of Natural History. Gaffney's suggestions were particularly helpful and he graciously provided us with references to important literature. We also benefitted from the hospitality of Joaquin Moratalla who showed the Enciso tracksite to one of us (M.G.L.). Jeff Pittman helped make the mold from which replica CU 197.3 was made.

REFERENCES

Anderson, O. J., and Lucas, S. G., 1996, The base of the Morrison Formation (Upper Jurassic) of northwestern New Mexico and adjacent areas, *in* Morales, Michael, editor, The continental Jurassic: Museum of Northern Arizona Bulletin 60, p. 443-456.

Bennett, S. C., 1997, Terrestrial locomotion of pterosaurs: a reconstruction based on *Pteraichnus* trackways: Journal of Vertebrate Paleontology, v. 17, p. 104-113.

Bernier, Paul, 1985, Un lagune tropicale au temps des dinosaures: Museum de Lyons, France, Centre National de la Recherche Scientifique, 136 p.

Bernier, Paul, Barale, Georges, Bourseau, J.-P., Buffetaut, Éric, Demathieu, Georges, Gaillard, Christian and Gall, J.-C., 1982, Trace nouvelle de locomotion de chélonien et figures d' émersion associees dans les calcaires lithographiques de Cerin (Kimméridgien Supérieur, Ain, France): Geobios, v. 15, p. 447-467.

Bernier, Paul, Barale, Georges, Bourseau, J.-P., Buffetaut, Éric, Demathieu, Georges, Gaillard, Christian, Gall, J.-C., and Wenz, Sylvie, 1984, Découverte de pistes de dinosaures sauteurs dans les calcaires lithographiques de Cerin (Kimméridgien Supérieur, Ain, France) implications paléoécologiques: Geobios, Memoires Specials, v. 8, p. 177-185.

Bird, R. T., 1939a, Untitled letter: Natural History, v. 43, p. 245.

—1939b, Thunder in his footsteps: Natural History, v. 43, p. 254-261.

Foster, J. R., and Lockley, M. G., 1997, Probable crocodilian tracks and traces from the Morrison Formation (Upper Jurassic) of eastern Utah: Ichnos, v. 5, p. 121-129.

Harris, J. D., 1998, Dinosaur footprints from Garden Park, Colorado, *in* Carpenter, Kenneth, Chure, D. J., and Kirkland, J. I., editors, Morrison Symposium volume: Modern Geology v. 23, p. 291-307.

Hatcher, J. B., 1903, Osteology of *Haplocanthosaurus*, with description of a new species, and remarks on the probable habits of the Sauropoda and the age and origin of the *Atlantosaurus* Beds: Memoirs of the Carnegie Museum, v. 2, p. 1-72.

Haubold, Hartmut, 1971, Ichnia amphibiorum et reptiliorum follilium: Handbuch der Paläeoherpetologie, tiel 18, 124 p.

Lockley, M. G., and Hunt, A. P., 1995, Dinosaur tracks and other fossil footprints of the western United States: New York, Columbia University Press, 338 p.

Lockley, M. G., Houck, K. J., and Prince, N. K., 1986, North America's largest dinosaur trackway site--implications for Morrison Formation paleoecology: Geological Society of America Bulletin, v. 97, p. 1163-1176.

Lockley, M. G., Logue, T. J., Moratalla, J. J., Hunt, A. P., Schultz, R. J., and Robinson, J. W., 1995, The fossil trackway *Pteraichnus* is pterosaurian, not crocodilian--implications for the global distribution of pterosaur tracks: Ichnos, v. 4, p. 7-20.

Lockley, M. G., and Mickelson, D. L., 1997, Dinosaur and pterosaur tracks in the Summerville and Bluff (Jurassic) beds of eastern Utah and northeastern Arizona: New Mexico Geological Society Guidebook, 48th Field Conference, Mesozoic Geology of the Four Corners Region, p. 133-138.

Marsh, O. C., 1899, Footprints of Jurassic dinosaurs: American Journal of Science, v. 7, p. 227-232.

Mazin, J.-M., Hantzpergue, Pierre, Lafaurie, Gérard, and Vignaud, Patrick, 1995, Des pistes de ptérosaures dans le Tithonien de Crayssac (Quercy, France): Comptes Rendus de l'Academie des Sciences de Paris, v. 321, p. 417-424.

Meyer, C. A., Lockley, M. G., Robinson, J. W., and Santos, V. F. d., 1994, A comparison of well-preserved sauropod tracks from the Late Jurassic of Portugal and the western United States--evidence and implications: Gaia, no. 10, p. 57-64.

Moratalla, J. J., 1993, Restos indirectos de dinosaurios del registro español-- paleoecologia de la Cuenca de Cameras (Jurasico Superior - Crectacio Inferior) y Paleontología del Cretacio Superior: Madrid, Universidad Autonoma, Facultad de Ciencias, Departmento de Biológía, Ph.D. thesis, v. I, 420 p.

Moratalla, J. J., Sanz, J. L., and Jimenez, Santiago, 1992, Hallazgo de nuevos tipos de huellas en La Rioja, Estrato: Revista Riojana de Arqueología, p. 63-66.

Padian, Kevin, and Olsen, P. E., 1984, The fossil trackway *Pteraichnus*-- not pterosaurian, but crocodilian: Journal of Paleontology, v. 58, p. 178-184.

Peterson, Fred, 1988, Stratigraphy and nomenclature of Middle and Upper Jurassic rocks, western Colorado Plateau, Utah and Arizona: U. S. Geological Survey Bulletin 1633-B, p. 13-56.

Prichard, P. C. H., 1979, Encyclopedia of turtles: Neptune, New Jersey, T. F. H. Publications., Inc. 895 p.

Schoff, S. L., and Stovall, J. W., 1943, Geology and groundwater resources of Cimarron County, Oklahoma: Oklahoma Geological Survey Bulletin 64, p. 1-317.

Stokes, W. L., 1957, Pterodactyl tracks from the Morrison Formation: Journal of Paleontology, v. 31, p. 952-954.

Thulborn, R. A., 1990, Dinosaur tracks: London, Chapman Hall, 410 p.

Unwin, D. M., 1997, Pterosaur tracks and the terrestrial ability of pterosaurs: Lethaia, v. 29, p. 373-386.

Walker, W. F., 1971, A structural and functional analysis of walking in the turtle, *Chrysemys picta marginata*: Journal of Morphology, v. 134: 195-214.

Zug, G. R., 1971, Buoyancy, locomotion, morphology of the pelvic girdle and hindlimb, and systematics of cryptodiran turtles: Miscellaneous Publications, Museum of Zoology, University of Michigan, no. 142, p. 1-98.

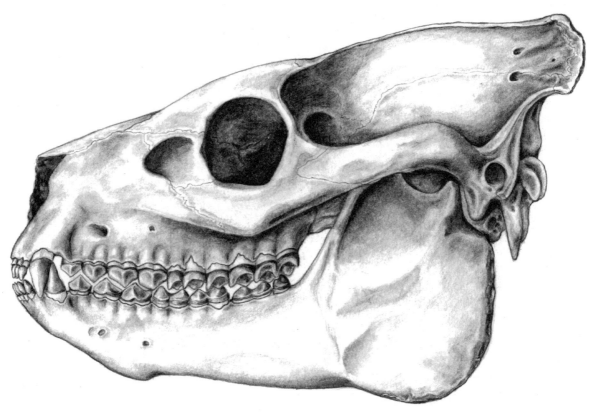

Brian Maebius © 1999

Oreodont

PRELIMINARY REPORT ON BORINGS IN JURASSIC DINOSAUR BONES: EVIDENCE FOR INVERTEBRATE-VERTEBRATE INTERACTIONS

Stephen T. Hasiotis

Department of Geological Sciences, Campus Box 250, University of Colorado at Boulder, Boulder, CO 80309
present address: Exxon Production Research Company, P.O. Box 2189, Houston, TX 77252-2189
Stephen.T.Hasiotis@Exxon.Sprint.com

Anthony R. Fiorillo

Dallas Museum of Natural History, Division of Collections and Research,
P.O. Box 150349, Dallas, TX 75315
fiorillo@mail.smu.edu

Rebecca R. Hanna

HC 58 Box 34B,
Choteau, MT 59422
rrl@3rivers.net

ABSTRACT

Circular- to elliptical-shaped borings on dinosaur bones from quarries in Utah and Wyoming indicate scavenging and reproductive behavior of partial puparia of dermestid beetle larvae (Coleoptera: Dermestidae) on subaerially exposed carcasses prior to burial. These ichnofossils represent not only the earliest evidence of this beetle by nearly 120 million years, but also record the recycling component of the food web and provide information about local paleoclimatic settings in Jurassic terrestrial ecosystems.

Borings occur on many skeletal elements of sauropods, stegosaurs, and theropods at Carnegie Quarry in Dinosaur National Monument (Utah), Cleveland Lloyd Quarry (Utah), "Big Al" Quarry (approximately 330 meters northeast of the famed Howe Quarry, Wyoming), and Bone Cabin Quarry (Wyoming). The borings are circular to elliptical in shape, range in diameter from 0.5 to 1 mm, 2.5 to 3 mm, and 4 to 5.0 mm, and form hemispherical pits in the surface of the bone. The density of borings in the skeletal elements ranges from densely bored (continuous areas of the surficial cortical bone are destroyed by overlapping pits), moderately bored (numerous non-overlapping pits), to slightly bored (just a few borings). The borings represent cocoon formation during the pupation stage of dermestid beetles, a transitional phase in the metamorphosis from larval to adult form.

Dermestid activity requires specific environmental conditions. The presence of these pupal chambers (borings) on the bones implies that: (1) the skeletons must have been partially covered by dried flesh; (2) the carcasses were above water and dry; and (3) carcasses had lain on the sediment surface, which allowed the dermestid infestation. During the period of infestation, the beetles and the carcasses had lain on the floodplain for varying amounts of time, which is indicated by the densities of overall borings in the skeletal elements.

INTRODUCTION

Compared to studies of Jurassic marine ichnofossils, Jurassic continental ichnofossil studies are for the most part nonexistent, with the exception of dinosaur tracks and trackways (for example, Gillette and Lockley, 1989; Lockley, 1991 and references therein). Little is known about the invertebrates of the continental Jurassic with the exception of terrestrial and freshwater aquatic bivalves, gastropods, ostracodes, and conchostrachans (Pang and Chen, 1996; Schudack, 1996; S. C. Good and E. E. Evanoff, personal communication, 1994). Even less is known about ichnofossils that record interactions between invertebrates, particularly insects, and vertebrates. Recent work, however, demonstrates that there is a diverse and abundant ichnofauna in marginal-marine, alluvial, and lacustrine deposits of the Jurassic Morrison Formation (for example, Hasiotis and Demko, 1996; Hasiotis, 1998).

Some of the more interesting Jurassic continental ichnofossil discoveries are of **borings** or **pitting** in dinosaur bones from a number of Morrison quarries in Utah and Wyoming. These traces are 0.5 mm to 5.0 mm in diameter, circular to elliptical in shape, and do not deeply penetrate the bone surface (figures 1-3). Recent

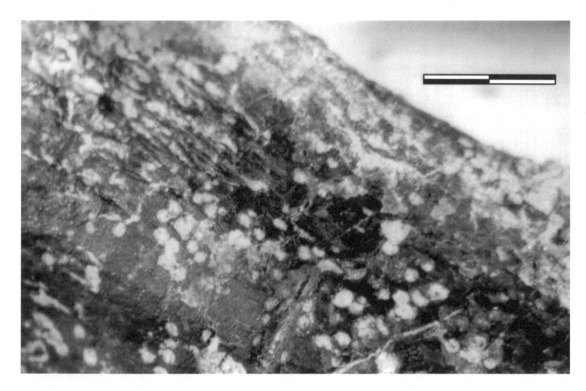

Figure 1. *Small borings on the surface of a dinosaur bone from Carnegie Quarry, Dinosaur National Monument, Utah. The density of borings in this photograph represents a moderately bored surface. Scale = 5 cm.*

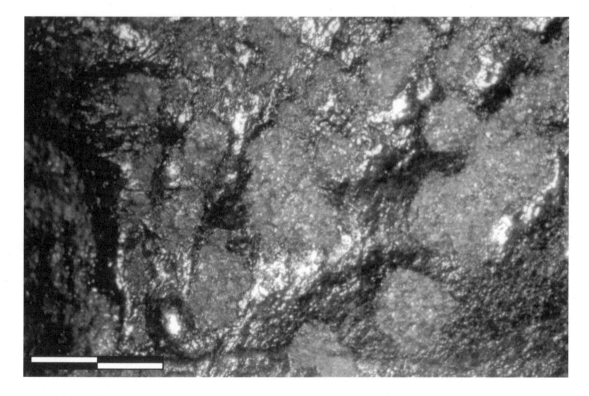

Figure 2. *Close-up view of borings on the surface of dinosaur bone from Carnegie Quarry, Dinosaur National Monument, Utah. Matrix fills the borings, indicating that this modification feature was in place before burial of the bone. The density of borings on this bone represents a densely bored surface. Scale = 5 cm.*

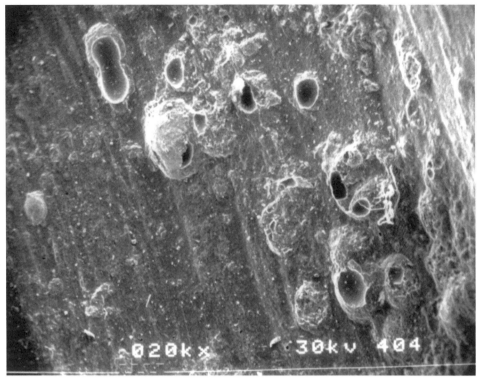

Figure 3. *Scanning electron microscope (SEM) photograph of a mold made from a bored bone surface at Carnegie Quarry, Dinosaur National Monument, Utah. Notice the semispherical (hemispherical) shape of the borings and the scratch marks along the surface of the borings that run as lines of longitude within these hemispheres. The bone surface represents a slightly bored surface. These hemispheres are approximately one millimeter in diameter. The SEM bar scale is 100 microns.*

work (Laws and others, 1996; Hasiotis and Fiorillo, 1997) suggests that these features may be borings attributed to the scavenging and reproductive interaction between specific saprophagous beetles (and their larvae) and dinosaur carcasses. These and other types of beetle borings and invertebrate ichnofossils are invaluable paleoecological and paleohydrological interpretational tools because they record the intimate interactions of decomposers in the food web and provide evidence on the probable season of scavaging in terrestrial ecosystems typically not recorded by body fossils or isotopes (for example, Hasiotis and Bown, 1992; Hasiotis, 1998).

The following abbreviations in this paper identify museums where specimens were examined and are stored: MOR 693, Museum of the Rockies (Montana State University, Bozeman) specimen number for the skeletal elements of "Big Al"; AMNH 600, American Museum of Natural History specimen number for the bones of an adult *Allosaurus* removed from the Carnegie Quarry (UT).

GEOLOGIC SETTING

The Morrison Formation, in the Rocky Mountain and the High Plains regions, ranges in thickness from about 100 to 300 meters (Peterson, 1994). The age of the Morrison is from latest Oxfordian (~156 Ma) to Tithonian

(~144 Ma) (Kowallis and others, 1996). Morrison stratigraphy commonly includes the Tidwell, Salt Wash, and Brushy Basin Members. The Tidwell and Salt Wash Members interfinger with the Bluff Sandstone and Junction Creek Sandstone Members, while the Salt Wash and lower Brushy Basin Members interfinger with the Recapture and Westwater Canyon Members in the Four Corners region (Peterson, 1994). In the northern Colorado Plateau area around Dinosaur National Monument, the basal unit in the Morrison is the Windy Hill Member.

The Morrison in the Colorado Plateau area is comprised of successions of sandstone, mudstone, and thin limestones (Peterson and Turner-Peterson, 1989; Peterson, 1994) that represent eolian, alluvial, and lacustrine deposition. The lowest part of the Morrison near Dinosaur National Monument records mudstone and sandstone deposition in a marginal-marine and tidal sequence (Peterson, 1994; Hasiotis and Demko, unpublished data). The Bluff Sandstone is a localized eolian deposit composed of fine-grained, well-sorted sandstones. The Salt Wash and Westwater Canyon Members were major alluvial complexes composed of vertically stacked sandstones and interbedded mudstones. The Brushy Basin Member contains interbedded sandstones, mudstones, and thin limestones deposited by alluvial and lacustrine systems, and is dominated by smectitic clays in its upper part (Turner and Fishman, 1991).

Bored dinosaur bones occur predominantly in quarries in the lower part of the Brushy Basin Member of the Morrison in Utah and Wyoming. These include the Cleveland Lloyd Quarry (UT), the Carnegie Quarry of Dinosaur National Monument (UT), the "Big Al" Quarry near the area of Howe Quarry (WY), and the Bone Cabin Quarry (WY). Various aspects of these quarries have been studied by several authors (Lawton, 1977; Fiorillo, 1994; Morris and others, 1996; Richmond and Morris, 1996). These assemblages of bones are generally attributed to congregation by flooding events and the miring of individuals in quagmires.

ICHNOFOSSIL EVIDENCE

Dinosaur bones exhibiting borings include the ischia, femora, tibiae, fibulae, metatarsals, scapulae, ribs, gastralia, and vertebrae of various sauropods, limb bones of *Stegosaurus*, and limb bones of *Allosaurus*. The borings show no preferred geographic distribution on the bone surface. In the Carnegie Quarry wall at Dinosaur National Monument, Hasiotis and Fiorillo (1997; unpublished data) observed that borings occur in nearly 40% of the skeletal elements. At the "Big Al" Quarry (MOR 693) the boring frequency was between 12 to15% (Laws and others, 1996). Estimates of bone-boring frequency from other quarries are currently unavailable.

On the bone surfaces, the plan-view shapes of the borings are predominantly circular, but elliptical borings are also present. They are preserved as molds (actual boring) and casts (fine-grain fill) within the bone and are shallow hemispheres (see figure 3) typically 0.01 to 4.0 mm in depth. On some of the bones, a few elliptical pits appear to be unfinished borings. The borings range from 0.5 to 1 mm, 2.5 to 3 mm, and 4 to 5.0 mm in diameter. Clusters of borings are random with no particular distribution between borings. Some skeletal elements contain both small and large borings, but the bone surfaces are always dominated by one size. The borings from the different quarries display similar diameters, shapes, and distributions across the bone surfaces. None of the dinosaur bones examined contain deep or fully penetrating holes or trails.

The skeletal elements exhibit various intensities of boring patterns. Skeletal elements are either: (1) **densely bored**, where continuous areas of the surficial cortical bone are destroyed by overlapping pits; (2) **moderately bored**, where numerous pits do not overlap; (3) **slightly bored**, where few borings are found together; or (4) are **unbored**. Where skeletal elements were removed from the quarries, typically only one side of bone contains borings. Only one of the bones examined, a tibia from an *Allosaurus* (AMNH 600), contains borings all around the bone.

SEM analysis of the borings from bones in the Carnegie and "Big Al" Quarries revealed excavated bone surfaces that contain scratch marks (figure 3). Some borings preserve incomplete scratch patterns that longitudinally and latitudinally contour the surface. The best preserved borings contain parallel sets of scratch marks and diagonally sweeping scratch patterns on the internal walls of the boring, which are 100 to 300 microns wide and up to 900 microns long. Some scratch patterns are triangular and often cross-cut each other. Under very high magnification, the grooves contain scratch patterns that appear as ridge and valleys which range in number from four to eight, and together are about 100 to 200 microns wide.

DISCUSSION

In taphonomy, bone modification is categorized as either geological (physical) or biological in origin. Bone modification features have been defined (Fiorillo, 1991a, b) as the result of any post-mortem, prediagenetic processes (for example, trampling, scavenging, and weathering) that alters the original morphology of the bone found in a living animal. Excluded from this definition are pathological processes (for example, arthritis, deformation from parasitism, and bone tumors). Also excluded are those geological processes which operate independent of those responsible for the formation of a particular bone quarry site (for example, compaction of surrounding sediment during lithification which can crush bone, or stress due to tectonic forces that can shear bones). Fossilization processes such as the "explosion" of bone cavities due to excessive mineral growth within the bone and bone dissolution are also excluded from this definition. The borings on the dinosaur bones discussed in this report are clearly biological in origin and resulted from bone modification due to the activity of adult and larval beetles after the death of the individuals, but prior to burial of some of the carcasses.

Based on size and morphology, the borings are attributable to behavior of beetles in either the families Dermestidae or the Histeridae. Species in these families eat flesh (Reed, 1958; Hinton, 1963; Payne, 1965; Payne and others, 1968; Timm, 1982; Smith, 1986; Martin and West, 1995) and possibly bore into the bones of carrion (R. E. Nelson personal communication, 1997) that the adults and larvae scavenge. However, each beetle species and other types of insects are found on carcasses at different stages in the decay process and play different roles in the decomposition of organic material (for example, Reed, 1958; Smith, 1986; Pickering and Bachman, 1997).

Histerid beetles are attracted to carrion that is moist to soupy, bloated, and decaying (Reed, 1958; Payne, 1965; Payne and others, 1968). They are thought to bore into the flesh of an animal and into the bones to get to the marrow tissue which is high in lipids and carbohydrates (R. E. Nelson personal communication, 1997). However, most often histerids are observed feeding on other coleopterous and dipterous insects, devouring their larvae (for example, Reed, 1958; Smith, 1986). As time progresses and new stages in the decay process evolve, these beetles are not associated with carrion that begins to dry out (Reed, 1958; Payne, 1965). When the carrion reaches a point where the moisture level is no longer high enough, the histerid beetles abandon the carcass. The borings of histerid beetles are thought to be large, 0.3 to 1.0 cm in diameter, and based on the mandible size, might be able to penetrate deeply into bone and form trails in and along the bone (R. E. Nelson, personal communication, 1997). We have found no references of histerid beetles boring into bone, however they may follow the paths of other insects in the flesh of the carrion (for example, Smith, 1986).

Dermestid beetles, on the other hand, are attracted to carrion that are drying out and have become leathery (Reed, 1958; Payne, 1965; Timm, 1982). They usually feed on skin, bone, hair, and feathers. Dermestids are most often observed feeding on dried muscular tissue. They bore holes into the skin and muscular tissue 2 to 5 mm in diameter that are used by the adults and the larvae to gain access into the interior of the carcass (Reed, 1958; Timm, 1982; Smith, 1986). These holes create pathways for the terminal stages in degradation (dry stage) of the carcass by other insects, mites, bacteria, and fungi (for example, Reed, 1958; Payne and others, 1968). When the larvae are ready to pupate to adults, they bore into hard tissues (or surfaces if nothing else is present) like bones and dried ligaments. Also, the larvae bore into bone for lipids and carbohydrates in the marrow. The calcium ingested by the larvae is used for the formation of a hard external exoskeleton during pupation (R. E. Timm, personal communication, 1996). Their borings can be numerous, variable in size, and circular to elliptical in shape. Although dermestid beetles are commonly used to prepare skeletons by removing dried flesh (Timm, 1982; Timm personal communication, 1996; Gillette personal communication, 1998), "nondestructive" species are employed and dermestid colonies of adults and larvae are kept in check; rarely does any dam-

age to the skeleton occur. However, if skeletons with thin bones (for example, scapulas, ribs, some skulls, etc.) are kept in dermestid colonies too long, these bones will be penetrated with holes or areas will be totally removed by the beetles.

The morphologic features of the borings in the dinosaur bones examined in this study suggest that the bones served as a substrate for pupation chambers of dermestid beetle larvae. The morphology of the borings is consistent with those features found in modern pupation borings constructed by beetle larvae in the Dermestidae. Modern and well documented late Tertiary fossil borings range from circular to elliptical in plan and cross-sectional views (Tobien, 1965; Martin and West, 1995, and references therein). Scratch patterns created by mandibular teeth have been observed in well-preserved modern and recently fossilized material. Well-preserved scratch patterns can also be observed in some of the borings from the Carnegie Quarry (figure 3) and the "Big Al" Quarry, that probably resulted from the mandibles of dermestid larvae during excavation of the boring. The detailed ridges and valleys probably reflect the morphology of the mandibular teeth, which were strong and heavily scleritized. And lastly, the shape of the borings probably represents half to a third of the pupal chamber, the remainder of which would have been positioned up into the dried muscular tissue or sticking up into the air above the bone surface.

Though there is no body fossil evidence of dermestid beetles prior to the Oligocene (Carpenter, 1992), the strikingly similar patterns in morphology and distribution of the borings in these dinosaur bones strongly suggest that species of the Dermestidae were present in the Jurassic. Thus, if the taxonomic assignment of the borings is correct, then the range of the Dermestidae is extended nearly 120 million years into the Jurassic.

Based on numerous other reports of modifications on bones, alternatives for the origin of the borings, including organic and inorganic possibilities, are discounted. For example, matrix is present in the borings (figures 1, 2), demonstrating that they were in place before burial and were not caused by preparation of the bones or by modern chemical activity. Similarly, there is no evidence to support fluvial abrasion or weathering of the bones as the cause of pitting prior to burial. Soil acidity due to low pH has been reported to result in cortical pitting (Andrews, 1990) and has been inferred for older fossil material (Fiorillo, 1998), but it is very unlikely that the acidity would result in such consistently recurring features as these borings (see Discussion). Gnawing by small mammals or reptiles is ruled out because these features are much smaller than toothmarks, are not elongate, do not exhibit serrated scrape marks, and no bone crushing is visible at the microscopic level. Stomach acid etching of bone may result in pitting but, as with soil acidity, it is highly unlikely that destruction of cortical bone would lead to the formation of well-defined pits. Rather, the acidity would etch pre-existing structures which are oriented longitudinally along the bone. Microorganisms like marine fungi, endolithic blue-green algae, and amoebic protozoans produce penetrations that are typically maze-like, interwoven tubules and spherules with highly variable diameters in microns (for example, Bromley, 1990; Fiorillo, 1998). These features are inconsistent with those borings found the Jurassic bones. Gastropod drill holes commonly occur on clam and snail shells (Carriker, 1969; Jones, 1969), but are more cylindrical and conical than cup-shaped, and exhibit microstructures that differ from those found in the bone borings. Insects other than dermestids, such as termites (Isoptera), ants, bees and wasps (Hymenoptera), other beetles (Coleoptera), and moths (Lepidoptera) are sometimes attracted to carrion, but do not burrow into flesh or bore into bone. Instead, they typically feed on larvae of other insects and mites, bury small pieces of carrion, feed on hairs and fur, are incidental to the carcass, or use pre-existing skeletal cavities as domiciles (Reed, 1958; Smith, 1986). Though it could be remotely possible that an unknown kind of beetle or insect not preserved as body fossils may have produced the Jurassic borings, the ichnologic evidence clearly indicates behavior and larval morphologies more closely allied to members of the Dermestidae than to any other beetle family or insect order.

In support of our dermestid beetle larvae interpretation is corroborating evidence from the position and condition of the skeletal elements in the "Big Al" and Carnegie Quarries. Skeletons in the "Big Al" Quarry were found in contorted positions (Laws and others, 1996). The skeleton of "Big Al" itself was oriented in an **opisthotonic position**, with the head and tail arched towards one another dorsally. Desiccation under prolonged hot and dry conditions (for example Payne, 1965; Coe, 1978; Smith, 1986; Weigelt, 1989) and subsequent contraction of the ligaments and tendons along the length of the spine after rigor mortis caused the skeleton to be in this position. Opisthotonic and other contorted positions are incurred during desiccation of carcasses. The skeletal elements that contain borings in Dinosaur National Monument are strings of articulated vertebrae and articulated limbs. The combined evidence of borings and articulated skeletal elements suggests that the carcasses were scavenged and desiccated on the floodplain before being swept up in flood waters and partially disarticulated by stream action prior to burial (Hasiotis and

Fiorillo, 1997). The ichnologic evidence from these and other quarries points to the carcasses reaching the dry stage of infestation prior to burial, and parallels similar arthropod successions on carcasses today (for example, Reed, 1958; Payne, 1965; Payne and others, 1968; Smith, 1986).

PALEOECOLOGIC IMPLICATIONS

When an animal of any size dies and is exposed to its surroundings, it is attacked almost immediately by other organisms (Smith, 1986; Pickering and Bachman, 1997). Besides scavaging animals and birds, necrophilous (dead-flesh eating) and saprophagous (feeding on dead or decaying) insects also arrive at the scene at various times throughout the five main stages of decay: (1) initial decay, (2) putrification, (3) black putrification, (4) butyric fermentation, and (5) dry decay (Smith, 1986). An ecological succession of insects results from changes in the attractive nature of a carcass that lead to the complete decomposition of the animal (Reed, 1958; Payne, 1965; Smith, 1986). The faunal succession and rate of decay of carcasses can either be accelerated or prolonged depending on temperature ranges, humidity and precipitation, exposure to light, geographical location and availability of necrophilous and saprophagous fauna, and seasonal variation or climate (Smith, 1986; Pickering and Bachman, 1997).

Dermestid beetle activity implies specific environmental conditions, and thus, the position and severity of bored skeletal elements in a quarry can be used to better constrain the reconstruction of the taphonomic history of each of the various quarries. The presence of the bone borings suggests that the individual carcasses were subaerially exposed for a specific amount of time with the seasonal conditions to allow the appropriate arthropod succession which lead to dermestid infestation (for example, Reed, 1958; Coe, 1978; Smith, 1986; Weigelt, 1989; Martin and West, 1995). For example, dermestid activity does not occur on submerged or moistened materials, and rapid burial of a carcass also prevents any activity. In the late decay and dry stages of a carcass when conditions are suitable, a modern dermestid female may lay 100 to 500 or more eggs in areas beneath desiccated skin or in shaded areas of the carcass (Payne, 1965; Timm, 1982; Smith, 1986; Martin and West, 1995). The eggs hatch into larvae anywhere between two and 10 days, and can grow to adulthood in six to nine weeks (Timm, 1982). If temperature and humidity are not optimal, and food is scarce, the larval period may be extended for years. A host of dermestid larvae can reduce the carcass of a horse or elephant over a period of a few weeks to months. At the appropriate time, when the larvae are ready to pupate, they bore into hard substrates (bone, or whatever is nearby) and lie dormant for one to two weeks. The dermestid larvae have the ability to bore through the hardest material including mortar, concrete, lead pipes, cables, electrical fuses, and wood (Timm, 1982). In 1593, dermestid beetles nearly sank a ship when hundreds of thousands of their larvae bored into the wooden hull after feeding on a cargo of dead penguins (Timm, 1982)!

Using modern data summarized by Smith (1986) for arthropod successions on carcasses and observations recorded by Timm (1982) for dermestid beetle life and reproductive histories as a proxy for the Jurassic beetles, the postmortem and burial histories are reconstructed in real time for dinosaur skeletons with dermestid borings. The size of a dinosaur does not pose a problem in the calculation of time because the study of Coe (1978) on elephant carcasses observed that a low diversity of tens of thousands of dipterous and coleopterous larvae could decimate a 3 to 6 ton carcass in three to six weeks. A preliminary reconstruction of the pre-burial taphonomy of the "Big Al" Quarry was produced using the beetle borings (Laws and others, 1996). When the sub-adult *Allosaurus* (MOR 693) perished, its carcass probably laid near to or in the dry river channel. Based on the eight densely pitted skeletal elements (the left and right pubic bones, right ischium, femur, tibia, fibula, metatarsal IV, and the left coracoid), and the moderate to slight pitting of the other elements, the carcass could have been exposed anywhere from nine to 18 weeks at a minimum. This interpretation is supported by the opisthotonic position of the skeleton which indicates that the carcass had desiccated before burial. Depending on when the animal perished during the dry season, the carcass may have been exposed for an additional two months. However, we assume that the estimation of 18 weeks is a more realistic figure considering the pre-mortem history assumed for the *Allosaurus*. In a reconstructed scenario, the *Allosaurus* most likely perished during the dry season (summer) from thirst, and possibly starvation, and had died very near to its source of water and food (for example, watering hole with associated prey; also see Weigelt, 1989). The fate of the *Allosaurus* is based on it being a sub-adult with no fatal pathologies and the lack of macro-scavenging evidence by other large dinosaurs or reptiles. The lack of such evidence (for example, toothmarks from gnawing or chewing) suggests death during highly stressed environmental and climatic conditions (for example, Weigelt, 1989). Based on the completeness and the position of the bones in the quarry, after a period spanning the fresh, bloated, decay, and dry stages of arthropod infestation, the carcass and its cargo of empty borings and puparia was presumably buried immediately--within a week after the start of the rainy season. If a carcass lingers on the surface for an extended period of time, its skeletal elements become disassociated and scattered by geological and biological processes (for example, Coe, 1978; Smith, 1986; Pickering and Bachman, 1997). Therefore, from the time of death, fresh to dry stages, including dermestid infestation and pupation, and burial, may have taken at least 10 to 19 weeks, or approximately 2.5 to five months. A maximum amount of time of exposure for the carcass prior to burial may have taken as long as nineteen to 27 weeks, or about five to seven months.

CONCLUSIONS

The role of recycling played by saprophagous insects is important today as it was in the Jurassic. If these insects were not actively dissembling carcasses, the decomposition and disintegration of the organic compounds into usable forms would take three to eight times as long or more (for example, Payne, 1965; Smith, 1986). The sauropod, stegosaur, and theropod bone boring evidence suggests that the Dermestidae were present in the Jurassic, extending their temporal range beyond the Oligocene nearly 120 million years. The Jurassic bone borings are also indirect evidence of the arthropod succession associated with the fresh-, bloated-, decay-, and dry-stages of carrion. The fossil record of many arthropods associated with carrion today, such as the Diptera (flies), Coleoptera (beetles), Hymenoptera (bees, wasps, ants), Hemiptera (bugs), Collembola (spring tails), and Diplura (millipedes, centipedes), originated around the Permo-Triassic or earlier (Carpenter, 1992). Thus, it is likely that necrophilous and saprophagous insects, including the Dermestidae, were very important recyclers of carrion and other organic matter in terrestrial ecosystems as far back as the Jurassic, and possibly as early as the Triassic. From the integration of ichnologic, paleontologic, and sedimentologic information, the postmortem-to-burial timing of carcasses can be better constrained and understood for the taphonomy of vertebrate quarries.

ACKNOWLEDGMENTS

We thank Dan Chure of Dinosaur National Monument for his assistance while the first two authors gathered data at the Carnegie Quarry. Hasiotis and Hanna thank Brent Breithaupt of the University of Wyoming Geological Museum for his help with data gathering related to the Howe Quarry. Hasiotis and Fiorillo thank Robert Nelson of Colby College for his thoughts on the taxonomic identification of the beetle responsible for the bone modification features. Hasiotis thanks Robert Timm of the University of Kansas for discussions and important information on dermestid borings on bones.

We also thank Thomas Bown (U. S. Geological Survey, retired), David Gillette (Utah Geological Survey), James Kirkland (Dinamation International Society), and Jared Morrow (University of Colorado, Boulder) for their comments and suggestions to the manuscript. Funding for part of this project was provided to Fiorillo by the National Science Foundation (DEB 9320133) and to Hasiotis by the National Park Service CA-1268-2-9005.

REFERENCES

Andrews, Peter, 1990, Owls, caves, and fossils: London, The Natural History Museum, 231 p.

Bromley, R. G., 1990, Trace fossils--biology and taphonomy: London, Unwin-Hyman Publishers, Special Topics in Paleontology, 280 p.

Carpenter, F. M., 1992, Superclass Hexapoda. Part R, Arthropoda 4. Treatise on invertebrate paleontology: Lawrence, Geological Society of America and the University of Kansas, 655 p.

Carriker, M. R., 1969, Excavation of boreholes by the gastropod, *Urosalpinx*--an analysis by light and scanning electron microscopy: American Zoologist, v. 9, p. 917-933.

Coe, Michael, 1978, The decomposition of elephant carcasses in the Tsavo (East) National Park, Kenya: Journal of Arid Environments, v. 1, p. 71-86.

Fiorillo, A. R., 1991a, Pattern and process in bone modification: Anthropologie, v. 29, no. 3, p. 151-161.

—1991b, Prey bone utilization by predatory dinosaurs: Palaeogeography, Palaeoclimatology, Palaeoecology, v. 88, p. 157-166.

—1994, Time resolution at Carnegie Quarry (Morrison Formation: Dinosaur National Monument, Utah)-- implications for dinosaur paleoecology: Contributions to Geology, University of Wyoming, v. 30, no. 2, p. 149-156.

—1998, Bone modification features on sauropod remains (Dinosauria) from the Freezeout Hills Quarry N (Morrison Formation) of southeastern Wyoming and their contribution to fine-scale paleoenvironmental interpretation: Modern Geology, Part 2, v. 23, p. 111-126.

Gillette, D. D., and Lockley, M. G., editors, 1989, Dinosaur tracks and traces: New York, Cambridge University Press, 454 p.

Hasiotis, S. T., 1998, In search of Jurassic continental trace fossils: Unlocking the mysteries of terrestrial and freshwater ecosytems. Modern Geology Special Paper, The Morrison Formation: An Interdisciplinary Study, Part 1, v. 22 (1-4), p. 451-459.

Hasiotis, S. T., and Bown, T. M., 1992, Invertebrate trace fossils--the backbone of continental ichnology, *in* Maples, C. G., and West, R. R., editors, Trace fossils--their paleobiological aspects: Paleontological Society Short Course, Number 5, p. 64-104.

Hasiotis, S. T., and Demko, T. M., 1996, Terrestrial and freshwater trace fossils, Upper Jurassic Morrison Formation, Colorado Plateau: Continental Jurassic Symposium, Museum of Northern Arizona, Number 60, p. 355-370.

Hasiotis, S. T., and Fiorillo, A. R., 1997, Dermestid beetle borings in sauropod and theropod dinosaur bones, Dinosaur National Monument, Utah-- keys to the taphonomy of a bone bed: Combined Rocky Mountain/Southcentral Geological Society of America Meeting, Abstracts with Program, El Paso, Texas, p. 13.

Hinton, H. E., 1963, A monograph of the beetles associated with stored products: British Museum of Natural History, 443 p.

Jones, M. L., 1969, Boring of shell by Caobangia in freshwater snails of Southeast Asia: American Zoologist, v. 9, p. 829-835.

Kowallis, B.J., Christiansen, E. H., Deino, A. L., Peterson, Fred, Turner, C. E., and Blakey, R. C., 1996, Implications of new high precision ^{40}Ar/^{39}Ar laser-microprobe ages for the Jurassic time scale: Continental Jurassic Symposium, Museum of Northern Arizona, Number 60, p. 7-8.

Laws, G. R., Hasiotis, S. T., Fiorillo, A. R., Chure, Daniel, Breithaupt, B. H., and Horner, John, 1996, The demise of a Jurassic dinosaur after death - three cheers for the dermestid beetle: Geological Society of America National Meeting, Abstracts with Program, v. 28, no. 7, p. 299.

Lawton, Robert, 1977, Taphonomy of the dinosaur quarry, Dinosaur National Monument: Contributions to Geology, University of Wyoming, v. 15, p. 119-126.

Lockley, M. G., 1991, Tracking dinosaurs--a new look at an ancient world: Cambridge, Cambridge University Press, 238 p.

Martin, L. D., and West, D. L., 1995, The recognition and use of dermistid (Insecta: Coleoptera) pupation chambers in paleoecology: Palaeogeography, Palaeoclimatology, Palaeoecology, v. 113, p. 303-310.

Morris, T. M., Richmond, D. R., and Grimshaw, S. D., 1996, Orientation of dinosaur bones in riverine environments-insights into sedimentary dynamics and taphonomy: Continental Jurassic symposium, Museum of Northern Arizona Bulletin 60, p. 521-530.

Pang, Quqing, and Chen, Anguo, 1996, The continental Jurassic and its Ostracoda in Northern China: Continental Jurassic symposium, Museum of Northern Arizona Bulletin 60, p. 343-352.

Payne, J. A., 1965, A summer carrion study of the baby pig *Sus scrofa* Linnaeus: Ecology, v. 46, no. 5, p. 592-602.

Payne, J. A., King, E. W., and Beinhart, George, 1968, Arthropod succession and decomposition of buried pigs: Nature, v. 219, p. 1180-1181.

Peterson, Fred, 1994, Sand dunes, sabkhas, streams, and shallow seas--Jurassic paleogeography in the southern part of the Western Interior Basin, *in* Caputo, M. V., Peterson, J. A., and Fronczyk, K. J., editors, Mesozoic systems of the Western Interior Region, USA: Denver, Colorado, Rocky Mountain Section SEPM, p. 233-272.

Peterson, Fred, and Turner-Peterson, C. E., 1989, Geology of the Colorado Plateau: International Geological Congress Field Trip Guidebook T130, 65 p.

Pickering, R. B., and Bachman, D. C., 1997, The use of forensic anthropology: New York, CRC Press, 170 p.

Richmond, D. R., and Morris, T. H., 1996, The Dinosaur death-trap of Cleveland- Lloyd Dinosaur Quarry, Emery County, Utah: Continental Jurassic Symposium, Museum of Northern Arizona Bulletin 60, p. 533-546.

Reed, H. B., Jr., 1958, A study of dog carcass communities in Tennessee, with special reference to the Insects: American Midland Naturalist, v. 59, no. 1, p. 213-245.

Schudack, M. E., 1996, Ostracode and charophyte biogeography in the continental Upper Jurassic of Europe and North America as influenced by plate tectonics and paleoclimate: Continental Jurassic Symposium, Museum of Northern Arizona Bulletin 60, p. 333-342.

Smith, K. G. V., 1986, A manual of forensic entomology: New York, Cornell University Press, 205 p.

Timm, R. M., 1982, Dermestids: Field Museum of Natural History Bulletin, v. 53, p. 14-18.

Tobien, Heinz, 1965, Insekten-Frasspuren an tertiaren und undpleistozanen Saugetier-Knochen: Senckenbergergiana Lethaea, v. 46, p. 441-451.

Turner, C. E., and Fishman, N. S., 1991, Jurassic Lake T'oo'dichi'--a large alkaline, saline lake, Morrison Formation, eastern Colorado Plateau: Geological Society of America Bulletin, v. 103, p. 538-558.

Weigelt, Johannes, 1989, Recent vertebrate carcasses and their paleobiological implications: Chicago, University of Chicago Press, 187 p.

DISTRIBUTION OF VERTEBRATE FAUNAS IN THE CEDAR MOUNTAIN FORMATION, EAST-CENTRAL UTAH

James I. Kirkland
Utah Geological Survey, Box 146100, Salt Lake City, UT 84114-6100

Richard L. Cifelli
Oklahoma Museum of Natural History, University of Oklahoma, Norman, OK 73019

Brooks B. Britt
Eccles Dinosaur Park, 1544 East Park Boulevard, Ogden, UT 84401

Donald L. Burge
College of Eastern Utah, Prehistoric Museum, 451 E. 400 N., Price, UT 84501

Frank L. DeCourten
Geology/ Earth Science, Sierra College, 5000 Rocklin Road, Rocklin, CA 95677

Jeffery G. Eaton
Department of Geology, Weber State University, Ogden, UT 84408-2507

J. Michael Parrish
Department of Biological Sciences, Northern Illinois University, DeKalb, IL 60115-2854

ABSTRACT

The Cedar Mountain Formation in east-central Utah preserves three distinct dinosaur-dominated vertebrate faunas in strata separated by unconformities. The oldest fauna is preserved in the basal Yellow Cat Member of the Cedar Mountain Formation in the area east of the San Rafael Swell and includes an abundant new genus of polacanthid ankylosaur related to *Polacanthus, Iguanodon ottingeri*, a sail-backed iguanodontid, a camarasaurid and titanosaurid sauropods, a new genus of theropod similar to *Ornitholestes*, and the giant dromaeosaurid *Utahraptor ostrommaysorum*. The polacanthid, iguanodontids, and titanosaurid indicate close temporal geographic ties to the Barremian of Europe, where similar dinosaurs occur. The Poison Strip Sandstone and Ruby Ranch Member preserve a fauna including the nodosaurid *Sauropelta*, the primitive iguanodontid *Tenontosaurus*?, sauropods assigned to *Pleurocoelus*, dromaeosaurid teeth, an unidentified large theropod, and *Acrocanthosaurus*. This fauna compares well with those documented from the Cloverly Formation, Arundel Formation, and Trinity Group characteristic of North America's apparently endemic Aptian-Albian dinosaur fauna. A sharp break from carbonate-nodule-bearing, non-smectitic strata to carbonaceous, highly smectitic strata marks the base of the Mussentuchit Member in the western San Rafael Swell region. This member is dated as straddling the Albian/Cenomanian boundary on palynological and radiometric age estimates. The preserved fauna includes a small nodosaurid *Animantarx ramaljonesi*, a small ornithopod, a primitive lambeosaurid hadrosaur, ceratopsian teeth, pachycephalosaur teeth, tiny sauropod teeth, a dromaeosaurid, cf. *Richardoestesia* teeth, cf. *Paronychodon* teeth, and an early tyrannosaurid. This fauna is remarkably similar to those of the Campanian and Maastrichtian of western North America. As the only likely ancestors of the hadrosaur and ceratopsian are from the Early Cretaceous of Asia, the dramatic shift to faunas typical of the North American Late Cretaceous is interpreted to be the result of opening migration corridors to and from Asia through Alaska at the end of the Early Cretaceous, when migration to eastern North America was still possible. The overlying middle to upper Cenomanian Dakota Formation preserves a dinosaur fauna much like that of the Mussentuchit fauna with the notable absence of sauropods. The fossil record in the Cedar Mountain Formation of east-central Utah can be divided as follows: (1) a basal Barremian iguanodontid-polacanthid fauna with European affinities predating common flowering plants; (2) a middle Aptian-middle Albian *Tenontosaurus-Pleurocoelus* fauna, perhaps representing an impoverished recovery fauna following a major Lower Cretaceous extinction event (endemic to North America); (3) an Albian-Cenomanian boundary fauna dominated by lambeosaurine hadrosaurids with Asian affinities, when flowering plants were co-dominant, which continued until the end of the Cretaceous.

INTRODUCTION

Historically, the Lower to "middle" Cretaceous terrestrial strata of the Cedar Mountain Formation have been considered to be largely unfossiliferous (Stokes, 1944, 1952; Young, 1960). The uppermost Cedar Mountain Formation in the western San Rafael Swell had been established as late Albian, based on palynomorphs, by Tschudy and others (1984). Ages based on freshwater bivalves, ostracodes, charophytes, and plants, while not as accurate, are compatible (Mitchell, 1956; Stokes, 1952; Young, 1960). The Cedar Mountain Formation has subsequently been considered as a homogenous Aptian-Albian unit in most regional studies (for example, Lawton, 1985, 1986; Heller and others, 1986; Heller and Paola, 1989; Baars and others, 1988).

Additionally, the North American terrestrial vertebrate record has been considered to be very poor overall for the "middle" Cretaceous, the notable exception being the Aptian-Albian Cloverly fauna of southern Montana (Ostrom, 1970). Largely correlative faunas are known from the Antlers Formation of Oklahoma, Arkansas, and northern Texas (Stovall and Langston, 1950; Langston, 1974, Cifelli and others, 1997a), the Paluxy and Twin Mountains Formations of central Texas (Langston, 1974; Winkler and others, 1989; 1990), and the Arundel Formation of Maryland (Gilmore, 1921; Kranz, 1989, 1996).

Recent research has indicated that there are three distinct faunas in the Cedar Mountain Formation of east-central Utah (Kirkland, 1996b; Kirkland and others, 1997). In addition to the fauna similar to the well known Cloverly fauna, there are both a distinct earlier and a later fauna. Improved biostratigraphic resolution within this time interval indicates a more complex regional history during the Early to "middle" Cretaceous than previously recognized.

THE CEDAR MOUNTAIN FORMATION AND ITS VERTEBRATE FAUNAS

The term Cedar Mountain Shale was designated by Stokes (1944) for the drab variegated slope-forming sedimentary rocks lying between the Buckhorn Conglomerate and the Dakota Formation, with a type section on the southwest flank of Cedar Mountain, Emery County, Utah. He characterized the Cedar Mountain Shale as having slopes covered with abundant carbonate nodules that are often septarized with agate, barite, and other fillings. Additionally, Stokes (1944) noted an abundance of elongate sandstone lenses (ribbon sandstones) that represent abandoned river channels. He also noted the presence of polished chert pebbles ("gastroliths").

Stokes (1952) renamed the formation the Cedar Mountain Formation and included the Buckhorn Conglomerate as its basal member (figure 1). His measured type section (section 9, T. 18 S., R.10 E. of the Salt Lake Base Line and Meridian) is 123.6 meters thick. He recognized that the Burro Canyon Formation of western Colorado (Stokes and Phoenix, 1948) was largely equivalent to the Cedar Mountain Formation and recommended using the Colorado River as the dividing line between these formations (Stokes, 1952).

Young (1960), recognizing the continuity of the two formations, proposed that the term Burro Canyon be abandoned in favor of Cedar Mountain Formation. This proposal has been ignored by subsequent authors (Craig, 1981). Young (1960) recognized several regionally extensive sandstones in the Cedar Mountain Formation that were useful for correlation (figure 1).

Based on correlations of regionally persistent sandstone units, Young (1960) proposed that calcareous mudstones assigned to the Cedar Mountain passed eastward into the carbonaceous sandstones and shales of his Naturita Formation. The more refined biostratigraphy developed by Kirkland and others (1997) permit more refined correlations across Utah that preclude correlating any sandstone bed within the Cedar Mountain Formation with any specific sandstone bed within the Dakota Formation to the east across central Utah. However, subsurface data presented by Molenaar and Cobban (1991) indicate that the upper Cedar Mountain Formation correlates with the upper Dakota Formation northwestward across the Uinta Basin. Young's (1960) sandstone correlations suffered from this lack of biostratigraphic control, but these regionally persistent sandstone units mark major breaks in sedimentation as indicated by the dramatic faunal changes documented herein. Thus Young's (1960) recognition of these sandstones represents a significant, if belatedly utilized, breakthrough in our understanding of the Cedar Mountain Formation.

In addition to the basal Buckhorn Conglomerate of the western San Rafael Swell, four additional members of the Cedar Mountain Formation have been defined (Kirkland and others, 1997). In ascending order, based on lithostratigraphic and biostratigraphic relationships, these are Yellow Cat Member, Poison Strip Sandstone, Ruby Ranch Member, and Mussentuchit Member (figure 1).

Buckhorn Conglomerate

The Buckhorn Conglomerate was defined as a formation by Stokes (1944) for exposures below the dam at Buckhorn Reservoir on the southwest flank of Cedar

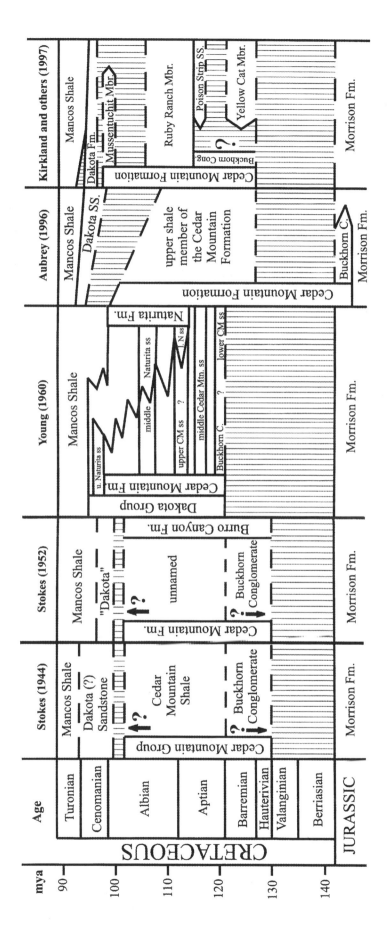

Figure 1. *History of nomenclature for Upper Jurassic through "middle" Cretaceous in east-central Utah. Time scale from Obradovich (1993). After Kirkland and others (1997).*

Mountain where its exposed thickness is 7.5 meters. At the type locality the pebbles have an average diameter of 3 centimeters and are composed mostly of black chert. The member is largely trough-crossbedded with flow directions to the northeast. The Buckhorn Conglomerate is best developed in the northern San Rafael Swell area. Because of its discontinuous nature, Stokes (1952) subsequently included the Buckhorn Conglomerate as the lower member of the Cedar Mountain Formation. Young (1960) also noted that the member is discontinuous and found that it could not be correlated to any specific sandstone east of the San Rafael Swell (figure 1).

Aubrey (1996, 1998) proposed that the Buckhorn Conglomerate is separated from the overlying strata of the Cedar Mountain Formation by a calcrete horizon and that it intertongues with the Morrison Formation and should be considered Upper Jurassic. Currie (1997) also recognized this calcrete horizon in the area of northeastern Utah and northwestern Colorado near Dinosaur National Monument and proposed that it was a sequence-bounding unconformity within the Lower Cretaceous. No fossils have been recovered from the Buckhorn Conglomerate beyond reworked late Paleozoic invertebrates and its correlation to the basal members of the Cedar Mountain Formation to the east is still problematic.

Yellow Cat Member

The Yellow Cat Member is exposed in the northern Paradox Basin in a belt extending from the west side of the ancestral Uncompahgre Uplift west of Dewey Bridge, Utah, to the east side of the San Rafael Swell (figure 2). At most exposures, the Yellow Cat Member extends from the basal calcrete of the Cedar Mountain Formation in this region (Aubrey, 1996, 1998; Kirkland and others, 1997) up to the base of a regionally extensive sandstone ledge (middle sandstone of Young, 1960; Poison Strip Sandstone of Kirkland and others, 1997). These sediments consist mostly of interbedded mudstone, with interbeds of sandstone and limestone. These mudstones tend to be mauve toward the base and pale green toward the top. They differ from those of the Morrison in being drabber and less strongly variegated. In addition, the mudstones in the Yellow Cat Member are not smectitic.

The basal calcrete is not always present and at some sites there is a shale-on-shale contact, although common polished chert pebbles ("gastroliths") are generally found at the best pick for the contact (Stokes, 1944; 1952) suggesting a deflation surface. At other sites, the basal calcrete is a complex of superimposed calcretes or there may be several calcretes and the contact is picked at the

top of the lowest calcrete above smectitic mudstones of the Brushy Basin Member of the Morrison Formation. Aubrey (1996, 1998) utilized the base of the calcrete as the base of the Cedar Mountain, however the basal surface is often gradational. His argument assumes that this calcrete represents a complex soil horizon developed on the Morrison paleosurface. However, while distinct soil features are recognized in many places, in other areas such as below the type section of the Ruby Ranch Member, overlying lucustrine sediments may be a control on the development these carbonates. The uppermost Morrison below the calcrete is often non-smectitic, root-mottled, and a brick red color, perhaps reflecting the period of exposure, oxidation, and soil formation between deposition of the Morrison Formation and the onset of Cedar Mountain deposition.

The type section of the Yellow Cat Member of the Cedar Mountain Formation is near the Gaston Quarry (figure 3) west of the Yellow Cat Road (Kirkland and others, 1997). At this site, the Cedar Mountain Formation is 45.9 meters thick and the basal Yellow Cat Member measures 24 meters thick. At 6.7 meters below the overlying Poison Strip Sandstone, there is an interval of limestone and shale interbeds which Young (1960, figure 6, section 37) used to mark the base of the Cedar Mountain Formation in this area. Therefore, a major portion of the Yellow Cat Member had been included in the Brushy Basin Member of the Morrison Formation.

The Yellow Cat fauna includes abundant specimens of a new genus of polacanthid ankylosaur related to *Polacanthus, Iguanodon ottingeri* (Galton and Jensen, 1979), perhaps a distinct genus of sail-backed iguanodontid, titanosaurid and camarasaurid sauropods, a new genus of theropod most similar to *Ornitholestes*, and the giant dromaeosaurid *Utahraptor ostrommaysorum* (Kirkland and others, 1991; Kirkland, Burge, Britt, and Blows, 1993; Kirkland and others, 1997; Kirkland and others, 1995; Kirkland, 1993, 1996a; Kirkland, Burge, and Gaston, 1993; Britt and others, 1996; Britt and Stadtman, 1997; Carpenter and others, 1996). In addition, turtles, crocodilians, and a sphenodontian have been recognized (Kirkland and others, 1997). Fish appear to be locally abundant, but have been identified only from isolated remains (table 1). Hybodont sharks have been identified on the basis of a small fragment of dorsal fin spine and several spiral coprolites rich in ganoid scales. Important vertebrate quarries in this member include Brigham Young University's Dalton Well Quarry (figure 4), which preserves a diverse fauna dominated by sauropods (Britt and others, 1996; Britt and Stadtman, 1997), and College of Eastern Utah Prehistoric Museum's Gaston Quarry (figure 3), which preserves a less

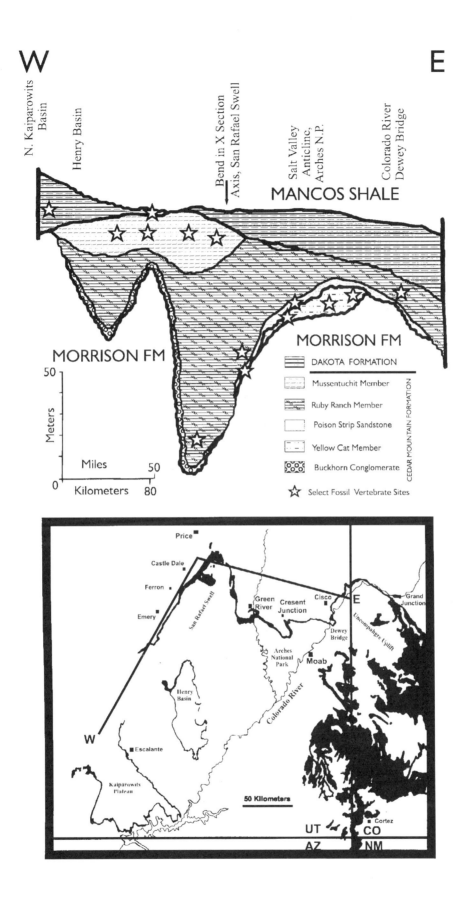

Figure 2. *Cross section showing the distribution of "middle" Cretaceous units across eastern Utah discussed in text. Modified after Kirkland and others (1997). Base map showing distribution of Cedar Mountain, Burro Canyon, and Dakota Formations modified after Young (1960).*

Distribution of Vertebrate Faunas - Kirkland, Cifelli, Britt, Burge, DeCourten, Eaton, Parrish

Figure 3. *Type area of Yellow Cat Member of the Cedar Mountain Formation above Yellow Cat Flat near College of Eastern Utah Prehistoric Museum's Gaston Quarry. Arrow indicates position of Gaston Quarry. Abbreviations: cal, calcrete; Cp, Poison Strip Sandstone; Cr, Ruby Ranch Member; Cy, Yellow Cat Member; D, Dakota Formation; Mor, Morrison Formation.*

Table 1. *Yellow Cat Fauna (see text for repositories)*

Class Osteichthyes
    Subclass Dipnoi
        Ceratodus undescribed new species
    Subclass Actinopterygia
        cf. *Semionotus* ? sp.
        cf. *Amia* sp.
Class Reptilia
    Order Chelonia
        cf. *Glyptops* sp.
    Order Rhynchocephalia
        cf. *Toxolophosaurus* sp.
    Order Crocodilia
        indeterminate teeth
    Order Theropoda
        Family Dromaeosauridae
            Utahraptor ostrommaysorum
        Family uncertain
            Nedcolbertia justinhofmanni
    Order Sauropoda
        Family Camarasauridae
            undescribed new genus
        Family Titanosauridae
            undescribed new genus
    Order Ornithopoda
        Family Iguanodontidae
            Iguanodon ottingeri
            undescribed new genus
    Order Ankylosauria
        Family Polacanthidae
            Gastonia burgei

diverse fauna dominated by polacanthid ankylosaurs. Both of these sites are in the upper third of the Yellow Cat Member. At the base of the Yellow Cat Member 1.5 kilometers east of the Gaston Quarry, one horizon has

yielded several isolated small theropod skeletons (figure 5) (Kirkland and others, 1997). Sites preserving isolated remains of iguanodontids, sauropods, and polacanthid ankylosaurs have also been found in the region by the Denver Museum of Natural History. Important collections of fossils from this interval are housed at the College of Eastern Utah Prehistoric Museum, Price, Utah; Earth Science Museum, Brigham Young University, Provo, Utah; Denver Museum of Natural History, Denver Colorado; and the Oklahoma Museum of Natural History, University of Oklahoma, Norman Oklahoma.

There is disagreement among the authors as to whether there are one or two iguanodontids in the Yellow Cat Member. Britt and Stadtman (1997) have proposed that the sail-backed iguanodontian is an adult specimen of *Iguanodon ottingeri* as both specimens occur together at the type locality. Kirkland and others (1997) have proposed that there are two iguanodontid taxa, a large sail-backed form and *I. ottingeri*; and a conservative small iguanodontian similar to or even conspecific with *I. lakotaensis* (Weishampel and Bjork, 1989). All the iguanodontid specimens collected at the Gaston Quarry and found as isolated specimens are similar to the type specimens of *I. ottingeri* and *I. lakotaensis*. Only further excavations will resolve this question.

The polacanthid ankylosaurs, iguanodontids, and titanosaurid sauropods indicate close temporal and geographic ties to the Barremian of Europe (Blows, 1993; Norman, 1988). This correlation is also supported by the presence of the charophyte *Nodosoclavator bradleyi*, which is not known in strata younger than Barremian (Niel Shudack, personal communication; Kirkland and

Figure 4. *The Brigham Young University's Dalton Wells Quarry indicated by D and brackets. Abbreviations: Cp, Poison Strip Sandstone; Mor, Morrison Formation.*

Figure 5. *College of Eastern Utah Prehistoric Museum's small theropod sites indicated by dots just to the east of the Gaston Quarry. Abbreviations: Cp, Poison Strip Sandstone; cal, calcrete.*

others, 1997). Furthermore, the dinosaurs indicate a close correlation with the Lakota Formation at Buffalo Gap, South Dakota (Kirkland, 1992; Kirkland, Burge, and Gaston, 1993; Kirkland and others, 1997; Lucas, 1993) (figure 6). Kirkland and others (1997) estimated that 20 to 25 million years of Earth history may be represented by the hiatus between Morrison and Cedar Mountain deposition based on radiometric age estimates at the top of the Morrison Formation (Kowallis and others; 1998) and the age of correlative dinosaur-bearing strata (Obradovich, 1993; Dyman and others, 1994).

The thickness of the Yellow Cat Member may vary by tens of meters over several kilometers of outcrop. Together with the observed differences in its basal contact, this lateral variation in thickness may in part reflect the topography of the erosional surface formed on the upper Jurassic strata during the earliest Cretaceous.

The distribution of the Yellow Cat Member provides an important constraint on the beginning of Sevier thrust-ing. Aubrey (1996, 1998) has postulated that thrusting may have begun in the Barremian based on the recognition of this basal Cedar Mountain fauna (Kirkland, 1992). As a rule, subsidence caused by loading in the proximal foreland basin is almost instantaneous geologically, (Turcotte and Schubert, 1982), indicating that age estimates from the sediment wedge formed proximal to the thrust belt provide a bracket for the beginning of thrusting. However, because the Barremian sediments of the Yellow Cat Member pinch out to the west (figure 2), they would seem to preclude the onset of Sevier thrusting until at least the Aptian and hence provide additional support to previously published dates for the onset of thrusting (Lawton, 1985, 1986; Heller and others, 1986; Heller and Paola, 1989).

The distribution of the Yellow Cat Member from the Uncompahgre Uplift to the San Rafael Swell is compatible with the proposal by Aubrey (1996) that the distribution of these sediments was controlled by salt tectonics

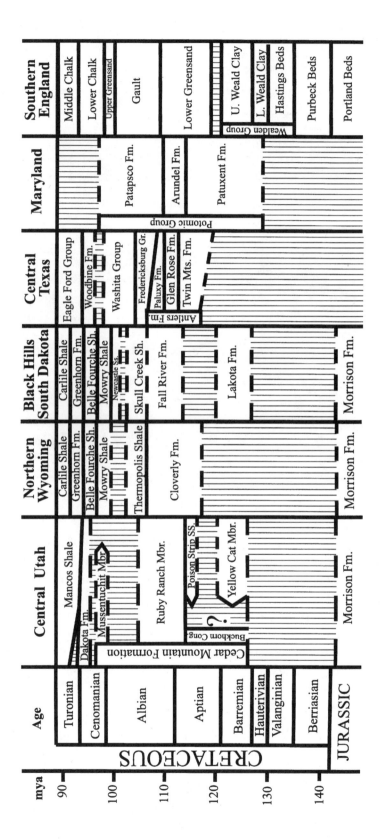

Figure 6. *Correlation chart showing age relationships of stratigraphic units discussed in text. Vertical lines denote unconformities. Time scale from Obradovich (1993). Data from Benton and Spencer (1995), Dyman and others (1994), Hancock and others (1993), and Winkler and others (1995). Modified after Kirkland and others (1997).*

Figure 7. *The Brigham Young University's Bodily's Nodosaur Site on west side of Arches National Park. Arrow points to site. Abbreviations: Cm, Mussentuchit Member; Cp, Poison Strip Sandstone; Cr, Ruby Ranch Member; Cy, Yellow Cat Member; D, Dakota Formation; Mor, Morrison Formation.*

during the Early Cretaceous as reported by Doelling (1988). Variation in local subsidence rates due to salt tectonics might help explain the rapid thinning and thickening observed in the Yellow Cat Member. Additionally, lacustrine sediments such as algal- and mudcracked limestones are common in the Yellow Cat Member (Britt and Stadtman, 1997; Kirkland and others, 1997). Lacustrine sediments are compatible with the formation of small basins due to salt tectonics.

The presence of numerous calcareous nodules representing paleosols indicates that the Yellow Cat Member was deposited under a semiarid monsoonal climate similar to that interpreted for the underlying Morrison Formation (Dodson and others, 1980, Wing and Sues, 1992). The widespread occurrence of viviparid snails, fish, freshwater turtles, and crocodilians suggest there may have been more standing water than indicated for the Late Jurassic of the Colorado Plateau (Dodson and others, 1980). The floras recorded for the Barremian are generally devoid of angiosperms other than a low diversity of pollen types, which first appear in the middle Barremian (Hughes and others, 1979). This would indicate that a flora dominated by non-flowering plants much like that of the of the Jurassic was present (Wing and Sues, 1992).

Poison Strip Sandstone

The cliff-forming middle Cedar Mountain sandstone unit of Young (1960) marks the top of the Yellow Cat Member in eastern Utah (figure 1). It commonly contains gray and white chert pebbles In some places there are several sandstones that are probably genetically related to each other, while rarely in other places there is only a thin crevasse splay or, locally, no sandstone at all. This

sandstone above the Yellow Cat Member has been named the Poison Strip Sandstone (Kirkland and others, 1997). It caps the escarpment exposing the upper Morrison Formation throughout the area from Green River, Utah to the Utah-Colorado border. This sandstone forms one of the most persistent and distinctive stratigraphic intervals in the entire Cedar Mountain Formation of eastern Utah. In some areas in the Poison Strip region south of Cisco, Utah, large scale (5 meters and greater) epsilon crossbedding indicates that a large, meandering river system was mostly responsible for its deposition.

The Poison Strip Sandstone is clearly equivalent to Young's (1960) middle Cedar Mountain sandstone east of the San Rafael Swell. However, the middle Sandstone unit as used by Young (1960) in the western San Rafael Swell area is well above sites preserving an Aptian-lower Albian fauna, such as at the Long Walk Quarry (DeCourten, 1991; Kirkland and others, 1997), and appears to be an unrelated sandstone of more limited extent. Without the biostratigraphic control provided by the vertebrate faunas preserved in the Cedar Mountain Formation, Young's (1960) miscorrelation of these sandstones across the San Rafael Swell is understandable.

Sedimentologically the Poison Strip Sandstone is clearly distinct from the trough cross-bedded conglomerate of the Buckhorn Member of the Cedar Mountain Formation in the San Rafael Swell area. Although apparently in the same stratigraphic positions, there is no means of correlation between the genetically distinct Buckhorn Conglomerate and the middle sandstone of Young (1960) in eastern Utah. In the western San Rafael Swell area, no fossils have been found in the Buckhorn Conglomerate at the base of the Cedar Mountain Formation; thus it impossible as yet to date the Buckhorn. Additionally, Currie (1997) describes the Buckhorn Conglomerate as representing an isolated river system flowing to the northeast from the San Rafael Swell across the extreme northwestern corner of Colorado into Wyoming.

The Poison Strip Sandstone is named for the typical exposures of this unit along the Poison Strip south-south-west of Cisco, Utah. The type section is on the southwest end of the Poison Strip east-northeast of the Ringtail Mine (Kirkland and other, 1997) (figure 4). The type section of the Poison Strip Sandstone measures 5.4 meters thick. The sandstone is fine- to medium-grained with matrix supported black, gray, and white chert pebbles, trough cross-bedded, and becomes slabby with pale greenish mudstone partings toward the top of the member. The Poison Strip Sandstone is economically significant in this area because it is the primary target in the Cisco Oil and Gas Field to the northeast (Larry Moyer, personal communication, 1995).

On the northeast side of Arches National Park, Bodily (1969) described a large ankylosaur as cf. *Hoplitosaurus* sp. from in, or just above this unit (figure 5). Coombs (1971) referred the taxon to the Cloverly nodosaurid ankylosaur, *Sauropelta*. Just north of this site a second specimen of *Sauropelta* was recently discovered by researchers from the Denver Museum of Natural History. These fossils indicate the Poison Strip Sandstone is close to the same age as the overlying Ruby Ranch Member, which also contains *Sauropelta*. The College of Eastern Utah Prehistoric Museum has recovered parts of an ornithopod from their Price River Quarry from a conglomeratic sandstone at the base of the Cedar Mountain Formation, southeast of Wellington, Utah (Burge, 1996). The ornithopod appears to represent *Tenontosaurus* and suggests that the conglomeratic sandstone southeast of Wellington correlates to the Poison Strip Sandstone. The sparse, small, black, gray, and white chert pebbles are also similar to those in the Poison Strip Sandstone. Large conifer logs and the cycads, *Cycadeoidea* and *Monanthasia* (William Tidwell, personal communication, 1997) are present locally within the Poison Strip Sandstone in the area around Arches National Park.

Ruby Ranch Member

The Ruby Ranch Member extends across the entire outcrop belt of the Cedar Mountain Formation and in strata assigned to the Burro Canyon Formation east of the Colorado River (figure 2). The Ruby Ranch Member overlies the Poison Strip Sandstone from at least the Utah-Colorado border region westward to the eastern San Rafael Swell and overlies the Buckhorn Conglomerate on the west side of the San Rafael Swell. From approximately the crest of the Salt Valley Anticline at

Arches National Park eastward, the upper contact of the Ruby Ranch Member is clearly with the base of the Dakota Formation. On the west side of the San Rafael Swell, a sharp break from carbonate nodule-bearing, non-smectitic strata to carbonaceous, highly smectitic strata marks the contact between the Ruby Ranch Member and the overlying Mussentuchit Member. A conglomerate unit rich in quartzite lies between these members along the northeastern side of the San Rafael Swell that is equivalent for the most part to Young's (1960) middle Naturita sandstone (Mark Kirschbaum, personal communication, 1996; Kirkland and others, 1997).

On the west side of Arches National Park a smectitic interval is present at the top of the Cedar Mountain Formation. This interval potentially correlates with the Mussentuchit Member of the western San Rafael Swell (figure 2). The report of a hadrosaur femur (Galton and Jensen, 1979) from this area may lend support to that correlation. Additionally, Brigham Young University's "Movie Valley" ankylosaur from the same area, may also be from this level based on the black color of the bones, which uniquely characterizes bones preserved in the Mussentuchit Member among units in the Cedar Mountain Formation.

The Ruby Ranch Member consists of drab, variegated mudstones with minor sandstone and limestone layers. Perhaps most characteristic of this interval are the abundant carbonate nodules that often are so abundant as to form a pavement covering the exposed slopes. The abundance of these nodules makes prospecting for fossils in this interval difficult. In addition, ribbon sandstone bodies holding up ridges that may extend for a kilometer or more are typical of this interval (Young, 1960; Harris, 1980; DeCourten, 1991; Kirkland and others, 1997). A substantial portion of the northwestward thickening observed in the Cedar Mountain Formation across the San Rafael Swell (for example, Stokes, 1952; Young, 1960) is represented by this interval. There is also a considerable thinning and thickening of this interval along the west side of the San Rafael Swell.

The type section of the Ruby Ranch Member is at the Ruby Ranch homestead site southwest of Crescent Junction, Utah (Kirkland and others, 1997). The basal contact is with the Poison Strip Sandstone and the upper contact is with the base of the Dakota Formation. The type section is 33.1 meters thick. At 2.1, 14, and 16.6 meters above the base, ribbon sandstones, whose thalweg and cross-bed orientations represent eastward-flowing rivers are present. Overall, the drab, variegated mudstones have a pale purplish surface expression. The upper 8.5 meters is a pale, greenish-gray color perhaps due to bleaching by the overlying Dakota Formation.

This upper interval also includes fewer, but larger carbonate nodules.

The Ruby Ranch fauna (table 2) includes the primitive iguanodontid *Tenontosaurus*?, the large nodosaur *Sauropelta*, a sauropod assigned to *Pleurocoelus* (= *Astrodon*), dromaeosaurid teeth, an unidentified large theropod, and *Acrocanthosaurus* (Weishampel and Weishampel, 1983; DeCourten, 1991; Kirkland and others, 1997). This fauna is the least known of the Cedar Mountain faunas. Important vertebrate sites in this member include the University of Utah's Long Walk Quarry near Castledale (DeCourten, 1991), the College of Eastern Utah's Price River 2 and KEM sites southeast of Wellington, Utah, and the Oklahoma Museum of Natural History's Hotel Mesa Quarry (figure 8) just to the east of the Colorado River, and thus what properly should be considered a Burro Canyon Formation site (Kirkland and others, 1997). The site, from which the *Tenontosaurus* specimens were collected on the west side of the San Rafael Swell (Weishampel and Weishampel, 1983), has not been relocated, but the carbonate matrix surrounding the specimens indicates they are from the Ruby Ranch Member. Important collections of fossils from this member are housed at the College of Eastern Utah Prehistoric Museum, Price, Utah; Earth Science Museum, Brigham Young University, Provo, Utah; and the Utah Museum of Natural History, University of Utah, Salt Lake City, Utah.

This fauna compares well with those documented from the Cloverly Formation, Arundel Formation, and Trinity Group characteristic of North America's apparently endemic Aptian-Lower Albian dinosaur fauna (Kirkland, 1996b; Kirkland and others, 1997). Determining the age of these sediments more precisely is impossible at this time.

The abundant calcareous nodules indicate that the Ruby Ranch Member was deposited under a semiarid monsoonal climate similar to that interpreted for the

Table 2. *Ruby Ranch Fauna (see text for repositories)*

Class Chondrichthyes
    Order Hybodontoidea
        Hybodus sp.

Class Reptilia
    Order Crocodilia
      indeterminate
    Order Theropoda
        Family Dromaeosauridae
            cf. *Deinonychus* sp.
        Family Allosauridae ?
           undescribed new genus
           cf. *Acrocanthosaurus* sp.
    Order Sauropoda
        Family Brachiosauridae
           Pleurocoelus sp. = *Astrodon* sp.
    Order Ornithopoda
        Family Iguanodontidae
           Tenontosaurus sp.
    Order Ankylosauria
        Family Nodosauridae
           cf. *Sauropelta* sp.

underlying Morrison Formation (Dodson and others, 1980, Wing and Sues, 1992). The Aptian-Albian pollen record indicates that angiosperms were becoming a significant part of western interior floras at this time (Wing and Sues, 1992).

Mussentuchit Member

A sharp break from carbonate-nodule-bearing, non-smectitic strata to carbonaceous, highly smectitic strata marks the base of the Mussentuchit Member. The dramatic increase in the volume of volcanic ash preserved in the Mussentuchit Member indicates a significant increase in volcanic activity to the west. The member is dated as straddling the Albian-Cenomanian boundary based on palynology (Nichols and Sweet, 1993), subsurface correlations (Molenaar and Cobban, 1991), and radiometric age estimates (Cifelli and others, 1997b).

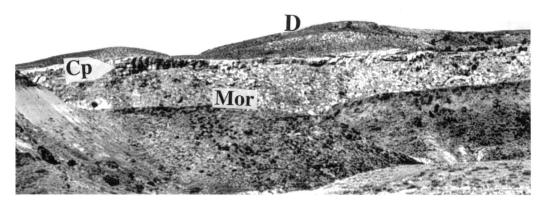

Figure 8. *Oklahoma Museum of Natural History's Hotel Mesa Site indicated by arrow looking east across the Colorado River. Abbreviations: Cp, Poison Strip Sandstone; D, Dakota Formation; Mor, Morrison Formation.*

Figure 9. *Type area of Mussentuchit Member of the Cedar Mountain Formation, Mussentuchit Wash near several of the Oklahoma Museum of Natural History's quarries. Dashed line indicates contact between Ruby Ranch and Mussentuchit Members. Abbreviations: Cb, Buckhorn Conglomerate; Cp, Poison Strip Sandstone; Cr, Ruby Ranch Member; Cy, Yellow Cat Member; D, Dakota Formation.*

Figure 10. *College of Eastern Utah Prehistoric Museum's Carol Site indicated by arrow northwest of Castledale, Utah. Abbreviations: Cr/Cm, contact between Ruby Ranch and Mussentuchit Members; D, Dakota Formation.*

Stokes (1944) included this member in the Cedar Mountain Shale. However, he described the Cedar Mountain as having abundant carbonate nodules and did not mention that, at the top of the unit, the formation may lack such nodules.

Locally in the area of the southwestern San Rafael Swell south of Interstate 70, sandstone lenses near the top of the Cedar Mountain Formation compare well with the more extensive sandstone ledge typically used to define the base of the Dakota Formation (Stokes, 1944). This transition suggests that the top of the Cedar Mountain Formation may represent a period of nearly continuous sedimentation including the more carbonaceous overlying Dakota Formation. In fact, Young (1960) included the Mussentuchit Member in his Naturita Formation (Dakota Formation). The dramatic shift in the

sedimentology and paleontology at the base of this interval suggests that perhaps the Mussentuchit Member would be better included as a basal member of the Dakota Formation; the authors of this paper are not in full agreement at to whether this member should be included in the Cedar Mountain Formation or in the Dakota Formation (Kirkland and others, 1997). However, including the Mussentuchit Member in the basal Dakota Formation would mean that nearly every fossiliferous horizon in the area of the western San Rafael Swell attributed to the Cedar Mountain Formation (Katich, 1951; Stokes, 1952; Thayne and others, 1983, 1985; Thayne and Tidwell, 1984; Tidwell and Thayne, 1985; Jensen, 1970; Eaton and Nelson, 1991; Cifelli, 1993; Kirkland and Burge, 1994; Cifelli and others, 1997b, this volume), would have to be attributed to the Dakota Formation.

The upper smectitic portion of the Cedar Mountain Formation was designated the Mussentuchit Member by Kirkland and others (1997) with its type section south of Mussentuchit Wash (figure 9). At the type section, the member is 25 meters thick. A thin, discontinuous sandstone marks the base, where the non-smectitic mudstone rich in carbonate nodules is replaced by highly smectitic, gray mudstone. Several thin lenticular sandstones and lignitic horizons are present in the type section. The top of the member is at the base of a thick buff sandstone that forms the basal unit of the Dakota Formation along most of the western San Rafael Swell. Locally to the east of Ferron Utah, the Dakota Formation is missing (figure 2) and a horizon of dark chert pebbles and cobbles marks the base of the overlying Mancos Shale (Eaton and others, 1990; Kirkland and others, 1997).

The preserved dinosaur fauna includes a small nodosaurid *Animantarx ramaljonesi*, a small iguanodontid ornithopod, a primitive lambeosaurid hadrosaur, ceratopsian teeth, pachycephalosaur teeth, tiny sauropod teeth, dromaeosaurid teeth, cf. *Richardoestesia* teeth, cf. *Paronychodon* teeth, and an early tyrannosaurid (Kirkland and Burge, 1994; Kirkland and Parrish, 1995; Burge, 1996; Carpenter and others, this volume). Teeth of a very small sauropod similar in morphology to those described as *Astrodon* are also present in this member marking the last occurrence of sauropods in North America prior to their reintroduction from South America in the late Maastrichtian (Lucas and Hunt, 1989). At the family level, this fauna is remarkably similar to those of the overlying Dakota Formation (Eaton and others, 1997) and those of the Campanian and Maastrichtian of western North America (Cifelli, Kirkland, and others, 1997b; Cifelli and others, this volume; Kirkland, 1996b; Kirkland and others, 1997). As the only likely ancestors of the hadrosaur, ceratopsian, and perhaps the tyrannosaurid are from the Early Cretaceous of Asia, the dramatic shift to faunas typical of the North American Late Cretaceous is interpreted to be the result of opening migration corridors to and from Asia through Alaska at the end of the Early Cretaceous, when migration to eastern North America was still possible (Kirkland, 1996b; Cifelli and others, 1997b).

Following an extensive screenwashing operation by the University of Oklahoma that resulted in thousands of catalogued specimens representing nearly 80 vertebrate taxa, Cifelli, Kirkland, Kirkland, and others (1997; and Cifelli and others, this volume, for complete faunal list) have characterized this fauna as the Mussentuchit local fauna for Mussentuchit Wash, where many of their best vertebrate sites are located.

In addition to the many important sites developed by the Oklahoma Museum of Natural History, a number of other important vertebrate sites have been developed in the Mussentuchit Member by other institutions. Most of these sites are from the area east of Ferron and Castle Dale, Utah and include the Carol Site (figure 10), the Rough Road Quarry, Jensen's egg site, and Robison's Eggshell Quarry (Jensen, 1970; Nelson and Crooks, 1987; Pomes, 1988; Eaton and Nelson, 1991; Jones and Burge, 1995; Burge, 1996). Important collections from these sites are housed at the College of Eastern Utah Prehistoric Museum, Price, Utah; Sternberg Museum, Hays, Kansas; University of Colorado Museum, Boulder, Colorado; University of California, Museum of Paleontology, Berkeley, California; Brigham Young University, Earth Science Museum, Provo, Utah; and the Oklahoma Museum of Natural History, Norman, Oklahoma.

The most common dinosaur from the Mussentuchit Member is a primitive hadrosaurid (Kirkland and Burge, 1994; Kirkland and others, 1997). Common hadrosaurid teeth from Cedar Mountain Formation sites on the west side of the San Rafael Swell were first noted by Parrish (1991), although the locality horizon was not indicated in that abstract. The senior author has determined this primitive hadrosaurid to be somewhat like *Telmatosaurus* (Weishampel and others, 1993) from the Upper Cretaceous of eastern Europe and a bit more advanced than the iguanodontid *Probactrosaurus* (Rozhdestvensky, 1967; Norman, 1990) from the Lower Cretaceous of central Asia. More research is needed to determine its systematic position relative to the Hadrosaurinae and Lambeosaurinae (Sereno, 1986; Horner, 1990; Weishampel and Horner, 1990). However, the material discovered to date suggests lambeosaurine affinities.

Molenaar and Cobban (1991) have demonstrated through subsurface relationships that the uppermost Cedar Mountain Formation may correlate to the Mowry Shale to the northeast and may thus be of basal Cenomanian age. The Albian-Cenomanian boundary, on the basis of non-marine palynomorphs, has been placed at the first occurrence of tricolporate pollen grains (for example *Nyssapollenites*, rare in marine rocks) and obligate tetrads (Singh, 1975; Nichols and Sweet, 1993). Tschudy and others (1984) did not encounter these palynomorphs in their samples from the upper Cedar Mountain Formation near Castle Dale, Utah. The occurrence of these palynomorphs is diachronous across Alberta (Nichols and Sweet, 1993). In addition, with the older placement of the Albian-Cenomanian boundary (Cobban and Kennedy, 1989) by ammonite correlations to the type areas in Europe, it is likely that the palynomorph datum (first occurrence of tricolpate and obligate tetrad pollen) is above the base of the Cenomanian (Nichols and Sweet, 1993).

A radiometric age estimate of 98.39 ± 0.07 million years B. P. (Cifelli, Kirkland, and others, 1997) places the fauna at, or just above, the Albian-Cenomanian boundary according to the most recent time scales for the Cretaceous, which have the boundary placed at 98.5 million years B. P. (Obradovich, 1993) or at 98.9 ± 0.6 million years B. P. (Gradstein and others, 1994). The date supports a correlation with the Mowry Shale to the northeast (figure 6).

The absence of calcareous nodules indicates that the Mussentuchit Member was deposited under a significantly wetter environment than were the lower members of the Cedar Mountain Formation. This wetter environment may be due to the transgression of the Mowry Sea into the area of the northeastern Uinta Basin (Wing and Sues, 1992). The North American plant record indicates that angiosperms were becoming a more important part of western interior floras at this time (Wing and Sues, 1992) and some of the earliest records of some angiosperm wood types are from this member (Tidwell, 1996).

A dramatic shift between Albian and middle Cenomanian faunas has been noted in Texas (Lee, 1995; Winkler and others, 1995). The new age estimates for the Mussentuchit Member indicate that this faunal turnover was even more dramatic than was previously thought. Thus, within the Cedar Mountain Formation there is a three-fold instead of a two-fold zonation of Cedar Mountain Formation based on dinosaurs (Kirkland, 1992, 1996b; Lucas, 1993): a basal Barremian iguanodont-polacanthid fauna with European affinities predating common flowering plants; a middle Aptian-middle Albian *Tenontosaurus-Pleurocoelus* fauna perhaps representing a depauperate fauna following a major Early Cretaceous extinction event (endemic to North America); and an upper latest Albian-lowest Cenomanian hadrosaur fauna with Asian affinities when flowering plants were co-dominant with gymnosperms. Biogeographic rather than floristic changes may account for most of the faunistic changes recorded at the end of the Albian as suggested by the dramatic shift to a dinosaur fauna dominated by taxa with an Asian ancestry (Kirkland, 1996b; Cifelli and others, 1997b, this volume).

CONCLUSIONS

Vertebrate fossils are present throughout the Cedar Mountain Formation of east-central Utah. It contains three distinct faunas, which are separated by intraformational unconformities. The recognition of these faunas combined with lithologic observations has permitted division of the Cedar Mountain Formation into five

members: the Buckhorn Conglomerate, the Yellow Cat Member, the Poison Strip Sandstone, the Ruby Ranch Member, and the Mussentuchit Member (Kirkland and others, 1997). Of these, only the Buckhorn Conglomerate has not yielded age-diagnostic fossils permitting its correlation with other strata.

The oldest fauna is preserved in the Yellow Cat Member and is dated as Barremian based on the occurrence of dinosaurs similar to those preserved in Barremian sediments of northwestern Europe, and based on the occurrence of charophytes not recorded in strata younger than Barremian. The middle fauna is preserved in the Poison Strip Sandstone and Ruby Ranch Member and is dated as broadly Aptian-Albian based on dinosaurs known to occur elsewhere in North America during the Aptian-Albian. The youngest fauna is preserved in the Mussentuchit Member and is precisely dated as overlapping the Albian/Cenomanian boundary at 98.39 ± 0.07 million years B. P. (Cifelli, Kirkland, and others, 1997).

The vertebrate faunas preserved in the Cedar Mountain Formation of east-central Utah provide a unique opportunity to study the transition of the terrestrial biota from an environment when angiosperms were rare until angiosperms were a major component of the flora. Additionally, these faunas record a shift from a Barremian fauna with European affinities to an Albian/Cenomanian fauna with Asian affinities. The transition from sediments largely devoid of carbonaceous material and containing abundant carbonate nodules, to sediments that are lignitic with no carbonate nodules, suggests increased rainfall in the region during the expansion of the Cretaceous Western Interior Seaway. Further research in the region is required to differentiate the relative effects of changes in the flora, climate, and biogeography on the terrestrial biota preserved in the Cedar Mountain Formation.

ACKNOWLEDGMENTS

We would like to thank the many people too numerous to count who have helped in the field, including many from the Utah Friends of Paleontology, Uncompahgre Plateau Paleontological Society, and the Western Interior Paleontological Society. Special thanks are extended to the Judd family of Castle Dale, Utah, the Jones family of Salt Lake City, Utah, the Gaston family of Knoxville, Tennessee, and the Corbett family of Raleigh, North Carolina. Robert Young of Grand Junction, Colorado is gratefully acknowledged for providing copies of his extensive field notes on the Cedar Mountain and Dakota Formations. Excavations were all undertaken under permits issued by the Bureau of Land

Management and the Utah School and Institutional Trust Lands Administration. Partial funding in support of this research was provided by the National Geographic Society (grants 4761-91 and 5021-92 to RLC; 5263-94 to JIK) and the National Science Foundation (grants BSR 8906992 and DEB 941094 to RLC). Special thanks are due to John Bird and Carl Limone, CEU Prehistoric Museum; Harold Bollan, Dinamation International Society; Randy Nydam, Oklahoma Museum of Natural History; Rod Scheetz, Museum of Western Colorado; Ken Stadtman, Brigham Young University; and Scott Madsen, Dinosaur National Monument for their skilled field assistance and preparation skills. Reviews of this manuscript by David D. Gillette, Louis L. Jacobs, and Mark Kirshbaum are gratefully acknowledged. Innumerable colleagues throughout our profession have aided this research with their knowledge, advice, encouragement, and camaraderie.

REFERENCES

Aubrey, W. M., 1996, Stratigraphic architecture and deformational history of Early Cretaceous Foreland Basin, eastern Utah and southwestern Colorado, *in* Huffman, A. C., Jr., Lund, W. R., and Godwin, L. H., editors, Geology and resources of the Paradox Basin: Utah Geological Association Guidebook 25, p. 211-220.

—1998, A newly discovered, widespread fluvial facies and unconformity marking the Upper Jurassic/Lower Cretaceous boundary, Colorado Plateau, *in* Carpenter, Kenneth, Chure, D. J., and Kirkland, J. I., editors, The Morrison Formation - an integrated study: Modern Geology, v. 22, p. 209-233.

Baars, D. L., and 15 others, 1988, Basins of the Rocky Mountain region, *in* Sloss, L. L., editor, Sedimentary cover -- North American craton, U. S.: Geological Society of America, The geology of North America, v. D-2, p. 109-220.

Benton, M. J., and Spencer, P. S., 1995, Fossil reptiles of Great Britain: New York, Chapman Hall, Inc., 386 p.

Blows, W. T., 1993, William Fox (1813-1881), a neglected dinosaur collector on the Isle of Wight: Archives of Natural History, v. 11, no. 2, p. 299-313.

Bodily, N. M., 1969, An armored dinosaur from the Lower Cretaceous of Utah: Brigham Young University Geology Studies, v. 16, no. 3, p. 557-580.

Britt, B. B., and Stadtman, K. L., 1997, Dalton Well Quarry, *in* Currie, P. J., and Padian, Kevin, editors, Encyclopedia of dinosaurs: San Diego, California, Academic Press, p. 165-166.

Britt, B. B., Stadtman, K. L., and Scheetz, R. D., 1996, The Early Cretaceous Dalton Wells dinosaur fauna and the earliest North American titanosaurid sauropod: Journal of Vertebrate Paleontology, v. 17, p. 24A.

Burge, D. L., 1996, New dinosaur discoveries in the Lower Cretaceous of southeastern Utah: Mesa, Arizona, Southwest Paleontological Society and Mesa Southwest Museum, Fossils of Arizona, v. 4., p. 85-105.

Carpenter, Kenneth, Kirkland, J. I., Miles, C. A., Cloward, K. C., and Burge, D. L., 1996, Evolutionary significance of new ankylosaurs (Dinosauria) from the Upper Jurassic and Lower Cretaceous, western Interior: Journal of Vertebrate Paleontology, v. 17, p. 25A.

Carpenter, Kenneth, Kirkland, J. I., Burge, D. L., and Bird, John, 1999, Stratigraphic distribution of ankylosaurs (Dinosauria: Ornithischia) in the Cedar Mountain Formation, Utah, *in* Gillette, D. D., editor, this volume.

Cifelli, R. L., 1993, Early Cretaceous mammal from North America and the evolution of marsupial dental characters: Proceedings of the National Academy of Science, USA, v. 90, p. 9413-9416.

Cifelli, R. L., Gardner, J. D., Nydam, R. L., and Brinkman, D. L., 1997, Additions to the vertebrate fauna of the Antlers Formation (Lower Cretaceous), southeastern Oklahoma: Oklahoma Geology Notes, v. 57, no. 4, p. 124-131.

Cifelli, R. L., Kirkland, J. I., Weil, Anne, Deinos, A. R., and Kowallis, B. J, 1997, High-precision ^{40}Ar/^{39}Ar geochronology and the advent of North America's Late Cretaceous terrestrial fauna: Proceedings National of the Academy of Science, USA, v. 97, p. 11163-11167.

Cifelli, R. L., Nydam, R. L., Weil, Anne, Gardner, J. D., Eaton, J. G., Kirkland, J. I., and Madsen, S. K., 1999, Medial Cretaceous vertebrates from the Cedar Mountain Formation, Emery County -- the Mussentuchit local fauna, *in* Gillette, D. D., editor, this volume.

Cobban, W. A., and Kennedy, W. J., 1989, The ammonite Metengonoceras Hyatt, 1903, from the Mowry Shale (Cretaceous) of Montana and Wyoming: U. S. Geological Survey Bulletin, v. 1787L, p. L1-L11.

Coombs, W. P., Jr., 1971, The Ankylosauria: New York, Columbia University, Ph. D. dissertation, 487 p.

Craig, L. C., 1981, Lower Cretaceous rocks, southwestern Colorado and southeastern Utah: Rocky Mountain Association of Geologists, 1981 Field Conference, p. 195-200.

Currie, B. S., 1997, Sequence stratigraphy of nonmarine Jurassic-Cretaceous rocks, central Cordilleran foreland-basin system: Geological Society of America Bulletin, v. 109, no. 9, p. 1206-1222.

DeCourten, F. L., 1991, New data on Early Cretaceous dinosaurs from Long Walk Quarry and Tracksite, Emery County, Utah, *in* Chidsey, T. C., Jr., editor, Geology of east-central Utah: Utah Geological Association Publication, v. 19, p. 311-324.

Dodson, P. A., Behrensmeyer, A. K., Bakker, R. T., and McIntosh, J. S., 1980, Taphonomy and paleoecology of dinosaur beds of the Jurassic Morrison Formation: Paleobiology, v. 6, p. 1567-1578.

Doelling, H. H., 1988, Geology of the Salt Valley Anticline and Arches National Park, *in* Doelling, H. H., Oviatt, C. G., and Huntoon, P. W., editors, Salt deformation in the Paradox Region: Utah Geological and Mineral Survey, Bulletin 122, p. 1-60.

Dyman, T. S., Merewether, E. A., Molenaar, C. M., Cobban, W. A., Obradovitch, J. D., Weimer, R. J., and Bryant, W. A., 1994, Stratigraphic transects for Cretaceous rocks, Rocky Mountain and Great Plains regions, *in* Caputo, M. V., Peterson, J. A., and Franczyk, K. J., editors, Mesozoic systems of the Rocky Mountain Region: Society of Sedimentary Geology, Denver, Colorado, p. 365-391.

Eaton, J. G. and Nelson, M. E., 1991, Multituberculate mammals from the Lower Cretaceous Cedar Mountain Formation, San Rafael Swell, Utah: Contributions to Geology, University of Wyoming, v. 29, p. 1-12.

Eaton, J. G., Kirkland, J. I., Hutchison, J. H., Denton, Robert, O'Neil, R. C., and Parrish, J. M., 1997, Nonmarine extinction across the Cenomanian-Turonian (C-T) boundary, southwestern Utah, with a comparison to the Cretaceous-Tertiary (K-T) extinction event: Geological Society of America Bulletin, v. 109, no. 5, p. 560-567.

Eaton, J. G., Kirkland, J. I., and Kauffman, E. G., 1990, Evidence and dating of mid-Cretaceous tectonic activity in the San Rafael Swell, Emery County, Utah: The Mountain Geologist, v. 27, no. 2, p. 39-45.

Galton, P. M., and Jensen, J. A., 1979, Remains of ornithopod dinosaurs from the Lower Cretaceous of North America: Brigham Young University Studies in Geology, v. 25, no. 1, p. 1-10.

Gilmore, C. W., 1921, The fauna of the Arundel Formation of Maryland: Proceedings of the United States National Museum, v. 59, p. 581-594.

Gradstein, F. M., Agterberg, F. P., Ogg, J. G., Hardenbol, Jan, van Veen, Paul, Thierry, Jacques, Huang, Zehui, 1994, A Mesozoic time scale: Journal of Geophysical Research, v. 99, no. B12, p. 24051-24074.

Hancock, J. M., Kennedy, W. J., and Cobban, W. A., 1993, A correlation of Upper Albian to basal Coniacian sequences of northwest Europe, Texas, and the United States Western Interior, *in* Caldwell, W. G. E., and Kauffman, E. G., editors, Evolution of the Western Interior Basin: Geological Association of Canada Special Paper, v. 39, p. 453-476.

Harris, D. R., 1980, Exhumed paleochannels in the Lower Cretaceous Cedar Mountain Formation near Green River, Utah: Brigham Young University Geology Studies, v. 27, pt. 1, p. 51-66.

Heller, P. L., Bowdler, S. S., Chambers, H. P., Coogan, J. C., Hagen, E. S., Shuster, M. W., and Winslow, N. S., 1986, Time of initial thrusting in the Sevier Orogenic belt: Geology, v. 14, p. 388-391.

Heller, P. L., and Paola, Carlo, 1989, The paradox of Lower Cretaceous gravels and the initiation of thrusting in the Sevier Orogenic belt, United States Western Interior: Geological Society of America Bulletin, v. 101, no. 6, p. 864-975.

Horner, J. R., 1990, Evidence of diphyletic origination of the hadrosaurian (Reptilia: Ornithischia) dinosaurs, *in* Carpenter, Kenneth, and Currie, P. J., editors, Dinosaur systematics -- perspectives and approaches: New York, Cambridge University Press, p. 179-187.

Hughes, N. F., Drewry, G. E., and Laing, J. F., 1979, Barremian earliest angiosperm pollen: Paleontology, v. 22, p. 513-535.

Jensen, J. A., 1970, Fossil eggs from the Lower Cretaceous of Utah: Brigham Young University Geology Studies, v. 17, no. 1, p. 51-66.

Jones, Ramal, and Burge, D. L., 1995, Radiological surveying as a method for mapping dinosaur bone sites: Journal of Vertebrate Paleontology, v. 15, 38A.

Katich, P. J., 1951, Occurrence of *Tempskya* in the Lower Cretaceous of the Western Interior: Journal of Paleontology, v. 26, no. 4, p. 677.

Kirkland, J. I., 1992, Dinosaurs define a two-fold Lower Cretaceous zonation of the Cedar Mountain Formation, central Utah: Geological Society of America Abstracts and Program, v. 24, no. 6, p. 22.

—1993, Polacanthid nodosaurs from the Upper Jurassic and Lower Cretaceous of the east-central Colorado Plateau: Journal of Vertebrate Paleontology, v. 13, 44A-45A.

—1996a, Reconstruction of polacanthid ankylosaurs based on new discoveries from the Late Jurassic and Early Cretaceous, *in* Wolberg, D. L., and Stump, E., editors, Dinofest International Symposium April 18-21, 1996: Tempe, Arizona State University, p. 67.

—1996b, Biogeography of North America's Mid-Cretaceous dinosaur faunas -- losing European ties and the first great Asian-North American interchange: Journal of Vertebrate Paleontology, v. 16, p. 45A.

Kirkland, J. I., Britt, B. B., Burge, D. L., Carpenter, Kenneth, Cifelli, R. L., DeCourten, F. L., Eaton, J. G., Hasiotis, Stephen., Lawton, T. F., 1997, Lower to Middle Cretaceous dinosaur faunas of the central Colorado Plateau; A key to understanding 35 million years of tectonics, evolution, and biogeography: Brigham Young University Geology Studies, v, 42, part II, p. 69-103.

Kirkland, J. I., Britt, B. B., Madsen, S. K., and Burge, D. L., 1995, A small theropod from the basal Cedar Mountain Formation (Lower Cretaceous, Barremian) of eastern Utah: Journal of Vertebrate Paleontology, v. 15, p. 39A.

Kirkland, J. I., and Burge, D. L., 1994, A large primitive hadrosaur from the Lower Cretaceous of Utah: Journal of Vertebrate Paleontology, v. 14, p. 32A.

Kirkland, J. I., Burge, D. L., Britt, B. B., and Blows, W. T., 1993, The earliest Cretaceous (Barremian ?) dinosaur fauna found to date on the Colorado Plateau: Journal of Vertebrate Paleontology, v. 13, 45A.

Kirkland, J. I., Burge, D. L., and Gaston, Robert, 1993, A large dromaeosaur (Theropoda) from the Lower Cretaceous of Utah: Hunteria, v. 2, no. 10, p. 1-16.

Kirkland, J. I., Carpenter, Kenneth, and Burge, D. L., 1991, A nodosaur with a distinct sacral shield of fused armor from the lower Cretaceous of east-central Utah: Journal of Vertebrate

Paleontology, v. 11, p. 40A.

Kirkland, J. I., and Parrish, J. M., 1995, Theropod teeth from the lower and middle Cretaceous of Utah: Journal of Vertebrate Paleontology, v. 15, p. 39A.

Kowallis, Bart, Deino, A. R., Peterson, Fred, and Turner, Christine, 1998, High precision radiometric dating of the Morrison Formation, *in* Carpenter, Kenneth, Chure, D. J., and Kirkland, J. I., editors, The Morrison Formation - an integrated study: Modern Geology, v. 22, p. 235-260.

Kranz, P. M., 1989, Dinosaurs in Maryland: Maryland Geological Survey Educational Series, no. 6, 34 p.

—1996, Notes on sedimentary iron ores of Maryland and their dinosaurian fauna: Maryland Geological Survey, Special Publication, no. 3, p. 87-115.

Langston, Wann, 1974, Nonmammalian Comanchean tetrapods: Geoscience and Man, v. 3, p. 77-102.

Lawton, T. F., 1985, Style and timing of frontal structures, thrust belt, central Utah: American Association of Petroleum Geologists Bulletin, v. 69, p. 1145-1159.

—1986, Compositional trends within a clastic wedge adjacent to a fold-thrust belt, Indianola Group, central Utah, U.S.A.: Special Publications International Association of Sedimentologists, v. 8, p. 411-423.

Lee, Y. -N., 1995, Mid-Cretaceous archosaur faunal changes in Texas, *in* Sun, Ailing, and Wang, Yuanqing, editors, Sixth symposium on Mesozoic terrestrial ecosystems and biota, short papers: Beijing, China Ocean Press, p. 175-177.

Lucas, S. G., 1993, Vertebrate biochronology of the Jurassic-Cretaceous boundary, North American western interior: Modern Geology, v. 18, p. 371-390.

Lucas, S. G., and Hunt, A. P., 1989, *Alamosaurus* and the sauropod hiatus in the Cretaceous of the North American western interior, *in* Farlow, J. O., editor, Paleobiology of the dinosaurs: Geological Society of America Special Paper, no. 238, p. 75-86.

Mitchell, J. G., 1956, Charophytes as a guide to distinguishing between Lower Cretaceous and Upper Jurassic continental sediments in the subsurface, *in* Peterson, J. A., editor, Geology and economic deposits of east-central Utah: Intermountain Association of Petroleum Geologists, seventh annual field Conference, p. 105-112.

Molenaar, C. M., and Cobban, W. A., 1991, Middle Cretaceous stratigraphy on the south and east sides of the Uinta Basin, northeastern Utah and northwestern Colorado: U.S. Geological Survey Bulletin, v. 1787, p. P1-P34.

Nelson, M. E., and Crooks, D. M., 1987, Stratigraphy and paleontology of the Cedar Mountain Formation (Lower Cretaceous), eastern Emery County, Utah, *in* Averett, W. R., editor, Paleontology of the Dinosaur Triangle--guidebook for 1987 field trip: Grand Junction, Colorado, Museum of Western Colorado, p. 55-63.

Nichols, D. J., and Sweet, A. R., 1993, Biostratigraphy of Upper Cretaceous non-marine palynofloras in a north-south transect of the Western Interior Basin, *in* Caldwell, W. G. E., and Kauffman, E. G., editors, Evolution of the Western Interior Basin: Geological Association of Canada Special Paper, v. 39, p. 539-584.

Norman, D. B., 1988, Wealden dinosaur biostratigraphy, *in* Currie, P. J., and Koster, E. H., editors, Fourth Symposium on Mesozoic Ecosystems, Short Papers: Drumheller, Alberta, Occasional Paper of the Tyrrell Museum of Palaeontology, v. 3, p. 165-170.

—1990, A review of *Vectisaurus valdensis*, with comments on the family Iguanodontidae, *in* Carpenter, Kenneth, and Currie, P. J., editors, Dinosaur systematics-- Perspectives and Approaches: New York, Cambridge University Press, p. 147-161.

Obradovich, John, 1993, A Cretaceous time scale, *in* Caldwell, W. G. E., and Kauffman, E. G., editors, Evolution of the Western Interior Basin: Geological Association of Canada Special Paper, v. 39, p. 379-396.

Ostrom, J. H., 1970, Stratigraphy and paleontology of the Cloverly Formation (Lower Cretaceous) of the Bighorn Basin area, Wyoming and Montana: New Haven, Yale University, Peabody Museum of Natural History Bulletin, v. 350, 234 p.

Parrish, J. M., 1991, Diversity and evolution of dinosaurs in the Cretaceous of the Kaiparowits Plateau, Utah: Journal of Vertebrate Paleontology, v. 11, p. 50A.

Pomes, M. L., 1988, Stratigraphy, paleontology, and paleogeography of lower vertebrates from the Cedar Mountain Formation (Lower Cretaceous), Emery County, Utah: Hays, Kansas, Fort Hays State University, M.S. thesis, 87 p.

Rozhdestvensky, A. K., 1967, New Iguanodonts from central Asia: International Geology Review, v. 9, no. 4, p. 556-566.

Sereno, P. C., 1986, Phylogeny of the bird-hipped dinosaurs (Order Ornithischia): National Geographic Research, v. 2, p. 234-256.

Singh, Chaitanya, 1975, Stratigraphic significance of early angiosperm pollen in the mid-Cretaceous strata of Alberta, *in* Caldwell, W. G. E., editor, The Cretaceous System in the Western Interior of North America: Geological Association of Canada Special Paper, v. 13, p. 365-389.

Stokes, W. L., 1944, Morrison and related deposits in the Colorado Plateau: Geological Society of America Bulletin, v. 55, p. 951-992.

—1952, Lower Cretaceous in Colorado Plateau: American Association of Petroleum Geologists Bulletin, v. 36, p. 1766-1776.

Stokes, W. L., and Phoenix, D. A., 1948, Geology of the Egnar-Gypsum Valley area, San Miguel and Montrose Counties, Colorado: U. S. Geological Survey Preliminary Map 93, Oil and Gas Inventory Survey.

Stovall, J. W., and Langston, Wann, Jr., 1950, *Acrocanthosaurus atokensis*, a new genus and species of Lower Cretaceous Theropoda from Oklahoma: The American Midland Naturalist, v. 43, no. 3, p. 696-728.

Thayne, G. F., and Tidwell, W. D., 1984, Flora of the Lower Cretaceous Cedar Mountain Formation of Utah and Colorado, Part II. *Mesembrioxylon stokesi*: Great Basin Naturalist, v. 44, no. 2, p. 257-262.

Thayne, G. F., Tidwell, W. D., and Stokes, W. L., 1983, Flora of the Lower Cretaceous Cedar Mountain Formation of Utah and Colorado, Part I. *Paraphyllanthoxylon utahense*: Great Basin Naturalist, v. 43, no. 3, p. 394-402.

—1985, Flora of the Lower Cretaceous Cedar Mountain Formation of Utah and Colorado, Part III. *Icacinoxylon pittiense* n. sp.: American Journal of Botany, v. 72, no. 2, p. 175-180.

Tidwell, W. D., 1996, Cretaceous floras of east-central Utah and western Colorado -- a review, *in* Herendeen, P. S., Johnson, Kurt, Tidwell, W. D., and Ash, S. R., editors, Guidebook for Paleozoic, Mesozoic, and Cenozoic excursion of Utah and Colorado - the fifth annual paleobotanical conference: Provo, Brigham Young University, p. 57-72.

Tidwell, W. D., and Thayne, G. F., 1985, Flora of the Lower Cretaceous Cedar Mountain Formation of Utah and Colorado, Part IV. *Palaeopiceoxylon thinosus* (Protopinaceae): The Southwestern Naturalist, v. 30, no. 4, p. 525-532.

Tschudy, R. H., Tschudy, B. D., and Craig, L. C., 1984, Palynological evaluation of Cedar Mountain and Burro Canyon Formations, Colorado Plateau: U. S. Geological Survey Professional Paper, v. 1281, p. 1-21.

Turcotte, E. L. and Schubert, George, 1982, Geodynamics: New York, John Wiley and Sons Inc., 450 p.

Weishampel, D. B., and Bjork, P. R., 1989, The first indisputable remains of *Iguanodon* (Ornithischia: Ornithopoda) from North America -- *Iguanodon lakotaensis*, sp. nov.: Journal of Vertebrate Paleontology, v. 9, no. 1, p. 56-66.

Weishampel, D. B., and Horner, J. R., 1990, Hadrosauridae, *in* Weishampel, D. B., Dodson, Peter, and Osmolska, Halszka, editors, The Dinosauria: Berkeley, University of California Press, p. 534-561.

Weishampel, D. B., and Weishampel, J. B., 1983, Annotated localities of ornithopod dinosaurs - implications to Mesozoic paleobiogeography: Mosasaur, v. 1, p. 43-87.

Weishampel, D. B., Norman, D. B., Grigorescu, Dan, 1993, *Telmatosaurus transsylvanicus* from the Late Cretaceous of Romania -- the most basal hadrosaurid dinosaur: Palaeontology, v. 36, no. 2, p. 361-385.

Wing, S. L., and Sues, H-. D., 1992, Mesozoic and early Cenozoic terrestrial ecosystems, *in* Behrensmeyer, A. K., Damuth, J. D., DiMichele, W. A., Potts, Richard, Sues, H-. D., and Wing, S. L., editors, Terrestrial ecosystems through time - evolutionary paleoecology of terrestrial plants and animals: Chicago, Illinois, The University of Chicago Press, p. 327-416.

Winkler, D. A., Murry, P. A, and Jacobs, L. L., 1989, Vertebrate paleontology of the Trinity Group, Lower Cretaceous of central Texas, *in* Winkler, D. A., Murry, P. A., and Jacobs, L. L., editors, Field guide to the vertebrate paleontology of the Trinity Group, Lower Cretaceous of central Texas: Dallas, Institute for the Study of the Earth and Man, Southern Methodist University, p. 1-22.

—1990, Early Cretaceous (Comanchean) vertebrates of central Texas: Journal of Vertebrate Paleontology, v. 10, no. 1, p. 95-116.

Winkler, D. A., Jacobs, L. L., Lee, Y. -N., and Murry, P. A., 1995, Sea level fluctuations and terrestrial faunal change in north-central Texas, *in* Sun, Ailing, and Wang, Yaunqing, editors, Sixth symposium on Mesozoic terrestrial ecosystems and biota, short papers: Beijing, China Ocean Press, p. 175-177.

Young, R. G., 1960, Dakota Group of the Colorado Plateau: American Association of Petroleum Geologists Bulletin, v. 44, no. 2, p. 156-194.

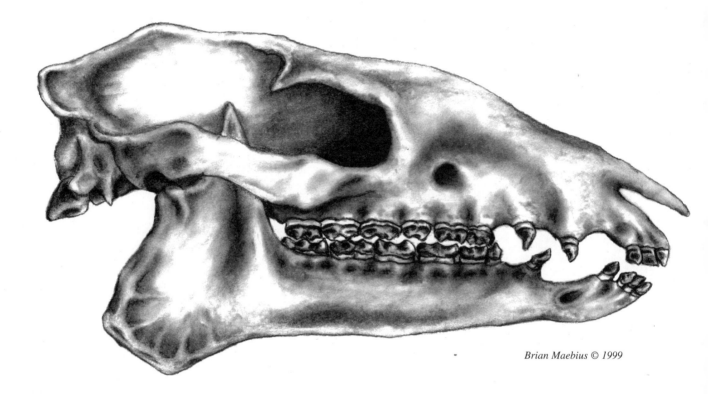

Brian Maebius © 1999

Eohippus

MEDIAL CRETACEOUS VERTEBRATES FROM THE CEDAR MOUNTAIN FORMATION, EMERY COUNTY, UTAH: THE MUSSENTUCHIT LOCAL FAUNA

Richard L. Cifelli
Oklahoma Museum of Natural History and Department of Zoology, University of Oklahoma, Norman, Oklahoma 73019

Randall L. Nydam
Oklahoma Museum of Natural History and Department of Zoology, University of Oklahoma, Norman, Oklahoma 73019

James D. Gardner
Department of Biological Sciences and Laboratory for Vertebrate Paleontology, University of Alberta, Edmonton, Alberta, Canada T6G 2E9

Anne Weil
Department of Integrative Biology, University of California, Berkeley, California 94720

Jeffrey G. Eaton
Department of Geosciences, Weber State University, 2507 University Circle, Ogden, Utah 84408

James I. Kirkland
Utah Geological Survey, Box 146100, Salt Lake City, UT 84114-6100

Scott K. Madsen
Dinosaur National Monument, P. O. Box 128, Jensen, Utah 84035

ABSTRACT

The upper Cedar Mountain Formation, Emery County, Utah, has yielded a rich vertebrate fauna including nearly 80 taxa of Chondrichthyes, Osteichthyes, Lissamphibia, Reptilia, Aves, and Mammalia. High-precision radiometric dating has established the age of the fauna as latest Albian-earliest Cenomanian, placing it on the Early-Late Cretaceous boundary. Although most of the taxa remain to be studied in detail, the dense paleontologic sampling and high diversity of the fauna, coupled with the fact that its age is well established, suggest that it will provide a benchmark for study of terrestrial biota in North America during this key time interval, which corresponds to the early radiation of angiosperm plants.

The vertebrate assemblage from the upper Cedar Mountain Formation, herein named the Mussentuchit local fauna for the area that has produced most of the known sites, is clearly of Late Cretaceous aspect, indicating that the broad pattern of faunal composition for the last half of the Cretaceous in North America was established by the beginning of that epoch. Accordingly, the Mussentuchit local fauna includes a number of first North American or global appearances, notably varanoid lizards; hadrosaurid, tyrannosaurid, and pachycephalosaurid dinosaurs; marsupial mammals; and snakes. Also present are representatives of a number of archaic groups, including the last sauropod in North America (prior to reintroduction through immigration from South America in the latest Cretaceous); triconodont and symmetrodont mammals; and several other taxa, such as the turtle *Glyptops*.

The Mussentuchit local fauna differs from Early Cretaceous assemblages of North America and Europe, and instead shares a number of taxa with Asia: although the continent of origin cannot be confidently established for many of the groups from the Mussentuchit local fauna, existing evidence suggests an Asian origin for some of the fauna, at least. The herbivore fauna is dominated by one extremely abundant hadrosaurid; diversity of large-bodied herbivores is low, in contrast to succeeding faunas of the Campanian and Maastrichtian.

INTRODUCTION

Introductory Remarks

The Cedar Mountain Formation, named for terrigenous sedimentary rocks lying between the Dakota and Morrison Formations (Stokes, 1944, 1952), is broadly exposed in central and eastern Utah; eastward, the unit is laterally contiguous with the Burro Canyon Formation of western Colorado (see Stokes and Phoenix, 1948; Tschudy and others, 1984; Mateer and others, 1992). Two units of the Cedar Mountain Formation are generally recognized, a lower Buckhorn Conglomerate (which is variable in presence and thickness) and an overlying, unnamed "shale" member (Stokes, 1952; Hale and Van de Graaf, 1964). This upper member is 116 meters thick in the type area, near Castle Dale, Emery County, though generally thinner elsewhere. It is comprised of drab, variegated mudstones, deposited on broad alluvial floodplains, together with thin channel sandstones (Young, 1960; Harris, 1980; Eaton and others, 1990). In places, the mudstones are bentonitic (Young, 1960; Kowallis and others, 1986). The lower part of the upper member of the Cedar Mountain Formation, where it is present, is characterized by abundant horizons containing caliche nodules (for example, see Nelson and Crooks, 1987), presumably representing seasonally dry paleosols. By contrast, the upper part of the "shale" member generally lacks nodular zones and instead has rare carbonaceous layers (see Tschudy and others, 1984), with occasional occurrences of amber.

Superpositional evidence has long favored a predominantly Lower Cretaceous correlation for the Cedar Mountain Formation (for example, Stokes, 1952), and limited biostratigraphic evidence, in the form of freshwater invertebrates (Scott, 1987), palynomorphs (Tschudy and others, 1984), and vertebrates (see below) seemed to uphold this view. However, it has also been long established that a significant time period lies between the Morrison Formation (an Upper Jurassic unit) and the Dakota Formation (of Cenomanian age), which bound the Cedar Mountain Formation, and simple calculations make it clear that complete representation of nearly 50 Ma in less than 150 meters of section is highly unlikely. Recent evidence suggests the possibility of three separate dinosaur faunas in the Cedar Mountain, separated by significant hiatuses (Kirkland, 1996; Kirkland and others, this volume)--one from a lowest part of the unit (perhaps equivalent, in part, to the Buckhorn Conglomerate) present only east of the San Rafael Swell, one from the lower, nodular zone in the upper member of the Cedar Mountain Formation, and the last from the upper part of that unit. Our contribution is focused strictly on the vertebrate fauna of the upper part of the upper member of the Cedar Mountain Formation. Large-scale collecting efforts, focused on a narrow stratigraphic interval about 10-20 meters below the contact with the overlying Dakota Formation, have been conducted in the Cedar Mountain Formation in Emery County, Utah, for the past ten years, resulting in a densely sampled fauna. Radiometric dates associated with the vertebrate fauna establish its

age as latest Albian-earliest Cenomanian (Cifelli, Kirkland, and others, 1997). Herein we describe the geographic, geologic, and stratigraphic context of this fauna, and present the preliminary results of work in progress on its constituent taxa.

Previous Work

Vertebrate Paleontology

Although the occurrence of fossil vertebrates in the Cedar Mountain Formation had been noted by Stokes (1944, 1952), the first published report describing such materials is that of Bodily (1969), who recorded a nodosaurid dinosaur from near Arches National Monument, in what is now interpreted to be the lower part of the Cedar Mountain Formation. Further work in the region was undertaken by paleontologists from Brigham Young University, who made a large collection of dinosaurs in the same part of the section from Dalton Well--a site that is under active investigation by researchers from Brigham Young University and the Museum of Western Colorado. The only described material we are aware of from this site belongs to the ornithopod *Iguanodon* (see Galton and Jensen, 1979), but Britt and Stadtman (1996) report a number of other taxa, including a second ornithopod, a small nodosaur, three theropods, and two sauropods. Recent investigations in the lowest Cedar Mountain Formation east of Arches National Monument have resulted in the discovery of several dinosaurian taxa, of which only *Utahraptor* has yet been described (Kirkland and others, 1993; see Kirkland and others, this volume). The most substantial assemblage from the lower part of the upper member of the Cedar Mountain Formation is that of the Long Walk Quarry, east of Castle Dale, Emery County, which has been under investigation by paleontologists from the Utah Museum of Natural History. The material is mostly undescribed, but the site evidently includes a massive accumulation of a sauropod, perhaps *Pleurocoelus*, and a theropod possibly similar to *Acrocanthosaurus* (DeCourten, 1991).

The most notable early report of fossil vertebrates from the upper part of the upper member of the Cedar Mountain Formation is that of Jensen (1970), who recorded the presence of several types of dinosaur eggshell from southeast of Castle Dale. In 1983, paleontological investigations in the upper Cedar Mountain Formation were independently begun by one of us (JGE, then of the University of Colorado) and by M. E. Nelson (then of Fort Hays State University). As a result, several preliminary investigations on the paleontology and stratigraphy of the unit were produced and/or published

(Nelson and Crooks, 1987; Pomes, 1988; Eaton and others, 1990; Eaton and Nelson, 1991). The primary sites worked by these parties lie east of Castle Dale and Ferron, Emery County, including Rough Road Quarry and Robison's Eggshell Quarry--the latter of which has been worked by a number of investigators, including Anthony Fiorillo (then of the Carnegie Museum of Natural History) in 1991 (this volume) and us in 1992.

Age

There are no published reports that provide direct evidence as to the age of the Buckhorn Conglomerate and the lower part of the shale member of the Cedar Mountain Formation. Stokes' original interpretation of a Lower Cretaceous correlation for the Cedar Mountain Formation was based largely on plant macrofossils said to be abundant in other Lower Cretaceous units, such as the Cloverly Formation (Stokes, 1952). At about the same time, Katich (1951) reported several other fossils from the type locality, including a fern, undetermined ostracodes, and a bivalve believed to be of Aptian age. Among the many plant macrofossils reported from the Cedar Mountain Formation, perhaps the most noteworthy are remains of angiosperm wood (Thayne and others, 1983, 1985), recovered from localities in the upper part of the upper member, east of Castle Dale and Ferron. Early angiosperms were generally low-statured; even with the younger age now interpreted for the upper part of the Cedar Mountain Formation (Cifelli, Kirkland, and others, 1997; see below), this is some of the oldest evidence for substantial woody tissue in flowering plants (Wing and Tiffney, 1987).

Scott (1987) reported on freshwater bivalves from the upper part of the Cedar Mountain Formation, which he believed to be indicative of a middle Albian age. A diverse assemblage of palynomorphs, also from the upper part of the unit east of Castle Dale, was described by Tschudy and others (1984). These authors considered the flora to be of late Albian age, somewhat younger than an assemblage obtained from the Burro Canyon Formation, basing their interpretation on the appearance of tricolporate pollen as a datum for the Upper Cretaceous. Nichols and Sweet (1993) indicated that tricolporates have a diachronous appearance in the Western Interior, and suggested that the assemblage reported by Tschudy and others (1984) may be from lower Cenomanian rocks.

Kowallis and others (1986) reported a 101 Ma age peak and a 106 Ma conventional age, based on fission-track dating of detrital zircons from what was interpreted to be the Cedar Mountain Formation near Capitol Reef National Park; these determinations are now considered unreliable (B. J. Kowallis, written communication, 1994). The most recent geochronologic evidence for the age of the upper part of the Cedar Mountain Formation, presented by Cifelli, Kirkland, and others (1997), is summarized below.

Abbreviations and Conventions

Abbreviations for institutions cited in the text: BYU, Brigham Young University, Provo, Utah; CMNH, Carnegie Museum of Natural History, Pittsburgh, Pennsylvania; FHSM, Fort Hays State University, Sternberg Museum, Fort Hays, Kansas; MNA, Museum of Northern Arizona, Flagstaff, Arizona; OMNH, Oklahoma Museum of Natural History, University of Oklahoma, Norman, Oklahoma; UCM, Museum, University of Colorado, Boulder, Colorado; UMNH, Utah Museum of Natural History, University of Utah, Salt Lake City, Utah. Other conventions: AP, anteroposterior tooth length; CT, computed tomography; LB, lingual-buccal tooth width; m, meters; Ma, millions of years before present.

VERTEBRATE PALEONTOLOGY OF THE UPPER CEDAR MOUNTAIN FORMATION

Methods; Geographic and Stratigraphic Distribution

The fauna reported herein was recovered as a result of a large-scale collecting program by the OMNH and includes most of the fossils collected between 1990 and 1996, although processing of some material remains incomplete at this writing. Also included are mammalian fossils obtained by one of us (JGE) while at UCM, and non-multituberculate mammal specimens collected under the direction of Michael Nelson while at FHSM. Virtually all mapped outcrops of the Cedar Mountain Formation in the State of Utah were prospected during the course of these investigations. Repeated attempts to find significant accumulations of microvertebrates in the lower and middle part of the unit were continually frustrated, whereas the upper part of the "shale" member was repeatedly found to be productive, particularly in Emery County. Here the outcrop of the Cedar Mountain Formation, like that of other Mesozoic units that are exposed in the area, follows the flanks of the main structural feature of the county, the San Rafael Swell (figure 1). Collecting was conducted at 31 sites, including two worked by previous investigators; most sites are near the headwaters of Mussentuchit Wash, for which the local fauna reported herein is named (figure 1). Collecting involved quarry-

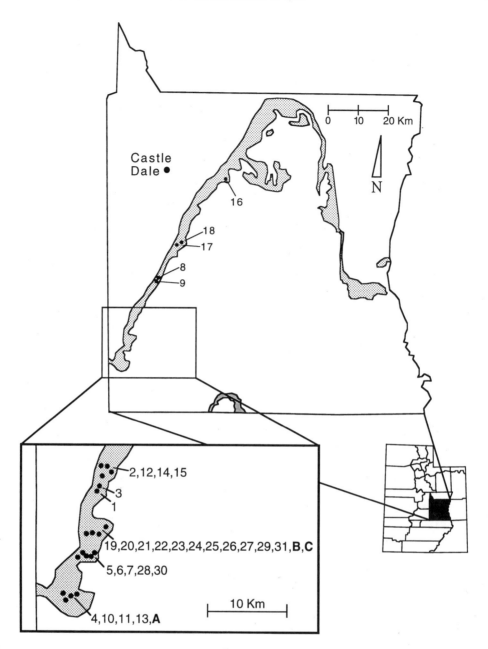

Figure 1. *Emery County, Utah, showing exposure of the Cedar Mountain Formation (after Nelson and Crooks, 1987) and approximate positions of OMNH fossil localities in the upper part of the "shale" member. Sites shown in inset, lower left, are in the immediate vicinity of Mussentuchit Wash; tight clustering of sites 19-27, 29, and 31 precludes separate plotting of each at this scale. Bold-faced letters A-C refer to positions of measured sections shown in figure 2 and described in the appendix. OMNH site numbers (see figure 2 for stratigraphic placement of representative sites): 1, V213; 2, V214; 3, V234, 4, V235; 5, V236; 6, V237; 7, V238; 8, V239; 9, V240; 10, V694; 11, V695; 12, V696; 13, V794; 14, V795; 15, V796; 16, V801 (=FHSM locality RRQ or Rough Road Quarry; see Nelson and Crooks, 1987; Eaton and Nelson, 1991); 17, V820 (=REQ or Robison's Eggshell Quarry; see Nelson and Crooks, 1987; Eaton and Nelson, 1991; Fiorillo, this volume); 18, V823 (=MNA locality 1072; see Eaton and Nelson, 1991); 19, V824; 20, V825; 21, V826; 22, V827; 23, V828; 24, V847; 25, V864; 26, V865; 27, V866; 28, V867; 29, V868; 30, V869; 31, V870.*

ing for macrovertebrates and a combination of quarrying and underwater screenwashing, with associated concentration and recovery techniques, for microvertebrates (Cifelli and others, 1996; Madsen, 1996). Articulated remains of macrovertebrates are rare in the upper part of the Cedar Mountain Formation. Accumulations of large bone generally include representation of several taxa, with occasional association of elements belonging to single individuals. In general, the bone is highly friable;

original condition varies from pristine to highly water worn. Microvertebrate specimens are similarly variable in preservation; at the most productive site, OMNH V695, abundant dissociated teeth occur together with dentulous jaws and, rarely, skulls and articulated postcrania. Most of the microvertebrate and macrovertebrate localities appear to represent lag concentration of both channel- and floodplain-derived materials, left in overbank deposits, although oxbow and other paleoenvironments are also represented.

Sections were measured so as to include the positions of all major localities; three sections through the principal sites in the Mussentuchit Wash area, including dated ash horizons, are shown in figure 2 (see also Nelson and Crooks, 1987) and are described in the appendix. All sites fall within a narrow stratigraphic interval, 10 to 20 meters below the contact with the overlying Dakota Formation (see figure 3). Laterally discontinuous, bentonitic horizons representing volcanic ashes occur sporadically in the upper part of the upper member of the Cedar Mountain Formation. One such horizon was discovered immediately overlying the top of the bone hori-

zon at the most productive site, OMNH V695 (figure 4; see also section A, figures 1, 2). Another such horizon, probably but not certainly representing the same volcanic event (see Cifelli, Kirkland, and others, 1997) occurs in association with another locality about 6 km to the northeast, in the same part of the stratigraphic column (section C, figures 1, 2). Sanidine crystals extracted from these horizons, including a total of four individual samples, were submitted for radiometric dating using the single-crystal $^{40}Ar/^{39}Ar$ single-crystal laser fusion method. The determinations are strongly concordant and indicate a mean age of 98.39 ± 0.07 Ma for the ash horizon and, by implication, for the associated fauna of the uppermost

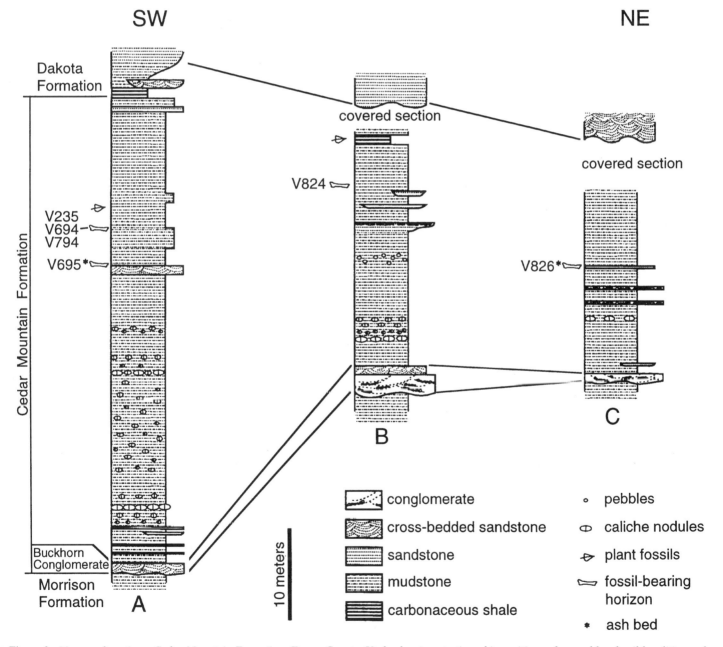

Figure 2. *Measured sections, Cedar Mountain Formation, Emery County, Utah, showing stratigraphic positions of several key fossil localities and dated ash samples (Cifelli, Kirkland, and others, 1997) in the area of Mussentuchit Wash. See figure 1 for approximate geographic positions of sites and measured sections, and the appendix for descriptions of the sections.*

Figure 3. *OMNH microvertebrate locality V868, Mussentuchit Wash area, upper Cedar Mountain Formation, Emery County, Utah. The locality lies approximately in the center of the photograph. The relatively homogenous character of the mudstones in the upper part of the unit is apparent; the overlying Dakota Formation forms the resistant cap to the ridge in the background.*

Figure 4. *OMNH microvertebrate quarry V695, Mussentuchit Wash area, upper Cedar Mountain Formation, Emery County, Utah. V695 has produced a number of the more informative microvertebrate specimens (see, for example, Cifelli, 1993a; Cifelli and Nydam, 1995) from the unit. The dated ash horizon (Cifelli, Kirkland, and others, 1997) is indicated by an arrow.*

tion and possibly representing the same volcanic event) have been identified in several other places, notably in association with a newly discovered and highly productive microsite (OMNH V868; figure 3); additional radiometric determinations are not yet available.

The Mussentuchit Local Fauna

Nearly 80 taxa of fossil vertebrates are now known from the upper part of the Cedar Mountain Formation (table 1). Because all of these are based on specimens from localities with a narrow stratigraphic and geographic focus, we refer to this assemblage as the Mussentuchit local fauna. We do this in order to promote precision of reference in making comparisons with other faunas, to avoid lumping of (or confusion with) temporally or geographically dissimilar assemblages, and to aid in future development of a biostratigraphic framework (see, for example, Savage and Russell, 1983; Woodburne, 1987; Rowe and others, 1992). Work on recovery and preparation of these fossils is still ongoing, and the following comments are offered in the form of a preliminary report. Level of resolution for taxonomic identification is highly variable and, in many cases, low. This is due partly to inadequate representation of diagnostic morphology but also to the fact that the time period represented by the Mussentuchit local fauna is otherwise virtually unrepresented elsewhere, and that significant hiatuses (about 10 Ma; see Jacobs and others, 1991) separate it from other reasonably well-known faunas, such as those of the Cloverly Formation, Montana and Wyoming (Ostrom, 1970) and the Trinity

Cedar Mountain Formation (Cifelli, Kirkland, and others, 1997). This age is not significantly different from the Albian-Cenomanian (Early- Late Cretaceous) boundary, currently placed at 98.5 Ma (Obradovich, 1993) and 98.9 ± 0.6 Ma (Gradstein and others, 1995). Since these dates were obtained, ash horizons (in the same part of the sec-

Group, northern Texas (Winkler and others, 1990). Many taxa are probably new, an expectation that is supported in the few cases in which detailed study has been undertaken (for example, Cifelli and Madsen, 1998). The faunal list for the Mussentuchit local fauna (table 1) is based on

Table 1. *Vertebrates of the upper part of the Cedar Mountain Formation: the Mussentuchit local fauna.*

Chondrichthyes
    Hybodontiformes
        Hybodontidae
           Hybodus sp.
        Polyacrodontidae
           Polyacrodus parvidens
           Lissodus spp. (2)
    Orectolobiformes
        Orectolobidae
           n. gen. & spp. (2)
    Rajiformes
        Ischyrhiza sp.
    Myliobatiformes
        cf. *Baibisha* n. sp.

Osteichthyes
    Neopterygii, indet.
        gen. & spp. (2) indet.
    Lepisosteiformes
        ?Lepisosteidae
           gen. & sp. indet.
    Pycnodontiformes
        ?Pycnodontidae
           gen. & spp. (2) indet.
    Amiiformes, indet.
        gen. & sp. indet.
    Dipnoi
        Ceratodontidae
           Ceratodus sp.

Lissamphibia
    Incertae sedis
        Albanerpetontidae
           cf. *Albanerpeton arthridion*
           gen. & sp. indet.
    Caudata
        Scapherpetontidae
           gen. & spp. (2) indet.
    Anura
        Family indet.
           gen. & spp. (4) indet.

Reptilia
    Testudines
        Baenidae
           gen. & sp. indet.
        Pleurosternidae
           Naomichelys sp.
        Glyptopsidae
           Glyptops sp.
    Squamata
        Family indet.
           n. gen. & sp.
        Teiidae
           cf. *Peneteius* sp.
           gen. & sp. Polyglyphanodontinae.
        ?Scincidae
           gen. & spp. (2) indet.
        ?Paramacellodidae
           gen. & sp. indet.
        ?Necrosauridae
           gen. & sp. indet.
        ?Helodermatidae
           n. gen. & sp.
    Serpentes
        Aniliidae
           Coniophis sp.

Crocodilia
    Bernissartiidae
        Bernissartia sp.
    Goniopholididae
        cf. *Dakotasuchus* sp.
        Polydectes sp.
    Atoposauridae
        gen. & sp. indet.

    Teleosauridae
        Machimosaurus sp.
        gen. & sp. indet.
    Pholidosauridae
        gen. & sp. indet.

Dinosauria
    Dromaeosaurinae
        gen. & sp. indet.
    Veloceraptorinae
        gen. & sp. indet.
    Troodontidae
        gen. & sp. indet.
        cf. *Paronychodon* sp.
    Family indet.
        cf. *Richardoestesia* sp.
    Tyrannosauridae
        cf. *Alectrosaurus* sp.
    ?Brachiosauridae
        cf. *Astrodon* sp.
    Hadrosauridae
        n. gen. & sp.
    Hypsilophodontidae
        cf. *Zephyrosaurus* sp.
        gen. & spp. (2) indet.
    Pachycephalosauridae
        gen. & sp. indet.
    Neoceratopsia
        gen. & sp. indet.

Avialae
    ?Hesperornithiformes
        gen. & sp. indet.
    Order indet
        gen. & sp. indet.

Mammalia
    Triconodonta
        Triconodontidae
           Astroconodon n. sp.
           n. gen. and spp. (2)

Multituberculata
    Suborder *incertae sedis*
        Family indet.
           n. gen. & sp.
    Suborder Ptilodontoidea
        Family indet.
           Paracimexomys robisoni
           P. n. sp. (small)
           P. n. sp. (large)
           ?*P. bestia*
           ?*P.* sp., cf. ?*P. bestia*
           ?*P.* n. sp.
           n. gen. and sp.

Symmetrodonta
    Spalacotheriidae
        Spalacotheridium n. sp.
        Symmetrodontoides sp.
        n. gen. & sp.

Tribotheria
    Picopsidae
        gen. & sp. indet
    Pappotheriidae
        n. gen. & spp. (2)
    Family indet.
        n. gen. & sp.

Order indet.
    Family indet.
        Kokopellia juddi

Marsupialia
    gen. & spp. (2) indet.

more than 5,000 catalogued specimens in the collection of the OMNH, supplemented by some of the mammalian fossils deposited at the UCM and the FHSM (see Eaton and Nelson, 1991). Basic data for the OMNH catalog, which includes all of the taxa reported herein, may be accessed through the OMNH web site: www.omnh.ou.edu.

Chondrichthyes

Several of the chondrichthyans known from the Mussentuchit local fauna are widely ranging, relatively undiagnostic taxa (for example, Hybodontiformes); *Lissodus* is relatively common, but *Hybodus* is also known. Notable occurrences include a new genus of Orectilobiformes, representing (to our knowledge) the earliest appearance of the Orectolobidae; and the rajiform *Ischyrhiza*, which is typical of Late Cretaceous assemblages and makes its first global appearance in this fauna. Also noteworthy is the presence of a myliobatiform remarkably similar to *Baibisha*, otherwise known from slightly younger rocks in central Asia (see Nessov and others, 1994) and, possibly, the somewhat older Paluxy Formation of Texas (Kirkland, unpublished data).

Osteichthyes

The dipnoan *Ceratodus*, common in earlier assemblages, is represented by extremely rare dental plates in the Mussentuchit local fauna; the last occurrence of this relict taxon is in the overlying Dakota Formation (Kirkland, 1987; Eaton and others, this volume). Actinopterygians are represented by abundant scales and vertebrae, and rare skull bones; several specimens, such as OMNH 30173 (from OMNH locality V695), include articulated scales. Despite the abundant material collected to date, actinopterygians remain the most poorly understood component of the Mussentuchit local fauna. Most of the scales resemble those of lepisosteids and semionotids in being ganoid and more or less rhomboidal in outline. In view of Wilson and Chalifa's (1989) observations about the taxonomic reliability of ganoid scales, we conservatively identify these, for the present, as "Neopterygii, indeterminate." A second neopterygian is probably represented by a tiny, rhomboid, ganoid scale, OMNH 33921, with a serrated posterior margin. All actinopterygian vertebrae collected this far from the upper part of the Cedar Mountain Formation are amphicoelous, but they vary markedly in size and preserved morphology. To what extent these differences reflect taxonomic, individual, or ontogenetic variation awaits further analysis. Lepisosteid fishes, so abundant and characteristic of Late Cretaceous and Early Tertiary assemblages of North America, are tentatively recognized from the Mussentu-

chit local fauna on the basis of isolated teeth; teeth also possibly belonging to Lepisosteidae are known from the somewhat older Trinity Group, Texas (Thurmond, 1974; Kirkland, unpublished data; but see cautionary note by Winkler and others, 1990). Given the fact that diagnostic materials, such as opistocoelous vertebrae (which are unique to lepisosteids among actinopterygians) have yet to be recovered from either unit, however, we emphasize that inclusion of Lepisosteidae in both faunas is highly tentative.

Specimens include jaws and teeth representing at least two kinds of pycnodontiforms, an extinct group of marine and freshwater fish characterized by a pavement-like durophagous dentition (for example, Nursall, 1996a,b). We tentatively refer these taxa to the Pycnodontidae; they are similar to certain freshwater taxa known from the Morrison and Dakota formations of the Western Interior (Kirkland, 1998). A diverse assemblage of Early Cretaceous pycnodontiforms has been described from the Trinity Group, Texas (Thurmond, 1974), but detailed comparisons with the material from the Mussentuchit local fauna remain to be made.

Additional tooth-bearing palatal and marginal bones have conical teeth. One indeterminate dentary fragment, OMNH 29794, preserves a single row of five subthecodont teeth and is perforated labially by several nutritive foramina. A nearly complete right dentary, OMNH 31059, bears a single row of 13 elongate, conical teeth and a prominent "coronoid process." Prepared in lingual view, the fossil jaw resembles dentaries of the extant amiiform *Amia calva*. Slightly older amiiform jaws (Thurmond, 1974) and vertebrae (Bryant, 1987) have been reported from freshwater and marine deposits of the Trinity Group, and the group as a whole is known back into the Jurassic (Grande, 1996). Given that the taxa listed in table 1 almost certainly underestimate the diversity of actinopterygians in the Mussentuchit local fauna, comparisons with other fish assemblages from the Early and Late Cretaceous of the Western Interior are best deferred at present.

Lissamphibia

Lissamphibians are represented in the Cedar Mountain Formation by isolated elements and rare, incomplete skeletons. Preliminary work suggests that four taxa of indeterminate frogs, two taxa of probable scapherpetontid salamanders, and two albanerpetontid taxa are present, making this one of the most taxonomically diverse lissamphibian assemblages yet reported from the mid-Cretaceous.

The most productive site for frogs in the Cedar Mountain Formation, OMNH V695, has yielded isolated humeri, vertebrae, maxillae, squamosals, and frontoparietals, as well as two incomplete skulls and an incomplete vertebral column with an associated ilium and humerus. The articulated specimens are currently being prepared, and they should prove useful both for associating isolated bones and determining the higher level affinities of at least some of the frogs represented in the collection. Preliminary study of fossils prepared to date suggests that these frogs were at an archaeobatrachian level of organization and that a moderately diverse assemblage is represented (Gardner, 1995). The most compelling evidence for the latter suggestion is the presence of four maxillary morphs. These morphs differ in a variety of features (for example, absolute sizes, proportions, ornamentation, lingual morphologies, and inferred patterns of contact with other bones), which we suspect are indicative of at least species-level differences. Similar maxillae from elsewhere have been referred to the Pelobatidae *sensu lato*, Discoglossidae *sensu lato*, and Gobiatidae (for example, Roĉek and Nessov, 1993; Gubin, 1993, 1996).

Based on a limited number of dentaries and one trunk vertebra from OMNH V695, Gardner (1994) reported the occurrence of a batrachosauroidid salamander in the Cedar Mountain Formation. With the discovery, from this same quarry, of better preserved examples of these elements, as well as two atlantes, it is evident that these fossils are more likely referable to the Scapherpetontidae, a family of paedomorphic salamanders known from the Campanian to early Eocene of North America (for example, Estes, 1964, 1965, 1969a, 1981; Naylor, 1983; Naylor and Krause, 1981) and from rocks of suspected latest Albian to Campanian age in Middle Asia (Nessov, 1981, 1988). Dentaries and vertebrae of batrachosauroidids and scapherpetontids are similar (for example, Estes, 1969a, 1981; Naylor, 1983; Naylor and Krause, 1981), but as these two families are currently considered to be only distantly related (for example, Estes, 1981; Naylor and Krause, 1981; Duellman and Trueb, 1986) and these resemblances appear to be largely convergent. The largest dentaries (OMNH 27130, 27394, 27401, 27888, and 28086) resemble those of other scapherpetontids in being elongate, lacking a dental gutter, in having a Meckelian groove that is elongate anteriorly and deep posteriorly, and in the presence of an anteriorly directed foramen below the posterior end of the tooth row. Among known taxa, they most closely resemble dentaries of *Piceoerpeton* (Paleocene to Eocene, North America; Naylor and Krause, 1981, figure 3), especially in having a shallow, anteriorly acuminate external depression and nonpedicellate teeth. Trunk vertebrae resemble those of both batrachosauroidids and

scapherpetontids in having prominent, widely divergent rib-bearing processes, an elongate, thin neural spine, and a markedly elongate hyperapophyseal spine (Estes, 1969a; Naylor and Krause, 1981), but they more closely resemble trunk vertebrae of unequivocal scapherpetontids in having amphicoelous centra (they are opisthocoelous in most batrachosauroidids) and cotyles that are not infilled with calcified tissue (cotyles are infilled in batrachosauroidids) (Estes, 1969a; Naylor and Krause, 1981). Two atlantal centra (OMNH 33919, 33920) are tentatively referred to the Scapherpetontidae based on their dorsoventrally compressed anterior cotyles, presence of an odontoid process, and lack of calcified tissues infilling the posterior cotyle (Naylor, 1983). OMNH 33919 resembles atlantes of *Piceoerpeton* (Naylor and Krause, 1981, figure 1I-K) and cf. *Piceoerpeton* (Maastrichtian, North America; Naylor, 1983, figures 1, 2A) in having a reduced odontoid process and deeply concave anterior cotyles that are subcircular in anterior outline; whereas OMNH 33920 resembles atlantes of *Lisserpeton* (Campanian to Paleocene, North America; Estes, 1965: figures 2a, b) in having the anterior cotyles short and broad in anterior outline, odontoid process not constricted at its base, and posterior cotyle deeply conical interiorly and laterally compressed in posterior outline. If the dentaries and vertebrae described above from OMNH V695 are correctly identified, these represent the geologically oldest North American scapherpetontids. Differences such as those noted above between the two atlantes are usually considered diagnostic at the specific or generic level, suggesting the presence of two probable scapherpetontid taxa in the Cedar Mountain Formation.

Jaws of albanerpetontids, a group of superficially salamander-like, Middle Jurassic to Miocene probable lissamphibians (Fox and Naylor, 1982; McGowan and Evans, 1995) are readily identified by their highly pleurodont, nonpedicellate, chisel-like, and faintly tricuspid teeth. Dentaries and premaxillae have been collected from various sites in the Cedar Mountain Formation, with several of the former bones preserving the interlocking symphysial prongs that are unique for albanerpetontids. Although most of the jaws are too fragmentary to be identified below the familial level, the best preserved specimens indicate that two albanerpetontid taxa are present. The first of these is represented by three tiny, isolated premaxillae (OMNH 27375, 27979, and 27980), which in their preserved morphologies and small size compare favorably with the holotype (Estes, 1969b, figure 2C-E) and referred premaxillae of *Albanerpeton arthridion*, a species otherwise known from the early to mid-Albian Antlers Formation of Texas (Fox and Naylor, 1982) and Oklahoma (Cifelli, Gardner, and others, 1997; Gardner, unpublished data). The second taxon is known by a relatively large dentary (OMNH 27413) and a pair of large, fused premaxillae (OMNH 26222). These jaws are similar to certain of the dentaries and premaxillae referred by Fox and Naylor (1982, figures 2d,e, 4a) to *A. galaktion* (early Campanian, Alberta), but the jaws from the Cedar Mountain Formation almost certainly represent a previously undescribed albanerpetontid species (Gardner, unpublished data).

Testudines

Turtles of the Mussentuchit local fauna are unremarkable. The archaic genus *Glyptops*, abundant in the underlying Morrison Formation, is also known from the overlying Dakota Formation, in which it makes its last appearance (Eaton and others, this volume). The pleurosternid *Naomichelys*, first described from the Aptian-Albian Cloverly Formation of Montana (Hay, 1908) and later reported from the penecontemporaneous (see Jacobs and others, 1991) Trinity Group of Texas (Ostrom, 1970; Langston, 1974), is commonly encountered in the uppermost Cedar Mountain Formation. This turtle, with its distinctive, pustulate ornamentation, was thought to be of biostratigraphic utility because of its distribution in the Cloverly Formation and Trinity Group (Ostrom, 1970); however, based on OMNH collections, it has a broad range in Cretaceous rocks of the Kaiparowits region, southern Utah, where it makes its last appearance in the lower Campanian Wahweap Formation (Eaton and others, this volume). In addition, *Naomichelys* has been reported from the Campanian (Milk River, Foremost Formations) of Alberta (Brinkman and Nicholls, 1991).

Squamata

The lizards of the Cedar Mountain Formation have previously been reported on only briefly (Cifelli and Nydam, 1995; Nydam, 1995) and their study is in progress by one of us (RLN). Materials recovered to date include jaws and jaw fragments, isolated teeth, vertebrae, limb elements, and isolated osteoderms. No complete skulls or skeletons have been recovered and articulated materials are limited to a series of three trunk vertebrae (OMNH 28125) and a broken dentary with an articulated splenial (OMNH 28069). In general the lizard fauna of the Cedar Mountain Formation is moderately diverse and is composed of taxonomic groups that are known from other North American Cretaceous microvertebrate faunas, though none of the taxa recovered can be assigned to known genera or species. The composition (at least on a family level) of the lizards of the Cedar Mountain Formation compares more closely to that of

significantly younger North American Late Cretaceous lizard faunas (see, for example, Estes, 1964; Estes and others, 1969; Estes and Berberian, 1970; Armstrong-Zeigler, 1980; Rowe and others, 1992; Gao and Fox, 1996) than to slightly older Early Cretaceous faunas (for example, Winkler and others, 1990), although the Early Cretaceous record is less well known. The lizard groups recognized from the Cedar Mountain Formation include the ?Paramacellodidae, Scincidae, Teiidae, ?Helodermatidae, and ?Polyglyphanodontinae.

The most abundant lizard in the Cedar Mountain Formation is a teiid known from nearly all of the sites in which microvertebrates have been collected. Assignment to the Teiidae is based on the widely open Meckelian fossa and associated hypertrophied splenial of the mandible, wide sulcus dentalis, thick deposits of cementum, and sub-circular resorbtion pits at the base of teeth (Estes and others, 1988; Gao and Fox, 1991). Most significant of known morphology in this lizard is the tooth structure, in which there are conical, recurved anterior teeth and transversely oriented, molariform, bicuspid posterior teeth. This tooth pattern is similar to that of Late Cretaceous *Peneteius* from the Hell Creek Formation (Estes, 1969c, 1983) and modern *Dicrodon* and *Teius* from South America. The fact that this teiid appears in localities worked both extensively (V695) and minimally (V801) indicates that the abundance of the fossils of this lizard is most likely reflective of its real abundance and not of a collecting bias. It should be noted here that the bicuspid pattern of posterior teeth in this lizard was previously believed to be restricted to only two, unrelated Cretaceous teiids, *Peneteius* and *Polyglyphanodon* (Estes, 1969c, 1983), with the former being viewed as the possible ancestor of the modern genera *Dicrodon* and *Teius*. However, the teiid of the Mussentuchit local fauna and other teiids now known from various Late Cretaceous faunas indicate that this pattern was widespread in teiids throughout the last half of the Cretaceous (Nydam, work in progress).

Another teiid from the Cedar Mountain Formation is known from only one specimen (OMNH 28067), a broken dentary from locality V695. Again, the specimen is identified as a teiid based on the morphology of the dentary and teeth (see above). The teeth of this lizard are anteriorly unicuspid and conical, and weakly tricuspid in the posterior part of the toothrow. This tooth pattern is common among North American Late Cretaceous teiids and has been described in such taxa as *Chamops, Leptochamops, Meniscognathus* (Estes, 1964, 1983; Gao and Fox, 1996), *Socognathus, Sphenosiagon*, and *Gerontoseps* (Gao and Fox, 1991, 1996; but see Denton and O'Neil, 1995 for a brief contrasting view of the taxonomic status of the latter three taxa). However, the abraded condition of the teeth and generally poor preservation of the dentary precludes any immediate assessment of the relationship of OMNH 28067 to other teiids.

The presence of a possible polyglyphanodontine teiid in the Mussentuchit local fauna is suggested by two specimens, a jaw fragment with a single tooth (OMNH 29771) and an isolated tooth (OMNH 32629), both from locality V239. Like polyglyphanodontines described from the Maastrichtian age North Horn Formation (Gilmore, 1942, 1943, 1946), the tooth of OMNH 29771 superficially appears to be thecodont or even acrodont. Fortunately, the jaw has been broken in such a way as to demonstrate a pleurodont attachment of the tooth to the lateral parapet of the jaw; moreover, the tooth base is covered with a heavy deposit of cementum. Assignment of OMNH 29771 and 32629 to the Teiidae is based on the heavy deposit of cementum at the base of the tooth. The tooth morphology of the taxon from the Cedar Mountain Formation is surprisingly similar to that of the large teiid *Polyglyphanodon* from the North Horn Formation (Gilmore, 1942). Like *Polyglyphanodon*, the teeth are transversely expanded, constricted at the base, and have a lingual and a labial apex connected by a crest. Unlike *Polyglyphanodon*, however, the crest connecting the apices forms a shallow "V" instead of a horizontal ridge in anterior view. Also, OMNH 29771 has anterior and posterior ridges that circumscribe shallow anterior and posterior semicircles and border shallow basins on either side of the central crest. Because of postdepositional abrasion these ridges are not completely preserved on OMNH 32629. Although similar in shape to *Polyglyphanodon*, these specimens are from an animal much smaller in size (see Gilmore, 1942, for an estimation of the size of *Polyglyphanodon*).

The presence of a polyglyphanodontine lizard in the Mussentuchit local fauna would represent the earliest record for the group, which is otherwise restricted to the Campanian and Maastrichtian of North America (Estes, 1983) and ?Campanian of Mongolia (Estes, 1983; Sulimski, 1975). Unfortunately, the material on hand is not nearly complete enough to support more than a tentative assignment to the Polyglyphanodontinae (in the sense of Estes, 1983). Materials currently under study indicate that polyglyphanodontines may also occur in older Late Cretaceous faunas (Turonian, southern Utah) than previously thought, suggesting that this group may have an extensive North American temporal record (Nydam, this volume).

Three specimens (OMNH 27381, 27388, and 27711) from locality V695 are referred to Scincidae. These specimens, possibly representing at least two taxa, do not compare readily to known Cretaceous taxa and referral to Scincidae is tentative. One of the specimens, OMNH 27711, is a broken right maxilla with low crowned teeth. The general appearance of this specimen is similar to that of *Eumeces*; however, this would extend the earliest record of this genus from the Oligocene to the medial Cretaceous, a doubtful prospect based on the current record of Cretaceous scincids. The lack of material that can be confidently assigned to Scincidae is not surprising in view of the globally poor Mesozoic fossil record of this group (Estes, 1983).

Not nearly as abundant as the teiid with bicuspid posterior teeth, but also widespread in the formation, are two species of scincomorph lizards tentatively referred to the Paramacellodidae. These taxa are most common in locality V868, but also are known from four other localities. Placement in the Scincomorpha is supported by the well-developed, albeit small, subdental gutter and subdental shelf as well as the thick cementum at the bases of the teeth. The crowns of the teeth are striated lingually and have an apex posterior to the midline of the shaft of the tooth which is formed by an anterior cutting edge that is longer than the posterior cutting edge. These two cutting edges turn medially towards the apex and form a posteromedially directed "v" in occlusal view. The teeth are also slightly rotated posteriorly around their long axes such that the anterior edges are exposed medially and the posterior edges are exposed laterally. This tooth morphology has been recognized as diagnostic of Anguidae (Gauthier, 1982; Estes and others, 1988), but has also been reported for taxa in the Scincidae (Gao and Fox, 1996) and Paramacellodidae (Broschinski and Sigogneau-Russell, 1996). The presence of a subdental shelf and subdental gutter clearly indicate that the Mussentuchit lizards are scincomorphan and thus eliminate the possibility of anguid affinities. Broschinski and Sigogneau-Russell (1996) describe the teeth of *Paramacellodus* as having a small, secondary apex (formed by the distal junction of two of the lingual striae) which is offset from the more labial, primary apex. These two cusps are connected by a small, transverse carina. The teeth of the Mussentuchit scincomorphs have a similar construction and are therefore referred to the ?Paramacellodidae. The reference is tentative, however, pending the resolution of relationships between Paramacellodidae and Cordylidae (see Estes, 1983). The two species of the Mussentuchit local fauna are distinguished primarily on the basis of morphological differences in the teeth. Species A is the best represented of the two; a complete dentary (OMNH 33889) is known from locality V868. The teeth of this species form a more acute apex in lateral view, bear an offset anterior cutting edge, and have weak labial striations on the crowns. The crown of species B in lateral view is blunt and the lingual striations of the crown are well developed. Formal description of both taxa is presently underway by one of the authors (RLN).

The possible existence of a helodermatid varanoid in the Cedar Mountain Formation was first suggested by Cifelli and Nydam (1995) in their description of a partial maxilla with widely spaced, plicidentine teeth, and osteoderms fused to the exterior surface of the maxilla. Since then, a partial dentary referable to the same taxon has been recovered from the same locality (V695), and further description and systematic work are in progress. This adds to the lizard fauna a taxon that presumably incorporated vertebrate prey in its diet, whereas the rest of the lizards are interpreted as having been insectivorous. The earliest published record of Helodermatidae is generally considered to be that of Lancian *Paraderma*. Assuming the material from the Cedar Mountain is correctly referred, it represents a significant increase in the temporal range of this group and thus begins to fill the gap between terrestrial and aquatic varanoids (see Carroll and deBraga, 1992, for discussion of the fossil record of these groups; see also Caldwell and others, 1995, for an alternative hypothesis of relationships among advanced anguimorphs).

In addition to the possible helodermatid, field work has resulted in the recovery of a single osteoderm (OMNH 28460) that is similar to those described for the varanoid *Necrosaurus* (Fejéráry, 1918, 1935; Estes, 1983). The osteoderm is unornamented, elongate, and strongly arched. Unlike similar osteoderms described for *Necrosaurus*, this osteoderm is large and has smooth, regular edges. The possibility that this osteoderm belongs to the aforementioned ?helodermatid is unlikely due to the lack of similar ornamentation on the fused osteoderms of the maxilla of that taxon. Placement in Crocodilia is also dismissed for the lack of the characteristic pit and ridge sculpturing common to that group. Because of the lack of additional, more diagnostic materials, a taxonomic assignment for the osteoderm is withheld at this time, although it can be tentatively considered to be indicative of a necrosaurian-grade varanoid.

As with most of the taxa of the Mussentuchit local fauna, the lizards described herein are more characteristic of described Late Cretaceous than Early Cretaceous faunas (see citations above). This is interesting because the Mussentuchit local fauna is not substantially younger than the more primitive assemblage described from the Trinity Group of Texas (Winkler and others, 1990). Investigations are underway to determine the extent to which the evolution of angiosperms may have con-

tributed to the apparent rapid change in lizard faunas (Nydam, work in progress). It should also be stressed that faunal comparisons are, perforce, based on a very limited fossil record.

Two snake vertebrae, OMNH 33250 and 33251, from OMNH V695 and V867, respectively, are referable to the primitive, anilioid-grade alethinophidian *Coniophis*. This genus previously was known from the Campanian to Eocene of North America, South America, and Europe (for example, Rage, 1984, 1987, 1988; Albino, 1996). OMNH 33250 and 33251 are of paleobiogeographic interest, because they are among the geologically oldest snake fossils known from anywhere in the world and they represent the oldest occurrence of snakes in the New World by at least 10 Ma (Gardner and Cifelli, 1999).

Crocodilia

At least seven taxa of crocodilians are represented in the Mussentuchit local fauna; most of these are known only by incredibly abundant, isolated teeth, but several skulls and some articulated postcranial materials are known: much of this is not yet prepared, and none of it has been studied; hence, the provisional identifications presented herein are based solely on the dentition. *Bernissartia*, best known from the Early Cretaceous of Europe (for example, Buffetaut and Ford, 1979), has also been reported from the Aptian-Albian of Texas (Winkler and others, 1990); apparently, however, *Bernissartia*-like crocodilians with a durophagous dentition are widely distributed in the Cretaceous of the southern Western Interior, ranging through the Dakota, Straight Cliffs, and Wahweap Formations in southern Utah (Eaton and others, this volume). Probable first occurrences in the Mussentuchit local fauna include the goniopholidids cf. *Dakotasuchus* and *Polydectes*; the record of the teleosaurid *Machimosaurus* (based on rare but very distinctive teeth) is a probable last occurrence.

Dinosauria

A diverse array of Theropoda is present in the fauna; at least six taxa, most of which are small coelurosaurs, are known. Each theropod taxon is represented by isolated teeth; in addition, isolated postcranials are known for several taxa, and a partial associated skeleton is known for one of the dromaeosaurids. Among coelurosaurs, the records of Dromaeosaurinae, Troodontidae, cf. *Paronychodon*, and cf. *Richardoestesia* represent first occurrences. Most noteworthy among theropods is a tyrannosaurid similar to *Alectrosaurus*, otherwise known from the Late Cretaceous of Asia (Gilmore, 1933); this family is first recorded from the

Early Cretaceous of southeast Asia (Buffetaut and others, 1996).

A ?brachiosaurid sauropod is represented by small teeth (less than 1 cm in crown length) morphologically indistinguishable from those of *Astrodon* (see summaries by Lull, 1911; Gilmore, 1921; Ostrom, 1970; Langston, 1974). *Astrodon* (and its probable synonym, *Pleurocoelus*) is a broadly distributed but generally rare taxon in the Early Cretaceous of North America, and is known from the Arundel Formation, Trinity Group, Cloverly Formation, and the lower part of the "shale" member of the Cedar Mountain Formation. The taxon in the Mussentuchit local fauna apparently represents the last North American record of Sauropoda, prior to their brief reappearance (in the form of the titanosaurid *Alamosaurus*) in Maastrichtian rocks of the Southwest -- presumably through immigration from South America (see Lehman, 1987; Lucas and Hunt, 1989). Interestingly, all known specimens of the sauropod from the upper Cedar Mountain Formation are from extremely small individuals: either some sampling bias has favored the representation of juveniles alone, or the taxon itself was remarkably small, by sauropod standards. Given the intense sampling (including use of both microvertebrate and macrovertebrate recovery techniques) and the abundance of localities in the upper part of the Cedar Mountain Formation, with representation of several different depositional (and presumably paleoenvironmental) settings, we consider this second interpretation to be at least viable, if not favorable.

The most abundant dinosaur -- and for that matter, the most abundant vertebrate represented by anything other than isolated teeth -- from the Mussentuchit local fauna is a hadrosaurid (Kirkland, 1994), represented by several incomplete skeletons, cranial material, jaws, and innumerable isolated teeth. This probable new genus is the oldest member of the family. The majority of specimens represent small, immature individuals, suggesting high mortality rates for younger members of the species, frequenting of the area by this taxon during time intervals corresponding to certain early, ontogenetic growth stages, or some other unknown factor(s). Three small, hypsilophodontid ornithopods are also present in the fauna; of these, one is similar to *Zephyrosaurus*, otherwise known from the Cloverly Formation of Montana (Sues, 1980). The Mussentuchit local fauna includes a nodosaurid (based on teeth) similar to *Pawpawsaurus*, which was described from upper Albian rocks of Texas (Lee, 1996). Marginocephalia are represented by a neoceratopsian and a pachycephalosaur, both tentatively recognized on the basis of isolated teeth. Assuming correct identification, the latter is of interest in representing the

first North American appearance of the group; the oldest pachycephalosaur, *Yaverlandia*, is from the Barremian of the Isle of Wight (Galton, 1971). The neoceratopsian also deserves comment because of its geologic age: only two, somewhat ambiguous occurrences may antedate it; one includes skeletal material from the Albian Wayan Formation, Idaho (Weishampel, 1990), the other is based on an enigmatic tooth recently collected from the Arundel Formation, Maryland (Kranz, 1996), of similar age.

At least two dental morphs of Avialae are present in the fauna; one of these appears referable to the Hesperornithiformes. These teeth have bulbous bases and rare serrations; they compare closely with hesperornithiform teeth from the Dinosaur Park Formation, Canada (Kirkland, unpublished data). The great abundance of these teeth (which superficially look like hypsilophodont premaxillary teeth) supports their tentative allocation to Hesperornithiformes as the most parsimonious identification. The earliest record of this group of toothed diving birds is generally considered to be *Enaliornis*, from the Early Cretaceous of England (for example, Unwin, 1993; Feduccia, 1996); the genus is also tentatively recorded from the Cenomanian Greenhorn Formation, Kansas. Additional hesperornithiform birds are known from marine units spanning the Turonian through Campanian of North America. If the teeth from the Cedar Mountain Formation are correctly identified, they represent only the second occurrence in nonmarine rocks on the continent -- the other being a report of *Hesperornis* in the Campanian of Canada (Fox, 1974). In Asia, Hesperornithiformes appear somewhat later, and are known from the Santonian through ?Maastrichtian; some of the Asian occurrences are also from nonmarine units (Kurochkin, 1995).

Remains of fossil eggs have long been known from the upper part of the Cedar Mountain Formation, but their identification is uncertain (for example, Jensen, 1970). Hirsch (written communication, 1996) examined material from a number of the OMNH localities and reported that all eggs are of the dinosauroid-spherulitic type, with protolaterospherulitic and angustiprismatic morphotypes being most common (see Hirsch and Quinn, 1990 for explanation of terminology and classification schemes). These types are found among Ornithopoda; the protolaterospherulitic structural morphotype is known for Hadrosauridae. Though a taxonomic referral of eggshell materials from the upper Cedar Mountain Formation cannot be made at this time, these data suggest that some, at least, may belong to the extremely abundant hadrosaurid known from the Mussentuchit local fauna. There is also the suggestion of a distinct pattern to the geographic distribution of eggshell within the upper part of the Cedar Mountain Formation. Although isolated eggshell fragments can be found practically wherever this part of the unit is exposed, extremely dense, largely monotypic concentrations (suggesting proximity to a colonial nesting site) seem to be limited to the western side of the San Rafael Swell. Sites have been noted as far north as Castle Dale (Jensen, 1970) and Ferron (Fiorillo, this volume), Emery County, but denser spacing of sites occurs south of this, from OMNH locality V239 to near locality V868. This apparent distribution may reflect sampling bias, sedimentological or depositional factors, or, perhaps, preferential selection of nesting sites. Further investigation is clearly warranted.

Mammalia: Multituberculata

The sample of multituberculate specimens on which Eaton and Nelson (1991) based their systematic discussion was relatively small and from localities all within the upper few meters of the formation. Collections made subsequently by Cifelli and currently under study by Eaton are much larger and appear to include at least eight multituberculate taxa. These new collections will vastly improve our knowledge of the Early Cretaceous evolution of multituberculates in the Western Interior. This report represents the results of a cursory examination of the OMNH material (by Eaton) and is based largely on first molars.

Eaton and Nelson (1991) described as *incertae sedis* a single, peculiar m1 (FHSM 10350; figure 1A) that has very broad, U-shaped valleys between the cusps in the same row. The new OMNH material includes more specimens of this morphologic style, including some extremely strange molar forms unlike any published multituberculates of any age. These peculiar teeth may represent a previously unrecognized clade of multituberculates, perhaps distinct at the level of suborder.

Virtually all of the remaining specimens are at a "*Paracimexomys*" grade of evolution in that cusp counts are low, cusps are primarily pyramidal to sub-pyramidal (not crescentic) in occlusal view, and the internal cusp row on M1s is poorly developed. Current diagnoses would place most of these specimens within the genus *Paracimexomys*. However, the concept of this taxon is based largely on primitive characteristics expressed in a Maastrichtian form on which the type of the genus is based (Archibald, 1982). There is a vast range of subtle morphologic variation within these specimens that will take time to analyze and interpret. This subtle morphologic variation may mark the initial divergence from a *Paracimexomys*-like ancestor that possibly (but not demonstrably) gave rise to many later Cretaceous multi-tuberculate taxa.

The OMNH sample includes a variety of species (as many as six, including those referred to the genus with doubt) of *Paracimexomys*, including at least one species distinctly smaller than *Paracimexomys robisoni* (Eaton and Nelson, 1991, table 1). Specimens of this small taxon are similar in size to what Eaton and Nelson (1991) described as ?*Paracimexomys* n. sp. B. However, the latter taxon does not have the cusp arrangement characteristic of other species of *Paracimexomys* (alternation of cusp position between the internal and external cusp rows). This suggests that these two small taxa from the Mussentuchit local fauna will probably be found to belong in different genera when study and analysis is completed.

Eaton and Nelson (1991) described a large taxon as *Paracimexomys bestia* based on an m1, two p4s, and an m2. Many large M1s in the OMNH sample are morphologically what might be expected in this taxon. These M1s are primitive in having either no internal cusp row or only a single, labially appressed cusp on the lingual side of the tooth; however, they are smaller than would be expected for M1s of *P. bestia*. The m1 of *P. bestia* (AP=2.7; LB=1.7, Eaton and Nelson, 1991, table 1) is larger than these upper molars (mean AP=2.4; mean LB=1.4), whereas the reverse is generally true of multituberculates. This suggests the presence of a taxon smaller than, but similar to, *P. bestia*. The primitive nature of the M1s (cusp formula 3:4:1-0) and strong anterior divergence of the cup rows raises question about the placement of *P. bestia* within *Paracimexomys*, and that assignment is questioned in the revised faunal list presented here (table 1).

Also of interest in the large OMNH sample are M1s that have a distinct internal cusp row bearing at least two cusps that connect to the posterior part of the second cusp of the medial row (which has four cusps). The overall cusp formula of the M1s is low (3:4:2), as in *Paracimexomys*. The M1s are approximately the same size as those of *Paracimexomys robisoni* (Eaton and Nelson, 1991, table 1), but the internal cusp row is much better developed than in described specimens of *Paracimexomys*. The internal cusp row is about half the length of the tooth, a condition similar to that found in *Cimexomys* (for example, Archibald, 1982), but these M1s are otherwise quite unlike the latter in cusp shape and position. These specimens also have deep pits in the valleys between cusp rows and cusps are coarsely ribbed at their bases. This suggests a taxon is present in the Cedar Mountain Formation that is distinct from *Paracimexomys* and all other known multituberculate genera.

Multituberculates from the Cedar Mountain Formation represent part of the transition from Late Jurassic to Late Cretaceous forms, and the analysis of this fauna is critical to understanding the relationships of all later multituberculates. With the possible exception of the morphologically divergent taxon mentioned above, all taxa appear to be referable to Ptilodontoidea (Cimolodonta of Simmons, 1993), which are prevalent in North American faunas of the Late Cretaceous and early Tertiary.

Mammalia: Triconodonta, Symmetrodonta, and Tribosphenida

Triconodonta: Triconodonts, most characteristic of Jurassic faunas (see Simpson, 1928, 1929; Jenkins and Crompton, 1979), are rare elements of North American Cretaceous assemblages: until recently, one species each had been described from the Trinity Group, Texas (Patterson, 1951; Slaughter, 1969); the upper Milk River Formation, Alberta (Fox, 1969, 1976); and the Cloverly Formation, Montana (Jenkins and Schaff, 1988). In this context, the presence of three species of Triconodontidae in the Mussentuchit local fauna appears somewhat surprising. Although triconodonts clearly were minor elements of North American Late Cretaceous faunas (only one species, represented by only two specimens, is known; Fox, 1969, 1976), low diversity in the Early and medial Cretaceous may simply reflect a sampling bias: recent work suggests the presence of as many as four species of triconodonts in the Cloverly Formation (Cifelli, Wible, and Jenkins, 1998). North American Cretaceous triconodontids appear to form a monophyletic clade with respect to the remainder of the family; the three species from the Mussentuchit local fauna are placed in separate genera (Cifelli and Madsen, 1998). The smallest species appears to be referable to the Aptian-Albian genus *Astroconodon*; another is congeneric with a species belonging to a genus being described from the Aptian-Albian Cloverly Formation (Cifelli, Wible, and Jenkins, 1998). The remaining species is astonishingly large (approximately equivalent in size to *Gobiconodon* from the Cloverly Formation; Jenkins and Schaff, 1988), by the standards of Mesozoic mammals, and is placed in a new, monotypic genus. The large size and presumed predaceous habits of this last species suggest that, as with the varanoid squamate noted above, it probably incorporated vertebrate prey in its diet.

Symmetrodonta: By the Cretaceous, symmetrodonts were also archaic, relictual taxa (for example, see Cassiliano and Clemens, 1979). In North America, most known taxa are referred to the Spalacotheriidae, with one species each being known from the following units:

lower Campanian Wahweap Formation (Cifelli and Madsen, 1986), Utah; the upper Milk River Formation (Fox, 1976), Alberta; Aptian-Albian Trinity Group (Patterson, 1956), Texas; Aptian-Albian Cloverly Formation, Wyoming (Cifelli, unpublished data); and Santonian John Henry Member, Straight Cliffs Formation, Utah (Eaton, 1991; Eaton and others, this volume). Two species are known from the Turonian Smoky Hollow Member, Straight Cliffs Formation, Utah (Cifelli, 1990; Eaton and others, this volume). Three species, all Spalacotheriidae, are present in the Mussentuchit local fauna: one is tentatively referred to *Symmetrodontoides* (a first occurrence of a genus that is otherwise known from the Turonian through early Campanian of Utah and the Campanian of Alberta), and a second is referable to *Spalacotheridium* (also a first occurrence; the only other record of the genus is from the Turonian of Utah). The third species of spalacotheriid is large by symmetrodont standards and may be referable to a new genus (Cifelli and Madsen, unpublished data). Small teeth of very primitive aspect, resembling those of both triconodonts and tinodontid or kuehneotheriid symmetrodonts (see Fox, 1984), are rather abundant at several sites, and are present in one jaw from OMNH V695. It is possible that these small teeth represent deciduous premolars of spalacotheriid symmetrodonts (similar teeth, though rare in occurrence, also are know from almost all other sites which have produced adult remains of spalacotheriids in North America; they are lacking from sites which have not yielded specimens of adult symmetrodonts). The abundance of these specimens suggests high juvenile mortality, delayed replacement of deciduous premolars by permanent teeth, or other, unknown factors in one or more species of Spalacotheriidae from the Mussentuchit local fauna.

Tribosphenida: Tribosphenic mammals of the Mussentuchit local fauna have not yet received detailed study. The only taxon published thus far is *Kokopellia juddi*, a marsupial-like mammal known from reasonably good material (Cifelli, 1993a). This species is probably the most abundant tribosphenic mammal in the upper part of the Cedar Mountain Formation, and new materials show that four lower incisors (perhaps the primitive count for Tribosphenida; Clemens and Lillegraven, 1986) were present. Two taxa present in the fauna appear to be bona fide marsupials, judged by the tight apposition of hypoconulid to metaconid on lower molars (see Clemens, 1979). As many as four other tribosphenic mammals of the Mussentuchit local fauna cannot be confidently allied with either Eutheria or Marsupialia, and fall into the awkwardly named category, "therians of metatherian-eutherian grade" (Patterson, 1956; see reviews by Kielan-Jaworowska and others, 1979; Cifelli, 1993b). One (see Nelson and Crooks, 1987, figure 8A) is similar to the aberrant *Picopsis*, first described from the lower Campanian Milk River Formation, Alberta (Fox, 1980), but with possible relatives known from the Turonian Smoky Hollow Member, Straight Cliffs Formation, Utah, and, perhaps, the Maastrichtian Lance Formation, Wyoming (Cifelli, 1990). If these poorly known taxa represent a divergent but phylogenetically related group of tribosphenic mammals, the Mussentichit local fauna represents the first appearance of this clade.

Two other tribosphenic mammals are similar in general appearance to Pappotheriidae, known from the Lower Cretaceous of Texas and Oklahoma (Butler, 1978; Cifelli, 1997). A final therian of metatherian-eutherian grade from the Mussentuchit local fauna is a large taxon with somewhat bulbous, inflated molars; morphologically, it is vaguely reminiscent of *Dakotadens*, from the Dakota Formation of southern Utah (Eaton, 1993; Eaton and others, this volume).

DISCUSSION AND CONCLUSIONS

As noted previously (Cifelli, Kirkland, and others, 1997), the fauna from the upper part of the "shale" member, Cedar Mountain Formation, is rather different from other known assemblages, with only about one-third of the genera surely being known from elsewhere -- a result that is predictable in view of the fact that the Mussentuchit local fauna lies within an otherwise poorly known time interval. Also unsurprisingly, almost half of the taxa represent stratigraphic range extensions. The majority of these are for taxa or groups otherwise known from the Late Cretaceous, indicating that the Mussentuchit local fauna resembles assemblages of that epoch more closely than it does those of the Early Cretaceous or older intervals. Most noteworthy of last appearances is that of the small ?brachiosaurid recorded in the fauna. Negative evidence must always be interpreted with caution, and dinosaur faunas of slightly younger age in North America are poorly known (see, for example, summary by Eaton and others, this volume). Nonetheless, it is clear that a significant "sauropod hiatus" (Lucas and Hunt, 1989) separates this occurrence from the ephemeral presence of the titanosaurid *Alamosaurus* in the latter half of the Maastrichtian of North America (Lehman, 1987). The limited evidence now available suggests that the little (possibly dwarfed) sauropod from Mussentuchit approximates the North American upper stratigraphic limit for this group of usually enormous dinosaurs that dominated the continent's faunas in the Upper Jurassic.

A brachiosaurid said to be of similar age has recently been reported from Arizona (McCord and Tegowski, 1996).

First North American or global appearances include three chondrichthyans, scapherpetontid salamanders, two lizards (including a possible relative of Helodermatidae), Serpentes, five taxa of theropods, several ornithopods, and several taxa of mammals. Of these, the most notable is Hadrosauridae, a group that was to become remarkably diverse and well-represented in Late Cretaceous faunas of North America (for example, Weishampel and Horner, 1990). Well-known earlier assemblages, such as those of the Cloverly Formation and the Trinity Group, are dominated by the basal iguanodontian *Tenontosaurus* (for example, Ostrom, 1970; D. L. Brinkman, oral communication, 1997) which, like hadrosaurs, was probably a low-level browser and possessed a sophisticated masticatory apparatus (for example, Weishampel, 1984) -- hence the paleobiological significance of this replacement among herbivores is unclear. Diversity of extremely large-bodied herbivores is rather low in the Mussentuchit local fauna, as it generally is in other mid-Cretaceous assemblages -- a situation quite different from what is encountered in the Late Jurassic and Late Cretaceous (Wing and Tiffney, 1987; Cifelli, Kirkland, and others, 1997).

Temporal distribution, phylogenetic relationships, or both are suggestive of an Asian origin for a number of the taxa appearing in the Mussentuchit local fauna, an hypothesis that is consistent with existing data based on plate tectonics and marine invertebrates (Cifelli, Kirkland, and others, 1997). Taxa with a possible Asian origin include scapherpetontid salamanders and a number of the dinosaurs, including Troodontidae, Tyrannosauridae, Hadrosauridae, and (depending on the veracity of reported Early Cretaceous occurrences in North America) Neoceratopsia. The myliobatiform cf. *Baibisha* first appears in North America: it is possible that it immigrated to Asia (as may also be the case for Hesperornithiformes, which also appear earlier in North America than they do in Asia). Other taxa in the Mussentuchit local fauna are represented by older relatives or proximate sister taxa in Europe or Africa (*Coniophis*, Pachycephalosauria, Hesperornithiformes), highlighting the complexity of global biogeography in the Cretaceous.

ACKNOWLEDGMENTS

We are most grateful to Michael Nelson for his generosity in making his localities and fossils available to us for study, and to D. L. Brinkman and D. A. Winkler for providing helpful review comments on an earlier version of the manuscript. Our thanks go also to the Judd family of Castle Dale, Utah, for their unwavering help with so many aspects of field work; to E. M. Larson, E. Miller, K. S. Smith, and other individuals too numerous to mention for help in the field and lab; and to Tom Rasmussen for the continuing cooperation of the U.S. BLM. For access to specimens we thank J. Bolt and W. F. Simpson (Field Museum of Natural History). JIK is grateful to D. Burge (College of Eastern Utah Prehistoric Museum) and R. and C. Jones for cooperation in field activities. Figure 1 was drafted by Coral McCallister, and K. S. Smith supplied the photographs reproduced herein. Partial funding for support of this research was provided by the National Geographic Society (grants 4761-91 and 5021-92 to RLC; 5263-94 to JIK) and the National Science Foundation (grants BSR 8906992 and DEB 9401094 to RLC); RLN acknowledges financial support from Sigma Xi, the American Federation of Mineralogical Societies, the Graduate Student Senate of the University of Oklahoma, and the Department of Zoology of the University of Oklahoma. JDG's part in this study has been supported by a Field Museum of Natural History Visiting Scholar Grant, a University of Alberta Ph.D. Dissertation Fellowship, and N. J. Marklund.

REFERENCES

Albino, A. M., 1996, The South American fossil Squamata (Reptilia: Lepidosauria): Münchner Geowissenschaftliche Abhandlungen A, v. 30, no. 1, p. 185-202.

Archibald, J. D., 1982, A study of Mammalia and geology across the Cretaceous-Tertiary boundary in Garfield County, Montana: University of California Publications in Geological Sciences, v. 122, p. 1-286.

Armstrong-Zeigler, J. G., 1980, Amphibia and Reptilia from the Campanian of New Mexico: Fieldiana Geology, new series, v. 4, p. 1-39.

Bodily, N. M., 1969, An armored dinosaur from the Lower Cretaceous of Utah: Brigham Young University Geological Studies, v. 16, p. 35-60.

Britt, B. B., and Stadtman, K. L., 1996, The Early Cretaceous Dalton Wells dinosaur fauna and the earliest North American titanosaurid sauropod, *in* Abstracts with Program, 56th Annual Meeting, Society of Vertebrate Paleontology, New York: Journal of Vertebrate Paleontology, v. 16, supplement to no. 3, p. 24A.

Brinkman, D. B., and Nicholls, E. L., 1991, Upper Cretaceous nonmarine turtle assemblages from western Canada, *in* Program and Abstracts, Canadian Paleontology Conference I and Pander Society Meeting: Vancouver, University of British Columbia, p. 19.

Broschinski, Annette, and Sigogneau-Russell, Denise, 1996, Remarkable lizard remains from the Lower Cretaceous of Anoual (Morocco): Annales de Paléontologie, v. 82, p. 147-175.

Bryant, L. J., 1987, A new genus and species of Amiidae (Holostei; Osteichthyes) from the Late Cretaceous of North America, with comments on the phylogeny of the Amiidae: Journal of Vertebrate Paleontology, v. 7, p. 349-361.

Buffetaut, Eric, and Ford, R. L. E., 1979, The crocodilian *Bernissartia* in the Wealden of the Island of Wight: Palaeontology, v. 22, p. 905-912.

Buffetaut, Eric, Suteethorn, Varavudh, and Tong, Haiyan, 1996, The earliest known tyrannosaur from the Lower Cretaceous of Thailand: Nature, v. 381, p. 689-691.

Butler, P. M., 1978, A new interpretation of the mammalian teeth of tribosphenic pattern from the Albian of Texas: Breviora, Museum of Comparative Zoology, no. 446, p. 1-27.

Caldwell, M. W., Carroll, R. L., and Kaiser, Hinrich, 1995, The pectoral girdle and forelimb of *Carsosaurus marchesetti* (Aigialosauridae), with a preliminary phylogenetic analysis of mosasauroids and varanoids: Journal of Vertebrate Paleontology, v. 15, p. 516-531.

Carroll, R. L., and deBraga, Michael, 1992, *Aigialosaurs*--mid-Cretaceous varanoid lizards: Journal of Vertebrate Paleontology, v. 12, p. 66-86.

Cassiliano, M. L., and Clemens, W. A., Jr., Symmetrodonta, *in* Lillegraven, J. A., Kielan- Jaworowska, Zofia, and Clemens, W. A., Jr., editors, Mesozoic mammals-- the first two-thirds of mammalian history: Berkeley, University of California Press, p. 150-161.

Cifelli, R. L., 1990, Cretaceous mammals of southern Utah. III. Therian mammals from the Turonian: Journal of Vertebrate Paleontology, v. 10, p. 332-345.

—1993a, Early Cretaceous mammal from North America and the evolution of marsupial dental characters: Proceedings, National Academy of Sciences, USA, v. 90, p. 9413-9416.

—1993b, Theria of metatherian-eutherian grade and the origin of marsupials, *in* Szalay, F. S., Novacek, M. J., and McKenna, M. C., editors, Mammal phylogeny, volume 1. Mesozoic differentiation, multituberculates, monotremes, early therians, and marsupials: New York, Springer-Verlag, p. 205-215.

—1997, First notice on Mesozoic mammals from Oklahoma: Oklahoma Geology Notes, v. 57, p. 4-17.

Cifelli, R. L., Gardner, J. D., Nydam, R. L., and Brinkman, D. L., 1997, Additions to the vertebrate fauna of the Antlers Formation (Lower Cretaceous), southeastern Oklahoma: Oklahoma Geology Notes, v. 57, p. 124-131.

Cifelli, R. L., Kirkland, J. I., Weil, Anne, Deino, A. L., and Kowallis, B. J., 1997, High-precision $^{40}Ar/^{39}Ar$ geochronology and the advent of North America's Late Cretaceous terrestrial fauna: Proceedings, National Acadademy of Sciences USA, v. 94, p. 11163-11167.

Cifelli, R. L., and Madsen, S. K., 1986, An Upper Cretaceous symmetrodont (Mammalia) from southern Utah: Journal of Vertebrate Paleontology, v. 6, p. 258-263.

—1998, Triconodont mammals from the medial Cretaceous of Utah: Journal of Vertebrate Paleontology, v. 18, p. 403-411.

Cifelli, R. L., and Muizon, Christian de, 1997, Dentition and jaw of *Kokopellia juddi*, a primitive marsupial or near-marsupial from the medial Cretaceous of Utah: Journal of Mammalian Evolution, v. 4, p. 241-258.

Cifelli, R. L., Madsen, S. K., and Larson, E. M., 1996, Screenwashing and associated recovery techniques for the recovery of microvertebrate fossils: Oklahoma Geological Survey Special Publication no. 96-4, p. 1-24.

Cifelli, R. L., and Nydam, R. L., 1995, Primitive, helodermatid-like platynotan from the Early Cretaceous of Utah: Herpetologica, v. 51, p. 286-291.

Cifelli, R. L., Wible, J. R., and Jenkins, F. A., Jr., 1998, Triconodont mammals from the Cloverly Formation (Lower Cretaceous) of Montana and Wyoming: Journal of Vertebrate Paleontology, v. 18, p. 237-241.

Clemens, W. A., Jr., 1979, Marsupialia, *in* Lillegraven, J. A., Kielan-Jaworowska, Zofia, and Clemens, W. A., Jr., editors, Mesozoic mammals--the first two-thirds of mammalian history: Berkeley, University of California Press, p. 192-220.

Clemens, W. A., Jr., and Lillegraven, J. A., 1986, New Late Cretaceous, North American advanced therian mammals that fit neither the marsupial nor eutherian molds: Contributions to Geology, University of Wyoming, Special Paper no. 3, p. 55-85.

Decourten, F. L., 1991, New data on Early Cretaceous dinosaurs from the Long Walk Quarry and tracksite, Emery County, Utah: Utah Geological Association Publication no. 19, p. 311-324.

Denton, R. K., and O'Neill, R. C., 1995, *Prototeius stageri*, gen. et sp. nov., a new teiid lizard from the Upper Cretaceous Marshalltown Formation of New Jersey, with a preliminary phylogenetic revision of the Teiidae: Journal of Vertebrate Paleontology, v. 15, p. 235-253.

Duellman, W. E., and Trueb, Linda, 1986, Biology of amphibians: New York, McGraw-Hill Inc., 670 p.

Eaton, J. G., 1991, Biostratigraphic framework for Upper Cretaceous rocks of the Kaiparowits Plateau, southern Utah, *in* Nations, J. D., and Eaton, J. G., editors, Stratigraphy, depositional environments, and sedimentary tectonics of the western margin, Cretaceous Western Interior Seaway: Geological Society of America, Special Paper no. 260, p. 47-63.

—1993, Therian mammals from the Cenomanian (Upper Cretaceous) Dakota Formation, southwestern Utah: Journal of Vertebrate Paleontology, v. 13, p. 105-124.

Eaton, J. G., Kirkland, J. I., and Kauffman, E. G., 1990, Evidence and dating of mid-Cretaceous tectonic activity in the San Rafael Swell, Emery County, Utah: Mountain Geologist, v. 27, p. 39-45.

Eaton, J. G., and Nelson, M. E., 1991, Multituberculate mammals from the Lower Cretaceous Cedar Mountain Formation, San Rafael Swell, Utah: Contributions to Geology, University of Wyoming, v. 29, p. 1-12.

Estes, Richard, 1964, Fossil vertebrates from the Late Cretaceous Lance Formation, eastern Wyoming: University of California Publications in Geology, v. 49, p. 1-180.

—1965, A new fossil salamander from Montana and Wyoming: Copeia, v. 1965, no. 1, p. 90-95.

—1969a, The Batrachosauroididae and Scapherpetontidae, Late Cretaceous and Early Cenozoic salamanders: Copeia, v. 1969, no. 2, p. 225-234.

—1969b, Prosirenidae, a new family of fossil salamanders: Nature, v. 224, p. 87-88.

---1969c, Relationships of two Cretaceous lizards (Sauria, Teiidae): Breviora, no. 328, p. 1-8.

—1981, Gymnophiona, Caudata--handbuch der paläoherpetologie, part 2: Stuttgart, Gustav Fischer Verlag, 115 p.

—1983, Sauria terrestria, Amphisbania--handbuch der paläoherpetologie, Part 10A: Stuttgart, Gustav Fischer Verlag, 249 p.

Estes, Richard, and Berberian, Paul, 1970, Paleoecology of a Late Cretaceous vertebrate community from Montana: Breviora, no. 343, p. 1-35.

Estes Richard, Berberian, Paul, and Meszoely, C. A. M., 1969, Lower vertebrates from the Late Cretaceous Hell Creek Formation, McCone County, Montana: Breviora, no. 337, p. 1-33.

Estes, R., Quieroz, Kevin de, and Gauthier, Jacques, 1988, Phylogenetic relationships within Squamata, *in* Estes, Richard, and Pregill, Gregory, editors, Phylogenetic relationships of the lizard families: Stanford, Stanford University Press, p. 119-281.

Feduccia, Alan, 1996, The origin and evolution of birds: New Haven, Yale University Press, 420 p.

Fejéráry, Baron G. J. de, 1918, Contributions to a monograph on fossil Varanidae and on Megalanidae: Annales Historico-Naturales Musei Nationales Hungarici, v. 16, p. 341-467.

—1935, Further contributions to a monograph on the Megalanidae and fossil Varanidae--with notes on Recent varanines: Annales Historico-Naturales Musei Nationales Hungarici, v. 29, p. 1-130.

Fox, R. C., 1969, Studies of Late Cretaceous vertebrates III--a triconodont mammal from Alberta: Canadian Journal of Zoology, v. 47, p. 1253-1256.

—1974, A middle Campanian, nonmarine occurrence of the Cretaceous toothed bird *Hesperornis*: Canadian Journal of Earth Sciences, v. 11, p. 1335-1338.

—1976, Additions to the mammalian local fauna from the upper Milk River Formation (Upper Cretaceous), Alberta: Canadian Journal of Earth Sciences, v. 13, p. 1105-1118

—1980, *Picopsis pattersoni*, n. gen. and sp., an unusual therian from the Upper Cretaceous of Alberta, and the classification of primitive tribosphenic mammals: Canadian Journal of Earth Sciences, v. 17, p. 1489-1498.

—1984, A primitive, "obtuse-angled" symmetrodont (Mammalia) from the Upper Cretaceous of Alberta: Canadian Journal of Earth Sciences, v. 21, p. 1204-1207.

Fox, R. C., and Naylor, B. G., 1982, A reconsideration of the relationships of the fossil amphibian *Albanerpeton*: Canadian Journal of Earth Sciences, v. 19, no. 1, p. 118-128.

Galton, P. M., 1971, A primitive dome-headed dinosaur (Ornithischia: Pachycephalosauridae) from the Lower Cretaceous of England, and the function of the dome in pachycephalosaurids: Journal of Paleontology, v. 45, p. 40-47.

Galton, P. M., and Jensen, J. A., 1979, Remains of ornithopod dinosaurs from the Lower Cretaceous of North America: Brigham Young University Geological Studies, v. 25, p. 1-10.

Gao, Keqin, and Fox, R. C., 1991, New teiid lizards from the upper Cretaceous Oldman Formation (Judithian) of southwestern Alberta, Canada, with a review of the Cretaceous record of teiids: Annals of the Carnegie Museum, v. 60, p. 145-162.

—1996, Taxonomy and evolution of Late Cretaceous lizards (Reptilia: Squamata) from western Canada: Bulletin of the Carnegie Museum of Natural History, v. 33, p. 1-107.

Gardner, J. D., 1994, Amphibians from the Lower Cretaceous (Albian) Cedar Mountain Formation, Emery County, Utah: Journal of Vertebrate Paleontology, v. 14, supplement to no. 3, p. 26A.

—1995, Lower Cretaceous anurans from Texas and Utah: Journal of Vertebrate Paleontology, v. 15, supplement to no. 3, p. 31A.

Gardner, J. D., and Cifelli, R. L., 1999, A primitive snake from the mid-Cretaceous of Utah, U.S.A.-- the geologically oldest snake from the New World: Special Papers in Palaeontology, v. 60, p. 87-100.

Gauthier, J. A., 1982, Fossil xenosaurid and anguid lizards from the early Eocene Wasatch Formation, southeast Wyoming, and a revision of the Anguioidea: Contributions to Geology, University of Wyoming, v. 21, p. 7-54.

Gilmore, C. W., 1921, The fauna of the Arundel Formation of Maryland: Proceedings of the U. S. National Museum, v. 59, p. 581-594.

—1933, On the dinosaurian fauna of the Iren Dabasu Formation: Bulletin of the American Museum of Natural History, v. 67, p. 23-78.

—1942, Osteology of *Polyglyphanodon*, an Upper Cretaceous lizard from Utah: Proceedings of the U. S. National Museum, v. 92, p. 229-265.

—1943, Osteology of Upper Cretaceous lizards from Utah, with a description of a new species: Proceedings of the U. S. National Museum, v. 93, p. 209-214.

—1946, Reptilian fauna of the North Horn Formation of central Utah: U.S. Geological Survey Professional Papers, no. 210-C, p. 29-53.

Gradstein, F. M., Agterberg, F. P., Ogg, J. G., Hardenbol, Jan, Van Veen, Paul, Thierry, Jacques, and Zehui, Huang, 1995, A Triassic, Jurassic and Cretaceous time scale, *in* Berggren, W. A., Kent, D. V., Aubry, M.-P., and Hardenbol, Jan, editors, Geochronology, time scales and global stratigraphic correlation: SEPM (Society for Sedimentary Geology) Special Publication no. 54, Tulsa, p. 95-126.

Grande, Lance, 1996, Using the extant *Amia calva* to test the monophyly of Mesozoic groups of fishes, *in* Arratia, Gloria, and Viohl, Günter, editors, Mesozoic fishes--systematics and paleoecology: München, Verlag Dr. Friedrich Pfeil, p. 181-189.

Gubin, Y. M., 1993, Cretaceous tailless amphibians from Mongolia: Paleontological Journal, v. 17, no. 1, p. 63-69.

—1996, First find of a pelobatid (Anura) from the Paleogene of Mongolia: Paleontologicheskii Zhurnal, v. 30, no. 5. p. 571-574.

Hale, L. A., and Van de Graaf, F. R., 1964, Cretaceous stratigraphy and facies patterns--northeastern Utah and adjacent areas, *in* Sabatka, E. F., editor, Geology and mineral resources of the Uinta Basin: Guidebook of the Intermountain Association of Petroleum Geologists, 13th Annual Field Conference, p. 115-138.

Harris, D. R., 1980, Exhumed paleochannels in the Lower Cretaceous Cedar Mountain Formation near Green River, Utah: Brigham Young University Geology Studies, v. 27, p. 51-66.

Hay, O. P., 1908, The fossil turtles of North America: Carnegie Institute of Washington, Publication no. 75, 568 p.

Hirsch, K. F., and Quinn, Betty, 1990, Eggs and eggshell fragments from the Upper Cretaceous Two Medicine Formation of Montana: Journal of Vertebrate Paleontology, v. 10, p. 491-511.

Jacobs, L. L., Winkler, D. A., and Murry, P. A., 1991, On the age and correlation of the Trinity mammals, Early Cretaceous of Texas, USA: Newsletters on Stratigraphy, v. 24, p. 35-43.

Jenkins, F. A., Jr., and Crompton, A. W., 1979, Triconodonta, *in* Lillegraven, J. A., Kielan- Jaworowska, Zophia, and Clemens, W. A., Jr., editors, Mesozoic mammals--the first two-thirds of mammalian history: Berkeley, University of California Press, p. 74-90.

Jenkins, F. A., Jr., and Schaff, C. R., 1988, The Early Cretaceous mammal *Gobiconodon* (Mammalia, Triconodonta) from the Cloverly Formation in Montana: Journal of Vertebrate Paleontology, v. 8, p. 1-24.

Jensen, J. A., 1970, Fossil eggs in the Lower Cretaceous of Utah: Brigham Young University Geology Studies, v. 17, p. 51-65.

Katich, P. J., 1951, Recent evidence for Lower Cretaceous deposits in Colorado Plateau: Bulletin of the American Association of Petroleum Geologists, v. 35, p. 2093-2094.

Kielan-Jaworowska, Zofia, Eaton, J. G., and Bown, T. M., 1979, Theria of metatherian-eutherian grade, *in* Lillegraven, J. A., Kielan-Jaworowska, Zofia, and Clemens, W. A., Jr., editors, Mesozoic mammals--the first two-thirds of mammalian history: Berkeley, University of California Press, p. 182-191.

Kirkland, J. I., 1987, Upper Jurassic and Cretaceous lungfish tooth plates from the Western Interior, the last dipnoan faunas of North America: Hunteria, v. 2, no. 2, 16 p.

—1994, A large primitive hadrosaur from the Lower Cretaceous of Utah: Journal of Vertebrate Paleontology, v. 14, supplement to no. 3, p. 32A.

—1996, Biogeography of western North America's mid-Cretaceous dinosaur faunas--losing European ties and the first great Asian-North American interchange: Journal of Vertebrate Paleontology, v. 16, supplement to no.3, p. 45A.

—1998, Morrison fishes, *in* Carpenter, Kenneth, Chure, D. J., and Kirkland, J. I., editors, The Upper Jurassic Morrison Formation--an interdisciplinary study: Modern Geology, v. 22, part 1, p. 503-533.

Kirkland, J. I., Burge, Donald, and Gaston, Robert, 1993, A large dromaeosaur (Theropoda) from the Lower Cretaceous of eastern Utah: Hunteria, v. 2, no. 10, p. 1-16.

Kowallis, B. J., Heaton, J. S., and Bringhurst, Kelly, 1986, Fission-track dating of volcanically-derived sedimentary rocks: Geology, v. 14, p. 19-22.

Kranz, P. M., 1996, Notes on the sedimentary iron ores of Maryland and their dinosaurian fauna, *in* Brezinski, D. K., and Reger, J. P., editors, Studies in Maryland paleontology in commemoration of the centennial of the Maryland Geological Survey: Maryland Geological Survey, Special Publication no. 3, p. 87-115.

Kurochkin, E. N., 1995, The assemblage of the Cretaceous birds in Asia, *in* Ailing Sun and Yuanqing Wang, editors, Sixth symposium on Mesozoic terrestrial ecosystems: Beijing, China Ocean Press, p. 203-208.

Langston, Wann, Jr., 1974, Nonmammalian Comanchean tetrapods: Geoscience and Man, v. 8, p. 77-102.

Lee, Y.-N., 1996, A new nodosaurid ankylosaur (Dinosauria: Ornithischia) from the Paw Paw Formation (late Albian) of Texas: Journal of Vertebrate Paleontology, v. 16, p. 232-245.

Lehman, T. M., 1987, Late Maastrichtian paleoenvironments and dinosaur biogeography in the western interior of North America: Palaeogeography, Palaeoclimatology, Palaeoecology, v. 60, p. 189-217.

Lucas, S. G., and Hunt, A. P., 1989, *Alamosaurus* and the sauropod hiatus in the Cretaceous of the North American Western Interior, *in* Farlow, J. O., editor, Paleobiology of the dinosaurs: Geological Society of America Special Paper, no. 238, p. 75-86.

Lull, R. S., 1911, The reptilian fauna of the Arundel Formation; systematic paleontology of the Lower Cretaceous deposits of Maryland: Maryland Geological Survey, Lower Cretaceous Volume, p. 174-178, 183-211.

Madsen, S. K., 1996, Some techniques and procedures for microvertebrate preparation: Oklahoma Geological Survey, Special Publication no. 96-4, p. 25-36.

Mateer, N. J., Lucas, S. G., and Hunt, A. P., 1992, Nonmarine Jurassic-Cretaceous boundary in western North America, *in* Mateer, N. J., and Chen, Pei-Ji, editors, Aspects of nonmarine Cretaceous geology: Beijing, China Ocean Press, p. 15-30.

McCord, R. D., III, and Tegowski, B. J., 1996, Mesozoic vertebrates of Arizona. II. Cretaceous, *in* Fossils of Arizona, v. 4: 1996 Proceedings of the Southwest Paleontological Society and Mesa Southwest Museum, Mesa, p. 45-54.

McGowan, Chris, and Evans, S. E., 1995, Albanerpetontid amphibians from the Cretaceous of Spain: Nature, v. 373, p. 143-145.

Naylor, B. G., 1983, New salamander (Amphibia: Caudata) atlantes from the Upper Cretaceous of North America: Journal of Paleontology, v. 57, no. 1, p. 48-52.

Naylor, B. G., and Krause, D. W., 1981, *Piceoerpeton*, a giant Early Tertiary salamander from western North America: Journal of Paleontology, v. 55, no. 3, p. 507-523.

Nelson, M. E., and Crooks, D. M., 1987, Stratigraphy and paleontology of the Cedar Mountain Formation (Lower Cretaceous), eastern Emery County, Utah, *in* Paleontology of the Dinosaur Triangle--guidebook for 1987 field trip: Grand Junction, Museum of Western Colorado, p. 55-63.

Nessov, L. A., 1981, Cretaceous salamanders and frogs of Kizylkum Desert [In Russian]: Trudy Zoologicheskogo Instituta, Akademiya Nauk SSSR, v. 101, p. 57-88.

—1988, Late Mesozoic amphibians and lizards of Soviet Middle Asia: Acta Zoologica Cracoviensia, v. 31, no. 14, p. 475-486.

Nessov, L. A., Sigogneau-Russell, Denise, and Russell, D. E., 1994, A survey of Cretaceous tribosphenic mammals from middle Asia (Uzbekistan, Kazakhstan and Tadjikistan), of their geological setting, age and faunal environment: Palaeovertebrata, v. 23, p. 51-92.

Nichols, D. J., and Sweet, A. R., 1993, Biostratigraphy of Upper Cretaceous non-marine palynofloras in a north-south transect of the Western Interior Basin, *in* Caldwell, W. G. E., and Kauffman, E. G., editors, Evolution of the Western Interior Basin: Geological Association of Canada Special Paper no. 39, p. 539-584.

Nursall, R. J., 1996a, Distribution and ecology of pycnodont fishes, *in* Arratia, Gloria, and Viohl, Günter, editors, Mesozoic Fishes--Systematics and Paleoecology: München, Verlag Dr. Friedrich Pfeil, p. 115-124.

—1996b, The phylogeny of pycnodont fishes, *in* Arratia, Gloria, and Viohl, Günter, editors, Mesozoic fishes--systematics and paleoecology: München, Verlag Dr. Friedrich Pfeil, p. 125- 152.

Nydam, R. L., 1995, Lizards from the Early Cretaceous of central Utah: Journal of Vertebrate Paleontology, v. 15, supplement to no. 3, p. 47A.

Obradovich, J. D., 1993, A Cretaceous time scale, *in* Caldwell, W. G. E., and Kauffman, E. G., editors, Evolution of the Western Interior Basin: Geological Association of Canada Special Paper no. 39, p. 379-396.

Ostrom, J. H., 1970, Stratigraphy and paleontology of the Cloverly Formation (Lower Cretaceous) of the Bighorn Basin area, Wyoming and Montana: Peabody Museum of Natural History, Bulletin, v. 35, p. 1-234.

Patterson, Bryan, 1951, Early Cretaceous mammals from northern Texas: American Journal of Science, v. 249, p. 31-46.

—1956, Early Cretaceous mammals and the evolution of mammalian molar teeth: Fieldiana, Geology, v. 13, p. 1-105.

Pomes, M. L., 1988, Stratigraphy, paleontology, and paleobiogeography of lower vertebrates from the Cedar Mountain Formation (Lower Cretaceous), Emery County, Utah: Hays, Kansas, Fort Hays State University, M. S. thesis, 87 p.

Rage, J.-C., 1984, Serpentes, *in* Wellnhofer, Peter, editor, Encyclopedia of paleoherpetology: Stuttgart, Gustav Fischer Verlag, Part 11, p. 1-80.

—1987, Fossil history, *in* Seigel, R. A., Collins, J. T., and Novak, S. S., editors, Snakes-- ecology and evolutionary biology: New York, McGraw-Hill Inc., p. 51-76.

—1988, Le gisement du Bretou (Phosphorites du Quercy, Tarn-et-Garonne, France) et sa faune de vertébrés de l'Eocène supérieur I-- amphibiens et reptiles: Palaeontographica Abt. A, v. 205, no.

1-6, p. 3-27.

Retallack, G. J., 1988, Field recognition of paleosols, *in* Reinhart, Juergen, and Sigleo, W. R., editors, paleosols and weathering through geologic time--principles and applications: Geological Society of America, Special Paper no. 216, p. 1-20.

Roĉek Zbynék, and Nessov, L. A., 1993, Cretaceous anurans from central Asia: Palaeontographica Abt. A, v. 226, no. 1-3, p. 1-54.

Rowe, T. B., Cifelli, R. L., Lehman, T. M., and Weil, Anne, 1992, The Campanian Terlingua local fauna, with a summary of other vertebrates from the Aguja Formation, trans-Pecos Texas: Journal of Vertebrate Paleontology, v. 12, p. 472-493.

Savage, D. E., and Russell, D. E., 1983, Mammalian paleofaunas of the World: London, Addison-Wesley Publishing Company, 432 p.

Scott, R. W., 1987, The bivalve *Musculiopsis* MacNeil in Lower Cretaceous non-marine strata, Rocky Mountains: Contributions to Geology, University of Wyoming, v. 25, p. 29-33.

Simmons, N. B., 1993, Phylogeny of Multituberculata, *in* Szalay, F. S., Novacek, M. J., and McKenna, M. C., editors, Mammal phylogeny, volume 1--Mesozoic differentiation, multituberculates, monotremes, early therians, and marsupials: New York, Springer-Verlag, p. 146-164.

Simpson, G. G., 1928, A Catalogue of the Mesozoic Mammalia in the Geological Department of the British Museum: British Museum (Natural History), London, 215 p.

—1929, American Mesozoic Mammalia: Memoirs of the Peabody Museum of Natural History, v. 3, 235 p.

Slaughter, Bob, 1969, *Astroconodon*, the Cretaceous triconodont: Journal of Mammalogy, v. 50, p. 102-107.

Stokes, W. L., 1944, Morrison Formation and related deposits in and adjacent to the Colorado Plateau: Bulletin of the Geological Society of America, v. 55, p. 951-992.

—1952, Lower Cretaceous in Colorado Plateau: GSA Bulletin, v. 36, p. 1766-1776.

Stokes, W. L., and Phoenix, D. A., 1948, Geology of the Egnar-Gypsum Valley area, San Miguel and Montrose Counties, Colorado: U. S. Geological Survey Oil and Gas Investigations Preliminary Map 93.

Sues, H.-D., 1980, Anatomy and relationships of a new hysilophodont dinosaur from the Lower Cretaceous of North America: Palaeontographica, Abt. A, v. 169, p. 51-72.

Sulimski, A., 1975, Macrocephalosauridae and Polyglyphanodontidae (Sauria) from the Late Cretaceous of Mongolia: Palaeontologica Polonica, v. 33, p. 25-102.

Thayne, G. F., Tidwell, W. D., and Stokes, W. L., 1983, Flora of the Cretaceous Cedar Mountain Formation of Utah and Colorado, part I-- *Paraphyllanthoxylon utahense*: Great Basin Naturalist, v. 43, p. 394-402.

—1985, Flora of the Cretaceous Cedar Mountain Formation of Utah and Colorado, part III-- *Icacinoxylon pittiense*, n. sp.: American Journal of Botany, v. 72, p. 175-181.

Thurmond, J. T., 1974, Lower vertebrate faunas of the Trinity Division in north-central Texas: Geoscience and Man, v. 8, p. 103-129.

Tschudy, R. H., Tschudy, B. D., and Craig, L. C., 1984, Palynological evaluation of the Cedar Mountain and Burro Canyon formations, Colorado Plateau: U.S. Geological Survey Professional Paper no. 1281, 21 p.

Unwin, D. M., 1993, Aves, *in* Benton, M. J., editor, The fossil record 2: London, Chapman and Hall, p. 717-737.

Weishampel, D. B., 1984, Evolution of jaw mechanisms in ornithopod dinosaurs: Advances in Anatomy, Embryology and Cell Biology, v. 87, p. 1-110.

—1990, New ornithischian dinosaur material from the Wayan Formation (Lower Cretaceous) of eastern Idaho: Journal of Vertebrate Paleontology, v. 10, supplement to no. 3, p. 48A.

Weishampel, D. B., and Horner, J. R., 1990, Hadrosauridae, *in* Weishampel, D. B., Dodson, Peter, and Osmólska, Halszka, editors, The Dinosauria: Berkeley, University of California Press, p. 534-561.

Wilson, M. V. H., and Chalifa, Yael, 1989, Fossil marine actinopterygian fishes from the Kaskapau Formation (Upper Cretaceous: Turonian) near Watino, Alberta: Canadian Journal of Earth Sciences, v. 26, p. 2604-2620.

Wing, S. L., and Tiffney, B. H., 1987, The reciprocal interaction of angiosperm evolution and tetrapod herbivory: Review of Palaeobotany and Palynology, v. 50, p. 179-210.

Winkler, D. A., Murry, P. A., and Jacobs, L. L., 1990, Early Cretaceous (Comanchean) vertebrates of central Texas: Journal of Vertebrate Paleontology, v. 10, p. 95-116.

Woodburne, M. O., editor, 1987, Cenozoic mammals of North America--geochronology and biostratigraphy: Berkeley, University of California Press, 336 p.

Young, R. G., 1960, Dakota Group of Colorado Plateau: Bulletin of the American Association of Petroleum Geologists, v. 44, p. 156-194.

APPENDIX: MEASURED SECTIONS

The three measured sections described below all lie in the immediate area of Mussentuchit Wash; see figure 1 for approximate locations and figure 2 for graphic depiction of sections. Classification of pedogenic calcretes and caliches is based on Retallack's (1988, p. 16) "Stages of carbonate accumulation in paleosols." Color descriptions are subjective.

The Cedar Mountain Formation in this area was deposited in three distinct environmental regimes: the first is the fluvial depositional environment that produced the basal Buckhorn Conglomerate (unit 1 in Section A, units 1 and 2 in Section B, and unit 1 in Section C). Above the Buckhorn Conglomerate, however, the prevalence of carbonate nodules and cemented carbonate horizons suggests that paleosols formed in a semi-arid environment make up the lower part of the Cedar Mountain Formation (units 2-18 in Section A, units 3-7 in Section B, and units 2-4 in Section C). In contrast, the presence of sand lenses, channel sands, carbonaceous shale and apparently floodplain-derived fossil deposits in the upper part of the formation, which completely lacks carbonate nodules, indicates a substantial environmental shift toward a wetter, more fluvially influenced depositional regime.

Section A: (Measured on S-facing slope; includes OMNH localities V235, 694, 695, 794)

Unit	Section Height	Description	Thickness
31	56-57 m	Siltstone, sandy, rapidly grading to resistant, medium-grained sandstone of the Dakota Formation.	1.0 m
30	55-56 m	Mudstone, clayey, light grey, small sand channels. Sandstone fine to medium grain size with some large mud rip-up clasts, chunks of carbonized wood.	1.0 m
29	54.5-55 m	Carbonaceous shale, plant hash, mud stringers, some sulfur and secondary gypsum present, weathers brown to purple.	0.5 m
28	53.4-54.5 m	Siltstone, grey, very sandy.	1.1 m
27	52.8-53.4 m	Sandstone, fine grained, grey.	0.6 m
26	43.3-52.8 m	Mudstone, light grey to greenish grey, weathered more than a meter into the slope in places. At about 47 m some iron staining, mudstone darker.	9.5 m
25	43-43.3 m	Sandy siltstone to fine sandstone, plant hash and carbonized wood common, mud clasts about 1 cm in diameter near the top of the interval.	0.3 m
24	41.7-43 m	Siltstone, light grey, with some very thin, discontinuous, non-resistant sandstone.	1.3 m
23	41-41.7 m	Level of OMNH localities V235, V240, V794. This horizon is variably fossiliferous along the outcrop. V235 was not exposed, so thickness of the productive layer was not measured. The productive layer at V240 and V794 is 60-70 cm thick, grey, silty, with plant debris, small bone fragments, and teeth.	0.7 m
22	37.73-41 m	Siltstone, light grey, with very thin, discontinuous, non-resistant sandstone.	3.27 m
21	37.7-37.73 m	Ash, occurs above bone at OMNH V695.	0.03 m
20	37-37.7 m	Siltstone, light grey, with very thin, discontinuous, non-resistant sandstone.	0.7 m
19	36.2-37 m	Sandstone, fine grained, color grey weathering brown to brownish red, thickness variable 30-70 cm. Variably resistant, a channel sand with low-angle tabular cross-bedding, continuous across the outcrop, holds up a slope break between light grey and dark grey mudstone, with mud weathered over it in places. 36.7 m: OMNH V695 quarry bottom.	0.8 m
18	28.6-36.2 m	Mudstone, grey with dark brown veining at about 32.5 m, no nodules, smooth pebbles of up to 1 cm diameter size on surface, but none found in place.	7.6 m
17	28.5-28.6 m	Mudstone, with yellow round and ovoid carbonate nodules of golfball to baseball size and stained yellow (Stage II carbonate accumulation).	0.1 m

Unit	Section Height	Description	Thickness
16	25.8- 28.5 m	Mudstone, grey and greenish grey with orange staining, varying silt content, no nodules, no bedding.	2.7 m
15	23.75-25.8 m	Mudstone with scattered carbonate nodules (Stage II carbonate accumulation).	3.0 m
14	23.75 m	Calcrete: a layer of large ovoid nodules, with cement in some places forming a continuous horizon (Stage III carbonate accumulation).	0.05 m
13	13.2-23.75 m	Mudstone, greenish grey and grey weathering to light grey. Caliche nodules (Stage II carbonate accumulation) of varying shapes, sizes, and colors throughout the interval: at 13.2 m a layer with ovoid nodules of yellow color measuring about 14 cm x 10 cm x 3 cm. Above this nodules are smaller and scattered. At 14.5 m nodules are similarly large and ovoid, weathering to reddish brown or yellowish brown where exposed. Between 14.5 m and about 18 m nodules are scattered, round or ovoid, 5-10 cm in diameter, and mixed with rounded smooth pebbles. Fewer nodules occur in the 18-18.5 m interval. They are again very numerous at 18.5 m, but decrease in size toward the top of the interval.	10.55 m
12	9-13.2 m	Mudstone, light grey with limonitic staining. Slopes covered with fragmentary nodules, probably from upsection.	4.1 m
11	9 m	Mudstone, including a layer of caliche nodules that are round and up to 10 cm in diameter (Stage II carbonate accumulation).	0.1 m
10	7.65-9 m	Mudstone, color grey-green.	1.35 m
9	7.5-7.65 m	Calcrete: Stage IV carbonate accumulation, hard, resistant, white, weathering into nodules. Appears to be a sandstone from a distance.	0.15 m
8	5.6-7.5 m	Mudstone, becoming more greenish in color higher in the interval. Abundant caliche: nodules small pebble-sized at the base, increasing to golf ball size. At 7 m there is a thin horizon in which carbonate cements the silt and mudstone (Stage III carbonate accumulation). Above this horizon there is more mudstone with large nodules.	1.9 m
7	5.4-5.6 m	Sandstone, fine to medium grained, buff color weathering to reddish brown, variable thickness and probably discontinuous, erosive base.	0.2 m
6	3.85-5.4 m	Mudstone.	1.55
5	3.75-3.85 m	Sandstone, fine grained with hard carbonate cement, not resistant.	0.1 m
4	2.6-3.75 m	Fine siltstone or mudstone, deeply weathered, buff color.	1.15 m
3	2.5-2.6 m	Sandstone, medium grainsize, thin and discontinuous, grey color, flaky weathering, trough cross-beds.	0.1 m
2	1.1-2.5 m	Siltstone, heavily weathered.	1.4 m
1	0-1.1 m	Sandstone, fine to medium grain size, thickness variable to maximum of approximately 3 m, grey color weathering buff, channels with cross-beds. Resistant, forming ledges between surrounding silts.	1.1 m

Section B (Measured through OMNH V824)

Unit	Section Height	Description	Thickness
16	31 m	Base of resistant, medium-grained sandstone, typical of the Dakota Formation.	
15	29.2-31 m	Section covered by slabs of Dakota Formation sandstone that have come down as surface float.	1.8 m
14	28-29.2 m	Mudstone, light grey.	1.2 m

Unit	Section Height	Description	Thickness
13	27.2-28 m	Carbonaceous shale with abundant plant hash, in places verging on impure lignite with some sub-bituminous seams. Secondary gypsum present. Dark brown color, weathers out light brown.	0.8 m
12	21.3-27.2 m	Mudstone, grey with some patches of iron staining, lenses of fine grey sand, cross-bedded, weathering out grey and flaky.	5.9 m

OMNH V824 at 23 m.

Unit	Section Height	Description	Thickness
11	20.9-21.3 m	Sandstone, thickness variable to maximum 40 cm. A long lens, extending about 200 feet N-S. Fine- to medium grained sand, resistant and highly visible, grey weathering to reddish brown.	0.4 m
10	18.2-20.9 m	Mudstone, light grey, sharp contact with underlying conglomerate.	2.7 m
9	17.5-18.2 m	Mudstone, coarsens upward over 50 cm to a microconglomerate at 18 m. Microconglomerate dark brown, discontinuous, contains silt, fine sand, mud clasts, tiny pebbles, plant fragments, and rare stream-worn bone.	0.7 m
8	11.7-17.5 m	Mudstone, light grey. Smooth pebbles range in size up to 2 cm diameter, occur first in surface float at about 14 m, are sparsely and randomly distributed in the mudstone between about 15-16 m.	5.8 m
7	11.5-11.7 m	Siltstone, very light grey, hard carbonate cement, holds up slope break, weathers out nodular.	0.2 m
6	8-11.5 m	Mudstone, light greenish grey, small caliche nodules sparse up to 10 m and absent above.	3.5 m
5	6-8 m	Mudstone, light greenish grey, fining upward within the interval. Caliche nodules between 6-7 m numerous and small, and then increase in size within interval (Stage II carbonate accumulation).	2.0 m
4	5.9-6 m	Siltstone or fine sandstone, carbonate cement with no visible crystalline structure, lighter color than surrounding mudstone, hard but not resistant, tiny organic fragments present.	0.1 m
3	3-5.9 m	Mudstone, light grey, variable sand content. At 4 m some lenses of fine sand with carbonate cement, no identifiable sedimentary structures. Fines upward slightly within the interval, secondary gypsum occurring above 5 m.	2.9
2	2-3 m	Sandstone, medium grain size, trough cross-bedded, not resistant.	1.0 m
1	0-2 m	Conglomerate, holds up a wide bench over an unstable cliff of Morrison Formation muds, thickness highly variable, trough cross-bedding, weathers reddish.	2.0 m

Section C

Unit	Section Height	Description	Thickness
17	27.5 m	Base of resistant, medium-grained sandstone typical of the Dakota Formation.	
16	21.75-27.5 m	Section covered by slabs of the Dakota Formation sandstone that have come down as surface float.	5.75 m
15	14-21.75 m	Mudstone, light to dark grey, substantial secondary gypsum.	7.75 m
14	13.4-14 m	Mudstone, light grey, fragmentary dinosaur bone.	0.6 m
13	13-13.4 m	Ash, white, porous, weathered near the surface, discontinuous over distance of less than 2 m.	0.4 m
12	12.9-13 m	Mudstone, grey.	0.1 m

Medial Cretaceous Vertebrates - Cifelli, Nydam, Gardner, Weil, Eaton, Kirkland, Madsen

Unit	Section Height	Description	Thickness
11	12.8-12.9 m	Sandstone, light tan weathering to reddish brown; black to dark grey, mostly fragmentary dinosaur bone weathering out (OMNH V826).	0.1 m
10	12.5-12.8 m	Mudstone, light grey.	0.3 m
9	11.5-12.5 m	Sandstone, thickness variable to maximum of 2 m, laterally discontinuous.	1.0 m
8	10.28-11.5 m	Mudstone, light grey.	1.25 m
7	10.25-10.28 m	Conglomerate, identical to that described for the interval 8.75- 8.77.	0.03 m
6	8.77-10.25 m	Mudstone, light greenish-grey.	1.48 m
5	8.75-8.77 m	Conglomerate, 2-5 cm thick, clasts small pebble size, few of cobble size, no visible cross-bedding, laterally continuous for at least 30 m, not resistant, source of many pebbles in surface float downslope.	0.02 m
4	7.3-8.75 m	Mudstone, light greenish-grey.	1.45 m
3	6.5-7.3 m	Mudstone, light grey; at 7 m and again at 7.3 m large ovoid caliche nodules greater than 15 cm length, distributed on apparently horizontal surfaces (Stage II carbonate accumulation).	0.8 m
2	1-6.5 m	Mudstone, light grey to greenish grey, occasional ovoid streamworn rocks up to 8 cm length, lenses of fine sandstone in the lower part of the interval, no other visible sedimentary structures.	5.5 m
1	0-1 m	Conglomerate, clasts of coarse sand size to up to 5 cm diameter, trough cross-bedding, weathers reddish, highly variable in thickness but thinning to the E; to the W it holds up a steep slope of the underlying Morrison Formation, and its dip slope forms the floor of a small valley.	1.0 m

ANKYLOSAURS (DINOSAURIA: ORNITHISCHIA) OF THE CEDAR MOUNTAIN FORMATION, UTAH, AND THEIR STRATIGRAPHIC DISTRIBUTION

Kenneth Carpenter

Department of Earth Sciences, Denver Museum of Natural History, 2001 Colorado Blvd., Denver, CO 80205

James I. Kirkland

Utah Geological Survey, Box 146100, Salt Lake City, UT 84114-6100

Donald Burge and John Bird

Prehistoric Museum, College of Eastern Utah, Price, UT 84501

ABSTRACT

Ankylosaurs are relatively common in the Cedar Mountain Formation and include (1) *Gastonia burgei*, (2) *Sauropelta* sp., and (3) *Animantarx ramaljonesi* new genus, new species. *Animantarx ramaljonesi* is characterized by a highly domed cranium, very small postorbital "horns," moderately developed lateral notch in the skull roof for the lateral temporal fenestra, indistinguishable pattern of armor on the skull roof, small quadratojugal "horn," elongated coracoid that is about 63% of the scapula length, a high shoulder on the deltopectoral crest, and an oblique ridge on anterolateral surface of the femur below the lesser trochanter.

The Cedar Mountain ankylosaurs appear to be restricted to distinct stratigraphic units: *Gastonia burgei* to the Yellow Cat Member, *Sauropelta* sp. to the Poison Strip Sandstone, and *Animantarx ramaljonesi* to the Mussentuchit Member. Provisionally, such a distribution supports a threefold division of the Cedar Mountain dinosaur faunas. The diversity of ankylosaurs in the Cedar Mountain is the highest of any Lower Cretaceous formation and may eventually provide important information about the evolution and adaptive radiation of these dinosaurs.

INTRODUCTION

The dinosaur fauna of the Lower Cretaceous Cedar Mountain Formation of eastern Utah has only recently been investigated in any detail (Cifelli and others, 1997; Kirkland and others, 1997). Alpha systematics for most of the dinosaur taxa are presently under study and only brief descriptions have thus far appeared (for example, Bodily, 1969; Nelson and Crooks, 1987; DeCourten, 1991; Kirkland and others, 1993; Burge, 1996). Part of this work in the Cedar Mountain seeks to better clarify the evolution of Early Cretaceous ankylosaurs in North America from their antecedents in the Late Jurassic (Kirkland, 1993; Kirkland and others 1991; Carpenter and others, 1996). These Late Jurassic forms have only recently been discovered in the Morrison Formation, and include *Mymoorapelta maysi* (Kirkland and Carpenter, 1994; Kirkland and others, 1998) and an unnamed new genus (Carpenter and others, 1996). These two taxa share certain features in common with *Gastonia* from the Cedar Mountain Formation (Kirkland, 1993). Footprints from the Cedar Mountain Formation purported to be those of ankylosaurs are described by Lockley and others (this volume). The specimens described below came from a band of the Cedar Mountain Formation that extends east-west, south of the Book Cliffs in northern Grand and Emery Counties, Utah (figure 1).

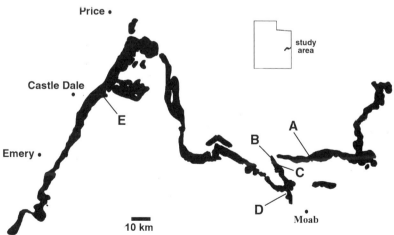

Figure 1. *Locations for ankylosaurs in the Cedar Mountain Formation, Utah. A, Gaston Quarry; B, Jim's Ankylosaur; C, Bodily Site; D, Dalton Well; E, Carol Site; F, Mussentuchit Wash. See text for taxa.*

ABBREVIATIONS

CEUM, Prehistoric Museum, College of Eastern Utah, Price, Utah; DMNH, Denver Museum of Natural History, Denver, Colorado; BYU, Brigham Young University, Provo, Utah; Earth Science Museum, Brigham Young University, Provo, Utah.

SYSTEMATIC PALEONTOLOGY
Order Ankylosauria
Family Nodosauridae
Animantarx new genus

Holotype

CEUM 6228, partial skull and right mandible (figures 2 and 3), cervical and dorsal vertebrae (figure 4), ribs, both scapula-coracoids (figure 5A-C), fragment of sternal plate, right humerus (figure 5D, E), left ilium with ischium (figure 6A, B), left femur (figure 6C, D).

Etymology

"Animant" Latin for "living" and "arx" Latin for fortress or citadel. The name is based on Richard Swann Lull's observation regarding ankylosaurs, that "[a]s an animated citadel, these animals must have been practically unassailable. . . " (Lull, 1914).

Type Locality

Carol Site (42EM366V), Mussentuchit Member, Cedar Mountain Formation, Utah (figure 1). Exact locality data on file at CEUM.

Diagnosis

Parietal region highly domed as in *Struthiosaurus, Pawpawsaurus*, and *Silvisaurus*, vs. moderately domed as in *Sauropelta* and *Panoplosaurus*, and slightly domed as in *Edmontonia*; postorbital "horns" very small, vs. prominent as in *Pawpawsaurus*, and absent as in *Sauropelta, Edmontonia, Silvisaurus, Panoplosaurus*, and *Struthiosaurus*. In dorsal view, lateral notch in skull roof for lateral temporal fenestra moderately developed as in *Edmontonia*, vs. well developed as in *Pawpawsaurus*, or absent as in *Silvisaurus*. Armor pattern of skull roof indistinguishable as in *Silvisaurus* and *Gastonia*, vs. well-developed pattern in all other nodosaurids. Quadratojugal "horn" small, rounded as in *Niobrarasaurus*, vs. large and pointed as in *Sauropelta*, and large and rounded as in *Pawpawsaurus* and *Silvisaurus*. Exoccipitals and supraoccipital form prominent dorsal and lateral rim to foramen magnum as in *Struthiosaurus*, vs. absent or moderately developed rim as in other nodosaurids.

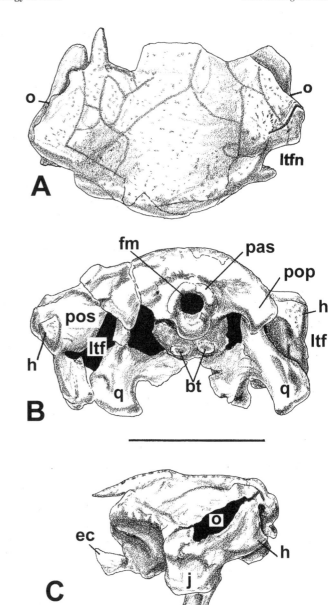

Figure 2. *Cranial elements of* Animantarx ramaljonesi *new genus and new species: A, posterior part of cranium in dorsal, B, posterior, and C, left lateral views. Abbreviations: bt - basipterygoid tubera, ec - ectopterygoid, fm - foramen magnum, h- horn on the postorbital, j - jugal horn, ltf - lateral temporal fenestra, lftn - lateral temporal fenestra notch, o - orbit, pas - proatlas shelf, pop - paraccipital process, pos - postoccural shelf, q - quadrate. Scale = 10 cm.*

Armor on mandible restricted to half the mandible length, vs. 3/4 as in *Edmontonia* and *Panoplosaurus*; armor is not prominent as in Silvisaurus, vs. very prominent in *Sauropelta, Edmontonia*, and *Panoplosaurus*. Coracoid elongated, about 63% of scapula in length similar to *Panoplosaurus* (62%), vs. 27% as in *Sauropelta*. Humerus very slender-shafted as in other nodosaurids, but shoulder of deltopectoral crest very high, near level of humeral head, in contrast with all other nodosaurids. Oblique ridge on anterolateral surface of femur below lesser trochanter as in *Texasetes*.

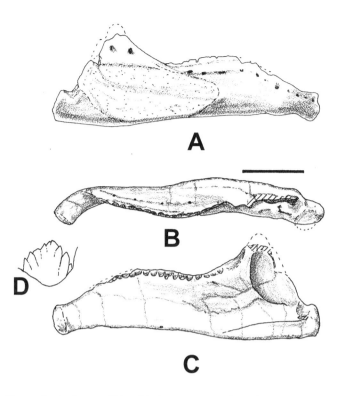

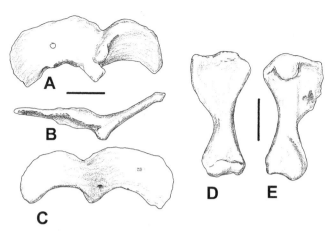

Figure 5. *Left scapula and co-ossified coracoid (A, B, C) and right humerus D, E) of* Animantarx ramaljonesi *new genus and new species: A, left lateral, B, dorsal, and C, medial views of scapula and co-ossified coracoids; scale = 10 cm. D, right humerus of* Animantarx ramaljonesi *new genus and new species: A, anterior, and B, posterior views of right humerus; scale = 10 cm.*

Figure 3. *Right mandible of* Animantarx ramaljonesi *new genus and new species: A, right lateral, B, occlusal, and C, left medial views. Scale = 10 cm. D, dentary tooth 16 in medial view.*

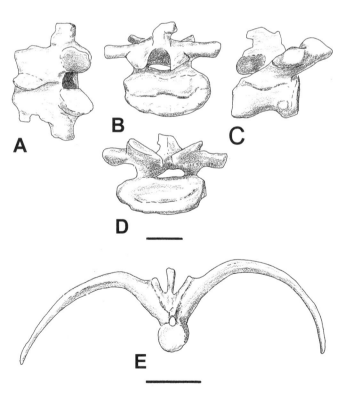

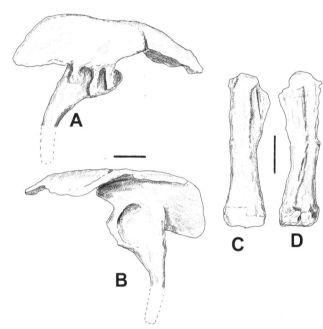

Figure 6. *Left ilium with co-ossified ischium (A, B) and right femur (C, D) of* Animantarx ramaljonesi *new genus and new species: A, medial, and B, lateral views of ilium with co-ossified ischium; scale = 10 cm. Right femur in C, anterior and D, posterior views of right femur; scale = 10 cm.*

Animantarx ramaljonesi new species

Etymology

Named for Ramal Jones who discovered the specimen using a modified scintillometer in an area with no bones exposed (see Jones and Burge, 1995).

Holotype

CEUM 6228R, as for the genus.

Diagnosis

As for the genus.

Figure 4. *Cervical vertebra of* Animantarx ramaljonesi *new genus and new species: A, dorsal, B, posterior, C, right lateral, and D, anterior views; scale = 2 cm. E, posterior dorsal with co-ossified rib in anterior view; scale = 10 cm.*

Discussion

Measurements of the holotype are given in table 1. The specimen was briefly described by one of us as a *Pawpawsaurus*-like nodosaurid (Burge, 1996). The skull is incomplete just anterior to the orbits (figure 2). What remains has suffered considerable distortion so that the orbit on the left side is reduced to a greatly elongated oval; the orbit of the right side is also distorted, although to a lesser degree. The distortion of the skull has displaced the postorbital horns on both sides, although not as much on the right (not illustrated). In addition, the shaft of the left quadrate is fractured and pushed forward, distorting the lateral temporal fenestra. The right quadrate has been pushed against the postocular shelf on that side reducing the lateral temporal fenestra to a slit. Both pterygoid processes of the quadrates have been displaced posteriorly, especially the right. A reconstruction of the skull is shown in figure 7.

Table 1. *Measurements (cm) of the holotype of* Animantarx ramaljonesi *CEUM 6228R..*

1. Maximum skull width across postorbital dermal scutes	20.4
2. Skull width across paroccipital processes	13.2
3. Left scapula midline length	~24
4. Left coracoid midline width	~15.5
5. Left humerus length	29.8
6. Right femur length	41.5

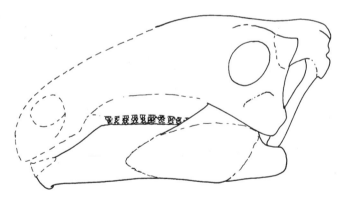

Figure 7. *Reconstructed skull of* Animantarx ramaljonesi *new genus and new species in left lateral view. Skull is estimated to be about 25 cm long.*

The skull shows the high doming of the forehead region between the orbits as in *Silvisaurus*. The armor pattern on the skull roof is difficult to determine because of numerous fractures. Nevertheless, a prominent central plate typical of most nodosaurids is present on the cranial roof. A postorbital horn is present as in *Pawpawsaurus*, although it is small; it is very large in *Pawpawsaurus* and absent in *Silvisaurus*. The armored jugal is small and rounded, whereas it is very large and prominent in both Pawpawsaurus and *Silvisaurus*. Further-

more, the surface of the skull between the lateral temporal fenestra and orbit is narrow, whereas it is very broad in both *Pawpawsaurus* and *Silvisaurus*. The underside of the skull roof shows conclusively that the supratemporal fenestra in nodosaurids is closed by bone (probably from the squamosal) and not simply roofed over by armor. A similar observation for ankylosaurids was previously made by Tumanova (1987) based on *Talurus*.

The right mandible is complete, although most of the teeth are absent (figure 3A-C). In profile, the mandible is long and low, with the characteristic sigmoidal shape of nodosaurids. The osteoderm co-ossified to the lateral surface is not well demarcated, but its presence can be inferred from the grooved and pitted surface texture. Unlike *Panoplosaurus* and *Edmontonia*, where the armor covers 3/4 or more of the mandible, it is confined to the posterior half of the mandible in *Animantarx*. The coronoid process is damaged, but appears to be low. The mandibular fossa is present on the medial side of the process. This fossa (figure 3C) is not as large as it is in *Panoplosaurus* and *Edmontonia*, nor is it closed off posteriorly as in those nodosaurids. There are about 19 tooth positions, with the crown of replacement teeth seen at positions 6, 8, 10, 13, 14, 16, and 17. The most complete crown visible is the medial side of number 16. The anteroposterior length is ~5.25 mm; it has 4 or 5 denticles on the anterior edge and two or three visible on the posterior edge (figure 3D). In dorsal view, the tooth row is medially arced (figure 3B) to conform with the hourglass-shaped palate that characterizes nodosaurids. The symphysis is edentulous and is almost vertical (80°), whereas it is angled about 30° in *Silvisaurus*, 45° in *Edmontonia*, and 50° in *Panoplosaurus* and *Sauropelta*. The articular is missing a small corner medially, nevertheless, the quadrate glenoid retains its plesiomorphic position in line with the axis of the mandible (figure 3B). In *Sauropelta*, for example, it is medially offset, a condition considered apomorphic. No trace of the Meckelian groove is seen on the edentulous portion of the dental ramus. Such a groove is seen in *Sauropelta*. Most of the sutures on the medial side can not be discerned with the exception of that between the angular and prearticular.

The postcrania indicate an individual about the same size as *Texasestes pleurohalio* Coombs (1995). Most of the cervicals are badly crushed and damaged; the least damaged of which is illustrated in figure 4A-D. The vertebrae resemble those of *Texasetes*, except that the centrum is not quite as concave ventrally. Such a concavity is unusual among nodosaurids and may be a synapomorphy shared by *Animantarx* and *Texasetes*. The parapophysis is low on the anterior sides of the centrum indicating that the vertebra is an anterior third(?) or fourth(?) cervical. The neural spine does not appear to have been a tall, thin blade as in *Sauropelta* and *Silvisaurus*, but is short and thick, a feature also seen in *Struthiosaurus* (Nopcsa, 1929). There is a deep concavity between the postzygapophyses, a feature seen in a few other nodosaurids, such as *Mymoorapelta*.

Four dorsal vertebrae are present, each with co-ossified rib, and thus are posterior-most dorsals; one is illustrated in figure 4E. The maximum rib-to-rib width is 63 centimeters. The transverse processes are angled steeply upwards, about 55°-60°, about the same for *Sauropelta*; the same angle is only 30° in *Edmontonia*, and 45° in *Silvisaurus* (Eaton, 1960). The top of the neural spine is as tall, or only slightly taller than the transverse processes and is only a little expanded laterally in marked contrast to *Sauropelta*.

Both left and right scapula and coracoids are present. The scapula and coracoid are co-ossified (figure 5A-C). The scapula is very unusual among nodosaurids in its small size as compared with the coracoid. The coracoid-to-scapula-ratio is about 62.5%, about the same (62%) as that for *Panoplosaurus* (Sternberg, 1921), whereas it is 27% in *Sauropelta* (Carpenter, 1984). The scapular blade is dorsoventrally arced and tapers distally. In most nodosaurids the scapula is straighter and the distal end is sightly rounded (for example, *Struthiosaurus*, and *Sauropelta*). The pseudoacromion process is a prominent, elongated knob located low on the scapular blade, just above the posterior portion of the glenoid. Dorsal to the process, the scapula has a neck separating the dorsal process or expansion from the scapular blade. At this neck, the scapula bends medially about 38° (figure 5B). The dorsal plate above the glenoid is taller in *Texasetes*. Although the coracoid-scapula ratio is about the same as that of *Panoplosaurus*, the scapula differs in that the pseudoacromion process and neck arc more posteriorly located. The coracoid is very elongated as it is many nodosaurids, especially that of *Panoplosaurus* and *Texasetes*. The coracoid foramen is large and located dorsal to the anterior rim of the glenoid. The anteroventral corner of the coracoid is thin, whereas it is very thick in *Texasetes*.

A complete right humerus is present, although badly crushed (figure 5D,E). It is 87% the scapula-coracoid length, whereas it is 80% in *Sauropelta* (Carpenter, 1984), and 75% in *Panoplosaurus* (Sternberg, 1921). Proximally, the inner tubercle is small, as in *Texasetes*, whereas it is large in *Sauropelta* and very large and well developed in *Panoplosaurus* (Russell, 1940). The lateral, or greater tubercle on the dorsal edge of the deltopectoral crest is slightly below the humeral head and it projects upwardly. In *Panoplosaurus* and *Sauropelta*, the greater tubercle is considerably below the humeral head.

The left ilium (figure 6A,B) lacks the anteriormost portion of the preacetabular blade. What remains is folded ventromedially, suggesting that the anterior part of the blade was bent ventrolaterally as in *Mymoorapelta* (see Kirkland and Carpenter, 1994). The fragments of three sacral ribs are attached to the medial side of the ilium. A partial ischium is fused to the ilium and together they form the acetabulum. The ischium bends anteriorly just above the break. How much is missing is unknown. The base of the pubis may be fused to the ischium, but this can not be determined for certain.

The left femur of *Animantarx* is badly crushed and damaged (figure 6C,D). It is not possible to determine if the lesser and fourth trochanters were present or, if present, how well developed they were. There is a distinct oblique ridge on the lateral side, now exposed on the anterior surface due to crushing. A similar ridge is present in *Texasetes*, where it extends anterodistally to the base of the lesser trochanter. The distal condyles of the femur are damaged in *Animantarx*, but the fibular condyle seems more equal in size to the tibial condyle. In all other nodosaurids, the fibular condyle is significantly smaller.

cf. *Sauropelta* sp.

Material

BYU 245, caudals and associated armor (figure 8); BYU 9430, five dorsals, ribs, and armor; DMNH 34586, armor and rib.

Localities

Bodily Quarry (State of Utah locality 42Gr003VP), Movie Valley Locality, and Jim's Ankylosaur Quarry; Poison Strip Sandstone, Cedar Mountain Formation, Grand County, Utah (figure 1).

Discussion

Bodily (1969) reported the discovery of a nodosaurid (BYU 245) in what is now known as the Poison Strip Sandstone . He referred it to *Hoplitosaurus*? sp. based on similarities of the armor with those of *Hoplitosaurus marshi* (Lucas, 1902). Pereda-Superbiola (1994) tentatively referred the Bodily specimen to *Polacanthus* on the basis of Bodily's description. We, however, conclude from a restudy of the material (figure 3E), that the specimen should be referred to the nodosaurid *Sauropelta* sp. The lateral triangular plates resemble those of both the polacanthines and *Sauropelta*. However, the large size of the individual and the structure of the caudals is most similar to that of *Sauropelta* (figures 8A,B vs. C,D). Although the tops of the neural spines are swollen, the

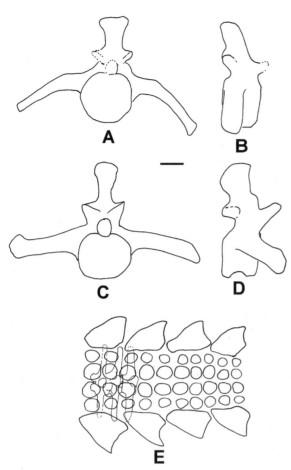

Figure 8. *Anterior caudal vertebrae of* Sauropelta sp. *(BYU 245) in A, posterior and B, right lateral view; and* Sauropelta edwardsi *in C, anterior, and D, right lateral view. Note the greater posterior expansion of the neural spine in D vs. B. Although A and C probably represent different caudal positions, more distal caudals of* Sauropelta edwardsi *show the same posterior expansion of the neural spine. E, tentative reconstruction of the anterior caudal vertebrae (light lines) and armor (dark lines) of* Sauropelta sp. *The reconstruction does not attempt to compensate for oval cross section of tail. More distal caudals and armor not shown. Scale for A-D = 5 cm. A modified from Bodily (1969), C and D modified from Ostrom (1970).*

spines are not expanded along their entire posterior length as in *Sauropelta edwardsi*. The taxonomic significance of this difference is not fully known at this time, but may indicate a new species of *Sauropelta*. The caudal ribs are also more horizontal in *Sauropelta* sp. than in *S. edwardsi*, and may also be taxonomically significant.

The other fragments of ankylosaur are tentatively identified as *Sauropelta* on the basis of armor and large size. Future study may change these assignments.

FAMILY ANKYLOSAURIDAE
SUBFAMILY POLACANTHINAE

Gastonia burgei: Kirkland 1998

Material

Hundreds of bones, including a complete skull, to be

described and listed elsewhere (Kirkland, 1998).

Locality

Gaston Quarry (State of Utah locality 42Gr184V), and Dalton Well Quarry (State of Utah locality 42Gr001V), Yellowcat Member, Cedar Mountain Formation, Grand County, Utah (figure 1). Exact locality data on file at the College of Eastern Utah, Price, Utah, Brigham Young University, Provo, Utah, and Museum of Western Colorado, Grand Junction, Colorado.

Discussion

This primitive ankylosaurid is represented by several hundred bones at the Gaston Quarry and by lesser numbers at the nearby Dalton Well Quarry. This ankylosaurid may also be represented by isolated bones found elsewhere in the Yellowcat Member in eastern Utah. All of this material is described in detail elsewhere by one of us (Kirkland, 1998). At the Gaston Quarry, at least four individuals of this ankylosaurid are represented based on ischia. Two partial skulls and one complete skull have also been found (figure 9A-C). The skull is almost as wide as it is long. It has cranial horns in the posterolateral corner of the skull roof similar to those in typical Late Cretaceous ankylosaurids (for example, *Ankylosaurus*). These horns and underlying bone have shifted posteriorly to almost obliterate the lateral temporal notch on the skull roof. In this feature, the Cedar Mountain ankylosaurid is intermediate between the distinct notch seen in the skull of *Gargoyleosaurus* from the Upper Jurassic (Carpenter and others, 1998) and the absence of the notch in the Lower Cretaceous *Shamosaurus*. The armor pattern on the skull roof cannot be determined; however the armor does not extend over the premaxillary beak. The external nares retain their plesiomorphic position and open laterally. As yet no mandible is known; thus, the height of the coronoid, development of the mandibular fossa, and extent of the lateral armor are unknown.

The body armor is most similar to that of *Polacanthus foxi* (Wealden Formation, Isle of Wight), especially in the fusion of the sacral armor together into a sheet over the dorsal surface of the ilium (Kirkland and others, 1991), and in the large, keeled plates along the sides of the body (figure 9D). Differences with other ankylosaurids warrant it being in a separate subfamily, Polacanthinae, along with the Cedar Mountain genus. The Polacanthinae differs from the other ankylosaurid subfamilies, Shamosaurinae and Ankylosaurinae, in the projecting shoulder spines, and sacral armor fused to the ilium. Other differences will be elaborated elsewhere by JIK (in preparation). A preliminary reconstruction of this primitive ankylosaurid is presented in figure 9D.

STRATIGRAPHIC DISTRIBUTION OF ANKYLOSAURS IN THE CEDAR MOUNTAIN FORMATION

The Cedar Mountain Formation has recently been divided into several members (Kirkland and others 1997): Yellow Cat Member, Poison Strip Sandstone, Ruby Ranch Member, and Mussentuchit Member. The Buckhorn Conglomerate, present in the San Rafael Swell, is believed to be equivalent to the Yellow Cat and Poison Strip Sandstone of the Paradox Basin. The ankylosaurs of the Cedar Mountain Formation seem to be confined stratigraphically as described below.

Yellowcat Member

The Yellow Cat Member appears to be confined to the Paradox Basin, where it was deposited in structural lows caused by the collapse of salt anticlines (Kirkland and others, 1997). The polacanthine ankylosaurid, *Gastonia*, is represented by several hundred bones at the Gaston and Dalton Well dinosaur quarries. These quarries are about at the same stratigraphic level in the Yellow Cat Member, although there are major differences in the composition of their faunas (Kirkland and others,

1993; Burge, 1996; Britt, 1997; Kirkland and others, 1997). The occurrence of a polacanthine suggests a Barremian age for the Yellow Cat Member. This age conclusion is based upon the occurrence of *Polacanthus foxi* in the Wessex and Vectis Formations (Wealden Group) of England (Benton and Spencer, 1995), and *Hoplitosaurus marshi* in the Lakota Formation of South Dakota (Pereda-Superbiola, 1994).

Poison Strip Sandstone

The most complete specimen from the Poison Strip Sandstone is the *Sauropelta* described by Bodily (1969) from just west of Arches National Monument. Other specimens referable to *Sauropelta* sp. also occur along the north and west sides of Arches National Park (BYU 9430, DMNH 34586). *Sauropelta* suggests that the Poison Strip Sandstone is Aptian-Albian age because it is also present in the Cloverly Formation of Montana and Wyoming (Ostrom, 1970).

Ruby Ranch Member

Except for the possible occurrence of *Sauropelta* sp. at the base of the Ruby Ranch mentioned above (BYU

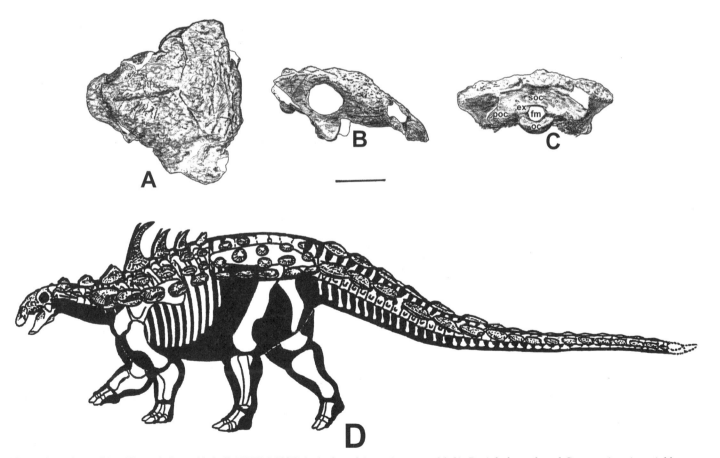

Figure 9. *Polacanthine* (Gastonia burgei) *skull (CEUM 1307) in A, dorsal (anterior toward left), B, right lateral, and C, posterior views (abbreviations: ex- exoccipital; fm - foramen magnum; oc - occipital condyle; poc - paroccipital process; soc - supraoccipital); scale = 10 cm. D, life restoration in lateral view by Tracy Ford.*

9430), the only other remains found are some very large teeth referable to *Sauropelta* collected near the Cleveland-Lloyd dinosaur quarry, Emery County, Utah (Kirkland and others, 1997). To date, the dinosaurs of the Ruby Ranch Member remain the least known from the Cedar Mountain. The few taxa known suggest that the Ruby Ranch correlates with the Cloverly Formation of Montana and Wyoming (Kirkland and others, 1997).

Mussentuchit Member

Ankylosaur remains from the Mussentuchit Member include unidentifiable isolated teeth and the partial skull and skeleton of *Animantarx ramaljonesi*. *Animantarx* was collected from just above the base of the Mussentuchit Member near the San Rafael Swell. Isolated nodosaurid teeth from the middle of the Mussentuchit Member have been recovered from the east side of the San Rafael Swell, but their taxonomic identity has not yet been determined. Similarities between *Animantarx*, *Pawpawsaurus* (Lee, 1996), and *Texasetes* (Coombs, 1995) from the Late Albian of Texas, and *Silvisaurus* from the Early Cenomanian of Kansas, suggest a Late Albian or Early Cenomanian age for the Mussentuchit Member. Such an age conclusion is supported by other lines of evidence, including a radiometric date of 98.39 ± 0.07 million years ago (Cifelli and others 1997; see also discussion in Kirkland and others, 1997).

DISCUSSION

The armor-plated ankylosaurs were one of the more successful groups of dinosaurs. They first appeared during the Middle Jurassic and survived about 115 million years, becoming extinct at the end of the Cretaceous. Ankylosaurs have been divided into two families: the non-spined, tail-clubbed Ankylosauridae and the spined, non-tail-clubbed Nodosauridae (Coombs and Maryanska, 1990; Carpenter, 1997a,b). The origin of the two families is not clear because supposed representatives from the Middle Jurassic are fragmentary (Carpenter and others, in preparation). During their subsequent evolution ankylosaurs remained rare until the Early Cretaceous when nodosaurid diversity peaked and relative abundance increased. Ankylosaurids evidently remained rare until the Late Cretaceous when they apparently reached peak diversity and abundance. Why these two different peaks occurred is presently under study by one of us (KC). Nevertheless, the abundance and distribution of ankylosaurs in the Cedar Mountain Formation suggest that, at least regionally, ankylosaurs can be used bio-stratigraphically.

Originally, one of us (JIK) suggested the presence of

two distinct dinosaur faunas in the Cedar Mountain Formation (Kirkland, 1992). Subsequent work, however, has modified this interpretation and three successive faunas are now recognized (Kirkland and others, 1997). The stratigraphic distribution of the ankylosaurs (figure 10) support this new interpretation. Ankylosaurs are the most common dinosaur of the upper part of the Yellowcat Member and Poison Strip Sandstone of the Cedar Mountain Formation, but are rare in other members. This scarcity may be an artifact of insufficient collecting in the middle and upper parts of the Cedar Mountain, a hypothesis we are now testing. Nevertheless, ankylosaur dinosaurs indicate a three-fold division of the Cedar Mountain dinosaur faunas and suggest that the formation spans at least the last half of the Lower Cretaceous. Work in progress seeks to determine the maximum age of the lowermost part of the Cedar Mountain Formation.

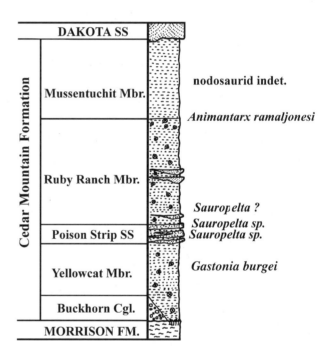

Figure 10. *Stratigraphic distribution of ankylosaurs in the Cedar Mountain Formation, eastern Utah. Stratigraphic nomenclature for the Cedar Mountain from Kirkland and others (1997).*

ACKNOWLEDGMENTS

We thank Kenneth Stadtman, Brigham Young University, for giving us access to the Cedar Mountain ankylosaur material under his care. Thanks to all those who assisted in the excavation of the specimens used in this study. Dale Russell, Matt Vickaryous, and David Gillette provided review comments that are greatly appreciated. Finally, it is always a pleasure to have the assistance of Ben Creisler in proposing creative names for dinosaurs; he suggested the name *Animantarx*

REFERENCES

Benton, M. J., and Spencer, P. S., 1995, Fossil reptiles of Great Britain: London, Chapman and Hall, 386 p.

Bodily, N. M., 1969, An armored dinosaur from the Lower Cretaceous of Utah: Brigham Young University Geology Studies, v. 16, p. 35-60.

Blows, William, 1987, The armoured dinosaur *Polacanthus foxi* from the Lower Cretaceous of the Isle of Wight: Palaeontology, v. 30, p. 557-580.

Britt, B. B., 1997, The Dalton Wells [sic] fauna (Cedar Mountain Formation) - a rare window into the little known world of Early Cretaceous dinosaurs in North America: Geological Society of America Abstracts with Programs, v. 29, p. A105.

Burge, Donald, 1996, New dinosaur discoveries in the Lower Cretaceous of southeastern Utah: Mesa Museum, Fossils of Arizona Proceedings, v. 4, p. 85-105.

Carpenter, Kenneth, 1984, Skeletal reconstruction and life restoration of *Sauropelta* (Ankylosauria: Nodosauridae) from the Cretaceous of North America: Canadian Journal of Earth Sciences, v. 21, p. 1491-1498.

—1997a, Ankylosauria, *in* Currie, P. J., and Padian, Kevin, editors, The encyclopedia of dinosaurs: San Diego, Academic Press, p. 16-20.

—1997b, Ankylosaurs, *in* Farlow, James, and Brett-Surman, Michael, editors, The complete dinosaur: Bloomington, Indiana University Press, p. 308-316.

Carpenter, K., Kirkland, J., Miles, C., Cloward, K., and Burge, D., 1996, Evolutionary significance of new ankylosaurs (Dinosauria) from the Upper Jurassic and Lower Cretaceous, Western Interior: Journal of Vertebrate Paleontology, v. 19, p. 25A.

Carpenter, Kenneth, Miles, Clifford, and Cloward, Karen, 1998, Skull of a Jurassic Onkylosaur (Dinosauria), Nature, v. 393, p. 782-783.

Cifelli, R. L., Kirkland, J. I., Weil, Anne, Deino, A. L., and Kowallis, Bart, 1997, High-precision $^{40}Ar/^{39}Ar$ geochronology and the advent of North America's Late Cretaceous terrestrial fauna: Proceedings of the National Academy of Sciences, v. 94, p. 11163-11167.

Coombs, Walter, 1995, A new nodosaurid ankylosaur (Dinosauria: Ornithischia) from the Lower Cretaceous of Texas: Journal of Vertebrate Paleontology, v. 15, p 298-312.

Coombs, Walter, and Maryanska, Teresa, 1990, Ankylosauria, *in* Weishampel, David, Dodson, Peter, and Osmolska, Halska, editors, The dinosauria: Berkeley, University of California Press, p. 456-483.

DeCourten, F. L., 1991, New data on Early Cretaceous dinosaurs from the Long Walk Quarry and tracksite, Emery County, Utah: Utah Geological Association Publication, v. 19, p. 311-324.

Eaton, T. H., 1960, A new armored dinosaur from the Cretaceous of Kansas: University of Kansas Paleontological Contribution, aricle 8, p. 1-24.

Jones, R. D., and Burge, Donald, 1995, Radiological surveying as a method for mapping dinosaur bone sites: Journal of Vertebrate Paleontology, v. 15, p. 38A.

Kirkland, J. I., 1992, Dinosaurs define a two-fold Lower Cretaceous zonation of the Cedar Mountain Formation, central Utah: Geological Society of America, Abstracts and Programs, v. 24, p. 22.

—1993, Polacanthid nodosaurs from the Upper Jurassic and Lower Cretaceous of the east-central Colorado Plateau: Journal of Vertebrate Paleontology, v. 13, p. 44A 45A.

Kirkland, James, I., 1998, A polacanthine ankylosaur (Ornithiscia: Dinosauria) from the Early Cretaceous (Barremian) of eastern

Utah, *in* Lucas, S.G., Kirkland, JI, and Estap, J.W., editors, Lower and Middle Cretaceous terrestrial ecosystems: New Mexico Museum of Natural History and Science Bulletin, v. 14, p. 271-281.

Kirkland, J. I., Britt, Brooks, Burge, D. L., Carpenter, Ken, Cifelli, Richard, DeCourten, Frank, Eaton, Jeffrey, Hasiotis, Steve, and Lawton, Tim, 1997, Lower to Middle Cretaceous dinosaur faunas of the central Colorado Plateau - a key to understanding 35 million years of tectonics, sedimentology, evolution, and biogeography: Brigham Young University, Geology Studies, v. 12, pt. 2, p. 69-103.

Kirkland, J. I., Burge, Donald, and Gaston, Robert, 1993, A large dromaeosaur (Theropoda) from the Lower Cretaceous of eastern Utah: Hunteria, v. 2, no. 10, p. 1-16.

Kirkland, J. I., and Carpenter, Kenneth, 1994, North America's first pre-Cretaceous ankylosaur (Dinosauria) from the Upper Jurassic Morrison Formation of western Colorado: Brigham Young University Geology Studies, v. 40, p. 25-42.

Kirkland, J. I., Carpenter, Kenneth, and Burge, Donald, 1991, A nodosaur with distinctive sacral shield of fused armor from the Lower Cretaceous of east-central Utah: Journal of Vertebrate Paleontology, v. 11, p. 40A.

Kirkland, J. I., Carpenter, Kenneth, Hunt, A. P., and Scheetz, R. D., 1998, Ankylosaur (Dinosauria) specimens from the Upper Jurassic Morrison Formation, *in* Carpenter, Kenneth, Chure, Daniel, and Kirkland, J. I., editors, The Morrison Formation - an interdisciplinary study: Modern Geology, p. 145-177.

Lee, Yuong-Nam, 1996, A new nodosaurid ankylosaur (Dinosauria: Ornithischia) from the Paw Paw Formation (Late Albian) of Texas: Journal of Vertebrate Paleontology, v. 16, p. 232-345.

Lockley, Martin, Kirkland, James, DeCourten, Frank, and Hasiotis, Steve, 1998, Dinosaur tracks from the Cedar Mountain Formation of Eastern Utah - a preliminary report: this volume.

Lucas, F. A., 1902, A new generic name for *Stegosaurus marshi*: Science, v. 16, p. 435.

Lull, R. S., 1914, Rulers of the Mesozoic: Yale Review, v. 3, p. 352-363.

Nelson, M. E., and Crooks, D. M., 1987, Stratigraphy and paleontology of the Cedar Mountain Formation (Lower Cretaceous), eastern Emery County, Utah, *in* Averett, W.R., editor, Paleontology and geology of the Dinosaur Triangle: Grand Junction, Colorado, Museum of Western Colorado, p. 55-63.

Nopcsa, Frederick, 1929, Dinosaurierreste aus Siebenbügen: Geologica Hungarica, Series Palaeontologica, v. 4, p. 1-76.

Ostrom, J. H., 1970, Stratigraphy and paleontology of the Cloverly Formation (Lower Cretaceous) of the Bighorn Basin area, Wyoming and Montana: Peabody Museum of Natural History Bulletin, v. 35, p. 1-234.

Pereda-Superbiola, Xavier, 1994, *Polacanthus* (Ornithischia, Ankylosauria), a transatlantic armoured dinosaur from the Early Cretaceous of Europe and North America: Palaeontographica, part A, v. 232, p. 133-159.

Russell, Loris, 1940, *Edmontonia rugosidens* (Gilmore), an armoured dinosaur from the Belly River Series of Alberta: University of Toronto Studies, Geological Series, v. 43, p. 3-27.

Sternberg, C. M., 1921, A supplemental study of *Panoplosaurus mirus*: Transactions of the Royal Society of Canada, v. 15, p. 93-102.

Tumanova, Tatyana, 1987, Pantsirny'e dinozavry' Mongolii: Sovmestnaya Sovetsno-Mongolskaya Paleontologicheskaya Ekspeditsiya Trudy', v. 32, p. 1-77.

Brian Maebius © 1999

Lepisosteus

DINOSAUR TRACKS FROM THE CEDAR MOUNTAIN FORMATION OF EASTERN UTAH: A PRELIMINARY REPORT

Martin G. Lockley
Geology Department, University of Colorado at Denver, PO Box 173364, Denver CO 80217-3364

James I. Kirkland
Utah Geological Survey, Box 146100, Salt Lake City, UT 84114-6100

Frank L. DeCourten
Geology-Earth Science Department, Sierra College, 5000 Rocklin Road, Rocklin, CA 95677

Brooks B. Britt
Museum of Western Colorado, Box 20000, Grand Junction, Colorado 81501

Stephen T. Hasiotis
Department of Geological Sciences, Campus Box 250, University of Colorado at Boulder, Boulder, CO 80309
present address: Exxon Production Research Company, P.O. Box 2189, Houston, TX 77252-2189
Stephen.T.Hasiotis@Exxon.Sprint.com

ABSTRACT

Dinosaur tracks from five different geographic sites in the Cedar Mountain Formation, are associated with three distinct stratigraphic levels (members) spanning the Barremian to the Albian-Cenomanian boundary. The most common track types appear to be those of large ornithopods, but tracks attributable to theropods, sauropods and ankylosaurs are also present, though they are not evenly distributed throughout the formation. The ankylosaur tracks appear to be the first reported from the United States. Current evidence suggests that footprints from the Cedar Mountain Formation are distinct from those in both the underlying Morrison Formation and the overlying Dakota Group. Given that five sites have been discovered without a systematic search, the potential for further track discoveries in this formation is promising.

INTRODUCTION

In recent years dinosaur tracks have been reported from a number of different localities in the Cedar Mountain Formation (Anonymous, 1989; DeCourten, 1990, 1991; Lockley and Hunt, 1994). These publications, however have given minimal information on the tracks and their stratigraphic context. Recent work on skeletal remains from this formation has demonstrated the presence of at least three distinct faunas (Kirkland, 1996) which can be assigned to three different members (Kirkland and others, 1997). The purpose of this paper, therefore, is to summarize all known tracksites in the Cedar mountain Formation, put them in their stratigraphic context, and assess the diversity of track types currently known.

We note that the Cedar Mountain and its constituent members are variable in vertical thickness and lateral lithofacies composition (figure 1), as described by Kirkland and others (1997), who identify four members in ascending stratigraphic order as follows: the Yellow Cat Member, the Poison Strip Member, the Ruby Ranch Member and the Mussentuchit Member. Tracks are known from three of these members and described below.

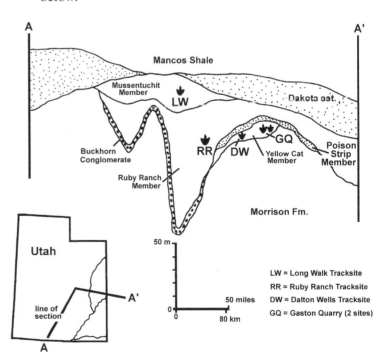

Figure 1. *Simplified cross section of the Cedar Mountain Formation in eastern Utah, showing the stratigraphic location of dinosaur tracksites. Modified after Kirkland and others (1997).*

DESCRIPTION OF TRACKSITES

Yellow Cat Member

Tracks are known from three localities near the base of the Cedar Mountain Formation. The first location, at Dalton Wells, about 18 kilometers due south of Thompson Springs, reveals a thin strip of bedding plane, about three to five meters wide and 30 meters long, on which approximately 10 tracks are preserved, mainly as nondescript indentations (figure 2). One track however, is clearly that of a theropod dinosaur, and measures approximately 37 centimeters long by 25 centimeters wide. This is the only convincing example of a theropod track from this interval. In the late summer of 1997, a single cast of a sauropod pes was recovered from the base of the track-bearing bed (figure 2). This track has yet to be transported from the field camp to the Museum of Western Colorado, and so still lacks a specimen number. However photographs and measurements have been taken to establish a record, and a description will be published in due course. In the meantime a preliminary description is given below in order to unequivocally establish its sauropod affinity through comparison with the tracks of other large quadrupedal dinosaurs.

Tracks have also been reported from the Gaston Quarry, approximately 12 kilometers southeast of Thompson Springs. These tracks are associated with bone beds in the Yellow Cat Member that have produced a fauna of probably Barremian age. Most of the tracks are associated with a trampled surface and so are not diagnostic. Large, circular, dish-shaped indentations, up to about 50 centimeters in diameter, are possibly of sauropod affinity, and may form part of a trackway. These tracks however, reveal no toe impressions indicative of foot morphology, and so could have been made by any large dinosaur, though the recently discovered Dalton Wells sauropod track, described below, establishes the presence of such large trackmakers in the Yellow Cat Member.

One small tridactyl print recovered from the site (figure 3C) indicates the presence of a biped (theropod or ornithopod with a foot approximately 12 cm long by 11 cm wide). A replica of this track (CU-MWC 199.4) was placed in the University of Colorado at Denver-Museum of Western Colorado joint collection.

Just east of Gaston Quarry three casts of large ornithopod tracks have been recovered from a sandstone bed in the Yellow Cat Member. Two of these casts are housed in the collections of the College of Eastern Utah (figure 3). Based on general morphology (tridactyl foot, broad-toed impressions and generally symmetric shape), we infer that these tracks are those of large ornithopods, probably iguanodontids. The tracks (figure 3A, B) measure 47 centimeters long and 38 centimeters wide, and 44 centimeters long by 40 centimeters wide, respectively. Usually ornithopod tracks are as long, or longer than wide, but any dinosaur track may be slightly elongated in the direction of progression, that is, parallel to foot length, and there is the slight possibility that the more elongate of the two tracks is attributable to a theropod. The tracks are comparable in size and shape to natural casts of ornithopod tracks from the Long Walk Quarry, and from various other Cretaceous sites.

Ruby Ranch Member

A single track from the Ruby Ranch Member is recorded from the type area (figure 3D). The track is impressed as a natural mold within an exfoliated sandstone unit. The track is tridactyl with a very broad heel impression, but narrow tear-drop-shaped toe impressions, which curve to the right, suggest some slippage of the foot or distortion of the sediment during or after the footprint was registered. The length is 21 centimeters and width 23 centimeters, and the size and morphology are similar to ornithopod tracks from the small end of the size range of ornithopod footprints found in the Dakota Group (Lockley and others, 1992).

Mussentuchit Member

The largest and most diagnostic sample of tracks known from the Cedar Mountain Formation, comes from the Long Walk Quarry area. Preliminary reports on this site (Anonymous, 1989; DeCourten, 1990, 1991) mention the footprints and

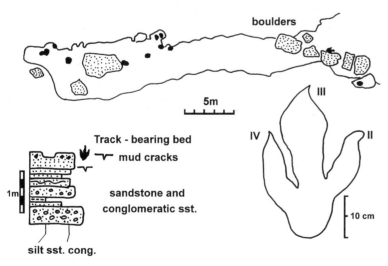

Figure 2. *Map of dinosaur tracksite at Dalton Wells, with detail of theropod track.*

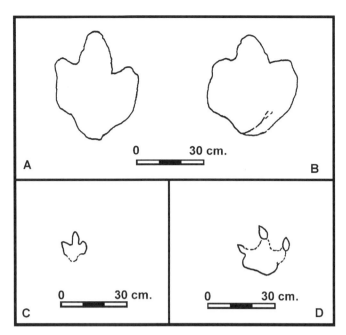

Figure 3. *Tracks from the Gaston Quarry (A-C) and Ruby Ranch area (D): A,B, two natural casts of large ornithopod tracks (upper right and left) from Yellow Cat Member; C, small tridactyl track from main quarry (Yellow Cat Member); D, tridactyl track from Ruby Ranch Member, Ruby Ranch area. All tracks drawn to same scale.*

illustrate some briefly. The best preserved tracks occur as natural casts, and display both tridactyl and tetradactyl morphologies (figure 4A-D). Two tridactyl tracks (figure 4A, B) measure about 37 centimeters long and 33 centimeters wide, and 36 centimeters long by 40 centimeters wide, respectively, and both reveal broad toes and a generally symmetrical appearance typical of large ornithopod tracks. Two tetradactyl tracks (figure 4C, D) measure 42 centimeters long by 37 centimeters wide, and 30 centimeters long by 25 centimeters wide, respectively, and most closely resemble *Tetrapodosaurus* (Sternberg, 1932) among footprints known from the Cretaceous of North America. Although originally attributed to ceratopsians by Sternberg (1932) *Tetrapodosaurus* originates from the Aptian-age Gething Formation of British Columbia, and has been reinterpreted, on morphological and stratigraphic grounds, as ankylosaurian in origin (Carpenter, 1984). Assuming an ankylosaurian origin for these tracks, then they are the first reported from the United States.

The argument for an ankylosaur origin for the Long Walk tracks is substantiated by consideration of the known and predicted track morphology, and stratigraphic distribution documented for the footprints of other large quadrupedal dinosaurs. Among the ornithischians, large Cretaceous ornithopods have only three toes (figure 4A, B). Stegosaur tracks are virtually unknown, but they also have a three-toed pes, and ceratopsian tracks are presently known only from the latest Cretaceous (Maas-

trichtian) as reported by Lockley and Hunt (1994, 1995a,b). Among the saurischians, the only large quadrupeds known from the Cretaceous are the sauropods. As revealed in figure 4E, the only known sauropod track from the Cedar Mountain Formation is pentadactyl, and is much larger (footprint length 80 cm, width 65 cm) than the others.

DISCUSSION

The general importance of the track discoveries reported herein is that they fill a large gap in the ichnological record. Until now little was known of the vertebrate track record between the Late Jurassic Morrison Formation and the latest Albian-Cenomanian Dakota Formation (Lockley and Hunt, 1995b). Most tracksites in the Dakota Formation are located east of the Colorado Front range and are slightly younger than the Dakota on the Colorado Plateau to the west. Previous reference to the Cedar Mountain vertebrate ichnofauna was restricted to the reports of DeCourten (1990,1991) and Lockley and Hunt (1994, 1995a) which mention only ornithopod tracks from the Gaston and the Long Walk quarries. In

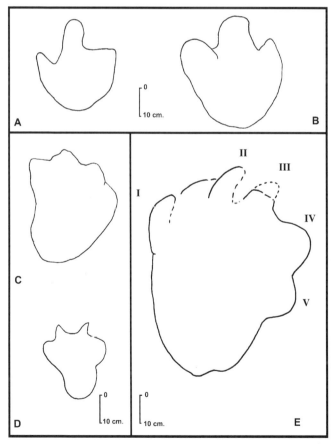

Figure 4. *Tracks from the Long Walk Quarry area (A-D) and Dalton Wells (E). A, B, large ornithopod tracks; C, D, below probable ankylosaur tracks are the first reported from the United States, note tetradactyl morphology; E, sauropod pes track, note pentadactyl morphology. All tracks drawn to same scale.*

this regard it should be noted that Lockley and Hunt (1994, 1995a) illustrated track casts that resemble those of large ornithopods, from the Cleveland-Lloyd Quarry area (Kantor and others, 1995), implying a Cretaceous age and stratigraphic position in the Cedar Mountain Formation. These tracks, however, are controversial with respect to their age and affinity, and have recently been interpreted as stegosaurian in origin (Bakker, 1996). They are probably from the Morrison Formation, not the Cedar Mountain Formation, though the age and stratigraphic location of this contact is uncertain in some areas, and thus controversial. This subject however is outside the scope of this paper.

It is clear that all important tracksite discoveries in the Cedar Mountain Formation, including the Dalton Wells site, appear to be made as a byproduct of digging for skeletal material. The identification and discovery of ankylosaur and sauropod tracks from the Long Walk and Dalton Wells quarries, respectively, are herein presented unequivocally for the first time. Such reports provide good examples of these "accidental" discoveries, which supplement previous reports of ornithopod ichnites. Clearly there is much to learn about the spatial and temporal distribution of tracks in the Cedar Mountain Formation, especially as paleontologists have yet to make deliberate efforts to search for ichnological evidence. Recent work also suggests that we are only just beginning to understand the lithostratigraphy, faunas and age of the formation (Kirkland, 1996; Kirkland and others, 1997).

At this stage it is hard to determine if there are any significant differences in the ichnofaunas discovered to date, but this may be due to the small sample size. The most common element appears to be ornithopod tracks, and at present there is no obvious difference between natural casts recovered from the lowest member (Yellow Cat) and the upper member (Mussentuchit), except that the Yellow Cat ichnofauna contains associated sauropod tracks, whereas to the best of our knowledge the Mussentuchit ichnofauna does not. It is possible that the absence of sauropod tracks in the Mussentuchit is a reflection of the age of this unit (Late Albian to Early Cenomanian) (Kirkland, 1996; Kirkland and others, 1997). If this age assignment is correct, then the Mussentuchit ichnofauna may represent an animal community that was extant during the early part of the so-called "sauropod hiatus" (Lucas and Hunt, 1989), a time (Cenomanian to Campanian) when sauropods appear to be absent from North America.

The most significant ichnological find in the Cedar Mountain Formation appears to be the tetradactyl tracks attributed to ankylosaurs (figure 4), which are evidently the first reported from the United States. Given that the only known ankylosaur tracks from North America (*Tetrapodosaurus* from the Gething Formation of Canada) are Aptian in age, it is evident that the Cedar Mountain tracks represent a site that is significantly younger, that is, close to the Albian-Cenomanian boundary. Although a large sample of tracks of the same age are known from the Dakota Group of the Colorado Front Range area, none are attributable to ankylosaurs. Thus it is tempting to conclude that the Mussentuchit tracks represent a different paleocommunity.

The Cedar Mountain ichnofaunas apparently have little in common with known ichnofaunas from the Barremian-early Cenomanian of western North America. For example, there is no indication that the Cedar Mountain ichnofauna has an obvious overall similarity to the Aptian Gething Formation of western Canada (Sternberg, 1932; Currie, 1989, and references therein), though the equivalent Cedar Mountain interval is poorly known. Similarly, there is no obvious similarity to the ichnofauna from the Lakota Group of the Black Hills region (Anderson, 1939), though this ichnofauna is also poorly known. Ichnofaunas that are time-equivalent to the Albian-Cenomanian Mussentuchit ichnofauna bear no obvious relationship to either the Albian sauropod-theropod-dominated ichnofaunas of Texas (see Lockley and Hunt, 1995a, and references therein) or to the younger (latest Albian to Early Cenomanian) Dakota Group ichnofaunas (Lockley and others, 1992; Lockley and Hunt, 1994). It is possible that this younger ichnofauna shares some elements in common with the Cenomanian Dunvegan Formation of Canada, which also contains ankylosaur tracks (Currie, 1989; Guy Plint, written communication, 1997).

Further work on the Lower to Middle Cretaceous tracks of both western Canada and the western U.S.A. is necessary to obtain a larger sample size and a better understanding of recurrent patterns in the composition of ichnofaunas. Such data should reveal the extent to which time-equivalent faunas are ichnostratigraphically similar, or whether there are regional (paleobiogeographic or paleoecologic) differences.

ACKNOWLEDGMENTS

We thank Philip Currie, Richard McCrea and Guy Plint for providing valuable information on Lower and "mid" Cretaceous ichnofaunas from Canada. We also thank Julianne Snider, Geoff Omvig and the offices of University of Colorado at Denver, Dinosaur Trackers Research Group, respectively, for assistance with the preparation of illustrations, and partial support of travel to field locations.

Notes added in proof: In addition to the five tracksites reported herein, a sixth was discovered in October 1998 by the senior authors (Lockley, M.G., and Kirkland, J.I.) near the base of the Mussentuchit Member, at Mussentuchit Wash. Tracks at this site consist of, at least, two well-preserved tridactyl, ornithopod track casts, one of which measures about 50 cm long by 55 cm wide.

Recent reports also indicate that ankylosaur tracks are now known from three formations in North America (McCrea and Currie, 1998; McCrea and others, 1998). The Cedar Mountain occurrences, however, remain the first documented in the United States.

REFERENCES

Anderson, S. M., 1939, Dinosaur tracks in the Lakota sandstone of the eastern Black Hills, South Dakota: Journal of Paleontology, v. 3, p. 361-364.

Anonymous, 1989, Work at Quarry Progresses During 1989: Utah Museum of Natural History, v. 21, no. 3, (no page number).

Bakker, R. T., 1996, The real Jurassic park--dinosaurs and habitats at Como Bluff, Wyoming, *in* Morales, Michael, editor, The continental Jurassic: Museum of Northern Arizona, p. 35-49.

Carpenter, Kenneth, 1984, Skeletal reconstructions and life restorations of *Sauropelta* and *Paleoscincus* (Ankylosauria: Nodosauridae) from the Cretaceous of North America: Canadian Journal of Earth Sciences, v. 21, p. 1491-1498.

Currie, P. J., 1989, Dinosaur footprints of western Canada, *in* Gillette, D. D., and Lockley, M. G., editors, Dinosaur tracks and traces: Cambridge, Cambridge University Press, p. 293-300.

DeCourten, F. L., 1990, The Long Walk quarry--a new horizon in dinosaur research: Canyon Legacy, Dan O'Laurie Museum, Moab, Utah. v. 2, p. 15-22.

—1991, New data on Early Cretaceous dinosaurs from the Long Walk quarry and tracksite, Emery County, Utah *in* Chidsey, T. C., editor, Geology of east central Utah: Utah Geological Association Publication, no. 19, p. 311-324.

Kantor, D. C., Byers, C. W., and Nadon, G. C., 1995, The upper Brushy Basin Member and Buckhorn Conglomerate at the Cleveland-Lloyd Quarry--transition from an anastomosed to a braided fluvial deposit: Geological Society of America Abstracts with Program, v. 27, p. 277.

Kirkland, K. I., 1996, Biogeography of western North America's mid-Cretaceous dinosaur faunas--losing European ties and the first great Asian-North American interchange: Journal of Vertebrate Paleontology, v. 16, p. 45A.

Kirkland, J. I., Britt, B. B., Burge, D.L., Carpenter, Kenneth, Cifelli, Richard, DeCourten, Frank, Eaton, J. G., Hasiotis, S. T., Kirshbaum, Mark, and Lawton, Timothy, 1997, Lower to Middle Cretaceous dinosaur faunas of the central Colorado Plateau--a key to understanding 35 million years of tectonics, sedimentology, evo-

lution and biogeography: Brigham Young University Geology Studies, v. 42, part 2, p. 69-103.

Lockley, M. G., Holbrook, John, Hunt, A. P., Matsukawa, M., and Meyer, C., 1992, The dinosaur freeway--a preliminary report on the Cretaceous megatracksite, Dakota Group, Rocky Mountain Front Range and High Plains, Colorado, Oklahoma and New Mexico, *in* Flores, Romeo, editor, Mesozoic of the Western Interior: Society of Economic Paleontologists and Mineralogists, Midyear Meeting Field Trip Guidebook, p. 39-54.

Lockley, M. G., and Hunt, A. P., 1994, A review of vertebrate ichnofaunas of the Western Interior United States--evidence and implications, *in* Caputo, M. V., Peterson, J. A., and Franczyk, K. J., editors, Mesozoic systems of the Rocky Mountain region, United States: Society of Economic Paleontologists and Mineralogists, p. 95-108.

__1995a, Dinosaur tracks and other fossil footprints of the western United States: New York, Columbia University Press, 338 p.

—1995b, Ceratopsid tracks and associated ichnofauna from the Laramie Formation (Upper Cretaceous, Maastrichtian) of Colorado: Journal of Vertebrate Paleontology, v. 15, p. 592-614.

Lucas, S. G., and Hunt, A. P., 1989, Alamosaurus and the sauropod hiatus in the Cretaceous of the North American Western Interior, *in* Farlow, J. O., editor, Paleobiology of the dinosaurs: Geological Society of America Special Paper, no. 238, p. 75-85.

McCrea, Richard T., and Currie, Philip J. 1998, A preliminary report on dinosaur tracksites in the lower Cretaceous (Albian) Gates Formation near Grande Cache, Alberta, *in* Lucas, S.G., Kirkland, J.I., and Estep, J.W., editors, Lower and Middle Cretaceous terrestrial ecosystems: New Mexico Museum of Natural History and Science Bulletin No. 14, p.155-162.

McCrea, Richard T, Lockley, Martin G., and Plint, A. Guy, 1998, A summary of purported ankylosaur track occurrences: Journal of Vertebrate Paleontology, 18 (Supplement to No. 3): 62A.

Sternberg, C. M., 1932, Dinosaur tracks from Peace River, British Columbia: Annual Report, National Museum of Canada (for 1930), p. 59-85.

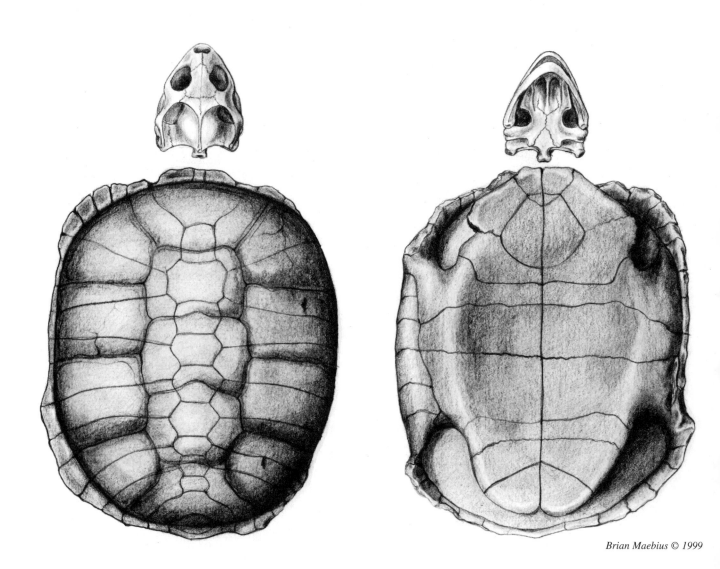

Brian Maebius © 1999

Eocene turtle

NON-MAMMALIAN MICROVERTEBRATE REMAINS FROM THE ROBISON EGGSHELL SITE, CEDAR MOUNTAIN FORMATION (LOWER CRETACEOUS), EMERY COUNTY, UTAH

Anthony R. Fiorillo
Dallas Museum of Natural History
P.O. Box 150349
Dallas, TX 75315
email: fiorillo@mail.smu.edu

ABSTRACT

The Robison Eggshell Site is located in the Lower Cretaceous Cedar Mountain Formation of Emery County, Utah. Previous published work on the non-mammalian remains from this site has been of a very broad taxonomic nature.

This report documents the presence of several taxa previously unrecorded at this site. Taxonomic diversity is greatest among the fishes, but theropod dinosaurs and crocodiles are well represented. Minor components of the fauna include a lizard, a frog, and turtles. This assemblage likely was derived from or near freshwater streams or rivers.

INTRODUCTION

The successful application of screenwash procedures to the recovery of microvertebrate fossil remains from the Tertiary (Hibbard, 1949) has warranted application of screenwash techniques to various other parts of the geologic column. For the Cretaceous Period, screenwash efforts have provided tremendous insights into the diversity and biogeography of a variety of taxa, ranging from fishes to mammals (Archibald, 1982; Cifelli, 1990a, 1990b, 1990c, 1990d, 1994; Clemens, 1964; Eaton and Nelson, 1991; Fiorillo, 1989; Lillegraven, 1969; Lillegraven and McKenna, 1986; Rowe and others, 1992; Sahni, 1972; Winkler and others, 1990), although the vast majority of the published work has centered on the Upper Cretaceous.

The purpose of this report is to add to the growing body of knowledge of the taxonomic diversity and biogeography of taxa in the Lower Cretaceous Cedar Mountain Formation. The Robison Eggshell Site (Nelson and Crooks, 1987), also called the Egg Shell Quarry (Nelson and Madsen, 1985), is perhaps best known for its reptilian eggshells and fossil mammals. In addition, teeth of teleosts and crocodiles have been mentioned (Nelson and Madsen, 1985). The crocodilian component of this fauna has been described in much more detail by Pomes (1988). More recent screenwash operations at this site by a small Carnegie Museum of Natural History field party in 1991 have shown the locality contains an abundant and diverse fauna of lower vertebrates. Eaton and Nelson (1991) have reported in great detail on the mammal fauna from this locality, and others in western Emery County, Utah. This paper focuses on the non-mammalian microvertebrate remains from the Robison Eggshell Site.

CEDAR MOUNTAIN FORMATION BACKGROUND

The Lower Cretaceous Cedar Mountain Formation is extensively exposed in the San Rafael Swell of eastern Utah and adjacent areas. In most places it unconformably overlies the Upper Jurassic Morrison Formation. The Cedar Mountain Formation marks the beginning of the Sevier Orogeny in central Utah according to Weiss and Roche (1988), a period of fold thrust deformation and arc magmatism in the western cordillera region of North America (Livacarri, 1991). Aubrey (1989), in contrast, has suggested that tectonism on the southern Colorado Plateau was active during the Jurassic as well. Based on a lack of tricoporate pollen, Tschudy and others (1984) considered the uppermost part of the Cedar Mountain Formation as late Albian in age. Eaton and Nelson (1991) concluded that the entire formation may be late Albian in age. Scott (1987) considered the unit to be slightly older, perhaps middle Albian in age, based on the distribution of the freshwater bivalve *Musculiopsis*, throughout the Rocky Mountain region and the Great Basin. The Dakota Sandstone (Aubrey, 1989) overlies the Cedar Mountain Formation in south-central Utah.

According to Stokes (1952), the lower member of

the Cedar Mountain Formation is the coarse-grained
Buckhorn Conglomerate; the unnamed main body of
the Cedar Mountain Formation is composed of massive, medium-gray siltstones with occasional lenses
of sandstone (Nelson and Crooks, 1987). More
recently, Kirkland and others (1997), and Kirkland
and others, this volume, have identified several
unconformities in the Cedar Mountain Formation.
Kirkland and associates have defined several members for this formation along the western side of the
San Rafael Swell; the Mussentuchit Member is the
youngest of these members and contains the Robison
Eggshell Site (J. I. Kirkland, personal communication). Pomes (1988) placed the Robison Eggshell
Site 10-15 meters below the contact with the overlying Dakota Sandstone. My observations during
screenwash operations place this site closer to 10
meters below the contact.

The Cedar Mountain Formation is well known
for its vertebrate fossils (Bodily, 1969; Galton and
Jensen, 1975, 1979; Tidwell and others, 1983; Nelson and Crooks, 1987; Eaton and Nelson, 1991;
DeCourten, 1991; Kirkland and others, 1997). Much
of the non-dinosaurian fauna is known from
microvertebrate localities and includes taxa of fishes,
turtles, crocodiles, and mammals (Nelson and
Crooks, 1987; Eaton and Nelson, 1991; Kirkland and
others, 1997). The dinosaur fauna includes large and
small theropods, sauropods, iguanodontids, and
ankylosaurids (Weishampel, 1990; Kirkland and others, 1997). Also, among the dinosaur remains are
locally abundant fragments of eggshells (Jensen,
1970; Tidwell and others, 1983; Nelson and Crooks,
1987).

Associated with this locality are a variety of plant
remains (Tidwell and others, 1983). These plants indicate that the sediments of the Robison Eggshell Site were
deposited under subtropical to tropical conditions.

In 1990, Steve Robison of the U.S. Forest Service
showed me a fossiliferous vertebrate locality (figure 1)
he had found several years earlier in the Cedar Mountain
Formation of Emery County while having a picnic with
his family. In 1991, I returned to the site with a small
crew to screenwash this locality. We screenwashed
approximately one quarter metric ton of sediment.
Pomes (1988) described a measured section containing
this locality. According to Pomes (1988), the Robison
Eggshell Site is within a variable siltstone-mudstone
interval approximately 5 meters thick. All specimens
discussed in this report are housed at the Carnegie Museum of Natural History (CM). Precise locality data, refer-
enced as the Robison Eggshell Site, are available either

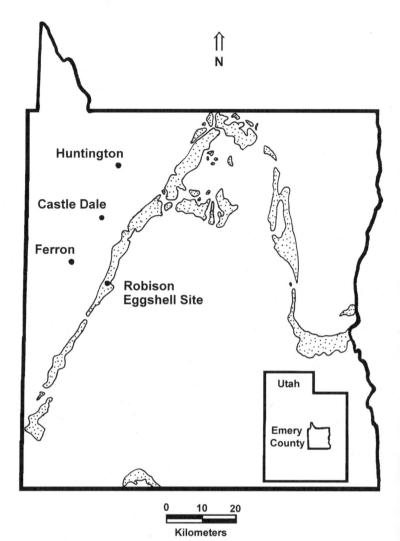

Figure 1. *Location of Robison Eggshell Site. Cedar Mountain Formation outcrop pattern, shown as lightly stippled shapes, adapted from Eaton and Nelson
(1991).*

through the author, the Section of Vertebrate Fossils at
the Carnegie Museum of Natural History, or based on the
earlier work by Nelson and others, at the Sternberg Memorial Museum at Fort Hays State University. Eggshell
collections from this locality (studied by the late Karl
Hirsch) are also housed at the University of Colorado
Museum in Boulder.

VERTEBRATE FAUNA

The fauna from the Robison Eggshell Site is summarized in table 1. Details of the fauna are elaborated on
below.

Fishes

By far the most diverse component of the fauna is
the fishes. At least seven types of fish have been identified, virtually all of which are represented solely by teeth.
Both the cartilaginous and bony fishes are common.

Table 1. *List of non-mammalian taxa recovered from screen-wash operations at the Robison Eggshell Site in the Lower Cretaceous Cedar Mountain Formation of Emery County, Utah. Specimens housed at the Carnegie Museum of Natural History.*

Class Chondrichthyes
    Order Hybodontiformes
        Hybodus sp.
    Order Rajiformes
        Pseudohypolophus sp.
    Order Orectolobiformes
        Cretorectolobus sp.
Class Osteichthyes
    Order Salmoniformes
        Enchodus sp.
    Order Semionotiformes
        Lepidotes sp.
    Order Amiiformes
        amiiform, indeterminate
    Order Pycnodontiformes
        pycnodontid, indeterminate
Class Amphibia
    Order Anura
        anuran, indeterminate
Class Reptilia
    Order Chelonia
        Naomichelys sp.
        trionychid, indeterminate
    Order Squamata
        Lacertilia, indeterminate
    Order Crocodylia
        ?Atoposauridae
        ?Pholidosauridae
        ?*Bernissartia* sp.
    Order Saurischia
        "*Paronychodon*" (Dromaeosauridae)
        aff. Theropod "A"
        Dromaeosaurinae
        Velociraptorinae
        Theropoda, indeterminate
    Order Ornithischia
        Ornithopoda, indeterminate

Of the cartilaginous fishes, teeth belonging to the ray *Pseudohypolophus* are the most common (CM 71579). They are hexagonal to rhombic in occlusal view, forming flat, crushing plates in the mouth, and have a prominent groove that bisects the tooth in the direction of the short axis. A weak ridge that runs along the long axis of the tooth is present on the crowns of some teeth. Thurmond (1971) considered ?*Hypolophus*, the genus later named *Pseudohypolophus* by Cappetta and Case (1975), an indicator of marine or brackish waters.

An uncommon component of the fish fauna are fragmentary teeth (CM 71580) attributed to the genus *Hybodus* (figure 2). The parts of the teeth represented are conical crowns with robust striae. Thurmond (1971) differentiated anterior and lateral teeth based on these striae. On anterior teeth the striae extend approximately half way up the main cusp of the tooth, while on lateral

teeth the striae may extend from base to tip with some striae bifurcating at the base (Thurmond, 1971). Though the very tip of one of these teeth from the Robison Eggshell Site is missing, the striae extend along the entire length of the cusp, indicating these are lateral teeth.

Figure 2. *Partial* Hybodus *tooth (CM 71580), side view. Scale bar equals 1 mm.*

One very small tooth, exhibiting a single narrow cusp with proportionately long, low shoulders, can be attributed to the genus *Cretorectolobus* (CM 71581). Welton and Farish (1993) described both *Cretorectolobus* and *Squatina* from the Cretaceous of Texas, noting that presence of a nutrient groove in the root of the tooth separates the former from the latter taxon. Though poorly preserved, the root on this specimen from the Robison Eggshell Site has a nutrient groove.

Indeterminate chondrichthian dermal ossicles (CM 71582) also are present in very small numbers.

The most common identifiable fish remains are teeth assigned to *Lepidotes* (figure 3A). These teeth (CM 71583) have a smooth, hemisphere-shaped enamel cap with a bony base or pedestal. In addition, two teeth of a second tooth type (CM 71584) have a proportionately long base and a small, conical enamel cap. Bilelo (1969), and Estes and Sanchiz (1982) discerned two tooth morphologies for *Lepidotes*, a conical tooth type and a hemispherical tooth type. The hemispherical teeth are from the palatine, while the conical teeth figured by Estes and Sanchiz (1982) are marginal or pharyngeal teeth. The hemispherical teeth (CM 71583) from the Robison Eggshell Site are clearly palatal teeth while the two conical teeth (CM 71584) are probably marginal teeth. The smooth surface of the crowns of the hemispherical teeth indicates a moderate amount of wear. Enamel scales attributable to semionotiform fish are common at the Robison Eggshell Site and most likely belong to *Lepidotes*.

An amiiform fish (CM 71585), represented in small numbers by isolated teeth (figure 3B), is similar to the Late Cretaceous amiiform *Melvius* (Bryant, 1987). However, the basic tooth morphology of this genus may be present in other amiiform fish such as *Kindleia* (Bryant,

1989). The teeth from the Robison Eggshell Site have a broadly conical enamel cap overlying a bony pedestal. Based on the limited taxonomic utility of amiiform teeth, the teeth from the Robison Eggshell Site are assigned to the order Amiiformes, genus indeterminate.

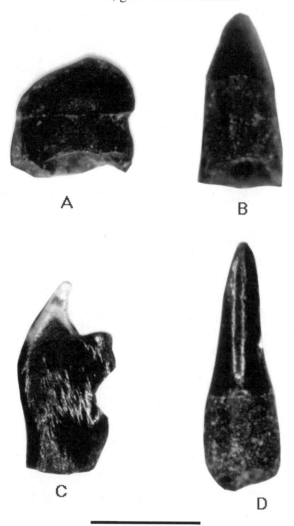

Figure 3. *Assorted osteichthyan teeth. A.* Lepidotes *tooth (CM 71583). B. amiiform tooth (CM 71585). C. pycnodont tooth (CM 71586). D.* Enchodus *tooth (CM 71587). All teeth are shown in lateral view. Scale bar equals 1 mm.*

In their report on Early Cretaceous lower vertebrates from Spain, Estes and Sanchiz (1982) identified two forms of pycnodont teeth. One form was rounded and approximately 2 mm in diameter. The second form was much smaller (1 mm or less) and graded into a more pronounced falcate type, and was considered as marginal or branchial. No teeth of the first type were obtained from the Robison Eggshell Site but three teeth of the latter type (CM 71586) were recovered (figure 3C). Although Thurmond (1974) made taxonomic determinations of pycnodont teeth, I follow Estes and Sanchiz (1982) in their belief that generic identifications are not possible.

One tooth (CM 71587, figure 3D) is similar to the *Enchodus* specimens of McNulty and Slaughter (1968) and Winkler and others (1990) from the Lower Cretaceous of Texas. This tooth is slender, somewhat conical, and slightly recurved, with a pronounced root.

In addition to the teeth discussed above, a small sample of unidentified osteichthyan centra was recovered from the site.

Amphibians

An anuran premaxilla (CM 71588, figure 4) from this site is roughly triangular and has not been fused either to the other premaxilla or to the maxilla. The pars dentalis is present, but lacks teeth. The alary process is nearly vertical. The bone has an irregular pattern of sculpting on its external side. On the internal side is a prominent ledge of bone above the tooth row, the pars palatina (Trueb, 1973). Above the pars palatina is a projection that is probably the palatine process. In many salamanders the premaxillae are paired and the pars palatina is absent (Duellman and Trueb, 1986). The presence of the palatine process in this specimen indicates that it is a frog.

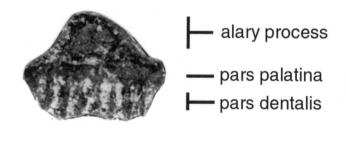

Figure 4. *Anuran premaxilla (CM 71588), medial view. Scale bar equals 1 mm.*

Reptiles

Turtles

Most of the turtle material is fragmentary and unsculpted, rendering taxonomic identification largely fruitless. However, due to the diagnostic pustular or beaded sculpture on the carapace and plastron of *Naomichelys*, CM 71589 allows identification of this genus at the Robison Eggshell Site. *Naomichelys* is typically an uncommon member in rocks of this age. Fragmentary remains of this turtle have been reported from the Trinity Group of Texas (Thurmond, 1974; Langston, 1974).

Figure 5. Trionychid neural (CM 71590), ventral (left) and dorsal (right) views. Scale bar equals 1 mm.

CM 71590 is a nearly complete neural (figure 5) belonging to a juvenile trionychid. This specimen is 4 mm by 4 mm in size, with sutures on three of the four sides, and displays the sculpting pattern typical of trionychid turtles. Meylan (1987) pointed out that the number of neurals in trionychids ranges from three to 10, but that a more typical series consists of nine neurals. Given this criterion, and assuming that this neural belongs to a typical trionychid with nine neurals, the approximate minimum carapace anterior-posterior length of this juvenile was 36 mm. This size range is only slightly larger than modern North American trionychid hatchlings.

Lizards

One isolated dentary fragment of a lizard (CM 71591) was recovered from this screenwashing. The specimen lacks complete teeth, but the alveoli are closely spaced. There is no evidence of a Meckelian groove. Because it otherwise lacks diagnostic features, it is listed in table 1 as Lacertilia indeterminate.

Crocodiles

Crocodile teeth are the most abundant, non-eggshell remains found at the Robison Eggshell Site. A large number of the teeth (CM 71592) have a corroded appearance (figure 6).

Teeth among one subset (CM 71593) are flattened mediolaterally and have a distinctive pattern of fine striations connecting the posterior and anterior crests (figure 7). Lateral striations

Figure 6. Indeterminate crocodile tooth (CM 71592). Note the heavy pitting on the surface. Scale bar equals 1 mm.

form a fan pattern that originates at the tip of the crown and expands toward the root. I follow Estes and Sanchiz (1982) in their tentative assignment of teeth matching this description to the family Atoposauridae.

Teeth in a second, larger subset are elongated, button-shaped, and typically exhibit heavy apical wear. Estes and Sanchiz (1982) and Winkler and others (1990) described teeth identical to these and assigned, or tentatively assigned, them to the Bernissartiidae.

Teeth belonging to the third and largest subset have proportionately heavy ridges running from the apex to the root (for example, CM 71595, figure 8). These teeth do not exhibit lateral compression and are typically only 5 mm or less in crown height. I follow Estes and Sanchiz (1982), who described similar teeth and questionably referred them to the Pholidosauridae.

Dinosaurs

Dinosaurs from the Robison Eggshell Site are known from teeth, tooth fragments, and eggshell fragments. Many of these eggshell fragments (CM 71596) are elongatoolithid according to the morphological classification of Mikhailov and others (1994), who reasoned that this type is either theropod or avian. Other eggshell fragments from the site are spheroolithid (CM 71597, sensu Mikhailov and others, 1994), and likely are ornithopods.

Most of the remaining teeth from the site are those of unidentifiable ornithopods. Recent work on theropod teeth from the Late Cretaceous of North America (for example, Currie and others, 1990; Fiorillo and Currie,

Figure 7. ?Atoposaurid crocodile tooth (CM 71593). Scale bar equals 1 mm.

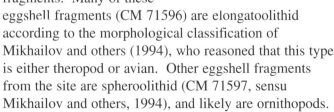

Figure 8. ?Pholidosaurid crocodile tooth (CM 71595). Scale bar equals 1 mm.

1994) has shown the utility of theropod teeth for taxonomic identifications. Based on the previous work of these other workers, it is possible to provide some degree of taxonomic resolution, at the subfamily level, to the theropod fauna of the Robison Eggshell Site. I hesitate to assign Late Cretaceous generic names to these taxa given the large amount of geologic time between these animals and those of the Early Cretaceous Robison Eggshell Site.

Most of the teeth recovered from the Robison Eggshell Site are fragmentary, but some yield valuable diagnostic characteristics. A large subset of teeth and fragments (CM 71598) are laterally compressed with labiolingual broad, chisel-like denticles. The denticles are simple and do not possess the apically oriented hook of velociraptorine dromaeosaurids. These teeth can be attributed to the subfamily Dromaeosaurinae (Dromaeosauridae).

Two strongly recurved teeth (CM 71599) in the sample also exhibit a pronounced lateral compression and have anterior carinae that lack denticles, while the denticles on the posterior carinae are taller than wide, narrow, and tend to be straight with a slight apically oriented hook. Following Currie and others (1990) and Fiorillo and Currie (1994), these two teeth are assigned to the subfamily Velociraptorinae (Dromaeosauridae).

One small tooth from this site (CM 71399) has both the anterior and posterior carinae on the lingual side of the tooth. The top half of the tooth is missing but the cross section of the tooth is decidedly D-shaped. This morphology is similar to that normally associated with tyrannosaurid premaxillary teeth (Currie and others, 1990, figure 8.6 R,S, V, W; Holtz, 1994), an unlikely taxonomic assignment for this specimen given the spatial distribution of tyrannosaurids (Holtz, 1994). However, Madsen (1974) tentatively assigned *Stokesosaurus* from the Upper Jurassic Morrison Formation of Utah to the Tyrannosauridae and Kirkland and Parrish (1995) reported tyrannosaurid teeth from the Cedar Mountain Formation in Utah.

One large tooth fragment (CM 72650), exhibiting a characteristic flattened side with longitudinal ridges (Currie and others, 1990), can be assigned to "*Paronychodon*." Currie and others (1990) summarized the history of this taxon and concluded that the serrated versions of this tooth form represent abnormalities in tooth development, perhaps due to prolonged contact to the medial wall of the tooth socket. Although the denticle-bearing parts of the carinae are missing on the Robison Eggshell specimen, the shape of the cross section at the proximal end of the tooth is similar to that of dromaeosaurids (Currie and others, 1990, figure 8.1N).

Therefore, following the "*Paronychodon*" assignments of Currie and others (1990), this tooth is tentatively assigned to "*Paronychodon*" (Dromaeosauridae).

One other theropod tooth fragment of interest (CM 72651) is a portion of a carina. The size and shape indicates that this fragment belonged to a much larger tooth. The denticles have a longer labiolingual axis than proximodistal axis, a characteristic of most large theropods (Fiorillo and Currie, 1994). There is no indication of a blood groove on this specimen and there is a strong similarity between this tooth fragment and those described from the Late Cretaceous as Theropod "A" by Fiorillo and Currie (1994). Based on the fragmentary nature of this specimen and the unknown taxonomic affinities of the material described by Fiorillo and Currie (1994), this specimen is listed in table 1 as aff. Theropod "A".

The last dinosaur specimen of interest is an edentulous partial jaw (CM 72652, figure 9). Based on the thecodont alveoli, the lack of ornamentation on the lateral side, and the deep, gracile nature and overall shape of the tooth sockets, I tentatively assign this jaw to the Ornithopoda. Its size indicates that is was a neonate.

Figure 9. *Jaw fragment attributed to the Ornithopoda, lingual view (CM 72652). Three and one half alveoli are visible on the specimen (highlighted by arrows). Scale bar equals 1 mm.*

Maxwell and Horner (1994) discussed the significance of neonate dinosaurian remains from the Cloverly Formation of Montana. Their paper constituted the first report of neonate dinosaurs from the Early Cretaceous of North America. They correctly pointed out that a more intensive exploration of the Cloverly Formation should yield more information on the reproductive behavior of ornithopod dinosaurs. The discovery of this specimen, the second report of neonate dinosaurs from the Early Cretaceous, emphasizes the need for a more intensive search for neonate dinosaurian material not only in the

Cloverly Formation (Maxwell and Horner, 1994), but also in the Cedar Mountain Formation.

The surface texture of most of the ornithopod teeth in the Robison Eggshell Site appears to be corroded, presumably due to a high pH environment such as a digestive tract. This pattern of corrosion was the result of either predation by another vertebrate, or by the individuals themselves swallowing their own teeth during the tooth replacement cycle. In contrast, only a few of the theropod teeth showed similar signs of corrosion.

PALEOENVIRONMENTAL INTERPRETATION OF THE FAUNA

The fauna recovered from this site resembles the Galve fossil assemblage from Spain (Estes and Sanchiz, 1982), and to a lesser extent the fauna reported from central Texas by Winkler and others (1990). Notable differences with the Galve assemblage are that the Robison Eggshell Site has higher taxonomic diversity in fishes, while amphibian specimens in the Galve assemblage are sufficiently diagnostic to allow a finer taxonomic resolution. The Robison Eggshell site has a greater taxonomic diversity of dinosaurs than the other two faunas.

Estes and Sanchiz (1982) concluded that the Galve fauna was derived from, or near, freshwater streams and rivers. Sediments of the Cedar Mountain Formation were deposited on a broad alluvial floodplain with no evidence of marine or brackish water facies (Eaton and others, 1990). Paleogeographic reconstruction for the Cedar Mountain Formation shows stream flow to have been from west to east (Elder and Kirkland, 1994). The nearest marine depositional realm was the Chihuahua Trough, a marine arm of the early Gulf of Mexico (Dickinson and others, 1989; Elder and Kirkland, 1994), which extended from southern Arizona through central and southern Texas.

The fauna from Robison Eggshell Site is similar to the Galve fauna of Spain (table 2). Both faunas accumulated under similar paleoenvironmental conditions, but some interesting anomalies in the Robison Eggshell Site fauna are consistent with the expected fauna given the regional depositional setting. For example, Thurmond (1971) suggested that the occurrence of *Hybodus* indicates brackish waters. Estes and Sanchiz (1982) considered *Hybodus* as marine, but pointed out that the genus had successfully migrated into freshwater environments by the Early Cretaceous. They also pointed out similar problems with pycnodontids and *Lepidotes* but, unlike their discussion on *Hybodus*, offered no further discussion for these other fishes. Based on the presence of

frogs and salamanders, Estes and Sanchiz (1982) argued that the Galve assemblage was only peripherally associated with marine environments. With respect to faunas containing assemblages with mixed environmental indicators, Winkler and others (1990) suggested that perhaps fish with marine affinities could tolerate fresh water and moved up rivers away from marine environments. The paleogeographic reconstruction of the Cedar Mountain Formation of Elder and Kirkland (1994) requires that the Robison Eggshell Site is nonmarine. Given the distance of the Robison Eggshell Site from any body of marine or brackish water, it seems that simple freshwater tolerance is not the answer to a paleoenvironmental reconstruction involving fish with suspect paleosalinity affinities. Therefore, the problematic fish taxa at the Robison Eggshell Site may represent a greater range in environmental conditions of these taxa than presently recognized.

CONCLUSIONS

Early reports on the fauna from the Robison Eggshell Site in the Cedar Mountain Formation of Emery County, Utah focused on fossil mammals, with only scant attention to non-mammalian remains.

This report documents the presence of several non-mammalian taxa previously unrecorded at this site. Taxonomic diversity is greatest among the fishes and reptiles. Amphibians are not well represented. Based on previous interpretations of the paleoenvironmental affinities of some of these taxa in other contemporary faunas, the Robison Eggshell Site assemblage seems to contain faunal abnormalities. However, paleogeographic reconstructions of the Cedar Mountain Formation indicate that this fossil assemblage was likely derived from marginally freshwater streams and rivers, and that the paleoenvironmental interpretations for the anomalous taxa deserve reconsideration.

ACKNOWLEDGMENTS

Foremost, I thank Steve Robison for showing me the eggshell site that he and his family discovered during the course of their picnic. Also, Susan Dawson, Richard Blob, and Susan Ruth provided valuable assistance in the field. David D. Gillette, Michael E. Nelson, and Steve Robison provided constructive reviews that greatly helped in the rewriting of this manuscript. I am grateful to Ben Hong for his help with the tedious microscope work in the lab. I also thank Dale Winkler for discussions regarding Early Cretaceous faunas of Texas, James I. Kirkland for discussions regarding the stratigraphic position of the Robison Eggshell Site, and Dan Chure for discussions on the possible occurrences of Late Jurassic

Table 2. *Generic (or higher taxonomic rank) list of Early Cretaceous non-mammalian taxa recovered from Robison Eggshell Site (RES) discussed in this report and in Pomes (1988: designated in this table by an * following the X) compared to those from central Texas (Central Texas, Winkler and others, 1990), and Galve, Spain (Estes and Sanchiz, 1982). Taxa are listed as presented in their respective reports with the exception of reference to material with affinities to the Coeluridae by both Pomes (1988) and Estes and Sanchiz (1982). As a taxonomic group, the name Coeluridae is problematic; these materials are listed here as Theropoda indeterminate. The occurrence of* Naomichelys *for central Texas is from Thurmond (1974) and Langston (1974).*

	RES	Central Texas	Galve
Class Chondrichthyes			
Order Hybodontiformes			
Lissodus sp.		X	
Lonchidion sp.			X
Hybodus sp.	X	X	
cf. *Hylaeobatis*		X	
Order Batoidea			
Dasyatidae sp.	X*		
Order Rajiformes			
Rhinobates sp.		X	
Pseudohypolophus sp.	X	X	
Order Orectolobiformes			
Cretorectolobus sp.	X		
Order Lamniformes			
Leptostyrax sp.		X	
Class Osteichthyes			
Order Ceratodontiformes			
Ceratodus sp.		X	
Order Pycnodontiformes			
Gyronchus sp.		X	
Nonaphalgodus sp.		X	
Callodus sp.		X	
Paramicrodon sp.		X	
Palaeobalistum sp.		X	
Proscincetes sp.		X	
Coelodus sp.		X	
pycnodontid, indeterminate	X	X	X
Order Semionotiformes			
Lepidotes sp.	X	X	X
Order Amiiformes			
Macrepistius sp.		X	
amiiform, indeterminate	X	X	X
Order Salmoniformes			
Enchodus sp.	X	X	
Class Amphibia			
Order Caudata			
Prosiren sp.		X	
Albanerpeton sp.			X
Galverpeton sp.			X
Caudata, indeterminate		X	
Order Anura			
Eodiscoglossus sp.			X
Discoglossidae?, indeterminate		X	
anuran, indeterminate	X	X	
Class Reptilia			
Order Chelonia			
Naomichelys sp.	X		
trionychid, indeterminate	X		
testudines, indeterminate		X	
Order Squamata			
Teiinae?, indeterminate		X	
Anguidae?, indeterminate		X	
Lacertilia, indeterminate	X	X	X
Order Crocodylia			
?*Bernissartia* sp.	X	X	X
Theriosuchus sp.	X*		
?Atoposauridae	X	X	X
Goniopholis sp.	X*		
Polydectes sp.	X*		
?Pholidosauridae	X	X	X
Machimosaurus sp.	X*		
Crocodylia, indeterminate		X	
Order Saurischia			
"*Paronychodon*" (Dromaeosauridae)	X		
Aff. Theropod "A"	X		
Dromaeosaurinae	X		
Velociraptorinae	X		
cf. Dromaeosauridae, indeterminate		X	
Theropoda, indeterminate	X	X	X
Sauropoda, indeterminate		X	
Order Ornithischia			
Tenontosaurus? sp.		X	
Aff. *Echinodon*			X
Hypsilophodontidae, indeterminate		X	X
Ornithopoda, indeterminate	X		

and Early Cretaceous tyrannosaurids. Amy Henrici was helpful in discussions regarding Mesozoic and Tertiary frogs. Gail Manning provided assistance in photographing the specimens illustrated in this report. Paul Krutak provided me access to Pomes (1988), and John Foster provided details of the localities of figured University of Colorado specimens studied by Karl Hirsch. Cooperation of the U. S. Bureau of Land Management in securing the necessary permit for collecting is also appreciated. Fieldwork for this project was sponsored by the M. Graham Netting and O'Neil funds from the Carnegie Museum of Natural History.

REFERENCES

Archibald, J. D., 1982, A study of Mammalia and geology across the Cretaceous-Tertiary boundary in Garfield County, Montana: University of California Publications in Geological Sciences, v. 122, p. 1-286.

Aubrey, W. M., 1989, Mid-Cretaceous alluvial-plain incision related to eustasy, southeastern Colorado Plateau: Geological Society of America Bulletin, v. 101, p. 443-449.

Bilelo, M. M., 1969, The fossil fish *Lepidotes* in the Paluxy Formation, north-central Texas: American Midland Naturalist, v. 81, p. 405-411.

Bodily, N. M., 1969, An armored dinosaur from the Lower Cretaceous of Utah: Brigham Young University Geology Studies, v. 16, p. 35-60.

Bryant, L. J., 1987, A new genus and species of Amiidae (Holostei; Osteichthyes) from the Late Cretaceous of North America, with comments on the phylogeny of the Amiidae: Journal of Vertebrate Paleontology, v. 7, p. 349-361.

—1989, Non-dinosaurian lower vertebrates across the Cretaceous-Tertiary boundary in northeastern Montana: University of California Publications in Geological Sciences, v. 134, p. 1-107.

Cappetta, Henri, and Case, J. A., 1975, Selaciens nouveaux du Cretace du Texas: Geobios, v. 8, p. 303-307.

Cifelli, R. L., 1990a, Cretaceous mammals of southern Utah. I. Marsupials from the Kaiparowits Formation (Judithian): Journal of Vertebrate Paleontology, v. 10, p. 295-319.

—1990b, Cretaceous mammals of southern Utah. II. Marsupials and marsupial-like mammals from the Wahweap Formation (early Campanian): Journal of Vertebrate Paleontology, v. 10, p. 320-331.

—1990c, Cretaceous mammals of southern Utah. III. Therian mammals from the Turonian (early Late Cretaceous): Journal of Vertebrate Paleontology, v. 10, p. 332-345.

—1990d, Cretaceous mammals of southern Utah. IV. Eutherian mammals from the Wahweap (Aquilan) and Kaiparowits (Judithian) Formations: Journal of Vertebrate Paleontology, v. 10, p. 346-360.

—1994, Therian mammals of the Terlingua local fauna (Judithian), Aguja Formation, Big Bend of the Rio Grande, Texas: Contributions to Geology, University of Wyoming, v. 30, p. 117-136.

Clemens, W. A., 1964, Fossil mammals of the type Lance Formation, Wyoming. Part I. Introduction and Multituberculata: University of California Publications in Geological Sciences, no. 48, p. 1-105.

Currie, P. J., Rigby, J. K., Jr., and Sloan, Robert, 1990, Theropod teeth from the Judith River Formation of southern Alberta, Canada, *in* Carpenter, Kenneth, and Currie, P. J., editors, Dinosaur systematics--approaches and perspectives: New York, Cambridge University Press, p. 107-125.

DeCourten, F. L., 1991, The Long Walk Quarry and tracksite--unveiling the mysterious Early Cretaceous of the Dinosaur Triangle region, *in* Averett, W. R., editor, Guidebook for dinosaur quarries and tracksites tour: Grand Junction, Grand Junction Geological Society, p. 19-25.

Dickinson, W. R., Fiorillo, A. R., Hall, D. L., Monreal, Rogelio, Potochnik, A. R., and Swift, P. N., 1989, Cretaceous strata of southern Arizona, *in* Jenney, J. P., and Reynolds, S. J., editors, Geologic evolution of Arizona: Tucson, Arizona Geological Society Digest, v. 17, p. 447-461.

Duellman, W. E., and Trueb, Linda, 1986, Biology of amphibians: New York, McGraw-Hill, Inc., 670 p.

Eaton, J. G., Kirkland, J. I., and Kauffman, E. G., 1990, Evidence and dating of mid-Cretaceous tectonic activity in the San Rafael Swell, Emery County, Utah: The Mountain Geologist, v. 27, p. 39-45.

Eaton, J. G., and Nelson, M. E., 1991, Multituberculate mammals from the Lower Cretaceous Cedar Mountain Formation, San Rafael Swell, Utah: Contributions to Geology, University of Wyoming, v. 29, no. 1, p. 1-12.

Elder, W. P., and Kirkland, J. I., 1994, Cretaceous paleogeography of the southern Western Interior region, *in* Caputo, M. V., Peterson, J. A., and Franczyk, K. J., editors, Mesozoic systems of the Rocky Mountain Region, USA: Denver, SEPM (Society for Sedimentary Geology), p. 415-440.

Estes, Richard, and Sanchiz, Borja, 1982, Early Cretaceous lower vertebrates from Galve (Teruel), Spain: Journal of Vertebrate Paleontology, v. 2, p. 21-39.

Fiorillo, A. R., 1989, The vertebrate fauna from the Judith River Formation (Late Cretaceous) of Wheatland and Golden Valley Counties, Montana: The Mosasaur, v. 4, p. 127-142.

Fiorillo, A. R., and Currie, P .J., 1994, Theropod teeth from the Judith River Formation (Upper Cretaceous) of south-central Montana: Journal of Vertebrate Paleontology, v. 14, p. 74-80.

Galton, P. M., and Jensen, J. A., 1975, *Hypsilophodon* and *Iguanodon* from the Lower Cretaceous of North America: Nature, v. 257, p. 668-669.

—1979, Remains of ornithopod dinosaurs from the Lower Cretaceous of North America: Brigham Young University Geology Studies, v. 15, p. 1-10.

Hibbard, C. W., 1949, Techniques of collecting micro-vertebrate fossils: University of Michigan, Contributions to the Museum of Paleontology, v. 8, p. 7-19.

Holtz, T. R., Jr., 1994, The phylogenetic position of the Tyrannosauridae-implications for theropod systematics: Journal of Paleontology, v. 68, p. 1100-1117.

Jensen, J. A., 1970, Fossil eggs in the Lower Cretaceous of Utah: Brigham Young University Geology Studies, v. 17, p. 51-66.

Kirkland, J, I., and Parrish, J. M., 1995, Theropod teeth from the Lower and Middle Cretaceous of Utah: Journal of Vertebrate Paleontology, v. 15, supplement to 3, p. 39A.

Kirkland, J. I., Britt, Brooks, Burge, D. L., Carpenter, Ken, Cifelli, Richard, DeCourten, Frank, Eaton, Jeffrey, Hasiotis, Steve, and Lawton, Tim, 1997, Lower to Middle Cretaceous dinosaur faunas of the Central Colorado Plateau: a key to understanding 35 million years of tectonics, sedimentology, evolution and biogeography, *in* Link, P. K., and Kowallis, B. J., editors, Mesozoic to Recent geology of Utah: Brigham Young University Geology Studies, v. 42, p. 69-103.

Langston, W. L., Jr., 1974, Nonmammalian Comanchean tetrapods: Geoscience and Man, v. 8, p. 77-102.

Lillegraven, J. A., 1969, Latest Cretaceous mammals of upper part of Edmonton Formation of Alberta, Canada, and review of marsupial-placental dichotomy in mammalian evolution: University of Kansas, Paleontological Contributions, no. 50, p. 1-122.

Lillegraven, J. A., and McKenna, M. C., 1986, Fossil mammals from the "Mesaverde" Formation (Late Cretaceous, Judithian) of the Bighorn and Wind River basins, Wyoming, with definitions of Late Cretaceous land-mammal "ages": American Museum Novitates, no. 2840, p. 1-68.

Livacarri, R. F., 1991, Role of crustal thickening and extensional collapse in the tectonic evolution of the Sevier-Laramide orogeny, western United States: Geology, v. 19, p. 1104-1107.

Madsen, J. H., Jr., 1974, A new theropod dinosaur from the Upper Jurassic of Utah: Journal of Paleontology, v. 48, p. 27-31.

Maxwell, W. D., and Horner, J. R., 1994, Neonate dinosaurian remains and dinosaurian eggshell from the Cloverly Formation, Montana: Journal of Vertebrate Paleontology, v. 14, p. 143-146.

McNulty, C. L., and Slaughter, B. H., 1968, Locality 3. Stratigraphy of the Woodbine Formation Tarrant County, Texas: Field Trip Guidebook, Second Annual Meeting, South-Central Section, Geological Society of America, p. 68-73.

Meylan, P. A., 1987, The phylogenetic relationships of soft-shelled turtles (Family Trionychidae): Bulletin of the American Museum of Natural History, v. 186, p. 1-101.

Mikhailov, Konstantin, Sabath, Karol, and Kurzanov, Sergey, 1994, Eggs and nests from the Cretaceous of Mongolia, *in* Carpenter, Kenneth, Hirsch, K. F., and Horner, J. R., editors, Dinosaur eggs and babies: Cambridge, Cambridge University Press, p. 88-115.

Nelson, M. E., and Crooks, D. M., 1987, Stratigraphy and paleontology of the Cedar Mountain Formation (Lower Cretaceous), eastern Emery County, Utah, *in* Averett, W.R., editor, Paleontology and geology of the Dinosaur Triangle: Grand Junction, Museum of Western Colorado, p. 55-63.

Nelson, M. E., and Madsen, J. H., Jr., 1985, Early Cretaceous mammals from central Utah: Geological Society of America Abstracts with Programs, v. 17, no. 4, p. 258.

Pomes, M. L., 1988, Stratigraphy, paleontology, and paleobiogeography of lower vertebrates from the Cedar Mountain Formation (Lower Cretaceous), Emery County, Utah: Hays, Kansas, Fort Hays State University, M.S. thesis, 86 p.

Rowe, Tim, Cifelli, R. L., Lehman, T. M., and Weil, Anne, 1992, The Campanian Terlingua local fauna, with a summary of other vertebrates from the Aguja Formation, Trans-Pecos Texas: Journal of Vertebrate Paleontology, v. 12, p. 472-493.

Sahni, Ashok, 1972, The vertebrate fauna of the Judith River Formation, Montana: American Museum of Natural History Bulletin, v. 147, p. 321-412.

Scott, R. W., 1987, The bivalve, *Musculiopsis* MacNeil, in Lower Cretaceous non-marine strata, Rocky Mountains: Contributions to Geology, University of Wyoming, v. 25, p. 29-33.

Stokes, W. L., 1952, Lower Cretaceous in Colorado Plateau: American Association of Petroleum Geologists Bulletin, v. 36, p. 1766-1776.

Thurmond, J. T., 1971, Cartilaginous fishes of the Trinity Group and related rocks (Lower Cretaceous) of north central Texas: Southeastern Geology, v. 13, p. 207-227.

—1974, Lower vertebrate faunas of the Trinity Division in north-central Texas. Geoscience and Man, v. 8, p. 103-129.

Tidwell, W. D., Britt, Brooks, and Robison, Steve, 1983, Paleoecology of a small Lower Cretaceous swamp near Ferron, Utah: Geological Society of America Abstracts with Programs, v. 15, no. 5, p. 286.

Trueb, Linda, 1973, Bones, frogs, and evolution, *in* Vial, J. L., editor, Evolutionary biology of the anurans: Columbia, University of Missouri Press, p. 65-132.

Tschudy, R. H., Tschudy, B .F., and Craig, L. C., 1984, Palynological evaluation of Cedar Mountain and Burro Canyon Formations, Colorado Plateau: U. S. Geological Survey Professional Paper 1281, p. 1-24.

Weishampel, D. B., 1990, Dinosaurian distribution, *in* Weishampel, D. B., Dodson, Peter, and Osmolska, Halszka, editors, The Dinosauria: Berkeley, University of California Press, p. 63-139.

Weiss, M. P., and Roche, M. G., 1988, The Cedar Mountain Formation (Lower Cretaceous) in the Gunnison Plateau, central Utah, *in* Schmidt, C. J., and Perry, W. J., editors, Interaction of the Rocky Mountain Foreland and the Cordilleran Thrust Belt: Geological Society of America Memoir 171, p. 557-569.

Welton, B. J., and Farish, R. F., 1993, The collector's guide to fossil sharks and rays from the Cretaceous of Texas: Lewisville, Texas, Before Time, 204 p.

Winkler, D. A., Murry, P. A., and Jacobs, L. L., 1990, Early Cretaceous (Comanchean) vertebrates of central Texas: Journal of Vertebrate Paleontology, v. 10, p. 95-116.

OCCURRENCE AND BIOSTRATIGRAPHIC FRAMEWORK OF A PLESIOSAUR FROM THE UPPER CRETACEOUS TROPIC SHALE OF SOUTHWESTERN UTAH

David D. Gillette*, Martha C. Hayden, and Alan L. Titus**
Utah Geological Survey, P.O. Box 146100, Salt Lake City , UT 84114-6100
*present address: Museum of Northern Arizona, 3101 Fort Valley Road, Flagstaff, AZ 86001
David.Gillette@nau.edu
**present address: Department of Physical Sciences, College of Southern Idaho, Twin Falls, ID 83301
atitus@evergreen2.csi.cc.id.us

ABSTRACT

In 1990, a heavy equipment operator discovered the partial skeleton of a large plesiosaur at a site in Kane County, Utah, in the lower part of the Upper Cretaceous Tropic Shale. Paleontologists from the Utah Division of State History immediately excavated the skeleton. The specimen consists primarily of vertebrae, two sections in articulation and several isolated elements, all from the trunk and tail region. The skeleton was in the upper portion of the *Sciponoceras gracile* Ammonoid Biozone (also called the *Euomphaloceras septemseriatum* Biozone), middle-upper Cenomanian Stage. This is the first articulated Cretaceous plesiosaur material from Utah, and only the second one found in the state.

INTRODUCTION

Mesozoic marine reptiles are rare in Utah. This preliminary report of the recovery in 1990 of a partial skeleton of a plesiosaur from the Upper Cretaceous Tropic Shale in Kane County, southern Utah, documents the first articulated Cretaceous plesiosaur to be found in the state. In the same year, Bilbey and others (1990) reported the recovery of several vertebrae of a plesiosaur from the Upper Jurassic Redwater Member of the Stump Formation, north of Vernal, in Uintah County, northeastern Utah. The plesiosaur from the Tropic Shale was associated with invertebrate fossils that provide firm biostratigraphic control of its occurrence.

One abbreviation has been adopted in the following text: UMNH, Utah Museum of Natural History, University of Utah Paleontology Collections.

Discovery

Bob Harris and Mark Johnson, both of Delta, Utah, discovered the skeleton in June, 1990 while mining at the site with heavy equipment for septarian concretions. They immediately contacted one of us (DDG) at the Utah Division of State History, which sponsored the

excavation of the skeleton on July 13-15, 1990. The site was at the base of a vertical cut in the Tropic Shale and the bones had to be excavated and removed without delay so that mining activities could resume. Some of the vertebrae had been displaced by the backhoe operations. The excavation team recovered the vertebral column (figures 1 and 2) in two sections of articulated vertebrae that were partially displaced by faulting. The two sections were removed in two large plaster jackets, plus the set of isolated vertebrae that had been disturbed, two isolated plesiosaur teeth, and a single "paddle" bone.

Figure 1. *The Muddy Creek plesiosaur in excavation. The skeleton is partially exposed at the base of a vertical cut in the Tropic Shale. The square is one meter on a side. The view is oblique to the axis of the skeleton, from the proximal caudals (nearest the viewer) to the basal cervicals (farthest from the viewer) in the distance.*

Figure 2. *The Muddy Creek plesiosaur in excavation, side view, anterior to left. Precise identification of vertebral positions must await laboratory preparation. Scale is one meter square; note also the rock hammer. The two lines of vertebrae were displaced, presumably by minor faulting.*

One plaster jacket, which has not yet been prepared, may contain sacral and/or pelvic elements. All of these elements presumably came from one individual skeleton. Identification of the specimen, which has not been sufficiently prepared for study, will depend upon the presence of the pelvic and sacral elements. Invertebrates and shark teeth are also associated with the skeleton, both within the limestone nodules and in the surrounding shale matrix.

Location

The site (figure 3) is located near Muddy Creek, a tributary of the East Fork of the Virgin River near Mount Carmel and Orderville, Kane County, Utah (Utah Geological Survey locality 42Ka008VI). It is on a state mineral lease section (N$\frac{1}{2}$ NE$\frac{1}{4}$NW$\frac{1}{4}$ section 36, T.40 S., R.8 W., Salt Lake Base Line and Meridian) that was leased to Gerald "Wiley" Berry of TETLA Septarians, when the skeleton was discovered.

DESCRIPTION
Systematic Paleontology

CLASS Reptilia
ORDER Plesiosauria
?SUPERFAMILY Pliosauroidea
GENUS and SPECIES Indeterminate

UMNH Accession No. 96.10, partial skeleton from the tail and trunk region, consisting of two sections of vertebrae in articulation, one with approximately 18 ver-

tebrae, the other with approximately 30 vertebrae; isolated vertebrae, two teeth, a paddle bone, and additional unidentified elements.

Osteology

The osteology of the bones is obscured at present. The vertebrae are typically plesiosaurian, and because of their large size, are tentatively assigned to the superfamily Pliosauroidea, the short-necked plesiosaurs in the classification of Carroll (1988). Additional study of the osteology must await full preparation of the skeleton.

STRATIGRAPHIC POSITION AND AGE

A stratigraphic section for the lower portion of the Tropic Shale at Muddy Creek is given in figure 4. The specimen was discovered immediately below a layer containing septarian nodules (yellow calcite crystals in limestone nodules mined as gemstones). The bones are encased in limestone nodules, and have been only partially prepared for curation. Well preserved invertebrate fossils are found throughout the shale and in the limestone concretions.

We have recovered biostratigraphically significant ammonoids from below, at, and above the plesiosaur skeletal horizon. The lower horizon, located approximately one meter below the skeleton, consists of a single band of 0.3 - 0.5 meter diameter, medium gray, non-septarian, spheroidal, micrite concretions. New data collected by one of us (ALT) indicates this interval is the lower

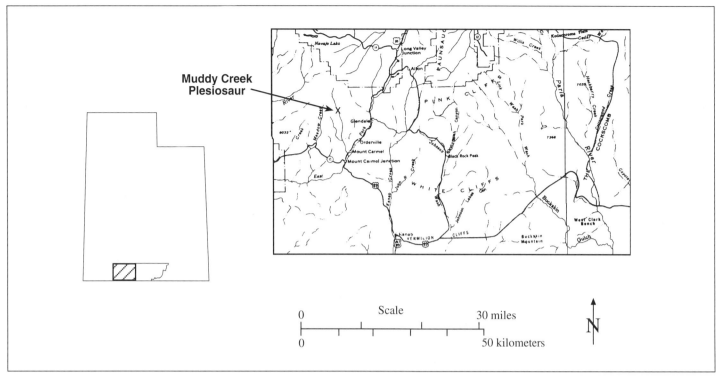

Figure 3. *Location of the Muddy Creek plesiosaur site, showing the western half (cross-hatch) of Kane County (outlined), southern Utah.*

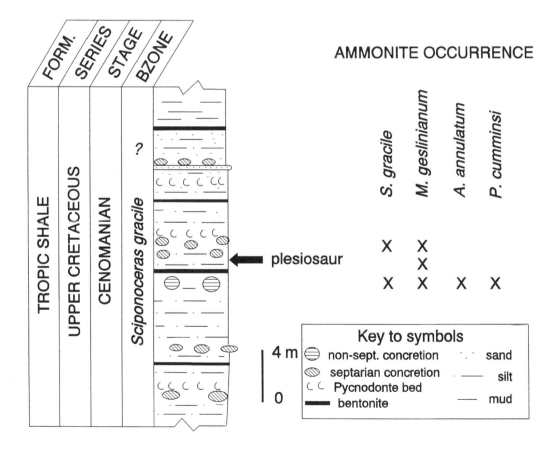

Figure 4. *Stratigraphic section for the lower portion of the Tropic Shale at Muddy Creek, Kane County, Utah. Base of the column starts at the base of the Tropic Shale. The plesiosaur horizon and ammonoid occurrences are also shown. Abbreviations are as follows: FORM. - Formation; BZONE - Biozone; S. - Sciponoceras; M. - Metoicoceras; A. - Allocrioceras; P. - Placenticeras. Modified from Elder (1991).*

portion of limestone unit 4 of Elder (1991). A single large ammonite or inoceramid is usually located at the core of the concretions, while smaller invertebrate shells are concentrated near the margins of the concretions. Macroinvertebrates identified from collections made at this interval by one of the authors (ALT) and Mark Johnson at the Muddy Creek locality include *Turritella whitei* Stanton, *Inoceramus pictus* Sowerby, and the ammonites *Placenticeras cumminsi* Cragin, *Sciponoceras gracile* (Shumard) and *Metoicoceras geslinianum* (d'Orbigny). Swensen (1962) reported the heteromorph *Allocrioceras annulatum* (Shumard) from the same concretionary level. *Metoicoceras geslinianum* from this horizon show the same strong dimorphism documented for this species by Wright and Kennedy (1981) and Kennedy (1988), with macroconchs (previously referred to *M. whitei* Hyatt) being more compressed in cross section and having reduced ornament in all ontogenetic stages. Microconchs (previously referred to *M. ornatum* Moreman) have slightly wider cross sections and bear more prominent juvenile (diameter less than 3 cm) nodes and clavi.

The higher horizon starts approximately 0.4 meters above the level of the skeleton and consists of a one-meter-thick interval of mudstone with 0.3 meter diameter, oval, tan-weathering, medium-gray, frequently hollow septarians. Macroinvertebrates identified from the concretions include *Turritella whitei* Stanton, cardioid and nuculoid bivalves, and the ammonites *Metoicoceras geslinianum* (d'Orbigny) and *Sciponoceras gracile* (Shumard). Unfortunately, most of the ammonoid phragmacones are crushed, although identification is still possible. This interval represents the upper portion of limestone 4 of Elder (1991) which is much thicker at Muddy Creek than to the east.

Macroinvertebrates identified from mudstones at approximately the same stratigraphic horizon as the plesiosaur include two crushed macroconchs of *Metoicoceras geslinianum* associated with *Pycnodonte newberryi* (Stanton) and *Turritella whitei* Stanton.

The standard middle Cenomanian-middle Turonian ammonoid zonation for the U.S. Western Interior is given in figure 5. All ammonites described above are diagnostic of the widespread *Sciponoceras gracile* Ammonoid Biozone (also called the *Euomphaloceras septemseriatum* Biozone), middle-upper Cenomanian Stage (Kennedy, 1988; Elder, 1989; Kirkland, 1996). The *S. gracile* Biozone coincides with the early part of a late Cenomanian-early Turonian transgression that peaked in

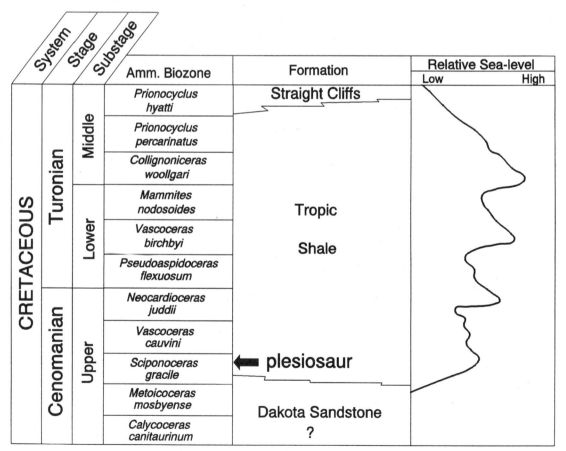

Figure 5. *Early Late Cretaceous lithostratigraphic and biostratigraphic framework for the Muddy Creek plesiosaur locality showing relative sea-level history. Ammonoid biozonation based on Kennedy (1988).*

the earliest mid-Turonian (figure 5). Nearly all significant Cenomanian-age vertebrate finds in the Tropic Shale are from the limestone 4 horizon.

DISCUSSION

Because the plesiosaur skeleton did not include paddles or cranial bones, its identity will not be possible until additional specimens from this level are recovered. The occurrence of a plesiosaur in the Tropic Shale in southern Utah is not surprising. Although this is the first documented occurrence of plesiosaur remains from the Tropic Shale in Utah, isolated plesiosaur vertebrae have been reported in this formation (Tilton, 1991), but cannot be verified by curated specimens.

In addition, roughly equivalent strata of the Mancos Shale in western Colorado and northern Arizona have yielded the remains of additional plesiosaur specimens and a mosasaur. In 1987, a short-necked "pliosauroid" plesiosaur was collected by the Museum of Western Colorado, Grand Junction. This specimen is from the top of the Mancos Shale, about three meters below the base of the Castlegate Sandstone, from Prairie Canyon, Garfield County, Colorado, approximately one km east of the Utah-Colorado border (Carter, 1991). Irby (1995) and Elliott and others (1997) reported the collection of plesiosaurs from the Mancos Shale in northern Arizona. Also from the Mancos Shale of western Colorado is a partially articulated mosasaur skeleton that was collected by Brigham Young University (Kass, 1995; and this volume).

ACKNOWLEDGMENTS

Members of the Utah Friends of Paleontology assisted with the excavation. Gerald Berry of Orderville, Utah, and Robert Harris and Mark Johnson, both of Delta, Utah, notified us of the discovery and provided heavy equipment on site that helped remove the skeleton. Mark Johnson also kindly provided invertebrate specimens for study. Michael S. Kass reviewed the manuscript and made valuable suggestions for improvement.

REFERENCES

Bilbey, S. A., Hall, J. E., and Welles, S. P., 1990, Pliosaurian plesiosaurs found in the Red Water Member of the Stump Formation (Jurassic, Oxfordian) of northeastern Utah: Journal of Vertebrate Paleontology, v. 10, p. 14A.

Carroll, R. L., 1988, Vertebrate paleontology and evolution: New York, W. H. Freeman and Company, 698 p.

Carter, B. R., 1991, A plesiosaur from the upper Mancos Shale, *in* Averett, Walter, editor, Guidebook for dinosaur quarries and tracksites tour, western Colorado and eastern Utah: Grand Junction, Museum of Western Colorado, p. 51.

Elder, W. P., 1989, Molluscan extinction patterns across the Cenomanian-Turonian Stage boundary in the western interior of the United States: Paleobiology, v. 15. p. 299-320.

—1991, Molluscan paleoecology and sedimentation patterns of the Cenomanian-Turonian extinction interval in the southern Colorado Plateau region, *in* Nations, J. D., and Eaton, J. G., editors, Stratigraphy, depositional environments, and sedimentary tectonics of the western margin, Cretaceous Western Interior Seaway: Geological Society of America Special Paper 260, p. 113-137.

Elliott, D. K, Irby, G. V., and Hutchison, J. H., 1997, *Desmatochelys lowi*, a marine turtle from the Upper Cretaceous, *in* Callaway, J. M., and Nicholls, E. L., editors, Ancient marine reptiles: San Diego, Academic Press, p. 243-258.

Irby, G. V., 1995, Marine reptiles from the Cretaceous Mancos Shale, Black Mesa, northeastern Arizona: Proceedings of the Third Annual Symposium, Fossils of Arizona, Mesa Southwest Museum, p. 75-80.

Kass, M. S., 1995, A new mosasaur from the Mancos Shale of Delta County, Colorado: Provo, Utah, Brigham Young University, M. S. thesis, 145 p.

Kennedy, W. J., 1988, Late Cenomanian and Turonian ammonite faunas from north-east and central Texas -- special papers in palaeontology no. 39: London, The Palaeontological Association, 131 p.

Kirkland, J. I., 1996, Paleontology of the Greenhorn Cyclothem (Cretaceous: Late Cenomanian to Middle Turonian) at Black Mesa, northeastern Arizona: New Mexico Museum of Natural History and Science Bulletin 9, 132 p.

Molenaar, C. M., 1983, Major depositional cycles and regional correlations of Upper Cretaceous rocks, southern Colorado Plateau and adjacent areas, *in* Reynolds, M. W., and Dolly, E. D., editors, Mesozoic paleogeography of the west-central United States: Rocky Mountain Section of the Society of Economic Paleontologists and Mineralogists, p. 201-224.

Swensen, A. J., 1962, Anisoceratidae and Hamitidae (Ammonoidea) from the Cretaceous of Texas and Utah: Brigham Young University Geology Studies, v. 9, p. 53-82.

Tilton, T.L., 1991, Upper Cretaceous stratigraphy of the southern Paunsaugunt Plateau, Kane County, Utah: Salt Lake City, University of Utah, Ph.D. dissertation, 162 p.

Wright, C. W., and Kennedy, W. J., 1981, The Ammonoidea of the Plenus Marls and the Middle Chalk: London, Palaeontographical Society Monograph, 148 p.

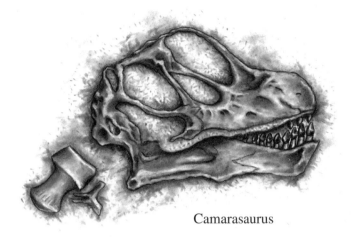

Camarasaurus

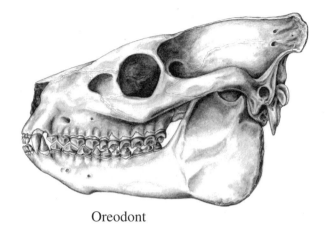

Oreodont

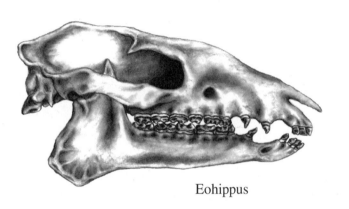

Eohippus

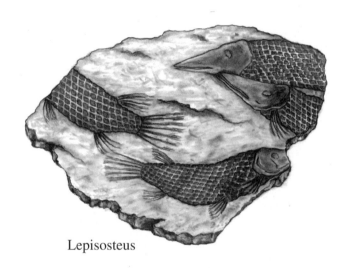

Lepisosteus

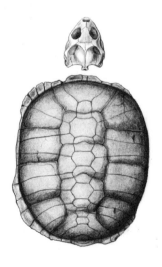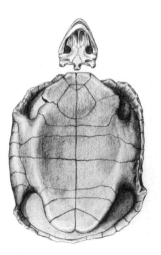

Eocene turtle

Brian Maebius © 1999

PROGNATHODON STADTMANI: (MOSASAURIDAE) A NEW SPECIES FROM THE MANCOS SHALE (LOWER CAMPANIAN) OF WESTERN COLORADO

Michael S. Kass

Department of Natural Sciences/Continuing Education, Salt Lake Community College, Salt Lake City, UT 84124

and

Utah Museum of Natural History, University of Utah, Salt Lake City, UT 84112

ABSTRACT

The osteology and stratigraphic position of a new specimen of mosasaur, BYU 13082, collected in 1975 near Cedaredge, Colorado from the Mancos "B" member of the Mancos Shale, is described in detail. This specimen is assigned to the genus *Prognathodon* and appears to be a new species based on differences in the shape of the coronoid, and in the edentulous anterior projection of the dentaries. The mosasaur carcass was buried or sank rapidly after death through the water column, as shown by preservation of major skull elements in association with a partially articulated vertebral column. This Mancos Shale mosasaur was found in a thinly laminated, dark gray siltstone, suggesting an off-shore deposit in relatively deep, quiet water. The associated faunal assemblage includes two types of sharks, inoceramid bivalves, and *Baculites*. The invertebrates indicate an open marine shelf and date the mosasaur site to the early Campanian *Scaphites hippocrepis* Zone.

INTRODUCTION

BYU 13082 is an associated skeleton of a single, partially articulated, large, adult mosasaur. There are adequate characters present to place this specimen within the genus *Prognathodon*, and sufficient distinctive features to describe it as a new species. Taxonomic classification of the three subfamilies of mosasaurs is based on cranial and vertebral characters (Russell, 1967; Lucas and Reser, 1981), as well as on the humerus and manus (Bell, 1993). The most diagnostic characters are in the premaxilla, teeth, and quadrate, reflecting an adaptation to the marine environment involving specialized foraging strategies (Bell, 1993). Generic diagnostic characteristics preserved in BYU 13082 include: the degree of development of the premaxillary rostrum (microrhynchous condition), size of the dentary, moderately procumbent anterior teeth in the dentary, number and type of marginal and pterygoid teeth, and presence of haemal peduncles or chevrons fused to the caudal vertebrae. This mosasaur appears to be a new species of *Prognathodon* based on differences in the shape of the coronoid, and in the edentulous anterior projection of the dentaries. This conclusion is further supported by the stratigraphic position in the Early Campanian whereas all other described *Prognathodon* specimens are from Late Campanian or Maastrichtian deposits.

Mosasaur fossils are very common on the eastern side of the Western Interior Seaway, where they are an important constituent in the tetrapod fauna. By contrast, mosasaur remains have seldom been reported from the Rocky Mountain region (Kues and Lucas, 1985). The new mosasaur described in this paper is from the Mancos Shale of Colorado. This formation is noted for its paucity of vertebrate fossil remains (Wolny and others, 1990; Carter, 1991; Hunt and Lucas 1993; Irby and others, 1994). Limited taphonomic data allow some inferences to be drawn from the fossil locality. The mosasaur was discovered by a high-school freshman, Gary Thompson, on April 1, 1975. He reported his find to a local science teacher, Richard Jones. Excavation of the specimen commenced a couple of days after Richard Jones notified paleontologist James Jensen of Brigham Young Univer- sity.

Institutional Abbreviations

BYU, Brigham Young University, Provo, Utah; CM, Canterbury Museum, Christchurch, New Zealand; FMNH, Field Museum of Natural History, Chicago, Illinois; IRSNB, Institut Royal des Sciences Naturelles de Belgique, Brussels, Belgium; KU, University of Kansas, Lawrence, Kansas; NJGS, New Jersey Geological Survey, Newark, New Jersey; NZGS, New Zealand Geological Survey, Lower Hutt, New Zealand; SDSM, South Dakota School of Mines, Rapid City, South Dakota; and UNM, University of New Mexico, Albuquerque, New Mexico.

GEOLOGY
Introduction

The basal Cretaceous strata (figure 1) in western Colorado consist of the predominately progradational nonmarine Dakota Group which intertongues eastward with the overlying transgressive marine Mancos Shale. Overlying the Mancos are marginal marine and nonmarine rocks of the Mesa Verde Group. In Delta County, Colorado, where the mosasaur fossil was discovered, the relatively non-resistant Mancos Shale forms a broad strike valley between the Book Cliffs to the north and northeast and the Uncompahgre Plateau to the southwest

(figure 2). Deposits of the upper part of the Mancos Shale dip gently (3 to 7 degrees) to the northeast off the Uncompahgre into the Piceance Creek Basin (Young, 1960).

The Mancos Shale was named by Cross (1899) for exposures in the Mancos Valley of southwest Colorado. The Mancos is primarily composed of dark gray to greenish shale with some sandy layers, limestone and calcareous nodules that were deposited offshore in the Western Interior Seaway during the Late Cretaceous. The matrix that entombed the specimen consists of calcareous silt and very fine sand which gives the matrix around the specimen a gritty texture. In thin-section the matrix is an argillaceous, medium-to-coarse siltstone

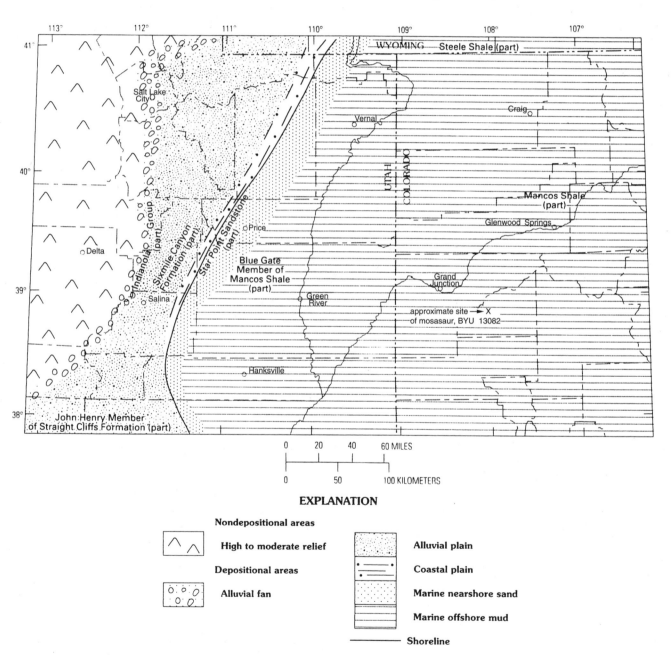

EXPLANATION

Nondepositional areas

High to moderate relief

Depositional areas

Alluvial fan

Alluvial plain

Coastal plain

Marine nearshore sand

Marine offshore mud

—— Shoreline

Figure 1. Paleogeographic reconstruction of the relative position of the strand line during the early Campanian, Scaphites hippocrepis *fauna Zone. This reconstruction illustrates the initial stage of the gradual shoreline regression that continued throughout the rest of the Campanian in the map area (after Francyzyk and others, 1992). X - approximate site of mosasaur BYU 13082.*

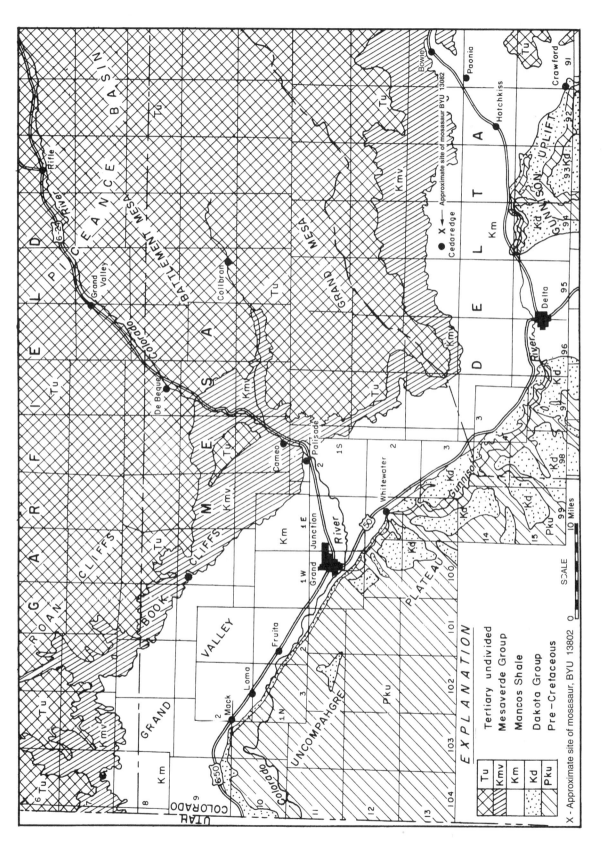

Figure 2. *Generalized geology of the Grand Junction-Cedaredge area of western Colorado (modified from Young, 1959). X - Approximate site of mosasaur, BYU 13082.*

composed of 60% to 70% quartz grains. The quartz grains measure 20 to 40 microns (.02-.04 mm) in diameter, and the grains composing the silty matrix are about half that size. This unit has been described as a sandy shale (Young, 1959). For a description of the depositional environment see Kass (1995).

Stratigraphy

The Mancos of western Colorado has a maximum thickness of 1,219 meters (Hail, 1972), with zones of sandy shale and calcareous concretions. Only the upper 305 meters of the Mancos is exposed at the base of the Book Cliffs (Mesa Verde Group) south of Grand Junction (Young, 1960), where it is divided into five members. In ascending order they have been designated the Tununk Shale, Ferron Sandstone, Blue Gate Shale, Emery Sandstone, and Masuk Shale (Cobban, 1976). However, the Masuk, which has its type section in nonmarine deposits of the Henry Mountains, is younger than the marine shales above the Emery (Molenaar, 1983; Cole, 1987) and the unit above the Emery has been referred to as the upper Blue Gate Member of the Mancos Shale (Fouch and others, 1983). The Mancos grades upward and into the Star Point Sandstone (Mesa Verde Group) which represents the initial Campanian regression in this part of the basin. The lowest unit of the Star Point is designated the Panther Tongue. East of the Wasatch Plateau the Panther Tongue pinches out into the upper Blue Gate Shale (Cole, 1987). The Panther Tongue has been assigned to the *Scaphites hippocrepis* Zone, based on marine ostracodes (Fouch and others, 1983). The upper Blue Gate Shale consists of open-marine deposits in the Price, Utah area, but lateral equivalents are generally not named farther to the east (Cole, 1987). Because stratigraphic relationships of late Santonian-early Campanian-age deposits from Utah to Colorado are still unclear, the term Mancos "B" is used for equivalent age rocks in this part of Colorado (Franczyk and others, 1992). The Mancos "B" is an informal stratigraphic unit of subsurface usage (Kellogg, 1977; Fouch and others, 1983; Cole, 1987) whose age, lithologic composition, stratigraphic contacts, and extent are not well defined, but are likely to be of the *S. hippocrepis* Zone (Franczyk and others, 1992). The Mancos "B" has been interpreted as prograding shelf sediments which encountered a sea-bottom shoal, probably related to the incipient uplift of the Douglas Creek Arch, and is thus correlated more to the Blackhawk Formation than to the Emery Member of the Mancos (Cole, 1987). This shoaling produced a slightly higher energy regime which winnowed the mud from the sand. It is this concentration of

sand that is commonly referred to as the Mancos "B" (Kellogg, 1977; Cole, 1987). The mosasaur site closely matches the description of the Mancos "B" in time-stratigraphic position and lithology. Cole and others (personal communication, 1994) have proposed naming the sand-shale facies (Mancos "B") between the marine-mudrock facies of the lower and upper Blue Gate Shale of western Colorado as the Praire Canyon Member of the Mancos Shale. The *Scaphites hippocrepis* Zone probably correlates with the lower half of this new member (R. G. Young, personal communication, 1994).

ASSOCIATED FAUNA AND AGE

The Mancos sediment in the immediate vicinity of the skeleton was barren of organic remains except for some plant debris. Numerous casts and internal molds of bivalves (figure 3) found at and above the mosasaur site have been identified as *Platyceramus cycloides* (Wegner) and *Endocostea* (*Inoceramus*) *balticus* Bohm (W. A. Cobban, personal communication, 1994). Calcareous concretions containing *Baculites aquilaensis* were found at the approximate mosasaur site, and above the site two specimens of *Baculites haresi* were recovered (figure 3). This particular faunal assemblage is suggestive of the range zone of *Scaphites hippocrepis* (W.A. Cobban, personal communication, 1994). The *S. hippocrepis* Fauna Zone has been radiometrically dated at 81.71 ± 0.34 million years ago (Obradovich, 1993).

Found in the matrix during preparation of the field jacket containing the pygal and caudal vertebrae of BYU 13082 were three lateral cusps of an odontaspid or lamnoid shark, tentatively identitifed as *Cretolamna* sp. (G.R. Case, personal communication, 1993), a fourth cusp of an unidentitifed lamnoid shark which has a different morphology than the other cuspids, and one fairly complete anterolateral tooth of *Squalicorax pristodontus* (Bilelo, 1969; Cappetta and Case, 1975; Lauginiger and Harstein, 1983; Cappetta, 1987; Welton and Farish, 1993). There is some utility using *Squalicorax* teeth for low-resolution biostratigraphy (Schwimmer and Williams, 1991) with the lowest stratigraphic range of *S. pristodontus* in the Campanian (Lauginiger and Hartstein, 1983; Cappetta, 1987) or Santonian (Bilelo, 1969). For elaboration of the biostratigraphy and paleoecology of the mosasaur site, and the western side of the Late Cretaceous Seaway see Kass (1995).

METHODS

The fossil bones of BYU 13082 were collected in 1975, and I prepared it seventeen years later, utilizing conventional laboratory techniques.

Figure 3. *Inoceramid fossils found in association with BYU 13082. A,* Platyceramus cyloides *(Wegner). B,* Endocostea (Inoceramus) balticus. Baculites *fossils found in association with BYU 13082. C,* Baculites aquilaensis *Reeside; D,* Baculites aquilaensis *Reeside, E,* Baculites aquilaensis *Reeside; F,* Baculites haresi *Reeside; G,* Baculites haresi *Reeside. Scale bar equals 2.5 cm.*

made with illustrations available in the literature. A skeleton of a modern monitor lizard, *Varanus salvator* (Laurenti), a sister taxon with the family Mosasauridae, was also used for identification of some of the fossil bones.

I subjected a sample of bone to x-ray diffraction analysis, then weighed it and treated with a 10% hydrochloric acid to dissolve the carbonate. For the remaining material I washed, centrifuged, dried, and reweighed it to obtain the mineralogical composition of the fossil bone. I also used a qualitative x-ray fluoresence scan to analyze the relative chemistry of solid bone taken from the centrum of the mosasaur, porous bone taken from the rib, and the enclosing matrix.

The matrix around BYU 13082 was thin-sectioned and easily dissaggregated to study the lithology. Both thin-section and individual grains were examined using a binocular dissection microscope for microfossils for biostratigraphic analysis. Grain-size and composition of the lithology of the mosasaur site has been discussed above.

SYSTEMATIC PALEONTOLOGY

Order SQUAMATA Oppel, 1811
Family MOSASAURIDAE Gervais, 1853
Subfamily PLIOPLATECARPINAE
(Dollo, 1884) Williston, 1897
Tribe PROGNATHODONTINI Russell, 1967
Genus PROGNATHODON Dollo, 1889
***Prognathodon stadtmani* new species**

Etymology

In honor of Kenneth Stadtman, Curator of the BYU Earth Science Museum, for his extensive work in paleontology.

Diagnosis

Small premaxillary rostrum, massively proportioned jaws with strong concavity of the dental margin, heavy dentition. Twelve teeth in maxilla and 14 teeth in dentary. Teeth smooth, bicarinate, and broadly ovate in cross section. Very large pterygoid with dentition almost as large as marginal teeth. Coronoid massive with large medial and anterior/posterior wing and an intermediately developed posterolateral wing. Vertebrae procoelus with articulating surfaces of the vertebrae wider than deep and elliptical in outline. Absence of zygosphenes and zygantra on dorsal vertebrae. Chevrons fused to caudal centra.

I measured the bones of the specimen and entered the dimensions into a data base along with descriptions, notes on preservation, general observations and comparisons to other mosasaurs at the New Jersey State Museum and the American Museum of Natural History, and the relevant literature. Osteological comparisons were

Type Specimen

BYU 13082, incomplete skull including both pre-maxillae and maxillae, nearly complete right and left mandibles consisting of dentaries, splenials, angulars, surangulars, and prearticulars; complete left coronoid and fragment of right coronoid; nearly complete left pterygoid; nearly complete left palatine; fragment of frontal; fragment of postorbitalfrontal; incomplete post-cranial skeleton consisting of posteriormost dorsal and pygal vertebrae, intermediate and terminal caudal verte-brae, and ribs.

Type Horizon and Locality

Upper part of Mancos Shale, Upper Blue Gate Member, early Campanian. The site is located NW$\frac{1}{4}$NW$\frac{1}{4}$ section 28, T.13S., R.94W., in a roadcut on Cedar Mesa about 0.3 kilometers east of Main Street in the town of Cedaredge, Delta County, Colorado. The Mancos has disconformable upper contacts with Pleistocene alluvial gravels, apparently the remains of old stream terraces (Kent, 1965), and basalt boulders derived from the flows capping Grand Mesa of Bull Lake age (Hail, 1972).

DESCRIPTION

Cranial Skeleton

Skull

The typical mosasaur skull is narrow, elongate, and dorsoventrally compressed which forms a long tapering snout. The skull of BYU 13082 is broad and stout with relatively short jaws typical of *Prognathodon* mosasaurs. *Prognathodon* skulls generally resemble those of *Mosasaurus* in the shape of the head, although the anteri-or portion of the muzzle is deeper and more bluntly ter-minated.

Premaxilla

For descriptive purposes the premaxillae of *P. stadt-mani* may be divided into a broad, anterior tooth-bearing apex and a relatively slender internarial bar (figure 4). The premaxillae appear to terminate directly in front of the anteriormost tooth. There are four teeth in the pre-maxillae of *Prognathodon*, but only three are present in BYU 13082, including the right posterior tooth which is procumbent, left anteriormost tooth, and a small replace-ment tooth in the left posterior alveolus. No observable foramina are evident in the premaxillae of BYU 13082 which have been described in other specimens of this genus as an irregular row paralleling the dorsal midline (Russell, 1967). This condition in BYU 13082 might be due to poor fossilization. The internarial bar arises from a triangular base enclosed between the anterior wings of the maxilla on the dorsal surface of the skull. In cross section, the internarial bar exhibits the shape of an invert-ed triangle. The descending keel probably supported a cartilaginous internasal septum posteroventrally, as in *Varanus* (Russell, 1967). The internarial bar is constrict-ed between the external nares. The external nares com-mence between the third and fourth maxillary teeth.

Maxilla

The maxillae are very massive and stout (figure 4). A ventral, longitudinally flattened buttress houses the conduit for the maxillary artery and the maxillary divi-sion of the trigeminal nerve. The ventral border of the buttress is straight and supports the tooth bases. All teeth in the maxilla have been heavily reconstructed during prior preparation, obscuring most of the details of the dentition. The best preserved teeth appear to be similar to the dentary teeth. The terminal branches of the maxil-lary nerve emerge through a row of oval foramina which extend in a straight line 25 mm above the probable gum line on the lateral surface of the maxillae as observed by Russell (1967) on other specimens of mosasaurs. The more anterior foramina are extremely small and have been obscured by both poor fossilization and the earlier plaster reconstruction on the maxillae. All foramina face in the same direction and open posteroventrally. The largest foramen present is the posteriormost one which measures 20 mm in length and 5 mm in height. These foramina appear to lead into a small, shallow longitudi-nal canal along the dorsolateral edge of the alveoli. The right maxilla tooth count is 11 while the left maxilla tooth count is 12. The difference in tooth count is due to an additional tooth erupting on the left maxilla where it tapers to a posterior point. The right maxilla was broken anterior to this taper, so it appears to have had the same total number of teeth as the left maxilla. The three most anterior teeth in the right maxilla are procumbent. All the teeth are preserved on the right maxilla except for alveolus 8 which contains just the bulbous base of that tooth, and alveolus 10 which is represented by a large erupting tooth. The left maxilla dentition is not as well preserved. Teeth in alveoli 1, 5, 6, 10, and 11 are broken and incomplete, alveoli 2, 7, 8, and 9 contain just the bulbous bases of the teeth, and alveolus 12 has an erupt-ing tooth.

Frontal

Only the posterior portion of the frontal is preserved before the enclosing shaft of the most posterior portion of the internarial bar (figure 5). The most posterior part of the frontal-parietal suture establishing the mesokinetic axis is not preserved. The large, irregular fragment of

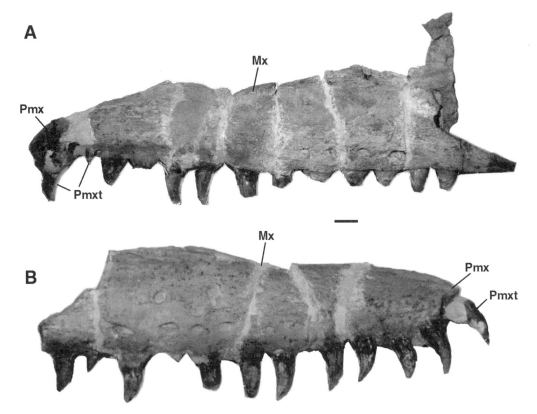

Figure 4. *Premaxilla and maxilla of the holotype of* Prognathodon stadtmani, *new species, (BYU 13082). A, Left premaxilla and maxilla lateral view. B, right premaxilla and maxilla lateral view. Pmx - premaxilla; Mx - maxilla; Pmxt - premaxilla teeth. Scale bar equals 5 cm.*

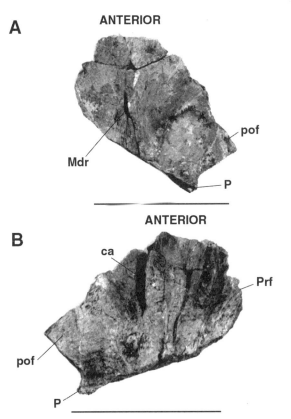

Figure 5. *Frontal of the holotype of* Prognathodon stadtmani, *new species (BYU 13082). A, dorsal view. B, ventral view. Mdr - median dorsal ridge; pof - postorbitalfrontal; Prf - prefrontal or suture for prefrontal; P - parietal or suture for parietal; ca - canal. Scale bar equals 7 cm.*

the frontal is solidly fused along the midline of the skull. In dorsal view the frontal forms a wide, flattened plate with a weakly developed median dorsal ridge that is not sharply defined.

On the ventral side of the frontal, a triangular excavation represents the sutures for the prefrontals. It lies lateral to the impressions of the olfactory tract along the ventral midline. A closed semitubular canal expands slightly, presumably for reception of the olfactory lobes. The outline of the cerebral hemispheres is not clearly defined over the posterior ventral surface of the frontal, and the posterior portion of the channel showing the position of the cerebral hemispheres is not preserved for *P. stadtmani*, as in other described mosasaur specimens. On the posterolateral corner of the right ventral surface, a suture marks the contacts of the postorbitalfrontal. This smooth suture extends medially about one-half the distance from the edge of the frontal to its midline.

Postorbitalfrontal

The postorbitals and postfrontals are co-ossified in BYU 13082 to form a single four-pronged element, the typical condition found in mosasaurs, and similar to that found in *Varanus* (Camp, 1942; Russell, 1967). The posttorbitalfrontal of BYU 13082 is represented by a small right fragment and a larger left fragment. The left postorbitalfrontal is broken anterior to the suture that forms the contact with the frontal and parietal. The main body of the left fragment of the postorbitalfrontal consists of the dorsally exposed surface of a process that extends anteriorly along the lateral edge of the frontal and bounds the orbit posterodorsally. The main body of the postorbital is expanded laterally into a broad triangular ala. The external apex of the ala is curved ventrally but appears to be broken just anterior to the suture with the dorsolateral surface of the jugal. Only the anterior portion of a long "slender" process that would fit into a deep groove on the dorsal edge of the squamosal is present. This long process to the squamosal forms the anterolateral boundary of the supratemporal fenestra as described by Russell (1967), and Lingham-Soliar and Nolf (1989). The face of the postorbitalfrontal lying beneath the posterolateral corner of the frontal is smooth.

Parietal

A very small fragment of the right anterior portion of the fused parietal appears to be preserved in contact with the frontal.

Palatine

The left palatine is preserved with the dorsal side cemented by matrix onto the posterodorsal side of the right maxilla. The palatine is a small, edentulous, rectangular plate of bone anterior to the pterygoids, wedged between the maxillae laterally, and the vomer anteriorly. The posterodorsal surface of the palatine slopes up from its posterior termination to form a J-shaped ridge. The ventral surface of the palatine, a posterolateral projection, has a V- or possibly W-shaped ridge that forms the termination boundary with the anteromedial process from the pterygoid.

Coronoid

Both coronoids are present. The right coronoid is badly eroded with only the most anterior portion present. The left coronoid is essentially complete (figure 6). The prominent coronoid is a long, saddle-shaped bone in *P. stadtmani*. A well-defined contact between the coronoid and the dorsal surface of the surangular in an anterior position that is enclosed in a deep ventral sulcus showed it would have been firmly sutured. A well-defined contact between the lateral wall of the surangular and surface of the coronoid clearly defines this position. The anterior end of the coronoid is rounded and cleft along the midline. Laterally the coronoid is considerably flattened and particularly deep posteriorly. The dorsal surface is smoothly convex transversely and is narrow from side to side with the edges rounding smoothly onto the lateral and medial sides. From about the mid-point of

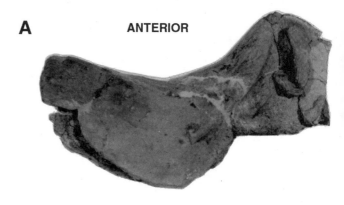

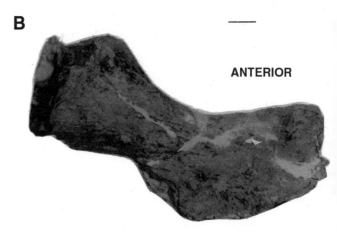

Figure 6. *Left coronoid of the holotype of* Prognathodon stadtmani, *new species (BYU 13082). A, lateral view. B, medial view. Scale bar equals 5 cm.*

the bone, the dorsal margin extends horizontally towards the anterior termination. The anterior wall of the coronoid eminence sweeps up at about an angle of 75 degrees from the horizontal to a point; the angle is less sharp than in *P. solvayi* (Lingham-Soliar and Nolf, 1989), but is similar to that of *P. giganteus* and *P. overtoni* (SDSM 3393). The coronoid eminence appears to descend posteriorly in a gradual fashion but does not appear to contact the dorsal edge of the surangular. The medial anterior/posterior wing is large and broad, covering the anterodorsal edge of the angular. The lateral wing is only intermediately developed posteriorly. Horizontal scarring on the posteromedial surface marks the points of tendinous insertions for the M. adductor externus muscles. The anterior process of the coronoid appears to have projected forward above the surangular and abutted against a small process on the posterodorsal surface of the dentary.

Pterygoid

The left pterygoid is a very stout bone in BYU

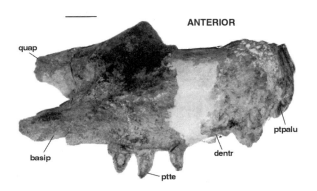

Figure 7. *Left pterygoid of the holotype of* Prognathodon stadtmani, *new species (BYU 13082). Lateral view. dentr - dentary ramus; basip - basisphenoid process of the pterygoid; quap - quadratic process of the pterygoid; ptpalus - utural union between pterygoid and palatine; ptte - pterygoid teeth. Scale bar equals 5 cm.*

13082 (figure 7). The pterygoid is a tetraradiate bone, sending processes to the palatine anteriorly, the ectopterygoid laterally, and the quadrate posteriorly, forming syndesmoses with these bones (Callison, 1967). The pterygoid also contacts the epipterygoid dorsally and the basipterygoid process medially. The main body of the pterygoid is a short, dorsoventrally flattened column terminating posteriorly in the basisphenoid process which is broken off, as is the process leading to the palatine. Breaks in these regions of the palatine are common in mosasaur fossils because both the basisphenoid and palatine processes are frequently flattened and slender (Soliar, 1988). The anterior portion is incomplete: the preserved element terminates anteriorly in an oval shape. The pterygoid anteriorly must have been firmly buttressed against the palatine but the contact is rarely preserved in mosasaur fossils (Russell, 1967).

The ectopterygoid process is short and projects anteriorly from the main body of the pterygoid at an acute angle. The base of the ectopterygoid process is fairly wide, with the distal end curved slightly posteriorly. A lunate sulcus is present on the posterodorsal face of the ectopterygoidal process. The process arises ventrally from a broad base in common with the quadratic ramus. The quadratic ramus is also broken off near the base of the main body of the pterygoid.

On the ventral surface of the pterygoid, a broad tooth-bearing segment extends over half the overall length of the bone, and is well preserved. A row of teeth bent in a gently recurving line extends from the medial base of the basisphenoid process to the anteroexternal termination of the bone. The tooth row, which is probably complete, supports six pterygoid teeth; four teeth are complete, one is partially preserved, and the anteriormost one is broken at the base. The preserved pterygoid teeth of BYU 13082 are large and stout with slight posteriorly recurved tips. No carinae are visible.

Mandibular Skeleton

Dentary

The dentary of BYU 13082 is a particularly stout bone (figure 8), as in all members of the genus *Prognathodon*. A striking feature is the strong concavity of the dorsal dental margin. The dentary projects beyond the front of the base of the first dentary tooth base by approximately 26 mm on the left dentary and 20 mm on the right dentary. The mandibular symphysis is not fused but in life was held together by ligaments.

A dorsal row of moderately pronounced foramina extends along almost the entire length of the dental ramus above the midpoint of the bone, the row curves upward anteriorly and posteriorly to parallel the dorsal margin of the bone just above a ridge that was presumably the gum line.

Splenial

Ventral to the dentary is a long, laterally compressed bone that tapers anteriorly, extending approximately 2/3 the length of the dentary, with the medial ala of the splenial sheathing the mandibular channel. The splenial extends just past the posterior extremity of the dentary. It makes contact with the anterior tuberous process of the angular by a fairly shallow, laterally compressed articulating surface which forms a moderately weak ball-and-socket joint. This articulation has a nearly subrectangular outline.

Angular

Behind the midjaw hinge, the posterior portion of the lower jaw is composed of four bones. Largest of these four bones is the angular which forms the entire ventral margin. Based on Russell's text-figure 90 (1967, p. 166) an estimated 10.5 cm is missing from the posterior end of the angular. The tuberous process of the angular forms a vertically moveable joint with the splenial. The articulation surface is somewhat taller than broad. The medial wing of the angular is overlapped from above by the surangular.

Surangular

The surangular is a long, laterally flattened bone in BYU 13082, tapering and pointed anteriorly. This condition is generally present in most squamates and nonsquamate lepidosaurs (Estes and others, 1988). Based on Russell's text-figure 90 (1967), an estimated 11 cm are missing from the posterior end of the surangular anterior to the retroarticular process on both mandibles. The surangular ends abruptly just above the splenio-angular articulation. The upper posterior part of the lateral surface extends back of the dentary and above the angular

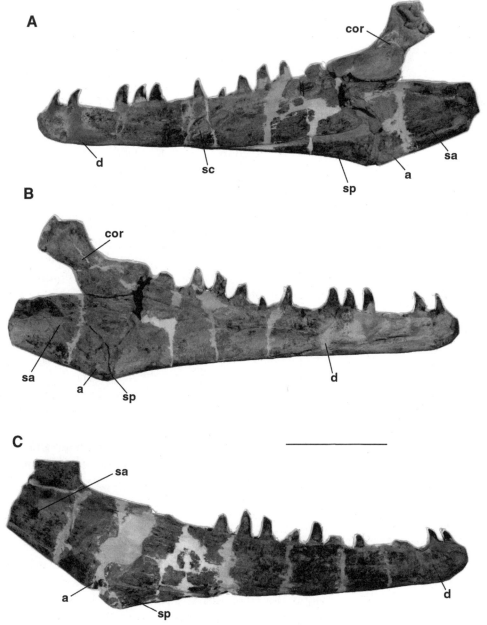

Figure 8. Mandibles of the holotype of Prognathodon stadtmani, *new species (BYU 13082). A, Left mandible lateral view. B, left mandible medial view. C, right mandible lateral view. cor - coronoid; sa - surangular; a - angular; d - dentary; sp - splenial; sc - scar. Scale bar equals 10 cm.*

face of the lower jaw. Posteriorly it is fused with the inner surface of the articular. It is overlapped from below by the medial wing of the angular and bounded above superficially by the coronoid. The anterior end of the prearticular is an extremely thin sheet of bone which extends forward medially between the surangular above and the angular below, into the mandibular foramen of the anterior segment of the jaw between the splenial and dentary. The prearticular crosses the gap between the surangular and the dentary, and terminates between the posterior ends of both the dentary and the splenial. Posteriorly the bone extends backward, forming the ventral margin of the mandible uniting with the articular to form the retroarticular process which is not preserved in BYU 13082, but has been described by Gregory (1951) for other mosasaurs. Russell (1967) described the retroarticular process as being rectangular in shape for *Prognathodon*.

Dentition

Large teeth, in various stages of replacement, entirely fill the alveolar margins of the upper and lower jaws. The marginal teeth of BYU 13082 each have a large bulbous base that is clearly marked off from the stout, bicarinate, and generally smooth enamel-clad crown.

to form most of the lateral wall of the large, deep adductor fossa. The adductor fossa opens dorsally, anterior to the articular area, which has not been preserved in BYU 13082. A posterior portion of the lateral wall on the right surangular shows that the bone becomes laterally compressed, and probably rose to form a ventral posterolateral buttress for the coronoid, as it is illustrated in several reconstructions of *Prognathodon*. The lateral wall of the surangular is considerably higher than the inner, medial wall formed by the prearticular.

Prearticular

The prearticular is a major element of the inner sur-

Incipient faceting is present on some teeth. The crowns are large, slightly recurved posteromedially, and divided into lingual and buccal surfaces by distinct longitudinal carinae which serve as cutting edges. Minute serrations are present along the carinae. The edges are aligned parallel to the length of the jaw.

The marginal dentition appears to be more or less uniform in size along the jaw ramus of the maxilla and the dentary except for the two anteriormost teeth in each dentary which are distinctly smaller. The teeth are slightly compressed, robust, and triangular-cone shaped in lateral profile. In cross section the teeth are broadly ovate.

All the teeth are arranged in a single row in each mandibular ramus. In the left dentary, alveoli 3, 4, and 14 are empty and alveolus 8 contains just the bulbous base of the tooth. In the right dentary, alveoli 3, 13, and 14 are empty and irregular in shape, indicating pre-mortem loss of the old tooth and post-mortem loss of its replacement. The teeth lost after death are in various stages of development that is consistent with a wave-replacement system. Reptile teeth are replaced sequentially as a function of time rather then of need (Romer, 1956). In mosasaurs, replacement waves proceed from the front of the jaws posteriorly, alternatingly affecting even and odd numbered teeth (Edmund, 1960).

On the right dentary, alveoli 9 and 13 have replacement teeth erupting, and alveolus 7 has just the tip projecting up from the ramus. The replacement teeth were more compressed and possess sharply pointed tips. These resorption pits are on the posterolingual aspect, and much the same size from anterior to posterior.

Tooth implantation is subthecodont, with a loose attachment of the teeth in their swollen base. Subthecodont dentition is typical of mosasaurs, and a modification from pleurodont dentition characteristic of most lizards (Romer, 1956) . The teeth are situated in a longitudinal groove of the dentary with a low, inner lingual wall and high, outer labial wall. Within this groove there are shallow sockets separated by a transverse bony septa connecting inner and outer walls. The teeth may be further cemented to the bone of the high outer wall of the dental groove. This dental anatomy differs slightly from the true thecodont condition in that each tooth has a long cylindrical root sheathed in a well-formed socket of bone. Growth of the lower inner wall and associated deepening of the tooth sockets lead to typical thecodont roots set in deep sockets.

Postcranial Skeleton

The vertebral column of *Prognathodon stadtmani* is divided into three regions, the cervical, dorsal, and caudal. This is typical for mosasaurs as well as most reptiles. Posterior cervical vertebrae do not show clear distinctions from the anterior dorsal vertebrae in mosasaurs (Williston, 1898). It does not appear that cervical vertebrae are preserved for BYU 13082. The vertebrae in this specimen are procoelous, the usual condition in mosa-saurs, but they are badly eroded, obscuring many features.

Dorsal Vertebrae

The dorsal column may be arbitrarily divided into an anterior thoracic series bearing long ribs

and a posterior lumbar series with short ribs (Russell, 1967).

Seventeen articulated vertebrae, representing the dorsal series (table 1), were in one plaster field jacket. The total number of dorsal vertebrae is unknown for BYU 13082. In the lumbar region, the synapophyses, formed jointly by the neural arch and centrum, move to a more central position on the anterolateral surface of the centrum preceeding the single sacrum or first pygal vertebrae of mosasaurs (Romer, 1956; Russell, 1967). The central position of the synapophysis and depressions under the synapophysis form a flat keel on the ventral side of the centra, which indicate that the dorsal vertebrae belong immediately anterior to the sacrum in BYU 13082. The neural arches and dorsal spines are badly eroded and poorly preserved in the entire series. The anterior eight vertebrae are broken across the centrum, obscuring the articulating surfaces of the adjoining centra.

Fusion of condyle to cotyle of the vertebrae is of unclear etiology, but there is no additional ossification which would be evidence of pathology. The posterior vertebrae in this series have a suggestion of a rudimentary postzygapophyses, indicated by swelling on the posterodorsal portion of the neural arch. A pair of corresponding small excavations located above the neural canal on either side of the neural spine on the non-fused vertebra 15 could represent points of tendinous attachment. No zygosphenes or zygantra are present.

Caudal Vertebrae

The caudal vertebral column of mosasaurs may be divided into three regions, a proximal (basal) region where vertebrae lack haemal arches but possess transverse processes, called "pygals" by Williston (1898), an intermediate region where they possess haemal arches and transverse processes, and a terminal region where haemal arches are present and transverse processes are absent (Russell, 1967). There are 26 caudal vertebrae present for BYU 13082 (table 2): 5 from the basal pygal section; 20 from the intermediate section (figure 9); and

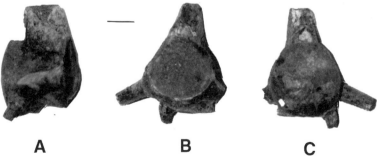

A **B** **C**

Figure 9. *Caudal vertebrae (V24) of the holotype of* Prognathodon stadtmani, *new species (BYU 13082). A, lateral view. B, anterior view. C, posterior view. Scale bar equals 5 cm.*

Table 1. *Measurements of the 17 dorsal vertebrae known for the holotype of* P. stadtmani *(BYU 13082). The vertebrae were numbered sequentially (A-V1-V16) in the field jacket during preparation and were articulated, representing a true consecutive series. Vertebra A represents only the posterior facet of the centrum fused onto the anterior facet of vertebrae 1 and was not numbered in the jacket. All measurements in millimeters. Abbreviations: W=width (measured at widest point between the transverse processes). H=height (measured at the highest point between neural canal and ventral articulating surface). Length of centrum was measured on ventral side between the anterior facet and the posterior facet. D=damaged. NIL=not present. a=approximate value.*

Vertebrae no.	Position	Anterior Facet of Centrum		Posterior Facet of Centrum		Length of Centrum Between Articulations	Haemal Arch	Fusion of Vertebrae	Condition of Vertebrae
		H	W	H	W				
A	Dorsal	D	D	a71	77	D	D	Fused on Posterior Facet of Vertebra	Anterior Portion Missing
V1	Dorsal	a71	77	D	73	90	NIL	Fused	Broken Through Centrum
V2	Dorsal	D	73	D	D	90	NIL	Fused	Broken Through Centrum
V3	Dorsal	D	D	D	D	90	NIL	Fused	Broken Through Centrum
V4	Dorsal	D	D	73	72	90	NIL	Fused	Broken Through Centrum
V5	Dorsal	73	72	D	D	a90	NIL	Fused	Broken Through Centrum
V6	Dorsal	D	D	a71	75	D	NIL	Fused	Broken Through Centrum
V7	Dorsal	a71	75	a66	a80	D	NIL	Fused	Broken Through Centrum
V8	Dorsal	a66	a80	72	70	84	NIL	—	Broken Through Centrum
V9	Dorsal	D	D	a73	a70	a90	NIL	—	Broken Through Centrum
V10	Dorsal	a67	a68	D	D	a71	NIL	—	Broken Through Centrum
V11	Dorsal	D	D	66	61	D	NIL	—	Broken Through Centrum
V12	Dorsal	D	D	72	65	D	NIL	—	Broken by Anterior Facet
V13	Dorsal	a90	D	71	66	86	NIL	—	—
V14	Dorsal	72	68	69	68	83	NIL	—	—
V15	Dorsal	a80	75	73	63	81	NIL	—	—
V16	Dorsal	a81	a69	D	D	D	D	—	Posterior Portion Missing

Table 2. *Detailed measurements of the pygal and caudal vertebrae known for the holotype of* P. stadtmani *(BYU 13082). Although the vertebrae have been numbered sequentially (V17-V42) only the pygal series (V20-V24) were articulated, representing a true consecutive series. Vertebrae 43 represents the best preserved distal caudal vertebrae from the mosasaur for comparison. All measurements in millimeters. Abbreviations: W=width (measured at widest point between the transverse processes). H=height (measured at the highest point between neural canal and ventral articulating surface). Length of centrum was measured on ventral side between the anterior facet and the posterior facet. P=eroded stumps of haemal arch present. NIL=not present. NS=partial neural spine present. a=approximate value.*

Vertebrae no.	Position	Anterior Facet of Centrum		Posterior Facet of Centrum		Length of Centrum Between Articulations	Haemal Arch	Fusion of Vertebrae	Condition of Vertebrae
		H	W	H	W				
V17	Caudal	D	D	58	56	a59	P	----	NS/Very Badly Eroded
V18	Caudal	59	a49	63	57	60	P	----	----
V19	Pygal	67	71	66	65	77	NIL	----	Dorsal Surface Eroded
V20	Pygal	67	71	65	69	72	NIL	----	Dorsal Surface Eroded
V21	Pygal	65	67	69	66	66	NIL	----	Dorsal Surface Eroded
V22	Pygal	68	71	69	71	65	NIL	----	NS
V23	Pygal	67	a62	64	68	61	NIL	----	NS
V24	Caudal	69	73	70	66	59	P	----	NS
V25	Caudal	70	67	a69	65`	60	P	----	NS
V26	Caudal	D	D	D	D	D	D	----	NS/Ventral and Right Side Badly Eroded
V27	Caudal	75	67	69	65	56	P	----	NS
V28	Caudal	D	D	70	67	61	P	----	NS
V29	Caudal	70	68	D	D	D	P	Fused	NS/Broken Through Centrum
V30	Caudal	72	69	D	63	67	P	Fused	Badly Eroded
V31	Caudal	D	D	a57	55	a56	P	----	NS
V32	Caudal	D	D	63	63	63	P	----	----
V33	Caudal	D	D	61	57	a55	P	----	Dorsal Surface Eroded
V34	Caudal	60	61	57	59	50	P - Well Preserved	----	NS
V35	Caudal	D	D	51	55	a49	P	----	NS/Badly Eroded
V36	Caudal	D	D	62	62	56	P - Well Preserved	----	Dorsal Surface Missing
V37	Caudal	a59	a51	59	56	53	P	----	NS but eroded
V38	Caudal	D	D	61	57	54	P	----	Dorsal Surface Eroded
V39	Caudal	57	a50	56	56	50	P	----	NS
V40	Terminal Caudal	57	29	56	47	54	P	----	NS
V41	Caudal	61	60	D	D	48	P	----	NS
V42	Caudal	64	48	60	57	55	P	----	NS
V43	Caudal	a25	16	21	16	18	P - Well Preserved	----	NS

one from the terminal section. Only the pygal vertebrae were articulated; the remaining caudal vertebrae were disarticulated but in association with each other.

The eroded stumps of chevron bones are present along the entire post-pygal region of the tail and fuse on either side of the ventral midline nearer to the posterior margin of the centrum than to the anterior. The few preserved neural spines in the caudals are tall, laterally broad, parallelogram in shape, and posteriorly directed. The neural spines taper posteriorly. The neural spine of the distal vertebra is nearly vertical behind the center of the tail at its base, and then has a marked posterior inclination at the tip.

The articulated pygals are distinguished by long, broad, dorsoventrally flattened transverse processess which form a narrow alae of bone. The single distal vertebra (table 2-V40) is distinguished from the intermediate region by a small nubbin of bone that represents the vestigial remains of the transverse process. Five additional vertebrae from the terminal series were found in a block separate from the other verebrae, and are very small, procoelous, and lack transverse processes. Two of the three associated vertebrae are very fragmentary, but the best preserved vertebra (table 2, no. 43) has well preserved, fused haemal arches that are about equal in length to the dorsal spine height. The preserved articulating surfaces are clearly oval-shaped and deeper than wide.

Ribs

The ribs are fairly slender and preservation is quite poor. There are two fragmentary long ribs and many (100+) smaller fragments. In mosasaurs as in other lizards, the ribs are single-headed (Romer, 1956), but this condition can not be determined for BYU 13082. The ribs are cancellous beneath a layer of laminar bone.

DISCUSSION

Comparisons

Because the Mancos Shale mosasaur has fused haemal arches, all of the Tylosaurinae and most Plioplatecarpinae may be removed from consideration in assessing its relationships. Fusion of the chevrons to the caudal centra is diagnostic of the subfamily Mosasaurinae, *Prognathodon* mosasaurs, and *Dollosaurus* (Iakovlev, 1901, cited in Russell, 1967; also cited in Lingham-Soliar and Nolf, 1989; Tsaregradsky, 1935, cited in Camp, 1942). The premaxilla exhibits the typical microrhynchous condition (broad and stout) for Plioplatecarpinae, and appears to have been blunt anteriorly.

The number of marginal and pterygoid teeth for *P. stadtmani* is reduced relative to other mosasaur genera, and is generically diagnostic (Russell, 1967; Kues and Lucas, 1985). The generally smooth teeth of the Mancos Shale mosasaur are massive, triangular in profile, and have an uncompressed cross section. In contrast, the teeth of relatively common mosasaurine genera *Clidastes* and *Mosasaurus* are generally narrow, strongly recurved, and laterally compressed. The prismatic condition of *Mosasaurus* teeth is very diagnostic (Russell, 1967), while the massive, deep jaw of BYU 13082 is much larger than the slender dentary of *Clidastes*. Therefore, on the basis of the microrhynchous condition of the premaxillae, tooth features, large massive dentaries, and fused haemal arches on the caudal vertebrae, BYU 13082 is assigned to *Prognathodon* rather than any genus within Mosasaurinae.

Russell (1967) published estimated lengths from Dollo's (1904) measurements for *P. solvayi* at 6 meters (19.5 feet), and *P. giganteus* at 10 meters (32.8 feet). Based on his calculations that the given length of the jaw equals 10% of the body length, the specimen of *Prognathodon* described herein is estimated to be 10.5 meters (34.4 feet) long. Dimensions of the cranial elements of BYU 13082 and all other known *Prognathodon* mosasaurs that have been published are provided in table 3.

P. stadtmani has six pterygoid teeth extending over half the overall length of the bone, as in *P. solvayi* (Lingham-Soliar and Nolf, 1989). Russell (1967) mentioned seven teeth in the pterygoid in his diagnosis for *Prognathodon*. As few as six pterygoid teeth have been described for aff. *P. overtoni* (NZGS, CD 535; Wiffen, 1990) while Welles and Gregg (1971) described eight pterygoid teeth for *Prognathodon waiparaensis*, as does Lingham-Soliar and Nolf (1989) for *Prognathodon solvayi*. The size of the pterygoid teeth in BYU 13082 is large, consistant with Williston's (1898) observation that the size of the pterygoid teeth is, "very large, agreeing with the most striking character of the genus *Prognathosaurus*."

A large foramen penetrates the flange of bone in front of the basisphenoid notch which supports the ectopterygoid and quadratic process on the pterygoid is an autopomorphic character for *Prognathodon overtoni* (G. L. Bell, personal communication, 1994). *P. stadtmani* is clearly not this species of *Prognathodon* as it does not share this character with *P. overtoni*. The short ectopterygoid process of the pterygoid is typical for Mosasauridae, and the acute angle that it projects from the main body of the pterygoid is similar to *Platecarpus* (Russell, 1967).

Prognathodon species show a degree of variation in

Table 3. *Comparisons of cranial measurements and elements in known* Prognathodon *species. The distance between the first and sixth tooth in a dentition is measured from the anterior base of the first tooth to the posterior base of the sixth tooth. The length of the dentary is measured from its anterior tip to the posterior apex of the aveolar margin of the bone. All measurements in millimeters (modified from Russell, 1967; Lingham-Soliar and Nolf, 1989; Wiffen, 1990); e, estimated values, approximate values between brackets. Data for* P. overtoni *(KU 950 and SDSM 3393) from Williston 1898 and Russell 1967;* P. rapax *(NJGS 9827) from Russell 1967; FMNH PR 165 from Russell 1970;* P. waiparaensis *(CM zfr 108) from Welles and Gregg 1971;* P. solvayi *(IRSNB R33) and* P. giganteus *(IRSNB R106) from Lingham-Soliar and Nolf 1989; NZGS, CD535 (aff.* P. over-toni*) from Wiffen 1990.*

Measurements	BYU 13082	FMNH PR 165	P. overtoni (SDSM 3393)	P. overtoni (KU 950)	P. rapax (NJGS 9827)	P. solvayi (IRSNB R33)	NZGS CD/535	P. giganteus (IRSNB R106)	P. waiparaensis (CM zfr 108)
Length of skull along mid-line			702			600	680	e.850	e.1110
Width of frontals between orbits			(188)			137		e.250	
Length between 1st and 6th max. tooth	270 (R) 260 (L)		167	222		132	135	(245)	138
Length between 1st and 6th dentary tooth	230 (R) 240 (L)	252 (R) 246 (L)	167	193		122		(235)	
Length of lower jaw	e.1050 (R) e.1110 (L)		867	1146		660	e.800	(1150)	
Length of dentary	660 (R) 690 (L)		472	650		350		(610)	570
Height of quadrate		139	119	145	135	90	115	(130-140)	140
Number of maxilla teeth	12		12	10-11		12	13		11-12
Number of dentary teeth	14		14	12-13		13	13-14		13
Maxilla length	(575)								530
Enamel surface of teeth	Smooth, incipient facets on some teeth	Strongly faceted	Smooth	Smooth	Smooth	Strongly faceted	Faceted	Smooth	Strongly faceted on some teeth
Frontal length							155		250

tooth count. BYU 13082 has 12 teeth in the maxilla and 14 teeth in the dentary, the same count that is described for *P. overtoni* (SDSM 3393) and *Brachysaurus* (=*Prognathodon overtoni*; KU 950) by Williston (1897). Williston (1898) subsequently stated that *P. overtoni* (KU 950) had ten, probably 11 maxillary teeth and 12 or 13 teeth for the dentary. Welles and Gregg (1971) also gave a contradictory count for the maxillary teeth in *P. waiparaensis*, either 11 (p. 69) or 12 (p. 58) and 13 for the dentary. *P. solvayi* has 12 maxillary teeth and 13 dentary teeth (Lingham-Soliar and Nolf, 1989). *Dollosaurus* has 12 (?) for the maxilla and 13 for the dentary (Russell, 1967).

The smooth enamel surfaces of the teeth of BYU 13082 are similar to *Prognathodon overtoni*, *Prognathodon rapax*, and *Prognathodon giganteus* while the marginal teeth of the *Prognathodon* sp.(FMNH PR 165), *Prognathodon solvayi*, and aff. *P. overtoni* (NZGS, CD 535) have facets on their teeth (Russell, 1970; Lingham-Soliar and Nolf, 1989; Wiffen, 1990). For *P. waiparaensis* the enamel surfaces of the teeth are usually smooth, but a few teeth have well-developed facets (Welles and Gregg, 1971). The facets are vertical ridges that form prismatic ornamentation on the teeth. The marginal teeth

are somewhat inflated and become distinctly fatter toward the posterior of the jaw for *P. overtoni* (Russell, 1967; Bell, 1993) and for *P. solvayi* (Lingham-Soliar and Nolf, 1989). The teeth for *P. rapax* are also swollen immediately distal to the tooth-base (Bell, 1993). Except for the smaller size of the two anteriormost teeth in the jaws, the dentition for BYU 13082 is homodont, the teeth not noticeably inflated. The cone-shape type of dentition is considered a plesiomorphic character for *Prognathodon* (G.L. Bell, personal communication, 1993). Minute serrations on the carinae of the marginal dentition for *P. stadtmani* are present. Serrations are visible in the newly erupted teeth in *Prognathodon overtoni* (SDSM 3393) and *Prognathodon waiparaensis* (Welles and Gregg, 1971; Nicholls, 1988). This should not be considered a definitive character, as serrations have been reported for tylosaurine teeth (Thurmond, 1969), *Hainosaurus* and *Mosasaurus dekayi* (Nicholls, 1988).

The concave upper border of the dentary of BYU 13082 is similar to "Prognathodon" FMNH PR 165 (Russell, 1970) and to *Prognathodon solvayi*, but lacks the highly procumbent teeth (Lingham-Soliar and Nolf, 1989) of both these mosasaurs. The moderately procumbent anterior teeth of BYU 13082 differ from the nonprocumbent nature of the anterior teeth described for *P. overtoni* (SDSM 3393; Russell, 1967). Williston (1898) described the concave upper border of the dentary as campylorhynchous. The anterior edentulous projection of the dentary of *P. stadtmani* differs from other described *Prognathodon* specimens. The usual condition for *Prognathodon* is that anteriorly the dentary terminates immediately in front of the first tooth (Russell, 1967). Kues and Lucas (1985) have described a mosasaur (UMN LK-2) from the Lewis Shale which they refer to *Prognathodon* with a rounded, edentulous anterior end of the dentary that projects 45 mm beyond the front of the first tooth base. The subrectangular articulation of the splenial for BYU 13082 is similar to that described for *P. overtoni* and *P. rapax* (Bell, 1993).

The coronoid is generally well developed in these genera of mosasaurs, particularly in *Prognathodon solvayi* (Lingham-Soliar and Nolf, 1989) and *P. waiparaensis* (Welles and Gregg, 1971). The shape of the coronoid of BYU 13082 differs by having a much deeper bowing in dorsal profile than other published illustrations of this element for other *Prognathodon* specimens. Russell (1967), Lingham-Soliar and Nolf (1989), and Bell (1993) described a "C"-shaped or shallow excavation on the posteromedial side of the coronoid process in which the segment of the bodenaponeurosis connecting the M. pseudotemporalis superficialis with the coronoid may have inserted, but this excavation is not present on the coronoid for BYU 13082 and is interpreted as a plesiomorphic condition for this species of *Prognathodon* (G.L. Bell, personal communication, 1994). The relatively short medial flange does not appear to contact the angular, a condition that is also considered a plesiomorphic character for *P. stadtmani* (G.L. Bell, personal communication, 1994). The contact of the coronoid with the dentary is similar to that of *Prognathodon overtoni* (SDSM 3393; Russell, 1967). For *P. solvayi*, the process on the posterodorsal surface of the dentary is absent and contact between the coronoid and the dentary was unlikely (Lingham-Soliar and Nolf, 1989). An incipient posterior process on the dentary in KU 950 suggests a contact intermediate between that of *P. overtoni* (SDSM 3393) and *P. solvayi*. This character is considered an early stage of a character reversal in mosasaurs, similar to that of *Varanus* (Lingham-Soliar and Nolf, 1989). This character reversal is also present as a separate autapomorphic condition in *Mosasaurus hoffmanni* (Lingham-Soliar and Nolf, 1989).

The centra of the pygals are considerably longer than those illustrated for *Prognathodon solvayi* (Lingham-Soliar and Nolf 1989). The cloaca in living reptiles is ventral to the pygals (Williston, 1898,1925). The central

articulations in the intermediate caudal vertebrae are round to broadly subtriangular in outline as in *Clidastes, Plotosaurus, Platecarpus*, and *Tylosaurus*, but does not conform to the subhexagonal description of *Prognathodon* (Russell, 1967). That the zygosphenes and zygantra are absent in BYU 13082 agrees with Russell's diagnosis (1967) of the genus. However, large functional zygosphenes and zygantra are described for the Belgium *P. solvayi* and *P. giganteus* (Lingham-Soliar and Nolf, 1989). In addition, the North American *P. rapax* (Bell, 1993), the New Zealand *P. waiparaensis* (Welles and Gregg, 1971), and *Dollosaurus* from Russia (Russell, 1967; Lingham-Soliar and Nolf, 1989) also have these articulations.

TAPHONOMY

BYU 13082 is in a fairly good state of preservation. However, an unknown part of the fossil was lost during excavation of an earth-fill pit by a backhoe that initially exposed the fossil as described in a 1975 newspaper account in the Delta County Independent (Marshall, 1975). The anterior portion of the skull and the posteriormost dorsal vertebrae are present. Because fossil skulls of mosasaurs are often firmly attached to the vertebral column (Williston, 1898), it seems reasonable to assume that the backhoe cut through the posterior portion of the skull, the cervical vertebrae, and an unknown number of anterior dorsal vertebrae. A two-day salvage operation was undertaken to rescue the remaining skeleton, which did not leave time for preparation of a quarry map to record the accurate relative position of the bones. Field notes were not taken during the excavation. Thus, the exact taphonomic context of the remains is impossible to determine.

BYU 13082 is an associated skeleton of a single, partially articulated, large adult representing an attritional mortality thanatocoensis for the site. The anterior portion of the muzzle suffered considerable lateral compression with portions of the internarial bar pushed underneath the right maxilla due to overburden pressure. The more massive bones resisted compaction. The dorsal surface of the left palatine was cemented onto the posterodorsal surface of the right maxilla.

The bone is pale buff in color and has a soft, powdery surface. This powdery bone surface may be due to prolonged exposure to sea water, or to marine algae encrusting the bone surface (Martill, 1987), although no evidence of marine algae encrusting the fossil has been observed. The carcass provided the soft sea-floor a hard substrate for a limited number of encrusting bivalves, as did the sedimentary matrix of thinly laminated homogenous silt, suggesting a constant supply of particles rather than sudden burial (Sato, 1997) of the mosasaur remains.

The lack of cementation in the sediment surrounding the bone may be another explanation for the soft condition and color of the bones. The Mancos "B" has low porosity (average 10-11%) and low permeability (average 0.7 md) (Kellogg, 1977) which would prevent ground water from percolating through the sediment and thus retard permineralization of the bone. No mineralization of the voids in the ribs has taken place.

No definitive cause of death is apparent from the remains of the animal or the encasing sediments. The animal either died where the carcass was buried, or it presumably sank rapidly through the water column soon after death. The carcass arrived on the sea floor relatively intact, evidently with soft connective tissue present, which served to hold most of the skeleton together.

Actuopaleontological studies of large marine mammals that died from natural causes show that animals with high fat content drift for weeks on the surface of the sea while the majority with low fat content sink to the sea floor (Schafer, 1972). Floating carcasses quickly begin to shed their heavier body parts as skin and connective tissue decompose. The skull and loosely attached lower jaws would be among the first skeletal elements to be lost from the rest of the carcass (Schafer, 1972; Hogler, 1992) due to wind- and current-driven transport. The buoyancy of air-breathing Mesozoic marine reptiles is currently being debated on the basis of bone histology and density (Taylor, 1987,1994; McGowen, 1992; Hua and de Buffrenil, 1996; Sheldon, 1997), and analogs with modern sea-snakes and marine Indopacific crocodiles (Wade, 1984). The preserved ribs of mosasaurs have not been reported to exhibit pachyostosis, with the possible exception of *Platecarpus* (Sheldon, 1994,1997) and some specimens of *Plioplatecarpus* (Holmes, 1996).

The cancellous condition of the ribs, termed adiposity, is associated with weight reduction. They were possibly impregnated with fat, increasing the buoyancy of the animal (Russell, 1967). The lower density of BYU 13082 suggests that this mosasaur was much more conservative in energy requirements; the lower bone density could have assisted in rapid acceleration toward prey (Lingham-Soliar, 1992). This condition has previously been described only in *Tylosaurus* (Russell, 1967; Carroll, 1985; Lingham-Soliar, 1992) and *Moanasaurus mangahouangae* (Wiffen, 1980), a possible junior synonym of *Mosasaurus* (Wright, 1989). Cancellous bones cannot just be considered an artifact of large size, with a correlation to weight reduction, because an equally large mosasaur, *Mosasaurus hoffmani*, lacks cancellous bones (Lingham-Soliar, 1992). Williston (1925) related cancellous bones as an adaptation for deep-diving for some mosasaurs.

Several hypotheses have been discussed with regard to partitioning of the water column by mosasaurs into coastal shallow-water, deeper open-sea, and deep-diving habitats (Camp, 1923). Within the wide adaptive zone that mosasaurs occupied, there were probably several adaptive grades between the various genera, which indicates correspondingly different swimming and predatory habits (Russell, 1967). This may be reflected to a degree by the body size, proportions, and amount of ossification of the post-cranial skeleton for the three subfamilies of Mosasauridae. Specific differences in details of mosasaur anatomy (Williston, 1898,1914; Camp, 1942; Kauffman and Kesling, 1960; Russell, 1967; Lingham-Soliar and Nolf, 1989; Martin and Rothschild, 1989; Lingham-Soliar, 1991,1992; Rothschild and Martin, 1993; Sheldon, 1994,1997) have been discussed in this ecological context. The various hypotheses are highly conjectural, and have been contradictory and inconclusive. The relative distance between the recovery site of BYU 13082 in relation to the paleoshoreline, the taphofacies, and the cancellous condition of the bones suggests an open-sea and possibly deep-diving habitat for *P. stadtmani*.

The abundance of complete and articulated marine reptile fossils suggests that the hydrodynamic behavior of these animals was a tendency toward negative buoyancy when dead which allowed the corpses to sink at death (Martill, 1987; Hogler, 1992,1994). A rough measure of the time between death and final deposition in a marine environment is the degree of completeness of the specimen (Hogler, 1992); and this is also an index to the paleobathymetry (Allison and others, 1991). Coherent parts of 17 interlocking vertebrae remained articulated for BYU 13082, and the first eight are fused condyle to cotyle. This fusion is probably an artifact of fossilization rather than ontogeny or pathology. Fusion of fragments as a consequence of fossilization has been described in *Platecarpus coryphaeus*, *Goronyosaurus nigeriensis* (Soliar, 1988), and *Hainosaurus pembinensis* (Nicholls, 1988). Five pygal vertebrae were also articulated, but twisted 180 degrees in association with the following vertebrae from the intermediate section of the tail. The smaller elements of the tail became disarticulated as they were probably less tightly bound together by bony processes, axial muscles, tendons, and ligaments than the anterior portion of the vertebral column (Lucas and Reser, 1981). The lack of smaller terminal caudals indicates that they were carried or moved some distance from the rest of the remains as would have been the case if current activity was responsible for reworking (Martill,

1985). Thus, the taphonomic inference from the hydrologic incompatibility in size difference between the smaller terminal caudals and the larger caudal bones strongly suggests an untransported (autochthonous) burial. This is consistent with the lithofacies of a thinly laminated siltstone. Some of these smaller terminal caudal vertebrae may have been carried away from the rest of the carcass by scavengers. However, no apparent scavenger grooves or bite marks are present on the skeletal remains.

No associated girdles and appendages were found with BYU 13082, a condition that is not uncommon for mosasaur taphonomy. Scavenging has been invoked as a plausible mechanism for paddle and pelvic elements being removed from mosasaur remains (Lucas and Reser, 1981; Hawkins, 1990).

The associated sharks teeth could represent gut contents, organic debris present in the sediment where the carcass came to rest, or scavenging. The enamel on the teeth shows no evidence of being de-calicified by stomach acids in the digestive tract. No other shark elements, such as scales or spines, are present that would indicate the mosasaur had recently fed on a shark prior to its death. This would eliminate the possiblity of the teeth as stomach contents, and would indicate that the mosasaur carcass either settled on organic debris including the shark teeth that were already present where it came to rest after death, or as evidence of scavenging of the carcass. Indirect evidence of scavenging by *Squalicorax* is the anomalous abundances in situ of *Squalicorax* teeth in association with larger fossil vertebrate carcasses as compared to background occurrences (Schwimmer and others, 1997; D.R. Schwimmer, personal communication, 1993; Schwimmer and Williams, 1991). There is direct evidence of predation by *Cretolamna* and by considerably smaller *Squalicorax* on several taxa of much larger mosasaurs in the Kansas seas (Martin and Rothschild, 1989; Rothschild and Martin, 1993), but there is no direct evidence of this predator-prey relationship in the preserved skeletal remains of *Prognathodon stadtmani*.

CONCLUSIONS

Vertebrate fossils are sparse in the marine Mancos Shale despite the extensive geographic and temporal range of this formation. Its vertebrate fauna is therefore poorly known. Data derived from this study will help illuminate part of this little-described fauna.

The location of the mosasaur site was in excess of 161 km (100 miles) from the presumed early Campanian paleoshoreline (see figure 1). Due to the low-energy environment, the remains of BYU 13082 are sufficiently well preserved to allow for generic and species identification. The skeletal remains of one large adult were recovered from the site. The occurrence in isolation from other large mosasaurs indicates a solitary death, and an attritional mortality thanatocoensis for the site. The presence of large, heavy elements and articulated vertebrae indicates that the carcass of *P. stadtmani*, like many other contemporaneous marine reptiles, had a tendency to sink to the seafloor at death. This individual might have died in situ in a low-energy depositional environment. This suggestion is supported by sedimentary analysis of the rock at the site, and suggests a preference for a deeper, open-sea environment for this mosasaur.

ACKNOWLEDGMENTS

I wish to express my appreciation to the many people and institutions who have assisted me in this study. Wade E. Miller and David D. Gillette supervised this manuscript. Their constructive criticism greatly improved the manuscript. I am much indebted to Kenneth L. Stadtman, curator at the BYU Earth Science Museum, and Dee A. Hall, preparator at this same institution for their enthusiastic support of all aspects of this study; both were integral to its completion. David Parris and Barbara Grandstaff of the New Jersey State Museum are gratefully acknowledged for their kind assistance while I was conducting initial research at the New Jersey State Museum. Teo Lingham-Soliar, Gordon Bell, and Kevin Bylund supplied many pieces of hard-to-find literature. G.L. Bell was particularly generous with his time involving lengthy discussions with regard to this study. James Jensen, Richard Jones, and Rod and Michael Scheetz were responsible for collecting the specimen. Richard Jones was instrumental in assisting me to relocate the mosasaur site. J. Keith Rigby, Dana Griffen, David Tingey, and Carma Bylund gave technical assistance. I would also like to thank Kris Mortenson, Jo Wixom, Nathan Heard, Lindy Glenn, Jennie Dalton , and Charlie McClellan. Funding for this study was provided in part by a grant from the Utah Division of State History, and the Society of Vertebrate Paleontology Richard Estes Memorial Award (1993).

REFERENCES

Allison, P. A.; Smith, C. R.; Kobeicht, Helmut; Demming, J. W.; and Bennett, B. A., 1991, Deep water taphonomy of vertebrate carcasses -- a whale skeleton in the bathyal Santa Catalina Basin: Paleobiology, v. 17., no.1, p. 78-89.

Bell, G. L., Jr., 1993, A phylogenetic revision of Mosasauroidea (Squamata): Austin, University of Texas, Ph.D. dissertation, 293 p.

Bilelo, M. A. M., 1969, The fossil shark genus *Squalicorax* in north-central Texas: Texas Journal of Science, v. 20, no.4, p. 339-348.

Callison, George, 1967, Intracranial mobility in Kansas mosasaurs: University of Kansas Paleontological Contributions, Paper 26, p. 1-15.

Camp, C. L., 1923, Classification of the lizards: American Museum of Natural History Bulletin 48, p. 289-481.

—1942, California mosasaurs: University of California Memoirs, v. 13, no. 1, p. 1-68.

Cappetta, Henri, 1987, Chondrichthyes 11: Mesozoic and Cenozoic Elasmobranchii, *in* Schultze, H-P., editor, Handbook of paleoichthyology 3B: Stuttgart, New York, Gustav Fischer Verlag, p. 109-110.

Cappetta, Henri, and Case, G. R., 1975, Contribution to the study of the selachians from Monmouth Group (Campanian-Maestrichtian) of New Jersey: Palaeontographica, Abteilung A 151, p. 1-46.

Carroll, R. L., 1985, Evolutionary constraints in aquatic diapsid reptiles - evolutionary case histories from the fossil record: London, England, The Paleontological Association, Special papers in palaeontology, v. 33, p. 145-155.

Carter, B. R., 1991, A plesiosaur from the Upper Mancos Shale, *in* Averett, W.R., editor, Guidebook for dinosaur quarries and tracksites tour - Western Colorado and eastern Utah: Grand Junction Geological Society, Grand Junction, Colorado, p. 51.

Cobban, W. A., 1976, Ammonite record from the Mancos Shale of the Castle Valley-Price-Woodside area, east-central Utah: Brigham Young University Geology Studies, v. 2, no. 3, p. 117-128.

Cole, R. D., 1987, Cretaceous rocks of the dinosaur triangle, *in* Averett, W. R., editor, Dinosaur triangle paleontological field trip: Grand Junction, Colorado, Grand Junction Geological Society, p. 21-35.

Cross, Whitman, 1899, Telluride Folio, Colorado, U. S. Geological Survey, Geological Atlas, 39 p., 3 sheets of illustrations, 4 maps, Folio 57.

Dollo, Louis, 1904, Les mosasauriens de la Belgique: Bulletin de la societe belge de Geologie, de Paleontologie et Hydrologie, v. 4, p. 207-216.

Edmund, A.G., 1960, Tooth replacement phenomena in the lower vertebrates: Royal Ontario Museum of Life Sciences Division Contribution, v. 52, p. 87-91

Estes, Richard; de Queiroz, Kevin; and Gauthier, Jacques, 1988, Phylogenetic relationships within Squamata, *in* Estes, Richard, and Pregill, Gregory, editors, Phylogenetic relationships of the lizard families-essays commemorating Charles L. Camp. Stanford, California, Stanford University Press, p. 119-280.

Fouch, T. D.; Lawton, T. F.; Nicholls, D. J.; Cashion, W. B.; and Cobban, W. A., 1983, Patterns and timing of synorogenic sedimentation in Upper Cretaceous rocks of central and northeast Utah, *in* Reynolds, M. W., and Dolly, E. D., editors, Mesozoic paleogeography of the west-central United States: Rocky Mountain Section, Society of Economic Paleontologists and Mineralogists, p. 305-336.

Franczyk, K. J., Fouch, T. D., Johnson, R. C., Molenaar, C. M., and Cobban, W. A., 1992, Cretaceous and Tertiary paleogeographic reconstructions for the Unita-Piceance Basin study area, Colorado and Utah: U. S. Geological Survey Bulletin 1787-Q, p. Q1-Q37.

Gregory, J. T., 1951, Convergent evolution-the jaws of *Hesperornis* and the mosasaur: Evolution, v. 5, no. 4, p. 345-354.

Hail, W. J., Jr., 1972, Reconnaissance geologic map of the Cedaredge area, Delta County, Colorado: U.S. Geological Survey Miscellaneous Geologic Investigations Map I-697, scale 1:48000.

Hawkins, W. B, Jr., 1990, Taphonomy of an Upper Cretaceous (Maastrichtian) mosasaur, Briggs, Alabama Society of Vertebrate Paleontology, 50th Annual Meeting, Abstracts of Papers: Journal of Vertebrate Paleontology, v. 9, p. 26A.

Hogler, J. A., 1992, Taphonomy and paleoecology of *Shinosaurus popularis* (Reptilia: Ichthyosauria): Palaios, v. 7, no. 1, p. 108-117.

—1994, Speculations on the role of marine reptile deadfalls in Mesozoic deep-sea paleoecology: Palaios, v. 9, no. 1, p. 42-47.

Holmes, Robert, 1996, *Plioplatecarpus primaevus* (Mosasauridae) from the Bearpaw Formation (Campanian, Upper Cretaceous) of the North American Western Interior Seaway: Journal of Vertebrate Paleontology, v. 16, no. 4, p. 673-687.

Hua, Stephanie, and deBuffrenil, Vivian, 1996, Bone histology as a clue in the interpretation of functional adaptations in the Thalattosuchia (Reptilia, Crocodylia): Journal of Vertebrate Paleontology, v. 16, no. 4, p. 703-717.

Hunt, A. P., and Lucas, S. G., 1993, Cretaceous vertebrates of New Mexico, *in* Lucas, S. G., and Zidek, Jiri, editors, Vertebrate paleontology in New Mexico: New Mexico Museum of Natural History and Science Bulletin, v. 2, p. 77-90.

Irby, G. V.; Elliott, D. K.; and Hutchison, J. H., 1994, New material of the Cretaceous turtle *Desmatochelys lowi*: Journal of Vertebrate Paleontology, v. 14, p. 31A.

Kass, M. S., 1995, A new mosasaur from the Mancos Shale of Delta County, Colorado: Provo, Utah, Brigham Young University, M.S. thesis, 145 p.

Kauffman, E. G., and Kesling, R. V., 1960, An Upper Cretaceous ammonite bitten by a mosasaur: Contributions from the Museum of Paleontology, The University of Michigan, v. 15, no. 9, p. 193-248.

Kellogg, H. E., 1977, Geology and petroleum of the Mancos B Formation, Douglas Creek area, Colorado and Utah, *in* Veal, H. K. , editor, Exploration frontiers of the Central and Southern Rockies: Rocky Mountain Association of Geologists Symposium, p. 167-179.

Kent, H.C., 1965, Biostratigraphy of the Lower Mancos Shale (Cretaceous) in northwestern Colorado: Boulder, University of Colorado, Ph. D. dissertation, 162 p.

Kues, B. S., and Lucas, S. G., 1985, Mosasaur remains from the Lewis Shale (Upper Cretaceous), S.W. Colorado: Journal of Paleontology, v. 59, no. 6, p. 1395-1400.

Lauginiger, E. M., and Hartstein, E. F., 1983, A guide to fossil sharks, skates, and rays from the Chesapeake and Delaware canal area, Delaware: Delaware Geological Survey Open- File Report 21, p. 33-35.

Lingham-Soliar, Theagarten, 1991, Mosasaurs from the Upper Cretaceous of Niger: Palaeontology, v. 34, p. 653-670.

—1992, The tylosaurine mosasaurs (Reptilia, Mosasauridae) from the Upper Cretaceous of Europe and Africa: Bulletin de L'Institut Royal des Sciences Naturelles de Belgique, v. 62, p. 171-194.

Lingham-Soliar, Theagarten, and Nolf, Dirk, 1989, The mosasaur *Prognathodon* (Reptilia, Mosasauridae) from the Upper Cretaceous of Belgium: Bulletin de L'Institut Royal des Sciences Naturelles de Belgique, v. 59, p. 137-190.

Lucas, S. G., and Reser, P. K., 1981, A mosasaur from the Lewis Shale (Upper Cretaceous), northwestern New Mexico: New Mexico Geology, v. 3, no. 3, p. 37-40.

Marshall, Murial, 1975, Bones discovered near Cedaredge: Delta County Independent, v. 92, no. 22, 8 p.

Martill, D. M., 1985, The preservation of marine vertebrates in the Lower Oxford Clay (Jurassic) of central England: Philosophical Transactions of the Royal Society of London B, v. 311, p. 155-165.

—1987, Taphonomic and diagenetic case study of a partially articulated ichthyosaur: Palaeontology, v. 30, no. 3, p. 543-555.

Martin, L. D., and Rothschild, B. M., 1989, Paleopathology and diving mosasaurs: American Scientist, v. 77, p. 460-467.

McGowan, Christopher, 1992, The ichthyosaurian tail--sharks do not provide an appropriate analogue: Palaeontology, v. 35, no. 3, p. 555-570.

Molenaar, C.M., 1983, Major depositional cycles and regional correlations of Upper Cretaceous rocks, southern Colorado Plateau and adjacent areas, *in* Reynolds, M. W., and Dolly, E.D., editors, Mesozoic paleogeography of west-central United States: Rocky Mountain Section, Society of Economic Paleontologists and Mineralogists, p. 201-224.

Nicholls, E. L., 1988, The first record of the mosasaur *Hainosaurus* (Reptilia: Lacertilia) from North America: Canadian Journal of Earth Science, v. 25, p. 1564-1570.

Obradovich, J. D., 1993, A Cretaceous time scale, *in* Caldwell, W. G. E., and Kauffman, E. G., editors, Evolution of the Western Interior Basin: Geological Association of Canada Special Paper 39, p. 379-396.

Romer, A. S., 1956, Osteology of the reptiles: Chicago, Illinois, The University of Chicago Press, 772 p.

Rothschild, B. M., and Martin, L. D., 1993, Paleopathology--disease in the fossil record: Boca Raton, Florida, CRC Press, Inc., 386 p.

Russell, D. A., 1967, Systematics and morphology of American mosasaurs (Reptilia, Sauria): Peabody Museum of Natural History Bulletin, v. 23, p. 1-237.

—1970, The vertebrate fauna of the Selma Formation of Alabama--the mosasaurs: Fieldiana Geology Memoirs, v. 3, no. 7, p. 363-380.

Sato, Tamaki, 1997, Taphonomy of a plesiosaurian fossil from Hokkaido, Japan: Journal of Vertebrate Paleontology, v. 17, p. 73A.

Schafer, Wilhelm, 1972, Ecology and paleoecology of marine environments: Chicago, Illinois, The University of Chicago Press, 568 p.

Schwimmer, D. R.; Stewart, J. D.; and Williams, G. D., 1997, Scavenging by sharks of the genus *Squalicorax* in the Late Cretaceous of North America: Palaios, v. 12, p. 71-83.

Schwimmer, D. R., and Williams, G. D., 1991, Evidence of scavenging by the selachian *Squalicorax kaupi* in the Upper Cretaceous marine sediments of the eastern Gulf Coastal Plain: Journal of Vertebrate Paleontology, v. 11, p. 55A.

Sheldon, M. A., 1994, Ecological implications of mosasaur bone microstructure: Journal of Vertebrate Paleontology, v. 14, p. 45A.

—1997, Ecological implications of mosasaur bone microstructure, *in* Callaway, J. M., and Nicholls, E. L., editors, Ancient marine reptiles, Academic Press, p. 333-354.

Soliar, Theagarten, 1988, The mosasaur *Goronyosaurus* from the upper Cretaceous of Sokoto State, Nigeria: Palaeontology, v. 31, no. 3, p. 747-762.

Taylor, M. A., 1987, Reinterpretation of ichthyosaur swimming and buoyancy: Palaeontology, v. 3 0, p. 531-535.

—1994, Convergent evolution in marine tetrapods: Journal of Vertebrate Paleontology, v. 14, p. 49A.

Thurmond, J. T., 1969, Notes on mosasaurs from Texas: Texas Journal of Science, v. 21, p. 69-80.

Wade, Mary, 1984, *Platypterygius australis*, an Australian Cretaceous ichthyosaur: Lethaia, v. 17, p. 99-113.

Welles, S. P., and Gregg, D. R., 1971, Late Cretaceous marine reptiles of New Zealand: Records of the Canterbury Museum, v. 9, no. 1, p. 1-111.

Welton, B. J., and Farish, R. F., 1993, The collector's guide to fossil sharks and rays from the Cretaceous of Texas: Dallas, Texas, Before Time, 204 p.

Wiffen, Joan, 1980, *Moanasaurus*, a new genus of marine reptile (Family Mosasauridae) from the Upper Cretaceous of North Island, N. Z.: New Zealand Journal of Geology and Geophysics, v. 23, p. 507-528.

—1990, New mosasaurs (Reptilia:Family Mosasauridae) from the Upper Cretaceous of North Island, New Zealand: New Zealand Journal of Geology and Geophysics, v. 33, p. 67-85.

Williston, S.W., 1897, *Brachysaurus*, a new genus of mosasaurs: Kansas University Quarterly, v. 6, no. 2, p. 95-98.

—1898, Mosasaurs: University Geology Survey, Kansas, v. 4, p. 83-221.

—1914, Water reptiles of the past and present: Chicago, Illinois, The University of Chicago Press, 251 p.

—1925, The osteology of the reptiles: Cambridge, Massachusetts, Cambridge, Harvard University Press, 300 p.

Wolny, D. G.; Armstrong, H. J.; and Kirkland, J. I., 1990, Hadrosaur skeleton from the Mancos Shale, W. Colorado: Journal of Vertebrate Paleontology, v. 10, p. 50A.

Wright, K. R., 1989, On the taxonomic status of *Moanasaurus mangahouangae* Wiffen (Squamata:Mosasauridae): Journal of Paleontology, v. 63, no. 1, p. 126-127.

Young, R. G., 1959, Cretaceous deposits of the Grand Junction area, Garfield, Mesa, and Delta Counties, Colorado, *in* Haun, J. D., and Weimer, R. J., editors, Symposium on Cretaceous rocks of Colorado and adjacent areas: Denver, Colorado, Eleventh Field Conference Washakie, Sand Wash, and Piceance Basins, Rocky Mountain Association of Geologists, p. 17-25.

—1960, Mancos Shale and Mesaverde group of Palisade area, *in* Weimer, R. J., and Haun, J. D., editors, Guide to the geology of Colorado: Geological Society of America. Rocky Mountain Association of Geologists, Colorado Scientific Society, p. 85-86.

HADROSAUR SKIN IMPRESSIONS FROM THE UPPER CRETACEOUS NESLEN FORMATION, BOOK CLIFFS, UTAH: MORPHOLOGY AND PALEOENVIRONMENTAL CONTEXT

Brian G. Anderson
Mesa Southwest Museum, 53 North MacDonald, Mesa, Arizona 85201
present address: Brown and Caldwell, 380 East Park Center Boulevard, Boise, ID 83706

Reese E. Barrick
Department of Marine, Earth and Atmospheric Sciences,
North Carolina State University, Raleigh, North Carolina 27695

Mary L. Droser
Department of Earth Sciences, University of California, Riverside, California 92521

Kenneth L. Stadtman
Earth Sciences Museum, Brigham Young University, Provo, Utah 85602

ABSTRACT

A well-preserved hadrosaur skeleton with skin impressions from the Upper Cretaceous Neslen Formation, east-central Utah, provides an unique window into the dermal morphology of these dinosaurs. The integument is characterized by polygonal and ovate to rounded tubercles, most of which exhibit radiating grooves extending from the top to the base of each tubercle. Three size ranges of tubercles are recognized: small (1 to 3 mm), medium (3 to 8 mm), and large (10 to 23 mm). There is minimal variation in tubercle size along the flank of the individual, with the mean long axis varying from 7 to 8 mm on the tail and 6 to 7 mm along the torso; while the short axis varies from 5 to 6 mm on both the tail and torso regions. Dorsal tubercles tend to be largest, with a patch corresponding to the pelvis area up to 23 mm in size. The integument along the dorsal surface also exhibits lower tubercle density than observed laterally along the tail. Several specimens likely from the ventral surface exhibit rounded tubercles isolated within a homogenous background of smaller polygonal forms. Osteological studies have yet to be performed; however, comparison with descriptions of other hadrosaurs with preserved skin impressions suggests the integument morphology is comparable to that of several gryposaurs.

The hadrosaur remains are preserved within a laterally discontinuous, very fine-grained calcareous sandstone. Sedimentologic and stratigraphic evidence indicate that deposition, and hence burial of the carcass, occurred within a low-energy environment. The lenticular geometry and overall progradational facies succession are consistent with a fluvio-estuarine system. This interpretation is further supported by the presence of *Teredolites* and rare *Rhizocorallium* directly overlying and surrounding the hadrosaur. The fossil assemblage also includes variably preserved woody debris, suggesting that the depositional system formed part of a poorly drained coastal floodplain. We believe this paleoenvironment, along with the fine grain size and stability of the substrate, were key to the preservational quality of the impressions.

INTRODUCTION

The biology of dinosaurs has been studied extensively for more than a century; yet very little is known about their external appearance due to taphonomic biases in the ancient environment. Necrotic processes such as scavenging and bacterial decay typically destroy soft parts prior to final burial and lithification, and thus soft tissues of terrestrial vertebrates are rare in the fossil record. There is no known evidence of organically preserved dinosaur skin, other than kerogenous film inferred as the degradation product of ornithischian epidermis from the Lower Jurassic of England (Martill, 1991). Rather, much of our understanding of dinosaur skin morphology, albeit only cursory, has come from impressions of the integument.

Of the dinosaur skin impressions that occur with diagnostic skeletal material, the majority are from hadrosaurs (Brown, 1917; Gilmore, 1946; Lull and Wright, 1942; Parks, 1920; Sternberg, 1925), with the most complete and famous specimens of *Edmontosaurus annectens* collected by Charles Sternberg in 1908. Other impressions of hadrosaur integument have been reported but were never described because the material was destroyed during extraction of the skeleton (Lull and Wright, 1942). Hadrosaur skin impressions are also occasionally found within footprints (Currie and others, 1992) and tail segments (Horner, 1984). Based on descriptions of these previously reported hadrosaurian skin impressions, the only commonality is that the integument consists of non-imbricating scales with tubercles and there is no indication of dermal ossicles.

Herein we report on a hadrosaur skeleton preserved with skin impressions from the Upper Cretaceous Neslen Formation of east-central Utah (figure 1). This specimen is the first dinosaur reported from the Neslen. More than two square meters of integument are preserved in situ with a partially articulated postcranial skeleton, as well as dentition which are diagnostic of hadrosaurs. This direct association of the skin impressions with the bones, along with the fine-scale preservation of discrete dermal features, represents an unparalleled opportunity to examine the variability in skin morphology of a single individual. The objectives of this paper are: (1) to document the integument morphology corresponding to specific regions of the body; (2) to delineate the paleoenvironmental context in which the original carcass was buried; and (3) to provide a comparison with earlier descriptions of hadrosaur skin impressions.

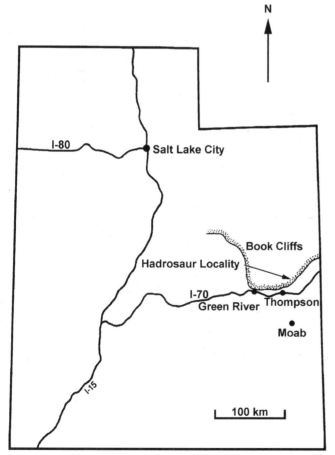

Figure 1. *Map of Utah showing the hadrosaur locality. Stippled pattern denotes the Book Cliffs escarpment. Exact locality information is on file at Mesa Southwest Museum and BYU Earth Sciences Museum.*

GEOLOGIC AND STRATIGRAPHIC SETTING

From Green River, Utah to the Utah-Colorado border, the Book Cliffs form a continuous southward-facing escarpment comprised of Cretaceous through Eocene strata. The Sevier Orogeny resulted in the formation of highlands in western Utah by Late Cretaceous, resulting in a foreland basin directly to the east that includes the Book Cliffs area (Hintze, 1988). During the Cretaceous, sediments derived from the highlands were deposited in the basin, which by Turonian time was occupied by a shallow epicontinental sea that extended from the Gulf of Mexico to the Arctic Ocean (Williams and Stelck, 1975). Sediments comprising the Neslen Formation were deposited along the western edge of the seaway during the latter Campanian. Deposition continued throughout the remainder of the Cretaceous and into the early Tertiary (Fouch and others, 1983).

The Neslen Formation consists of mudstone, siltstone, sandstone, and coal with an average thickness of 106 meters (Willis, 1986). Previous work by Pitman and others (1987) and Willis (1986) recognized the Neslen as a nonmarine succession with a dominant fluvial component. The base of the formation is demarcated by a regionally extensive unconformity, which is considered to form the bounding surface of a high-resolution stratigraphic sequence (Van Wagoner and others, 1990). The skin impressions and skeletal elements occur in the lower member of the Neslen Formation approximately 12 meters above the unconformity.

The fossil material is preserved in a 1.5 meter thick, coarsening-upward succession of buff-colored, very fine- to fine-grained sandstone interbedded with carbonaceous siltstone and mudstone (figure 2). Individual sandstone beds range from 5 to 50 centimeters thick, and are laterally discontinuous. Primary sedimentary structures include small-scale trough cross-stratification and wavy laminae; however, some of the original fabric has been altered by biogenic reworking. The impressions occur primarily along a plane between two sandstone beds 10 centimeters above the base of the measured section shown in figure 2. Several isolated patches of impressions are preserved in the overlying sandstone unit that contains the skeleton.

FIELD AND LABORATORY METHODS

Because this study is dependent on understanding where the skin impressions occur in relation to the body, the hadrosaur was excavated by removing blocks of the

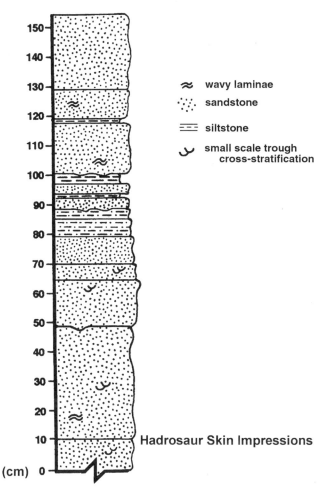

Figure 2. Generalized stratigraphic section of the hadrosaur skin impressions within the lower member of the Campanian Neslen Formation. The measured section begins approximately 12 meters above the basal contact of the formation.

sandstone containing the impression surface and skeletal elements, rather than attempting to jacket the specimen. During excavation, skeletal elements identified were mapped in relation to the outcrop surface and stratigraphic position above the skin impression surface. Sedimentologic analyses were conducted at a centimeter-scale as the blocks were removed. Trace fossil occurrences were documented according to stratigraphic position relative to the skeleton. Selected trace fossil specimens were collected for ichnotaxonomic and paleoenvironmental study.

The excavated blocks were reassembled for further examination at the Brigham Young University (BYU) Earth Sciences Museum, the repository for the material (BYU specimen no. 13258). Tubercle measurements were made to the nearest millimeter using a dial-caliper. As most tubercles are polygonal or ovate, the widest (long axis) and narrowest (short axis) dimensions were selected for analysis. Twenty-five tubercles were measured from impression surfaces corresponding to the following body regions: mid-caudal, proximal caudal,

pelvis, mid-torso, anterior torso, and dorsal surface. Tubercle density was assessed by counting the number of tubercles within a unit area of 25 square centimeters. For each body region, three independent counts were made on randomly selected areas of each impression panel. Statistical averages were calculated for the long and short axes, as well as the number of tubercles per unit area. Presence and number of radiating grooves were also noted for exceptionally preserved tubercles.

INTEGUMENT MORPHOLOGY AND PRESERVATIONAL STYLE

The skin impressions are characterized by a distinct mammillate morphology. Discrete tubercles are evident in all of the specimens examined. In terms of shape, most tubercles are five- to six-sided polygonal forms (figure 3A). A wide range of tubercle dimensions is recognized; however, it is possible to group the sizes into three categories: small (1 to 3 mm), medium (3 to 8 mm), and large (10 to 23 mm). The large tubercles tend to be ovate to rounded and are up to 4 mm in relief. Medium and large forms typically exhibit radiating grooves extending from the top to the base of each tubercle. Most commonly the number of grooves per tubercle is 8 or 12, with a maximum of 22 observed on a large, rounded tubercle. The distribution of tubercle patterns across a single impression surface varies considerably. On several of the specimens examined, large forms occur occasionally in clustered groups of 4 to 6 or are isolated within a background of small and medium tubercles. Distances between a single large tubercle from its nearest neighbor varies between 9 and 53 centimeters.

Mean tubercle dimensions and number per unit area are provided in table 1. Excluding large tubercles, the mean long and short axes vary from 5 to 7 millimeters and 4 to 5 millimeters, respectively. Tubercle dimensions and density are similar along the side of the individual from the distal tail to the anterior torso. The mean long axes of tubercles vary from 7 to 8 millimeters on the tail and 6 to 7 millimeters along the torso, whereas the mean short axes vary from 5 to 6 millimeters on both the tail and torso regions. These size ranges are similar to tubercles on the pelvis, which have mean long and short axes of 7 and 5 millimeters. The mean number of tubercles within a unit area is from 87 to 99 and 92 to 133 at the tail and torso, respectively. On the pelvic region the mean tubercle density is 88 per 25 square centimeters.

There are two exceptions to the relatively homogenous tubercle size along the flank. The first example is a section of the integument from the dorsal position near

Table 1. Tubercle densities and dimensions for specific body regions. N = total number of observations, R = range of values.

Body Region	Mean Tubercle Density (#/25 cm^2)	Mean Long Axis (mm) N = 25	Mean Short Axis (mm) N = 25	Mean Long Axis Excluding Large Tubercles (mm) N = 25	Mean Short Axis Excluding Large Tubercles (mm) N = 25
mid-caudal	99	7 R = 2 - 19	6 R = 2 - 17	6 R = 2 - 10	5 R = 2 - 8
proximal caudal	87	8 R = 2 - 15	5 R = 2 - 11	7 R = 2 - 11	5 R = 2 - 7
pelvis	88	7 R = 3 - 15	5 R = 2 - 12	6 R = 3 - 9	5 R = 2 - 8
mid-torso	92	6 R = 3 - 10	5 R = 2 - 6	6 R = 3 - 10	5 R = 2 - 6
anterior torso	133	7 R = 4 - 17	6 R = 3 - 16	5 R = 4 - 7	4 R = 3 - 5
dorsal surface	27	13 R = 7 - 23	10 R = 5 - 16	------	------

the pelvic region, where tubercles have mean long and short axes of 13 and 10 millimeters, with only 27 tubercles per unit area. Thus, while tubercles along the sides of the animal appear to be generally small with minimal heterogeneity, the dorsal area appears to have been covered by tubercles approximately double the size. Secondly, there is a pattern of small polygonal tubercles which are found in several samples collected as float at the base of the outcrop. A rounded tubercle occurs within a background of these smaller forms in one of the specimens examined (figure 3B). Considering that the skeleton is positioned in outcrop with the ventral side exposed, and the presence of external molds likely representing distal rib elements directly above the skin impression surface, it is reasonable to infer that these specimens correspond to the ventral surface. Hence, tubercle size appears to generally increase from the ventral to the dorsal surface with only minimal anterior to posterior variation in the integument morphology.

The majority of skin impressions are preserved as one continuous surface at the interface of two sandstone beds, although isolated patches are also found above the skeleton. Preservation of the skin impressions occurs in both positive and negative-relief, with the latter representing the original substrate surface in which the skin impressions formed. The positive impressions are found along the sole of the overlying sandstone bed, and thus represent a cast of the negative-relief surface. The positive surface therefore closely mimics the texture of the epidermis; whereas the shape of the scales are delineated by the negative-relief impressions (figure 3C). Additionally, several specimens exhibit folded impression surfaces, which correspond to locations of the skeletal ele-

ments and ossified tendons, but there is no clear evidence to determine if they are biologic or a taphonomic consequence. On some of the impression folds, particularly those which are wrapped over bone material or are recumbent, the tubercles appear imbricated normal to the fold axis.

The skeletal remains are situated directly above the bedding plane containing the impressions. Figure 4 shows the skeletal elements identified during excavation relative to the outcrop face. The extent of preservation spans from the axial region to the mid-caudal section of the animal. Disarticulated cranial elements, such as the dentary, surangular and quadrate, occur along the bedding plane, but there is no corresponding integument preserved. Ossified tendons are located between the vertebrae and skin impressions in the caudal section.

PALEOENVIRONMENTAL CONTEXT OF SKIN IMPRESSIONS

Abundant *Teredolites* and woody debris overlic and are concentrated around the hadrosaur remains (figure 5). These borings, along with variably preserved xylic remains, provide evidence of a log-ground (Savrda, 1991) positioned directly above the hadrosaur. Borings assigned to *T. clavatus* are commonly club-shaped and appear to represent boring activities normal to the dominant wood grain direction. *Teredolites longissimus* tend to be slightly tapering cylindrical forms that occur parallel to the wood grain. In some instances, the xylic substrate in which the borings were produced is entirely absent, with the *Teredolites* preserved as internal molds of the original borehole infilled by sediment.

Figure 3. *Hadrosaur integument morphologies (BYU specimen no. 13258). A, Positive-relief skin impressions characterized by polygonal tubercles. The largest forms tend to be ovate to rounded. B, Rounded tubercle with radiating grooves occurring in a background of homogeneous smaller tubercles. C, Negative-relief skin impressions. One square on graph paper equals 1 millimeter (specimens whitened with ammonium chloride).*

The lenticular geometry and overall progradational facies succession are consistent with a meandering distributary channel. Based on the types of ichnotaxa present, it is reasonable to infer that the channel was situated in the distal portion of a coastal floodplain. *Teredolites* borings are known to be produced in logs found in modern marginal and fully marine environments (Kelly and Bromley, 1984). We envision that the channel was situated in a poorly drained coastal floodplain, considering the disposition and taphonomic variability of the woody debris (Behrensmeyer and others, 1992).

The disparity between bone size and matrix grain size precludes the possibility for bedload transport of the hadrosaur material with contemporaneous sedimentation (Fiorillo and May, 1995). Rather, we suggest that the carcass floated to its position within the channel. Physical reworking of the carcass was minimal once it came to rest on the substrate, as the majority of the skeletal remains are articulated. The substrate was most likely stabilized before the carcass was deposited, otherwise it would have been too fluid for preserving fine-scale morphologic details of the integument, such as the radial grooves on the medium and large tubercles (Anderson and Barrick, 1996).

CONCLUSIONS

The paucity of preserved dinosaur skin impressions has limited our understanding of the external appearance of these animals. Discoveries such as this one present rare opportunities to examine hadrosaurian integument at a fine scale. The Neslen hadrosaur exhibits two distinctly different impression morphologies: (1) polygonal-shaped tubercles and larger ovate to rounded forms with radiating grooves; and (2) a homogeneous pattern of small polygonal tubercles, some of which also contain isolated rounded tubercles. The former morphology occurs on one side of the tail region of the animal studied. Based on associated bone material and ossified tendons, the small tubercles likely correlate to the ventral surface. These forms may represent the distal-axial to proximal-caudal section on the ventral side, since the impressions are preserved as folded surfaces with ossified tendons, and are separate from the principal

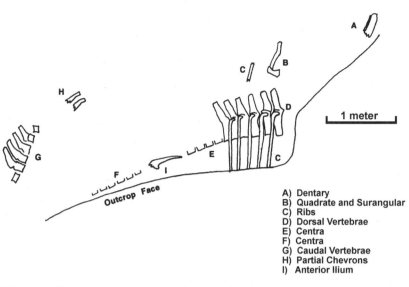

A) Dentary
B) Quadrate and Surangular
C) Ribs
D) Dorsal Vertebrae
E) Centra
F) Centra
G) Caudal Vertebrae
H) Partial Chevrons
I) Anterior Ilium

Figure 4. *Plan-view map of skeletal elements identified in outcrop.*

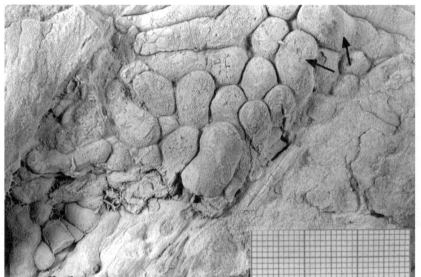

Figure 5. *Cluster of* Teredolites clavatus. *Note diagnostic club shape of the borings, as indicated by the arrows. The* Teredolites *occur in association with carbonaceous plant material directly above the hadrosaur skeleton. One square on graph paper equals 1 millimeter (specimen whitened with ammonium chloride).*

impression surface along the bedding plane.

Based on comparison with other descriptions of hadrosaur integument, the undifferentiated pattern of polygonal tubercles of relatively uniform size is similar to *Corythosaurus casuarius, Parasaurolophus walkeri, Lambeosaurus lambei and* an unnamed gryposaur (= "*Kritosaurus*" *incurvimanus*) (Lull and Wright, 1942). Additionally, the small tubercles interpreted to be from the abdominal region resemble the "ground" tubercles of "*Kritosaurus*" *incurvimanus* (Lull and Wright, 1942). As is the case for *Corythosaurus casuarius* and *Lambeosaurus lambei*, polygonal tubercles are dominant on the tail and pelvis, but these specimens lack the large ovate to circular forms. These large tubercles have been

reported from a specimen originally referred to as "*Trachodon*" *marginatus* by Lambe (1914) and later considered *nomina dubia* (Weishampel and Horner, 1990). Although osteological descriptions have not yet been completed to determine the taxonomic affinity of the Neslen hadrosaur, comparison with these earlier descriptions suggests the integument morphology most closely resembles that of the gryposaurs, which occur in Campanian strata from New Mexico to Alberta, Canada.

An analysis of lithofacies containing the hadrosaur remains suggests that burial of the carcass occurred in a meandering distributary channel situated within the distal portion of a coastal floodplain. The presence of *Teredolites* borings indicate there was some degree of marine influence in the ancient environment, which is consistent with a distributary system in close proximity to the depositional-shoreline break. The relatively low physical energy level within this setting, as is associated with modern fluvio-estuarine environments, provided a very fine-grained substrate that had a cohesive quality capable of mimicking the fine dermal features of the skin tissue. We believe that these physical characteristics were requisite to the quality of preservation. Had the substrate been coarser grained or over-saturated, the ability of the sediment to record the integument morphology would be greatly diminished. These features of the sediment, in relation to the carcass mass, are of primary importance in understanding the role of the substrate in preserving the skin impressions.

Unlike the hadrosaur specimens described by Osborn (1912) and Gilmore (1946), this example of skin impression preservation does not appear to represent complete mummification. Although patches of skin impressions are found above the skeleton, only one side of the integument is continuously preserved as impressions. Moreover, the skin impressions do not tend to drape over the skeletal remains, as would be predicted if the carcass had been subjected to considerable desiccation. Indeed, several centimeters of sediment occur between the bone and impressions, which discounts the possibility for significant subaerial desiccation prior to deposition. Moreover, complete dessication would result in greater density of the carcass due to the loss of body fluids. A mummified carcass would therefore, likely be transported as bedload. The mass of the dinosaur compared to the sediment grain size, as well as the articulated nature of skeleton, suggests that the carcass was instead transported via flotation.

The Neslen hadrosaur skin impressions truly represent an unique preservational environment that has not yet been fully investigated. However, the paleoenvironmental context in which the impressions were preserved is only one aspect of the taphonomic story; early diagenesis is another. The diagenetic effects should be examined in future studies to determine what role cementation of the substrate may have played in the fossilization process.

ACKNOWLEDGMENTS

This research was supported by the University of California Research Expeditions Program (UREP), Mesa Southwest Museum and a grant to Anderson from the Geological Society of America. We thank David B. Weishampel and David D. Gillette for reviewing an earlier version of the manuscript. We are indebted to the UREP participants who helped us with the excavation, and the Utah Army National Guard for providing helicopter transport of the specimen. Field work was made possible by the gracious support of Dorothy Droser, Vincent Droser and Dee Hall.

REFERENCES

Anderson, B. G., and Barrick, R. E., 1996, Petrographic and geochemical analysis of hadrosaur skin impressions, *in* Boaz, Debra, Dierking, Peggy, Dornan, Michael, McGeorge, Rose, and Tegowski, B. J., editors, Proceedings of the Fourth Annual Fossils of Arizona Symposium: Mesa, Mesa Southwest Museum, v. 4, p. 121-134.

Behrensmeyer, A. K., Damuth, J. D., DiMichele, W. A., Potts, Richard, Sues, H. D., and Wing, S. L., 1992, Terrestrial ecosystems through time: Chicago, University of Chicago Press, 568 p.

Brown, Barnum, 1917, A complete skeleton of the horned dinosaur *Monoclonius*, and description of a second skeleton showing skin impressions: Bulletin of the American Museum of Natural History, v. 37, p. 281-306.

Currie, P. C., Nadon, G. C., and Lockley, M. G., 1992, Dinosaur footprints with skin impressions from the Cretaceous of Alberta and Colorado: Canadian Journal of Earth Science, v. 28, p. 102-115.

Fiorillo, A. R., and May, Cathleen, 1995, Depositional environment of the first dinosaur remains from the Morrison Formation (Upper Jurassic) of Curecanti National Recreation Area (Southwest Colorado): Geological Society of America Abstracts with Programs, v. 27, no. 4, p. 11.

Fouch, T. D., Lawton, T. F., Nichols, D. J., Cashion, W. B., and Cobban, W. A., 1983, Patterns and timing of synorogenic sedimentation in Upper Cretaceous rocks of central and northeast Utah, *in* Reynolds, M. W., and Dolly, E. D., editors, Mesozoic paleogeography of the west-central United States, Rocky Mountain Paleogeography Symposium 2: Rocky Mountain Section of Economic Paleontologists and Mineralogists, p. 305-336.

Gilmore, C. W., 1946, Notes on some recently mounted reptile fossil skeletons in the United States National Museum: Proceedings of the U. S. National Museum, v. 96, p. 195-203.

Hintze, L. F., 1988, Geologic history of Utah: Brigham Young University Geology Studies, Special Publication 7, 202 p.

Horner, J. R., 1984, A "segmented" epidermal tail frill in a species of hadrosaurian dinosaur: Journal of Paleontology, v. 58, p. 270-271.

Kelly, S. R. A., and Bromley, R. G., 1984, Ichnological nomenclature of clavate borings: Palaeontology, v. 27, p. 793-807.

Lambe, L. M., 1914, On the fore-limb of a carnivorous dinosaur from the Belly River Formation of Alberta, and a new genus of Ceratopsia from the same horizon, with remarks on the integument of some Cretaceous herbivorous dinosaurs: Ottawa Naturalist, v. 27, no. 10, p. 129-135.

Lull, R. S., and Wright, N. E., 1942, Hadrosaurian dinosaurs of North America: Geological Society of America Special Paper 40, 242 p., 31 plates.

Martill, D. M., 1991, Organically preserved dinosaur skin: taphonomic and biological implications: Modern Geology, v. 16, p. 61-68.

Osborn, J. F., 1912, Integument of the iguanodont dinosaur *Trachodon*: American Museum of Natural History Memoir, New Series, v. 1, p. 33-54.

Parks, W. A., 1920, The osteology of the trachodont dinosaur *Kritosaurus incurvimanus*: University of Toronto, Studies in Geology no. 11, 74 p.

Pitman, J. K., Franczyk, K. J., and Anders, D. E., 1987, Marine and nonmarine gas-bearing rocks in Upper Cretaceous Blackhawk and Neslen Formations, eastern Uinta Basin-- sedimentology, diagenesis and source rock potential: American Association of Petroleum Geologists Bulletin, v. 71, p. 76-94.

Savrda, C. E., 1991, *Teredolites*, wood substrates, and sea-level dynamics: Geology, v. 19, p. 905-908.

Sternberg, C. M., 1925, Integument of *Chasmosaurus belli*: Canadian Field-Naturalist, v. 39, p. 108-110.

Van Wagoner, J. C., Mitchum, R. M., Campion, K. M., Rahmanian, V. D., 1990, Siliciclastic sequence stratigraphy in well logs, cores and outcrops: American Association of Petroleum Geologists, Methods in Exploration Series Number 7, 55 p.

Weishampel, D. B., and Horner, J. R., 1990, Hadrosauridae, *in* Weishampel, D. B., Dodson, Peter, and Osmolska, Halszka, editors, The Dinosauria: Berkeley, University of California Press, p. 534-561.

Williams, G. D., and Stelck, C. R., 1975, Speculations on the Cretaceous paleogeography of North America, *in* Caldwell, W. G. E., editor, The Cretaceous System in the Western Interior of North America: Geological Association of Canada, Special Paper 13, p. 1-20.

Willis, G. C., 1986, Geology, depositional environment, and coal resources of the Sego Canyon 7.5-Minute Quadrangle, near Green River, east central Utah: Brigham Young University Geology Studies, v. 33, p. 175-208.

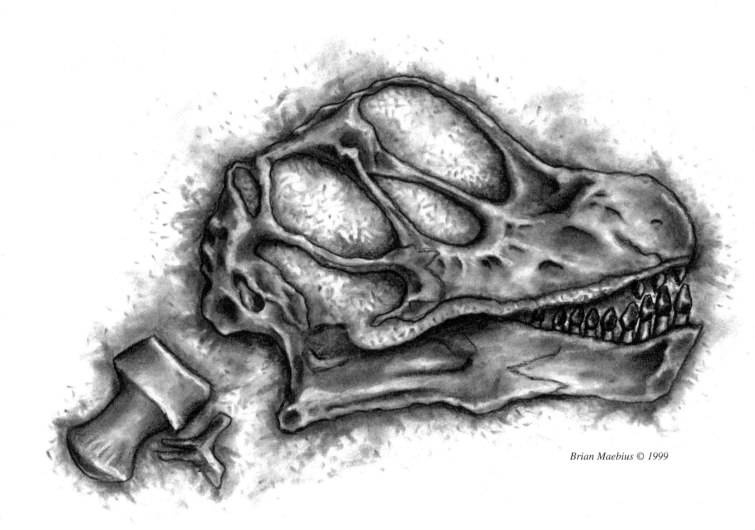

Brian Maebius © 1999

Camarasaurus

POLYGLYPHANODONTINAE (SQUAMATA:TEIIDAE) FROM THE MEDIAL AND LATE CRETACEOUS: NEW TAXA FROM UTAH, U.S.A. AND BAJA CALIFORNIA DEL NORTE, MEXICO

Randall L. Nydam
Oklahoma Museum of Natural History and Department of Zoology,
University of Oklahoma, Norman, Oklahoma 73019
rlnydam@ou.edu (e-mail)

ABSTRACT

Isolated lizard teeth from the upper Albian part of the Cedar Mountain Formation and the Turonian part of the Straight Cliffs Formation, both in Utah, and from the upper Campanian "El Gallo Formation" in Baja California del Norte closely resemble described teeth of the North American Maastrichtian polyglyphanodontines *Polyglyphanodon* (1 species) and *Paraglyphanodon* (2 species), but differ from the Asian genera (Santonian-Campanian; Mongolia) in being transversely oriented and medially expanded. Apart from these generalized similarities, the new teeth are distinctive from the three described North American taxa. A new genus and a new species are named for the teeth from Utah and a second species of *Polyglyphanodon* is erected for the teeth from Baja California del Norte. The new fossils extend the record of the Polyglyphanodontinae back to the medial Cretaceous and indicate that the unusual tooth morphology found in *Polyglyphanodon* and *Paraglyphanodon*: (1) was not derived from Late Cretaceous Mongolian polyglyphanodontines, (2) is much more archaic than previously believed, and (3) represents a stable pattern that underwent little apparent change during the mid- and Late Cretaceous. The extended record of North American polyglyphanodontine lizards with this characteristic tooth morphology and the temporally limited record of Asian polyglyphanodontines with vastly different tooth morphologies, indicates that the North American and Asian Polyglyphanodontinae diverged early in their history, perhaps as a result of an Early Cretaceous faunal exchange between the continents, and existed as separately evolving groups during the latter half of the Cretaceous. Although there is no direct evidence as to what the diet of these lizards may have been, the stable tooth morphology of the North American polyglyphanodontines was possibly associated with omnivory and/or herbivory.

INTRODUCTION

Introductory Remarks

The Cretaceous Period is an important time in the evolution of lizards, as indicated by, but not restricted to, the fossil record of North American and Asian lizards. It is during this period that many of the modern lizard families first appear in the fossil record. These geologically oldest occurrences include the Anguidae (Gilmore, 1928), Cordylidae, (Gao, 1994), Gekkonidae (Alifanov, 1992), Helodermatidae (Estes, 1964), Iguanidae (Gao and Fox, 1996), Scincidae (Estes, 1964), Teiidae (Marsh, 1892; Gilmore, 1940), Xantusiidae (Miller, 1997), and Varanidae (Gilmore, 1928). Many Cretaceous lizard taxa are represented by isolated jaws and vertebrae, which complicates their taxonomic identification. On rare occasions, more nearly complete material, even complete skeletons, have been recovered. Such is the case for most of the taxa referred to the Polyglyphanodontinae.

The Polyglyphanodontinae is a primitive group of teiids (Estes, 1983) which includes taxa from the Late Cretaceous (figure 1) of North America (Gilmore,1940, 1942, 1943a) and Mongolia (Gilmore, 1943a; Sulimski, 1972, 1975, 1978). The group is diagnosed by a variety of characteristics associated with the skull: fusion of the supratemporal and squamosal, contact of vomers and pterygoids, and a large and extensive postorbital (Estes, 1983). Most taxa in this group are large lizards with massive skulls, which may account for the unusually good fossil record of the group. One of the unique features of the Polyglyphanodontinae is the diverse array of tooth patterns exhibited in the different taxa (see Estes, 1983 for a review and figures of the known tooth types). Tooth morphologies found in the Mongolian taxa include the following: leaf-shaped, polycuspate teeth (for example, *Darchansaurus*, *Erdenetesaurus*, and *Macrocephalosaurus*); large, bulbous, durophagous-type teeth (for

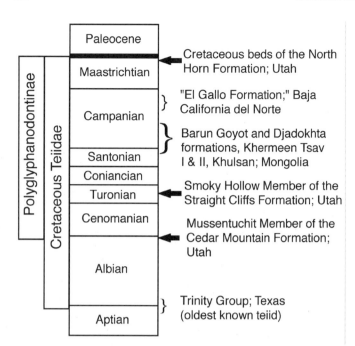

Figure 1. *Geologic time scale showing the relative ages of the rock units which are known to produce polyglyphanodontine material as well as the oldest record of a teiid. The left side of the time scale shows the known ranges for the Teiidae and the teiid subfamily, Polyglyphanodontinae during the Cretaceous. All teiids went extinct in Asia and North America at the K/T boundary (Estes, 1983).*

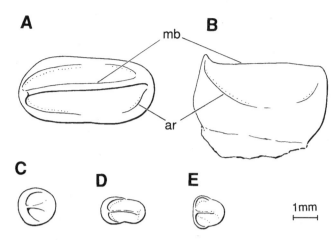

Figure 2. *Teeth of polyglyphanodontines from the North Horn Formation. A-C based on OMNH 33460. A and B, posterior tooth of* Polyglyphanodon sternbergi, *occlusal and anterior views, respectively. C, occlusal view of anterior tooth of* P. sternbergi. *D, occlusal view of right dentary tooth of* Paraglyphanodon gazini, *redrawn from Gilmore (1943a). E, occlusal view of right dentary tooth of* P. utahensis, *redrawn from Gilmore (1940). All occlusal views are oriented with anterior toward bottom of the page and in all figures medial is toward right side of the page. Abbreviations: ar-accessory ridge, mb-main blade.*

example, *Adamisaurus*); and slightly rotated (=obliquely oriented), chisel-like, teeth with polycuspate crowns (for example, *Cherminsaurus*). By contrast, teeth in the North American taxa *Polyglyphanodon* and *Paraglyphanodon* (figure 2) are transversely oriented and medially expanded with chisel-like crowns. In addition to medial expansion, the teeth of *P. utahensis* are also anteroposteriorly expanded on the lateral side.

Work by crews of the Oklahoma Museum of Natural History and the Museum of Northern Arizona in rocks of the medial and Upper Cretaceous of Utah has resulted in the recovery of fossils of numerous vertebrate taxa (Cifelli, 1990a-d, 1993; Cifelli and Eaton, 1987; Cifelli and Johanson, 1994; Cifelli and Nydam, 1995; Cifelli and Madsen, 1998; Cifelli and Muizon, 1998; Cifelli and others, 1997; Cifelli and others, 1998a; Eaton and Cifelli, 1988; Gardner, 1994, 1995; Gardner and Cifelli, 1999; Kirkland and Parrish, 1995; Nydam, 1995, 1997). Among the polyglyphanodontine specimens collected was an incomplete topotypic skeleton of *Polyglyphanodon sternbergi* from the North Horn Formation (Maastrichtian). Also collected were geologically older, isolated teeth of a new genus from the upper Albian part of the Cedar Mountain Formation and the Turonian part of the Straight Cliffs Formation. In addition, a fossil jaw fragment and isolated teeth collected by crews of the Los Angeles County Museum from the "El Gallo Formation" in Baja California del Norte resemble those of *Poly-*

glyphanodon sternbergi, but are referable to a new species in the genus.

Most Cretaceous lizards, especially those from North America, are diagnosed primarily on the basis of jaw and dental characteristics, largely because these are typically the only elements recovered. Teeth alone are rarely used to diagnose higher taxonomic groups of lizards, which is understandable because in many lizard groups teeth can be similar and, when isolated, difficult to distinguish without clarification from associated skeletal material. However, transversely oriented teeth, like those reported herein, are rare in lizards and all occurrences are restricted to the Teiidae. The only other taxa besides *Polyglyphanodon* and *Paraglyphanodon* described as having a transverse tooth orientation are *Peneteius* from the Maastrichtian of Montana (Estes, 1969) and the extant South American teiids *Teius* and *Dicrodon* (Presch, 1974). Transversely oriented teeth that are also medially expanded are only known to occur in *Polyglyphanodon* and *Paraglyphanodon*. Although modified differently in specimens from each horizon, the new taxa described herein share this transversely oriented, medially expanded tooth pattern, indicating that they belong to the Polyglyphanodontinae, extending the North American record of this group over 30 million years back to the medial Cretaceous. The new material presented here also indicates that during this 30+ million year record the tooth morphology in North American polyglyphanodontines remained relatively stable. I believe taxonomic assignment for the taxa described herein is justified because formally naming these new lizards appropriately reflects the diversity in the fossil record.

The goals of this paper are: (1) to describe the new taxa from the Cedar Mountain, Straight Cliffs, and "El Gallo" formations; (2) to discuss the evolutionary history of dental morphology in the Polyglyphanodontinae; and (3) to examine aspects of polyglyphanodontine biogeography and biology in light of the new fossils.

Previous Work

Polyglyphanodontine lizards were first described by Gilmore (1940, 1942, 1943a) from the Upper Cretaceous North Horn Formation, Emery County, Utah. These taxa include: *Polyglyphanodon sternbergi*, a species of large lizard known from nearly 50 topotypic skeletons, some nearly complete (Gilmore, 1940, 1942); and *Paraglyphanodon utahensis* and *P. gazini*, two species of smaller lizards each known from fragmentary cranial material (Gilmore, 1940, 1943a). Based on these two genera, Gilmore (1942) erected the family Polyglyphanodontidae which he allied with the Iguanidae. Hoffstetter (1955) and Estes (1964, 1969) subsequently argued that *Polyglyphanodon* and *Paraglyphanodon* are more closely allied with the Teiidae.

Asian polyglyphanodontines are only known from the upper Cretaceous of Mongolia (Gilmore, 1943b; Sulimski, 1972, 1975). As with their North American counterparts, the Asian taxa were originally referred to various families. *Macrocephalosaurus ferrugenous* (Gilmore, 1943b) was placed in the Agamidae as was *Adamisaurus magnidentatus* (Sulimski, 1972). Later, Sulimski (1978) erected *Adamisaurus* as the type genus of the monotypic scincomorph family Adamisauridae. Sulimski (1975) then referred *M. ferrugenous* and the newly discovered taxa *M. chulsanensis*, *M. gilmorei*, and *Darchansaurus estesi* to his newly erected Macrocephalosauridae. In addition, Sulimski (1975), following the example of Hoffstetter (1955) and Estes, (1964, 1969), transferred the Polyglyphanodontidae (sensu Gilmore, 1942) to the Scincomorpha and assigned the Mongolian taxa *Cherminsaurus kozlowskii* and *Erdenetesaurus robinsonae* to the family.

In his comprehensive review of fossil lizards, Estes (1983) re-evaluated the relationships of all of the taxa listed above. He considered *Adamisaurus, Cherminsaurus, Darchansaurus, Erdenetesaurus, Macrocephalosaurus, Paraglyphanodon, Polyglyphanodon*, and the aberrant taxon *Haptosphenus placodon* to all be closely related and included these genera within a new teiid subfamily, the Polyglyphanodontinae. The Polyglyphanodontinae has remained relatively unchanged since its establishment; however, two recent studies deserve comment.

In examining the phylogenetic position of the Upper Cretaceous teiid *Prototeius*, from the Marshalltown Formation in New Jersey, Denton and O'Neil (1995) concluded that the Polyglyphanodontinae is paraphyletic. However, their results are difficult to evaluate since their phylogenetic analysis included only three of the eight known polyglyphanodontine genera. More recently, Gao and Fox (1996) questioned the placement of *Haptosphenus* in the Polyglyphanodontinae and suggested that it may be more closely allied with the teiid subfamily Tupinambinae (sensu Estes and others, 1988; and Sullivan and Estes, 1997) based on similarities with the modern South American tupinambinine *Dracaena*.

Abbreviations and Conventions

Abbreviations for institutions cited in the text: IGM, Instituto de Geología de la Universidad Nacional Autonoma de Mexico, Mexico City; LACM, Los Angeles County Museum, Los Angeles; LAV, vertebrate paleontology locality, Los Angeles County Museum, Los Angeles; MNA, Museum of Northern Arizona, Flagstaff; MVZ, Museum of Vertebrate Zoology, University of California, Berkeley; OMNH, Oklahoma Museum of Natural History, University of Oklahoma, Norman; USNM, Museum of Natural History, Smithsonian Institution, Washington. Other conventions: Gr., Greek; Ma, millions of years before present; SEM, scanning electron microscopy; SVL, snout-vent-length; W/L, ratio of mediolateral width to anteroposterior length.

MATERIALS AND METHODS

Fossils from the Cedar Mountain and Straight Cliffs Formations were collected by quarrying and underwater screenwashing following the methods described by Cifelli and others (1996a). The classification used in this report follows that of Estes (1983). Comparative material used in this study includes *Dicrodon guttalatum* (MVZ 85401) and *Teius teyou* (MVZ 92989). Measurements of the greatest mediolateral width and anteroposterior length, as well as the ratio of the two measures (for example, W/L values), are used to demonstrate the size and relative shapes of the teeth reported herein.

For SEM figures specimens were secured to aluminum mounts and sputter coated with gold paladium in an Hummer VI Sputtering System (Anatech, Ltd.) at 10 mA for 90 seconds under a vacuum of approximately 57 mtorr. Micrographs were taken with an ETEC Autoscan scanning electron microscope at 20 kV, 15 mm working distance, using a 100 μm final aperture. Images were recorded on Polaroid 660 positive/negative film.

GEOLOGICAL SETTING

The isolated polyglyphanodontine teeth (OMNH 29771 and 32629) from the Cedar Mountain Formation were recovered from OMNH locality V239, 7 kilometers east of Moore, Emery County, Utah (figure 3) during the 1992 field season. Locality V239 is in the Mussentuchit Member (sensu Kirkland and others, 1997), or uppermost beds, of the Cedar Mountain Formation. This part of the formation is a variegated, terrestrial deposit composed primarily of bentonitic mudstones with interbedded channel sands, caliche, and cherts (Stokes, 1944; Tschudy and others, 1984). The Mussentuchit Member lies unconformably above the caliche-covered slopes of the Ruby Ranch Member (Kirkland and others, 1997) of the Cedar Mountain Formation and unconformably below the Dakota Sandstone. Tschudy and others (1984, p. 10-11) stated that palynomorphs from the Cedar Mountain Formation "eliminates the possibility of Cenomanian age" and shows the age to be "clearly of late or latest Albian." More recent work by Molenaar and Cobban (1991) on regional Cretaceous deposits in Utah indicates the age of

the uppermost part of the Cedar Mountain Formation, in the Uinta Basin (northeast of the localities reported here) to be Cenomanian. However, they also report that in the region of the OMNH localities the Cenomanian part of the Cedar Mountain Formation has been removed by truncation by the Dakota Sandstone. The best constrained date for the upper mudstones of the Cedar Mountain Formation is a recently reported $^{40}Ar/^{39}Ar$ age estimate of about 98.4 million yr B.P. (latest Albian) of a volcanic ash from a fossil-bearing locality that is laterally equivalent and geographically close to V239 (Cifelli and others, 1997). For a review of the paleontology of the Cedar Mountain Formation see Cifelli and others (1998a).

The polyglyphanodontine tooth (OMNH 25386) from the Straight Cliffs Formation was recovered in 1990 from OMNH locality V4 (=MNA locality 1003-1), Garfield County, Utah (figure 3). The Straight Cliffs Formation lies between the underlying Tropic Shale and the overlying Wahweap Formation in the Kaiparowits Plateau region of southern Utah. Peterson (1969) divided the Straight Cliffs Formation into four members; in ascending stratigraphic order these are the Tibbett Canyon, Smoky Hollow, John Henry, and Drip Tank Members. These members were deposited in marine and terrestrial environments from the Turonian through Campanian. Locality V4 is in the Smoky Hollow Member, which consists primarily of terrigenous rocks interpreted to be Turonian in age based on laterally equivalent invertebrate horizons (Peterson, 1969) and palynological evidence (Orlansky, 1971). At the level of locality OMNH V4, the depositional environment of the Smoky Hollow Member is interpreted as primarily fluvial/floodplain (Peterson, 1969). For a complete review of the Straight Cliffs Formation see Eaton (1991).

Based on the taxonomic diversity and number of vertebrate fossils recovered from both the Cedar Mountain and Straight Cliffs Formations, the rarity of fossils of the polyglyphanodontine taxa described below likely reflects the scarcity of these lizards in their respective paleoenvironments.

The partial skeleton of *Polyglyphanodon sternbergi* was collected in 1994 from the type locality (=OMNH V811; figure 3) in the Late Cretaceous (Maastrictian) part of the North Horn Formation (Gilmore, 1946) which has yielded nearly 50 topotypic skeletons of this taxon (Estes, 1983). The North Horn Formation consists of predominantly terrigenous deposits which span the K/T boundary in the Wasatch Plateau (Spieker, 1960). For a review of the paleontology of the North Horn Formation see Cifelli and others (1998b).

Jaw fragments and broken limb elements of a polyg-

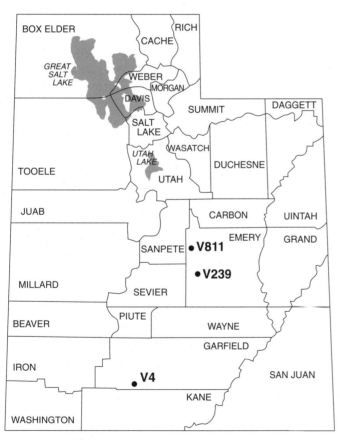

Figure 3. *OMNH localities in Utah from which fossils of polyglyphanodontine lizards have been recovered. V4, Smoky Hollow Member of the Straight Cliffs Formation, Garfield County; V239, Mussentuchit Member of the Cedar Mountain Formation, Emery County; V811 (=type locality for* Polyglyphanodon sternbergi, Paraglyphanodon gazini, *and* P. utahaensis), *North Horn Formation, Emery County.*

lyphanodontine from Baja California del Norte were collected by crews from the LACM working in the "El Gallo Formation" in 1970 and 1973. This unit has not yet been formally described and can only be referred to informally. The "El Gallo Formation" is believed to represent an upper Cretaceous (late Campanian) terrestrial deposit (see Lillegraven, 1972). Other vertebrates associated with the polyglyphanodontine material include a small diversity of mammals, amphibians, and fish (Lillegraven, 1972, 1976; Clemens and others, 1979) as well as dinosaurs and turtles (S. A. McLeod, personal communication). All of the fossils collected in the "El Gallo Formation" were originally curated into the collections at the LACM, but are now housed in the collections at the IGM.

SYSTEMATIC PALEONTOLOGY
Order Squamata Oppel 1811
Family Teiidae Gray 1827
Subfamily Polyglyphanodontinae Estes 1983
Genus *Polyglyphanodon* Gilmore 1940

Prior to this paper, *Polyglyphanodon* was known only by the type species, *P. sternbergi*. *Polyglyphanodon* is diagnosed by numerous cranial characters (Estes, 1983), the most distinguishing of which is the transversely widened, anteroposteriorly compressed (=high W/L value) teeth of the posterior part of the tooth row (Gilmore, 1942, Estes, 1983; my figures 5E,F and 6A,B herein).

Polyglyphanodon bajaensis new species, figure 4

Holotype

IGM 6965 (=LACM 58008; figure 4C), posterior tooth.

Hypodigm

IGM 6965 (holotype), posterior tooth; IGM 6963 (=LACM 57869; figure 4A), anterior right dentary fragment with two teeth and a broken base of a third tooth; IGM 6964 (=LACM 57877; figure 4B), posterior tooth; IGM 6966 (=LACM 58011; figure 4D), posteriormost tooth.

Horizon and Locality

Middle one-third of the upper Campanian "El Gallo Formation," Baja California del Norte, Mexico. LACM localities LAV-7170 (IGM 6963, 6965, 6966) and LAV-7172 (IGM 6964). Both localities are near the village of El Rosario (see Lillegraven, 1972, figure 1).

Diagnosis

Differs from *Polyglyphanodon sternbergi* in having posterior teeth that are bicuspid with a cusp on the medial side of the tooth as well as on the on the lateral side, lateral and medial cusps connected by a central U-shaped main blade, and well-defined anterior and posterior accessory blades. The main and accessory blades border shallow basins on the anterior and posterior sides of the tooth crown. The anterior teeth differ from *P. sternbergi* in that they are oval in occlusal view and weakly expanded medially.

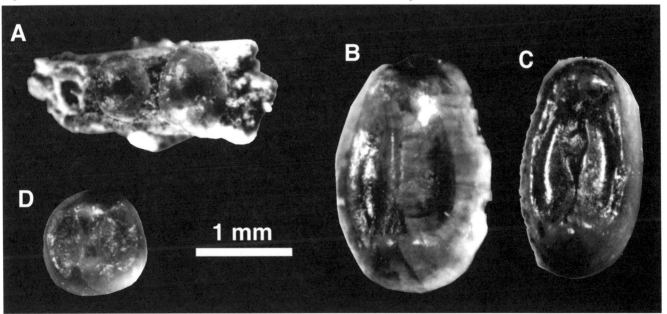

Figure 4. *Occlusal views of teeth of* Polyglyphanodon bajaensis *new species, from the "El Gallo Formation," Baja California del Norte, Mexico.* A, IGM 6963, anterior dentary fragment; B, IGM 6964, posterior tooth; C, IGM 6965, transverse tooth, holotype; D, IGM 6966, posteriormost tooth. Scale bar =1 mm.

Description

Positions for each tooth in *Polyglyphanodon bajaensis* can be inferred by comparison to teeth preserved in jaws of *P. sternbergi*, *Paraglyphanodon gazini*, and the extant teiids *Teius teyou* and *Dicrodon guttalatum*. The two teeth on IGM 6963 are identified as anterior teeth with the broken base in the anteriormost position. In occlusal view these teeth are ovoid with the medial side wider than the lateral. These teeth are also small (tooth next to broken base: 0.83 mm wide, 0.71 mm long, W/L 1.17; more posterior tooth: 0.98 mm wide, 1.19 mm long, W/L 1.21). Both lack the bi-concave medial surface seen in the anterior teeth of *P. sternbergi*. IGM 6964 and IGM 6965, identified as teeth from the posterior part of the tooth row, resemble posterior teeth of *P. sternbergi* in being medially expanded and anteroposteriorly compressed. These teeth differ, however, from posterior teeth of *P. sternbergi* in being bicuspid and possessing well-defined accessory blades, anterior and posterior basins, and a wide, shallow U-shaped main blade which is predominantly horizontal, but turns towards the apices on medial and lateral sides of the teeth. The main blade on IGM 6965 is unusual in that it bifurcates in the center of the tooth, forming a small, oval basin in the middle of the blade. I cannot determine whether this is a diagnostic or pathologic condition. IGM 6964 is the only specimen from locality LAV 7172 and is the largest (2.62 mm wide, 1.86 mm long, W/L 1.41) of the four teeth from Baja California del Norte. This tooth differs from IGM 6965 (2.50 mm wide, 1.43 mm long, W/L 1.75) in having a smaller W/L value and one side (medial?) of the tooth more anteroposteriorly expanded than the other. A small bicuspid tooth, IGM 6966, is symmetrical rather than medialy expanded (1.07 mm wide, 1.07 mm long, W/L 1.0). This tooth also has well-defined lateral and medial cusps, anterior and posterior accessory blades, and a narrow, U-shaped, main blade. Based on comparison with the teeth of *P. sternbergi* (Gilmore, 1940: figure 19) I tentatively assign this tooth a posteriormost position in the tooth row.

Remarks

The *Polyglyphanodon bajaensis* material was originally referred to *Polyglyphanodon sternbergi* as unnumbered and undescribed IGM specimens by Estes (1983). The similarities in tooth morphology between *Polyglyphanodon bajaensis* and the teeth of *P. sternbergi* support, in part, Estes's (1983) placement of this taxon in the genus *Polyglyphanodon*, but not his assignment to *P. sternbergi*. The specimens are referred to *Polyglyphanodon* based on dental characteristics shared with *P. sternbergi*: conical anterior teeth, posterior teeth great-

ly anteroposteriorly compressed (resulting in a high W/L value), a predominantly horizontal main blade on posterior teeth, and posteriormost tooth bicuspid though not transversely expanded (variable in *P. sternbergi*, see below).

Dicothodon new genus

Type Species

Dicothodon moorensis new species.

Etymology

Di, Gr., two; *kothos*, Gr., cup; *odous*, Gr., tooth; in reference to the basins on either side of the V-shaped blade on the occlusal surface of the tooth.

Diagnosis

Teeth differ from *Polyglyphanodon* and *Paraglyphanodon* in having the medial and lateral cusps connected by a V-shaped main blade rather than a U-shaped main blade (for example, *Polyglyphanodon bajaensis*) or horizontal ridge (for example, *P. sternbergi*, *Paraglyphanodon*), and medial part of crown expanded anteroposteriorly in relation to the lateral part giving the tooth an egg-like oval shape in occlusal view.

Remarks

The material described below is too limited to permit a phylogenetic analysis and it is, therefore, impossible to eliminate the possibility that the new teeth represent a convergent evolution of this unusual tooth pattern. This interpretation could be supported by the same morphological evidence used to place the Utah taxa in a new genus (the V-shaped main blade as well as the strongly developed accessory blades). However, it is less parsimonious that such striking similarities in such an unusual and rare tooth morphology among these taxa could be other than by phylogenetic relatedness.

Dicothodon moorensis new species, figures 5A, B; 6A, B, C

Etymology

Named for the town of Moore, Utah, which is close to the holotype locality.

Holotype

OMNH 29771, dentary fragment with one complete tooth and the broken base of another tooth.

Hypodigm

OMNH 29771 (holotype; figures 5A, B; 6A, B) and OMNH 32629, isolated tooth (figure 6C).

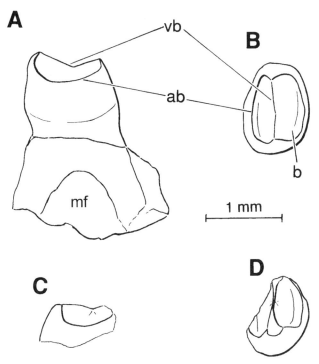

Figure 5. Dicothodon *new genus from the Cretaceous of Utah. A and B, OMNH 29771, holotype of* Dicothodon moorensis *new species, from the Cedar Mountain Formation, Emery County, mesiodistal and occlusal views, respectively. C and D, OMNH 25386,* Dicothodon *sp. from the Straight Cliffs Formation, Garfield County, mesiodistal and occlusal views, respectively. Abbreviations: ab-accessory blade, mf-Meckelian fossa, vb-V-shaped main blade.*

Horizon and Locality

Upper Albian Mussentuchit Member, Cedar Mountain Formation, OMNH locality V239.

Diagnosis

Same as for the genus.

Description

Of the two teeth recovered, only OMNH 29771 is complete and is still attached to a fragment of the dentary. The tooth is medially expanded, anteroposteriorly compressed, and moderate in size (1.65 mm wide and 1.25 mm long, W/L 1.32). The tooth-jaw contact in OMNH 29771 is similar to that seen in *Polyglyphanodon sternbergi* in superficially appearing to be acrodont. However, broken surfaces on the anterior and posterior sides of the jaw fragment show that the implantation was subpleurodont (sensu Gao and Fox, 1996). Below the crown, the tooth is obscured by heavy deposits of cementum, which also appears to fill the sulcus dentalis and the space between the teeth. The body of the tooth is bulbous, widens medially, and is constricted below the crown. There are two cusps on the tooth, one labial and one lingual. The labial cusp is taller and narrower than the lingual cusp, and bears two weak sulci on its lateral surface. These sulci run vertically down either side of

the cusp and terminate above the base. A main, V-shaped blade runs between the two cusps. The medial arm of the blade is short and set at about a 20° angle between the lingual cusp and the base of the "V." The lateral arm of the blade is longer and set at about a 45° angle between the labial cusp and the base of the "V." The anterior and posterior sides of the crown have well-defined ridges, which will henceforth be referred to as accessory blades. These accessory blades originate at the apices of the cusps, are lunate (semicircular) in mesiodistal view and run around the crown below the level of the V-shaped blade, defining the outer borders of the occlusal surface of the tooth. The accessory blades and the V-shaped blade border small, lunate basins on anterior and posterior sides of the tooth. One of these basins is smaller than the other and may represent the posterior side of the tooth, assuming that this taxon follows the same pattern as seen in *Polyglyphanodon sternbergi* (see below).

The second tooth, OMNH 32629, differs slightly from OMNH 29771. These differences include a reduced degree of widening of the medial part of the tooth crown, a more acute angle in the V-shaped blade, the lateral and medial arms of the V-shaped blade equal in length, cusps equal in height, and the basins on either side of the V-shaped blade lower down on the crown and with steeper sides (the basins do not appear to be deeper than those on OMNH 29771). The accessory blades in OMNH 32629 are eroded, but it is evident that they were not as tall those on OMNH 29771. Lastly, OMNH 32629 (1.77 mm wide, 1.24 mm length, L/W 1.43) either came from a slightly larger individual than OMNH 29771 or represents a different position in the tooth row of a similar sized animal. Most of the differences between the two specimens are minor and, when compared to tooth sets of *Polyglyphanodon sternbergi* and the extant teiids, *Dicrodon* and *Teius*, appear to be related to either positional differences along the jaw or ontogenetic variation.

Dicothodon sp., figures 5C,D; 6D

Referred Specimen

OMNH 25386, isolated tooth.

Horizon and Locality

Smoky Hollow Member of the Straight Cliffs Formation, Garfield County, Utah; late Turonian. OMNH locality V4.

Description

OMNH 25386 is an isolated tooth which is broken such that most of one cusp and about half of one of the basins is missing. This tooth resembles the teeth described above for *Dicothodon moorensis* as follows: the tooth is transversely oriented, medially expanded, and anteroposteriorly compressed; there is a lateral and medial cusp connected by a main V-shaped blade; and there are anterior and posterior accessory blades that border lunate basins. Aside from these similarities in general morphology, OMNH 25386 shows features that may distinguish it from *D. moorensis*: a more symmetrical shape in occlusal and a smaller size (width 1.43 mm vs. 1.65 mm; length 1.03 mm vs. 1.25 mm) than both OMNH 29771 and OMNH 32629. Also, the more complete of the accessory blades on OMNH 25386 differs from those of *D. moorensis* in having a nearly horizontal central portion that abruptly becomes vertically directed on the medial and lateral ends, resulting in a more rectangular (as opposed to lunate) shaped blade and a basin that is more constrained to the center of the tooth. Lastly, the better preserved cusp on OMNH 25386 has a prominent, apical wear facet. The pattern of tooth attachment and amount of cementum cannot be determined in OMNH 25386 as no jaw material is known.

Remarks

The V-shaped and accessory blades as well as the associated basins clearly show that OMNH 25386 belongs in the new genus *Dicothodon*. However, differences in size, age, and accessory blade structure may indicate the specimen from the Straight Cliffs Formation is a new taxon. However, I have refrained from designating a new species because better material is needed to eliminate the possibility of these differences being due to ontogeny or positional differences in the tooth row.

Comparisons

OMNH 33460 is an incomplete topotypic skeleton of *Polyglyphanodon sternbergi* consisting of associated cranial (braincase, quadrate, mandible) and post-cranial (broken humerus, ulna, broken radius, broken femur, assorted phalanges, and an articulated series of four distal caudal vertebrae) material. The osteology of *Polyglyphanodon sternbergi* is well documented from the numerous skeletons previously collected and now housed at the USNM (Gilmore, 1942; Estes, 1983). Although previously described by Gilmore (1942), I will briefly discuss the morphology of the teeth (figures 2A, B, C, and 6E, F) of

P. sternbergi because the new taxa are based on comparative differences with these elements. Also, additional features of the teeth of *P. sternbergi*, based on examination of teeth on OMNH 33460, are discussed below.

Anterior teeth (figure 2C) in the maxilla and dentary of *Polyglyphanodon sternbergi* differ from those of most teiids (for example, *Tupinambis*, Rieppel, 1980; figure 7A) in not being recurved. Instead, the anterior teeth in *P. sternbergi* are blocky, unrecurved, and have a conical outline in lateral view. The lateral surface of these teeth is strongly convex and the medial surface is weakly concave with a low vertical ridge that extends about half way down the crown from the apex. This vertical ridge separates the medial surface of the anterior teeth into two concave lingual surfaces in much the same way the main blade on the teeth of the posterior tooth row separates two semicircular surfaces.

The posterior part of the maxillary and dentary tooth rows in *P. sternbergi* consists of a series of transversely oriented, parallel, chisel-like teeth (Gilmore, 1942; figure 2A, B herein). These teeth are larger (3.75 mm wide, 1.62 mm long; topotypic tooth from OMNH 33460; figures 6E, F) and show more extreme medial expansion and anteroposterior compression (W/L 2.31, same tooth) than those described above for the new taxa. The posterior teeth have a small lateral cusp, but no medial cusp. The horizontal main blade between the medial and lateral sides of the tooth traces a weak, sigmoidal curve in

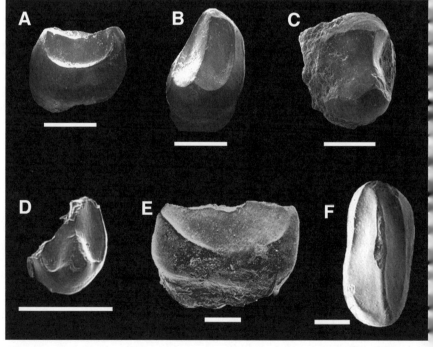

Figure 6. *Polyglyphanodontine teeth from Utah. A-B, OMNH 29771,* Dicothodon moorensis, *mesiodistal and oblique lingual views, respectively; C, OMNH 32629,* D. moorensis, *occlusal view; D, OMNH 25386* Dicothodon sp., *occlusal view; E and F, OMNH 33460* Polyglyphanodon sternbergi Gilmore 1940, *North Horn Formation, Emery County, Utah, 2nd to last left dentary tooth from topotypic skeleton (lateral cusp broken off), anterior and occlusal views, respectively. All scale bars =1 mm.*

occlusal view (contra Gilmore, 1942). To either side (anterior and posterior) of the main blade are low, semi-circular, accessory ridges that define the periphery of the occlusal surface. There are no basins between the main blade and accessory ridges in most of the teeth of the posterior tooth row (the anterior and posterior faces of the crown are steep, lunate-shaped surfaces), however, the second to last tooth in the right mandible of OMNH 33460 (figure 5E, F) has incipient basins medially and laterally not evident in the other teeth of the same jaw. The posterior surface on the chisel-like teeth are smaller than the anterior one. The last tooth in the maxilla and dentary of *P. sternbergi* was described by Gilmore (1942) as conical (that is, not expanded transversely) with a small vertical ridge on the center of the medial surface. However, in his figures (Gilmore, 1942: figures 19 and 21) only the last maxillary tooth has this morphology. The last dentary tooth remains slightly expanded transversely, and thus resembles the anteriormost chisel-like tooth in the tooth row. Likewise, the last dentary tooth in OMNH 33460 is nearly identical to the five anterior teeth in being conical and having a weakly concave medial surface. Apparently the morphology of the last tooth in the tooth row of *P. sternbergi* varies between being unicuspid to transversely expanded and chisel-like.

Dicothodon moorensis, Dicothodon sp., *Polyglyphanodon bajaensis*, and *P. sternbergi* all posses teeth that are transversely oriented, medially expanded, and bear a main, central ridge or blade and semicircular accessory structures (blades or low ridges) that define the perimeter of the occlusal surface. Variations in this design separate the new taxa from one another and from *P. sternbergi* (see above).

The primary difference between the new taxa and *P. sternbergi* is size of the teeth. As seen by comparison of the scale bars in figure 6, teeth of *P. sternbergi* are up to twice as large as those of the new taxa. Teeth of the two species of *Dicothodon* further differ from those of *P. sternbergi* in having a V-shaped, main blade instead of the horizontal ridge seen in the teeth of *P. sternbergi*. The shallow, U-shaped main blade of *P. bajaensis* also differentiates teeth in this species from those of *P. sternbergi*. Accessory structures on the teeth of *P. sternbergi* are low ridges and not the well-developed blades seen on the teeth of the new taxa. In teeth of *Dicothodon* and *P. bajaensis*, there are small basins between these accessory blades and the main blades (both V- and U-shaped). The symmetrical, bicuspid tooth (IGM 6966) of *P. bajaensis* is nearly identical to the last tooth in the maxillary tooth row of *P. sternbergi* (see Gilmore, 1942: figure 19).

Gilmore (1940, 1943a) described two other lizards,

Paraglyphanodon gazini and *P. utahensis*, from the holotype locality of *Polyglyphanodon sternbergi*. Although smaller, the teeth of *Paraglyphanodon gazini* (figure 2D) are nearly identical to those of *Polyglyphanodon sternbergi*. The other taxon found in the North Horn Formation is *Paraglyphanodon utahensis* (figure 2E). This lizard has teeth that are triangular in occlusal view as opposed to transversely expanded. Except for size, the morphological comparisons between the new taxa and *Paraglyphanodon gazini* are much the same as with *Polyglyphanodon sternbergi*. However, none of the new taxa compare favorably, in dental morphology, with *Paraglyphanodon utahensis*, except for the shared presence of a transversely oriented ridge in the center of the teeth.

The disparity of size and similarity in tooth structure, in addition to the direct association of these three taxa of lizards from the North Horn Formation (all from the same locality), led Estes (1969, 1983) to suggest that the two species of *Paraglyphanodon* represent ontogenetically younger specimens of *Polyglyphanodon sternbergi*, rather than distinct taxa. This could be supported by a figure of *Paraglyphanodon gazini* (Gilmore, 1943a, figure 7) that shows the enlarged orbits and reduced tooth row (= reduced snout length) associated with juvenile lizards (and most vertebrates). Although speculation on the ontogenetic relationships of these taxa is shared by others (for example, Cifelli and others, 1998b), such a relationship has not yet been convincingly demonstrated. Because of the uncertain status of the relationship between *Polyglyphanodon sternbergi* and the two species of *Paraglyphanodon*, comparisons between the latter and the new taxa may not bear the same weight as comparisons with former

DISCUSSION

History of the Cretaceous Teiidae

The earliest record of the Teiidae are two dentary fragments from the Aptian-Albian of Texas (Winkler and others, 1990). New teiid jaws from the uppermost Albian Cedar Mountain Formation in the collections of the OMNH (two as yet undescribed taxa and *Dicothodon moorensis*) represent three distinct grades of tooth morphology, suggesting that diversification of the family was well underway by the medial Cretaceous. The Upper Cretaceous fossil record of the Teiidae includes numerous morphologically and taxonomically diverse taxa from North America and Asia (Marsh, 1892; Gilmore, 1940, 1943a, 1943b; Estes, 1964, 1969, 1983; Sulimski, 1972, 1975; Gao and Fox, 1991, 1996; Denton and

O'Neil, 1995). In North America, Cretaceous teiids are known to occur from Baja California (this report) to New Jersey (Denton and O'Neil, 1995). Most records, however, are from the extensively worked deposits of west-central North America (Marsh, 1892; Gilmore, 1940, 1943a; Estes, 1964, 1969, 1983; Gao and Fox, 1991, 1996). Asian teiids are restricted to the polyglyphanodontines from the Upper Cretaceous of Mongolia (Sulimski, 1972, 1975). To some degree the high diversity of teiids (including Polyglyphanodontinae) during the Late Cretaceous can be explained by a bias towards collecting in horizons of this age. However, recent work in Lower Cretaceous deposits (Winkler and others, 1990; Kirkland and others, 1997; Cifelli and others, 1998a) has not revealed a similar diversity for older teiids. The polyglyphanodontines parallel other teiids in having had their greatest diversity during the Late Cretaceous. All teiids in the northern hemisphere appear to have gone extinct at the end of the Cretaceous.

Dental Evolution in the Polyglyphanodontinae

As mentioned above, the majority of Cretaceous specimens that make up the fossil record of the Teiidae are jaws and jaw fragments. Many of the characteristics used to diagnose the Teiidae are found in these jaws; for example, Meckelian fossa widely open to the symphysis to accommodate a hypertrophied splenial, replacement teeth develop in subcircular replacement pits at the base of the teeth, and heavy deposits of cementum at tooth bases (Estes and others, 1988; Gao and Fox, 1991, 1996). For many of the Cretaceous teiid taxa, the morphology of the teeth in these jaws is considered diagnostic at the genus and/or species level (Estes, 1983; Gao and Fox, 1991, 1996). As a group, the Teiidae are unusual in the high diversity of tooth types represented in the various taxa, a diversity that was even greater during the Cretaceous.

The oldest known teiid (Aptian-Albian of Texas) has unicuspid, conical teeth (Winkler and others, 1990). Based on these specimens and the iterative occurrence of this morphology in numerous Late Cretaceous teiids, Gao and Fox (1991) proposed that this was the primitive tooth pattern for teiids. This is further supported by widespread occurrence of this simple tooth pattern in Gekkonidae and Pygopodidae (theoretical outgroups to the Teiidae; Estes and others, 1988). By the medial and Late Cretaceous, teiids exhibit a wide array of tooth morphologies. Three dental patterns are evident among the Late Cretaceous, non-polyglyphanodontine teiids: (1) "ancestral-type" with unicuspid and conical teeth (for example, *Gerontoseps, Socognathus, Sphenosiagon*, and

Stypodontosaurus); (2) "normal-type" with anteroposteriorly oriented teeth with bi- or tricuspid crowns (e.g., *Chamops, Glyptogenys, Haptosphenus, Leptochamops*, and *Meniscognathus*); or (3) "transverse-type" with transversely oriented, bicuspid crown (for example, *Peneteius*, undescribed taxon from the Cedar Mountain Formation). *Peneteius* and *Polyglyphanodon sternbergi* share a transverse orientation, however, the teeth of *Peneteius* are otherwise distinct; expanded medially (Estes, 1969) and multicuspate (Nydam and others, unpublished data). *Peneteius* is not considered a polyglyphanodontine (Estes, 1969, 1983; personal observation). As with the Mesozoic teiids, the "normal-type" tooth pattern is also the most common tooth pattern of modern teiids, with the exception of *Dicrodon* and *Teius* which have transversely oriented teeth. An evolutionary pattern of teiid tooth types in the Cretaceous is not clear as all three morphotypes listed above are known to occur at the same horizon (Estes, 1983; Gao and Fox, 1991, 1996). Unlike the rest of the Cretaceous Teiidae, the Polyglyphanodontinae exhibit even more diverse and unusual dental patterns.

The Mongolian polyglyphanodontines exhibit three tooth patterns: (1) leaf-shaped, polycuspate teeth (for example, *Darchansaurus, Erdenetesaurus*, and *Macrocephalosaurus*); large, bulbous, conical teeth (for example, *Adamisaurus*); and obliquely oriented, polycuspate, blade-like teeth (for example, *Cherminsaurus*). The most common tooth pattern of the Mongolian taxa is the leaf-shaped, polycuspate morphology found in a majority of the taxa. This pattern is similar to that found in modern herbivorous lizards such as Iguanidae (sensu Frost and Etheridge, 1989). The conical teeth of *Adamisaurus* are the closest in form to the presumed primitive teiid tooth pattern. However, it is quite possible that this tooth morphology was secondarily derived in association with the development of a durophagus diet (see below). The most unusual dentition of the Mongolian polyglyphanodontines occurs in *Cherminsaurus* (Sulimski, 1975, figure 14A) which has horizontal, polycuspate, and diagonally rotated teeth. The pattern of dental evolution within the Mongolian Polyglyphanodontinae remains uncertain.

The North American Polyglyphanodontines all have chisel-like teeth which are transversely oriented, medially expanded, and anteroposteriorly compressed (except for *Paraglyphanodon utahensis*). The age of *Dicothodon moorensis* demonstrates that this morphology was established by the end of the Early Cretaceous. The iteration of this tooth pattern in *Dicothodon* sp., *Polyglyphanodon bajaensis*, and *P. sternbergi* shows that this morphology underwent only minor changes (i.e., shape of main blade and extent of accessory blades) throughout the rest of the Cretaceous. Without a phylogenetic analysis it is not certain that these differences actually represent the apparent trend in the North American polyglyphanodontines towards more chisel-like teeth.

In his evaluation of the relationships between the taxa from North America and Mongolia, Estes (1983, p. 80) interpreted the obliquely oriented teeth in *Cherminsaurus* (Campanian; Mongolia) as "demonstrating a trend towards transverse orientation of teeth that culminated in the Maastrichtian North American *Polyglyphanodon* and *Paraglyphanodon*," implying that the tooth morphology of *Cherminsaurus* is ancestral to that of *P. sternbergi*. The discovery of the new North American polyglyphanodontine taxa requires that this scenario be re-examined. *Dicothodon moorensis* (upper Albian) and *Dicothodon* sp. (Turonian) are the geologically oldest polyglyphanodontine lizards and both taxa exhibit tooth morphologies similar to that of *Polyglyphanodon*. As such, *Dicothodon* would be a more likely ancestor of *Polyglyphanodon* than *Cherminsaurus*. Following the same criteria used by Estes (1983), the age and tooth morphology of *Dicothodon* could be interpreted to imply that *Cherminsaurus* represents a transitional form in the evolution of the Mongolian taxa from the older North American taxa. However, both Estes' scenario and its reverse have some difficulties. First, the oldest taxon is not necessarily the most primitive and a phylogenetic analysis is required to establish character polarity and identify evolutionary trends; as mentioned already, the new material described here is insufficient for such an analysis. Second, the teeth of both the Mongolian and the North American taxa appear to be "derived" with respect to the supposed primitive teiid dental condition (see above) as well as with respect to each other, indicating that the time of divergence between the Mongolian and North American lineages predates *Dicothodon moorensis*. The best approach at this point would be to recognize both the Asian and North American taxa as representing two groups of polyglyphanodontine lizards that diverged from each other some time prior to the medial Cretaceous. Following the convention of placing the point of origin of a group at the location of the oldest known specimen (Humphries, 1992), the polyglyphanodontines appear to have originated in North America, but without a better understanding of the Early Cretaceous of Asia broad statements such as this remain speculative.

Recent work examining the fossil record of the late Early and medial Cretaceous of North America indicates that a faunal exchange (predominantly from east to west) between Asia and North America was active during the time between the Barremian and Cenomanian (Kirkland and others, 1997). Assuming that the present record reflects the actual temporal and geographic distribution of the Polyglyphanodontinae, this group would represent only the second vertebrate record (the first being the Cretaceous shark *Baibisha*; Cifelli and others, this volume) of a west-to-east dispersal during the Early Cretaceous faunal exchange.

Dietary Interpretations of the Polyglyphanodontinae

In modern lizards it is possible to associate the dental patterns of some taxa with their diet, particularly if the diet is specialized. Lizards with specialized diets (for example, herbivory, vertebrate carnivory, durophagy) commonly have the most derived and distinguishable teeth. Good examples of this are extant taxa such as the herbivorous iguanid *Iguana iguana*, the carnivorous varanid *Varanus komodoensis*, and the durophagous teiid *Dracaena guianensis*. In some cases, similarity in diet may result in highly similar tooth morphologies in otherwise unrelated taxa. Such is the case with the extant taxa *Iguana iguana* and the skink *Corucia zebrata*. These animals have nearly identical leaf-shaped, polycuspate teeth (Montanucci, 1968; personal observation) and both are herbivores (Rand, 1990; Parker, 1983). Since these two lizards are not closely related they must have independently/convergently evolved similar diets and dentition. Because we can observe the habits of modern taxa we can determine the correlations between diet and morphology (at least in many of the specialized taxa) and use these correlations as modern analogs to aid in interpreting the diets of fossil lizards, assuming we find similar patterns.

Polyglyphanodon sternbergi is immediately distinguishable by its large size and unusual dentition. The transverse orientation and medial expansion, characteristic of the teeth of the North American polyglyphanodontines, also occur in *Trilophosaurus*, a primitive archosaur from the Triassic (Gregory, 1945; Demar and Bolt, 1981). Demar and Bolt (1981) identify the chisel-like teeth, alternating occlusion, and weak wear facets on some teeth, in addition to the likely presence of a horny beak, as evidence that *Trilophosaurus* was an herbivore, supporting an earlier conclusion of Gregory (1945). Gilmore's reconstruction (1942) of *Polyglyphanodon sternbergi* shows an interlocking or alternating pattern of maxillary and dentary teeth similar to that of *Trilophosaurus*. He interpreted this tooth morphology and jaw reconstruction to "indicate quite conclusively that *Polyglyphanodon* was herbivorous in diet" (Gilmore, 1942, p. 265). One line of evidence that supports the possibility of *P. sternbergi* having been herbivorous is its large size. Based on the energetic requirements of lizards and energy available from plant material, Pough (1973) determined that in order for a lizard to be able to sustain itself through herbivory it would need to have a minimum SVL of 15 cm. The SVL of *P. sternbergi* is approximately 45 cm (from Gilmore, 1942), well over the minimum needed to effectively exploit plant material as a food source.

Gao and Fox (1996, p. 44) described *Polyglyphanodon sternbergi* as having "greatly expanded crushing teeth" implying a durophagous diet. A durophagous diet involves an animal crushing hard food items with teeth that are usually broad and flat which results in various degrees of apical wear on the teeth. There are no reports of apical wear on the chisel-like teeth of any of the material of *P. sternbergi* described by Gilmore (1942) and no wear is evident on the teeth of OMNH 33460. However, a jaw fragment of a polyglyphanodontine with two teeth (OMNH 27683) was recovered from the Cretaceous part of the North Horn Formation. Both of the teeth have wear facets indicating abrasive occlusion of teeth. The specimen (possibly one of the species of *Paraglyphanodon*) is currently involved in a study of the possible ontogenetic relationships of *Polyglyphanodon* and *Paraglyphanodon* (Nydam and Caldwell, unpublished data). The chisel-like shape of the teeth of *Polyglyphanodon sternbergi* and the manner in which they are securely cemented to the jaw suggest that they were used to process tough food items that could be sliced, most likely tough vegetation. As such, I tentatively accept Gilmore's (1942) interpretation of an herbivorous diet for *Polyglyphanodon sternbergi*. The interpretation of the diets of the polyglyphanodontine lizards from Mongolia are less ambiguous.

Three of the Mongolian taxa, *Macrocephalosaurus*, *Darchansaurus*, and *Erdenetesaurus*, possess teeth that are similar in structure to modern herbivorous lizards such as *Iguana iguana* and *Corucia zebrata*. *Macrocephalosaurus ferrugenous* is difficult to interpret because the teeth of the specimen are worn and denticles may or not have been present (Sulimski, 1975; Estes, 1983). Estes's (1983) conclusion that these lizards were either herbivores or omnivores is reasonable, though I speculate that the close similarity in dental pattern to the Iguanidae makes a stronger case for herbivory. *Adamisaurus* (Sulimski, 1972) has teeth of durophagous design (large, bluntly conical), similar to those found in the molluscivorous modern skink *Tiliqua*. The teeth of *Adamisaurus* also have a reduced tooth count similar to that of the extant durophagous amphisbaenid, *Amphisbaena ridleyi* (Pregill, 1984). *Adamisaurus* was most likely durophagous and may have been a molluscovore. The teeth of *Cherminsaurus* are unusual and there is no modern analogue with which to compare and infer a possible diet. However, the presence of multiple small cusps on the teeth of *Cherminsaurus* imply possible herbivory.

The diets of *Dicothodon moorensis*, *Dicothodon* sp., and *Polyglyphanodon bajaensis* are the most difficult to interpret. Although similar to the teeth of *P. sternbergi*, the differences in the shape of the main blade and the presence of accessory ridges preclude an automatic assignment of herbivory to these taxa. The material is too limited to determine the SVL of the animals so their possible energetic requirements are also indeterminate. In *Trilophosaurus*, Demar and Bolt (1981) believed that the juveniles were carnivorous because of the presence of sharp cusps on the teeth. The teeth of *Dicothodon moorensis*, *Dicothodon* sp., and *P. bajaensis* are more cuspate than those of *P. sternbergi*, but these cusps are not tall and sharp as would be expected for a carnivore or insectivore, or as seen in *Trilophosaurus* (Demar and Bolt, 1981: figure 6). Comparison with modern, transversely bicuspid teiids (*Dicrodon* and *Teius*, figure 7)

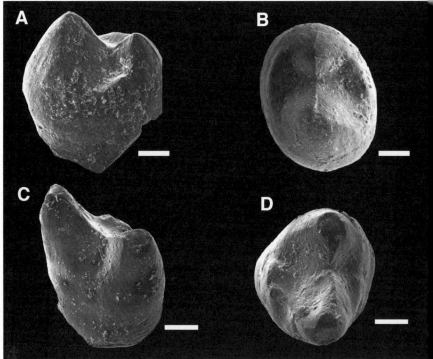

Figure 7. *Transversely oriented bicuspid teeth of extant teiids. A and B,* Dicrodon guttalatum, *coastal Peru, MVZ 85401, posterior tooth from right maxilla, posterior and occlusal views, respectively. B and C,* Teius teyou, *south-central South America, posterior tooth from left maxilla, anterior and occlusal views, respectively.*

does not clarify the situation. Of the two genera, *Dicrodon holmbergi* is the only completely herbivorous species (Holmberg, 1957). *Dicrodon guttalatum* is primarily insectivorous, but is known to take flowers when available (J. Dixon, personal communication). *Teius oculatus* (Alcosta and others, 1991) and *T. teyou* (Milstead, 1961) are reported to be insectivorous. Based on this information, there is no iterative dietary trend, or adaptation, associated with the transversely oriented teeth of *Teius* and *Dicrodon*. Although only speculative, the cuspate morphology of the teeth in the new polyglyphanodontine taxa, in addition to the similarities in morphology to the possibly herbivorous *P. sternbergi*, make it likely that *Dicothodon moorensis*, *Dicothodon* sp., and *Polyglyphanodon bajaensis* were omnivores. More complete material may help clarify this interpretation.

CONCLUSIONS

The discovery of the Albian *Dicothodon moorensis* and Turonian *Dicothodon* sp. of Utah, and the Campanian *Polyglyphanodon bajaensis* in Baja California del Norte, considerably extend the record of the Polyglyphanodontinae in North America. More importantly, these new taxa demonstrate that the unique morphology of transversely oriented, medially expanded teeth became established much earlier than previously believed. This morphology was also very stable, showing only minor changes over a history of more than 30 million years.

Contrary to previous interpretations, it now appears that the transversely oriented, medially expanded teeth found in the North American polyglyphanodontines did not evolve from any of the known Asian polyglyphanodontine taxa. Instead, the taxa in Mongolia and North American most likely represent a divergence within the Polyglyphanodontinae sometime during the Early Cretaceous. The differences in tooth morphologies between the Asian and North American polyglyphanodontine taxa, as well as the apparent endemism of these taxa to their respective continents, suggest that after diverging these groups remained separated throughout the medial and Late Cretaceous. Although the morphologies are different, tooth patterns in taxa from both continents appear to be adapted for omnivory/herbivory.

ACKNOWLEDGMENTS

I would like to thank D. A. Winkler and J. D. Gardner for their comments in reviews of an earlier version of manuscript. R. L. Cifelli, N. J. Czaplewski, G. D. Schnell, and L. J. Vitt provided useful comments and discussion during the early phases of this project. I would also like to thank E. Sanders for preparation of the *Polyglyphanodon sternbergi* material, E. M. Larson, E. Miller, and C. Miller for picking of concentrate recovered from the Cedar Mountain and Straight Cliffs Formations. N. J. Czaplewski prepared figures 2 and 5. Special thanks go to M. Perrilliat at the IGU for providing the photographs for figure 4, S. McLeod at the LACM for providing collection data for the *Polyglyphanodon bajaensis* specimens, and H. Greene at the MVZ for loan of the *Dicrodon* and *Teius* specimens. SEM images were taken at the Samuel Roberts Noble Electron Microscopy Laboratory at the University of Oklahoma. Funding for this project was made possible by grants and scholarships to the author from Sigma Xi and the Graduate Student Senate of the University of Oklahoma, the American Federation of Mineralogical Societies, and Dinamation International Society (Ying Chang Scholarship) as well as by National Geographic Society Grants 4762-91 and 5021-92 and National Science Foundation grant DEB 9401094 to R. L. Cifelli.

REFERENCES

Alcosta, J. C., Avila, R. A. and Martori, Ricardo, 1991, Ecología trófica de *Teius oculatus* (Sauria: Teiidae) en el sur de la provincia de Córdoba (Argentina) -- Composición, variacion anual y estacional de la dieta: Cuadernos de Herpetologia v. 6, p. 12-22.

Alifanov, V. R., 1992, The oldest gecko (Lacertilia, Gekkonidae) from the Lower Cretaceous of Mongolia: Paleontological Journal, v. 1992, p. 128-131.

Cifelli, R. L., 1990a, Cretaceous mammals of southern Utah. I. Marsupial mammals from the Kaiparowits Formation (Judithian): Journal of Vertebrate Paleontology, v. 10, p. 295-319.

—1990b, Cretaceous mammals of southern Utah. II. Marsupials and marsupial-like mammals from the Wahweap (Aquilan) and Kaiparowits (Judithian) formations: Journal of Vertebrate Paleontology, v. 10, p. 320-331.

—1990c, Cretaceous mammals of southern Utah. III. Therian mammals from the Turonian (early Late Cretaceous): Journal of Vertebrate Paleontology, v. 10, p. 332-345.

—1990d, Cretaceous mammals of southern Utah. IV. Eutherians from the Wahweap (Aquilan) and Kaiparowits (Judithian) formations: Journal of Vertebrate Paleontology, v. 10, p. 346-360.

—1993, Early Cretaceous mammal from North America and the evolution of marsupial dental characters: Proceedings of the National Academy of Sciences USA, v. 90, p. 9413-9416.

Cifelli, R. L., and Eaton, J. G., 1987, Marsupial from the earliest Late Cretaceous of Western US: Nature, v. 325, p. 520-522.

Cifelli, R. L., and Johanson, Zerina, 1994, New marsupial from the Upper Cretaceous of Utah: Journal of Vertebrate Paleontology, v. 14, p. 292-295.

Cifelli, R. L., Kirkland, J. I., Weil, Anne, Deino, A. L., and Kowallis, B. J., 1997, High-precision $^{40}Ar/^{39}Ar$ geochronology and the advent of North America's Late Cretaceous terrestrial fauna: Proceedings of the National Academy of Sciences USA, v. 94, p. 11163-11167.

Cifelli, R. L., and Madsen, S. K., Triconodont mammals from the medial Cretaceous of Utah: Journal of Vertebrate Paleontology, 1998.

Cifelli, R. L., Madsen, S. K., and Larson, E. M., 1996a, Screenwashing and associated techniques for the recovery of microvertebrate fossils, *in* Cifelli, R. L., editor, Techniques for recovery and preparation of microvertebrate fossils: Oklahoma Geological Survey Special Publication 96-4, p. 1-24.

Cifelli, R. L, and Muizon, Christian, Marsupial mammal from the Upper Cretaceous North Horn Formation, central Utah: Journal of Paleontology, 1998.

Cifelli, R. L, and Nydam, R. L., 1995, Primitive, helodermatid-like platynotan from the Early Cretaceous of Utah: Herpetologica, v. 51, p.286-291.

Cifelli, R. L., Nydam, R. L., Eaton, J. G., Gardner, J. D., and Kirkland, J. I., 1999, Vertebrate faunas of the North Horn Formation (Upper Cretaceous-Lower Paleocene), Emery and Sanpete Counties, in Gillette, D. D., editor, this volume.

Cifelli, R. L., Nydam, R. L., Gardner, J. D., Weil, Anne, Eaton, J. G., Kirkland, J. I., and Madsen, S. K., 1999, Medial Cretaceous vertebrates from the Cedar Mountain Formation, Emery County, Utah-- the Mussentuchit local fauna, *in* Gillette, D. D., editor, this volume.

Cifelli, R. L, Rowe, T. B., Luckett, W. P., Banta, James, Reyes, Reuben, and Howes, R. I., 1996, Fossil evidence for the origin of the marsupial pattern of tooth replacement: Nature, v. 379, p. 715-718.

Clemens, W. A., Jr., Lillegraven, J. A., Lindsay, E. H., and Simpson, G. G., 1979, Where when, and what--a survey of known Mesozoic mammal distribution, *in* Lillegraven, J. A., Kielan-Jaworowska, Zophia, and Clemens, W. A., Jr., editors, Mesozoic mammals--the first two-thirds of mammalian history: Berkeley, University of California Press, p. 7-58.

Demar, Robert, and Bolt, J. R., 1981, Dentitional organization and function in a Triassic reptile: Journal of Paleontology, v. 55, p. 967-984.

Denton, R. K., and O'Neil, R. C., 1995, *Prototeius stageri*, gen. et sp.

nov., a new teiid lizard from the Upper Cretaceous Marshalltown Formation of New Jersey, with a preliminary phylogenetic revision of the Teiidae: Journal of Vertebrate Paleontology, v. 15, p. 235-253.

Eaton, J. G., 1991, Biostratigraphic framework for the Upper Cretaceous rocks of the Kaiparowits Plateau, southern Utah, *in* Nations, J. D., and Eaton, J. G, editors, Stratigraphy, depositional environments, and sedimentary tectonics of the western margin, Cretaceous Western Interior Seaway: Geological Society of America Special Paper 260, p.47-63.

Eaton, J. G., and Cifelli, R. L., 1988, Preliminary report on Late Cretaceous mammals of the Kaiparowits Plateau, southern Utah: Contributions to Geology, University of Wyoming, v. 26, p. 45-55.

Estes, Richard, 1964, Fossil vertebres from the Late Cretaceous Lance Formation, eastern Wyoming: University of California Publications in Geological Sciences, v. 49, p. 1-186.

—1969, Relationships of two Cretaceous lizards (Sauria, Teiidae): Breviora, no. 317, p. 1-8.

—1983, Handbuch der Paläoherpetologie, Part 10A, Sauria Terrestria, Amphisbænia: Stuttgart, Gustav Fischer Verlag, 249 p.

Estes, Richard, de Queiroz, Kevin, Gauthier, J. A., 1988, Phylogenetic relationships within Squamata, *in* Estes, Richard and Pregill, Gregory, editors, Phylogenetic relationships of the lizard families--essay commemoration Charles L. Camp: Stanford, Stanford University Press, p. 119-281.

Frost, D. R., and Etheridge, Richard, 1989, A phylogenetic analysis and taxonomy of iguanian lizards (Reptilia: Squamata): University of Kansas Museum of Natural History Miscellaneous Publications, v. 81, p. 1-165.

Gao, Keqin, 1994, First discovery of Late Cretaceous cordylids (Squamata) from Madagascar: Journal of Vertebrate Paleontology, v. 14, supplement to no. 3, p. 26A.

Gao, Keqin, and Fox, R. C., 1991, New teiid lizards from the Upper Cretaceous Oldman Formation (Judithian) of southeastern Alberta, Canada, with a review of the Cretaceous record of teiids: Annals of Carnegie Museum, v. 60, p. 145-162.

—1996, Taxonomy and evolution of Late Cretaceous lizards (Reptilia: Squamata) from western Canada, Bulletin of the Carnegie Museum of Natural History, v. 33, p. 1-107.

Gardner, J. D., 1994, Amphibians from the Lower Cretaceous (Albian) Cedar Mountain Formation, Emery County, Utah: Journal of Vertebrate Paleontology, v. 14, supplement to no. 3, p. 26A.

—1995, Lower Cretaceous anurans from Texas and Utah: Journal of Vertebrate Paleontology, v. 15, supplement to no. 3, p. 31A.

Gardner, J. D., and Cifelli, R. L, A primitive snake from the mid-Cretaceous of Utah--the geologically oldest snake from the New World, *in* Unwin, David, editor, Cretaceous fossil vertebrates--Special Papers in Palaeontology, in press.

Gilmore, C. W., 1928, Fossil lizards of North America: National Academy of Sciences Memoir, v. 22, p. 1-201.

—1940, New fossil lizards from the Upper Cretaceous of Utah: Smithsonian Miscellaneous Collections, v. 99, p. 1-3.

—1942, Osteology of *Polyglyphanodon*, an Upper Cretaceous lizard from Utah: Proceedings of the United States National Museum, v. 92, p. 229-265.

—1943a, Osteology of Upper Cretaceous lizards from Utah, with a description of a new species: Proceedings of the United States National Museum, v. 93, p. 209-214.

—1943b, Fossil lizards of Mongolia: Bulletin of the American Museum of Natural History, v. 81, p. 361-384.

—1946, Reptilian fauna of the North Horn Formation of central Utah: U.S. Geological Survey Professional Paper, no. 210-C, p. 29-53.

Gregory, J. T., 1945, Osteology and relationships of *Trilophosaurus*: University of Texas Publications, no. 4401, p. 273-359.

Hoffstetter, Robert, 1955, Squamates de type moderne: Traité de Paleontologie, v. 5, p. 606-662.

Holmberg, A. R., 1957, Lizard hunts on the North coast of Peru: Fieldiana-Anthropology, v. 36, p. 203-220.

Humphries, C. J., 1992, Cladistic biogeography, *in* Forey, P. L, Humphries, C. J., Kitching, I. L., Scotland, R. W., Siebert, D. J., and Williams, D. M., editors, Cladistics: a practical course in systematics: Oxford, Clarendon Press, p. 137-169.

Kirkland, J. I., and Parrish, J. M., 1995, Theropod teeth from the Lower and middle Cretaceous of Utah: Journal of Vertebrate Paleontology, v. 15, supplement to no. 3, p. 39A.

Kirkland, J. I., Britt, Brooks, Burge, D. L., Carpenter, Kenneth, Cifelli, R. L., Decourten, Frank, Eaton, J. G., Hasiotis, Steve, and Lawton, Tim, 1997, Lower to Middle Cretaceous dinosaur faunas of the central Colorado Plateau--a key to understanding 35 million years of tectonics, sedimentology, evolution and biogeography: Brigham Young University Geology Studies, v. 42, p. 69-103.

Lillegraven, J. A., 1972, Preliminary report on Late Cretaceous Mammals from the El Gallo Formation, Baja California Del Norte, Mexico: Los Angeles County Museum Contributions in Science, no. 232, p. 1-11.

—1976, A new genus of therian mammal from the Late Cretaceous "El Gallo Formation," Baja California, Mexico: Journal of Paleontology, v. 50, p. 437-443.

Marsh, Othniel, 1892, Notice of new reptiles from the Laramie Formation: American Journal of Science, v. 43, p. 449-453.

Miller, M. S., 1997, Squamates of the Campanian Terlingua local fauna, Brewster County, Texas: Austin, University of Texas, M.S. thesis, 98 p.

Milstead, W. M., 1961, Notes on teiid lizards in southern Brazil: Copeia, v. 1964, p. 493-495.

Molenaar, C. M., and Cobban, W. A., 1991, Middle Cretaceous stratigraphy on the south and east sides of the Uinta Basin, northeastern Utah and northwestern Colorado: U. S. Geological Survey Bulletin, v. 1787, chapter P, p. P1-P34.

Montanucci, R. R., 1968, Comparative dentition in four iguanid lizards: Herpetologica, v. 24, p. 305-315.

Nydam, R. L., 1995, Lizards from the Early Cretaceous of central Utah: Journal of Vertebrate Paleontology, v. 15, supplement to no. 3, p. 47A.

—1997, Polyglyphanodontinae (Squamata: Teiidae) teeth across the Cretaceous of Utah-- a 33 million year record of this unusual lizard group in North America: Journal of Vertebrate Paleontology, v. 17, supplement to no. 3, p. 67A.

Orlansky, Ralf, 1971, Palynology of the Upper Cretaceous Straight Cliffs Sandstone, Garfield County, Utah: Utah Geological and Mineralogical Survey Bulletin, no. 89, p. 1-57.

Parker, Fred, 1983, The prehensile-tailed skink (*Corucia zebrata*) on Bougainville Island, Papua New Guinea, *in* Rhodin, A. G. and Miyata, Kenneth, editors, Advances in herpetology and evolutionary biology--essays in honor of Ernest E. Williams: Museum of Comparative Zoology, Cambridge, Harvard University, p. 435-440.

Peterson, Fred, 1969, Four new members of the Upper Cretaceous Straight Cliffs Formation in southeastern Kaiparowits region, Kane County, Utah: U. S. Geological Survey Bulletin, no. 1274-J, p. 1-28.

Pough, F. H., 1973, Lizard energetics and diet: Ecology, v. 54, p. 837-844.

Pregill, Gregory, 1984, Durophagous feeding adaptations in an amphisbaenid: Journal of Herpetology, v. 18, p. 186-191.

Presch, William, 1974, A survey of the dentition of the macroteiid lizards (Teiidae: Lacertilia): Herpetologica, v. 30, p. 344-349.

Rand, A. S., 1990, The diet of a generalized folivore: *Iguana iguana* in Panama: Journal of Herpetology, v. 24, p. 211-214.

Rieppel, Olivier, 1980, The trigeminal jaw adductor musculature of *Tupinambis*, with comments on the phylogenetic relationships of the Teiidae (Reptilia, Lacertilia): Zoological Journal of the Linnean Society, v. 69, p. 1-29.

Spieker, E. M., 1960, The Cretaceous-Tertiary boundary in Utah: International Geological Congress, part 5, p. 14-24.

Stokes, W. L., 1944, Morrison Formation and related deposits in and adjacent to the Colorado Plateau: Bulletin of the Geological Society of America, v. 55, p. 951-992.

Sulimski, Andrzej, 1972, *Adamisaurus magnidentatus* n. gen., n. sp. (Sauria) from the Upper Cretaceous of Mongolia: Palaeontologica Polonica, v. 27, p. 33-40.

—1975, Macrocephalosauridae and Polyglyphanodontidae (Sauria) from the Late Cretaceous of Mongolia: Palaeontologica Polonica, v. 33, p. 25-102.

—1978, New data on the genus *Adamisaurus* 1972 (Sauria) from the Upper Cretaceous of Mongolia: Palaeontologica Polonica, v. 38, p. 43-56.

Sullivan, R. M., and Estes, Richard, 1997, A reassessment of the fossil Tupinambinae, *in* Kay, R. F., Madden, R. H., Cifelli, R. L., and Flynn, J. J., editors, Vertebrate paleontology in the Neotropics, the Miocene fauna of La Venta, Colombia: Washington, D.C., Smithsonian Institution, p.100-112.

Tschudy, R. H., Tschudy, B. D., and Craig, L. C., 1984, Palynological evaluations of Cedar Mountain and Burro Canyon formations, Colorado Plateau: U. S. Geological.Survey Professional Paper 1281, p. 1-19.

Winkler, D. A., Murry, P. A., and Jacobs, L. L., 1990, Early Cretaceous (Comanchean) vertebrates of central Texas: Journal of Vertebrate Paleontology. v. 10, p. 95-116.

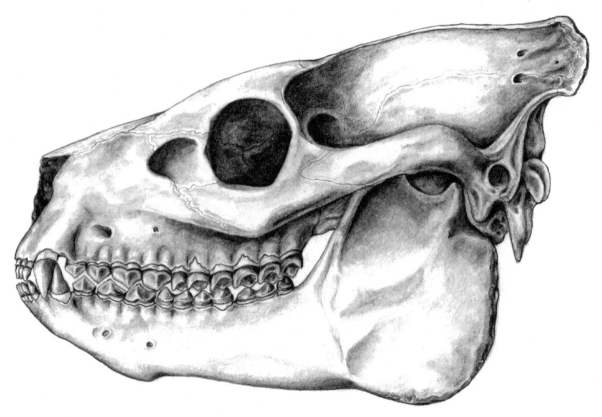

Brian Maebius © 1999

Oreodont

DINOSAUR TEETH FROM THE UPPER CRETACEOUS (TURONIAN-JUDITHIAN) OF SOUTHERN UTAH

J. Michael Parrish
Department of Biological Sciences
Northern Illinois University
DeKalb, Illinois 60115

ABSTRACT

Knowledge of Upper Cretaceous dinosaurs of southern Utah has grown slowly during the past two decades. Dinosaur teeth occur with microvertebrate faunas that have been recovered by paleontologists conducting faunal studies in the Straight Cliffs (Turonian-Coniacian), Wahweap (early Campanian), and Kaiparowits (late Campanian) Formations. Identification of the dinosaur teeth recovered from these formations allows a preliminary estimate of diversity, biostratigraphy, and occurrence of dinosaurs in these Late Cretaceous vertebrate faunas.

INTRODUCTION

Knowledge of the Late Cretaceous dinosaur faunas of the Rocky Mountain region of the U. S. and southwestern Canada is extensive. Much less intensively studied, and therefore less completely understood, is the evolution and biostratigraphy of the dinosaurs of southern Utah, the other region of North America from which a reasonably complete section of Upper Cretaceous continental strata is known. In the last fifteen years or so, Jeff Eaton (Weber State University, Ogden, Utah), Richard Cifelli (Oklahoma State Museum), and their crews have collected matrix and sieved for microvertebrates throughout the continental Cretaceous of the Kaiparowits Plateau (see other papers by Cifelli, Eaton, and their colleagues, this volume). This report summarizes the dinosaur tooth faunas known to date from the Straight Cliffs (Turonian-?Coniacian), Wahweap (early Campanian), and Kaipirowits (late Campanian) Formations from the Kaipirowits Plateau, based on collections housed at the University of Colorado Museum, Boulder, Colorado; the Museum of Northern Arizona, Flagstaff, Arizona; and the Oklahoma Museum of Natural History, Norman, Oklahoma. Because most of the material is represented by isolated teeth, diversity can only be estimated at the family or, in some cases, the subfamily level (for example, Currie and others, 1990; Parrish and Eaton, 1991). Nonetheless, these collections give a good overview of the diversity and gross patterns of faunal evolution in southern Utah during the Late Cretaceous. Faunal data are presented in tabular form, and in stratigraphic order.

Abbreviations: MNA, Museum of Northern Arizona, Flagstaff, Arizona; OMNH, Oklahoma Museum of Natural History, Norman, Oklahoma; UCM, University of Colorado Museum, Boulder, Colorado.

BIOSTRATIGRAPHY/SYSTEMATIC PALEONTOLOGY

Straight Cliffs Formation (Turonian-?Coniacian), Kaiparowits Plateau, Utah

The Straight Cliffs Formation is represented by 300 to 500 meters of continental sediments dominated by sandstones (Eaton, 1991). It consists of four members, of which the second (Smoky Hollow Member) and third (John Henry Member) have yielded dinosaur tooth faunas.

Smoky Hollow Member (Middle to Late Turonian)

The Smoky Hollow Member ranges from 7 to 55 meters in thickness, and consists of interbedded sandstones, mudstones, carbonaceous mudstones, and coals. The dinosaur teeth come from the middle of three beds in the member, the Barren Beds (Eaton, 1991).

Ornithischia
    Ornithopoda
        Hadrosauridae (OMNH 21492, 25427, 21506, 21508, 21510, 20862, 23710, 23862, 23863, 23697, 24443-24447)
        Hypsilophodontidae , cf. *Thescelosaurus* (OMNH 21512, 24313, 25418)
    Thyreophora
        Ankylosauria
            Ankylosauridae (OMNH 23681)
            Nodosauridae (OMNH 21711, 24448)
Saurischia
    Theropoda
        Dromaeosauridae
            Dromaeosaurinae (OMNH 23712, 25422, 24437, 24438, 25420).

Velociraptorinae (MNA 994, OMNH
24439, 24441, 24442).
Tyrannosauridae (OMNH 24125, 24436).
Family indeterminate, cf. *Paranychodon* (MNA
995, OMNH 24451, 25415).
Family indeterminate, cf. *Aublysodon*
(OMNH 21518, 21524)

John Henry Member (Coanacian-Santonian)

The John Henry Member overlies the Smoky Hollow, and consists of 200 to 340 meters of interbedded
sandstones, mudstones, carbonaceous mudstones, and
coals. The lower part of the member includes marine
sediments, particularly in the northeast part of the basin
(Peterson, 1969).

Ornithischia
Ankylosauria
Ankylosauridae (OMNH 21243)
Nodosauridae (OMNH 21671)
Ornithopoda
Hadrosauridae (MNA HC-2, PC-1, OMNH
21540, 21675, 21895)
Saurischia
Theropoda
Dromaeosauridae
Velociraptorinae (OMNH 21238, 21673).

Wahweap Formation (Early Campanian: Aquilan), Kaipirowits Plateau

The Wahweap Formation is a sequence 360 to 460
meters thick of continental sandstones and mudstones
(Eaton, 1991). It consists of four members: Lower, Middle, Upper, and Capping Sandstone; the dinosaur teeth
come from the Upper Member.

Ornithischia
Ankylosauria
Nodosauridae (OMNH 21280 (part), 21992,
24278)
Ankylosauridae (OMNH 21280 (part), 21858,
24276)
Ornithopoda
Hadrosauridae (UCM 8603, 8605, 8618, MNA DR-2,
NB 11, NB 12, OMNH 21279, 21319,
21396, 21944, 21602, 21617, 21986,
23657, 24264, 24271)
Hypsilophodontidae
cf. *Thescelosaurus* (OMNH 21813, 24281)

Saurischia
Theropoda
Dromaeosauridae
Dromaeosaurinae (MNA NB-9, OMNH
21222, 21318, 21230, 21281, 21335,
21340, 21395, 21868, 21991, 23636,
24307, 24308, 24327)
Veloceraptorinae (UCM 8613)
Family indeterminate
cf. *Aublysodon* (OMNH 24309 (part))
Troodontidae
cf. *Troodon* (OMNH 21988, 24237)
Tyrannosauridae (OMNH 23635)

Kaiparowits Formation - (Late Campanian: Judithian)

At its thickest, the Kaiparowits Formation consists of
about 850 meters of continental sandstones and mudstones. It contains an abundant fossil fauna and paly-
noflora, particularly in the interval between 170 and 740
meters from the base of the formation (Eaton, 1991). The
Kaipirowits demonstrates the greatest diversity and abundance of dinosaur teeth among the Cretaceous formations
of the Kaipirowits Plateau.

Ornithischia
Ankylosauria
Nodosauridae (UCM 83240, 83263, OMNH
24471, 21190)
Ankylosauridae (UCM 8319, 8330, 83240 (part),
8659 (part), 8667 (part), OMNH 21118,
24112)
Ornithopoda
Hadrosauridae (UCM 8368, 83237, 83238,
83239 (part), 83240 (part), 83244, 83245,
83246, 83247, 83249 (part), 83251 (part),
83252, 83253, 83258, 83261, 83263, 83264,
8626, 8462, 8647, 8653, 8660 (part), 8662,
8663, 8664, 8667 (part), 8671, 8672, 8673,
8675, 8676, 8679, 8680, 8690, MNA FB-1,
HM-6, HM-8, OMNH 21248, 21738,
21743, 21748, 21825, 21847, 23745, 23596,
23613, 23614, 23745, 23753, 23848, 23849,
23850, 23856, 23988, 24000, 24003, 24165,
24292, 24772, 24773, 24774, 24775)
Marginocephalia
Ceratopsia
Ceratopsidae (UCM 83239 (part), 83251
(part), 8659 (part), OMNH 21253,
21823, 23858, 24001, 24002, 24476)

Saurischia
Sauropoda (OMNH 23984, 24382)
Theropoda
Dromaeosauridae
Veloceraptorinae (UCM 8312, 83240 (part),
8642 (part), 8655, 8659 (part), 8663,
MNA HM-6, OMNH 21240, 24158)
Dromeosaurinae (UCM 83240, 8659
(part),OMNH 21117, 23178, 23527,
23595, 23608, 23854, 23875, 23969-
23975, 24157, 24159, 24160, 23851,
23565 (part , 24381)
Troodontidae (UCM 83253, 8659 (part),
OMNH 21958)
Tyrannosauridae (UCM 8304, 83239, 8626,
8642 (part), 8647, 8659, 8671, MNA
HM-6 (part), OMNH 21960, 21961)
Family indeterminate
cf. *Paranychodon* (UCM 8304, OMNH
24161, 24164)
cf. *Richardoestesia* (UCM 8656)

DISCUSSION

At the level of resolution afforded by tooth analysis, differences in dinosaur taxa among these formations appear to reflect sampling more than distinct evolutionary patterns. Although tyrannosaurids and ceratopsians appear at the top of the sequence considered in this paper, both are also known from the Cedar Mountain Formation (Albian) from central Utah (Kirkland and Parrish, 1995). The greatest diversity of tooth forms comes from the two formations with the greatest abundance of teeth, the Cedar Mountain and Kaipirowits.

ACKNOWLEDGMENTS

The material was collected by field parties led by Jeff Eaton and Rich Cifelli from 1983-1991. I am indebted to them for providing this material for study. I benefitted from discussions with Cifelli, Eaton, Ken Carpenter, Phil Currie, Jim Kirkland, and Lou Jacobs.

REFERENCES

Currie, P. J., Rigby, J. K., Jr., and Sloan, R. E., 1990, Theropod teeth from the Judith River Formation of Southern Alberta, Canada, *in* Carpenter, Kenneth, and Currie, P. J., editors, Dinosaur systematics: Cambridge, Cambridge University Press, p.107-126.

Eaton, J. G. 1991, Biostratigraphic framework for the Upper Cretaceous rocks of the Kaipirowits Plateau, southern Utah: Geological Society of America Special Paper, v. 260, p. 47-63.

Kirkland, J. I., and Parrish, J. M., 1995, Theropod teeth from the Lower and middle Cretaceous of Utah: Journal of Vertebrate Paleontology, v. 14, p. 39A.

Parrish, J. M., and Eaton, J. G., 1991, Diversity and evolution of dinosaurs in the Cretaceous of the Kaipirowits Plateau, Utah: Journal of Vertebrate Paleontology, v. 11, p. 50A.

Peterson, Fred, 1969, Cretaceous sedimentation and tectonism in the southeastern Kaipirowits region: U. S. Geological Survey Open File Report, 259 p.

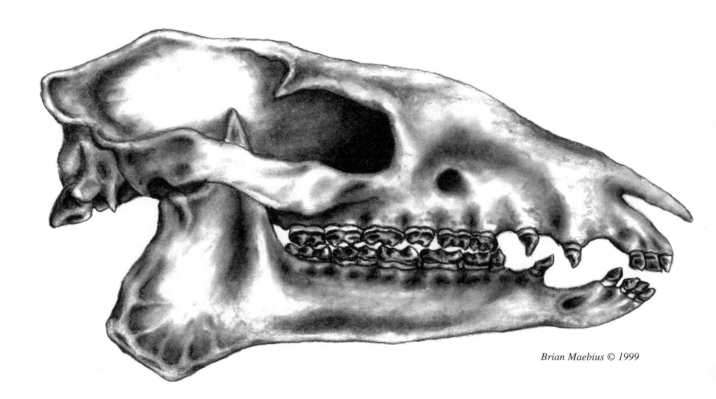

Brian Maebius © 1999

Eohippus

VERTEBRATE PALEONTOLOGY OF THE UPPER CRETACEOUS ROCKS OF THE MARKAGUNT PLATEAU, SOUTHWESTERN UTAH

Jeffrey G. Eaton
Department of Geological Sciences
Weber State University
Ogden, Utah 84408-2507

Steve Diem and J. David Archibald
Department of Biology
San Diego State University
San Diego, California 92182-4614

Christopher Schierup
Department of Biological Sciences
Northern Illinois University
Dekalb, IL 60115

Heidi Munk
Department of Geological Sciences
Weber State University
Ogden, Utah 84408-2507

ABSTRACT

A series of vertebrate localities have been discovered in the Cretaceous strata overlying the regressive sandstone (Tibbet Canyon Member) of the Straight Cliffs Formation in Cedar Canyon, western Markagunt Plateau. The lower 50 meters produces a brackish-water community of vertebrate and invertebrate taxa equivalent to those recovered from the base of the Smoky Hollow Member (middle or late Turonian) of the Straight Cliffs Formation in the region of the Kaiparowits Plateau to the east. Above the brackish sequence is 600 meters of lithologically similar fluvial deposits. The two lowest localities in this part of the sequence may mark the transgression recorded in the John Henry Member of the Straight Cliffs Formation (Coniacian) in the region of the Kaiparowits Plateau. Another locality, 150 meters higher in section, contains a fauna that is most closely comparable to that of the Milk River fauna of Canada and is Santonian in age based on palynomorphs. A locality present at the top of the Cretaceous section has yielded a small fauna that is inadequate for age determination. The fauna from this locality is unusual in containing pediomyid marsupials, a family not previously reported from the Cretaceous of southern Utah.

INTRODUCTION

The Markagunt Plateau (figure 1) is bounded on the east by the Sevier fault system, to the south by the Kolob Terrace which descends into the magnificent canyons of Zion National Park, and to the west by the Hurricane fault system which marks the transition from the Colorado Plateau physiographic province to the Basin and Range. Most of the plateau consists of Cretaceous strata capped by Tertiary volcanics.

Outcrops are limited on the Markagunt Plateau (relative to southwestern Utah in general) due to the relatively high amount of annual precipitation. It is possibly for this reason that no fossil vertebrates have been reported previously from this area. Eaton first located significant microvertebrate localities in Cretaceous strata during the 1991 field season and was joined by Archibald during the 1992 field season. Some work has been done on the Markagunt Plateau during every subsequent field season. Schierup joined the research project during the 1996 field season to study the dinosaur teeth as part of a senior thesis at the University of Michigan, Flint; and Munk has begun a study of the squamates from Locality 10 as part of an undergraduate research project. Eaton reports on the therian mammals and Diem and Archibald on multituberculate mammals herein. This preliminary report is the first on vertebrates from the Markagunt Plateau. All specimens are catalogued in the collections of the Utah Museum of Natural History (UMNH), Salt Lake City, and all localities are recorded in UMNH locality files.

STRATIGRAPHY

The Cretaceous strata present along the western margin of the Markagunt Plateau (Cedar Canyon) has the Dakota Formation at its base, overlain by an unusually thick and clastic-rich section of the Tropic Shale (Gustason, 1989). This section is rich in clastics due to large volumes of material derived from an active thrust belt associated with the Sevier orogenic event about 50 kilometers to the west (Eaton and Nations, 1991). Above the Tropic Shale are very thick sets of regressive sandstones equivalent to the Tibbet Canyon Member of the Straight Cliffs Formation to the east in the Kaiparowits Plateau region. Although these and overlying rocks are considered here to represent the Straight Cliffs Formation, none of the member names have been applied on the Markagunt Plateau and there is considerable contention regarding the units represented in the Cretaceous sequence.

Gregory (1950a, 1950b), who pioneered Cretaceous stratigraphic nomenclature in southwestern Utah, considered the section on the Markagunt Plateau to contain the full complement of Cretaceous units that is found on the Kaiparowits Plateau to the east (Dakota, Tropic, Straight Cliffs, Wahweap, and Kaiparowits Formations). Cashion's (1967) map of the southern margin of the Markagunt Plateau indicates a very thin Straight Cliffs Formation overlain by a thick section of undifferentiated Wahweap and Kaiparowits Formations. A later map covering the same area by Doelling and Davis (1989) also shows a very thin Straight Cliffs Formation overlain by a thick section of Wahweap Formation which is, in turn, overlain by a thin section of the Kaiparowits Formation. None of these publications provide lithostratigraphic justifications for the formational designations or any basis for biotratigraphic or chronologic equivalency of units.

On the Markagunt Plateau (specifically Cedar Canyon, east of Cedar City, figure 1), there is a distinct lithologic break above the regressive sandstone which is equivalent to the Tibbet Canyon Member of the Straight Cliffs Formation to the east. This sandstone is mapped as the Straight Cliffs Formation by Cashion (1967) and Doelling and Davis (1989). Overlying the sandstone is approximately 50 meters of sandstones and organic-rich mudstones that contain abundant brackish-water faunas and some vertebrates (UMNH VP Locality 66, figure 2; also see Eaton and others, 1997). This sequence is

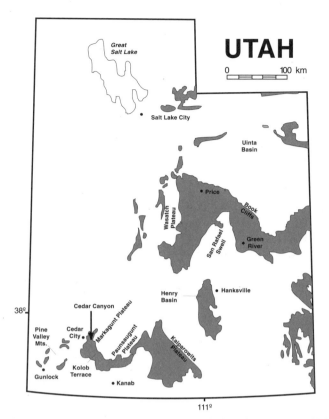

Figure 1. *Cretaceous outcrop map of Utah (based on Hintze, 1974) showing the geographic position of the Markagunt Plateau. Arrow indicates location of Cedar Canyon where these faunas have been recovered.*

included in the Wahweap Formation on Cashion's (1967) and Doelling and Davis's (1989) maps, but the Wahweap Formation contains no brackish mollusks (Eaton, 1987, 1991) and we believe these strata to be equivalent to the lower part of the Smoky Hollow Member of the Straight Cliffs Formation, which contains almost identical molluscan faunas in the Kaiparowits Plateau region (Museum of Northern Arizona Locality 996 in figure 2, Eaton and others, 1997). Two hundred meters above the brackish water deposits, floodplain mudstones contain a locality (UMNH Locality 8, figure 2) that produces an abundance of shark and ray teeth similar to those recovered from the John Henry Member of the Straight Cliffs Formation to the east on the Kaiparowits Plateau. The presence of "freshwater" vertebrates such as sharks and rays requires some access to brackish or marine water (Eaton and others, 1997). The closest approach of the seaway after the Greenhorn regression (marked by the Tibbet Canyon Member) was during deposition of the John Henry Member, which developed a strand line in the middle of the Kaiparowits Plateau (Eaton, 1991) about 110 kilometers to the east. Immediately prior to and after John Henry Member deposition the strand line was well to the east of the Henry Mountains (Eaton, 1987; also see paper on the Kaiparowits Plateau, this volume).

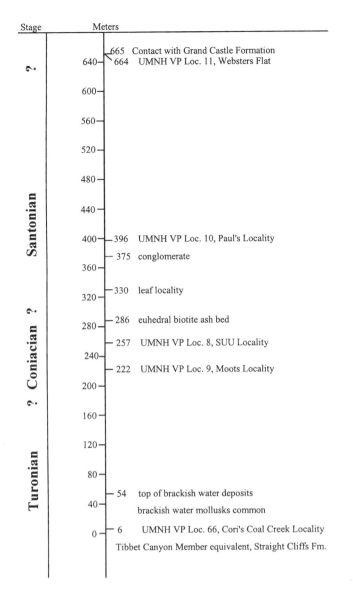

Figure 2. *The stratigraphic position of marker beds and fossil localities in the Cretaceous section of Cedar Canyon above the regressive sandstone equivalent to the Tibbet Canyon Member of the Straight Cliffs Formation.*

The 600 meters of Cretaceous strata (figure 2) overlying the brackish water deposits are lithologically indistinguishable. The strata consist of variegated mudstones and channel sandstones and we have been unable to find lithologic characteristics or breaks which allow us to distinguish the Straight Cliffs, Wahweap, or Kaiparowits lithologies as defined in their type areas. About 375 meters above the top of the regressive sandstone (figure 2) is a conglomerate (the only one observed in the section) which Edward G. Sable (U.S. Geological Survey, personal communications, 1994) considers to represent the uppermost member of the Straight Cliffs Formation (the Drip Tank Member). If this equivalency is correct, then most of the remaining 275 meters of Cretaceous strata should be equivalent to the Wahweap Formation.

One of the localities discussed here, UMNH VP Locality 10, is 20 meters above the conglomerate (figure 2) and contains a diverse fauna that will have a direct bearing on the correlation of the conglomerate.

Nichols (1997), in a study of the palynomorphs from the Cretaceous section in Cedar Canyon, suggested that the Cretaceous section is no younger than Santonian. The age of the Wahweap Formation is considered to be early Campanian based on comparison to the Milk River mammalian fauna (Eaton and Cifelli, 1988; Eaton, 1991), but there has been no study of the palynomorphs from the Wahweap Formation on which to base a direct comparison. Furthermore, Dennis Braman (personal communication, 1997) considers the upper part of the Milk River Formation (lower part of the Deadhorse Coulee Member from which the Milk River fauna was collected) to be latest Santonian in age. As such, it is currently difficult to distinguish late Santonian or early Campanian ages based on vertebrates alone.

The section is lithologically similar to the top where there is another vertebrate locality, UMNH VP Locality 11 (figure 2). This locality should serve as an upper age constraint for the Cretaceous rocks present on the Markagunt Plateau. The uppermost Cretaceous rocks are unconformably overlain by the Grand Castle Formation, of Paleocene age (Goldstrand, 1994).

Cretaceous rocks of the Iron Springs Formation are present in fault-bounded canyons to the north of Cedar Canyon and Cedar Breaks National Monument. How these two quite lithologically different and, at least in part, age-equivalent Cretaceous sequences lie in such close geographic proximity is unknown. These sections found along the northwestern margin of the Markagunt Plateau are discussed in the chapter on the Iron Springs Formation in this volume.

VERTEBRATE FAUNAS AND AGE

The localities in this 600-meter sequence of lithologically similar rocks are discussed in ascending stratigraphic order (figure 2). Over this range of thickness it is likely that at least some of these localities represent different stages. Most study to date has addressed the mammals, and other groups are listed as "unstudied" so that researchers are aware that these are available for study.

UMNH VP Locality 66

Locality 66 (see figure 2; table 1) occurs just above the Tibbet Canyon Member equivalent of the Straight Cliffs Formation. It contains abundant brackish molluscs and marks an embayment formed behind the regressing beaches (Tibbet Canyon Member) of the Greenhorn Sea. Regression of the Greenhorn cycle occurs in the middle-late Turonian (Eaton, 1991) and the mollusks are comparable to those found in the base of the Smoky Hollow Member of the Straight Cliffs Formation to the east along the western margin of the Kaiparowits Plateau (Eaton and others, 1997). For this reason, we are confident of a Turonian (middle?) age for this locality.

Table 1. *Vertebrate Fauna of UMNH VP Locality 66, Cori's Crow Creek Brackish Site.*

Class Condrichthyes
   Order Rajiformes
      Suborder Rhinobatoidei
         Family indet.
         Family incertae sedis
            Ptychotrygon sp.

Class Osteichthyes (unstudied)

UMNH VP Localities 8 and 9

Dating of the overlying localities is considerably more difficult. Locality 9 (table 2) is more than 200 meters above Locality 66 and is notable for its lack of brackish influence in its fauna. Only a single shark tooth has been recovered from the locality. This is in direct contrast to the abundant sharks (particularly *Hybodus*) found in Locality 8 (table 3), 35 meters above Locality 9 (figure 2). This is similar to the pattern found for vertebrate sites of the Smoky Hollow Member on the Kaiparowits Plateau (middle or late Turonian; Eaton, 1991) which show little brackish influence and in which shark teeth are very rare. Subsequent marine transgression occurs early in the Coniacian as recorded in the John Henry Member of the Straight Cliffs Formation, with a north-south oriented strandline stabilizing in about the middle of the present Kaiparowits Plateau during the Santonian (Eaton, 1991). The vertebrate localities in the John Henry Member demonstrate strong brackish affinities (Eaton and Cifelli, 1988) and contain abundant sharks. For this reason it is thought that Locality 9 may represent the late Turonian or early Coniacian and Locality 8 may mark the transgression of the epeiric seaway during the Coniacian.

UMNH VP Locality 10

Locality 10 is 140 meters above Locality 8 and it is difficult to establish the age of this fauna. Some 75 isolated teeth and tooth fragments of multituberculates have

---

Table 2. *Vertebrate Fauna of UMNH VP Locality 9, Moots Locality.*

Class Condrichthyes (unstudied)
Class Osteichthyes (unstudied)
   Order Lepisosteiformes
      Family Lepisosteidae
         cf. *Lepisosteus* sp. indet.
Class Reptilia
   Order Chelonia (unstudied)
      Family incertae sedis
         cf. *Naomichelys* sp.
   Order Squamata (unstudied)
   Order Crocodylia (unstudied)
Class Mammalia
   Order Marsupialia
      Family Alphadontidae
         Alphadon sp.

Table 3. *Vertebrate Fauna of UMNH VP Locality 8, SUU Locality.*

Class Chondrichthyes
   Order Hybodontiformes
      Family Hybodontidae
         Hybodus sp.
      Family Polyacrodontidae
         Lissodus sp.
      Family Ginglymostomatidae
         cf. *Cantioscyllium* sp.
   Suborder Rhinbatoidea indet.
Class Osteichthyes (unstudied)
Class Reptilia
   Order Chelonia (unstudied)
   Order Crocodylia (unstudied)
   Order Squamata (unstudied)
   Subclass Dinosauria (unstudied)
Class Mammalia
   Order Multituberculata indet.
   Order Marsupialia
      Family Alphadontidae
         Alphadon indet.

---

been recovered to date from the locality (table 4). Of these, 36 are complete enough to be referred to genus. These teeth represent p4, m1, m2, M1, and M2. Only three partial and one complete P4's have been recovered and, because of their fragmentary nature, reference to a lower taxon was not attempted.

Two left m1's (UMNH VP 5615 and VP 6914) and, less certainly, an m2 (UMNH VP 5613) and an M2 (UMNH VP 5620), may be referable to *Cimolomys*. Although comparable in width, the two m1's from Paul's Locality are only 70% the length of the smallest m1's of either *C. clarki* or *C. gracilis* (Montellano, 1992). The greater width of these two m1's results at least in part from a narrow, minutely cuspidate cingulum along the posterolabial and anterolabial margins of these teeth. Clemens (1963) reported a similarly positioned postero-

Table 4. *Vertebrate Fauna of UMNH VP Locality 10, Paul's Locality.*

Class Condrichthyes (unstudied)

Class Osteichthyes (unstudied)
Order Clupeiformes
  Family Elopidae indet.

Class Reptilia
Order Chelonia (unstudied)
  Family Neurankylidae
    Compsemys sp.
  Family incertae sedis
    Naomichelys sp.

Order Squamata
  Family Teiidae
    Chamops segnis Gilmore, 1928
    Leptochamops denticulatus (Gilmore, 1928)
    Meniscognathus sp., cf. *M. altmoni* Estes, 1964
  Family Anquidae
    Odaxosaurus sp., cf. *O. piger* (Gilmore, 1928)
  Family Scinidae
    Contogenys sp., cf. *C. sloani* Estes, 1969
  Family incertae sedis
    Litakis gilmori Estes, 1964
Subclass Dinosauria

Order Saurishchia
  Suborder Theropoda
    Family ?Dromaeosauridae indet.
    Family ?Tyrannosauridae
      ?Aublysodon sp.
      ?Tyrannosauridae indet.
  Suborder Ornithopoda
    Family Hadrosauridae indet.

Class Mammalia
Order Multituberculata
  Family Cimolomyidae
    ?Cimolomys undescribed sp.
    Meniscoessus intermedius Fox, 1976
  Family Cimolodontidae
    Cimolodon nitidus Marsh, 1889
    Cimolodon similis Fox, 1971
    Cimolodon sp., aff. *C. similis* Fox, 1971
  Family incertae sedis
    Paracimexomys undescribed sp.
    Bryceomys undescribed sp.

Order Symmetrodonta
  Family Spalacotheriidae
    Symmetrodontoides sp.
Order Marsupialia
  Family Alphadontidae
    Alphadon undescribed sp. A
    Alphadon undescribed sp. B
  Family Pediomyidae
    undescribed gen.(?) and sp.
Order incertae sedis
  Family Picopsidae
    cf. *Picopsis* sp.

labial expansion or cingulum on a majority of m1's of *C. gracilis* from the Lance Formation. Fox (1971, figure 6d) referred several m1's to *?Cimolomys* sp. and noted that "on the labial side of the crown [at the level of the anterior root] some teeth display a swelling" (Fox, 1971, p. 931). Eaton (1987) noted a similar "shelf" on an m1 that he referred to *C. similis* (p. 161, figure 55A) and an m1 referred to ?Cimolomyid gen. & sp. indet. (p. 165, figure 56G).

The cusp formula for both m1's is 6:4 with a small, distinct cuspule anterior to the first external cusp on at least the better preserved specimen UMNH VP 6914. The anteriormost internal cusp is significantly shorter (height) and smaller (at base) that the other 3 internal cusps, which are approximately similar in size. The cusps on these two m1's are quite closely spaced as in *C. clarki* and *C. gracilis*, but are somewhat less crescentic. The m2 and M2 are quite worn and were referred to the two m1's only on the basis of size.

A partial left M1 (UMNH VP 5101) seems best referred to *Meniscoessus intermedius*. About two-thirds of the crown is present, with the anterior third being the part that is missing. In the posterior two-thirds that are preserved, the only differences that could be detected between UMNH VP 5101 and the M1 of *Meniscoessus intermedius* figured by Fox (1976, figure 3), are a slightly longer internal row and a more fully divided posteriormost cusp in the external row (UMNH VP 5101 is about 90% of the width of the M1 of *Meniscoessus intermedius* reported by Fox, 1976). UMNH VP 5101 possesses accessory cusps, which is characteristic of, but not restricted to, species of *Meniscoessus*. *Meniscoessus intermedius* is restricted to the Judithian (Fox, 1976, Oldman Formation; Lillegraven and McKenna, 1986, "Mesaverde" Formation) and possibly the "Edmontonian" (Flynn, 1986, Fruitland Formation).

A p4 (UMNH VP 5106) lacking only the roots and the bottom margin of the anteroventral lobe, and a right M1 (UMNH VP 5917) resemble comparable teeth referred to *Cimolodon nitidus*. UMNH VP 5106 has 12 serrations, 10 labial external ridges, and 10 internal ridges; wear may have obliterated one or, possibly, two additional labial ridges. These numbers, along with the size and high arcuate shape of UMNH VP 5106, place it well within the norms of p4's of *Cimolodon nitidus* known from Lancian localities (Clemens, 1963; Lillegraven, 1969; Archibald 1982). For the most part, this is also true of the M1 (UMNH VP 5917). This tooth falls near the upper size range of *C. nitidus* and has a cusp formula of 7:6:5+. The only way in which this is somewhat atypical for M1's of *C. nitidus* is the lower medial cusp count of six. The anteriormost medial cusp is grooved, suggesting the beginning of separation into two cusps. Clemens (1963) noted that, if the internal cusp row is notably longer than 50% of the medial row, the internal row has a constriction near the midpoint of the tooth. Anterior to this constriction, the internal row is composed of very small cuspules. This is the case in UMNH VP 5917. *Cimolodon nitidus* is restricted to Lancian local faunas. It has also been described from the St. Mary River Formation (Sloan and Russell, 1974) and is present in the Williams Fork Formation (Diem, personal observation), both of which are questionably "Edmontonian" in age.

The following teeth are referred to *Cimolodon similis*: right p4 (UMNH VP 6915); right m1 (UMNH VP 6911); right m2 (UMNH VP 6911); right M1 (UMNH VP 6912), anterior half M1 (UMNH VP 6910), and left M1 (UMNH VP 6916); left M2 (UMNH VP 6929). The p4, UMNH VP 6915, has 12 serrations, 10 external ridges, and 10 internal ridges. Wear may have obliterated one or, possibly, two additional labial ridges. These numbers and the high arcuate shape of UMNH VP 6915 are similar to the two p4's assigned to *C. similis* by Fox (1971). UMNH VP 6915 is, however, about 10% larger than the largest (and type) of the two p4's referred to *C. similis* and the smallest p4 referred to *C. electus* (Fox, 1971). Cusp formulae of the above specimens are as follows, 6?:3 for m1, 4:2 for m2, 5:6:3 for two M1's, and R?:3:3? for M2. These are in general agreement with the formulae given by Fox (1971) except that in the Utah specimens: m1 has one less internal row cusp; M1 has one less medial and one less internal row cusp; and M2 may have one less internal row cusp, but this single M2 has considerable dental attrition. All of the Utah molars match or are within 10% of the sizes for comparable molars for given *C. similis* by Fox (1971), except for the length of the single Utah M2, which is about 15% shorter. The descriptions of teeth of *C. similis* given by Fox (1971) match those of the Utah specimens in so far as they can be compared. *Cimolodon similis* is restricted to Aquilan local faunas.

The m1 (VP 6911) displays the same "shelf" (the appearance is the result of the anterolabial and posterolabial cingula) as seen on the larger m1's referred to *?Cimolomys* sp. (UMNH VP 5615 and VP 6914). These three molars are similar, except for the one less internal cusp on VP 6911. The additional anterior cusp on UMNH VP 5615 and UMNH VP 6914 is significantly smaller than the other 3 internal cusps (which are all approximately equal in height and size). The presence of this cusp/cuspule seems correlated with size. Thus, these 3 m1's may not belong to two separate genera, but possibly to two differently sized species within the same genus. We are more confident that UMNH VP 6911 has been correctly identified as *C. similis*, it seems possible that what we call *?Cimolomys* above may be another species of *Cimolodon*.

The following teeth share similarities with *Cimolodon similis*: worn right p4 lacking the very upper margin (UMNH VP 7428); anterior half of a right p4 (UMNH VP 6913); right m1 (UMNH VP 5111); two right (UMNH VP 6908, VP 6925) and one left (UMNH VP 6922) m2's; two right M1's (UMNH VP 5110, VP 6917); three left M2's (UMNH VP 5636, VP 6903, VP 6906). Neither p4 is complete, but the number of serrations is estimated as 12. The number of serrations relative to size and the relatively high arcuate profile suggest that these p4's more likely belong to a species of *Cimolodon* than a taxon such as *Paracimexomys* or *Cimexomys*. The estimated sizes of these p4's would place them at the lowest end of the size range (only two teeth) reported by Fox (1971) for *C. similis*, thus they might be referable to *C. similis*, which is more positively identified from Locality 10. The one p4 (UMNH VP 6915) referred to *C. similis* from Locality 10 is, however, 20% larger than either of the other two partial p4's (UMNH VP 6913 and VP 7429). Thus, we hesitate to include these smaller p4's in the *C. similis* sample, although they may be large enough to be included. UMNH VP 6913 is very similar to the cast of MNA (Museum of Northern Arizona) V6347 (described in Eaton, 1995), which was assigned to genus and species undetermined. The relative height of the first, second, and third serrations may fall within the range of variation of *C. similis*, but more comparisons are required.

Cusp formulae of the above specimens is as follows, 6:4 for m1, 3-4:2 for two m2's, 4-5:6:R-5(4 very small) for two M1's, and 1:3:3 for three M2's. With two exceptions, these cusp formulae are the same or less by one than those given previously for *C. similis* from Locality 10. The two exceptions in *Cimolodon* sp., aff. *C. similis* are the presence of four rather than three internal row cusps on m1's and the presence of one cusp with as many as four small cuspules on the internal cusp row of M1. All of the molars assigned to *Cimolodon* sp., aff. *C. similis* range from 55 to 65% of the size of the comparable molars in *C. similis* from both Locality 10 and Alberta (Fox, 1971).

The M1's of *Cimolodon* sp., aff. *C. similis* from Locality 10 were compared to a photograph kindly provided by Anne Weil (written communication, 1996) of an M1 of an unpublished new genus and species from the Terlingua local fauna, Big Bend, Texas. The Terlingua local fauna is regarded as middle Campanian (Judithian) in age (Rowe and others, 1992). More detailed comparisons are required, but *Cimolodon* sp., aff. *C. similis* from Locality 10 and the new genus and species from Texas may be the same. One notable difference between the M1's from Locality 10 and the M1 from Texas is the internal row of cusps; UMNH VP 5110 and VP 6917 have poorly defined cusps (more reminiscent of a ridge), whereas the M1 from the Terlingua local fauna has four well-defined cusps on the internal row. The poorly defined cusps and the anterior convergence of the medial and external row of cusps may indicate affinities with *Cimexomys* rather than *Cimolodon*. There is very little doubt (when uppers and lowers are occluded) that the M1's and m1 herein referred to *Cimolodon* sp., aff. *C. similis* are from the same species; UMNH VP 5110 and VP 5111 may be from the same individual.

A species of *Paracimexomys* is represented at Paul's Locality by a partial left p4 (UMNH VP 7430), one left (UMNH VP 5631) and three right (UMNH VP 5180, VP 5623, VP 6907) m1's, a complete left M1 (UMNH VP 6944) and the posterior half of a left M1 (UMNH VP 5163); and one left (UMNH VP 6920) and one right M2 (UMNH VP 5614). The partial left p4 lacks the very posterior end. It has eight serrations preserved; there could have been as many as 10. This p4 is about 10% smaller than the two partial p4's referred to *Cimolodon* sp., aff. *C. similis*. It appears to have a slightly less arcuate profile. On the basis of its smaller size and less arcuate profile, it is referred to *Paracimexomys*, although referral to *Cimexomys* is also possible. Cusp formulae of the above specimens are as follows: 4:3 for four m1's, 3:4:1 for one M1, 1:3:4? for two M2's. These cusp formulae are the same as comparable teeth of *Paracimexomys* sp., cf. *P. robisoni* and *Paracimexomys* sp. from the upper Cenomanian Dakota Formation of Utah (Eaton, 1995) and comparable teeth of *Paracimexomys* sp., cf. *P. robisoni* from the middle or upper Turonian Smoky Hollow Member of Utah (Eaton, 1995), and are the same or lower (especially M1) than for other, later species of *Paracimexomys* (Archibald, 1982; Montellano, 1992). The teeth from Locality 10 are about 25% larger than those from the Dakota Formation, about the same size as those from the Smoky Hollow Member, but are about 20% smaller than the next larger species, *P. priscus*. The specimens from Locality 10 cannot be referred to any named species of *Paracimexomys* without expanding known size ranges or cusp formulae for these species. These differences suggest that an undescribed species of *Paracimexomys* is present at Locality 10 and may be the same species as present in the Turonian Smoky Hollow Member.

A lower left m1 (UMNH VP 6933) and m2 (UMNH VP 6918) are referable to *Bryceomys*. The slightly worn m1 has a cusp formula 5:3 and the slightly worn m2 has a cusp formula of ?3:2. The uncertainty in cusp formula is caused by slight wear of the posteriormost, ridge-like cusp in the external row. If unworn, there might be an additional cusp, resulting in a count of four for the external row. Of the two species of *Bryceomys* named by Eaton (1995), *B. fumosus* and *B. hadrosus*, the specimens from Locality 10 most closely resemble m1's and m2's referred to *B. hadrosus*. On m1's of *B. hadrosus* (and to a lesser extent in *B. fumosus*) and in UMNH VP 6933 the penultimate and ultimate posterior cusps in the exterior row are incompletely divided and are smaller than the preceding cusps in the same row. Also, on m1's of *B. hadrosus* (and to a lesser extent in *B. fumosus*) and on UMNH VP 6933, the first cusp in the external row is smaller, more conical, and positioned lower than the other cusps in either rows. The m2, UMNH VP 6918, is less confidently referred to *Bryceomys*. It lacks the very small posterior third cusp seen in the internal row on the m2 referred to *B. hadrosus*. Although referable to *Bryceomys*, the specimens from Locality 10 are 20% larger than comparable teeth of *B. fumosus*, but 25% smaller than comparable teeth referred to *B. hadrosus*. These considerable differences in size suggest that an undescribed, intermediate-sized species of *Bryceomys* is present at Locality 10.

The multituberculates from Locality 10 probably represent seven different taxa. Six of the taxa offer conflicting age assessments for Paul's Locality, while the seventh, ?*Cimolomys* undescribed sp. is not of any aid for age assessment. An early Campanian (Aquilan) or older age is suggested by the presence of an undescribed species of *Bryceomys*, a genus known from only the middle or late Turonian (Eaton, 1995; but there are possible younger occurrences, see papers on the Kaiparowits and Paunsaugunt plateaus, this volume). *Cimolodon similis* is known from only the early Campanian (Aquilan) of Alberta (Fox, 1971). The undescribed species of *Paracimexomys* has teeth similar to those from the middle or late Turonian of Utah (Eaton, 1995). A middle Campanian (Judithian) age is suggested by the presence of *Meniscoessus intermedius* known from only the middle Campanian (Judithian) of Alberta (Fox, 1976) and Wyoming (Lillegraven and McKenna, 1986), and possibly from the late Campanian/early Maastrichtian ("Edmontonian") of New Mexico (Flynn, 1986). *Cimolodon* sp., aff. *C. similis* may be known elsewhere from the middle Campanian (Judithian) of Texas (represented by a new genus and species, Anne Weil, personal communication, 1996). A late Maastrichtian (Lancian) age is suggested by the presence of *Cimolodon nitidus*, best documented from Wyoming (Clemens, 1963), Montana (Archibald, 1982), and Alberta (Lillegraven, 1969), but also reported from the "Edmontonian" (Sloan and Russell, 1974; Diem, personal observation). Except for the probable occurrence of *Cimolodon nitidus*, the other multituberculate taxa argue for an age bracketed by the early through middle Campanian (Aquilan - Judithian), but possibly closer to an early Campanian (Aquilan) age.

There are relatively few complete therian molars from this locality and three of them are of symmetrodonts. Symmetrodonts have been previously reported from the Smoky Hollow Member (Cifelli, 1990) through the Wahweap Formation (Cifelli and Madsen, 1986) of southern Utah. In the paper on the Kaiparowits Formation in this volume, a single symmetrodont lower molar is reported, but symmetrodonts must be extremely rare in the Kaiparowits Formation considering the huge volumes of Kaiparowits matrix that have been processed relative to any other unit (see Eaton and Cifelli, 1988).

A single pediomyid upper tooth is present in Locality 10. This tooth (UMNH VP 5140, figure 3A) looks somewhat like what has traditionally been figured as a DP3 in Clemens (1966) and Lillegraven (1969); however, this tooth is strongly rooted and may actually represent a very primitive M1. The occurrence of pediomyids in this sequence is further discussed below.

Two species of *Alphadon* are present in the fauna and are represented by both upper and lower molars. Stylar cusp C is completely absent in the upper molars of the larger species and cusp C and D are subequal and small in the smaller species.

A single upper molar (UMNH VP 5144, figure 3B) very similar to *Picopsis* as described by Fox (1980) from the early Campanian Milk River Formation is known from Locality 10. This taxon is also reported from the Smoky Hollow Member of the Straight Cliffs Formation (see Kaiparowits Plateau chapter in this volume).

This fauna compares most closely to the Milk River fauna (Aquilan North American Land-Mammal "Age") based on the common occurrence of symmetrodonts, the presence of *Cimolodon similis*, *Picopsis*, species of *Paracimexomys* and *Bryceomys* similar to Turonian

forms, and the co-occurrence of the turtle *Naomichelys*, which has brackish affinities and is unknown from the Kaiparowits Formation (it is most common in the John Henry Member of the Straight Cliffs Formation), and *Compsemys* which is unknown until the Wahweap Formation (see Kaiparowits Plateau paper, this volume). The Wahweap fauna was considered to be early Campanian in age, but Nichol's (1997) palynomorph study suggests that Locality 10 is well within the Santonian. This suggests that either the Wahweap Formation is, at least in part, Santonian in age or that the fauna from Locality 10 is older than that recovered from the Wahweap Formation. Additional studies, particularly of the palynomorphs from the Wahweap Formation, will be needed to resolve these discrepancies.

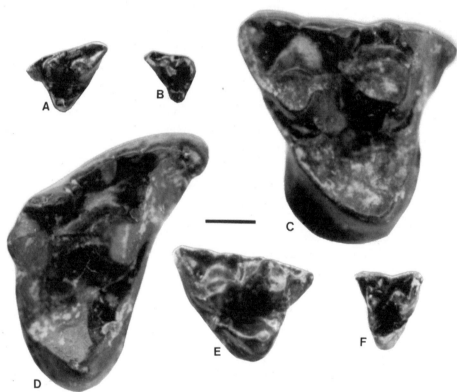

Figure 3. *A. UMNH VP 5140, Locality 10, pediomyid, LDP3?; B. UMNH VP 5144, Locality 10, cf.* Picopis *sp. upper molar; C. UMNH VP 5632, Locality 11, pediomyid, RM2?; D. UMNH VP 5634, Locality 11, RM4; E. UMNH VP 6594, Locality 11, pediomyid, RDP3?; F. UMNH VP 5634, Locality 11, cf.* Iqualadelphis *sp., upper molar. Scale bar = 1 mm.*

UMNH VP Locality 11

Locality 11, at the top of the Cretaceous section (figure 2), is even more difficult to assess age based on the vertebrate fauna (table 5). Two of the teeth from Locality 11 are included as ornithopods in the faunal list but may actually represent ceratopsians. This would represent the first occurrence of ceratopsians in the section

Table 5. *Vertebrate Fauna of UMNH Locality 11 - Websters Flat Locality.*

Class Reptilia
    Order Squamata
        Family Parasaniwidae
            Parasaniwa sp., cf. *P. wyomingensis* Gilmore, 1928
    Order Saurischia
      Suborder Theropoda
        Family ?Dromaeosauridae indet.
      Suborder Ornithopoda
        Family Hadrosauridae indet.
        Family ?Ankylosauridae indet.
Class Mammalia
    Order Multituberculata indet.
    Order Marsupialia
        Family Alphadontidae
            Alphadon sp., cf. *A. sahnii* Lillegraven and McKenna, 1986
            Alphadon sp., cf. *A. attaragos* Lillegraven and McKenna, 1986
        Family Pediomyidae
            cf. *Pediomys* undescribed sp.
        Family incertae sedis
            cf. *Iqualadelphis* sp.

and possibly imply equivalence to Wahweap or younger rocks (see Kaiparowits Plateau chapter).

Only five specimens of multituberculates have been recovered to date from Locality 11: UMNH VP 6902 is a right m2; UMNH VP 6900 and VP 6901 are left M2's; UMNH VP 6898 is the posterior half of a left M1; and UMNH VP 5102 is a fragment of a left P4. None of the specimens are very diagnostic and thus are not useful in suggesting an age for Locality 11.

The two species of *Alphadon* are of little biostratigraphic help. A taxon closest to *A. attaragos* is represented here by a very small upper molar (UMNH VP 6892, AP=1.44; LB=1.43). The type of this species is a lower molar and the species is diagnosed principally by its small size (Lillegraven and McKenna, 1986). Compared to the specimen of *A. attaragos* described by Cifelli (1990) from the Kaiparowits Formation, this taxon appears to be slightly smaller, the stylar cusps are more poorly developed, the stylar shelf is more compressed, stylar cusp C is absent, and the conules are smaller and closer to the protocone. Two other specimens (UMNH VP 5635 - M3?, UMNH VP 6897 - m2?) are morphologically very much like *A. sahnii* but are distinctly smaller.

At least one taxon of pediomyid not referable to any described taxon has been recovered from Locality 11. We are very wary of the homology between alphadontid stylar cusp nomenclature and that of pediomyids, but the issue is important particularly in regards to Fox's (1987a) assessment of pediomyid relationships. On an upper molar of the pediomyid (UMNH VP 5632, figure 3C) there are two small, subequal cuspules buccal to the paracone (stylar cusps in "B" position) and a small cus-

pule directly posterobuccal to the paracone. There is a large, well-developed cusp (tallest of the stylar cusp series) in approximately the "C" position. There are two small swellings posterior to the cusp in the "C" position. An M4 of the same taxon (and possibly the same individual) has also been recovered (UMNH VP 5634, figure 3D) which has a series of five well-developed stylar cusps.

A possible DP3 of the same species of pediomyid has also been recovered (UMNH VP 6594, figure 3E). The tooth is much longer anteroposteriorly (2.89 mm) than it is linguobuccally (2.34 mm). Unusual on this specimen is that the paracone, even though the tip is broken, appears to have been both taller and larger than the metacone. There is a very narrow stylar shelf buccal to the paracone. A single stylar cusp is present just posterior to the centrocrista notch (approximately in the "C" position). Another cusp is present posterolabial to the metacone (in the "D" position?).

Although these teeth appear to represent pediomyids, and closer to Milk River pediomyids (based on illustrations in Fox, 1987a) than to Lancian pediomyids, the stylar cusp in the "C" position is problematic. These pediomyids are not at all like *Pediomys elegans* which Fox (1987a) suggested may not be a true pediomyid because of the presence of the stylar cusp in the "C" position. As such, these specimens could represent primitive pediomyids if stylar cusp "C" is an ancestral condition (favored here), or derived pediomyids if the absence of a cusp in the "C" position is the primitive condition.

Pediomyids are unrecorded from the Kaiparowits Plateau region (see this volume) and it is peculiar that pediomyids are relatively well represented in this very small sample from the Markagunt Plateau. This may indicate paleoecologic controls on the distribution of pediomyids.

A single upper molar (UMNH VP 5634, figure 3F) from Locality 11 is very much like *Iqualadelphis* described by Fox (1987b) from the early Campanian Milk River Formation. In Johanson's (1993) revised diagnosis of the genus it is indicated that stylar cusp A is higher and larger on the occlusal surface than is stylar cusp B. In this regard only is the specimen from Locality 11 different, its stylar cusp A is distinctly lower than stylar cusp B.

The therians in this fauna do not compare closely to those described from elsewhere and the multituberculates provide no age-diagnostic data. For these reasons we consider it premature to provide an age assessment for Locality 11; however, the presence of *Iqualadelphis* may indicate that the fauna is older than those known from the Kaiparowits Formation (Judithian).

CONCLUSIONS

The 650 meters of nonmarine Upper Cretaceous strata on the Markagunt Plateau contain significant vertebrate localities. The fauna recovered from these localities appear to span the Turonian through the early(?) Campanian. The composition of these faunas is different from those of the better known age-equivalent faunas of the Kaiparowits Plateau region to the east and may provide insights regarding paleoecologic controls on the distribution of taxa as well as chronologic range extensions for many taxa,

ACKNOWLEDGMENTS

The U.S.D.A. Forest Service, and in particular Marion Jacklin, have been very supportive of our research. Two of our localities are on Southern Utah University land and their help and the assistance of Fred Lohrengel II and his students, particularly Ellen Seeley, is appreciated. Discussions with Dave Moore, Edward Sable, and Florian Maldonado of the U.S. Geological Survey were very helpful. David Ward contributed much to our quarrying and matrix processing techniques. Many of Eaton's students including Angie Nebeker, Shawn Willsey, Cori Yordi; and Dave Archibald's students Matthew Colbert, Paul Majors, Darren Barton, and Annette Harshman contributed a tremendous amount of work to this project. The Petroleum Research Fund of the American Chemical Society (30989-BG8 to Eaton) has funded this research. Richard Cifelli provided a very helpful review of the manuscript.

REFERENCES

Archibald, J. D., 1982, A study of Mammalia and geology across the Cretaceous-Tertiary boundary in Garfield County, Montana: University of California Publications in Geological Sciences, v. 122, p. 1-286.

Cashion, W. B., 1967, Geologic map of the south flank of the Markagunt Plateau, northwest Kane County, Utah: U. S. Geological Survey, Miscellaneous Geologic Investigations Map I-494, scale 1:62,500.

Cifelli, R. L., 1990, Cretaceous mammals of southern Utah. III. Therian mammals from the Turonian (early Late Cretaceous): Journal of Vertebrate Paleontology, v. 10, p. 332-345.

Cifelli, R. L., and Madsen, S. K., 1986, An Upper Cretaceous symmetrodont (Mammalia) from southern Utah: Journal of Vertebrate Paleontology, v. 6, p. 258-263.

Clemens, W. A., 1963, Fossil mammals of the type Lance Formation, Wyoming. Part I. Introduction and Multituberculata: University of California Publications in Geological Sciences, p. 1-102.

—1966, Fossil mammals of the type Lance Formation. Part II. Marsupialia: University of California Publications in Geological Sciences, v. 62, p. 1-122.

Doelling, H. H., and Davis, F. D., 1989, The geology of Kane County, Utah: Utah Geological and Mineral Survey Bulletin 124, 192 p., 10 pl.

Eaton, J. G., 1987, Stratigraphy, depositional environments, and age of Cretaceous mammal-bearing rocks in Utah, and systematics of the Multituberculata (Mammalia): Boulder, University of Colorado, Ph.D. dissertation, 308 p.

—1991, Biostratigraphic framework for the Upper Cretaceous rocks of the Kaiparowits Plateau, southern Utah: *in* Nations, J.D., and Eaton, J.G., editors, Stratigraphy, depositional environments, and sedimentary tectonics of the western margin, Cretaceous Western Interior Seaway: Geological Society of America Special Paper 260, p. 47-63

—1995, Cenomanian and Turonian (early Late Cretaceous) multituberculate mammals from southwestern Utah: Journal of Vertebrate Paleontology, v. 15, p. 761-784.

Eaton, J. G., and Cifelli, R. L., 1988, Preliminary report on Late Cretaceous mammals of the Kaiparowits Plateau, southern Utah: University of Wyoming, Contributions to Geology, v. 26, p. 45-55.

Eaton, J. G., Kirkland, J. I., Hutchison, J. H., Denton, Robert, O'Neill, R. C., and Parrish, J. M., 1997, Nonmarine extinction across the Cenomanian-Turonian boundary, southwestern Utah, with a comparison to the Cretaceous-Tertiary extinction event: Geological Society of America Bulletin, v. 109, p. 560-567.

Eaton, J. G., and Nations, J. D., 1991, Introduction; tectonic setting along the margin of the Cretaceous Western Interior Seaway, southwestern Utah and northern Arizona, *in* Nations, J. D., and Eaton, J. G., editors, Stratigraphy, depositional environments, and sedimentary tectonics of the western margin, Cretaceous Western Interior Seaway: Geological Society of America Special Paper 260, p. 1-8.

Flynn, L.J., 1986, Late Cretaceous mammal horizons from the San Juan Basin, New Mexico: American Museum Novitates, no. 2845, p. 1-30.

Fox, R.C., 1971, Early Campanian multituberculates (Mammalia: Allotheria) from the upper Milk River Formation, Alberta: Canadian Journal of Earth Sciences, v. 8, p. 916-938.

—1976, Cretaceous mammals (*Meniscoessus intermedius*, new species, and *Alphadon* sp.) from the lowermost Oldman Formation, Alberta: Canadian Journal of Earth Sciences, v. 13, p. 1216-1222.

—1980, *Picopsis pattersoni*, n. gen. and sp., an unusual therian mammal from the Upper Cretaceous of Alberta, and the classification of primitive tribosphenic mammals: Canadian Journal of Earth Sciences, v. 17, p. 1489-1498.

—1987a, Palaeontology and the early evolution of the marsupials, *in* Archer, Michael, editor, Possums and oppossums-- studies in evolution; Sidney, Surrey Beatty & Sons and the Royal Zoological Society of New South Wales, p. 161-169.

—1987b, An ancestral marsupial and its implications for early marsupial evolution, *in* Currie, P. J., and Koster, E. H., editors, Fourth symposium on Mesozoic terrestrial ecosystems: Occasional Paper of the Tyrrell Museum of Palaeontology, no. 3, p. 101-105.

Gregory, H. E., 1950a, Geology of eastern Iron County, Utah: Utah Geological and Mineralogical Survey Bulletin 37, 153 p.

—1950b, Geology and geography of the Zion Park Region, Utah and Arizona: U.S. Geological Survey Professional Paper 220, 200 p.

Goldstrand, P. M., 1994, Tectonic development of Upper Cretaceous to Eocene strata of southwestern Utah: Geological Society of America Bulletin, v. 106, p. 145-154.

Gustason, E. R., 1989, Stratigraphy and sedimentology of the middle Cretaceous (Albian-Cenomanian) Dakota formation, southwestern Utah: Boulder, University of Colorado, Ph.D. dissertation, 376 p.

Hintze, L. F., 1974, Geologic map of Utah: Brigham Young University Geology Studies Special Publication 2.

Johanson, Zerina, 1993, A revision of the Late Cretaceous (Campanian) marsupial *Iqualadelphis lactea*, Fox, 1987: Journal of Vertebrate Paleontology, v. 13, p. 373-377.

Lillegraven, J. A., 1969, Latest Cretaceous mammals of the upper part of Edmonton Formation of Alberta, Canada, and review of the marsupial-placental dichotomy in mammalian evolution: Paleontological Contributions, University of Kansas 50 (Vertebrata 12), p. 1-122.

Lillegraven, J. A., and McKenna, M. C., 1986, Fossil mammals from the "Mesaverde" Formation (Late Cretaceous, Judithian) of the Bighorn and Wind River Basins, Wyoming, with definitions of Late Cretaceous North American Land-Mammal "ages": American Museum Novitates, no. 2840, p. 1-68.

Montellano, Marisol, 1992, Mammalian fauna of the Judith River Formation (Late Cretaceous, Judithian), north-central Montana: University of California Publications in Geological Sciences, v. 136, p. 1-115.

Nichols, D. J., 1997, Palynology and ages of some Upper Cretaceous formations in the Markagunt and northwestern Kaiparowits plateaus, southwestern Utah, *in* Maldonado, Florian and Nealey, L. D., editors, Geologic studies in the Basin and Range-Colorado Plateau transition in southeastern Nevada, southwestern Utah, and northwestern Arizona, 1995: U.S. Geological Survey Bulletin 2153-E, p. 81-95.

Rowe, T. B., Cifelli, R. L., Lehman, T. M., and Weil, Anne, 1992, The Campanian Terlingua fauna, with a summary of other vertebrates from the Aquja Formation, Trans-Pecos Texas: Journal of Vertebrate Paleontology, v. 12, p. 472-493.

Sloan, R. E., and Russell, L. S., 1974, Mammals from the St. Mary River Formation (Cretaceous) of southwestern Alberta: Life Sciences Contributions, Royal Ontario Museum, v. 95, p. 1-21.

Brian Maebius © 1999

Lepisosteus

VERTEBRATE PALEONTOLOGY OF THE PAUNSAUGUNT PLATEAU, UPPER CRETACEOUS, SOUTHWESTERN UTAH

Jeffrey G. Eaton
Department of Geosciences
Weber State University
Ogden, UT 84408-2507

ABSTRACT

Vertebrate fossils have been recovered primarily from the stratigraphically highest Upper Cretaceous rocks on the Paunsaugunt Plateau, southern Utah. The fauna includes dinosaurs, crocodilians, turtles, lizards, and a mammalian fauna of moderate diversity; however, no chondrichthians have been recovered. The horizons that produced the vertebrate fauna have been variously referred to either the Wahweap or Kaiparowits Formations. Comparison of the mammals to those of the Wahweap and Kaiparowits Formations supports correlation with the latter. The relatively common occurrence of ceratopsian teeth, the turtle *Compsemys*, along with the absence of sharks also suggest correlation with Kaiparowits Formation faunas. Further work is required to make this correlation with certainty.

INTRODUCTION

The Paunsaugunt Plateau of southern Utah is located south of the Sevier Plateau and is bounded to the east by the Paunsaugunt fault system and to the west by the Sand Pass and Sevier fault systems (figures 1 and 2) (Eaton and others, 1993). The southern margin of the plateau is an erosional scarp formed above the Skutumpah Terrace. The Plateau is dominated by the pink and white rocks of the Claron Formation which form the resistant caprocks of the plateau and the spires and cliffs of Bryce Canyon National Park along the eastern margin of the Plateau.

Below the colorful cliff-forming rocks of the Tertiary Claron Formation is a problematic series of Upper Cretaceous rocks. The Paunsaugunt Plateau contains less than half the thickness (approximately 900 m) of Cretaceous rocks that are present immediately to the east on the Kaiparowits Plateau (approximately 2000 m) (Eaton and others, 1993). Critical to interpretation of regional tectonics is why the Cretaceous sequence on the Paunsaugunt Plateau is so much thinner than that of the Kaiparowits Plateau.

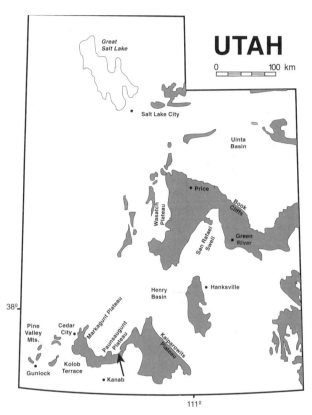

Figure 1. *Cretaceous outcrop map of Utah (based on Hintze, 1974), with arrow indicating the geographic location of the Paunsaugunt Plateau.*

STRATIGRAPHY

The presence of the Dakota Formation, Tropic Shale, and the Tibbet Canyon, Smoky Hollow, and John Henry Members of the Straight Cliffs Formation has been documented on the Paunsaugunt Plateau (Gregory, 1951; Eaton, 1993a; 1993b; Eaton and others, 1993). Difficulties arise in interpreting the equivalency of the uppermost Cretaceous rocks on the Paunsaugunt Plateau. Gregory (1951) was unable to distinguish the Straight Cliffs Formation from the Wahweap Formation and mapped them as a single unit (Ksw). Gregory (1951) placed a conglomerate high in the Cretaceous section at the base of the Kaiparowits Formation and considered it to lie unconformably on top of the combined Straight Cliffs-

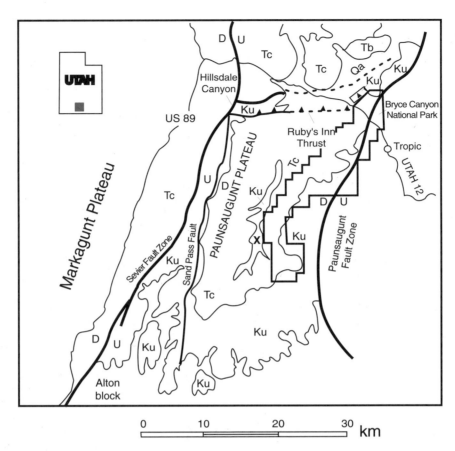

Figure 2. *Map of the Paunsaugunt Plateau area showing the major faults, distribution of undifferentiated Cretaceous formations (Ku), the Claron Formation (Cl), Tertiary basalts and other volcanics (Tb), Quaternary alluvium (Qa), and the area from which most of the Cretaceous vertebrates have been recovered (indicated by the X) (modified from Eaton, 1993a).*

Wahweap formations (Ksw). Overlying the conglomerate are gray and variegated mudstones and sandstones that Gregory included, along with the basal conglomerate, in the Kaiparowits Formation. Doelling and Davis (1989) also maintained that the Kaiparowits Formation is present on the Paunsaugunt Plateau (and to the west) and suggested that the Straight Cliffs Formation is very thin (30-80 m) on the plateau but provided no justification for this hypothesis.

Bowers (1990) and Tilton (1991) suggested that the conglomerate did not represent an unconformity at the base of the Kaiparowits Formation, but was rather the uppermost member of the Straight Cliffs Formation, the Drip Tank Member, which can be conglomeratic on the Kaiparowits Plateau (Eaton, 1991). Both Bowers (1990) and Tilton (1991) suggested that the beds immediately overlying the conglomerate belong to the lower part of the Wahweap Formation rather than to the Kaiparowits Formation. This is certainly the most parsimonious explanation as it requires only a single erosional unconformity prior to deposition of Tertiary rocks.

Goldstrand (1994), Goldstrand and others (1993), and Eaton and others (1993) suggested that the Kaiparowits Formation may be present on the plateau based on comparisons of sandstone petrology between the uppermost rocks of the Paunsaugunt and Kaiparowits Plateaus. Eaton and others (1993) suggested several possible scenarios that might preserve a remnant of the Kaiparowits Formation on the Paunsaugunt Plateau, and all of these scenarios require a major unconformity within the Cretaceous sequence on that plateau that is either absent or undetected on the adjacent Kaiparowits Plateau.

An attempt to compare the mammalian fauna recovered from the uppermost Cretaceous rocks of the Paunsaugunt Plateau to faunas from the Wahweap and Kaiparowits Formations on the Kaiparowits Plateau yielded equivocal results (Eaton, 1993a). Eaton (1993a) tentatively suggested that the fauna argues for a correlation with the fauna of the Kaiparowits Formation rather than that of the Wahweap Formation.

VERTEBRATE FAUNA

Vertebrate localities are common throughout the Cretaceous sequence on the Paunsaugunt Plateau; however, access is extremely limited and few localities have been screen-washed for vertebrates.

Vertebrates have been recovered from the Dakota

Formation along the western margin of the plateau near the town of Alton, and the mammals recovered from that locality (Museum of Northern Arizona [MNA] Locality 939) have been described in Eaton (1993b, 1995).

No vertebrates have been recovered from the Smoky Hollow Member of the Straight Cliffs Formation around the margins of the plateau, but fossils are relatively common from stratigraphically higher rocks variously interpreted to represent the Straight Cliffs or Wahweap Formations, particularly in the area of Bryce Canyon National Park (Eaton, 1994). There is no vehicular access to any of these localities as most are high on roadless cliff faces. As such, surface collection of crocodylian, dinosaur, and turtle scrap are common, but small, biostratigraphically useful materials have not been recovered until recently. A single test screen-washing of a small sample from a locality within Bryce Canyon National Park yielded microvertebrate fossils including a partial upper molar of a marsupial (Eaton, 1994). During the 1997 field season, a locality was discovered in what is unquestionably the Wahweap Formation within Bryce Canyon National Park. Eighteen sacks of matrix were hauled by backpack from this locality and processed, but at the time of this writing only a small amount of the concentrate has been picked. The material recovered to date includes mammals (a pediomyid marsupial and a multituberculate with teeth smaller than, but morphologically similar to those of *Cimolodon similis*), dinosaur, sharks, rays, turtles, and herptiles. This material will be curated into the collections at the Utah Museum of Natural History (UMNH VP Locality 77).

The vertebrate fauna described by Eaton (1993a) is from the top of the plateau in an erosional window cut through the Claron Formation into the uppermost Cretaceous rocks (figure 2). Approximately 2,000 kilograms of matrix were processed for microvertebrates. The recovered fauna includes material of dinosaurs, herptiles, and mammals which are housed at the Museum of Northern Arizona, Flagstaff (mostly from MNA Localities 1073 and 1074). An additional 4,000 kg were processed during the 1997 field season and will be curated into the collections at the Utah Museum of Natural History in Salt Lake City (mostly from UMNH VP Locality 61). The results of the 1997 field season are not included here.

Among the material discovered to date, not a single shark or ray tooth has been recovered. The turtle *Compsemys* is relatively abundant as are ceratopsian teeth. Only the mammals have been studied in detail and the list presented in table 1 is essentially the same as that presented in Eaton (1993a).

Differing from the original faunal list is the question

mark preceding *Cimexomys gregoryi*. Eaton (1995) noted the similarity of this taxon to *Bryceomys* described from the Smoky Hollow Member of the Straight Cliffs Formation. More material of the Paunsaugunt Plateau taxon would be required to confirm this synonymy.

AGE AND CORRELATION OF THE FAUNA

Eaton (1993a) considered the fauna more likely to be equivalent to a Kaiparowits (most closely correlative to the Judithian Land-Mammal "Age") than to a Wahweap (most closely correlative to the Aquilan Land-Mammal "Age") fauna. The species of *Alphadon* and *Mesodma* appear to be even younger than those known from the Kaiparowits Formation. Unfortunately, many of these species are based primarily on size and it is now clear (see paper on the Markagunt Plateau in this volume) that species of *Alphadon* and *Mesodma* appear to have had a wide range of sizes throughout the Late Cretaceous and that size alone is not a reliable taxonomic guide. *Turgidodon* was described from the Kaiparowits Formation by Cifelli (1990) and is unknown from the Wahweap Formation. This supports correlation of the fauna to that of the Kaiparowits Formation.

The presence of *Symmetrodontoides foxi* originally argued strongly against correlation to Kaiparowits faunas as symmetrodonts were completely unknown from the Kaiparowits Formation, and the type of this species was recovered from the Wahweap Formation. However, a

---

Table 1. *Mammals from the uppermost Cretaceous rocks of the Paunsaugunt Plateau.*

Class Mammalia
Order Multituberculata
Suborder Ptilodontoidea
Family Neoplagiaulacidae
Mesodma sp., cf. *M. formosa*
Mesodma sp., cf. *M. hensleighi*
Mesodma sp.
Family Cimolodontidae
Cimolodon sp., cf. *C. nitidus*
?*Cimolodon* sp.
Family Cimolomyidae
Cimolomys milliensis
Suborder and Family, incertae sedis
?*Cimexomys gregoryi*
Paracimexomys sp.
Order Symmetrodonta
Family Spalacotheriidae
Symmetrodontoides foxi
Order Marsupialia
Family Alphadontidae
Alphadon sp., cf. *A. wilsoni*
Alphadon sp., cf. *A. russelli*
Alphadon sp., cf. *A. attaragos*
Turgidodon sp. indet.

single symmetrodont tooth (probably *Symmetrodontoides)* has now been reported from the Kaiparowits Formation (in this volume).

The complete absence of sharks and rays suggests that the seaway was well to the east. The sea was at its greatest distance from the area (during the time represented by Cretaceous strata on the Kaiparowits Plateau) during deposition of the Kaiparowits Formation and sharks are unknown from that formation except near the base. Teeth of ceratopsian dinosaurs are relatively common in the uppermost Cretaceous beds of the Paunsaugunt Plateau. Although ceratopsians may have an older record (see both the Kaiparowits Plateau and Iron Springs Formation papers in this volume), they are not found commonly in this region until after deposition of the Wahweap Formation.

So in the years that have followed the original description of the fauna from the Paunsaugunt Plateau (Eaton, 1993a), the age of this fauna still remains somewhat equivocal. Localities were revisited during the 1996 and 1997 field seasons by Eaton and his students and work is planned over the next several field seasons to help resolve the age of this fauna.

The thinning of the Cretaceous section across the Paunsaugunt Plateau remains a mystery. The thinning occurs 130-150 kilometers from the thrust belt and may reflect a short wavelength forebulge associated with a zone of crustal weakness (Eaton and others, 1997); however, this is only one of many possible hypotheses and further work is needed.

CONCLUSIONS

Most of the vertebrates recovered from the Paunsaugunt Plateau are from the stratigraphically highest Cretaceous rocks. The age of the fauna is as yet uncertain, but it is either correlative to those of the Wahweap or Kaiparowits Formations (approximately correlative to the Aquilan and Judithian, respectively). Correlation with the latter is the most likely, based on the similarity of mammalian taxa to the fauna from the Kaiparowits Formation, the occurrence of abundant ceratopsian teeth along with the turtle *Compsemys*, and the absence of sharks or rays.

ACKNOWLEDGMENTS

The U.S.D.A. Forest Service, particularly Marion Jacklin, have been very helpful in all aspects of our research on the Paunsaugunt Plateau. Bryce Canyon National Park, particularly Richard Bryant, and the Bryce Canyon Natural History Association have aided our research within Bryce Canyon National Park. Jared Morrow, Patrick Goldstrand, Terry Tilton, William Bowers, and Ed Sable have all made contributions to my understanding of the plateau. The Petroleum Research Fund of the American Chemical Society (30989-GB8) is funding our current work on the plateau. I thank Anne Weil for her helpful review of the manuscript.

REFERENCES

Bowers, W. E., 1990, Geologic map of Bryce Canyon National Park and vicinity, southwestern Utah: U. S. Geological Survey Miscellaneous Investigation Series Map I-2108.

Cifelli, R. L., 1990, Cretaceous mammals of southern Utah. I. Marsupials from the Kaiparowits Formation (Judithian): Journal of Vertebrate Paleontology, v. 10, p. 295-319.

Doelling, H. H., and Davis, F. D., 1989, The geology of Kane County, Utah: Utah Geological and Mineral Survey Bulletin 124, 192 p., 10 pl., geologic map scale 1:100,000.

Eaton, J. G., 1991, Biostratigraphic framework for the Upper Cretaceous rocks of the Kaiparowits Plateau, southern Utah, *in* Nations, J. D., and Eaton, J. G., editors., Stratigraphy, depositional environments, and sedimentary tectonics of the western margin, Cretaceous Western Interior Seaway: Geological Society of America Special Paper 260, p. 47-63.

—1993a, Mammalian paleontology and correlation of the uppermost Cretaceous rocks of the Paunsaugunt Plateau, *in* Morales, Michael, editor, Aspects of Mesozoic geology and paleontology of the Colorado Plateau: Museum of Northern Arizona Bulletin 59, p. 163-180.

—1993b, Therian mammals from the Cenomanian (Upper Cretaceous) Dakota Formation, southwestern Utah: Journal of Vertebrate Paleontology, v. 13, p. 105-124.

—1994, Vertebrate paleontology of Cretaceous rocks in Bryce Canyon National Park, Utah (abstract): Geological Society of America, Rocky Mountain Section, Abstracts with Programs, v. 26, p. 12.

—1995, Cenomanian and Turonian (early Late Cretaceous) multituberculate mammals from southwestern Utah: Journal of Vertebrate Paleontology, v. 15, p. 761-784.

Eaton, J. G., Goldstrand, P.M., and Morrow, J., 1993, Composition and stratigraphic interpretation of Cretaceous strata of the Paunsaugunt Plateau, Utah, *in* Morales, M., editors, Aspects of Mesozoic geology and paleontology of the Colorado Plateau: Museum of Northern Arizona Bulletin 59, p. 153-162.

Eaton, J. G., Willsey, S. P., Yonkee, W. A., Tilton, T. L., and White, T. S., 1997, The Geometry of the Late Cretaceous Sevier foreland basin, southwestern Utah: Geological Society of America, Abstracts with Programs, v. 29, p. A-278.

Goldstrand, P. M., 1994, Tectonic development of Upper Cretaceous to Eocene strata of southwestern Utah: Geological Society of America Bulletin, v. 106, p. 145-154.

Goldstrand, P. M., Trexler, J. D., Kowallis, B. J., and Eaton, J. G., 1993, Late Cretaceous to early Tertiary tectonostratigraphy of southwest Utah, *in* Morales, Michael, editor, Aspects of Mesozoic geology and paleontology of the Colorado Plateau: Museum of Northern Arizona Bulletin 59, p. 181-191.

Gregory, H. E., 1951, The geology and geography of the Paunsaugunt Region, Utah: U. S. Geological Survey Professional Paper 226, 116 p.

Hintze, L. F., 1974, Geologic Map of Utah: Brigham Young University Geology Studies Special Publication 2.

Tilton, T. L., 1991, Upper Cretaceous stratigraphy of the southern Paunsaugunt Plateau, Kane County, Utah: Salt Lake City, The University of Utah, Ph.D. dissertation, 162 p.

VERTEBRATE PALEONTOLOGY OF THE IRON SPRINGS FORMATION, UPPER CRETACEOUS, SOUTHWESTERN UTAH

Jeffrey G. Eaton
Department of Geosciences
Weber State University
Ogden, UT 84408-2507

ABSTRACT

The Iron Springs Formation is a thick (~1,000 m) Upper Cretaceous sequence, consisting predominantly of sandstones, present in southwestern Utah. Vertebrates have recently been recovered from this formation in four areas: the Pine Valley Mountains, north of the Pine Valley Mountains, near the town of Gunlock, and Parowan Canyon. Currently the fauna is of relatively low diversity and includes specimens of dinosaurs, fishes, crocodilians, turtles, and mammals (both multituberculates and marsupials). The material recovered to date is not age diagnostic but suggests a range from Cenomanian to Santonian.

INTRODUCTION

Exposures of the Iron Springs Formation are present in southwestern Utah along the northwest margin of the Markagunt Plateau, the Pine Valley mountains region, and the area around the town of Gunlock (figure 1). The formation represents proximal deposits derived from Sevier orogenic thrust faults and consists of approximately 1,000 meters of fluvial sandstone, conglomerate, mudstones, and rare lacustrine carbonate rocks (Fillmore, 1991). In some areas, thick coal deposits are present low in the formation (Cook, 1957). Mudstones commonly contain shaley plant-bearing carbonaceous horizons. No vertebrates have been reported previously from the formation.

The formation is of Late Cretaceous age (for example, Hintze, 1986), but which stages are represented by the formation is still an open question. The sequence appears to be a proximal equivalent, at least in part, to the Upper Cretaceous sequences present on the Markagunt, Paunsaugunt, and Kaiparowits plateaus (see Eaton and Nations, 1991). Brackish water molluscan faunas located approximately 300 meters from the base of the section in the Pine Valley Mountains probably indicate maximum transgression of the Greenhorn Sea and sug-

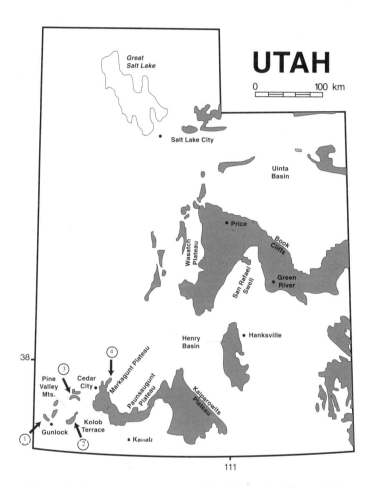

Figure 1. *Cretaceous outcrop map of Utah (based on Hintze, 1974) indicating where vertebrate fossils have been recovered from the Iron Springs Formation: 1) Gunlock area; 2) Pine Valley Mountains; 3) north of Pine Valley Mountains; and 4) Parowan Canyon.*

gest the lower third of the formation is no younger than late Cenomanian or early Turonian (Eaton and others, 1997). Eaton and Nations (1991) suggested that subsidence may have been very rapid adjacent to the Sevier orogenic belt early in the Late Cretaceous (Cenomanian through Santonian) and the major axis of subsidence may have migrated eastward to the Kaiparowits Plateau region by the Campanian. In their schematic cross section (Eaton and Nations, 1991, figure 5) it is implied that the Iron Springs may be no younger than Santonian in age.

Examination of the Iron Springs Formation for vertebrates was initiated by Eaton during the late 1980s. Eaton and James Kirkland undertook the first serious prospecting of the formation in the fall of 1990 during which bone scrap was discovered in the Gunlock area (figure 1); several localities including microvertebrate sites and a dinosaur locality were found on the west side of the Pine Valley Mountains. In 1992 some dinosaur material was recovered from high in the Iron Springs Formation in the Gunlock area. Small collections have been generated from the microvertebrate localities using screenwashing techniques. The fossils recovered from this early phase of research are housed at the Museum of Northern Arizona (MNA) in Flagstaff.

In the 1993 field season vertebrate fossils were recovered from a single locality in the Iron Springs Formation from Parowan Canyon and along the northwest margin of the Markagunt Plateau (figure 1). This locality yielded abundant turtle and fish. During the 1996 field season, two more vertebrate localities were found in Parowan Canyon that yielded sparse microvertebrate remains and ostracodes when screenwashed. The collections generated since 1993 are housed in the Utah Museum of Natural History (UMNH) in Salt Lake City. Additional mollusk and paleobotanical localities have also been recorded.

This report represents the first published record of vertebrates from the Iron Springs Formation. The study of the vertebrate fauna is very preliminary and further work within the formation is scheduled for future field seasons.

VERTEBRATE FAUNA

The Iron Springs Formation is thick (approximately 1,000 m; Fillmore, 1991) and the amount of time represented by the formation is unknown other than it appears to be restricted to the Upper Cretaceous. The outcrop areas are geographically disjunct and are often deformed by folding, faulting, and thrusting. In many areas the base of the formation is not exposed. The formation also contains little in the way of diagnostic marker beds that would aid in correlation of disjunct sections except for a distinctive layer of euhedral biotite ash independently discovered by Eaton and Florian Maldonado (U. S. Geological Survey, Denver). Several samples from different areas have been submitted for fingerprinting and isotopic dating but the analyses are not yet completed so it is unknown whether these ashes represent one or more events.

Because of the problem of correlation of the different outcrop areas of the Iron Springs Formation, each area where fossils were discovered will be discussed separately so that their stratigraphic position within the formation is not necessarily considered to imply chronologic equivalency.

Gunlock Area

The westernmost exposures of the formation abut Sevier thrust faults in the Gunlock area (figure 1). The section in this area is poorly fossiliferous. Vertebrate fossils are rare although trace fossils (usually insect burrows or nests) are commonly preserved. The only significant vertebrate fossil locality (MNA Locality 1416) from this area is near the top of the Iron Springs Formation. It produced mostly toe bones of a neoceratopsian dinosaur (identified by Michael Parrish, Northern Illinois University). Neoceratopsians are generally considered not to have appeared before the Campanian in North America (Dodson and Currie, 1990) and that seems to be consistent with the record on the Kaiparowits Plateau farther east (see Kaiparowits Plateau paper, this volume). However, knowledge of older Cretaceous dinosaurian faunas is poor in North America and Wolfe and others (1997) have reported a neoceratopsian from the Turonian of New Mexico.

Pine Valley Mountains

A few pieces of dermal armor from an ankylosaurian dinosaur were recovered from the west side of the Pine Valley Mountains (MNA Locality 1229) by Eaton and James Kirkland in 1990-91 at a site brought to our attention by Patrick Goldstrand (then at University of Nevada, Reno). Ankylosaurs occur throughout the Cretaceous of North America and this discovery is of little biostratigraphic significance.

A microvertebrate site (MNA Locality 1221) was discovered on the east side of the Pine Valley Mountains directly overlying a several-meter-thick sequence of sandstones and mudstones that contain a diverse brackish water molluscan fauna. It is likely that this very western occurrence of brackish deposits and faunas is associated with maximum transgression of the Greenhorn Sea in latest Cenomanian or earliest Turonian (Eaton and others, 1997). The locality contains at least two taxa of chondrichthians, *Hybodus* sp. and ?*Lissodus* sp. Tooth fragments indicate the presence of marsupials and multituberculates in the fauna. The only identifiable mammal from the locality is an m2 of the multituberculate *Bryceomys*. *Bryceomys* has been reported previously (Eaton, 1995) only from the Smoky Hollow Member of the Straight Cliffs Formation in the Kaiparowits Plateau region where the unit is of middle or late Turonian age. However, another taxon described by Eaton (1993) as *Cimexomys gregoryi*, from the stratigraphically highest Cretaceous rocks on the Paunsaugunt Plateau (age also uncertain, see Paunsaugunt paper in this volume), may be more properly assigned to *Bryceomys*.

Another microvertebrate site (MNA Locality 1230; UMNH Locality 12), near the top of the Iron Springs Formation at the north end of the Pine Valley Mountains, east of the town of Pinto, contains a large, unidentified rhinobatoid ray, several taxa of turtles including one comparable to *Naomichelys* sp., abundant fish and crocodiles, several kinds of dinosaur teeth including a theropod, a troodontid, and an ankylosaur(?). Tooth fragments indicate the presence of the marsupial *Alphadon*. A well-preserved first molar of the multituberculate *Paracimexomys* sp., cf. *P. priscus* was also recovered as well as that of another unidentified taxon of multituberculate. The type of *P. priscus* was described by Lillegraven (1969) from Maastrichtian deposits. The specimen from the Iron Springs Formation is too small to represent *P. priscus* which it resembles morphologically and is closer to the size range of *P. robisoni* known from both the Cedar Mountain and Dakota Formations (Eaton and Nelson, 1991; Eaton, 1995) and provides little in the way of age constraints.

Parowan Canyon

The Iron Springs Formation is also exposed in fault-bounded blocks in Parowan Canyon along the northwestern margin of the Markagunt Plateau. It is typical of Iron Springs in being dominated by thick braided stream deposits with very thin interbedded mudstones. Exactly why the Iron Springs Formation is present in that area is uncertain. Less than 20 kilometers to the south the Cretaceous sequence consists of the Dakota, Tropic, and Straight Cliffs Formations (and possibly other stratigraphically higher units, see the paper on the Markagunt Plateau in this volume) that are lithologically very different from the Iron Springs Formation. No areas of lithologic gradation have been observed; the Cretaceous sequence in both areas is capped by the Grand Castle Formation (Paleocene age; see Goldstrand, 1994), and at least part of these sequences appear to be chronologic equivalents (see below and the Markagunt Plateau paper, this volume).

Several localities are known from the Iron Springs Formation in Parowan Canyon. Three of these localities (UMNH VP Localities 6, 62, and 64) are in similar stratigraphic positions about 300 meters below the top of the formation (the base is not exposed in the canyon). Two of the localities (UMNH VP Localities 6, 62) contain

unidentified turtle fragments as well as cf. *Naomichelys* sp., a taxon which generally occurs near, or in association with, brackish waters (J. Howard Hutchison, personal communication, 1986; and see Eaton, 1990). This fragmentary turtle material is identical to shell fragments recovered from the Smoky Hollow Member of the Straight Cliffs Formation (of middle or late Turonian age) on the Kaiparowits Plateau. It is unknown if this indicates temporal or ecologic equivalence. However, *Naomichelys* is rare in the Wahweap Formation and absent in the Kaiparowits Formation to the east. This suggests that the locality is pre-Campanian. Also found at these localities are sharks (cf. *Cantioscyllium* sp.), fragments of fish including *Lepisosteus* sp., unidentified crocodiles, and multituberculate tooth fragments and premolars.

The other locality in Parowan Canyon (UMNH VP Locality 64) occurs at the very top of the Iron Springs section. Only a small sample of matrix has been screen-washed, but it has yielded delicately preserved vertebrates including a multituberculate maxillary fragment with two premolars. It has also yielded two trigonids of *Alphadon*-like lower molars, shark teeth, numerous crocodile teeth, ostracodes, and a single theropod dinosaur tooth (dromaeosaurid?). Considerable work remains to be done on this important locality.

AGE OF THE IRON SPRINGS FORMATION

There is no evidence of rocks older than the upper Cenomanian deposited in the Sevier foreland basin, and deposition begins at that time across the basin as represented by the Dakota Formation (Eaton, 1991). There is as of yet no other basis for providing a bottom limit on the age of the Iron Springs Formation. Maximum transgression of the Greenhorn Sea is recorded in the Pine Valley Mountains (Eaton and others, 1997) more than 300 meters above the base of the Iron Springs Formation, suggesting that the lower 300 meters of the formation is Cenomanian is age. Localities near the top of the Iron Springs Formation contain relatively abundant remains of turtles similar to *Naomichelys* which are rare in the early Campanian rocks of the Wahweap Formation and absent in the Kaiparowits Formation to the east. The apparent brackish water affinities of these turtles and the common presence of shark teeth suggest the Western Interior Sea was not far away. The sea underwent a major regression at the end of the Santonian with the strandline shifting more than 200 kilometers east of where the sediments of the Iron Springs Formation were being deposited.

The close proximity of the seaway suggested by the common presence of sharks and a taxon of turtle with brackish water affinities indicates that the Iron Springs Formation is no younger than Santonian. A tentative correlation of the Iron Springs Formation to other Cretaceous sequences in southwestern Utah is shown in figure 2.

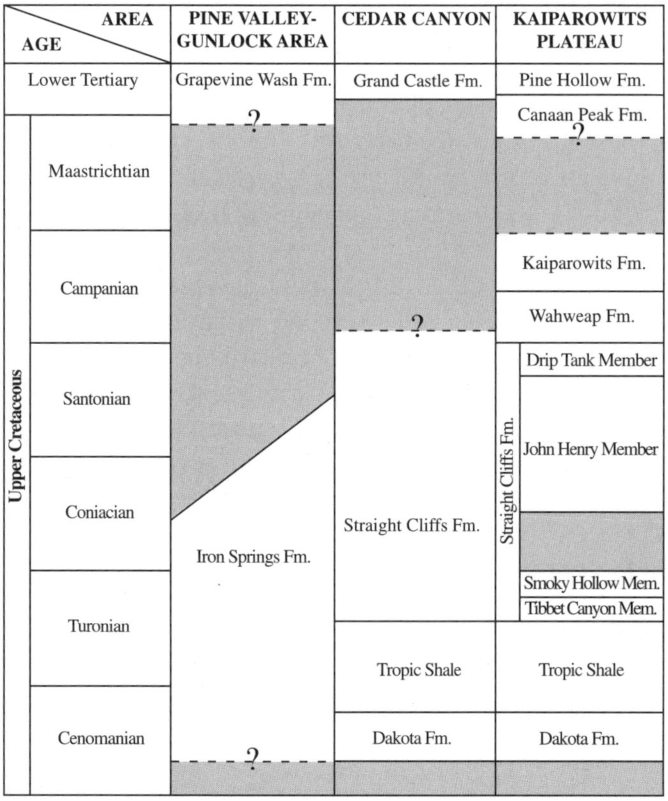

Figure 2. *Tentative correlation of the Iron Springs Formation to other Upper Cretaceous strata in southwestern Utah. Shaded areas indicate unconformities.*

CONCLUSIONS

Although the Iron Springs Formation has produced a relatively limited diversity of vertebrate taxa, it has the potential to produce significant and important fossil material. Of particular interest is the position of the formation adjacent to the Sevier orogenic thrust belt. The faunas recovered from this area will represent upland faunas relative to the coastal or lowland floodplains samples recovered from the Kaiparowits Plateau region well to the east. The fauna has the potential to reveal aspects of regional paleoecology and paleoclimatology particularly when studied in concert with invertebrate faunas and floras. The formation is tentatively considered to range from the Cenomanian through the Santonian based on regional basinal history and evidence of the proximity of the Western Interior Sea.

ACKNOWLEDGMENTS

I have been helped in the field by James Kirkland, Jared Morrow, William Little, J. David Archibald and his students. Discussions with Florian Maldonado and Patrick Goldstrand were very helpful. Funding for this research has been provided by the National Science Foundation (EAR-9004560) and the Petroleum Research Fund of the American Chemical Society (30989-GB8). The cooperation of the Bureau of Land Management and the U.S.D.A. Forest Service is greatly appreciated, especially that of Marion Jacklin who has taken a sincere interest in our research. Don Lofgren made a significant contribution to this paper as a result of his thorough and constructive review of the manuscript.

REFERENCES

Cook, E. F., 1957, Geology of the Pine Valley Mountains: Utah Geological and Mineralogical Survey Bulletin 58, 111 p.

Dodson, Peter, and Currie, P. J., 1990, Neoceratopsia, *in* Weishampel, D. B., Dodson, Peter, and Osmolska, Halszka, editors, Dinosauria: Berkeley, University of California Press, p. 593-618.

Eaton, J. G., 1990, Stratigraphic revision of the Campanian (Upper Cretaceous) rocks of the Henry Basin, Utah: The Mountain Geologist, v. 27, p. 27-38.

—1991, Biostratigraphic framework of the Upper Cretaceous rocks of the Kaiparowits Plateau, southern Utah, *in* Nations, J. D., and Eaton, J. G., editors, Stratigraphy, depositional environments, and sedimentary tectonics of the western margin, Cretaceous Western Interior Seaway: Geological Society of America Special Paper 260, p. 47-63.

—1993, Mammalian paleontology and correlation of uppermost Cretaceous rocks of the Paunsaugunt Plateau, Utah, *in* Morales, Michael, editor, Aspects of Mesozoic geology and paleontology of the Colorado Plateau, southern Utah: Museum of Northern Arizona Bulletin 59, p. 163-180.

—1995, Cenomanian and Turonian (early Late Cretaceous) multituberculate mammals from southwestern Utah: Journal of Vertebrate Paleontology, v. 15, p. 761-784.

Eaton, J. G., Kirkland, J. I., Hutchison, J. H., Denton, Robert, O'Neill, R. C., and Parrish, J. M., 1997, Nonmarine extinction across the Cenomanian-Turonian (C-T) boundary, southwestern Utah, with a comparison to the Cretaceous-Tertiary (K-T) extinction event: Geological Society of America Bulletin, v. 109, p. 560-567.

Eaton, J. G., and Nations, J. D., 1991, Introduction; tectonic setting along the margin of the Cretaceous Western Interior Seaway, southwestern Utah and northern Arizona, *in* Nations, J. D., and Eaton, J. G., editors, Stratigraphy, depositional environments, and sedimentary tectonics of the Western Margin, Cretaceous Western Seaway: Geological Society of America Special Paper 20, p. 1-8.

Eaton, J. G., and Nelson, M. E., 1991, Multituberculate mammals from the Lower Cretaceous Cedar Mountain Formation, San Rafael Swell, Utah: Contributions to Geology, University of Wyoming, v. 29, p. 1-12.

Fillmore, R. P., 1991, Tectonic influence on sedimentation in the southern Sevier foreland, Iron Springs Formation (Upper Cretaceous), southwestern Utah, *in* Nations, J. D., and Eaton, J. G., editors, Stratigraphy, depositional environments, and sedimentary tectonics of the Western Margin, Cretaceous Western Interior Seaway: Geological Society of America Special Paper 260, p. 9-25.

Goldstrand, P. M., 1994, Tectonic development of Upper Cretaceous to Eocene strata of southwestern Utah: Geological Society of America Bulletin, v. 106, p. 145-154.

Hintze, L. F., 1974, Geologic map of Utah: Brigham Young University Geology Studies, Special Publication 2, scale 1:500,000.

—1986, Stratigraphy and structure of the Beaver Dam Mountains, southwestern Utah, *in* Griffin, D.T., and Phillips, W.R., editors, Thrusting and extensional structures and mineralization in the Beaver Dam Mountains, southwestern Utah: Utah Geological Association Publication 15, p. 1-36.

Lillegraven, J. A., 1969, Latest Cretaceous mammals of the upper part of the Edmonton Formation of Alberta, Canada, and a review of the marsupial-placental dichotomy in mammalian evolution: Paleontological Contributions, University of Kansas 50 (Vertebrata 12), p. 1-122.

Wolfe, D. G., Kirkland, J. I., Denton, Robert, and Anderson, B. G., 1997, A new terrestrial vertebrate record from the Moreno Hill Formation (Turonian, Cretaceous), west-central New Mexico: Journal of Vertebrate Paleontology, supplement to No. 3, p. 85A-86A.

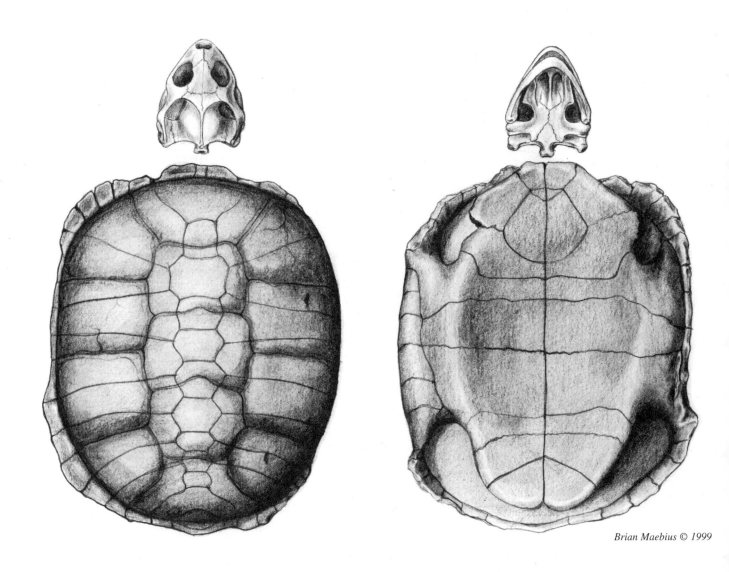

Brian Maebius © 1999

Eocene turtle

CRETACEOUS VERTEBRATE FAUNAS FROM THE KAIPAROWITS PLATEAU, SOUTH-CENTRAL UTAH

Jeffrey G. Eaton
Department of Geosciences
Weber State University
Ogden, Utah 84408-2507
jeaton@weber.edu

Richard L. Cifelli
Oklahoma Museum of Natural History and Department of Zoology
University of Oklahoma
Norman, Oklahoma 73019
rlc@ou.edu

J. Howard Hutchison
Museum of Paleontology
University of California
Berkeley, CA 94720

James I. Kirkland
Utah Geological Survey
Box 146100
Salt Lake City, UT 84114-6100

J. Michael Parrish
Department of Biological Sciences
Northern Dekalb University
Dekalb, Illinois 60115
mparrish@niu.edu

ABSTRACT

Abundant vertebrate fossils have been recovered throughout the several-kilometer-thick sequence of Upper Cretaceous strata present on the Kaiparowits Plateau. The late Cenomanian fauna from the Dakota Formation retains some Late Jurassic elements (*Glyptops* sp., *Ceratodus* sp., *Lepidotes* sp.) and the first diverse metatherian fauna. The late(?) Turonian Smoky Hollow Member of the Straight Cliffs Formation has a diverse vertebrate fauna entirely of Late Cretaceous aspect. Brackish elements are rare in this fauna due to a regression eastward of the epicontinental sea. The John Henry Member of the Straight Cliffs Formation marks a return of the epicontinental seaway into the region in the Coniacian and Santonian and contains a rich brackish fauna but only a limited record of the more fully terrestrial animals such as mammals and dinosaurs. The seaway again withdrew from the region in the late Santonian or early Campanian and the fauna is preserved in the nonmarine Wahweap Formation that correlates closely to the Milk River fauna of Canada and records the oldest certain record of eutherians in the region if not in North America. The overlying Kaiparowits Formation (Campanian, Judithian) contains the richest and most diverse record in the Late Cretaceous sequence of the Kaiparowits Plateau. The epicontinental seaway was well to the east and the formation contains a dominantly nonmarine fauna. Included in this diverse vertebrate fauna is the first occurrence of the insectivore *Gypsonictops* sp. and kinosternoid turtles.

INTRODUCTION

The Kaiparowits Plateau (figure 1) contains a thick (2 km) sequence of Upper Cretaceous, largely nonmarine rocks spanning the Cenomanian through Campanian stages (figure 2) (Gregory and Moore, 1931; Peterson, 1969a, 1969b; Eaton, 1991). The sequence formed in the foreland basin of the Sevier orogenic belt with detritus shed principally from the west and southwest (Eaton and Nations, 1991). The Cretaceous Western Interior Seaway advanced into the area from the east during the late Cenomanian. Although deeper waters withdrew from the

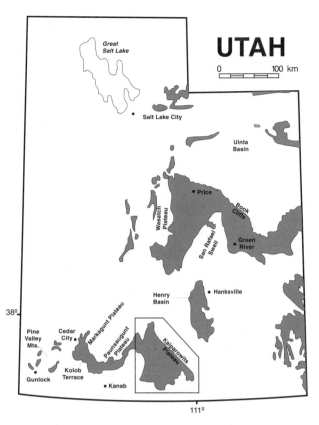

Figure 1. *Cretaceous outcrop map of Utah (based on Hintze, 1974) showing the geographic location of the Kaiparowits Plateau.*

STAGE	FORMATION	MEMBER	THICKNESS, m
Campanian	Kaiparowits		855
	Wahweap	capping ss	357-458
		upper	
?		middle	
Santonian		lower	
	Straight Cliffs	Drip Tank	295-493
Coniacian		John Henry	
Turonian		Smoky Hollow	
		Tibbet Canyon	
	Tropic Shale		186-215
Cenomanian	Dakota	upper	4-51
		middle	
		lower	

Figure 2. *Generalized stratigraphy and ages of Cretaceous units of the Kaiparowits Plateau (modified from Eaton, 1991).*

area in the Middle Turonian, there was strong marine influence on depositional sequences along the eastern margin of the plateau through the Santonian. By the Campanian, the epicontinental sea had withdrawn to a position well east of the Henry Mountains (figure 1), and there are no brackish water or marine environments recorded in the Campanian rocks of the plateau (Eaton, 1991).

The stratigraphic sequence (figure 2) on the east side of the plateau is only interrupted by marine deposits during the late Cenomanian to middle Turonian. The rest of the sequence is nonmarine and represents one of the thicker nonmarine Cenomanian-Campanian sequences in the world.

Several early reports (for example, Gregory and Moore, 1931) mention the existence of fossil vertebrates in the Cretaceous sequence of the Kaiparowits region (also see Cifelli 1990a, 1990b, for references) but, until recently, the sequence was generally regarded as barren by paleontologists. Serious work on the vertebrates in the Kaiparowits region began in the 1982-1983 field seasons when parties led by Richard Cifelli (then at the Museum of Northern Arizona) and Jeffrey Eaton (then a graduate student at the University of Colorado, Boulder) began prospecting and large-scale screenwashing for microvertebrates. The last summary paper on the fauna

of the plateau was Eaton and Cifelli (1988) and this paper represents a significant update of that preliminary report. Data were extracted from unpublished catalogues, manuscripts in preparation, comments and notes placed with specimens by a plethora of workers, and the published literature including Cifelli (1990a, 1990b, 1990c, 1990d, 1990e), Cifelli and Johanson (1994), Cifelli and Madsen (1986), Cifelli and Eaton (1987), Eaton (1987, 1993, 1995), Eaton and others (1997), Hutchison (1993), and Parrish and Eaton (1991).

Eaton was responsible for all of the multituberculate identifications and the therians from the Dakota Formation. Cifelli was responsible for all therians other than those reported from the Dakota Formation and for providing general taxonomic information on the collections housed at the Oklahoma Museum of Natural History. Hutchison has reviewed all of the turtle occurrences on the plateau, some of the marine chondrichthians from the John Henry Member of the Straight Cliffs Formation, and the bird and a few of the dinosaurs from the Kaiparowits Formation. Kirkland identified most of the nonmarine and marine chondrichthians and some of the osteichthians. Parrish reviewed most of the dinosaur material, but not all.

We also gratefully acknowledge identifications of taxa by workers who are not authors on this paper. The amphibians and squamates from the Dakota Formation and the Smoky Hollow Member of the Straight Cliffs Formation were identified by Robert Denton and Robert O'Neill (New Jersey State Museum); those recovered from the Kaiparowits Formation were identified by Robert McCord (Arizona State University); specimens from other units are only preliminarily identified and are less reliable. The crocodilians are still unstudied and probably represent the most problematic group in terms of consistency of identification.

There is considerable variation in this report as to the diversity within formations and the level of taxonomic resolution, particularly for the lower vertebrates. This is a result both of inherent variability of the fossil content of units within the sequence and the degree to which each group has been studied.

The collections upon which this report is based are housed at the Oklahoma Museum of Natural History and the Museum of Northern Arizona. Data regarding these collections may be obtained from collection managers at those institutions.

VERTEBRATE FAUNAS

Dakota Formation

The basal unit of the Cretaceous sequence rests on an unconformity of significant duration cut into the middle Jurassic Entrada Formation on the western side of the plateau and into the Upper Jurassic Morrison Formation on the eastern side. All existing evidence suggests the entire Dakota Formation is of late Cenomanian age (Eaton, 1991; 1995).

The Dakota Formation contains fluvial, paludal, lacustrine, brackish water, and marine environments. Most of the material described here was recovered from floodplain deposits, and although localities have been found in other paleoenvironments, particularly lacustrine, little work has been done on those faunas.

The fauna of the Dakota Formation (table 1) marks a transition between older faunas and those characteristic of the Late Cretaceous. Certain archaic relics of the

Jurassic such as the turtle *Glyptops* sp., and the fishes *Lepidotes* sp. and *Ceratodus* sp. are present in the fauna along with the first relatively diverse assemblage of metatherian mammals (Eaton, 1991). The dinosaurs are of relatively low diversity and dinosaur remains (even teeth recovered by screenwashing) are relatively rare in sampled localities.

Straight Cliffs Formation

The Straight Cliffs Formation spans the middle Turonian through the Santonian and is divided into four distinct members (Peterson, 1969a). The stratigraphy is summarized in Eaton (1991).

Tibbet Canyon Member

The Straight Cliffs Formation records the epicontinental sea regression in the middle Turonian Tibbet Canyon Member. The member is dominated by sandstones which represent lower shore face overlain by upper shore face deposits. The most common vertebrates recovered from this unit are sharks, but screenwashing of two deltaic localities in the upper part of the member resulted in the recovery of other vertebrates including mammals.

There has been little study of the recovered specimens from this member which includes sharks, rays, lepisosteid fishes, crocodiles, and fragmentary teeth of marsupials. Identified chondrichthians include *Chiloscyllium greeni*, *Squalicorax falcatus*, *Scapanorhynchus raphiodon*, and *Ceratodus semiplicatus*.

Smoky Hollow Member

The seaway temporarily withdrew to somewhere east of the Kaiparowits Plateau during deposition of the overlying Smoky Hollow Member. This member contains coal and some brackish paludal deposits in its basal part following the retreating shoreline eastward. The lower brackish parts have only been sampled for vertebrates in the Markagunt Plateau region (see Eaton, Diem, and others, this volume), but would undoubtedly produce brackish water fish faunas in the Kaiparowits region. The upper part of the member contains both lacustrine and floodplain paleoenvironments and has produced abundant microvertebrates.

The fauna of the Smoky Hollow Member (table 2) does not contain any of the archaic elements present in the Dakota fauna (e.g., *Lepidotes* sp., *Ceratodus* sp., *Glyptops* sp.) and is completely Late Cretaceous in composition.

Table 1. *Vertebrate fauna from the Dakota Formation.*

Class Chondrichthyes
    Order Hybodontiformes
        Family Hybodontidae
            Hybodus n. sp.
        Family Polyacrodontidae
            Lissodus n. sp.
    Order Rajiformes
        Family Rhynobatidae
            cf. *Myledaphus* n. sp.
Class Osteichthyes
    Order Periridiformes
        Family Colobodontidae
            cf. *Colobodus* sp.
    Order Semionotiformes
        Family Semionotidae
            Lepidotes n. sp.
            cf. *Semionotus* n. sp.
            cf. *Dapedius*? sp.
    Order Pycnodontiformes
        Family Pycnodontidae indet.
    Order Amiiformes
        Family Amiidae indet.
    Order Dipnoi
        Family Ceratodontidae
            Ceratodus gustasoni Kirkland, 1987
Class Amphibia
    Order Urodela
        Family Prosirenoidea
            cf. *Albanerpeton* sp.
        Family Batrachosauroididae
            cf. *Batrachosauroides* sp.
Class Reptilia
    Order Chelonia
        Family Pleurosternidae
            Glyptops sp.
        Family ?Pleurosternidae indet.
        Family Baenidae
            cf. *Dinochelys* sp.
            Baenidae gen. & sp. indet.
        Family incertae sedis
            cf. *Naomichelys* sp.
    Order Squamata
        Family Scincidae indet.
        Family Cordylidae indet.
        Family Teiidae indet.
        Family Paramacellodidae
            cf. *Saurilodon* sp.
        Family incertae sedis
            gen. & sp. indet.
        Family Anguidae indet.
    Order Crocodylia
        Family Pholidosauridae
            Teleorhinus sp.
        Family Goniopholidae
            Goniopholis sp.
        Family ?Bernissartiidae indet.
    Subclass Dinosauria
    Order Saurischia
        Family Dromaeosauridae
            Velociraptorinae indet.
            Dromaeosaurinae indet.
        Family Troodontidae
            cf. *Troodon* sp.
        Family incertae sedis
            cf. *Richardoestesia* sp.
            cf. *Paranychodon* sp.
        Family Tyrannosauridae indet.
    Order Ornithischia
        Family Nodosauridae indet.
        Family ?Ankylosauridae (or Pachycephalosauria) indet.
        Family Hadrosauridae indet.
        Family Hypsolophodontidae indet.
Class Mammalia
    Order Multituberculata
        Family Cimolodontidae
            Cimolodon sp., cf. *C. similis* Fox, 1971
        Family ?Taeniolabidoidea indet.
        Family incertae sedis
            Paracimexomys sp., cf. *P. robisoni* Eaton & Nelson, 1991
            Dakotamys malcolmi Eaton, 1995
    Order Symmetrodonta
        Family Spalacotheriidae indet.
    Order Marsupialia
        Family incertae sedis

            Dakotadens morrowi Eaton, 1993
        Family Alphadontidae
            Alphadon clemensi Eaton, 1993
            Alphadon lillegraveni Eaton, 1993
            Protalphadon sp.
        Family ?Stagodontidae
            Pariadens kirklandi Cifelli & Eaton, 1987

Table 2. *Vertebrate fauna of the Smoky Hollow Member of the Straight Cliffs Formation.*

Class Chondrichthyes
    Order Hybodontiformes
        Family Hybodontidae
            Hybodus n. sp.
        Family Polyacrodontidae
            Lissodus sp.
    Order Rajiformes
        Family Sclerorhynchidae
            Ischyrhiza sp., cf. *I. avonicola* Estes, 1964
        Family Rhynobatidae
            cf. *Myledaphus* n. sp.
    Order Orectolobiformes
        Family ?Ginglymostomatidae
            Squatirhina sp.
Class Osteichthyes
    Order Palaeonisciformes
        Family Platysomidae
            Platysomus? sp.
    Order Pycnodontiformes
        Family Pycnodontidae indet.
    Order Amiiformes
        Family Amiidae indet.
            Melvius sp.
            Amiidae indet.
    Order Lepisosteiformes
        Family Lepisosteidae
            Lepisosteus sp.
    Order Elopiformes
        Family Elopidae indet.
Class Amphibia
    Order Urodela
        Family Prosirenoidea
            cf. *Albanerpeton* sp.
        Family Batrachosauridae
            cf. *Batrachosauroides* sp.
    Order Anura
        Family Discoglossidae
            Scotiphryne postulosa Estes, 1969
        Family Pelobatidae
            Eopelobates sp.
Class Reptilia
    Order Chelonia
        Family Pelomedusidae
            Bothremys sp.
            cf. *Bothremys* sp.
        Family Baenidae indet.
        Family Pleurosternidae?
            Compsemys sp.
        Family ?Adocidae indet.
        Family Trionychidae indet.
        Family Chelydridae
            n. gen. & sp.
        Family incertae sedis
            cf. *Naomichelys* sp.
    Order Squamata
        Family Teiidae
            Chamops sp.
            Polyglyphanodon sp.
        Family Scincidae
            Contogenys sloani Estes, 1969
            Contogenys sp.
            Scincidae indet.
        Family Teiidae indet.
        Family incertae sedis
            gen. & sp. indet.
        Family Dorsetisauridae
            cf. *Dorsetisaurus* sp.
        Family Anguidae
            Odaxosaurus piger (Gilmore, 1928)
            cf. *Odaxosaurus* sp.
        Family Necrosauridae indet.
        Family incertae sedis
            gen. & sp. indet.

Order Crocodylia
   Family Pholidosauridae
     ?Teleorhinus sp.
   Family Goniopholidae indet.
   Family ?Bernissartiidae
     cf. *Bernissartia* sp.
     ?Bernissartiidae indet.
   Family Crocodylia
     Leidyosuchus sp.
     Brachychampsa sp.
Order Pterosauria
   Family indet.
Subclass Dinosauria
   Order Saurischia
     Family Dromaeosauridae
       Velociraptorinae indet.
       Dromaeosaurinae indet.
     Family Troodontidae indet.
     Family incertae sedis
       cf. *Richardoestesia* sp.
       cf. *Aublysodon* sp.
   Order Ornithischia
     Family ?Ankylosauridae indet.
     Family Nodosauridae indet.
     Family Hypsilophodontidae indet.
     Family Hadrosauridae indet.

Class Mammalia
   Order Multituberculata
     Family Cimolodontidae indet.
     Family ?Taeniolabididae indet.
     Family incertae sedis
       Paracimexomys sp., cf. *P. robisoni* Eaton & Nelson, 1991
       Bryceomys fumosus Eaton, 1995
       B. hadrosus Eaton, 1995
   Order Symmetrodonta
     Family Spalacotheriidae
       Spalacotheridium mckennai Cifelli, 1990
       Symmetrodontoides oligodontos Cifelli, 1990
   Order incertae sedis
     Family Picopsidae
       Picopsis sp.
   Order Marsupialia
     Family incertae sedis
       Dakotadens sp.
     Family Didelphidae
       Alphadon sp.
       Protalphadon sp.
       Anchistodelphys delicatus Cifelli, 1990
     Family ?Stagodontidae indet.
   Order Eutheria? indet.

John Henry Member

There was a significant transgression of the seaway that began in the mid-Coniacian and by the Santonian the strand line was established in the middle of the Kaiparowits Plateau (Eaton, 1991). Minor fluctuations in relative sea level occur throughout John Henry deposition, but in general the John Henry Member is primarily marine along the eastern margin of the plateau and brackish water to nonmarine along the western margin. Because of Cifelli's and Eaton's interest in mammals, most of the localities that have been worked are from the west side of the plateau (except for some of the sharks which were collected by Hutchison from the eastern part of the plateau). There is a large brackish component to the fauna (table 3) due to the nearby influences of the seaway, and mammals and other fully terrestrial components of the fauna are relatively rare in this member.

Drip Tank Member

The uppermost member of the Straight Cliffs Formation is the Drip Tank Member. It is composed predomi-

---

Table 3. *Vertebrate fauna from the John Henry Member of the Straight Cliffs Formation.*

Class Chondrichthyes
   Order Lamniformes
     Family Lamnidae
       Squalicorax sp., cf. *S. falcatus* (Agassiz, 1843)
     Family Mitsukurinidae
       Scapanorhynchus sp.
   Order Hybodontiformes
     Family Polyacrodontidae
       Lissodus sp.
     Family Hybodontidae
       Hybodus sp.
     Family Ptychodontidae
       Ptychodus mortoni Agassiz, 1843
   Order Orectolobiformes
     Family Brachaeluridae
       Chiloscyllium? sp.
     Family ?Ginglymostomatidae
       Squatirhina sp.
   Order Rajiformes
     Family Rhynobatidae
       cf. *Myledaphus* n. sp.
     Family Sclerorhynchidae
       Ischyrhiza sp.
     Family incertae sedis
       Ptychotrygon sp., cf. *P. triangularis* Reuss, 1845
       Pseudohypolophus sp.
Class Osteichthys
   Order Lepisosteiformes
     Family Lepisosteidae
       Lepisosteus sp.
       Atractosteus sp.
   Order Amiiformes
     Family Amiidae
       Amia sp.
       Melvius sp.
   Order Elopiformes
     Family ?Phyllodontidae
       Paralbula sp.
   Order Perciformes
     Family Palaeolabriadae
       Palaeolabrus sp.
Class Amphibia
   Order Urodela
     Family Prosirenoidea
       Albanerpeton sp.
   Order Anura indet.
Class Reptilia
   Order Chelonia
     Family Pelomedusidae
       Bothremys? sp.
     Family Baenidae
       "*Baena*" *nodosa*? Gilmore, 1916
       Baenidae indet.
     Family Adocidae
       Adocus sp.
     Family Trionychidae
       cf. *Aspideretes* sp.
     Family Nanhsiungchelyidae
       Basilemys sp.
     Family incertae sedis
       Naomichelys sp.
   Order Squamata
     Family Teiidae indet.
     Family Anguidae
       Odaxosaurus piger (Gilmore, 1928)
     Family Varanidae indet.
   Order Crocodylia
     Family Goniopholidae indet.
     Family Atoposauridae indet.
     Family Bernissartidae
       Bernissartia sp.
   Subclass Dinosauria
     Order Saurischia
       Family Dromaeosauridae
         Velociraptorinae indet.
         Dromaeosaurinae indet.
     Order Ornithischia
       Family Fabrosauridae(?) indet.
       Family Ankylosauridae indet.
       Family Hadrosauridae indet.
Class Mammalia
   Order Multituberculata
     Family Cimolodontidae

Cimolodon sp., cf. *C. similis* Fox, 1971
Family incertae sedis
     Paracimexomys n. sp.
Order Symmetrodonta
     Family Spalacotheriidae
         Symmetrodontoides sp.
Order Marsupialia
     Family Peradectidae indet.
     Family Stagodontidae indet.

nantly of sandstones deposited by braided and meandering streams (Eaton, 1991). Rare thin layers of mudstones are also present. Only water-worn fragments of turtle and crocodile have been recovered from this member. There is no basis for dating this member other than stratigraphic position.

Wahweap Formation

The sediments of the Wahweap Formation were deposited predominantly by meandering streams during the early part of the Campanian. The formation is overall not very fossiliferous, with the most productive known horizons occurring in basal lag deposits of streams. There is no evidence of either brackish water or marine deposits in the formation, as the seaway had retreated well to the east by the Campanian (Eaton, 1987; 1991). The early Campanian age is based in part on the similarity of the fauna to that reported by Fox (1971) from the Milk River Formation of Canada. The Wahweap is also correlative to the Masuk Formation to the east (Peterson and Kirk, 1975) from which palynomorphs indicate a post-Santonian age and mollusks in the underlying Blue Gate Member of the Mancos Shale indicate an age for the upper part of the member close the Santonian-Campanian boundary (Eaton, 1990).

We are following the standard application of ammonite-based zonal terminology developed by Cobban (e.g., 1993); however, a recent challenge to the orthodox correlation of North American ammonites to European stages was presented by Leahy and Lerbekmo (1995). If their evaluation is correct, then both the Milk River and Wahweap faunas may be late Santonian in age or span the Santonian-Campanian boundary.

The Wahweap fauna (table 4) is notable for the first definite occurrence of eutherian mammals in the region and, assuming contemporaneity with the upper Milk River Formation of Alberta, this occurrence represents the oldest unambiguous record of eutherians from North America, although specimens in the Smoky Hollow Member of the Straight Cliffs Formation (table 2, Order Eutheria? indet.) hint at a much earlier occurrence.

Kaiparowits Formation

This formation represents more than 800 m of Cam-

Table 4. *Vertebrate Fauna of the Wahweap Formation.*

Class Chondrichthyes
     Order Hybodontiformes
         Family Polyacrodontidae
             Lissodus sp.
         Family Hybodontidae
             Hybodus sp.
     Order Rajiformes
         Family Sclerorhynchidae
             Ischyrhiza avonicola Estes, 1964
             Ischyrhiza sp.
         Family Rhynobatidae
             cf. *Myledaphus* n. sp.
     Order Orectolobiformes
         Family Brachaeluridae
             cf. *Cantioscyllium* n. sp.
         Family ?Ginglymostomatidae
             Squatirhina sp.
Class Osteichthys
     Order Lepisosteiformes
         Family Lepisosteidae
             Lepisosteus sp.
             Astractosteus sp.
     Order Amiiformes
         Family Amiidae
             Amia sp.
             Melvius sp.
     Order Elopiformes
         Family ?Phyllodontidae
             Paralbula sp., cf. *P. casei* Estes, 1969
             Paralbula sp.
     Order Perdiformes
         Family Palaeolabridae
             Palaeolabrus sp.
Class Amphibia
     Order Urodela
         Family Batrachosauroididae
             Opisthotriton? sp.
     Order Anura indet.
Class Reptilia
     Order Chelonia
         Family Baenidae
             Baena nodosa Gilmore, 1916
         Family Pleurosternidae?
             Compsemys sp.
         Family Adocidae
             Adocus sp.
         Family Trionychidae
             cf. *Aspideretes* sp.
         Family Nanhsiungchelyidae
             Basilemys sp.
         Family incertae sedis
             Naomichelys sp.
     Order Squamata
         Family Anguidae indet.
         Family Varanidae indet.
     Order Crocodylia
         Family Atoposauridae? indet.
         Family Bernissartiidae
             Bernissartia sp.
         Family Crocodylidae
             Brachychampsa sp.
   Subclass Dinosauria
     Order Saurischia
         Family Dromaeosauridae
             Dromaeosaurinae indet.
             Velociraptorinae indet.
         Family Troodontidae
             Troodon sp.
         Family Tyrannosauridae indet.
     Order Ornithischia
         Family Hadrosauridae indet.
         Suborder Ankylosauria indet.
         Family Nodosauridae? indet.
         Suborder Ceratopsia? indet.
Class Mammalia
     Order Multituberculata
         Family Neoplagiaulacidae
             Mesodma sp., cf. *M. formosa* (Marsh, 1889)
             ?*Mesodma* sp.
         Family Cimolodontidae
             Cimolodon similis Fox, 1971
             Cimolodon electus Fox, 1971
             Cimolodon sp.
             ?*Cimolodon* sp.

Family Cimolomyidae
  Cimolomys sp., cf. *C. clarki* Sahni, 1972
  Cimolomys n. sp.
  ?Meniscoessus sp.
Family ?Cimolomyidae indet.
Family incertae sedis
  Cimexomys sp., cf. *C. antiquus* Fox, 1971
  Paracimexomys n. sp.
  Paracimexomys sp.
Order uncertain
  Family incertae sedis
    Zygiocuspis goldingi Cifelli, 1994
Order Symmetrodonta
  Family Spalacotheriidae
    Symmetrodontoides foxi Cifelli & Madsen, 1986
Order Marsupialia
  Family Peradectidae
    Protalphadon crebreforme Cifelli, 1990
    Alphadon sp.
  Family incertae sedis
    Iugomortiferum thoringtoni Cifelli, 1990
    cf. *Iugomortiferum* n. sp.
    gen. & sp. indet.
    Anchistodelphys archibaldi Cifelli, 1990
    Anchistodelphys sp.
Order Insectivora
  Family ?Nyctitheriidae
    Paranyctoides spp.

---

panian strata deposited by large rivers with broad alluvial floodplains (Eaton, 1991). Localities occur in the sandstones associated with rivers, and mudstones associated with floodplain and lacustrine environments. The Kaiparowits Formation is the most fossiliferous of Cretaceous units on the plateau.

Fossils are most common in the lower half of the formation. Eaton and Cifelli (1988) suggested that this might be an artifact of extensive badlands being well developed in the lower part of the formation, while the upper part has limited access due to steep topography controlled by the overlying Canaan Peak and Claron Formations. Although this may in part be true, work in subsequent years (by Eaton and Hutchison) suggests the upper part is actually not as fossiliferous as the lower.

When the preliminary report was published, there was an attempt made to separate the fauna of this thick formation into lower and upper faunas, but it is evident from Eaton and Cifelli (1988) that there is no significant faunal distinction; however, there is some indication of up-section change in the fauna including the first occurrences of *Paranyctoides* sp., *Gypsonictops* spp. and some marsupials such as *Alphadon attaragos* in the upper part of the section. Nonetheless, it appears this thick formation was deposited relatively quickly in a rapidly subsiding basin (Eaton, 1991).

The age of the fauna is determined mostly by palynomorphs (see Eaton, 1991; Nichols, 1997) and the lack of diagnostic Maastrichtian mammals. The stratigraphically highest locality from which significant amounts of matrix have been processed is about 200 m below the top of the formation so it is unknown if the Kaiparowits Formation could cross the Campanian-Maastrichtian boundary, but palynomorph samples (see Eaton, 1991, figure

16) appear to be Campanian in age and lack diagnostic Maastrichtian taxa (Farabee, 1991).

Perhaps most distinctive of the Kaiparowits fauna (table 5) is the first appearance of the insectivore *Gypsonictops* sp. which may be a good index fossil for the beginning of the Judithian North American Land-Mammal "Age" (see Cifelli, 1994). Among the turtles, kinosternoids and baenid *Boremys* sp. first appear, and the pleurosternid *Compsemys* is common. Sharks become much rarer, with *Ischyrhiza* sp. and *Hybodus* sp. known only from a single locality near the base of the formation (locality FB1 in Eaton and Cifelli, 1988, figure 3). The multituberculates are still very tentatively identified and do not differ greatly from the list presented in Eaton (1987). Subsequent, almost annual, collection from the Kaiparowits Formation over the past decade has made the ongoing revision of the multituberculates increasingly complex. Multituberculates from the Wahweap compare closely to forms described from the Milk River Formation, but the Kaiparowits taxa do not compare well to any fauna and include many new forms.

Table 5. *Vertebrate fauna of the Kaiparowits Formation.*

Class Chondrichthyes
  Order Hybodontiformes
    Family Hybodontidae
      Hybodus sp.
    Family Polyacrodontidae
      Lissodus sp.
  Order Rajiformes
    Family Sclerorhynchidae
      Ischyrhiza sp.
    Family Rhynobatidae
      Myledaphus bipartis Cope, 1876
  Order Orectolobiformes
    Family Brachaeluridae
      Brachaelurus? sp.
    Family ?Ginglymostomatidae
      Squatirhina sp.
Class Osteichthys
  Order Semionotiformes
    Family Lepisosteidae
      Lepisosteus sp.
  Order Amiiformes
    Family Amiidae
      Amia sp.
      Melvius sp.
  Order Elopiformes
    Family ?Phyllodontidae
      Paralbula sp.
  Order Perciformes
    Family Palaeolabridae
      Palaeolabrus sp.
  Order Acipenseriformes
    Family Acipenseridae
      Acipenser sp.
  Order Elopiformes
    Family Elopidae indet.
Class Amphibia
  Order Urodela
    Family Prosirenoidea
      Albanerpeton sp., cf. *A. nexuosus* Estes, 1981
      Albanerpeton sp.
    Family Scapherpetontidae n. gen. & sp.
    Family Sirenidae
      Habrosaurus dilatus Gilmore, 1928
  Order Anura
    Family Discoglossidae
      Scotiphryne pustulosa Estes, 1969
    Family Pelobatidae
      Eopelobates sp.

Class Reptilia
    Order Chelonia
        Family Baenidae
            Boremys pulchra Lambe, 1906
            Baena nodosa Gilmore, 1916
        Family Pleurosternidae?
            Compsemys victa Leidy, 1856
        Family Neurankylidae
            Neurankylus sp.
        Superfamily Kinosternoidea n. gen. & sp.
        Family Adocidae
            Adocus sp.
        Family Trionychidae
            cf. *Aspideretes* sp.
        Family Nanhsiungchelyidae
            Basilemys sp.
        Family incertae sedis
            Naomichelys sp.
        Family Chelydridae indet.
    Order Squamata
        Family Teiidae
            Chamops segnis Marsh, 1892
            Leptochamops denticulatus (Gilmore, 1928)
            Meniscognathus altimani Estes, 1969
            Paraglyphanodon gazini Gilmore, 1943
            cf. *Polyglyphanodon* n. sp.
        Family Anguidae
            Odaxosaurus piger (Gilmore, 1928)
            cf. *Odaxosaurus* n. sp.
            Anguidae n. gen.? & sp.
        Family Xenosauridae
            Exostinus sp.
        Family Parasaniwidae
            Parasaniwa wyomingensis Gilmore, 1928
            Parasaniwa sp.
        Family ?Helodermatidae indet.
        Family incertae sedis
            Litakis sp.
      Suborder Serpentes indet.
    Order Crocodylia
        Family Bernissartidae
            Bernissartia sp.
         Family Crocodylidae
            Brachychampsa sp.
        Family Goniopholidae indet.
    Subclass Dinosauria
    Order Saurischia
        Family Dromaeosauridae
            Velociraptorinae indet.
            Dromaeosaurinae indet.
        Family Troodontidae
            Troodon sp.
        Family Ornithomimidae
            Ornithomimus velox Marsh, 1890
        Family Tyrannosauridae indet.
    Order Ornithischia
        Family Nodosauridae
        Family Ankylosauridae
            Euoplocephalus sp.
        Family Hadrosauridae
            Parasaurolophus sp., cf. *P. cyrtocristatus* Ostrom, 1961
        Family Pachycephalosauridae
            Stegoceras sp.
        Family Ceratopsidae indet.
Class Aves
    Order Enantiornithiformes
        Family Avisauridae
            Avisaurus n. sp.
Class Mammalia
    Order Multituberculata
        Family Neoplagiaulacidae
            Mesodma n. sp., cf. *M. hensleighi* Lille graven, 1969
            Mesodma sp., cf. *M. senecta* Fox, 1971 or *M. thompsoni* Clemens, 1964
            Mesodma sp., cf. *M. formosa* (Marsh, 1889)
            Mesodma n. sp. A
            Mesodma n. sp. B
        Family Cimolodontidae
            Cimolodon sp., cf. *C. similis* Fox, 1971
            Cimolodon sp., cf. *C. nitidus* Marsh, 1889
            Cimolodon n. sp. A
            Cimolodon n. sp. B
        Family Cimolomyidae
            cf. *Cimolomys* n. sp.
            cf. *Bryceomys* n. sp.
            Cimolomys n. sp. A
            Cimolomys n. sp. B

            Meniscoessus sp.
        Family incertae sedis
            Cimexomys sp., cf. *C. judithae* Sahni, 1972
            Paracimexomys spp.
    Order Symmetrodonta
        Family Spalacotheriidae
            Symmetrodontoides sp.
    Order Marsupialia
        Family Peradectidae
            Aenigmadelphys archeri Cifelli and Johanson, 1994
            Protalphadon wahweapensis Cifelli, 1990
            Turgidodon lillegraveni Cifelli, 1990
            Turgidodon sp., cf. *T. lillegraveni* Cifelli, 1990
            Turgidodon madseni Cifelli, 1990
            Turgidodon sp.
            Alphadon halleyi Sahni, 1972
            Alphadon sahnii Lillegraven & McKenna, 1986
            Alphadon sp. cf. *A. sahnii* Lillegraven & McKenna, 1986
            Alphadon attaragos Lillegraven & McKenna, 1986
    Order Insectivora
        Family Leptictidae
            Gypsonictops spp.
        Family Palaeoryctidae
            Cimolestes sp.
        Family ?Nyctitheriidae
            Paranyctoides spp.
    Order uncertain
        Family incertae sedis
            Avitotherium utahensis Cifelli, 1990

CONCLUSIONS

The Kaiparowits Plateau contains a remarkable record of vertebrate evolution from the late Cenomanian through the Campanian. The enormous number of specimens recovered from the plateau include many new taxa and new temporal and geographic occurrences. Mammals have been the most studied of the classes and an enormous amount of work remains to be done on the lower vertebrates. New recently discovered localities that appear to be very productive suggest that the collections reported on here mark only the beginning.

ACKNOWLEDGMENTS

The Bureau of Land Management is thanked for their consistent help with permitting. Malcolm C. McKenna provided initial support for research on the plateau. This research was supported by grants from the National Science Foundation (BSR 8507598, 8796225, 8906992 to Cifelli; EAR-9004560 to Eaton); the National Geographic Society (3965-88 to Eaton; 2881-84 to Cifelli), and the Annie M. Alexander Endowment to the University of California Museum of Paleontology. We thank Phillip Murry and Thomas Williamson for their helpful reviews.

REFERENCES

Cifelli, R. L., 1990a, Cretaceous mammals of southern Utah. I. Marsupials from the Kaiparowits Formation (Judithian): Journal of Vertebrate Paleontology, v. 10, p. 295-319.

—1990b, Cretaceous mammals of southern Utah. II. Marsupials and marsupial-like mammals from the Wahweap Formation (early Campanian): Journal of Vertebrate Paleontology, v. 10, p. 320-331.

—1990c, Cretaceous mammals of southern Utah. III. Therian mammals from the Turonian (early Late Cretaceous): Journal of Vertebrate Paleontology, v. 10., p. 332-345.

—1990d, Cretaceous mammals of southern Utah. IV. Eutherian mammals from the Wahweap (Aquilan) and Kaiparowits (Judithian) formations: Journal of Vertebrate Paleontology, v. 10, p. 346-360.

—1990e, A primitive higher mammal from the Late Cretaceous of southern Utah: Journal of Mammalogy, v. 71, p. 343-350.

—1994, Therian mammals of the Terlingua local fauna (Judithian), Aguja Formation, Big Bend of the Rio Grande, Texas: Contributions to Geology, University of Wyoming, v. 30, p. 117-136.

Cifelli, R. L., and Eaton, J. G., 1987, Marsupial from the earliest Late Cretaceous of western U. S.: Nature, v. 325, p. 520-522.

Cifelli, R. L., and Johanson, Zerina, 1994, New marsupial from the Upper Cretaceous of Utah: Journal of Vertebrate Paleontology, v. 14, p. 292-295.

Cifelli, R. L., and Madsen, S. K., 1986, An Upper Cretaceous symmetrodont (Mammalia) from southern Utah: Journal of Vertebrate Paleontology, v. 6, p. 258-263.

Cobban, W. A., 1993, Diversity and distribution of Late Cretaceous ammonites, Western Interior, United States, *in* Caldwell, W. G. E., and Kauffman, E. G., editors, Evolution of the Western Interior Basin: Geological Association of Canada, Special Paper 39, p. 435-451.

Eaton, J. G., 1987, Stratigraphy, depositional environments, and age of Cretaceous mammal-bearing rocks in Utah, and systematics of the Multituberculata: Boulder, University of Colorado, Ph.D, dissertation, 315 p.

—1990, Stratigraphic revision of Campanian (Upper Cretaceous) rocks of the Henry Basin, Utah: The Mountain Geologist, v. 27, p. 27-38.

—1991, Biostratigraphic framework for Upper Cretaceous rocks of the Kaiparowits Plateau, southern Utah, *in* Nations, J. D., and Eaton, J. G., editors, Stratigraphy, depositional environments, and sedimentary tectonics of the western margin, Cretaceous Western Interior Seaway: Geological Society of America Special Paper 260, p. 47-63.

—1993, Therian mammals of the Cenomanian (Late Cretaceous) Dakota Formation, southwestern Utah: Journal of Vertebrate Paleontology, v. 13, p. 105-124.

—1995, Cenomanian and Turonian (early Late Cretaceous) multituberculate mammals from southwestern Utah: Journal of Vertebrate Paleontology, v. 15, p. 761-784.

Eaton, J. G., and Cifelli, R. L., 1988, Preliminary report on Late Cretaceous mammals of the Kaiparowits Plateau, southern Utah: Contributions to Geology, The University of Wyoming, v. 26, p. 45-55.

Eaton, J. G., Kirkland, J. I., Hutchison, J. H., Denton, Robert, O'Neill, R. C., and Parrish, J. M., 1997, Nonmarine extinction across the Cenomanian-Turonian (C-T) boundary, southwestern Utah, with a comparison to the Cretaceous-Tertiary (K-T) extinction event: Geological Society of American Bulletin, v. 109, no. 5.

Eaton, J. G., and Nations, J. D., 1991, Introduction-- tectonic setting along the margin of the Cretaceous Western Interior Seaway, southwestern Utah and northern Arizona, in Nations, J. D., and Eaton, J. G., editors, Stratigraphy, depositional environments, and sedimentary tectonics of the western margin, Cretaceous Western Interior Seaway: Geological Society of America Special Paper 260, p. 1-8.

Farabee, M. J., 1991, Palynology of the upper Kaiparowits Formation (Upper Cretaceous, Campanian) in southcentral Utah: Georgia Journal of Science, v. 49, p. 34-35.

Fox, R. C., 1971, Marsupial mammals from the early Campanian Milk River Formation, Alberta, Canada, in Kermack, D. M., and Kermack, K. A., editors, Early mammals: Zoological Journal of the Linnean Society 50, supplement 1, p. 145-164.

Gregory, H. E., and Moore, R. C., 1931, The Kaiparowits region; geographic and geologic reconnaissance of parts of Utah and Arizona: U. S. Geological Survey Professional Paper 164, 161 p.

Hintze, L. F., 1974, Geologic map of Utah: Brigham Young University Geology Studies Special Publication 2.

Hutchison, J. H., 1993, *Avisaurus*-- a "dinosaur" grows wings: Journal of Vertebrate Paleontology, v. 13, p. 43A.

Leahy, G. D., and Lerbekmo, J. F., 1995, Macrofossil magnetostratigraphy for the upper Santonian - lower Campanian interval in the Western Interior of North America: comparisons with European stage boundaries and planktonic foraminiferal zonal boundaries: Canadian Journal of Earth Sciences, v. 32, p. 247-260.

Nichols, D. J., 1997, Palynology and ages of some Upper Cretaceous formations in the Markagunt and northwestern Kaiparowits plateaus, southwestern Utah, in Maldonado, Florian, and Nealey, L. D., editors, Geologic studies of the Basin and Range-Colorado Plateau transition in southeastern Nevada, southwestern Utah, and northwestern Arizona, 1995: U. S. Geological Survey Bulletin 2153, p. 81-95.

Parrish, J. M., and Eaton, J. G., 1991, Diversity and evolution of dinosaurs in the Cretaceous of the Kaiparowits Plateau, Utah: Journal of Vertebrate Paleontology, v. 11, p. 50A.

Peterson, Fred, 1969a, Four new members of the Upper Cretaceous Straight Cliffs Formation in southeastern Kaiparowits region, Kane County, Utah: U. S. Geological Survey Bulletin 1274-J, p. 1-28.

—1969b, Cretaceous sedimentation and tectonism in the southeastern Kaiparowits region: U. S. Geological Survey Open-File Report, 259 p.

Peterson, Fred, and Kirk, A. R., 1977, Correlation of Cretaceous rocks in San Juan, Black Mesa, Kaiparowits, and Henry basins, southern Colorado Plateau, in Fassett, J. E., editor, San Juan Basin III, northwestern New Mexico: New Mexico Geological Society Guidebook, 28th Field Conference, p. 167-178.

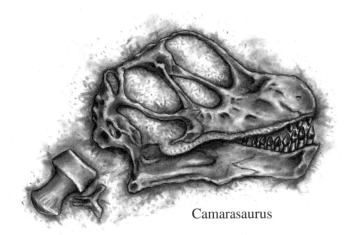

Camarasaurus

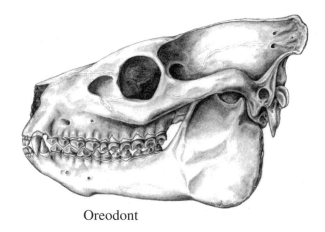

Oreodont

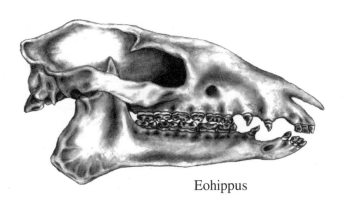

Eohippus

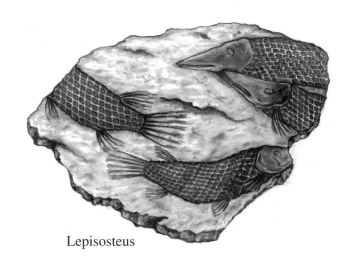

Lepisosteus

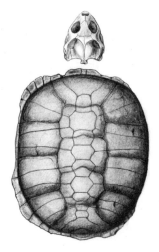
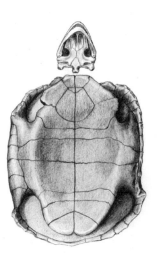

Eocene turtle

Brian Maebius © 1999

PTEROSAUR AND BIRD TRACKS FROM A NEW LATE CRETACEOUS LOCALITY IN UTAH

Martin G. Lockley
Geology Department,
University of Colorado at Denver,
P.O. Box 173364, Denver, Colorado 80217

ABSTRACT

Tracks resembling those of the ichnogenus *Pteraichnus* and attributable to pterosaurs have recently been discovered in the North Horn Formation (Late Cretaceous, Maastrichtian) of Emery County, Utah. The tracks are moderately well preserved, but not of sufficient quality to make a more precise ichnotaxonomic assignment. The tracks are the youngest pterosaur footprints known. They are also smaller than most other pterosaurian ichnites of Cretaceous age, thus adding to the growing diversity of pterosaur footprints known from this time period. This discovery confirms a growing number of recent reports that pterosaur tracks are quite abundant and indicative of quadrupedal progression on land. Small bird tracks are also known from the same locality, and represent the first discovery, and second published report, of pterosaur and bird tracks from the same stratigraphic horizon. The paleoecological implications of such co-occurrences are considered.

INTRODUCTION

Since Stokes (1957) first named the fossil trackway *Pteraichnus*, from the Jurassic Morrison Formation, and attributed them to pterosaurs, these tracks have been controversial. Padian and Olsen (1984) argued that Stokes was incorrect in his interpretation and that *Pteraichnus* is attributable to a crocodilian, a conclusion which implies that no pterosaur tracks are known (Unwin, 1989; Padian and Rayner, 1993). This conclusion has recently been challenged by the discovery and re-evaluation of a large amount of *Pteraichnus* material (Lockley and others, 1995, 1997; Lockley and Unwin, 1996; Bennett, 1997, Unwin, 1997; Wright and others, 1997). This material strongly suggests that Stokes was correct in his interpretation of *Pteraichnus* as pterosaurian, and that pterosaur tracks are, in fact, widespread in North America and Europe in the Jurassic and Cretaceous. The purpose of this paper is to present evidence of a new Cretaceous locality where pterosaur tracks are common, and to compare this new material with that known from other Cretaceous sites.

LOCALITY AND GEOLOGIC SETTING

The tracks were first discovered by Mark Donivan at a locality in the vicinity of Cottonwood Creek, about 10 miles northwest of Castle Dale, in Emery County, Utah. Sedimentary rocks in this area comprise a part of the Late Cretaceous (Maastrichtian) North Horn Formation, and typically consist of terriginous sandstones, siltstones, mudstones and coals that are rich in plant remains and trace fossils but lacking in an abundant body fossil record.

According to Franzyck and Pitman (1991) and references therein, the North Horn Formation in this region is assigned a Maastrichtian age. It represents a sandstone-dominated alluvial facies in the lower part, grading up into a silt- and mud-dominated alluvial facies that becomes lacustrine in the upper part.

MATERIAL

The material discussed herein consists of five slabs of fine-grained light olive gray sandstone (5Y 6/1 on GSA rock color chart) capped by a medium dark gray (color = N4) mud drape. Original unnumbered specimens of the pterosaur tracks are housed in the Dinosaur Museum, Blanding, Utah, with locality data. These specimens have been replicated for the joint University of Colorado at Denver-Museum of Western Colorado (CU-MWC) collection and assigned the numbers cited below. The tracks occur in association with the mud-draped surfaces which are also covered with small-scale invertebrate traces. Two of the slabs represent parts and counterparts of the same surface (CU-MWC 217), and allow us to study the tracks both as impressions (molds of the foot) and as fillings or natural casts. Thus the five slabs represent four different areas of track-bearing surface (figures 1-3), all from the same stratigraphic level.

The pterosaur track specimens (four slabs) expose a total surface area of about 3000 cm^2 or 0.3 m^2 (approximately 20 x 30 cm, 30 x 40 cm and 30 x 40 cm, respectively). Collectively these three surfaces reveal a total of between 25 and 30 individual footprints ranging from well preserved to poorly preserved examples. This den-

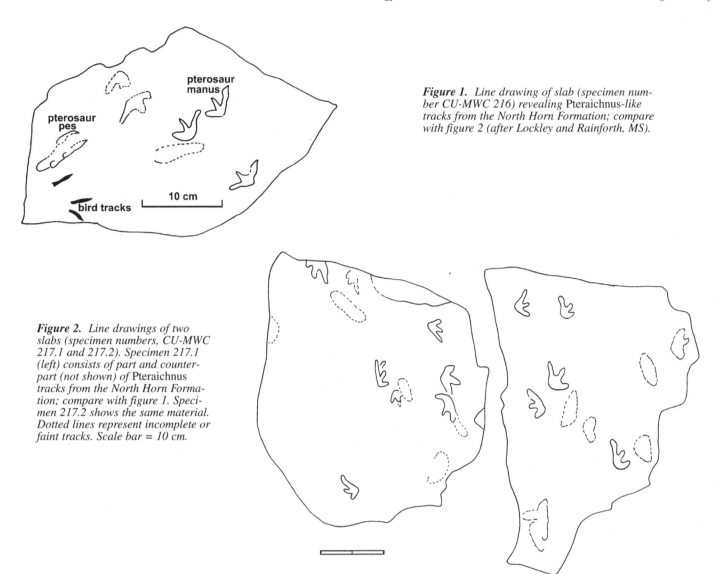

Figure 1. *Line drawing of slab (specimen number CU-MWC 216) revealing* Pteraichnus-*like tracks from the North Horn Formation; compare with figure 2 (after Lockley and Rainforth, MS).*

Figure 2. *Line drawings of two slabs (specimen numbers, CU-MWC 217.1 and 217.2). Specimen 217.1 (left) consists of part and counterpart (not shown) of* Pteraichnus *tracks from the North Horn Formation; compare with figure 1. Specimen 217.2 shows the same material. Dotted lines represent incomplete or faint tracks. Scale bar = 10 cm.*

sity of tracks corresponds to about 100 per m². One slab (CU-MWC 216) reveals traces that may be interpreted as partial bird tracks (figure 1) and represents the first discovery of bird and pterosaur tracks on the same surface (Lockley and Rainforth, in press). Recently a second discovery of bird and pterosaur tracks on the same surface was reported from the Cretaceous of Korea (Lockley and others, 1997).

It is evident that the most common and well-preserved track morphology is an asymmetrical three-toed (tridactyl) footprint that represents the typical *Pteraichnus* manus morphology. These tracks show a relatively narrow range in size: 4 to 5 cm in maximum length by 2.5 to 3.5 cm in width (N = 13). Two additional specimens appear slightly smaller (measuring about 3.5 cm in length by 2.0 to 2.5 cm in width), though some of the variation in size may be due to variable quality of preservation rather than substantial size differences.

Only one track is easily recognized as a typical

Pteraichnus-like pes footprint (figure 1). This track measures 7 cm long by 2.5 cm wide, and is the right size to correspond to the footprints of an animal with manus tracks in the size range described above. Other elongate impressions with the same general shape and size are probably also pes tracks. Their orientation and position relative to manus tracks (that is situated near a manus track, and with the long axis parallel or at a low angle to the manus track) also suggest that the pes and manus tracks are associated in trackway segments. Unfortunately however, we have not yet found any long segments of continuous trackway, or examples of manus-pes sets in which the pes tracks are well preserved.

One slab (CU-MWC 218) has been recovered that reveals only bird tracks (figure 3). The slab is approximately 20 x 15 cm and reveals about 30 small tracks, of which about seven are moderately well preserved. The estimated density is therefore approximately 1000 tracks per square meter (Lockley and others, 1992). These

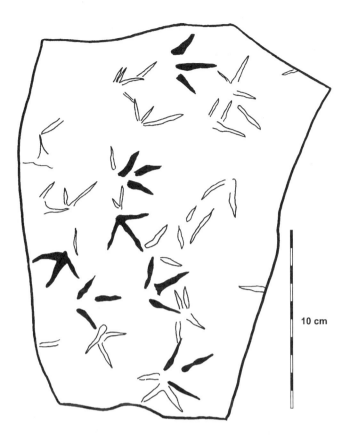

Figure 3. *Line drawing of slab (specimen CU-MWC 216) with bird tracks from the North Horn Formation.*

tracks are approximately 3 cm long by 3.5 cm wide, and are clearly different from the three morphotypes reported by Robison (1991). Thus at least four bird track types are known from the Blackhawk and North Horn Formations (Lockley and Rainforth, in press).

COMPARISON WITH OTHER PTERO-SAURIAN ICHNITES

Probable pterosaur tracks from the Blackhawk Formation were first reported as possible bird tracks by Parker and Balsley (1989), but later reinterpreted as pterosaurian in affinity (Lockley and others, 1995; Lockley and Rainforth, in press). These tracks are larger than the *Pteraichnus*-like footprints described herein, and perhaps should be assigned to a different ichnotaxon. However, no work has been done on the actual material, which is situated in a coal mine, so further detailed analysis of the tracks is not possible. Furthermore, the absence of pes tracks in what appears to be a manus-only assemblage, argues against premature naming of a new ichnotaxon.

Pterosaur tracks assigned to the ichnogenus *Purbeckopus* have recently been identified and re-described from the Cretaceous of England (Wright and others, 1997). This ichnogenus is characterized by pes tracks that vary

from 187 to 225 mm in length and 98 to 123 mm in width. Apart from the larger size, the *Purbeckopus* pes is evidently much wider (52-55% as wide as long) than the elongate tracks described herein (35% as wide as long). Thus it is clear that there are several footprint morphotypes that fall under the general heading of pterosaur tracks. The North Horn footprints described herein clearly have a very elongate foot, and in this respect, as well as size, resemble *Pteraichnus*, and not *Purbeckopus* or the large morphotype from the Blackhawk Formation. When compared with recently discovered pterosaur tracks from the Cretaceous of Korea (Lockley and others, 1997) that measure up to 35 cm in length, which represents a *Quetzacoatalus*-sized species with a distinctive trace of metatarsal V, the North Horn tracks represent a diminutive trackmaker.

Thus it can be argued that in the short time that the pterosaur tracks debate has been reopened (1995-1997) it is already apparent that there are at least four distinct pterosaur track morphotypes known from the Cretaceous. These include, in ascending stratigraphic order: *Purbeckopus*, a medium-sized morphotype from England; an unnamed giant ichnite from Korea; a medium-sized large form from the Blackhawk Formation of Utah (Parker and Balsley, 1989); and the small *Pteraichnus*-like ichnite described herein from the North Horn Formation. This list excludes various additional poorly preserved ichnites from Spain (Lockley and others, 1995) that might be considered morphologically distinct from those referred to above.

It is noteworthy that the North Horn tracks are *Pteraichnus*-like in morphology and size, because the body fossil record of latest Cretaceous (Maastrichtian) pterosaurs is dominated by species much larger than anything that could have made such small tracks (David Unwin, written communication, 1997). The identification of these footprints as being similar to the Jurassic ichnogenus *Pteraichnus* does not imply that the trackmakers belonged to the same genus or species, or that the footprints should be formally assigned to this ichnogenus. Experience has taught ichnologists that the premature naming of tracks, without reference to adequate supplies of well-preserved material (Baird, 1957), can lead to future problems. It is for precisely this reason that I use the term *Pteraichnus*-like, and not *Pteraichnus sensu stricto*. In this way, pending further ichnological study, the use of a Jurassic ichnogenus name is not formally extended to the Cretaceous. The nature of ichnological material is such that it is sometimes inadvisable to put precise labels on material that is not highly distinctive, well preserved, and represented by large samples. For this reason, it would be desirable to find more, and better preserved material before commenting further on the ichnotaxonomic affinity of this material.

IMPLICATIONS OF THE NORTH HORN ASSEMBLAGE FOR PTEROSAUR ICHNOLOGY

The pterosaur tracks discovery is significant for several other reasons. First, the Cretaceous track record of pterosaurs is presently somewhat sketchy in terms of quality of trackways, and completeness of material. As summarized by Lockley and others (1995), only one complete trackway is known from the Cretaceous of Spain (Moratalla, 1993), though there are also a handful of other localities that have yielded tracks with the general *Pteraichnus*-like manus morphology. Thus the North Horn locality adds another site to the patchy Cretaceous record.

The North Horn site is also important in that, after the Spanish site, it provides a second Cretaceous example of an assemblage containing pes tracks. A third example was recently reported from England (Wright and others, 1997), and a fourth from South Korea (Lockley and others, 1997). As noted by Lockley and others (1995), most Cretaceous sites have so far only yielded assemblages with manus tracks. This is because, in virtually all known examples of *Pteraichnus*, manus tracks are more deeply impressed than pes tracks. Indeed this feature is characteristic of *Pteraichnus* tracks and helps identify them as such. The reasons for the disparity in depth between manus and pes tracks pertains to the distinctive anatomy of pterosaurs, which have a large front end (that is, well-developed forelimbs and flight muscles, and large head) in relation to their diminutive hind quarters. In fact their hind limbs (pes) may, in some cases, exert such slight pressure on the substrate, in relation to the manus, as to be undetectable after the process of fossilization (Lockley and others, 1995).

There appears to be an alignment of manus tracks in two opposite directions. Such alignments have been noticed in other samples, but not studied in detail. The lack of study is in part owing to the fact that pterosaur tracks have largely been ignored until very recently, due to the previously widespread but mistaken belief that *Pteraichnus* was made by a crocodilian. Now that *Pteraichnus* and other pterosaurian tracks have been confidently identified as pterosaurian by many authors (Logue, 1994; Lockley and others, 1995, 1997; Lockley and Unwin, 1996; Bennett, 1997; Unwin, 1997), we hope that the trackway samples can be studied in detail and that more material can be collected from all accessible sites, including the one described herein.

PALEOECOLOGICAL CONSIDERATIONS

The pterosaur and bird tracks, described herein, are moderately abundant and representative of a high density of footprints in a small area. As has been discussed elsewhere (Lockley and others 1992), high bird track densities are characteristic of shorebird footprint assemblages, and probably reflect high activity levels and relatively high abundance of birds in a localized area. Although pterosaur track densities have not been studied in detail, there are many Jurassic sites where the density is high (Lockley and others, 1995). The North Horn assemblage also suggests an abundance of trackmakers in a small area, though the sample is too small for this inference to be certain. Nevertheless the evidence points to the possibility of high densities of pterosaurs congregating, or flocking in certain areas.

The co-occurrence of tracks of small pterosaurs and small birds in the North Horn assemblage can be compared and contrasted with the co-occurrence of tracks of large pterosaurs and small birds in the Cretaceous of Korea. The largest Cretaceous pterosaurs were much larger that the largest known birds, possibly leading to the inference that birds and pterosaurs occupied different niches, or even that pterosaurs might have preyed on smaller birds (Lockley and others, 1995). The co-occurrence of tracks in the North Horn however suggests some level of coexistence, or mixing in the same habitat, and would presumably argue against extreme niche partitioning either by body size or geographical location. In short, despite the preponderance of body fossil and trace fossil evidence for large pterosaurs and small birds in various different Cretaceous paleoenvironments, the North Horn assemblage provides evidence for co-existence of small species belonging to both groups. Again, more evidence is needed to take such inferences any further.

We may conclude, however, that the North Horn tracksite is similar to all other known Cretaceous pterosaur tracksites in being associated with a freshwater depositional environment (Lockley and Rainforth, in press). About 27 pterosaur tracksites are known from around the world. Almost all the Jurassic sites represent marginal marine, or marine shoreline environments, whereas all the Cretaceous tracksites (now totaling about ten localities) represent freshwater environments. It is too early to tell if this represents a significant pattern, though, based on body fossils, it has been suggested that, during the Cretaceous, pterosaurs began to inhabit more terrestrial environments (Bakurina and Unwin, 1995). The track record evidently supports such an assertion.

ACKNOWLEDGMENTS

Special thanks go to Marc Donivan, of Salt Lake City who discovered the tracks while working for the Dinosaur Museum, Blanding. Thanks to David Unwin and Joanna Wright, Bristol University, England for their helpful reviews and for useful discussion. Thanks also to Emma Rainforth for help with preparation of the illustrations.

REFERENCES

Baird, Donald, 1957, Triassic reptile footprint faunules from Milford, New Jersey: Bulletin of the Museum of Comparative Zoology, Harvard University, v. 117, p. 449-520.

Bakhurina, N. N., and Unwin, D. M., 1995, A survey of pterosaurs from the Jurassic and Cretaceous of the former Soviet Union and Mongolia: Historical Biology, v. 10, p. 197- 245.

Bennett, Christopher, 1997, Terrestrial locomotion of pterosaurs--a reconstruction based on *Pteraichnus* trackways: Journal of Vertebrate Paleontology, v. 17, p. 104-113.

Franczyk, K. J., and Pitman, J. K., 1991, Latest Cretaceous nonmarine depositional systems in the Wasatch Plateau area--reflections of foreland to intermontane basin transition, *in* Chidsey, T. C., Jr. editor, Geology of east-central Utah: Salt Lake City, Utah Geological Association Publication, v. 19, p. 77-93.

Lockley, M. G., and Unwin, David, 1996, The case for *Pteraichnus* as a common pterosaurian track--evidence, implications and controversy; Journal of Vertebrate Paleontology, v. 16, p. 48A

Lockley, M. G., and Rainforth, E. C., The track record of Mesozoic birds and pterosaurs--an ichnological perspective, *in* Chiappe, Luis, and Witmer, Larry, editors, Mesozoic birds: Berkeley, University of California Press (in press).

Lockley, M. G., Logue, T. J., Moratalla, J. J., Hunt, A. P., Schultz, R. J., and Robinson, J. W. 1995, The fossil trackway *Pteraichnus* is pterosaurian, not crocodilian--implications for the global distribution of pterosaurs tracks: Ichnos, v. 4, p. 7-20.

Lockley, M. G., Yang, S-Y., Matsukawa, Masaki, Fleming, R. F., and Lim, S-K, 1992, The track record of Mesozoic birds--evidence and implications: Philosophical Transactions of the Royal Society of London, v. 336, p. 113-134.

Lockley, M. G., Huh, Min, Lim, S-K., Yang, S-Y., Chun, S. S., and Unwin, D. M., 1997, First report of pterosaur tracks from Asia, Chollanam Province Korea: International Dinosaur Symposium for the Uhangri Dinosaur Center and Theme Park in Korea, Chollanam Province and Haenam County, Korea, p. 52-67.

Logue, T. J., 1994, Alcova, Wyoming tracks of *Pteraichnus saltwashensis* made by pterosaurs: Geological Society of America, Abstracts with Program, South Central Section, v. 26, no. 1, p. 10.

Moratalla, J. J., 1993, Restos indirectos de dinosaurios del registro espanol--paleoicnologia de la Cuenca de Cameros (Jurassico superior-Cretacico inferior) y Paleoologia del Cretacico superior: Madrid, Universidad Autonoma de Madrid, Ph.D. thesis, 727 p.

Padian, Kevin, and Olsen, P. E., 1984, The fossil trackway *Pteraichnus*--not pterosaurian, but crocodilian: Journal of Paleontology, v. 58, p. 178-184.

Padian, Kevin, and Rayner, J. M. V., 1993, The wings of pterosaurs: American Journal of Science, v. 273, p. 91-166.

Parker, Lee, and Balsley, John, 1989, Coal mines as localities for studying trace fossils, *in* Gillette, D. D., and Lockley, M. G., editors, Dinosaur tracks and traces: Cambridge, Cambridge University Press, p. 353-359.

Robison, S. F., 1991, Bird and frog tracks from the Late Cretaceous Blackhawk Formation in east central Utah, *in* Chidsey, T. C. Jr., editor, Geology of east-central Utah: Salt Lake City, Utah Geological Association Publication, v. 19, p. 325-334.

Stokes, W. L. 1957, Pterodactyl tracks from the Morrison Formation: Journal of Paleontology, v. 31, p. 952-954.

Unwin, D. M., 1989, A predictive method for the identification of vertebrate ichnites and its application to pterosaur tracks, *in* Gillette, D. D., and Lockley, M. G., editors, Dinosaur tracks and traces: Cambridge, Cambridge University Press, p. 259-274.

—1997, Pterosaur tracks and the terrestrial ability of pterosaurs: Lethaia, v. 29, p. 373-386.

Wright, J. L., Unwin, D. M., Lockley, M. G., and Rainforth, E. C., 1997, Pterosaur tracks from the Purbeck Limestone Formation of Dorset, England: Proceedings of the Geologists' Association, v. 108, p. 39-48.

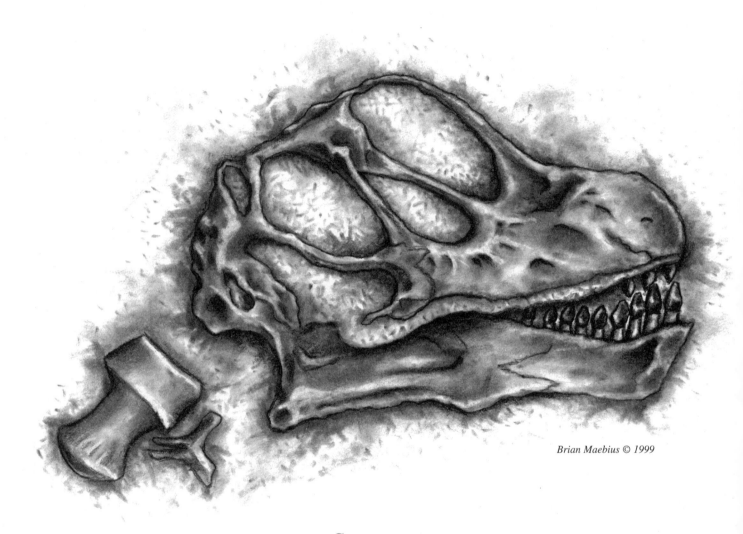

Brian Maebius © 1999

Camarasaurus

EGGS AND EGGSHELL FROM THE UPPER CRETACEOUS NORTH HORN FORMATION, CENTRAL UTAH

Emily S. Bray

University of Colorado Museum, Geology Section, Campus Box 315, Boulder, CO 80309-0315

ABSTRACT

The eggshell in this study is from the Upper Cretaceous (Maastrichtian) portion of the North Horn Formation. Two oogenera and five oospecies new to the Western Interior of North America are established. A morphotype new to the dinosauroid prismatic basic type, designated as spheruprismatic, has a mammillary layer to continuous layer ratio of 1:1. *Spheruprismatoolithus condensus*, new oogenus and oospecies, is known from thousands of eggshell fragments including the shells from a weathered nesting site. Eggs contained in a nest of *Prismatoolithus jenseni*, a new oospecies, are less elongate than other prismatoolithid eggs and the shell unit structure typical for *Prismatoolithus*. From abundant eggshell fragments of the ornithoid ratite morphotype, a microstructure characteristic of the eggs of theropod dinosaurs is established: *Spongioolithus hirschi* with a dispersituberculate sculpture pattern and a mammillary layer thinner than that of other elongatoolithid eggshell. The first evidence within North America of eggshell of dinosauroid-spherulitic basic type and angustispherulitic morphotype is represented by *Ovaloolithus utahensis* and *Ovaloolithus tenuisus*, new oospecies. Eggshell of this oogenus has previously been described from the Upper Cretaceous of China and Mongolia and is associated with ornithopod dinosaurs. *Ovaloolithus utahensis* and *O. tenuisus* exhibit a smooth outer surface. Additionally, general descriptions of two types of eggshell of dinosauroid-spherulitic basic type, *Spheroolithus* oospecies indeterminate, one of prolatospherulitic morphotype, and another much thinner than most *Spheroolithus* eggshell, are both found as surface float material. A specimen lacking a distinguishing structure is assessed as a questionable eggshell of undetermined affinity. An abbreviated review of eggshell structure and current use of parataxonomic classification of eggshell are also discussed.

INTRODUCTION

The North Horn Formation of central Utah, dominated by fluvial and lacustrine deposits, spans the Cretaceous-Tertiary boundary (Spieker, 1946). The fauna of the Upper Cretaceous portion is known to include the reptilians Crocodilia, Chelonia, Squamata, Rhynchocephalia, Saurischian and Ornithischian dinosaurs, and the actinopterygian fish, *Lepisosteus* (Gilmore, 1946; see also Cifelli and others, this volume; and Difley and Ekdale, this volume).

This study focuses on the abundant eggshells of dinosaurian origin found throughout the Upper Cretaceous portion of the North Horn Formation. The variety of eggshell indicates a diversity of dinosaurs existed. The fossil skeletal remains found to date do not substantiate this diversity. The taxonomic groups represented by different eggshell morphotypes consist of ornithopods, represented by angustispherulitic and prolatospherulitic morphotypes, and of theropods, represented by the ratite and prismatic morphotypes (figure 1).

The eggshell described in this study represents morphotypes, oogenera and oospecies new to North America and to the Upper Cretaceous. Two of these morphotypes, prolatospherulitic and ratite, are known from the Upper Cretaceous of Montana. A third morphotype, the dinosaur-prismatic, is known from both Montana and Alberta (Hirsch and Quinn, 1990; Zelenitsky and Hills, 1996). Prismatic eggshell of Late Cretaceous age is also known from China, Mongolia, and France (Zhao and Li, 1993; Mikhailov, 1994a; Vianey-Liaud and Crochet, 1993). The angustispherulitic morphotype is known from the Upper Cretaceous of China and Mongolia (Zhao, 1979; Mikhailov, 1994b). The ratite morphotype is known from the Upper Cretaceous of China, Mongolia, and North America (Zhao, 1975: Mikhailov, 1994a; Norell and others, 1994; Hirsch and Quinn, 1990).

The significance of the fossil eggs lies in the expression of direct evidence of the biological demands of a given taxon (see Mikhailov and others, 1996). Eggshell, though widely regarded as a trace fossil, conveys specific information regarding the biological activity of an organism. Anatomical and physiological constraints determine the characteristics of the amniotic egg. These constraints differ among amniotes. The insights gained from the analysis of eggshell structure can be used to enhance phylogenetic correlation, particularly with regard to extinct taxa.

BASIC TYPES OF EGGSHELL ORGANIZATION		STRUCTURAL MORPHOTYPES	PORE SYSTEM	PARATAXONOMIC OOFAMILIES	TAXONOMIC GROUPS
Testudoid		Spherorigidis Spheruflexibilis		Testudoolithidae Testudooflexoolithidae	Chelonia
Geckoid		Geckonoid	Rete-canaliculate	Gekkoolithidae	Gekkota
Crocodiloid		Crocodiloid		Krokolithidae	Crocodylia
Dinosauroid-spherulitic		Prolatospherulitic	Prolato- and rimo-canaliculate	Spheroolithidae	Ornithopoda (hadrosaurine embryos)
		Angustispherulitic	Rimo-prolato and angusti-canaliculate	Ovaloolithidae	?Ornithopoda
		Discretispherulitic (Tubospherulitic)	Tubo-canaliculate	Megaloolithidae	?Sauropoda ?Ornithischia
		Filispherulitic (Multispherulitic)	Multi-canaliculate	Faveoloolithidae	?Sauropoda
		Dendrospherulitic	Prolato-canaliculate	Dendroolithidae	?Sauropoda ?Ornithopoda
			Prolato-canaliculate	Dictyoolithidae	?Sauropoda
Dinosauroid-prismatic		Prismatic	Angusti-canaliculate	Prismatoolithidae	Theropoda (Troodontid embryos)
			Obliqui-canaliculate		
		Spheruprismatic	Angusti-canaliculate		
Ornithoid		Ratite	Angusti-canaliculate	Elongatoolithidae	Theropoda (Oviraptorid embryo)
			Angusti-canaliculate	Laevisoolithidae	?Theropoda ?Enantiornithids
			Angusti-canaliculate	Oblongoolithidae	
			Angusti-canaliculate	Medioolithidae	?Palaeognathae
			Angusti-canaliculate	Struthiolithidae	Struthionidae
			Angusti-canaliculate	Ornitholithidae	?Diatrymatidae
		Prismatic ("neognathe")	Angusti-canaliculate		Neognathae and Volant Paleognathous
				Gobioolithidae	

Figure 1. *Correlation chart showing the basic types of eggshell organization, eggshell structural morphotypes and diagrammatic representations, characteristic pore systems, parataxonomic oofamilies, and the representative taxonomic groups.*

ABBREVIATIONS

BYUVP, Brigham Young University Vertebrate Paleontology, Provo, UT; DINO, Dinosaur National Monument, Jensen, UT; HEC, Hirsch eggshell catalogue at the University of Colorado Museum, Boulder, CO; MWC, Museum of Western Colorado, Grand Junction, CO; PIN, Paleontological Institute of the Russian Academy of Sciences, Moscow; UCM, University of Colorado Museum, Boulder, CO; UCMP, University of California Museum of Paleontology, Berkeley, CA.

CL, continuous layer; CLM, cathodoluminescence microscopy; EL, elongation index; H:W, height to width ratio; ML, mammillary layer; PL, polarizing light microscopy; SEM, scanning electron microscopy; SL, squamatic layer; TL, transmitted light microscopy.

METHODS AND MATERIAL

All eggshells were cleaned ultrasonically in deionized distilled water and dried. The radial thickness was measured with a micrometer. Eggshells were prepared in radial thin section and examined by transmitted and polarized light microscopy. Cathodoluminescence microscopy (CLM) was applied to thin sections for the detection of diagenetic alteration and recrystallization. Fragments of eggshell were also mounted on stubs and viewed under the scanning electron microscope for inner, outer, and radial shell views. These techniques have been described in Packard (1980) and Hirsch (1983). The technical terminology of eggshell anatomy follows Mikhailov (1991), Hirsch (1994a), and Mikhailov and others (1996).

All material is catalogued at the University of Colorado Museum unless otherwise noted. Eggshell specimens used in thin section and SEM analyses are also catalogued in the Hirsch eggshell catalogue (HEC) of the University of Colorado, Boulder. All material represents specimens found both in situ and from the surface.

EGGSHELL STRUCTURE:
AN ABBREVIATED REVIEW

Amniote eggshell is composed of biocrystalline calcite or aragonite. The structure and organization of the shell units are determined by the anatomical constraints and physiological and structural demands of the egg laying species. The research on recent avian, crocodile, and testudoid eggshell (Romanoff and Romanoff, 1949; Simkiss and Tyler, 1957; Tyler and Simkiss, 1959; Tyler, 1964, 1969; Erben, 1970; Packard, 1980; Packard and others, 1984; Packard and Hirsch, 1986; Hirsch, 1983, 1985, 1996; Mikhailov, 1987a,b, 1992, 1995) has shown that these taxa each exhibit unique and particular eggshell structures. This taxonomic specificity of recent eggshell structure allows us to extend the phylogenetic continuity of eggshell and to evaluate extinct groups, such as dinosaurs, employing the same logic as we do with those of extant groups.

The interpretation of fossil eggshell is dominated by our knowledge of recent eggshell structure. The correlation of eggshell structure with representative taxa is aided by the rare finds of embryonic skeletal remains within eggs (Horner and Makela, 1979; Horner and Weishampel 1988, 1996; Norell and others, 1994). Such finds, combined with a formation's representative fauna and the associated skeletal remains found at egg localities, have enabled us in some cases to correlate the eggshell structures of extinct taxa to their taxonomic representatives. This study deals with such interpretations.

The study of recent and fossil eggshell has created a general grouping of eggshell into basic or primary types based on the ultrastructure of the individual shell units of the eggshell. There are six basic types of eggshell organization: testudoid, geckoid, crocodiloid, dinosauroid-spherulitic, dinosauroid-prismatic, and ornithoid (figure 1). The basic types are subdivided into structural morphotypes that express variations within the structure of the individual shell units of the basic type groups. To further enhance the particulars of the structural morphotypes, the types of pore systems are also incorporated as diagnostic criteria. Currently there are 13 recognized structural morphotypes.

The laying down of the shell layer begins from an organic core secreted on the outer layer of the shell membrane from which the nucleation of individual calcite crystals begins. This point of penetration of the shell membrane by crystalline calcite is called the basal cap or basal plate group. From this point of growth, spherulites grow in all directions. Due to ionic conditions and restrictions by the shell membrane the spherulites grow most freely in an outward direction, initiating growth of the shell unit (Simkiss, 1968). The formation of the egg is affected by many parameters: chemistry, physiology, anatomical and structural constraints, and environmental dictates all contribute to its uniquely taxonomic manifestation.

To define the crystalline structure of the calcitic growth of an egg, analysis of the ultrastructural organization is required. This fine structure, resulting from the interaction of organic and inorganic components, is created by both the horizontal and vertical growth of the shell unit. As shown in figure 2, the structural compo-

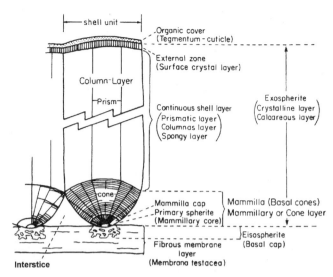

Figure 2. *Diagram of the structure of a shell unit and corresponding structural terminology (modified from Hirsch, 1979).*

nents of the shell unit consist of a basal cap that adheres to the shell membrane, the eisospherite, and the mammillary core, cap, and cone layer consisting of radial (or radial tabular) ultrastructure. Above the mammillae lies the continuous shell layer that varies in ultrastructural composition according to its taxonomic origin.

Dinosauroid-spherulitic eggshells have a continuous radiation of radial tabular ultrastructure from their origins in the mammillae and throughout the shell units to the outer surface. Dinosauroid-prismatic eggshells have an organic core and radial tabular ultrastructure at their base, with a prismatic, more tabular, ultrastructure in the upper, or continuous, region of the shells. The vertical boundaries between the narrow shell units are evident in prismatic eggshell. Ratite eggshells are composed of an organic core, a mammillary layer of calcite radial (and/or tabular), and an overlying squamatic ultrastructural layer. The transition between these two ultrastructural zones is marked by a visible change in structure and the upper vertical boundaries between shell units are indistinguishable.

CLASSIFICATION OF EGGSHELL: CURRENT STATUS

Over the last twenty five years a formal system for classifying fossil eggs has taken shape. This system was initiated by Chinese paleontologists (Young, 1954, 1965; Zhao and Jiang, 1974; Zhao, 1975, 1979) and has recently been modified to incorporate the structural morphotypes and pore systems that are representative of basic types of eggshell organization (Mikhailov, 1991; Hirsch and Quinn, 1990; Hirsch, 1994a,b). Recently an informal proposal for the parataxonomic classification of fos-

sil eggs and eggshell has been proposed (Mikhailov and others, 1996). This proposal advocates the use of binomial nomenclature, the names often being descriptive of the egg or structure of the eggshell, and independent of correlation to representative taxa. The intent of this system is to standardize the criteria used for fossil egg classification. The prefix "oo" (for egg) is recommended to precede the family, genus, and species categorization and to designate the use of parataxonomic classification. The criteria for oofamily classification are egg shape, structural morphotype, pore system, and sculpturing of the shells' outer surface. For oogenus, the egg shape, variation within the morphotype, the pore system, and variation in the surface sculpturing are the desired criteria. The oospecies criteria include egg size, range of eggshell thickness, external pore pattern, and details of the sculpturing on the shells' outer surface.

To be certain of the correlation of a zoological taxon with a particular eggshell structure, it is necessary to have identifiable skeletal remains within an egg. Such evidence is, however, rare in the fossil record. To date there are only five egg types containing identifiable embryonic skeletal remains. These types of eggs are: (1) the ornithoid ratite morphotype with oviraptorids (Norell and others, 1994); (2) the dinosauroid-prismatic morphotype containing troodontids (Horner and Weishampel, 1988, 1996); and (3) the dinosauroid-spherulitic, prolatospherulitic morphotype, associated with hadrosaurids (Horner and Makela, 1979; Horner, 1994). Eggs from China that contain embryos include an emyid embryo in an egg of testudoid basic type, and what is thought to be a therizinosaur embryo in an egg of dinosauroid-spherulitic basic type (Cohen and others, 1995).

SYSTEMATIC PALEONTOLOGY

Basic Type: Dinosauroid-prismatic
Morphotype: Prismatic
Oofamily Prismatoolithidae Hirsch 1994
Oogenus *Prismatoolithus* Zhao & Li 1993
Oospecies *Prismatoolithus jenseni*, new oospecies

Holotype
BYUVP 9481, partial nest containing three eggs.

Etymology
Named after James Jensen, discoverer of these eggs.

Diagnosis
Egg shape elongate ovoid; outer surface smooth, no sculpturing; pore pattern circular, small, singular and

oval to elongate; shell thickness ranges from 0.83 mm to 1.16 mm.

Material

Holotype BYU 9481 and UCM 73464, HEC 437 (representing the eggshell removed from holotype eggs 1, 2, and 3).

Type Locality and Horizon

UCM L73464, Sauropod Locality (locality #1, Gilmore, 1946); Emery County, Utah, U.S.A.; North Horn Formation, Maastrichtian.

Referred Material

HEC 761; HEC 829-1, 2, 3; HEC 831-1 from the Lizard locality, Emery County, Utah (locality #3 of Dragon Valley, Gilmore, 1946). HEC 767-4, 5 from the Sauropod locality. Material totals more than 100 eggshell fragments.

Description

Eggs are of dinosauroid-prismatic basic type, prismatic morphotype, with an angusticanaliculate pore system. Three eggs, nearly intact, were found in situ embedded in a hard, resistant sandstone (figure 3A). The three eggs vary in size and condition. Egg 1 is embedded in the sandstone and missing one pole, measuring 75 x 60 mm. Egg 2 is compressed, resting on its long axis, incomplete and measuring 140 x 75 mm. Egg 3 is partially restored, measuring 70 x 66 mm. The nest size is 400 x 200 mm, with the eggs arranged in a semi-circular pattern and two standing vertically. The number of pore openings per 1.0 cm^2 for single, circular pores averages 11, and for oval elongated pore openings averages 39 (figure 3B). The oval to elongated pores are oriented in a linear pattern across the outer surface and are positioned close together; the thickness of these shell fragments averages 1.10 mm. The single, circular pores are fewer in number and are widely spaced. Fragments with this type of pore opening have a shell thickness averaging 0.91 mm. Few eggshell fragments of *P. jenseni* have both types of pore openings; most shells are dominated by one or another type of pore opening. It is likely that the type of pore openings differ from the equator of the egg to the poles and this difference is evident in the egg fragments collected. The pore system is angusticanaliculate (figure 3 C,D). The shell units are slender, well defined, and typical for prismatoolithid eggshell (figure 3 E,F). The mammillae of all specimens are worn due to weathering (figure 3 E).

Comparison

Prismatoolithus jenseni eggshell differs in egg shape, eggshell thickness, and alignment of pores from that of the *Prismatoolithus*

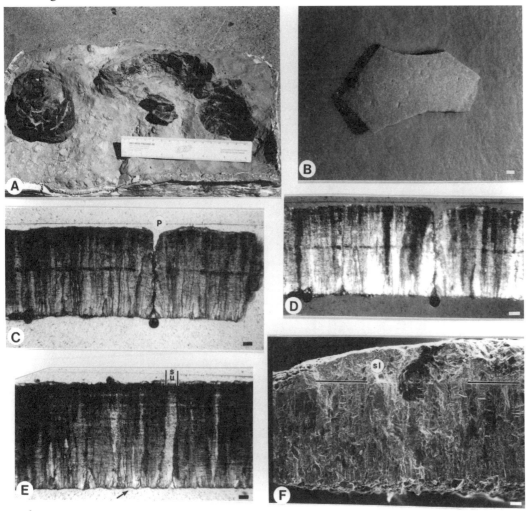

Figure 3. *Thin section and SEM radial photos in all figures have outer surface at top of photo. A-F, Prismatoolithus jenseni, new oospecies BYUVP 9481. A, nest containing three eggs; photo scale in mm. B, outer surface of eggshell showing elongate and oval pore openings; bar =1 mm. C, thin section under TL of angusticaliculate pore canal (p). D, as in (C) under PL showing columnar extinction of shells' narrow units. E, under TL showing narrow shell units (su) and worn mammillae (arrow). F, SEM photo showing ultrastructure of prismatic shell units; lines demarcate post-depositional secondary layer (sl) on outer shell surface.). C-F, bar = 100µ m.*

holotype, *Prismatoolithus gebiensis* (Zhao and Li, 1993). *Prismatoolithus gebiensis* is also of Late Cretaceous age, from the Djadokhta Formation of Bayan Manduhu, Inner Mongolia. The eggs of *Prismatoolithus jenseni*, though incomplete, appear less elongate than those of *P. gebiensis* with elongation indexes (EL) of 1.86 and 2.4, respectively. The prismatic eggshell of Montana's Two Medicine Formation are most similar in size and shape to the prismatic eggs of *P. gebiensis* with an average EL of 2.27 (Hirsch and Quinn, 1990). The eggshell of *P. jenseni* averages slightly thicker (up to 1.16 mm) than that of *P. gebiensis* (0.7-0.9 mm) and of the Two Medicine prismatic (0.8-0.9 mm) and *P. levis* of Alberta (0.7-1.0 mm). The pore openings of *P. jenseni* are of two different shapes, and the linear orientation of the oval to elongate pores is not found in other prismatoolithid eggshell. The ML:CL of 1:6, 1:7 is comparable in all specimens.

Discussion

This eggshell is found in the lower to middle portions of the North Horn and at numerous localities. Of the sampled shells, preservation is generally good, yet the nest eggs have the poorest outer surface preservation. Eggs of prismatoolithid morphotype have been described from Upper Cretaceous deposits of Montana, Inner Mongolia, France, Mongolia, and Alberta (Hirsch and Quinn, 1990; Zhao, 1993; Vianey-Liaud and Crochet, 1993; Mikhailov, 1994a; Zelenitsky and Hills, 1996) and from the Upper Jurassic of Utah and Colorado (Hirsch, 1994b). Initially Montana's eggs were diagnosed as those of the hypsilophodont *Orodromeus makelai* (Horner and Weishampel, 1988) from embryonic remains within an egg. This diagnoses was later revised to *Troodon* sp., cf. *formosus* (Horner and Weishampel, 1996).

Basic Type: Dinosauroid-prismatic
Morphotype: Spheruprismatic
Oofamily Prismatoolithidae   Hirsch 1994
Oogenus *Spheruprismatoolithus* new oogenus

Type Species

Spheruprismatoolithus condensus, new oospecies.

Etymology

Refers to the structure of shell units, having extended characteristics of the spherulitic ("spheru") portion in a prismatic eggshell ("prismatic").

Diagnosis

Outer surface sculpturing contoured with linear ridges and nodes in a longitudinal pattern; pore openings singular, circular, some slit-like; ratio of mammillary layer (spherulitic) to continuous layer (prismatic) nearly 1:1.

Known Distribution

North Horn Formation, Utah; Two Medicine Formation, Montana.

Discussion

The distinctive feature of this eggshell is the ratio of the ML:CL which is 1:1 (figure 4A,B). Prismatoolithid eggshell from other localities have greater ML:CL ratios: Montana,1:5; China, 1:3; Alberta, 1:6 to 1:8. The outer surface of the shell has nodes, coalescing nodes and low, undulating ridges, of dominantly ramotuberculate sculpturing.

Oospecies *Spheruprismatoolithus condensus* new oospecies

Holotype

UCM 47627.

Etymology

Latin, "condensus," dense, thick, refers to the increased proportion of spherulitic region of the shell.

Diagnosis

Shell thickness ranges from 0.66 mm to 0.94 mm; sculpturing of undulating ridges and nodes, some coalescing; ramotuberculate to dispersituberculate sculpturing; pore pattern small, single, circular, angusticanaliculate, and, paired larger, oval to elongate, irregularly shaped, rimocanaliculate pores.

Material

Holotype UMC 47627, and HEC 289 consisting of 270 fragments weathering out of a hole 5.5 cm in diameter.

Type Locality And Horizon

UCM L79059, Mudbank Site 1.2; Emery County, Utah; North Horn Formation, Maastrichtian.

Referred Material

HEC 832-1,2,3 from Lizard locality weathered nest site, fragments numbering thousands. From the Upper Cretaceous Two Medicine Formation of Montana: HEC 374-3R, Missel Site N= 25; HEC 619A, Eileens Nest N= 75; HEC 581-2, Microsite ; HEC 624-5, Red Bone; HEC 622-6, Lisa's Canyon. HEC 787-6 from the Upper Cretaceous Judith River Formations Long Time Waiting site, Hill County, Montana, has a shell thickness of 0.5 mm to 0.6 mm.

Figure 4. A-G, Spheruprismatoolithus condensus, *new oogenus and oospecies UCM 47627. A, radial thin section under TL showing 1:1 ratio of mammillary layer (ml) to prismatic layer (pl). B, as in (A) under PL with shell unit (su) height to width ratio of 2:1, sweeping extinction in mammillary layer and columnar extinction in prismatic layer. A-B bar = 100 μm. C-E, outer surface of eggshell; bar = 1 mm. C, linearituberculate sculpturing. D, sagentotuberculate sculpturing. E, dispersituberculate sculpturing. F-G, horizontal accretion lines paralleling contour of shells' outer surface (arrows), bar = 100μ m.*

Description

The eggshell is of dinosauroid-prismatic basic type. The structural morphotype differs from the prismatic morphotype by the comparative thickness of the spherulitic and prismatic regions of the shell; *S. condensus* has a ML:CL of 1:1 whereas other prismatoolithus eggshells average a ML:CL of 1:5. This significant deviation necessitates the establishment of a new morphotype, spheruprismatic.

The outer surface of the shell has sculpturing of unidirectional linear ridges and short, irregular, discontinuous coalescing ridges, as well as individual nodes and coalescing nodes (figure 4 C,D,E). The eggshell is generally thin, less than 0.90 mm, and consists of a thick radiating spherulitic mammillary layer that is overlain by the prismatic layer with a ML:CL ratio of 1:1. Shell units are broad, tightly abutting, and have a height-to-width ratio of 2:1 (figure 4 B). Accretion lines are horizontal, undulating, and reflective of the sculpturing on the outer shell surface (figure 4 F,G). Pore openings are singular and appear either circular or oval to elongate and are located on the ridges, on the flattened shell surfaces, and at the bases of nodes. The average number of nodes per cm^2 is 20. Organic cores are visible in some specimens. Mammillae are generally well preserved whereas the outer surfaces of many fragments show weathering. Most fragments have curvature.

Comparison

S. condensus differs from other *Prismatoolithidae* shells by the ML:CL ratio of 1:1, the height to width ratio of 2:1, and by the outer surface sculpturing of the shell. The outer surfaces of described *Prismatoolithus* eggs are smooth.

Discussion

The site of a weathered nest containing abundant *S. condensus* eggshell, combined with the material comprising the holotype, has allowed for calculation of an estimated egg diameter of 61 mm, and possible egg size of 50-68 mm x 60-70 mm. All fragments have strong curvature indicating a possible spheroidal egg. All eggshell fragments were found in situ.

Basic Type: Ornithoid
Morphotype: Ratite
Oofamily Elongatoolithidae Zhao 1975
Oogenus *Spongioolithus* new oogenus

Type Species

Spongioolithus hirschi new oospecies.

Etymology

Named for the squamatic region of the eggshell that in the past has often been referred to as the spongy layer of the avian eggshell.

Diagnosis

Sculpturing of outer surface linearituberculate and dispersituberculate; pore system angusticanaliculate; reduced ratio of ML:CL. Known distribution- North Horn Formation, Utah; Two Medicine Formation, Montana.

***Spongioolithus hirschi* new oospecies**

Holotype

UCM 47620.

Etymology

Named in honor of the late Karl F. Hirsch, whose work on amniotic eggshell greatly advanced the structural classification of fossil eggshell.

Diagnosis

Outer surface sculpturing of single nodes, discontinuous ridges, coalescing nodes and ridges, dispersituberculate and linearituberculate sculpturing; pores single, circular, angusticanaliculate; shell thickness with sculpturing ranges from 1.20 mm to 1.55 mm.

Material

Holotype, UCM 47620, HEC 246, 413 fragments.

Type Locality And Horizon

UCM L79058, One Egg Locality, Emery County, Utah; North Horn Formation, Maastrichtian.

Referred Material

HEC 296 from section 4 Site 7, 45 fragments; HEC 759, Kitchen Locality, 19 fragments; HEC 762-1, Sauropod Locality, 13 fragments; HEC 763, Sauropod Locality, 6 fragments; HEC 79, Sauropod Locality (UCMP 88127); HEC 765, Sauropod One Egg, 9 fragments; HEC 766, Pond Locality; HEC 80, Lizard locality, and HEC 77, North Horn Mountain; HEC 78 (UCMP specimen 88124); all localities in Emery County, Utah.

Description

Eggshell of ornithoid ratite morphotype. ML:CL ratio 1:7. The sculpturing consists of thin, high, sharp ridges with linear orientation. The ridges become discontinuous, irregular, and coalesce into right-angled patterns (figure 5 A,B). The shell thickness of these fragments ranges from 1.34 mm to 1.55 mm. The nodes are distinct and individual, but do coalesce in some fragments. Shell fragments of this type range in thickness from 1.20 mm to 1.52 mm. The pore openings are singular, circular, average 25 to 30 per cm^2, and are located at the bases of nodes or in between nodes (figure 5 C). The number of nodes per cm^2 averages 50. Some fragments have elongated nodes that are oriented in linear rows. The fragments with coalescing nodes tend to have fewer pore openings. Mammillae are generally well preserved (figure 5 D). The change in ultrastructure of radial calcite in the mammillary layer to squamatic in the continuous layer is noted visibly in thin section and SEM radial views (figure 5 E,F).

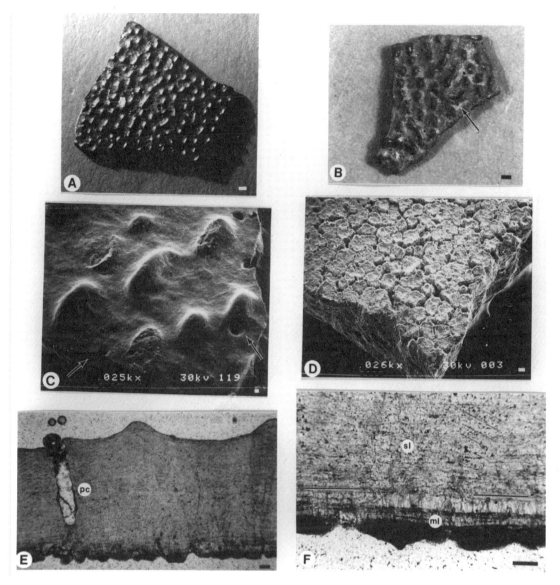

Figure 5. *A-F, Spongioolithus hirschi, UCM 47620. A-C, outer surface of eggshell. A, dispersituberculate sculpturing. B, dispersituberculate sculpturing and coalescing nodes; arrow points to circular pore openings. A-B, bar = 1 mm. C, SEM photo of nodes and angusticanaliculate pore openings (arrows). D, mammillae of shells' inner surface. E-F, thin section under TL in radial view. E, note nodes in cross section, partial pore canal (pc). F, horizontal lines mark change in structure from the mammillary layer (ml) to squamatic layer (sl). C-F, bar = 100μ m.*

Comparison

The sculpturing of elongatoolithid eggshell is highly variable and *S. hirschi* demonstrates this trait. The thinness of the mammillary layer of *S. hirschi* is less than in most elongatoolithid shells. *Spongioolithus hirschi* has a ML:CL ratio of 1:7 whereas elongatoolithid shells average 1:3 to 1:5 (figure 5 E).

Discussion

Most elongatoolithid eggs are dominated by linearituberculate sculpturing, whereas *S. hirschi* is dominated by dispersituberculate sculpturing. The reduced ML:CL is distinctive for *S. hirschi*. Fragments of this type were found in situ.

Basic type: Dinosauroid-spherulitic
Morphotype: Angustispherulitic
Oofamily Ovaloolithidae Mikhailov 1991
Oogenus *Ovaloolithus* Zhao 1979
Oospecies *Ovaloolithus utahensis* new oospecies

Holotype

UCM 47621.

Etymology

For the state in which the eggshell is found, Utah, U.S.A.

Diagnosis

Eggshell with smooth outer surface, no sculpturing;

pore openings small, single, and closely paired circular; pore system angusticaniculate; shell thickness ranges from 1.42 mm to 1.68 mm.

Material

Holotype UCM 47621, HEC 247-1.

Type Locality And Horizon

UCM L79058, Emery County, Utah; North Horn Formation, Maastrichtian.

Referred Material

Specimens from Emery County, Utah include: Site 3 locality, HEC 247-1 and 247-3 and All Over locality, HEC 247-4, 247-5, 247-6, 247-7. HEC 880-1, 2, 3, and 4 from North Horn Mountain, Emery County, Utah. Sauropod locality; Emery County, Utah, HEC 767-6, and HEC 764-1. Total number is greater than 300 fragments. All fragments have curvature.

Description

The eggshell is of dinosauroid-spherulitic basic type, and angustispherulitic morphotype. The pore system is angusticaniculate with single circular and paired circular pore openings (figure 6 A). Single circular pore openings average 22 -38 per cm^2; circular paired pores average 14-25 per cm^2. The shell units are vertically compact and closely abutting (figure 6 B). Height-to-width ratio of shell units averages 7:1. The outward radiation of crystallites within the shell unit begins at one-third to one-half of the eggshell thickness. In radial section, the distinction between shell units becomes less obvious approaching the outer surface of shell (figure 6 C,D). Radiation of the micro-fine fanning, spherulitic, radial tabular ultrastructure is most apparent when viewed under

the SEM at high magnification (figure 6 E,F). The mammillae are worn, closely positioned, and show some cratering (figure 6 E).

Comparison

Ovaloolithus utahensis is widely distributed throughout the lower North Horn Formation and in the lower coal sequence. Eggshell of this angustispherulitic morphotype have been described from Upper Cretaceous deposits of China and Mongolia. However, the smooth shell surface of *O. utahensis* is unique and the shell is thinner than most ovaloolithid eggshell.

From China, the *Ovaloolithus* type species, *O. chinkangkouensis* (Zhao and Jiang, 1974), was originally

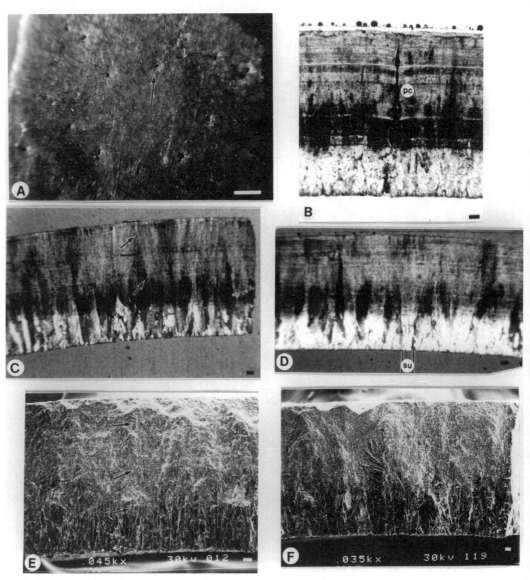

Figure 6. *A-F, Ovaloolithus utahensis, UCM 47621. A, outer surface of shell with single and closely paired circular pore openings (arrow) . A, bar = 1 mm;. B, thin section under TL with angusticaniculate pore canal (pc); note color differential in mammillae preservation (white) present in all specimens. C-D, thin section under TL showing fine outward radiation of spherulitic structure in upper region of shell unit (arrows) and narrow shell units (su). E-F, SEM radial view photos; note extended mammillary layer and slender shell units. The lack of distinct separation between individual shell units in upper portions of shell unit give appearance of differing structures although radiation of spherulitic structure does continue throughout (arrows). B-F, bar = 100μ m.*

described as composed of four types (*Oolithes chinkangkouensis*, types A-D) having complex sagentotuberculate sculpturing, rimocanaliculate pores, and a thicker eggshell ranging 2.2-2.85 mm, averaging 2.7 mm. Zhao (1979) established the oogenus *Ovaloolithus*, assigning the four varieties of *Oolithes chinkangkouensis* as *Ovaloolithus* oospecies. Mikhailov (1991) established the oofamily Ovaloolithidae. *Ovaloolithus tristriatus*, previously type B from *O. chinkangkouensis* (Zhao and Jiang, 1974), has a thickness of 1.7-2.6 mm and a slightly undulating sculpturing. *Ovaloolithus mixtistriatus*, described by Zhao (1979), and formerly *Oolithes chinkangkouensis* type C (Zhao and Jiang, 1974), is a spheroidal egg 88.4 x 67.9 mm. Eggshell thickness ranges from 1.7 mm 2.6 mm, averaging 2.1 mm. *Ovaloolithus monostriatus*- (Zhao, 1979), formerly *Oolithes chinkangkouensis* type D (Zhao, 1974) consists of spheroidal eggs 88.4 x 67.9 mm. Shell thickness ranges from 1.7 mm to 2.6 mm, averaging 2.1 mm. *Ovaloolithus laminadermus* (Zhao and Jiang, 1974, V788) has an eggshell thickness range of 0.6 mm to 1.2 mm, averaging 0.9 mm. The sculpturing is described as undulating. The shell units are tightly abutting and pore system is angusticanaliculate. *Ovaloolithus dinornithoides*-PIN4231-1 described by Mikhailov (1994b) from the Upper Cretaceous Nemegt Formation, Altan Ula III Locality, Southern Gobi, Mongolia, has an eggshell thickness range of 1.1 mm to 1.8 mm. The eggs are oval with an EL of 1.2->1.3. The outer surface sculpturing is a microscopic version of *O. chinkangkouensis* which is described as complexly sculptured sagentotuberculate. The pore system is rimocanaliculate.

Discussion

Most described *Ovaloolithus* have sagentotuberculate sculpturing, whereas the outer surface of *O. utahensis* is smooth. Accretion lines extend horizontally throughout the shell from mammillae to the outer surface and curve slightly downward at intersection with the pore canals (figure 6 B). Mammillae are closely spaced and shell units are tightly abutting. The number of pore openings present varies across the surface of the shell; some fragments have very few pore openings. All fragments (even sized less than 0.50 cm^2) have noticeable curvature. The eggshell fragments were found in situ and as surface float.

Oospecies *Ovaloolithus tenuisus* new oospecies

Holotype

UMC 73463.

Etymology

Latin, thin, referring to the thinness of the eggshell.

Diagnosis

Eggshell thickness ranges from 0.43 mm to 0.58 mm; outer surface smooth, no sculpturing; pore openings small, circular, singular, and a very few closely paired, angusticanaliculate pore system.

Material

Holotype UCM 73355; HEC 247-2.

Type Locality And Horizon

UCM L79058, Site 3 locality; Emery County, Utah; North Horn Formation, Maastrichtian.

Referred Material

Section 4 All Over locality; Emery County, Utah, more than 100 eggshell fragments.

Description

Eggshell is of dinosauroid-spherulitic basic type, angustispherulitic morphotype. Height-to-width ratio of the shell units is 8:1. The majority of fragments are small with small circular pore openings averaging 20 singular, and 5 paired per 0.5 cm^2. The mammillae are closely spaced and shell units are closely abutting. Distinct radial tabular ultrastructure is visible extending from mammillae throughout shell units, with slight fanning curvature of spherulitic structure beginning at one-third of the distance from the mammillae (figure 7 A).

Comparison

Ovaloolithus tenuisus is similar to *O. utahensis* in having a smooth outer surface, close abutment of individual shell units, and a point at which the radial tabular ultrastructure curves outward as it nears the mid-point of the shell (figure 7B,C). *Ovaloolithus tenuisus* is thinner than any other *Ovaloolithus* oospecies, the next thinnest being *O. laminadermus* at 0.6 mm to 1.2 mm thick.

Discussion

The unique features of this eggshell are its thinness and smooth outer surface which distinguish it from most *Ovaloolithus*. The difference in eggshell thickness between *O. tenuisus* (0.43-0.58 mm) and *O. utahensis* (1.51-1.82 mm) cannot be assumed as the thinning of eggshell due to weathering since the preservation of the outer surface and pore openings show no significant weathering. The pore openings have fewer paired openings than *O. utahensis* and pore system is angusticanaliculate (figure 7 D). Shell fragments, although small, do not exhibit significant curvature as do those of *O. utahensis*. Eggshell fragments were found in situ and as sur-

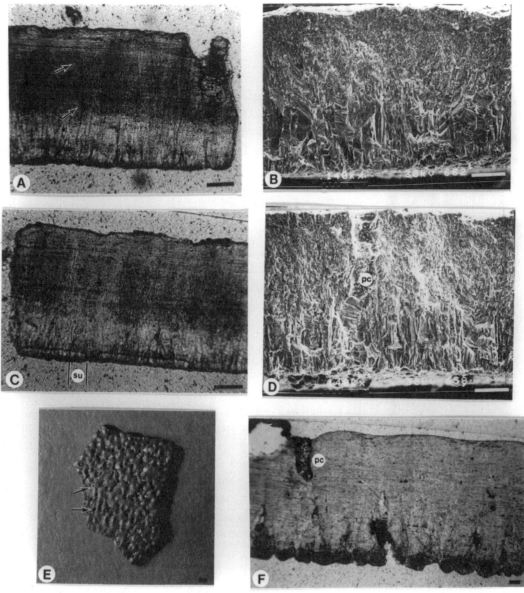

Figure 7. *A-D,* Ovaloolithus tenuisus, *new oospecies, UCM 73463; radial views. A, note outward radiation of spherulitic structure in upper portion of shell units (arrows). B, SEM radial view of structure. C, note narrow shell units, more distinct in mammillae than in upper shell unit (su). D, SEM micrograph with bisecting pore canal (pc). A-D, bar = 100μ m. E-F, Spheroolithus species indeterminate, UCM 73461. E, Outer surface of eggshell with sagentotuberculate sculpturing and pore openings (arrows), bar = 1 mm. F, radial thin section under TL with partial pore canal (pc), bar = 100μ m.*

Locality And Horizon

Lizard locality, (Locality 3 of Gilmore, 1946); Emery County, Utah, North Horn Formation, Upper Cretaceous, Maastrichtian.

Referred Material

Spheroolithid eggshell of the Two Medicine and Saint Mary River Formations of Montana.

Description

Eggshell thickness ranges from 1.27 mm to 1.37 mm. The sculpturing is sagentotuberculate, of low undulating ridges (averaging 3 per cm²) with linear orientation (figure 7 E). The pore system is rimocanaliculate and prolatocanaliculate. Pore openings are single and paired circular, and elongate slits that are situated in the depressions or valleys of the outer surface (figure 7 F). Single pores (large and small) average 42 per cm², paired average 15 per cm², and elongate average 14 per cm². The eggshell is of dinosauroid-spherulitic basic type, prolatospherulitic morphotype. Many fragments are weathered, reducing original height of ridges. Large interstices and pore canal openings between mammillae create voids between the shell units (figure 8 A). The shell units abut in the upper half of the shell unit. Shell units widen near outer surface in the characteristic "fanning" pattern of Spheroolithidae (figure 8 B). The height-to-width ratio of shell units is 2:1. Horizontal accretion lines are apparent in radial thin section and dip downward at intersection with the pore canals.

Comparison

Spheroolithid eggshell is known from Upper Cretaceous deposits of China (Young, 1959; Zhao and Jiang,

face float. These two *Ovaloolithus* oospecies share the same stratigraphic range, the lower North Horn Formation and are found in close proximity laterally and geographically.

Basic Type: Dinosauroid-spherulitic
Morphotype: Prolatospherulitic
Oofamily Spheroolithidae Zhao 1979
Oogenus *Spheroolithus* Zhao 1979
***Spheroolithus* oospecies indeterminate**

Material

UCM 73461, HEC 760 consisting of more than 17 fragments.

1974), Mongolia (Mikhailov, 1994b), and North America (Hirsch and Quinn, 1990). The North Horn *Spheroolithus* oospecies indeterminate is very similar in structure and sculpturing to the spherulitic shells of the Upper Cretaceous Two Medicine Formation of Montana. The Montana shells are thinner (averaging 1.0 mm) and are associated with the hadrosaur *Maiasaura peeblesorum* by hatchlings and eggs in nests (Horner and Makela, 1979; Hirsch and Quinn, 1990).

Discussion

This eggshell is weathered, wearing down the sculpturing on the outer surface. Details of the original sagentotuberculate sculpturing are not well preserved. The mammillae are slightly weathered, however, the large interstices between mammillae are visible in hand specimens and in radial thin section. Eggshell was found as surface float. This spheroolithid eggshell morphotype has been correlated to hadrosaurs (Hirsch and Quinn, 1990). From North Horn Mountain, hadrosaur remains have been excavated and the skeletons are comparable in size to that of *Kritosaurus* or *Parasaurolophus* (Gilmore, 1946).

Oogenus *Spheroolithus* oospecies indeterminate

Material

UCM 73462, HEC 830-1,2, consisting of 3 fragments.

Locality And Horizon

Lizard locality (Locality 3 of Gilmore, 1946); Emery County, Utah; North Horn Formation, Maastrichtian.

Referred Material

None.

Description

The eggshell has fine sagentotubercualte sculpturing (figure 8 C). The pores are of two types; single, circular, and short elongate. The shell thickness ranges from 0.58 mm to 0.82 mm. The vertical boundaries between shell units are well defined, and the radiating spherulitic crystalline structure is visible in radial thin section (figure 8 D). Horizontal accretion lines are present and contour the shape of the shell units. The mammillae are well preserved in some specimens (figure 8 E). The thinness of this eggshell and characteristics of shell units distinguish it from other spheroolithid eggshells.

Comparison

Eggshell is similar in structure to spherulitic shell

DINO 14731/HEC770-1 (shell thickness 0.22-0.53 mm) and MWCLoc5/HEC630-1 (thickness of 0.30-0.34 mm; Bray and Hirsch, in press) from the Upper Jurassic Morrison Formation. Both shells have nodose sculpturing which is not present on the North Horn eggshell.

Discussion

Because this eggshell type is represented by only three fragments, the material is not of sufficient quantity to assign parataxonomic status. The degree of weathering and recrystallization is significant, requiring analysis of additional material to enable classification.

In addition to the above described eggshell, there is an eggshell-like form (UCM73484/HEC830-1,2;764) of uncertain origin which is widespread throughout the North Horn Formation. Although it appears eggshell-like, no microstructure can be distinguished to verify that it is an eggshell. The outer surface is fractured with polygons, giving it a "cracked" appearance (figure 8 F). There are abundant single, circular openings which appear very pore-like. In radial thin section these openings are seen to extend throughout the thickness of the specimen (figure 8G). No structure is clearly visible in radial thin sections or when viewed at higher magnifications under scanning electron microscopy except for a radiating pattern stemming from the lower portion of the specimen (figure 8H). Elemental analysis by microprobe EDS shows a 98.42% by weight calcium content which would be expected for eggshell.

CONCLUSION

The eggs and eggshell of the North Horn Formation include a new morphotype, new oogenera and oospecies, and an oogenus new to the Western Interior of North America. The significance of these finds is a broadening of Late Cretaceous eggshell diversity within the Western Interior, providing an increased potential for direct comparison of Late Cretaceous eggshell material world wide.

Fossil eggs can yield important evidence indicating the type of fauna that inhabited a region. It is possible that nesting horizons may be preserved whereas adult, juvenile, or hatchling remains are absent. As the discoveries of embryos in fossil eggs and the research of recent eggshell have shown, it is possible to extend some phylogenetic correlation of fossil eggshell to representative extinct taxon. In regions where notable fossil skeletal remains are poorly represented, correlations based upon the fossil egg record can be a helpful indicator of faunal diversity.

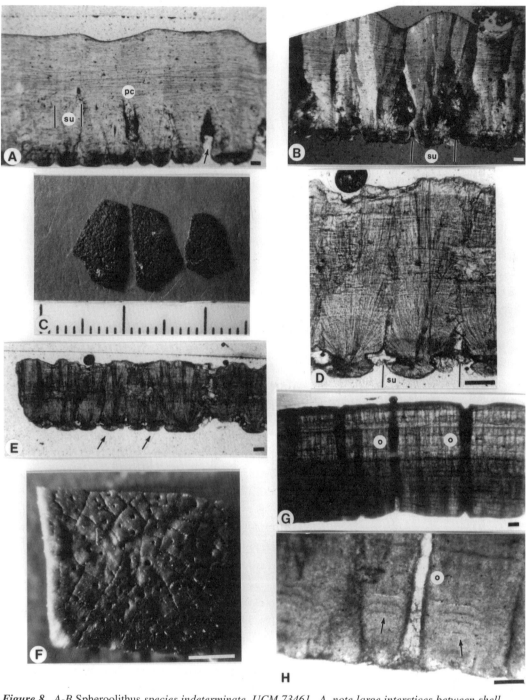

The author is deeply indebted to Karl for the many years of understudy and friendship. Karl passed away on June 1, 1996. His presence is sorely missed. That this study was possible is tribute to Karl's dedication, love, and perseverance in the seeking out of fossil egg remains throughout the western interior of North America.

Thanks are given to Steve Robison who assisted Karl on many of his field excursions in the North Horn and to whom Karl was most grateful. To Judith Harris, Konstantin Mikhailov, and Michael Thomas for their input and critical reviews of earlier versions of this manuscript and to Hans-Peter Schultze, Steve Robison and Dave Gillette for their final reviews of this manuscript. To John Drexler, University of Colorado Geology Department, and Bob McGrew, Colorado School of Mines, for their assistance with SEM and CL use and microprobe data, and to Paul Boni, University of Colorado Geology Department, for his assistance with XRD and mineralogical analysis. To James Jensen for his discovery of the *Prismatoolithus* eggs. To Ken Statman of Brigham Young University for assistance and access to specimens of concern to this study. To the Utah Museum of Natural History

Figure 8. *A-B* Spheroolithus *species indeterminate, UCM 73461. A, note large interstices between shell units (arrow) and distinct, separate shell units (su); partial pore canal (pc). B, thin section under PL showing characteristic fanning extinction pattern of spherulitic structure and distinction of individual shell units (su), bar = 100 µm. C-E,* Spheroolithus *species indeterminate, UCM 73462. C, Outer surface of eggshell with fine sagentotuberculate sculpturing; scale in mm. D-E, Radial thin section, TL, bar = 100µ m. D, note distinct shell units (su) and radiating spherulitic structure (arrows). E, note well-preserved mammillae (arrows) and radiating spherulitic structure of distinct shell units. F-H, eggshell-like form, UCM 73484. F, outer surface showing polygonal cracks and circular openings; bar = 1 mm. G, radial thin section under TL showing bisecting openings (o). H, radial thin section, TL, showing opening (o) and slight upward radiating structure (arrows). G-H bar = 100µ m.*

ACKNOWLEDGMENTS

The material analyzed in this study was collected, in large part, by the late Karl F. Hirsch. Research of this material was carried out by the author at Karl's request.

and their volunteers, and to Rose Difley, University of Utah, for her collaborative efforts with regard to eggshell finds. This study was supported by the University of Colorado Museum and by personal funds.

REFERENCES

Bray, E. S, and Hirsch, K. F., in press, Eggshell from the Upper Jurassic Morrison Formation: Modern Geology, Special Paper.

Cohen, Simon, Cruickshank, Arthur, Joysey, Ken, Manning, Terry, and Upchurch, Paul, 1995, The dinosaur egg and embryo project, exhibition guide: Rock Art, Leicester, 16 p.

Erben, H. K., 1970, Ultrastrukturen und Mineralisation rezenter und fossiler Eischalen bei Vogeln und Reptilien: Biomineralisation, v.1, p. 1-65.

Gilmore, C. W., 1940, New fossil lizards from the Upper Cretaceous of Utah: Smithsonian Miscellaneous Collection, v. 99, p. 1-3.

—1946, Reptilian fauna of the North Horn Formation of Central Utah: U. S. Geological Survey Professional Paper, 210-C, p. 29-53.

Hirsch, K. F., 1979, The oldest vertebrate egg: Journal of Vertebrate Paleontology, v. 53, no. 5, p. 1068-1084.

—1983, Contemporary and fossil chelonian eggshells: Copeia, 1983 no. 2, p. 382-397.

—1985, Fossil crocodilian eggs from the Eocene of Colorado: Journal of Paleontology, v. 59, no. 3, p. 531-542.

—1994a, The fossil record of vertebrate eggs, in Donovan, S.K., editor, The paleobiology of trace fossils: John Wiley and Sons, London, p. 269-294.

—1994b, Upper Jurassic eggshells from the Western Interior of North America, in Carpenter, Kenneth, Hirsch, K.F., and Horner, J.R., editors, Dinosaur eggs and babies: Cambridge, Cambridge University Press, p. 137-150.

—1996, Parataxonomic classification of fossil chelonian and gecko eggs: Journal of Vertebrate Paleontology, v. 16, no. 4, p. 752-762.

Hirsch, K. F., and Quinn, Betty, 1990, Eggs and eggshell fragments from the Upper Cretaceous Two Medicine Formation of Montana: Journal of Vertebrate Paleontology, v. 10, no. 4, p. 491-511.

Horner, J. R., 1994, Comparative taphonomy of some dinosaur and extant bird colonial nesting grounds, in Carpenter, Kenneth, Hirsch, K.F., and Horner, J.R., editors, Dinosaur eggs and babies: Cambridge, Cambridge University Press, p. 116-123.

Horner, J. R., and Makela, Robert, 1979, Nest of juvenile provides evidence of family structure among dinosaurs: Nature, v. 282, p. 296-299.

Horner, J. R., and Weishampel, D. B., 1988, A comparative embryological study of two ornithischian dinosaurs: Nature, v. 332, p. 256-257.

—1996, A comparative embryological study of two ornithischian dinosaurs: Nature, v. 332, p. 103.

Mikhailov, K. E. 1987a, Some aspects of the structure of the shell of the egg: Paleontological Journal, v. 21 no. 3, p. 54 61.

—1987b, The principle structure of the avian egg-shell: data of SEM studies: Acta Zoologica Cracovienzia, v. 30, no. 5, p. 193-238.

—1991, Classification of fossil eggshells of amniotic vertebrates: Acta Paleontologica Polonica , v. 36, no. 2, p. 193-238.

—1992, The microstructure of avian and dinosaurian eggshell-- phylogenetic implications, in Campbell , K. E., editor, Papers in avian paleontology honoring Pierce Brodkorb: Natural History Museum Los Angeles County, Science Series, 36, p. 361-373.

—1994a, Theropod and protoceratopsian dinosaur eggs from the Cretaceous of Mongolia and Kazakhstan: Palcontological Journal, v. 28, no. 2, p. 101-120.

—1994b, Eggs of sauropod and ornithopod dinosaurs from the Cretaceous deposits of Mongolia: Paleontological Journal, v. 28 , no. 3, p. 141-159.

—1995, Eggshell structure in the Shoebill and pelecaniform birds-- comparison with hammerkop, herons, ibises and storks: Canadian Journal of Zoology, v. 73, p. 1754-1770.

Mikhailov, K.E., Bray, E.S., and Hirsch, K.F., 1996, Parataxonomy of fossil egg remains (Veterovata)-- principles and applications: Journal of Vertebrate Paleontology, v. 16, no. 4, p. 763-769.

Norell, M.A., Clark, J.M., Demberelyin, Dashzeveg, Rhinchen, Barsbold, Chiappe, L.M., Davidson, A.R., McKenna, M.C., Altangerel, Perle, and Novacek, M.J., 1994, A theropod dinosaur embryo and the affinities of the Flaming Cliffs dinosaur eggs: Science, v. 226, p. 779-782.

Packard, M. J., 1980, Ultrastructural morphology of the shell and shell membranes of eggs of common snapping turtles (Chelydra serpentina): Journal of Morphology, v. 165, p. 187- 204.

Packard, M. J., and Hirsch K. F., 1986, Scanning electron microscopy of eggshell of contemporary reptiles: Scanning Electron Microscopy, v. 4, p. 1581-1590.

Packard, M. J., and Hirsch, K. F., and Iverson, J. B., 1984, Structure of shells from eggs of kinosternid turtles: Journal of Morphology, v. 18, p. 9-20.

Romanoff, A. L., and Romanoff, A. J., 1949, The avian egg: John Wiley and Sons, New York, 918 p.

Simkiss, Kenneth, 1968, The structure and formation of the shell and shell membranes, in Carter, T. C., editor, Egg quality--a study of the hen's egg: Oliver and Boyd Limited, p. 3-25.

Simkiss, Kenneth, and Tyler, Cyril, 1957, A histochemical study of the organic matrix of hen egg-shells: Quarterly Journal of Microscopical Science, v. 98, no. 1, pp. 19-28.

Spieker, E. M., 1946, Late Mesozoic and Early Cenozoic history of central Utah: U. S. Geological Survey Professional Paper 205-D, p. 117-161.

Tyler, Cyril, 1964, Wilhelm von Nathusius (1821-1899) on avian eggshells, a translated and edited version of his work: Berkshire Printing Company, p. 1-104, 18 plates.

—1969, Avian egg shells--their structure and characteristics, in Felts, W. J. L., and Harrison, R. J., editors, International review of general and experimental zoology: New York, Academic Press, p. 82-130.

Tyler, Cyril, and Simkiss, Kenneth, 1959, A study of the egg shells of ratite birds: Proceedings of the Zoological Society of London, v. 133, p. 201-243.

Vianey-Liaud, Monique, and Crochet, J. Y., 1993, Dinosaur eggshells from the Late Cretaceous of Languedoc (southern France): Revue de Paleobiologie, Geneve, v. 7, p.237-249.

Vianey-Liaud, Monique, Mallan, Pascale, Buscail, Olivier, and Montgelard, Claudine, 1994, Review of French eggshells--morphology, structure, mineral and organic composition, in Carpenter, Kenneth, Hirsch, K. F., Horner, J. R, editors, Dinosaur eggs and babies: Cambridge, Cambridge University Press, p. 151-183.

Young, C. C., 1954, Fossil reptilian eggs from Laiyang, Shantung, China: Scientia Sinica, v. 3, p. 505-522.

—1959, On a new fossil egg from Laiyang, Shantung: Vertebrata PalAsiatica v. 3, no. 1, p. 34-38.

1965, Fossil eggs from Nanhsiung, Kwangtung and Kanchou, Kiangsi: Vertebrata PalAsiatica, v. 9, no. 2, p. 141-170.

Zelenitsky, D. K., and Hills, L. V., 1996, An egg clutch of Prismatoolithus levis oosp. nov. from the Oldman Formation (Upper Cretaceous), Devil's Coulee, southern Alberta: Canadian Journal of Earth Science, v. 33, p. 1127-1131.

—1975, The microstructure of dinosaurian eggshells of Nanhsiung Basin, Guangdong Province: Vertebrata PalAsiatica, v. 13, no. 2, p. 105-117.

—1979, The advancement of research on the dinosaurian eggs in China, in Institute of Vertebrate Paleontology, Paleoanthropology and Nanjing Institute of Paleontology, editors, Mesozoic and Cenozoic red beds in Southern China: Beijing, Science Press, p. 330-340.

—1993, Structure, formation and evolutionary trends of dinosaur eggshells, in Kobayashi, I., Mutvei, Harry, Sahni, Ashok, editors, Structure, formation, and evolution of fossil hard tissues: Tokai University Press, Tokyo, p. 195-212.

Zhao, Z. K., and Jiang, Y. K., 1974, Microscopic studies on the dinosaurian eggshells from Laiyang, Shangtung Province: Scientia Sinica, v. 17, p. 73-83.

Zhao, Z. K., and Li, Rong, 1993, First record of Late Cretaceous hypsilophodontid eggs from Bayan Manduhu, Inner Mongolia: Vertebrata PalAsiatica, v. 31, no. 2, p. 77-84.

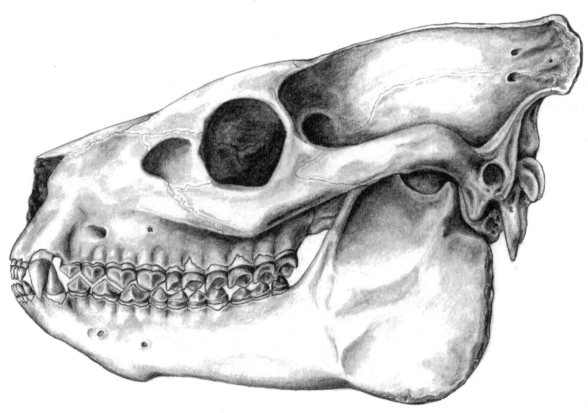

Brian Maebius © 1999

Oreodont

VERTEBRATE FAUNAS OF THE NORTH HORN FORMATION (UPPER CRETACEOUS-LOWER PALEOCENE), EMERY AND SANPETE COUNTIES, UTAH

Richard L. Cifelli
Oklahoma Museum of Natural History and Department of Zoology, University of Oklahoma, Norman, Oklahoma 73019

Randall L. Nydam
Oklahoma Museum of Natural History and Department of Zoology, University of Oklahoma, Norman, Oklahoma 73019

Jeffrey G. Eaton
Department of Geosciences, Weber State University, 2507 University Circle, Ogden, Utah 84408

James D. Gardner
Department of Biological Sciences and Laboratory for Vertebrate Paleontology, University of Alberta, Edmonton, Alberta, Canada T6G 2E9

James I. Kirkland
Utah Geological Survey, Box 146100, Salt Lake City, UT 84114-6100

ABSTRACT

We review herein the vertebrate faunas of the North Horn Formation, Emery and Sanpete Counties. Though the unit is correlated with the Upper Cretaceous through the lower Paleocene, a marked taxonomic hiatus separates the contained Cretaceous and Paleocene assemblages. Also, there exists no evidence that the North Horn Formation includes the K/T boundary, as has been previously suggested, despite the inability of geologists to locate an unconformity in the appropriate part of the section. The Cretaceous fauna, which includes about 40 taxa, is clearly of Lancian aspect; most diagnostic in this regard are the dinosaurs *Torosaurus latus* and *Alamosaurus sanjuanensis*, the multituberculate *Mesodma* cf. *M. hensleighi*, and the marsupial *Pediomys hatcheri*, which are otherwise known only from Lancian assemblages. *Alamosaurus* is of particular interest because of its apparently abrupt appearance (presumably as an immigrant) in the North American Late Cretaceous and because of its geographic restriction to faunas of the southwest. The most commonly encountered taxon in the Cretaceous part of the North Horn Formation is the teiid squamate *Polyglaphanodon*, elsewhere known from the Campanian of Baja California and thus conceivably also endemic to the southwest. Paleocene faunas of the North Horn Formation are more diverse, collectively including more than 70 taxa. Three distinct assemblages, the Gas Tank, Wagon Road, and Dragon local faunas, are recognized; these are referred to as Pu2, Pu3, and To1, respectively, and are considered to be of early but not earliest Paleocene age. Unsurprisingly, these faunas compare most closely with respective faunas of comparable age from the San Juan Basin, New Mexico; they are dominated by arctocyonid, periptychid, and mioclaenid condylarths.

INTRODUCTION

The North Horn Formation, exposed on the east side of the Wasatch Plateau in central Utah but probably with a broader distribution, including the Uinta Basin (Hintze, 1988), is of interest because it has produced the only well-sampled Lancian and Paleocene (Puercan, Torrejonian) vertebrate faunas in Utah. In this context, the faunas of the North Horn Formation are of biogeographic significance: the Paleocene assemblages lie geographically between more-or-less temporally equivalent faunas known from the San Juan Basin, New Mexico (for example, Matthew, 1937) and more northerly areas, such as the Bighorn Basin, Wyoming (see, for example, Van Valen, 1978); the Cretaceous assemblage is one of only a few Lancian faunas known from the southwest (for example, Clemens and others, 1979; Weishampel, 1990). Furthermore, the Late Cretaceous and early Tertiary fossils from the North Horn Formation have sparked interest in the unit because of the implication that it may be one of only a few terrigenous formations to include the Cretaceous/Tertiary boundary (for example, Spieker, 1960).

Since the initial description of Cretaceous and Paleocene vertebrates from the North Horn Formation in the 1930s and early 1940s, various additions to the faunas have appeared in a variety of publications, and taxonomy has been updated for many of the early reports, with the result that there exists no general compendia for the vertebrate assemblages. The purpose of this account is to provide faunal lists for the North Horn Formation based on existing literature and supplemented by newly collected materials resulting from our own, previously unpublished investigations.

Previous Work

Fossil vertebrates were discovered in the North Horn Formation by E. M. Spieker and J. B. Reeside of the U. S. Geological Survey, who apparently found dinosaur bones on the southwest face of North Horn Mountain itself, as well as indeterminate mammalian remains (from what later proved to be the Paleocene part of the unit) about 3 miles to the west, on Wagon Road Ridge, in 1934 and 1935, respectively (Spieker, 1960). The discoveries were of sufficient interest to arouse the curiosity of C. W. Gilmore, then a senior paleontologist with the United States National Museum, who explored and collected in the unit during the summer of 1937 (Gilmore, 1938a). Gilmore's field crew recovered a number of significant fossils that summer, including an incomplete skeleton of *Alamosaurus sanjuanensis* (Gilmore, 1938b, 1946), relatively complete remains of *Polyglyphanodon sternbergi* and another lizard (Gilmore, 1940, 1942a), and fossils of what proved to be Paleocene mammals (Gazin, 1938a). Gilmore's younger colleague and then relatively new curator at the United States National Museum, C. L. Gazin, led expeditions for the subsequent three field seasons (Gazin, 1938b, 1939a, 1941a; Gilmore, 1946). Among the many specimens obtained were further dinosaurs, lizards, and other reptiles from the Cretaceous part of the unit (Gilmore, 1942b, 1943a, 1946), as well as Paleocene mammals. The site of the Spieker/Reeside mammal discovery proved unproductive; instead, Gazin's crew obtained relatively diverse faunas, first from Dragon Canyon (Gazin, 1939b) and, later, from a second site, which included a distinct, older assemblage he named the Wagonroad fauna (Gazin, 1941b). The Dragon Canyon fauna became the basis for the "Dragonian" Land Mammal Age (Wood and others, 1941), which is now included in the Torrejonian Land Mammal Age (Archibald and others, 1987).

The next significant collecting in the North Horn Formation was undertaken by field parties led by M. C. McKenna in the 1950s and 1960s, based first at the University of California, Berkeley, and, later, the American Museum of Natural History. The most notable discoveries from these expeditions include: additional Paleocene mammals from known localities (for example, MacIntyre, 1966); an assemblage from Gas Tank Hill (said by

Robison, 1986, to be the same locality as that reported by Spieker, 1960; some of the taxa collected were published by Van Valen, 1978), which is older than Wagon Road fauna; and the Lancian mammal *Pediomys hatcheri* from the Cretaceous part of the North Horn Formation (Clemens, 1961). In the 1970s, teams from Brigham Young University and the University of Arizona worked in the North Horn Formation, the latter collecting magnetic samples as well as fossils (Tomida and Butler, 1980; Tomida, 1981, 1982; Archibald and others, 1983; Robison, 1986). Later parties to work the unit include the University of Utah and the Oklahoma Museum of Natural History, both of which obtained microvertebrates (Cifelli and others, 1995; Cifelli, Rowe, and others, 1996); small collections from the North Horn Formation are reported to be in other repositories as well.

Abbreviations

BYU, Brigham Young University; OMNH, Oklahoma Museum of Natural History, University of Oklahoma; UMNH, Utah Museum of Natural History, University of Utah; USNM, U. S. National Museum of Natural History, Smithsonian Institution.

VERTEBRATE ASSEMBLAGES OF THE NORTH HORN FORMATION

Cretaceous Vertebrates

The major reported finds of Cretaceous vertebrates from the North Horn Formation all derive from two major areas: the immediate vicinity of North Horn Mountain itself, and exposures in a faulted block to the south, in Dragon Canyon (figure 1, table 1). Most of the more nearly complete dinosaur material was collected from the former area (for example, Gilmore, 1946), whereas the latter includes the famous lizard quarries, from which abundant articulated specimens of *Polyglyphanodon* were obtained. Curiously, *Polyglyphanodon* is abundant (albeit not as well preserved) virtually everywhere the appropriate part of the section is exposed; eggshell, presumed to be dinosaurian, is also abundant in the Cretaceous part of the North Horn Formation (for example, Jensen, 1966). The most significant additions to the fauna since Gilmore's (1946) summary of the reptilian fauna (which was published posthumously and was incomplete even at the time of publication, omitting some of the author's own publications--notably Gilmore, 1942b, 1943a) are microvertebrates, collected from both of the main exposures of the Cretaceous part of the

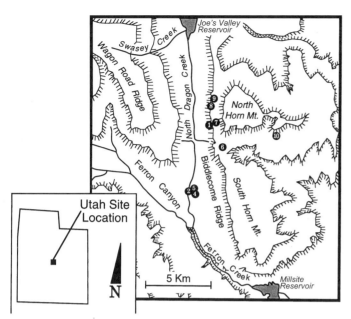

Figure 1. *Geographic distribution of fossil vertebrate localities, Cretaceous part, North Horn Formation, Emery County. Numbers are keyed to taxonomic listings in table 1 (number 3, not plotted, refers to area around North Horn Mountain, exact locality unknown).*

Table 1. *Vertebrate fauna from the Cretaceous part of the North Horn Formation; footnotes refer to literature citations given below; site numbers are keyed to those in figure 1. New identifications (footnote 1) are based on specimens deposited at OMNH and UMNH, indicated as (O) and (U), respectively, following taxon name. OMNH specimen data can be accessed through the OMNH home page: www.omnh.ou.edu.*

Chondrichthyes
Batoidea
　Family indet.
　　gen. and sp. indet.[1]　1 (O)
　Sclerorhynchidae
　　Ischyrhiza sp.[1]　1 (O)
　Dasyatidae
　　Myledaphis bipartus[1]　1 (O)
Galeomorpha
　Orectolobidae
　　Squatirhina americana[1]　1 (O)

Osteichthyes
Lepisosteidae
　Lepisosteus sp.[1]　1,2 (O)
Amiidae
　gen. and sp. indet.[1]　3 (O)
Pycnodontidae
　gen. and sp. indet.[1]　1 (O)
Family indet.
　gen. and sp. indet.[1]　1 (O)

Lissamphibia
Anura
　gen. and sp. indet.[1]　2 (O)

Reptilia
Testudines[2]
　Dermatemyidae
　　Basilemys sp.[3]　3
　　Adocus sp.[3]　5

Trionychidae
　"*Aspideretes*" sp.[3,4]　5
Family uncertain
　Compsemys sp.[3]　5
Squamata
　Teiidae
　　Polyglyphanodon sternbergi[1,3]　1, 3-5 (O)
　　Paraglyphanodon utahensis[3]　3
　　Paraglyphanodon gazini[5]　3
　　cf. *Leptochamops* sp.[1]　5
　Family indet.
　　gen. and sp. indet.[1]　5
Eosuchia
　Champsosauridae
　　Champsosaurus sp.[3]　5
Crocodilia
　?Atoposauridae
　　gen. and sp. indet.[1]　1-3 (O)
　　gen. and sp. indet.[1]　1 (O)
　?Pholidosauridae
　　gen. and sp. indet.[1]　2 (O)
　Crocodylidae
　　cf. *Allognathosuchus* sp.[1]　3 (O)
　　cf. *Leidyosuchus* sp.[1]　3 (O)
Theropoda
　gen. and sp. indet.[1,3]　2,3 (O)
　Tyrannosauridae
　　gen. and sp. indet.[3]　3
　Troodontidae
　　gen. and sp. indet.[1]　3 (O)
Sauropoda
　Alamosaurus sanjuanensis[3]　6
Ornithopoda
　Hadrosauridae
　　gen. and sp. indet.[1,3]　3 (O)
　　gen. and sp. indet.[3]　6,7
?Ankylosauria
　Pinasuchus mantiensis[6]　4
Ceratopsia
　Torosaurus latus[3,7]　8
　Ceratopsidae, gen. and sp. indet.[3]　9,10

Mammalia
Multituberculata
　Mesodma sp., cf. *M. hensleighi*[1]　2 (U)
　Cimolomys sp.[1]　2 (U)
　Paracimexomys sp.[1]　2 (U)
Marsupialia
　Alphadon sp.[1,8]　2,4 (O)
　Pediomys sp.[1]　2 (O)
　Pediomys hatcheri[9]　3
Eutheria
　gen. and sp. indet.[1]　2 (O, U)
　Proteutheria, gen. and sp. indet.[1]　2 (O, U)

[1]This study; [2]we follow the classification of Hutchison and Archibald, 1986; [3]Gilmore, 1946; [4]name used in quotes, following Meylan's (1987) restriction of this genus to living species; [5]Gilmore, 1943a; [6]Gilmore, 1942b; [7]originally listed (Gilmore, 1946) as *Arrhinoceratops*? *utahensis* and later transferred to *Torosaurus* by Lawson, 1976 (see also Lehman, 1980); we follow the taxonomy of Dodson and Currie, 1990; [8]Cifelli and others, 1996; [9]Clemens, 1961.

North Horn Formation. These were obtained through standard quarrying and underwater screenwashing techniques (see Cifelli, Madsen, and Larson, 1996).

Fishes and Amphibians

Scales and teeth of a lepisosteid fish, referred to *Lepisosteus*, are commonly encountered virtually throughout the North Horn Formation, as they are elsewhere in Upper Cretaceous and Lower Tertiary rock units of the Western Interior. Similarly, the other fishes recently recovered (*Ischyrhiza, Myledaphis, Squatirhina*, and an unidentified chondrithyan; Amiidae, Pycnodontidae, and an unidentified osteichthyan; table 1), predominantly from a microvertebrate site, are common elements of North American Late Cretaceous communities (see, for example, Estes, 1964) and are of little biogeographic or biostratigraphic utility.

Though only one anuran is positively known from the Cretaceous part of the North Horn Formation, this taxon merits special comment because it is represented by the only articulated frog specimen from the Lancian of North America (the four nominal species of North American Cretaceous frogs are based on isolated elements from Lancian sites in Wyoming and Montana). The specimen in question is OMNH 27756, collected in 1993 from OMNH locality V812. This previously undescribed specimen consists of the incomplete skull, most of the vertebral column, and a crushed left ilium and femur of a metamorphosed frog with a snout-vent length no greater than 25 mm. Although incompletely prepared, this specimen reveals enough detail to permit some preliminary comments about its identity. OMNH 27756 exhibits no features that are unequivocally diagnostic for any anuran family, but it clearly differs from each of the four named species of North American Lancian frogs as follows: from the palaeobatrachid *Palaeobatrachus occidentalis* Estes and Sanchíz 1982 (Lance Formation) in lacking a dorsal tubercle on the ilium; from the discoglossid *Paradiscoglossus americanus* Estes and Sanchíz 1982 (Lance Formation) in lacking a dorsal crest on the ilium; and from the discoglossid *Scotiophryne pustulosa* Estes 1969 (Hell Creek and Lance Formations) and the incertae sedis frog *Theatonius lancensis* Fox 1976 (Lance Formation) in having skull bones that are ornamented externally with pits and ridges (skull ornament pustulate in *S. pustulosa* and *T. lancensis*). OMNH 27756 has a dentulous premaxilla, suggesting that the maxilla also bore teeth in this specimen. This differs from the condition in *T. lancensis*, in which the maxilla is edentulous. Some of the ilia and skull bones from the Hell Creek and Lance Formations that Estes and Sanchíz (1982; see also Estes, 1964) iden-

tified as *Eopelobates* sp. (Pelobatidae sensu lato) resemble homologous bones in OMNH 27756, but the significance, if any, of these resemblances awaits further preparation and study of OMNH 27756.

Testudines, Squamata, and Eosuchia

The turtles recorded by Gilmore (1946) from the Cretaceous of the North Horn Formation, *Basilemys, Adocus, Compsemys*, and "*Aspideretes*" (cf. Meylan, 1987; see note in our table 1), are common elements of Lancian faunas (for example, Estes, 1964). Gilmore (1946) compared the turtle assemblage with that of the Naashoibito Member of the Kirtland Shale (Ojo Alamo Sandstone of earlier authors; see Gilmore, 1946; Lehman, 1981). With the possible exception of *Compsemys* (see below), these taxa (and the eosuchian *Champsosaurus*) are widely ranging, both geographically and biostratigraphically, and their presence in the Cretaceous part of the North Horn Formation is both predictable and relatively uninformative. It is worth noting, however, that turtle assemblages of both the Cretaceous and Paleocene parts of the North Horn Formation appear impoverished in comparison to those of the Hell Creek and Tullock Formations (see Hutchison and Archibald, 1986).

Gilmore (1940, 1942a, 1943a) described three squamates from the Cretaceous part of the North Horn Formation: *Polyglyphanodon sternbergi, Paraglyphanodon utahensis,* and *P. gazini*. We agree with Estes' (1983) suggestion that the latter two species probably represent growth stages of *Polyglyphanodon sternbergi*, but that existing materials are inadequate to settle the issue with certainty. A large number of relatively complete, sometimes articulated skeletons of *P. sternbergi* have been recovered from two closely spaced sites in Dragon Canyon; as noted above, the species occurs in abundance elsewhere in the unit. Previously placed in its own family (Gilmore, 1942a) but now referred to the Teiidae (Estes, 1983), *P. sternbergi* was a very large lizard (snout-vent length of approximately 50 cm, estimated from Gilmore, 1942a) that is believed to have been herbivorous (Gilmore, 1942a). If this dietary interpretation is correct, *Polyglyphanodon* filled a niche now occupied by Iguanidae (sensu Frost and Etheridge, 1989)-- and, indeed, Gilmore (1942a) found this species to be remarkably iguanid-like, except for the dentition. The closest ecological equivalent would probably be *Ctenosauria*, a large, primarily terrestrial iguanid that inhabits the neotropics. Another teiid, represented by fragmentary jaws, is present in the fauna; we tentatively refer it to *Leptochamops*, which is known from both Lancian and Judithian assemblages, including the Lance (Estes,

1964), Hell Creek (Estes and others, 1969), Fruitland (Armstrong-Ziegler, 1980), Frenchman, and Oldman Formations (Gao and Fox, 1996).

Archosauria

Gilmore (1946) listed the Recent crocodilian *Crocodylus* in the Cretaceous part of the North Horn Formation, which is almost certainly incorrect; based on isolated teeth, at least five crocodilians appear to be present. Several taxa (?Atoposauridae, Pholidosauridae) are found in earlier faunas (cf. Cifelli and others, 1997). The latest Cretaceous and early Tertiary (see Lehman, 1981) genus *Allognathosuchus* is tentatively recognized on the basis of teeth of durophagous design with constricted bases, and other teeth with pointed, laterally compressed crowns lacking basal constrictions. Teeth tentatively referred to Atoposauridae are pointed and laterally compressed, with constricted bases and lingual striae that flare onto the carinae (a feature lacking in *Allognathosuchus*). Teeth tentatively referred to Pholidosauridae are long and gracile.

A problematic reptile from the Cretaceous part of the North Horn Formation is *Pinasuchus mantiensis*, described by Gilmore (1942b) from the "lizard locality" in Dragon Canyon. Gilmore tentatively referred this small, puzzling animal to the Crocodilia on the basis of thecodont dentition and dermal armor, though he noted that the weakly amphicoelous vertebrae and highly ornate armor with elongate spines are features unlike the conditions seen in most contemporary members of the order. No additional materials of *Pinasuchus* have surfaced, and we can add nothing to Gilmore's (1942b) assessment of its relationship, except to note that Kenneth Carpenter (written communication, 1997) has observed some faint resemblances to the ?goniopholidid crocodilian *Eutretauranosuchus*, from the Upper Jurassic Morrison Formation of Colorado.

At least three theropods (including an unidentified tyrannosaurid) and two hadrosaurids are known from the unit; we are not aware of any diagnostic material that has emerged since Gilmore's original descriptions (1946). Gilmore (1946) also described a new ceratopsian, tentatively referred to *Arrhinoceratops* as *A.? utahensis*, and noted at least one other ceratopsian in the fauna. *A.? utahensis* was transferred to *Torosaurus* by Lawson (1976), who described material he referred to *T. utahensis* from the Javelina Formation of the Big Bend region, Texas. Lawson (1976) suggested that *T. utahensis* was a species of southern distribution and that the closely related *T. latus* was its northern counterpart. This suggestion was followed by Lehman (1981), who tentatively also recognized *T. utahensis* from the Naashoibito Member of

the Kirtland Shale, San Juan Basin, New Mexico. Dodson and Currie (1990), however, regard the two species as synonymous.

The most celebrated dinosaur from the Cretaceous part of the North Horn Formation is the titanosaurid sauropod *Alamosaurus sanjuanensis*, represented by a partial skeleton (Gilmore, 1938b, 1946). This species is also known farther to the southwest, from other units believed to be of Maastrichtian age, including the Naashoibito Member of the Kirtland Shale, New Mexico (Gilmore, 1922; see also Lehman, 1981; Mateer, 1981); the Javelina Formation, Texas (Lawson, 1976; Lehman, 1987); the McRae Formation, New Mexico, and, possibly (specimens have not yet been described), the Evanston Formation, Wyoming (see Lehman, 1987; Lucas and Hunt, 1989).

Mammalia

The first mammal to be described from the Cretaceous part of the North Horn Formation is the Lancian marsupial *Pediomys hatcheri*, which Clemens (1961) reported from Gilmore's "lizard locality" in Dragon Canyon; Clemens and others (1979) also reported that a multituberculate ultimate lower premolar (which has not been described) was collected from the same site. An extraordinarily complete mandible of a juvenile individual (see Cifelli, Rowe, and others, 1996) of *Alphadon* was collected at the nearby, second USNM lizard locality by an OMNH field party. The specimen represents a taxon smaller than other Lancian species of the genus and is referred to *A. eatoni*, known only from the North Horn Formation (Cifelli and Muizon, 1998).

The most diverse assemblage of mammals from the Cretaceous part of the North Horn Formation comes from a locality on the flank of North Horn Mountain itself, which has been worked by parties from both UMNH and OMNH, using underwater screenwashing. The material is very fragmentary, but at least six taxa are represented. Multituberculates include *Cimolomys* sp., *Paracimexomys* sp. (both of which are widely ranging genera, both geographically and temporally; see Archibald, 1982; Eaton, 1995), and *Mesodma* sp., cf. *M. hensleighi*, which is encountered in most Lancian faunas in the Western Interior (Lillegraven and McKenna, 1986). Two species of *Alphadon* are present, one of which represents an individual approximately the size of *A. eatoni* from Dragon Canyon (see Cifelli, Rowe, and others, 1996; Cifelli and Muizon, 1998). The other species is larger and is similar to *A. sahnii* (see Cifelli, 1990) in size. Also present is an extremely small species of *Pediomys*, similar in size to *P. krejcii* or *P. prokrejcii* from the Lancian and Judithian, respectively. Eutherians include a taxon represented by a trigonid of a lower molar similar to those of *Avitotherium* and *Paranyctoides,* and a small, palaeoryctoid-like insectivore, represented by a fragmentary ultimate upper premolar.

Paleocene Vertebrates

Paleocene vertebrates from the North Horn Formation have received much more extensive study and published treatment than those from the Cretaceous part of the unit, and for this reason we confine our remarks to literature summary and review of problematic taxa or occurrences. Gazin's (1941b) definitive treatment of Paleocene mammals from this unit was based on specimens from two localities. The Dragon fauna included materials from the original site in Dragon Canyon and an upper level at a second site. A lower level at this latter area produced fossils referred by Gazin (1941b) to an older assemblage, which he named the Wagonroad fauna, and the site has been called by this same name in the literature (for example, Robison, 1986). The choice of name is unfelicitous, as the site is not on or near Wagon Road Ridge (the geographic source of the name); moreover, some confusion arises because the original discovery of (practically indeterminate) Paleocene mammals in the North Horn Formation was on Wagon Road Ridge (see Gazin, 1941b), and these are likely to belong to the third Paleocene assemblage from the unit, the Gas Tank fauna (Robison, 1986). The site in question lies below Elk Horn Flats and just east of an area locally called The Kitchen, a name that appears on maps and is therefore more appropriate for the site itself. Dragon mammals have not been recovered from this area by subsequent workers (see Tomida and Butler, 1980). The Kitchen remains the only known locality for fossils attributed to the Wagonroad fauna; Robison (1986) described fossils from a third locality (Sage Flat) for the Dragon fauna, and recorded five localities (Gas Tank Hill, Dairy Creek, Blue Lake, Jason Spring, and Ferron Mountain) yielding mammals that he referred to the Gas Tank fauna. We follow Robison's (1986) referral of these sites to three distinct assemblages, and simply list taxa by fauna in table 2.

Table 2. *Vertebrate fauna from the Paleocene part of the North Horn Formation. Footnotes denote references and explanations given below; letters following taxa refer to local faunas as defined by Robison (1986) and emended by Cifelli and others (1995); land-mammal age subdivisions follow Archibald and others, 1987: GT, Gas Tank (Pu2); W, Wagon Road (Pu3); D, Dragon (To1).*

Osteichthyes
　Lepisosteidae
　　Lepisosteus sp. GT,W,D[1,2]

Reptilia
　Testudines
　　Dermatemyidae
　　　Hoplochelys sp. GT,W,D[2]
　　Trionychidae
　　　"*Trionyx*" sp. GT,D[2,3]
　　　?*Plastomenus* sp. GT[2]
　　Family uncertain
　　　Compsemys victa GT,W,D[2]
　Squamata
　　Anguidae
　　　cf. *Proxestops jepseni* GT,D[1,2]
　　　gen. and sp. indet. D[2]
　Eosuchia
　　Champsosauridae
　　　Champsosaurus sp. GT,W[1,2]
　Crocodilia
　　Crocodylidae
　　　cf. *Allognathosuchus* GT,W,D[2]
　　　cf. *Leidyosuchus* GT,W,D[1,2]

Mammalia
　Multituberculata
　　Taeniolabididae
　　　Catopsalis utahensis D[4]
　　　Taeniolabis sp. W[4]
　　　cf. *T. taoensis* GT[2]
　　Ptilodontidae
　　　?*Ptilodus* sp. D[2]
　　　Ptilodus ferronensis D[4]
　　　Ptilodus sp, cf. *P. tsosiensis* GT[2]
　　　gen and sp. indet. D,W[2,5]
　　Neoplagiaulacidae
　　　Neoplagiaulax macintyrei D[2]
　　　Parectypodus sp. D[5]
　Marsupialia
　　Didelphidae
　　　gen. and sp. indet. D[5]
　Proteutheria
　　fam., gen. and sp. indet. GT[2]
　　Pantolestidae
　　　?*Propalaeosinopa* sp. D[6]
　　　gen. and sp. indet. D[4]
　　Pentacodontidae
　　　Aphronorus simpsoni D[4]
　　Mixodectidae
　　　Dracontolestes aphanatus D[4,7]
　　　gen. and sp. indet. D[4]
　　　gen. and sp. indet. W[4]
　　Palaeoryctidae
　　　Acmeodon D[8]
　　Leptictidae
　　　Myrmecoboides sp. D[2]
　Taeniodonta
　　Stylinodontidae
　　　gen. and sp. indet. W,D[2,4,9]
　　　Onychodectes sp., cf. *O. tisonensis* W[2]
　　　Conoryctella dragonensis D[4]
　Primates
　　Paromomyidae
　　　Paromomys sp., cf. *P. depressidens* D[2]
　　　?*Palaechthon* sp. D[2,5]
　　　gen. and sp. indet. W[5]

Picrodontidae
   Draconodus apertus D[10]
Carnivora
  Miacidae
    Protictis haydenianus D[7,11]
    Bryanictis sp. D[2,12]
Condylarthra
  Arctocyonidae
    Loxolophus sp. W,D[2,4]
    L. pentacus GT,D[2]
    L. spiekeri D[4,13]
    Loxolophus sp., cf. *L. spiekeri* GT[2]
    Oxyclaenus pugnax GT[2]
    O. piercei D[4]
    O. sp. W[4]
    Chriacus sp. D[2]
    C. truncatus D[2]
    Chriacus sp., cf. *C. baldwini* D[5]
    Mimotricentes sp. D[2]
    M. subtrigonus D[2]
    M. elassus D[5,14]
    Desmatoclaenus hermaeus GT,W,D[2,4,6]
    Goniacodon sp. D[5]
    Oxytomodon perissum D[4,14]
  Periptychidae
    Ectoconus sp. GT[2]
    Ectoconus ditrigonus GT[2,5]
    E. symbolus W,GT[2,4]
    Carsioptychus coarctatus GT[2,15]
    C. hamaxitus GT,W[2,4]
    Carsioptychus sp., cf. *C. hamaxitus* D[2]
    Periptychus gilmorei D[4]
    Anisonchus sp D[2]
    A. athelas GT,W[2,16]
    A. onostus GT,D[2,4]
    A. dracus D[3]
    A. oligistus D,W[2,4,17]
    Haploconus sp. GT,W[2]
    H. elachistus GT,W[2,4]
    H. inopinatus D[4]
    Conacodon utahensis GT,W[2]
    Oxyacodon sp. GT[2]
    O. apiculatus GT[18]
    O. ferronensis GT[18]
    O. marshater W[16]
  Mioclaenidae
    Promioclaenus sp. D[2]
    P. acolytus GT[2]
    P. wilsoni GT[2]
    P. lemuroides D[2]
    Litaletes sternbergi D[4]
    L. disjunctus D[2]
    L. gazini GT[2,19]
    Ellipsodon grangeri D[2]
    ?E. sp. W[4]
    Protoselene griphus D[4]

[1]This study; [2]Robison, 1986; [3]name used in quotes following Meylan's (1987) restriction of the genus to a living species; [4]Gazin, 1941b; [5]Tomida and Butler, 1980; [6]Cifelli and others, 1995; [7]see Szalay, 1969; [8]see Van Valen, 1966; [9]Tomida and Butler (1980, p. 792) list "near *Psittacotherium*", which may or may not refer to the same taxon; [10]Tomida, 1982; [11]MacIntyre, 1966; [12]placed by Flynn and Galiano (1982) in *Protictis*; we follow Gingerich and Winkler (1985) in recognizing *Bryanictis* as distinct; [13]including *Protogonodon biatheles*; see Van Valen, 1978; [14]taxonomy follows Cifelli, 1983; [15]genus founded by Simpson (1936) and synonymized with *Periptychus* by Van Valen, 1978; we follow Archibald and others, 1987, in recognizing *Carsioptychus* as distinct; [16]Van Valen, 1978; [17]referred by Rigby (1981) to *Gillisonchus*, a junior synonym of *Mithrandir* Van Valen, 1978; see Cifelli, 1983; [18]Archibald and others, 1983; [19]emended from *Litaletes "gazinensis"* in Robison, 1986, p. 129.

In addition to the recognition of a third Paleocene fauna from the North Horn Formation (Robison, 1986; Archibald and others, 1987), a number of additions and taxonomic changes have been made to the faunas described by Gazin (1941b). Robison (1986) was the first to provide a comprehensive list of lower vertebrates from the Paleocene part of the North Horn Formation; even with more recent additions, the roster of included taxa is unremarkable (table 1). Among multituberculates, notable recent records include cf. *Taeniolabis taoensis* from the Gas Tank fauna and *Neoplagiaulax macintyrei* from the Dragon fauna (Robison, 1986). The former is otherwise known from the *Taeniolabis taoensis/Periptychis* zone (Pu3; Archibald and others, 1987). *Neoplagiaulax macintyrei* was originally described from Mammalon Hill, Betonnie Tsosie Wash, in the San Juan Basin (Sloan, 1981; this author indicates that specimens from this locality are from the "*Hemithlaeus* zone," which is conventionally regarded as Pu2; but Archibald and others, 1987, tentatively referred the site to Pu3). Another multituberculate, *Parectypodus*, previously unknown from the Dragon fauna, proves (as a result of screenwashing) to be the most abundant mammal present at the main site in Dragon Canyon (Tomida and Butler, 1980). Tomida and Butler (1980) also recorded the presence of an unidentified didelphid marsupial, hitherto unknown from the Dragon fauna, at the same site in Dragon Canyon, but this occurrence is unsurprising in view of the extended range of this group in the Paleogene of North America.

Of the non-ungulate eutherians, the pantolestid *Propalaeosinopa*, which elsewhere appears first in To3 faunas (Archibald and others, 1987), has been tentatively reported from the Dragon fauna (Cifelli and others, 1995); another proteutherian, *Myrmecoboides* (elsewhere known from To3 through To5; Archibald and others, 1987) was included by Gazin (1941b) in this fauna as well. Remains of several primates have been recovered from Paleocene sites in the North Horn Formation; of these, *Draconodus apertus* is endemic to the Dragon fauna (Tomida, 1982). The occurrence of *Paromomys* and *Palaechthon* in the same fauna (Tomida and Butler, 1980; Robison, 1986) is predictable in view of their temporal distribution elsewhere, but the presence of a paromomyid in the Wagonroad fauna (Tomida and Butler, 1980) is notable in that, aside from *Purgatorious*, it represents the earliest occurence of the family. Robison (1986) also reported the carnivoran *Bryanictis* sp. from the Dragon fauna; this genus is otherwise found in deposits of To3 and, possibly, Ti1 age (J. J. Flynn, written communication, 1997).

The condylarth families Arctocyonidae, Periptychidae, and Mioclaenidae are represented by numerous taxa in the Paleocene faunas of the North Horn Formation. Since Gazin's (1941b) work, the principal additions to knowledge of ungulates from this unit have been by Van Valen (1978), Tomida and Butler (1980), Archibald and others (1983), Robison (1986), and Cifelli and others (1995); Van Valen (1978) and Archibald and others (1983) made significant emendations to taxonomy. The most biostratigraphically noteworthy addition is the recognition by Robison (1986) of *Carsioptychus* (otherwise known from Pu2 to Pu3; Archibald and others, 1987) in the Dragon fauna. Robison's summary listing (1986, table 1, p. 92) includes "*Periptychus* cf. *P. hamaxitus*" (which we refer to *Carsioptychus*, following arguments presented by Archibald and others, 1987) in this fauna based on a specimen from the Sage Flat locality. The only such specimen in the hypodigm is an M2 referred to as BYU 3834, but in the discussion on the same page (Robison, 1986, p. 110) said to be BYU 3801. Robison's (1986) referral was said to have been tentative because of this species' similarity in upper molar structure to that of "*P.*" *coarctatus*, now also referred to *Carsioptychus*; hence generic referral is unaffected by this uncertainty.

DISCUSSION AND CONCLUSIONS

Recent collecting has more than doubled the known taxonomic diversity from the Cretaceous part of the North Horn Formation, an outcome which underscores the importance of supplementing traditional prospecting methods with underwater screenwashing, in order to obtain the most complete fossil sampling possible (see, for example, McKenna, 1962; Cifelli, Madsen, and Larson, 1996). Though most of the specimens obtained through screenwashing are fragmentary (because many of the productive horizons in the Cretaceous part of the North Horn Formation are well indurated and difficult to wash), another result of recent work has been the recovery of extremely well-preserved microvertebrate fossils—such as an articulated frog and a relatively complete mammal jaw—through quarrying methods. Both of these collecting strategies suggest that there is considerable

potential for obtaining morphologically informative specimens from the North Horn Formation.

As previously indicated (for example, Lawson, 1976; Lucas and Hunt, 1989), the Cretaceous part of the North Horn Formation has a fauna of Lancian aspect and is of Maastrichtian, probably late Maastrichtian (Lehman, 1987), age. Most important in this regard are the occurrences of the ceratopsian *Torosaurus latus* and the titanosaurid *Alamosaurus sanjuanensis*, which are restricted to the Lancian. In the San Juan Basin, New Mexico (Lehman, 1981) and the Big Bend, Texas (Lawson, 1976), units bearing these taxa (Naashoibito Member of the Kirtland Shale and Javelina Formation, respectively) are underlain by other, dinosaur-bearing units that are faunally distinct (Lawson, 1976; Lehman, 1981). *Alamosaurus* appeared suddenly in the latest Cretaceous of North America, probably as a result of immigration from South America (Lucas and Hunt, 1989). As suggested by Sloan (1969) and detailed by Lehman (1987), the Lancian of western North America was characterized by biogeographic zonation owing to distinct paleoenvironmental and sedimentary provinciality; the *Alamosaurus* fauna appears to have been distributed in semiarid intermontane basins south of about 35° north latitude.

The teiid lizard *Polyglyphanodon*, not previously mentioned in connection with biogeographic provinciality in the Late Cretaceous of North America, deserves some commentary here because of its great abundance in the Cretaceous part of the North Horn Formation and its apparent absence in more northerly faunas of North America. In this connection, we note that Estes (1983) considered *Haptosphenus* (from the Lance Formation) as a possible relative of *Polyglyphanodon*. Gao and Fox (1996), however, tentatively referred *Haptosphenus* to the Teiinae and suggested that it may be morphologically convergent on modern *Dracaena*. At least five genera and seven species of lizards probably related to *Polyglyphanodon* are known from Upper Cretaceous rocks (Baron Goyot, Djadochtha, Nemegt Formations; Khermeen Tsav I and Khermeen Tsav II beds) of Mongolia (Gilmore, 1943b; Sulimski, 1972, 1975, 1978), and Estes (1983) reported remains of *P. sternbergi* from the "El Gallo Formation" of Baja California del Norte, Mexico, which is correlated with the Campanian on the basis of marine invertebrates (Clemens and others, 1979; see also Lillegraven, 1972, 1976). In addition, work in progress by one of us (RLN) suggests the presence of related taxa in rocks of Albian/Cenomanian and Turonian age in central and southern Utah, respectively (see Cifelli and others, this volume; Eaton and others, this volume). From these data it appears likely that polyglyphanodontine teiids had become distinct by the mid-Cretaceous; though the continent of origin is unclear, existing evidence suggests a southern distribution in the Late Cretaceous of North America. *Polyglyphanodon*-like lizards have not yet been reported from Upper Cretaceous units of New Mexico or Texas, but this may be an artifact of sampling.

Another biogeographically interesting taxon present in the Cretaceous part of the North Horn Formation is the turtle *Compsemys*. This taxon has a geographically widespread distribution in the Lancian. It has not, to our knowledge, been reported from older faunas in the central and northern part of the Western Interior. However, *Compsemys* has been recorded from the Hunter Wash local fauna of the San Juan Basin, New Mexico, which is of Campanian age (Lehman, 1981), and it is also tentatively recognized from several pre-Lancian units in southern Utah (Eaton and others, this volume). This suggests that *Compsemys* may have had a southern distribution through the Campanian, before becoming more widely distributed in the Lancian.

The most significant recent contributions to knowledge of Paleocene vertebrates from the North Horn Formation have been the recognition of the Gas Tank fauna, which -- thanks to the efforts of Robison (1986) -- is now represented by fossil assemblages from five localities, and the development of greater understanding in the age of the faunas. Based on a combination of biostratigraphic and paleomagnetic evidence, Tomida and Butler (1980) considered the Wagonroad fauna to be Puercan, or slightly younger than otherwise-known Puercan, and the Dragon fauna to be slightly older than the then-known Torrejonian of the San Juan Basin (as implied in the recognition of a "Dragonian" Land Mammal Age by Wood and others, 1941). Subsequent work, including the discovery of a correlative horizon in the San Juan Basin, together with detailed comparison of the faunas, led to recognition of the Dragon fauna as the earliest subdivision of the Torrejonian (Tomida, 1981). In a comprehensive treatment of Paleocene land mammal ages, Archibald and others (1987) supported this assessment, referring the Dragon fauna to To1. These authors tentatively recognized the Wagonroad fauna as late Puercan (Pu3?) and the Gas Tank fauna, only just then becoming known, as belonging to the preceding subdivision of the Puercan (Pu2?). Tomida and Butler (1980) placed the Wagonroad fauna in the younger part of chron 28N and the older part of chron 27R, and the Dragon fauna in the younger part of chron 27N and the older part of chron 26R. These authors considered the Torrejonian in the San Juan Basin to correlate with chrons 26R to 26N; the Puercan was placed in chron 28N (Tomida, 1981). Archibald and others (1987) referred the entire Puercan

to the younger part of chron 29R and possibly the whole of chron 29N, placing the Wagonroad fauna in the upper part of chron 29N and the earliest part of the Torrejonian (To1), including the Dragon fauna, in chron 28N. These views were upheld by Prothero (1995), who placed the Puercan in the youngest part of chron 29R and the entirety of chron 29N, and To1 in chron 28N.

Although the compositions of the assemblages from the North Horn Formation are generally consistent with the correlations indicated above, several problematic occurrences should be noted. The Gas Tank fauna was tentatively regarded as Pu2 based on the absence of the taeniolabidid multituberculate *Taeniolabis taoensis* (which is found in the younger Wagonroad fauna and which is restricted to Pu3 in the San Juan Basin; Archibald and others, 1987); however, Robison (1986) reported a specimen possibly referable to *T. taoensis* from the Ferron Mountain locality (which is assigned to the Gas Tank fauna). Similarly, Archibald and others (1987) distinguished Puercan from Torrejonian faunas partially on the occurrence of different genera of large periptychid condylarths, with *Carsioptychus* being present in the Puercan and *Periptychus* in the *Torrejonian*: Robison's report of *Carsioptychus* sp., cf. *C. hamaxitus* in the Dragon fauna, based on a specimen from Sage Flat (see above), is enigmatic in this respect. Other noteworthy occurrences in the Dragon fauna are *Neoplagiaulax macintyrei* (elsewhere known only from Pu3 of the San Juan Basin); ?*Propaleosinopa*, *Bryanictis*, and *Myrmecoboides* (which elsewhere make their first appearance in To3); and *Draconodus*, which represents the earliest record of Picrodontidae. The dermatemyid turtle *Hoplochelys* occurs in all three Paleocene faunas of the North Horn Formation (Robison, 1986); this taxon is otherwise known from the Puercan (and possibly Lancian; Lehman, 1981) through Torrejonian of the San Juan Basin (Gilmore, 1919) but not, as far as we are aware, from more northerly assemblages in Wyoming, Montana, and Canada.

The North Horn Formation has long been known to include rocks of both Cretaceous and Paleocene age, based on included vertebrate faunas. On this basis, it might be inferred that the Cretaceous/Tertiary boundary is included or represented in the unit. Spieker (1960) believed this to be the case, basing his argument on the perception that the sequence within the North Horn Formation is uninterrupted and that fossil mammals said by him to be of "earliest Paleocene" (Spieker, 1960, p. 18) age were found within 35 feet, stratigraphically, of dinosaur fossils. The Paleocene mammals in question, including *Desmatoclaenus* sp., *Ectoconus* sp., cf. *E. majusculus*, and *Anisonchus* sp., cf. *A. oligistus*, are from the Gas Tank locality (Robison, 1986), which is referred to Pu2?. Magnetostratigraphic data summarized above suggests that both the Pu2 and Pu3 interval-zones occur in magnetic polarity chron 29N, which is considered to range from 64.1 to 64.6 million years ago (Berggren and others, 1995). The age of the Cretaceous part of the North Horn Formation is imprecisely understood, but presumably it is older than the K/T boundary, which occurs in the younger part of Chron C29R, at about 65 million years ago (see Archibald, 1990; Archibald and Lofgren, 1990; Berggren and others, 1995). Furthermore, the fauna of the Cretaceous part of the North Horn Formation bears much stronger similarity to assemblages of Lancian age than to Bug Creek (interpreted to be transitional between Lancian and Puercan; Archibald and Lofgren, 1990) or Puercan faunas. The youngest part of the Lancian is interpreted (Archibald and Lofgren, 1990) as occurring within Chron 30n and the older part of Chron 29R, or about 65.5 to 67 million years ago (Gradstein and others, 1995). Hence a gap of at least 1 million years, and perhaps as much as 2-3 million years separates the ages of known vertebrate fossils from the Creta-

ceous and Paleocene parts of the North Horn Formation. There is no evidence that vertebrate fossils of intervening age exist in the unit nor, for that matter, that the intervening period is represented in the North Horn Formation.

ACKNOWLEDGMENTS

We thank J. D. Archibald, J. J. Flynn, Kenneth Carpenter, Daniel Brinkman, and D. J. Chure for information, advice, and/or helpful comments on an earlier version of this manuscript, and Dale Harber for the support and cooperation of the U.S. Forest Service. For access to comparative specimens we thank P. C. Holroyd (University of California Museum of Paleontology), Charlotte Holton (American Museum of Natural History), and C. R. Schaff (Museum of Comparative Zoology, Harvard University). Figure 1 was drafted by Coral McCallister. Partial support for this research was provided by grants to RLC from the National Geographic Society (4761-92, 5021-93) and the National Science Foundation (DEB 9401094); JDG's part in this study has been supported by a University of Alberta Ph.D. Dissertation Fellowship and N. J. Marklund.

REFERENCES

Archibald, J. D., 1982, A study of Mammalia and geology across the Cretaceous-Tertiary boundary in Garfield County, Montana: University of California Publications in Geological Sciences, v. 22, 286 p.

—1990, Vertebrate biochronology in the uppermost Cretaceous and lowermost Paleogene of North America, in Krassilov, V. A., editor, International symposium on non-marine correlation: International Geological Correlation Program, Project no. 245, Alma Alta, p. 7.

Archibald, J. D., Clemens, W. A., Gingerich, P. D., Krause, D. W., Lindsay, E. H., and Rose, K. D., 1987, First North American land mammal ages of the Cenozoic Era, in Woodburne, M. O., editor, Cenozoic mammals of North America--geochronology and biostratigraphy: University of California Press, Berkeley, p. 24-76.

Archibald, J. D., and Lofgren, D. L., 1990, Mammalian zonation near the Cretaceous-Tertiary boundary, in Bown, T. M., and Rose, K. D., editors, Dawn of the age of mammals in the northern part of the Rocky Mountain Interior: Geological Society of America, Special Paper no. 243, p. 31-50.

Archibald, J. D., Rigby, J. K., Jr., and Robison, S. F., 1983, Systematic revision of *Oxyacodon* (Condylarthra, Periptychidae) and a description of *O. ferronensis* n. sp.: Journal of Paleontology, v. 57, p. 53-72.

Armstrong-Ziegler, J. G., 1980, Amphibia and Reptilia from the Campanian of New Mexico: Fieldiana, Geology, n. s., v. 4, p. 1-39.

Berggren, W. A., Kent, D. V., Swisher, C. C., III, and Aubry, M.-P., 1995, A revised Cenozoic geochronology and chronostratigraphy, in Berggren, W. A., Kent, D. V., Aubry, M.-P., and Hardenbol, Jan, editors, Geochronology, time scales and global stratigraphic correlation: Tulsa, SEPM (Society for Sedimentary Geology) Special Publication no. 54, p. 129-212.

Butler, R. F., and Lindsay, E. H., 1985, Mineralogy of magnetic minerals and revised magnetic polarity stratigraphy of continental

sediments, San Juan Basin, New Mexico: Journal of Geology, v. 94, p. 535-554.

Cifelli, R. L., 1983, The origin and affinities of the South American Condylarthra and Early Tertiary Litopterna (Mammalia): American Museum Novitates no. 2772, 49 p.

—1990, Cretaceous mammals of southern Utah. I. Marsupials from the Kaiparowits Formation (Judithian): Journal of Vertebrate Paleontology, v. 10, p. 295-319.

Cifelli, R. L., Czaplewski, N. J., and Rose, K. D., 1995, Additions to knowledge of Paleocene mammals from the North Horn Formation, central Utah: Great Basin Naturalist, v. 55, p. 304-314.

Cifelli, R. L., Kirkland, J. I., Weil, Anne, Deino, A. R., Kowallis, B. J., 1997, High-precision ^{40}Ar/^{39}Ar geochronology and the advent of North America's Late Cretaceous terrestrial fauna: Proceedings, National Academy of Sciences USA, v. 94, p. 11163-11167.

Cifelli, R. L., Madsen, S. K., and Larson, E. M., 1996, Screenwashing and associated techniques for the recovery of microvertebrate fossils in Cifelli, R. L., editor, Techniques for recovery and preparation of microvertebrate fossils: Oklahoma Geological Survey Special Publication no. 96-4, p. 1-24.

Cifelli, R. L., and Muizon, Christian de, 1998, Marsupial mammal from the Upper Cretaceous North Horn Formation, central Utah: Journal of Paleontology, v. 72, p. 532-538.

Cifelli, R. L., Rowe, T. B., Luckett, W. P., Banta, James, Reyes, Ruben, and Howes, R. I., 1996, Fossil evidence for the origin of the marsupial pattern of tooth replacement: Nature, v. 379, p. 715-718.

Clemens, W. A., 1961, A Late Cretaceous mammal from Dragon Canyon, Utah: Journal of Paleontology, v. 35, p. 578-579.

Clemens, W. A., Jr., Lillegraven, J. A., Lindsay, E. H., and Simpson, G. G., 1979, Where, when, and what--a survey of known Mesozoic mammal distribution, in Lillegraven, J. A., Kielan-Jaworowska, Zofia, and Clemens, W. A., editors, Mesozoic mammals--the first two-thirds of mammalian history: Berkeley,

University of California Press, p. 7-58.

Dodson, Peter, and Currie, P. J., 1990, Neoceratopsia, *in* Weishampel, D. B., Dodson, Peter, and Osmólska, Halszka, editors, The dinosauria: Berkeley, University of California Press, p. 593-618.

Eaton, J. G., 1995, Cenomanian and Turonian (early Late Cretaceous) multituberculate mammals from southwestern Utah: Journal of Vertebrate Paleontology, v. 15, p. 761-784.

Estes, Richard, 1964, Fossil vertebrates from the Late Cretaceous Lance Formation eastern Wyoming: University of California Publications in Geological Sciences, v. 49, 180 p.

—1969, A new fossil discoglossid frog from Montana and Wyoming: Breviora, no. 328, p. 1-7.

—1983, Handbuch der Paläoherpetologie. Part 10A--Sauria Terrestria, Amphisbaenia: Stuttgart, Gustav Fischer Verlag, 249 p.

Estes, Richard, Berberian, Paul, and Meszoely, C. A. M., 1969, Lower vertebrates from the Late Cretaceous Hell Creek Formation, McCone County, Montana: Breviora no. 337, 33 p.

Estes, Richard, and Sanchíz, Borja, 1982, New discoglossid and palaeobatrachid frogs from the Late Cretaceous of Wyoming and Montana, and a review of other frogs from the Lance and Hell Creek formations: Journal of Vertebrate Paleontology, v. 2, p. 9-20.

Flynn, J. J., and Galiano, Henry, 1982, Phylogeny of early Tertiary Carnivora, with a description of a new species of *Protictis* from the middle Eocene of Wyoming: American Museum Novitates, no. 2725, 64 p.

Fox, R. C., 1976, An edentulous frog (*Theatonius lancensis*, new genus and species) from the Upper Cretaceous Lance Formation of Wyoming: Canadian Journal of Earth Sciences, v. 13, p. 1486-1490.

Frost, D. R., and Etheridge, Richard, 1989, A phylogenetic analysis and taxonomy of iguanian lizard families (Reptilia: Squamata): Miscellaneous Publications, University of Kansas Museum of Natural History, v. 81, 65 p.

Gao, Keqin, and Fox, R. C., 1996, Taxonomy and evolution of Late Cretaceous lizards (Reptilia: Squamata) from western Canada: Bulletin of the Carnegie Museum of Natural History no. 33, 107 p.

Gazin, C. L., 1938a, A Paleocene mammalian fauna from central Utah: Journal of the Washington Academy of Sciences, v. 28, p. 271-277.

—1938b, Ancient mammals of Utah: Exploration and Field-work of the Smithsonian Institution in 1938, p. 25-28.

—1939a, The third expedition to central Utah in search of dinosaurs and extinct mammals: Exploration and Field-work of the Smithsonian Institution in 1939, p. 5-8.

—1939b, A further contribution to the Dragon Paleocene fauna of Utah: Journal of the Washington Academy of Sciences, v. 29, p. 273-286.

—1941a, Trailing extinct animals in central Utah and the Bridger Basin of Wyoming: Explorations and Field-work of the Smithsonian Institution in 1940, p. 5-8.

—1941b, The mammalian faunas of the Paleocene of central Utah, with notes on the geology: Proceedings of the United States National Museum, v. 91, p. 1-53.

Gilmore, C. W., 1919, Reptilian faunas of the Torrejon, Puerco, and underlying Upper Cretaceous formations of San Juan County, New Mexico: U.S. Geological Survey Professional Paper no.119, 68 p.

—1922, A new sauropod dinosaur from the Ojo Alamo Formation of New Mexico: Smithsonian Miscellaneous Collections, v. 72, p. 1-9.

—1938a, Fossil hunting in Utah and Arizona: Explorations and Field-work of the Smithsonian Institution in 1937, p. 1-4.

—1938b, Sauropod dinosaur remains from the Upper Cretaceous: Science, v. 87, p. 299.

—1940, New fossil lizards from the Upper Cretaceous of Utah: Smithsonian Miscellaneous Collections, v. 99, p. 1-3.

—1942a, Osteology of *Polyglyphanodon*, an Upper Cretaceous lizard from Utah: Proceedings of the United States National Museum, v. 92, p. 229-265.

—1942b, A new fossil reptile from the Upper Cretaceous of Utah:

Proceedings of the United States National Museum, v. 93, p. 109-114.

—1943a, Osteology of Upper Cretaceous lizards from Utah, with a description of a new species: Proceedings of the United States National Museum, v. 93, p. 209-214.

—1943b, Fossil lizards of Mongolia: Bulletin of the American Museum of Natural History, v. 81, p. 361-383.

—1946, Reptilian fauna of the North Horn Formation of central Utah: United States Geological Survey Professional Paper no. 210-C, p. 29-53.

Gingerich, P. D., and Winkler, D. A., 1985, Systematics of Paleocene Viverravidae (Mammalia, Carnivora) in the Bighorn and Clark's Fork basins, Wyoming: Contributions from the Museum of Paleontology, University of Michigan, v. 27, p. 87-128.

Gradstein, F. M., Agterberg, F. P., Ogg, J. G., Hardenbol, Jan, Van Veen, Paul, Thierry, Jacques, and Zehui, Huang, 1995, A Triassic, Jurassic and Cretaceous time scale, *in* Berggren, W. A., Kent, D. V., Aubry, M.-P., and Hardenbol, Jan, editors, Geochronology, time scales and global stratigraphic correlation: Tulsa, SEPM (Society for Sedimentary Geology) Special Publication no. 54, p. 95-126.

Hintze, L. H., 1988, Geological History of Utah: Provo, Brigham Young University Geology Series, Special Publication no. 7, 202 p.

Hutchison, J. H., 1982, Turtle, crocodilian, and champsosaur diversity changes in the Cenozoic of the north-central region of western United States: Palaeogeography, Palaeoclimatology, Palaeoecology, v. 37, p. 149-164.

Hutchison, J. H., and Archibald, J. D., 1986, Diversity of turtles across the Cretaceous/Tertiary boundary in northeastern Montana: Palaeogeography, Palaeoclimatology, Palaeoecology, v. 55, p. 1-22.

Jensen, J. A., 1966, Dinosaur eggs from the Upper Cretaceous North Horn Formation of central Utah: Brigham Young University Geology Studies, v. 13, p. 55-67.

Lawson, D. A., 1976, *Tyrannosaurus* and *Torosaurus*, Maastrichtian dinosaurs from trans-Pecos Texas: Journal of Paleontology, v. 50, p. 158-164.

Lehman, T. M., 1981, The Alamo Wash Local Fauna--a new look at the old Ojo Alamo fauna, *in* Lucas, S. G., Rigby, J. K., Jr., and Kues, Barry, editors, Advances in San Juan Basin paleontology: Albuquerque, University of New Mexico Press, p. 189-221.

—1987, Late Maastrichtian paleoenvironments and dinosaur biogeography in the western interior of North America: Palaeogeography, Palaeoclimatology, Palaeoecology, v. 60, p. 189-217.

Lillegraven, J. A., 1972, Preliminary report on Late Cretaceous mammals from the El Gallo Formation, Baja California del Norte, Mexico: Contributions to Science, Natural History Museum of Los Angeles County, no. 232, 11 p.

—1976, A new genus of therian mammal from the Late Cretaceous "El Gallo Formation," Baja California, Mexico: Journal of Paleontology, v. 50, p. 437-443.

Lillegraven, J. A., and McKenna, M. C., 1986, Fossil mammals from the "Mesaverde" Formation (Late Cretaceous, Judithian) of the Bighorn and Wind River basins, Wyoming, with definitions of Late Cretaceous North American land-mammal "ages": American Museum Novitates, no. 2840, 68 p.

Lucas, S. G., and Hunt, A. P., 1989, *Alamosaurus* and the sauropod hiatus in the Cretaceous of the North American Western Interior, *in* Farlow, J. O., editor, Paleobiology of the dinosaurs: Geological Society of America Special Paper, no. 238, p. 75-86.

MacIntyre, G. T., 1966, The Miacidae (Mammalia, Carnivora). Part 1. The systematics of *Ictidopappus* and *Protictis*: Bulletin of the American Museum of Natural History, v. 131, p. 115-210.

Mateer, N. J., 1981, The reptilian megafauna from the Kirtland Shale (Late Cretaceous) of the San Juan Basin, New Mexico, *in* Lucas, S. G., Rigby, J. K., Jr., and Kues, Barry, editors, Advances in San Juan Basin paleontology: Albuquerque, University of New Mexico Press, p. 49-75.

Matthew, W. D., 1937, Paleocene faunas of the San Juan Basin, New Mexico: Transactions, American Philosophical Society, v. 30, 510 p.

McKenna, M. C., 1962, Collecting small fossils by washing and screening: Curator, v. 5, p. 221-235.

Meylan, P. A., 1987, The phylogenetic relationships of soft-shelled turtles (Family Trionychidae): Bulletin of the American Museum of Natural History, v. 186, p. 1-101.

Prothero, D. R., 1995, Geochronology and magnetostratigraphy of Paleogene North American land mammal "ages", *in* Berggren, W. A., Kent, D. V., Aubry, M.-P., and Hardenbol, Jan, editors, Geochronology, time scales and global stratigraphic correlation: Tulsa, SEPM (Society for Sedimentary Geology) Special Publication no. 54, p. 305-314.

Rigby, J. K., Jr., 1981, A skeleton of *Gillisonchus gillianus* (Mammalia: Condylarthra) from the early Paleocene (Puercan) Ojo Alamo Sandstone, San Juan Basin, New Mexico, with comments on the local stratigraphy of Betonnie Tsosie Wash, *in* Lucas, S. G., Rigby, J. K., Jr., and Kues, Barry, editors, Advances in San Juan Basin paleontology: Albuquerque, University of New Mexico Press, p. 221-235.

Robison, S. F., 1986, Paleocene (Puercan-Torrejonian) mammalian faunas of the North Horn Formation, central Utah: Brigham Young University Geology Studies, v. 33, p. 87-133.

Simpson, G. G., 1936, *Carsioptychus*, new name for *Plagioptychus* Matthew, *nec* Matheron: American Journal of Science, ser. 5, v. 32, p. 234.

Sloan, R. E., 1969, Cretaceous and Paleocene terrestrial communities of western North America: Proceedings of the North American Paleontological Convention, part E, p. 427-453.

—1981, Systematics of Paleocene multituberculates from the San Juan Basin, New Mexico, *in* Lucas, S. G., Rigby, J. K., Jr., and Kues, Barry, editors, Advances in San Juan Basin paleontology: Albuquerque, University of New Mexico Press, p. 127-160.

Spieker, E. M., 1960, The Cretaceous-Tertiary boundary in Utah: International Geological Congress, Report of the 21st Session, part 5, p. 14-24.

Sulimski, Andrzej., 1972, *Adamisaurus magnidentatus* n. gen., n. sp. (Sauria) from the Upper Cretaceous of Mongolia: Palaeontologica Polonica, v. 27, p. 33-40.

—1975, Macrocephalosauridae and Polyglyphanodontidae (Sauria) from the Late Cretaceous of Mongolia: Palaeontologica Polonica, v. 33, p. 25-102.

—1978, New data on the genus *Adamisaurus* Sulimski 1972 (Sauria) from the Upper Cretaceous of Mongolia: Palaeontologica Polonica, v. 38, p. 43-56.

Szalay, F. S., 1969, Mixodectidae, Microsyopidae, and the insectivore-primate transition: Bulletin of the American Museum of Natural History, v. 140, p. 193-330.

Tomida, Yukimitsu, 1981, "Dragonian" fossils from the San Juan Basin and status of the "Dragonian" land mammal "age," *in* Lucas, S. G., Rigby, J. K., Jr., and Kues, Barry, editors, Advances in San Juan Basin paleontology: Albuquerque, University of New Mexico Press, p. 222-241.

—1982, A new genus of picrodontid primate from the Paleocene of Utah: Folia Primatologica, v. 37, p. 37-43.

Tomida, Yukimitsu, and Butler, R. F., 1980, Dragonian mammals and Paleocene magnetic polarity stratigraphy North Horn Formation, central Utah: American Journal of Science, v. 280, p. 787-811.

Van Valen, Leigh, 1966, Deltatheridia, a new order of mammals: Bulletin of the American Museum of Natural History, v.132, p. 1-126.

—1978, The beginning of the age of mammals: Evolutionary Theory, v. 4, p. 45-80.

Weishampel, D. B., 1990, Dinosaur distribution, *in* Weishampel, D. B., Dodson, Peter, and Osmólska, Halszka, editors, The Dinosauria: Berkeley, University of California Press, p. 63-140.

Wood, H. E., Chaney, R. W., Clark, John, Colbert, E. H., Jepsen, G. L., Reeside, J. B., and Stock, Chester, 1941, Nomenclature and correlation of the North American continental Tertiary: Bulletin of the Geological Society of America, v. 52, p. 1-48.

BIOSTRATIGRAPHIC ASPECTS OF THE CRETACEOUS-TERTIARY (KT) BOUNDARY INTERVAL AT NORTH HORN MOUNTAIN, EMERY COUNTY, UTAH

Rose Difley and A. A. Ekdale

Department of Geology and Geophysics, University of Utah, Salt Lake City, Utah 84112
(difley@1-d-e-a.com) (ekdale@mail.mines.utah.edu)

ABSTRACT

Because it is thought to contain one of the most complete North American sections spanning the Cretaceous-Tertiary (KT) boundary, North Horn Mountain may be an important key to unlocking the chronostratigraphic puzzles of the KT interval in Utah. This study employed physical stratigraphy and paleontology in an attempt to define the interval containing the KT boundary at the type section of the North Horn Formation at North Horn Mountain, Emery County, Utah.

The KT boundary in central Utah occurs within a prominent coal sequence in the 404-meter-thick North Horn Formation at North Horn Mountain. Although the boundary has not yet been precisely placed, it can be recognized within a stratigraphic interval of a few meters in the North Horn Formation in this area on the basis of fossil remains of dinosaurs, charophytes, ostracodes, and pollen. Current biostratigraphic information indicates that the KT boundary interval occurs within at least a few meters of the stratigraphically highest Cretaceous dinosaur fossils, which occur at a level of about 199 meters above the base of the formation at the type section.

INTRODUCTION

The Cretaceous-Tertiary (KT) boundary interval in central Utah occurs within the North Horn Formation, which is well exposed on the Wasatch Plateau of central Utah. The North Horn Formation reflects essentially continuous sedimentation across the era boundary, thus yielding a relatively complete boundary interval.

No obvious sedimentologic break separates the lower units (uppermost Cretaceous) and the upper units (lowermost Paleocene) of the North Horn Formation. Cretaceous dinosaurs and Tertiary mammals do not occur in close enough stratigraphic proximity to be useful in dividing the units at North Horn Mountain (Spieker, 1960). The degree of precision needed for locating the KT boundary is difficult to obtain, because sedimentary units that comprise the North Horn Formation units are not laterally persistent (Spieker, 1949).

The KT boundary horizon in Utah has not been defined as precisely as that at a number of other localities in the western United States and nearby provinces of Canada. Because of the difficulty of defining the KT boundary in Utah on the basis of fossils, the boundary has not often been noted in the literature alongside other KT boundaries in the Western Interior of North America. Information from previously published and current paleontologic investigations allow us to locate the boundary interval within a few meters at most. The growing store of data on Utah's KT boundary should be added to the worldwide picture of this important transition in earth history.

Previous Work

There have been several prior attempts to locate the KT boundary at North Horn Mountain, Emery County, Utah. Spieker (1949) reported that careful and repeated searches by experienced researchers revealed no discernible break in sedimentation or any paleontologic KT boundary indicator at North Horn Mountain. At Flagstaff Peak, 16 kilometers south of North Horn Mountain, Spieker (1960) reported the occurrence of abundant dinosaur bone material about 11 meters stratigraphically below the horizon where three taxa of Tertiary mammal remains were found, but these occurrences were separated laterally by about 0.8 kilometer. Spieker placed the KT boundary within the 11-meter interval, but this interval could not be traced beyond the sites where the fossils were located.

In 1965, J. R. Bushman measured and sampled North Horn Mountain for palynomorphs (Lohrengel, 1969). His objective was not to locate the boundary precisely (J. R. Bushman, verbal communication, 1994), but rather to compare the palynology of the North Horn Formation with its equivalent, the Kaiparowits Formation in southern Utah. Bushman bracketed a 1.5-meter interval that he believed to contain the KT boundary (J. C. Hinshaw, verbal and written communication, 1991) based on his pollen results that were supplemented by oil company analyses (J. R. Bushman, verbal communication, 1994; unpublished information).

In 1981, J. C. Hinshaw resampled Bushman's bracketed interval for both pollen and iridium, but he was unable to locate the iridium anomaly he sought or to find typical Maastrichtian palynomorphs (J. C. Hinshaw, verbal communication, 1991, 1994). He did find a horizon abundant in Paleocene palynomorphs. Neither Bushman's nor Hinshaw's studies were published formally.

A number of other paleontologic investigations relevant to the North Horn Formation, but not specifically seeking the KT boundary, were conducted at North Horn Mountain and elsewhere. Griesbach and MacAlpine (1973) noted some of the assemblages of fossil invertebrates, microfossils and palynomorphs of the North Horn Formation at North Horn Mountain. Peck and Forester (1979) reported the stratigraphic relationship of the Cretaceous charophyte *Platychara compressa*, which also occurs at North Horn Mountain, to other Cretaceous fossils of the North Horn Formation in Wales Canyon, Sanpete County. R. M. Forester (verbal communication, 1993) believes *P. compressa* to be a strictly Cretaceous charophyte. He concurs with Griesbach and MacAlpine (1973), who noted that *Aclistochara compressa* (=*P. compressa*) was associated stratigraphically with dinosaur levels at North Horn Mountain and therefore was Cretaceous in age. The stratigraphic relationships of *P. compressa*, palynomorphs and other fossils in the North Horn Formation of Price River Canyon, Carbon County, were reported by Fouch and others (1987) who considered the occurrence of *P. compressa* to indicate a Cretaceous age for the interval that contained it.

Beginning in 1993, H. J. Hansen conducted a detailed stratigraphic study of the coal sequence and a portion of the underlying subunit near the middle of the North Horn Formation at North Horn Mountain. Based on the stratigraphic record of magnetic susceptibility of the sediment deposited throughout the KT transition, he suggested that the KT boundary occurs at a level 184 meters above the base of the formation, which is positioned about 20 meters below the contact between the upper and lower coal sequence at North Horn Mountain (Hansen, 1995; Hansen and others, 1996).

Abbreviations

KT, Cretaceous-Tertiary.

UUGG, University of Utah, Department of Geology and
    Geophysics.

UMNH, Utah Museum of Natural History, vertebrate
    paleontology.

Location

North Horn Mountain is located on the eastern edge of the Wasatch Plateau, west of the San Rafael Swell, in Emery County, Utah (figure 1). It is bounded on the north by Straight Canyon, on the east by the Castle Valley, on the south by South Horn Mountain, and on the west by North Dragon Canyon, which is formed by a major regional fault system, the north-south-trending Joes Valley Graben.

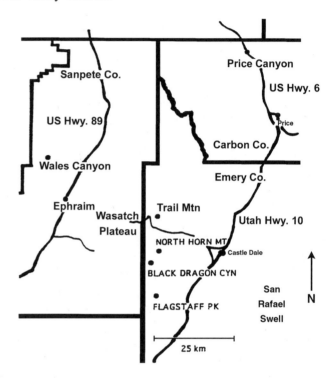

Figure 1. *Location of study areas of North Horn Formation in central Utah.*

Methods

Field work for this study of the North Horn Formation was carried out during the summers of 1991 to 1997. The primary study area was North Horn Mountain (sections 3, 4, 33, 34, 35, and 36, T.18S. and T.19S., R.6E., Salt Lake Base Line and Meridian (SLBM)). The North Horn Formation was examined in several other areas for comparison to the type section. These were North Dragon Canyon (section 29, T18S., R.6E., SLBM), Black Dragon Canyon (sections 7, 8, and 17, T.19S., R.6E., SLBM), Trail Mountain (sections 34 and 35, T.17S., R.6E., SLBM), Flagstaff Peak (sections 29 and 30, T.20S., R.6E., SLBM), Wales Canyon (section 26, T.15S., R.2E., SLBM), and Price Canyon (sections 16 and 21, T.11S., R.9E., SLBM). All sites are in Emery, Sanpete and Carbon Counties, Utah.

Field methods initially included preliminary reconnaissance by foot and surface collecting of miscellaneous fossils. Stratigraphic sections were measured using standard techniques. Marker beds were staked for future reference. Vertebrate remains were collected from the surface, and soil and bedrock were sampled to recover microfossils and invertebrates.

Lab work included screening and picking microfossils. Palynology methods included washing the rock sample, crushing in a mortar, digesting the rock in HCl and HF, followed by sieving out the palynomorphs for staining and mounting on glass slides. The slides were scanned using a petrographic microscope at 10X and photographed at 40X. Bone and coal samples were thin-sectioned. Specimens were compared with those in published literature and in research collections in the Department of Geology and Geophysics at the University of Utah, the Utah Museum of Natural History, the Earth Science Museum of Brigham Young University, and the Royal Tyrrell Museum in Alberta, Canada. Living aquatic ostracodes were observed and studied for comparison.

STRATIGRAPHIC SEQUENCE

The KT boundary occurs near the middle of the 404-meter-thick North Horn Formation, at North Horn Mountain, where it is divided into three informal units, the lower variegated unit, the coal sequence and the upper variegated unit (figure 2). Only the coal sequence is of interest here since it is the unit that contains the KT boundary (figure 3). The coal sequence, so called because of its dark high-organic and coaly deposits, is the middle unit of the three main units in the formation. At North Horn Mountain, it is situated stratigraphically from 160 to 237 meters above the base of the formation. There the coal sequence is 77 meters thick and it is divided into two subunits, the lower coal sequence and the upper coal sequence, 45 and 32 meters thick, respectively (figure 4). The lower coal sequence chiefly consists of thinly bedded, high-organic rocks and carbonate rocks interbedded with sandstones and thin coals. Sandstones are more prominent in the upper coal sequence, where they are interbedded with organic deposits and mudrocks. The high-organic, lower subunit is dark. At North Horn Mountain it is readily distinguished from the lighter colored upper subunit, which contains prominent yellow sandstone beds (figure 3).

The coal sequence represents a paleoenvironment of shallow ephemeral lakes and streams dissecting swampy

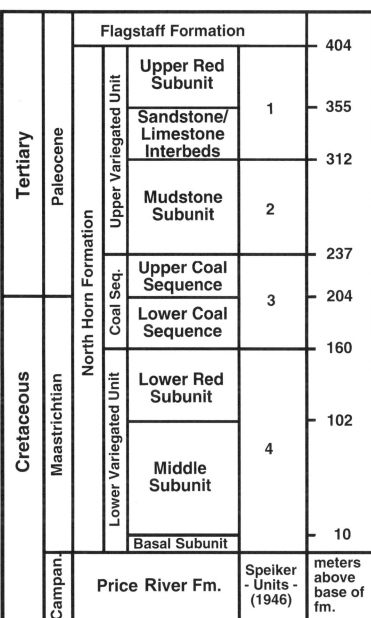

Figure 2. *Idealized stratigraphic column of the North Horn Formation at North Horn Mountain.*

wetlands (Franczyk and Pitman, 1991) in a tectonically subsiding basin (Lawton and others, 1990). North Horn Mountain is situated about 35 kilometers east-southeast of the Sanpete Valley anticline (Stanley and Collinson, 1979) and about 35 kilometers west-northwest of the San Rafael Swell. These two structures represent a paleohighland that bounded a lowland basin into which sediments that now comprise North Horn Mountain were being deposited. No structural evidence is available to indicate that the distance between these two ancient highlands has changed since the Cretaceous. The depositional basin probably underwent a slow, steady subsidence accompanied by sedimentation, resulting in a complete stratigraphic section at the type locality.

Figure 3. West face of North Horn Mountain, showing the coal sequence in the upper half of the section.

The type section of the North Horn Formation is considered continuous, because no large hiatus above the

Figure 4. KT interval on west face of North Horn Mountain. A, distant view with level of lithologic change shown; B, close-up of box in A, arrow shows limestone bed with highest eggshells.

lowest subunit of the lower variegated unit is known (figure 2). Some pauses in sedimentation, during which subaerial weathering occurred, is suggested by the presence of horizons of caliche which record episodes of soil formation as was elsewhere similarly suggested to Mikhailov and others (1994). Caliche horizons that represent paleopedogenesis occur throughout most of the middle subunit of the lower variegated unit. However, no caliche deposits have been noted in the lower coal sequence, the subunit in which the KT boundary occurs. No other evidence of hiatuses was noted in this subunit. For these reasons, we believe that the North Horn Formation at North Horn Mountain contains a relatively complete history of geologic events across this important era boundary in central Utah.

EVIDENCE OF THE KT BOUNDARY INTERVAL

Other KT boundary sites in western North America north of Texas are associated with a series of coal deposits that indicate a wet climate at the KT transition (Sweet and Braman, 1992). The lithology of the coal sequence at North Horn Mountain suggests a paleoenvironment similar to that of several other North American KT boundary sites.

Although there is no obvious and distinctive KT boundary layer at North Horn Mountain, like the distinctive clay layers reported in numerous marine sequences around the world, Upper Cretaceous fossils help define the interval containing the era boundary in Utah. The lower coal sequence contains the stratigraphically highest dinosaur bone and highest dinosaur eggshells in the section. Two strictly Cretaceous charophytes last appear a few meters below the highest dinosaur eggshells. No strictly Cretaceous pollen is currently known above the last dinosaur eggshells. Other fossils, such as turtles, fish, crocodiles, ostracodes, gastropods and bivalves are found throughout the coal sequence, and the taxa are known to cross the KT boundary. Certain other fossil taxa that never cross, or are only rarely known to cross the KT boundary at other localities (for example, some of the same ostracode species in China), also last appear in the lower coal sequence at North Horn Mountain.

Since 1934 when Spieker (1936) first located dinosaur fossils at North Horn Mountain, geologists have recognized that the KT boundary was contained within the North Horn Formation (Spieker, 1946), but its exact stratigraphic position has remained undefined. Gazin (1941) placed the KT boundary at the base of Spieker's

(1946) unit 2, (termed the 'upper variegated unit' here) (figure 2) in the Joes Valley-North Horn Mountain area because it was the unit in which Paleocene mammals occurred.

At nearby Flagstaff Peak, Spieker (1960) placed the KT boundary within an 11-meter interval between the occurrences of the stratigraphically highest dinosaur fossils and lowest Paleocene mammal fossils. Because Flagstaff Peak is 16 kilometers distant from North Horn Mountain, and because key beds of the North Horn Formation are not laterally persistent, Spieker was unable to trace this interval beyond the local area. At North Horn Mountain, Spieker (1949) placed the KT boundary within an approximately 180-meter interval he termed a "no-man's-land" of neither distinctly Cretaceous nor distinctly Paleocene fossils. He found no dinosaur remains in either the coal sequence or in the upper part of the lower variegated unit. Nor did he find Paleocene mammal remains near Black Dragon and North Dragon Canyons in beds lower than those that are correlative with the upper variegated unit of North Horn Mountain (Gazin's map in Gilmore, 1946).

In the 1930s when Spieker (1936, 1956) discovered that the North Horn Formation spans the KT boundary, biostratigraphic relationships and/or aspects of several fossil groups of the North Horn Formation were unknown or poorly known. As a result, precise KT placement could not be determined paleontologically (Spieker, 1949). Last appearances of individual fossils or assemblage changes are better understood today.

Dinosaurs

Dinosaur fossils are rare in the coal sequence, but they are present. The stratigraphically highest bone of undoubted dinosaur origin is located 174 meters above the base of the formation at North Horn Mountain.

Three types of eggshells, all of which exhibit diagnostic characteristics of dinosaur eggshells (following the criteria of Mikhailov and others, 1996), occur in the coal sequence (figure 5). These include the following eggshell types: (1) Type 1, which has widely spaced single round pores on a smooth surface and a shell thickness of 0.7 to 0.9 millimeters (same as dinosauroid-spherulitic/angustispherulitic morphotype of Mikhailov and others; E. S. Bray, verbal communication, 1997); (2) Type 2, which has irregularly shaped, closely spaced, single pores on a finely stippled to weakly crenulated surface, and a shell thickness of 0.9 to 1.1 millimeters (may be the same as ?dinosauroid-spherulitic/?spherulitic morphotype; E. S. Bray, verbal communication, 1997); (3) Smooth mixed type, which has a smooth sur-

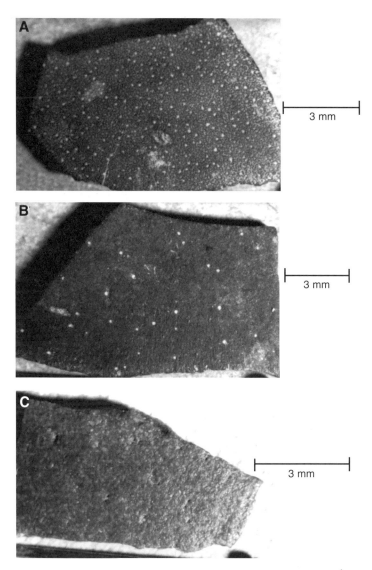

Figure 5. *Dinosaur eggshell fragments from North Horn Mountain. A, Type 2 (UMNH VP7501) from lower coal sequence. B, Type 1 (UMNH VP7503) from lower coal sequence. C, Smooth mixed (UMNH VP7505) from lower variegated unit of the same type found in the coal sequence.*

face with a mixture of single and paired pores, which are arranged parallel to the lengthwise axis of the egg, and a shell thickness of 0.5 to 1.5 millimeters (same as dinosauroid-prismatic/ prismatic morphotype of Mikhailov and others, 1996).

The highest in situ eggshells are entirely of a single variety (type 2). Type 2 eggshells consistently occur near the base of a limestone bed 199 meters above the base of the formation at North Horn Mountain (figure 6; see also figure 4). The other two dinosaur eggshells, smooth mixed and type 1, last appear in the coal sequence at 173 and 187 meters, respectively, above the base of the formation at North Horn Mountain (figure 7).

Analysis of bulk soil and bedding samples from several levels shows a few small eggshell fragments in the soil samples at the level of, or lower than, the highest

Figure 6. *Two eggshell fragments in situ in limestone bed five meters below the lithologic change between the lower and upper coal sequences.*

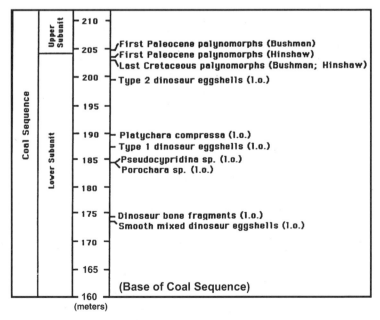

Figure 7. *Cretaceous last occurrences and Paleocene first occurrences of important fossil groups.*

eggshell-bearing limestone bed. There are no eggshell fragments as high as the contact between the upper and lower coal sequences. A single microscopic fragment of the highest bedded shell, type 2, was found on the surface about a meter above the eggshell-bearing limestone bed, but this fragment may have been displaced by natural processes.

Dinosaur bone and eggshell material are relatively rare in the coal sequence. Eggshells occur at different levels in the coal sequence and are associated with different rock types. It is unlikely that the highest eggshell material has been reworked by fluvial processes, since it occurs in a lacustrine limestone, and no proximity to paleochannels has been noted. The overall paleogeographic setting of North Horn Mountain is near the center of a low-gradient basin, located about 35 kilometers from highlands to the northwest and southeast. Distance from known paleo-highland areas, and lack of evidence of proximal upland areas from which fossil material could have been derived, makes reworking a less tenable option. Many of the eggshells occur with gastropods and bivalves, which are not likely to have been reworked appreciably in the lacustrine setting.

In the highest eggshell-bearing bed, we traced type 2 eggshells laterally for about 0.8 kilometer at the same stratigraphic level. Type 2 eggshells also occur in limestone in association with molluscan material at the base of the coal sequence at North Horn Mountain and in Price Canyon. At one site at North Horn Mountain, sufficient type 2 eggshell material occurred in a small volume of limestone to represent most of a single egg. Type 2 eggshells also are found at the same stratigraphic level at Trail Mountain, north of the type section.

Dinosaurs that laid type 2 eggs probably preferred nest sites in lacustrine or swampy settings situated close enough to shorelines that whole eggs or fragments occasionally were carried into the water. The closely spaced pores of type 2 eggshells may indicate a special adaptation to wet environments. High porosity of eggshells is considered to be an indication of a nesting site in a low-oxygen, high-humidity environment (Mikhailov and others, 1994). The adaptation of a high-porosity eggshell could enable an embryo in an egg laid in moist areas to obtain sufficient oxygen for survival. It is less likely that specially adapted type 2 eggshell material represents reworked material, since it usually appears in deposits of the North Horn Formation that are easily attributed to moist environments, such as lacustrine and swampy areas. This situation is true at both North Horn Mountain and its probable stratigraphic equivalent in Price River Canyon.

The stratigraphically next highest eggshells at North Horn Mountain are type 1 and smooth mixed varieties. These types of shells are less abundant throughout the lower coal sequence at North Horn Mountain than are type 2 eggshells, except in stratigraphic levels more closely associated with channel deposits. Smooth mixed eggshells are the least abundant eggshell type in the coal sequence at North Horn Mountain. In Price Canyon, the lacustrine sequence, a probable equivalent of the coal sequence at North Horn Mountain, passes stratigraphically upward into fluvial channel sandstones interbedded with variegated mudstone, where lacustrine wackestones are less abundant. In these levels in Price Canyon, the numbers of type 2 eggshells are surpassed by type 1 eggshells, and smooth mixed eggshells are nearly as numerous. Proportions of observed eggshells may reflect relative numbers of dinosaurs that lived in proximal lacustrine-swampy areas versus those that preferred fluvially-dominated areas. A number of isolated shell fragments both in the coal sequence at North Horn Mountain and in Price River Canyon are abraided, in contrast to unabraided shell fragments of a single type in one location at North Horn Mountain. The unabraided eggshells may be attributed to a single crushed egg whose clustered fragments were stacked together, indicating that the fragments of the egg were not widely separated by reworking. The shell fragments with an abraided appearance, rather than indicating reworking at a much later time, may simply reflect the wet environment of deposition, where some dissolution of the shell in water could have occurred before burial, as similarly described elsewhere by Mikhailov and others (1994).

All three eggshell types are associated with the charophyte species *Platychara compressa* (figure 8) in the lower coal sequence at North Horn Mountain. Type 2 eggshells and *P. compressa* have been observed in the same stratigraphic levels at Trail Mountain as those at North Horn Mountain. In Price River Canyon, all three coal sequence dinosaur eggshells also appear with undoubted dinosaur bone material at the same stratigraphic levels as does *P. compressa*. *Platychara compressa* is found in the basal 50 meters of the North Horn Formation of Price River Canyon up to (but not above) the unconformity between the Maastrichtian and Middle Paleocene (Fouch and others, 1987). In addition, a stratigraphic association between eggshells and *P. compressa* was noted in Wales Canyon (Peck and Forester, 1979), where eggshells were reported above *P. compressa* near a former mine opening that was in wackestone strata similar to the rock types in Price River Canyon and at North Horn Mountain.

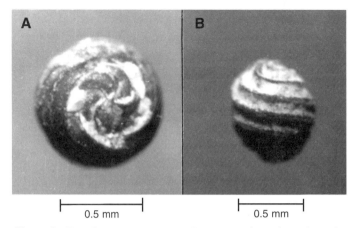

Figure 8. *Two characteristic Upper Cretaceous charophytes from the lower coal sequence. A,* Platychara compressa *(UUGG 1998.1.1471). B,* Porochara *(UUGG 1998.1.1472).*

The eggshells and *P. compressa* occur with other fossils at North Horn Mountain. The fossils include other charophytes, which we identified as *Porochara* sp. (figure 8), *Strobilochara* sp. and *Retusochara* sp. (following criteria of R. M. Forester, verbal communication, 1994). Also occurring in this assemblage are ostracodes, which we identified as *Bisulcocypridea* ?*nyensis* and *Pseudocypridina* sp., cf. *P. longa* sp. (figure 9; following the criteria of F. M. Swain, written communication, 1994), and gastropods, which we identified as *Lioplacodes* sp. and *Physa* sp. (based on comparisons with descriptions in LaRocque, 1960). A similar assemblage occurs in the same intervals as the three egg-shell types in the basal 50 meters of the North Horn Formation in Price River Canyon

Figure 9. Pseudocypridina *(UUGG 1998.1.1470), a characteristic Upper Cretaceous ostracode from the lower coal sequence.*

Dinosaurs that laid type 2 eggs probably inhabited shallow lake margins and swampy or marshy areas. This type eggshell has been found in gastropod-rich limestones at North Horn Mountain and Price River Canyon. Fouch and others (1987) indicated that the paleoenvironment represented by the first 30 meters of the Price River Canyon section was a marginal, littoral or shallow lacustrine setting. The gastropod-eggshell association at North Horn Mountain may indicate a similar setting. The occurrence of eggshells at the same stratigraphic levels as *Physa* sp. suggests a very shallow lacustrine environment, since *Physa* is an air-breathing snail that likely lived on plants that grew in shallow lake margins (LaRocque, 1960).

The highest bedded eggshells at North Horn Mountain were found in a yellow limestone that shows color mottling and pseudo-microkarstic textures. This unit contains rounded and angular intraclasts and evidence of root traces. Features such as these are interpreted by Alonso Zarza and others (1992) as evidence of a low-energy, palustrine environment and subaerial exposure resulting from very shallow water depths. Similarly they are interpreted by Platt (1989) as sediments subjected to repeated wetting and drying. We interpret the portion of the limestone that contains eggshells as representing an environment having energy sufficient only for local reworking (for example, from the shore into shallow water depths). The limestone color changes from yellow to gray immediately above the eggshell level, a change that could indicate a higher organic content that resulted from increased water depth accompanied by anoxic conditions following the disappearance of the eggshells.

It seems unlikely that eggshell material could be reworked and still maintain similar associations with other fossils in more than one locality. The same fossil associations occur in localities separated by up to 80 kilometers, as is the case between North Horn and Trail Mountains and Price River Canyon. These common fossil associations probably represent non-reworked fossil remains recovered from sediments of widely separated localities, where they were originally deposited in similar environments that were preferred by the plants and animals that lived there.

Charophytes

The charophytes *Platychara compressa* and *Porochara* sp. (figure 8) do not cross the KT boundary (R. M. Forester, verbal communication, 1994). *Platychara compressa* disappears ten meters stratigraphically below the highest in situ dinosaur eggshells at 189 meters above the base of the formation at North Horn Mountain. *Porochara* sp. last appears at 184 meters above the base of the formation there, one meter below *P. compressa*. A change in proportions in the morphology of *P. compressa* fossils occurs before their disappearance in the coal sequence (R. M. Forester, verbal communication, 1994). As *P. compressa*, which is compressed through its poles, nears the KT boundary, its polar diameter typically increases.

Ostracodes

The ostracodes of North Horn Mountain were stud-

ied as environmental indicators rather than as biostratigraphic indices, but we found that they are more diverse and occur more commonly in the KT interval than in other parts of the section. Several ostracode taxa occur in the KT interval, the most common of which are *Pseudocypridina* sp., cf. *P. longa* (figure 9) and *Cypridea (Bisulcocypridea) bisulcata*. *Bisulcocypridea* occurs in the Maastrichtian portion (basal 50 meters) of the North Horn Formation of Price Canyon (Fouch and others, 1987). The species of this ostracode genus change across the KT boundary from the interval between the base of the coal sequence and the contact between the upper and lower coal sequences (160 to 204 meters above base at North Horn Mountain). Brouwers and DeDeckker (1996) describe similar changes in *Bisulcocypridea* elsewhere in the Western Interior.

Pseudocypridina sp., cf. *P. longa* is common in the Maastrichtian levels, and it disappears, or is seen only rarely after the KT boundary in China (F. M. Swain, written communication, 1994). This pattern is similar to the distribution of *Pseudocypridina* at North Horn Mountain, where it is common in the lowest part of the coal sequence. It occurs in anomalously high numbers relative to its numbers elsewhere in the sequence or relative to numbers of other ostracode species in limestone at 181 meters above the base of the formation at North Horn Mountain, but it has not been noted above 184 meters (figure 7), about 20 meters below the upper/ lower coal sequence contact.

Pollen

The studies of J. R. Bushman (unpublished information; J. C. Hinshaw, verbal communication, 1991) indicated that the KT boundary might occur within a particular 1.5-meter thick interval. We determined this interval to be situated at 204 meters from the base of the formation at North Horn Mountain (figure 7). Bushman determined a Paleocene age for a sample at this interval and a Cretaceous age for another sample that was 1.5 meters lower. Hinshaw closely resampled Bushman's interval for pollen and analyzed several samples geochemically in a search for iridium. He found neither typical Cretaceous palynomorphs (for example, *Aquilapollenites*, *Wodehouseia*, or *Proteacidites*) nor iridium, but his results did show an abrupt palynological assemblage change in samples which were interpreted to be of Paleocene age. The samples indicated a change from a moist lowland pollen assemblage that included "a few herbaceous pollen and unique spores...that are restricted to the Cretaceous," to a pollen assemblage containing arboreal hardwoods of taxa "known from the Paleocene, but not from the Cretaceous" (J. C. Hinshaw, written communication, 1991).

We sampled at a site 0.8 kilometer north of Hinshaw's site, beginning at Hinshaw's levels and dropping down to and including the limestone bed that contains the stratigraphically highest type 2 eggshells. Most of the samples from this interval contain palynomorphs, but they are barren in the eggshell-containing limestone bed itself.

Although some of our palynomorphs were the same as those from Price River Canyon (Fouch and others, 1987), no distinctly Cretaceous pollen occur in our samples. D. J. Nichols (written communication, 1995) saw no distinctly Cretaceous species in micrographs of some of the palynomorphs recovered from two levels of our sampled interval.

Our palynofacies and lithofacies indicate a change from a lacustrine and swamp environment to a floodplain environment at approximately the same horizon where Hinshaw and Bushman placed the KT boundary. Bushman's age determinations were made by palynologists at an oil company, and the data on which those determinations were based are unavailable. Since no distinctly Cretaceous or Paleocene palynomorphs have been recovered by either Hinshaw or us, serious questions remain as to whether the palynofacies changes are the result of evolution (extinction) or merely local environment fluctuations. Whatever the cause of the environment change at the lower/upper coal sequence contact, environmental conditions never returned to those of the lower coal sequence, but the new conditions begun at the lower/upper coal sequence contact endured to produce an additional 32 meters of deposition that lasted to the end of the coal sequence.

The pollen study is incomplete. The pollen assemblage across the KT boundary in central Utah is poorly known, and it may vary significantly from those assemblages recognized as indicators of a Cretaceous age from other KT boundaries north, south and east of central Utah. With the exception of *Balmeisporites*, Fouch and others (1987) did not report an assemblage of palynomorphs that is considered typically Maastrichtian from the North Horn Formation in Price River Canyon. Griesbach and MacAlpine (1973) reported typical Maastrichtian pollen assemblages containing *Aquilapollenites*, *Balmeisporites* and *Proteacidites* from stratigraphic levels at North Horn Mountain that were associated with dinosaur bones. The field work of Griesbach was completed in the early 1950s (Frederick Griesbach, verbal communication, 1992), when dinosaurs were known only from lower levels in the formation (Spieker, 1949). This suggests that perhaps all palynomorphs in an assemblage

that has been hitherto recognized elsewhere as typical Maastrichtian do not extend as high as the KT boundary at North Horn Mountain.

Shocked Quartz

In an effort to determine the presence of possible shocked quartz crystals in KT beds, samples from two levels in the coal sequence (near the contact between the upper and lower coal sequence and an interval about 20 meters below the contact) were thin-sectioned and examined by John Lyons and Charles Officer. Microscopic deformation features in quartz grains were found at both levels, but John Lyons (written communication, 1995) suggested that the type of deformation had a volcanic or tectonic origin.

CONCLUSIONS

The proximity of the KT interval is indicated by the last stratigraphic occurrences of the Cretaceous charophyte fossils, *Platychara compressa* and *Porochara* sp., and by changes in the ostracode assemblage over a range of about 18 meters below the upper/lower coal sequence contact. The last appearance of undoubted dinosaur bones is at 174 meters above the base of the formation at North Horn Mountain, and the last appearance of dinosaur eggshells is at 199 meters above the base of the formation there. Immediately beneath the bone is the last appearance of the smooth mixed eggshells, which were extremely rare at that level. The last type 1 and type 2 eggshells occur 15 and 25 meters, respectively, above the bone.

Several fossil groups disappear one by one in the lower coal sequence in a pattern typical of gradual extinction (Archibald, 1996). Changes in the composition of a particular faunal assemblage or the disappearance of any single fossil group would be inconclusive by itself. However, the preponderance of evidence indicates that sufficient changes in diverse fossil groups occurred in this stratigraphic interval to indicate proximity to the KT boundary. It is entirely conceivable that the KT boundary is located at a level in the section where pollen indicate an environmental change. If so, the local environmental change merely may have coincided with and disguised a much larger environmental change across the KT boundary. If this horizon represents the KT boundary, our biostratigraphic data indicate that the last Cretaceous groups at North Horn Mountain, which were present only a few meters below, were no longer represented by fossils at the boundary.

The KT boundary horizon appears to be positioned within a prominent coal sequence in the interval between 199 meters and 204 meters above the base of the North Horn Formation at North Horn Mountain. Until additional paleontologic data (for example, from fossil pollen) and/or other pertinent information (for example, a recognizable horizon of shocked quartz and/or anomalously high iridium concentration) are available, a more precise placement of the KT boundary in the North Horn Mountain section is not likely.

ACKNOWLEDGMENTS

Partial financial support of this project was provided by Utah Mineral Leasing Funds and the Utah Historical Society. We thank the following people for their significant contributions to this project: Paul Ames, Jess R. Bushman, Billy J. Dye, Deborah Fulkerson, Hans Jørgen Hansen, Martha Hayden, Jerald Hinshaw, Fred Lohrengel, John Lyons, Fred E. May, Doug J. Nichols, Charles Officer, Earl T. Peterson, Raivo Puusemp, Steve Robison, Quintin Sahratian, Craig Sanders, C. D. Stephenson, Peter Toft, John E. Welsh, and Brad Wolverton. We thank Dennis Bramble, Emily Bray, Elizabeth Brouwers, Richard M. Forester, Janet Gillette, David Gillette, the late Karl Hirsch, and Frederick M. Swain, for their valuable assistance in fossil identifications. However, we assume full responsibility for the accuracy of identifications reported herein. We especially thank John, Aleta, Seth, and Thea Difley for field assistance and for general support throughout the entire project.

REFERENCES

Alonso Zarza, A. M., Calvo, J. P., and Garcia del Cura, M. A., 1992, Palustrine sedimentation and associated features -- grainification and pseudo-microkarst -- in the middle Miocene (Intermediate Unit) of the Madrid Basin, Spain: Sedimentary Geology, v. 76, p. 43-61.

Archibald, J. D., 1996, Dinosaur extinction and the end of an era -- what the fossils say: New York, Columbia University Press, 237 p.

Brouwers, E. M., and DeDeckker, Patrick, 1996, Earliest origins of northern hemisphere temperate non-marine ostracode taxa -- evolutionary development and survival through the Cretaceous-Tertiary boundary mass-extinction event, *in* Keller, Gerta, and MacLeod, Norman, editors, Cretaceous-Tertiary mass extinctions - biotic and environmental changes: New York, W. W. Norton and Company, p. 205-229.

Fouch, T. D., Hanley, J. H., Forester, R. M., Pitman, J. K. and Nichols, D. J., 1987, Chart showing lithology, mineralogy and paleontology of the nonmarine North Horn Formation and Flagstaff Member of the Green River Formation, Price Canyon, central Utah: U. S. Geological Survey Map I-1797-A.

Franczyk, K. J., and Pitman, J. K., 1991, Latest Cretaceous nonmarine depositional systems in the Wasatch Plateau area -- reflections of foreland to intermontane basin transition, *in* Chidsey, T. C., Jr., editor, Geology of east-central Utah: Salt Lake City, Utah Geological Association Publication 19, p. 77-93.

Gazin, C. L., 1941, The mammalian faunas of the Paleocene of central Utah, with notes on the geology: Washington, D. C., Proceedings of the National Museum, v. 91, no. 3121, p. 1-53.

Gilmore, C. W., 1946, Reptilian fauna of the North Horn Formation of Central Utah: U. S. Geological Survey Professional Paper 210-C, p. 29-53.

Griesbach, F. R., and MacAlpine, S. A., 1973, Reconnaissance palynology and micropaleontology of the Late Cretaceous-Early Tertiary, North Horn Formation, central Utah [abstract]: Geological Society of America Abstracts with Programs, v. 5, no. 6, p. 483.

Hansen, H. J., 1995, Excursion to Stevns Klint: Copenhagen, the 6th International Nannoplankton Association Conference, Copenhagen, 1995, Field Guide - Stevns-Klint, 8 p.

Hansen, H. J., Toft, Peter, Mohabey, D. M., and Sarkar, A., 1996, Lameta age - dating the main pulse of the Deccan Traps volcanism: Gondwana Geological Magazine, Special v. 2, p. 365-374.

LaRocque, Aurele, 1960, Molluscan faunas of the Flagstaff Formation of central Utah: Geological Society of America Memoir 78, 100 p.

Lawton, T. F., Franczyk, K. J., and Pitman, J. K., 1990, Latest Creta-ceous-Paleogene basin development and resultant sedimentation patterns in the thrust belt and broken foreland of central Utah [abstract]: American Association of Petroleum Geologists Bulletin, v. 74, no. 5, p. 701.

Lohrengel, C. F., 1969, Palynology of the Kaiparowits Formation, Garfield County, Utah: Brigham Young University Geology Studies, v. 16, part 3, p. 61-180.

Mikhailov, Konstantin, Sabath, Karol and Kurzanov, Sergey, 1994, Eggs and nests from the Cretaceous of Mongolia, *in* Carpenter, Kenneth, Hirsch, K. F., and Horner, J. R., editors, Dinosaur eggs and babies: New York, Cambridge University Press, p. 88-115.

Mikhailov, Konstantin, Bray, E. S., and Hirsch, K. F., 1996, Parataxonomy of fossil egg remains (Veterovata) -- principles and applications: Journal of Paleontology, v. 16, no. 4, p. 763-769.

Platt, N. H., 1989, Lacustrine carbonates and pedogenesis -- sedimentology and origin of palustrine deposits from the Early Cretaceous Rupelo Formation, W Cameros Basin, N Spain: Sedimentology, v. 36, p. 665-684.

Peck, R. E., and Forester, R. M., 1979, The genus *Platychara* from the western hemisphere: Review of Palaeobotany and Palynology, v. 28, p. 223-236.

Spieker, E. M., 1936, The orogenic history of central Utah: Science, v. 83, no. 2142, p. 62-63.

—1946, Late Mesozoic and Early Cenozoic history of central Utah: U. S. Geological Survey Professional Paper 205-D, p. 117-161.

—1949, Transition between the Colorado plateaus and the Great Basin in central Utah, Guidebook to the geology of Utah 4: Salt Lake City, Utah Geological Society, 106 p.

—1956, Mountain building chronology and nature of geologic time scale: American Association of Petroleum Geologists Bulletin, v. 40, no. 8, p. 1769-1815.

—1960, The Cretaceous-Tertiary boundary in Utah: International Geological Conference Report of 21st Session, Norden 1960, p. 14-24.

Stanley, K. O., and Collinson, J. W., 1979, Depositional history of Paleocene-Lower Eocene Flagstaff Limestone and coeval rocks, central Utah: American Association of Petroleum Geologists Bulletin, v. 63, no. 3, p. 311-323.

Sweet, A. R., and Braman, D. R., 1992, The K-T boundary and contiguous strata in western Canada - interactions between paleoenvironments and palynological assemblages: Cretaceous Research, v. 13, no.1, p. 31-79.

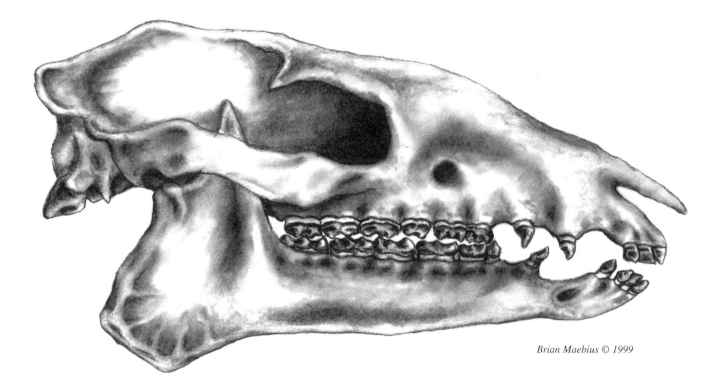

Brian Maebius © 1999

Eohippus

CENOZOIC ERA

MAMMALS OF THE MIDDLE EOCENE UINTA FORMATION

D. Tab Rasmussen
Department of Anthropology, Washington University, St. Louis, Missouri 63130

Glenn C. Conroy
Department of Anthropology, Washington University, St. Louis, Missouri 63130

Anthony R. Friscia
Department of Biology, University of California, Los Angeles, California 90024

K. Elizabeth Townsend
Department of Anthropology, Washington University, St. Louis, Missouri 63130

Mary D. Kinkel
Department of Anatomy, Northeastern Ohio Universities College of Medicine, Rootstown, Ohio, 44272

ABSTRACT

Fossil mammals from the Uinta Formation, Uinta Basin, northeastern Utah, served as the primary basis for establishing the Uintan North American Land Mammal "Age." These Uintan mammals still remain of central importance in understanding mammalian evolution and paleoecology of the middle Eocene in North America. The Uintan fauna represents a transition between the relatively stable, tropical conditions of the earlier Eocene, and the more arid and cooler conditions of the later Eocene. Among the key mammalian events during the Uintan are the appearance and radiation of selenodont artiodactyls, and the great family-level diversification of rodents. Less spectacular radiations involved carnivorans and rhinoceratoid perissodactyls. Other mammalian groups were experiencing extinction or reductions in diversity, including uintatheres, hyopsodontid condylarths, and North American primates. A typical Uintan community was dominated by the selendont artiodactyls *Protoreodon* and *Leptotragulus*; by several different perissodacyl groups, including brontotheres, tapirs, the horse *Epihippus*, and both amynodont and hyracodont rhinos; and by a characteristic assemblage of abundant rodents, most notably the cylindrodontid *Pareumys*, the sciuravid *Sciuravus*, and the ischyromyid *Leptotomus*. While these taxa are consistently present and common through time and space, other mammals are unevenly distributed through the stratigraphic section or among localities, indicating taphonomic and collecting biases (especially for the smallest taxa) or paleoecological specializations.

INTRODUCTION

Fossils from the Uinta Formation (UF) of northeastern Utah have played a prominent role in our understanding of middle Eocene mammalian evolution in North America. O. C. Marsh of the Yale Peabody Museum first explored the fossil-bearing terrestrial sediments of the Uinta Basin in 1870 (Betts, 1871; Marsh, 1875a, 1875b). He collected fossil mammals from gray badlands near the White River that clearly belong to today's UF (figure 1). This same area was collected more extensively by Francis Speir in the 1880s, working for Princeton University. Speir's fossils were studied by the great paleontologists W. B. Scott and H. F. Osborn, who produced the first substantive publications on UF mammals (Scott and Osborn, 1887, 1890).

The work of Scott and Osborn showed that the fauna of the UF represented a distinct time period in the evolution of North American mammals, later formalized as the Uintan Land Mammal "Age" (LMA). Initially, the Uintan LMA was believed to be latest Eocene. Now it is positioned squarely in the middle Eocene, following the Wasatchian and Bridgerian LMAs, and preceding the Duchesnean and Chadronian LMAs. Although the collections of fossil mammals from Utah originally stood as the centerpiece of the Uintan LMA, mammals of similar age have been found also in California, Texas, Wyoming, and other places (Black and Dawson, 1966; Storer, 1984; Walsh, 1996a; Westgate, 1990; Wilson, 1986).

The Uintan LMA has received significantly less attention than the four other Eocene LMAs. The Wasatchian, Bridgerian, and Chadronian LMAs are

Figure 1. *Typical outcrop of the Uinta Formation showing good exposure and low erosional relief of the soft mudstones and siltstones, with steeper, horizontally banded exposures rising in the background. Recent expeditions have logged over 150 vertebrate localities, including this one a few miles northeast of where O. C. Marsh first commented on the abundance of fossil turtles near the junction of the White and Green Rivers in 1870.*

made to Uintan faunas elsewhere in North America. It is not our purpose to provide a formal, revised taxonomic list of UF mammals by stratigraphic level, as this has been accomplished by Walsh (1996a).

REGIONAL GEOLOGICAL HISTORY

Utah has been near sea level for most of its Phanerozoic geologic history, only rising much above that level over the last hundred million years or so during the Sevier and Laramide orogenic events. Far earlier than these two events, sometime between about 1,000 and 600 Ma, an unusual east-west basin or trench (aulacogen) developed along the trend of the present Uinta Mountains in which some 25,000 feet of sandstone and shale accumulated. During the so-called Laramide uplift in the early Cenozoic (~66 - 37 Ma), the rise of the Uinta Mountains was linked to downwarping of an adjacent asymmetrical synclinal basin, the Uinta Basin. The Uinta Mountain-Basin couplet is the largest Laramide structure in Utah. Laramide uplift of the Uinta Mountains ended after deposition of the Uinta and Duchesne River Formations (Hintze, 1988).

known by more extensive collections, and have been targets of much more research than the Uintan. Fossils of the Duchesnean LMA are less common than those of the Uintan but, in part because of this scarcity, the Duchesnean's status as an LMA has been controversial, and it has therefore received more than its share of attention (Lucas, 1992; Rasmussen and others, 1999).

The UF has not been systematically collected for many decades. Since the Carnegie Museum field trips through the first half of the century (Douglass, 1910; Peterson, 1919; Kay, 1957; Dawson, 1966), only brief visits have been made to the UF, usually by museums interested in obtaining a sample of the typical fauna for their collections. Because most of the work on the UF occurred during an era that emphasized the discovery of large mammals (for example, the brontotheres), the smaller mammals from the formation remained underrepresented in collections. Partly for this reason, a series of annual expeditions to the UF was initiated in 1993 by Washington University (WU), St. Louis, which focused on finding smaller taxa, such as primates, insectivores, proteutheres, and rodents (figure 2).

The purposes of this review are to introduce the reader to the mammalian faunas of the UF and to provide an update on current field research on this formation. The first section provides an overview of the geological framework and reviews what is known of climate and paleoenvironments. Subsequent sections summarize the mammals in a paleobiological framework rather than a formal systematic one. Finally, brief comparisons are

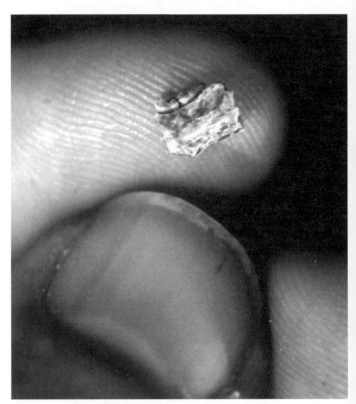

Figure 2. *Mandible with m2-3 (CM 69899) of a new species of Trogolemur, a diminutive anaptomorphine primate. Recent WU expeditions have concentrated on the recovery of small mammals which were relatively neglected in the early fieldwork in the basin.*

The UF consists of sandstone paleochannels and overbank siltstone and mudstone deposits that accumulated on the distributary delta of a lake occupying the basin (figure 3)(Kay, 1934; Grande, 1984; Hamblin, 1987). Traditionally, the formation is divided into three sequential lithologic units, Uinta A, B and C (Osborn, 1895, 1929). Uinta A has rarely yielded fossil mammals and its relationship to the Bridgerian-Uintan boundary remains uncertain (Dane, 1954; Walsh, 1996b). Our understanding of the UF fauna is based almost entirely on fossils from Uinta B and C. The Uinta B fauna is best known from material collected at White River Pocket, a loosely circumscribed region just southeast of the junction of the White River and the Green River, while the Uinta C fauna is known best by collections made at the large sprawling region called Myton Pocket, west of the Green River (Hamblin, 1987). Our work has been restricted to a region well east of the Green River, on land administered by the U.S. Bureau of Land Management (figure 4). The repository for the newly collected material is the Carnegie Museum of Natural History (CM) of Pittsburgh (chosen because of its historically important collections from the basin).

Within the Uinta Basin the Bridgerian/Uintan boundary is currently dated to about 46 Ma (Chron C20r; Prothero, 1996; Prothero and Swisher, 1992). Poorly fossiliferous Uinta A is in sediments of normal polarity and is presently dated to about 46.3 to 47.8 Ma (Chron C21n). Most of Uinta B is reversed polarity and dates to about 43.8 to 46.3 Ma (Chron C20r) although a short normal zone spanning upper Uinta B and lower Uinta C probably correlates with Chron C20n (42.5 - 43.8 Ma). The upper part of Uinta C and lowermost Duchesne River Formation (Anderson and Picard, 1972) are reversed polarity and date to about 41.4 to 42.5 Ma (C19r). The Uintan/Duchesnean boundary occurs within a poorly fossiliferous span in the middle part of the Duchesne River Formation and lies within Chron C18n. The earliest Duchesnean faunas first occur above the Lapoint Ash (about ~40 Ma). The Duchesnean-Chadronian transition is about 37 Ma (Chron C16n).

The mammals of the UF are typically divided into two distinct faunas, early Uintan (based on mammals from Uinta B) and late Uintan (based on mammals from

Figure 3. *Sandstone channels (eroding as blocks in the upper right) and mudstones/siltstones (eroding as guttered slopes) of the Uinta Formation. Many parts of the formation show paleosol development and some freshwater limestone units do occur. The deposits in this photograph of Uinta C are predominantly bright orange and red, which mainly occur high in the section; most of the formation consists of reduced, drabber gray, greens, and browns. A collector in the lower left provides scale.*

Figure 4. *View to the northwest across Devil's Playground, an area of well-developed badlands in the drainage of Kennedy Wash. This and our other collecting areas are on land administered by the BLM.*

Uinta C). This simple dichotomy has been usefully applied to the UF because most mammalian fossils have been recovered from one of the two major localities, White River Pocket of Uinta B, and Myton Pocket of Uinta C. However, there are presently several unresolved difficulties with stratigraphic control and faunal comparisons among key localities in the UF and elsewhere (Prothero and Swisher, 1992; Walsh, 1996a, b). Current field work in the basin has sampled a much more complete section and well over 150 mammal localities have been logged spanning a deep stratigraphic section. Measuring the section is underway.

PALEOCLIMATES AND ENVIRONMENTS

Reconstruction of Eocene climates is based on abundant paleobotanical, paleogeographical, and paleontological evidence. The late Paleogene was a critical period in earth history in that major changes in both ocean circulation and global climate occurred over an approximately 10 million year interval spanning the middle Eocene to the early Oligocene (the Eocene/Oligocene boundary is now taken to be 34 Ma) (Swisher and Prothero, 1990; Berggren and others, 1992; Berggren and Prothero, 1992). The Eocene, particularly the earlier part, was in general a time of warm, wet climates, without great extremes of temperature. These warming trends, which began in the Paleocene, gradually continued into the middle Eocene, which may have been the time of greatest tropicality of the whole Cenozoic. After the middle Eocene, the period of relative tropicality in northern latitudes ended and gradual cooling commenced. By the late Eocene, the climate became drier and more seasonal and the succeeding Oligocene was even cooler, drier, and more arid.

Analyses of early Tertiary floras have been particularly valuable in detailing these trends (Wing, 1987; Wolfe, 1978, 1992). Eocene floras have been recovered from many regions of the world. In general, these floras include a large number of plants characteristic of tropical rain forests today. One of the most extensive Eocene paleobotanical faunas in North America is from the Pacific Northwest dating to some 50 to 34 Ma. This flora contains numerous leaf species with liana-like leaves or driptips (pointed tips to facilitate water runoff), typical of vegetation that grows under abundant year-round precipitation. Not only do these Paleogene floras provide unequivocal evidence that the early and middle Eocene was the warmest part of the Tertiary, but also that mean annual temperature ranges decreased during this same period to about half that of today (latitudinal temperature gradients along the western coast of North America were also about half of what they are today). This overall warming trend was not unidirectional, but was interrupted by at least two cooler intervals during this period (even the cool intervals are still estimated to have been about 4° C warmer than at present).

Three Eocene-Oligocene Rocky Mountain floristic stages have been identified by Wing (1987). The early Eocene (Wasatchian and early Bridgerian) is character-

ized by subtropical and paratropical paleofloras of broad-leaved, evergreen, and deciduous forests up to about 60° N. latitude. In the later Bridgerian and Uintan these paleofloras were replaced by more open subtropical vegetation; by the late Eocene and Oligocene, the paleofloras were dominated by a mixture of conifers and broad-leafed deciduous forms.

Abundant evidence indicates that this period of relative tropicality came to an end after the middle Eocene, after which a time of gradual cooling commenced and mean annual temperature ranges began to increase (Gazin, 1958; Hutchison, 1992; Stucky, 1992). By the late Eocene the climate was becoming drier and more seasonal and the global belt of tropical rain forest was becoming modified, reduced, and ultimately interrupted.

The configuration of Paleogene landmasses and oceans was very different from that of today. As might be expected, these changing land configurations had dramatic affects on both Eocene climate and mammalian biogeography. There were extensive intercontinental mammal migrations between Europe and North America in the early Paleogene, including hyaenodontid creodonts, primates, artiodactyls, perissodactyls, and other mammal groups. In fact, before Europe and North America began rifting apart by the middle Eocene, more than 40 mammalian genera were shared in common between the Wasatchian of North America and the Ypresian of Europe. In addition, at least 16 mammalian genera were common to North America, Europe, and Asia (Savage and Russell, 1983; Stucky, 1992).

Major Paleogene tectonic activities such as continental drift and the Laramide orogeny not only had significant biogeographical consequences, but also profound climatic influences as well. Together they certainly contributed to the developing seasonality and climatic deterioration which began in the later Eocene and continued into the Oligocene. For example, climatic models demonstrate that increasing the height of mountain ranges produces drier continental conditions leeward of the mountains and wetter conditions windward of the mountains. In addition, surface temperatures generally decrease in areas which experience increased elevations (Sloan and Barron, 1992).

The climatic deterioration of the Eocene-Oligocene was influenced in large measure by plate tectonic movements involving Antarctica and Australia. During the early Eocene the southern oceans were comparatively warm and Antarctica was largely unglaciated. However, Antarctic sea ice may have begun to form when Australia began its northward drift from Antarctica in the Paleogene. Major ice sheets in Antarctica were in evidence by late Oligocene times but indirect evidence suggests that continental ice may have been developing there earlier. One suggestion is that the development of the East Antarctic ice sheet was triggered by the opening of a seaway between Antarctica and Australia during the Late Cretaceous or early Paleogene. This would have permitted the transportation of moist air over Antarctica with the resulting precipitation leading to the formation of Antarctic ice sheets (Bartek and others, 1992). As a consequence of this new open seaway in the Antarctic, ocean water temperatures dropped rapidly and ultimately contributed to global climatic cooling. Detailed oxygen-isotope studies reveal that both surface and deep ocean waters experienced sharp temperature drops during the early Tertiary, with particularly marked cooling near the Eocene-Oligocene boundary. Benthic foraminiferal $\delta^{18}0$ values increased by nearly 3 parts per thousand during the middle Eocene and early Oligocene, reflecting the largest climate change of the entire Cenozoic. Much of this change must be ascribed to both deep-water cooling and to development of ice sheets (Kennett, 1977; Miller, 1992). Dramatic biotic changes occurred in both marine and non-marine invertebrate and vertebrate faunas that reflect this series of worldwide climatic changes near the Eocene-Oligocene boundary (Evanoff and others, 1992; Stucky, 1992). For example, during this time some 60 percent of Europe's mammalian genera, including most primates, became extinct (the so-called "Grand Coupure"), as did nearly 80 percent of planktic foraminifera (Keller and others, 1992).

THE UINTA FORMATION MAMMALS

Faunal lists for the UF have been published often over the decades, usually not based on extensive revision of the faunas, but rather handed down with slight modifications from some earlier published list. The best Uinta mammal list is the one compiled by Walsh (1996a). The following descriptions of UF mammals are less concerned with precise taxonomic details and stratigraphic occurrence than with the general paleobiology of the Uintan mammals. The goal is to provide the reader with an overview of mammalian diversity and adaptation in a Rocky Mountain fauna on the brink of the climatic deterioration that led to the loss of tropical habitats in the region.

PRIMITIVE MAMMALS

Marsupials

Marsupials are an important component of Eocene mammal faunas worldwide. Two taxa are represented in the UF, both recorded for the first time in the 1990s. Most of the teeth recovered so far can be referred to *Herpetotherium marsupium*, a small-bodied didelphid marsupial. We follow Rothecker and Storer (1996) in transferring the species from *Peratherium*, a very similar early Eocene genus (Crochet, 1977; Eberle and Storer, 1995). The didelphids are one of the longest-lived of mammalian families, first appearing in the Cretaceous and still living today in the form of the abundant and diverse Neotropical opossums. Small-bodied opossums are typically insectivorous to omnivorous, with a primitive, generalized body shape, grasping hands and feet, and a semi-prehensile tail. The best living analogs of *Herpetotherium* may be the modern mouse opossums of the genus *Marmosa*. The UF species, *H. marsupium*, is otherwise known from middle to late Eocene deposits in the Rocky Mountain region and contemporary deposits of Europe (Crochet, 1977; Walsh, 1996a). Another genus of didelphid, *Peradectes*, is represented in the UF by a single upper molar found in 1996.

Proteutheres

The mammalian order Proteutheria, as construed here, contains several distinct families of primitive mammals that have eluded understanding of their precise phylogenetic position (Romer, 1966; Butler, 1972). There is no compelling evidence to suggest that the families included form a natural group.

Pantolestids are an enigmatic group of mammals that retain relatively primitive structure of the molars. The lower molars have a low, short talonid basin, and a high trigonid basin that differs from those of insectivores in the loss of the paraconid. The upper molars generally resemble the insectivore pattern except for the absence of a stylar shelf on the buccal margin. Pantolestids also differ from most insectivores in their relatively larger body size. Specimens of crushed skeletons found in the middle Eocene lake beds of Messel, Germany, show a long, short-limbed body, a long powerful tail suggesting swimming, and short, heavily clawed, broad hands and feet (Koenigswald, 1980). Gut contents from the Messel pantolestids indicate a diet consisting partly of fish. The overall view that emerges is of a semi-aquatic mammal perhaps similar in ways to a modern mink. The Uinta specimens of this family probably represent four species, differing from each other in size and the degree of inflation of the lower molar cusps. None are known by very complete material.

A genus of mammals that has been affiliated sometimes with the true pantolestids is *Simidectes*, a relatively large-bodied (raccoon-sized) carnivorous mammal known only from the Uintan LMA. It was initially described from the Uinta Basin as a genus of creodont (Peterson, 1919). Later researchers excluded it from Creodonta (Coombs, 1971) and have placed it in Proteutheria or Condylarthra. Gingerich (1981, 1982) recognized Wasatchian forms from Wyoming related to *Simidectes* and compared these favorably to a mammalian family in China called Didymoconidae, which may be related in turn to the Mesonychia, a group of large-bodied predatory mammals (see below). In our collections, *Simidectes* is only represented in the uppermost part of the UF and the lower strata of the Duchesne River Formation, where it is a common member of the fauna. Evidence of early Uintan relatives in the Rocky Mountain region is lacking. Related species of *Simidectes* occur in the Uintan and Duchesnean of southern California and Texas (Walsh, 1996a). The Wasatchian genus, *Wyolestes*, remains the earliest possible member of the group in North America.

Taxonomic uncertainties aside, *Simidectes* clearly represents a formidable predator of the Uintan fauna. The animal had large, robust canines, and simple, serrated shearing premolars. The molars superficially resemble the carnassials of creodonts, with a prominent, bladed trigonid and a low talonid. The talonids differ from those of creodonts in lacking a basin; instead, they are simple, slightly curved crests dropping off the back of the tooth. Shearing and slicing functions clearly predominate over grinding. The dental structure of *Simidectes* approaches that of "hypercarnivores" (van Valkenburgh, 1991), an ecomorphological designation containing mammals which are specialized on animal prey to the point of lacking grinding talonids, such as most hyaenodontine creodonts and felids.

The final group of proteutheres known from the UF are members of the family Apatemyidae, which like most proteutheres, have a checkered taxonomic history (West, 1973). The primate-like lower molars, with small trigonids and broad talonid basins, along with the enlarged, procumbent pair of incisors, are similarities shared with the Plesiadapiformes, an ordinal level group that is itself of uncertain taxonomic status. (Although true plesiadapiforms of Uintan age have been found elsewhere in North America, none are yet known from the UF.) Traditionally placed in the order Primates, the plesiadapiforms have been suggested as belonging to Dermoptera or have been separated off as their own order. Apatemyids, in turn, have recently been considered only dubiously associated with Plesiadapiformes. Raising an order Apatotheria for them has become common (Russell and others, 1979).

The ecomorphological adaptations of apatemyids had long been a mystery until a beautifully preserved skeleton of one from the Messel Lake beds solved that issue (Koenigswald, 1987). The hand of the Messel apatemyid has a bizarrely elongated finger with a pointed claw at the tip. This feature, in tandem with the massive, elongated incisors, suggests a special adaptational similarity to the living striped possum of Australia (*Dactylopsila*) and an odd primate, the aye-aye (*Daubentonia*) from Madagascar (Cartmill, 1974). Both of these extant mammals use their chisel-like incisors to gouge and pry tree bark, and then use the elongated finger to ream beetle larvae out of the tunnels they bore in wood (Erickson, 1995). This is the same food source relied upon by modern woodpeckers; there are no woodpeckers in Australasia, Madagascar, or in the Eocene.

Matthew (1921) first described an apatemyid from the UF based on a nearly complete skull found in a block of sandstone. This served as the basis for a new taxon, *Stehlinella uintensis* (Matthew, 1929a). The WU expeditions have retrieved several additional jaws representing the same species from stratigraphically low in the UF.

Insectivores

Mammals of the order Insectivora have long been a problematic group, continually under suspicion for polyphyly (Gregory, 1910; Van Valen, 1967; Butler, 1972; Krishtalka, 1976). However, once some groups have been stripped away and moved to the unnatural Proteutheria, then a streamlined order Insectivora (or the order Lipotyphla of some authors) appears to be monophyletic. The two primary divisions within Insectivora are the suborders Erinaceomorpha (the hedgehogs and their relatives) and the Soricomorpha (today represented by shrews and moles)(Butler, 1972; Krishtalka, 1976). While Soricomorpha was certainly present during Uintan times, a fossil record for them has failed to turn up in the UF. All insectivore jaws and teeth that are identifiable represent erinaceomorphs of the Eocene family Dormaaliidae (formerly not distinct from Adapisoricidae).

A unique insectivore from the UF is *Talpavus duplus*, a hedgehog-sized species known by a single lower jaw with p4-m3 (Krishtalka, 1976). This animal has a mesiodistally compressed trigonid and a short, broad talonid, attributes that characterize many of the early Tertiary erinaceomorphs. *T. duplus* has very trenchant occlusal features, suggesting that it was primarily insectivorous. We have failed to turn up any new diagnostic specimens of *T. duplus*, but have found several specimens of two related genera: isolated teeth of the widespread genus *Scenopagus*, and some jaws and teeth of a new genus of dormaaliid. This new hedgehog is characterized by its larger size and less trenchant tooth morphology, in addition to technical details of tooth structure. The new genus differs substantially from comparably large, common erinaceomorphs of the Uintan in southern California (Walsh, 1998).

The notoriously poor preservation of small teeth in the UF is nowhere more frustrating than in the case of the insectivores. We have recovered many specimens of small edentulous jaws that suggest insectivores are an important and diverse part of the fauna, but the delicate and prismatic structure of insectivore teeth is very susceptible to fracturing in the poorly mineralized Uinta samples (in contrast to the more durable, compact shape of the equally small teeth of the rodent *Microparamys*, for example). We are still awaiting discovery of the micromammal site that will illuminate insectivore diversity in the UF.

Primates

Primates are generally not considered under a heading of "primitive mammals" but that is because of vanity. In the structure of the dentition and appendicular skeleton, Eocene primates are indeed primitive in most respects when contrasted with rodents, lagomorphs, carnivorous mammals, and many ungulates. The Eocene was a time of great primate abundance and diversity throughout much of the world, but by Uintan times primates were dwindling in North America, apparently in association with the deterioration of tropical climates and arboreal habitats. One of several important faunal contrasts distinguishing the Uintan LMA from the earlier Wasatchian and Bridgerian LMAs is the great reduction in primate diversity, and the complete absence of the familiar, large-bodied notharctines in the Rocky Mountain region (although there is a southern California record; Gunnell, 1995).

All primates of the UF belong to the family Omomyidae, a diverse group of tarsioids represented in North America by two subfamilies. The early Eocene of North America was dominated by the anaptomorphines, which like the notharctines, show a sharp drop in abundance and diversity at the end of the Bridger LMA. The anaptomorphines were very small-bodied (some less than 100 grams in body mass), leaping, insectivorous primates. These represent the earliest known diverse radiation of true primates in the world. By the Uintan, however, the group was nearly extinct. The only post-Bridger record of the subfamily is the tiny genus *Trogolemur*, known best from the Bridgerian of Wyoming and Nevada. *Trogolemur* is unique in having an extremely long, procumbent, hook-tipped lower incisor -- the root of which

extends far back under the molar series -- which suggests a unique specialization for food procurement (Emry, 1990). We have recovered the first specimens of *Trogolemur* from the UF, which represents a species distinct from the Bridger taxa (figure 2). Younger records of *Trogolemur* come from the Duchesnean of Saskatchewan (Storer, 1996).

The remaining UF primates belong to the subfamily Omomyinae. While populations and diversity of anaptomorphines and notharctines crashed before the Uintan, the omomyines show remarkable diversification into new ecomorphological types. For the first time in North American omomyids, we see the acquisition of larger body size (up to that of living Malagasy lemurs) and the advent of dental specializations indicating an almost exclusively herbivorous diet. Three genera are known from the UF: *Chipetaia, Ourayia*, and *Macrotarsius* (Gazin, 1958; Robinson, 1968; Krishtalka, 1978; Rasmussen, 1996). *Chipetaia lamporea* is a moderate-sized primate (about 1000 grams) with low-crowned, heavily crenulated molars adapted for grinding functions, such as crushing resistant nuts and seeds (figure 5). It has been found only in the lower part of the formation. Lemursized *Ourayia* is represented by two species from the UF, *O. uintensis* of the early Uintan and *O. hopsoni* of the late Uintan. Both are clearly frugivorous species, with low, broad occlusal relief on the molars. The new WU expeditions have increased the sample size for both species, including the first upper and anterior teeth. *Macrotarsius* is known in the UF from a single, excellent specimen of upper and lower jaws, the type of *M. jepseni*. This species, identical in size to *O. uintensis*, has more sharply crested teeth than *Ourayia* and apparently represents a more folivorous animal. The first postcranial elements of Uintan omomyines (*Chipetaia* and *Ourayia*) are now under study; they indicate arboreal, leaping habits.

RODENTS, LAGOMORPHS and TAENIODONTS

These divergent mammalian orders are considered here together under one heading for no more sophisticated reason than that they all have prominent gnawing incisors at the front of their jaws. There is no special phylogenetic link among these groups.

Rodents

The Uintan was a time of spectacular radiation among the rodents (Dawson, 1977; Korth, 1994). In-

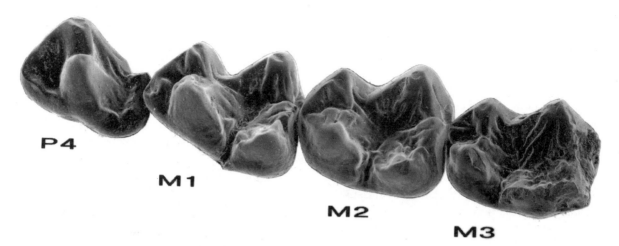

Figure 5. *Right mandibular dentition (p3-m1, CM 69804; m2-3, CM 69800) of* Chipetaia lamporea, *an omomyine primate with heavy, crenulated enamel on the molars, indicating an adaptation for grinding resistant seeds or nuts. Scanning electron micrograph by G. Michael Veith.*

deed, the origin of today's dominant position of rodents among the world's mammals in terms of both abundance and diversity can be traced to the Uintan. Rodents are a common but not particularly diverse part of earlier Eocene faunas. It is only in the latest Bridgerian and early Uintan that North American rodents explode into great taxonomic diversity that reflects adaptive specializations in body size, diet, and locomotion. Although Uintan rodent diversity pales in comparison to that of modern rodents, it is important to keep diversity in comparative perspective. The UF rodents span a size range from *Microparamys*, tinier than most insectivores of the formation, to *Ischyrotomus eugenei*, a species larger than the local Eocene horses.

The most primitive of the UF rodents are the primitive ischyromyids (Wood, 1962). The species in this family have a generalized, somewhat squirrel-like dentition that remains remarkably conservative during the Eocene. The most commonly found ischyromyids from the UF are relatively large, marmot-sized *Leptotomus leptodus* of the early Uintan, and *L. mytonensis* of the later Uintan. These two ischyromyids have relatively long and narrow lower molars, and lightly built jaws. A substantial number of postcranial elements of this genus have now been retrieved but paleobiological analyses of the material are still pending. The long, narrow tooth morphology of *Leptotomus* is also shared with several smaller, squirrel-sized ischyromyids, *Reithroparamys gidleyi* and *Uintamys sciuroides*. These two taxa have remained enigmatic due to fragmentary representation in the fossil record and small sample sizes; the new material that we have collected is more complete and will lead to some taxonomic revision.

Another taxonomic cluster of UF ischyromyids departs from the dental structure of *Leptotomus* in having short, square, heavily built lower cheek teeth. One genus

is characterized by very smooth, thick enamel (*Ischyrotomus*), while another has heavily corrugated, crenulated enamel (*Thisbemys*). Each of these two genera is represented by multiple, poorly understood species in the UF. The largest rodent in the entire fauna is *Ischyrotomus eugenei*, previously known by two badly worn lower jaws and some isolated incisor fragments, but now represented by more complete material including a partial cranium and entire upper dentition.

A final rodent often affiliated with the ischyromyids, but probably distinct at the family level, is *Microparamys*, represented in the UF by a species similar or identical to *M. dubius* (Dawson, 1966, 1973). The isolated cheek teeth of these rodents are only a fraction of a millimeter in length; several have been collected from the surface and by screenwashing sediment from rich micromammal sites. The occlusal morphology of these miniature rodents is unusual for being very flat and simple; clearly, there was minimal slicing function, which suggests that arthropods with resistant exoskeletons and fibrous plant products were not an integral part of the diet. A crushed skeleton of *Microparamys* from Messel, Germany, shows a vole-like animal characterized by very short limbs (Koenigswald and others, 1992).

An entirely distinct rodent family in the UF is the Sciuravidae, represented by several species of *Sciuravus* (Burke, 1937; Dawson, 1966). These are hyper-bunodont rodents with inflated, quadrate cheek teeth, indicating a frugivorous diet. Species in the UF include small (mouse-sized) *S. altidens*, medium-sized *S. popi* (figure 6), and finally a new, large species (rat-sized) from the upper part of the UF. The sciuravids are among the most common mammals of the UF, being a regular part of the fauna at most sites that have yielded small mammals.

A genus of much smaller, bunodont, quadrate-

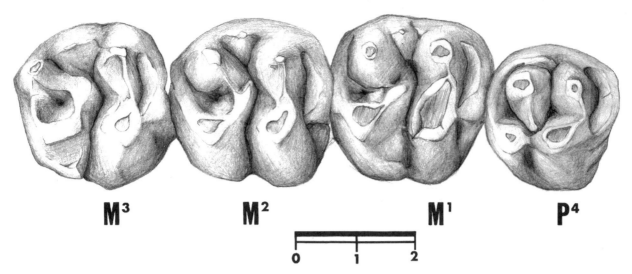

Figure 6. *Right maxillary dentition (P4-M3, CM 69881) of* Sciuravus popi, *a bunodont sciuravid rodent. This is the first complete upper cheek dentition known for the species. Scale bar = 2 mm. Drawing by Janet Lo.*

toothed rodents has now also been recorded from the UF for the first time. This genus is also known from Badwater Creek, Wyoming (M. R. Dawson, personal communication). Similar forms have been found in Uintan deposits of Texas (Walton, 1993) and southern California (Chiment and Korth, 1997). The California rodents (*Metanoiamys*) are considered to be early eomyids, a family not found in the UF. The Rocky Mountain genus has some general adaptive similarities to *Sciuravus*, if not a true taxonomic affiliation. The taxon is being described by M. R. Dawson. Another small, obscure, but very interesting rodent from the UF is *Janimus rhinophilos* (Dawson, 1966), still known only from the type specimen found embedded in matrix stuck to a rhino bone. *Janimus* is a taxonomic enigma; it seems to be a small seed eater, judging from the ridged grinding surface of the only known lower molars.

The most abundant of all mammals in the UF are rodents of the family Cylindrodontidae (Emry and Korth, 1996). The UF taxa are relatively small-bodied (mouse-sized) lophodont rodents. The dental structure suggests a diet of resistant plant fibers and/or seeds. The smallest cylindrodontid of the formation is *Pareumys grangeri*; hundreds of specimens have been found (figure 7). Given the certain collecting bias against finding these small rodents, it seems likely that *P. grangeri* was the most common mammal in the living Uintan fauna. A slightly larger species, *P. milleri*, is also present in the formation, along with one new record of a similar cylindrodontid, *Spurimus selbyi*, otherwise recorded only from Badwater Creek, Wyoming.

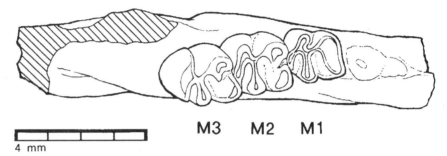

Figure 7. *Left mandibular dentition (m1-3, CM 69898) of* Pareumys grangeri, *a very common lophodont rodent of the Uinta Formation. Bar scale = 4 mm.*

Among the most adaptively divergent of the Uintan rodents is *Protoptychus hatcheri*, a small-bodied mammal which had, by Eocene standards, unusually high-crowned, lophodont molars (Wahlert, 1973). Its limb proportions and morphology indicate specialized, leaping locomotion. Most knowledge of *Protoptychus* comes from late Bridgerian deposits in Wyoming (Turnbull, 1991). Only a few dental and associated postcranial elements have been found by the WU expeditions from low in the stratigraphic section.

Lagomorphs

The order Lagomorpha is characterized today by the ubiquitous rabbit. *Mytonolagus* is the only known representative of the group in the UF (Burke, 1934; Dawson, 1970), often dubiously placed in the extant family Leporidae. *Mytonolagus* surely predates the split of the two living families, Leporidae and Ochotonidae. The appearance of *Mytonolagus* during the middle Eocene is the first evidence of rabbits in the New World (Black and Dawson, 1966). Lagomorphs initially evolved in Asia and subsequently migrated to North America. Specimens of *Mytonolagus* and other Eocene lagomorphs have been found in Utah, Wyoming, and Saskatchewan, yet none have been found in the Uintan assemblages of southern California (Walsh, 1996a). Black and Dawson (1966) posited that this indicates the environments of the montane regions of North America were more favorable because of similarities to the Asian habitats.

Specimens of *Mytonolagus* were initially discovered in Myton Pocket, of Uinta C levels. The WU expeditions have produced few new specimens of *Mytonolagus*, our only substantive addition to knowledge of *Mytonolagus* being the recovery of a fused distal tibiofibula that displays morphology similar to that of a modern rabbit: leaping behavior was already established in the Eocene.

Taeniodonts

The genus *Stylinodon*, a rare member of the UF fauna, is a late representative of the bizarre early Tertiary order, Taeniodontia (Matthew, 1937). These animals resemble rodents and lagomorphs in having an enlarged, continuously growing pair of incisors (lateral incisors in taeniodonts, central incisors in rodents, a double pair in lagomorphs), but they differ from those groups in being large, robust animals -- in fact, they rank as one of the largest mammals of the UF, along with uintatheres, brontotheres, and aquatic rhinos. Taeniodonts further differ from rodents and lagomorphs in having simple, peg-like cheek teeth that also grow from a persistent pulp. The bear-sized postcranium of *Stylinodon* has stout, heavily built limbs and clawed feet (Romer, 1966).

CARNIVOROUS MAMMALS

Early Tertiary carnivorous mammals can be divided into three orders, the extinct Creodonta and Mesonychia, and the true Carnivora, which contains today's modern carnivore families. In addition, there is the enigmatic, racoon-sized meat-eater, *Simidectes* (described above under Proteutheria). Each of the three carnivorous orders discussed here had wide temporal and spatial distributions in the Tertiary and were major components of all continental paleofaunas. Since study began on these groups their definitions and content have often changed, but currently there is a widely accepted taxonomic and phylogenetic arrangement that classifies each group as distinct at the ordinal level.

Creodonts

The order Creodonta is widely held as the closest relative of the true Carnivora, together forming a supra-ordinal group, the Ferae (MacIntyre, 1966). Recent work has suggested that Ferae may not be a natural classification, because creodonts only show superficial resemblances to the Carnivora, and that creodonts may themselves be polyphyletic (Fox and Youzwshyn, 1994; Polly, 1996). The creodonts have their specialized shearing teeth (the carnassials) variably located within the molar series, either M1/m2 or M2/m3, and in some cases both (Polly, 1996). Creodonts arose in the late Paleocene and at least one species survived into the early Pliocene. The emphasis on shearing in the entire molar tooth battery, and the accompanying lack of plasticity, has been suggested as a key to the creodonts' subsequent replacement worldwide by true carnivorans, whose more generalized molar dentition, adapted for both shearing and grinding, allowed for a more varied adaptive radiation (Ewer, 1973).

The first creodont described from the Uinta Basin was an edentulous jaw attributed to *Hyaenodon* (Osborn, 1895). This specimen was later assigned to *Oxyaenodon dysodus* (Wortman, 1901-02), and another specimen was attributed to a different species of the same genus, *O. dysclerus* (Peterson, 1919). Van Valen (1966) found the two species to be synonymous, but removed the specimen originally assigned to *Hyaendon* to a new species, *O. wortmani*. Specimens collected by the recent WU expeditions include a skeleton of *O. dysodus* with fore- and hindlimbs, some of the axial skeleton, and much of the cranium and dentition.

The strangest and the most problematical creodont from the UF is *Apatelurus kayi* (Scott, 1938), known from associated right and left mandibles. Although clearly a hypercarnivore in adaptation, *A. kayi* displays a unique suite of taxonomic features. The posterior dentition resembles derived hyaenodontid creodonts, such as *Hyaenodon*, with a large, blade-like m2 bearing only two main cusps, and lacking an m3. Anteriorly, the ramus is expanded dorsoventrally with a large symphysis, in many ways resembling a saber-toothed cat. A low mandibular condyle also lends itself to the saber-toothed adaptation. Our lone new specimen of the genus, an isolated lower tooth, differs in size from the type of *A. kayi* and may represent a distinct species.

Two other species of creodonts are also known from the UF. *Mimocyon longipes* was originally placed in the Miacidae (Peterson, 1919), but was later recognized as a creodont after more specimens were found in Wyoming, and renamed *Proviverra longipes* (Dawson, 1980). *M. longipes* is unique among Uintan creodonts in retaining large, well-developed talonid basins on the carnassials. This suggests a more generalized diet than seen in the other taxa. *Limnocyon potens* (formerly *L. douglassi*;

Peterson, 1919) is a larger animal than the other two genera, and a recently collected mandible has been assigned to this species. Finally, we have recovered the first record of a very small-bodied creodont in the UF, based on one specimen representing a weasel-sized animal similar in comparable features to early Eocene *Prototomus*.

Carnivorans

Carnivorans are characterized by a single set of carnassials placed farther forward in the jaw (P4/m1) than is the case for creodonts (Flynn and Galiano, 1982; Wozencraft, 1989). Early true carnivores from the Paleocene and Eocene traditionally have been divided into two families, the Miacidae and the Viverravidae. The viverravids have a distribution from the early Paleocene to the middle Eocene, while the miacids are strictly an Eocene group. Carnivores attributable to modern families begin to show up in the fossil record of the early Oligocene (Martin, 1989). This suggests that the radiation of primitive carnivorans into modern suborders occurred in the middle to late Eocene. This makes the Uintan an important time in carnivore evolution, and it is here that we should start to find a diversification not previously seen in Carnivora.

The first Uinta Basin carnivore found was *Amphicyon vulpinum*, later amended to *Miacis vulpinus*, the type of which has been lost (Scott and Osborn, 1887, 1890). Two other species of *Miacis* have been added subsequently to the fauna, *M. uintensis* (Osborn, 1895) and *M. gracilis* (Clark, 1939). The latter species is perhaps near the ancestry of the canid subfamily Hesperocyoninae (Bryant, 1992; Wang, 1994; Wang and Tedford, 1994). Another small miacid recorded from the UF, *Procynodictis vulpiceps* (Wortman and Matthew, 1899), is a widely distributed species also known from Texas and Wyoming (Westgate, 1990; Dawson, 1980; Eaton, 1985). All of these relatively small miacids range in size from weasels to skunks. Finally, there is a new, tiny miacid known only by a single lower molar that is smaller even than the *Prototomus*-like creodont.

Larger carnivores are also known from the UF, but their taxonomic history is complex. Wortman and Matthew (1899) described a large species (about the size of a small bear), *Prodaphaenus scotti*, which they thought was related to *Uintacyon* of the earlier Bridger Basin deposits (Wortman, 1901-02). Later authors transferred the species to that genus as *U. scotti* (Thorpe, 1923a). Finds in Saskatchewan led to a major revision of the genus (Bryant, 1992), which revived Matthew's (1909) previously ignored subgenus *Miocyon* for the Uinta Basin species (as well as for other earlier and later

species found elsewhere in North America). New finds of this genus by the WU expeditions, including mandibular and maxillary dentitions, along with some postcrania (figure 8), demonstrate two distinct but similar morphologies within the assemblage. The taxon represents an interesting suite of dental characters, including a deep mandibular ramus, a large m1 with a broad talonid basin, and an extremely low-crowned but large m2. Together these attributes suggest an emphasis on grinding, and possibly a dietary hard-object component, a dental adaptation not previously known among early carnivores.

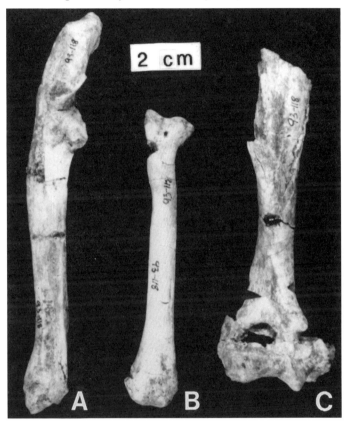

Figure 8. *Right forelimb bones (A, ulna; B, radius; C, humerus; CM 6989/) of a large miacid,* Miocyon. *White bar = 2 cm.*

Peterson (1919) described another miacid, a bit smaller than *Miocyon*, which he assigned to *Prodaphaenus robustus*. After additional specimens were collected from California sites, the species was reassigned to the genus *Tapocyon* (Stock, 1934a). A new specimen with a complete m1 shows much greater disparity in the size of the trigonid and talonid than in *Miocyon*. Thus, *T. robusta* has a dental structure more typical of the smaller Eocene miacids, but the large trigonid suggests a more cat-like diet (Dawson, 1980).

Mesonychids

Mesonychians are only distantly related to the other groups of Uintan predators. They are actually considered to be an ungulate group, with certain members lying near the ancestry of modern Cetacea (whales and dolphins; Thewissen, 1994; Thewissen and others, 1994). Despite their apparent ungulate affinities, the dentition of mesonychians distinguishes them as having a carnivorous component to their diet. The best-studied form postcranially is *Pachyaena* of the early Eocene; its skeleton indicates a relatively unspecialized cursorial animal, comparable in some ways to the running style of modern tapirs (O'Leary and Rose, 1995; Rose and O'Leary, 1995). The mesonychians easily outsized all other UF meat-eaters, having formidable, heavy jaws up to 20 centimeters in length.

Mesonychians are represented in the UF by one genus, *Harpagolestes*, with at least one and possibly more species. *H. uintensis*, the first species described, was originally assigned to the genus *Mesonyx* (Scott, 1888), but was reclassified when its affiliation with Bridgerian *H. macrocephalus* was recognized (Matthew, 1909). Two other species, *H. leotensis* and *H. brevipes* have been described, both based on very fragmentary material (Peterson, 1931a; Thorpe, 1923b). Few new specimens have been found in recent years, which given their large size, suggests that they were not an abundant component of the Uintan fauna.

UNGULATES

Uintatheres

Despite bearing the name "Uinta," these animals are actually quite rare in the UF. Only a few specimens are known, all from the lower part of the formation, and our work has turned up no additional specimens. Knowledge of uintatheres, classified in the order Dinocerata, comes principally from late Bridgerian deposits in Wyoming. The uintatheres were huge, rhino-sized herbivores, with massive, heavily horned heads (Wheeler, 1961). They are one of several enigmatic groups of early Tertiary herbivores that do not show any obvious relationship to later ungulate taxa. The dentition is distinctive, not resembling the teeth found in any other mammalian order. The UF records the latest surviving uintatheres in North America, *Uintatherium* and *Eobasileus*.

Hyopsodontids

The genus *Hyopsodus* is probably the most abundant and widespread mammal of the early Eocene in the Rocky Mountain region. The genus is also found in the early Eocene of Europe, Mongolia, and China. *Hyopsodus* first appears in the Clarkforkian LMA and persists into the Uintan, a period of some 17 million years (Cande and Kent, 1992). The WU expeditions have recovered many new specimens of *Hyopsodus uintensis* (Krishtalka, 1979), the only species known from the UF (figure 9). Compared to earlier species of the genus, *H. uintensis* has more quadrate (rather than rounded) molar margins, and the cusps are more inflated, while at the same time exhibiting greater crest development. This trend toward lophodonty is the most distinctive dental attribute of *H. uintensis*, and has been considered an adaptation to increased amounts of coarse plant material in the diet. Gazin (1968) noted that the dental changes coincided

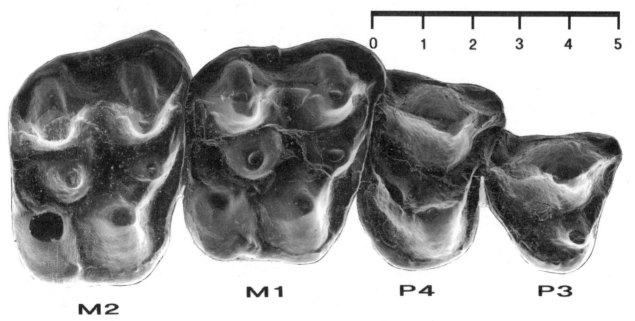

Figure 9. *Right maxillary dentition (P3-M2; CM 69826) of the condylarth,* Hyopsodus uintensis, *one of the signature mammals of the North American early to middle Eocene. Bar scale = 5 mm. Scanning electron micrograph by G. Michael Veith.*

with the onset of a more arid climate during the middle Eocene, which he suggested was associated with a shift towards coarser, more fibrous vegetation.

The molar structure of *H. uintensis* exhibits the same basic cusp arrangement and morphology seen in the homacodont artiodactyls, a group of small-bodied artiodactyls that underwent an evolutionary radiation in the Uintan (see below). This raises the question of whether the decrease in diversity of *Hyopsodus* is associated with the rise and radiation of the homacodonts, a group that may have competed with them in small-bodied, forest-floor herbivorous niches.

Perissodactyls

The fossil record of the Perissodactyla begins in the early Eocene in Asia, North America, and Europe. Perissodactyls probably originated in Asia and migrated to North America via the Bering Strait (McKenna and others, 1989; Prothero and Schoch, 1989). Subsequent to reaching North America, the perissodactyls underwent a tremendous radiation. Three major groups have been identified in North America: Hippomorpha, represented by equids; Moropomorpha, which includes tapiroids, rhinocerotoids and chalicotheres; and Titanotheriomorpha, the brontotheres (Hooker, 1989). Each of these groups is represented in the UF.

Equids are represented in the UF by one genus with two species, *Epihippus gracilis* and *E. uintensis*. Fossils are relatively fragmentary, and little has been published on *Epihippus*, especially compared to the attention given to other fossil horses (MacFadden, 1992). In his classic review of horse evolution, Matthew (1929b) recognized *Epihippus* as being on the main line leading to modern horses, and this assessment is still accepted. *Epihippus* is distinguished from the earlier *Orohippus* by several specialized dental characteristics. Significant among these is increased molarization of the premolars. The third and fourth premolars are molariform and the second premolar is somewhat molariform. In *Orohippus*, only the fourth premolar is fully molariform. *Epihippus*, like its immediate predecessors, has four digits on its forelimb and three on its hindlimb. However, unlike the earlier horses, the middle digit of the hindlimb is enlarged compared to the flanking digits. This is the first indication of the equid trend towards increased dominance of the middle digit.

The Rhinocerotoidea are the most diverse group of perissodactyls and are represented by four genera in the UF (Radinsky, 1966, 1967). These are *Amynodon*, a large-bodied aquatic animal (family Amynodontidae); *Triplopus* and *Epitriplopus*, small gracile "racing rhinos"

(family Hyracodontidae); and *Uintaceras*, a recently described form lying near the ancestry of true rhinocerotoids (Holbrook and Lucas, 1997). Amynodontids are distinguished from other rhinos by a shortened face and enlarged upper and lower canines. The lower canines are procumbent, causing them to shear anterior to the vertical upper canines and producing a wear pattern unique to amynodontids (Wall, 1989). The postcanine diastema is reduced and the premolar series is shortened; the molars are massive, sharply crested teeth.

The Uinta hyracodonts, *Triplopus* and *Epitriplopus*, are smaller (greyhound-sized) cursorial mammals. The metapodials are elongated and laterally compressed. Dentally, they differ from other rhinos in having the ectoloph of M3 confluent with the metaloph (Radinsky, 1969). *Epitriplopus* differs from *Triplopus* in having greater hypsodonty and more molarized premolars. There are two or more species of each genus recognized in the UF, but little taxonomic work has been done in recent decades. Like the amynodonts, the hyracodonts are known from Asia as well as North America.

The final UF rhino is the recently described genus *Uintaceras* (Holbrook and Lucas, 1997). This taxon closely resembles the familiar North American *Hyrachyus* and Asian *Forstercooperia* in the structure of the lower molars, but new specimens of upper dentitions and partial crania indicate that *Uintaceras* is distinct. It is possibly a very primitive true rhino. *Uintaceras* is rare in the UF, with one lower jaw known from Uinta A and other material of perhaps a distinct species coming from the upper part of the formation.

Tapiroids are represented in the UF by two genera, *Isectolophus* and *Colodon* (Radinsky, 1963; Schoch, 1989). The most common of the two is *Isectolophus*, a primitive, bunolophodont genus of moderate size. *Colodon* is infrequently found in the formation, but we do have several nice specimens of the genus from Uinta C. *Colodon* differs from *Isectolophus* in having smaller, squarer molars with lophs that are precisely perpendicular to the tooth row (rather than oblique).

The chalicotheres are an unusual group of perissodactyls. They have a number of strange attributes, perhaps the most distinct being that they have large hook-like claws. Early workers mistakenly identified chalicothere postcrania as edentates or pangolins, before it was recognized that they were associated with perissodactyl dentitions. Chalicotheres were long-armed knuckle-walkers, showing some similarities to giant ground sloths and to gorillas (Coombs, 1989). Because of their W-shaped ectolophs, the chalicotheres were long considered allied with the horses and brontotheres in Hippomorpha, but Radinsky (1964) argued that the hippomorph W-shaped ectoloph evolved independently in chalicotheres. The Chalicotherioidea are now considered moropomorphs (Hooker, 1989). The UF chalicothere is *Eomoropus*, one of the earliest and structurally most primitive members of the group. It is very rare in the formation, with only a small handful of specimens recorded.

The final group of perissodactyls in the UF are the brontotheres (or titanotheres). Later brontotheres are known for their massive size and the huge sweeping horns on their heads (Osborn, 1929). The brontotheres of the middle Eocene, however, were small (cow-sized) compared to their descendants in the Oligocene, and the Uintan taxa further differed from the later forms in lacking horns (Douglass, 1910). A total of at least eight genera have been described from the UF, but this total is certainly too great. Recent revisions are helping to clarify brontothere systematics (Mader, 1989), but work remains to be done on the UF species.

Artiodactyls

Artiodactyls represent one of the largest components of the UF mammalian fauna. Earlier in the Eocene, perissodactyls were more abundant and had greater diversity than artiodactyls, but in the Uintan LMA the trend began to reverse (Gazin, 1955; Black and Dawson, 1966). During this period, great diversification is seen in dental adaptations, most notably in the origin and radiation of the selenodont artiodactyls. At the same time, there was also increasing diversity of bunodont artiodactyls, as well as the retention of very primitive artiodactyl groups that had been present in North America

since the Wasatchian LMA. The Uintan was a golden age of the order Artiodactyla, a time when they established their dominance as the most diverse and successful ungulates of the Cenozoic.

Among the UF artiodactyls, the ones that represent taxonomic holdovers from the earliest Eocene are the diacodexine dichobunids, which retain very generalized molar structure. Only one genus of this group is found in the UF, *Auxontodon*, known by just a few dental specimens from Uinta C. Two other groups of non-selenodont artiodactyls are also represented: the small-bodied homacodonts and the massive *Achaenodon*. Homacodonts are common in the UF. There are five genera, each characterized by small size, quadrate lower teeth, and five or six-cusped upper molars. In terms of their dental structure, they show an interesting combination of bunodont and "selenodont" features. In fact, one species from the UF, *Mesomeryx grangeri*, has been suggested as a possible direct ancestor of the true selenodont family, Hypertragulidae (Stock, 1934b). Within the UF, we have recovered fossils of *Mesomeryx* low in the section, the slightly larger *Bunomeryx* through the middle part of the section, and the largest genus, *Pentacemylus*, apparently restricted to the highest levels. Two other, rarer genera also occur, *Hylomeryx* and *Mytonomeryx*. All five taxa can be distinguished mainly on the basis of details of upper molar structure. The most important new finds we have made of this group are postcranial elements of *Mesomeryx*, a tiny animal the size of a cottontail rabbit (figure 10). Analysis of these postcrania suggests that the animal was a cursorial quadruped that lacked the saltatory specializations seen in *Diacodexis*, an early Eocene dichobunid (Townsend and Rasmussen, 1995;

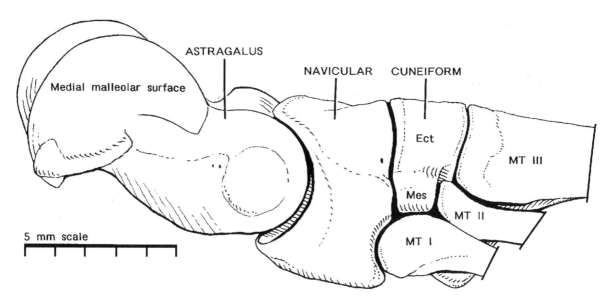

Figure 10. *Left tarsus of the small homacodont artiodactyl,* Mesomeryx grangeri, *based on several unassociated specimens collected at locality WU-18 in Uinta B. The ecto- and mesocuneiforms are fused and the medial two metatarsals are reduced in size compared to the metatarsal for digit III.*

Mammals of the Middle Eocene Unita Formation - Rasmussen, Conroy, Friscia, Townsend, Kinkel

Rose, 1982). Like many other Eocene artiodactyls, *Mesomeryx* retains several primitive locomotor features, such as pentadactyly, and unfused ulna and radius.

The largest of the UF artiodactyls, and the last of the non-selenodont forms, is *Achaenodon*, a massive, heavy-jawed animal with remarkably bunodont, pig-like molars. The genus has been placed in its own family, Achaenodontidae (Coombs and Coombs, 1977). In a general adaptive sense, *Achaenodon* resembles other large-bodied "pig-like" artiodactyls of the early Tertiary, such as helohyids and entelodonts, but it is not clear how *Achaenodon* and these other forms are phylogenetically related to each other. In the UF, material of *Achaenodon* is found in the sheets of coarse, golden "*Amynodon* sandstones," which also preserve the remains of other large-bodied mammals such as the brontotheres and amynodontid rhinos.

One of the most important evolutionary events of the Uintan LMA is the adaptive radiation of true selenodont artiodactyls (Scott, 1898, 1899). These animals are characterized by the sharp-edged, crescentic crests and cusps on their upper and lower molars, which apparently serve to slice up leafy vegetation. The UF selenodonts are classified in three families: Agriochoeridae, Oromerycidae, and Protoceratidae. The agriochoerids of the UF are *Protoreodon* and *Diplobunops* (Peterson, 1931b). *Protoreodon* is the most commonly found mammal in the UF. It is characterized by a caniniform p1, a closed tooth row, and a short, deep mandible. The molars are relatively shorter and broader than those of the other UF selenodonts, and they bear accessory cuspules (a metastylid on the lower molars and a paraconule on the uppers). Postcranially, *Protoreodon* is quite generalized, without the cursorial specializations seen in some of the early diacodexines (Rose, 1985) or in later selenodonts. *Diplobunops* differs from *Protoreodon* primarily in the robustness of the limbs. The species level systematics of *Protoreodon* remain complex; new metrical analyses of *Protoreodon* from controlled stratigraphic levels indicate that there is no notable sexual dimorphism; this suggests that the variation present in the pooled samples really does represent taxonomic diversity in time and space.

The family Oromerycidae is represented in the UF by a few rare genera (*Oromeryx*, *Malaquiferus*), and by the better known genus, *Protylopus*. Oromerycid molars are relatively longer, narrower, and more high-crowned than those of the agriochoerids. They lack the caniniform p1 and the accessory cuspules. The most important feature of the oromerycids is their relatively specialized postcranium, with elongated, gracile limbs and reduction of lateral digits. *Protylopus* remains uncommon in the UF collections, although it is a common and diverse

genus in beds of comparable age in southern California (Golz, 1976).

The family Protoceratidae is represented in the UF by two genera: *Leptotragulus* and *Leptoreodon*. They differ from agriochoerids in having very shallow, elongated lower jaws with notable diastemata on either side of the canine, and in lacking molar accessory cuspules. The two leptotraguline genera are very similar to each other, distinguished mainly by differences in premolar morphology (possible synonymy of the two has been mentioned by most systematists working with the group, but the formal deed remains undone). *Leptotragulus proavus* is the most common species of leptotraguline in the UF, and is the second most common artiodactyl, after *Protoreodon*. Smaller species of *Leptotragulus* occur higher, near the contact with the overlying Duchesne River Formation. *Leptotragulus* is similar in size, tooth morphology, and body build to living chevrotains (family Tragulidae) of tropical Africa and Asia (Janis, 1984). Chevrotains are browsers that live in forested environments; aspects of their diet, ranging behavior and social interactions have been interpreted as primitive based in part on their resemblances to many early Tertiary artiodactyls.

THE UINTAN FAUNAL COMMUNITY

What would be the mammalian fauna that a visitor would encounter in the Eocene of the Uinta Basin? Ignoring the rare taxa or the ones limited to isolated localities, the following overview constructs a typical fauna based on relatively common taxa that are regularly found at multiple localities.

The small-bodied insectivores would be dominated by hedgehog-like dormaaliids and small didelphid marsupials. Arboreal insect-eaters would include apatemyids and, at least in some areas, the small anaptomorphine, *Trogolemur*. A semi-aquatic insect- and fish-eater found in the Uinta Basin was a fairly large pantolestid. The main mammalian predators of the community would have been an interesting mixture of skunk-sized animals of widely differing taxonomic affiliations: the creodont *Oxyaenodon*, the miacid *Tapocyon*, and the proteuthere *Simidectes*. The less common larger predators included the miacid *Miocyon*, and the mesonychid, *Harpagolestes*.

The herbivores included a broad diversity of forms. The homacodont artiodactyls, along with the condylarth *Hyopsodus*, were apparently forest floor omnivores. Arboreal herbivores included the lemur-sized tarsioid primates of the genus *Ourayia*. Medium-sized browsers included *Epihippus*, *Protoreodon*, *Leptotragulus*, and less commonly, small oromerycids, the latter probably being one of the most cursorial of the Uinta mammals. The browser most highly specialized to a leafy diet would have been the hyracodont rhinos, *Triplopus* and especially *Epitriplopus*, both of which were also specialized cursors. Other moderate-sized herbivores that may have had a more generalized diet include the tapirs, *Isectolophus* and *Colodon*. The largest-bodied herbivores of the Uintan communities would have been the ubiquitous brontotheres, the aquatic rhino *Amynodon*, and the pig-like *Achaeonodon*.

Rodents were an important part of the fauna, but the postcranial adaptations and ecological relationships of the rodents remain very poorly understood. The typical Uintan forms included tiny vole-shaped *Microparamys*, the mouse-sized *Pareumys* eating fibrous material, the squirrel-sized *Sciuravus* eating fruit, and large-bodied *Leptotomus* and *Ischyrotomus*. Paleobiological analysis of this early, diverse rodent fauna should shed light on the adaptive radiation of the order Rodentia.

From the point of view of taxonomic representation within the mammalian faunas, the small mammals of the UF contrast markedly with the small mammals of Uintan beds in southern California. Omomyid primates from California are represented by at least seven genera, including small-bodied forms such as *Dyseolemur* and *Washakius*. *Hyopsodus* is common in Utah but absent from southern California, while conversely, the dormaaliid insectivores *Proterixoides* and *Sespedectes* are common in southern California but not in Utah. The differences in the small mammal faunas between California and Utah cannot be entirely ascribed to collecting bias, but rather represent real biogeographic patterns that reflect continental paleoecological differences (Walsh, 1996a; Rasmussen and Townsend, 1995). There is greater faunal similarity between the UF mammals and those of later Rocky Mountain faunas (such as Badwater

Creek faunas) than between UF and coeval Californian or Texan faunas (table 1). The faunal provincialism of the later Eocene emphasized by Storer (1996) was already being established during Uintan times.

Table 1. *Faunal resemblance index comparing the Uinta B and C small mammals to Uintan mammals in California and Wyoming.*

Simpson Coefficient = 100 x (shared taxa/small sample)

Uinta B small mammals compared to:	Families	Genera	Species
Early Uintan, California	73	47	5
Late Uintan, California	73	53	5
Latest Uintan, Wyoming	91	75	14

Uinta C small mammals compared to:	Families	Genera	Species
Early Uintan, California	82	41	6
Late Uintan, California	82	47	6
Latest Uintan, Wyoming	100	65	28

ACKNOWLEDGMENTS

The Uinta Basin field work is conducted under permits granted by BLM. We thank Blaine Phillips of the BLM's Vernal District, and Alden Hamblin and Sue Ann Bilbey of the Utah Field House, Vernal, for their help and input into the field operations. We also thank Hatch River Expeditions and the Chevron employees of Redwash for their logistic support in the basin. For advice and insight about the mammals we thank Mary Dawson, Alan Tabrum and Chris Beard, of the Carnegie Museum, Steve Walsh of the San Diego Museum of Natural History, and J.G.M. Thewissen of Northwestern Ohio Universities College of Medicine. The paper benefited from the critical review and editing provided by David Gillette, Donald Prothero, and Peter Robinson. We also acknowledge the skills and helpful contributions of WU students Janet Lo and Becky Speckman.

REFERENCES

Anderson, D. W., and Picard, M. D., 1972, Stratigraphy of the Duchesne River Formation (Eocene-Oligocene?), northern Uinta Basin, northeastern Utah: Utah Geological and Mineralogical Survey Bulletin, v. 97, p. 1-23.

Bartek, L. R., Cirbus Sloan, Lisa, Anderson, J. B., and Ross, M. I., 1992, Evidence from the Antarctic continental margin of late Paleogene ice sheets--a manifestation of plate reorganization and synchronous changes in atmospheric circulation over the emerging southern ocean?, *in* Prothero, D. R., and Berggren, W. A., editors, Eocene-Oligocene climatic and biotic evolution: Princeton, New Jersey, Princeton University Press, p. 131-159.

Berggren, W. A., and Prothero, D. R., 1992, Eocene and Oligocene climatic and biotic evolution-- an overview, *in* Prothero, D. R. and Berggren, W. A., editors, Eocene-Oligocene climatic and biotic evolution: Princeton, New Jersey, Princeton University Press, p. 1-28.

Berggren, W. A., Kent, D. V., Obradovich, J. D., and Swisher, C. C., 1992, Toward a revised Paleogene geochronology, *in* Prothero, D. R., and Berggren, W. A., editors, Eocene-Oligocene climatic and biotic evolution: Princeton, New Jersey, Princeton University Press, p. 29-45.

Betts, C. W., 1871, The Yale College expedition of 1870: Harper's New Monthly Magazine, v. 43, p. 663-671.

Black, C. C., and Dawson, M. R., 1966, A review of late Eocene mammalian faunas from North America: American Journal of Science, v. 264, p. 321-349.

Bryant, H. N., 1992, The Carnivora of the Lac Pelletier Lower Fauna (Eocene: Duchesnean), Cypress Hills Formation, Saskatchewan: Journal of Paleontology, v. 66, p. 847-855.

Burke, J. J., 1934, *Mytonolagus*, a new leporine genus from the Uinta Eocene series in Utah: Annals of Carnegie Museum, v. 23, p. 399-420.

—1937, A new *Sciuravus* from Utah: Annals of Carnegie Museum, v. 27, p. 1-9.

Butler, P. M., 1972, The problem of insectivore classification, *in* Joysey, K. A., and Kemp, T. S., editors, Studies in vertebrate evolution: Edinburgh, Oliver and Boyd, p. 253-265.

Cande, S. C., and Kent, D. V., 1992, A new geomagnetic polarity timescale for the late Cretaceous and Cenozoic: Journal of Geophysical Research, v. 97, p. 13917-13951.

Carroll, R. L., 1988, Vertebrate paleontology and evolution, New York, W. H. Freeman and Company, 698 p.

Cartmill, Matt, 1974, *Daubentonia*, *Dactylopsila*, woodpeckers and klinorhynchy, *in* Martin, R. D., and Doyle, G. A., editors, Prosimian biology: London, Duckworth, p. 655-669.

Chiment, J. J., and Korth, W. W., 1997, A new genus of eomyid rodent (Mammalia) from the Eocene (Uintan-Duchesnean) of southern California: Journal of Vertebrate Paleontology, v. 16, p. 116 124.

Clark, James, 1939, *Miacis gracilis*, a new carnivore from the Uinta Eocene (Utah): Annals of Carnegie Museum, v. 27, p. 349-370.

Coombs, M. C., 1971, Status of *Simidectes* (Insectivora, Pantolestoidea) of the late Eocene of North America: American Museum Novitates, v. 2455, p. 1-41.

—1989, Interrelationships and diversity in the Chalicotheriidae, *in* Prothero, D.R., and Schoch, R. M., editors, The evolution of perissodactyls: New York, Oxford University Press, p. 438-457.

Coombs, M. C., and Coombs, W. D., 1977, Dentition of *Gobiohyus* and a reevaluation of the Helohyidae (Artiodactyla): Journal of Mammalogy, v. 58, p.291-308.

Crochet, J.-Y., 1977, Les Didelphidae (Marsupiocarnivora, Marsupialia) holarctiques tertiares: Comptes-Rendus Hébdomadaires des Séances de L'Académie des Sciences, Paris, séries D, t. 24, p. 357-360.

Dane, C. H., 1954, Stratigraphic and facies relationships of the upper part of the Green River Formation and lower part of the Uinta Formation in Duchesne, Uintah, and Wasatch Counties, Utah: American Association of Petroleum Geologists Bulletin, v. 38, p. 405-425.

Dawson, M. R., 1966, Additional late Eocene rodents (Mammalia) from the Uinta Basin, Utah: Annals of Carnegie Museum, v. 38, p. 97-114.

—1970, Paleontology and geology of the Badwater Creek area, central Wyoming, part 6, the leporid *Mytonolagus* (Mammalia, Lagomorpha): Annals of Carnegie Museum, v. 41, p. 215-230.

—1973, Paleontology and geology of the Badwater Creek area, central Wyoming, part 8, the rodent *Microparamys* (Mammalia): Annals of Carnegie Museum, v. 45, p. 145-150.

—1977, Late Eocene rodent radiations--North America, Europe and Asia: Geobios, Mémoire Spécial, t. 1, p. 195-209.

—1980, Paleontology and geology of the Badwater Creek area, central Wyoming. Part 20. The Late Eocene Creodonta and Carnivora: Annals of Carnegie Museum, v. 49, p. 79-91.

Douglass, Earl, 1910, Preliminary description of some new titanotheres from the Uinta deposits: Annals of Carnegie Museum, v. 6, p. 304-313.

Eaton, J. G., 1985, Paleontology and correlation of the Eocene Tepee Trail and Wiggins Formations in the North Fork of Owl Creek area, southeastern Absaroka Range, Hot Springs County, Wyoming: Journal of Vertebrate Paleontology, v. 5, p. 345-370.

Eberle, Jaelyn, and Storer, J. E., 1995, *Herpetotherium valens* (Lambe), a didelphid marsupial from the Calf Creek local fauna (Chadronian), Saskatchewan: Journal of Vertebrate Paleontology, v. 15, p. 785-794.

Emry, R. J., 1990, Mammals of the Bridgerian (Middle Eocene) Elderberry Canyon local fauna of eastern Nevada: Geological Society of America Special Paper, v. 243, p. 187-210.

Emry, R. J., and Korth, W. W., 1996, Cylindrodontidae, *in* Prothero, D. R., and Emry, R. J., editors, The terrestrial Eocene-Oligocene transition in North America: Cambridge, England, Cambridge University Press, p. 399-416.

Erickson, C. J., 1995, Perspectives on percussive foraging in the aye-aye (*Daubentonia madagascariensis*), *in* Alterman, Lon, Doyle, G. A., and Izard, M. K., editors, Creatures of the dark: New York, Plenum Press, p. 251-260.

Evanoff, Emmett, Prothero, D. R., and Lander, R. H., 1992, Eocene-Oligocene climatic change in North America--the White River Formation near Douglas, east-central Wyoming, *in* Prothero, D. R., and Berggren, W. A., editors, Eocene-Oligocene climatic and biotic evolution: Princeton, New Jersey, Princeton University Press, p. 116-130.

Ewer, R. F., 1973, The Carnivores: Ithaca, Cornell University Press, 494 p.

Flynn, J. J., and Galiano, Henry, 1982, Phylogeny of early Tertiary Carnivora, with a description of a new species of *Prosictis* from the Middle Eocene of northwestern Wyoming: American Museum Novitates, v. 2725, p. 1-64.

Fox, R. C., and Youzwshyn, G. P., 1994, New primitive carnivorans (Mammalia) from the Paleocene of western Canada, and their bearing on relationships of the order: Journal of Vertebrate Paleontology, v. 14, p. 382-404.

Gazin, C. L., 1955, A review of the upper Eocene Artiodactyla of North America: Smithsonian Miscellaneous Collections, v. 128, no. 8, p. 1-95.

—1958, A review of the middle and upper Eocene primates of North America: Smithsonian Miscellaneous Collections, v. 136, p. 1-112.

—1968, A study of the Eocene condylarthran mammal *Hyopsodus*: Smithsonian Miscellaneous Collections, v. 153, p. 1-90.

Gingerich, P. D., 1981, Radiation of early Cenozoic Didymoconidae (Condylarthra, Mesonychia) in Asia, with a new genus from the early Eocene of western North America: Journal of Mammalogy, v. 62, p. 526-538.

—1982, Second species of *Wyolestes* (Condylarthra, Mesonychia) from the early Eocene of western North America: Journal of Mammalogy, v. 63, p. 706-709.

Golz, D. J., 1976, Eocene Artiodactyla of southern California: Natural History Museum of Los Angeles County, Science Bulletin, v. 26, p. 1-85.

Grande, Lance, 1984, Paleontology of the Green River Formation, with a review of the fish fauna: The Geological Survey of Wyoming, Bulletin, v. 63, p. 1-333.

Gregory, W. K., 1910, The orders of mammals: Bulletin of the American Museum of Natural History, v. 27, p. 1-524.

Gunnell, G.F., 1995, New notharctine (Primates, Adapiformes) skull from the Uintan (Middle Eocene) of San Diego County, California: American Journal of Physical Anthropology, v. 98, p. 447-470.

Hamblin, A. H., 1987, Paleogeography and paleoecology of the Myton Pocket, Uinta Basin, Utah (Uinta Formation -- Upper Eocene): Brigham Young University Geology Studies, v. 34, p. 33-60.

Hintze, L. F., 1988, Geological history of Utah: Brigham Young University Geology Studies, v. 20, no. 3, p. 1-181.

Holbrook, L. T., and Lucas, S. G., 1997, A new genus of rhinocerotoid from the Eocene of Utah and the status of North American "*Forstercooperia*": Journal of Vertebrate Paleontology, v. 17, p. 384-396.

Hooker, J. J., 1989, Character polarities in early perissodactyls and their significance for *Hyracotherium* and infraordinal relationships, *in* Prothero, D. R., and Schoch, R. M., editors, The evolution of perissodactyls: New York, Oxford University Press, p. 79-101.

Hutchison, J. H., 1992, Western North American reptile and amphibian record across the Eocene-Oligocene boundary and its climatic implications, *in* Prothero, D. R., and Berggren, W. A., editors, Eocene-Oligocene climatic and biotic evolution: Princeton, New Jersey, Princeton University Press, p. 451-463.

Janis, Christine, 1984, Tragulids as living fossils, *in* Eldredge, Niles, and Stanley, S. M., editors, Living fossils: New York, Springer Verlag, p. 87-94.

Kay, J. L., 1934, The Tertiary formations of the Uinta Basin, Utah: Annals of Carnegie Museum, v. 23, p. 357-371.

—1957, The Eocene vertebrates of the Uinta Basin, Utah, *in* Seal, O. G., editor, Guidebook to the geology of the Uinta Basin: Intermountain Association of Petroleum Geologists, p. 110-114.

Keller, Gerta, MacLeod, Norman, and Barrera, Enriqueta, 1992, Eocene-Oligocene faunal turnover in planktonic foraminifera, and Antarctic glaciation, *in* Prothero, D. R., and Berggren, W. A., editors, Eocene-Oligocene climatic and biotic evolution: Princeton, New Jersey, Princeton University Press, p. 218-244.

Kennett, J. P., 1977, Cenozoic evolution of Antarctic glaciation, the circum-Antarctic ocean, and their impact on global paleoceanography: Journal of Geophysical Research, v. 82, p. 3843-3860.

Koenigswald, Wighart von, 1980, Das Skelett eines Pantolestiden (Proteutheria, Mammalia) aus dem mittleren Eozän von Messel bei Darmstadt: Paläontologie Zeitschrift, v. 54, p. 267-287.

—1987, The ecological niche of early Tertiary apatemyids -- an extinct group of mammals: Nature, v. 326, p. 595-597.

Koenigswald, Wighart von, Storch, Gerhard, and Richter, Gotthard, 1992, Rodents -- at the start of a great career, *in* Schaal, Stephan, and Ziegler, Willi, editors, Messel: Oxford, Clarendon Press, p. 219-222.

Korth, W. W., 1994, The Tertiary record of rodents in North America: New York, Plenum Press.

Krishtalka, Leonard, 1976, Early Tertiary Adapisoricidae and Erinaceidae (Mammalia, Insectivora) of North America: Bulletin of the Carnegie Museum of Natural History, v. 1, p. 1-40.

—1978, Paleontology and geology of the Badwater Creek area, central Wyoming, part 15, review of the late Eocene primates from Wyoming and Utah, and the Plesitarsiiformes: Annals of Carnegie Museum, v. 47, p. 335-360.

—1979, Paleontology and geology of the Badwater Creek area, central Wyoming, part 18, revision of late Eocene *Hyopsodus*: Annals of Carnegie Museum, v. 48, p. 377-389.

Lucas, S. G., 1992, Redefinition of the Duchesnean Land Mammal "Age", late Eocene of western North America, *in* Prothero, D. R., and Berggren, W. A., editors, Eocene-Oligocene climatic and biotic evolution: Princeton, New Jersey, Princeton University Press, p. 88-105.

MacFadden, B. J., 1992, Fossil horses: systematics, paleobiology, and evolution of the Family Equidae: Cambridge, England, Cambridge University Press.

MacIntyre, G. T., 1966, The Miacidae (Mammalia, Carnivora), part 1, the systematics of *Ictidopappus* and *Protictis*: Bulletin of the American Museum of Natural History, v. 131, p. 115-210.

Mader, B. J., 1989, The Brontotheriida-- a systematic revision and preliminary phylogeny of North American genera, *in* Prothero, D. R., and Schoch, R. M., editors, The evolution of the Perissodactyla: New York, Oxford University Press, p. 458-484.

Marsh, O. C., 1875a, Ancient lake basins of the Rocky Mountain region: American Journal of Science and Arts, v. 9, p. 49-52.

—1875b, Notice of new Tertiary mammals, IV: American Journal of Science and Arts, Third Series, v. 9, p. 239-250.

Martin, L. D., 1989, Fossil history of the terrestrial Carnivora, *in* Gittleman, J. L., editor, Carnivore behavior, ecology, and evolution: Ithaca, New York, Cornell University Press, p. 536-568.

Matthew, W. D., 1909, The Carnivora and Insectivora of the Bridger Basin, Middle Eocene: Memoirs of the American Museum of Natural History, v. 9, p. 291-567.

—1921, *Stehlinius*, a new Eocene insectivore, American Museum Novitates, v. 14, p. 1-5.

—1929a, Preoccupied names: Journal of Mammalogy, v. 10, p. 171.

—1929b, The evolution of the horse -- a record and its interpretation: Quarterly Review of Biology, v. 1, p. 139-185.

—1937, Paleocene faunas of the San Juan Basin, New Mexico: Transactions of the American Philosophical Society, v. 30, p. 1-65.

McKenna, M. C., Chow Minchen, Suyin Ting, and Luo Zhexi, 1989, *Radinskya yupingae*, a perissodactyl-like mammal from the late Paleocene of China, *in* Prothero, D. R., and Schoch, R. M., editors, The evolution of perissodactyls: New York, Oxford University Press, p. 24-36.

Miller, K. G., 1992, Middle Eocene to Oligocene stable isotopes, climate and deep-water history-- the terminal Eocene event?, *in* Prothero, D. R., and Berggren, W. A., editors, Eocene-Oligocene climatic and biotic evolution: Princeton, New Jersey, Princeton University Press, p. 160-177.

O'Leary, M. A., and Rose, K. D., 1995, Postcranial skeleton of the early Eocene mesonychid *Pachyaena* (Mammalia: Mesonychia): Journal of Vertebrate Paleontology, v. 15, p. 401- 430.

Osborn, H. F., 1895, Fossil animals of the Uinta Basin, expedition of 1894: Bulletin of the American Museum of Natural History, v. 7, p. 71-105.

—1929, The titanotheres of ancient Wyoming, Dakota and Nebraska: Monograph of the U. S. Geological Survey, v. 55, p. 1-953.

Peterson, O. A., 1919, Report upon the material discovered in the Upper Eocene of the Uinta Basin by Earl Douglas in the years 1908-1909, and by O. A. Peterson in 1912: Annals of Carnegie Museum, v. 12, p. 40-141.

—1931a, New mesonychids from the Uinta: Annals of Carnegie Museum, v. 20, p. 333-339.

—1931b, Two new species of agriochoerids: Annals of Carnegie Museum, v. 20, p. 333-339.

Polly, P. D., 1996, Skeleton of *Gazinocyon vulpeculus*, gen. et comb. nov., and the cladistic relationships of Hyaenodontidae (Eutheria, Mammalia): Journal of Vertebrate Paleontology, v. 16, p. 303-319.

Prothero, D. R., 1996, Magnetic stratigraphy and biostratigraphy of the Middle Eocene Uinta Formation, Uinta Basin, Utah, *in* Prothero, D. R., and Emry, R. J., editors, The terrestrial Eocene-Oligocene transition in North America: Cambridge, England, Cambridge University Press, p. 3-24.

Prothero, D. R., and Schoch, R.M., 1989, Origin and evolution of the Perissodactyla--summary and synthesis, *in* Prothero, D. R., and Schoch, R. M., editors, The evolution of perissodactyls: New York, Oxford University Press, p. 504-529.

Prothero, D. R., and Swisher, C. C., 1992, Magnetostratigraphy and geochronology of the terrestrial Eocene-Oligocene transition in North America, *in* Prothero, D. R., and Berggren, W. A., editors, Eocene-Oligocene climatic and biotic evolution: Princeton, New Jersey, Princeton University Press, p. 46-73.

Radinsky, L. B., 1963, Origin and early evolution of North American Tapiroidea: Bulletin of the Peabody Museum of Natural History, v. 17, p. 1-106.

—1964, *Paleomoropus*, a new early Eocene chalicothere (Mammalia,

Perissodactyla), and a revision of Eocene chalicotheres: American Museum Novitates, v. 2179, p. 1-28.

—1966, The families of Rhinocerotoidea (Mammalia, Perissodactyla): Journal of Mammalogy, v. 47, p. 631-639.

—1967, Revision of the hyracodontid rhinocerotoids: Bulletin of the American Museum of Natural History, v. 136, p. 1-45.

—1969, The early evolution of the Perissodactyla: Evolution, v. 23, p. 308-328.

Rasmussen, D. T., 1996, A new Middle Eocene omomyine primate from the Uinta Basin, Utah: Journal of Human Evolution, v. 31, p. 75-87.

Rasmussen, D. T., and Townsend, K. E., 1995, New small-bodied mammals from the Uinta Formation, Uintah Basin, Utah, contrast with the coeval small mammals of California: Journal of Vertebrate Paleontology, v. 15, no. 3, p. 49A [abstract].

Rasmussen, D. T., Hamblin, A. H., and Tabrum, A. R., 1999, The mammals of the Duchesne River Formation, *in* Gillette, D. D., editor, this volume.

Robinson, Peter, 1968, The paleontology and geology of the Badwater Creek area, central Wyoming, part 4, late Eocene primates from Badwater, Wyoming, with a discussion of material from Utah: Annals of Carnegie Museum, v. 39, p. 307-326.

Romer, A. S., 1966, Vertebrate paleontology (3rd edition): Chicago, University of Chicago Press, 468 p.

Rose, K. D., 1982, Skeleton of *Diacodexis*, oldest known artiodactyl: Science, v. 216, p. 621-623.

—1985, Comparative osteology of North American dichobunid artiodactyls: Journal of Paleontology, v. 59, p. 1203-1226.

Rose, K. D., and O'Leary, M. A., 1995, The manus of *Pachyaena gigantea* (Mammalia: Mesonychia): Journal of Vertebrate Paleontology, v. 15, p. 855-859.

Rothecker, Jennifer, and Storer, J. E., 1996, The marsupial of the Lac Pelletier Lower Fauna, Middle Eocene (Duchesnean) of Saskatchewan: Journal of Vertebrate Paleontology, v. 16, p. 770-774.

Russell, D. E., Godinot, Marc, Louis, Pierre, and Savage, D. E., 1979, Apatotheria (Mammalia) de l'Éocène inférieur de France et de Belgique. Bulletin de la Musée Nationale d'Histoire Naturelle, v. 3, p. 203-243.

Savage, D. E., and Russell, D. E., 1983, Mammalian paleofaunas of the World: London, Addison-Wesley.

Schoch, R. M., 1989, A review of the tapiroids, *in* Prothero, D. R., and Schoch, R. M., editors, The evolution of perissodactyls: Oxford, Oxford University Press, p. 298-320.

Scott, W. B., 1888, On some new and little known creodonts: Journal of the Academy of Natural Sciences of Philadelphia, v. 9, p. 155-185.

—1898, Preliminary note on the selenodont artiodactyls of the Uinta Formation: Proceedings of the American Philosophical Society, v. 37, p. 73-81.

—1899, The selenodont artiodactyls of the Uinta Eocene: Transactions of the Wagner Free Institute of Science, Philadelphia, v. 6, p. 15-121.

—1938, Problematical cat-like mandible from the Uinta Eocene, *Apataelurus kayi* Scott: Annals of Carnegie Museum, v. 27, p. 113-120.

Scott, W. B., and Osborn, H. F., 1887, Preliminary report of the vertebrate fossils from the Uinta Formation, collected by the Princeton expedition of 1886: Proceedings of the American Philosophical Society, v. 1887, p. 255-264.

—1890, The Mammalia of the Uinta Formation: Transactions of the American Philosophical Society, v. 16, p. 461-572.

Sloan, L. C., and Barron, E. J., 1992, Paleogene climatic evolution--a climate model investigation of the influence of continental elevation and sea-surface temperature upon continental climate, *in* Prothero, D. R., and Berggren, W. A., editors, Eocene-Oligocene climatic and biotic evolution: Princeton, New Jersey, Princeton University Press, p. 202-217.

Stock, Chester, 1934a, New Creodonta from the Sespe Upper Eocene, California: Proceedings of the National Academy of Sciences, v. 20, p. 423-427.

Stock, Chester, 1934b, A hypertragulid from the Sespe uppermost

Eocene, California: Proceedings of the National Academy of Sciences, v. 20, p. 625-629.

Storer, J. E., 1984, Mammals of the Swift Current Creek local fauna (Eocene, Uintan, Saskatchewan): Saskatchewan Museum of Natural History Contributions, v. 7, p. 1-158.

—1996, Eocene-Oligocene faunas of the Cypress Hills Formation, Saskatchewan, *in* Prothero, D. R., and Emry, R. J., editors, The terrestrial Eocene-Oligocene transition in North America: Cambridge, England, Cambridge University Press, p. 240-261.

Stucky, R. K., 1992, Mammalian faunas in North America of Bridgerian to early Arikareean "ages" (Eocene and Oligocene), *in* Prothero, D. R., and Berggren, W. A., editors, Eocene-Oligocene climatic and biotic evolution: Princeton, N.J., Princeton University Press, p. 464-493.

Swisher, C. C., and Prothero, D. R., 1990, Single-crystal ^{40}Ar/^{39}Ar dating of the Eocene-Oligocene transition in North America: Science, v. 249, p. 760-762.

Thewissen, J. G. M., 1994, Phylogenetic aspects of cetacean origins--a morphological perspective: Journal of Mammalian Evolution, v. 2, p. 157-184.

Thewissen, J. G. M., Hussain, S. T., and Arif, M., 1994, Fossil evidence for the origin of aquatic locomotion in archaeocete whales: Science, v. 263, p. 210-212.

Thorpe, M. R., 1923a, Notes on the Bridger (Eocene) Carnivora: American Journal of Science, v. 5, p. 23-39.

—1923b, New species of Uinta Carnivora from White River, Utah: American Journal of Science, v. 5, p. 218-225.

Townsend, K. E., and Rasmussen, D. T. 1995, Skeletal remains of the small artiodactyl, *Mesomeryx grangeri*, from the Uinta Formation, Uintah Basin, Utah: Journal of Vertebrate Paleontology, v. 15, no. 3, p. 57A.

Turnbull, W. D., 1991, *Protoptychus hatcheri* Scott, 1895 -- the mammalian faunas of the Washakie Formation, Eocene age, of southern Wyoming, part II: Fieldiana Geology, v. 21, p. 1-33.

Van Valen, Lee, 1966, Deltatheridia, a new order of mammals: Bulletin of the American Museum of Natural History, v. 132, p. 1-126.

—1967, New Paleocene insectivores and insectivore classification: Bulletin of the American Museum of Natural History, v. 135, no. 5, p. 217-284.

Van Valkenburgh, Blaire, 1991, Iterative evolution of hypercarnivory in canids (Mammalia: Carnivora) -- evolutionary interaction among sympatric predators: Paleobiology, v. 17, p. 340-362.

Wahlert, J. H., 1973, *Protoptychus*, a hystricomorphous rodent from the late Eocene of North America: Breviora, v. 419, p. 1-14.

Wall, W. P., 1989, The phylogenetic history and adaptive radiation of the Amynodontidae, *in* Prothero, D. R., and Schoch, R. M., editors, The evolution of perissodactyls: Oxford, Oxford University Press, p. 341-354.

Walsh, S. L., 1996a, Middle Eocene mammalian faunas of San Diego County, California, *in* Prothero, D. R., and Emry, R. J., editors, The terrestrial Eocene-Oligocene transition in North America: Cambridge, England, Cambridge University Press, p. 75-119.

—1996b, Theoretical biochronology, the Bridgerian-Uintan boundary and the "Shoshonian Subage" of the Uintan, *in* Prothero, D. R., and Emry, R. J., editors, The terrestrial Eocene-Oligocene transition in North America: Cambridge, England, Cambridge University Press, p. 52-74.

—1998, Notes on the anterior dentition and skull of *Proterixoides* (Mammalia: Insectivora: Dormaaliidae), and a new dormaaliid genus from the early Uintan (Middle Eocene) of southern California: Proceedings of the San Diego Society of Natural History, v. 34, p. 1-26.

Walton, A. H., 1993, *Pauromys* and other small Sciuravidae (Mammalia: Rodentia) from the middle Eocene of Texas: Journal of Vertebrate Paleontology, v. 13, p. 243-261.

Wang, Xiaoming, 1994, Phylogenetic systematics of the Hesperocyoninae (Carnivora: Canidae): Bulletin of the American Museum of Natural History, v. 221, p. 1-207.

Wang, Xiaoming and Tedford, R. H., 1994, The status of genus *Nothocyon* Matthew, 1899 (Carnivora)--an arctoid not a canid: Journal of Vertebrate Paleontology, v. 12, p. 23-229.

West, R. M., 1973, Review of the North American Eocene and Oligocene Apatemyidae (Mammalia--Insectivora): Museum of Texas Tech University Special Publication, v. 3, p. 1-42.

Westgate, J. W., 1990, Uintan land mammals (excluding rodents) from an estuarine facies of the Laredo Formation (Middle Eocene, Claiborne Group), Webb County, Texas: Journal of Paleontology, v. 64, p. 454-468.

Wheeler, W. H., 1961, Revision of the uintatheres: Yale Peabody Museum of Natural History Bulletin, v. 14, p. 1-93.

Wilson, J. A., 1986, Stratigraphic occurrence and correlation of early Tertiary vertebrate faunas, Trans-Pecos Texas -- Agua Fria-Green Valley areas: Journal of Vertebrate Paleontology, v. 6, p. 350-373.

Wing, S. L., 1987, Eocene and Oligocene floras and vegetation of the Rocky Mountains: Annals of the Missouri Botanical Garden, v. 274, p. 748-784.

Wolfe, J. A., 1978, A paleobotanical interpretation of Tertiary climates in the Northern Hemisphere: American Scientist, v. 66, p. 694-703.

—1992, Climatic, floristic, and vegetational changes near the Eocene/Oligocene boundary in North America, *in* Prothero, D.

R., and Berggren, W. A., editors, Eocene-Oligocene climatic and biotic evolution: Princeton, N.J., Princeton University Press, p. 421-436.

Wood, A. E., 1962, The early Tertiary rodents of the family Paramyidae: Transactions of the American Philosophical Society, v. 52, p. 1-261.

Wortman, J. L., 1901-1902, Studies of Eocene Mammalia in the Marsh Collection, Peabody Museum--part 1. Carnivora: American Journal of Science, v. 11 (1901), p. 333-348, 437-448; v.12 (1901), p. 143-154, 193-206, 281-296, 377-382, 421-432; v. 13 (1902), p. 39-46, 115-128, 197-206, 433-448; v. 14 (1902), p. 17-23.

Wortman, J. L., and Matthew, W. D., 1899, The ancestry of certain members of the Canidae, the Viverridae, and Procyonidae: Bulletin of the American Museum of Natural History, v. 12, p. 109-139.

Wozencraft, W. C., 1989, Phylogeny of the recent Carnivora, *in* Gittleman, J. L., editor, Carnivora behavior, ecology, and evolution: Ithaca, New York, Cornell University Press, p. 495-535.

THE MAMMALS OF THE EOCENE DUCHESNE RIVER FORMATION

D. Tab Rasmussen

Department of Anthropology, Washington University, One Brookings Drive, St. Louis, MO 63130

Alden H. Hamblin

Grand Staircase/Escalante NationalMonument, 337 South Main Street, Cedar City, UT 84720

Alan R. Tabrum

Section of Vertebrate Paleontology, Carnegie Museum of Natural History, 4400 Forbes Avenue, Pittsburgh, PA 15213

ABSTRACT

Mammalian fossils from the Duchesne River Formation (DRF), Uinta Basin, Utah, are sparse, but they have played a prominent role in the development of North American mammalian biochronology. Recent work in the field and restudy of the available museum collections provide the basis for a revision of the mammalian faunal list of the DRF. The following taxa can be documented to occur in the Lapoint Member of the DRF: *Centetodon* sp.; *Pareumys guensbergi*; *Protadjidaumo typus*; *Hessolestes ultimus*; *Hyaenodon* sp., cf. *H. vetus*; Carnivora, genus and species indeterminate; *Colodon* sp.; *Hyracodon medius*; rhinocerotid, genus and species indeterminate; *Duchesnehippus intermedius*; *Duchesneodus uintensis*; *Brachyhyops wyomingensis*; *Protoreodon* sp., cf. *P. pumilus*; *Agriochoerus maximus*; *Poabromylus kayi*; and *Simimeryx minutus*. The mammals of the two lower members of the DRF, the Dry Gulch Creek Member and the Brennan Basin Member, are also discussed and revised. The formerly controversial Duchesnean Land Mammal Age (LMA) is now widely accepted as a distinct LMA based principally on mammalian fossils from other parts of North America, but the DRF mammals remain important as the type assemblage of the Duchesnean LMA as well as for understanding faunal provincialism and climatic change through the late Eocene.

INTRODUCTION

Paleontological fieldwork in western North America during the latter part of the 19th century yielded an enormous amount of information about mammalian evolution during much of the Eocene epoch. Fossils from the Bighorn and Bridger Basins of Wyoming, and from the Uinta Formation of Utah, were abundant, readily collected, and eagerly studied from 1870 onward. The faunas from these three classic mammal-producing basins and from other sites in the Rocky Mountains led to the recognition of three sequential but related mammalian faunas that were considered to represent early, middle, and late Eocene time. Half a century later, these successive faunas were codified as the Wasatchian, Bridgerian, and Uintan "Provincial Ages" now known as "Land-Mammal Ages" or LMA (Wood and others, 1941). Contemporaneous fieldwork in the Great Plains region produced the abundant and beautifully preserved mammals from the White River Badlands of South Dakota and Nebraska, which manifested significantly younger mammalian faunas than those from the Rocky Mountain basins. The oldest of the Great Plains faunas, from the Chadron Formation, were considered to be of early Oligocene age (Chadronian LMA). The hiatus between the Eocene mammals of the Rockies and those of the Chadron remained for many years a great, yawning gap in the North American terrestrial record. The first important paleontological discovery to begin filling this gap was made by J. L. Kay of the Carnegie Museum (CM), who located and worked a quarry rich in brontothere bones in what is now the Duchesne River Formation (DRF) in the northern Uinta Basin, Utah. The new finds were announced by O. A. Peterson (1931a,b,c), who concluded that the fauna from Kay's quarry was "perfectly transitional" (Peterson, 1931c, p. 62) between the Uinta Formation mammals and those from the Chadron Formation of the White River Group. Peterson and Kay (1931, p. 296) reported that the new quarry was "certainly representative of a post-Eocene or basal Oligocene deposit." Other mammals found in Kay's brontothere quarry, or at other localities in the same horizon of the DRF, included a mesonychid, a creodont, hyracodontids, an insectivore, a rodent, and both bunodont and selenodont artiodactyls (Peterson, 1931b, 1931c, 1934; Burke, 1934).

The quarry Kay discovered was in what were then called the "upper red beds" of the Uinta Basin. Prior to Kay's work, fossil mammals from the Uinta Basin had been recovered only from the lower, predominantly gray badlands of the Uinta Formation (Rasmussen and others, 1999). The upper red beds, although extensively exposed in the Uinta Basin, were typically devoid of fossil mammals. At the suggestion of W. B. Scott, the name "Duchesne Formation" was proposed for the red beds (Peterson, 1931c), but was later emended to Duchesne River Formation, the original name being preoccupied (Kay, 1934). After the initial discovery of Kay's brontothere quarry, further effort was directed toward other parts of the red beds. Fossils were found in three broadly defined lithological horizons. The lowest of these was called the "Randlett Horizon," the intermediate level was called the "Halfway Horizon," while the uppermost beds containing Kay's quarry were called the "Lapoint Horizon" (Kay, 1934). Shortly thereafter, the mammals from the DRF provided the basis for establishing the Duchesnean Provincial "Age" (Wood and others, 1941). The fauna from all three horizons was summarized and revised by Scott (1945), who regarded the entire fauna as pertaining to the "Duchesne River Oligocene." Later, only those mammals from the Lapoint Member were considered to be representative of the Duchesnean LMA (Clark and others, 1967).

Since activity at Kay's quarry ended, very few mammalian fossils have been recovered from the DRF. Limited fieldwork was conducted by Mary Dawson for the CM and by Thomas Guensburg for the Field Museum of Natural History (FMNH) in the late 1960s and early 1970s, with one new rodent being described (Black, 1970). Dee Hall of Maeser, Utah, collected a few specimens in the 1970s for the Smithsonian Institution (Emry, 1981). In more recent years, the Utah Field House (UFH) and Washington University, St. Louis (WU), have collected in the region. Formal systematic work is currently in progress. However, despite limited gains in knowledge of the fauna, the mammals of the DRF continue to figure prominently in regional and continental assessments of biostratigraphy and mammalian evolution.

Despite the small number of specimens that have been described from the DRF, much information repeated in the literature still conveys errors about the taxonomic representation or stratigraphic position of the key DRF fossils. Some of these errors apparently stemmed from an imprecise reading of Scott's (1945) monograph, which described material not only from the differ-

ent members of the DRF but also fossils from the Beaver Divide area of Wyoming. Minor errors have been perpetuated in some faunal lists (for example, Black and Dawson, 1966; Anderson and Picard, 1972) and the most recent faunal lists continue to pass on inaccurate information (for example, Lucas, 1992; Prothero, 1996a). The principal purposes of the current paper are to clarify the type Duchesnean fauna, to compile an updated faunal list for the lower member of the DRF, and to provide preliminary reports of a few additions to the DRF's mammalian fauna.

STRATIGRAPHY

The DRF consists primarily of reddish sandstones and mudstones that were deposited in a broad east-west swath across the northern part of the Uinta Basin (figure 1). Analysis of paleocurrent data shows drainage patterns from north to south, indicating that source materials from the Uinta Mountains were being deposited along the northern margin of the Uinta Basin (Anderson and Picard, 1972). Four lithologic members are recognized within the formation, three bearing mammalian fossils (Anderson and Picard, 1972). The stratigraphically lowest of these is the Brennan Basin Member (including the old Randlett Horizon plus the lowest part of the Halfway Horizon), which ranges in thickness from about 220 to 600 meters. It is characterized by pale reddish and yellowish sandstones with some conglomerates and mudstones (figure 2)(Anderson and Picard, 1972). Mammals are more common in this member than in the other three members. The fauna from the Brennan Basin Member is best regarded as late Uintan in age (Gazin, 1955).

Figure 1. *A party of collectors from the Utah Field House, Vernal, and Washington University, St. Louis, explores the Brennan Basin Member of the Duchesne River Formation in Uintah County. These exposures are on land administered by the Utah BLM. The view is to the southeast across the east part of the Uinta Basin.*

The next youngest unit is the Dry Gulch Creek Member (equivalent to the upper part of the old Halfway Horizon), ranging in thickness from about 150 to 200 meters. Lithologically, this member is characterized by a higher proportion of fine-grained rocks than the Brennan Basin Member. The sandstones are reddish brown in color, and the mudstones are brown, yellow, and gray (Anderson and Picard, 1972). The mammalian fauna from this member is particularly sparse, with only a few specimens known. The affinities of the Dry Gulch Creek fauna remain uncertain, although new material reported here suggests a close relationship to the stratigraphically higher Lapoint fauna.

The overlying Lapoint Member apparently ranges between 70 and 320 meters in thickness, and is the type sequence for the Duchesnean mammal fauna (Anderson and Picard, 1972). Lithologically, the most distinctive characteristic of this member is the occurrence of fine-grained, bentonitic mudstones; these occur along with the typical DRF red sandstones, conglomerates, and siltstones (Anderson and Picard, 1972). The Lapoint mammals come primarily from the "Titanothere Quarry" (Peterson, 1931a) found by J. L. Kay and worked by CM parties. Only a few isolated mammal finds have been made elsewhere in the Lapoint Member. The lowermost bentonitic bed in the member is a pale gray unit called the Lapoint Tuff; K/Ar and ^{40}Ar/^{39}Ar age estimates from the tuff indicate an age of about 40 Ma (McDowell and others, 1973; Prothero and Swisher, 1992).

The stratigraphically highest member of the DRF is the Starr Flat Member, a coarse clastic unit spottily represented along the southern flanks of the Uinta Mountains (Anderson and Picard, 1972). Mammals have not been found in this member.

THE TYPE DUCHESNEAN FAUNA

The mammalian fauna of the Lapoint Member is summarized in table 1. While most of these records are unambiguous, the literature proves that other cases are confusing, and we attempt to clarify as much of this as we can.

The hyracodontid specimens collected from the DRF continue to vex faunal listers. Peterson (1931c) described a lower jaw with p3-m2 of a robust hyracodontid (which he considered to be an amynodontid) that he named *Mesamynodon medius*. This specimen came from Kay's "Titanothere Quarry" in the Lapoint Member. In an inexplicable display of dullness, Peterson (1934) granted the same species nomen ("*medius*") three years later to another new species of hyracodontid, *Epitriplopus medius*, based on an upper dentition from the old

Table 1. Mammals of the Lapoint Member, Duchesne River Formation.

Taxon	Reference
Insectivora	
Centetodon sp.	Peterson, 1934
Rodentia	
Pareumys guensbergi	Black, 1970
Protadjidaumo typus	Burke, 1934
Mesonychia	
Hessolestes ultimus	Peterson, 1931b
Creodonta	
Hyaenodon sp., cf. *H. vetus*	Peterson, 1931c
Carnivora	
Genus and species indeterminate	Emry, 1981
Perissodactyla	
Colodon sp.	New record (CM)
Hyracodon medius	Peterson, 1931c
Rhinocerotid, indeterminate genus and species	New record (CM)
Duchesnehippus intermedius	New record (CM)
Duchesneodus uintensis	Peterson, 1931a
Artiodactyla	
Brachyhyops wyomingensis	Gazin, 1956
Protoreodon sp., cf. *P. pumilus*	New record (CM, WU)
Agriochoerus maximus	Emry, 1981
Simimeryx minutus	Peterson, 1934
Poabromylus kayi	Peterson, 1931c

Randlett Horizon (= Brennan Basin Member). Scott (1945) properly identified *Mesamynodon medius* as a hyracodontid, but some subsequent authors have apparently been confused by the name "medius" and have listed *Epitriplopus medius* as coming from the Lapoint Member (for example, Lucas, 1992; Prothero, 1996a). In fact, Peterson's *Mesamynodon medius* is actually synonymous with another large-bodied, robust hyracodont also described by Peterson (1934), *Hyracodon primus*. This latter species was based on a fragmentary P4-M2 found "one-half mile north of the Vernal-Lapoint road, about fourteen miles west of Vernal, Utah" (Peterson, 1934, p. 388). This locality is unambiguously in the Lapoint Member. Unfortunately, confusion was introduced when Scott (1945, p. 248) faultily transcribed the above locality data by deleting all the words from "north" to "miles", thus yielding "$^1/_2$ mile W. of Vernal, Utah", a site that could only place the fossil low in the DRF near Asphalt Ridge, the upturned rim of the depositional basin (and then only if the DRF were stretched westward quite a bit). The specimen is comparable in size to the lower jaw of *Mesamynodon medius*, and the two are morphologically compatible. Scott (1945) recognized the synonymy of the two, as did Emry (1981), who nevertheless listed both taxa. Scott believed the species to be generi-

Figure 2. *The contact between the stratigraphically lower Uinta Formation, characterized by slope-forming mudstones and siltstones, and the Brennan Basin Member of the Duchesne River Formation, characterized by ledge-forming sandstones, as exposed near Randlett, Uintah County. The black arrow points to the approximate contact between formations.*

cally distinct from *Hyracodon*, thereby choosing the designation *Mesamynodon medius* for the animal. Authors who have doubted the generic distinction from *Hyracodon* have used inappropriately the junior synonym of the species, *Hyracodon primus* (Wilson and Schiebout, 1984; Prothero, 1996a, 1996b). The correct name for the hyracodontid of the Lapoint Member is *Hyracodon medius*, at least until such time as it can be shown to be generically distinct from *Hyracodon* (in which case the genus *Mesamynodon* would be available). This species is entirely different from the gracile hyracodontid of the Brennan Basin Member, *Epitriplopus medius*, which is unknown in the Lapoint Member.

Another point of confusion surrounds the faunal affinities of the DRF horse described by Peterson (1931c) as *Epihippus* (*Duchesnehippus*) *intermedius*. We accept *Duchesnehippus* as a valid genus. The single published specimen of *D. intermedius* , a lower jaw with p3-m3, is one of the few mammalian specimens ever found in the Dry Gulch Creek Member. This specimen was described (Peterson, 1931c) many years before the stratigraphic revision of the formation was completed by Anderson and Picard (1972). Our field reconaissance of the locality data provided by Peterson (1931c, p. 67) fully supports Anderson and Picard (1972) in placing the specimen in the Dry Gulch Creek Member. While some authors have been content to associate the Dry Gulch specimen with the Lapoint fauna as part of the "type" Duchesnean (for example, Lucas, 1992), others have rejected this move (Tedford, 1970). We now have independent evidence that tends to support such an allo-

cation. A partial lower cheek tooth of an equid from the Lapoint Member agrees in size, robustness, and crown height with the teeth of the holotype of *D. intermedius*. This specimen affords some support for the argument that *Duchesnehippus*, morphologically intermediate between Uintan *Epihippus* and Chadronian *Mesohippus*, was a component of the Lapoint fauna.

Another undescribed specimen in the CM collection from Kay's brontothere quarry is a lower jaw fragment with p4-m1 of the tapiroid, *Colodon*. This specimen is larger than any Uintan specimens of *Colodon* and falls within the size range of the late Duchesnean and early Chadronian species *C. stovalli* (Wilson and Schiebout, 1984), and at the small end of the size range of White River *C. occidentalis* (Radinsky, 1963). This is the first record of a tapir from the Lapoint Member.

Although *Protoreodon* has been reported previously from the Lapoint fauna (Gazin, 1955; Kay, 1957; Tedford, 1970) this record has been ignored by most workers. Among the new specimens we have collected from the Lapoint fauna are several teeth and partial jaws of *Protoreodon* sp., cf. *P. pumilus*. The best preserved of these teeth, an unassociated dp4 and two poorly preserved lower molars, match in detail the homologous teeth in CM specimens of *Protoreodon pumilus* from Myton Pocket. Three additional undescribed Lapoint specimens in the CM collections (CM 3011, 12009 and 23653) also appear to pertain to this species. Size and shape comparisons indicate that the new specimens and

Figure 3. *A right mandible of* Uintaceras *photographed in situ in the Brennan Basin Member of the Duchesne River Formation. The mandibular symphysis is visible on the far left, as are the outlines of p2-m3. This Utah Field House specimen comprises the first record of the genus for the formation.*

the CM material together represent a single species of *Protoreodon* in the Lapoint Member. None of the Lapoint dental elements known at this time can be distinguished specifically from *P. pumilus* of Myton Pocket. *Protoreodon* is abundant in faunas of Uintan age, is well represented in other faunas of Duchesnean age elsewhere in North America, and persists into the early Chadronian (Wilson, 1971, 1986; Golz, 1976).

Another taxon that sometimes appears listed as part of the Duchesnean fauna is *Eosictis avinoffi*, based on the type partial maxilla containing a sharp caniniform tooth and some anterior premolars. Scott (1945) concluded that the specimen belonged to a sabertooth cat; later tentative suggestions are that it is an agriochoerid or an amphicyonid (Gustafson, 1986). The fossil is frustratingly incomplete. The locality information available on the specimen ("west fork of Halfway Hollow") is insufficient to determine whether it came from the Dry Gulch Creek or Lapoint Member, but it was certainly not collected from the Brennan Basin Member. Considering the taxonomic and stratigraphic uncertainty surrounding the specimen, we have not included it in our faunal lists.

THE FAUNA OF THE BRENNAN BASIN MEMBER

The mammals of the old Randlett Horizon and lower part of the Halfway Horizon, now together referred to as the Brennan Basin Member of the DRF, have received relatively little attention. Most work on DRF mammals has focused on the Lapoint material. The Brennan Basin Member is broadly exposed in the Uinta Basin, and it contains several productive localities, some worked by the early expeditions and others found during the recent UFH and WU projects (figure 3). In addition, there are several undescribed and largely unprepared fossils from the Brennan Basin Member in the CM collection that have now been examined. Some of the taxa represented by these unpublished specimens were listed as part of the "Randlett" fauna by Black and Dawson (1966).

First, the stratigraphic assignment of *Megalamynodon regalis* H. E. Wood, 1945 (in Scott, 1945) should be clarified. This species was originally cited as coming from the Halfway Horizon, and was listed as part of the Halfway fauna by Black and Dawson (1966). The three known specimens were quarried by J. L. Kay from a single locality "one mile north and west of Twelve Mile Bridge on U. S. Highway No. 40, twelve miles southwest of Vernal" (Wood, in Scott, 1945, p. 251). A field check revealed that this locality must be located within the Brennan Basin Member. Thus, with the taxonomic and

geographic uncertainties associated with *Eosictis*, the only mammal known to derive from the Dry Gulch Creek Member is *Duchesnehippus intermedius*.

Black and Dawson (1966) listed *Amynodon* as occurring in the Randlett Horizon, a record that cannot be substantiated (Wilson and Schiebout, 1981). It is possible that this was a mistaken reference to material of *Megalamynodon*. Black and Dawson (1966) also listed *Protadjidaumo* as being present in the Randlett Horizon, but there are no catalogued specimens of *Protadjidaumo* from this horizon in the CM collection, and the record appears to be in error.

Table 2. *Mammals of the Brennan Basin Member, Duchesne River Formation.*

Taxon	Reference
Proteutheria	
Simidectes sp., cf. *S. magnus*	New record (UFH)
Rodentia	
Pareumys sp., aff. *P. milleri*	New record (WU)
Mytonomys robustus	Burke, 1934
Lagomorpha	
Mytonolagus sp.	Burke, 1933
Perissodactyla	
Dilophodon leotanus	Peterson, 1931c
Megalamynodon regalis	Scott, 1945
Epitriplopus medius	Peterson, 1934
Uintaceras sp.	New record (UFH)
Duchesneodus new species	Black & Dawson, 1966
brontothere, new genus and species	New record (WU)
Artiodactyla	
Pentacymelus progressus	Peterson, 1931c
Protoreodon pumilus	Peterson, 1934
Protoreodon primus	Peterson, 1934
Diplobunops crassus	Peterson, 1934
Leptotragulus proavus	Gazin, 1955
Leptotragulinae, indeterminate genus and species	New records (WU)
Oromerycidae, indeterminate genus and species	New record (UFH)

The Brennan Basin Member contains a fauna that is intermediate between mammalian faunas of classic Uinta C and the Lapoint Member of the DRF. Most Brennan Basin taxa compare most closely to Uinta C mammals, but in contrast, the brontothere *Duchesneodus* is typical of the Lapoint. Two sets of globular upper incisors, two unassociated upper canines, and an associated set of upper premolars from both sides of a single individual, are catalogued together as CM 9174 and appear to represent an undescribed species of *Duchesneodus*. This genus is a geographically widespread brontothere and has been identified as the key index fossil of the Duchesnean LMA (Lucas and Schoch, 1982, 1989; Lucas, 1992).

THE DUCHESNEAN LAND MAMMAL AGE

The Duchesnean LMA has endured a checkered history, with some early researchers recognizing it as a legitimate Eocene LMA, while others have rejected it (for example, Wilson, 1978). Some authors regarded the Duchesnean as late Eocene in age, while others preferred to call it early Oligocene. Lucas (1992, p. 88) observed that the Duchesnean "has either been questioned, abandoned, subdivided or defended." Its pivotal chronological position near the perceived Eocene-Oligocene boundary in North America for many years made mammals of Duchesnean age particularly important for questions of continental faunal turnover and climatic change. The main obstacle preventing ready acceptance of the Duchesnean as a distinct land mammal age was "the low taxonomic diversity and small number of specimens of fossil mammals from the Lapoint fauna of the Duchesne River Formation, usually considered the 'type' fauna of the Duchesnean LMA" (Lucas, 1992, p. 91).

In recent years, there has been widespread acceptance of the Duchesnean LMA (for example, Prothero and Berggren, 1992; Prothero and Emry, 1996, and the papers therein). Much of this stems from work in other parts of North America, particularly investigations in Saskatchewan (Storer, 1996), southern California (Kelly, 1990; Walsh, 1996), and Texas (Wilson, 1984, 1986), where much richer mammalian faunas have been found. Additional Duchesnean localities have been recognized in South Dakota (Bjork, 1967), New Mexico (Lucas, 1982, 1992), Oregon (Hanson, 1996), and Montana (Tabrum and others, 1996). However, it would be unfortunate if knowledge of the Duchesnean in these other areas led to a slowdown of efforts in the Uinta Basin to recover more mammals from the "type fauna." As Storer (1996) has pointed out, the Duchesnean was a time of increasing provincialism in North America. Climatic heterogeneity, faunal fragmentation, and adaptive radiation during this time period seem to have followed different patterns than during the preceding North American LMAs, and larger samples from Utah will be critical for assessing the evolution of the Rocky Mountain mammalian faunas during the later part of the Eocene.

ACKNOWLEDGMENTS

For valuable information and help in putting together this manuscript we thank Dee Hall, Mary Dawson, and Beth Townsend. We thank David Gillette, Spencer Lucas, and Anthony Friscia for their careful reviews of the manuscript. Field collectors who have suffered on the nearly barren Lapoint outcrops include Townsend, Friscia, Glenn Conroy, Jennifer Rehg, Mary Kinkel, Suellen Gauld, and Jonathan Lesser. Field work was conducted under the auspices of the Utah BLM; we would especially like to thank Blaine Phillips of the BLM's Vernal office.

REFERENCES

Anderson, D. W., and Picard, M. D., 1972, Stratigraphy of the Duchesne River Formation (Eocene-Oligocene?), northern Uinta Basin, northeastern Utah: Utah Geological and Mineralogical Survey Bulletin 97, p. 1-28.

Bjork, P. R., 1967, Latest Eocene vertebrates from northwestern South Dakota: Journal of Paleontology, v. 41, p. 227-236.

Black, C. C., 1970, A new *Pareumys* (Rodentia: Cylindrodontidae) from the Duchesne River Formation, Utah: Fieldiana, Geology, v. 17, p. 453-459.

Black, C. C., and Dawson, M. R., 1966, A review of late Eocene mammalian faunas from North America: American Journal of Science, v. 264, p. 321-349.

Burke, J. J., 1933, Eocene Lagomorpha: Science, v. 77, p. 191.

---1934, New Duchesne River rodents and a preliminary survey of the Adjidaumidae: Annals of the Carnegie Museum, v. 23, p. 391-398.

Clark, John, Beerbower, J. R., and Kietzke, K. K., 1967, Oligocene sedimentation, stratigraphy, paleoecology and paleoclimatology in the Big Badlands of South Dakota: Fieldiana, Geology Memoirs, v. 5, p. 1-158.

Emry, R. J., 1981, Additions to the mammalian fauna of the type Duchesnean, with comments on the status of the Duchesnean "Age": Journal of Paleontology, v. 55, p. 563-570.

Gazin, C. L., 1955, A review of the upper Eocene Artiodactyla of North America: Smithsonian Miscellaneous Collections, v. 128, no. 8, p. 1-96.

---1956, The geology and vertebrate paleontology of Upper Eocene strata in the northwestern part of the Wind River Basin, Wyoming, part 2--the mammalian fauna of the Badwater area: Smithsonian Miscellaneous Collections, v. 131, no. 8, p. 1-35.

Golz, D. J., 1976, Eocene Artiodactyla of southern California: Natural History Museum of Los Angeles County, Science Bulletin, v. 26, p. 1-85.

Gustafson, E. P., 1986, Carnivorous mammals of the late Eocene and early Oligocene of Trans-Pecos Texas: Texas Memorial Museum Bulletin, v. 33, p. 1-66.

Hanson, C. B., 1996, Stratigraphy and vertebrate faunas of the Bridgerian-Duchesnean Clarno Formation, north-central Oregon, *in* Prothero, D. R., and Emry, R. J., editors, The Terrestrial Eocene-Oligocene Transition in North America: Cambridge, England, Cambridge University Press, p. 206-239.

Kay, J. L., 1934, The Tertiary formations of the Uinta Basin, Utah: Annals of Carnegie Museum, v. 23, p. 357-371.

—1957, The Eocene vertebrates of the Uinta Basin, Utah, *in* Seal, O.

G., editor, Guidebook to the geology of the Uinta Basin: Intermountain Association of Petroleum Geologists, p. 110-114.

Kelly, T. S., 1990, Biostratigraphy of Uintan and Duchesnean land mammal assemblages from the middle member of the Sespe Formation, Simi Valley, California: Contributions in Science, Natural History Museum of Los Angeles County, v. 419, p. 1-42.

Lucas, S. G., 1982, Vertebrate paleontology, stratigraphy and biostratigraphy of Eocene Galisteo Formation, north-central New Mexico: New Mexico Bureau of Mines and Mineral Resources Circular, v. 186, p. 1-34.

—1992, Redefinition of the Duchesnean Land Mammal "Age", Late Eocene of western North America, *in* Prothero, D. R., and Berggren, W. A., editors, Eocene-Oligocene climatic and biotic evolution: Princeton, New Jersey, Princeton University Press, p. 88-105.

Lucas, S. G., and Schoch, R. M., 1982, *Duchesneodus*, a new name for some titanotheres (Perissodactyla, Brontotheriidae) from the late Eocene of western North America: Journal of Paleontology, v. 56, p. 1018-1023.

—1989, Taxonomy of *Duchesneodus* (Brontotheriidae) from the late Eocene of North America, *in* Prothero, D. R., and Schoch, R. M., editors, The evolution of perissodactyls: New York, Oxford University Press, p. 490-503.

McDowell, F. W., Wilson, J. A., and Clark, John, 1973, K-Ar dates for biotite from two paleontologically significant localities--Duchesne River Formation, Utah, and Chadron Formation, South Dakota: Isochron/West, v. 7, p. 11-12.

Peterson, O. A., 1931a, New species of the genus *Teleodus* from the upper Uinta of northeastern Utah: Annals of Carnegie Museum, v. 20, p. 307-312.

—1931b, New mesonychids from the Uinta: Annals of Carnegie Museum, v. 20, p. 333-339.

—1931c, New species from the Oligocene of the Uinta: Annals of Carnegie Museum, v. 21, p. 61-78.

—1934, List of species and description of new material from the Duchesne River Oligocene, Uinta Basin, Utah: Annals of Carnegie Museum, v. 23, p. 373-389.

Peterson, O. A., and Kay, J. L., 1931, The Upper Uinta Formation of northeastern Utah: Annals of Carnegie Museum, v. 20, p. 293-306.

Prothero, D. R., 1996a, Magnetic stratigraphy and biostratigraphy of the middle Eocene Uinta Formation, Uinta Basin, Utah, *in* Prothero, D. R., and Emry, R. J., editors, The terrestrial Eocene-Oligocene transition in North America: Cambridge, England, Cambridge University Press, p. 3-24.

—1996b, Hyracodontidae, *in* Prothero, D. R., and Emry, R. J., editors, The terrestrial Eocene-Oligocene transition in North America: Cambridge, England, Cambridge University Press, p. 652-663.

Prothero, D. R., and Berggren, W. A., editors, 1992, Eocene-Oligocene climatic and biotic evolution: Princeton, New Jersey, Princeton University Press.

Prothero, D. R., and Emry, R. J., editors, 1996, The terrestrial Eocene-Oligocene transition in North America: Cambridge, England, Cambridge University Press, 688 p.

Prothero, D. R., and Swisher, C. C., III, 1992, Magnetostratigraphy and geochronology of the terrestrial Eocene-Oligocene transition in North America, *in* Prothero, D. R., and Berggren, W. A., editors, Eocene-Oligocene climatic and biotic evolution: Princeton, New Jersey, Princeton University Press, p. 46-73.

Radinsky, L. B., 1963, Origin and early evolution of North American Tapiroidea: Bulletin of the Peabody Museum of Natural History, v. 17, p. 1-106.

Rasmussen, D. T., Conroy, G. C., Friscia, A. R., Townsend, K. E., and Kinkel, M. D., 1999, Mammals of the Middle Eocene Uinta Formation, *in* Gillette, D. D., editor, this volume.

Scott, W. B., 1945, The Mammalia of the Duchesne River Oligocene: Transactions of the American Philosophical Society, v. 34, p. 209-253.

Storer, J. E., 1996, Eocene-Oligocene faunas of the Cypress Hills Formation, Saskatchewan, *in* Prothero, D. R., and Emry, R. J., editors, The terrestrial Eocene-Oligocene transition in North America: Cambridge, England, Cambridge University Press, p. 240-261.

Tabrum, A. R., Prothero, D. R., and Garcia, Daniel, 1996, Magnetostratigraphy and biostratigraphy of the Eocene-Oligocene transition, southwestern Montana, *in* Prothero, D. R., and Emry, R. J., editors, The terrestrial Eocene-Oligocene transition in North America: Cambridge, England, Cambridge University Press, p. 278-311.

Tedford, R. H., 1970, Principles and practices of mammalian geochronology in North America: Proceedings of the North American Paleontological Convention, part F, p. 666-703.

Walsh, S. L., 1996, Middle Eocene mammalian faunas of San Diego County, California, *in* Prothero, D. R., and Emry, R. J., editors, The terrestrial Eocene-Oligocene transition in North America: Cambridge, England, Cambridge University Press, p. 75-119.

Wilson, J. A., 1971, Early Tertiary vertebrate faunas, Trans-Pecos Texas--Agriochoeridae and Merycoidodontidae: Texas Memorial Museum Bulletin, v. 18, p. 1-83.

—1978, Stratigraphic occurrence and correlation of early Tertiary vertebrate faunas, Trans-Pecos Texas, Part 1--Vieja area: Texas Memorial Museum Bulletin, v. 25, p. 1-42.

—1984, Vertebrate faunas 49 to 36 million years ago and additions to the species of *Leptoreodon* (Mammalia: Artiodacytla) found in Texas: Journal of Vertebrate Paleontology, v. 4, p. 199-207.

—1986, Stratigraphic occurrence and correlation of early Tertiary vertebrate faunas, Trans-Pecos Texas--Agua Fria-Green Valley areas: Journal of Vertebrate Paleontology, v. 6, p. 350-373.

Wilson, J. A., and Schiebout, Judith, 1981, Early Tertiary vertebrate faunas, Trans-Pecos Texas--Amynodontidae: The Pearce-Sellards Series, Texas Memorial Museum, v. 33, p. 1-62.

—1984, Early Tertiary vertebrate faunas, Trans-Pecos Texas--Ceratomorpha less Amynododontidae: Pearce-Sellards Series, Texas Memorial Museum, v. 39, p. 1-47.

Wood, H. E., II, Chaney, R. W., Clark, John, Colbert, E. H., Jepsen, G. L., Reeside, J. B., Jr., and Stock, Chester, 1941, Nomenclature and correlation of the North American continental Tertiary: Geological Society of America Bulletin, v. 52, p. 1-48.

Brian Maebius © 1999

Lepisosteus

MIDDLE EOCENE VERTEBRATES FROM THE UINTA BASIN, UTAH, AND THEIR RELATIONSHIP WITH FAUNAS FROM THE SOUTHERN GREEN RIVER BASIN, WYOMING

Gregg F. Gunnell
Museum of Paleontology, University of Michigan, Ann Arbor, MI 48109-1079

William S. Bartels
Department of Geology, Albion College, Albion, MI 49224

ABSTRACT

Fossil vertebrates from the Uinta Basin in northeastern Utah and the Green River Basin in southwestern Wyoming have been known for over 125 years. Despite close geographic proximity, there is little time overlap in the sequences of rock units containing terrestrial faunas in the two basins. The fluvial Uinta Formation preserves fossils from the Uintan Land Mammal Age (late middle Eocene) in Utah while the fluvial Wasatch and Bridger Formations preserve fossils from the Bridgerian Land Mammal Age (early middle Eocene) in Wyoming. Uintan mammal faunas are dominated by perissodactyls (34 species), artiodactyls (26 species), and rodents (17 species). Bridgerian mammal faunas are dominated by primates (8 species in Bridgerian Zone Br1, 10 in Br2, and 11 in Br3), rodents (7, 19, and 11 species, respectively), and perissodactyls (4, 10, and 14 species, respectively). Primates virtually disappeared by the Uintan, reflecting a change from closed, subtropical climatic conditions in the Bridgerian to more open, temperate, and seasonal climates in the Uintan.

The only well-documented record of a Bridgerian assemblage from the Uinta Basin is at Powder Wash located in the lacustrine Green River Formation. Comparisons of this faunal assemblage with the Green River Basin record indicate an early to middle Bridgerian age for Powder Wash. Confounding this age assessment is the fact that the Powder Wash assemblage is taphonomically biased towards smaller sized animals. Important biostratigraphic index taxa are missing, including brontotheriid perissodactyls and emydid turtles, especially *Echmatemys*. Additionally, Powder Wash may represent a basin-margin fauna, further obscuring its temporal relationships. Biostratigraphic zonation of Tertiary Land Mammal Ages has been based almost exclusively on basin-center assemblages, making correlation with basin margin samples difficult.

INTRODUCTION

Large-scale changes in climate occurred during the middle Eocene (~ 50 to 40 Ma) with Cenozoic maximum mean annual temperatures being reached at the beginning of the middle Eocene accompanied by widespread subtropical environments (Wing and others, 1991; Dettman and Lohmann, 1993; Wing and Greenwood, 1993; Gunnell and others, 1995; Williams and Bartels, 1995; Bartels and Williams, 1996). Cooling occurred towards the end of the middle Eocene with replacement of subtropical floral regimes with more seasonal, temperate floral regimes (Collinson, 1992; Hutchison, 1992; Miller, 1992; Wolfe, 1992). Associated with these changes in paleoclimate and paleohabitat were changes in vertebrate faunas as documented in the fossil record. In North America, the middle Eocene includes the Bridgerian and Uintan Land Mammal Ages.

North American Bridgerian faunas are best represented in the southern Green River Basin of southwestern Wyoming from the Bridger Formation. Bridgerian- age sediments also crop out in fewer extensively distributed beds in several other areas along the Rocky Mountain corridor. Fossil vertebrates of Bridgerian age have been known for over 140 years and large collections of Bridgerian vertebrates have been amassed by several institutions. Uintan faunas are well represented in the Uinta Basin in northeastern Utah from the Uinta Formation. Uintan-age sediments are also known from the eastern Wind River Basin and the Washakie Basin in Wyoming, the southern coastal areas of California near San Diego and Los Angeles, western Texas, and the central plains of Canada in Saskatchewan, as well as a few other isolated localities in the Rockies.

The Uinta and southern Green River basins are adjacent to one another, separated by the east-west-oriented Uinta Mountains along the state border between Utah and Wyoming. Despite relatively close geographic proximity, there is little time overlap in the terrestrial faunal records from the two basins (Doi, 1990; Evanoff and others, 1994). Most of Bridgerian time is represented by lacustrine deposition (Green River Formation) in the Uinta Basin whereas the fluvial Wasatch and Bridger Formations interfinger with the lacustrine Green River Formation throughout the southern Green River Basin during the Bridgerian. The onset of significant Eocene fluvial deposition in the Uinta Basin begins near the Bridgerian/Uintan boundary and is represented by the Uinta Formation. Uintan-age sediments are virtually unknown in the Green River Basin west of the Rock Springs uplift.

The purpose of this paper is twofold: first, to provide a brief overview of Bridgerian and Uintan vertebrate faunas and to discuss the general trends in reptilian and mammalian diversity through the two land mammal ages; and second, to examine the one well-known Bridgerian faunal sample from the Uinta Basin, that from the Powder Wash locality, and to compare this assemblage with those from the Bridgerian of the Green River Basin. Powder Wash has generally been considered to be early Bridgerian in age, younger than Gardnerbuttean (Br0) but perhaps older than Bridgerian Br2 (Krishtalka and Stucky, 1984). Direct comparison of the assemblage from Powder Wash with early Bridgerian faunas from the Green River Basin has been hampered in the past by the lack of good faunal samples from the Bridgerian interval known as "Bridger A" (Bridgerian Zone Br1, Gunnell and Bartels, 1994). A joint project by the University of Michigan, Albion College, and California State University at Sacramento in the southern Green River Basin has produced a large sample of fossil vertebrates from Bridgerian Zone Br1 (Gunnell and Bartels, 1994; Gunnell, 1998). These fossils have facilitated a new comparison between the Powder Wash assemblage and those from the Green River Basin.

The Powder Wash locality is situated on the eastern margin of the Uinta Basin along the flank of Raven Ridge in the Douglas Creek Member of the Green River Formation (Dawson, 1968). According to Cashion (in Dawson, 1968, p. 327) the Bridgerian "Powder Wash mammal locality is 270 feet stratigraphically below the Mahogany oil-shale bed" and, according to Dawson (1968, p. 327), is "near the lower part of the Green River Formation as it is developed in the eastern Uinta Basin." No complete systematic treatment of all vertebrate fossils from Powder Wash is available but several parts of the mammalian fauna have been examined in detail (Gazin, 1958; Wood, 1962; Dawson, 1968; Gazin, 1968; Burke, 1969; Szalay, 1969, 1976; Krishtalka, 1976a,b; West, 1979; Lillegraven and others, 1981). A revised faunal

list for Powder Wash mammals and a brief discussion of the reptiles was provided by Krishtalka and Stucky (1984). This list has been augmented by a more thorough review of the reptilian taxa and a reassessment of the mammalian assemblage from Powder Wash.

BRIDGERIAN FAUNAS - GREEN RIVER BASIN

Much of what is known of middle Eocene terrestrial vertebrate faunas from North America is based on the fossil record from the Bridger Formation in the southern Green River Basin of Wyoming. Leidy (1869, 1870), Marsh (1871, 1872a, 1872b), Cope (1882, 1884), and Hay (1908) were among the first workers to publish accounts of vertebrate fossils from the Bridger Formation. In a 1909 monograph on the southern Green River Basin ("Bridger Basin"), Matthew proposed a five-part division of the Bridger Formation, designating these intervals A through E. The lowest 200 meters of the Bridger Formation represents interval A (Bridgerian Zone Br1, Gunnell and Bartels, 1994). The Bridger A interval was viewed by Matthew (1909) as poorly fossiliferous, at least in terms of mammals. Interval B (Bridgerian Zone Br2, Gunnell and Bartels, 1994) represents the succeeding 150 meters of the Bridger Formation and is abundantly fossiliferous with many thousands of vertebrate specimens having been collected from these classic Bridger B beds. Bridger B is separated from the C interval by the laterally extensive and relatively thick Sage Creek White Layer (calcareous limestone), while interval D is separated from Bridger C by the laterally extensive, calcareous Lone Tree White Layer. Bridger intervals C and D (Bridgerian Zone Br3, Gunnell and Bartels, 1994) together represent approximately 300 meters of section. Interval E, originally viewed as essentially non-fossiliferous by Matthew but now known to have a relatively extensive, though poorly distributed, vertebrate fauna (West and Hutchison, 1981; Evanoff and others, 1994), represents approximately the upper 50 meters of the Bridger Formation in the Green River Basin.

Mammalian faunas from Bridger C and D differ in content and composition from those in Bridger B (Matthew, 1909; Gazin, 1976). Wood (1934) proposed grouping Matthew's intervals A and B into the Black's Fork "Member" of the Bridger Formation, based on faunal differences between this interval and those of Bridger C and D (termed the Twin Butte "Member" by Wood). The terms Blacksforkian and Twinbuttean have been used to designate land mammal subages of the Bridgerian Land Mammal Age (Krishtalka and others, 1987).

Tables 1 through 3 provide faunal lists of mammals from each Bridgerian Biostratigraphic Zone (Br1 through Br3). Figure 1 shows the diversity of the more common orders of Bridgerian mammals as reflected by the number of species contained within each order. In Br1 the most diverse orders are primates with eight species and rodents with seven, but none of the seven more common orders really dominates the fauna. By Br2, rodents have become the most diverse order of mammals being represented by 19 species, followed by carnivores with twelve species. Perissodactyls, primates, and creodonts are all equally diverse being represented by 10 species each. In Br3, perissodactyls have become the most diverse order being represented by 14 species, while primates and rodents are equally diverse being represented by 11 species.

Overall, the Bridgerian can be typified by the relatively large numbers of primates, rodents, and perissodactyls present throughout the sequence. None of the orders present in the Bridgerian are new occurrences compared to the earlier Eocene (Wasatchian Land Mammal Age) but many of the genera and species are new compared to the Wasatchian (Gunnell, 1998). In addition, while Bridgerian orders may not be new occurrences, many of their relative diversities have changed dramatically from the Wasatchian to the Bridgerian. For instance, the Order Condylarthra (*sensu lato*) is one of the most common elements of Wasatchian faunas in general, both in species diversity and in relative abundance. Condylarths are still relatively abundant in the Bridgerian (the hyopsodontid condylarth *Hyopsodus* is the most common fossil mammal found in Br2), but their species diversity has been greatly reduced compared to the Wasatchian (one species in Br1, two in Br2, and three in Br3).

Table 1. *Faunal list of mammals from Bridgerian Biostratigraphic Zone Br1, southern Green River Basin.*

Mammalia
　Marsupialia
　　Didelphidae
　　　Peratherium marsupium
　　　Peratherium innominatum
　　　Peratherium knighti
　　　Peratherium sp.
　　　Peradectes chesteri
　　　Cf. *Armintodelphys* sp.
　Proteutheria
　　Apatemyidae
　　　Apatemys bellulus
　　Pantolestidae
　　　Pantolestes longicaudus
　Insectivora
　　Sespedectidae
　　　Scenopagus priscus
　　　Scenopagus edenensis
　　　Scenopagus curtidens
　　Geolabididae
　　　Centetodon bembicophagus
　　Nyctitheriidae
　　　Nyctitherium serotinum

?Primates
　Microsyopidae
　　Microsyops sp., cf. *M. elegans*
Primates
　Notharctidae
　　Notharctus robinsoni
　　Smilodectes mcgrewi
　Omomyidae
　　Anaptomorphus westi
　　Cf. *Gazinius amplus*
　　Trogolemur sp., cf. *T. amplior*
　　Uintanius sp., cf. *U. rutherfurdi*
　　Washakius insignis
　　Omomys carteri
Tillodontia
　Esthonychidae
　　Trogosus sp.
Taeniodonta
　Stylinodontidae
　　Stylinodon mirus
　　Stylinodon inexplicatus
Palaeanodonta (Order Uncertain)
　Metacheiromyidae
　　Metacheiromys sp.
　　Brachianodon westorum
　Epoicotheriidae
　　Tetrapassalus sp.
Rodentia
　Paramyidae
　　Paramys delicatus
　　Paramys delicatior
　　Leptotomus parvus
　　Leptotomus grandis
　　Thisbemys plicatus
　　Microparamys sp., cf. *M. minutus*
　Sciuravidae
　　Sciuravus nitidus
Creodonta
　Oxyaenidae
　　Patriofelis sp., cf. *P. ulta*
　Hyaenodontidae
　　Sinopa rapax
　　Sinopa minor
　　Thinocyon sp., cf. *T. velox*
　　Limnocyon sp.
Carnivora
　Viverravidae
　　Viverravus minutus
　　Viverravus gracilis
　Miacidae
　　Miacis parvivorus
　　Uintacyon vorax
　　Vulpavus sp., cf. *V. palustris*
　　Vulpavus farsonensis
Condylarthra
　Hyopsodontidae
　　Hyopsodus minusculus
Dinocerata
　Uintatheriidae
　　Bathyopsis middleswarti
Perissodactyla
　Equidae
　　Orohippus sp., cf. *O. pumilus*
　Brontotheriidae
　　Palaeosyops fontinalis
　Helaletidae
　　Helaletes nanus
　　Hyrachyus sp.
Artiodactyla
　Homacodontidae
　　Microsus cuspidatus
　　Antiacodon sp., cf. *A. pygmaeus*

Table 2. *Faunal list of mammals from Bridgerian Biostratigraphic Zone Br2, southern Green River Basin only.*

Mammalia
　Marsupialia
　　Didelphidae
　　　Peratherium marsupium
　　　Peratherium innominatum
　Proteutheria
　　Apatemyidae
　　　Apatemys bellus

        Apatemys bellulus
        Apatemys rodens
    Pantolestidae
        Pantolestes elegans
        Pantolestes longicaudus
Insectivora
    Family Uncertain
        Entomolestes grangeri
    Sespedectidae
        Scenopagus edenensis
        Scenopagus priscus
    Geolabididae
        Centetodon bembicophagus
        Centetodon pulcher
    Nyctitheriidae
        Nyctitherium serotinum
        Nyctitherium dasypelix
        Nyctitherium velox
?Primates
    Microsyopidae
        Microsyops elegans
Primates
    Notharctidae
        Notharctus tenebrosus
        Notharctus pugnax
        Smilodectes gracilis
    Omomyidae
        Trogolemur myodes
        Anaptomorphus aemulus
        Omomys carteri
        Washakius insignis
        Uintanius ameghini
        Wyomomys bridgeri
        Hemiacodon gracilis
Tillodontia
    Esthonychidae
        Trogosus castoridens
        Trogosus hyracoides
        Tillodon fodiens
Taeniodonta
    Stylinodontidae
        Stylinodon mirus
Palaeanodonta (Order Uncertain)
    Metacheiromyidae
        Metacheiromys marshi
        Metacheiromys dasypus
        Metacheiromys tatusia
    Epoicotheriidae
        Tetrapassalus proius
Rodentia
    Paramyidae
        Paramys delicatus
        Paramys delicatior
        Reithroparamys delicatissimus
        Pseudotomus robustus
        Pseudotomus hians
        Microparamys minutus
        Leptotomus parvus
        Leptotomus grandis
        Thisbemys corrugatus
        Thisbemys plicatus
        Ischyrotomus horribilis
        Ischyrotomus oweni
        Ischyrotomus superbus
    Sciuravidae
        Sciuravus nitidus
        Sciuravus bridgeri
        Pauromys perditus
    Cylindrodontidae
        Mysops minimus
        Mysops parvus
        Mysops fraternus
Creodonta
    Oxyaenidae
        Patriofelis ulta
    Hyaenodontidae
        Limnocyon verus
        Thinocyon velox
        Thinocyon mustelinus
        Sinopa rapax
        Sinopa grangeri
        Sinopa minor
        Sinopa major
        Tritemnodon agilis
        Machaeroides eothen
Carnivora

    Viverravidae
        Viverravus gracilis
        Viverravus sicarius
        Viverravus minutus
    Miacidae
        Miacis parvivorus
        Vulpavus palustris
        Vulpavus profectus
        Vulpavus ovatus
        Palaearctonyx meadi
        Oödectes herpestoides
        Oödectes proximus
        Uintacyon edax
        Uintacyon vorax
Condylarthra
    Hyopsodontidae
        Hyopsodus paulus
        Hyopsodus minusculus
Perissodactyla
    Equidae
        Orohippus pumilus
        Orohippus major
        Orohippus progressus
    Brontotheriidae
        Palaeosyops paludosus
        Palaeosyops major
        Limnohyops priscus
    Helaletidae
        Helaletes nanus
        Hyrachyus modestus
        Hyrachyus eximius
        Hyrachyus affinis
Artiodactyla
    Homacodontidae
        Microsus cuspidatus
        Antiacodon pygmaeus
        Helohyus plicodon
Mesonychia
    Mesonychidae
        Mesonyx obtusidens
        Harpagolestes macrocephalus

Table 3. *Faunal list of mammals from Bridgerian Biostratigraphic Zone Br3, southern Green River Basin only.*

Marsupialia
    Didelphidae
        Peratherium marsupium
        Peratherium innominatum
Proteutheria
    Palaeoryctidae
        Didelphodus altidens
    Leptictidae
        Hypictops syntaphus
    Pantolestidae
        Pantolestes longicaudus
        Pantolestes elegans
        Pantolestes natans
        Pantolestes phocipes
    Apatemyidae
        Apatemys bellus
        Apatemys bellulus
        Apatemys rodens
Insectivora
    Nyctitheriidae
        Nyctitherium velox
        Pontifactor bestiola
    Sespedectidae
        Scenopagus priscus
    Geolabididae
        Centetodon pulcher
?Primates
    Microsyopidae
        Microsyops annectens
        Uintasorex parvulus
Primates
    Notharctidae
        Notharctus robustior
        Smilodectes gracilis
    Omomyidae
        Omomys carteri
        Hemiacodon gracilis
        Washakius insignis
        Ageitodendron matthewi

Sphacorhysis burntforkensis
Gazinius bowni
Anaptomorphus aemulus
Trogolemur myodes
Uintanius ameghini
Taeniodonta
    Stylinodontidae
        Stylinodon mirus

Palaeanodonta (Order Uncertain)
    Metacheiromyidae
        Metacheiromys osborni
Rodentia
    Paramyidae
        Paramys delicatus
        Paramys delicatior
        Thisbemys corrugatus
        Leptotomus bridgerensis
        Reithroparamys matthewi
    Cylindrodontidae
        Mysops parvus
        Mysops fraternus
    Sciuravidae
        Sciuravus nitidus
        Tillomys senex
        Taxymys lucaris
        Pauromys schaubi
Mesonychia
    Mesonychidae
        Synoplotherium vorax
Creodonta
    Oxyaenidae
        Patriofelis ferox
    Hyaenodontidae
        Thinocyon medius
Carnivora
    Viverravidae
        Viverravus gracilis

Miacidae
    Miacis sylvestris
    Miacis hargeri
    Uintacyon jugulans
Condylarthra
    Hyopsodontidae
        Hyopsodus marshi
        Hyopsodus despiciens
        Hyopsodus lepidus
Dinocerata
    Uintatheriidae
        Uintatherium anceps
Perissodactyla
    Equidae
        Orohippus agilis
        Orohippus sylvaticus
        Orohippus progressus
    Brontotheriidae
        Palaeosyops robustus
        Telmatherium validum
        Telmatherium cultridens
        Manteoceras manteoceras
        Mesatirhinus megarhinus
        Mesatirhinus petersoni
    Isectolophidae
        Parisectolophus latidens
    Helaletidae
        Helaletes intermedius
        Dilophodon minusculus
        Hyrachyus eximius
        Hyrachyus princeps
Artiodactyla
    Dichobunidae
        Homacodon vagans
        Antiacodon venustus
        Helohyus lentus
        Helohyus validus
        Helohyus milleri

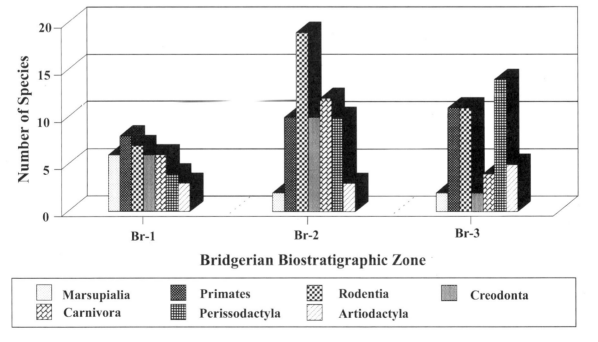

Figure 1. *Ordinal diversity expressed as number of species for the seven most diverse orders of Bridgerian mammals from Bridgerian Biostratigraphic Zones Br1 through Br3.*

Middle Eocene Vertebrates from the Unita Basin - Gunnell, Bartels

UINTAN FAUNAS -- UINTA BASIN

The Uinta Basin in northeastern Utah preserves one of the best records of Uintan-age mammals known in North America. Marsh (1870) reported the first vertebrate fossils from the Uinta Basin and Scott and Osborn (1890) offered the first systematic treatment of fossil mammals from the Uinta Formation followed by the work of Peterson (1919). Osborn (1929) revised the stratigraphic nomenclature of the Uinta Formation recognizing three intervals, designated Uinta A through C (Osborn actually subdivided Uinta B into B1 and B2). Wood (1934) proposed the Wagonhound Member of the Uinta Formation for the lower part of the sequence including Uinta A and B and the Myton Member for the upper sequence including Uinta C. Peterson (1932) and Kay (1934) separated the Duchesne River Formation from the Uinta Formation which underlies it and this, in turn, was made the type section of the Duschesnean Land Mammal Age by the Wood Committee (Wood and others, 1941). The Uintan Land Mammal Age is based on the mammalian faunas from the Uinta Formation in Utah (for more complete historical reviews of Uinta Basin geology and paleontology see Rasmussen and others, this volume).

Table 4 provides a faunal list of mammals from a combined sample of faunas from Uinta A through C. Figure 2 shows the diversity of the more common orders of Uintan mammals as reflected by the number of species contained within each order. For the whole of the Uintan, perissodactyls (34 species) and artiodactyls (26 species) are the most diverse orders of mammals with rodents somewhat less diverse (17 species) and carnivores (6 species), creodonts (4 species), and primates (4 species) even less so. Lagomorphs appear in the fossil record in the Uintan, an order that was not present in the Bridgerian.

Table 4. *Faunal list of mammals from Uinta A through C, Uinta Basin only.*

Lagomorpha
   Leporidae
      Mytonolagus petersoni
Proteutheria
   Apatemyidae
      Stehlinella uintensis
Taeniodonta
   Stylinodontidae
      Stylinodon mirus
Creodonta
   Hyaenodontidae
      Limnocyon douglassi
      Limnocyon potens
      Oxyaenodon dysclerus
      Apataelurus kayi
Carnivora
   Miacidae
      Miacis gracilis
      Miacis longipes
      Tapocyon robustus

      Prodaphaenus scotti
      Procynodictis vulpiceps
      Eosictis avinoffi
Primates
   Omomyidae
      Ourayia uintensis
      Ourayia hopsoni
      Trogolemur sp.
      Chipetaia lamporea
Dinocerata
   Uintatheriidae
      Uintatherium anceps
      Eobasileus cornutus
Artiodactyla
   Dichobunidae
      Pentacemylus leotensis
      Pentacemylus progressus
      Mytonomeryx scotti
      Hylomeryx quadricuspis
      Hylomeryx annectens
      Bunomeryx elegans
      Bunomeryx montanus
      Mesomeryx grangeri
      Achaenodon insolens
      Achaenodon robustus
      Achaenodon uitense
   Agriochoeridae
      Protoreodon pumilus
      Protoreodon parvus
      Protoreodon paradoxicus
      Protoreodon minor
      Protoreodon petersoni
      Diplobunops matthewi
      Diplobunops crassus
      Diplobunops vanhouteni
   Protoceratidae
      Leptotragulus proavus
      Leptotragulus medius
      Leptotragulus clarki
   Camelidae
      Oromeryx plicatus
      Poëbrodon kayi
      Protylopus petersoni
      Protylopus? annectens
Mesonychia
   Mesonychidae
      Harpagolestes breviceps
      Harpagolestes uintensis
      Harpagolestes leotensis
Condylarthra
   Hyopsodontidae
      Hyopsodus paulus
      Hyopsodus uintensis
Perissodactyla
   Equidae
      Epihippus gracilis
      Epihippus parvus
      Epihippus uintensis
      Epihippus intermedius
   Brontotheriidae
      Metarhinus earlei
      Metarhinus riparius
      Rhadinorhinus abbotti
      Rhadinorhinus diploconus
      Sphenocoelus uintensis
      Dolichorhinus longiceps
      Dolichorhinus intermedius
      Dolichorhinus heterodon
      Sthenodectes incisivus
      Sthenodectes priscus
      Manteoceras uintensis
      Protitanotherium emarginatum
      Diplacodon progressum
      Diplacodon elatum
      Eotitanotherium osborni
      Telmatherium altidens
      Heterotitanops parvus
   Isectolophidae
      Isectolophus annectens
      Isectolophus cuspidens
   Helaletidae
      Dilophodon leotanus
   Amynodontidae
      Amynodon advenum
      Amynodon intermedius
   Hyracodontidae

Triplopus cubitalis
Triplopus implicatus
Triplopus? douglassi
Triplopus rhinocerinus
Triplopus obliquidens
Forstercooperia grandis
Epitriplopus uintensis
Chalicotheriidae
Eomoropus annectens
Rodentia
Paramyidae
Ischyrotomus petersoni
Ischyrotomus compressidens
Ischyrotomus eugenei
Leptotomus mytonensis
Leptotomus sciuroides

Microparamys dubius
Reithroparamys gidleyi
Mytonomys robustus
Thisbemys uintensis
Thisbemys medius
Janimus rhinophilus
Sciuravidae
Sciuravus altidens
Sciuravus popi
Cylindrodontidae
Pareumys grangeri
Pareumys milleri
Pareumys? troxelli
Protoptychidae
Protoptychus hatcheri

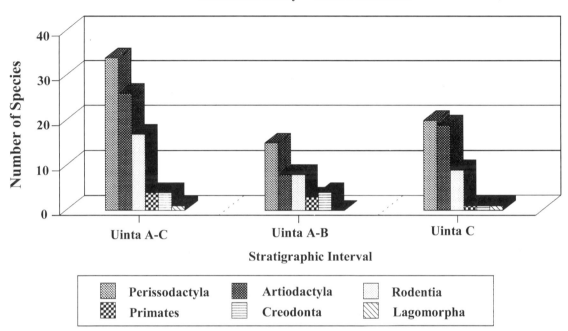

Figure 2. *Ordinal diversity expressed as number of species for six orders of Uintan mammals from Uintan intervals A-C.*

Examining Uinta A-B (Uinta A remains relatively poorly represented) and Uinta C separately reveals the following ordinal diversity patterns (figure 2). Perissodactyls are the most diverse order in the early Uintan (15 species) with rodents and artiodactyls being the next most diverse (8 species each). No other order is represented by more than four species. In the late Uintan (Uinta C), perissodactyls (20 species) and artiodactyls (19 species) are nearly equally diverse with rodents the next most diverse (9 species) followed by carnivores (6 species). No other order is represented by more than a single species. Lagomorphs make their first appearance in Uinta C in the Uinta Basin. These dramatic changes in vertebrate faunal composition late in the Uintan may well reflect a change from the relatively closed vegetation and warm subtropical climates characteristic of the middle Eocene to more open conditions and a more temperate and seasonal climate just prior to the late Eocene.

Figure 3 compares Bridgerian diversity for four mammalian orders (Primates, Rodentia, Perissodactyla, Artiodactyla) with that of the Uintan. For primates, ordinal species diversity remains relatively constant throughout the Bridgerian (from 8 to 11 species) then drops rapidly to three species in the early Uintan and one in the later Uintan. Except for a relatively large jump in species diversity in Br2, rodents remain relatively consistent throughout the Bridgerian and Uintan (ranging from diversities of 7 to 11 species). Perissodactyls show a steady increase in specific diversity beginning with four species in Br1 and ending with twenty species in Uinta C. Artiodactyls remain at relatively low diversities throughout the Bridgerian (3 to 5 species) but experience an increase in the Uintan from eight species in Uinta A-B to 19 species in Uinta C. A general trend toward more species of artiodactyls and perissodactyls and decreasing numbers of primate species can be seen from the Bridgerian through the Uintan.

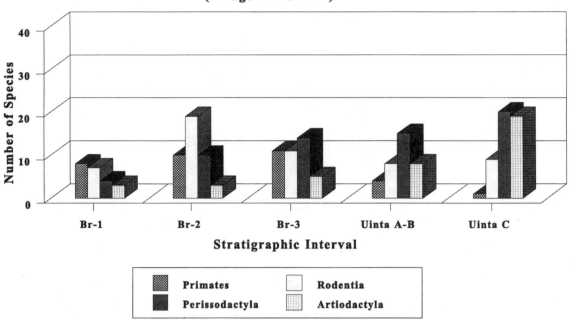

Figure 3. *Ordinal diversity expressed as number of species for four mammalian orders compared by Bridgerian and Uintan biostratigraphic intervals.*

POWDER WASH VERTEBRATE ASSEMBLAGE

Tables 5 and 6 provide faunal lists of reptiles and mammals from Powder Wash (adapted in part from Krishtalka and Stucky, 1984). Figure 4 shows mammalian ordinal diversity at Powder Wash compared with those of Bridgerian Zones Br1 through Br3 from the Green River Basin. Superficially, the Powder Wash diversity profile for Primates, Rodentia, Perissodactyla, and Artiodactyla resembles that of Br1 most closely. However, this may be somewhat deceiving because the Powder Wash fauna as a whole is biased against large mammals (Krishtalka and Stucky, 1984). The most specifically diverse order at Powder Wash is Insectivora with 10 species. In general, small mammals are the most common elements found at Powder Wash with proteutherians (6 species) and marsupials (4 species) being relatively common. Of the 57 mammalian species recognized at Powder Wash, none could be considered to represent large mammals and only a small number (*Trogosus, Hyrachyus, Hyracotherium, Uintacyon major, Helaletes nanus, Patriofelis,* and perhaps *Sinopa grangeri*) could be considered medium-sized mammals. There are no records of brontotheriids or uintatheriids from Powder Wash yet the former are common, almost ubiquitous, elements of most Bridgerian vertebrate assemblages and the latter, while not common, are usually present in Br1

and Br3 assemblages. The size and taxonomic biases of the Powder Wash assemblage are further discussed below.

Figure 5 compares the taxonomic composition of the Powder Wash mammalian fauna with those of Br0 (Gardnerbuttean, earliest Bridgerian) through Br3 using the Simpson Coefficient of Faunal Similarity. Both Br1 and Br2 are quite similar to Powder Wash at the generic level, while Br2 has the highest similarity coefficient at the species level. Examining the taxonomic composition of the Powder Wash mammals more closely reveals some interesting details.

Among Powder Wash marsupials, most taxa range from at least the latest Wasatchian (Lostcabinian) to or through the Uintan and, in the case of the two *Peratherium* species, are known earlier in the Wasatchian as well (Krishtalka and Stucky, 1983b). *Armintodelphys* is known only from Powder Wash, from three localities in the Lostcabinian and Gardnerbuttean of the Wind River Basin (Krishtalka and Stucky, 1983a), and from two localities in Br1 from the southern Green River Basin (Gunnell, 1998). The presence of *Armintodelphys* in Bridgerian Zone Br1 supports Krishtalka and Stucky's (1984) contention that Powder Wash may be best correlated with the earliest Bridgerian, postdating the Gardnerbuttean.

Most of the insectivorous taxa (insectivores, proteutherians, chiropterans) are relatively uninformative biostratigraphically. Most occur over rather broad time ranges or are poorly known and only one, *Palaeictops*

Table 5. *Faunal list of reptiles from Powder Wash and vicinity (adapted from Krishtalka and Stucky, 1984). Taxa denoted with a plus (+) are also known from Powder Springs localities, those with an asterisk (*) are known exclusively from Powder Springs.*

Testudines
    Trionychidae
        Gen. and Sp. indet.+
    Emydidae
        Echmatemys sp.*
    Testudinidae
        Hadrianus sp.*
Lacertilia
    Iguanidae
        Parasauromalus olseni+
        Parasauromalus sp.
    Agamidae
        Tinosaurus stenodon
    Xantusiidae
        Paleoxantusia sp.
    Anguidae
        Glyptosaurus sylvestris+
        Xestops vagans
        Eodiploglossus borealis
    Varanidae
        Saniwa sp.+
Serpentes
    Booidea
        Gen. and Sp. indet.

Crocodylia
    Alligatoridae
        Procaimanoidea kayi+
        Cf. *Allognathosuchus* sp.*
    Crocodylidae
        Gen. and Sp. indet.*
    Pristichampsidae
        Pristichampsus vorax+
    Caimanidae
        Diplocynodon sp.*

Table 6. *Faunal list of mammals from Powder Wash (adapted from Krishtalka and Stucky, 1984).*

Marsupialia
    Didelphidae
        Peratherium marsupium
        Peratherium innominatum
        Peradectes chesteri
        Armintodelphys dawsoni
Proteutheria
    Apatemyidae
        Apatemys sp., cf. *A. rodens*
        Apatemys sp., cf. *A. bellus*
        Apatemys sp., cf. *A. bellulus*
    Pantolestidae
        Pantolestes sp., cf. *P. longicaudus*
    Leptictidae
        Palaeictops bridgeri
Insectivora
    Sespedectidae
        Scenopagus edenensis
        Scenopagus priscus
        Talpavus nitidus
        Talpavus sp., cf. *T. nitidus*
        Crypholestes sp.
    Nyctitheriidae
        Nyctitherium serotinum
    Geolabididae
        Centetodon pulcher
        Centetodon bembicophagus
    Family Uncertain
        "*Eoryctes*" sp.
        Aethomylus simplicidens
Chiroptera
    Family Uncertain
        Cf. *Ageina* sp.
Primates?
    Microsyopidae
        Uintasorex sp., cf. *U. parvulus*
        Microsyops sp., cf. *M. elegans*
Primates
    Omomyidae
        Utahia kayi
        Anaptomorphus aemulus
        Omomys carteri
        Omomys lloydi
        Uintanius ameghini
    Notharctidae
        Smilodectes sp., cf. *S. gracilis*
        Notharctus sp., cf. *N. tenebrosus*
Tillodontia

    Esthonychidae
        Trogosus sp.
Condylarthra
    Hyopsodontidae
        Hyopsodus paulus
        Hyopsodus minusculus
Creodonta
    Oxyaenidae
        Patriofelis sp.
    Hyaenodontidae
        Sinopa grangeri
        Sinopa minor
        Tritemnodon sp., cf. *T. gracilis*
        Tritemnodon sp., cf. *T. whitiae*
        Limnocyon sp., cf. *L. verus*
        ?*Proviverroides* sp.
Carnivora
    Viverravidae
        Viverravus minutus
        Viverravus gracilis
        Viverravus sicarius
    Miacidae
        Miacis sp., cf. *M. parvivorus*
        Uintacyon sp., cf. *U. major*
        ?*Oödectes* sp.
Perissodactyla
    Equidae
        Hyracotherium vassaciense
    Isectolophidae
        Isectolophus sp., cf. *I. latidens*
    Helaletidae
        Helaletes nanus
        Hyrachyus modestus
Artiodactyla
    Homacodontidae
        Antiacodon pygmaeus
Mesonychia
    Mesonychidae
        Mesonyx sp.
Rodentia
    Paramyidae
        Paramys near *P. delicatus*
        Pseudotomus near *P. robustus*
        Microparamys minutus
    Sciuravidae
        Sciuravus eucristadens
        Sciuravid sp.
        Pauromys sp.

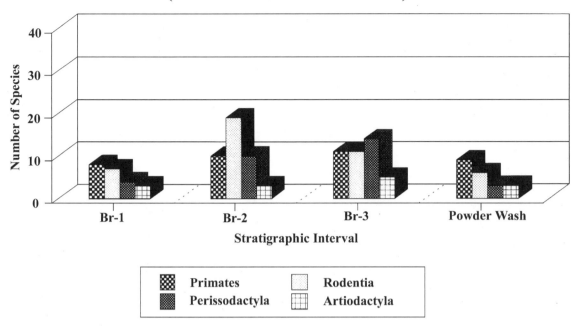

Figure 4. *Ordinal diversity expressed as number of species for four mammalian orders comparing Powder Wash with Bridgerian Biostratigraphic Zones Br1 through Br3.*

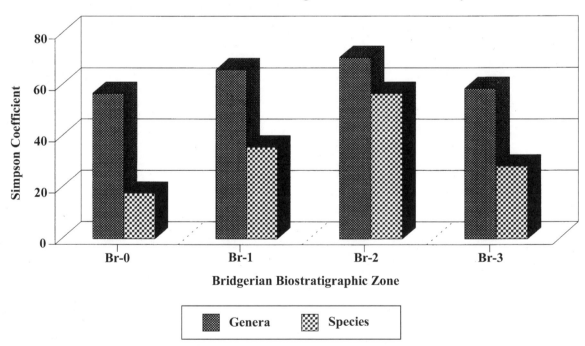

Figure 5. *Comparison of Powder Wash assemblage with Bridgerian Biostratigraphic Zones Br0 through Br3 at the species and generic levels using the Simpson Coefficient (SC) of Faunal Similarity (Simpson, 1943; Flynn, 1986). SC = C/N₁ x 100, where C = the number of taxa (at any chosen taxonomic level) shared between two faunas or samples and N₁ = the total number of taxa present (at the same taxonomic level as C) in the smaller fauna or sample. Note relatively high SC for Powder Wash genera with Br1 and Br2 and relatively high SC for Powder Wash species with Br2.*

bridgeri, presently is restricted to a single time interval, Bridgerian Zone Br3. *Palaeictops bridgeri* is only known from Powder Wash and Tabernacle Butte (McGrew and others, 1959; McKenna and others, 1962), the latter traditionally having been interpreted as late Bridgerian (Br3) in age (McGrew and others, 1959). However, the Bridgerian record of *Palaeictops* and leptictids in general is so poor that these two isolated occurrences probably have little biostratigraphic importance.

Among primates and primate-like taxa, only the questionably assigned *Notharctus* sp., cf. *N. tenebrosus* may be of biostratigraphic significance as this taxon probably is restricted to Bridgerian Zone Br2. However, the Powder Wash sample of *Notharctus* is very limited making taxonomic identification tenuous. The other notharctine primate at Powder Wash, *Smilodectes* sp., cf. *S. gracilis*, is known from Br2 and Br3 in the Green River Basin but is much more common from the former. It is possible that the Powder Wash *Smilodectes* material represents a new species as the specimens are at the small end of the size range for *S. gracilis* and differ morphologically in the construction of their lower fourth premolars (better developed talonids with small but distinct entoconids present). Further analysis will be required to make this determination.

The microsyopid *Uintasorex* sp., cf. *U. parvulus*, once thought to be restricted to Bridgerian Zone Br3 is now known also from Br2 (UM collections), but is much more abundant in Br3 deposits (*U. parvalus* also is relatively common in the early Bridgerian of the Washakie Basin, Peter Robinson, personal communication, 1997). *Utahia* is only known from Powder Wash by a small number of specimens and from a single specimen from the Lostcabinian of the Green River Basin north of Big Piney, Wyoming (Gazin, 1962). The taxonomic identity of the Big Piney specimen is somewhat doubtful and *Utahia* is so poorly represented that no biostratigraphic implications can be garnered from these two records.

Among the remaining taxa known from Powder Wash only a few may provide important biostratigraphic information. The creodont *Sinopa grangeri* is restricted to Bridgerian Zone Br2 in the Green River Basin but the systematics of Bridgerian hyaenodontids are such that taxonomic assignments are rather ambiguous. The perissodactyl *Hyracotherium vassaciense* is only known from the Lostcabinian and Gardnerbuttean outside of Powder Wash. Krishtalka and Stucky (1984) state that the assignment of the Powder Wash equid specimens to this genus is based on the lack of the upper molar mesostyle diagnostic of *Orohippus*, the later Bridgerian descendant of *Hyracotherium*. However, upper molar mesostyles are variably present in *Orohippus* (Kitts, 1957; Gunnell,

1998) so that this character state alone does not suffice to distinguish between *Hyracotherium* and *Orohippus* and renders equivocal the biostratigraphic importance of the Powder Wash equids. The paramyid rodent *Pseudotomus robustus* and the isectolophid tapiroid *Isectolophus latidens* are both restricted to Br2 in the Green River Basin. Their possible presence in the Powder Wash faunal sample may prove to be a useful biostratigraphic indicator when better material becomes available for a more complete systematic treatment. The mesonychid *Mesonyx* and the viverravid carnivore *Viverravus sicarius* are known from Br2 but not Br1 in the Green River Basin. However, both are present in Br0 (Robinson, 1966; John-Paul Zonneveld and others, in preparation) such that their absence from Br1 is probably a preservational artifact.

POWDER WASH DEPOSITION AND TAPHONOMY

The depositional history of the Powder Wash locality has not been studied in great detail. The geographic position of Powder Wash along the northeastern margin of the Uinta Basin may play a role in making a direct time correlation difficult. It is becoming clear that faunal assemblages sampled from marginal basin areas differ in content and composition from time-equivalent samples from basin depocenters (Gunnell, 1995, 1997; Bartels, 1993, 1994). Basin-margin sedimentary systems sample faunas from a different suite of paleohabitats than that of the basin center. These differing paleohabitats and, perhaps, varying habitat utilization of vertebrate taxa in basin-margin environments, may account for many of the dissimilarities documented between basin-margin and basin-center faunal assemblages. Since the biostratigraphy of Tertiary Land Mammal Ages is based almost exclusively on basin-center assemblages, correlation of basin-margin assemblages to established biostratigraphic zones is problematical.

It is possible that Powder Wash represents a basin-margin assemblage. Further study of the assemblage and a careful analysis of the depositional history of the Powder Wash deposits are necessary before a full understanding of the Powder Wash fauna can be reached.

The Powder Wash assemblage has a very strong taphonomic bias toward small terrestrial animals. The assemblage is dominated, both in terms of diversity and relative abundance, by insectivores, rodents, small primates, and iguanids and other small lizards. This bias is further indicated by the presence of snakes and isolated teeth of the highly terrestrial crocodylian *Pristichampsus*, and the virtual absences of large mammals, turtles, and other crocodylians. Fish (represented almost exclusively by gar scales and isolated teeth) and amphibians are also exceedingly rare.

The size bias appears to be largely hydraulic. The Power Wash matrix is a uniformly muddy, fine-grained sublitharenite. The preponderance of vertebrate remains are small dentaries and isolated teeth, with small maxillae (and other skull elements), vertebrae, and long bones comprising the remainder of the sample. This association of hard, dense, bony elements in a sandstone suggests a lag deposit within a channel or splay. Since the geometry and stratigraphic sequence of the deposit has not been examined by the authors, the type of channel cannot be determined, but the grain size, matrix, and vertebrate assemblage would suggest a small meandering stream channel, a lake-margin (deltaic) distributary channel, or the basal portion of a crevasse splay.

The terrestrial bias would suggest ultimate derivation of the assemblage from extra-channel environments such as alluvial-fan interfluves or the floodplain of a meandering stream. Without additional microstratigraphic analyses, however, further speculation on the taphonomy of the deposit would be premature.

Collecting biases in the Powder Wash sample itself are probably insignificant since larger taxa would have been recovered if present and remains of all vertebrate classes are well represented (if unevenly distributed). Several taxa are known exclusively from the nearby Powder Springs localities and suggest that a more thorough collection of these adjacent sites would provide a clearer picture of the age and composition of the fauna extant in the eastern margin of the Uinta basin at that time.

CONCLUSIONS

Krishtalka and Stucky (1984) argued for an early Bridgerian age for Powder Wash based on the co-occurrence of *Palaeictops bridgeri, Talpavus nitidus, Pantolestes, Nyctitherium*, two species of *Centetodon, Omomys, Smilodectes, Anaptomorphus, Uintanius, Helaletes, Hyrachyus, Trogosus, Antiacodon*, and *Sciuravus*. They noted that, based on these co-occurrences, the Powder Wash fauna could correlate with either "Bridger A or B."

Krishtalka and Stucky (1984) suggested that the presence of *Notharctus* sp., cf. *N. tenebrosus, Anaptomorphus aemulus, Microparamys minutus*, and *Pseudotomus* sp., cf. *P. robustus* may indicate that Powder Wash is correlative with Bridger B (Br2) because all of these taxa are restricted to that interval in the southern Green River Basin. In fact, *Anaptomorphus aemulus* also is known from the later Bridgerian (Br3, Bridger C, see

Gunnell, 1995) and *Microparamys minutus* occurs in Br1 (Gunnell, 1998). It is difficult to evaluate the importance of the tentatively referred species of *Notharctus*. Br1 contains a larger species of *Notharctus* (*N. robinsoni*, see Gingerich, 1979; Gunnell, 1998) while the Powder Wash *Notharctus* specimens are smaller than is typical for those representing *N. tenebrosus*. However, the presence of *Pseudotomus, Isectolophus*, and *Sinopa grangeri* in the Powder Wash fauna do suggest a slightly later correlation than Br1 as all of these taxa are unknown from that interval at present, occurring first in Br2 in the southern Green River Basin.

Other mammalian taxa present at Powder Wash make a secure correlation difficult. As noted above, *Armintodelphys* is not known from sediments later than Br1, while *Palaeictops bridgeri* does not occur before Br3 elsewhere. Both of these taxa are poorly represented such that their biostratigraphic importance remains dubious. *Uintasorex parvulus*, while known from Br2 is much more common in later occurring sediments (Br3) which might indicate a slightly later age for Powder Wash.

The reptiles preserved at Powder Wash and Powder Springs provide little indication of the precise age of the fauna. Each of the taxa present in the sample range from the Wasatchian through at least the middle Bridgerian (Br2). Despite the strong bias toward small terrestrial forms, the general appearance of the assemblage (abundance of *Pristichampsus* relative to other crocodylian teeth, great diversity and abundance of lizards) is reminiscent of middle Bridgerian (Br2) assemblages. This faunal composition is, however, also indicative of basin-margin conditions. Without a more diagnostic assemblage of large reptiles, particularly the emydid turtle *Echmatemys*, there is little hope of further refinement of a Bridgerian age for Powder Wash from the reptile material.

Changes in vertebrate faunas that occur through the middle Eocene in North America can be documented by studying the faunal assemblages from the southern Green River and Uinta Basins. The early part of the middle Eocene (Bridgerian) can be typified faunally as subtropical with a relatively high number of primates being a key element in this interpretation. In the Uintan, the number of perissodactyls continued to increase from the high number reached by the end of the Bridgerian and artiodactyls underwent a large increase in diversity from the early to late Uintan. In conjunction with this, primate diversity decreased dramatically through the Uintan. These documented changes in vertebrate diversity patterns indicate that subtropical conditions gave way to more open, seasonal, temperate conditions by the later part of the Uintan. The southern Green River and Uinta Basins will continue to play a key role in the development of a better understanding of the changes that occurred through the middle Eocene in North America.

ACKNOWLEDGMENTS

We would like to thank D. D. Gillette for the invita-

tion to participate in this volume. We thank M. R. Dawson, K. C. Beard, and A. R. Tabrum for the opportunity to study the Powder Wash assemblage housed at the Carnegie Museum of Natural History. We thank Peter Robinson for reading and improving an earlier version of this manuscript.

REFERENCES

Bartels, W.S., 1993, Niche separation of fluvial and lacustrine reptiles from the Eocene Green River and Bridger Formations of Wyoming: Journal of Vertebrate Paleontology, v. 13, p. 25A.

—1994, Laramide basin-fill evolution and long-term patterns of terrestrial vertebrate preservation: Geological Society of America, Abstracts with Programs, v. 26, p. 3-4.

Bartels, W. S., and Williams, E. M., 1996, Paleocene and Eocene climatic estimates for the northern Rocky Mountains - A comparison of proxy indicators: Journal of Vertebrate Paleontology, v. 16, p. 21A.

Burke, J. J., 1969, An antiacodont from the Green River Eocene of Utah: Kirtlandia, v. 5, p. 1-7.

Collinson, M. E., 1992, Vegetational and floristic changes around the Eocene/Oligocene in western and central Europe, *in* Prothero, D. R., and Berggren, W. A., editors, Eocene-Oligocene climatic and biotic evolution: Princeton, Princeton University Press, p. 437-450.

Cope, E. D., 1882, The reptiles of the American Eocene: American Naturalist, v. 16, p. 979-993.

—1884, The Vertebrata of the Tertiary formations of the West: Report of the United States Geological Survey of the Territories, v. 3, p. 1-1009.

Dawson, M. R., 1968, Middle Eocene rodents (Mammalia) from northeastern Utah: Annals of the Carnegie Museum, v. 39, p. 327-370.

Dettman, D. L., and Lohmann, K. C., 1993, Seasonal change in Paleogene surface water $\delta^{18}O$- Fresh-water bivalves of western North America: Geophysical Monographs 78, p. 153-163.

Doi, Kentaro, 1990, Geology, and paleontology of two primate families of the Raven Ridge, northwestern Colorado and northeastern Utah: Boulder, University of Colorado, MS thesis, 215 p.

Evanoff, Emmett, Robinson, Peter, Murphey, P. C., Kron, D. G., Engard, Donna, and Monaco, Patricia, 1994, An early Uintan fauna from Bridger E: Journal of Vertebrate Paleontology, v. 14, p. 24A.

Flynn, J. J., 1986, Faunal provinces and the Simpson Coefficient: Contributions to Geology, University of Wyoming, Special Paper 3, p. 317-338.

Gazin, C. L., 1958, A review of Middle and Upper Eocene primates of North America: Smithsonian Miscellaneous Collections 136, 112 p.

—1962, A further study of the Lower Eocene mammal faunas of southwestern Wyoming: Smithsonian Miscellaneous Collections 144, 98 p.

—1968, A study of the Eocene condylarthran mammal *Hyopsodus*: Smithsonian Miscellaneous Collections 153, 90 p.

—1976, Mammalian faunal zones of the Bridger Middle Eocene: Smithsonian Contributions to Paleobiology 26, p. 1-25.

Gingerich, P. D., 1979, Phylogeny of middle Eocene Adapidae (Mammalia, Primates) in North America- *Smilodectes* and *Notharctus*: Journal of Paleontology, v. 53, p. 153-163.

Gunnell, G. F., 1995, Omomyid primates (Tarsiiformes) from the Bridger Formation, middle Eocene, southern Green River Basin, Wyoming: Journal of Human Evolution, v. 28, p. 147-187.

—1997, Wasatchian-Bridgerian (Eocene) paleoecology of the western interior of North America - changing paleoenvironments and taxonomic composition of omomyid (Tarsiiformes) primates: Jour-

nal of Human Evolution, v. 32, p. 105-132.

—1998, Mammalian fauna from the lower Bridger Formation (Bridger A, Early Middle Eocene), of the southern Green River Basin, Wyoming: Contributions from the Museum of Paleontology, University of Michigan, v. 30, p. 83-130.

Gunnell, G. F., and Bartels, W. S., 1994, Early Bridgerian (middle Eocene) vertebrate paleontology and paleoecology of the southern Green River Basin, Wyoming: Contributions to Geology, University of Wyoming, v. 30, p. 57-70.

Gunnell, G. F., Morgan, M. E., Maas, M. E., and Gingerich, P. D., 1995, Comparative paleoecology of Paleogene and Neogene mammalian faunas - trophic structure and composition: Palaeogeography, Palaeoclimatology, Palaeoecology, v. 115, p. 265-286.

Hay, O.P., 1908, Fossil turtles of North America: Carnegie Institution of Washington, v. 75, p. 1-568.

Hutchison, J. H., 1992, Western North American reptile and amphibian record across the Eocene/Oligocene boundary and its climatic implications, *in* Prothero, D. R., and Berggren, W. A., editors, Eocene-Oligocene climatic and biotic evolution: Princeton, Princeton University Press, p. 451-463.

Kay, J. J., 1934, The Tertiary formations of the Uinta Basin, Utah: Annals of the Carnegie Museum, v. 23, p. 357-371.

Kitts, D. B., 1957, A revision of the genus *Orohippus* (Perissodactyla, Equidae): American Museum Novitates 1864, 40 p.

Krishtalka, Leonard, 1976a, Early Tertiary Adapisoricidae and Erinaceidae (Mammalia, Insectivora) of North America: Carnegie Museum of Natural History Bulletin 1, 40 p.

—1976b, North American Nyctitheriidae (Mammalia, Insectivora): Annals of the Carnegie Museum, v. 46, p. 7-28.

Krishtalka, Leonard, and Stucky, R. K., 1983a, Revision of the Wind River faunas, early Eocene of central Wyoming. Part 3. Marsupialia: Annals of the Carnegie Museum, v. 52, p. 205-228.

—1983b, Paleocene and Eocene marsupials of North America: Annals of the Carnegie Museum, v. 52, p. 229-263.

—1984, Middle Eocene marsupials (Mammalia) from northeastern Utah and the mammalian fauna from Powder Wash: Annals of the Carnegie Museum, v. 53, p. 31-45.

Krishtalka, Leonard, West, R. M., Black, C. C., Dawson, M. R., Flynn, J. J., Turnbull, W. D., Stucky, R. K., McKenna, M. C., Bown, T. M., Golz, D. J., and Lillegraven, J. A., 1987, Eocene (Wasatchian through Duchesnean) biochronology of North America, *in* Woodburne, M. O., editor, Cenozoic mammals of North America--geochronology and biostratigraphy: Berkeley and Los Angeles, University of California Press, p. 77-117.

Leidy, Joseph, 1869, Notice of some extinct vertebrates from Wyoming and Dakota: Proceedings of the Academy of Natural Sciences of Philadelphia, v. 21, p. 63-67.

—1870, [Descriptions of *Palaeosyops paludosus, Microsus cuspidatus*, and *Notharctus tenebrosus*]: Proceedings of the Academy of Natural Sciences of Philadelphia, v. 22, p. 113-114.

Lillegraven, J. A., McKenna, M. C., and Krishtalka, Leonard, 1981, Evolutionary relationships of middle Eocene and younger species of *Centetodon* (Mammalia, Insectivora, Geolabididae) with a description of the dentition of *Ankylodon* (Adapisoricidae): University of Wyoming Publications 45, 115 p.

Marsh, O. C., 1870, Professor Marsh's Rocky Mountain expedition-

Discovery of the Mauvaises Terres Formation in Colorado: American Journal of Science, 2nd Series, v. 50, p. 292.

—1871, Notice of some new fossil reptiles from the Cretaceous and Tertiary formations: American Journal of Science and Arts, v. 3, p. 447-459.

—1872a, Preliminary description of new Tertiary mammals. Parts I-IV: American Journal of Science and Arts, v. 4, p. 122-128, 202-224.

—1872b, Preliminary description of new Tertiary reptiles. Part I: American Journal of Science and Arts, v. 4, p. 298-309.

Matthew, W. D., 1909, The Carnivora and Insectivora of the Bridger Basin, middle Eocene: American Museum of Natura History Memoir 9, p. 291-567.

McGrew, P. O., Berman, J. E., Hecht, M. K., Hummel, J. M., Simpson, G. G., and Wood, A. E., 1959, The geology and paleontology of the Elk Mountain and Tabernacle Butte area, Wyoming: Bulletin of the American Museum of Natural History, v. 117, p. 117-176.

McKenna, M. C., Robinson, Peter, and Taylor, D. W., 1962, Notes on Eocene Mammalia and Mollusca from Tabernacle Butte, Wyoming: American Museum Novitates 2102, 33 p.

Miller, K. G., 1992, Middle Eocene to Oligocene stable isotopes, climate, and deep-water history-- the terminal Eocene event?, *in* Prothero, D. R., and Berggren, W. A., editors, Eocene-Oligocene climatic and biotic evolution: Princeton, Princeton University Press, p. 160-177.

Osborn, H. F., 1929, The Titanotheres of ancient Wyoming, Dakota, and Nebraska: U. S. Geological Survey Monograph 55, v. I and II, 953 p.

Peterson, O. A., 1919, Report upon the material discovered in the upper Eocene of the Uinta Basin by Earl Douglas in the years 1908-1909, then by O. A. Peterson in 1912: Annals of the Carnegie Museum, v. 12, p. 40-168.

—1932, New species from the Oligocene of the Uinta: Annals of the Carnegie Museum, v. 21, p. 61-78.

Robinson, Peter, 1966, Fossil Mammalia of the Huerfano Formation, Eocene, of Colorado: Bulletin, Peabody Museum of Natural History, Yale University, v. 21, 95 p.

Scott, W. B., and Osborn, H. F., 1890, The Mammalia of the Uinta Formation: Transactions of the American Philosophical Society, new series, v. 16, p. 461-572.

Simpson, G. G., 1943, Mammals and the nature of continents: American Journal of Science, v. 241, p. 1-31.

Szalay, F. S., 1969, Uintasoricinae, a new subfamily of early Tertiary mammals (?Primates): American Museum Novitates 2363, 36 p.

—1976, Systematics of the Omomyidae (Tarsiiformes, Primates) taxonomy, phylogeny, and adaptations: Bulletin of the American Museum of Natural History, v. 156, p. 157-450.

West, R. M., 1979, Paleontology and geology of the Bridger Formation, southern Green River Basin, southwestern Wyoming. Part 3. Notes on *Hyopsodus*: Milwaukee Public Museum Contributions in Biology and Geology, v. 25, 52 p.

West, R. M., and Hutchison, J. H., 1981, Geology and paleontology of the Bridger Formation, southern Green River Basin, southwestern Wyoming. Part 6. The fauna and correlation of Bridger E: Milwaukee Public Museum Contributions in Biology and Geology, v. 46, 8 p.

Williams, E. M., and Bartels, W. S., 1995, Geographic Information System analysis of the distribution of Recent vertebrates with respect to climate and its potential for generating quantitative paleoclimatic estimates: Journal of Vertebrate Paleontology, v.15, p. 60A.

Wing, S. L., Bown, T. M., and Obradovich, J. D., 1991, Early Eocene biotic and climatic change in interior western North America: Geology, v. 19, p. 1189-1192.

Wing, S. L., and Greenwood, D. R., 1993, Fossils and fossil climate-the case for equable continental interiors in the Eocene: Philosophical Transactions, Royal Society of London, v. 341, p. 243-252.

Wolfe, J. A., 1992, Climatic, floristic, and vegetational changes near the Eocene/Oligocene boundary in North America, *in* Prothero, D. R., and Berggren, W. A., editors, Eocene-Oligocene climatic and biotic evolution: Princeton, Princeton University Press, p. 421-436.

Wood, A. E., 1962, The early Tertiary rodents of the family Paramyidae: Transactions of the American Philosophical Society, new series, v. 52, p. 1-261.

Wood, H. E., 1934, Revision of the Hyrachyidae: Bulletin of the American Museum of Natural History, v. 67, p. 181-295.

Wood, H. E., Chaney, R. W., Clark, John, Colbert, E. H., Jepsen, G. L., Reeside, Jr., J. B., and Stock, Chester, 1941, Nomenclature and correlation of the North American continental Tertiary: Bulletin of the Geological Society of America, v. 52, p. 1-48.

VERTEBRATE FOOTPRINTS IN THE DUCHESNE RIVER AND UINTA FORMATIONS (MIDDLE TO LATE EOCENE), UINTA BASIN, UTAH

Alden H. Hamblin
Grand Staircase - Escalante National Monument
337 South Main, Suite 010, Cedar City, Utah 84720

William A. S. Sarjeant
Department of Geological Sciences, University of Saskatchewan
114 Science Place, Saskatoon, Saskatchewan, Canada S7N 5E2

David A. E. Spalding
1105 Ogden Road, RR #1, Pender Island, British Columbia, Canada V0N 2M1

ABSTRACT

Vertebrate footprints are reported confidently from eight sites, and more questionably from two other sites, in the Uinta Basin, Utah. Nine are in the Uinta Formation (middle to late Eocene) and one in the Duchesne River Formation (late Eocene). The trackmakers range from small mammals and birds to medium or large ungulates (probably including amynodonts and brontotheres). These 10 sites illustrate the potential for discovering additional tracks in the Uinta and Duchesne River Formations.

INTRODUCTION

Fossil vertebrate footprints have been identified with varying degrees of confidence, from a number of sites in the Tertiary formations of the Uinta Basin. Ten such sites are briefly discussed in this paper (figure 1), nine being in the Uinta Formation (middle to late Eocene) and one in the Duchesne River Formation (late Eocene). About half of these sites were first discovered and recorded, by the first author or others during paleontological surveys associated with petroleum activities in the Uinta Basin (Hamblin, 1994). The three authors together visited several of these sites during May, 1995 and prepared maps of the more important sites. Our results indicate the potential for additional footprint research in these formations in the Uinta Basin.

A number of reptile track sites have been recorded from the Mesozoic rocks along the foot of the Uinta Mountains over the past 50 years (Peabody, 1948; Untermann and Untermann, 1949, 1954; Lockley, Conrad, Paquette, and Hamblin, 1992; Lockley, Conrad, Paquette, and Farlow, 1992; Hamblin and Bilbey, 1999). In contrast, as Lockley and Hunt (1995) noted, very little has been published on footprints of Tertiary age from North America. One of the earliest reports of Uinta Basin Tertiary tracks was of footprints of birds from the Green River Formation (Curry, 1957). Erickson (1967) likewise reported tracks from the Green River Formation. Lockley and Hunt (1995) noted that tracks (particularly of birds) had been extensively collected from that formation, discussing several other occurrences. They also described a slab of rock at the Utah Museum of Natural History which exhibited large and small mammal footprints as well as bird tracks. This slab came from the Red Creek area of the western Uinta Basin and is listed as from the Uinta Formation (James H. Madsen, Jr., personal communication to A.A.H.). However, recent mapping and stratigraphic studies by Bryant and others (1989) and Bryant (1992) would place it in the Duchesne River Formation, as redefined by them. If this is the case, no fossil footprints or track sites have been described hitherto from the Uinta Formation.

The first extended study of Tertiary mammal and bird footprints from North America was by Scrivner and Bottjer (1986), on Neogene tracks from Death Valley, California. Subsequently, Sarjeant and Langston (1994) described a rich ichnofauna from the Chadronian (late Eocene) of west Texas, which includes avian footprints comparable to those reported in this paper. A series of

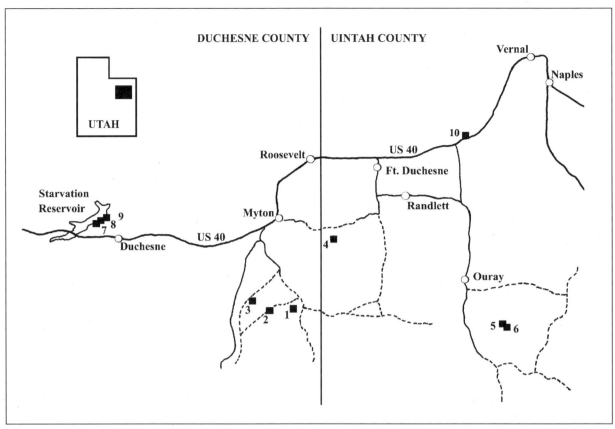

Figure 1. *Footprint localities in Duchesne River and Uinta Formations of northeastern Utah.*

studies on vertebrate footprints from the Tertiary of California is presently undergoing publication (Sarjeant and Reynolds, 1997a, b). However, none of the mammalian footprint morphotypes reported in those papers corresponds to any of the morphotypes encountered in the Uinta Basin.

Most of the sites discussed in this paper were at first only tentatively identified on the basis of the presence either of round indentations on upper rock surfaces or of round bulges on undersurfaces; these were provisionally interpreted respectively as molds or casts of footprints. The identity of some of these is beyond question, as in the case of bird footprints. The fact that several of these features line up in a possible left-right trackway pattern indicates their footprint character. In other instances, however, the lack of any clear pattern in a mass of indentations or the isolation of the structures means that, though these may also represent the footprints of large mammals, the evidence for their identity is much more tenuous.

GEOLOGIC SETTING

The Uinta Basin is a broad, east-west-trending basin south of the Uinta Mountains in northeastern Utah. It covers approximately 31,100 square kilometers, with ele-

vations ranging from 1,500 to 2,100 meters. It forms both a topographic basin and a structural basin. The axis of the structural basin parallels the mountains, near the foot of their southern flank.

The principal drainage systems are formed by the east-flowing Duchesne River and its tributaries and by the west-flowing White River and its tributaries. Both of these major streams enter the south-flowing Green River near Ouray, Utah. The Green River flows south through the Book Cliffs out of the Uinta Basin.

Exposures within the Uinta Basin consist mostly of middle and late Eocene sediments. In some areas, these sediments exceed 3,000 meters in thickness (Hintze, 1988). Geological formations dating back to Precambrian time are exposed in the Uinta Mountains north of the Basin.

With the advent of the Laramide Orogeny in the Late Cretaceous (ca. 70 million years ago), uplifts forming the Rocky Mountains commenced. The largest Laramide structure in Utah is the Uinta Mountain anticline (Hintze, 1988). Basins were formed adjacent to this anticline, several being occupied by large freshwater lakes. On the south side of the Uinta Mountains, Lake Uinta constituted the environment in which the Green River Formation (middle Eocene) and parts of the Uinta Formation (late Eocene) were deposited. Fluvial sediments intertongue with and overlie the lacustrine deposits.

By late Eocene time, Lake Uinta had diminished in areal extent. Conditions fluctuated between lacustrine and fluvial, tending to become more fluvial as this epoch approached its end. The Uinta and Duchesne River Formations were deposited during this time. The Uinta Formation is exposed in an approximately 130 kilometer long east-west band in the central part of the Uinta Basin which ranges from 19 to 24 kilometers wide in a north-south direction (Peterson and Kay, 1931). The Uinta Formation is composed of alternating beds of shale, siltstone and lenticular sandstone, with occasional beds of limestone. It is within these sediments that the bulk of middle and late Eocene vertebrate fossil material-bones and trace-fossils - occur in the Uinta Basin.

The Duchesne River Formation, which overlies the Uinta Formation, is almost entirely fluvial in origin. It is composed of reddish brown to tan sediments, consisting of interbedded claystone, sandstone and conglomerate. The Duchesne River Formation sediments were derived primarily from the ancestral Uinta Mountains (Andersen and Picard, 1972) and form an outcrop band along the foot of the Uinta Mountains.

The age of the Duchesne River Formation has been debated for years. This argument has been settled recently (at least for the central and eastern Uinta Basin; see Bryant and others, 1989) by means of geochronometric and biochronologic evidence (Prothero and Swisher, 1992, 1996); the Duchesne River Formation is now firmly placed in the late Eocene. On the western side of the Uinta Basin, Bryant and others (1989) and Bryant (1992) extend what they refer to as the Duchesne River Formation back to the Paleocene. No outcrops of the Uinta Formation have been reported east of Starvation Reservoir.

TRACK SITES

Site 42DC194TV - Castle Peak Pocket

Site 42DC194TV is discussed first because it exemplifies a site at which the initial record of footprints was dubious, but was verified by later discoveries. This site is in the lower Uinta Formation and is located 16 kilometers south of Myton, Utah (NE1/4 NW1/4 section 8, T.9S., R.17E., Salt Lake Base Line and Meridian).

Initially, surveys at an oil well location and access road had identified fossil mammal bones; crocodilian teeth, bones and armor fragments; and turtle bones and carapace fragments, in the immediate area of the proposed development. Several round indentations, 7.5 to 10 centimeters in diameter, occur in a sandstone cropping out in a small gully northeast of the proposed well location. These were recorded as being possible tracks but, because of limited exposure and their small number, the identification was considered questionable.

Construction of an oil well pit at this location was monitored for paleontological purposes, not because of the possible footprints, but because of the amount of osteological material in the area. The monitoring revealed a few turtle carapace fragments. However, when pit construction required blasting of a thick (up to 2.5 m) sandstone layer, the resultant blocks proved to have large footprints on them (figure 2a-c). The construction workers set aside several large slabs for preservation and later study.

Depending on how the rock surfaces separated, the footprints could be seen as both indentations (molds in exposed surfaces) and bulges (casts on the under-surface of the overlying bed). One slab had bulges on one side and indentations on the other (figure 2a, b). The five large slabs, numbered A-E were mapped by the first author and show a complex pattern of footprints (figures 3A-E). Another slab, F, exhibits a single imprint measuring 23 by 28 centimeters which appears to display three large toes (figure 3F). Most of the other casts or molds did not show definite digits. Criss-crossing trackways make it difficult to determine the gait of the trackmakers with any confidence.

The sandstone blocks with the tracks appear to form part of the same sandstone layer noted in the original discovery.

Subsequent to the first author's mapping and photographing of the blocks, all three authors visited this locality. After examining the blocks, the first two authors became engaged in recovering a turtle carapace from a dry stream bed. The slope beyond also continued the outcrop of the Uinta Formation. While walking up it, the third author found himself looking down a row of more than twenty stone disks arranged in a left-right pattern (figure 2d). This unusual row of stone disks has been interpreted as coarse sand filling in the footprints of a large mammal crossing a mudflat. Recent erosion had exhumed the harder sandstone pads as the soft matrix eroded away from around them. This remarkable discovery is reported in detail elsewhere (Hamblin and others, 1998). Since very vulnerable to collectors or vandals, the disks have been removed and transferred to the Utah Field House of Natural History, Vernal, where it is hoped they will be shortly on display.

Owing to the large size of the various footprints found at this site, large ungulates (brontotheres, amynodonts, or uintatheres) appear likely candidates as trackmakers.

Figure 2a

Figure 2b

Figure 2c

Figure 2d

Figure 2. *Mammalian footprints from the lower Uinta Formation, Castle Peak Pocket; a-b: molds 2a and casts 2b on either side of the same block; c: closeup of a footprint; d: the 'Spalding' track: a row of weathered-out stone disks representing the trackway of a large animal.*

42DC130T - Castle Peak Draw Northwest

This small track site no longer exists. It was located southwest of Myton, Utah on an oil service road which later became the location for an underground pipeline (SW^1/$_4$ section 11, T.9S., R.16E., Salt Lake Base Line and Meridian). It consisted of a slab with possibly as many as nine small footprints, exposed on a surface that had been cleared for the road (figure 4). Four of the footprints appeared to line up in a left-right pattern,

forming part of a trackway. The slab was discovered late one afternoon just before sundown; the imprints were barely discernible the following day, when the light was overhead.

Each footprint is 6 centimeters in diameter, the pace being about 30 centimeters. No clear indications of toes or hooves were discerned, although several appear to be overstep impressions (both pedal and manual). The trackmaker might be any of a number of dog-sized animals, possibly a carnivore, an artiodactyl or a small

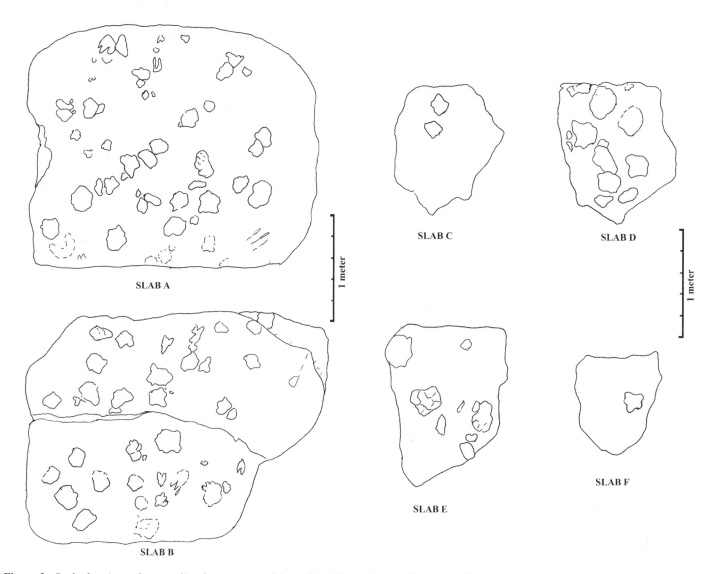

Figure 3. *Scale drawings of mammalian footprints on slabs at Castle Peak Pocket. See text for discussion.*

perissodactyl (horse or tapir).

Because this spot was to be destroyed by a pipeline trench, a rubber mold was made of the footprints and is stored at the Utah Field House of Natural History, Vernal. The site was monitored during trench excavation, but no additional tracks were found.

Site 42DC177TIVP - Wells Draw East

This track site is located 14.5 kilometers south and 6 kilometers west of Myton, Utah (NW1/4 section 4, T.9S., R.16E., Salt Lake Base Line and Meridian). The footprints occur in a limestone bed. The limestone layer also contains a few freshwater gastropods and ostracodes, as well as bird bone fragments. About 10 centimeters above the limestone layer is a thin-bedded sandstone with plant debris.

There appear to be at least three trackways of large mammals (amynodonts or brontotheres). They consist of sets of four to nine footprints, preserved as molds in the limestone surface (figure 5). The footprints are 60 to 90 centimeters apart and are round to oblong in shape, maximum elongation being perpendicular to the trackway midline. Average footprint diameter is about 20 centimeters (figure 5).

Site 42UN003 - Myton Pocket

These footprints occur as casts on the underside of a channel sandstone in the Myton Pocket (SW1/4 section 6, T.4S., R.1E., Uintah Base Line and Meridian). It should be stressed that land in the Myton Pocket is owned by the Ute Indian Tribe and one must have permission from the Tribe to visit this area. The square grid in figure 6 measures 1 x 1 meter. These bulges - surely casts of

Figure 4. *Mammalian footprints from the lower Uinta Formation, Castle Peak Draw Northwest.*

Figure 5. *Mammalian footprints from the lower Uinta Formation, Wells Draw East; a: looking north, along a series of tracks; b: looking south; three footprints may be seen.*

Figure 6. *Mammalian footprints casts on the underside of a channel sandstone, Myton Pocket.*

footprints - appear to form a left-right pattern in the bottom of an ancient stream channel. Other similar casts were seen in the immediate area.

An amynodont would be a good candidate for the trackmaker here. Osborn (1929) referred to *Amynodon* as "the aquatic rhinoceros," in that its habits and habitat are considered to have been similar to that of the modern hippopotamus, which spends most of its time in streams. However, it remains possible that some other large mammal, such as a brontothere, made the tracks.

Site 42UN805T - Ute Tribe, Cottonwood Wash #1

This site is likewise located on Tribal land; it is located in the NW¼ section 20, T.9S., R.21E., Salt Lake Base Line and Meridian. The tracks at this site consist of impressions in a sandstone layer along the side of a stream channel. Figures 7 and 8 comprise a scale drawing and photos of the site. The scale drawing (figure 7) was prepared by the three authors during a visit to the site with Tribal representative Leo Tapoof. It shows the tracks of at least three mammals, moving on a NNE - SSE line, and of at least two others crossing their path at right angles. Both manual and pedal imprints have a length and breadth of nearly equal dimensions and exhibit nothing to indicate front or back. Fifty-two footprints were measured, showing a range of 6 to 26 centimeters length and 6 to 24 centimeters breadth; averages are 16 centimeters length and 13 centimeters breadth. It appears likely that all the trackmakers belonged to a sin-

Figure 8. *Mammalian footprints at Cottonwood Wash tracksite no. 1; a, overall view; b, closeup of footprints.*

gle species. The considerable range of dimensions makes it likely that individuals of different ages (and thus, of different foot sizes) were present. There is nothing, however, to indicate the presence of more than one species and indeed, on average, the footprints at this site are all of medium size. They could have been made by any of a number of different ungulates, including small rhinoceroses, brontotheres and amynodonts.

Site 42UN866T - Ute Tribe, Cottonwood Wash #2

This sixth site also occurs on Ute Tribal land (at SE¼ section 20, T.9S., R.21E., Salt Lake Base Line and Meridian). The tracks occur in the bottom of a present-day stream channel, where erosion has exposed a layer of sandstone. There are two sections of tracks, separated by alluvium and eroded rock debris (see sketch map, figure 9). The distribution of the footprints in the two sections is shown on figures 10 and 11; they are illustrated on figure 12. The scale drawings were again prepared by the authors during a visit to the site with Leo Tapoof.

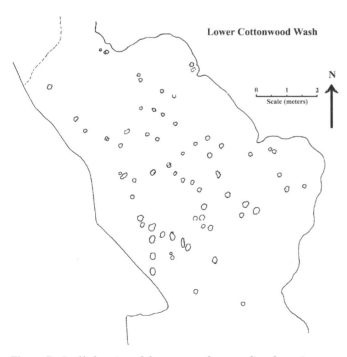

Figure 7. *Scale drawing of the pattern of mammalian footprints at Cottonwood Wash tracksite no. 1.*

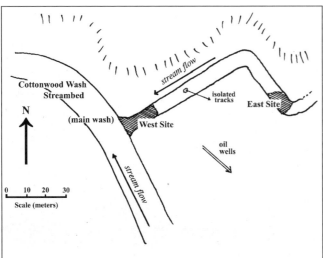

Figure 9. *Sketch map of Cottonwood Wash tracksite no. 2, showing the two exposures of the Uinta Formation in which abundant mammalian footprints occur.*

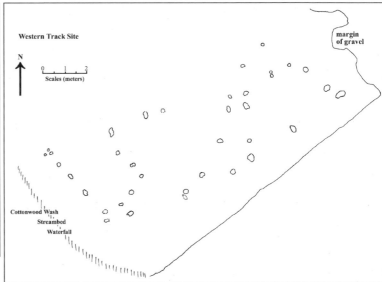

Figure 10. *Scale drawing of the west section, Cottonwood Wash tracksite.*

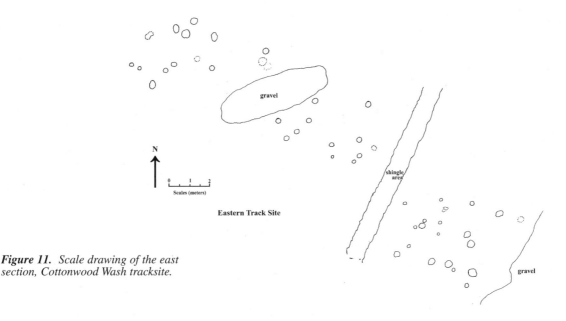

Figure 11. *Scale drawing of the east section, Cottonwood Wash tracksite.*

At the western end (figure 10), tracks of at least two types may be seen, one large and the other smaller. Twenty-seven footprints were measured. The smaller forms, represented by 9 footprints, measured 10 to 16 centimeters in length, average 14 centimeters; and 8 to 14 centimeters in breadth, average 10 centimeters. The remaining footprints, certainly representing more than one individual, ranged in length from 16 to 42 centimeters, average 26 centimeters; and in breadth from 15 to 30 centimeters, average 20 centimeters. The animals were moving in a circuitous fashion, as if feeding on vegetation of small height.

The pattern at the eastern end (figure 11) is less clear, but appears to indicate at least two large mammals and one that was smaller. Thirty-five footprints were measured. The length of the smaller footprints, 11 of which were measured, ranges from 12 to 19 centimeters, average 15 centimeters; and their breadth from 10 to 16 centimeters, average 13 centimeters. The length of the larger footprints ranges from 18 to 45 centimeters, average 32 centimeters; and their breadth from 16 to 40 centimeters, average 27 centimeters - a range larger than that seen at the western track site.

The larger tracks at these sites are surely those of ungulates, from their symmetry; it was again not possible to distinguish front from back. Amynodonts, brontotheres or uintatheres are all possible trackmakers. The smaller tracks, from their close association with the larger ones, may well represent juveniles of the same species.

Figure 12. *Mammalian footprints at Cottonwood tracksite no. 2; a, general view of the west section, looking downstream; b, two footprints from the west section in closeup.*

Site 42DC260VIT - Juniper Point East

This locality comprises a slab of sandstone found on a small hillside near the Juniper Point area at Starvation Reservoir (NE1/4 section 27, T.3S., R.5W., Salt Lake Base Line and Meridian), an area mapped by Bryant (1992) as Uinta Formation. The slab measures approximately 46 x 95 centimeters and exhibits at least six bird footprints (figure 13). These have a length of between 11 to 12 centimeters and a span between digits of 15 to 20 centimeters; the track pattern could not be discerned. The footprints compare well with *Gruipeda maxima* Panin and Avram (1962, p. 465, plate 13, figure 25); the trackmaker was probably a member of the Ciconiiformes (the herons and allies).

Site 42DC261PVT - Juniper Point West

This track site consists of a number of rocks washed out along the shore line of Starvation Reservoir (NW1/4 and NE 1/4 section 27, T.3S., R.5W., Salt Lake Base Line and Meridian). It is mapped as Uinta Formation by

Figure 13. *Bird tracks (*Gruipeda maxima *Panin and Avram) in a slab from Juniper Point East, probably from the Uinta Formation.*

Bryant (1992), but has the appearance of a tongue of the Green River Formation, consisting of green shales and sandstones.

Three blocks were found which present quite obvious tracks. The first block (figure 14a) has a small trackway of three bird footprints, each about 3 centimeters in length and almost 4 centimeters in span from digit tip to digit tip, plus an isolated print of the same type. These footprints are closely comparable with *Avipeda* aff. *phoenix* of Sarjeant and Langston (1994, p. 13, plates 9, 14, text-figures 10-11). There is also one larger bird footprint, about 7 centimeters in length and about 10 centimeters in span; this compares well with *Gruipeda intermedia* Panin (1965, p. 147, figure 3). Both types of footprints would have been made by shorebirds, but the constancy of footprint type makes closer identification of such birds impossible.

The second block (figure 14b) exhibits two tracks as bulges (casts) on the underside; these measure about 12 centimeters in length and 13 centimeters in span. They appear attributable to *Fuscinapeda texana* Sarjeant and Langston (1994, p. 15-16, plate 10, text-figures 12-13), considered to have been probably made by a member of the Ciconiiformes (the herons and allies).

The third block (figure 14c) has a rather odd mammalian footprint with three digits; it is again preserved as a cast on the undersurface of the rock. Its length is about 11.5 centimeters, its breadth about 7.5 centimeters. No similar footprints have been yet described; the trackmaker may have been an early horse or tapir.

Site 42DC270VPT - Southwest of Park Headquarters

A rock exposure in a shallow gully southwest of the Starvation State Park headquarters presents a number of

*Figure 14. Bird and mammal footprints from Juniper Point West, probably from the Uinta Formation. a, bird footprints (*Gruipeda intermedia *Panin), b, bird footprints (*Fuscinapeda texana *Sarjeant and Langston), c, mammalian footprint, probably of a perissodactyl.*

circular depressions filled with sediment from the layer above. They vary from 14 to 20 centimeters in diameter (figure 15).

The depressions were too numerous, and the gully bottom too narrow, to distinguish any trackways, but the area around the site could quite readily be cleared

Figure 15. The pattern of depressions (perhaps footprints?) southwest of park headquarters, Starvation State Park; a, oblique view; b, near-vertical view.

to expose a large flat surface, upon which their pattern might be determined. Footprints of this size - if indeed these are footprints - might have been made by amynodonts or brontotheres.

Site 42UN567T - West of Halfway Hollow, North of US 40

This site is in the Brennan Basin Member of the Duchesne River Formation. The location is about 16 km southwest of Vernal, Utah (NW 1/4 section 4, T.6S., R.20E., Salt Lake Base Line and Meridian). It consists of two or three possible footprint molds in the surface of a sandstone block and two possible footprints visible in vertical cross section. Figures 16a and 16b show the two

Figure 16. *Depressions in the Brennan Basin Member of the Duchesne River Formation, west of Half-way Hollow, resembling mammalian footprints; a, closeup of one depression; b, oblique view of surface; c, sectional view showing deformation of sand layers.*

footprint-like depressions in the sandstone block; one of these has three lobes, apparently representing three-hooved toes. If this interpretation is correct, the trackmaker was possibly an amynodont or some other medium-sized perissodactyl.

Cross sections of the molds (figure 16c) show vertical deformation of the layers of sand, similar to those seen in tracks described by Loope (1986).

CONCLUSIONS

These 10 sites illustrate the potential for discovering vertebrate footprints in the Uinta and Duchesne River Formations. Several other, more dubious sites have also been documented by the first author. Much more work is needed to properly evaluate all of these sites. However, the present information indicates an Eocene fauna comprising, at least, large and medium-size ungulates (probably including amynodonts and brontotheres), large wading birds and smaller shorebirds.

Researchers working in the Tertiary formations of the Uinta Basin should be aware of the potential of discovering footprints while undertaking surveys and other geological work.

ACKNOWLEDGMENTS

The work of the first author (A. H. H.) was undertaken during his employment at the Utah Field House of Natural History State Park, Vernal, Utah. That of the second author (W. A. S. S.) was undertaken while on sabbatical leave from the University of Saskatchewan. We would all like to offer our thanks to Mrs. Linda Dietz, research assistant to W. A. S. S., for aid in the preparation of the footprint site maps, and to the members of the Ute Tribe for permission to undertake geological studies on their lands.

REFERENCES

Andersen, D. W., and Picard, M. D., 1972, Stratigraphy of the Duchesne River Formation (Eocene-Oligocene?), northern Uinta Basin, northeastern Utah: Utah Geological and Mineralogical Survey Bulletin, v. 97, 29 p.

Bryant, Bruce, 1992, Geologic and structure maps of the Salt Lake City 1° X 2° Quadrangle, Utah and Wyoming: U.S. Geological Survey Miscellaneous Investigations Series, Map I-1997, scale 1:125,000.

Bryant, Bruce, Naeser, C. W., Marvin, R. F., and Mehnert, H. H., 1989, Upper Cretaceous and Paleogene sedimentary rocks and isotopic ages of Paleogene Tuffs, Uinta Basin, Utah: U.S. Geological Survey Bulletin 1787J, 22 p.

Curry, H. D., 1957, Fossil tracks of Eocene vertebrates, southwestern Uinta Basin, Utah: Eighth Annual Field Conference, Intermountain Association of Petroleum Geologists, p. 42-47.

Erickson, B. R., 1967, Fossil bird tracks from Utah: Museum Observer, v. 5, p. 6-12.

Hamblin, A. H., 1987, Paleogeography and paleoecology of the Myton Pocket, Uinta Basin, Utah (Uinta Formation - Upper Eocene): Brigham Young University Geology Studies, v. 34, p. 33-60.

—1994, Paleontology report of well location and access road on PGandE 21~8H, NE/NW sec. 8, T9S, R17E, SLB and M, Duchesne County, Utah: Ogden, Utah, unpublished report for Sagebrush Archaeological Consultants.

Hamblin, A. H., and Bilbey, S. A., 1999, Track site in Navajo-Nugget Sandstone, Red Fleet Reservoir, Uintah Co., Utah, *in* Gillette, D. D., editor, this volume.

Hamblin, A. H., Sarjeant, W. A. S., and Spalding, D. A. E., 1998, A remarkable mammal trackway in the Uinta Formation (Late Eocene) of Utah: Brigham Young University Geology Studies, v. 43, p. 9-18.

Hintze, L. F., 1988, Geologic history of Utah: Brigham Young University Geology Studies, Special Publication, no. 7, 202 p.

Kay, J. L., 1934, The Tertiary formations of the Uinta Basin, Utah: Carnegie Museum Annals, v. 23, p. 357-372.

Lockley, M. G., Conrad, Kelly, Paquette, Michelle, and Hamblin, A. H., 1992, Late Triassic vertebrate tracks in the Dinosaur National Monument area, *in* Wilson, J. R., editor, Field guide to geological excursions in Utah and adjacent areas of Nevada, Idaho, and Wyoming: Utah Geological Survey, Miscellaneous Publication, no. 92-3, p. 383-390.

Lockley, M. G., Conrad, Kelly, Paquette, Michelle, and Farlow, J. O., Jr., 1992, Distribution and significance of Mesozoic vertebrate trace fossils in Dinosaur National Monument: Sixteenth Annual Report of the National Park Service Research Center, University of Wyoming, p. 74-85.

Lockley, M. G., and Hunt, A. P., 1995, Dinosaur tracks and other fossil footprints of the western United States: New York, Columbia University Press, 338 p.

Loope, D. B., 1986, Recognizing and utilizing vertebrate tracks in the cross section: Cenozoic hoofprints from Nebraska: Palaios, v. 1, p. 141-151.

Osborn, H. F., 1929, The titanotheres of ancient Wyoming, Dakota and Nebraska: U.S. Geological Survey Monograph 55, 953 p.

Panin, N., 1965, Coexistence de traces de pas de vertébrés et des mécanoglyphes dans la molasse Miocène des Carpates Orientales: Revue Roumaine de Géologie, Géophysique et Géographie, v. 9, p. 141-163.

Panin, N., and Avram, E., 1962, Noe urme de vertebrate in Mioconul Subcaptatilor Romineşti: Studii şi Cercetări de Geologie, v. 7, p. 455-484.

Peabody, F. E., 1948, Reptile and amphibian trackways from the Lower Triassic Moenkopi Formation of Arizona and Utah: University of California Bulletin of Geological Science, v. 28, p. 295-468.

Peterson, O. A., 1895, Fossil mammals of the Uinta Basin, *in* Expedition of 1895: Bulletin of the American Museum of Natural History, v. 7, p. 71-105.

Peterson O. A., and Kay, J. L., 1931, The Upper Uinta Formation of northeastern Utah: Carnegie Museum Annals, v. 20, p. 293-306.

Prothero, D. R., and Swisher, C. C., III, 1992, Magnetostratigraphy and geochronology of terrestrial Eocene-Oligocene transition in North America, *in* Prothero, D. R., and Berggren, W. A., editors, Eocene-Oligocene climatic and biotic evolution: Princeton, New Jersey, Princeton University Press, p. 46-74.

—1996, Magnetic stratigraphy and biostratigraphy of the Middle Eocene Uinta Formation, Uinta Basin, Utah, *in* Prothero, D. R. and Emry, R. J., editors, The Terrestrial Eocene-Oligocene transition in North America: New York, Cambridge University Press, p. 3-24.

Sarjeant, W. A. S., and Langston, Wann, Jr., 1994, Vertebrate footprints and invertebrate traces from the Chadronian (Late Eocene) of Trans-Pecos Texas: Texas Memorial Museum Bulletin, no. 36, 86 p.

Sarjeant, W. A. S., and Reynolds, R. E., 1997a, Camelid and horse footprints from the Miocene of California: San Bernardino County Museum Association Quarterly (in press).

—1997b, Bird footprints from the Miocene of California: San Bernardino County Museum Association Quarterly (in press).

Scrivner, P. J., and Bottjer, D. J., 1986, Neogene avian and mammalian tracks from Death Valley National Monument, California-their context, classification and preservation: Palaeogeography, Palaeoclimatology, Palaeoecology, v. 57, p. 285-331.

Untermann, G. E., and Untermann, B. R., 1949, Geology of Green and Yampa River Canyons and vicinity, Dinosaur National Monument, Utah and Colorado: Bulletin of the American Association of Petroleum Geologists, v. 33, p. 683-394.

Untermann, G. E., and Untermann, B. R., 1954, Geology of Dinosaur National Monument and vicinity, Utah Colorado: Utah Geological and Mineral Survey Bulletin 42, 228 p.

COMMENTS ON AMPHIBIANS FROM THE GREEN RIVER FORMATION, WITH A DESCRIPTION OF A FOSSIL TADPOLE

James D. Gardner

Department of Biological Sciences and Laboratory for Vertebrate Paleontology,
University of Alberta, Edmonton, Alberta, Canada T6G 2E9
E-mail:gardner@odum.biology.ualberta.ca

ABSTRACT

Eocene lacustrine sediments of the Green River Formation, western United States (U. S.), have yielded several amphibian fossils, including skeletons of metamorphosed salamanders and frogs. An indeterminate, pond-type tadpole described herein from Utah is the second amphibian fossil to be described in detail from the Green River Formation and the only larval specimen reported from these deposits. The small sample of amphibian fossils now available from the Green River Formation demonstrates that this unit is a potentially important source of fossils for documenting and interpreting the history of North American Eocene amphibians.

INTRODUCTION

The Green River Formation is a series of predominantly lacustrine deposits exposed in southwestern Wyoming, northeastern Utah, and northwestern Colorado (MacGinitie, 1969, figure 1; here, figure 1). These sediments were deposited in three lake basins (Fossil Lake and lakes Gosiute, and Uinta), under warm temperate to subtropical conditions from the late Paleocene (Clarkforkian) to late Eocene (Uintan) (Bradley, 1931, 1964; MacGinitie, 1969; McGrew and Casilliano, 1975; Grande, 1984, 1994; Grande and Buchheim, 1994). The Green River Formation is justifiably famous for having yielded abundant, well-preserved fossils of Eocene plants, invertebrates, and fishes, and a limited number of tetrapod fossils (see Grande, 1984, and references therein). Compared to other tetrapods, amphibians are poorly represented in the Green River Formation. The only published fossils from these deposits are: a presumably metamorphosed frog from Wyoming that was briefly described by Cope (1882, 1883); two metamorphosed frogs, one each from Wyoming and Colorado, briefly discussed and figured by Grande (1984); and an articulated salamander skeleton from Wyoming that was briefly discussed and figured by Grande and Buchheim (1994). Recently discovered fossils of a metamorphosed frog in Colorado and a tadpole in Utah add to the small, but growing list of amphibian fossils from the Green River Formation. As amphibians are not well known from contemporaneous deposits elsewhere in North America, fossils from the Green River Formation are potentially useful for examining the evolutionary history of North American amphibians during the Eocene Epoch. Here I review and comment on the amphibians from the Green River Formation and describe the fossil tadpole from Utah.

Institutional abbreviations used in this paper are: Black Hills Institute of Geological Research, Hill City, South Dakota (BHI-GR); Natural History Museum [formerly the British Museum (Natural History)], London (BMNH); Carnegie Museum of Natural History, Pittsburgh (CM); Denver Museum of Natural History, Denver (DMNH); Field Museum of Natural History, Chicago (FMNH); and University of Florida, Gainesville (UF). Stratigraphic nomenclature and age estimates for members in the Green River Formation follow Grande (1984, figure I.5). Terminology for localities "F-2," "G-1, G-3, and G-4," and "U-2" follows Grande (1984) and for separate "F-2" quarries follows Grande and Buchheim (1994, appendix).

LOCALITIES

At least eight localities in the Green River Formation have yielded amphibian fossils (figure 1). In alphabetical order, these sites are: *DMNH locality 304* (= "site B" of Dayvault and others, 1995), upper Eocene Parachute Creek Member, "Lake Uinta," Rio Blanco County, Colorado (Logan Ivy, written communication, 1996); *F-2*, includes several quarries, such as F-2H, that are geographically and stratigraphically close to one another (Grande and Buchheim, 1994, figure 4 and appendix), lower Eocene Fossil Butte Member, "Fossil Lake," Lincoln County, Wyoming (Grande, 1984; Grande and Buchheim, 1994); *G-1*, middle Eocene Laney Member, "Lake Gosiute," Lincoln County, Wyoming (Grande, 1984, 1994); *G-3* (= "Petrified Fish Cut" locality of Hay-

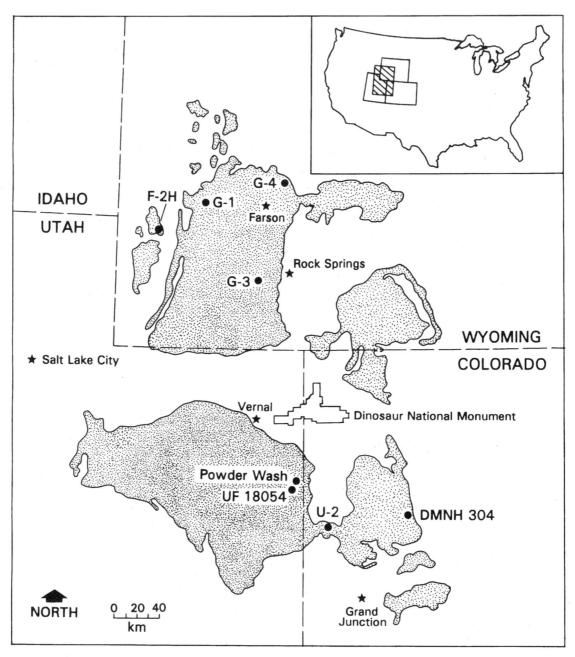

Figure 1. *Map depicting outcrops of the Green River Formation (stippled) and localities (solid circles) that have yielded amphibian fossils (modified from Grande, 1984, figure I.4; Grande and Buchheim, 1994, figures 1B, 4). Map in upper right of the continental United States depicts area (cross-hatched) shown in larger map. See text and cited references for information on localities.*

den, 1872), middle Eocene Laney Member, "Lake Gosiute," Sweetwater County, Wyoming (Grande, 1984, 1994); *G-4*, middle Eocene Laney Member, "Lake Gosiute," Sweetwater County, Wyoming (Grande, 1984, 1994); *UF locality 18054*, upper Eocene Evacuation Creek Member, "Lake Uinta," Uintah County, Utah (see below); *U-2* (= "Raydome" locality of Durden and Rose, 1978), upper Eocene Parachute Creek Member, "Lake Uinta," Douglas Pass, Garfield and Rio Blanco counties, Colorado (Durden and Rose, 1978; Grande, 1984); and *Powder Wash locality* (= "Powder Springs" locality of

Gazin, 1958), middle Eocene Douglas Creek Member, "Lake Uintah," Uintah County, Utah (Dawson, 1968).

AMPHIBIAN FOSSILS PREVIOUSLY REPORTED FROM THE GREEN RIVER FORMATION

According to Grande (1984), fragmentary fossils of salamanders have been collected by private collectors at localities G-1, U-2, and unspecified F-2 sites. None of these specimens have been described, and they evidently remain in private collections. The only other salamander fossil that I am aware of from the Green River Formation is a nearly complete, articulated skeleton, FMNH PR1810, of an amphiumid (Grande and Buchheim, 1994, figure 14A) from locality F-2H. This fossil pertains to a new genus (Rieppel and Grande, 1998) and it is the most nearly complete fossil amphiumid yet discovered; hence it may provide insights into the intra- and interfamilial relationships of the Amphiumidae. The discovery of an amphiumid fossil in the Green River Formation is consistent with the documented temporal and paleobiogeographic range of this family, which elsewhere is known from the Campanian to Miocene of the Western Interior and Pleistocene to Recent of the southeastern U. S. (Estes, 1969, 1981; Duellman and Trueb, 1986). The F-2 localities are interpreted as occurring in nearshore lacustrine deposits (Grande and Buchheim, 1994), suggesting that FMNH PR1810 was collected from a depositional environment similar to the shallow, quiet, murky waters favored by extant amphiumids (Baker, 1945; Salthe, 1973a, b; Conant, 1975).

Fossils of frogs are somewhat better represented than those of salamanders in the Green River Formation. The earliest report of a frog from this unit was by Cope (1882, 1883), who provided the following account (Cope, 1882, p. 979): "The vertebral column and part of the cranium of a probably incompletely developed tailless batrachian, were procured by Dr. F. V. Hayden, from the fish shales of the Green River epoch, from near Green River City, Wyoming. They are not sufficiently characteristic to enable me to determine the relation of the species to known forms." I can add nothing to Cope's description and interpretation because this fossil has never been figured and I have not been able to locate it in any museum collection. Given that Cope occasionally described fossils from private collections (E. B. Daeschler, verbal communication, 1996), this frog fossil may not have been deposited in an institutional collection. Grande's (1984) suggestion that this specimen may have been collected from locality G-3 seems reasonable because this site is located about three kilometers west of Green River, Wyoming, and it was the source for many of the fish fossils that Hayden supplied to Cope (Knight, 1955). This frog fossil is historically interesting, because it was the first amphibian fossil to be reported from the Green River Formation and at the time of its description it was the geologically oldest known anuran fossil.

Grande (1984) reported two additional frog fossils from the Green River Formation. Specimen BHI-GR 123 is an exquisitely preserved fossil of an articulated, metamorphosed frog (Grande, 1984, figure III.1a) from locality G-4. Like many of the vertebrate fossils from G-4 (Grande, 1984), BHI-GR 123 is preserved largely as a natural cast. Grande (1984) identified this specimen as a probable new species of *Eopelobates*, a pelobatoid (*sensu* Ford and Cannatella, 1993) genus that is reliably known from the early Eocene to Pliocene of North America and Eurasia (Estes, 1970; Henrici, 1994). Lance Grande and D. C. Cannatella will describe this fossil elsewhere (Lance Grande, verbal communication, 1996). The second frog reported by Grande (1984) consists of the part (private collection) and counterpart (BMNH uncatalogued specimen) of the skin impressions of a small, metamorphosed frog (Grande, 1984, figure III.1b) from locality U-2. Grande (1984) suggested that this frog may also be referable to *Eopelobates*.

Johnson and Stucky (1995, p. 112-113) recently figured a moderately well preserved, incomplete skeleton of a metamorphosed frog, DMNH 15013, from DMNH locality 304. Although this locality has produced abundant fossils of plants and arthropods (Dayvault and others, 1995), to my knowledge DMNH 15013 is the only vertebrate fossil from this site. This fossil is currently on display in the DMNH's "Prehistoric Journey" gallery (Logan Ivy, written communication, 1996).

Grande (1984) and Krishtalka and Stucky (1984) reported unidentified amphibian fossils in the CM collections from the Powder Wash locality, a richly fossiliferous site most notable for its taxonomically diverse assemblage of early Bridgerian mammals (see Krishtalka and Stucky, 1984, and references therein). Finally, it is worth noting that because the Green River Formation has been worked by private and commercial collectors since at least the late 1800's (Hesse, 1939; Grande, 1984), additional amphibian fossils not considered here exist in private collections (Lance Grande, written communication, 1997).

A FOSSIL TADPOLE, PREVIOUSLY UNKNOWN FROM THE GREEN RIVER FORMATION

Systematic Paleontology

Anura *incertae sedis*

Specimen

UF 143200, incomplete body fossil (figure 2).

Horizon and Locality

Middle Eocene Evacuation Creek Member, Green River Formation; UF locality 18054, fossil "Lake Uinta," near the ghost town of Watson, Uintah County, Utah (figure 1). Locality coordinates are on file at the UF. This

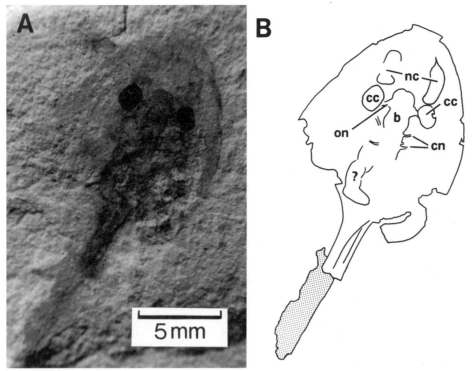

Figure 2. *Anura* incertae sedis*; tadpole fossil, UF 143200, from the upper Eocene Evacuation Creek Member, Green River Formation, Utah. A, photograph and B, camera lucida interpretive drawing of fossil. Anterior of fossil is towards upper right. Abbreviations: b = brain; cc = choroid coat of eye; cn = unidentified cranial nerves; nc = nasal capsule; on = optic nerve; and ? = unidentified structure that may represent part of the intestine. Stippled area is indistinct smear that probably represents the distal part of the tail.*

indistinct traces in the snout region (see figure 2A) may represent other structures of the mouth (Ronald Altig, written communication, 1997), but I have not been able to interpret these with any confidence. Traces of internal structures that can be reliably identified are: the choroid coat of the large paired eyes, the brain, several pairs of cranial nerves, and the nasal capsules.

Discussion

I identify UF 143200 as a tadpole based on its large ovoid body, elongate and laterally compressed tail, and traces of the internal structures listed above. More diagnostic tadpole features, such as a spiracle, tightly coiled intestine, keratinous oral denticles and beak, 11 or fewer trunk vertebrae, and ossified, characteristically shaped exoccipitals, frontoparietals, and parasphenoid are not preserved in UF 143200. Many of the soft and skeletal features noted above, whether preserved or not in UF 143200, have been described by Špinar (1972), Estes and others (1978), and Wassersug and Wake (1995) in exceptionally well-preserved tadpole fossils from the Old World.

I cannot determine the familial or generic identity of UF 143200 because features such as the form and arrangement of mouthparts, the positions of the mouth, vent, and spiracle, and the shape of the tail, which are diagnostic at lower taxonomic levels for tadpoles (see Orton, 1952, 1957; Altig, 1970; Lynch, 1973; Starrett, 1973; Sokol, 1975; Wassersug, 1980), are not preserved or cannot confidently be identified in the fossil. The lack of oral sensory barbels, if not a preservational artifact, excludes UF 143200 from the Palaeobatrachidae, Pipidae, and Rhinophrynidae because larvae in these families have oral barbels (Lynch, 1973). The body shape and dorsally placed eyes also exclude UF 143200 from the latter two families (Ronald Altig, written communication, 1997). The specimen's large ovoid body is typical of a generalized pond-type tadpole (Duellman and Trueb, 1986, figure 6-12), a form found in at least ten families of frogs (Duellman and Trueb, 1986). Among North America anuran families having pond-type tadpoles, UF 143200 most closely resembles pelobatid *sensu lato*, bufonid, and ranid tadpoles (for example, Stebbins, 1985,

locality has also yielded a modest collection of undescribed fossil plants (S. R. Manchester, written communication, 1996) and insects.

Desciption

Specimen UF 143200 is preserved on a 14 x 14 cm slab of fine-grained, horizontally and finely laminated, buff-colored shale, on the same bedding plane, or nearly so, with a fossil of an ichneumonoid wasp (J. H. Acorn, verbal communication, 1994). The former fossil is dorsoventrally flattened and preserved as a carbonized film of soft tissues that lacks any trace of bone (figure 2A). This soft-bodied preservation is typical of vertebrate fossils from some "Lake Uinta" sites (Grande, 1984), and does not indicate that UF 143200 died before its skeleton began ossifying. The outline of UF 143200 is incomplete, but it clearly represents an animal with a rotund, ovoid body that is narrower anteriorly than posteriorly and a narrow, evidently elongate, laterally compressed tail that is incomplete distally (figure 2B). The fossil is about 18.5 mm long, although the animal was undoubtedly longer when alive. No limbs are evident. Anteriorly, a short flap of tissue, probably part of the oral disc, extends beyond the remainder of the body's outline, suggesting that the mouth was more or less terminal (Ronald Altig, written communication, 1997). Dark,

figures 37, 38, and 40) in having large, dorsally placed eyes that are located well medial to the lateral margins of the head, but it cannot reliably be referred to any of these families. Bufonids and ranids are unknown in North America until the Miocene (Holman, 1995), but there are several reports of Eocene pelobatids from the continent (Hecht, 1959; Holman, 1968; Estes, 1970; Golz and Lillegraven, 1977), including two metamorphosed specimens (Grande, 1984, figures III.1a, b) from the Green River Formation.

A variety of schemes may be used to estimate a tadpole's relative age, based on its ontogenetic stage of development (see Duellman and Trueb, 1986, table 5-6). Gosner's (1960) table of development is most appropriate for staging UF 143200 because his scheme is not species-specific and it is based on external features. The latter is an important consideration because some developmental tables rely at least in part on ossification sequences, information that is not accessible for UF 143200. If the absence of hind limbs from UF 143200 is real and not an artifact of preservation – for example, limbs drifted away or obscured by body – then the tadpole apparently died relatively early in its development, prior to Gosner's (1960) stages 30 to 35 when hind limbs become prominent. By contrast, most previously described fossil tadpoles are later stage individuals that bear prominent hind- and forelimbs (however, see Špinar, 1972, text figure 73; Estes and others, 1978, figure 12; Wassersug and Wake, 1995, figures 1 and 2).

The relatively large and ovoid body of UF 143200 suggests that this individual was a pond-type tadpole adapted to life in relatively still water, conditions that were probably the norm in fossil "Lake Uinta." The dorsally placed eyes further suggest that this tadpole was primarily benthic. In the absence of any well-preserved mouthparts or branchial arches, nothing can be interpreted about the feeding strategy of this individual.

Specimen UF 143200 and the associated wasp are relatively intact and undistorted. Comparisons with decay sequences of carcasses of extant metamorphosed frogs (Wuttke, 1983) and insects (Martínez-Delclòs and Martinell, 1993) in freshwater suggest that the tadpole and wasp were buried rapidly after death, prior to the onset of substantial decay and disturbance by scavengers. The fine-grained, horizontally laminated shale in which these fossils are preserved suggests deposition in relatively quiet water, such as in a lake or on a floodplain (Picard and High, 1972). Both of these depositional environments are represented in the Green River Formation and have yielded well-preserved vertebrate fossils (Grande, 1984; Ferber and Wells, 1995). The absence on the slab of mudcracks or raindrops suggests that the sediments were submerged, and the lack of ripple marks, which are sedimentological structures formed by waves (Bucher, 1919), suggests that deposition probably occurred somewhat offshore below the wave base. An offshore depositional model for UF 143200 is also supported by observations that vertebrate carcasses in lacustrine sediments tend to be more nearly complete in offshore deposits, whereas those in nearshore environments are typically disarticulated and scattered by waves and scavengers (Wilson, 1980, 1993; Ferber and Wells, 1995).

Fossil tadpoles are rare, and they are reliably known only from the Cretaceous and Eocene to Miocene (Gardner, 1996). The discovery in the Green River Formation of a fossil tadpole, the only larval amphibian reported from these deposits, is consequently notable, although it is not unexpected because fossils of metamorphosed frogs have been collected from other sites in the unit. The only other North American fossil tadpoles are late-stage rhinophrynids from the middle to upper Eocene Wagon Bed Formation, Wyoming (Henrici, 1991), and undescribed, possible pelodytids from the middle Miocene Elko shales, Nevada (T. M. Cavender, personal communication to A. C. Henrici, in Henrici, 1994, p. 157).

CONCLUSIONS

The small number of amphibian fossils that have been collected from the Green River Formation demonstrate that this unit is a potentially important source of fossils for interpreting the Eocene history of North American amphibians. Discoveries of articulated skeletons of salamanders and frogs, fossils that are rare in other North American Eocene deposits, are particularly encouraging because such well-preserved fossils typically provide a wealth of phylogenetic information. The co-occurrence of fossils of larval and metamorphosed amphibians in the Green River Formation is also of interest because both life stages can contribute to our understanding of life histories and phylogenies. Further exploration of the Green River Formation will undoubtedly yield additional amphibian fossils of scientific interest.

ACKNOWLEDGMENTS

I thank A. G. Gardner for riding shotgun on our road trip to Gainesville; Vic Call for unwittingly bringing UF 143200 to my attention; S. R. Manchester and S. D. Webb for the loan of UF 143200 and locality information; J. H. Acorn for identifying the wasp; Logan Ivy for information about DMNH 15013; M. W. Webb for swiftly delivering a critical photocopy; G. E. Ball, E. B. Daeschler, R. C. Fox, A. C. Henrici, S. R. Manchester, B. G. Naylor, R. J. Wassersug, and M. V. H. Wilson for their comments on the many earlier versions of this paper, and Ronald Altig and Lance Grande for their reviews of the submitted version; and D. D. Gillette for the opportunity to participate in this volume. Funding has been provided to me by a University of Alberta Ph. D. Recruitment Scholarship and Dissertation Fellowship, Province of Alberta Scholarship, an Andrew Stewart Memorial Prize, and some indulgent relatives. I thank N. J. Marklund for all her support.

REFERENCES

Altig, Ronald, 1970, A key to the tadpoles of the continental United States and Canada: Herpetologica, v. 26, no. 2, p. 180-207.

Baker, C. L., 1945, The natural history and morphology of Amphiumidae: Journal of the Tennessee Academy of Science, v. 20, no. 1, p. 55-91.

Bradley, W. H., 1931, Origin and microfossils of the oil shale of the Green River Formation of Colorado and Utah: United States Geological Survey Professional Paper 168, p. 1-56.

—1964, Geology of Green River Formation and associated Eocene rocks in southwestern Wyoming and adjacent parts of Colorado and Utah: United States Geological Survey Professional Paper 496-A, p. 1-86.

Bucher, W. H., 1919, On ripples and related sedimentary surface forms and their paleogeographic interpretation. Part I. The origin of ripples and related sedimentary surface forms: American Journal of Science, series 4, v. 47, no. 279, p. 149-210.

Conant, Roger, 1975, A field guide to reptiles and amphibians of eastern and central North America, 2nd Edition: Boston, Houghton Mifflin Co., 429 p.

Cope, E. D., 1882, The reptiles of the American Eocene: American Naturalist, v. 16, no. 12, p. 979-993.

—1883, The Vertebrata of the Tertiary formations of the West: United States Geological Survey of the Territories, v. 3, p. 1-1009.

Dawson, M. R., 1968, Middle Eocene rodents (Mammalia) from northeastern Utah: Annals of Carnegie Museum, v. 39, p. 327-370.

Dayvault, R. D., Codington, L. A., Kohls, David, Hawes, W. D., and Ott, P. M., 1995, Fossil insects and spiders from three locations in the Green River Formation of the Piceance Creek Basin, Colorado: The Green River Formation in Piceance Creek and Eastern Uinta Basins Field Trip Guidebook, Grand Junction Geological Society, p. 97-115.

Duellman, W. E., and Trueb, Linda, 1986, Biology of Amphibians: New York, McGraw-Hill, Inc., 670 p.

Durden, C. J., and Rose, Hugh, 1978, Butterflies from the middle Eocene: the earliest occurrence of fossil Papilionoidea (Lepidoptera): The Peace-Sellards Series, Texas Memorial Museum, no. 29, p. 1-25.

Estes, Richard, 1969, The fossil record of amphiumid salamanders: Breviora, no. 322, p. 1-11.

—1970, New fossil pelobatid frogs and a review of the genus *Eopelobates*: Bulletin of the Museum of Comparative Zoology, v. 139, no. 6, p. 293-340.

—1981, Gymnophiona, Caudata, *in* Wellnhofer, Peter, editor, Encyclopedia of paleoherpetology, v. 2: Stuttgart, Gustav Fischer Verlag, p. 115.

Estes, Richard, Špinar, Z. V., and Nevo, Eviator, 1978, Early Cretaceous pipid tadpoles from Israel (Amphibia: Anura): Herpetologica, v. 34, no. 4, p. 374-393.

Ferber, C. T., and Wells, N. A., 1995, Paleolimnology and taphonomy of some fish deposits in "Fossil" and "Uinta" lakes of the Eocene Green River Formation, Utah and Wyoming: Palaeogeography, Palaeoclimatology, Palaeoecology, v. 117, no. 3-4, p. 185-210.

Ford, L. S., and Cannatella, D. C., 1993, The major clades of frogs: Herpetological Monographs, v. 7, p. 94-117.

Gardner, J. D., 1996, Comments on the fossil record of tadpoles: Abstracts of Papers, 56th Annual Meeting, Society of Vertebrate Paleontology, Journal of Vertebrate Paleontology, v. 16 (supplement to no. 3), p. 36A.

Gazin, C. L., 1958, A review of the middle and upper Eocene primates of North America: Smithsonian Miscellaneous Collections, v. 136, no. 1, p. 1-112.

Golz, D. J., and Lillegraven, J. A., 1977, Summary of known occurrences of terrestrial vertebrates from Eocene strata of southern California: Contributions to Geology, University of Wyoming, v. 15, no. 1, p. 43-65.

Gosner, K. L., 1960, A simplified table for staging anuran embryos and larvae with notes on identification: Herpetologica, v. 16, no. 3, p. 183-190.

Grande, Lance, 1984, Paleontology of the Green River Formation, with a review of the fish fauna, 2nd edition: Geological Survey of Wyoming Bulletin 63, p. 1-333.

—1994, Studies of paleoenvironments and historical biogeography in the Fossil Butte and Laney members of the Green River Formation: Contributions to Geology, University of Wyoming, v. 30, no. 1, p. 15-32.

Grande, Lance, and Buchheim, H. P., 1994, Paleontological and sedimentological variation in early Eocene Fossil Lake: Contributions to Geology, University of Wyoming, v. 30, no. 1, p. 33-56.

Hayden, F. V., 1872, Preliminary report of the United States Geological Survey of Wyoming and portions of contiguous territories: United States Geological and Geographical Survey of the Territories, Fourth Annual Report, p. 511.

Hecht, M. K., 1959, Amphibians and reptiles, *in* McGrew, P. O., Berman, J. E., Hecht, M. K., Hummel, J. M., Simpson, G. G., and Wood, A. E., authors, The geology and paleontology of the Elk Mountain and Tabernacle Butte area, Wyoming: Bulletin of the American Museum of Natural History, v. 117, no. 3, p. 130-146.

Henrici, A. C., 1991, *Chelomophrynus bayi* (Amphibia, Anura, Rhinophrynidae), a new genus and species from the middle Eocene of Wyoming: ontogeny and relationships: Annals of Carnegie Museum, v. 60, no. 2, p. 97-144.

—1994, *Tephrodytes brassicarvalis*, new genus and species (Anura: Pelodytidae), from the Arikareean Cabbage Patch Beds of Montana, USA, and pelodytid-pelobatid relationships: Annals of Carnegie Museum, v. 63, no. 2, p. 155-183.

Hesse, C. J., 1939, Fossil fish localities in the Green River Eocene of Wyoming: The Scientific Monthly, v. 48 (February), p. 147-151.

Holman, J. A., 1968, Lower Oligocene amphibians from Saskatchewan: Quarterly Journal of the Florida Academy of Sciences, v. 31, no. 4, p. 273-289.

—1995, Pleistocene amphibians and reptiles in North America: New York, Oxford University Press, 243 p.

Johnson, K. R., and Stucky, R. K., 1995, Prehistoric journey; a history of life on Earth: Boulder, Roberts Rhinehart Publishers, 144 p.

Knight, S. H., 1955, Review of the early geological explorations of the Green River Basin area 1812-1879: Wyoming Geological Association Guidebook, Tenth Annual Field Conference, p. 10-18.

Krishtalka, Leonard, and Stucky, R. K., 1984, Middle Eocene marsupials (Mammalia) from northeastern Utah, and the mammalian fauna from Powder Wash: Annals of Carnegie Museum, v. 53, p. 31-45.

Lynch, J. D., 1973, The transition from archaic to advanced frogs, *in* Vial, J. L., editor, Evolutionary biology of the anurans; contemporary research on major problems: Columbia, University of Missouri Press, p. 133-182.

MacGinitie, H. D., 1969, The Eocene Green River flora of northwestern Colorado and northeastern Utah: University of California Publications in Geological Sciences, v. 83, p. 1-140.

Martínez-Delclòs, Xavier, and Martinell, Jordi, 1993, Insect taphonomy experiments. Their application to the Cretaceous outcrops of lithographic limestones from Spain: Kaupia, Darmstädter Beiträge zur Naturgeschichte, v. 2, p. 133-144.

McGrew, P. O., and Casilliano, Michael, 1975, The geologic history of Fossil Butte National Monument and Fossil Basin: National Park Service Occasional Paper 3, p. 1-37.

Orton, G. L., 1952, Key to the genera of tadpoles in the United States and Canada: American Midland Naturalist, v. 47, no. 2, p. 382-395.

—1957, The bearing of larval evolution on some problems in frog classification: Systematic Zoology, v. 6, no. 2, p. 79-86.

Picard, M. D., and High, L. R., Jr., 1972, Criteria for recognizing lacustrine rocks, *in* Rigby, J. K., and Hamblin, W. K., editors, Recognition of ancient sedimentary environments: Society of Economic Paleontologists and Mineralogists Special Publication 16, p. 108-145.

Rieppel, Olivier, and Grande, Lance, 1998, A well-preserved fossil amphiumid (Lissamphibia: Caudata) from the Eocene Green River Formation of Wyoming: Journal of Vertebrate Paleontology, v. 18, no. 4, p. 700-708.

Salthe, S. N., 1973a, *Amphiuma means*: Catalogue of American Amphibians and Reptiles, no. 148, p. 1-2.

—1973b, *Amphiuma tridactylum*: Catalogue of American Amphibians and Reptiles, no. 149, p. 1-2.

Sokol, O. M., 1975, The phylogeny of anuran larvae: a new look: Copeia, v. 1975, no. 1, p. 1-23.

Špinar, Z. V., 1972, Tertiary frogs from central Europe: The Hague, W. Junk, p. 253.

Starrett, P. H., 1973, Evolutionary patterns in larval morphology, *in* Vial, J. L., editor, Evolutionary biology of the anurans; contemporary research on major problems: Columbia, University of Missouri Press, p. 251-271.

Stebbins, R. C., 1985, A field guide to western reptiles and amphibians, 2nd Edition: Boston, Houghton Mifflin Co., 336 p.

Wassersug, R. J., 1980, Internal oral features of larvae from eight anuran families: functional, systematic, evolutionary and ecological considerations: University of Kansas Museum of Natural History Miscellaneous Publication no. 68, p. 1-146.

Wassersug, R. J., and Wake, D. B., 1995, Fossil tadpoles from the Miocene of Turkey: Alytes, v. 12, no. 4, p. 145-157.

Wilson, M. V. H., 1980, Eocene lake environments: depth and distance-from-shore variation in fish, insect, and plant assemblages: Palaeogeography, Paleoclimatology, Palaeoecology, v. 32, no. 1, p. 21-44.

—1993, Calibration of Eocene varves at Horsefly, British Columbia, Canada, and temporal distribution of specimens of the Eocene fish *Amyzon aggregatum* Wilson: Kaupia, Darmstädter Beiträge zur Naturgeschichte, v. 2, p. 27-38.

Wuttke, Michael, 1983, Aktuopaläontologische studien über den zerfall von wirbeltieren. teil I – Anura: Senckenbergiana lethaea, v. 64, no. 5-6, p. 529-560.

Note added in press:

Since this paper was accepted for publication, Rieppel and Grande (1998) have formally erected the amphiumid skeleton (FMNH) PR1810) as the holotype and only speciman of the new genus and species *Paleoamphiuma tetradactylum*.

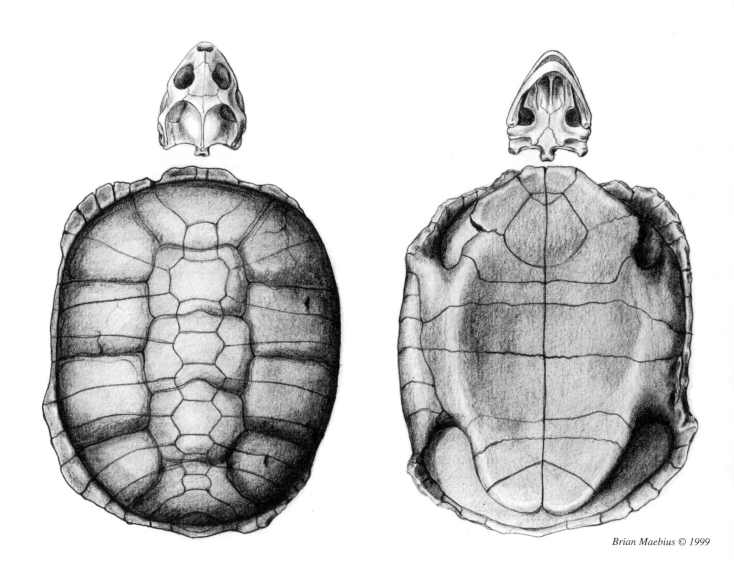

Brian Maebius © 1999

Eocene turtle

VERTEBRATES OF THE TURTLE BASIN LOCAL FAUNA, MIDDLE EOCENE, SEVIER PLATEAU, SOUTH-CENTRAL UTAH

Jeffrey G. Eaton
Department of Geosciences, Weber State University, Ogden, UT 84408-2507

J. Howard Hutchison and Patricia A. Holroyd
Museum of Paleontology, University of California, Berkeley, CA 94720

William W. Korth
Rochester Institute of Vertebrate Paleontology, 928 Whalen Road, Penfield NY 14526

Patrick M. Goldstrand
Midas Joint Venture, HC66, Box 125, Midas, NV 89414

ABSTRACT

The Turtle Basin local fauna, assignable to the Duchesnean North American Land Mammal Age, is here described from the Sevier Plateau of southern Utah. The Turtle Basin local fauna is dominated by aquatic faunal elements, especially chelonians, with rarer records of artiodactyls, a diverse rodent fauna, perissodactyls, and various fish taxa. The combined occurrence of the Uintan to Duchesnean rodents *Griphomys* and *Metanoiamys*, a heliscomyid and a new species of *Litoyoderimys* more primitive than Chadronian forms, and the Duchesnean and later anthracotheriids *Aepinacodon* and *Heptacodon* are the basis for a Duchesnean age for the Turtle Basin local fauna. The fauna is distinctive among Duchesnean faunas in including latest records of North American freshwater rays (Dasyatidae), and several turtles (*Plastomenus* sp., *Raptemys* n. sp., *Echmatemys* n. sp., and a new genus of derived chelydrid).

INTRODUCTION

The Sevier Plateau (figure 1) of Garfield and Kane Counties, southern Utah, is bounded on the east by the Paunsaugunt fault system, separating it from the Aquarius Plateau; to the south by the topographically lower Paunsaugunt Plateau; and to the west by the Sevier fault system, separating it from the Markagunt Plateau. The stratigraphic sequence on the plateau consists primarily of early Tertiary carbonates grading upward into volcanics, although faulted Cretaceous sequences are present at the southern margin of the plateau. The lowest Tertiary unit on the Sevier Plateau is the Claron Formation, which forms the picturesque pink and white cliffs of the region, including Bryce Canyon National Park. The Claron Formation consists predominantly of carbonates, mudstones, sandstones, and conglomerates. Only rare invertebrates and palynomorphs have been recovered. These fossils suggest an Late Paleocene to early Eocene age for the lower part of the formation (Goldstrand and others, 1993; Goldstrand, 1994).

Overlying the Claron Formation is a thick (approximately 250 m) sequence of volcaniclastic rocks (figure 2) with a complex nomenclatural history. Gregory (1944, 1945, 1949, 1950) applied the name "Brian Head Formation" to those rocks he considered equivalent to ones exposed in the type area on the Markagunt Plateau to the west. The formation was poorly defined and included several rock units that were subsequently recognized as distinct and removed from the "Brian Head Formation." Problems were noted by Threet (1952a, 1952b), Anderson (1971) and Judy (1974). The name was formally abandoned by Anderson and Rowley (1975).

This sequence of volcaniclastic rocks has been given informal names such as the "variegated sandstone member" and the "white tuffaceous sandstone" by Bowers (1972) in the Aquarius Plateau area or included within the Claron Formation on the Sevier Plateau (Rowley and others, 1987). Sable and Maldonado (1997) reinstate and redefine the Brian Head Formation based on a type section exposed on the Markagunt Plateau and refer the sequence of rocks on the Sevier Plateau to that formation. The term Brian Head Formation will be used in quotes here due to uncertainties in the correlation of this unit from the type area.

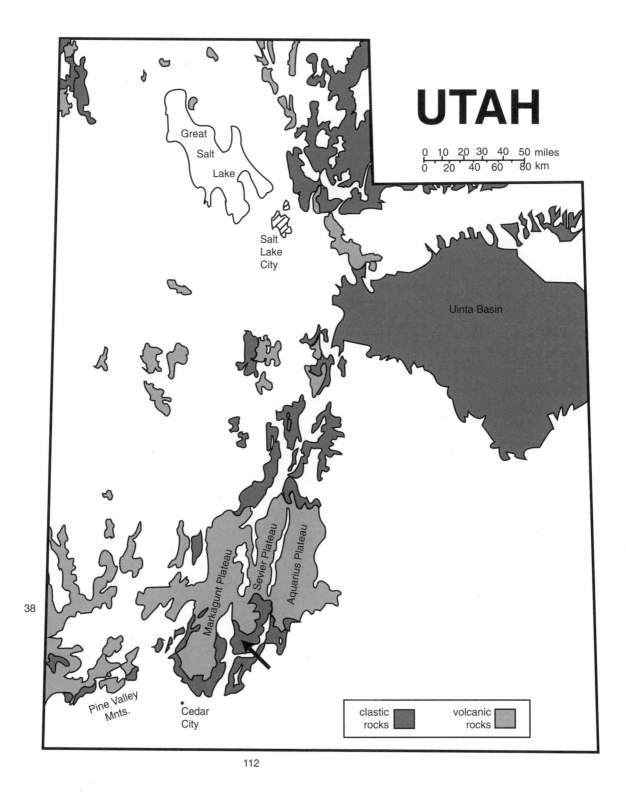

Figure 1. *Tertiary outcrop map of Utah (based on Hintze, 1974) indicating geographic location of the Sevier, Markagunt, and Aquarius plateaus. Arrow indicates location of the Turtle Basin local fauna.*

Turtle Basin Local Fauna - Eaton, Hutchison, Holroyd, Korth, Goldstrand

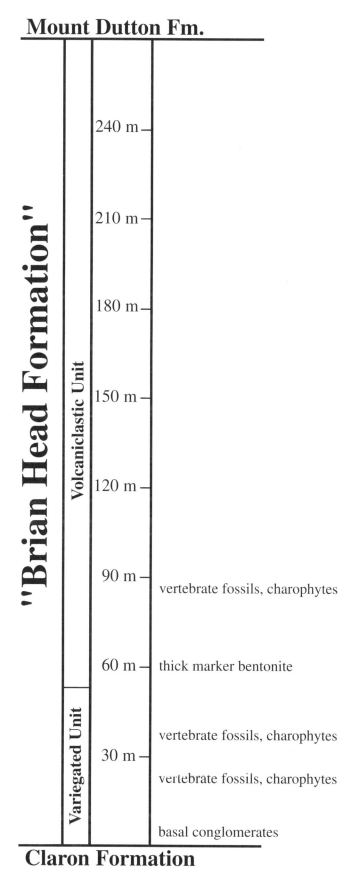

Figure 2. Generalized stratigraphic section of the "Brian Head Formation" on the Sevier Plateau indicating informal stratigraphic units and approximate stratigraphic position of fossil localities and marker beds.

Overlying the "Brian Head Formation" is a thick (~1000 m), complex sequence of volcanic flows, tuffs, and lahars of the Mount Dutton Formation. A radiometric date from near the base of the unit indicates an Oligocene age (32 Ma; Rowley and others, 1994).

STRATIGRAPHY

The "Brian Head Formation" on the Sevier Plateau is separated from the underlying Claron Formation by a conglomerate of quartzite and chert pebbles which float in a carbonate mud matrix. This conglomerate is widespread and highly variable in thickness and appears to infill a paleotopographic surface. The conglomerate is overlain by a sequence of variegated mudstones, bentonitic mudstones, fine-grained sandstones, and thin limestone beds. Sandstones from the variegated unit consist primarily of quartz and chert with some feldspar (Goldstrand and Eaton, 1996). Volcanic influence is restricted to bentonitic contributions to the mudstones. This unit, informally referred to as the "variegated unit" (see figure 2), is variable in thickness but averages about 50 meters and represents a series of lake and associated facies deposits laid down over a relatively short interval of time.

Overlying the variegated unit is a thick (200 m) unit dominated by volcaniclastic sandstones and conglomerates informally referred to as the "volcaniclastic unit" (figure 2). The sandstones are compositionally markedly different from those of the variegated unit as they are dominated by felsic and intermediate volcanic fragments suggesting a more proximal relationship to active volcanism than was the case for the variegated unit. Thin mudstones and bentonitic layers are present in the volcaniclastic unit.

Most of the fossils recovered to date have been from the variegated unit. It contains abundant charophytes, and more rarely ostracodes and gastropods. Among the vertebrates, turtle remains are the most abundant. The fossils are recovered from a sequence of lacustrine mudstones probably representing a single lake system. Fossils have also been recovered from lacustrine localities low in the volcaniclastic unit (figure 2). The turtles and rodents recovered from the variegated unit and low in the volcaniclastic unit represent the same taxa and are likely to be approximately of the same age.

VERTEBRATE FAUNA

Fossil vertebrates are common in the variegated unit, and collections are dominated by abundant turtle remains. Other lower vertebrates include bony fishes, a ray, a bird, and an alligator. Mammalian fossils are rare in surface collections, and most mammalian taxa were recovered through screenwashing. A preliminary faunal list is provided in table 1. Large surface-collected vertebrate materials (turtles and ungulates) are housed at the Museum of Paleontology, University of California, Berkeley. Small vertebrate material recovered by screenwashing (rodent and ray teeth) are housed at the Utah Museum of Natural History, Salt Lake City.

The composition of the lower vertebrate fauna reflects a lakeshore paleoenvironment. Fish are present, and the turtle and crocodilian fauna is entirely aquatic. The mix of chelonian taxa is unique and incorporates late members of earlier Eocene lineages and derived members of others. The fauna is also unusual in the absence of terrestrial turtles (testudinids), taxa preferring river channels (baenids), and kinosternids found in other Duchesnean faunas (Hutchison, 1996).

An undescribed genus of chelydrid turtles shares derived features of the shell with the Neogene members of the family. These include inflation of the peripherals, thinning and reduction of the carapace and plastron, serration of the posterior peripherals, and prominent development of carinae and knobs on the carapace, the latter suggesting *Macroclemmys*. The oldest known *Macroclemmys* are Miocene.

Two trionychids are known from this fauna. The plastominine *Plastomenus* sp. represents the latest record of the genus, elsewhere known only as late as Bridgerian. The trionychine lacks a preneural and is probably allied with *Apalone*, the extant North American genus. The dermatemydid *Baptemys* undescribed species is derived by comparison to the previous latest known species, *B. wyomingensis* Leidy, 1870 from the Uintan (Shoshonian) of the Rocky Mountain states. This undescribed species exhibits a broadening of the plastron and development of a xiphiplastral notch continuing the trend seen in the earlier species toward the extant *Dermatemys*.

Three batagurids are present and all represent new species. Two belong to genera known earlier, while one may represent a new genus. *Echmatemys* is the most abundant turtle in the fauna and outnumbers all others combined. The *Echmatemys* from the fauna is comparable to Wasatchian species in size, reversing the general trend for size increase seen from the Wasatchian through Uintan (Hutchison, 1992). This is also the latest confirmed record of the genus *Echmatemys* in North America. The second, small batagurid is related to "*Rhinoclemmys*" *morrisiae* Hay, 1908, a species known only from the Fowkes and Bridger Formations of Wyoming which may be as late as Shoshonian. The third batagurid

Table 1. *Preliminary vertebrate faunal list, Turtle Basin local fauna.*

Chondrichthyes
　　Myliobatiformes
　　　　Dasyatidae?, unidentified

Osteichthyes
　　Amiiformes
　　　　Amiidae
　　　　　　Amia uintensis
　　Salmoniformes
　　　　Esocidae, unidentified
　　Lepisosteiformes
　　　　Lepisosteidae, unidentified
　　Cypriniformes
　　　　cf. Catostomidae
　　Siluriformes
　　　　Ictaluridae, unidentified

Osteichthyes, unidentified

Reptilia
　　Chelonia
　　　　Chelydridae, undescribed genus
　　　　Bataguridae
　　　　　　Echmatemys undescribed species
　　　　　　"*Rhinoclemys*" undescribed species
　　　　　　genus unidentified
　　　　Dermatemydidae
　　　　　　Baptemys undescribed species
　　　　Carettochelyidae
　　　　　　Anosteira sp. or *Pseudanosteira* sp.
　　　　Trionychidae
　　　　　　Apalone sp.
　　　　　　Plastomenus sp.
　　Crocodylia
　　　　Alligatoridae
　　　　　　Alligator sp.
Aves
　　Neornithes, unidentified
Mammalia
　　Marsupialia
　　　　Peradectidae, unidentified
　　Rodentia
　　　　Eomyidae
　　　　　　Litoyoderimys undescribed species
　　　　　　Metanoiamys sp., cf. *M. lacus*
　　　　　　Protadjidaumo sp.
　　　　　　Paradjidaumo sp., cf. *P. alberti*
　　　　Heteromyidae
　　　　　　undescribed genus and species
　　　　Geomyoidea?
　　　　　　Griphomys alecer
　　Artiodactyla
　　　　Anthracotheriidae
　　　　　　Aepinacodon sp.
　　　　　　Heptacodon sp.
　　Perissodactyla
　　　　Brontotheriidae, unidentified
　　　　Helaletidae?, unidentified
　　Carnivora, unidentified

may represent a new genus and is the largest batagurid in the fauna.

A large, broad-snouted *Alligator* is the only crocodylian. It approaches the size of the extant North American *Alligator*. Fish remains are present, but not common. The ray is unusual and clearly new, but its relationships are obscure. It could bear some relationship to the only genus of freshwater ray known from the Eocene of the Western Interior, *Heliobatis*; however, the strong, paired prong-like cusps are unlike anything seen in *Heliobatis*.

Very small rodent teeth are the most common mammalian element produced by screenwashing. The recovered eomyids include *Protadjidaumo* sp. which is only known from the Uintan or Duchesnean; *Metanoiamys* sp., cf. *M. lacus*, a taxon known from the Duchesnean of Saskatchewan, Canada; *Paradjidaumo* sp., cf. *P. alberti* known from near the Duchesnean-Chadronian boundary of British Columbia; and an undescribed species of *Litoyoderimys* more primitive than known Chadronian species. An undescribed genus of heliscomyid is present that is more primitive than the Chadronian genus *Heliscomys*. The possible geomyid *Griphomys alecer* is known from the Uintan and Duchesnean of California (Chiment and Korth, 1996).

Two anthracotheriid artiodactyls are present. The more common is a large, medium-crowned species that is probably best assigned to *Aepinacodon*. Until further preparation is completed, it is not possible to determine whether these fossils represent a new species of the genus. A second genus, *Heptacodon*, is represented by a single poorly preserved maxilla.

AGE AND BIOSTRATIGRAPHIC RELATIONSHIPS

The age of the vertebrate fauna can be constrained from several lines of evidence. Charophytes from the variegated unit (based on comparisons with European charophyte zonations) suggest a lower Paleocene to middle Eocene age (Feist and others, 1997). A lower limit for the age of the vertebrate fauna can be obtained from the late Paleocene to early Eocene age for the underlying Claron Formation. An upper limit can be derived based on K/Ar dates from the overlying volcaniclastics. These dates, from presumably coeval rocks to the west, range from 32 to 34 million years ago (Sable and Maldonado, 1997) and those from the top of the type section of the Brian Head Formation range from 29 to 32 million years ago (Rowley and others, 1994). Based on a revised age for the Eocene-Oligocene boundary of approximately 33.5 million years ago (Berggren and others, 1995), the volcaniclastic unit of the upper part of the "Brian Head Formation" is latest Eocene to earliest Oligocene in age. Although the K/Ar dates provide a broad upper boundary for the age of the vertebrate fauna, their utility for dating the fauna itself is limited. The variegated unit does not occur in either of the sections for which K/Ar dates are available, nor is the stratigraphic correlation between the volcaniclastic rocks of the Markagunt and Sevier Plateaus clear. However, these varying lines of evidence (age range of underlying rocks and overlying rocks, age range of charophytes) are consistent with a middle to late Eocene age for the vertebrate fauna of the variegated unit.

The vertebrate fauna itself provides several biostratigraphic clues. Many of the chelonian taxa (for example, *Echmatemys, Plastomenus, Baptemys*) range throughout most of the Eocene, but are not definitely known in the Chadronian. Morphologically, most of the species found in the Turtle Basin local fauna are derived with respect to Uintan members of these genera. None of the distinctive Chadronian emydids are present (Hutchison, 1996). Another, *Apalone*, is more typically known from the Chadronian, and the chelydrid is more derived than other known members in the Eocene. The chelonians strongly suggest a post-Uintan, pre-Chadronian age, that is, the Duchesnean Land Mammal Age

The combination of mammalian taxa also indicates a Duchesnean age. The anthracotheriids, *Heptacodon* and *Aepinacodon*, first appear in North America in the Duchesnean (Storer, 1983; Hanson, 1996) and persist through the early Oligocene (MacDonald, 1956). Unfortunately, anthracotheriid material is rare in the Duchesnean and Chadronian, so adequate comparisons among species cannot be made.

The rodents also strongly support a Duchesnean age. *Metanoiamys* sp., cf. *M. lacus* is known from the Chadronian; *Griphomys acer* and *Ptotadjidaumo* sp. range from the Uintan through the Duchesnean; *Paradjidaumo* sp., cf. *P. alberti* is close to a taxon known from the Duchesnean-Chadronian boundary; and the new species of *Litoyoderimys* and new genus and species of heliscomid are more primitive than Chadronian forms.

Recently, the entire Duchesnean North American Land Mammal Age was shifted into the middle Eocene subepoch and the Chadronian/Duchesnean boundary to be approximately coincident with the middle/late Eocene boundary, based on new data on the magnetostratigraphy and radiometric ages of critical vertebrate-bearing stratigraphic sections (Prothero, 1995). An assignment of the Turtle Basin local fauna to the Duchesnean would thus be consistent with the limited charophyte data as well as the morphology and ranges of the vertebrate taxa.

SUMMARY

The vertebrate fauna recovered from low in the "Brian Head Formation" on the Sevier Plateau, south-central Utah, the Turtle Basin local fauna, suggests lacustrine paleoenvironments developed locally during the Duchesnean (end of the middle Eocene). The fauna is dominated by aquatic taxa such as turtles, alligatorids, and fish in association with charophytes, ostracodes, and gastropods. The Turtle Basin local fauna represents an unusual association of taxa both from chronologic, geographic, and paleoecologic perspectives.

ACKNOWLEDGMENTS

The authors would like to thank the U. S. Forest Service, in particularly Marion Jacklin, Carlton Guillette, and Evan Boshell, for their cooperation in our investigations in the Dixie National Forest. We appreciate discussions in the field with Ed Sable and Florian Maldonado of the U. S. Geological Survey, and John Anderson (formerly of Kent State University, now retired). Tab Rasmussen is thanked for his review of the manuscript.

REFERENCES

Anderson, J. J., 1971, Geology of the southwestern high plateaus of Utah - Bear Valley Formation, an Oligocene-Miocene volcanic arenite: Geological Society of America Bulletin, v. 82, p. 1179-1205.

Anderson J. J., and Rowley, P. D., 1975, Cenozoic geology of southwestern high plateaus of Utah, *in* Anderson, J. J., Rowley, P. D., Fleck, R. V., and Nairn, A. E. M., editors, Cenozoic geology of the southwestern high plateaus of Utah: Geological Society of America Special Paper 160, p. 151.

Berggren, W.A., Kent, D.V., Swisher, C.C., III, and Aubry, M.-P., 1995, A revised Cenozoic geochronology and chronostratigraphy, *in* Berggren, W.A., Kent, D.V., Aubry, M.-P., and Hardenbol, Jan, editors, Geochronology, time scales and global stratigraphic correlation: SEPM Special Publication no. 54, p. 129-212.

Bowers, W. E., 1972, The Canaan Peak, Pine Hollow, and Wasatch Formations in the Table Cliff region, Garfield County, Utah: U.S. Geological Survey Bulletin 1331-B, 39 p.

Chiment, J. J., and Korth, W. W., 1996, A new genus of eomyid rodent (Mammalia) from the Eocene (Uintan-Duchesnean) of southern California: Journal of Vertebrate Paleontology, v. 16, p. 116-124.

Feist, Monique, Eaton, J. G., Brouwers, E. M., and Maldonado, Florian, 1997, Significance of charophytes from the Lower Tertiary variegated and volcaniclastic units, Brian Head Formation, Casto Canyon area, southern Sevier Plateau, southwestern Utah, *in* Maldonado, Florian, and Nealey, L. D., editors, Geologic studies in the Basin and Range-Colorado Plateau transition in southeastern Nevada, southwestern Utah, and northwestern Arizona, 1995: U.S. Geological Survey Bulletin 2153-B, p. 29-37.

Goldstrand, P. M., 1994, Tectonic development of Upper Cretaceous to Eocene strata of southwestern Utah: Geological Society of America Bulletin, v. 106, p. 145-154.

Goldstrand, P. M., and Eaton, J. G., 1996, Upper Eocene-Oligocene(?) depositional systems and basin development, southern Utah: Rocky Mountain Section, Geological Society of America, Abstracts with Programs, v. 28, p. 69.

Goldstrand, P. M., Trexler, J. H., Jr., Kowallis, B. J., and Eaton, J. G., 1993, Late Cretaceous to early Tertiary tectonostratigraphy of southwest Utah, *in* Morales, Michael, editor, Aspects of Mesozoic geology and paleontology of the Colorado Plateau: Museum of Northern Arizona Bulletin 59, p. 181-191.

Gregory, H. E., 1944, Geologic observations in the upper Sevier River Valley, Utah: American Journal of Science, v. 242, p. 577-607.

—1945, Post-Wasatch Tertiary formations in southwestern Utah: Journal of Geology, v. 53, p. 105-115.

—1949, Geologic and geographic reconnaissance of eastern Markagunt Plateau, Utah: Geological Society of America Bulletin, v. 60, p. 969-998.

—1950, Geology of eastern Iron Country, Utah: Utah Geological and Mineralogical Survey Bulletin 37, 153 p.

Hanson, C. B., 1996, Stratigraphy and vertebrate faunas of the Bridgerian-Duchesnean Clarno Formation, north-central Oregon, *in* Prothero, D. R. and Emry, R. J., editors, The terrestrial Eocene-Oligocene transition in North America: New York, Cambridge University Press, p. 206-239.

Hintze, L. F., 1974, Geologic map of Utah: Brigham Young University Geology Studies, Special Publication 2.

Hutchison, J. H., 1992, Western North American reptile and amphibian record across the Eocene/Oligocene boundary and its climatic implications, *in* Prothero, D. R. and Berggren, W. A., editors, Eocene-Oligocene climatic and biotic evolution: Princeton, New Jersey, Princeton University Press, p. 451-463.

—1996, Testudines, *in* Prothero, D. R. and Emry, R. J., editors, The terrestrial Eocene-Oligocene transition in North America: New York, Cambridge University Press, p. 337-353.

Judy, J. R., 1974, Geologic evolution of the west-central Markagunt Plateau, Utah: Kent, Ohio, Kent State University, M.S. thesis, 154 p.

MacDonald, J. R., 1956, The North American anthracotheres: Journal of Paleontology, v. 30, no. 3, p. 615-645.

Prothero, D. R., 1995, Geochronology and magnetostratigraphy of Paleogene North American Land Mammal "Ages" -- an update, *in* Berggren, W. A., Kent, D. V., Aubry, M.-P., and Hardenbol, Jan, editors, Geochronology time scales and global stratigraphic correlation: SEPM Special Publication No. 54, p. 305-316.

Rowley, P. D., Mehnert, H. H., Naeser, C. W., Snee, L. W., Cunningham, C. G., Steven, T. A., Anderson, J. J., Sable, E. G., and Anderson, R. E., 1994, Isotopic ages and stratigraphy of Cenozoic rocks of the Marysvale volcanic field and adjacent areas, west-central Utah: U.S. Geological Survey Bulletin 2071, 35 p.

Rowley, P.D., Hereford, Richard, and Williams, V. S., 1987, Geologic map of the Adams Head-Johns Valley area, southern Sevier Plateau, Garfield County, Utah: U. S. Geological Survey Miscellaneous Investigation Series Map I-1798, scale 1:50,000.

Sable, E. G., and Maldonado, Florian, 1997, The Brian Head Formation (revised) and selected Tertiary sedimentary rock units, Markagunt Plateau and adjacent areas, southwestern Utah, *in* Maldonado, Florian, and Nealey, L. D., editors, Geologic studies in the Basin and Range-Colorado Plateau transition in southeastern Nevada, southwestern Utah, northwestern Arizona, 1995: U. S. Geological Survey Bulletin 2153-A, p. 7-26.

Storer, J. E., 1983, A new species of the artiodactyl *Heptacodon* from the Cypress Hills Formation, Lac Pelletier, Saskatchewan: Canadian Journal of Earth Sciences, v. 20, p.1344-1347.

Threet, R. L., 1952a, Geology of the Red Hills area, Iron County, Utah: Seattle, University of Washington, Ph.D. dissertation 7310, 107 p.

—1952b, Some problems of the Brian Head (Tertiary) Formation in southwestern Utah: Geological Society of America Bulletin, v. 63, p. 1386.

LATE TERTIARY BASINS AND VERTEBRATE FAUNAS ALONG THE NEVADA-UTAH BORDER

Robert E. Reynolds
San Bernardino County Museum, Earth Sciences Section, 2024 Orange Tree Lane, Redlands, CA 92374

Everett H. Lindsay
University of Arizona, Department of Geological Sciences, Tucson, AZ, 85721

ABSTRACT

Depositional basins in eastern Nevada near the Utah border contain fossil vertebrate faunas that help constrain the timing of basin development. The oldest basins were developed by extensional tectonics that signal the development of the western margin of Utah's Colorado Plateau, while the younger basins may have been developed by erosion related to the expanding Colorado River/Virgin River drainage system in southwestern Utah and southeastern Nevada. The basins, from the oldest to youngest, are the Muddy Creek Basin, considered late Clarendonian through Hemphillian Land Mammal Ages; the Spring Valley Basin, considered Hemphillian Land Mammal Age; and the Meadow Valley Basin, considered Blancan Land Mammal Age. The older basins contain faunas that consist of large mammal remains. The White Narrows Formation of early Blancan Land Mammal Age sits in a graben within the Muddy Creek Formation at Moapa. Both the White Narrows Formation and the Panaca Formation in Meadow Valley Basin have large mammals and abundant small mammal faunas that suggest a Blancan Land Mammal Age.

INTRODUCTION

The sedimentary basins in eastern Nevada provide a number of local faunas with potential for producing biostratigraphic age control for the development and filling of basins that lie to the west of Utah's spectacular Colorado Plateau. In an attempt to make order of the tantalizing pieces, collections in a number of museums were reviewed and field work was conducted by the University of Arizona and the San Bernardino County Museum from 1992 to 1997.

Institutional abbreviations are as follows: AMNH, American Museum of Natural History; LACM, Los Angeles County Museum of Natural History; MNA, Museum of Northern Arizona; SBCM, San Bernardino County; UALP, University of Arizona Laboratory of Paleontology; UCMP, University of California Museum of Paleontology, Berkeley Museum.

Taxa listed in the tables are based on specimens housed at the AMNH, SBCM, UCMP, and UALP.

PREVIOUS WORK

Immediately west of the Utah border in southern Nevada (figure 1), the generally flat-lying sediments in Meadow Valley and Muddy Valley (along Muddy Creek) were placed in a relative stratigraphic framework by Stock (1921), based on field investigations made in 1919. These and similar deposits in Nevada had previously been identified as late Cenozoic (for example, Pliocene or Pleistocene) by Spurr (1903) based on reconnaissance mapping, and by Carpenter (1915) based on hydrology-geomorphology of the deposits. Stock (1921) characterized the deposits in Meadow and Muddy Valleys as dominantly red-brown, light brown or green, poorly indurated to well indurated sands, silts, and clays with minor quantities of gravels and tuffs; they are usually flat-lying or show slight deformation; sands may be thin bedded and/or cross bedded.

Stock (1921) called the Meadow Valley deposits the Panaca beds and assigned an early Pliocene age (now considered late Miocene, Hemphillian Land Mammal Age) based on the horse, rhino, and camel remains (UCMP repository) he identified from the Panaca beds. Stock (1921, p. 257) called the deposits in Muddy Valley the Muddy Valley beds and considered them to be slightly older than the Panaca beds although the fossils at his disposal were not very diagnostic. MacDonald and Pelletier (1956) made a comprehensive review of the Pliocene mammal faunas of Nevada; they were less precise, placing the Panaca fauna (from the Panaca beds) in either Clarendonian (late Miocene) or Hemphillian (early Pliocene) Land Mammal Age, and the Muddy Valley fauna in the Barstovian (middle Miocene) or Clarendon-

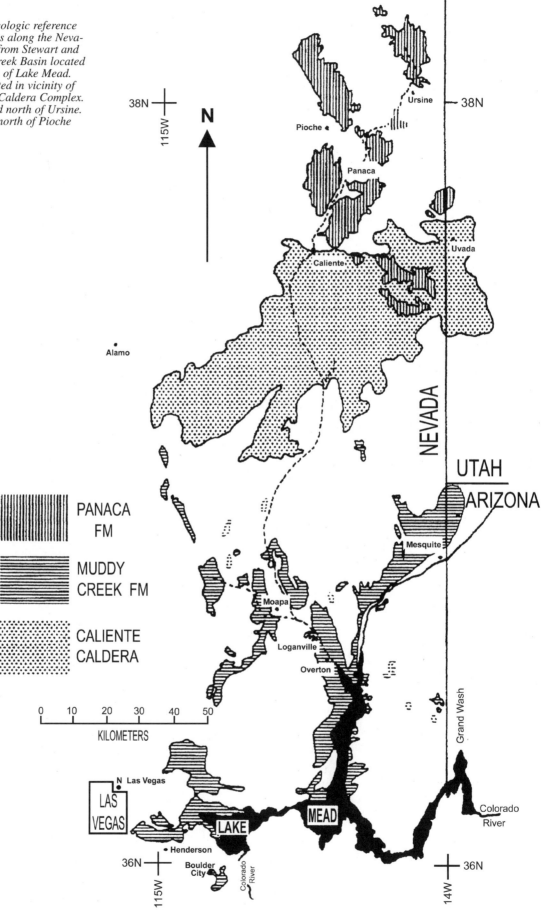

Figure 1. *Location and geologic reference map for late Tertiary basins along the Nevada/Utah border (modified from Stewart and Carlson, 1978). Muddy Creek Basin located in vicinity of Moapa, north of Lake Mead. Meadow Valley Basin located in vicinity of Panaca, north of Caliente Caldera Complex. Spring Valley Basin located north of Ursine. Lake Valley Basin located north of Pioche (west of Spring Valley).*

ian (late Miocene) Land Mammal Age, based on basically the same fossil record studied earlier by Stock.

The Panaca Formation was mapped by Phoenix (1948), primarily to evaluate the hydrologic potential of the deposits in Meadow Valley. A more extensive and detailed study of the Panaca Formation was published by Ekren and others (1977), who identified the limits of the Panaca Formation within Lincoln County, and related it to underlying deposits and overlying alluvium or colluvium. Ekren and others (1977, p. 3) characterized the Panaca Formation as "flat-stratified tuffaceous siltstones, sandstones, and mudstones, and local thin beds of diatomite or diatomite-like ash, and gravel." The older fluvial sands and gravels of Ekren and others (1977) probably include some of the strata mapped as the Panaca Formation by Phoenix (1948). Phoenix estimated total thickness of the Panaca Formation as greater than 427 meters; in Meadow Valley, where it is best developed, maximum relief of the Panaca Formation is more than 300 meters. There is a slight initial dip to the Panaca Formation in Meadow Valley, suggesting its maximum thickness is between 300 and 400 meters in that area. Ekren and others (1977) also recognized the Panaca Formation in Spring Valley, northeast of Meadow Valley. They identified no significant difference in the Panaca Formation throughout Lincoln County. Our initial impression is that sediments in Spring Valley seem more tuffaceous and slightly older relative to those in Meadow Valley.

Field parties from the American Museum of Natural History in New York collected fossils from Meadow Valley and Spring Valley in 1940-1941 (Hazen and Gentry) and in 1961 (Galusha and Emry). They accumulated many more fossils, which revised earlier interpretations of the age of these deposits. Many of the fossils collected from Meadow Valley and Spring Valley in the American Museum repository are still unpublished; to date, some of the AMNH small mammals were published by May (1981), Repenning (1987), and White (1987, 1991). These small mammals indicate that most if not all of the Panaca Formation in Meadow Valley can be assigned to the Blancan Land Mammal Age (Pliocene). More recently, Mou (1996a, b) described additional small mammal fossils from the Panaca Formation, suggesting that a sequence of sites from these deposits should preserve a significant record of phyletic evolution among the rodent fossils.

GEOLOGIC SETTING

For the last 10 years geologists have been studying the structure and chronology of late Tertiary basins in the western Basin and Range area, searching for a better understanding of the cessation or dissipation of crustal extension in the Basin and Range Physiographic Province. Meadow Valley and Muddy Valley offer important clues to the tectonic history of the Basin and Range. They are separated by the Caliente Caldera Complex, which is an extensive volcanic dome of nested calderas that formed between about 24 and 13 million years ago (Rowley and others, 1995). According to current interpretations, the Caliente Caldera Complex formed during a late episode of subduction that preceded crustal extension in the Basin and Range Physiographic Province; quenching of this volcanism is thought to coincide, more or less, with the beginning of crustal extension. Age estimates from ash-flow tuffs found within sediments that filled newly formed basins constrain the timing of basin formation and filling (Taylor and others, 1989). Basins with flat-lying sediments (for example, Meadow Valley and Muddy Valley) are considered post-extension, having formed during (or subsequent to) the latest interval of tectonic extension. Many of these basins are being mapped to provide useful data on the timing of crustal extension (Rowley and Shroba, 1991; Rowley and others, 1994). Thus, flat-lying sedimentary deposits north and south of the Caliente Caldera Complex should be younger than about 10 million years. The ash-flow tuffs in Meadow Valley and Muddy Valley are generally considered as being derived from volcanism in distant areas (for example, the late Tertiary volcanic center in southern Idaho) where volcanism continued subsequent to quenching in the Caliente Caldera Complex.

Muddy Creek Formation

The Muddy Creek Formation was deposited in a series of small basins that coalesced into a single large basin which now includes the area from Henderson on the southwest, Mesquite on the northeast, Coyote Spring Valley on the northwest, and the Grand Wash Cliffs on the southeast (Longwell and others, 1965; Lucchita, 1979), an area approaching 5,000 square miles. The Muddy Creek Formation sits unconformably on the Horse Spring Formation, and on the red sandstone unit of Bohannon (Bohannon, 1984; Wallin and others, 1993). Crustal extension that caused tilting of the Horse Spring Formation is constrained by deposition of the flat-lying Muddy Creek sediments. The youngest age estimate on the Horse Spring Formation is 15.9 million years ago. Structural tilting ended prior to the deposition of the flat-lying Muddy Creek Formation where early age estimates are as old as 11.6 million years (Beard, 1993) or 10.4 million years (Wallin and others, 1993).

The Muddy Creek Formation is the youngest basin-filling deposit to form prior to through-flowing drainage in the lower Colorado River system (Lucchita, 1979). Age estimates for early deposition of the Muddy Creek Formation are not precise and span a period of about one to three million years [for example, 11.4 million years, 10.6 million years, 8.5 million years for basalt of Calville Mesa (Duebendorfer and Wallin, 1991; Anderson 1973, 1978); fission track age estimates of 11.6 to 10.8 million years from the south side of Grand Wash (Bohannon, 1984) and age estimates of 11.9 million years to 10.46 million years on the underlying red sandstone unit of Bohannon (1984)].

Deposition in Muddy Basin continued at least until the flows of the Fortification Basalt member of the Muddy Creek Formation which is as young as or younger than the Hualapai limestone member of the Muddy Creek Formation (Lucchita, 1979). Age estimates on the Fortification Basalt, south of Henderson, range from 4.9 to 5.85 million years (Lucchita, 1979; Anderson, 1978; Damon and others, 1978; D. L. Schmidt, personal communication to R. E. Reynolds, 1994). Age estimates near the top of the Muddy Creek Formation located to the northeast are 5.9 million years at Table Mountain (D. L. Schmidt, personal communication to R. E. Reynolds, 1992) and 4.73 million years from the north side of Grand Wash (Reynolds and others, 1986).

The Bouse Formation, a brackish estuarian embayment to the south of the Muddy Creek Formation along the Colorado River trough, provides age estimates of 5.47 ± 0.20 million years (Damon and others, 1978). Lucchita (1979) suggested that the Bouse embayment did not receive fresh waters of a through-flowing drainage system until after that time. D. L. Schmidt (personal communication to R. E. Reynolds, 1994) indicated that the age of the first Colorado River alluvium in the overlying Imperial Formation is estimated at 4.3 million years, thus providing limits to the development of a through-flowing drainage.

Faunas of the Muddy Creek Formation

The taxa from the Muddy Creek Formation (table 1) reinforce the Hemphillian age of this formation.

Stock (1921) assigned a Miocene age to the Muddy Creek Formation near the type area at Overton based on scanty vertebrate remains including camels. Ted Galusha from the AMNH Frick Labs discovered a more complete Muddy Creek fauna at Juanita Springs in Arizona, southwest of Mesquite, Nevada (Robert Evander written communication to R. E. Reynolds via R. H. Tedford, 1997).

Table 1. *Mammals of the Muddy Creek fauna.*

Taxon	Land Mammal Ages*		
	C	H	B
Carnivora			
Aelurodon sp. cf. *A. validus* (lg. dog)		x	
?*Indarctos* sp. (bear)		x	
Perissodactyla			
Equinae gen. indet.			
Artiodactyla			
Megatylopus sp. (large camel)	x	x	x
"*Megatylopus*" sp. (large camel)	x	x	x
Alforjas sp. (camel)	x	x	
Hemiauchenia sp. (llama)	x	x	x
Texoceros sp. (pronghorn)	x	x	
Neotragoceras sp. (bovid)		x	

Notes: AMNH and SBCM specimen repositories. The Muddy Creek faunas are assigned to the Hemphillian Land Mammal Age.

  * Abbreviations C = Clarendonian, H = Hemphillian, B = Blancan

The camel *Alforjas* sp. (SBCM L2745-133) and ?*Neotragoceras* sp. (SBCM L2743-32) come from within or west of Mesquite, Nevada. Although certain taxa range through long periods of time, *Aelurodon validus*, ?*Indarctos* sp. (AMNH repository), and ?*Neotragoceras* sp. (SBCM repository) are restricted to the Hemphillian Land Mammal Age, and these are found at localities in the middle and upper portions of the section in eastern exposures (Robert Evander written communication to R. E. Reynolds via R. H. Tedford, 1997). The Muddy Creek assemblage (AMNH repository) is mid-Hemphillian and therefore older than the fauna from the Panaca Formation in Spring Valley.

All of the taxa recorded from Muddy Valley (table 1) and Spring Valley (table 2) are known from Hemphillian faunas, although several genera (for example, *Canis* sp., *Felis* sp., *Megatylopus* sp., and *Hemiauchenia* sp.) span both Hemphillian and Blancan time. We assign the fauna from Muddy Valley and Spring Valley to Hemphillian Land Mammal Age.

White Narrows Formation

The White Narrows member of the Muddy Creek Formation (Gardner, 1968) has been elevated to formation status (Schmidt and others, 1996). This formation fills a north-striking graben with pond and lacustrine sediments, carbonates, and fluvial sand. A fauna (table 3) from near the base of the section contains small mammal fossils that suggest an age estimate approximating the transition from the late Miocene Hemphillian Land Mammal Age to the Pliocene Blancan Land Mammal Age.

Fauna of the White Narrows Formation

Only two fish and selected mammalian taxa are list-

Table 2. *Mammals of the Spring Valley fauna.*

Taxon	Land Mammal Ages*		
	C	**H**	**B**
Carnivora			
Pliotaxidea sp. (badger)		x	
Vulpes stenognathus (fox)		x	
"*Canis*" *davisi* (dog)		x	
Canis sp. (dog)		x	x
Felis sp. (cat)		x	x
Machairodus sp. (stabbing cat)		x	
PERISSODACTYLA			
Dinohippus sp. (primitive horse)		x	
Teleoceras sp. (rhino)		x	
ARTIODACTYLA			
Megatylopus sp. (large camel)		x	x
Hemiauchenia sp. (llama)		x	x
Hexobelomeryx sp. (pronghorn)		x	
Texoceros sp.		x	

Note: This fauna, including taxa compiled by Mou (1996a,b) and R.H. Tedford (personal communication), is assigned to the Hemphillian Land Mammal Age. None of these taxa constrain the Spring Valley fauna to early or late Hemphillian but they are probably more common in late Hemphillian. Specimens are in the AMNH repository.

     * Abbreviations C = Clarendonian, H = Hemphillian, B = Blancan

Table 3. *Mammals of the White Narrows fauna.*

Taxon	Land Mammal Ages*			
	C	**H**	**B**	**I**
Pisces				
Catastomatidae (sucker)				
Archoplites sp. (perch)				
Insectivora				
Antrozous sp. (bat)	x			
Myotis sp. (bat)	x			
Sorex sp. (shrew)			x	
Sorex sp. sm. (shrew)			x	
Rodentia				
Paranychomys sp. (small) cf. *P. lemredfieldi* (jumping mouse)		x		
Copemys sp. (small) cf. *C. vasquezi* (deer mouse)		x		
Peromyscus valensis (deer mouse)		x		
Repomys sp. (small) cf. *R. gustleyi* (rat)		x		
Calomys (*Bensonomys*) cf. (*B.*) *arizonae* (mouse)			x	
Calomys (*Bensonomys*) cf. (*B.*) *coffeyi* (mouse)		x		
Neotoma (*Paraneotoma*) sp. (small) cf. *N.* (*P.*) *vaughani* (woodrat)			x	
Perognathus sp. (pocket mouse)	x	x	x	x
Prodipodomys (undescribed species) (small) (kangaroo rat)		x	x	
Dipodomys gidleyi (kangaroo rat)			x	
Oregonomys sp. cf. *O. sargenti* (pocket mouse)		x		
Carnivora				
Bassariscus sp. (ring-tail)	x	x	x	

Note: Specimens are in the SBCM repository. Based on the presence of six Hemphillian indicator species and two Blancan indicator species, the White Narrows fauna is assigned to the earliest Blancan Land Mammal Age.

     *Abbreviations C=Clarendonian, H=Hemphillian, B=Blancan, I= rvingtonian.

ed for the White Narrows fauna (table 3). The fauna also contains gastropods, ostracodes, fish, frog and toad, lizards and snakes, and birds. The rodents are particularly helpful in determining the age of the White Narrows fauna. Of those that are restricted temporally, six are known only from the Hemphillian Land Mammal Age and three are known only from the Blancan Land Mammal Age. This suggests that the basal (Schmidt and others, 1996) White Narrows Formation was deposited around 4.7 million years ago (Woodburne and Swisher, 1995), although C. A. Repenning (p. 15, in Schmidt and others, 1996) suggests a younger age based on the presence of one taxon, *Neotoma* (*Paraneotoma*) sp., cf. *P. vaughani* (SBCM repository), and its affinities to *P. vaughani* from the Verde Formation of Arizona (Czaplewski, 1990, MNA repository). However, the *P. vaughani* material from the White Narrows Formation is smaller and perhaps less derived than the material from the Verde Formation, and is associated with two other taxa restricted to the Blancan and six taxa restricted to the Hemphillian.

The large fishes (SBCM repository) from this site are important because they are consistent with the depositional environment of the White Narrows Formation as a through-flowing drainage reaching the Colorado River system.

Panaca Formation

The Panaca Formation is exposed in Meadow Valley, Spring Valley, and Lake Valley, all located north of the Caliente Caldera Complex (see figure 1). The Panaca Formation, like the Muddy Creek Formation, is interpreted as basin fill developed in several small, adjacent, extensional basins that possibly coalesced during an early period of interior drainage. Deflation and erosion proceeded after integration of through drainage (Ekren and others, 1977). These basin-fill deposits are generally flat-lying, and are derived primarily from adjacent uplands which are comprised primarily of Miocene rhyolitic or dacitic ash-flow tuffs and breccias, or Paleozoic limestones. The age of the Tertiary volcanics is highly variable; some had been interpreted as Oligocene (Ekren and others, 1977) but many of the ages have been revised (Rowley and others, 1994) and are now all considered Miocene. The Leach Canyon Formation, the oldest ash-flow tuff in the vicinity of Caliente Caldera Complex, is now interpreted to be 23.8 million years (Rowley and others, 1995); most of the other ash-flow tuffs in this area yielded age estimates younger than 20 million years. Volcanic ashes are also frequently encountered in the upper part of the Panaca Formation in

Meadow Valley; these ashes have been difficult to date, primarily because the grain size is minimal. Rowley and Shroba (1991) reviewed the frustrating attempts to estimate the ages of these ashes; they concluded that none of the ashes in Meadow Valley are older than about 2.1 million years.

Meadow Valley and Spring Valley have been connected by Meadow Valley Wash, whereas Lake Valley is still nearly a playa. Lake Valley is drained by Patterson Wash, a minor wash at its southern end that joins Meadow Wash in Condor Canyon between Meadow Valley and Spring Valley. Consequently, exposures of the Panaca Formation are best developed in Meadow Valley, which is down slope relative to Spring Valley, and exposures are minimal in Lake Valley. Blank and Kucks (1989) presented gravity data from these areas that indicate considerable thickness of sediment in each of these basins. We interpret the oldest exposed strata of the Panaca Formation in Meadow Valley as organic-rich silts (carbonaceous siltstone) at the base of the section north of Panaca. These organic-rich silts are overlain by a thick sequence of mollusc and ostracode-bearing silts and sands found only in the vicinity of Panaca that probably represent local ponding associated with elevation of the water table. Numerous springs in the vicinity of Panaca are currently active. These mollusc and ostracode-bearing silts and sands in the vicinity of Panaca have given rise to interpretations that the Panaca Formation is partly or dominantly lacustrine (Phoenix, 1948; Ekren and others, 1977); similar deposits have not been found in Spring Valley where the Panaca Formation is presumably equivalent or older.

Abundant fossil sites are recorded from the Panaca Formation in Meadow Valley where exposures are more plentiful. Golgotha Hill is the only site to yield identifiable vertebrate fossils in Spring Valley. Vertebrate fossils are unknown from Lake Valley, where exposures are minimal. The Golgotha Hill fossil site was discovered and collected by Gentry and Hazen for the Childs Frick collection at the AMNH in 1940; these are the best Hemphillian fossils known from the Panaca Formation. Gentry and Hazen reported (letter from Gentry to Childs Frick in AMNH archives) that fossils at Golgotha Hill came from a channel sand deposit, with fossils frequently coated by thick calcitic (or gypsiferous) concretions. These sands are interbedded with several white volcanic ashes; they occur in the upper half of a 40-meter-thick section of the Panaca Formation on the east side of Spring Valley. Sands and ashes are found in the Panaca Formation in Meadow Valley; however, most of the fossil sites in Meadow Valley are from strata located stratigraphically below volcanic ash beds, and all of the

Meadow Valley sites are considered Blancan, younger than the fossil sites from Spring Valley.

Thus, the geologic context of vertebrate fossils and ashes in Meadow Valley and Spring Valley suggests a sequential development in these intermontane basins and sequential deposition of volcanic ashes within the Panaca Formation. It appears that vertebrates lived (and volcanic ashes rained down) in Spring Valley as much as three million years before similar events occurred in Meadow Valley. Most, if not all, of the volcanic ashes now exposed in Meadow Valley were laid down after deposition of fossil vertebrates.

Fauna of the Panaca Formation in Spring Valley

The taxa from the Panaca Formation in Spring Valley are listed in table 2. As noted previously, the taxa con-sist of Hemphillian or perhaps late Hemphillian indicators. This suggests that deposition in Spring Valley (Panaca Formation) started as deposition in Muddy Valley (Muddy Creek Formation) was culminating. Deposition of the Panaca Formation in Spring Valley preceded most deposition in Meadow Valley. A single specimen of *Teleoceras* sp. from Meadow Valley, discussed below, suggests that deposition in both basins was contemporaneous only during latest Hemphillian time.

Fauna of the Panaca Formation in Meadow Valley

The fauna from the Panaca Formation in Meadow Valley is listed in table 4. Stock (1921) discussed and illustrated specimen UCMP 24093 from LACM locality 3546 near Panaca, that he identified as a proximal phalanx on digit 3 of a rhinocerotid, possibly *Teleoceras*.

Taxon	C	H	B
Table 4. *Mammals of the Meadow Valley fauna.*			
Taxon	\<Land Mammal Ages*\> C	H	B
INSECTIVORA			
Notiosorex sp. (shrew)		x	x
LAGOMORPHA			
Hypolagus edensis (cottontail)		x	x
Hypolagus ringoldensis (cottontail)		x	x
Lepoides lepoides (jack rabbit)		x	x
Pewelagus dawsoni (small rabbit)			x
Nekrolagus progressus (rabbit)			x
RODENTIA			
Perognathus sp. (pocket mouse)		x	x
Prodipodomys sp. (kangaroo rat)		x	x
Repomys panacaensis (mouse)			x
Repomys sp. (mouse)		x	x
small cricetine rodent		x	x
Neotoma sp. (pack rat)			x
Ophiomys mcknighti (vole)			x
Ophiomys magilli (primitive vole)			x
Ondatra sp. (muskrat)			x
CARNIVORA			
Bassariscus sp. (ring-tail)		x	x
?Martinogale (skunk)		x	
Taxidea sp. (badger)			x
Canis lepophagus (dog)			x
Borophagus sp. cf. *B. diversidens* (dog)			x
Felis sp. (cat)		x	x
PROBOSCIDEA			
?Cuvieronius (gomphothere)			x
PERISSODACTYLA			
Dinohippus sp. (primitive horse)		x	
Equus (*Dolichohippus*) sp. cf. *E.* (*D.*) *simplicidens* (horse)			x
Equus (*Hemionus*) sp. (horse)			x
?Teleoceras sp.		?	
ARTIODACTYLA			
Platygonus sp. (peccary)		x	x
Megatylopus sp. (large camel)		x	x
Hemiauchenia sp. (llama)		x	x
Caprini undescribed genus			

Note: Taxa from Meadow Valley (SBCM, AMNH, UALP, UCMP repositories) are consistent with the Blancan Land Mammal Age except for the occurrence low in the section of *Teleoceras* sp. (UCMP repository) which is normally thought to be restricted to the Hemphillian Land Mammal Age.

* Abbreviations C = Clarendonian, H = Hemphillian, B = Blancan

Rhinocerotids are unknown from Blancan deposits. The specimen (UCMP 24093) has been reviewed by the authors and we agree with Stock's identification that it represents rhinocerotid, indicating that one site in Meadow Valley is Hemphillian. We conclude that the remainder of the fauna from Meadow Valley is Blancan, but do not rule out the potential for some sites within the section to produce Hemphillian mammals.

The composite Meadow Valley Fauna from the Panaca Formation is important because it contains both large and small mammals that help constrain the age of the basin development. The large mammals that are identified to a specific level — *Equus* (*Dolichohippus*) sp., cf. *E.* (*D.*) *simplicidens, Borophagus* sp., cf. *B. diversidens, Canis lepophagus* (AMNH repository) — are restricted to the Blancan Land Mammal Age and were recovered from exposures higher in the section than where the Hemphillian ?*Teleoceras* sp. was reported.

The only taxa on our faunal list from Meadow Valley (table 4) that are not recorded from Blancan faunas are ?*Martinogale* and *Dinohippus*, although several genera (for example, *Notiosorex, Hypolagus, Lepoides, Perognathus, Prodipodomys, Repomys, Bassariscus, Canis, Felis, Megatylopus*, and *Hemiauchenia*) are recorded from both Hemphillian and Blancan faunas.

The small mammals have been partially reviewed by Mou (1996a,b). Certain rabbit species and rodent genera span the Hemphillian and Blancan Land Mammal Ages. However, two rabbits (*P. dawsoni, N. progressus*), the cricetids and microtines (*R. panacaensis, O. mcknighti, O. magilli*, and *Ondatra* sp.) (AMNH, SBCM, UALP repositories), are restricted to the Blancan. Thus, the basal portion of the Panaca Formation in Meadow Valley has a single specimen identified as rhinoceros that suggests a late Hemphillian age. The remainder of the section contains taxa that span long periods of time and are restricted to the Blancan Land Mammal Age.

GEOLOGICAL HISTORY

The filling of selected basins along the eastern Nevada boundary has a bearing on interpretations of the end of extensional tectonics and the development of the western margin of the Colorado Plateau in Utah. Age estimates of around 11 million years (Bohannon, 1984) on the lower section of the Muddy Creek Formation suggest extension ended prior to that time. The Muddy Creek basin continued filling through approximately five million years ago (Lucchita, 1979; Damon and others, 1978). The fauna from the middle Muddy Creek section is mid-Hemphillian. The fauna from Spring Valley is

more derived (Robert Evander written communication to R.E. Reynolds via R.H. Tedford, 1997), and thus perhaps late Hemphillian (6 to 5 million years). These two basins, the Muddy Creek to the south and Spring Valley to the north, apparently ceased filling by about five million years ago. The topographic relief in western Utah and eastern Nevada that includes the Colorado Plateau margin may have been well developed by this time.

These late Miocene basins near the Utah-Nevada border reflect closed drainage systems with no through-flowing drainage until about five million years ago. To the south, in the Colorado River trough, the brackish, estuarine Bouse Formation (Metzger, 1968; Smith, 1970; Metzger and others, 1973) was present at 5.47 ± 0.2 million years (Damon and others, 1978). Additional interpretations of Bouse environment and relation to the structure of the Colorado River trough is provided by Buising (1992, 1993) and Spencer and Patchett (1997).

The White Narrows Formation, with a fauna estimated at approximately 4.7 million years, indicates a through-flowing drainage system dissecting the Muddy Creek Formation. The large fish (suckers and perch) reinforce the connection with a major river. Age estimates on basalt flows (Lucchita, 1979; Damon and others, 1978) in channels within the Muddy Creek Formation indicate that incision was older in the southwest (5.9 - 5.2 million years ago). Additionally, Lucchita (1979) reported a basalt in the Colorado River Valley near Grand Wash that is located within 105 meters of the present river grade. The basalt, estimated at 3.8 million years (Damon and others, 1978), indicates rapid downcutting by the river during one to one-half million years of time.

Age estimates for filling of Meadow Valley basin (that is, the Panaca Formation) range from approximately five million years ago to one million years ago. It appears that the Muddy Creek branch of the Virgin River arm of the Colorado River was not integrated (cut through the Caliente Caldera to drain Meadow Valley) until as recently as about one million years ago. This inference is based in part on relatively extensive, although discontinuous, ash beds in the Meadow Valley basin estimated at younger than 2.1 million years ago (approximately 1.2 to 0.8 million years ago according to P. D. Rowley, personal communication to E. H. Lindsay, 1996). The oldest exposures of the Panaca Formation in Meadow Valley are dominantly high-energy slope wash at the margins (mostly southern margin) of the valley. They are overlain by low-energy lacustrine sediments (silts and diatomites) which are best developed in the northern part of the basin near the town of Panaca. Aggradation and deflation must have kept pace during much of the low-energy depositional history of the Panaca Formation, with sediment transport mainly toward the center of the basin. The most pronounced physical relief in Meadow Valley is at Cathedral Gorge, on the northwest flank of the basin, where 20 to 30-meter-high cliff faces or spires are placed in a broad, flat valley. Meadow Valley Wash drops about 97 meters from Condor Canyon in the north to Indian Cove in the south, a distance of about 21.5 kilometers. Meadow Valley is relatively broad but not flat, and there is no profound physical relief. Integration of drainage did not result in an abrupt shift of base level; alluvial fans on the basin margin are still supplying sediment to a relatively low-energy, through-flowing stream, Meadow Valley Wash. While the Colorado River was cutting the Grand Canyon upstream from the Virgin River, there was relatively little downcutting in Meadow Valley.

SUMMARY

Mammal faunas and radiometric age estimates from late Tertiary basins in eastern Nevada provide a time-transitional picture of structural and depositional events. Major extensional tectonism ceased by about 12 million years and, presumably, the relief of Utah's spectacular Colorado Plateau was developed by this time. First the Muddy Basin and then Spring and Lake Basins filled during the late Miocene Hemphillian Land Mammal Age. Meadow Basin in eastern Nevada continued to fill during the Pliocene Blancan Land Mammal Age. However, in southern Nevada, faunas with large fish indicate downcutting by the Colorado River system by about 4.7 million years in the early Blancan Land Mammal Age. Rapid downcutting continued on the Colorado River system through the Pliocene. However, basins north of the Caliente Caldera were not integrated into that drainage system until approximately the last one million years.

ACKNOWLEDGMENTS

The authors wish to thank curators and staff at the AMNH and UCMP for access to and direction within the vertebrate fossil collections. Dwight Schmidt, U. S. Geological Survey, provided insight and inspiration in regard to the Muddy Creek Formation. Of special importance to note are the great number of field, wash site, and laboratory hours put in by volunteers and students of the SBCM and UALP, without whose help the collections of specimens that is the basis for this report would not have been possible.

REFERENCES

Anderson, R. E., 1973, Large-magnitude, late Tertiary strike-slip faulting north of Lake Mead, Nevada: U. S. Geological Survey Professional Paper 794, 18 p.

—1978, Geologic map of the Black Canyon 15' quadrangle, Mojave County, Arizona and Clark County, Nevada: U. S. Geological Survey Geologic Quadrangle Map GQ-1394, scale 1:62,500.

Beard, S. L., 1993, Tertiary stratigraphy of the South Virgin Mountains, southeast Nevada, and the Grand Wash Trough, northwest Arizona, *in* Sherrod, D. R., and Nielson, J. E., editors, U. S. Geological Survey Bulletin 2053, p. 29-32.

Blank, H. R., and Kucks, R. P., 1989, Preliminary aeromagnetic, gravity, and generalized geologic maps of the U.S.G.S. Basin and Range - Colorado Plateau transition zone study area in southwestern Utah, southeastern Nevada, and northwestern Arizona (the "BARCO" project): U. S. Geological Survey Open-File Report 89-432, 16 p., scale 1:250,000.

Bohannon, R. G., 1984, Nonmarine sedimentary rocks of Tertiary age in the Lake Mead region, southeastern Nevada and northwestern Arizona: U. S. Geological Survey Professional Paper 1259, 72 p.

Buising, A. V., 1992, The Bouse Formation and bracketing units, southeastern California and western Arizona, *in* Reynolds, R. E., compiler, Old routes to the Colorado: San Bernardino County Museum Special Publication v. 92-2, p. 103.

—1993, Stratigraphic overview of the Bouse Formation and gravels of the Colorado River, Riverside Mountains, Eastern Vidal Valley, and Mesquite Mountains areas, California and Arizona, *in* Sherrod, D. R., and Nielson, J. E., editors, Tertiary stratigraphy of highly extended terranes, California, Arizona, and Nevada: U. S. Geological Survey Bulletin 2053, 250 p.

Carpenter, Eugene, 1915, Ground water in southeastern Nevada: U. S. Geological Survey, Water-Supply Paper 365, p. 1-86.

Czaplewski, N. J., 1990, The Verde local fauna--small vertebrate fossils from the Verde Formation, Arizona: San Bernardino County Museum Association Quarterly, v. 37, no. 3, 39 p.

Damon, P. E., Shafiqullah, M. J., and Scarborough, R. B., 1978, Revised chronology for critical stages in the evolution of the lower Colorado River: Geological Society of America, Abstracts with Programs v. 10, no. 3, p. 101-102.

Duebendorfer, E. W., and Wallin, E. T., 1991, Basin development and syntectonic sedimentation associated with kinematically coupled strike-slip and detachment faulting, southern Nevada: Geology, v. 19, p. 87-90.

Ekren, E. B., Orkild, P. P., Sargent, K. A., and Dixon, G. L., 1977, Geologic map of Lincoln County, Nevada: U. S. Geological Survey Miscellaneous Investigations Map I-1041, scale 1:250,000.

Gardner, L. R., 1968, The Quaternary geology of the Moapa Valley, Clark County, Nevada: University Park, Pennsylvania State University, Ph.D. dissertation, 162 p.

Longwell, C. R., Pampeyan, E. H., Bowyer, Ben, and Roberts, R. J., 1965, Geology and mineral deposits of Clark County, Nevada: Nevada Bureau of Mines Bulletin 62, 218 p.

Lucchita, Ivo, 1979, Late Cenozoic uplift of the southwestern Colorado Plateau and adjacent lower Colorado River region, *in* McGetchin, T. R., and Merrill R. B., editors, Plateau uplift - mode and mechanism: Tectono Physics: v. 61, p. 63-95.

MacDonald, J. R., and Pelletier, W. J., 1956, The Pliocene mammalian faunas of Nevada, U. S. A.: Section VII (Paleontologia, Taxonomia y Evolucion), Congress Geologico International, XX Sesion, p. 365-388.

May, S. R., 1981, *Repomys* (Mammalia: Rodentia, gen. nov.) from the late Neogene of California and Nevada: Journal of Vertebrate Paleontology, v. 1, no. 2, p. 219-230.

Metzger, D. G., 1968, The Bouse Formation (Pliocene) of the Parker-Blyth-Cibola area, Arizona and California: U. S. Geological Survey Professional Paper 600-D p. D126-D136.

Metzger, D. G., Loeltz, O. J., and Ireland, Burdge, 1973, Geohydrology of the Needles area, Arizona, California, and Nevada: U. S. Geological Survey Professional Paper, 486G, 130 p.

Mou, Yun, 1996a, A new arvicoline species (Mammalia: Rodentia) from the Pliocene Panaca Formation, southeast Nevada in punctuated chaos in the Northeastern Mojave Desert: San Bernardino County Museum Association Quarterly, v. 43, no.1,2, 158 p.

—1996b, *Mimomys* and *Repomys* (Rodentia: Cricetidae) from the Pliocene Panaca Formation, southeast Nevada: Journal of Vertebrate Paleontology, v. 16, no. 3, p 55A.

Phoenix, D. A., 1948, Geology and ground water on the Meadow Valley Wash drainage area, Nevada, above the vicinity of Caliente: Nevada, Office of State Engineer, Water Resources Bulletin, v. 7, p. 1-117.

Repenning, C. A., 1987, Biochronology of the microtine rodents of the United States, *in* Woodburne, M.O., editor, Cenozoic mammals of North America — geochronology and biostratigraphy: Berkeley, University of California Press, 336 p.

Reynolds, S. J., Florence, F. P., Welty, J. W., Roddy, M. S., Currier, D. A., Anderson, A. V., Keith, S. B., 1986, Compilation of radiometric age determination in Arizona: Arizona Bureau of Geology and Mineral Technology Bulletin 197, 258 p.

Rowley, P. D., Nealey, L. D., Unruh, D. N., Snee, L. W., Mehnert, H. H., Anderson, R. E., and Gromme, C. S., 1995, Stratigraphy of Miocene ash-flow tuffs in and near the Caliente Caldera Complex, southeastern Nevada and southwestern Utah: U. S. Geological Survey Bulletin 2056B: p. 47-88.

Rowley, P. D., and Shroba, R. R., 1991, Geologic map of the Indian Cove Quadrangle, Lincoln County, Nevada: U. S. Geological Survey Map GQ-1701, scale 1:24,000.

Rowley P. D., Shroba, R. R., Simonds, P. W., Burke, K. J., Axen, G. J., and Olmore, S. D., 1994, Geologic map of the Chief Mountain quadrangle, Lincoln County, Nevada: U. S. Geological Survey Map GQ-1781, scale 1:24,000.

Schmidt, D. L., Page, W. R., and Workman, J. B., 1996, Preliminary geologic map of the Moapa West quadrangle, Clark County, Nevada: U. S. Geological Survey Open File Report [Number], p. 96-521, scale 1:24,000.

Smith, P. B., 1970, New evidence for Pliocene marine embayment along the lower Colorado River area, California and Arizona: Geological Society of American Bulletin, v. 81, p. 1411-1420.

Spencer, J. E., and Patchett, P. J., 1997, Sr isotope evidence for a lacustrine origin for the upper Miocene to Pliocene Bouse Formation, lower Colorado River trough and implications for timing of Colorado Plateau uplift: Geological Society of American Bulletin, v. 109, p. 767-778.

Stewart, J. H., and Carlson, J. E., 1978, Geologic map of Nevada: U. S. Geological Survey in cooperation with the Nevada Bureau of Mines and Geology.

Stock, Chester, 1921, Later Cenozoic mammalian remains from Meadow Valley Region, southeastern Nevada: American Journal of Science, v. 2, p. 250-264.

Spurr, J. E., 1903, Descriptive geology of Nevada south of the fortieth parallel and adjacent portions of California: U. S. Geological Survey Bulletin 208: p. 15-229.

Taylor, W. J., Bartley, J. M., Lux, D. R., and Axen, G. J., 1989, Timing of Tertiary extension in the Railroad Valley-Pioche transect, Nevada--constraints from Ar/Ar ages of volcanic rocks: Journal of Geophysical Research, v. 94, no. 66, p. 7757-7774.

Tedford, R. H., Skinner, M. F., Fields, R. W., Rensberger, J. M., Whistler, D. P., Galusha, Ted, Taylor, B. E., MacDonald, J. R., and Webb, S. D, 1987, Faunal succession and biochronology of the Arikaarean through Hemphillian interval (late Oligocene through earliest Pliocene epochs) in North America, *in* Woodburne, M. O., editor, Cenozoic mammals of North America — geochronology and biostratigraphy: Berkeley, University of California Press, p. 153-210.

Wallin, E. T., Duebendorfor, E. M., and Smith, E. I., 1993, Tertiary stratigraphy of the Lake Mead Region: PN 33-35, in U. S. Geological Survey Bulletin 2053, 250 p.

White, J. A., 1987, The Archaeolaginae (Mammalia: Lagomorpha) of North American, excluding Archaeolagus and Panolax: Journal of Vertebrate Paleontology, v. 7 (4), p. 425-450.

—1991, North American Leporinae (Mammalia: Lagomorpha) from late Miocene (Clarendonian) to latest Pliocene (Blancan): Journal of Vertebrate Paleontology, v. 11 (1), p. 67-89.

Woodburne, M. O., and Swisher III, C. C., 1995, Land mammal high-resolution geochronology, intercontinental overland dispersal, sea level, climate and vicariance--geochronology, time scales, and global stratigraphic correlation, Society of Economic Paleontologists and Mineralogists Special Publication No. 54, p. 335-364.

A PRELIMINARY REPORT OF A NEW CLARENDONIAN (LATE MIOCENE) MAMMALIAN FAUNA FROM NORTHWESTERN UTAH

Allen R. Tedrow

Division of Paleontology, Idaho Museum of Natural History, Campus Box 8096, Idaho State University, Pocatello, Idaho 83209-8096

Steven F. Robison

Division of Geology, Caribou National Forest, 250 South Fourth Avenue, Pocatello, Idaho 83201

ABSTRACT

A small faunal assemblage containing fossil mammals, fish and molluscs was recovered from late Miocene (Clarendonian Land Mammal Age) sediments of the Salt Lake Formation in Box Elder County, Utah. Preliminary assessment of this material suggests that the Fish Lake Valley fauna of western Nevada is closely correlative. The as yet meager fauna includes the mammals *Hesperolagomys*, *Eucastor*, and *Copemys*.

INTRODUCTION

Introductory Remarks

Vertebrate fossils were recovered from the Salt Lake Formation roughly 35 kilometers (22 miles) southeast of the town of Grouse Creek (figure 1), Box Elder County, in extreme northwestern Utah. Located at the northern limits of the Great Salt Lake Desert, the terrain is predominantly low, rolling hills and shallow, dry washes. Sparse desert vegetation in the area reveals numerous fault-bounded exposures of predominantly fine-grained sands, silts, and clays.

Geologic Setting

Overview

The rocks along the southern flanks of the Grouse Creek Mountains are comprised of a cluster of late Eocene to early Miocene granitic bodies and several allochthonous sheets of variably metamorphosed early to late Paleozoic rocks. These rocks juxtapose and/or are thrust over thick, folded, late Miocene sediments composed predominantly of volcanoclastic and allochthonous debris (Armstrong, 1970; Compton and others, 1977) deposited prior to the onset of basin and range faulting. Compton and others (1977) suggested that cooling and sagging within the pluton(s) produced broad late Miocene basins.

Salt Lake Formation

Late Miocene deposits in the vicinity of Grouse Creek are mapped as Salt Lake Formation or Group (Mapel and Hail, 1956; Blue, 1960) a name which has been variously applied to a lithologically diverse assemblage of Cenozoic deposits in northern Utah, southern Idaho, and restricted portions of northeastern Nevada. The term Salt Lake Group was first used by Hayden (1869) for Tertiary deposits in Salt Lake and Weber Valleys. The Weber Valley beds were later referred to the Norwood Tuff by Eardley (1944), a late Eocene deposit which has yielded brontothere remains and a K-Ar date (recalibrated from Evernden and others, 1964) of 38.5 Ma. Nevertheless, the name Salt Lake Formation or Group is still applied to mid- and late Tertiary rocks in the Bonneville Basin and adjacent areas. Although as McClellan (1976) pointed out, beds from Eocene through Pleistocene age have been assigned to the Salt Lake Formation (Group) by various workers, a medial to late Miocene age is defensible on the basis of radiometric dates and floral and faunal analyses.

Several factors have contributed to the confusion surrounding recognition of the Salt Lake Formation, but it is partially due to the highly variable nature of the rocks referred to the Salt Lake Formation which include lacustrine siltstones, shales, and limestones; fluvial sands, silts, and conglomerates; reworked volcanic tuffs; and waterlain tuffs; and interbedded rhyolites, basalts and tuffs. Contemporaneous deposits in adjacent basins are comprised predominantly of locally derived material and may therefore be distinct lithologically. Because these deposits are scattered in numerous intermountain basins, direct correlation is often difficult if not impossible. Further confounding our knowledge of the Salt Lake Formation is the generally scattered occurrence of outcrops, a high level of postdepositional faulting region-

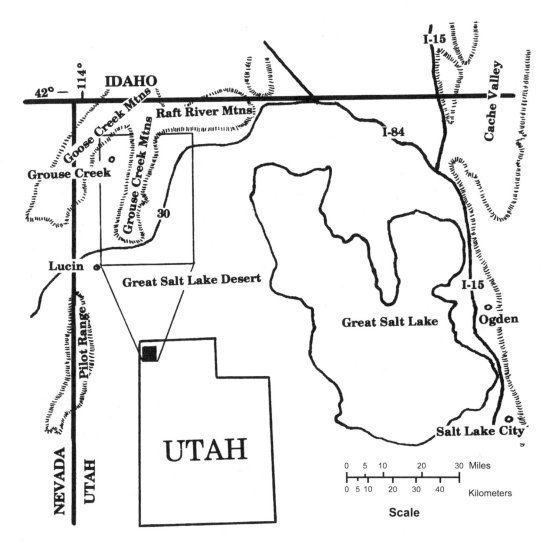

Figure 1. *Map of northern Utah and surrounding areas described in the text. Outlined region represents the general area currently under study by the authors. Locality data concerning IMNH 1123 and 1124 are on file at the Idaho Museum of Natural History.*

ally producing incomplete sequences, and a general lack of age-diagnostic fossils recovered to date.

Previous Work

The Salt Lake Formation in the Cache Valley area of northern Utah and southeastern Idaho has been more closely examined [Keller, 1952; Williams (in Smith, 1953); Adamson and others, 1955; Williams, 1962] than in the present study area. Working primarily within the southern Cache Valley, Williams (1962) demoted the Salt Lake Group to formation status, dividing over 760 meters (2,500 feet) of the formation into three members: (1) a lower conglomerate, (2) a middle tuffaceous unit, and (3) an upper conglomerate and sandstone unit.

Fossils are not commonly found in the Salt Lake Formation and most of the published accounts are mainly from within the Cache Valley area. Yen (1947), Swain

(1947) and Brown (1949) described fossil molluscs, ostracodes and plants, respectively. McClellan (1977) described the fish fauna from the Salt Lake Formation near Cache Valley, and reported on fossil fish and mammals from the Grouse Creek Valley, Utah area, about 40 kilometers (25 miles) northwest of our study area. McClellan (1976) assigned the beds a Barstovian age (table 1) based on the presence of *Liodontia, Cupidinimus, Merychippus, Hypohippus, Merycodus,* and *Merriamoceros.* These beds may in fact be as old as late Hemingfordian but can be no younger than early Barstovian, because the temporal range of *Merriamoceros* is resitricted to that interval. Taylor (1985) has noted the occurrence of Miocene freshwater molluscs from the western flanks of the Grouse Creek Mountains and adjacent areas. Fossil plants from the southern margin of the Grouse Creek Mountains are currently under study by Daniel I. Axelrod (verbal communication, 1997).

Table 1. *Relationship of North American Land Mammal Ages to later Tertiary Epochs.*

EPOCH	MA*	NORTH AMERICAN LAND MAMMAL AGE
Pliocene		Blancan
	— 4.8 —	
	— 8.5 —	Hemphillian
		Clarendonian
	— 11 —	
Miocene		Barstovian
	— 16 —	
		Hemingfordian
	— 20 —	
	— 24 —	Arikarean
Oligocene		

*Age and dates from Tedford and others (1987)

No formal subdivision has been attempted for the Salt Lake Formation in extreme northwestern Utah. Blue (1960) mapped nearly 915 meters (3,000 feet) of Tertiary rocks on the northeast and northwest flanks of the Pilot Range, near Lucin; the majority of these he referred to the Salt Lake Formation. These beds had been previously described by Van Houten (1956) as belonging to the "eastern sedimentary sequence," a somewhat localized but lithologically distinct group comprised of sandstone, limestone, mudstone and Paleozoic-pebble conglomerate distributed across eastern Nevada and northeastern Utah. Van Houten (1956) recognized an overlying "vitric tuff unit" present throughout Nevada and extending into southern Idaho and northwestern Utah. According to Blue (1960) this conspicuous, lightly colored sequence of tuff, reworked ash, sandstone, calcareous siltstone, and fine pebble conglomerate reaches a thickness of 152 meters (500 feet) near Lucin. Blue (1960) regarded the "vitric tuff unit" a mappable unit distinct from the Salt Lake Formation and retained Van Houten's informal name. More recent work on these same beds has yielded K-Ar dates ranging from 12.0 Ma (Hillhouse, 1983 in Miller, 1984) to 8.6 Ma (Armstrong, 1970). Interestingly, many of these later works have not included assignment of these deposits to any particular formation.

Throughout Nevada, these rocks are collectively known by various formational names, including Esmeralda, Humboldt, and Truckee. Fossil mammal assemblages indicating Barstovian through Clarendonian ages are most common (Macdonald, 1949; Clark and others, 1964; Mawby, 1965; Suthard, 1966) in these deposits. However, while faunas from the Humboldt Formation in eastern Nevada remain for the most part undescribed,

younger, Hemphillian faunas have been recognized therein by R. H. Tedford (C. C. Swisher, verbal communication, 1998).

Williams and others (1982) recognized over 760 meters (2500 feet) of Salt Lake Formation within the Raft River Valley of south-central Idaho, roughly 50 kilometers (32 miles) northeast of Grouse Creek. Radiometric data indicate that this largely tuffaceous sequence ranges from approximately 11 to 7 Ma.

Precisely how any of these beds from other areas relate to recognized members of the Salt Lake Formation in the Cache Valley is not known. To the best of our knowledge, there has been no systematic attempt at radiometric age determination of the Salt Lake Formation within this, the type area. Futhermore, the presently available fossil data based largely on fish and invertebrates do not provide a reliable basis for correlation. Smith and Nash (1976) demonstrated that ash beds within widely separated outcrops of the Salt Lake Formation could be correlated with one another. Their most thoroughly sampled section, in the Goose Creek Mountains, can be correlated with the Lucin and Grouse Creek sections and with ash beds in south-central Idaho.

Abbreviations

IMNH (Idaho Museum of Natural History) designates both fossil localities and fossil specimens. Dental measurements were recorded in millimeters (mm) using a Gaertner measuring microscope. Abbreviatons for dental measurements are as follows: A-P, anteroposterior length; Tra, anterior transverse width; Trp, posterior transverse width; Tr, maximum transverse width. Kilometers are abbreviated as km. Age-dates are abbreviated as Ma (Mega-annum).

Occurrence of Fossils

The fossils at Scrappy Hill are contained within roughly one vertical meter of strata in which at least two productive horizons (localities) have been identified. The rabbit horizon (figure 2) has produced essentially all the diagnostic material. The subadjacent ungulate horizon has yielded an ungulate skull, but it is so badly weathered and fragmented as to preclude more detailed study. In fact, of the mammalian fossils collected, only

Figure 2. *Photograph showing terrain and IMNH 1123 and 1124. Rabbit horizon (IMNH 1123) indicated by the vertical arrow. Ungulate horizon (IMNH 1124) indicated by the horizontal arrow.*

those from the rabbit horizon are complete enough to warrant description. Fossil molluscs and fish have been recovered from both horizons and will be described in a later paper, but these are not likely to provide any greater temporal resolution than that supplied by the mammalian taxa. Additionally, fossil leaves and wood (conifer and angiosperm) are present about one-half kilometer from Scrappy Hill, and additional, although as yet only fragmentary, mammalian remains have been recovered there in immediately adjacent strata. The mammalian material from the plant locality is not discussed in this paper. Much additional fieldwork will be required to determine the stratigraphic relationships between these two areas because numerous faults with undetermined vertical displacement have been observed between them.

The beds at Scrappy Hill are well below the late Pleistocene Lake Bonneville highstand as indicated by terraces which onlap adjacent, topographically higher hillsides. In fact, molluscs of Bonneville age and perhaps fish appear to be draped upon these demonstrably older (Clarendonian) deposits.

The sediments of the rabbit horizon are grey clays having numerous, ribbon-like iron oxide stringers which impart a yellowish tone to the surrounding sediments when leached. Abundant in this horizon are small pebble to sand-size gypsum crystals, thin shelled molluscs (Bonneville type), and iron oxide replaced gastropods and bivalves. Immediately below, the ungulate horizon contains somber grey silty clays which lighten upward and contain numerous carbonized root traces (compressions), tiny Bonneville molluscs and flat ironstone concretions.

SYSTEMATIC PALEONTOGY
Class Mammalia
Order Lagomorpha
Family Leporidae
Genus *Hesperolagomys* Clark and others, 1964
Hesperolagomys galbreathi Clark and others, 1964
(figure 3, a-e, table 2)

Referred Specimens

IMNH 15871, RM^{1or2}; IMNH 15870, isolated lower molariform; IMNH 15869, isolated lower molariform, ?M$_1$

Horizon

Rabbit horizon (IMNH 1123)

Description

The upper molar has a deep and persistant internal hypostria which nearly reaches the crescentic valley. The anterior loph extends farther medially than posterior loph and has greater enamel thickness. The crescentic valley is cement-filled and roughly w-shaped. This valley opens through a narrow, somewhat tortuous, passage in the posterior loph but would close with little additional wear. Buccal roots are strongly developed. The buccal margin of tooth has an acute occlusal outline.

IMNH 15869 is a rooted, left lower molariform having the trigonid more transversely elongate and antero-posteriorly compressed than the talonid. Enamel is thickest on the posterior and anterolabial faces of both the trigonid and talonid. The talonid narrows greatly as

Table 2. *Dimensions (mm) of three molar teeth of* Hespero-lagomys galbreathi *from the Rabbit horizon, Salt Lake Formation, Box Elder County, Utah.*

	IMNH 15869 LM$_x$	IMNH 15870 Lm$_x$	IMNH 15871 LM^{1or2}
A-P	1.63	1.58	1.31
Tra.	1.75	1.79	2.73
Trp.	1.44	1.23	1.86

it approaches the posterior face of the trigonid; a thin wafer of cement separates the two.

The other isolated molariform (IMNH 15870, figure 3, a-f), possibly a M$_2$, exhibits pronounced posterior curvature when viewed from the side. The posterior face of the talonid has a rounded contour bearing a slight remnant of an appression facet. As with IMNH 15869, both lingual and buccal folds are cement-filled. Neither of the lower molariforms has any suggestion of a posterolophid.

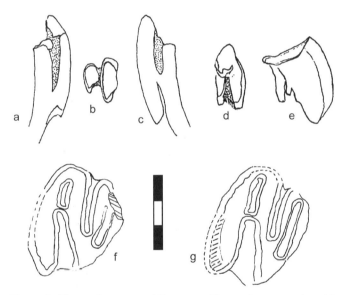

Figure 3. Hesperolagomys and Eucastor: Hesperolagomys gabreathi: *IMNH 15870, lower molariform teeth in a, lingual; b, occlusal; and c, buccal view; IMNH 15871 in d, occlusal; and e, posterior views.* Eucastor sp., cf. E. tortus: *f, IMNH 15872, ?M^1 and g, IMNH 15873, ?M^2. Scale bar equals three millimeters.*

Discussion

The material at hand is very similar in size and morphology to specimens of *Hesperolagomys galbreathi* from the early Clarendonian Fish Lake Valley fauna of western Nevada. The lower molariform teeth from Utah are distinguished from those of *Hesperolagomys fluviatilis* (Storer, 1970) from the Barstovian of Saskatchewan in having a very narrow connection of talonid to the trigonid, and in their much greater thickness of

enamel on the posterior faces of trigonids and talonids, whereas, in *H. fluviatilis*, the enamel thickness appears more uniformly distributed. Storer (1970) observed that the anterobuccal wall of the talonid outlined an acute angle or curve in *H. fluviatilis*. This condition is present in the least worn of our two available specimens, but is quite different in the other (figure 3b), suggesting that this feature may be a function of wear.

Order Rodentia
Family Castoridae
Genus *Eucastor* Leidy 1858
***Eucastor* sp., cf. *E. tortus* Leidy 1858**
(figure 3, f and g)

Referred Specimens

IMNH 15872, ?LM^1; IMNH 15873, ?LM^2.

Horizon

Rabbit horizon, IMNH 1123

Description

These teeth are in an early stage of wear. Both are broken away some distance above their roots and have minor damage to their crowns and sides. They also exhibit some evidence of fluvatile abrasion. The para- and metafossettes have formed and the mesoflexus is near closure. Metafossettes extend nearly to the lingual margin of the crown and on ?M^1 appears to have opened buccally due to wear. Parastriae persist as subtle but detectable furrows on the buccal surface into the most advanced stages of wear. Dimensions are (1) ?M^1, A-P: 4.8 mm; Tr.: 4.1 mm; (2) ?M^2, A-P: 3.4 mm; Tr: 4.5 mm.

Comparisons

These teeth can be distinguished from those of *Monosaulax pansus* by their greater degree of hypsodonty, shorter more transversely directed mesostriae, and less persistent metafossettes. The mesoflexus is more transversely directed than in *Eucastor dividerus* where it is deflected posteriorly, nearly surrounding the metafossette. In *Eucastor phillisi* from the Clarendonian of Kansas, the parafossette is evidently much shorter lived than in this material, judging by its small size compared to the great length of the mesostria (Wilson, 1968, Figure 15). In the Utah specimens, the mesofossette is late to develop, but its formation would be roughly coincident with the loss of the parafossette.

The specimens at hand closely resemble *Eucastor tortus* from Kansas (Hibbard, 1942) in nearly all features of their crown morphology. One striking difference, however, is the much more transversely elongate metafossette in the Utah specimens which extends from the posterolabial margin of the crown to beyond the lingual extent of the mesoflexus. In this respect they may be unique among all known populations of *Eucastor*.

Dorr and Wheeler (1964) referred to *Eucastor* sp., near *E. tortus* an isolated P[4] from what they considered Madison Valley Formation equivalent in southwestern Montana. This specimen was not figured nor were measurements provided, but it is described as having a metaflexus and extremely short metastria, which is consistent with Stirton's (1935) discussion of the P[4] in *Eucastor tortus*. Unfortunately, dental ontogenetic variation in the molar teeth of *E. tortus* is not adequately known. However, judging from the proximity of the metafossettes to the external border in the Utah specimens, it seems likely that a metaflexus would have been present in an earlier wear stage. While subsequent direct comparison of the Utah and Montana beavers might suggest that they are conspecific, a review of the genus *Eucastor* may be required to assign these teeth to a particular species.

Records of *Eucastor tortus* are common to the Barstovian through Hemphillian of the central Great Plains but apparently this species has not been reported west of the continental divide.

Family Cricetidae

Genus *Copemys* Wood 1936
Copemys sp., aff. *C. lindsayi* Dalquest and others, 1996

Referred Specimen

IMNH 15874, RM[1].

Horizon

Rabbit horizon, IMNH 1123.

Description

The specimen is an isolated, lightly worn M[1]. The protocone is farther anterior than is the paracone. The anterocone is long and vaguely bilobate. The buccal anterior valley (paraflexus) is occupied by a short, buccally directed ridge which terminates well before the buccal margin of the crown. A parastyle blocks buccal entrance to the anterior valley. A mesoloph is well developed but terminates short of the labial margin of the crown. Metacone connects to the posteroloph. Dimensions of this M[1] are: A-P: 2.09 mm; Tr.:1.28 mm.

Comparisons

Of the numerous described species of *Copemys*, the Grouse Creek specimen is most similar to (and in many respects intermediate between) the early Clarendonian *C. esmeraldensis* (Clark and others, 1964) and the medial to late Clarendonian *C. lindsayi* (Dalquest and others, 1996). It is similar to *C. lindsayi* in most aspects of crown morphology, notably: the bilobate condition of the anterocone; mesoloph and paralophule centered within valleys; presence of a parastyle; and opposite orientation of the paraflexus and protoflexus. With *Copemys esmeraldensis*, IMNH 15874 shares the strongly developed posteroloph and the union of the metacone with the posteroloph. The mesoloph is incomplete but partitions the median valley in IMNH 15874 rather than terminating at the metacone, as in *C. esmeraldensis*. There is no hint of a mesostyle (variably present in *C. lindsayi*), and a distinct parastyle is present. In size, IMNH 15874 is close to the reported range for *Copemys lindsayi* but is slightly longer.

Table 3. *Faunal list from Grouse Creek, Box Elder County, Utah. See text for discussion of rabbit horizon and ungulate horizon, respectively. Identifications of fossil molluscs and fish are tentative.*

Rabbit horizon - IMNH 1123
    Mollusca
        Gastropoda
            ?*Valvata utahensis*
        Pelecypoda
            ?*Pisidium* sp.
    Vertebrata
        Osteichthyes
            genus and species indeterminate
    Mammalia
        Lagomorpha
            Leporidae?
                Hesperolagomys galbreathi
        Rodentia
            Castoridae
                Eucastor sp., cf. *E. tortus*
        Rodentia
            Cricetidae
                Copemys sp., aff. *C. lindsayi*

Ungulate horizon IMNH 1124
    Mollusca
        Gastropoda
    Vertebrata
        Osteichthyes
        Cyprinidae
    Mammalia
        ?Artiodactyla

CONCLUSIONS

We assign a Clarendonian age to this scant fauna. Solely on the basis of the lagomorph, it seems that the closest faunal correlative is the Fish Lake Valley local fauna from the Esmeralda Formation of western Nevada (Hall, 1930; Clark and others, 1964; Mawby, 1965). The age of this fauna is given by Tedford and others (1987) as early Clarendonian and interbedded tuffs have yielded dates ranging from 11.4 to 11.8 Ma (Evernden and others, 1964). The Clarendonian Chalk Spring fauna (Macdonald, 1949) of northeastern Nevada, roughly 120 kilometers (75 miles) to the west, bears no real similarity to our scant collection. The Chalk Spring material may in fact represent both Hemphillian and Clarendonian ages based on the presence there of the early Hemphillian *Peromyscus antiquus* and *Eucastor lecontei* from the Clarendonian.

Further aquisition of fossil mammals and radiometric dates from the Grouse Creek area and from the Cache Valley should greatly enhance our understanding of the geologic history of the Bonneville Basin during much of Miocene time.

ACKNOWLEDGMENTS

Thanks to Brian Arnold for introducing SFR to the area and showing him the fossil plant locality. The authors wish to acknowledge a tremendous resource we have at IMNH, namely the R.A. Stirton Library. Sue Ann Bilbey (Utah Field House of Natural History State Park, Vernal Utah), Jon Baskin (Texas A and M at Kingsville, Texas), and Carl Swisher III (Berkeley Geochronology Center) kindly provided valuable reference material.

REFERENCES

Adamson, R. D., Hardy, C. T., and Williams, J. S., 1955, Tertiary rocks of Cache Valley, Utah and Idaho: Utah Geological Society Guidebook, no. 10, p. 1-22.

Armstrong, R. L., 1970, Geochronology of Tertiary igneous rocks, eastern Basin and Range province, western Utah, eastern Nevada, and vicinity, U.S.A.: Geochimica et Cosmochimica Acta, v. 34, p. 203-232.

Blue, D. M., 1960, Geology and ore deposits of the Lucin Mining District, Box Elder County, Utah, and Elko County, Nevada: Salt Lake City, University of Utah, M.S. thesis, 122 p.

Brown, R. W., 1949, Pliocene plants from Cache Valley, Utah: Journal of the Washington Academy of Sciences, v. 39, no. 7, p.224-229.

Clark, J. B., Dawson, M. R., and Wood, A. E., 1964, Fossil mammals from the lower Pliocene of Fish Lake Valley, Nevada: Bulletin of the Museum of Comparative Zoology, v. 131, no. 2, p. 27-63.

Compton, R. R., Todd, V. R., Zartman, R. E., and Naeser, C. W., 1977, Oligocene and Miocene metamorphism, folding, and faulting in northwestern Utah: Geological Society of America Bulletin, v. 88, p. 1237-1250.

Dalquest, W. W., Baskin, J. A., and Schultz, G. E., 1996, Fossil mammals from a late Miocene (Clarendonian) site in Beaver County, Oklahoma, *in* Genoways, H. H., and Baker, R. J., editors, Contributions in mammalogy--a memorial volume honoring Dr. Knox Jones, Jr.: Lubbock, Museum of Texas Tech University, p. 107-137.

Dorr, J. A., Jr., and W. H. Wheeler, 1964, Cenozoic paleontology, stratigraphy, and reconnaissance geology of the upper Ruby River Basin, southwestern Montana: University of Michigan, Contributions of the Museum of Paleontology, v.13, no.12, p. 297-339.

Eardley, A. J., 1944, Geology of the north-central Wasatch Mountains, Utah: Geological Society of America Bulletin, v. 55, no. 7, p. 819-894.

Evernden, J. F., Savage, D. E., Curtis, G. H., and James, G. T., 1964, Potassium-argon dates and the Cenozoic mammalian chronology of North America: American Journal of Science, v. 262, no. 2, p. 145-198.

Hall, E. R., 1930, Rodents and Lagomorphs from the late Tertiary of Fish Lake Valley, Nevada: University of California Publications, Bulletin of the Department of Geological Sciences, v. 19, p. 295-312.

Hayden, F. N., 1869, Preliminary field reports of the U. S. Geological Survey of Colorado and New Mexico: U. S. Geological survey of the territories, 3rd annual field report, 155 p.

Hibbard, C. W., 1942, The occurrence of *Eucastor tortus* Leidy in Phillips County, Kansas: Transactions Kansas Academy of Science, v. 45, p. 248-252.

Keller, A. S., 1952, Geology of the Mink Creek Region, Idaho: Salt Lake City, University of Utah, M. S. thesis.

Macdonald, J. R., 1949, A new Clarendonian fauna from northeastern Nevada, University of Califfornia Bulletin of the Department of Geological Sciences, v. 28, no. 7, p. 173-194.

Mapel, W. J., and Hail W. J., Jr., 1956, Teriary stratigraphy of the Goose Creek District, Idaho, and adjacent parts of Utah and Nevada: Utah Geological Society Guidebook, no.11, p. 1-16.

Mawby, J. E., 1965, Pliocene vertebrates and stratigraphy in Stewart and Ione Valleys, Nevada: Berkeley, University of California, Ph.D. dissertation.

McClellan, P. H., 1976, New evidence for the age of Cenozoic Salt Lake Beds in northeastern Great Basin: Bulletin of the American Association of Petroleum Geologists, v. 60, no. 12, p. 2185.

—1977, Paleontology and paleoecology of Neogene freshwater fishes from Salt Lake Beds, northern Utah: Berkeley, University of California, M.S. thesis, 243 p.

Miller, D. M., 1984, Sedimentary and igneous rocks of the Pilot Range and vicinity, Utah and Nevada: Utah Geological Association Publication 13, Geology of Northwest Utah, Southern Idaho and Northwest Nevada, p.45-63.

Smith, Neal, 1953, Tertiary stratigraphy of northern Utah and southeastern Idaho, Intermountain Association of Petroleum Geologists, 4th Annual Field Conference, p. 73-77.

Smith, R. P., and Nash, W. P., 1976, Chemical correlation of volcanic ash deposits in the Salt Lake Group, Utah, Idaho and Nevada: Journal of Sedimentary Petrology, v. 46, no. 4, p. 930-939.

Stirton, R. A., 1935, A review of the Tertiary beavers: University of California Publications, Bulletin of the Department of Geological Sciences, v. 23, no. 13, p. 391-458.

Storer, J. E., 1970, New rodents and lagomorphs from the Upper Miocene Wood Mountain Formation of southern Saskatchewan: Canadian Journal of Earth Science, v. 7, no. 4, p. 1125-1129.

Suthard, J. A., 1966, Stratigraphy and paleontology in Fish Lake Valley, Esmeralda County, Nevada: Riverside, University of California, M.S. thesis.

Swain, F. M., 1947, Tertiary non-marine Ostracoda from the Salt Lake Formation, northern Utah: Journal of Paleontology, v. 21, p. 518-528.

Taylor, D. W., 1985, Evolution of freshwater drainages and molluscs in western North America: *in* Smiley, C. J., editor, Late Cenozoic history of the Pacific Northwest: San Francisco, California, Pacific Division, American Asociation for the Advancement of Science, p. 265-321.

Tedford, R. H., Skinner, M. F., Fields, R. W., Rensberger, J. M., Whistler, D. P., Galusha, Theodore, Taylor, B. E., Macdonald, J. R., and Webb, S. D., 1987, Faunal succession and biochronology of the Arikareean through Hemphillian interval (late Oligocene through earliest Pliocene Epochs) in North America, *in* Woodburne, M. O., editor, Cenozoic mammals of North America: Berkeley and Los Angeles, University of California Press, p. 153-210.

Van Houten, F. B., 1956, Reconnaisance of Cenozoic sedimentary rocks of Nevada: American Association of Petroleum Geologists Bulletin, v. 40, no. 12, p. 2801-2825.

Williams, J. S., 1962, Lake Bonneville--geology of the southern Cache Valley, Utah: U. S. Geological Survey Professional Paper 257C, p. 131-152.

Williams, P. L., Covington, H. R., and Pierce, K. L., 1982, Cenozoic stratigraphy and tectonic evolution of the Raft River Basin, Idaho, *in* Bonnichsen, Bill, and Breckenridge, R. M., editors, Cenozoic geology of Idaho: Idaho Bureau of Mines and Geology Bulletin 26, p. 491- 504.

Wilson, R. L., 1968, Systematics and faunal analysis of a lower Pliocene vertebrate assemblage from Trego County, Kansas: University of Michigan, Contribution from the Museum of Paleontology, v. 22, no.7, p.75-126.

Yen, T. C., 1947, Pliocene freshwater molluscs from northern Utah: Journal of Paleontology, v. 21, p. 268-277.

AN ADDITIONAL OCCURRENCE OF *SIMOCYON* (MAMMALIA, CARNIVORA, PROCYONIDAE) IN NORTH AMERICA

Allen R. Tedrow

Division of Paleontology, Idaho Museum of Natural History, Campus Box 8096, Idaho State University, Pocatello, Idaho 83209-8096

Jon A. Baskin

Department of Geosciences, Texas A&M University at Kingsville, Kingsville, Texas 78363

Steven F. Robison

Division of Geology, Caribou National Forest, 250 South Fourth Avenue, Pocatello, Idaho 83201

ABSTRACT

A nearly complete lower jaw of the large procyonid *Simocyon* was collected from southeastern Idaho, 100 kilometers north of the Utah state line. *Simocyon* indicates that the age of the upper member of the Starlight Formation is late early Hemphillian (North American Land Mammal Age), approximately 7 Ma. This is the second recorded occurrence of this Eurasian immigrant in North America. The North American specimens of *Simocyon* are probably conspecific with the Old World *S. primigenius*. An astragalus from the Starlight Formation that is tentatively referred to *Simocyon* supports a possible sister group relationship for the Ailurinae and Simocyoninae and the inclusion of both these subfamilies in the Procyonidae.

Table 1. *Relationship of North American Land Mammal Ages to later Tertiary Epochs.*

EPOCH	MA*	NORTH AMERICAN LAND MAMMAL AGE
Pliocene		Blancan
	— 4.8 —	
	— 8.5 —	Hemphillian
		Clarendonian
	— 11 —	
Miocene		Barstovian
	— 16 —	
		Hemingfordian
	— 20 —	
	— 24 —	Arikareean
Oligocene		

*Age and dates from Tedford and others (1987)

INTRODUCTION

Introductory Remarks

This paper reports the second occurrence in North America of *Simocyon*, an unusual procyonid the size of a large dog. *Simocyon* is the first taxon to be described from an important Hemphillian Land Mammal Age (table 1) local fauna recovered from a gravel quarry near the town of Rockland, Power County, in southeastern Idaho.

In the New World, this genus has been reported previously only from the Hemphillian Rattlesnake Fauna of Oregon (Thorpe, 1921, 1922; Merriam and others, 1925). In the Old World, *Simocyon* is known from the Vallesian and Turolian of Europe (Savage and Russell, 1983) and the Baodean (Turolian equivalent) of China (Zdansky, 1924; Wang, 1995). Tedford and others (1987) include *Simocyon* among the immigrant taxa whose limited occurrence is indicative of the late early or medial Hemphillian (approximately 6-7 Ma). Presently, the precise timing of arrival(s) for these immigrant taxa is unclear because all taxa are not present at any one locality and because not all localities have independent chronologies associated (Tedford and others, 1987). A detailed geochronologic study of the Rockland site is currently in progress. These results combined with further, more detailed, stratigraphic and faunal analysis will add significantly to our knowledge of the late early Hemphillian age, and its endemic and immigrant constituents.

Geographic and Geologic Setting

The Rockland Valley lies immediately south of the

Snake River Plain in southeastern Idaho (figure 1). It is bounded by the Sublette Range on the west and the Deep Creek Mountains to the east. The Rockland Valley is filled with a heterogenous mix of basalts, rhyolitic tuff, ash, reworked ash, conglomerates, sands and silts which were mapped as Starlight Formation by Carr and Trimble (1963) and are considered to be of predominantly late Miocene age (Trimble and Carr, 1976; Tedrow, 1997). The ubiquitous drape of loess that blankets the valley effectively limits viewing of the Starlight Formation to roadcuts and gravel quarries. The northern part of the Rockland Valley contains numerous outcrops of basalts and bedded airfall and ash-flow tuffs assigned to the lower and middle members of the Starlight Formation. The majority of the middle member is comprised of the Tuff of Arbon Valley which has been dated at 9.6 Ma by Armstrong and others (1975).

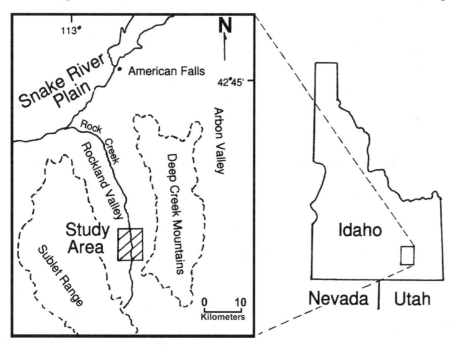

Figure 1. *Map of the general vicinity of the fossil locality.*

According to Trimble and Carr (1976), the upper member of the Starlight Formation is difficult to recognize except where its relationship to either the underlying Tuff of Arbon Valley or the overlying Neeley or Little Creek Formations can be observed. Nevertheless, several discontinuous and poorly exposed, coarse- to fine-grained interbedded sequences, representing the upper member are visible in isolated road cuts and gravel quarries throughout the southern part of the valley. To date, the age of these beds is not well understood, in part because few exposures have produced fossil vertebrates. While numerous ash beds in the area suggest good potential for radiometric work, reliable dates are lacking.

The term "Starlight Formation" has, in our opinion, been inconsistently applied throughout southeastern Idaho. Its deposition was at least partly contemporaneous with that of the lithologically similar Salt Lake Formation (or Group) which has been mapped in many of the surrounding valleys south of the eastern Snake River Plain. Both units are predominantly tuffaceous, and both incorporate a considerable amount of locally derived coarse clastic debris. Although the temporal and geographic limits of the Salt Lake Formation (or Group) are at present imperfectly understood (Tedrow and Robison, this volume), we suspect a close genetic relationship exists between ash beds in the Salt Lake and Starlight Formations.

Smith and Nash (1976) were successful in correlating ash beds from geographically disparate outcrops within the predominantly Miocene Salt Lake Formation on the basis of trace element variation within the contained glass. This approach to correlation has been underutilized, in our opinion, and has tremendous potential for correlating widely scattered outcrops of the Salt Lake Formation throughout Utah, eastern Nevada, and southern Idaho with ash beds in the contemporaneous Starlight Formation in southeastern Idaho.

Trimble and Carr (1976) report the presence of ?*Hipparion*, ?*Megatylopus*, and *Pliomastodon* from gravels in the southern portion of the Rockland Basin, roughly 10 kilometers north of the *Simocyon* locality. Unfortunately some of these remains are quite fragmentary and their precise locality is presently unknown. Recently, a specimen of the fossil mole *Scapanus* (*Xeroscapheus*) has been described (Tedrow, 1997) from a poorly exposed tuffaceous unit, in the vicinity of Trimble and Carr's locality. Based on stage of evolution, this specimen suggests an early Hemphillian age.

The specimen of *Simocyon* was recovered from a thick unit of tan-colored, reworked ash having little or no bedding, but with several discontinuous pebble stringers. This unit is less than 4 meters from the top of roughly a 15-meter sequence of ash (predominantly reworked), gravels, sands and clays (figure 2).

Vertebrate fossils have been collected throughout the sequence and the majority are awaiting further preparation and analysis. The *Simocyon* mandible was collected from a tan ash horizon that also contained specimens of fish, lizards, birds, rodents, insectivores and ungulates.

Figure 2. *Photograph of the sedimentary sequence exposed in the quarry with arrows indicating stratigraphic position of IMNH 15825 and IMNH 15840.*

None of the fossils from this horizon are well silicified and most of the smaller material is extremely fragile, making recovery and preparation quite difficult. Considering the preservation and completeness of some of these specimens, fluvial transport must have been very minimal. However, some minor splintering of the bone along the postromedial surface of the *Simocyon* mandible (figure 3) suggests that burial may have been deferred a short time.

Additional fauna from the Rockland Valley gravel quarry occurring below the tan ash horizon are tentatively identified as *Spermophilus* (*Otospermophilus*) sp., cf. *Microtoscoptes* (W. A. Akersten, personal communication, 1996), *Rhynchotherium edense*, *Prosthenops* sp., and *Megacamelus* sp..

An astragalus tentatively referred to *Simocyon* was recovered from very near the base of the sequence and suggests that the sediments within the quarry area are no older than early late Hemphillian (about 7 Ma). Previous age estimates of between 4 Ma and 150 Ka for a boulder deposit low in the quarry section by Ore and others (1996) are evidently in error.

Abbreviations

Measurements were recorded in millimeters (mm) using dial calipers. Age dates are abbreviated as Ma (Mega-annum) and Ka (Kilo-annum). Comparisons to fossil and recent skeletal material were based on specimens in the collections of the Idaho Museum of Natural History (IMNH), the Museum of Vertebrate Zoology (MVZ) at the University of California at Berkeley,

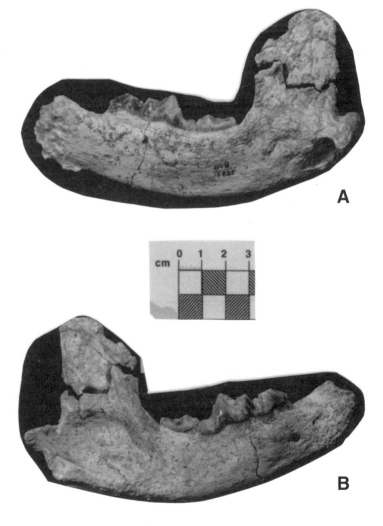

Figure 3. *IMNH 15825,* Simocyon *sp,. cf.* S. marshi; *right dentary in A, medial, and B, lateral views.*

British Museum of Natural History (BMNH), and the Yale Peabody Museum (YPM). Locality data given are approximate. Precise locality information is filed at the Idaho Museum of Natural History and is available to qualified researchers at the discretion of the curator in charge.

SYSTEMATIC PALEONTOLOGY
CLASS MAMMALIA
ORDER CARNIVORA

Family Procyonidae
Subfamily Simocyoninae

Discussion

In the past this group has been used as a taxonomic scrap basket that included many canids and amphicyonids with a trenchant talonid on the M_1. The subfamily Simocynoninae is used in the restricted sense of de Beaumont (1982, 1988) to include *Simocyon, Metarctos, Alopecocyon*, and at least some species of *Amphictis*. *Actiocyon* (Stock, 1947) is also referred to this subfamily. True simocyonines are poorly known and are tentatively included in the Procyonidae (Baskin, in press). Simocyonines are regarded as procyonids with a tendancy to develop an open trigonid with an anteriorly placed, blade-like paraconid on M_1.

Genus *Simocyon* Wagner, 1858

Genotypic Species

Simocyon robustus Wagner, 1858; junior synonym of *S. primigenius* (Roth & Wagner, 1854).

Referred Species

S. primigenius and *S. marshi*.

Characteristics

A large procyonid with P_1 reduced to absent and P_{2-3} absent. The M_1 is elongate, with an open carnassial blade, a small metaconid on the posterior flank of the large protoconid, a low trenchant hypoconid, a very slightly basined talonid, and the metaconid connected to the low internal cingulum of the talonid. The M_2 is very elongate.

Simocyon sp., cf. *S. marshi* (Thorpe, 1921)
(figures 3, 4, 5; table 2)

Referred material

IMNH 15825, right dentary with P_4-M_2.

Locality

IMNH V 853; Power County, Idaho.

Horizon and Age

Tan ash horizon, upper member Starlight Formation; ?late early Hemphillian.

Tentatively Referred

IMNH 15840, left astragalus.

Locality and Horizon

IMNH 1121; basal grit, upper member, Starlight Formation.

Description

IMNH 15825 is a complete right dentary with canine broken, P_1 alveolus, P_4-M_2 complete and no indication of M_3. The ventral margin of the mandible is curved. Maximum depth is below the posterior root of M_2. The angular process is slightly below the level of the tooth row. There are two mental foramina: a smaller one situated below the mid-point of the P_1-P_4 diastema; the second below the anterior root of P_4. What remains of the symphyseal region is very rugose. P_2 and P_3 are absent. The P_1 is represented by a small alveolus just posterior to the canine alveolus and is separated from the P_4 by a long diastema.

P_4 has a centrally located main cusp with a median ridge extending to the anterior margin. There is a prominent posterior accessory cusp. A posterior and posteroexternal cingulum is present. The posterointernal margin overlaps to the level of the posterior accessory cusp with the paraconid of M_1.

Table 2. *Measurements of* Simocyon. *YPM 10043 is the type of* S. marshi. *Measurements of the type (of* S. primegenius*) are estimated from the plate in de Beaumont (1964). Specimens BMNH 9033 and 9034 are also from Pikermi (measurements from Pilgrim, 1931). The BMNH prefixes were listed simply as "M" rather than BMNH in older publications.*

Simocyon marshi			*Simocyon primegenius*		
	IMNH 15825	YPM 10043	BMNH type	BMNH 9033	BMNH 9034
P_4 L	16.4	13.8	13.2	15.0	13.5
W	9.2	8.0	-	9.0	9.0
M_1 L	24.4	22.5	23.0	25.0	23.0
Wa	11.1	10.0	-	11.0	10.0
Wp	9.8	-	-	-	-
M_2 L	17.2	-	15.6	16.0	-
W	9.7	-	-	12.0	-
P_4 - M_2	53.6	50.6	47.7	-	-

The M_1 has an open, blade-like trigonid and a low, very slightly basined talonid. The protoconid is the largest and tallest cusp. The paraconid is situated anteriorly, more or less on the mid-axis of the tooth. The metaconid is small, relatively low, and closely appressed to the posterointernal margin of the protoconid and is connected to the low internal cingulum of the talonid. The hypoconid is a low, somewhat trenchant cusp with a slight anterior posterior crest, that occupies the external half of the talonid.

M_2 has low, rounded cusps, a relatively short anterior cingulum, and an extremely elongate talonid (length = 12.0 mm). The protoconid is slightly larger than the metaconid. These cusps are rather tightly appressed (figure 4) and are connected by a transverse ridge. The metaconid is slightly posterior to the protoconid. A low, lingually curving crest connects the protoconid, very small hypoconid, and posterior hypoconulid.

Tentatively referred to *Simocyon* is a left astragalus (IMNH 15840), collected from a coarse sand approximately 8 meters below the level of the jaw. This specimen (figure 5) is missing the medial one-third of the navicular facet. The distal portion of the malleolar tibial facet has been lost and no astragalar foramen is evident. The divergence of the neck, bearing the navicular facet, from the main body is roughly 36 degrees. The tibial trochlea is shallow. Its lateral and medial borders are essentially parallel. The insertion for the astragalo-fibular ligament is a clearly defined, somewhat lenticular depression having smooth margins. The fibular facet is shallow. The sustentacular facet is a sinuous surface, being convex near the astragalar neck and becoming concave proximally. The astragalocalcaneal (ectal) facet is unexcavated, having no raised borders. The interarticular sulcus opens into a broad embayment distoventrally which undercuts the ventrolateral portion of the navicular facet. The embayed region is walled-off from tibial trochlea by a ridge running from the lateral edge of the navicular facet to near the distal margin of the astragalocalcaneal facet.

Comparisons

Simocyon marshi was described as *Pliocyon marshi* (Thorpe, 1921) from a mandible with P_4-M_1 from the Hemphillian Rattlesnake Fauna of the John Day Basin of eastern Oregon. Noting that the genus name was preoccupied, Thorpe (1922) substituted the name *Araeocyon*. Thorpe (1921, 1922) nonetheless recognized a close relationship with the Old World *S. primigenius*. In addition to the holotype, two additional specimens from Rattlesnake are apparently referable to *S. marshi*. These include an M_1 assigned to *Canis* sp., cf. *C. davisi* and an M_2 assigned to Amphicyonidae or Ursidae (Merriam and others, 1925).

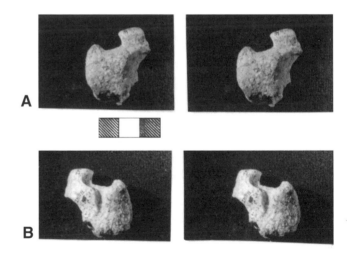

Figure 5. *Stereo photographs of astragalus referred to* Simocyon *sp. cf.* S. marshi *(IMNH 15840) in A, dorsal, and B, ventral views. Scale in centimeters.*

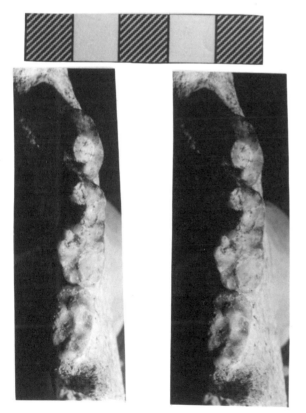

Figure 4. *Stereo photograph of right dentary of* Simocyon *sp., cf.* S. marshi *(IMNH 15840). Scale in centimeters.*

The Idaho specimen is larger and more robust than the holotype of *S. marshi* (Thorpe, 1921). Depth below the M_1 is 30.0 mm versus 26.0 mm. The mandible displays the same degree of outward curvature immediately anterior to P_4 noted in the Rattlesnake specimen. The M_1s are almost identical in size, but the P_4 of the Idaho specimen is about 15 percent longer. Differences between the Idaho and Oregon specimens are not significant and almost surely are the result of sexual dimorphism and/or individual variation.

Thorpe (1921, 1922) listed 10 characteristics, which he considered worthy of generic differentiation, distinguishing *S. marshi* from the holotype of *S. primigenius*. These include having two (not three) lower incisors, in possessing P$_1$, and in characteristics of the mandible and canine. Pilgrim (1931) synonymized *Araeocyon* with *Simocyon* and noted that there were few significant differences between *S. primigenius* and *S. marshi*. Using a larger sample from Pikermi (the type locality of *S. primigenius*), as well as the specimens from China described by Zdansky (1924), Pilgrim stated that most of the differences noted by Thorpe, such as the number of incisors, were probably the result of individual variation. Pilgrim (1931) nevertheless distinguished *S. primigenius* by its longer, more robust ramus and blunter muzzle, in which the incisors were less likely to be crowded or lost.

Simocyon primigenius and *S. marshi* are coeval and are certainly very closely related, perhaps even conspecific. The age of the Pikermi specimen is at the MN12/MN13 boundary, about 7 Ma. The Rattlesnake fauna is approximately 7 Ma (Tedford and others, 1987). The Idaho specimen adds further support to the conclusion that all these differences are probably the result of individual variation. Unfortunately, the North American material remains very limited and more must be obtained before a firm conclusion can be reached.

The referred astragalus displays several unique features when compared with astragali of various extant North American carnivorans. It is distinct from that of the Felidae in its relatively smaller and more cylindrical astragalar head, shallower tibial trochlea, and large unconfined astragalocalcaneal facet. Species of *Ursus* have relatively much larger navicular facets, an extremely short neck and the medial and lateral borders of the tibial trochlea are distally converging. IMNH 15840 bears little if any resemblance to modern *Canis*. The basic differences lie in the shape and orientation of the astragalar head and neck respectively, and in the condition of the astragalocalcaneal facet, which is deeply notched in *Canis*. With the mustelid *Martes* it shares a shallow tibial trochlea and a concavo-convex sustentacular facet but it differs dramatically in many other features including length and angle of divergence of the neck and

the configuration of navicular, fibular and astragalocalcaneal facets. IMNH 15840 shows considerable resemblance to *Procyon*, more so than with any of the taxa discussed above. However, IMNH 15840 is nearly identical with the Asian procyonid *Ailurus fulgens*. Aside from the smaller size of *Ailurus*, few features serve to distinguish the two. In *Ailurus* the distal surface of the lateral trochlea is less pronounced and the insertion for the astragalofibular ligament more distally positioned.

CONCLUSIONS

If, as it appears, this astragalus is indeed from *Simocyon*, it supports a sister group relationship of the Simocyoninae with the Ailurinae, and the inclusion of both these subfamilies in the Procyonidae (Baskin, in press). However, a study of the astragali of primitive ursoids is needed to determine polarity among these characteristics.

In the Old World, *Simocyon* is known from Spain to China; however, its distribution in North America is restricted to a few localities in the west. *Simocyon* had a short face, powerful jaws, and well-developed carnassials, all of which indicate a predaceous, hyaena-like mode of life. The arrival of *Simocyon* in North America coincided with the radiation of *Osteoborus*, a short-faced hyaena-like canid that is one of the most common carnivorans in Hemphillian (late Miocene) deposits. Some degree of competitive exclusion may therefore account for the rarity of *Simocyon* in North America. Given its restricted temporal range, the occurrence of *Simocyon* at both the base of the stratigraphic section and several meters from the top suggests that the entire intervening sequence was deposited in less (probably much less) than a million years.

ACKNOWLEDGMENTS

The authors gratefully acknowledge the efforts of the following field voluteers: Dean Mandiloff, Barbara and Frank Cochrane, Don Thoen, and Patrick Harapp. Elaine Anderson, Phil Bjork and David Gillette reviewed the manuscript and provided helpful suggestions. Thanks to James Patton (MVZ) for loan of material in his care. Thanks also for the friendly cooperation extended to us by the equipment operators of the Power County Highway Division.

REFERENCES

Armstrong, R. L.,Leeman, W. P., and Malde, H. E., 1975, K-Ar dating, Quaternary and Neogene volcanic rocks of the Snake River Plain, Idaho: American Journal of Science, v. 275, p. 224-251.

Baskin, J. A., Procyonidae--chapter 8, *in* Janis, Christine, editor, Evolution of Tertiary mammals of North America: Cambridge, Cambridge University Press, in press.

Beaumont, Gérard de, 1964, Essai sur la position taxonomique des genres *Alopecocyon* Viret et *Simocyon* Wagner (Carnivora): Eclogae geologicae Helvetiae, v. 57, p. 829-836.

—1982, Qu'est-ce que le *Plesictis leobensis* Redlich (mammifère, carnivore)?:Archives des Sciences (Genève), v. 35, p. 143-152.

—1988, Contributions à l'étude du gisement Miocène supérieur de Montredon (Hérault)-- les grands mammifères, 2 - Les carnivores: Montpellier, Palaeovertebrata, Mémoire extraordinaire 1988, p. 15-42, 5 plates.

Carr, W. J., and Trimble, D. E., 1963, Geology of the American Falls quadrangle, Idaho: U. S. Geological Survey Bulletin 1121-G, 44 p.

Merriam, J. C., Stock, Chester, and Moody, C. L., 1925, The Pliocene Rattlesnake Formation and fauna of eastern Oregon, with notes on the geology of the Rattlesnake and Mascall deposits: Carnegie Institution of Washington Publication 347. p. 43-92.

Ore, H. T., Reid, T. V. and Link, P. K., 1996, Pre-Bonneville-level catastrophic overflow of Plio-Pleistocene Lake Bonneville, south of Rockland, Idaho: Northwest Geology, v. 26, p.1-15.

Pilgrim, G. E., 1931, Catalogue of the Pontian Carnivora of Europe in the Department of Geology: London, British Museum (Natural History), 174 p.

Roth, Johannes, and Wagner, J. A., 1854, Die fossilen knochenüberriste von Pikermi in Griechenland: Abhandlungen der Königlich Bayerischen Akademie der Wissenschaften der München, v. 7, p. 371-464.

Savage, D. E., and Russell, D. E., 1983, Mammalian paleofaunas of the world: New York, Addison-Wesley, 432 p.

Smith, R. P., and Nash, W. P.,1976, Chemical correlation of volcanic ash deposits in the Salt Lake Group, Utah, Idaho and Nevada: Journal of Sedimentary Petrology, v.46, no. 4, p. 930-939.

Stock, Chester, 1947, A peculiar new carnivore from the Cuyama Miocene, California: Bulletin of the Southern California Academy of Sciences, v. 46, p. 84-89.

Tedford, R. H., Skinner, M. F., Fields, R. W., Rensberger, J. M., Whistler, D. P., Galusha, Theodore, Taylor, B. E., Macdonald, J. R., and Webb, S. D., 1987, Faunal succession and biochronology of the Arikareean through Hemphillian interval (late Oligocene through earliest Pliocene Epochs) in North America, *in* Woodburne, M. O., editor, Cenozoic mammals of North America: Berkeley and Los Angeles, University of California Press, p. 153-210.

Tedrow, A. R., 1997, The earliest fossil mole in Idaho: Tebiwa, v.26, p. 232-238.

Tedrow, A. R., Robison, S. F., Akersten, W. A., Korth, W. W. and Swisher, C. C. III., 1999, Preliminary report of a new Hemphillian fauna from southeastern Idaho: Part one, Geology and Rodentia: GSA abstracts with programs, v. 31, number 4, #14241, A58.

Thorpe, M. R., 1921, Two new fossil Carnivora: American Journal of Science, series 5, v. 1, p. 477-483.

—1922. *Araeocyon*, a probable Old World migrant: American Journal of Science, series 5, v. 3, p. 371-377.

Trimble, D. E., and Carr, W. J., 1976, Geology of the Rockland and Arbon Quadrangles, Power County, Idaho: U. S. Geological Survey Bulletin 1399, 115 p.

Wagner, J. A., 1858, Geschichte der Urwelt, mit besonderer Berücksichtigung der Menschenrassen und des mosaischen Schöpfungsberichtes, 2, Das Menschen Geschlecht und das Thier -- und Pflanzenreich der Urwelt, second edition: Leipzig, 528 p.

Wang, X-M., 1995, *Simocyon* and its bearing on the relationships of the red panda (*Ailurus*): Journal of Vertebrate Paleontology, v. 15, p. 59A.

Zdansky, Otto, 1924, Jungtertiäre Carnivoren aus China: Palaeontologia Sinica, Peking, Series C., v. 2, no. 1, p. 1-155.

Notes added in proof: A recently radiometric date of 8.14 Ma (Tedrow and others, 1999) from ash just above the *Simocyon* horizon indicates the earlier arrival of *Simocyon* in North America than previously recognized.

According to R.H. Tedford (written communicaition, 1998) a specimen of *Simocyon* has been recovered from unnamed beds in the vicinity of Carlin, Nevada.

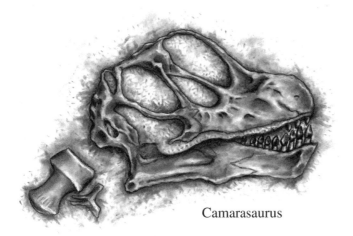

Camarasaurus

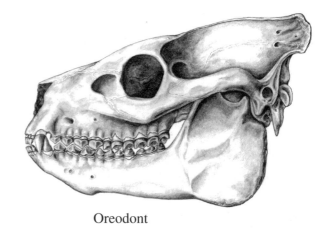

Oreodont

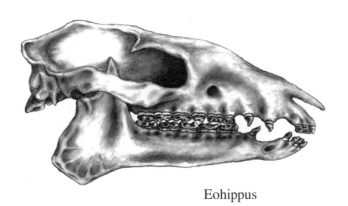

Eohippus

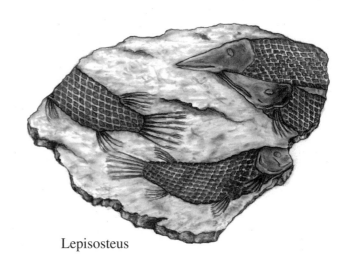

Lepisosteus

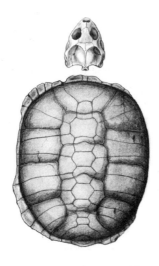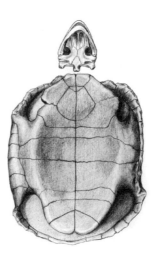

Eocene turtle

Brian Maebius © 1999

Medial Cretaceous Vertebrates - Cifelli, Nydam, Gardner, Weil, Eaton, Kirkland, Madsen

PRELIMINARY REPORT ON THE LITTLE DELL DAM FAUNA, SALT LAKE COUNTY, UTAH (MIDDLE PLEISTOCENE, IRVINGTONIAN LAND MAMMAL AGE)

David D. Gillette
Museum of Northern Arizona, 3101 North Fort Valley Road, Flagstaff, AZ 86001

Christopher J. Bell
Department of Geological Sciences, University of Texas at Austin, Austin, TX, 78712

Martha C. Hayden
Utah Geological Survey, P.O. Box 146100, Salt Lake City, UT 84114-6100

ABSTRACT

Vertebrate fossils recovered during construction of Little Dell Dam in Mountain Dell Canyon, 16 kilometers east of Salt Lake City, include large and small mammals from three sites. Among the large mammals are unidentifiable proboscideans and horses. The age of the fauna from one site (the proboscidean locality) cannot be established beyond Pleistocene. The small mammal faunas from the other sites (localities 1 and 2) include rodents that indicate probable Irvingtonian Land Mammal Age. The small mammal fauna from locality 2 appears to be at least 750,000 years old, and perhaps as old as 1.3 million years, making this fauna the oldest taxonomically diverse Pleistocene fauna in Utah.

INTRODUCTION

Fossils from the Little Dell Dam site were recovered as part of a salvage and mitigation effort during the construction of the Little Dell Dam in Mountain Dell Canyon of the Wasatch Range. The damsite is about 16 kilometers east of Salt Lake City, Utah, at an elevation of approximately 1,768 meters above sea level. The fossils were discovered upstream from the dam in 1992 by heavy equipment operators who initially found large bones in the alluvium. At first, the fossils were only curiosities and a few were collected by construction personnel. These were large bones of Pleistocene horses and proboscideans with tusk fragments.

As construction activities in the valley proceeded, engineering geologists recognized structural deformation of the alluvium that had disturbed several of the horizons along a high-angle fault. The antiquity of the fault, a matter related to dam safety, could not be confidently established on structural grounds alone. The engineering geologists recognized that the fossils might help determine the timing of the deformation, and called one of us (DDG) to ask for assistance. Personnel from the Utah Division of State History (now with the Utah Geological Survey) visited the site to identify fossils recovered up to that time and to determine the feasibility of collecting additional material.

During several subsequent visits, a team from the Utah Division of State History collected additional fossils, photographed the several localities where fossils were recovered, and took sediment samples for analysis. The U. S. Army Corps of Engineers, Sacramento Office, awarded the Utah Division of State History a grant to process the fossils and prepare them for research. The practical purpose of the grant was to facilitate an independent evaluation of the age of the fault. From a pale-

Figure 1. *Overview of the Little Dell Reservoir excavation.*

ontological standpoint, the fauna and flora represented the first Pleistocene biota from an intermediate elevation (approximately 1,768 meters above sea level) in the Wasatch Range, where only a few Pleistocene sites of consequence had previously been reported (Miller, 1976, 1987; Gillette and Madsen, 1992, 1993), all from higher elevations ranging from approximately 2,195 meters to 3,048 meters above sea level. Isolated fossils from the shorelines of Pleistocene Lake Bonneville (maximum elevation approximately 1554 meters above sea level) are relatively common, but are much younger (late Rancholabrean) than the fossils from the Little Dell Dam site. The Little Dell fossils proved to be much more abundant than originally anticipated, especially the bones and teeth of small vertebrates, some of which constitute the subject of this report. Herein, we present a preliminary taxonomic assessment of some of the small vertebrate fossils from the Little Dell Dam site and explore the biochronological age and significance of the site.

METHODS

All fossils were recovered from lacustrine and fluvial sediments in Mountain Dell Canyon, a tributary of Parley's Canyon immediately east of Salt Lake City. Fossils recovered from three localities at the Little Dell Dam site were isolated and curated in the fossil preparation laboratory of the Utah Division of State History. Preparation of small fossils involved removal of surrounding clay and silt with needles under a microscope, screenwashing with sieves with openings as small as 150 micrometers, sorting under a microscope, labeling, and repair of damaged specimens where possible. All fossils are sufficiently prepared for deposition in the permanent collections at the University of Utah Museum of Natural History. In addition to vertebrates, the fossils recovered from the site include plants, insects, and invertebrates.

Two radiocarbon age estimates were taken from materials contemporaneous with some of the fossils, as described by Fea (1993). Both age estimates are older than 35,000 years B.P. These are Beta 56197 (37,000 years B.P.), taken from basal gravels in the oldest of four fluvial channels (Shlemon, 1993), and Beta 55236 (greater than 39,000 years B.P.), from the base of an undisplaced fining-upward section of the next-to-oldest fluvial channel in Mountain Dell Canyon (Shlemon, 1993). Correlation of Shlemon's (1993) and Fea's (1993) four fluvial channels with the three fossil-yielding sites in the valley was not firmly established prior to filling of the reservoir, due to considerable construction-related disturbance of the sediments.

LOCALITIES

The Little Dell Dam site is in NW1/4 section 36, T.1N., R.2E., Salt Lake Base Line and Meridian, immediately upstream from Mountain Dell Reservoir in Mountain Dell Canyon. We identify the three fossil sites as the proboscidean locality (called the mastodon locality in engineering reports), locality 1, and locality 2. The proboscidean locality, first recognized by construction personnel, was situated in trench FT-5 of Fea (1993) and Schlemon (1993). Three sedimentary units defined at the proboscidean locality are an upper peat layer, a middle clay, and a basal gravel. Initial discoveries included a portion of a proboscidean tusk, postcranial bones from a large horse, and postcranial bones of an unidentified ungulate. A few small mammal bones, snails, and plants were also recovered from this site. The fossils were recovered from basal channel deposits of fluvial cycle 4 of Fea (1993), the oldest of four fluvial cycles recognized in that report. This site was approximately 550 meters upstream from localities 1 and 2.

Locality 1 was situated in trench FT-24 and locality 2 in trench FT-8 (Fea, 1993); disturbed and faulted sediments prevented confident correlation of these localities with the proboscidean locality. Stratigraphic relationships inferred from structural geology reported by Fea (1993) indicate a considerable age difference between these two sites and the proboscidean site; paleontological evidence accumulated thus far at least partly substantiates this conclusion (see below). Four sedimentary units were defined at locality 1: in descending order these are an upper clay, an upper peat, a middle clay, and a basal gravel. Two sedimentary units were defined at locality 2: in descending order, these are a lower peat (from which the majority of fossils were recovered) and a lower clay.

FAUNAS

The Proboscidean Locality

The fauna from the proboscidean locality includes several unidentifiable microtine rodent molar fragments from the upper peat unit. The middle clay unit produced the proboscidean tusk and bone fragments, limb bones and a tooth of *Equus* sp. (unidentified horse), several broken small mammal bones and tooth fragments, ostracodes, and seeds. The proboscidean material is insufficient to permit even generic identification, but neither mastodon nor mammoth are common in the Pleistocene of Utah. One confirmed record of mastodon, *Mammut americanum*, was reported by Miller (1987); several records of *Mammuthus* were previously reported from the state (Agenbroad, 1984; Agenbroad and Mead, 1989; Gillette and Madsen, 1993).

Locality 1

The upper peat unit of Locality 1 produced insect carapace fragments, an insect head, and a single molar fragment of a small sciurid rodent (probably the chipmunk, *Eutamias*) as well as several types of seeds and some large plant fragments. The middle clay unit of locality 1 produced: one fish vertebra; three squamate reptile vertebral fragments; several unidentifiable microtine rodent molar fragments; a molar fragment of *Neotoma* sp. (woodrat); a lower first molar of *Peromyscus* sp. (white-footed mouse); a lower first molar of *Lemmiscus curtatus* (sagebrush vole); a lower first molar of *Microtus paroperarius* (extinct vole); rib fragments, a humerus fragment, radius, ulna and foot bones of a Pleistocene horse *Equus* sp.; and several unidentified bones and bone fragments of large mammals. All of the small mammal remains from the middle clay unit are light yellowish-brown in color.

Locality 2

The lower clay unit of locality 2 yielded an insect carapace fragment, and two microtine rodent teeth, one an upper first molar, the other an upper third molar. Both molars are rooted and lack cementum in the reentrant angles; they probably represent the genus *Phenacomys* (heather vole). Several seeds and plant fragments were also collected.

The lower peat unit of locality 2 produced a diverse fauna including snails, an insect carapace and carapace fragments, a posterior jaw fragment of a soricid insectivore (identification beyond Soricidae [shrews] is not possible), a complete lower dentition of *Thomomys* sp. (pocket gopher), an isolated molar of a pocket mouse *Perognathus* sp. (*sensu lato*), several molars of *Peromyscus* sp. (deer mouse), one molar of *Spermophilus* sp. (ground squirrel), one molar of *Eutamias* sp., and three molars of an undetermined species of *Zapus* (jumping mouse). Although relatively few specimens are available, there is also a diverse fauna of microtine rodents represented in this unit. One isolated lower first molar is rooted, with cementum in the reentrant angles, and represents a specimen of the extinct microtine, *Mimomys* (*Cromeromys*) sp., cf. *M. dakotaensis*. *Allophaiomys pliocaenicus* (extinct meadow vole) is represented by an isolated lower first molar and also an associated partial upper and lower dentition that appears

to have been derived from a raptor regurgitation pellet. This associated dentition is preserved in a block of sediment that contains several such associations, representing at least three microtine rodent species. This block of sediment represents a very important discovery because associated upper and lower dentitions of most extinct North American microtine rodent species are unknown. In addition to the *Allophaiomys* remains, there is an associated lower dentition of a bog lemming, *Mictomys* sp. (that appears to represent either *M. meltoni* or *M. kansasensis*, but additional preparation and study will be required to determine precise species affinity of this material), and at least a lower right molar series of *Phenacomys* sp., cf. *P. gryci*. The lower first molar of the latter series is rooted, lacks cementum in the reentrant angles, has a posterior loop with five closed triangles and a dentine tract on the posterior loop that is much lower than that on the anterior cap (lower than that seen in *P. brachyodus*; Repenning and Grady, 1988). There is a slight asymmetry in length of the lingual and labial triangles, but it is not as pronounced as that seen in living representatives of *Phenacomys* and *Arborimus*. Two small molar fragments that lack cementum in the reentrant angles and show a pronounced asymmetry in length of the triangles may represent another species of *Phenacomys* in this fauna, but at present this cannot be confirmed. All of the small mammal specimens from the lower peat layer are dark brown or black in color.

DISCUSSION AND CONCLUSION

Biochronology

Although a biochronological age estimate more precise than "Pleistocene" cannot be made for the proboscidean locality based on the recovered fauna, both locality 1 and locality 2 contain species that indicate Irvingtonian North American Land Mammal Age (early to middle Pleistocene), although they do not appear to be contemporaneous. The differences in preservation of the small mammal remains (reflected primarily in the distinct differences in coloration) indicate a difference in taphonomic history of the two localities, and the taxonomic composition of the microtine rodent faunas suggests a difference in age, perhaps a significant one.

The two complete microtine rodent molars in locality 1 form the basis of the age estimate for this fauna. *Microtus paroperarius* is widespread in the central and eastern United States in the middle Pleistocene. It is present in several faunas reported to date between 830,000 and 840,000 years B.P., including Hamilton Cave, West Virginia (possibly the earliest occurrence, but specimens referred to *Microtus paroperarius* may represent population variants of *Lasiopodomys*; Repenning and Grady, 1988), Cumberland Cave, Maryland (Van der Meulen, 1978), the County Line fauna in Illinois (Miller and others, 1994), and the basal sections of the Hansen Bluff sequence in Colorado (Rogers and others, 1985; Repenning, 1992). The youngest occurrence is in Salamander Cave, South Dakota where it was recovered from sediments that may be as young as 252,000 years B.P. (Mead and others, 1996).

The *Lemmiscus curtatus* lower first molar from Little Dell locality 1 is a morphotype showing five closed triangles. This is the morphology typical of most living populations, but several fossil populations of *Lemmiscus* show only four closed triangles on the lower first molar (Repenning, 1992; Bell and Mead, 1998). The oldest published record of the five triangle morphotype is in the Pit fauna of Porcupine Cave in Colorado (Bell and Barnosky, in review) where it is found in reversed sediments older than 780,000 years B.P., and it persists to the present.

Taken together, these two rodents suggest that locality 1 at Little Dell is probably no younger than about 250,000 years B.P. and may be as old as 850,000 years B.P. At present a more precise age estimate cannot be made, but an Irvingtonian Land Mammal Age is relatively certain.

The microtine rodent fauna from locality 2 suggests a greater antiquity. *Allophaiomys pliocaenicus* first appears in North American faunas nearly contemporaneous with the lower boundary of the Olduvai magnetic polarity Chron at about 1.9 million years ago; the oldest record is from a drill core at the base of the Hansen Bluff sequence in Colorado (Repenning, 1992; Rogers and others, 1992). Additional early records are from the Java fauna in South Dakota (of undetermined age, but apparently early Irvingtonian; Martin, 1989; Repenning, 1992) and the Wellsch Valley fauna in Saskatchewan (also possibly earliest Irvingtonian; Churcher, 1984; Barendregt and others, 1991; Repenning, 1992). The only North American record of *A. pliocaenicus* that is potentially younger than 825,000 years B.P. (Repenning, 1992) is in the Pit sequence in Porcupine Cave, where it may be as young as 750,000 years B.P. (Bell and Barnosky, in review).

Mimomys (*Cromeromys*) is known from two species in North America. *Mimomys* (*Cromeromys*) *virginianus* was originally described from the Hamilton Cave fauna in West Virginia (Repenning and Grady, 1988) and a tentative identification was subsequently reported from the Pit locality in Porcupine Cave, Colorado (Bell and Barnosky, in review). *Mimomys dakotaensis* was

described from the Java fauna in South Dakota (Martin, 1989) and is only known from the type locality; referral of the Little Dell specimen to this species is tentative. The relationships between *M. virginianus* and *M. dakotaensis* are unknown, and they may be synonymous. The type material of *M. dakotaensis* only contains two lower first molars, at least one of which is broken (the second was listed, but not discussed; Martin, 1989). *Mimomys dakotaensis* was distinguished from *M. virginianus* by larger size (though only one specimen of *M. dakotaensis* was measured), a very well-developed dentine tract at the level of the *Mimomys* "kante" and by having significantly less cementum in the reentrant angles. The Little Dell specimen lacks a well-developed *Mimomys* "kante" and dentine tracts cannot be reliably discerned. Our referral of the specimen to *M. dakotaensis* is based on the small amount of cement in the reentrant angles.

The age of the Java fauna is problematic. It contains several species typically considered Blancan. Martin (1989) considered the fauna to be earliest Pleistocene. Repenning and others (1990, 1995) placed it in the Irvingtonian I microtine rodent division.

Phenacomys gryci was first described from the Fish Creek fauna in Alaska (Repenning and others, 1987), dating to approximately 2.4 million years B.P. Additional material was reported from 1.6 million years B.P. in the Froman Ferry sequence in Idaho (Repenning and others, 1995). Very advanced morphotypes referred to this species were recently identified from Cathedral Cave in Nevada (Bell, 1995) and in the Pit sequence of Porcupine Cave, dating to between 750,000 and 850,000 years B.P. (Bell and Barnosky, in review). The Little Dell material most closely resembles the specimens from Porcupine Cave; there is no *Mimomys* "kante" and only five closed triangles are present on the lower first molar.

The *Mictomys* material from Little Dell most closely resembles *M. kansasensis, M. meltoni*, or the *Mictomys* material from Snowville, Utah (Repenning, 1987; Repenning and Grady, 1988). The unique association preserved on the Little Dell slab is quite fragile and additional preparation will be required before a definitive species identification can be made. The most reliable way to distinguish *Mictomys* species may be the enamel microstructure, or schmelzmuster (von Koenigswald and Martin, 1984). Schmelzmuster has not been examined for the Little Dell material, or for the Snowville specimens, and only a few specimens of *M. kansasensis* and *M. meltoni* have been studied in this regard. The earliest record of *Mictomys kansasensis* is from the Sappa fauna in Nebraska, dated to approximately 1.3 million years B.P. (Lundelius and others, 1987). *Mictomys meltoni* or *M. kansasensis* was reported from Salamander Cave,

South Dakota, at an age possibly between approximately 323,000 years B.P. and 252,000 years B.P. (Mead and others, 1996).

Based on the present understanding of North American microtine rodent biochronology, the fauna from locality 2 at Little Dell appears to be no older than 1.3 million years B.P. and cannot be assumed to be younger than 750,000 years B.P. If this age is correct, the Little Dell fauna from locality 2 is the oldest taxonomically diverse Pleistocene fauna from Utah. The only other Irvingtonian microtine rodents reported from Utah are from the Snowville locality (*Mictomys* sp. and *Microtus* sp.; Repenning, 1987; Bell, 1998).

Biogeography

The principal paleontological significance of the Little Dell faunas lies in their age and elevation (approximately 1,768 meters above sea level). The sites are roughly 480 meters above the modern level of the Great Salt Lake and 900 to 1,200 meters below the highest valleys along the Wasatch Front. The Little Dell localities are the only middle elevation Pleistocene fossil localities in the Wasatch Mountains, and are among only a few in all the mountains of the American west. The Snowville, Utah locality (Repenning, 1987) is at an elevation of 1,619 meters, but produced only a few small mammal fossils. At an elevation of approximately 1,950 meters, the Silver Creek fauna (Miller 1976), close to the summit of Interstate 80 near Park City, Utah, is somewhat higher in elevation than Little Dell but is much younger in age. Three other late Pleistocene sites at comparable elevations in Utah (but with limited faunal and floral information) are the Huntington Dam mammoth site (elevation approximately 2,740 meters; Gillette and Madsen, 1992, 1993), the mastodon sinkhole site (elevation approximately 2,980 meters; Miller, 1987), and the Blonquist Rock Shelter (elevation approximately 2,125 meters; Nelson, 1988, 1989). The faunas and floras from these sites were reviewed by Gillette and Madsen (1992, 1993).

Many of the mammalian taxa represented in the Little Dell fauna are known from faunas both east and west of the Rocky Mountains during the Irvingtonian, but two important records deserve special note. Until recently, *Microtus paroperarius* and *Allophaiomys pliocaenicus* were unknown from faunas west of the Rocky Mountains (Repenning, 1992; Bell, 1998). The only western occurrence of these species was reported from Cathedral Cave in Nevada, an Irvingtonian fauna with no external age control (Bell, 1995). The records from Little Dell contribute significantly to our understanding of the microtine rodent faunal composition west of the Rocky Mountains during the Irvingtonian. The Eastern and Western United States faunal regions proposed by Fejfar and Repenning (1992) appear to be fairly well defined for much of the Blancan Land Mammal Age, but the distinction between them is less clear during the Irvingtonian. The presence of *Allophaiomys pliocaenicus* and *Microtus paroperarius* at Little Dell provides additional records substantiating the occurrence of these species west of the Rocky Mountains during the Pleistocene, and indicate a closer faunal similarity with the eastern United States during part of the Irvingtonian.

When additional preparation and stabilization of some of the more delicate vertebrate materials from Little Dell are completed, a more complete view of the fauna will be published. This, in combination with palynological analysis and a study of the insect and mollusk components of the fauna, will permit a preliminary assessment of the paleoenvironment of northern Utah in the early and middle Pleistocene.

ACKNOWLEDGMENTS

The Little Dell salvage project was supported in part by a contract from the Sacramento Office of the U.S. Army Corps of Engineers to the Division of State History, State of Utah. Kevin Jones and David B. Madsen assisted with collection of specimens and Carl Limone prepared the fossil material. We are grateful to Charles Repenning for discussions about the Little Dell microtines. Comments on an earlier versions of this report were provided by Charles Repenning and Geraldine Swartz.

REFERENCES

Agenbroad, L. D., 1984, New World mammoth distribution, *in* Martin, P. S., and Klein, R. G., editors, Quaternary extinctions -- a prehistoric revolution: Tucson, University of Arizona Press, p. 90-108.

Agenbroad, L. D., and Mead, J. I., 1989, Quaternary geochronology and distribution of *Mammuthus* on the Colorado Plateau: Geology, v. 17, p. 861-864.

Barendregt, R. W., Thomas, F. F., Irving, E., Baker, J., Stalker, A. Macs., and Churcher, C. S., 1991, Stratigraphy and paleomagnetism of the Jaw Face Section, Wellsch Valley site, Saskatchewan: Canadian Journal of Earth Sciences, v. 28, p. 1353-1364.

Bell, C. J., 1995, A middle Pleistocene (Irvingtonian) microtine rodent fauna from White Pine County, Nevada, and its implications for microtine rodent biochronology: Journal of Vertebrate Paleontology, v. 15, supp. 3, p. 18A.

—1998, North American Quaternary land mammal ages and the biochronology of North American microtine rodents, *in* Sowers, J. M., Noller, J. S., and Lettis, W. R., editors, Dating and earthquakes -- review of Quaternary geochronology and its implication to paleoseismology: Nuclear Regulatory Commission, NUREG/CR, v. 5562, p. 2-605 - 2-645.

Bell, C. J., and Barnosky, A. D., in review, The microtine rodents from the Pit Locality in Porcupine Cave, Park County, Colorado.

Bell, C. J., and Mead, J. I., 1998, Late Pleistocene microtine rodents from Snake Creek Burial Cave, White Pine County, Nevada: Great Basin Naturalist, v. 58, p. 82-86.

Churcher, C. S., 1984, Faunal correlations of Pleistocene deposits in western Canada, *in* Mahaney, W. C., editor, Correlation of Quaternary chronologies: Norwich, England, Geo Books, p. 145-158.

Fea, T. W., compiler, 1993, The age of faults in the reservoir borrow area -- Little Dell Dam, Utah: U.S. Army Corps of Engineers, Sacramento District, Office Report, April 1993, 17 p.

Fejfar, Oldrich, and Repenning, C. A., 1992, Holarctic dispersal of the arvicolids (Rodentia, Cricetidae), *in* von Koenigswald, Wighart, and Werdelin, Lars, editors, Mammalian migration and dispersal events in the European Quaternary: Courier Forschungsinstitut Senckenberg, v. 153, p. 205-212.

Gillette, D. D., and Madsen, D. B., 1992, The short-faced bear *Arctodus simus* from the late Quaternary in the Wasatch Mountains of central Utah: Journal of Vertebrate Paleontology, v. 12, p. 107-112.

—1993, The Columbian mammoth, *Mammuthus columbi*, from the Wasatch Mountains of central Utah: Journal of Paleontology, v. 67, p. 669-680.

von Koenigswald, W., and Martin, L. D., 1984, Revision of the fossil and Recent Lemminae (Rodentia, Mammalia), *in* Mengel, R. M., editor, Papers in vertebrate paleontology honoring Robert Warren Wilson: Carnegie Museum of Natural History special Publication, v. 9, p. 122-137.

Lundelius, E. L., Jr., Churcher, C. S., Downs, Theodore, Harington, C. R., Lindsay, E. H., Schultz, G. E., Semken, H. A., Webb, S. D., and Zakrzewski, R. J., 1987, The North American Quaternary sequence, *in* Woodburne, M. O., editor, Cenozoic mammals of North America -- geochronology and biostratigraphy: Berkeley, University of California Press, p. 211-235.

Martin, R. A., 1989, Arvicolid rodents of the early Pleistocene Java local fauna from north-central South Dakota: Journal of Vertebrate Paleontology, v. 9, p. 438-450.

Mead, J. I., Manganaro, C. A., Repenning, C. A., and Agenbroad, L. D., 1996, Early Rancholabrean mammals from Salamander Cave, Black Hills, South Dakota, *in* Stewart, K. M., and Seymour, K. L., editors, Palaeoecology and palaeoenvironments of Late Cenozoic mammals -- tributes to the career of C. S. (Rufus) Churcher: Toronto, University of Toronto Press, p. 458-482.

Miller, B. B., Graham, R. W., Morgan, A. V., Miller, N. G., McCoy, W. D., Palmer, D. F., Smith, A. J., and Pilny, J. J., 1994, A biota associated with Matuyama-age sediments in west-central Illinois: Quaternary Research, v. 41, p. 350-265.

Miller, W. E., 1976, Late Pleistocene vertebrates of the Silver Creek local fauna from north central Utah: Great Basin Naturalist, v. 36, p. 387-424.

—1987, *Mammut americanum*, Utah's first record of the American mastodon: Journal of Paleontology, v. 61, p. 168-183.

Nelson, M. E., 1988, A new cavity biota from northeastern Utah: Current Research in the Pleistocene, v. 5, p. 77-78.

—1989, New paleontological investigations at Blonquist Rock Shelter, Summit County, Utah: Current Research in the Pleistocene, v. 6, p. 77-78.

Repenning, C. A., 1987, Biochronology of the microtine rodents of the United States, *in* Woodburne, M. O., editor, Cenozoic mammals of North America -- geochronology and biostratigraphy: Berkeley, University of California Press, p. 236-268.

—1992, *Allophaiomys* and the age of the Olyor Suite, Krestovka Sections, Yakutia: U. S. Geological Survey Bulletin, v. 2037, p. 1-98.

Repenning, C. A., Brouwers, E. M., Carter, L. D., Marincovich, Louie, Jr., and Ager, T. A., 1987, The Beringian ancestry of *Phenacomys* (Rodentia: Cricetidae) and the beginning of the modern Arctic Ocean borderland biota: U. S. Geological Survey Bulletin, v. 1687, p. 1-31.

Repenning, C. A., Fejfar, Old_ich, and Heinrich, W.-D., 1990, Arvicolid rodent biochronology of the Northern Hemisphere, *in* Fejfar, Oldrich, and Heinrich, W.-D., editors, International symposium -- evolution, phylogeny and biostratigraphy of arvicolids (Rodentia, Mammalia): Rohanov, Czechoslovakia, Geological Survey, p. 385-418.

Repenning, C. A., and Grady, Frederick, 1988, The microtine rodents of the Cheetah Room fauna, Hamilton Cave, West Virginia, and the spontaneous origin of *Synaptomys*: U. S. Geological Survey Bulletin, v. 1853, p. 1-32.

Repenning, C. A., Weasma, T. R., and Scott, G. R., 1995, The early Pleistocene (latest Blancan - earliest Irvingtonian) Froman Ferry fauna and history of the Glenns Ferry Formation, southwestern Idaho: U. S. Geological Survey Bulletin, v. 2105, p. 1-86.

Rogers, K. L., Repenning, C. A., Forester, R. M., Larson, E. E., Hall, S. A., Smith, G. R., Anderson, Elaine, and Brown, T. J., 1985, Middle Pleistocene (Late Irvingtonian - Nebraskan) climatic changes in south-central Colorado: National Geographic Research, v. 1, p. 535-563.

Rogers, K. L., Larson, E. E., Smith, Gary, Katzman, Danny, Smith, G. R., Cerling, Thure, Wang, Yang, Baker, R. G., Lohmann, K. C., Repenning, C. A., Patterson, Penny, and Mackie, Gerald, 1992, Pliocene and Pleistocene geologic and climatic evolution in the San Luis Valley of south-central Colorado: Palaeogeography, Palaeoclimatology, Palaeoecology, v. 94, p. 55-86.

Shlemon, R. J., 1993, Estimated age of Late Quaternary fluvial channels, reservoir borrow area, Little Dell Dam, Utah, *in* Fea, T. W., compiler, The age of faults in the reservoir borrow area, Little Dell Dam, Utah: U.S. Army Corps of Engineers, Sacramento District, Office Report, April, 1993, 17 p., appendix B.

Van der Meulen, A. J., 1978, *Microtus* and *Pitymys* (Arvicolidae) from Cumberland Cave, Maryland, with a comparison of some New and Old World species: Annals of Carnegie Museum, v. 47, p. 101-145.

LATE QUATERNARY VERTEBRATE HISTORY OF THE GREAT BASIN

Timothy H. Heaton
Department of Earth Sciences, University of South Dakota, Vermillion, SD 57069

ABSTRACT

At the end of the Pleistocene Epoch the Great Basin was transformed from valleys of lakes and forests to valleys of salt flats and desert shrubs. Lake and cave deposits have provided a rich vertebrate history for the region. Great Basin fishes are highly endemic, and most Pleistocene species survive today in the remaining freshwater lakes and streams. About 30 species of Great Basin birds and mammals went extinct at the end of the Pleistocene, mostly large-bodied mammals. Surviving montane mammals, along with their plant counterparts, were driven to mountaintop refugia. Some have been extirpated from the Great Basin; others have undergone allopatric speciation. All these transitions can be causally linked to a warming climate at the end of the Pleistocene.

INTRODUCTION

The Great Basin covers nearly the entire state of Nevada as well as portions of all surrounding states including most of the western half of Utah. It was originally defined as the region between the Rocky Mountains and the Sierra Nevada that lacks external drainage, and by this definition its eastern boundary lies east of Salt Lake City where the Wasatch Mountains divide the Great Salt Lake and Colorado River drainages. Geologically the Great Basin is characterized by north-south- trending valleys and mountain ranges created by Basin and Range extension over the last 15 million years (Hunt, 1967). In this sense its eastern boundary lies along the Wasatch Front, while on the west it ends with similar abruptness at the base of the Sierra Nevada.

Climatically the Great Basin is the northernmost and coolest of the deserts of the American Southwest. Its broad valleys are covered mainly with xeric vegetation such as sagebrush, saltbush, shadscale, and annual grasses, and mountain front areas are characterized by pinyon-juniper woodland. Some playa areas are too salty to support any vegetation. The mountain ranges commonly rise high above the valley bottoms and have a series of elevation-controlled floral belts. A variety of pines, firs, and junipers (mostly with Rocky Mountain affinities) are found in the higher elevations (Wells, 1983), though some peaks extend well above timberline.

The dry conditions of the Great Basin have aided in the preservation of vertebrate fossils. Caves have developed in early Paleozoic limestone exposures around the base of many mountain ranges and commonly contain fossil deposits (Davis, 1990). Remains of larger mammals are sometimes found in late Pleistocene lake sediments. Quaternary fossils are virtually unknown from higher elevation areas, but the living faunas and floras of the mountain ranges provide important clues to the region's past. This paper provides a brief summary of what is currently understood about the Quaternary history of vertebrates in the Great Basin, focusing on Utah, and refers the reader to relevant literature.

THE GREAT SALT LAKE AND LAKE BONNEVILLE

What makes the Quaternary history of the Great Basin especially interesting is the stark contrast between past and present. Nothing in the Salt Lake City area symbolizes the desert conditions of the Great Basin more than Great Salt Lake and its islands and promontories formed by nearby mountain ranges. Having no outlet, the salt content in the lake varies from 5% during wet periods to over 27% (eight times saltier than the ocean) during dry periods. Great Salt Lakes's major water sources are the Bear River, which drains the northern Wasatch Mountains, the Weber River, which drains the western end of the Uinta Mountains, and the Jordan River, which flows north from Utah Lake and drains the southern and middle Wasatch Mountains. The high plateaus of central Utah drain westward via the Sevier River to the intermittent Sevier Dry Lake.

Lake terraces (including the high benches along the Wasatch Front) demonstrate that many of the valleys were occupied by sizeable lakes during the late Pleistocene. By far the largest of these was Lake Bonneville, which covered most of Utah's portion of the Great Basin and extended into Idaho and Nevada. Lake Bonneville began filling above the current Great Salt Lake level about 30,000 years ago and rose an average of two centimeters per year, reaching its maximum level of 1,545 meters (adjusted for rebound) about 15,300 years ago; it then dropped 100 meters by a catastrophic outlet to the north about 14,400 years ago and continued dropping by evaporation to its current level of 1,280 meters about 12,000 years ago, separating into several separate lakes in the process (Gilbert, 1890; Currey, 1990; Oviatt and others, 1992). More than a hundred pluvial lakes filled the valleys of Nevada during the late Pleistocene, the largest being Lake Lahontan of northwestern Nevada, and these lakes underwent fill and evaporation cycles similar to Lake Bonneville (Benson and others, 1990; Benson and others, 1992).

All Utah mountains over 3,000 meters in elevation were glaciated during the late Wisconsin glaciation which peaked about 18,000 years ago (Hintze, 1988). Of particular interest in the Salt Lake City area is Little Cottonwood Canyon, where a large valley glacier once flowed into Lake Bonneville (Richmond, 1964; Madsen and Currey, 1979). The plant fossil record of the Great Basin also shows radical differences from the modern climate (Thompson and Mead, 1982; Wells, 1983; Grayson, 1993). Limber pine and other conifers retreated to high elevations and were replaced by xeric vegetation about 11,000 years ago as the summers grew warmer (Rhode and Madsen, 1995).

NON-MAMMALIAN VERTEBRATES

Not surprisingly, the native fishes of the Great Basin exhibit low diversity and considerable endemism. The Great Salt Lake and many other saline basins currently contain no fish at all (Sigler and Sigler, 1987, 1994, 1996), but these areas contained freshwater lakes during the last glaciopluvial. Lake Bonneville sediments are not especially fossiliferous (see Nelson and Madsen, 1980), but Smith and others (1968) described two fish faunas containing seven species: cutthroat trout (*Salmo clarkii*), Bonneville cisco (*Prosopium gemmiferum*), Bonneville whitefish (*Prosopium spilonotus*), Utah chub (*Gila atraria*), Utah sucker (*Catostomus ardens*), mottled sculpin (*Cottus bairdii*), Bear Lake sculpin (*Cottus extensus*). This list comprises all but one species of the highly endemic living fauna of Bear Lake on the Utah-Idaho border. Smith and others (1968) considered the endemic Utah Lake sculpin (*Cottus echinatus*) to be a likely descendant of the Bear Lake sculpin (*C. extensus*) which has been

found in Lake Bonneville sediments dating to 13,000-11,000 years B.P. The Lake Lahontan basin has had a fish fauna distinct from the Lake Bonneville Basin throughout the Pleistocene (Smith, 1978, 1985), thus supporting the geologic evidence that no waterway has ever connected these two sides of the Great Basin.

Mead and others (1982) and Mead and others (1989) described reptile faunas from three caves along the Utah-Nevada border, and a number of other cave herpetofaunas have been described from elsewhere in Nevada (Brattstrom, 1958; Mead, 1985, 1988; Mead and others, 1983). The great majority of species recovered are also found living locally, though a few species such as chorus frog (cf. *Pseudacris triseriata*), short-horned lizard (*Phrynosoma douglassi*), and common kingsnake (*Lampropeltis getulus*) appear to have suffered a reduced range since the early Holocene, suggesting a drying and warming of the climate (Mead, 1985, 1988; Mead and others, 1989). Mead and Bell (1994) provided a summary of the Quaternary amphibian and reptile record of the Great Basin.

The largest fossil avifauna of the Great Basin is from Smith Creek Cave, located in eastern Nevada near the Utah border. Howard (1935, 1952) described a new species of eagle (*Spizaëtus willetti*) and giant raptor (*Teratornis incredibilis*) from this cave and reported about 50 species, six of which are extinct. Emslie and Heaton (1987) described about 30 avian taxa from nearby Crystal Ball Cave in western Utah including an extinct raptor (cf. *Teratornis merriami*), owl (*Bubo* sp., cf. *B. sinclairi*), and raven (*Corvus* sp., cf. *C. neomexicanus*). Also reported was the first record of caracara (*Polyborus plancus*) from the state of Utah. The substantial differences between these two avifaunas (located only 14 kilometers apart) were attributed to an earlier (full glacial) age for Crystal Ball Cave and the fact that it does not include a shelter suitable for raptor and vulture roosting as does Smith Creek Cave (Emslie and Heaton, 1987). Livingston (1991) provided a survey and analysis of utilization of birds by early peoples of the Great Basin.

LARGE MAMMALS

The Quaternary mammals of the Great Basin have received far more study than any other vertebrate group, and several papers have been devoted to summarizing what is known about them (Grayson, 1982, 1987, 1994; Heaton, 1990). In reviewing the mammalian history of the Great Basin since the last glaciation, it is useful to divide the species into two broad groups: (1) large-bodied species, the majority of which went extinct at the end of the Pleistocene, and (2) small-bodied species, many of which have undergone significant range shifts or extirpation in the region.

Table 1 lists extinct species that have been found in Late Quaternary sites of the Great Basin, and Grayson (1991, 1993, 1994) has provided a thorough description and analysis of these species. For additional species and new records see Quaternary papers by Gillette and colleagues, this volume. These 20 species represent about half of the mammalian taxa that went extinct in North America toward the end of the Pleistocene. *Martes nobilis*, an extinct species of marten once recognized from several Great Basin faunas, is now considered by Youngman and Schueler (1991) to be a synonym of *M. americana*, the living pine marten (for an opposing view see Grayson, 1984; Graham and Graham, 1994). If this is true then the only extinct species that can be considered small is the short-faced skunk (*Brachyprotoma brevimala*) from Crystal Ball Cave (Heaton, 1985, 1990). In addition, half of the surviving large mammals that have been reported from the Great Basin (beaver, wolf, black bear, grizzly bear, otter, lynx, wapiti, and bison) are now rare or extirpated. The only large mammals found in great numbers in the Great Basin today are coyote, fox, mountain lion, bobcat, mule deer, mountain sheep, pronghorn, and, ironically, wild European horses (Berger, 1986).

In western Utah most of the large mammal remains have been recovered from Lake Bonneville gravels (Nel-

son and Madsen, 1978, 1980, 1983, 1986, 1987a, 1987b; Miller, 1982), from Crystal Ball Cave (Heaton, 1985), and from the Wasatch Range just east of the Great Basin (Miller, 1976, 1987; Gillette and Madsen, 1992). The bulk of the productive cave sites of the Great Basin lie in Nevada and southern California (Grayson, 1982, 1987, 1993, 1994; Heaton, 1990).

The loss of so many species of large mammals has been attributed by different researchers to overkill by early human hunters and to climatic changes associated with the end of the Ice Age (see Grayson, 1991 for a thorough review). In the Great Basin, at least, the evidence weighs strongly in favor of the climatic hypothesis since the extinctions occurred coincident with a drastic drop in lake levels, with a turnover in valley vegetation, with the loss or severe range reduction of many surviving large mammals, and with many range reductions and systematic replacements among the small mammals (discussed below). Early human populations in the Great Basin appear never to have been large enough to have had a significant impact on regional mammal populations, and the only large mammals that appear to have been hunted in great numbers are mountain sheep (*Ovis canadensis*) and pronghorn (*Antilocapra americana*) which still survive (Grayson, 1993). Nevertheless it is puzzling that horses - one of the most common mammals in late Pleistocene faunas - went extinct but now thrive after re-introduction.

Table 1. *List of extinct mammals that lived in the Great Basin during the late Pleistocene and the number of sites from which fossils have been reported (after Grayson 1993, 1994, Heaton 1990, Mead and Lawler 1994).*

Scientific name	Common name	Sites	Utah
Megalonyx sp., cf. *M. jeffersonii*	Jefferson's Ground Sloth	1	
Nothrotheriops shastensis	Shasta Ground Sloth	5	
Glossotherium cf. *G. harlani*	Harlan's Ground Sloth	3	*
Canis sp., cf. *C. dirus*	Dire wolf	1	
Arctodus simus	Giant Short-faced Bear	3	*
Brachyprotoma brevimala	Short-faced Skunk	1	*
Smilodon sp., cf. *S. fatalis*	Saber-toothed Cat	4	*
Panthera atrox	American Lion	2	
Miracinonyx trumani	American Cheetah	1	
Mammut americanum	American Mastodon	2	*
Mammuthus columbi	Columbian Mammoth	10	*
Equus spp.	Horses	24	*
Platygonus sp., cf. *P. compressus*	Flat-headed Peccary	1	
Camelops hesternus	Yesterday's Camel	20	*
Hemiauchenia macrocephala	Large-headed Llama	7	*
Capromeryx minor	Diminutive Pronghorn	2	
Oreamnos harringtoni	Harrington's Mountain Goat	2	*
Eucerotherium sp.	Shrub Ox	2	
Bootherium bombifrons	Harlan's Muskox	2	*

SMALL MAMMALS

The fact that small mammals typically have small home ranges (unlike large mammals and birds) makes them ideal climatic indicators. Hall (1946) recognized that small montane mammals are restricted to mountaintops in the Great Basin, and he speculated that they might cross the desert valley barriers during wintertime. Brown (1971, 1978) applied island biogeographic techniques to these populations by measuring the size and spacing of montane islands (using 2,300 meters as the threshold elevation) throughout the Great Basin. He identified 19 distinct montane "islands" with isolated populations of montane mammals, and these species also range throughout the "mainland" populations of the Sierra Nevada and Rocky Mountains. Brown (1971, 1978) found that the number of species of small montane mammals correlates with island size but not with proximity to a mainland or another island (table 2). This non-equilibrium condition led Brown to conclude that such mammals are not colonizing the Great Basin mountains by dispersal under current conditions, but that these populations are instead relics from the late Pleistocene when lakes and coniferous forests extended across Great Basin valleys.

Grayson (1981, 1987, 1993) and Heaton (1990) derived a series of testable implications for the fossil record based on Brown's conclusions, most of which have been verified by paleontologists. Some modifications have had to be made in Brown's data and interpretations, however. Studies of modern mammals have increased the known diversity on a number of Great Basin mountain ranges, showing that part of the correlation between island size and diversity is an artifact of sampling bias (Grayson, 1993; Grayson and Livingston, 1989, 1993). It has also been shown that some small mammals considered to be montane (Nuttall's cottontail [*Sylvilagus nuttali*], bushy-tailed wood rat [*Neotoma cinerea*]) do appear to cross xeric valley barriers under some conditions (Grayson and Livingston, 1993; Grayson and others, 1996). But Brown's general conclusions about biogeographic isolation are still supported.

Such isolation even appears to have been the primary factor in the origin of several mammalian species endemic to mountain areas of the Great Basin and Mojave Desert such as Inyo shrew (*Sorex tenellus*), Palmer's chipmunk (*Tamias palmeri*), and white-eared pocket mouse (*Perognathus alticola*) (Hall, 1946; Heaton, 1990).

Cave sites and rock shelters have provided the primary late Pleistocene and early Holocene faunas that have allowed the history of Great Basin mammals to be understood (table 2). One important cluster of such caves occurs along the Utah-Nevada border on the east side of the Snake Range and in the adjacent Snake Valley. Crystal Ball Cave, the primary site within this cluster in Utah, is located in a hill 10 kilometers northeast of the Snake Range in a barren valley setting (Heaton, 1985, 1990). Yet the fossils from this cave are dominantly montane species such as pika (*Ochotona princeps*), marmot (*Marmota flaviventris*), and long-tailed vole (*Microtus longicaudus*) that currently inhabit only high mountaintops in the region. Also included are montane species such as snowshoe rabbit (*Lepus* sp., cf. *L. americanus*), meadow vole (*Microtus* sp., cf. *M. pennsylvanicus*), and pine marten (*Martes americana*) that have been completely extirpated from the Great Basin. This supports Brown's (1971, 1978) contention that montane mammals were able to move freely across Great Basin valleys during the last glacial interval. In some cases fossils from the cave even document the systematic replacement of one species by another (table 3). Desert species such as the desert wood rat (*Neotoma lepida*) and black-tailed jackrabbit (*Lepus californicus*) currently live in or around Crystal Ball Cave, but most of the fossils are of their montane counterparts that compete for a similar ecologic niche (Hall, 1946; Heaton, 1990).

The Crystal Ball Cave fauna has several unique components that distinguish it from other caves in the Great Basin. The fauna includes remains of two water-loving mammals, muskrat (*Ondatra zibethicus*) and mink (*Mustela* sp., cf. *M. vison*), as well as several species of fish. The occurrence of these water-loving species undoubtedly resulted from the close proximity of the

Table 2. List of small montane mammals found living in the Great Basin, the number of mountain ranges on which each is living today, and the number of valley and mountain late Pleistocene and early Holocene faunas that each has been found in (after Brown 1971, 1978, Grayson 1987, 1993, Heaton 1990).

Scientific name	Common name	Living Mtns	Fossil Valleys	Fossil Mtns
Sorex vagrans	Vagrant shrew	10	0	1
Sorex palustris	Water shrew	8	1	0
Ochotona princeps	Pika	5	12	10
Sylvilagus nuttallii	Nuttall's cottontail	14	4	0
Lepus townsendii	White-tailed jack rabbit	2	3	1
Eutamias amoenus	Yellow-pine chipmunk	1	1	0
Eutamias dorsalis	Cliff Chipmunk	17	2	1
Eutamias umbrinus	Uinta Chipmunk	17	0	2
Marmota flaviventris	Yellow-bellied marmot	13	11	3
Spermophilus beldingi	Belding's ground squirrel	3	0	2
Spermophilus lateralis	Golden-mantled ground squirrel	15	4	2
Neotoma cinerea	Bushy-tailed woodrat	18	4	4
Phenacomys intermedius	Heather vole	0	0	1
Microtus longicaudus	Long-tailed vole	13	2	2
Zapus princeps	Western jumping mouse	5	0	1
Martes americana	Pine marten	0	3	3
Mustela nivalis	Least weasel	0	1	0
Mustela erminea	Ermine	6	1	1
Gulo gulo	Wolverine	1	1	0

Table 3. *Systematic replacements among closely related species that occupy similar niches as documented at Crystal Ball Cave, Millard County, Utah (Heaton 1985, 1990). Only the desert species are found living in or around the cave today. Numbers indicate minimum number of individuals (MNI) for each species in the late Pleistocene fauna of the Crystal Ball Cave. Wood rats are particularly abundant because they live in the cave (and appear to be the main agent of fossil accumulation).*

Montane species		MNI		Desert species		MNI
Sylvilagus nuttallii	Nuttall's cottontail	4	>	*Sylvilagus audubonii*	Desert cottontail	0
Lepus townsendii	White-tailed jackrabbit	10	>	*Lepus californicus*	Black-tailed jackrabbit	1
Neotoma cinerea	Bushy-tailed wood rat	57	>	*Neotoma lepida*	Desert wood rat	3
Vulpes vulpes	Red fox	3	>	*Urocyon cinereoargenteus*	Gray fox	0

cave to Lake Bonneville (1.7 kilometers to the east at its highest level). Crystal Ball Cave is also unusual in containing large numbers of two desert-adapted species, Townsend's ground squirrel (*Spermophilus townsendii*) and sagebrush vole (*Lemmiscus curtatus*). Townsend's ground squirrel is by far the most abundantly represented species in the cave (minimum number of individuals = 288) even though it is not a common animal in the area today. The Sagebrush vole is the most abundant mouse-sized rodent (minimum number of individuals = 28), and it only lives in association with sagebrush (Heaton, 1985, 1990). Nearby Smith Creek Cave, by contrast, contains small numbers of five species of ground squirrels and lacks sagebrush vole (Mead and others, 1982). The abundance of these two species at Crystal Ball Cave, together with the montane and water-loving species, suggests that Snake Valley contained a diverse plant community during the last glacial interval. This supports the view proposed by Thompson and Mead (1982) and Mead and others (1982) that the Bonneville lakeshore area supported a mosaic of vegetation, including sagebrush, rather than being uniformly forested as proposed by Wells (1983).

Until recently all Quaternary fossil deposits of the Great Basin were reported to be latest Pleistocene and Holocene. Recent work by Bell (1993, 1995) has revealed an Irvingtonian fauna that has not yet been fully described (see also Gillette, Bell, and Hayden, this volume). The deposits of Cathedral Cave and lowest levels of Smith Creek Cave, both in Smith Creek Canyon near the Utah-Nevada border, now appear to represent a much older fauna than anything previously known from the Great Basin. At first the researchers (Mead and others, 1992; Bell, 1993) were mislead by an erroneously young uranium date and a rodent misidentification, but now the true significance of the fauna is being recognized. This fauna includes *Phenacomys* sp., cf. *P. gryci*, cf. *Mimomys*, *Microtus paroperarius*, *Microtus pennsylvanicus*, *Lemmiscus curtatus* and a new extinct species of *Lemmiscus*, *Terricola meadensis*, *Allophaiomys* sp., *Mictomys meltoni*, and several squirrels among the rodents; *Canis latrans*, *Martes americana*, *Mustela nigripes*, and *M. nivalis* among the carnivores; and a variety of shrews, bats, lagomorphs, and other mammals (Bell, 1993, 1995, and personal communication). Comparison of this fauna with that of Porcupine Cave in Colorado should give important insights into the middle Pleistocene mammalian history of the western United States.

SUMMARY

The Great Basin has undergone drastic climatic changes since the peak of late Wisconsin glaciation. During the Pleistocene cooler temperatures allowed closed basins to house pluvial lakes, and conifers that are now restricted to mountaintops were able to colonize lowland areas. Because of a warming climate, many vertebrates now live in relict populations both in lakes and on mountaintops. Over half of the large mammal species of the late Pleistocene Great Basin have gone extinct. Comparing late Pleistocene and early Holocene vertebrate faunas with living faunas has helped to unravel the complex changes that this portion of North America has undergone during the last 20,000 years.

ACKNOWLEDGMENTS

This paper was greatly improved by reviews from Elaine Anderson and David Gillette, as well as discussions with Christopher Bell, Donald Grayson, Jim Mead, and Wade Miller.

REFERENCES

Bell, C. J., 1993, A late Pleistocene mammalian fauna from Cathedral Cave, White Pine County, Nevada: Journal of Vertebrate Paleontology, v. 13, no. 3, p. 26A.

—1995, A middle Pleistocene (Irvingtonian) microtine rodent fauna from White Pine County, Nevada, and its implications for microtine rodent biochronology: Journal of Vertebrate Paleontology, v. 15, no. 3, p. 18A.

Benson, L. V., Currey, D. R., Lao, Y., Hostetler, S., 1992, Lake-size variations in the Lahontan and Bonneville basins between 13,000 and 9000 ^{14}C yr B.P.: Palaeogeography, Palaeoclimatology, Palaeoecology, v. 95, p. 19-32.

Benson, L. V., Currey, D. R., Dorn, R. I., Lajoie, K. R., Oviatt, C. G., Robinson, S. W., Smith, G. I., and Stein, S., 1990, Chronology of expansion and contraction of four Great Basin lake systems during the past 35,000 years: Palaeogeography, Palaeoclimatology, Palaeoecology, v. 78, p. 241-286.

Berger, Joel, 1986, Wild horses of the Great Basin-- social competition and population size: Chicago, University of Chicago Press, 326 p.

Brattstrom, B. H., 1958, Additions to the Pleistocene herpetofauna of Nevada: Herpetologica, v. 14, p. 36.

Brown, J. H., 1971, Mammals on mountaintops-- nonequilibrium insular biogeography: American Naturalist, v. 105, no. 945, p. 467-478.

—1978, The theory of insular biogeography and the distribution of boreal birds and mammals, *in* Harper, K. T., and Reveal, J. L., editors, Intermountain biogeography-- a symposium: Great Basin Naturalist Memoirs, v. 2, p. 209-227.

Currey, D. R., 1990, Quaternary paleolakes in the evolution of semi-desert basins, with special emphasis on Lake Bonneville and the Great Basin, U.S.A.: Palaeogeography, Palaeoclimatology, Palaeoecology, v. 76, p. 189-214.

Davis, O. K., 1990, Caves as sources of biotic remains in arid western North America: Palaeogeography, Palaeoclimatology, Palaeoecology, v. 76, p. 331-348.

Emslie, S. D., and Heaton, T. H., 1987, The late Pleistocene avifauna of Crystal Ball Cave, Utah: Journal of the Arizona-Nevada Academy of Science, vol. 21, no. 2, pp. 53-60.

Gilbert, G. K. 1890, Lake Bonneville: U.S. Geological Survey Monograph, 438 p.

Gillette, D. D., and Madsen, D. B., 1992, The short-faced bear *Arctodus simus* from the late Quaternary in the Wasatch Mountains of central Utah: Journal of Vertebrate Paleontology, v. 12, no. 1, p. 107-112.

Graham, R. W., and Graham, M. A., 1994, Late Quaternary distribution of *Martes* in North America, *in* Buskirk, S. W., Harestad, A. S., Raphael, M. G., and Powell, R. A., editors, Martins, sables, and rishers-- biology and conservation: Ithaca, New York, Cornell University Press, p. 26-58.

Grayson, D. K., 1981, A mid-Holocene record for the heather vole, *Phenacomys* cf. *intermedius*, in the central Great Basin and its biogeographic significance: Journal of Mammalogy, v. 62, p. 115-121.

—1982, Toward a history of Great Basin mammals during the past 15,000 years, *in* Madsen, D. B., and O'Connell, J. F., editors, Man and environment in the Great Basin: Society for American Archaeology Paper 2, p. 82-101.

—1984, The time of extinction and nature of adaptation of the noble martin, *Martes nobilis*, *in* Genoways, H. H., and Dawson, M. R., editors, Contributions in Quaternary vertebrate paleontology-- a volume in memorial to John E. Guilday: Special Publication of the Carnegie Museum of Natural History 8, p. 233-240.

—1987, The biogeographic history of small mammals in the Great Basin: observations on the last 20,000 years: Journal of Mammalogy, v. 68, no. 2, p. 359-375.

—1991, Late Pleistocene mammalian extinctions in North America-- taxonomy, chronology, and explanations: Journal of World Prehistory, v. 5, p. 193-231.

—1993, The desert's past-- a natural prehistory of the Great Basin: Washington, D. C., Smithsonian Institution Press, 356 p.

—1994, The extinct Late Pleistocene mammals of the Great Basin, *in* Harper, K. T., St. Clair, L. L., Thorne, K. H., and Hess, W. M., editors, Natural history of the Colorado Plateau and Great Basin: Niwot, University Press of Colorado, p. 55-85.

Grayson, D. K., and Livingston, S. D., 1989, High-elevation records for *Neotoma cinerea* in the White Mountains, California: Great Basin Naturalist, v. 49, no. 3, p. 392-395.

—1993, Missing mammals on Great Basin mountains-- Holocene extinctions and inadequate knowledge: Conservation Biology, v. 7, no. 3, p. 527-532.

Grayson, D. K., Livingston, S. D., Rickart, Eric, and Shaver, M. W., 1996, Biogeographic significance of low-elevation records for *Neotoma cinerea* from the northern Bonneville Basin, Utah: Great Basin Naturalist, v. 56, no. 3, p. 191-196.

Hall, E. R., 1946, Mammals of Nevada: University of California Press, Berkeley.

Heaton, T. H., 1985, Quaternary paleontology and paleoecology of Crystal Ball Cave, Millard County, Utah-- with emphasis on mammals and description of a new species of fossil skunk: Great Basin Naturalist, v. 45, no. 3, p. 337-390.

—1990, Quaternary mammals of the Great Basin: extinct giants, Pleistocene relics, and recent immigrants, *in* Ross, R. M., and Allmon, W. D., editors, Causes of evolution-- a paleontological perspective: Chicago, University of Chicago Press, p. 422-465.

Hintze, L. F., 1988, Geologic history of Utah: Brigham Young University Geology Studies Special Publication 7, 202 p.

Howard, Hildegarde, 1935, A new species of eagle from a Quaternary cave deposit in eastern Nevada: Condor, v. 37, p. 206-209.

—1952, The prehistoric avifauna of Smith Creek Cave, Nevada, with a description of a new gigantic raptor: Southern California Academy of Sciences Bulletin, v. 51, no. 2, p. 50-54.

Hunt, C. B., 1967, Physiography of the United States: San Francisco, W. H. Freeman and Co., 480 p.

Livingston, S. D., 1991, Aboriginal utilization of birds in the western Great Basin, *in* Purdue, J. R., Klipple, W. E., and Styles, B. W., editors, Beamers, bobwhites, and blue-points-- tributes to the career of Paul W. Parmalee: Illinois State Museum Scientific Papers 23, p. 341-357.

Madsen, D. B., and Currey., D. R., 1979, Late Quaternary glacial and vegetation changes, Little Cottonwood Canyon area, Wasatch Mountains, Utah: Quaternary Research, v. 12, p. 254-270.

Mead, J. I., 1985, Paleontology of Hidden Cave-- amphibians and reptiles, *in* Thomas, D. H., editor, The archaeology of Hidden Cave, Nevada: Anthropological Papers of the American Museum of Natural History, v. 61, p. 162-170.

—1988, Herpetofauna from Danger Cave, Last Supper Cave, and Hanging Rock Shelter, *in* Grayson, D. K. editor, Danger Cave, Last Supper Cave, and Hanging Rock Shelter-- the faunas: Anthropological Papers of the American Museum of Natural History, v. 66, no. 1, p. 116-124.

Mead, J. I., and Bell, C. J., 1994, Late Pleistocene and Holocene herpetofaunas of the Great Basin and Colorado Plateau, *in* Harper, K. T., St. Clair, L. L., Thorne, K. H., and Hess, W. M., editors, Natural history of the Colorado Plateau and Great Basin: Niwot, University Press of Colorado, p. 255-275.

Mead, J. I., Bell, C. J., and Murray, L. K., 1992, *Mictomys borealis* (northern bog lemming) and the Wisconsin paleoecology of the east-central Great Basin: Quaternary Research, v. 37, p. 229-238.

Mead, J. I., Grayson, D. K., and Casteel, R. W., 1983, Fish, amphibians, reptiles, and birds, *in* Thomas, D. H., editor, The archaeology of Monitor Valley. 2, Gatecliff Shelter: Anthropological Papers of the American Museum of Natural History, v. 59, p. 129-135.

Mead, J. I., Heaton, T. H., and Mead, E. M., 1989, Late Quaternary reptiles from two caves in the east-central Great Basin: Journal of Herpetology, vol. 23, no. 2, pp. 186-189.

Mead, J. I., and Lawler, M. C., 1994, Skull, mandible, and metapodials of the extinct Harrington's mountain goat (*Oreamnos harringtoni*): Journal of Vertebrate Paleontology, v. 14, no. 4, p. 562-576.

Mead, J. I., Thompson, R. S., and Van Devender, T. R., 1982, Late Wisconsinan and Holocene fauna from Smith Creek Canyon, Snake Range, Nevada: Transactions of the San Diego Society of Natural History, v. 20, no. 1, p. 1-26.

Miller, W. E., 1976, Late Pleistocene vertebrates of the Silver Creek local fauna from north central Utah: Great Basin Naturalist, v. 36, no. 4, p. 387-424.

—1982, Pleistocene vertebrates from the deposits of Lake Bonneville, Utah: National Geographic Research Reports, v. 14, p. 473-478.

—1987, *Mammut americanum*, Utah's first record of the American mastodon: Journal of Paleontology, v. 61, no. 1, p. 168-183.

Nelson, M. E., and Madsen, J. H., Jr., 1978, Late Pleistocene musk oxen from Utah: Transactions of the Kansas Academy of Sciences, v. 81, no. 4, p. 277-295.

—1980, A summary of Pleistocene, fossil vertebrate localities in the northern Bonneville Basin of Utah, *in* Gwynn, J. W., editor, Great Salt Lake: a scientific, historical and economic overview: Utah Geological and Mineral Survey Bulletin 116, p. 97-113.

—1983, A giant short-faced bear (*Arctodus simus*) from the Pleistocene of northern Utah: Transactions of the Kansas Academy of Sciences, v. 86, no. 1, p. 1-9.

—1986, Canids from the late Pleistocene of Utah: Great Basin Naturalist, v. 46, no. 3, p. 415-420.

—1987a, Occurrence of the musk ox, *Symbos cavifrons*, from southeastern Idaho and comments on the genus *Bootherium*: Great Basin Naturalist, v. 47, no. 2, p. 239-251.

—1987b, A review of Lake Bonneville shoreline faunas (late Pleistocene) of northern Utah, *in* Koop, R. S., and Cohenour, R. E., editors, Cenozoic geology of western Utah--sites for precious metal and hydrocarbon accumulation: Utah Geological Association Publication 16, p. 319-334.

Oviatt, C. G., Currey, D. R., and Sack, Dorothy, 1992, Radiocarbon chronology of Lake Bonneville, eastern Great Basin, USA: Palaeogeography, Palaeoclimatology, Palaeoecology, v. 99, p. 225-241.

Richmond, G. M., 1964, Glaciation of Little Cottonwood and Bells Canyons, Wasatch Mountains, Utah: U.S. Geological Survey Professional Paper 454-D, 41 p.

Rhode, David, and Madsen, D. B., 1995, Late Wisconsin/early Holocene vegetation in the Bonneville Basin: Quaternary Research, v. 44, p. 246-256.

Sigler, W. F., and Sigler, J. W., 1987, Fishes of the Great Basin: a Natural History: Reno, University of Nevada Press, 425 p.

—1994, Fishes of the Great Basin and the Colorado Plateau: past and present forms, *in* Harper, K. T., St. Clair, L. L., Thorne, K. H., and Hess, W. M., editors, Natural history of the Colorado Plateau and Great Basin: Niwot, University Press of Colorado, p. 163-208.

—1996, Fishes of Utah: Salt Lake City, University of Utah Press, 375 p.

Smith, G. R., 1978, Biogeography of intermountain fishes, *in* Harper, K. T., and Reveal, J. L., editors, Intermountain biogeography-- a symposium, Great Basin Naturalist Memoir, v. 2, p. 17-42.

—1985, Paleontology of Hidden Cave-- fish, *in* Thomas, D. H., editor, The archaeology of Hidden Cave, Nevada: Anthropological Papers of the American Museum of Natural History, v. 61, p. 171-178.

Smith, G. R., Stokes, W. L., and Horn, K. F., 1968, Some late Pleistocene fishes of Lake Bonneville: Copeia, v. 4, p. 807-816.

Thompson, R. S., and Mead, J. I., 1982, Late Quaternary environments and biogeography of the Great Basin: Quaternary Research, v. 17, p. 39-55.

Wells, P. V., 1983, Paleobiogeography of montane islands in the Great Basin since the last glaciopluvial: Ecological Monographs, v. 53, no. 4, p. 341-382.

Youngman, P. M., and Schueler, F. W., 1991, *Martes nobilis* is a synonym of *Martes americana*, not an extinct Pleistocene-Holocene species: Journal of Mammalogy, v. 72, no. 3, p. 567-577.

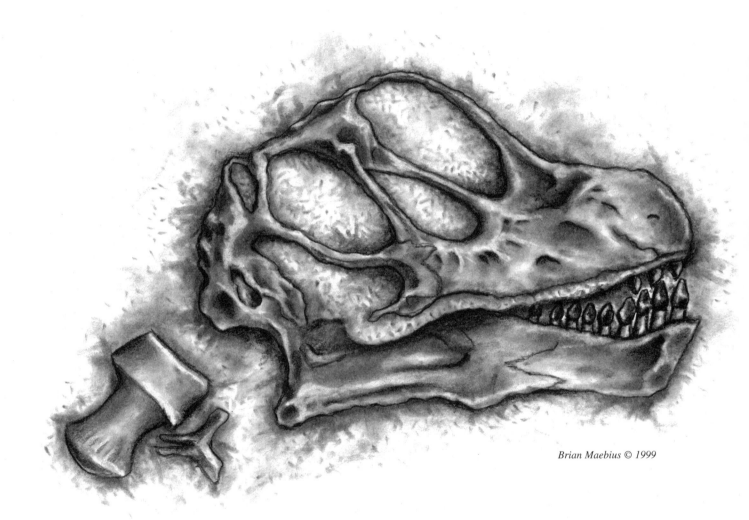

Brian Maebius © 1999

Camarasaurus

THE FIRST RECORD OF JEFFERSON'S GROUND SLOTH, *MEGALONYX JEFFERSONII*, IN UTAH (PLEISTOCENE, RANCHOLABREAN LAND MAMMAL AGE)

David D. Gillette
Museum of Northern Arizona, 3101 North Fort Valley Road, Flagstaff, AZ 86001

H. Gregory McDonald
Hagerman Fossil Beds National Monument, 221 North State Street, P.O. Box 570, Hagerman, ID 83332-0570

Martha C. Hayden
Utah Geological Survey, PO Box 146100, Salt Lake City, UT 84114-6100

ABSTRACT

The discovery of a partial skeleton of Jefferson's ground sloth, *Megalonyx jeffersoni*, near Orem, Utah County, Utah, is the first record of this genus in Utah. The site is in high-energy fluvial or lacustrine deposits at an elevation of 1439 meters. These sediments were deposited during or immediately after Lake Bonneville's Provo stillstand, approximately 14,300 yr B.P. The skeleton, apparently from a single adult individual, includes tooth fragments, ribs, partial manus, innominate, femur, tibia, and partial pes, most in articulation. This record of Late Pleistocene *Megalonyx* confirms the presence of this genus in the Great Basin during the Rancholabrean Land Mammal Age. Among several possible migration corridors, the late Pleistocene population represented by this individual probably originated from disperal through riparian habitats in the Snake River Plain that came close to, or were contiguous with, similar habitats extending from the northern margin of the Great Basin, along and near Lake Bonneville shorelines. A second, unstudied, ground sloth, tentatively identified as the same species, was discovered in 1997 only a few kilometers north of the Orem site.

INTRODUCTION

In the summer of 1991, Ron Robison of Orem, Utah, discovered fossil bones eroding from the edge of a slope near his home, where bicyclists had worn a path in unconsolidated sand and gravel. He collected several of the bones and identified the position of others still in place in the sediments. He showed the bones to his brother, paleontologist Steven Robison, who suspected they belonged to one of the genera of ground sloths that inhabited North America during the Pleistocene Epoch. Ron Robison called one of us (DDG) then at the office of the State Paleontologist at the Utah Division of State History to confirm identification of the bones.

Two of us (DDG and MCH) visited Ron Robison in Orem and corroborated his brother's determination. We identified the bones as those of Jefferson's ground sloth, *Megalonyx jeffersonii*, and examined the site (figures 1 and 2) to establish that there were additional bones in place. After gaining permission from the landowner to excavate the remaining bones, personnel from the Division of State History, the Utah Statewide Archaeological Society, and the Utah Friends of Paleontology conducted an excavation from August 29 to September 1, 1991. The excavation produced part of the skeleton of a single individual ground sloth that was embedded in coarse sand and gravel near a shoreline of Pleistocene Lake Bonneville.

The field crew excavated (figures 3 and 4) the bones by traditional burlap-and-plaster field methods, and simultaneously mapped and photographed them in place. Ribs, partial manus, pelvis, partial rear leg, and partial pes were in situ, in articulation. The excavation crew removed these bones in a manner that would preserve the articulation. Because the sand and gravel were unconsolidated, the bones were difficult to remove without being damaged by caving-in beneath the bones as the surrounding sediment was removed. Part of the pelvis collapsed during undercutting despite extraordinary care to prevent such loss in that critical phase of the excavation. Dry screen-sieving of debris on the slope beneath the site produced fragments of smaller bones and teeth, evidently accumulations of broken fragments that had been dislodged by bicyclists and pedestrian traffic.

During the excavation, the crew preserved the exposed bones with a solution of polyvinyl acetate and acetone, a hardener and consolidant. After excavation, preparators stabilized the bones at the paleontology laboratory of the Utah Division of State History.

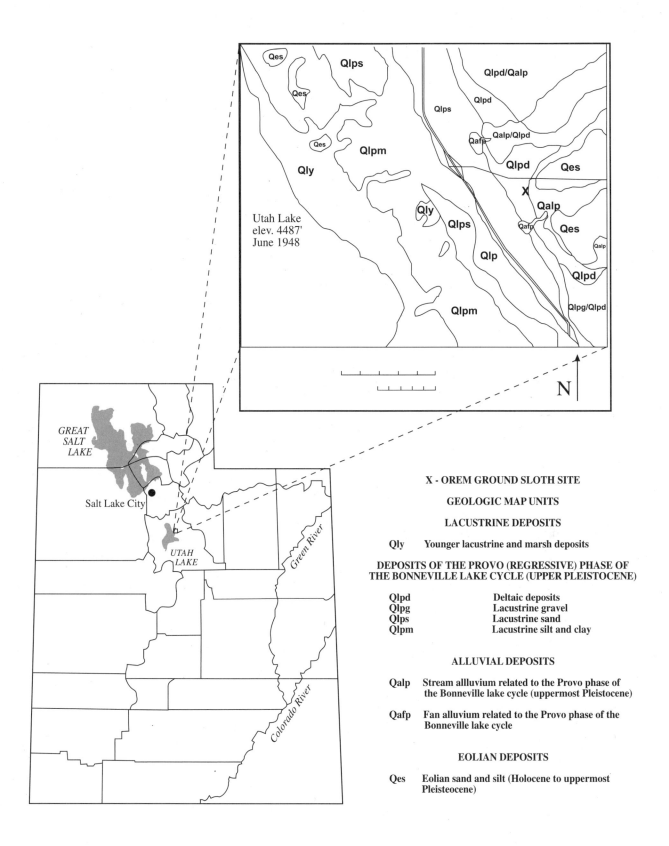

Figure 1. *Locality map of the Orem ground sloth excavation site showing local stratigraphy of Quaternary geologic units, after Machette (1992). All deposits in the area of the excavation are associated with the Provo phase of the Bonneville lake cycle, which dates to approximately 14,300 yr B.P.*

Figure 2. *Excavation in progress. The bones occurred at a level approximately two meters below the crest of the shoreline terrace, where the pickup truck is parked.*

Figure 3. *More excavation in progress showing the head of the femur of the Orem ground sloth and its geologic context; scale in centimeters and inches.*

Figure 4. *Partial ribcage of the Orem ground sloth in articulation, but upside down. Note the unbedded, coarse sand and gravel matrix; scale in centimeters and inches.*

ABBREVIATIONS

BYUVP, Brigham Young University Earth Science Museum, Provo, Utah, vertebrate paleontology; DMNH, Dayton Museum of Natural History, Dayton, Ohio; CM, Carnegie Museum of Natural History, Pittsburgh, PA; F:AM, Frick Collection, American Museum of Natural History, New York; IMNH, Idaho Museum of Natural History Vertebrate Paleontology Department, Pocatello, Idaho; LACM, Los Angeles County Museum, Los Angeles, California; MR, Museum of the Rockies, Montana State University, Bozeman, Montana; PPHM, Panhandle Plains Historical Museum, West Texas State University, Lubbock, Texas; SBCM, San Bernardino County Museum, San Bernardino, California; SMU, Southern Methodist University, Shuler Museum of Paleontology, Department of Geological Sciences, Dallas, Texas; TMM, Texas Memorial Museum, University of Texas, Austin, TX; UA, University of Arizona, Department of Geosciences; UCMP, University of California Museum of Paleontology, Berkeley, California; UF, University of Florida Museum of Natural History; USNM, United States National Museum, Smithsonian Institution, Washington, D. C.; UW, University of Washington Burke Museum, Seattle, Washington; and WTSU, West Texas State University, Canyon, Texas.

DESCRIPTION

Systematic Paleontology
CLASS Mammalia
ORDER Xenarthra
FAMILY Megalonychidae
GENUS *Megalonyx*
Megalonyx jeffersonii

Referred Specimen

BYUVP 13301, partial skeleton of an adult individual consisting of tooth fragments; seven ribs; digit III, right manus; partial right pes including: metatarsal II, with phalanges 1-3, and metatarsal III with associated sesamoids and phalanges 1-3; innominate; femur; tibia; patella; partial calcaneum; ecto-cuneiform; navicular; and other unidentified bone fragments. Diagnostic elements include the femur, tibia, and elements of the pes.

Locality

The site, Utah Geological Survey Locality 42Ut430V, is at the margin of an abandoned gravel quarry at an elevation of 1,439.6 meters above mean sea level. It is at 40° 16' 19" North latitude, 111° 42' 08" West longitude, about 100 meters south of the Water Conservancy District office building at 355 West University Parkway, Orem, Utah County, Utah (figure 1).

Stratigraphic Position and Age

The sand and gravel in which the skeleton was buried (figure 1) are deltaic deposits of the Provo (regressive) phase of the Bonneville lake cycle (upper Pleistocene), or stream alluvium related to the Provo phase of the Bonneville lake cycle (uppermost Pleistocene) (Machette, 1992). The site was in a coarse, ungraded and unbedded gravel, but with slight imbrication of the gravel clasts immediately adjacent to the bones that suggested high-energy fluvial sedimentation. The geologic situation, elevation, and topographic setting indicate the sediments were deposited during the Provo Shoreline stillstand of Lake Bonneville, approximately 14,300 yr B.P. (Oviatt and others, 1992), or slightly later if the gravels represent an aggrading fluvial channel deposited some time after regression of the Provo level. This age assignment is late Rancholabrean Land Mammal Age. Attempts to obtain a radiocarbon date were unsuccessful due to leaching of organics from the bone (Thomas Stafford, personal communication, 1996).

Previous Work

Previously thought to be absent from the Great Basin (Kurtén and Anderson, 1980), this is the first record of *Megalonyx jeffersonii* from Utah, a rather surprising circumstance in view of the relatively abundant record of Pleistocene mammals in the state (Jefferson and others, 1994). This record is also the first ground sloth in northern Utah in the vicinity of Pleistocene Lake Bonneville (Nelson and Madsen, 1987). The largest Pleistocene fauna known from northern Utah is from the Silver Creek locality (Miller, 1976), 109 km north of the Orem site and approximately 22 km directly east of the closest Lake Bonneville shoreline. The Silver Creek site is at a much higher elevation (approximately 1,950 m above sea level) in an alpine setting with a much older age (late Sangamon or early Wisconsin). The Silver Creek fauna includes the ground sloth *Paramylodon harlani*. The other genus of ground sloth recorded for Utah is *Nothrotheriops shastensis*, based on dung preserved in caves on the Colorado Plateau in the southern part of the state (Jefferson and others, 1994 and references therein).

Other Pleistocene fossil sites near Orem include several unpublished records of extinct muskoxen, *Bootherium bombifrons*, from approximately the same horizon.

Remains of Pleistocene vertebrates from the Bonneville Basin were reported as early as 1878. The mammalian fauna from Lake Bonneville now includes at least 16 species, with radiocarbon age estimates ranging from 20,000-10,000 yr B.P. This late Pleistocene assemblage includes Columbian mammoth, *Mammuthus columbi*; American mastodon, *Mammut americanum*, and associated megafauna (summarized by Nelson and Madsen, 1987). The majority of these finds are isolated elements such as skulls and metapodials, usually in deltaic sand and gravel. Articulated skeletons or associated material from a single individual, such as the sloth described herein, are rare in Lake Bonneville-age sediments.

OSTEOLOGY

Tooth Fragments

The fragments consist entirely of osteodentine characteristic of sloths. None of the fragments is sufficiently well preserved to indicate size or cross-sectional shape.

Manus

All three phalanges of the third digit of the right manus (figure 5) were recovered in articulation. As preserved, the joint between the ungual and second phalanx was in a condition of hyperflexion, with the long axis of phalanx 2 nearly at right angle to the long axis of the ungual phalanx, perhaps a rigor mortis condition of the digit. The contact between the two bones at this joint was tightly preserved and cannot be separated without damage to the bones. The articulation between the proximal and second phalanges was also tightly preserved. At both joints, the bones were broken during excavation, leaving portions of the bone in the articular facets.

Innominate

The right side of the pelvis appeared to be relatively complete during exposure of the skeleton, but was damaged during excavation. Most of the wing of the ilium (figure 6) is preserved, but lacks the acetabulum and the medial margin that connected with the sacral vertebrae. The dorsal margin of the iliac wing is nearly straight in profile from the lateral extremity inward for half its length, and curves gently toward the sacral arch. The anterior face is concave. The posterior face is slightly convex and marked with numerous ridges for muscles that converge toward the acetabulum. Many of the unidentified fragments in the collection of this specimen probably belong to the innominate.

Figure 5. *Digit III, right manus (left); and digit III, right pes (right) of the Orem ground sloth, both in medial view; scale in centimeters and inches. The ungual phalanx of digit III, pes, is incomplete.*

Figure 6. *Innominate of the Orem ground sloth, lateral view; scale in centimeters and inches. Upper margin of the innominate is not shown in this photograph.*

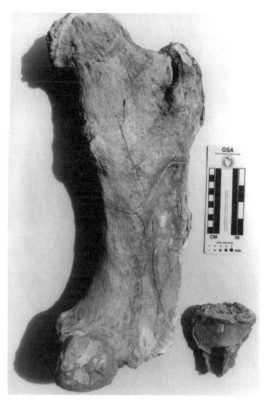

Figure 7. *Femur of the Orem ground sloth, anterior view, and patella (lower right), articular aspect showing the femoral facet; scale in centimeters and inches.*

Dimensions of the right iliac wing as preserved are: transverse length along the curve of the dorsal crest, 520 mm; straight line diameter between the two extremities of the dorsal crest, 448 mm; and dorsoventral diameter between lateral extremity of the iliac crest to the broken extremity of the acetabular neck, 270 mm.

Femur

The right femur of the Orem ground sloth (figure 7, table 1) is complete except for the lateral condyle of the distal extremity. Like other femora of *Megalonyx* and in contrast with the femur of *Nothrotheriops* (Stock, 1925), the distal articular facets of the Orem specimen lie in the same transverse plane as the shaft and proximal end. The prominent head, with a distinctive neck lacks the prominent fovea present in earlier species of *Megalonyx*. The prominent greater trochanter and relatively weak lesser trochanter distinguish the Orem femur from that of

Nothrotheriops as does the presence of a small third trochanter distinct from the lateral epicondyle. The inner epicondyle and the articular facet for the patella are not continuous in the Orem specimen, in that respect resembling the condition in *Nothrotheriops* and differing from that of *Paramylodon*. Dimensions of the Orem specimen are similar to those of other examples of *Megalonyx jeffersonii*, greater than those of other species such as *M. leptostomus* and *M. wheatleyi* (table 1), greater than those of *Nothrotheriops shastensis* provided by Stock (1925, p. 82, table 36), and somewhat smaller than the averages for twenty-six specimens of *Paramylodon harlani* (Stock, 1925, p. 171, table 86).

Patella

The right patella of the Orem ground sloth (figure 7, table 2) closely resembles the patella of *Megalonyx jeffersonii* (UCMP 22776) illustrated and described by Stock (1925, p. 106 and figure 46). Its nearly triangular shape and transversely expanded femoral facet differ from the patella of *Nothrotheriops*, which is nearly rectangular and has a narrow articular facet, and from the patella of *Paramylodon* which is more nearly oval (Stock, 1925). According to Stock (1925, p. 82), the articular facet of the patella of *Megalonyx* is concave dorsoventrally and nearly flat transversely; in the Orem

Table 1. *Dimensions (mm) of the femur of three species of the ground sloth* Megalonyx, *including the Orem specimen of* Megalonyx jeffersonii *(* = approximate dimension).*

Dimensions:
1. Length along medial side from top of head to distal surface of medial condyle.
2. Greatest transverse diameter of proximal end.
3. Mediolateral diameter of head.
4. Anteroposterior diameter of head.
5. Mediolateral diameter of distal end across epicondyles.
6. Transverse diameter of shaft proximal to epicondyles and distal to third trochanter.

	1	2	3	4	5	6
Megalonyx leptostomus						
LACM 55828, Ringhold, WA	411.0	152.3	74.9	79.0	158.0	94.3
Megalonyx wheatleyi						
F:AM 103-1986 field number, McLeod, FL	440.0	183.0	80.4	87.4	188.0	124.3
F:AM 102-1920 field number, McLeod, FL	417.7	—	85.3	—	201.5	—
Megalonyx jeffersonii						
BYU 13301, Orem, UT	505.0	225.2	115.1	108.6	224.7	159*
UCMP 56088, Irvington, CA	500.0	200*	108.5	116.5	212.5	146.1
IMNH 15171, American Falls Reservoir, ID	485.0	227.0	103.9	107.8	237.0	159.6
IMNH 17060, American Falls Reservoir, ID	478.0	216.2	102.3	109.9	231.0	142.9
IMNH 23034, American Falls Reservoir, ID	514.2	250.0	110.0	112.6	241.5	160.0
UW 20788, Seattle Tacoma Airport, WA	506.0	218.2	111.0	110.4	235.6	164.1
USNM 23737, Saltville, VA	525.6	—	106.7	112.0	238.2	—
SMU 60247, Moore Pit, Dallas, TX	413.3	—	83.2	82.0	184.0	—
USNM 64-R-15 6-7 field number, Valsequillo, Mexico	440.0	—	95.4	100.0	201.3	—
DMNH G-25928, Darke County, OH	617.1	268.0	130.0	133.4	283.3	192.0

Table 2. *Dimensions (mm) of the patella of* Megalonyx jeffersonii, *including the Orem specimen BYU 13301. Measurements of Rancho La Brea specimens after Stock (1925, p. 106). (+ denotes actual dimension to broken surface.)*

Dimensions:
1. Dorsoventral diameter
2. Transverse diameter
3. Dorsoventral diameter of femoral surface (articular facet)
4. Transverse diameter of femoral surface (articular facet)
5. Thickness through femoral surface

	1	2	3	4	5
BYUVP 13301, Orem, UT	105.1+	97.6+	60.6	89.2	51.7
UCMP 22776, Rancho La Brea, CA	106	99	52	97.6	42.2
LACM 6001-1, Rancho La Brea, CA	109	90.8	45.4	90	41

specimen the facet is concave dorsoventrally and convex transversely, agreeing in surface shape more with that of *Nothrotheriops*. Otherwise, the overall resemblance, proportions, and dimensions of the Orem specimen closely resemble those of the *Megalonyx* patella described by Stock (1925) from Rancho La Brea and by McDonald (1977) from other localities.

Tibia

The right tibia of the Orem ground sloth (figure 8, table 3) is complete except for medial and lateral margins of the proximal end. In overall osteology and dimensions this tibia resembles other tibiae of *Megalonyx jeffersonii* from nearby American Falls Reservoir in southern Idaho. The Orem tibia is similar in shape; the profile of the anterior surface when viewed from above is straight, a consequence of the great lateral expansion of the anterior tuberosity, and the anterior tuberosity for attachment of the patellar ligament is situated lateral to the inner articulating surface and directly

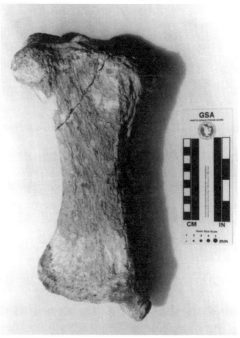

Figure 8. *Tibia of the Orem ground sloth, anterior view; scale in centimeters and inches.*

Table 3. *Dimensions (mm) of the tibia of three species of the ground sloth* Megalonyx, *including the Orem specimen of* Megalonyx jeffersonii *(* = approximate dimension).*

Dimensions:
1. Length from top of intercondylar spine to middle of astragalar surface.
2. Least width of shaft.
3. Mediolateral diameter of distal end.
4. Mediolateral diameter of proximal end from edge of medial condyle to tibial crest.
5. Anteroposterior diameter of proximal end from posterior edge of lateral condyle to anterior edge of medial condyle.

	1	2	3	4	5
Megalonyx leptostomus					
PPHM 1716, Cita Canyon, TX	237.6	47.2	104.4	134.0	—
WTSU unnumbered, Cita Canyon, TX	—	55.2	—	140.0	—
Megalonyx wheatleyi					
F:AM 103-1986 field number, McLeod FL	247.2	62.8	118.2	154.1	162.6
ANSP 15554, Port Kennedy Cave, PA	287.1	61.0	119.3	129*	116
ANSP 15555, Port Kennedy Cave, PA	268.7	62.0	123.3	166.9	—
ANSP 186, Port Kennedy Cave, PA	257.9	64.5	116.6	—	—
Megalonyx jeffersonii					
BYUVP 13301, Orem, UT	303*	81.3	149.4	172*	177.3
IMNH 1781, Acequia Gravel Pit, ID	333.1	88.0	163.1	198.0	194.1
IMNH 15170, America Falls Reservoir, ID	332.8	82.5	158.7	—	—
IMNH 149, American Falls Reservoir, ID	345.1	80.1	155.9	211.5	—
UF 21344, Aucilla River, FL	288.3	83.3	138.6	180*	—
UF 14888, Aucilla River, FL	—	—	146.3	185.4	174.3
CM 12528, Robinson Cave, TN	289.8	73.8	140.8	—	—
TMM 30967-1231, Ingleside, TX	272.8	62.7	128.5	173*	157
MR 002, Doedon Local Fauna, MT	—	78.8	156.8	192.4	189.6
UW 20788, Sea Tac, WA	282.6	71.5	142.6	184.6	201.0
UF 23569, Warm Mineral Springs, FL	276.2	66.6	123.5	175.9	182.0
DMNH G-25717, Darke County, OH	356.2	93.9	172.8	—	—

in front of the outer articulating surface. In articulation with the femur the overall form and shape resembles the tibia of *Megalonyx (*Stock, 1925): the transverse plane of the anterior surfaces of the shafts of the femur and tibia with the joint extended are in the same plane (not oblique as in *Nothrotheriops*), a consequence of only slight obliquity of the distal end of the femur with respect to the proximal end and the shaft. The distal extremity of the Orem tibia possesses the extreme development of the malleolus on the medial border seen in both *Nothrotheriops* and *Megalonyx*, but resembles *Megalonyx* in the possession of only a single tendinal groove on the posterior surface while *Nothrotheriops* has two. The articular surface for the astragalus is a single continuous surface and lacks the deep concavity for the odontoid process of the astragalus present in *Nothrotheriops* and *Paramylodon*. The greater size of the Orem specimen distinguishes it from the tibia of *M. wheatleyi* and *M. leptostomus* (table 3); its dimensions fall within the range of measurements provided by Stock (1925) for *Nothrotheriops shastensis* and McDonald (1977) for *Megalonyx jeffersonii*; the proportionally heavy shaft (minimum transverse diameter) in the Orem specimen approximates the dimension and proportions in *Megalonyx jeffersonii* reported by Stock (1925, p. 82, table 36).

Pes

Parts of the right pes are preserved and include the navicular, calcaneum, ectocuneiform, metatarsal II, metatarsal III, and phalanges 1-3 of digit III.

Navicular

The right navicular was broken into three pieces but when reassembled permits comparison with other *Megalonyx* naviculars. The astragalar articulation is convex as is typical in ground sloths, and parts of the articular facets for the ectocuneiform and mesocuneiform are preserved. The specimen compares well with that of *Megalonyx* illustrated by Leidy (1855, plate XIII, figures 7, 8). The plantar wall is incomplete but was well developed. Approximate measurements are dorsoventral length, 75.1 mm, and proximodistal thickness, 31.1 mm.

Calcaneum

A fragment of the articular end of the calcaneum of the Orem ground sloth includes the medial astragalar facet and the sustentacular facet. Not enough is preserved to be compared in detail with other ground sloths or to be measured for comparative dimensions.

Ectocuneiform

Although heavily weathered and abraded, the right ectocuneiform retains enough of its morphology to be identified, but does not warrant further description.

Metatarsal II

The morphology of right metatarsal II compares closely with that of other *Megalonyx jeffersonii* second metatarsals illustrated by Leidy (1855, plate 10, figures 2,6). It has a shallow concave facet for the mesocuneiform on the proximal end, and a flat oval facet for the first metatarsal medially. There is no distinct facet for the third metatarsal laterally. The distal end is asymmetrical with a well-developed shelf on the medial side of the carina but none on the lateral side.

Digit III, Pes

This digit (figure 5) includes the right metatarsal III, co-ossified phalanges 1 and 2, and the third (ungual) phalanx.

Metatarsal III

Although incomplete, this bone can be identified as the right third metatarsal. Because of its fragmentary nature, the third metatarsal can be made to articulate, but only crudely, with the proximal facet of the co-ossified proximal and second phalanges and associated ungual phalanx. Both sesamoids of the third digit of the pes were preserved as well.

Co-ossified Phalanges 1 and 2, Digit III, Pes

Fusion of the proximal and second phalanx in the third digit of the pes was one of the criteria used by McDonald (1977) to distinguish *Megalonyx jeffersonii* from earlier species of *Megalonyx* in which the two bones remain separated in adults. The two bones are distinct in juveniles of *Megalonyx jeffersonii* but become completely fused in adults with complete loss of any visible suture. The absence of any indication of the original separation of the two bones in this individual, along with the absence of any visible epiphyseal lines in the limb bones, supports the interpretation that these are the remains of an adult, mature individual.

Ungual Phalanx, Digit III, Pes

This bone lacks the distal tip and the dorsal portion of the articular surface. Enough is preserved of the articular surface to confirm its articulation with the co-ossi-fied phalanges.

Ribs and Unidentified Bones

In addition to the bones identified here, ribs, several additional unidentified bones, and fragments are included with this specimen. One is a phalanx of undetermined position.

ZOOGEOGRAPHY

Sloths are generally absent from the Great Basin and the few known records are confined to its margins. These include *Megalonyx, Nothrotheriops*, and *Paramylodon* at Manix Lake in southern California; *Megalonyx* and *Nothrotheriops* at Tule Springs in southern Nevada; and *Paramylodon* from Carson City (McDonald, 1996). The Orem record conforms to this general pattern of sloths living in habitat associated with the margin of the Great Basin and not the basin proper. The inference is that suitable habitat within the Great Basin was not generally available to support sloths, and their dispersal into the area was restricted to pathways that provided suitable habitat. The question is whether possible pathways of dispersal for *Megalonyx jeffersonii* into the Bonneville Basin can be identified. Two possible routes are a southern dispersal route northward from Manix Lake and Tule Springs, or a northern dispersal route southward from the Snake River Plain.

Stock (1925) considered *Megalonyx* to be a browser associated with woodland habitat; this interpretation has been followed by most subsequent researchers. In the eastern United States numerous sites containing *Megalonyx* are coastal but *Megalonyx* also ranged inland. The distribution of *Megalonyx* in western North America (figure 9) suggests a strong connection to gallery forests and riparian habitat associated with permanent water. Many of the inland sites, like the Orem locality which is on or near a shoreline of Lake Bonneville, are associated with pluvial lakes (for example, Lake Bonneville, Manix Lake, and Las Vegas Lake), while other sites seem to indicate an association with gallery forests along rivers. During the Rancholabrean, Lake Manix, for example, would have connected to coastal habitat via the then much larger Mojave River (Jefferson and others, 1982). This connection would have provided a corridor inland from the coast. McDonald and Anderson (1983) noted a similar association of *Megalonyx* with river deposits in Iowa. Sites on the Great Plains with *Megalonyx* are also often associated with fluvial deposits, which similarly seem to indicate that its dispersal from eastern wood-lands to the Great Plains was facilitated by gallery forests and riparian habitat.

The nearest concentration of localities with *Megalonyx* to the Orem site is on the Snake River Plain in southern Idaho. All late Pleistocene records of *Megalonyx jeffersonii* in Idaho are associated with fluvial and lacustrine deposits along the course of the Snake River (table 4). *Megalonyx* was present in Idaho since the Blancan Land Mammal Age where it is known from Hagerman (ca. 3.5 mya) (Gazin, 1935) and younger Blancan age sites. Its Blancan dispersal into southern Idaho was probably facilitated by gallery forests and riparian habitat along the former connection of the Snake River to the Sacramento River system (Taylor, 1960, 1985; Smith, 1981), prior to capture of the Snake River by the Columbia River system via Hells Canyon (Wheeler and Cook, 1954). Dispersal beyond the riparian habitat associated with the Snake River into other parts of Idaho was probably restricted by the surrounding dry steppe environment north of the Snake River. Dispersal to the south, however, would have been possible via contiguous or nearly contiguous habitats suitable for *Megalonyx* between the Snake River and the shores of Lake Bonneville.

During its highest stages, parts of Lake Bonneville extended into southern Idaho, decreasing the distance between the Snake River drainage and the Bonneville Basin. Despite the extensive existence of arid steppe habitat in the region, the persistence of these fluvial connections and their associated riparian vegetation would have provided habitat that would have supported populations of *Megalonyx* and facilitated its dispersal through otherwise inhospitable environments. One of these former connections between the Snake River Plain and the Bonneville Basin has been documented by Taylor (1960) based on the distribution of the freshwater clam, *Pisidium ultramontanum*; three snails: *Cariniflex newberryi*, *Valvata utahensis*, and *Stagnicola utahensis*; and the bony fish *Chasmistes*. Examination of modern and fossil records of these taxa provides evidence for the existence of a former aquatic connection via the Portneuf River through the Gentile Valley in southeastern Idaho into the Cache Valley of Utah (Taylor and Bright, 1987). This connection was eventually interrupted by the blockage of the Portneuf River drainage by lava flows, which at the same time diverted the Bear River south into the Cache Valley.

Another possible route from the Snake River Plain, where numerous faunas with *Megalonyx* have been found, into the Bonneville Basin is through the Portneuf Gap and via Marsh Valley. Overflow of Lake Bonneville at the time of its maximum height (Bonneville Shore-

Figure 9. *Distribution of* Megalonyx *in western North America. Numbers correspond to the site numbers listed in table 5.*

Table 4. *Megalonyx localities in southern Idaho and their elevations compared to the Orem Locality.*

LOCALITY	ELEVATION
Acequia Gravel Pit	1,272 m
American Falls Fauna	1,340 m
Dam Local Fauna	1,333 m
Duck Point Fauna	1,342 m
Massacre Rocks Fauna	1,324 m
Power County Landfill	1,327 m
Rainbow Beach	1,335 m
Orem	1,440 m

line), when the lake was at a level of 1,552 m, produced a river that flowed through Marsh Valley and onto the Snake River Plain via the Portneuf Gap. This river would have existed from the time maximum lake level was established around 16,000 years B.P. until the Bonneville flood around 14,400 years B.P. (Cerling, 1990). This river probably supported riparian habitat that in turn would have aided the dispersal of *Megalonyx* from the Snake River Plain, via Marsh Valley, into the Bonneville Basin, via the Cache Valley. During the maximum lake level (Bonneville Shoreline) riparian habitat along the narrow, steeply sloping eastern margin of the lake may have been minimal and restricted to canyons in the Wasatch Mountains. Following the overflow of Lake

Table 5. *Rancholabrean records of faunas with* Megalonyx *west of the Rocky Mountains. Unpublished records are listed by repository: IMNH VP, Idaho Museum of Natural History Vertebrate Paleontology Department; MR, Museum of the Rockies; SBCM, San Bernardino County Museum; UA, University of Arizona, Department of Geosciences. Numbers correspond to site numbers in figure 9.*

State / Province	Site Name	Reference
Alaska	1. Cripple Creek, North Star Borough	Stock, 1942
Arizona	2. Coconino Caverns, Coconino County	UA
	3. Shonto Spring, Navajo Co.	Gregory, 1917
California	4. San Pedro, Beacon and Second Streets, Los Angeles Co.	Lyon, 1938
	5. Campbell Hill and Twentynine Palms Gravel Pit, San Bernardino Co.	Jefferson, 1986
	6. Centinella Park, Los Angeles Co.	Miller, 1971
	7. Chandler Sand Pit, Los Angeles Co.	Jefferson , 1991
	8. Domenigoni Valley, Riverside Co.	SBCM
	9. Douglas City, Trinity Co.	Hay, 1927
	10. Emery Borrow Pit, Orange Co.	Miller, 1971
	11. Garber Farm, Stanislaus Co.	Jefferson, 1991
	12. Hawver Cave, Eldorado Co.	Stock, 1918
	13. Lake Manix, Camp Cady Fauna	Jefferson, 1987
	14. La Mirada, Coyote Creek, Los Angeles Co.	Miller, 1971
	15. Mercer Cave, Calaveras Co.	Sinclair, 1905; Harris, 1985
	16. Newport Bay Mesa, Orange Co.	Miller, 1971
	17. Potter Creek Cave, Shasta Co.	Sinclair, 1905
	18. Rancho La Brea, Los Angeles Co.	Stock, 1913, 1925
	19. Samwel Cave, Shasta Co.	Furlong, 1906
	20. Tracy Gravel Pit, San Joaquin Co.	Jefferson, 1991
Idaho	21. Acequia Gravel Pit, Minidoka Co.	McDonald, 1977
	22. American Falls Reservoir, Power Co.	McDonald, 1977; Hopkins and others, 1969
	23. Dam Local Fauna, Power Co.	Gazin, 1935; Barton, 1975
	24. Duck Point, Power Co.	Hearst, 1990
	25. Massacre Rocks, Power Co	IMNH VP
	26. Rainbow Beach, Power Co.	McDonald and Anderson, 1975
Montana	27. Doedon Local Fauna, Custer Co.	MR
New Mexico	28. Conkling Caverns, Dona Ana County	Conkling, 1932, Harris, 1993
Nevada	29. Tule Springs Locality 2, Clark Co.	Mawby, 1967
Utah	30. Orem, Utah County	this paper
Washington	31. SeaTac, King Co.	McDonald, 1977
	32. Wenatchee, Chelan Co.	Hay, 1921, 1927
Alberta	33. Edmonton	Burns and Young, 1994
	34. Medicine Hat	Harington, 1971
British Columbia	35. Quesnel Forks, Cariboo District	Cowan, 1941; Harington, 1971b
Northwest Territories	36. Lower Carp Lake	Stock and Richards, 1949
Saskatchewan	37. Sutherland	SkwaraWolf, 1981
Yukon	38. Old Crow Basin	Harington, 1970, 1971a
Nuevo Leon	39. San Josecito Cave	Stock, 1943
Puebla	40. Valsequillo	McDonald, 1977

Bonneville and subsequent lowering of the lake level there would have been a general increase in the area for the expansion of riparian habitat along the now wider, gently sloping lake margin which would have supported browsing megaherbivores such as *Megalonyx*, *Bootherium*, and *Mammut*.

Another possible access point into the Bonneville Basin from Marsh Valley would have been across the Malad Summit. At an elevation of 1,696 m, the Malad Summit is 262 meters above the floor of the Marsh Valley. Today a small stream system flows north from the Malad Summit to Marsh Valley, and Devil Creek flows south into the Bonneville Basin. Each of these stream systems probably existed in the past to some degree and would have supported a riparian habitat that in turn would have merged with the riparian zone existing around the periphery of Lake Bonneville. At the time of the Bonneville shoreline stillstand the vertical distance from the Malad Summit to the shoreline and its associated vegetation was reduced to 144 m, and by the time of the Provo shoreline stillstand (elevation = 1,446 m) the vertical distance would have increased to 250 m. As can be seen in table 4, the elevation of the Orem locality is actually higher than sites on the Snake River Plain. The slight elevational differences at the lower passes between the Snake River Plain and the Bonneville Basin were probably not an effective barrier to prevent disperal of *Megalonyx* from the Snake River Plain into the Bonneville Basin. The presence of *Megalonyx* in the Bonneville Basin probably represents an expansion of the Idaho population southward.

Although the distribution of *Megalonyx* and its close association with the margins of fluviatile and lacustrine systems seems correct, the specifics regarding the types of preferred vegetation for browse is still unknown. In the Bonneville Basin the primary source of information regarding the type of vegetation existing at the time of the Orem *Megalonyx* is limited to the western side of the basin (Rhode and Madsen, 1995). Analysis of vegetation preserved in packrat (*Neotoma* sp.) middens from low elevation sites permitted reconstruction of vegetation along the western margin of the lake. Between 14,000 and 13,000 years ago the lake margin supported montane brush vegetation dominated by sagebrush (*Artemisia* sect. *tridentata*), snowberry (*Symphoricarpos* sp.), and current (*Ribes* sp., cf. *R. velutinum*) along with herbaceous plants such as thistle (*Cirsium* sp., cf. *C. neomexicanum*) and ryegrass (*Elymus* sp.). Prostrate juniper (*Juniperus communis*) and mesophilic shrubby cinquefoil (*Potentilla fruticosa*) were also common in some localities. According to Rhode and Madsen (1995) this montane brush was similar in many respects to that now found in subalpine settings in the Great Basin. Whether this type of vegetation was present all around the periphery of the lake or extended northward into Idaho and the

Snake River Plain and is representative of the preferred habitat utilized by *Megalonyx* in the Bonneville Basin cannot be determined at this time. We are still left in the frustrating position of being able to discern broad patterns with regard to the distribution of this species but specifics remain elusive. We hope other sharp eyes will spot additional specimens that will aid in filling in the gaps.

Note added during manuscript preparation: Late in 1997 another ground sloth skeleton was recovered from a Lake Bonneville deposit. The site is only a few kilometers north of the Orem locality, immediately north of the Utah County - Salt Lake County border at the geographic feature known locally as "Point of the Mountain." The skeleton (curated in the Earth Science Museum, Brigham Young University) is tentatively identified as *Megalonyx jeffersonii*. This discovery does not change the conclusions presented in this paper. For more information on this skeleton, see Gillette and Miller, this volume.

ACKNOWLEDGMENTS

We are grateful for the support of our host institutions, the Utah Geological Survey and Hagerman Fossil Beds National Monument; also, the Utah Division of State History, Utah Statewide Archaeological Society, and Utah Friends of Paleontology. David B. Madsen assisted with interpretation of the stratigraphy. In addition we recognize the exceptional participation of Aaron Wignall, Candice Wignall, Robin Wignall, Steven Robison, Ron Robison, Jimmy Kirkman, and Brad Wolverton. We also thank James H. Madsen, Jr., and Michael Lowe who ably reviewed the manuscript.

REFERENCES

Barton, 1975, J. B., 1976, A late Pleistocene local fauna from American Falls, southeastern Idaho: Provo, Utah, Brigham Young University, M.S. thesis, 71 p.

Burns, J.A., and Young, R. R., 1994, Pleistocene mammals of the Edmonton area, Alberta--part I, the carnivores: Canadian Journal of Earth Sciences v. 31, no. 2, p. 393-400.

Cerling, T. E., 1990, Dating geomorphological surfaces using cosmogenic ^{3}He: Quaternary Research, v. 33, p. 148-156.

Conkling, R. P., 1932, Conkling Cavern--the discoveries in the Bone Cave at Bishop's Cap, New Mexico: West Texas Historical and Scientific Society Bulletin v. 44, p. 7-19.

Cowan, I. McT., 1941, Fossil and subfossil mammals from the Quaternary of British Colombia: Transactions of the Royal Society of Canada, 3rd series, v. 35, no. 4, p. 39-50.

Furlong, E. L., 1906, The exploration of Samwell Cave: American Journal of Science v. 22, no. 129, article 22, p. 235-247.

Gazin, C. L., 1935, Gravigrade sloth remains from the late Pliocene and Pleistocene of Idaho: Journal of Mammalogy, v. 15, p. 52-60.

Gregory, H. E., 1917, Geology of the Navajo Country, a reconnaissance of parts of Arizona, New Mexico, and Utah: U. S. Geological Survey Professional Paper 93, 161 p.

Harington, C. R., 1970, Ice age mammal research in the Yukon Territory and Alaska, *in* Smoth, R. A., and Smith, J. W., editors, Early man and environments in northwest North America: Calgary, University of Calgary Archaeological Association, p. 35-51.

—1971a, Ice age mammals in Canada: The Arctic Circular, v. 22, no. 2, p. 66-89.

—1971b, A Pleistocene mountain goat from British Colombia and comments on the dispersal history of Oreamnos: Canadian Journal of Earth Sciences 8(9):1081-1093.

Harris, A. H., 1985, Late Pleistocene vertebrate paleoecology of the West: Austin, University of Texas Press, 293 p.

—1993, Quaternary vertebrates of New Mexico, *in* Lucas, S. G., and Zidek, Jiri, editors, Vertebrate paleontology in New Mexico: Albuquerque, New Mexico Museum of Natural History and Science Bulletin 2, p. 179-197.

Hay, O. P., 1921, Descriptions of species of Pleistocene Vertebrata, types or specimens of most of which are preserved in the United States National Museum: Proceedings of the United States

National Museum, v. 59, p. 599-642.

—1927, The Pleistocene of the western region of North America and its vertebrated animals: Carnegie Institution of Washington Publications, no. 322A, 346 p.

Hearst, Jonena, 1990, Paleontology and depositional setting of the Duck Point local fauna (late Pleistocene: Rancholabrean) Power County, southeastern Idaho. Pocatello, Idaho State University, M.S. thesis, 275 p.

Hopkins, Marie, Bonnichsen, Robson, and Fortsch, D. E., 1969, The stratigraphic position and faunal associates of *Bison* (*Gigantobison*) *latifrons* in southeastern Idaho -- a progress report: Tebiwa, v. 12, p. 1-8.

Jefferson, G. T., 1986, Fossil vertebrates from the late Pleistocene sedimentary deposits in the San Bernardino and Little San Bernardino Mountains, *in* Kooser, M. A., and Reynolds, R. E., editors, Geology around the eastern San Bernardino Mountains: Santa Ana, Publications Inland Geological Society, v. 1, p. 77-80.

—1987, The Camp Cady local fauna-- paleoenvironment of the Lake Manix Basin: San Bernardino County Museum Association Quarterly v. 34, no. 3-4, p. 3-35.

—1991, A catalogue of Late Quaternary vertebrates from California--part two, mammals: Natural History Museum of Los Angeles County Technical Reports No. 7, 129 p.

Jefferson, G. T., Keaton, J. R., and Hamilton, Patrick, 1982, Manix Lake and Manix Fault field trip guide: Quarterly San Bernardino County Museum Association, v. 29, 47 p.

Jefferson, G. T., Miller, W. E., Nelson, M. E., and Madsen, Jr., J. H., 1994, Catalogue of late Quaternary vertebrates from Utah: Natural History Museum of Los Angeles County, Technical Report No. 9, 34 p.

Kurtén, Bjorn, and Anderson, Elaine, 1980, Pleistocene mammals of North America: New York, Columbia University Press, 442 p.

Leidy, Joseph, 1855, A memoir on the extinct sloth tribe of North America: Smithsonian Contributions to Knowledge, v. 7, p. 1-68.

Lyon, G. M., 1938, *Megalonyx milleri*, a new Pleistocene ground sloth from southern California: Transactions of the San Diego Society of Natural History, v. 9, no. 6, p. 15-30.

Machette, M. N., 1992, Surficial geologic map of the Wasatch fault zone, eastern part of Utah Valley, Utah County, and parts of Salt Lake and Juab Counties, Utah: U. S. Geological Survey Miscellaneous Investigations Series Map I-2095, scale 1:50,000.

Mawby, J. E., 1967, Fossil vertebrates of the Tule Spring site, Nevada -- Pleistocene studies in southern Nevada, part 2: Nevada State Museum Anthropology Papers, v. 13, p. 105-129.

McDonald, H. G., 1977, Description of the osteology of the extinct gravigrade edentate *Megalonyx* with observations on its ontogeny, phylogeny and functional anatomy: Gainesville, University of Florida, MS thesis, 328 p.

—1996, Biogeography and paleoecology of ground sloths in California, Arizona and Nevada: San Bernardino County Museum Quarterly, v. 43, no. 1-2, p. 61-65.

McDonald, H. G., and Anderson, D. C., 1983, A well-preserved ground sloth (*Megalonyx*) cranium from Turin, Monona County, Iowa: Proceedings Iowa Academy Science v. 90, p. 134-140.

McDonald, H. G., and Anderson, Elaine, 1975, A late Pleistocene vertebrate fauna from southeastern Idaho: Tebiwa v. 18, no. 1, p. 19-38.

McDonald, H. G., and Ray, C. E., 1990, The extinct sloth, *Megalonyx*, (Mammalia: Xenarthra) from the United States Mid-

Atlantic continental shelf.: Proceedings Biological Society Washington, v. 103, p. 1-5.

Miller, W. E., 1971, Pleistocene vertebrates of the Los Angeles Basin and vicinity (exclusive of Rancho La Brea): Bulletin of the Los Angeles County Museum of Natural History and Science no. 10, 124 p.

—1976, Late Pleistocene vertebrates of the Silver Creek local fauna from north central Utah: Great Basin Naturalist, v. 36, p. 387-424.

Nelson, M. E., and Madsen, Jr., J. H., 1987, A review of Lake Bonneville shoreline faunas (Late Pleistocene) of northern Utah, *in* Kopp, R. S., and Cohenour, R. E., editors, Cenozoic geology of western Utah, sites for precious metal and hydrocarbon accumulations: Utah Geological Association Publication 16, p. 318-333.

Oviatt, C. G., Currey, D. R., and Sack, Dorothy, 1992, Radiocarbon chronology of Lake Bonneville, eastern Great Basin, USA: Palaeogeography, Palaeoclimatology, Palaeoecology, v. 99, p. 225-241.

Rhode, David, and Madsen, D. B., 1995, Late Wisconsin/Early Holocene vegetation in the Bonneville Basin: Quaternary Research, v. 44, p. 246-256.

Sinclair, W. J., 1905, New Mammalia from the Quaternary Caves of California: University of California Publications, Department of Geological Sciences Bulletin, v. 4, p. 145-161.

SkwaraWolf, Theresa, 1981, Biostratigraphy and paleoecology of Pleistocene deposits (Riddell Member, Floral Formation, late Rancholabrean), Saskatoon, Canada: Canadian Journal of Earth Sciences, v. 18, no. 2, p. 311-322.

Smith, G. R., 1981, Late Cenozoic freshwater fishes of North America: Annual Review of Ecology and Systematics, v. 12, p. 163-193.

Stock, Chester, 1913, *Nothrotherium* and *Megalonyx* from the Pleistocene of southern California: University of California Publications, Department of Geological Sciences Bulletin, v. 7, p. 341-358.

—1918, The Pleistocene fauna of Hawver Cave: University of California Publications, Department of Geological Sciences Bulletin, v. 10, p. 461-515.

—1925, Cenozoic gravigrade edentates of western North America: Carnegie Institute of Washington Publication 331, 206 p.

—1942, A ground sloth in Alaska: Science v. 95, p. 552-553.

—1943, The cave of San Josecito, Mexico: Balch Graduate School of Geological Sciences, California Institute of Technology contribution no. 361, 8 p.

Stock, Chester, and Richards, 1949, A *Megalonyx* tooth from the Northwest Territories, Canada: Science, v. 1110, p. 709-710.

Taylor, D.W., 1960, Distribution of the freshwater clam *Pisidium ultramontanum*, a zoogeographic inquiry: American Journal Science, v. 258A, p. 325-334.

—1985, Evolution of freshwater drainages and molluscs in western North America, *in* Smiley, C.J., editor, Late Cenozoic history of the Pacific Northwest: San Francisco, American Association for the Advancement of Science, p. 265-321.

Taylor, D. W., and Bright, R. C., 1987, Drainage history of the Bonneville Basin, *in* Kopp, R. S., and Cohenour, R. E., editors, Cenozoic geology of western Utah, sites for precious metal and hydrocarbon accumulations: Utah Geological Association Publication 16, p. 239-256.

Wheeler, H. E., and Cook, E. F., 1954, Structural and stratigraphic significance of the Snake River capture, Idaho-Oregon: Journal of Geology, v. 62, p. 525-536.

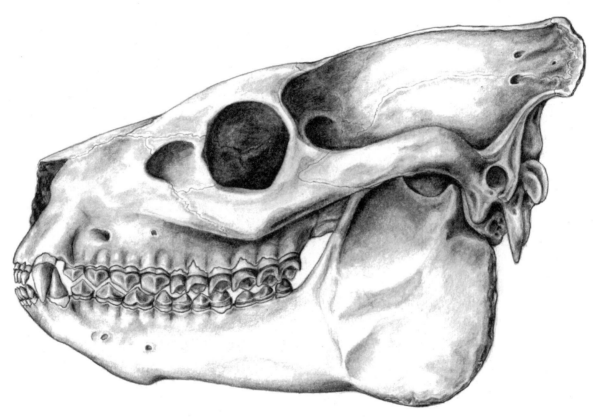

Brian Maebius © 1999

Oreodont

CATALOGUE OF NEW PLEISTOCENE MAMMALIAN SITES AND RECOVERED FOSSILS FROM UTAH

David D. Gillette
Utah Geological Survey, P.O. Box 146100, Salt Lake City, Utah 84114-6100
present address: Museum of Northern Arizona, 3101 North Fort Valley Road, Flagstaff, AZ 86001

Wade E. Miller
Department of Geology, Brigham Young University, Provo, Utah 84602

ABSTRACT

Discoveries of Pleistocene fossil vertebrates throughout Utah have produced significant new specimens that are important for research, exhibition, and education. These specimens have been collected from counties throughout the state, but most are from northern counties near the major population centers. The new records include a variety of species, mostly of large mammals, although several new sites have produced small vertebrates as well.

INTRODUCTION

Previous Catalogues

Paleontologists at Utah's museums, universities, and government agencies, such as the Utah Geological Survey, receive dozens of reports of new fossil discoveries every year. Some are from Pleistocene sites, often discovered by construction activities that involve disturbance of alluvial sediments in valleys throughout the state, or along Lake Bonneville shorelines in western Utah. Overall, the new records of Pleistocene vertebrates that have accumulated in the past two decades, added to the previously established catalogues of Pleistocene vertebrates in this state (Nelson and Madsen, 1980, 1987; Jefferson and others, 1994), represent a meager but growing record of the Pleistocene vertebrate fauna of Utah.

Nearly all records of Pleistocene vertebrates in Utah are from the latest Pleistocene (late Rancholabrean Land Mammal Age). The newly recognized middle Pleistocene fauna from Little Dell Dam, which is listed below and in Gillette and others (this volume), is the first record of fossil vertebrates from the Irvingtonian Land Mammal Age in Utah.

Explanation of Categories in the Catalogue

This catalogue of new Pleistocene mammal sites and newly discovered Pleistocene fossils from previously reported sites in Utah is organized alphabetically by county. Some Utah counties have few or no records of Pleistocene vertebrates while other counties have numerous sites. This geographically uneven distribution is surely an artifact of collection bias and proximity to population centers. All counties in Utah are likely to eventually produce important and in some places abundant records of Pleistocene vertebrates.

Discoveries are often made long before the fossils are brought to the attention of personnel at museums, universities, or government agencies, in which case the details might already have been lost or confounded. Determination of the date of discovery of fossils is often surprisingly difficult; this catalogue reports the most reliable date, but paleontologists who need to verify that information should consult with the repositories for additional details. We have listed the collectors according to the best information at hand, and we regret any omissions or mistakes. Accession numbers and catalogue numbers are devices used by museums to keep track of specimens and archival information; we provide that information here to facilitate research and inquiry by paleontologists who follow. Locality and site information are more fully explained below. Stratigraphic and geological records are generally more detailed than presented here, but we provide this summary information as a guide to the nature of the sites. Information provided under site description and specimen inventory is self explanatory. Additional information or comments pertinent to this catalogue that do not fit neatly into these categories is provided in notes as the final entry for some of the records.

Localities

The Utah Geological Survey maintains a locality data base for fossil sites in Utah. This data base is used for permit management, resource management, and research. The catalogue in this paper uses state locality numbers as assigned from that data base, where available. The numbering system follows the Smithsonian Institution data management organization that has been adopted by federal agencies for archaeological and paleontological record-keeping. Thus, for Utah paleontological site 42Ca210V, the prefix number "42" is the Smithsonian number universally applied for the state of Utah, and the letters that follow refer to County. In this case, "Ca" is the abbreviation for Cache County. The numbers that follow are the locality number applied by the Utah Geological Survey, in sequence as entered into the data base: 42Ca210 is the 210th paleontological site recorded for Cache County. The terminal letter that follows gives an indication of the kind of fossils found at the locality; in this case, the "V" identifies the site as bearing vertebrate fossils. Sites with "I," "b," or "t" as the terminal letter in this system identify invertebrate, paleobotanical, or trace fossil sites, respectively. In this paper, only vertebrate sites are listed. Accordingly, all have the terminal "V" following the site number. Because this volume is dedicated to vertebrate fossils, only those sites that have produced vertebrates are listed, and since this paper reports Pleistocene vertebrates only, sites from all other ages are excluded.

Paleontologists from a variety of institutions have conducted paleontological research in Utah. In some cases, their collections have not been assigned locality numbers, thus accounting for several entries in this catalogue that do not bear a Utah Paleontology Locality Number.

Abbreviations

BYU, Brigham Young University, Provo, Utah; N/A, not applicable; UGS, Utah Geological Survey; SUU, Southern Utah University, Cedar City, Utah; USGS, United States Geological Survey; UMNH, Utah Museum of Natural History, University of Utah, Salt Lake City.

HYRUM MAMMOTH TUSK, CACHE COUNTY

Taxon: *Mammuthus* sp.
Date collected: January 26, 1995
Collector: Joe Kirby, Cache County Road Superintendent

Accession number: UGS 95.1
Repository: UMNH
Specimen number: UMNH VP5314
UMNH accession number: UMNH 95.12
Utah paleontology locality number: 42Ca210V
Location: SE1/4NW1/4NW1/4 section 3, T. 10 N., R. 1 E., Salt Lake Base Line and Meridian; Logan 7.5' USGS quadrangle from a county-owned gravel pit northeast of Hyrum, Utah
Site description: Blacksmith Fork Delta of Lake Bonneville
Stratigraphy and geology: Bonneville Lake Cycle, Provo Shoreline, deltaic gravel deposits
Specimen inventory: Complete mammoth tusk, on display at the Utah State University Geology Department, Logan, Utah.

MUSK OX MANDIBLE, CACHE COUNTY

Taxon: *Bootherium bombifrons*
Date collected: 1996
Collector: Unknown
Accession number: UGS 96.4
Repository: UMNH
Specimen number: UMNH, unnumbered
Utah paleontology locality number: none
Location: Unknown
Site description: From an unknown gravel pit; specimen brought to Sue Morgan, Utah State University Geology Instructor
Stratigraphy and geology: Lake Bonneville gravel deposits
Specimen Inventory: Musk ox mandible.

SOUTHERN UTAH UNIVERSITY MAMMOTH JAW, IRON COUNTY

Taxon: *Mammuthus* sp., cf. *Mammuthus columbi*
Date collected: 1996
Collector: David Dial
Accession number: UGS 96.5
Repository: SUU
Specimen number: Unnumbered, SUU Physical Science Department
Utah paleontology locality number: 42In 066V
Location: Section 3, T. 36 S., R. 16 W., Salt Lake Base Line and Meridian; Beryl Junction 7.5' USGS quadrangle, 3.2 kilometers (2 miles) south of Beryl Junction in a gravel pit owned by Robert Holt, Enterprise, Utah
Site description: Pleistocene gravel

Stratigraphy and geology: Alluvial fan

Specimen inventory: Complete, but poorly preserved mammoth mandible with dentition; on display at Southern Utah State University, Cedar City, Utah

Notes: See Larson, this volume.

CRYSTAL BALL CAVE HORSE AND CAMEL, MILLARD COUNTY

Taxa: *Equus* sp., *Hemiauchenia* sp.

Date collected: February, 1990

Collector: Rod Horrocks

Repository: BYU

Accession number: Unnumbered

Specimen number: Unnumbered

Location: Crystal Ball Cave, 4.8 kilometers (3 miles) northwest of the community of Gandy, westernmost Millard County; exact location on file at repository

Site description: Cave situated in an outlier on the Utah-Nevada border

Stratigraphy and geology: Specimens collected from shallow trench dug in fine, basically unstratified sediments in cave floor

Specimen inventory: Second phalanx of small horse and first phalanx of a camel; horse is a small species

Notes: Both bones are well preserved; a thin coating of calcium carbonate covers much of the horse phalanx. Many hundreds of bones, Pleistocene to Recent, have been collected from Crystal Ball Cave. Its fauna has previously been reported and described (Miller, 1982; Heaton, 1985).

BEAR LAKE BABY MAMMOTH SITE, RICH COUNTY

Taxa: *Mammuthus columbi*, *Bootherium bombifrons*, and unidentified bovid

Date collected: September 30, 1992

Collector: Edwin and Linda Gledhill, Conrad Tanner

Accession number: Utah Geological Survey UGS 92.4

Repository: UMNH

Specimen number: UMNH, unnumbered

Utah paleontology locality number: 42Ri098V

Location: West side of Bear Lake, approximately 50 meters (163 feet) below the normal shoreline at an estimated elevation of 1,803 meters (5,910 feet). Location is east of Highway 30, about 5.6 kilometers (3.5 miles) south of Garden City and 9.6 kilometers (6 miles) north of Laketown, Rich County, Utah; NE1/4 section 3, T. 13 N., R. 5 E., Salt Lake Base Line and Meridian; Bear Lake South 7.5' USGS quadrangle

Site description: In 1992 the elevation of Bear Lake was lower than normal, exposing a 100- to 300-meter (328-984 feet) strip of beach east of the normal shoreline at this location. These beach deposits consist of coarse sand containing water-eroded cobbles 5 to 30 centimeters (2-12 inches) in diameter. A complete mandible of a baby Columbian mammoth and 14 bones of other taxa were discovered along this submerged beach near a spring. These bones may represent a total of four individuals: the year-old Columbian mammoth, two juvenile bovids (2 right maxillae), and a large bovid.

Stratigraphy and geology: Submerged spring deposits below modern shoreline of Bear Lake

Specimen inventory: UGS 92.4.1: sacrum, ?musk ox; UGS 92.4.2: unidentifiable fragment; UGS 92.4.3: cervical vertebra, ?musk ox (juvenile); UGS 92.4.4: cervical vertebra, ?musk ox; UGS 92.4.5: atlas, juvenile ?musk ox; UGS 92.4.6: ?fibula, distal end, baby mammoth; UGS 92.4.7: fragment; UGS 92.4.8: radius, distal end, ?bison; UGS 92.4.9: fragment from #12: ?musk ox mandible; UGS92.4.10: fragment; UGS92.4.11: atlas, ?musk ox; UGS92.4.12: right mandible, juvenile ?musk ox; UGS92.4.13: rib, ?bison; UGS92.4.14: right mandible, juvenile ?musk ox; UGS92.4.15: complete mandible of a baby Columbian mammoth, *Mammuthus columbi*, estimated age of one year.

BIGHORN SHEEP, RICH COUNTY

Taxon: *Ovis canadensis*

Date collected: 1996

Collector: Bert B. Moffitt

Repository: collector, now on loan to BYU

Accession number: N/A

Specimen number: N/A

Location: southeast portion of Bear Lake, Rich County, SE1/4 section 5, T. 13 N., R. 6 E., Salt Lake Base Line and Meridian; Bear Lake South 7.5' USGS quadrangle

Site description: Beneath mapped lake surface on the Bear Lake South quadrangle as of 1969; lake bottom sand and gravel

Stratigraphy and geology: Poorly sorted sand and gravel

Specimen inventory: Two specimens, including (1) posterior half of skull with both horn cores nearly complete; and (2) most of both horn cores with connecting portion of frontal bones.

Notes: The first is a well-preserved specimen with well-indurated sand adhered to auditory orifices, and sand and subrounded gravel inside braincase; calcium carbonate encrusts much of skull's basal surface; it is an adult female, as indicated by fusion of cranial elements and small horn cores. The second specimen is well preserved, but with some of posterior portion of horn cores missing; adhering to the sinus cavities and part of anterior part of horn cores is indurated sand and subrounded to subangular gravel; several partial gastropod shells also are affixed to the horn cores and in sinuses; it is a subadult or adult male based on bone fusion and large horn cores.

BEAR LAKE BISON, RICH COUNTY

Bison sp.

Date collected: 1995
Collector: Annalise Clayton
Repository: BYU
Accession number: Unnumbered
Specimen number: Unnumbered
Location: Bear Lake, Rich County
Site description: From lake sediments at low lake level
Stratigraphy and geology: Unknown
Specimen inventory: Small piece of right maxilla with M1-2.

BEAR LAKE MAMMOTH, RICH COUNTY

Mammuthus sp., cf. *Mammuthus columbi*

Date collected: July 2, 1990
Collector: Devro Sealy
Repository: In collector's possession
Accession number: N/A
Specimen number: N/A
Location: Southeast part of Bear Lake, Rich County
Site description: On lake bottom, collected by SCUBA diving
Stratigraphy and geology: Unknown
Specimen information: Distal two-thirds of humerus.

BEAR LAKE BISON, RICH COUNTY

Taxon: *Bison* sp.
Date collected: 1994
Collector: Bert B. Moffitt
Repository: Collector, now on loan to BYU
Accession number: Unnumbered
Specimen number: Unnumbered
Location: Southeast portion of Bear Lake, Rich County,

SE1/4 section 5, T. 13 N., R. 6 E., Salt Lake Base Line and Meridian
Site description: Beneath mapped lake surface
Stratigraphy and geology: Fine sand
Specimen information: Adult metatarsal, distal two-thirds of tibia, and midportion of femur shaft; juvenile middle portion of humerus
Notes: Bone cavities contain fine, poorly indurated gray sand.

LARK FAUNA, KENNECOTT COPPER MINE, SALT LAKE COUNTY

Taxa: *Camelops* sp., *Equus* sp. (2 species), *Tetrameryx* sp., *Neotoma* sp., *Microtus* sp., other unidentified rodents, rabbits, lizard, small unidentified vertebrates
Date collected: January 1994
Collector: Discovered by equipment operators for Kennecott contractors from W. W. Clyde Construction Company at Kennecott's ground-water reclamation project below the Bingham Canyon open-pit mine; collected by David D. Gillette and Martha Hayden with the assistance of the Utah Friends of Paleontology
Accession number: Utah Geological Survey UGS 94.1
Repository: UMNH
Specimen number: UMNH VP5192
Utah paleontology locality number: 42SL135V
Location: NW1/4NE1/4NE1/4 section 30, T. 30 S., R. 2 W., Salt Lake Base Line and Meridian; Lark 7.5' USGS quadrangle; elevation 1,717 meters (5,629 feet)
Site description: On a steep slope being modified for drainage control on the east side of the Kennecott mine, above the highstand of Lake Bonneville.
Stratigraphy and geology: Debris flow deposits, brown clays with an orange, oxidized lens containing low concentration of bones and weathered volcanic rock fragments. Bones were discovered in base of weathered, unconsolidated volcanic debris flow that accumulated in a broad paleochannel with a steep slope. The debris flow rested on a thick bed of consolidated volcanic rock. Original thickness of the debris flow was at least 10 meters (33 feet). These sediments were probably an unrecognized and unnamed formation, but it has been completely stripped away for drainage control. Age originally considered older than Lake Bonneville shoreline sediments, but faunal study to date has not confirmed any age older than Rancholabrean Land Mammal Age.
Specimen inventory: Mandible with nearly complete dentition of the antilocaprid; dental and post cranial

elements of the other taxa, including rodents and probably rabbits. By UGS accession number, including all fossils and samples, as follows: 94.1.1, horse mandible; 94.1.2, horse incisor; 94.1.3, tooth fragment, unidentified; 94.1.4, innominate, unidentified; 94.1.5, unidentified bone; 94.1.6, unidentified bone; 94.1.7, unidentified bone; 94.1.8, antilocaprid jaw fragment; 94.1.9, bone fragment, unidentified; 94.1.10, horse tooth; 94.1.11, unidentified phalanx; 94.1.12, camel phalanx; 94.1.13, camel phalanx; 94.1.14, camel tooth fragment; 94.1.15, bone fragments, unidentified; 94.1.16, tooth and bone fragment, unidentified; 94.1.17, bone fragments, unidentified; 94.1.18, rib fragments, unidentified; 94.1.19, horse mandible; 94.1.20, long bone fragment, unidentified; 94.1.21, horse teeth; 94.1.22, jaw fragment with teeth, unidentified; 94.1.23, patella, unidentified; 94.1.24, long bone fragments, unidentified; 94.1.25, long bone, unidentified; 94.1.26, sample bag #1; 94.1.27, sample bag #2; 94.1.28, sample bag #3; 94.1.29, sample bag #4; 94.1.30, sample bag #5; 94.1.31, small innominate, unidentified; 94.1.32, 3 articulated vertebrae, caudal or sacral, unidentified; 94.1.33, horse phalanx; 94.1.34, long thin rib, unidentified; 94.1.35, horse vertebrae; 94.1.36, ?wood; 94.1.37, horse phalanx I; 94.1.38, pollen sample #1, from sand lens; 94.1.39, pollen sample #2, from weathered volcanics; 94.1.40, pollen sample #3, partially oxidized layer of weathered volcanics; 94.1.41, horse mandible with teeth; 94.1.42, unidentified bone; 94.1.43, camel, phalanx; 94.1.44, large block of matrix, with possible calcaneum, unidentified; 94.1.45, rib fragment, unidentified; 94.1.46, rodent skull with teeth; 94.1.47, carbon/wood fragment; 94.1.48, carbon sample #2; 94.1.49, pollen sample; 94.1.50, ?plant fragments; 94.1.51, horse phalanx; 94.1.52, horse tooth fragments; 94.1.53, horse tooth; 94.1.54, horse tooth, upper molar; 94.1.55, horse terminal phalanx; 94.1.56, cervical vertebrae, unidentified; 94.1.57, horse astragalus; 94.1.58, horse tooth; 94.1.59, pos-terior part of horse mandible; miscellaneous bone fragments, unnumbered.

Notes: This fauna is currently under study. Fossil antilocaprids can be positively identified only on the basis of horn cores; in the absence of horn cores in this fauna, only a tentative identification as cf. *Tetrameryx* has been made. *Stockoceros* and *Hayoceros* are Pleistocene taxa that commonly have been placed in the genus *Tetrameryx*. The fauna contains at least two species of *Equus*, one large-size and one medium-size.

KENNECOTT HORSE METAPODIAL, SALT LAKE COUNTY

Taxon: *Equus* sp.
Date collected: June 7, 1990
Collector: Pat Fenderson
Accession number: UGS 90.4
Repository: UMNH
Specimen number: UMNH, unnumbered
Utah paleontology locality number: 42SL131V
Location: NW1/4SW1/4NE1/4 section 8, T. 3 S., R. 2 W., Salt Lake Base Line and Meridian; Lark 7.5' quadrangle; at a gravel pit on Kennecott property approximately 1.6 kilometers (1 mile) northeast of Copperton
Site description: Isolated specimen from gravel pit
Stratigraphy and geology: Lake Bonneville gravel
Specimen inventory: Horse metapodial
Notes: This site is different from the preceding and following localities.

KENNECOTT VERTEBRA AND EAR BONE, SALT LAKE COUNTY

Taxon: *Bootherium bombifrons*
Date collected: 1994
Collector: Russ Hubbard, Kennecott Plant Modernization Project
UGS accession number: UGS 94.3
Repository: UMNH
Specimen number: UMNH, unnumbered
Utah paleontology locality number: 42SL137V
Location: Unknown
Site description: Gravel quarry owned by Kennecott Copper Corporation
Stratigraphy and geology: Lake Bonneville gravel
Specimen inventory: Musk ox vertebra and ear bone
Note: This site is different from the preceding two localities.

HUNTSMAN MUSK OX SITE, SALT LAKE COUNTY

Taxon: *Bootherium bombifrons*
Date collected: July 13, 1994
Collector: Discovered by equipment operators Ray Goings and Jeff Moffet of Oakland Construction Company at building excavation site for Huntsman Chemical Corporation headquarters, 500 Huntsman Way, Research Park, Salt Lake City
Accession number: UGS 94.2

Repository: UMNH

Specimen number: UMNH VP5192

Utah paleontology locality number: 42SL136V

Location: section 3, T. 1 S., R. 1 E., Salt Lake Base Line and Meridian; Fort Douglas 7.5' USGS quadrangle; elevation 1,540 meters (5,048 feet); latitude 111° 49' 05" N., longitude 40° 45' 35" W.

Site description: Just below the Bonneville Shoreline Trail at the mouth of Georges Hollow

Stratigraphy and geology: Lake Bonneville, Bonneville Stage (highest lake level), transgressive shoreline, sand and gravel beach deposits

Specimen inventory: Musk ox, *Bootherium bombifrons*: partial skeleton of a single individual, including horn core; scapula; cervical vertebrae 5, 6, and 7; thoracic vertebrae 1, 2, and 3; metatarsal; and ribs.

STAKER MUSK OX SKULL, SALT LAKE COUNTY

Taxon: *Bootherium bombifrons*

Date collected: March 24, 1995

Collector: Kim Peterson

Accession number: UGS 95.2

Repository: UMNH

Specimen number: UMNH, unnumbered

Utah paleontology locality number: 42SL138V

Location: Center, section 27, T. 2 S., R. 2 W., Salt Lake Base Line and Meridian; Lark 7.5' USGS quadrangle; elevation 1,586 meters (5,200 feet); Staker Paving and Construction gravel pit on east side of Utah Highway 111 at 7400 South and north of junction with the Kennecott Mining Railroad line

Site description: Commercial gravel pit owned by Staker Paving and Construction Company, Inc.

Stratigraphy and geology: Lake Bonneville shoreline, Bonneville lake cycle

Specimen inventory: *Bootherium bombifrons* skull with horn cores; unidentified gastropods.

LITTLE DELL DAM SITE, SALT LAKE COUNTY

Taxa: Pleistocene fauna and flora

Date collected: September 11, 1992, and later in same year

Collector: David D. Gillette

Accession number: UGS 92.3

Repository: UMNH

Specimen number: UMNH unnumbered

Utah paleontology locality number: 42SL133V

Location: NW1/4 section 36, T. 1 N., R. 2 E., Salt Lake Base Line and Meridian; Mountain Dell 7.5' USGS quadrangle; Mountain Dell Dam construction excavation site; elevation 1,772 meters (5,813 feet)

Site description: see Gillette, Bell, and Hayden, this volume

Stratigraphy and geology: Quaternary alluvium, peat and clay, tentatively assigned to middle Pleistocene (Irvingtonian Land Mammal Age)

Specimen inventory: numerous taxa and specimens

Notes: See Gillette, Bell, and Hayden, this volume.

JORDAN NARROWS BISON, SALT LAKE COUNTY

Taxon: *Bison* sp.

Date collected: Unknown

Collector: Richard Trotter

Repository: BYU

Accession number: Unnumbered

Specimen number: Unnumbered

Utah paleontology locality number: 42LSL141V

Location: Section 23, T. 4 S., R. 1 W., Salt Lake Base Line and Meridian; Jordan Narrows 7.5' USGS quadrangle; southernmost Salt Lake County

Site description: Within large gravel pit of Geneva Rock Products

Stratigraphy and geology: Bones from poorly sorted sand 8 to 9 meters (26-30 feet) below original land surface

Specimen inventory: Much of a juvenile skeleton including portions of skull and mandible with dentition; bones with unfused epiphyses common, milk dentition with first and second molars in place

Notes: Although the skeleton was reported from the depth given above and collected in situ, it appears Recent in its state of preservation; therefore, age could be Pleistocene or Holocene.

JORDAN NARROWS GROUND SLOTH, DEER, MUSK OX, AND HORSE, SALT LAKE COUNTY

Taxa: *Megalonyx jeffersoni*, *Odocoileus* sp., *Bootherium bombifrons*, *Equus* sp.

Date collected: 1997

Collector: Joe Miller and Richard Trotter

Repository: BYU

Accession number: Unnumbered

Specimen number: BYU 11123, *Bootherium bombifrons*; others unnumbered

Utah paleontology locality number: 42SL140V

Location: Section 23, T. 4 S., R. 1 W., Salt Lake Base Line and Meridian; Jordan Narrows 7.5' USGS quadrangle; southernmost Salt Lake County

Site description: Within large gravel pit of Geneva Rock Products

Stratigraphy and geology: From poorly sorted sand unit overlying clay, 9 to 10 meters (30-33 feet) below original land surface

Specimen inventory: Numerous foot and incomplete limb elements of sloth; atlas of deer; major portion of skull with horn cores but lacking dentition (BYUVP 111213), right and left incomplete scapulae, proximal half of sacrum and nearly complete metatarsal of musk ox; half of tibia, proximal and medial phalanx of horse

Notes: Sloth bones are well preserved, but light weight, with no signs of permineralization.

MASTODON, HORSE, AND BISON SINK-HOLE SITE, SANPETE COUNTY

Taxa: *Mammut americanum, Equus* sp., and *Bison* sp.

Date collected: 1954 (few specimens), 1980 to 1981 (most specimens) for the mastodon; 1988 for the horse and bison

Collector: Keith Rigby (1954); Wade Miller and Kenneth Stadtman (1980-1981) for the mastodon; Steve Robison for the horse and bison

Repository: BYU

Accession number: unnumbered

Specimen number: BYUVP 4378, 4379 (mastodon); horse unnumbered; bison unnumbered

Location: About three kilometers (1.9 miles) west of Huntington Reservoir, adjacent to Skyline Drive, Sanpete County, exact locality information on file at repository

Site description: In 4 meter (13 feet) deep sinkhole on Wasatch Plateau

Stratigraphy and geology: Poorly indurated clay/mud to fine sandstone deposits in the sinkhole, which is a collapse feature in the Upper Cretaceous/lower Tertiary North Horn Formation

Specimen inventory: Mastodon material is from two individuals; BYUVP 4379 is a nearly complete skull and jaws with dentition, 16 vertebrae and parts or all of limb and foot elements; BYUVP 4378 is skull and jaw fragments with partial dentition and few postcranial bones. Horse material (unnumbered) includes one nearly complete incisor and one fragmentary incisor. Bison material (unnumbered) is a broken cheek tooth.

Notes: Specimens of both mastodon individuals are well preserved and represent young adults according to dentition, dental wear, and degree of fusion at epiphyses and sutures; at least one of the specimens (BYUVP 4379) is a male as indicated by the size of tusk alveoli. These specimens were reported by Miller (1981, 1987). The mastodon, bison, and horse were listed in Gillette and Madsen (1992, 1993).

OREM GROUND SLOTH SITE, UTAH COUNTY

Taxa: *Megalonyx jeffersoni*

Date collected: August 29 to September 1, 1991

Collector: Discovered by Ron Robison; collected by David D. Gillette and Utah Friends of Paleontology

UGS accession number: UGS 91.2

Repository: BYU

Specimen number: BYUVP 13301

Utah paleontology locality number: 42Ut430V

Location: SW1/4NE1/4 section 27, T. 6 S., R. 2 E., Salt Lake Base Line and Meridian; Orem 7.5' USGS quadrangle; elevation 1,444 meters (4,720 feet)

Site description: Abandoned gravel quarry south of Utah Water Conservancy District offices on south side of University Parkway, 1 kilometer (0.7 mile) east from I-15 exit 272, Orem, Utah

Stratigraphy and geology: Bonneville lake cycle, Provo shoreline, deltaic gravel from the Provo Canyon Delta

Specimen inventory: Jefferson's ground sloth, *Megalonyx jeffersoni*, partial skeleton

Notes: See Gillette, McDonald, and Hayden, this volume.

SPANISH FORK CANYON MUSK OX, UTAH COUNTY

Taxon: *Bootherium bombifrons*

Date collected: ?1996

Collector: Lyndon Brockbank

Repository: BYU

Accession number: unnumbered

Specimen number: unnumbered

Location: H. E. Davis Gravel Pit near mouth of Spanish Fork Canyon, Utah County

Site description: Gravel pit, found about 7 to 9 meters (23-29 feet) below original land surface

Stratigraphy and geology: Deltaic and alluvial deposits from Spanish Fork Canyon

Specimen inventory: Posterior portion of skull with one-third of left horn core and most of right horn core.

BIGHORN SHEEP, ?WESTERN UTAH

Taxon: *Ovis canadensis*
Date collected: Unknown
Collector: Unknown
Repository: BYU
Accession number: Unnumbered
Specimen number: Unnumbered
Location: ?Western Utah
Site description: Unknown
Stratigraphy and geology: Unknown
Specimen inventory: Most of both horn cores and connecting portion of frontals
Notes: This is a moderately well-preserved specimen, but with noticeably weathered surface and minor amounts of fine sediment in sinus cavities. Specimen could be Holocene. It is an adult male according to bone fusion and size of horn cores.

MAMMOTH, SITE UNKNOWN

Taxon: *Mammuthus* sp., cf. *Mammuthus columbi*
Date collected: Unknown
Collector: Unknown
Repository: BYU

Accession number: Unnumbered
Specimen number: Unnumbered
Location: ?Utah
Site description: Unknown
Stratigraphy and geology: unknown
Specimen inventory: About one half of lower third molar
Notes: This is a moderately well-preserved tooth of an adult according to tooth morphology and wear surface.

ACKNOWLEDGMENTS

Most new discoveries of Pleistocene fossils in Utah have been made at construction sites where alert workers recognized the bones and reported them to a museum, university, or government agency. The cooperation of these construction workers and others is essential to the continuing accumulation of fossils in our museums and universities. In addition, hobby collectors and amateur geologists often discover Pleistocene fossils that they report to responsible institutions. Without the good will and enthusiasm of construction workers, collectors, and others who are overcome with curiosity about their discoveries, our record of Pleistocene life would be skimpy indeed. To all these people, we give our heartfelt thanks.

REFERENCES

Gillette, D. D., Bell, C. J., and Hayden, M. C., 1998, Preliminary report on the Little Dell Dam fauna, Salt Lake County, Utah (Middle Pleistocene, Irvingtonian Land Mammal Age), *in* Gillette, D. D., editor, this volume.

Gillette, D. D., and Madsen, D. B., 1992, The short-faced bear *Arctodus simus* from the late Quaternary in the Wasatch Mountains of central Utah: Journal of Vertebrate Paleontology, v. 12, p. 107-112.

—1993, The Columbian mammoth, *Mammuthus columbi*, from the Wasatch Mountains of central Utah: Journal of Paleontology, v. 67, p. 669-680.

Gillette, D. D., McDonald, H. G., and Hayden, M. C., The first record of Jefferson's ground sloth, *Megalonyx jeffersonii*, in Utah (Pleistocene, Rancholabrean Land Mammal Age), *in* Gillette, D. D., editor, this volume.

Heaton, T. H., 1985, Quaternary paleontology and paleoecology of Crystal Ball Cave, Millard County, Utah-- with emphasis on mammals and description of a new species of fossil skunk: Great Basin Naturalist, v. 45, no. 3, p. 337-390.

Jefferson, G. T., Miller, W. E., Nelson, M. E., and Madsen, J. H., Jr., 1994, Catalogue of late Quaternary vertebrates from Utah: Natural History Museum of Los Angeles County, Technical Reports, v. 9, p. 1-34.

Larson, P. R., The Columbian Mammoth (*Mammuthus columbi*) from Escalante Valley, Iron County, Utah -- discovery and implications, *in* Gillette, D. D., editor, this volume.

Miller, W. E., 1981, *Mammut* from the Pleistocene of Utah: Geological Society of America, Abstracts, v. 13, no. 4, p. 220.

—1982, Pleistocene vertebrates from the deposits of Lake Bonneville, Utah: National Geographic Research Reports, v. 14, p. 473-478.

—1987, *Mammut americanum*, Utah's first record of the American mastodon: Journal of Paleontology, v. 61, no. 1, p. 168-183.

Nelson, M. E., and Madsen, J. H., Jr., 1980, A summary of Pleistocene fossil vertebrate localities in the northern Bonneville Basin of Utah, *in* Gwynn, J. W., editor, Great Salt Lake--a scientific, historical, and economic overview: Utah Geological and Mineral Survey Bulletin, v. 16, p. 97-113.

—1987, A review of Lake Bonneville shoreline faunas (late Pleistocene) of northern Utah, *in* Kopp, R. S., and Cohenour, R. E., editors, Symposium and field conference: Utah Geological Association Publication, v. 1, p. 319-333.

Note added in press: A *Bootherium bombifrons* braincase with right horn core was found in July, 1999 at the Geneva Rock Products, Inc., Bacchus Pit, Salt Lake City, Utah (425L 142V) from Lake Bonneville shore line sands (see Jordan Narrows entry on p. 528). Accession number UGS 99.3.

THE COLUMBIAN MAMMOTH (*MAMMUTHUS COLUMBI*) FROM ESCALANTE VALLEY, IRON COUNTY, UTAH -- DISCOVERY AND IMPLICATIONS

Paul R. Larson
Department of Physical Sciences
Southern Utah University
Cedar City, Utah 84720

ABSTRACT

In the Spring of 1996 a heavy equipment operator discovered the mandible, including teeth, of a mammoth (*Mammuthus* sp.) in a gravel pit near the town of Newcastle, Iron County, Utah. This is the first confirmed record of *Mammuthus* in Iron County. A radiocarbon age estimate for the bone is $28,670 \pm 260$ yr B.P. (Beta-109845). This paper describes the bone, its discovery, and the chronologic, spatial, and stratigraphic correlation between the bone and local geomorphology. The mammoth site lies in an area previously mapped as having been inundated by the waters of Lake Bonneville, but the bone predates the lake's highstand by 12,000 years.

INTRODUCTION

Discovery

David Dial, equipment operator for the Iron County Road Department discovered a mammoth mandible in the spring of 1996 in a privately owned gravel pit near Newcastle, Iron County, Utah. The poorly preserved lower jaw was upside down; fragments of the jaw and left molar separated from the main bone as it was removed from the gravel, while the main portion of the jaw survived undamaged with the right tooth intact. David D. Gillette, Utah State Paleontologist, examined the bone and tentatively identified it as *Mammuthus columbi*. He preserved and stabilized it in a solution of vinyl acetate, and it is now displayed on the campus of Southern Utah University, Cedar City, Utah. This is the first confirmed discovery of *Mammuthus* in Iron County.

Description of the Area

The Escalante Desert is in western Iron and northern Washington Counties, Utah (figure 1), approximately 70 kilometers west of Cedar City. This broad, arid to semi-arid valley contains several small settlements, irrigated agricultural land, and open rangeland. Valley dimensions are 100 kilometers from northeast to southwest, 62 kilometers east to west at its widest, and four kilometers east to west at its narrowest. Its long axis is oriented northeast-southwest. Valley floor gradients are as low as 0.65 meters per kilometer. The valley contains the main line of the Union Pacific Railroad extending from Salt Lake City, Utah, to Los Angeles, California.

The valley is bounded by mountains composed mostly of Tertiary volcanic rocks (Hintze, 1980). Elevations of the nearly level valley floor range from 1,545 meters near Lund to 1,675 meters near Modena. Sand dunes, small playas, and sabkhas are found in parts of the valley, and alluvial fans extend into the valley from all surrounding mountains. Alluvium associated with these fans can be traced horizontally for tens of kilometers.

Previous Work

The discovery of the Newcastle mammoth is the first documented discovery of this genus in Iron County, Utah (D. D. Gillette, personal communication, 1997). Occurrences of mammoth and mastodon in the Colorado Plateau area of southeastern Utah were documented by Nelson (1990). Gillette (1989) and Gillette and Madsen (1993) described a complete mammoth skeleton discovered on the Wasatch Plateau of north-central Utah in 1988, commonly referred to as the Huntington mammoth. Amino acid hydroxyproline extracted from the right zygoma of the Huntington mammoth skull provided a radiocarbon age estimate of $11,220 \pm 110$ yr B. P. (Gillette and Madsen, 1993). Miller (1987) described a mastodon discovered only three kilometers from the Huntington mammoth site, and Nelson (1990) documents the occurrence of mastodon throughout the Colorado Plateau of southeastern Utah.

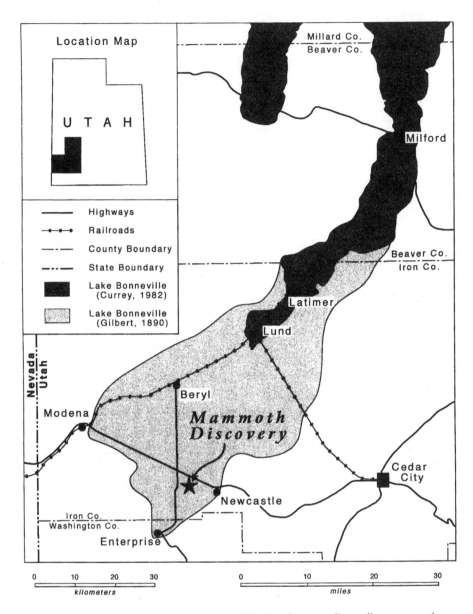

Figure 1. *Escalante Desert includes the shaded area from Enterprise to Milford and surrounding valley areas to the mountains on all sides.*

SYSTEMATIC PALEONTOLOGY

Order Proboscidea
Family Elephantidae
Mammuthus sp., cf. *M. columbi*

Material

Unnumbered lower jaw (figure 2), Southern Utah University, Cedar City, Utah, with dentition, from a mature adult. Right dentary complete, including M_3, except for the rear part of the jaw. Left ramus less complete, damaged somewhat at discovery. Left M_3 dislodged but complete. Collected by David Dial, equipment operator for the Iron County Road Department, Spring, 1996.

Locality

Utah Paleontology Locality No. 42In066v, section 3, T.36 S., R.16W., Salt Lake Base and Meridian, Iron County, Utah (Beryl Junction 7.5" USGS topographic quadrangle map), two miles southeast of Beryl Junction in a gravel pit owned by Robert Holt of Enterprise, Utah; surface elevation 1,580 meters.

Identification

Identification of the mandible as the Columbian mammoth, *Mammuthus* sp., cf. *M. columbi*, follows Miller (1971, 1976), Lundelius and others (1983), Agenbroad (1984), Agenbroad and Mead (1989), and Gillette and Madsen (1993). The mandible is not sufficiently preserved to determine the specific identity with confidence. Its age, osteology, and location are consistent with *M. columbi* (Miller, 1976), and less consistent for the imperial mammoth (*M. imperator*), the woolly mammoth (*M. primigenius*), and Jefferson's mammoth (*M. jeffersoni*). For a recent discussion on the nomenclatural and taxonomic issues related to mammoths in Utah, see Gillette and Madsen (1993) and references therein.

Specimen Description

The lower jaw came from a mature adult, and is nearly complete. Except for the rear part of the jaw, the right side is complete with molar firmly in place, as in life. The left molar was dislodged during discovery and is nearly complete. It is more severely weathered than the right molar but has some bone from the socket still attached. Occlusal surfaces measure 220 millimeters long and 90 millimeters wide.

This specimen is estimated to have been about 50 years of age, based on the amount of wear on tooth surfaces (figure 2). It was a large specimen, estimated at about 4.5 metric tons live weight. Gender cannot be determined, but because of its size it is assumed to have been a bull (D. D. Gillette, personal communication, 1997).

STRATIGRAPHY

The gravel pit in which the mammoth bone was found is part of an old alluvial fan complex (Ulrich and others, 1960) whose apex is 16 kilometers to the southwest of the pit. Alluvial features can be traced clearly on aerial photographs from the fan apex to and beyond the pit. Figure 3 shows the exposed sides of the gravel pit. Two alluvial strata are exposed in the pit. The lower stratum consists of a calcified, gravelly loamy sand; the gravel contains clasts three to five centimeters in diameter and smaller. It averages two meters or more in thickness. This is overlain by calcareous, fine sandy loam containing considerable fine gravel (Ulrich and others, 1960), which extends from the gravel bed to the surface. It varies in thickness from less than one meter to more than two meters. The gravels in the lower stratum are composed of Tertiary rhyolitic and dacitic ignimbrites with some quartzite which originated in the mountains surrounding the valley (Cook, 1965). The southern portion of the valley is thought to be a caldera which may be the source of the ignimbrites (C. F. Lohrengel, II and S. C. Hatfield, personal communication, 1998).

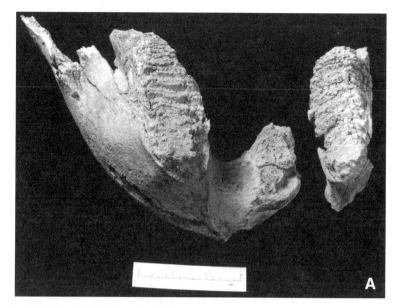

Figure 2. *Mandible and teeth of the Newcastle mammoth. A, front view showing the deep mandibular symphysis and occlusal surfaces of the right molar and detached left molar; scale is 15 centimeters. B, rear view of mandible and detached left molar. C, occlusal surface of right molar, anterior to left. Photograph by Karl Hugh.*

Figure 3. Exposed side of gravel pit showing gravel and overlying soil strata.

Mower (1982, plate 4) identified sediments stratigraphically below those exposed in the pit in well logs. Sands, gravels, and boulders, typical of alluvial fans, dominate the sequence. The two wells in closest proximity to the gravel pit are located 2.4 kilometers south and 5.1 kilometers north of the gravel pit, respectively. The southern well was 200 meters deep and the northern well was 215 meters deep. Maximum valley fill thickness is estimated at over 1,000 meters (Mower, 1982). Mower (1982) interpreted the stratigraphy penetrated by the wells to be typical of alluvial fan and valley-fill deposits.

RADIOCARBON DATING

Dating Procedure

It is difficult to obtain sufficient carbon to date old, badly contaminated, or severely weathered bone, or to identify the carbon as endogenous (Hedges and van Klinken, 1992). This problem occurred with the Newcastle mammoth. The bone is very severely weathered and has begun to crumble. Because the jaw was so poorly preserved it was treated with vinyl acetate as a hardener and stabilizer. Radiocarbon analyses were done by Beta Analytic, Inc., of Miami, Florida. Untreated bone fragments were not datable because all collagen had been removed by weathering. Tooth dentine was considered as an alternative, but the vinyl acetate preservative rendered them unsuitable for dating. An untreated fragment of tooth dentine was discovered in the personal collection of David Dial, which he graciously donated. This fragment had separated from the original specimen during discovery and collection. It was submitted for dating, with favorable results, although the carbon extracted

could not be positively identified as endogenous.

Standard accelerator mass spectrometry radiocarbon dating of collagen from the tooth fragment was favorable. According to the report (Beta-109845): "Clearly identifiable protein was not extracted from the sample. As you instructed, we analyzed the unidentifiable organics which were extracted. This carbon may, or may not, have been exogenous. ^{14}C content measurement and age calibration went normally." The ^{14}C conventional age is reported as 28,670 ± 260 yr B.P., and the $^{13}C/^{12}C$ ratio was -20.4‰.

Interpretation

D. D. Gillette (personal communication, 1997) and D. R. Currey (personal communication, 1997) reiterated the concern of Hedges and van Klinken (1992) that bone collagen may become easily contaminated with younger carbon. It generally, or probably always, yields age estimates younger than if uncontaminated. The real concern involves endogenous collagen versus exogenous organic that could have been introduced following the mammoth's death, especially in a very porous medium such as the gravels in which the mammoth was found. Introduction of exogenous organic would produce an anomalously young age estimate. Therefore, the age estimate obtained on the Newcastle mammoth is a minimum-limiting date. The bone had sufficient endogenous organics to produce an age estimate of 28,670 ± 260 yr B.P. Unless the bone had a complicated burial-reburial history, which is unlikely according to the condition of the bone, it is fairly safe to assign the same age to the sediments in which they were preserved (D. D. Gillette, personal communication, 1997). Based on the age of the mammoth, if the uppermost four meters of sediment observed at the pit accumulated in approximately 28,000 years, then alluvial sediments have been accumulating in this valley for possibly as long as 1.4 million years, assuming a similar sedimentation rate for the upper 200 meters of valley fill.

GEOMORPHIC SIGNIFICANCE OF MAMOTH DISCOVERY

G. K. Gilbert's (1890) classic Lake Bonneville monograph and map indicate that, at its highstand, the lake covered all of the Escalante Desert, including the town sites of Enterprise and Newcastle (figure 1). Subsequent researchers, including Donald R. Currey (1980, 1982, 1990, Currey and others, 1984) and Charles G. Oviatt (Oviatt and Currey, 1987), have mapped the entire shoreline of Lake Bonneville, a distance of over 3,000 kilometers, and determined that the lake did not extend as far south as indicated by Gilbert. The discovery of the mammoth in a setting that lacks lacustrine sediments at an elevation higher than the Bonneville Shoreline is consistent with their maps. The mammoth lived at least 28,000 ^{14}C years ago, long before the lake's highstand roughly 16,000 years ago.

SUMMARY AND CONCLUSIONS

A mammoth jawbone (*Mammuthus* sp., cf. *M. columbi*) was discovered in a gravel pit in western Iron County, Utah in the spring of 1996. This was the first discovery of a mammoth in Iron County. It consisted of the mandible with both molars attached, but the left molar became detached during recovery. The specimen was in poor condition, and was stabilized with a solution of vinyl acetate. The bone could not be radiocarbon dated due to its state of weathering, however, a tooth fragment provided an age estimate of 28,670 ± 260 yr B.P. (Beta-109845). The bone was discovered at a higher elevation than the maximum shoreline elevation for Lake Bonneville. The jawbone is now on display in the Science Building of Southern Utah University, Cedar City, Utah.

ACKNOWLEDGMENTS

David D. Gillette, Utah State Paleontologist, assisted in several phases of the research. He prepared the mammoth specimen for curation, identified it, and aided in obtaining and interpreting radiocarbon dating of the bone. Charles G. Oviatt, professor of geology at Kansas State University, and Donald R. Currey, professor of geography at the University of Utah, have conducted considerable research on the Lake Bonneville shoreline, including many days of field work in the Escalante Desert area. They graciously shared their findings with the author. Appreciation is also expressed to Robert L. Eves, professor of geology at Southern Utah University (SUU), for supplying topographic maps; to C. Frederick Lohrengel II, professor of geology at SUU, for valuable suggestions with the structure of the paper and field work assistance; to Stanley C. Hatfield, assistant professor of geology at SUU for help with mineral identification; to Alden H. Hamblin, paleontologist, Cedar City office, Bureau of Land Management, for assistance in selecting specimens for radiocarbon dating; and to Janet B. Seegmiller, SUU Sherratt Library Special Collections Coordinator, for assistance in archival research. Funding for this project was provided by a faculty development grant from the Center for Faculty Excellence, SUU, Thomas H. Cunningham, Director; the SUU Physical Science Department, Richard A. Dotson, Chair; and the SUU College of Science, B. Al Tait, Dean.

Note added in proof: Since the original discovery, pit operators have unearthed other specimens. These include part of a tusk, another jaw with teeth, and many small unidentified bone fragments. The poorly preserved tusk fragment containing the tip section measures 1.41 meters in length. Its elliptical cross section measures 14.0 by 15.5 centimeters. It is not possible to determine with certainty whether the tusk is from mammoth (*Mammuthus*) or mastodon (*Mammut*), but the tooth is from *Mammuthus*. Heavy equipment crushed the jaw, but we did save some tooth fragments. We cannot determine whether it was an upper or lower jaw nor whether the jaw and tusk came from the same or a different individual. They were found in the same stratum as the original discover, approximately 75 meters away.

Columbian Mammoth from Escalante Valley - P. R. Larson

REFERENCES

Agenbroad, L. D., 1984, New World mammoth distribution, *in* Martin, P. S., and Klein, R. G., editors, Quaternary extinctions, a prehistoric revolution: Tucson, University of Arizona Press, p. 90-108.

Agenbroad, L. D., and Mead, J. I., 1989, Quaternary geochronology and distribution of *Mammuthus* on the Colorado Plateau: Geology, v. 17, p. 861-864.

Cook, E. F., 1965, Stratigraphy of Tertiary volcanic rocks in eastern Nevada: Reno, Nevada Bureau of Mines Report II, MacKay School of Mines, University of Nevada, 61 p.

Currey, D. R., 1980, Coastal geomorphology of Great Salt Lake and vicinity: Utah Geological and Mineral Survey Bulletin 116, p. 69-82.

---1982, Lake Bonneville -- selected features of relevance to neotectonic analysis: U. S. Geological Survey Open-File Report 82-1070, 30 p.

---1990, Quaternary palaeolakes in the evolution of semidesert basins, with special emphasis on Lake Bonneville and the Great Basin, U. S. A: Palaeogeography, Palaeoclimatology, Palaeoecology, v. 76, p. 189-214.

Currey, D. R., Atwood, Genevieve, and Mabey, D. R., 1984, Major levels of Great Salt Lake and Lake Bonneville: Utah Geological and Mineral Survey Map 73, scale 1:750,000.

Gilbert, G. K., 1890, Lake Bonneville: U. S. Geological Survey Monograph 1, 438 p.

Gillette, D. D., 1989, The Huntington Mountain mammoth-- the last holdout?: Moab, Utah, Canyon Legacy- A Journal of the Dan O'Laurie Museum, v. 1, p. 3-8.

Gillette, D. D., and Madsen, D. B., 1993, The Columbian mammoth, *Mammuthus columbi*, from the Wasatch Mountains of central Utah: Journal of Paleontology v. 67, no. 4, p. 669-680.

Hedges, R. E. M., and van Klinken G. J., 1992, A review of current approaches in the pretreatment of bone for radiocarbon dating by AMS: Radiocarbon, v. 34, no. 3, p. 279-291.

Hintze, L. F., 1980, Geologic map of Utah: Salt Lake City, Utah Geological and Mineral Survey (1:500,000).

Lundelius, E. L., Jr., Graham, R. W., Anderson, Elaine, Guilday, John, Holman, J. A., Steadman, D. W., and Webb, S. D., 1983, Terrestrial vertebrate faunas, *in* Porter, S. C., editor, Late Quaternary environments of the United States, v. 1, The Late Pleistocene: Minneapolis, University of Minnesota Press, p. 311-353.

Miller, W. E., 1971, Pleistocene vertebrates of the Los Angeles basin and vicinity (exclusive of Rancho la Brea): Los Angeles County Museum Science Bulletin, v. 10, p. 1-24.

—1976, Late Pleistocene vertebrates of the Silver Creek local fauna from north central Utah: Great Basin Naturalist, v. 36, p. 387-424.

—1987, *Mammut americanum*, Utah's first record of the American mastodon: Journal of Paleontology, v. 61, p. 1668-183.

Mower, R. W., 1982, Hydrology of the Beryl-Enterprise areas, Escalante Desert, Utah, with emphasis on ground water: State of Utah, Department of Natural Resources, Technical Publication No. 73.

Nelson, Lisa, 1990, Ice age mammals of the Colorado Plateau: Flagstaff, Arizona, Northern Arizona University, 24 p.

Oviatt, C. G., and Currey, D. R., 1987, Pre-Bonneville Quaternary lakes in the Bonneville Basin, Utah, *in* Kopp, R. S., and Cohenour, R. E., editors, Cenozoic geology of western Utah-sites for precious metal and hydrocarbon accumulations: Utah Geological Association Publication 16, p. 257-263.

.Ulrich, R., Harper, W. G., and Schafer, G., 1960, Soil survey of the Beryl-Enterprise Area, Utah: U. S. Department of Agriculture, Soil Conservation Service, Washington, D. C., U. S. Government Printing Office, 75 p.

Columbian Mammoth from Escalante Valley - P. R. Larson

AN EARLY HOLOCENE, HIGH-ALTITUDE VERTEBRATE FAUNULE FROM CENTRAL UTAH

Kent S. Smith

Oklahoma Museum of Natural History and Department of Zoology, University of Oklahoma, Norman, Oklahoma 73019;
present address: Department of Biology, Oklahoma City Community College, 7777 South May Ave., Oklahoma City, Oklahoma 73159
(kssmith@ou.edu)

Richard L. Cifelli and Nicholas J. Czaplewski

Oklahoma Museum of Natural History and Department of Zoology, University of Oklahoma, Norman, Oklahoma 73019
(RLC@ou.edu; Nczaplewski@ou.edu)

ABSTRACT

High-altitude Quaternary vertebrate sites are extremely rare in the intermountain west, particularly for microvertebrates. Herein we describe a small microvertebrate fauna obtained through screenwashing rock from a site (Stevens Creek) on the east side of the Wasatch Plateau, Sanpete County. The site lies at an elevation of 2,658 m and thus represents the highest microvertebrate faunule known from the Quaternary of Utah. Radiocarbon dating on a sample of charcoal associated with the fossils yielded an age estimate of 8,330 ± 60 yr B.P., placing the fauna in the early Holocene. The assemblage includes at least ten taxa of reptiles and mammals. Three orders and six families of Mammalia are represented, including the first Quaternary records of the western jumping mouse (*Zapus princeps*) and the montane shrew (*Sorex monticolus*) for the state of Utah. No species are demonstrably shared with the only comparable and nearby site, Blonquist Rock Shelter, but this may be an artifact of sampling. Quaternary deposits in the Stevens Creek area include thinly bedded, fine-grained clastic material as well as coarser fluvial sediments. By contrast, the area is currently marked by a steep slope, rather arid environment, and a combination of colluvial and, locally, alluvial depositional processes. This suggests that the Quaternary sediments of Stevens Creek may have accumulated, in part, behind an ephemeral impoundment, perhaps formed by a beaver dam or small rockslide. In addition, certain members of the fossil fauna, including the montane shrew and the jumping mouse, suggest a local environment that was lusher and wetter than it is today. The mammalian assemblage is similar to that seen in the region today, suggesting that an essentially modern pattern of faunal composition may have been established by 8,330 yr B.P.

INTRODUCTION

Introductory Remarks and Previous Work

Holocene fossils can sometimes provide an important basis in helping to explain the historical biogeographic patterns behind the distributions of modern vertebrates (Grayson, 1987; Graham and others, 1987). The Wasatch Plateau is of special interest in this regard, as it lies on the margins of both the Great Basin and the Colorado Plateau (see, for example, Armstrong, 1977). Gillette and Madsen (1992, 1993) have suggested that the terminal Pleistocene of Utah may have harbored a distinctive, high-elevation fauna, some of whose constituents survived, if only briefly, the megafaunal extinctions that are believed to have occurred in North America between 10,000 and 12,000 yr B.P. (years before present) (Martin, 1984). In the context of this hypothesis, any new data bearing on the late Quaternary of the region represents a welcome addition to current knowledge. Unfortunately, early Holocene vertebrate faunas are not well represented in Utah; those from high elevations are rare throughout North America in general (Graham and others, 1994; Jefferson and others, 1994). Gillette and Madsen (1992) recorded only four high-elevation sites yielding late Quaternary fossils in Utah: the Silver Creek Junction fauna, Summit County, at 1,952 m (Miller, 1976); Blonquist Rockshelter, Summit County, at 2,106 m (Nelson, 1988; Nelson and others, 1989); the Huntington Dam site, Sanpete County, at 2,681 m (Gillette and Madsen, 1992); and the Sinkhole locality, Sanpete County, at 2,983 m (Miller, 1987). The Silver Creek Junction site dates to the middle Wisconsinan glacial age and has produced a relatively diverse fauna of about 30 taxa (Miller, 1976; Jefferson and others, 1994). The other three localities have radiocarbon age estimates spanning the Wisconsinan-Holocene boundary, and thus are more directly comparable in time (and presumably in paleoen-vironment) to the locality reported herein from Stevens Creek. The Huntington Dam site (Gillette and Madsen, 1989, 1993) has yielded two taxa of large mammals, the Columbian mammoth (*Mammuthus columbi*) and the giant short-faced bear (*Arctodus simus*); the Sinkhole has also produced only large mammals, including the American mastodon (*Mammut americanum*), *Bison* sp., and *Equus* sp. (Miller, 1981, 1987). By comparison, the assemblage from Blonquist Rockshelter, including more than 40 taxa, is much better sampled, particularly in terms of lower vertebrates and birds, although the few mammals known from that site have not been identified with precision (Nelson, 1988; Nelson and others, 1989; Jefferson and others, 1994).

The Stevens Creek site, Sanpete County (figures 1, 2, 3), was discovered in 1992 by the senior author in connection with reconnaissance of the eastern Wasatch Plateau for Pleistocene and early Holocene vertebrate fossils. Exposures of alluvium occur sporadically throughout the vicinity with the best occurring in stream drainages. Test samples were collected for screenwashing from eight sites; based on the results, efforts were focused on the single site reported herein, where additional collecting was conducted in 1993-4.

Methods

A total of 1,400 kg of sediment was collected from within a thinly banded zone (unit 4, bed b; see below) at the Stevens Creek site, based on the results of test sampling (small samples from other units proved to be non-fossiliferous). The sediment was subjected to underwater screenwashing in the field (Cifelli and others, 1996), and the concentrate was picked under a dissecting micro-scope at the OMNH (Oklahoma Museum of Natural History). More than 30 mammalian cheek teeth, two mammal jaws, one mammal maxillary fragment, two reptilian vertebrae, and numerous isolated postcranial elements were recovered, forming the basis for this report.

The fossiliferous horizon is also rich in snail shells and small carbon fragments. A sample of unweathered carbon was collected in situ from deep within the out-crop and submitted to Beta Analytic for dating (the gas-tropod shells were considered unsuitable for dating because the prevalence of carbonate rocks in the area might have induced contamination). The radiocarbon determination for this sample (Beta Analytic reference number 74806), using accelerated mass spectrometry, is 8,330 ± 60 yr B.P. The carbon is in the same horizon (unit 4, bed b, described below) as the fossils.

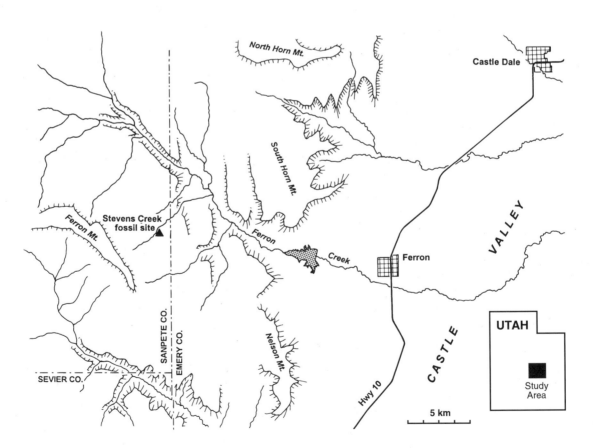

Figure 1. *Location map for Stevens Creek fossil site (OMNH V965), Sanpete County.*

The basis for identification of the fossils from Stevens Creek was comparison with specimens of Recent taxa, housed at the OMNH and MSU (Midwestern State University). The taxonomy of Wilson and Reeder (1993) has been adopted. Specimen measurements, in millimeters, were made with a microscope-mounted ocular micrometer, accurate to 0.01 mm.

DEPOSITIONAL SETTING

The site, OMNH V965, lies in the drainage of a small, ephemeral tributary of Stevens Creek, which in turn flows into Ferron Creek (figure 1); site elevation is 2,658 m above sea level. The local area slopes noticeably to the southeast; alluvial deposits are exposed in the drainages, where they have been subject to erosion (figure 2). Exposures typically occur as vertical faces or, as at the site, pillar-like erosional remnants at the margins of stream cuts, and are characterized by distinct banding. The lateral extent of these deposits cannot be determined because of overlying slope cover (in the form of colluvium and vegetation); similarly, the contact with the underlying bedrock is obscure. The maximum exposed thickness of these deposits is about 18 meters.

The sediments consist of moderately well-indurated fluvial clays and silts with associated gravel layers characterized by both pebbles and cobbles. The fine-grained sediments presumably are derived locally from Cretaceous and Paleocene sedimentary rock; most of the coarse clastic particles consist of limestone derived from the Flagstaff Limestone. The silts and clays are characterized by distinct bands ranging from buff to light brown to dark gray; individual beds are roughly horizontal and lenticular.

Figure 3. *Exposure of Quaternary sediments at OMNH locality V965; fossil specimens and carbon sample were obtained from within the banded zone (unit 4 in text), at the level of the pick.*

We identify five major units in the alluvial deposits at OMNH V965 (figure 3), as follows (from top to bottom; average thickness in parentheses): (1) topsoil (20 cm); (2) a white to buff-colored, indurated silt (13 cm); (3) a light grayish-brown silt with some clay layers and with irregular crossbedding (43 cm); (4) a zone comprised of seven lenticular layers (total thickness, 76 cm), including (from top to bottom) (a) gray silt (8 cm); (b) dark gray silt and clay with carbon flakes (5 cm; this is the horizon which produced both fossil vertebrates and the charcoal sample used for radiometric dating); (c) light gray-brown silt (10 cm); (d) dark gray silt (5 cm); (e) gravel with poorly sorted, subangular to subrounded pebble- to cobble-sized particles (4 cm); (f) dark gray silt and clay (23 cm); and (g) light grayish brown silt and clay with a pebble/cobble stringer near the base (18 cm); and (5) buff to bluish gray siltstone and claystone with a pebble/cobble stringer near the base (covered at the bottom; exposed thickness, 114 cm).

SYSTEMATIC PALEONTOLOGY

Order Squamata
Suborder Serpentes
Family Indeterminate

OMNH 55023 is a postcloacal vertebra lacking the pleurapophyses and hemapophyses. It can be identified as belonging to a snake based on the development of the hypapophysis. Unfortunately, no taxonomic identification can be made because postcloacal vertebrae are not generally diagnostic (see, for example, LaDuke, 1991).

Figure 2. *Drainage area of OMNH locality V965, showing exposures of Quaternary sediments in the vicinity; the position of the site is shown by a white arrow (view toward the northwest).*

Order Insectivora
Family Soricidae
Sorex monticolus Merriam, 1890
(montane shrew)

Soricidae are represented at OMNH V965 by a single tooth, OMNH 55014, a left p4. The specimen was compared with three species of *Sorex* that currently inhabit Utah (*S. vagrans, S. palustris, S. monticolus*). Of these, the fossil resembles *S. monticolus* in both size and morphology. *S. vagrans* is smaller than the other two species; both the fossil and recent *S. monticolus* differ from *S. palustris* in having a greater angle (in labial view) between the two cusps on p4. As far as we are aware, the specimen from Stevens Creek represents the first known occurrence of the montane shrew in the Quaternary of Utah (Jefferson and others, 1994). *S. monticolus* frequents aspen stands, willow thickets, gallery forests, and marshy areas (Fitzgerald and others, 1994).

Order Lagomorpha
Family Leporidae
Genus and Species unidentified

The sole specimen of a leporid from the Stevens Creek site is an incomplete cheektooth that belongs to either *Sylvilagus* or *Lepus*; the specimen (OMNH 55019) is too incomplete for more precise identification. Both jackrabbits and cottontails inhabit the Stevens Creek area today.

Order Rodentia
Family Sciuridae
Tamias ?minimus (Bachman, 1839) (least chipmunk)

OMNH 55017 (figure 4A), a left M3, was compared with *Tamias minimus, T. quadrivittatus, T. dorsalis,* and *T. townsendi.* Body size of *T. minimus* is reported to be less than that of *T. quadrivittatus* (Findley and others, 1975; Fitzgerald and others, 1994), but we found the M3 of the two species to be virtually identical in size. In terms of size (length= 1.30; width= 1.40) the specimen is appropriate for either *T. minimus* or *T. quadrivittatus;* it is tentatively referred to the former based on elevational differences in the distribution of living species (Findley and others, 1975), though both species range widely.

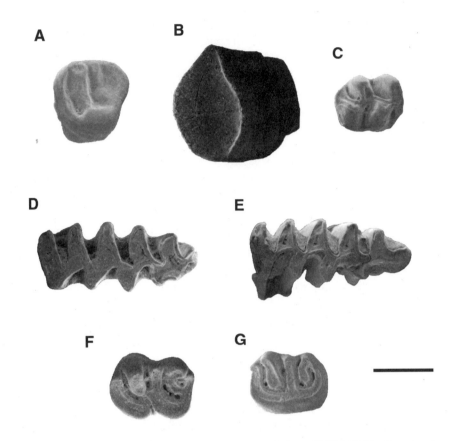

Figure 4. *Representative specimens of fossil mammals from OMNH V965; all occlusal views. A, OMNH 55017, M3, Tamias minimus; B, OMNH 55012, M1or 2, Thomomys talpoides; C, OMNH 55022, m2, ?Peromyscus sp.; D, OMNH 55008, m1, Phenacomys intermedius; E, OMNH 55003, m1, Microtus sp.; F, OMNH 55005, M1, Zapus princeps; G, OMNH 55006, M2, Zapus princeps. Scale bar = 1 mm.*

Spermophilus sp.

A heavily worn p4, OMNH 55018, clearly belongs to a ground squirrel, genus *Spermophilus,* but species identification is problematic. Five species of *Spermophilus* are found along the Wasatch Plateau today (Durrant, 1952), and at least three of these (*S. armatus, S. lateralis,* and *S. elegans*) have been observed by one of us (KSS) in the area. We are unable to identify the fossil on the basis of preserved morphology.

Family Geomyidae
Thomomys talpoides (Richardson, 1828)
(northern pocket gopher)

Two specimens, OMNH 55012 (M1or 2; figure 4B) and 55013 (left p4) are referred to the northern pocket gopher. Dalquest and Schultz (1992) provide the basis for identification of p4 in *Thomomys;* this tooth is also useful in establishing identity at the species level (Thaeler, 1980). The most important characteristics in this regard are the triangular-shaped anterior prism, the concave shape of the anterior enamel plate on the anterior prism, and the proximity of the anterior enamel plate to the lateral lingual plate. *Thomomys talpoides* occurs in most mountainous areas of Utah and evidently prefers areas of shallow, rocky soil in open pine forests and alpine meadows, usually near streams (Durrant, 1952).

Family Cricetidae
?*Peromyscus* sp.

Three unassociated specimens, OMNH 55020 (M3), 55021 (m2), and 55022 (m2; figure 4C) document the presence of a small cricetid in the Stevens Creek fauna. The teeth are too large to belong to either of the two species of *Reithrodontomys* that frequent the area today, *R. megalotis* and *R. montanus*. The specimens cannot be positively identified, but almost surely belong to one or more species of deer mouse, *Peromyscus*; according to Durrant (1952), two species are found at high elevations in the region today, *P. maniculatus* and *P. boylii*.

Phenacomys intermedius Merriam, 1889
(heather vole)

Four rooted cheekteeth are referred to this species: OMNH 55008 (m1; figure 4D), 55009 (M3), 55010 (m3), and 55011 (m2). Only two extant microtines in North America possess rooted cheekteeth as adults, *Clethrionomys* and *Phenacomys*; these are easily distinguished (teeth of *Clethrionomys* contain cementum in the angles of the reentrants, a feature lacking in *Phenacomys*; the latter genus has much deeper inner than outer reentrant angles on lower molars, whereas they are subequal in *Clethrionomys*). The specimens are indistinguishable from modern *P. intermedius*, which today is found in the Wasatch Range and Uinta Mountains of Utah (Durrant, 1952). This species has a fairly eclectic habitat preference, being found in both xeric and moist environments, but it is primarily a subalpine to alpine mammal (Fitzgerald and others, 1994). The heather vole no longer is distributed in the eastern U.S., though it is frequently found in Pleistocene faunas (Guilday and others, 1977); in Utah, it has been reported from the late Pleistocene Silver Creek fauna (Miller, 1976).

Microtus sp. (voles)

Three specimens from Stevens Creek, OMNH 55002 (dentary fragment with m1-2), 55003 (m1; figure 4E), and 55004 (maxilla fragment with M1) are referred to *Microtus*. The materials in hand are inadequate for species identification. Four species of *Microtus* currently live on the Wasatch Plateau: *M. pennsylvanicus*, *M. montanus*, *M. richardsoni*, and *M. longicaudus* (Durrant,

1952). Of these, *M. richardsoni* is the largest and can be eliminated on the basis of size, but we cannot distinguish among the remaining species on the basis of available teeth.

Family Dipodidae
Zapus princeps Allen, 1893
(western jumping mouse)

Three specimens from the Stevens Creek site are referred to the western jumping mouse, *Zapus princeps*: OMNH 55005 (M1; figure 4F), 55006 (M2; figure 4G), and 55007 (M3). *Zapus princeps* (which currently occurs in the area) can be distinguished from *Z. hudsonius* (which does not occur in Utah today, though it is found in Colorado) on the basis of size (for example, Hall and Kelson, 1959) and the fact that the primary folds of the upper cheekteeth meet in *Z. princeps*, whereas they do not in *Z. hudsonicus* (Jones, 1981). On both M1 and M2 the paracone is free; Jones (1981) has suggested that the coronal pattern is variable within *Z. princeps*, with the paracone being attached in interior populations and free in populations that are peripheral.

Although the western jumping mouse inhabits the area of Stevens Creek today (Durant, 1952), this is the first Quaternary record for the species in Utah, as far as we are aware (see, for example, Jefferson and others, 1994). *Z. princeps* apparently favors primarily wet, relatively open habitat that has dense cover (Dalquest, 1948).

DISCUSSION AND CONCLUSIONS

Poorly represented as it is, the faunule from Stevens Creek includes at least 10 vertebrate taxa, most of which are small mammals, and thus adds substantially to the meager record of Utah's high-elevation faunas from the late Quaternary - which, as noted above, is otherwise represented mostly by large mammals and birds. All of the taxa known are found in the area today (though one species, *Phenacomys intermedius*, is more commonly encountered in the northern part of the state, particularly the Uinta Mountains): hence evidence in hand suggests that an essentially modern pattern of faunal composition had been achieved - for small mammals, at least - by about 8,330 yr B.P. in the higher elevations of the eastern Wasatch Plateau. The Stevens Creek site is slightly younger than the nearby Huntington Dam and Sinkhole sites, which collectively have produced at least four taxa that subsequently went extinct (*Mammut americanum*, *Mammuthus columbi*, *Arctodus simus*, *Equus* sp.). It has been suggested that one or more of these large mammal taxa may have survived later in the region than the megafaunal extinctions which occurred in North America (Gillette and Madsen, 1992) and that they may have occupied Utah's high country on a seasonal basis (Gillette and Madsen, 1993). Limited sampling of the Stevens Creek fauna precludes any assessment as to whether one or more of these large mammals still inhabited the region in the early Holocene.

At present, the environment at the Stevens Creek site is rather arid; local drainages are ephemeral and flow during and after snowmelt or local rains. The stream channel at the site and others nearby are now moderately incised (perhaps an historic phenomenon related to increased runoff and erosion) and have a steep gradient. Beyond the streambanks, vegetation is sparse and consists of semiarid sage and grasses, with occasional scattered junipers; a stand of quaking aspen occurs upslope about 0.5 km from the site, and there is no riparian vegetation.

By contrast, both sedimentological and faunal evidence from the site suggests a local environment that was wetter and lusher at the time of deposition. The distribution of now-eroding alluvial sediments suggests that some unknown factor affected local base level early in the Holocene. Similarly, the clays and silts predominant in part of the section at the site suggest a relatively low-energy, wetter environment of deposition, perhaps a beaver pond or a shallow pond developed behind a dam temporarily created by a small rockslide. For example, Dalquest and others (1990) described ancient beaver dams in association with five Quaternary sites in northeastern New Mexico and the Oklahoma panhandle. They hypothesized ancient beaver dams based, in part, on lacustrine deposits in cutbacks of several high-gradient streams. Additionally, Smith (1992) reported on an ancient beaver dam from a late Holocene locality in southwest Oklahoma. Evidence for this beaver dam was based on a lens-shaped deposit containing gastropods and snail shells. Certain members of the vertebrate assemblage also suggest a wetter local environment during the early Holocene. *Sorex monticolus* apparently prefers moist habitat; in Manitoba, it frequents grass-sedge marsh and willow-alder fen (Wrigley and others, 1979). Western jumping mice occur in damp, dense growths of grass and forbs, especially along streams, ponds, and bogs (Burt and Grossenheider, 1964; Whitaker, 1980). None of the taxa from Stevens Creek appear in the only comparable nearby fauna, that of Blonquist Rockshelter (Nelson, 1988; Nelson and others, 1989), although this could be simply a sampling bias.

ACKNOWLEDGMENTS

The senior author thanks P. B. Smith for her help and companionship during the initial field reconnaissance conducted in 1992; we also thank K. G. Smith, R. L. Nydam, D. F. Schmidt, W. E. Sanders, and J. Hilliard. We are especially grateful to D. Harber of the U.S. Forest Service for showing us the field area, facilitating permits, and innumerable other courtesies. Access to collections of recent mammals was provided by W. W. Dalquest (Midwestern State University) and M. A. Mares (Oklahoma Museum of Natural History). The SEM photographs were taken by E. Miller. We thank D. D. Gillette and T. H. Heaton for reviewing an earlier version of this manuscript. This research was supported by awards to KSS from the Department of Zoology and the Graduate Student Senate, University of Oklahoma, and the Society of the Sigma Xi. Additional support was provided by grants from the National Geographic Society (4761-91, 5021-92) and the National Science Foundation (DEB 9401094) awarded to RLC.

REFERENCES

Armstrong, D. M., 1977, Distributional patterns of mammals in Utah: Great Basin Naturalist, v. 37, p. 457-474.

Burt, W. H., and Grossenheider, R. P., 1964, A Field Guide to the Mammals: Peterson Field Guide Series, Boston, Houghton Mifflin Co., 284 p.

Cifelli, R. L., Madsen, S. K., and Larson, E. M., 1996, Screenwashing and associated recovery techniques for the recovery of microvertebrates: Oklahoma Geological Survey Special Publication no. 96-4, p. 1-24.

Dalquest, W. W., 1948, Mammals of Washington State: University of Kansas Publications, Museum of Natural History, v. 2, p. 1-444.

Dalquest, W. W., and Schultz, G. E., 1992, Ice-Age Mammals of Northwest Texas: Midwestern State University Press, Wichita Falls, 309 p.

Dalquest, W. W., Stangl, F. B., Jr., and Kocurko, M. J., 1990, Zoogeographic implications of Holocene mammal remains from ancient beaver ponds in Oklahoma and New Mexico: Southwest Naturalist, v. 35, 2, p. 105-110.

Durrant, S. D., 1952, Mammals of Utah--taxonomy and distribution: University of Kansas Publications, Museum of Natural History, v. 6, p. 1-549.

Findley, J. S., Harris, A. H., Wilson, D. E., and Jones, Clyde, 1975, Mammals of New Mexico: Albuquerque, University of New Mexico Press, 360 p.

Fitzgerald, J. P., Meaney, C. A., and Armstrong, D. M., 1994, Mammals of Colorado: Boulder, Denver Museum of Natural History and the University of Colorado Press, 467. p.

Gillette, D. D., and Madsen, D. B., 1989, A late Quaternary mammoth from the Wasatch Plateau of central Utah: Abstracts of the Symposium on Southwestern Geology and Paleontology, Museum of Northern Arizona, Flagstaff, p. 9.

—1992, The short-faced bear *Arctodus simus* from the late Quaternary in the Wasatch Mountains of central Utah: Journal of Vertebrate Paleontology, v. 12, p. 107-112.

—1993, The Columbian mammoth, *Mammuthus columbi*, from the Wasatch Mountains of central Utah: Journal of Paleontology, v. 67, p. 669-680.

Graham, R. W., Lundelius, E. L., Jr., Graham, M. A., Stearley, R. L., Schroeder, E. K., Anderson, Elaine, Barnosky, A. D., Burns, J. A., Churcher, C. S., Grayson, D. K., Guthrie, R. D., Harington, C. R., Jefferson, G. T., Martin, L. D., McDonald, H. G., Morlan, R. E., Semken, H. A., Jr., Webb, S. D., and Wilson, M. C., 1994, FAUNMAP--A database documenting late Quaternary distributions of mammal species in the United States: Illinois State Museum Scientific Papers, v. 25, nos. 1-2, 690 p.

Graham, R. W., Semken, H. A., and Graham, M. A., editors, 1987, Late Quaternary Mammalian Biogeography and Environments of the Great Plains and Prairies: Illinois State Museum Scientific Papers, v. 22, 491 p.

Grayson, D. K., 1987, The biogeographic history of small mammals

in the Great Basin: observations on the last 20,000 years: Journal of Mammalogy, v. 68, p. 359-375.

Guilday, J. E., Parmalee, P. W., and Hamilton, H. W., 1977, The Clark's cave bone deposit and the late Pleistocene paleoecology of the central Appalachian Mountains of Virginia: Bulletin of the Carnegie Museum of Natural History, v. 2, p. 1-87.

Hall, E. R., and Kelson, K. R., 1959, The mammals of North America: New York, Ronald Press, v. 1-2, 1083 p.

Jefferson, G. T., Miller, W. E., Nelson, M. E., and Madsen, J. H., Jr., 1994, Catalogue of late Quaternary vertebrates from Utah: Natural History Museum of Los Angeles County, Technical Reports, no. 9, 34 p.

Jones, G. S., 1981, The systematics and biology of the genus *Zapus* (Mammalia, Rodentia, Zapodidae): Terre Haute, Indiana State University, Ph.D. dissertation, 569 p.

LaDuke, T. C., 1991, The fossil snakes of pit 91, Rancho La Brea, California: Natural History Museum of Los Angeles County, Contributions in Science no. 424, p. 1-28.

Martin, P. S., 1984, Prehistoric overkill--the global model, *in* Martin, P. S., and Klein, R. G., editors, Quaternary extinctions--a prehistoric revolution: Tucson, University of Arizona Press, p. 354-403.

Miller, W. E., 1976, Late Pleistocene vertebrates of the Silver Creek local fauna from north-central Utah: Great Basin Naturalist, v. 36, p. 387-424.

—1981, *Mammut* from the late Pleistocene of Utah--Utah's first mastodon record: Geological Society of America Special Paper, Abstracts with Programs, v. 13, p. 220.

—1987, *Mammut americanum*, Utah's first record of the American mastodon: Journal of Paleontology, v. 61, p. 168-183.

Nelson, M. E., 1988, A new cavity biota from northeastern Utah: Current Research in the Pleistocene, v. 5, p. 77-78.

Nelson, M. E., Dreiling, D. D., and Vandenberg, R. S., 1989, New paleontological investigations at Blonquist Rockshelter, Summit County, Utah: Current Research in the Pleistocene, v. 6, p. 77-78.

Smith, K. S., 1992, A Holocene mammalian fauna from Box Elder Creek, Caddo County, Oklahoma: Proceedings of the Oklahoma Academy of Science, v. 72, p. 39-44.

Thaeler, C. S., Jr., 1980, Chromosome number and systematic relations in the genus *Thomomys* (Rodentia: Geomyidae): Journal of Mammalogy, v. 61, p. 414-422.

Whitaker, J. O., 1980, The Audubon Society field guide to North American mammals: New York, Chanticleer press, 745 p.

Wilson, D. E., and Reeder, D. M., editors, 1993, Mammalian species of the world--a taxonomic and geographic reference 2nd ed.: Washington, D. C., Smithsonian Institution Press, 1206 p.

Wrigley, R. E., Dubois, J. E., and Copland, H. W., 1979, Habitat, abundance, and distribution of six species of shrews in Manitoba: Journal of Mammalogy, v. 60, p. 505-520.

AUTHOR INDEX

Keyed to paper number used in Table of Contents
(Bold # indicates initial author)
(First page of each paper is in parentheses)

KEY WORD INDEX